FISKE 2024
GUIDE TO
COLLEGES

FISKE GUIDE TO COLLEGES 2024

EDWARD B. FISKE

former Education Editor of
the *New York Times*

with Michelle Lecuyer
and
the *Fiske Guide to Colleges* staff

Published by Sourcebooks
P.O. Box 4410
Naperville, Illinois 60567-4410
(630) 961-3900
sourcebooks.com

Fortieth Edition

**Your comments and corrections
are welcome. Please send them to:**

Fiske Guide to Colleges
Email: editor@fiskeguide.com

Printed and bound in the United States of America.

BB 10 9 8 7 6 5 4 3 2 1

To Sunny

Contents

Index by State and Country

The colleges in this guide are listed alphabetically and cross-referenced for your convenience. Below is a list of the selected colleges grouped by state. Following this listing, you will find additional listings that categorize the colleges by their yearly costs of attendance and by the average debt accrued by students during their tenure at each school.

University of North Carolina at Chapel Hill, 503
University of North Carolina Wilmington, 506
North Carolina State University, 508
Wake Forest University, 744
Warren Wilson College, 747

OHIO
Antioch College, 25
Case Western Reserve, 126
University of Cincinnati, 144
University of Dayton, 205
Denison University, 213
Hiram College, 323
Kenyon College, 406
Miami University, 456
Oberlin College, 519
The Ohio State University, 527
Ohio University, 529
Ohio Wesleyan University, 532
Wittenberg University, 795
The College of Wooster, 799

OKLAHOMA
University of Oklahoma, 534
University of Tulsa, 717

OREGON
Lewis & Clark College, 420
University of Oregon, 539
Oregon State University, 542
Reed College, 582
Willamette University, 784

PENNSYLVANIA
Allegheny College, 13
Bryn Mawr College, 86
Bucknell University, 89
Carnegie Mellon University, 123
Dickinson College, 222
Drexel University, 227
Franklin & Marshall College, 266
Gettysburg College, 283
Haverford College, 315
Juniata College, 396
Lafayette College, 411
Lehigh University, 418
Muhlenberg College, 481
University of Pennsylvania, 546
Pennsylvania State University, 549

University of Pittsburgh, 554
Susquehanna University, 683
Swarthmore College, 685
Ursinus College, 722
Villanova University, 734
Washington and Jefferson College, 752

RHODE ISLAND
Brown University, 82
Providence College, 568
University of Rhode Island, 587
Rhode Island School of Design, 589

SOUTH CAROLINA
College of Charleston, 138
Clemson University, 164
Furman University, 268
Presbyterian College, 557
University of South Carolina, 650
Wofford College, 797

TENNESSEE
Rhodes College, 591
University of the South (Sewanee), 647
University of Tennessee Knoxville, 690
Vanderbilt University, 726

TEXAS
Austin College, 45
Baylor University, 58
University of Dallas, 197
Rice University, 594
Southern Methodist University, 654
Southwestern University, 657
University of Texas at Austin, 692
University of Texas at Dallas, 695
Texas A&M University, 697
Texas Christian University, 700
Texas Tech University, 702
Trinity University, 707

UTAH
Brigham Young University, 80
University of Utah, 724

VERMONT
Bennington College, 63
Champlain College, 133
Middlebury College, 464

Saint Michael's College, 626
University of Vermont, 731

VIRGINIA
George Mason University, 270
Hampden–Sydney College, 303
Hollins University, 330
James Madison University, 391
University of Mary Washington, 441
Randolph College, 577
University of Richmond, 596
University of Virginia, 736
Virginia Tech, 739
Washington and Lee University, 754
William & Mary, 787

WASHINGTON
The Evergreen State College, 249
Gonzaga University, 286
University of Puget Sound, 570
Seattle University, 640
University of Washington, 749
Whitman College, 780

WASHINGTON, D.C. (SEE DISTRICT OF COLUMBIA)

WEST VIRGINIA
West Virginia University, 771

WISCONSIN
Alverno College, 18
Beloit College, 60
Lawrence University, 415
Marquette University, 439
Ripon College, 599
University of Wisconsin–Madison, 792

CANADA
University of British Columbia, 358
McGill University, 360
Queen's University, 362
University of Toronto, 364

GREAT BRITAIN AND IRELAND
University of Aberdeen, 369
University of Edinburgh, 372
University of Glasgow, 375
University of St Andrews, 377
Trinity College Dublin, 381

Index by Price

	PUBLIC	PRIVATE
$$$$	More than $15,000	More than $60,000
$$$	$13,001–$15,000	$55,001–$60,000
$$	$10,500–$13,000	$47,000–$55,000
$	Less than $10,500	Less than $47,000

Price categories are based on current tuition and fees and do not include room, board, transportation, and other expenses.

PUBLIC COLLEGES AND UNIVERSITIES

PRIVATE COLLEGES AND UNIVERSITIES

INEXPENSIVE—$

University of Aberdeen*, 369
Adelphi University, 1
Agnes Scott College, 3
Alfred University, 10
Alma College, 15
Alverno College, 18
Antioch College, 25
College of the Atlantic, 40
Austin College, 45
Birmingham–Southern College, 68
Brigham Young University, 80
University of British Columbia*, 358
Butler University, 91
Calvin University, 118
Champlain College, 133
The Cooper Union, 188
University of Dallas, 197
University of Dayton, 205
Deep Springs College, 207
DePaul University, 217
Drew University, 225
Drexel University, 227
University of Edinburgh*, 372
Elon University, 238
Florida Institute of Technology, 256
Florida Southern College, 259
University of Glasgow*, 375
Gordon College, 288
Guilford College, 296
Hendrix College, 320
Hiram College, 323
Hollins University, 330
Hood College, 335
Hope College, 337
Houghton College, 339
Howard University, 342
The College of Idaho, 344
Loyola University New Orleans, 429
Manhattanville College, 436
Marquette University, 439
McGill University*, 360
Millsaps College, 467
Morehouse College, 36
Oglethorpe University, 524
Presbyterian College, 557
Prescott College, 559
Principia College, 565
Queen's University*, 362

Randolph College, 577
University of St Andrews*, 377
St. John's College, 616
Spelman College, 38
University of Toronto*, 364
Trinity College Dublin (Ire)*, 381
University of Tulsa, 717
Wabash College, 742
Warren Wilson College, 747
Wells College, 766
Wheaton College (IL), 775
Willamette University, 784
Wittenberg University, 795
Xavier University of Louisiana, 805

MODERATE—$$

Albion College, 8
Allegheny College, 13
American University, 20
Baylor University, 58
The Catholic University of America, 128
Centre College, 131
Clark University, 159
Clarkson University, 161
Cornell College, 191
DePauw University, 220
Earlham College, 234
Eckerd College, 236
Emerson College, 241
Eugene Lang College of Liberal Arts, 246
Fairfield University, 251
Gonzaga University, 286
Goucher College, 291
Gustavus Adolphus College, 298
Hampden–Sydney College, 303
Hampshire College, 306
Hartwick College, 308
Harvard University, 311
Hofstra University, 328
Illinois Institute of Technology, 348
Illinois Wesleyan University, 351
Ithaca College, 389
Juniata College, 396
Knox College, 408
Lake Forest College, 413
Lawrence University, 415
Loyola University Maryland, 425

Loyola Marymount University, 427
University of Miami (FL), 454
Ohio Wesleyan University, 532
University of the Pacific, 544
Quinnipiac University, 574
Rhodes College, 591
Rice University, 594
Ripon College, 599
Rochester Institute of Technology, 604
Rose–Hulman Institute of Technology, 608
College of Saint Benedict and Saint John's University, 613
Saint Louis University, 621
Saint Michael's College, 626
St. Olaf College, 628
University of San Diego, 630
University of San Francisco, 633
Seattle University, 640
University of the South (Sewanee), 647
Southwestern University, 657
Stetson University, 678
Susquehanna University, 683
Texas Christian University, 700
Trinity University (TX), 707
Washington and Jefferson College, 752
Washington College, 757
Westmont College, 773
Whittier College, 782
Wofford College, 797

EXPENSIVE—$$$

Babson College, 47
Bard College, 50
Beloit College, 60
Bentley University, 65
Brandeis University, 77
Bryn Mawr College, 86
California Institute of Technology, 115
Carnegie Mellon University, 123
Davidson College, 202
Denison University, 213
University of Denver, 215
Emory University, 244
Fordham University, 263

* These colleges are public institutions, but Americans and other non-Europeans
  should compare them in cost and academic quality to top U.S. privates.

Index by Average Debt

$$$$	More than $33,000
$$$	$28,301–$33,000
$$	$24,000–$28,300
$	Less than $24,000

Debt categories are based on the average amount of principal accumulated by each undergraduate who borrowed during their tenure as a student. Public and private institutions have been rated using the same criteria. Institutions for which data on average borrowing was unavailable have been omitted.

LOW AVERAGE DEBT—$

Amherst College, 22
Antioch College, 25
Barnard College, 53
Beloit College, 60
Boston College, 70
Bowdoin College, 75
Brigham Young University, 80
UC Berkeley, 96
UC Davis, 99
UC Irvine, 101
UC Los Angeles, 103
UC Riverside, 106
UC San Diego, 108
UC Santa Barbara, 111
UC Santa Cruz, 113
California Institute of Technology, 115
Carleton College, 120
Claremont McKenna College, 148
Colorado College, 174
Dartmouth College, 199
Davidson College, 202
Emerson College, 241
University of Florida, 254
Florida State University, 261
University of Georgia, 278
Grinnell College, 293
Guilford College, 296
Hamilton College, 301
Harvard University, 311
Haverford College, 315
University of Hawai'i at Mānoa, 318
University of Illinois at Urbana–
  Champaign, 346
The Johns Hopkins University, 393
Kenyon College, 406
Lehigh University, 418
Manhattanville College, 436

University of Miami (FL), 454
Middlebury College, 464
University of Minnesota Morris, 471
New College of Florida, 486
University of New Mexico, 496
University of North Carolina
  Asheville, 501
University of North Carolina at
  Chapel Hill, 503
Olin College of Engineering, 536
Pitzer College, 152
Pomona College, 154
Presbyterian College, 557
Princeton University, 561
Principia College, 565
Reed College, 582
Rensselaer Polytechnic Institute, 584
Rice University, 594
Santa Clara University, 635
Scripps College, 157
Smith College, 644
Stanford University, 659
SUNY–College at Geneseo, 671
Purchase College, SUNY, 673
SUNY–Stony Brook University, 675
Swarthmore College, 685
University of Texas at Austin, 692
University of Texas at Dallas, 695
University of Utah, 724
Vassar College, 729
University of Washington, 749
Washington University in St. Louis,
  760
Wellesley College, 763
Whitman College, 780
Williams College, 790
Xavier University of Louisiana, 805
Yale University, 807

MODERATE AVERAGE DEBT—$$

Alfred University, 10
University of Arizona, 27
Arizona State University, 30
University of Arkansas, 33
Bard College, 50
Bates College, 55
Bennington College, 63
Birmingham–Southern College, 68
Brown University, 82
Bryn Mawr College, 86
Case Western Reserve, 126
Centre College, 131
Chapman University, 136
University of Chicago, 141
University of Cincinnati, 144
Clarkson University, 161
Colby College, 166
Colgate University, 168
University of Colorado Boulder, 171
Colorado State University, 178
Columbia University, 180
University of Connecticut, 183
The Cooper Union, 188
Cornell University, 193
DePaul University, 217
DePauw University, 220
Dickinson College, 222
Drew University, 225
Duke University, 230
Earlham College, 234
Emory University, 244
Florida Southern College, 259
Franklin & Marshall College, 266
Georgetown University, 275
Georgia Institute of Technology, 281
Harvey Mudd College, 150

The Best Buys of 2024

Following is an alphabetical list of 20 colleges and universities that qualify as Best Buys based on the quality of their academic offerings in relation to the cost of attendance.
(See page xxi for an explanation of how Best Buys were identified.)

Public	Private
Arizona State University	Agnes Scott College
University of Florida	Alfred University
Georgia Institute of Technology	Beloit College
University of Maryland, Baltimore County	Centre College
University of New Mexico	The Cooper Union
University of North Carolina at Chapel Hill	Olin College of Engineering
Purdue University	Rice University
SUNY–Stony Brook University	Vanderbilt University
Truman State University	Warren Wilson College
University of Washington	Xavier University of Louisiana

Introduction

FISKE GUIDE TO COLLEGES—AND HOW TO USE IT

The 2024 edition of the *Fiske Guide to Colleges* is a revised and updated version of a book that has been a bestseller since it first appeared four decades ago and is universally regarded as the definitive college guide of its type. Features of the new edition include:

- Updated write-ups on more than 320 of the country's best and most interesting colleges and universities

- An index that categorizes the colleges according to how much debt, on average, students accumulate during their time at school

- A list of schools that no longer require the SAT or ACT of all applicants

- A "Sizing-Yourself-Up" questionnaire that will help you figure out what kind of school is best for you

- "A Guide for Preprofessionals," which lists colleges and universities strong in nine preprofessional areas

- A list of schools with strong programs for students with learning disabilities

- Designation of the 20 schools that constitute this year's Best Buys

- Statistical summaries that give you the numbers you need, but spare you those that you do not

- Authoritative ratings of each institution by academics, social life, and quality of life

- The unique "If You Apply To" feature, which summarizes vital information about each college's admission policies

- A section on top Canadian, British, and Irish universities that offer first-rate academics and are easily the equivalent of the flagship public institutions and elite privates in the U.S.—but much less expensive

Picking the right college—one that will coincide with your particular needs, goals, interests, talents, and personality—is one of the most important decisions any young person will ever make. It is also a major investment. Tuition and fees alone now run at least $10,000 per year at a typical public university and $38,000 per year at a typical private college, and the overall tab at the most selective and expensive schools tops $80,000 per year. Obviously, a major investment like that should be approached with as much information as possible.

That's where the *Fiske Guide to Colleges* fits in. It is a tool to help you make the most intelligent educational investment you can.

WHAT IS THE FISKE GUIDE TO COLLEGES?

Fiske Guide to Colleges mirrors a process familiar to any college-bound student and his or her family. If you are wondering whether to consider a particular college, it is logical to seek out friends or acquaintances who go there and ask them to tell you about their experiences. We have done exactly that—but on a far broader and more systematic basis than any individual or family could do alone.

In using the *Fiske Guide*, you should keep some special features in mind:

- The guide is **selective**. We have not tried to cover all four-year colleges and universities. Rather, we have chosen more than 320 of the "best and most interesting" of the country's 2,300 institutions—ones that students most want to know about—and written descriptive essays of 1,000 to 2,500 words about each of them.

- Since choosing a college is a matter of making a calculated and informed judgment, this guide is also **subjective**. It makes judgments about the strengths and weaknesses of each institution, and it contains a unique set of ratings of each college or university on the basis of academic strength, social life, and overall quality of life. No institution is a good fit for every student. The underlying assumption of the *Fiske Guide* is that each of the colleges chosen for inclusion is the right place for some students but not a good bet for others. Like finding the right spouse, college admissions is a matching process. You know your own interests and needs; the *Fiske Guide* will tell you something about those needs that each college seems to serve best.

- Finally, the *Fiske Guide* is **systematic**. Each write-up is carefully constructed to cover specific topics— from the academic climate and the makeup of the student body to the social scene—in a systematic order. This means that you can easily take a specific topic, such as the level of academic pressure or the role of fraternities and sororities on campus, and trace it through all of the colleges that interest you.

HOW THE COLLEGES WERE SELECTED

How do you single out the "best and most interesting" of those 2,300 four-year colleges in the United States? Obviously, many fine institutions are not included. Space limitations simply require that some hard decisions be made.

The selection was done with several broad principles in mind, beginning with academic quality. Depending on how you define the term, there are about 200 "selective" colleges and universities in the nation, and by and large these constitute the best institutions academically. All of these are included in the *Fiske Guide*. In addition, an effort was made to achieve geographic diversity and a balance of public and private schools. Special efforts were made to include a good selection of three types of institutions that seem to be enjoying special popularity at present: engineering and technical schools, those with a religious emphasis, and those with an environmental focus.

Finally, in a few cases, we exercised the journalist's prerogative of writing about schools that are simply interesting. The tiny College of the Atlantic, for example, would hardly qualify on the basis of a superior academic program or national significance, but it offers an unusual and fascinating brand of liberal arts within the context of environmental studies for those who seek it. Likewise, Deep Springs College, the only two-year school in the *Fiske Guide*, is a unique institution of intrinsic interest.

HOW THE *FISKE GUIDE* WAS COMPILED

Each college or university selected for inclusion in the *Fiske Guide to Colleges* was sent a questionnaire to be filled out and returned online. This questionnaire covered topics ranging from their perception of the institution's mission to the demographics of the student body. Administrators were also asked to recruit a small cross section of students to complete another electronic questionnaire with questions relating to what it is like to be a student at their particular college or university.

The questions for students, all open-ended and requiring short essays as responses, covered topics ranging from the accessibility of professors and the quality of housing and dining facilities to the type of nightlife and weekend entertainment available in the area. By and large, students responded enthusiastically to the challenge we offered them. The quality of the information in the write-ups is a tribute to their diligence and openness. American college students, we learned, are a candid lot. They are proud of their institutions, but also critical—in the positive sense of the word.

Other sources of information were also employed. Administrators were invited to send us any in-house research or other documents that would contribute to an understanding of the institution, and they were invited to comment on their write-up in the previous edition. Also, staff members have visited many of the colleges, and in some cases, additional information was solicited through published materials, such as the Common Data Set, telephone interviews, and other contacts with students and administrators.

The information from these various questionnaires was then incorporated into write-ups by staff members under the editorial direction of Edward B. Fiske, former education editor of the *New York Times*.

THE FORMAT

Each essay covers certain broad subjects in roughly the same order. They are as follows:

Campus setting	**Housing**
Academics	**Food**
Student body	**Social life**
Financial aid	**Extracurricular activities**

Certain topics are covered in all of the essays. The sections on academics, for example, always discuss the departments (or, in the case of large universities, schools) that are particularly strong or weak, while the sections on housing contain information on the types of accommodations offered (traditional dorms, suite- or apartment-style, single sex, gender neutral, etc.). Other topics, however, such as class size, the need for a car, or the number of volumes in the library, are mentioned only if they constitute a particular strength or weakness at that institution.

We paid particular attention to perennial and emerging issues such as underage drinking on campus, efforts by colleges to deal with growing concerns about mental health and sexual assault on campus, and initiatives aimed at increasing the socioeconomic, racial, and ethnic diversity of the student body. Also, we noted efforts that schools' administrations have been making to change or improve campus social and residential life through such measures as creating learning communities, restricting fraternities, and constructing new recreational facilities.

BEST BUYS

In the face of today's skyrocketing tuition rates, students and families in all economic circumstances are looking for ways to get the best value for their education dollar. To help out, the *Fiske Guide* has an "Index by Price" that groups public and private institutions into four price categories, as well as an "Index by Average Debt" that indicates how much debt students who borrow typically incur by the time they graduate.

We also designate 20 colleges and universities—10 public and 10 private—as this year's Best Buys, institutions where it is possible for students to enjoy a quality academic experience at a relatively low cost. Most of these schools fall into the low/moderate categories for price and average debt, and their academic ratings range from 3 to 5. Many qualify to be Best Buys because of innovative financial aid policies or a commitment to enroll a socioeconomically diverse student body. Look for the Best Buy graphic next to the college name. (An alphabetical list of all 2024 Best Buys appears on page xviii.)

STATISTICS

At the beginning of each write-up are some basic statistics about the college or university—ones that are the most relevant to applicants. These include the address, type of location (urban, small town, rural, etc.), enrollment, and male/female ratio. We report the relative cost of the school, the percentage of students receiving financial aid of any kind (including loans), the percentage of students who procure loans, and the average debt incurred by students. The percentage of incoming freshmen receiving Pell Grants is listed as an indication of the extent of socioeconomic diversity among the student body. Other statistics show the number of students who apply and the percentage of those who are accepted, the percentage of accepted students who enroll, the percentage of freshmen who graduate within six years, and the percentage of freshmen who return for their sophomore year. For convenience, we include the telephone number and email address of the admissions office, as well as the school's website.

Unlike some guides, we have intentionally not published figures on the student/faculty ratio because colleges use wildly different—and often self-serving—methods to calculate the ratio, thus making this particular statistic virtually meaningless.

Within the statistics, you will sometimes encounter the letters "N/A." In most cases, this means that the statistic was not available. In other cases, however, such as schools that do not accept federal financial aid or Pell Grants, it means "not applicable." The write-up should make it clear which meaning is the relevant one.

FISKE GUIDE POLICY REGARDING TEST SCORE RANGES

A special word needs to be said about the reporting of SAT and ACT test score ranges. Previous editions of the *Fiske Guide* regularly listed the range of scores for the middle half of enrolled freshmen—those between the 25th and 75th percentiles—on these tests for each college or university. We did so for two reasons: to help students assess their competitiveness as an applicant to a particular school and to give them a sense of how they might fit into the academic environment of the institution.

Several recent trends have now conspired to call into question the validity of admissions test data—and hence the reliability of using them for either purpose. Rather than publish inaccurate and misleading information, the *Fiske Guide*, beginning with the 2022 edition, has omitted any reporting of score ranges, at least for the foreseeable future. Such scores are, of course, readily available elsewhere on most college websites (search for "Common Data Set") or through the College Navigator feature of the National Center for Education Statistics website (www.nces.ed.gov/collegenavigator).

The most obvious recent challenge to the integrity of SAT and ACT score ranges has been the soaring number of colleges adopting admissions policies that are "test-optional" (meaning that applicants have the choice of whether or not to submit scores) or "test-blind" (meaning that colleges do not look at scores even if applicants submit them). By the spring of 2020, more than 1,000 of the 2,300 bachelor-degree-granting institutions in the U.S. fell into one of these categories, a trend that was accelerated by the COVID-19 pandemic, which caused the widespread closing of testing sites and deprived hundreds of thousands of applicants of an opportunity to take the tests. As a result, hundreds more colleges and universities have waived testing requirements for current applicants and have become effectively test-optional (see the section on SAT and ACT Optional Schools on pages xxxix–xli). How many of these colleges will adopt test-optional policies permanently or restore testing requirements in the long term remains to be seen.

Unless the published score ranges reflect the scores of *all* freshmen, not merely those who were able to take the tests and chose to submit scores, the usefulness of these score ranges for assessing both an applicant's chances of admission and where they would fit into the academic environment of the school is seriously compromised. Incomplete, and thus misleading, scores serve no one's interest. Moreover, since it is likely that many students who choose not to submit test results do so because they have relatively modest scores, the result is to inflate a school's reported score ranges (something that has not gone unnoticed by schools pondering whether to go test-optional). Artificially high score ranges may also discourage students who might otherwise qualify for admission from applying in the first place. (One mitigating factor is that some test-optional colleges do request and report the test scores of all incoming freshmen who took the tests after they have enrolled.)

Students applying to college in the next few years will be rightly concerned about how these trends will affect their chances of admission to a school of their choice. Such students should find comfort in the fact that, since well before the pandemic, selective colleges in general have been placing less and less emphasis on test scores in making admissions decisions. Based on their own experiences, they have concluded that the combination of two other metrics—the level and consistency of applicants' high school grades and the rigor of curriculum they pursued—is by far the most reliable means to assess applicants' abilities. Increasingly, test scores, if they are referenced at all, are viewed primarily as confirmation of these other metrics.

In this context, an effective strategy for college-bound high school students seeking to estimate their admissions prospects at competitive schools would be to focus on the two factors that we know to be keys to their chances of admission: high school grades and whether they took advantage of the most challenging course offerings at their school. The *Fiske Guide* includes exclusive academic ratings for each school (see the section on Academic Ratings on page xxvi) as well as information on admissions selectivity. A school might be "highly selective" (up to 25 percent of applicants accepted) or "selective" (26 to 50 percent). Students seeking to gauge whether they would fit into the academic environment of a particular school can consult the school's write-up for information on academic advising, tutoring and mentoring programs, freshman seminars, and other programs to ease the transition to college in the first year. They can also read what students have to say about the level of competitiveness or supportiveness of fellow students. Retention and graduation rates are other useful clues.

Debate over the future role of SAT and ACT scores in college admissions—and their value for individual applicants—is playing out in the context of some broader social issues, including the extent to which admissions policies of selective colleges inadvertently perpetuate structural racism and economic inequality. On August 24, 2017, the *New York Times* reported that, despite well-publicized efforts to the contrary, the proportion of Black and Hispanic/Latino students at public flagship, Ivy League, and other top colleges is actually *lower* than it was 35 years ago.

Critics cite numerous routine admissions policies at selective private colleges and universities as biased against first-generation students and those from ethnic and racial minority groups. These include preferential admissions for legacies (14 percent of Harvard undergraduates) and for recruited athletes in niche sports such as lacrosse, crew, or golf that are played primarily by students from privileged backgrounds. Other suspect practices include the strategic allocating of merit scholarships to maximize tuition revenue and rapidly increasing pressure on students to apply through early decision, thereby surrendering their ability to negotiate a better financial aid package.

The role that SAT and ACT scores play in college admissions is at the center of these discussions. There was a time when one could make a credible argument that, since the tests, especially the SAT, were not curriculum-oriented, they offered colleges an independent way to identify "diamonds in the rough"—talented applicants, especially those from underrepresented racial or ethnic groups or from disadvantaged backgrounds, whose abilities might otherwise have gone unnoticed. In some cases, this still happens, but the broader argument no longer holds water. The enormous expansion of the $1 billion test-prep industry that has grown up around admissions tests has now tipped the scales back in favor of privileged applicants with access to tutors and other sophisticated test prep and reduced the opportunities for those diamonds to glitter. Indeed, a wide body of research has shown that SAT and ACT scores track closely with socioeconomic data and may say more about a student's zip code than about their academic potential.

This problem has, of course, been exacerbated by the pandemic. Stories abound about well-to-do students flying to other states to take the SAT or ACT in hopes of gaining an edge in the admissions process. In another sign of mounting public pressure on these tests, the College Board, which sponsors the SAT, announced in January 2021 that it was scrapping the optional writing section of the SAT as well as its numerous subject area tests.

The decision to end the reporting of test score ranges in the *Fiske Guide* for the foreseeable future has been informed by all of the issues described above. How this policy might develop over the long term remains to be seen, as the role of tests in the admissions process itself continues to evolve. No one knows what role the SAT and ACT will play in the "new normal" when colleges must make decisions without the benefit of testing for a majority of their applicants.

COLLEGE COSTS

Tuition and fees are constantly increasing at American colleges, but for the most part, the cost of various institutions in relation to one another does not change. Rather than put in specific cost figures that would immediately become out of date, we have classified colleges into four groups ranging from inexpensive ($) to very expensive ($$$$) based on estimated costs of tuition and fees for the 2023–2024 academic year. The results for each college can be found in the "Index by Price" on pages xii–xiv. Separate scales were used for public and private institutions, and the ratings for the public institutions are based on the cost for residents of the state; out-of-staters should expect to pay more. If a public institution has a particularly low or high surcharge for out-of-staters, this is noted in the essay. The categories are defined as follows:

	PUBLIC	PRIVATE
$$$$	More than $15,000	More than $60,000
$$$	$13,001–$15,000	$55,001–$60,000
$$	$10,500–$13,000	$47,000–$55,000
$	Less than $10,500	Less than $47,000

In assessing the relative costs of various colleges and universities, it is important to keep in mind that the posted charges for tuition and fees are, in effect, "sticker prices." Every American who has ever walked into an automobile showroom knows that the price on the car window is not necessarily the amount they will end up paying, but rather the starting point for negotiations over matters such as trade-ins, financing terms, and so forth. The same rule applies to posted tuition and fee levels, especially at private colleges. Your cost at a particular college depends on a variety of factors, including your family's financial situation and how eager the school is for you to enroll. Some wealthy students will pay the full sticker price, but many others—often a substantial majority of others—will receive "discounts" in the form of merit- or need-based scholarships, loans, and other concessions. Likewise, students from disadvantaged backgrounds who manage to gain admission to expensive Ivy League or other elite universities can expect virtual free rides. Bottom line: don't write off a school that you really like simply because the published sticker price looks out of reach. You might end up paying less at an expensive school seeking to lure you with a generous financial aid package than you would at a school with lower tuition and fees but a smaller financial aid budget.

FINANCIAL AID

Since the first edition of the *Fiske Guide to Colleges* appeared, the problems of financing college have become increasingly complex, mainly because of the seemingly relentless rise in the cost of education and some significant trends in financial aid. There has been a gradual shift from need-based to merit-based scholarships that favor middle class students, as well as a tendency for schools to build higher loans and smaller outright grants into their financial aid packages. On the other hand, partly in response to public pressure to increase socioeconomic diversity among their student bodies, a number of both public and private universities have begun to substitute grants for loans and even to eliminate tuition for low- and some middle-income students. Some colleges advertise that they are "need-blind" in their admissions, meaning that they accept or reject applicants without reference to their financial situation, and also guarantee to meet the "demonstrated need" of all students whom they accept. "Demonstrated need" is itself a slippery term. In theory, the figure is determined when students and families fill out a needs-analysis form (e.g., the FAFSA and/or CSS Profile), which leads to an estimate of how much the family can afford to pay, frequently referred to as the "expected family contribution," or EFC. (Effective October 1, 2022, the FAFSA changed the term "expected family contribution" to "student aid index," or SAI.) Demonstrated need is then calculated by subtracting that figure from the cost at a particular institution.

In practice, however, what seems rather straightforward can be misleading. For one thing, colleges may make their own independent calculations about what families can afford to pay. Five different colleges may each give the same student five different numbers for what their demonstrated need is, and the differences can be significant. Some colleges say that they are need-blind in their admissions decisions but do not guarantee to provide the full financial aid required of all those who are accepted. Still others agree to meet the demonstrated need of all students, but they package their offers so that students they really want to enroll receive a higher percentage of their aid in the form of outright grants and a lower proportion in repayable loans. For example, if a school with a $50,000 annual price tag offers a financial aid package that includes $25,000 of grants and scholarships and $25,000 of "self-help" (institutional loans, Federal Direct Loans, a parent loan, or work study), that school can claim that it has met 100 percent of the student's demonstrated need, but at the end of four years, the student will still graduate with $100,000 of debt.

In order to test the sincerity of a school's promise to "meet 100 percent of demonstrated need," students might ask whether it has backed up that claim with other initiatives, such as replacing loans with grants in all financial aid packages (a welcome trend among many elite private colleges in recent years) or reducing or capping the amount of loans that families are expected to assume. Our write-ups often call attention to such initiatives. To get an idea whether the average student at a college graduates with a high amount of debt, check out our statistics on loans and debt (see "Student Loans and Average Debt Rating" on page xxv).

Students and parents should not assume that their family's six-figure annual income automatically disqualifies them from some kind of subsidized financial aid. In cases of doubt, they should fill out a needs-analysis form to determine their eligibility. Whether they qualify or not, they may be eligible for a variety of awards made without regard to financial need.

Inasmuch as need-based awards are universal at the colleges in this guide, the awards generally singled out for special mention in the write-ups in the *Fiske Guide to Colleges* are the merit scholarships. We have not mentioned awards of a purely local nature—restricted to residents of a particular county, for example—but college applicants should search out these awards through their guidance offices and the bulletins of the colleges that are of interest to them. Similarly, we have not duplicated the information on federally guaranteed loan programs that is readily available through both high school and college counseling offices; but we do cite novel and often less expensive variants of the federal loan programs that are offered by individual colleges.

For more information on the ever-changing financial aid scene, we suggest that you consult the companion book to this guide, the *Fiske Guide to Getting into the Right College*.

STUDENT LOANS AND AVERAGE DEBT RATING

In today's academic climate, it is common for students and/or their families to borrow funds to assist with paying tuition and other college expenses. Therefore, a potentially useful piece of information is the proportion of students at each school who find it necessary to procure loans to finance their education. The student loan percentage considers any loan program used by students at any time during their tenure at an institution. Included are institutional, state, Federal Direct, and private loans certified by an institution, excluding parent loans. To ensure the most accurate information, schools submitted this data for students comprising their last graduating class. When available, this data was confirmed using the Common Data Set.

For a variety of reasons, the average debt carried by graduating seniors varies greatly from college to college as well as from student to student. Nevertheless, when considering a particular school, many prospective students will find it useful to know how much debt is typically incurred by students at that school. Thus the 2024 *Fiske Guide* lists the Average Debt Rating (ADR) for each school as reported in each institution's Common Data Set. The ADR is based on the average amount of principal accumulated by each undergraduate who borrowed during their tenure as a student. Using $28,300 as the median, we have organized the schools into four categories from low average debt ($) to very high average debt ($$$$). Both public and private institutions were rated using the same criteria.

DEBT RATING	AVERAGE CUMULATIVE PRINCIPAL PER UNDERGRADUATE BORROWER
$$$$	More than $33,000
$$$	$28,301–$33,000
$$	$24,000–$28,300
$	Less than $24,000

As previously noted at the end of the discussion of college costs on page xxiii, it is important when thinking about the cost of college to keep in mind your particular financial situation. Even if a school has high average debt levels, students who qualify for substantial financial aid packages may end up with little or no debt.

RATINGS

Much of the fierce controversy that greeted the first edition of the *Fiske Guide to Colleges* four decades ago revolved around its unique system of rating colleges in three areas: academics, social life, and quality of life. In each case, the ratings are done on a system of one to five, with three considered normal for colleges included in the *Fiske Guide*. If a college receives a rating higher or lower than three in any category, the reasons should be apparent from the narrative description of that college.

Students and parents should keep in mind that these ratings are by design general in nature and inherently subjective. No complex institution can be described in terms of a single number or other symbol, and different people will have different views of how various institutions should be rated in the three categories. The ratings should not be viewed as either precise or infallible judgments about any given college. On the other hand, the ratings are a helpful tool in using this book. The core of the *Fiske Guide* is the essays on each of the colleges, and the ratings represent a summary—an index, if you will—that flows out of the write-ups. Our hope is that each student, having decided on the kind of configuration that suits their needs, will then thumb through the book looking for other institutions with a similar set of ratings. Please note that these are **ratings**, not **rankings**. Rankings that list schools in numerical order—#1, #2, #18, #52, etc.—have an abundance of methodological and other flaws, but their overarching problem is that they purport to answer the wrong question: "What is the best college?" From the point of view of a college-bound student, the relevant question is: **"What is the best college for me?"** The three categories, defined as follows, are academics, social life, and quality of life.

Academics ✍

This is a judgment about the overall academic climate of the institution, including its standing in the academic world, the quality of the faculty, the level of teaching and research, the academic ability of students, the quality of libraries and other facilities, and the level of academic seriousness among students and faculty members.

Although the same basic criteria have been applied to all institutions, it should be evident that an outstanding small liberal arts college will by definition differ significantly from an outstanding major public university. No one would expect the former to have massive library facilities, but one would look for a high-quality faculty that combines research with a good deal of attention to the individual needs of students. Likewise, public universities, because of their implicit commitment to serving a broad cross section of society, might have a broader range of curriculum offerings but somewhat lower retention and graduation rates than a large private counterpart. Readers may find the ratings most useful when comparing colleges and universities of the same type.

In general, an academics rating of three pens suggests that the institution is a solid one that easily meets the criteria for inclusion in a guide devoted to the "best and most interesting" colleges and universities in the nation. An academics rating of four pens suggests that the institution is above average even by these standards and that it has some particularly distinguishing academic feature, such as especially rich course offerings or an especially serious academic atmosphere. A rating of five pens for academics indicates that the college or university is among the handful of top institutions of its type in the nation by a broad variety of criteria. Those in the private sector will attract academically high-achieving students, and those in the public sector are invariably magnets for the top students in their states. All can be assumed to have outstanding faculties and other academic resources.

In response to the suggestion that the range of colleges within a single category has been too broad, we have introduced some half-steps into the ratings.

Social Life ☎

This is primarily a judgment about the amount of social life that is readily available. A rating of three telephones suggests a typical college social life, while four telephones means that students devote an above-average amount of time to socializing. It can be assumed that a college with a rating of five is something of a party school, which may or may not detract from the academic quality. Colleges with a rating below three have some impediment to a strong social life, such as geographic isolation, a high percentage of commuting students, or a disproportionate number of nerds who never leave the library. Once again, the reason should be evident from the write-up.

Quality of Life ★

This category grew out of the fact that schools with good academic credentials and plenty of social life may not, for one reason or another, be particularly wholesome places to spend four years. The term "quality of life" is one that has gained currency in social science circles, and, in most cases, the rating for a particular college will be similar to the academic and/or social ratings. The reader, though, should be alert to exceptions to this pattern. A liberal arts college, for example, might attract bright students who study hard during the week and party hard on weekends, and thus earn high ratings for both academics and social life. If the academic pressure is cutthroat rather than constructive, though, and the social system is exclusive or elitist, this college might get an apparently anomalous two stars for quality of life. By contrast, a small college with modest academic programs and relatively few organized social opportunities might have developed a strong sense of supportive community, have a beautiful campus, and be located near a wonderful city—and thus be rated four stars for quality of life. As in the other categories, the reason can be found in the essay to which the ratings point.

OVERLAPS

Most colleges and universities operate within fairly defined "niche markets." That is, they compete for students against other institutions with whom they share important characteristics, such as academic quality and mission, size, geographic location, and the overall tone and style of campus life. Not surprisingly, students who apply to

College X also tend to apply to the other institutions—often referred to as "peer institutions"—in its particular niche. For example, "alternative" colleges such as Bard, Bennington, Hampshire, Oberlin, Reed, and Sarah Lawrence share many common applications, as do those with an evangelical flavor, such as Calvin, Gordon, and Wheaton (IL).

As a service to readers, we ask each school to give us the names of the colleges or universities that they consider to be their closest peer institutions and those with which they share the most common applications, and these are listed in the "Overlaps" section at the end of each write-up. We encourage students who know they are interested in a particular school to check out its peer institutions—and perhaps then check out the "overlaps of the overlaps." This method of systematic browsing should yield a list of 15 or 20 schools that, based on the behavior of thousands of past applicants, would constitute a good starting point for your college search.

IF YOU APPLY TO

Another helpful feature is the "If You Apply To" section at the end of each write-up. This is designed for students who become seriously interested in a particular college and want to know more specifics about what it takes to get in. It begins by listing the admissions plans that the school offers: early decision, early action, and/or regular decision. If the college operates on a rolling-admissions basis—making decisions as the applications are received—this is also indicated.

Next, this section describes whether the school requires students to submit SAT or ACT scores. In response to the COVID-19 pandemic, many colleges and universities have temporarily waived their testing requirements. In such cases, the "If You Apply To" section advises students to check the school's website for the most up-to-date information regarding standardized test requirements. Additionally, we indicate whether the school accepts the Common Application and include information on any special instructions or unique components of the application that may be pertinent for students to know about.

For additional details about the application process, including ever-changing application deadlines, students should consult schools' websites, which will always contain the most complete and up-to-date information.

MOVING FORWARD

Students will find the *Fiske Guide* useful at various points in the college selection process—from deciding whether to visit a particular campus to selecting among institutions where they have been accepted. To make it easy to find a particular college, the write-ups are arranged in alphabetical order in the indexes. An "Index by State and Country," the "Index by Price," and the "Index by Average Debt" can be found on pages ix, xii, and xv, respectively.

While few people are likely to start reading at Adelphi and keep going until they reach Yale (though some tell us they do), we encourage you to browse. This country has an enormously rich and varied network of colleges and universities. There are dozens of institutions out there that can meet the needs of any particular student. Too many students approach the college selection process wearing blinders, limiting their sights to local institutions, the pet schools of their parents or guidance counselors, or ones they know only by possibly outdated reputations.

But applicants need not be bound by such limitations. Once you have decided on the type of school you think you want—a small liberal arts college, an engineering school, or whatever—we hope you will thumb through the book looking for similar institutions that might not have caught your eye. As already noted, one way to do this is to look at the overlaps of schools you like and then check out those schools' overlaps. Many students have found this worthwhile, and quite frankly, we view the widening of students' horizons about American higher education as one of the most important purposes of this book. Perhaps the most gratifying remark we hear comes when students tell us, as many have, that they are attending a school that they first heard about while browsing through the *Fiske Guide to Colleges*.

Picking a college is a tricky business. But given the current buyer's market, there is no reason why you should not be able to find the right one *for you*. That's what the *Fiske Guide to Colleges* is designed to help you do. Happy college hunting!

COLLEGE ADMISSION PLEDGES

The college admissions process can be stressful for students and family members alike. For some lighthearted relief, we invite you to check out our fanciful College Admissions Pledges on pages 820–21. Enjoy!

Sizing Yourself Up

The college search is a game of matchmaking. You have interests and needs; the colleges have programs to meet those needs. If all goes according to plan, you'll find the right one and live happily ever after——or at least for four years. It ought to be simple, but today's admissions process resembles a high-stakes obstacle course.

Many colleges are more interested in making a sale than they are in making a match. Under intense competitive pressure, many won't hesitate to sell you a bill of goods if they can get their hands on your tuition dollars. Guidance counselors generally mean well, but they are often under pressure to steer students toward prestigious schools regardless of whether the fit is right. Your friends won't be shy with advice on where to go, but their knowledge is generally limited to a small group of hot colleges that everyone is talking about. National publications rake in millions by playing on the public's fascination with rankings, but a close look at their criteria reveals that they are, for all practical purposes, measures of institutional wealth.

Before you find yourself spinning headlong on this merry-go-round, take a step back. This is your life and your college career. What are you looking for in a college? Think hard and don't answer right away. Before you throw yourself and your life history on the mercy of college admissions officers, you need to take some time to objectively and honestly evaluate your needs, likes and dislikes, strengths and weaknesses. What do you have to offer a college? What can a college do for you? Unlike the high school selection process, which is usually predetermined by your home address, family income, or religious affiliation, picking a college isn't a procedure you can brush off on your parents or guardians. You have to take some initiative. You're the best judge of how well each school fits your personal needs and academic goals.

We encourage you to view the college selection process as the first semester in your higher education. Life's transitions often call for extra energy and focus. The college search is no exception. For the first time, you'll be contemplating a life away from home that can unfold in any direction you choose. Visions of majors and careers will dance in your head as you sample various institutions of higher learning, each with hundreds of millions of dollars in academic resources; it is hard to imagine a better hands-on seminar in research and matchmaking than the college search. The main impact, however, will be measured by what you learn about yourself. Piqued by new worlds of learning and tested by the competition of the admissions process, you'll be pushed as never before to show your accomplishments, clarify your interests, and chart a course for the future. More than one parent has watched in amazement as an erstwhile teenager suddenly emerged as an adult during the course of a college tour. Be ready when your time comes.

DEVELOP YOUR CRITERIA

One strategy is to begin the search with a personal inventory of your own strengths and weaknesses and your "wish list" for a college. This method tends to work well for compulsive list-makers and other highly organized people. What sorts of things are you especially good at? Do you have a list of skills or interests that you would like to explore further? What sort of personality are you looking for in a college? Mainstream? Conservative? Offbeat? What about extracurriculars? If you are really into riding horses, you might include a strong equestrian program in your criteria. The main problem won't be thinking of qualities to look for—you could probably name dozens—but rather figuring out what criteria should play a defining role in your search. Serious students should think carefully about the intellectual climate they are seeking. At some schools, students routinely stay up until 3:00 a.m. discussing the value of deconstructing literary texts or the pros and cons of free trade. These same students would be viewed as geeks or weirdos on less cosmopolitan campuses. Athletes should take a hard look at whether they really want to play college ball and, if so, whether they want to go for an athletic scholarship or play at the less-pressured Division III level, where athletic prowess can give you an edge in getting accepted. Either way, intercollegiate sports require a huge time commitment.

Young women have an opportunity all to themselves—the chance to study at a women's college. The *Fiske Guide* profiles 10 such campuses, a vastly underappreciated resource on today's higher education scene. With small classes and strong encouragement from faculty, students at women's colleges move on to graduate study in significantly higher numbers than their counterparts at co-ed schools, especially in the natural sciences. Males seeking an all-male experience will find four options in the *Fiske Guide*.

Students with a firm career goal will want to look for a course of study that matches their needs. If you want to major in aerospace engineering, your search will be limited to schools that have the program. Outside of specialized areas like this, many applicants overestimate the importance of their anticipated major in choosing a college. If you're interested in a liberal arts field, your expected major should probably have little to do with your college selection. A big purpose of college is to develop interests and set goals. Most students change their intentions regarding a major at least two or three times before graduation, and once out in the working world, they often end up in jobs bearing no relation to their academic specialty. Even those with a firm career goal may not need as much specialization as they think at the undergraduate level. If you want to be a lawyer, don't worry yourself looking for something labeled "prelaw." Follow your interests, get the best liberal arts education available, and then apply to law school.

Naturally, it is never a bad idea to check out the department(s) of any likely major, and occasionally your choice of major will suggest a direction for your search. If you're really into national politics, it may make sense to look at some schools in or near Washington, D.C. If you think you're interested in a relatively specialized field, say, oceanography, then be sure to look for some colleges that are a good match for you and also have programs in oceanography. But for the most part, rumors about top-ranked departments in this or that should be no more than a tie-breaker between schools you like for more important reasons. There are good professors (and bad ones) in any department. You'll have plenty of time to figure out who is who once you've enrolled. Being undecided about your career path as a senior in high school is often a sign of intelligence. Don't feel bad if you have absolutely no idea what you're going to do when you "grow up." One of the reasons you'll be paying megabucks to the college of your choice is the prospect that it will expand your horizons and introduce you to fields that you never knew existed. Instead of worrying about particular departments, try to keep the focus on big-picture items, such as: What's the academic climate? How big are the freshman classes? Do I like it here? Are these my kind of people?

KEEP AN OPEN MIND

The biggest mistake of beginning applicants is hyperchoosiness. At the extreme is the "perfect-school syndrome," which comes in two basic forms.

In one category are the applicants who refuse to consider any school that doesn't have every little thing they want in a college. If you're one who begins the process with a detailed picture of Perfect U in mind, you may want to remember the oft-quoted advice, "Two out of three ain't bad." If a college seems to have most of the qualities you seek, give it a chance. You may come to realize that some things you thought were absolutely essential are really not that crucial after all.

The other strain of perfect-school syndrome is the applicant who gets stuck on a "dream" school at the beginning and then won't look anywhere else. With those 2,300 four-year colleges out there (not counting those in Canada and Great Britain), it is just a bit silly to insist that only one will meet your needs. Having a first choice is OK, but the whole purpose of the search is to consider new options and uncover new possibilities. A student who has only one dream school—especially if it is a highly selective one—could be headed for disappointment.

As you begin the college search, don't expect any quick revelations. The answers will unfold in due time. Our advice? Be patient. Set priorities. Keep an open mind. Reexamine priorities. Again, be patient.

To get the ball rolling, move on to the Sizing-Yourself-Up Survey.

FISKE'S SIZING-YOURSELF-UP SURVEY

With apologies to Socrates, knowing thyself is easier said than done. Most high school students can analyze a differential equation or a Shakespearean play with the greatest of ease, but when it comes to cataloging their own strengths, weaknesses, likes, and dislikes, many draw a blank. But self-knowledge is crucial to the matching process at the heart of a successful college search. The 30-item survey on the next page offers a simple way to get a handle on some crucial issues in college selection—and what sort of college may fit your preferences.

In the space beside each statement, rate your feelings on a scale of 1 to 10, with 10 = Strongly Agree, 1 = Strongly Disagree, and 5 = Not Sure/Don't Have Strong Feelings. (For instance, a rating of 7 would mean that you agree with the statement, but that the issue is a lower priority than those you rated 8, 9, or 10.) After you're done, read on to "Grading Yourself" to find out what it all means.

FISKE'S SIZING-YOURSELF-UP SURVEY

Size

____ 1. I enjoy participating in many activities.

____ 2. I would like to have a prominent place in my community.

____ 3. Individual attention from teachers is important to me.

____ 4. I learn best when I can speak out in class and ask questions.

____ 5. I am undecided about what I will study.

____ 6. I want to earn a Ph.D. in my chosen field of study.

____ 7. I learn best by listening and writing down what I hear.

____ 8. I would like to be in a place where I can be anonymous if I choose.

____ 9. I prefer devoting my time to one or two activities rather than many.

____ 10. I want to attend a college that most people have heard of.

____ 11. I am interested in a career-oriented major.

____ 12. I like to be on my own.

Location

____ 13. I prefer a college in a warm or hot climate.

____ 14. I prefer a college in a cool or cold climate.

____ 15. I want to be near the mountains.

____ 16. I want to be near a lake or ocean.

____ 17. I prefer to attend a college in a particular state or region.

____ 18. I prefer to attend a college near my family.

____ 19. I want city life within walking distance of my campus.

____ 20. I want city life within driving distance of my campus.

____ 21. I want my campus to be surrounded by natural beauty.

Academics and Extracurriculars

____ 22. I like to be surrounded by people who are freethinkers and nonconformists.

____ 23. I like the idea of joining a fraternity or sorority.

____ 24. I like rubbing shoulders with people who are bright and talented.

____ 25. I like being one of the smartest people in my class.

____ 26. I want to go to a prestigious college.

____ 27. I want to go to a college where I can get an excellent education.

____ 28. I want to try for an academic scholarship.

____ 29. I want a diverse college.

____ 30. I want a college where the students are serious about ideas.

Grading Yourself

Picking a college is not an exact science. People who are total opposites can be equally happy at the same college. Nevertheless, particular types tend to do better at some colleges than others. Each item in the survey is designed to test your feelings on an important issue related to college selection. "Sizing Up the Survey" (below) offers commentary on each item.

Taken together, your responses may help you construct a tentative blueprint for your college search. Statements 1–12 deal with the issue of size. Would you be happier at a large university or a small college? Here's the trick: Add the sum of your responses to questions 1–6. Then make a second tally of your responses to 7–12. If the sum of 1–6 is larger, you may want to consider a small college. If 7–12 is greater, then perhaps a big school would be more to your liking. If the totals are roughly equal, you should probably consider colleges of various sizes.

Statements 13–21 deal with location. The key in this section is the intensity of your feeling. If you replied to number 13 with a 10, does that mean you are going to look only at schools in warm climates? Think hard. If you consider only schools within a certain region or state, you'll be eliminating hundreds of possibilities. By examining your most intense responses—the 1s, 2s, 9s, and 10s—you'll be able to create a geographic profile of likely options.

Statements 22–30 deal with big-picture issues related to the character and personality of the college that may be in your future. As before, pay attention to your most intense responses. Read on for a look at the significance of each question.

SIZING UP THE SURVEY

1. **I enjoy participating in many activities.** Students at small colleges tend to have more opportunities to be involved in many activities. Fewer students means less competition for spots.

2. **I would like to have a prominent place in my community.** Student council presidents and other would-be leaders take note: it is easier to be a big fish if you're swimming in a small pond.

3. **Individual attention from teachers is important to me.** Small colleges generally offer more one-on-one with faculty in both the classroom and the laboratory.

4. **I learn best when I can speak out in class and ask questions.** Students who learn from interaction and participation would be well-advised to consider a small college.

5. **I am undecided about what I will study.** Small colleges generally offer more guidance and support to students who are undecided. The exception: students who are considering a preprofessional or highly specialized major.

6. **I want to earn a Ph.D. in my chosen field of study.** A higher percentage of students at selective small colleges earn a Ph.D. than those who attend large institutions of similar quality.

7. **I learn best by listening and writing down what I hear.** Students who prefer lecture courses will find more of them at large institutions.

8. **I would like to be in a place where I can be anonymous if I choose.** At a large university, the supply of new faces is never-ending. Students who have the initiative can always reinvent themselves.

9. **I prefer devoting my time to one or two activities rather than many.** Students who are passionate about one activity—say, writing for the college newspaper—will often find higher quality at a bigger school.

10. **I want to attend a college that most people have heard of.** Big schools have more name recognition because they're bigger and have Division I athletic programs. Even the finest small colleges are relatively anonymous among the general public.

11. **I am interested in a career-oriented major.** More large institutions offer business, engineering, nursing, etc., though some excellent small institutions do so as well (depending on the field).

12. **I like to be on my own.** A higher percentage of students live off campus at large schools, which are more likely to be in urban areas than their smaller counterparts.

13. **I prefer a college in a warm or hot climate.** Keep in mind that the Southeast and the Southwest have far different personalities (not to mention humidity levels).

14. **I prefer a college in a cool or cold climate.** Consider the Midwest, where there are many fine schools that are notably less selective than those in the Northeast.

15. **I want to be near the mountains.** You're probably thinking Colorado or Vermont, but don't zero in too quickly. States from Maine to Georgia and Arkansas to Arizona have easy access to mountains.

16. **I want to be near a lake or ocean.** Oceans are only on the coasts, but keep in mind the Great Lakes, the Finger Lakes, etc. Think about whether you want to be on the water or, say, within a two-hour drive.

17. **I prefer to attend a college in a particular state or region.** Geographical blinders limit options. Even if you think you want a certain area of the country, consider at least one college located elsewhere just to be sure.

18. **I prefer to attend a college near my family.** Unless you're planning to live with your parents or guardians, it may not matter whether your college is a two-hour drive or a two-hour plane ride.

19. **I want city life within walking distance of my campus.** Check out the neighborhood(s) surrounding your campus. Urban campuses—even in the same city—can be wildly different.

20. **I want city life within driving distance of my campus.** Unless you're a hard-core urban dweller, a suburban perch near a city may beat living in the thick of one. Does public transportation or a campus shuttle help students get around?

21. **I want my campus to be surrounded by natural beauty.** A college viewbook will take you only so far. To really know if you'll fall in love with the campus, visiting is a must.

22. **I like to be surrounded by people who are freethinkers and nonconformists.** Plenty of schools cater specifically to students who buck the mainstream. Talk to your counselor or browse the *Fiske Guide to Colleges* to find some.

23. **I like the idea of joining a fraternity or sorority.** Greek life is strongest at mainstream and conservative-leaning schools. Find out if there is a split between Greeks and non-Greeks.

24. **I like rubbing shoulders with people who are bright and talented.** This is perhaps the best reason to aim for a highly selective institution, especially if you're the type who rises to the level of the competition.

25. **I like being one of the smartest people in my class.** If so, maybe you should skip the highly selective rat race. Star students get the best a college has to offer.

26. **I want to go to a prestigious college.** There is nothing wrong with wanting prestige. Think honestly about how badly you want a big-name school and act accordingly.

27. **I want to go to a college where I can get an excellent education.** Throw out the *U.S. News* rankings and think about which colleges will best meet your needs as a student.

28. **I want to try for an academic scholarship.** Students in this category should consider less-selective alternatives. Scholarships are more likely if you rank high in the applicant pool.

29. **I want a diverse college.** All colleges pay lip service to diversity. To get the truth, see the campus for yourself and take a hard look at the student-body statistics in the *Fiske Guide*'s write-ups.

30. **I want a college where students are serious about ideas.** Don't assume that a college necessarily attracts true intellectuals merely because it is highly selective. Some top schools are known for their intellectual climate—and others for their lack of it.

A Guide for Preprofessionals

The lists that follow include colleges and universities with unusual strength in each of nine preprofessional areas: architecture, art/design, business, communications/journalism, engineering, film/television, dance, drama, and music. We also offer lists covering two of today's hottest interdisciplinary majors: environmental studies/science and international studies. In compiling the lists, we drew on data from the thousands of surveys used to compile the *Fiske Guide*. We examined the strongest majors at each college as reported in student and administrative questionnaires, and then weighed these against the selectivity and overall academic quality of each institution. After compiling tentative lists in each subject, we queried our counselors advisory group, listed on page 816, for additional suggestions and feedback. To make the lists as useful as possible, we have included some schools that do not receive full-length write-ups in the *Fiske Guide*. Moreover, while the lists are suggestive, they are by no means all-inclusive, and there are other institutions in the *Fiske Guide* that offer fine programs in these areas. Nevertheless, we hope the lists will be a starting place for students interested in these fields.

If you are planning a career in one of the subjects below, your college search may focus largely on finding the best programs for you in that particular area. But we also recommend that you shop for a school that will give you an adequate dose of liberal arts. For that matter, you might consider a double major (or minor) in a liberal arts field to complement your area of technical expertise. If you allow yourself to get too specialized too soon, you may end up as tomorrow's equivalent of the typewriter repairman. In a rapidly changing job market, nothing is so practical as the ability to read, write, and think.

ARCHITECTURE
Private Universities Strong in Architecture
Case Western Reserve
Carnegie Mellon University
The Catholic University of America
The Cooper Union
Cornell University
Drexel University
Howard University
Illinois Institute of Technology
Massachusetts Institute of Technology
University of Miami (FL)
Northeastern University
University of Notre Dame
Princeton University
Rensselaer Polytechnic Institute
Rice University
University of Southern California
Syracuse University
Tuskegee University
Tulane University
Washington University in St. Louis

Public Universities Strong in Architecture
University of Arizona
Arizona State University
University of Arkansas
Auburn University
UC Berkeley
California Polytechnic State University–San Luis Obispo
Clemson University
Georgia Institute of Technology
University of Illinois at Urbana–Champaign
University of Kansas
Kansas State University
Miami University (OH)
University of Michigan
North Carolina State University
University of Oregon
SUNY–University at Buffalo
University of Tennessee Knoxville
University of Texas at Austin
Virginia Tech
University of Washington

Arts-Oriented Architecture Programs
Barnard College
Bennington College
Hobart and William Smith Colleges
Pratt Institute
Rhode Island School of Design
Yale University

ART/DESIGN
Top Schools of Art and Design
Art Center College of Design
School of the Art Institute of Chicago
California College of the Arts
California Institute of the Arts
The Cooper Union
Kansas City Art Institute
Maryland Institute College of Art
Massachusetts College of Art and Design
Moore College of Art and Design
School of the Museum of Fine Arts (MA)
University of North Carolina School of the Arts
Otis College of Art and Design
Parsons School of Design
Pratt Institute
Rhode Island School of Design
Ringling College of Art and Design
San Francisco Art Institute

Large Universities Strong in Art or Design
Arizona State University
UC Davis
UC Irvine

UC Los Angeles
Carnegie Mellon University
Cornell University
DePaul University
Drexel University
Florida State University
The George Washington University
University of Kansas
University of Michigan
University of New Mexico
New York University
The Ohio State University
University of Oregon
Rochester Institute of Technology
University of Southern California
Southern Methodist University
Syracuse University
Texas Christian University
Washington University in St. Louis
Yale University

Small Colleges and Universities Strong in Art or Design

Alfred University
University of the Arts (PA)
Bard College
Barnard College
Bennington College
Birmingham–Southern College
Carleton College
Centre College
Champlain College
Emerson College
Eugene Lang College of Liberal Arts
Hampshire College
Loyola University New Orleans
University of North Carolina Asheville
Sarah Lawrence College
Scripps College
Skidmore College
Smith College
Southwestern University
Purchase College, SUNY
Vassar College
Westmont College
Wheaton College (MA)
Williams College

BUSINESS
Large Private Universities Strong in Business

American University
Baylor University
Boston College
Boston University
Brigham Young University
Carnegie Mellon University
Case Western Reserve
Chapman University
Cornell University
University of Denver
DePaul University
Drexel University
Elon University
Emory University
Fordham University
The George Washington University
Georgetown University
Gonzaga University
Hofstra University
Howard University
Lehigh University
Loyola Marymount University
Marquette University
Massachusetts Institute of Technology
University of Miami (FL)
New York University
Northeastern University
University of Notre Dame
University of the Pacific
University of Pennsylvania
Pepperdine University
Rensselaer Polytechnic Institute
Saint Louis University
University of San Diego
Santa Clara University
Seattle University
University of Southern California
Southern Methodist University
Syracuse University
Texas Christian University
Villanova University
Wake Forest University
Washington University in St. Louis

Public Universities Strong in Business

University of Arizona
University of Arkansas
UC Berkeley
University of Colorado Boulder
University of Connecticut
University of Florida
Florida State University
University of Georgia
University of Illinois at Urbana–Champaign
Indiana University
University of Iowa
James Madison University
University of Maryland
University of Massachusetts Amherst
Miami University (OH)
University of Michigan
Michigan State University
University of Minnesota
University of New Hampshire
University of North Carolina at Chapel Hill
North Carolina State University
The Ohio State University
University of Oregon
Pennsylvania State University
Purdue University
Queen's University (Can)
University of South Carolina
SUNY–University at Albany
SUNY–Binghamton University
SUNY–University at Buffalo
University of Tennessee Knoxville
University of Texas at Austin
Texas A&M University
University of Utah
University of Virginia
Virginia Tech
University of Washington
William & Mary
University of Wisconsin–Madison

Small Colleges and Universities Strong in Business

Austin College
Babson College
Bentley University
Bucknell University
Butler University
Clarkson University
Cornell College
DePauw University
Fairfield University

Franklin & Marshall College
Furman University
Guilford College
Illinois Wesleyan University
Ithaca College
Lake Forest College
Loyola University Maryland
Millsaps College
Morehouse College
Oglethorpe University
Ohio Wesleyan University
Providence College
University of Redlands
University of Richmond
College of Saint Benedict and
Saint John's University
Skidmore College
Stetson University
Susquehanna University
Trinity University (TX)
Washington and Lee University
Westmont College
Wofford College

COMMUNICATIONS/ JOURNALISM
Private Colleges and Universities Strong in Communications/Journalism
American University
Boston University
DePauw University
Elon University
Emerson College
Fordham University
The George Washington University
Hofstra University
Howard University
Ithaca College
Loyola University New Orleans
New York University
Northeastern University
Northwestern University
University of Pennsylvania
Pepperdine University
Quinnipiac University
University of San Francisco
University of Southern California
Stanford University
Syracuse University

Texas Christian University
Washington and Lee University

Public Universities Strong in Communications/Journalism
University of Alabama
Arizona State University
University of Florida
University of Georgia
University of Illinois at Urbana–Champaign
Indiana University
University of Kansas
University of Maryland
University of Missouri
University of Nebraska–Lincoln
University of North Carolina at Chapel Hill
Ohio University
University of Oregon
University of Texas at Austin
University of Wisconsin–Madison

ENGINEERING
Top Technical Institutes
California Institute of Technology
California Polytechnic State University–San Luis Obispo
Colorado School of Mines
The Cooper Union
Florida Institute of Technology
Georgia Institute of Technology
Illinois Institute of Technology
Massachusetts Institute of Technology
Michigan Technological University
New Mexico Institute of Mining and Technology
Rensselaer Polytechnic Institute
Rochester Institute of Technology
Rose–Hulman Institute of Technology
Stevens Institute of Technology
Worcester Polytechnic Institute

Large Private Universities Strong in Engineering
Boston University
Brigham Young University
Brown University
Carnegie Mellon University
Case Western Reserve

Columbia University
Cornell University
Dartmouth College
University of Denver
Drexel University
Duke University
The George Washington University
Gonzaga University
The Johns Hopkins University
Howard University
Lehigh University
Loyola Marymount University
Northeastern University
Northwestern University
University of Notre Dame
University of the Pacific
University of Pennsylvania
Princeton University
Rice University
University of Rochester
Saint Louis University
Santa Clara University
University of Southern California
Stanford University
Tufts University
Vanderbilt University
Villanova University
Washington University in St. Louis
Yale University

Public Universities Strong in Engineering
University of Arizona
Arizona State University
Auburn University
UC Berkeley
UC Davis
UC Irvine
UC Los Angeles
UC San Diego
UC Santa Barbara
Clemson University
University of Colorado Boulder
University of Connecticut
University of Delaware
University of Florida
University of Illinois at Urbana–Champaign
Iowa State University
University of Kansas
University of Maryland

University of Maryland, Baltimore County
University of Massachusetts Amherst
McGill University (Can)
University of Michigan
University of Minnesota
University of New Hampshire
New Jersey Institute of Technology
North Carolina State University
The Ohio State University
University of Oklahoma
Oregon State University
Pennsylvania State University
University of Pittsburgh
Purdue University
Queen's University (Can)
SUNY–Binghamton University
SUNY–University at Buffalo
SUNY–Stony Brook University
University of Tennessee Knoxville
University of Texas at Austin
University of Texas at Dallas
Texas A&M University
Texas Tech University
University of Toronto (Can)
University of Utah
University of Virginia
Virginia Tech
University of Washington
University of Waterloo
University of Wisconsin–Madison

Small Colleges and Universities Strong in Engineering

Alfred University
Bradley University
Bucknell University
Calvin University
Clarkson University
Harvey Mudd College
Lafayette College
Loyola University Maryland
Olin College of Engineering
Smith College
Swarthmore College
Trinity College (CT)
Trinity University (TX)
University of Tulsa
Tuskegee University
Union College

FILM/TELEVISION
Large Universities Strong in Film/Television

Boston College
UC Los Angeles
Chapman University
DePaul University
Drexel University
Elon University
Florida State University
Fordham University
Hofstra University
Indiana University
The Johns Hopkins University
Loyola Marymount University
University of Michigan
New York University
Northwestern University
Pennsylvania State University
Quinnipiac University
Rochester Institute of Technology
University of Southern California
Syracuse University
University of Texas at Austin

Small Colleges and Universities Strong in Film/Television

Bard College
California Institute of the Arts
Champlain College
Columbia College (CA)
Columbia College (IL)
Emerson College
Hampshire College
Hollins University
Ithaca College
Loyola University New Orleans
Occidental College
Rhode Island School of Design
Sarah Lawrence College
Purchase College, SUNY
Vassar College
Wesleyan University

PERFORMING ARTS—DANCE
Large Universities Strong in Dance

Arizona State University
UC Irvine
UC Los Angeles
Chapman University

Duke University
Florida State University
Fordham University
Indiana University
University of Iowa
New York University
The Ohio State University
University of Oregon
University of Southern California
Southern Methodist University
Texas Christian University
University of Utah

Small Colleges and Universities Strong in Dance

University of the Arts (PA)
Barnard College
Beloit College
Bennington College
Butler University
Connecticut College
Emerson College
Goucher College
Grinnell College
Hollins University
The Juilliard School
University of North Carolina School of the Arts
Oberlin College
St. Olaf College
Sarah Lawrence College
Skidmore College
Smith College
Purchase College, SUNY

PERFORMING ARTS—DRAMA
Large Universities Strong in Drama

Adelphi University
Boston University
Brandeis University
UC Irvine
UC Los Angeles
Carnegie Mellon University
Chapman University
DePaul University
Elon University
Florida State University
Fordham University
University of Iowa
Loyola Marymount University

University of Maryland, Baltimore
County
University of Minnesota
New York University
Northwestern University
University of Southern California
Southern Methodist University
Syracuse University
Texas Christian University
University of Washington
Yale University

Small Colleges and Universities Strong in Drama

Beloit College
Bennington College
Birmingham–Southern College
Columbia College (IL)
Connecticut College
Cornell College
Denison University
Drew University
Emerson College
Eugene Lang College of Liberal Arts
Grinnell College
Hollins University
Illinois Wesleyan University
Ithaca College
The Juilliard School
Kenyon College
Knox College
Muhlenberg College
University of North Carolina School
of the Arts
Oglethorpe University
Otterbein University
Rollins College
Sarah Lawrence College
Skidmore College
Purchase College, SUNY
Vassar College
Wabash College
Wheaton College (IL)
Willamette University

PERFORMING ARTS—MUSIC
Top Music Conservatories

Berklee College of Music
California Institute of the Arts
Cleveland Institute of Music
Curtis Institute of Music

The Juilliard School
Manhattan School of Music
New England Conservatory
University of North Carolina
School of the Arts
Peabody Conservatory
San Francisco Conservatory
of Music

Large Universities Strong in Music

University of Alabama
Arizona State University
Brandeis University
UC Irvine
UC Los Angeles
Carnegie Mellon University
Case Western Reserve
Chapman University
University of Cincinnati
University of Colorado Boulder
University of Denver
Florida State University
Indiana University
University of Iowa
Johns Hopkins University
University of Miami (FL)
University of Michigan
University of Nebraska–Lincoln
New York University
University of North Texas
Northwestern University
University of Oregon
Rice University
University of Rochester
University of Southern California
Southern Methodist University
Texas Tech University
University of Toronto (Can)
Vanderbilt University
Yale University

Small Colleges and Universities Strong in Music

Bard College
Bennington College
Birmingham–Southern College
Carleton College
The Catholic University of America
Denison University
DePauw University

Gettysburg College
Gustavus Adolphus College
Illinois Wesleyan University
Ithaca College
Lawrence University*
Loyola University New Orleans
University of North Carolina
Asheville
Oberlin College*
University of Redlands
College of Saint Benedict and
St. John's University
St. Mary's College of Maryland
St. Olaf College
Sarah Lawrence College
Scripps College
Skidmore College
Smith College
Purchase College, SUNY
Stetson University
Wesleyan University
Westmont College
Wheaton College (IL)
Wittenberg University

* These two schools are unusual because
they combine a world-class conservatory
with a top-notch liberal arts college.

ENVIRONMENTAL STUDIES/ SCIENCE

Allegheny College
American University
College of the Atlantic
Bard College
Bates College
Bowdoin College
Brown University
Bucknell University
UC Davis
UC Santa Barbara
UC Santa Cruz
Carleton College
University of Chicago
Clark University
Clarkson University
Colby College
Colgate University
University of Colorado Boulder
Colorado College
Connecticut College

Cornell University
Dartmouth College
Dickinson College
Eckerd College
The Evergreen State College
Florida Institute of Technology
Juniata College
McGill University (Can)
Middlebury College
University of Minnesota Morris
Mount Holyoke College
University of New Hampshire
University of North Carolina
   Asheville
Oberlin College
University of Oregon
Pitzer College
Prescott College
St. Lawrence University
Santa Clara University
University of the South (Sewanee)
Southwestern University
Stanford University
SUNY College of Environmental
   Science and Forestry
Purchase College, SUNY
Tulane University
University of Vermont
Warren Wilson College
University of Washington

Washington College
Wesleyan University
Whitman College
Williams College

INTERNATIONAL STUDIES
Allegheny College
American University
Boston College
Brandeis University
UC Santa Barbara
Carleton College
University of Chicago
Claremont McKenna College
Clark University
Colby College
Colorado State University
Connecticut College
University of Denver
Dickinson College
Drew University
Earlham College
Eckerd College
University of Edinburgh (UK)
The George Washington University
Georgetown University
University of Georgia
Goucher College
The Johns Hopkins University
Kalamazoo College

Lewis & Clark College
Macalester College
Middlebury College
University of Mississippi
Mount Holyoke College
New York University
University of North Carolina at
   Chapel Hill
Occidental College
University of the Pacific
Pomona College
Princeton University
University of Puget Sound
Rhodes College
University of Richmond
University of St Andrews (UK)
University of South Carolina
Stanford University
University of Toronto (Can)
Trinity College Dublin (Ire)
Tufts University
Tulane University
University of Utah
Vassar College
University of Virginia
William & Mary
The College of Wooster

Learning Disabilities

Accommodation for students with learning disabilities is one of the fastest-growing academic areas in higher education. Colleges and universities recognize that a significant segment of the population may be dealing with issues that qualify as learning disabilities, and the range of support services offered to such students is increasing. Assistance ranges from counseling services to accommodations such as tapes of lectures or extended time on exams.

Following are two lists—the first of major universities, the second of smaller colleges—that offer particularly strong services for LD students. If you qualify for such support, you should be diligent in checking out the services at each college on your list. If possible, pay a visit to the LD support office or have a phone conversation with one of the administrators. Since many such programs depend on the expertise of one or two people, the quality of the services can change abruptly with changes in staff.

Keep in mind also that many colleges are becoming increasingly skeptical of requests for LD services, especially when the initial diagnosis is made on the eve of the college search.

STRONG SUPPORT FOR STUDENTS WITH LEARNING DISABILITIES

Major Universities

American University
University of Arizona
Auburn University
Clark University
University of Colorado Boulder
University of Connecticut
University of Denver
DePaul University
Fairleigh Dickinson University
University of Georgia
Hofstra University
Northeastern University
Purdue University
Rochester Institute of Technology
Syracuse University
University of Vermont

Small Colleges

Bard College
Beacon College
Curry College
Landmark College
Lesley University
Loras College
Lynn University
Manhattanville College
Marist College
Marymount Manhattan College
Mercyhurst College
Mitchell College
Muskingum College
New England College
University of New England
St. Thomas Aquinas College (NY)
West Virginia Wesleyan College
Westminster College (MO)

SAT and ACT Optional Schools

Many years ago a small number of pioneering U.S. colleges and universities, most notably Bates and Bowdoin, decided that they would no longer require all applicants to submit SAT or ACT scores. They reasoned that there is a significant pool of bright students who can do quality academic work but who for one reason or another do not test well. A "test-optional" policy would allow schools to tap into this market.

Over the years the number of "test-optional" or, in some cases, "test-blind" schools has grown dramatically. The National Center for Fair and Open Testing (FairTest), a Cambridge, Massachusetts–based advocacy organization that is critical of standardized testing in general, has tracked this growth; by the fall of 2022, its website (www.fairtest.org) listed more than 1,800 such colleges and universities, many of which adopted this policy either temporarily or permanently in the wake of the COVID-19 pandemic. Reasons for this growing aversion to college admissions tests are many. The early test-optional schools have been happy with the way the policy has worked out. Numerous colleges—backed by a national commission headed by William Fitzsimmons, the dean of admissions and financial aid at Harvard University—have concluded that AP and International Baccalaureate exams, which are closely tied to curriculum, are more useful than SAT and ACT scores. And perhaps most importantly, the whole field of "test prep" has spiraled out of control. Students and parents alike are tired of the anxiety surrounding prep courses and the pressure to bolster the coffers of Kaplan or Princeton Review. Many admissions directors have concluded that SAT and ACT scores are little more than reflections of family wealth.

Until recently there was not much that students could do—especially if they hoped to be able to choose among a range of quality colleges. Over the last few years, however, a critical mass has emerged of quality liberal arts colleges and major state universities, many of which are described in the *Fiske Guide*, that are test-optional or test-flexible in the sense that they offer applicants a range of options for the tests they take. For the first time, students who wish to avoid getting involved in the admissions-test rat race can do so while still enjoying a range of colleges and universities from which to choose.

Accordingly, we now publish in the guide a list of those colleges and universities that are test-optional. We are not recommending that any particular student eschew college admissions tests and apply only to these schools. As a resource designed to help students and parents, we are simply pointing out that applicants now have that option.

In looking over the list below of test-optional colleges and universities described in the *Fiske Guide*, please keep a few things in mind. First, a significant proportion of the schools are large state universities or small liberal arts colleges. You won't find many other types, including the Ivies or flagship publics. Second, keep in mind that there are different ways of being test-optional. Some schools, for example, only exempt students who meet certain GPA or class-rank criteria, while others on the list may require other types of tests or supplemental components, like extra essay questions. At some schools, test-optional policies come with certain conditions, such as disqualifying students who choose not to submit test scores from consideration for merit-based scholarships or honors programs. Third, in response to the COVID-19 pandemic, many colleges and universities have temporarily waived their testing requirements, without committing to any permanent test-optional policies. Such schools are ***not included*** in the list that follows. **Since the test-optional field is changing daily, go to www.fairtest.org for updated information and, above all, confirm current policy with any school to which you are thinking of applying.**

Agnes Scott College
Allegheny College
American University
Antioch College
University of Arizona
Arizona State University
College of the Atlantic
Austin College
Bard College
Bates College
Beloit College
Bennington College
Birmingham–Southern College
Bowdoin College
Brandeis University
Bryn Mawr College
Butler University
UC Berkeley
UC Davis
UC Irvine
UC Los Angeles
UC Riverside
UC San Diego
UC Santa Barbara
UC Santa Cruz
Calvin University
The Catholic University of America
Champlain College
Chapman University
University of Chicago
Clark University
Colby College
University of Colorado Boulder
Colorado College

Colorado School of Mines
Colorado State University
Columbia University
Connecticut College
Cornell College
Davidson College
University of Dayton
Deep Springs College
Denison University
University of Denver
DePaul University
DePauw University
Dickinson College
Drew University
Earlham College
Emerson College
Eugene Lang College of Liberal Arts
The Evergreen State College
Fairfield University
Franklin & Marshall College
Furman University
George Mason University
The George Washington University
Gettysburg College
Gonzaga University
Gordon College
Goucher College
Grinnell College
Guilford College
Gustavus Adolphus College
Hampshire College
Hartwick College
Haverford College
Hendrix College

Hiram College
Hobart and William Smith Colleges
Hofstra University
Hollins University
College of the Holy Cross
Hood College
Hope College
Houghton College
The College of Idaho
University of Illinois at Urbana–Champaign
Illinois Institute of Technology
Illinois Wesleyan University
Indiana University
University of Iowa
Iowa State University
Ithaca College
James Madison University
Juniata College
Kalamazoo College
University of Kansas
Knox College
Lake Forest College
Lawrence University
Lewis & Clark College
Louisiana State University
Loyola University Maryland
Loyola University New Orleans
Macalester College
University of Maine
Manhattanville College
Marquette University
University of Mary Washington
Michigan State University

Millsaps College
Mount Holyoke College
Muhlenberg College
University of Nebraska–Lincoln
University of New Hampshire
University of New Mexico
Ohio University
Ohio Wesleyan University
University of Oregon
Oregon State University
University of the Pacific
Pitzer College
Presbyterian College
Prescott College
Providence College
University of Puget Sound
Quinnipiac University
Randolph College
University of Redlands
Rhode Island School of Design
Ripon College
University of Rochester

Rochester Institute of Technology
Rollins College
College of Saint Benedict and
   Saint John's University
St. John's College
St. Lawrence University
Saint Louis University
St. Mary's College of Maryland
Saint Michael's College
St. Olaf College
University of San Diego
University of San Francisco
Sarah Lawrence College
Scripps College
Seattle University
Skidmore College
Smith College
University of the South (Sewanee)
Southwestern University
SUNY–College at Geneseo
Purchase College, SUNY
Stetson University

Susquehanna University
Trinity College (CT)
Union College
Ursinus College
Wabash College
Wake Forest University
Warren Wilson College
University of Washington
Washington and Jefferson College
Washington College
Wells College
Wesleyan University
Wheaton College (MA)
Whitman College
Whittier College
Willamette University
William & Mary
Wittenberg University
Wofford College
The College of Wooster
Worcester Polytechnic Institute

A Note to the Reader

From its first edition 40 years ago, the *Fiske Guide* has sought, through coherent narrative essays, to capture the distinctive cultures and institutional personalities of the "best and most interesting" colleges in the country. The descriptions then become a tool for students to identify schools that would be a good match for their own interests, values, and learning styles.

The process of identifying and then applying to such schools has always been challenging, and COVID-19 has, if anything, made it more so.

The pandemic has forced changes in colleges' recruiting activities, enrollment projections, and financial aid budgets. On-campus visits and interviews have been curtailed, and prospective students have been left to speculate on the changing importance of familiar factors such as early decision, legacy status, and ability to pay. But there is some good news. In the midst of all this uncertainty, applicants seeking to identify a set of schools that might be a good fit for them would be wise to step back, take a deep breath, and consider the bigger picture.

The most striking feature of American higher education—unique among developed countries—is its astonishing diversity. There are about 2,300 nonprofit, baccalaureate-granting colleges and universities in the U.S., everything from small liberal arts colleges off the beaten path to world-class urban research universities, some public, some private. This potpourri ranges from schools that define themselves as historically Black, single-sex, evangelical, or Roman Catholic to those that focus on engineering, the environment, or a Great Books curriculum.

This diversity has other dimensions as well. Even schools that look similar at first glance are diverse in their own ways. Every college and university has its own unique culture and institutional personality—shaped, among other things, by its academic philosophy, social values, extracurricular resources, and perhaps most important, the narrative of its distinctive history. Think, for example, of the spirit of American ingenuity that informed Stanford's curricular foundations in science and engineering and found expression in the wide-open architectural style of its campus. Then compare it with the philosophical intellectualism that characterizes many of the older Eastern Ivies and continues to resonate in the centuries-old intimacy of a Harvard Yard. And while institutional personalities may gradually evolve, they remain surprisingly consistent over time. When Yale and Vassar went co-ed, each in its own way, the character of their student bodies and academic cultures did not noticeably change. To take an extreme example of such consistency, the fact that the University of Pennsylvania is a leader in service learning can be traced to the lingering influence of its founder, Benjamin Franklin, the ultimate pragmatist, who lived three centuries ago.

One inevitable consequence of the COVID-19 pandemic is that, for some schools, some of the specific information in this edition of the *Fiske Guide*—such as details related to residential and Greek life, study abroad, or intercollegiate athletics—may be out of date or, indeed, subject to future changes as yet unknown. But if history is a guide, the distinctive underlying institutional cultures of these colleges and universities will persist, even during this time of flux, and will eventually reassert themselves. We are confident that the narrative descriptions of colleges and universities in the pages that follow will remain as relevant as ever for high school students seeking to figure out where they fit into the diverse world of American higher education.

Edward B. Fiske
Chapel Hill, NC

Adelphi University

One South Avenue, Garden City, NY 11530

Situated in a comfortable Long Island suburb within shouting distance of Manhattan, Adelphi lets you taste urban life without being overwhelmed. Long established as an innovator in public health and the arts, Adelphi's strengths are professional programs grounded in the liberal arts. Almost all undergrads are New Yorkers, two-thirds are women, and 92 percent get some financial aid. Compare to Fairfield and Quinnipiac.

Think of Adelphi as a Gen Y of higher education. After going through a tumultuous time in the late 1990s, Adelphi began coming of age in 2002 thanks to new leadership and a revamped mission. Enrollment has grown, and nearly 100 new faculty have been hired in the last eight years. Student financial aid has been expanded, and Adelphi has a policy of keeping tuition lower than peer institutions. At the same time, the school has focused on reducing class sizes and creating more hands-on learning experiences. Students say that, as a result, there is a palpable sense of energy among students and faculty.

Founded in 1863 as a prep school in Brooklyn, Adelphi morphed into a coeducational college in 1896 and in 1928 moved to Garden City, where it occupies 75 acres in an attractive residential suburb that boasts a Gothic cathedral and lots of stately homes. The campus is registered as an arboretum. A $34 million renovation of the Harley University Center has added and enhanced dining and study areas, high-tech event spaces, an art gallery, and other amenities.

General education requirements include a 24-credit distribution in several liberal arts areas, as well as courses designed to develop skills in communication, quantitative reasoning, global learning and civic engagement, and information literacy. First-year students take part in a four-credit seminar that introduces them to college-level academics and life at Adelphi. All students are required to complete a capstone course or project. Adelphi's most popular majors have a decidedly preprofessional bent: nursing, psychology, biology, and management. Communication sciences and disorders, exercise science, and social work are traditional strengths. The fine and performing arts are also notable, especially the theater program. New majors include health sciences, international relations, and languages and cultures. Joint bachelor's/graduate degree programs have been established in a number of disciplines, including dentistry, law, physical therapy, engineering, and environmental studies. A B.S./M.B.A. program in the business of science prepares students for executive careers in pharmaceuticals, tech, and other industries.

"It's easy to form relationships with the instructors and network with them for future opportunities."

Adelphi has "a relaxed but still serious environment," says a communications major. "The students are generally working hard, but it never feels too intense." Forty-three percent of classes have fewer than 20 students. Despite an increase in faculty hiring, students complain that it can be hard to find open courses come registration time, and the quality of teaching can be hit or miss. Still, a criminal science major says, "It's easy to form relationships with the instructors and network with them for future opportunities." Adelphi's Learning Resource Program, for students with learning disabilities, is said to be well-staffed and effective, and Bridges

Website: www.adelphi.edu
Location: Suburban
Private
Total Enrollment: 6,233
Undergraduates: 4,939
Male/Female: 30/70
Financial Aid: 92%
Pell Grant: 30%
Expense: Pr $
Student Loans: 64%
Average Debt: $ $ $
Applicants: 16,084
Accepted: 77%
Enrolled: 11%
Grad in 6 Years: 73%
Returning Freshmen: 83%
Academics: ✍ ✍ ✍
Social: ☎ ☎
Q of L: ★ ★ ★
Admissions: (516) 877-3050
Email Address: admissions@adelphi.edu

Strong Programs:
Communication Sciences and Disorders
Exercise Science
Social Work
Theater
Nursing
Psychology
Biology
Management

to Adelphi is an award-winning program offering career development and academic support to students with autism spectrum disorder.

Adelphi has increased its emphasis on experiential learning and student engagement in recent years. The Levermore Global Scholars program, open to students in all majors, takes an interdisciplinary approach to addressing global issues through special seminars, cultural excursions, activities at the UN headquarters in New York City, and opportunities for internships, study abroad, and service projects. Overall, 9 percent of students study abroad, choosing from more than 100 programs. The Jaggar Community Fellows Program places about 60 undergrads in paid summer internships at local nonprofit organizations. Adelphi's Innovation Center research lab provides opportunities for students to collaborate with area businesses and nonprofits on business plans and consulting projects. The Honors College offers a rigorous liberal arts program and living/learning community for exceptional students.

Eighty-six percent of undergraduates hail from New York, while 4 percent arrive from foreign countries. A sophomore describes Adelphi students as "vibrant, outgoing, and dedicated." The student population reflects the university's proximity to the Big Apple: 9 percent are Black, 20 percent are Hispanic/Latino, 12 percent are Asian American, and 3 percent are multiracial. Minority representation is growing among

"Adelphi is very close to the city, so many students choose to go there and adventure."

Adelphi's faculty as well. School-sponsored series like Diversity Dialogue and Common Ground encourage students to share their experiences with diversity and respond to national events, but a sophomore says, "Students tend to keep their political opinions to themselves." Adelphi offers merit scholarships, worth an average of $20,800 each, to qualified students, and athletic scholarships are awarded in 23 sports.

Despite several "comfortable and well-maintained" residence halls, a mere 18 percent of all undergrads (including 31 percent of first-years) live in campus housing. Gender-inclusive options are available, as are two first-year living/learning communities. Many students reside in university-arranged, off-campus apartments in Garden City. Campus dining gets mixed reviews. Students report feeling safe on campus, and a sophomore says, "The school provides us with the resources we need to support one another and not be afraid to talk about sexual assault."

Adelphi has been bolstering on-campus social life with an increase in free weekend and late-night programming aimed at encouraging students to stick around on weekends, and students are active in more than 90 clubs and organizations. Greek life does play a role in the social scene, with 12 fraternities and sororities that attract 8 percent of the men and 16 percent of the women, respectively. Adelphi is a dry campus, and students say that the policy is strictly enforced. In the fall, students look forward to Spirit Weekend, while spring brings Pantherfest and the Spring Concert. One student describes Garden City as "a very safe, low-key residential neighborhood," if not a college town. About half of students get involved in community service. A junior says, "Adelphi is very close to the city, so many students choose to go there and adventure." The Center for Student Involvement offers discounted tickets to movies, Broadway shows, and professional sporting events.

Adelphi fields several competitive Division II teams (the Panthers). Women's lacrosse is a recent national champion, while baseball, softball, men's soccer, and women's basketball have been successful in the Northeast-10 Conference. Among the school's 11 club sports, ultimate Frisbee, soccer, Latin dance, and Bollywood dance are the most popular; half a dozen intramural sports are also available.

At Adelphi, signs of renewal are everywhere, from the campus facilities to the burgeoning enrollment. Although the university's lingering commuter heritage can leave some wanting for more social opportunities, most welcome the chance to play an active role in shaping not just their education, but the community as a

Overlaps

Fordham, Hofstra, Long Island University, Molloy, Pace, Fairfield, Quinnipiac

whole. Says a senior, "I really feel that all of our departments, as well as our students, work together to collaborate on new ideas, classes, events, and opportunities for the campus community."

If You Apply To ›

Adelphi: Early action, rolling admissions. Accepts the Common Application with supplement. Application includes optional question regarding gender identity. Please consult Adelphi's website for the most up-to-date information regarding standardized test requirements.

Agnes Scott College

BEST BUY

141 East College Avenue, Decatur, GA 30030

Combines the tree-lined seclusion of Decatur with the bustle of Atlanta. All-female school with exceptional facilities for a college of its size, Agnes Scott offers small classes, sisterhood, a richly diverse student body, and a more exciting location than some of its cohorts. Big emphasis on leadership and global learning. Socioeconomic diversity a priority.

Agnes Scott College, founded by Presbyterians in 1889, offers a small-town campus atmosphere and provides women with an intellectually challenging institution—absent the distractions of men. The college is known for its science and math programs, but it also produces skilled writers and artists and continues to be one of the South's leading women's schools. Faculty have become increasingly focused in recent years on designing a curriculum that cultivates globally aware women leaders. ASC's climate as a small, single-sex institution leads to close relationships with the faculty and very involved students—both academically and socially. "We believe in the power of women, of deep thinking, of honor, of social justice, of learning for the sake of learning," asserts one senior.

The Agnes Scott campus sits on 100 acres in the historic district of Decatur, just outside of Atlanta. The well-maintained Gothic and Victorian buildings are surrounded by gardens filled with rare shrubs, bushes, and trees—all evidence of thriving alumnae support. The Bullock Science Center includes an X-ray spectrometer, nuclear magnetic resonance imaging equipment, and a scanning tunneling microscope. As part of a campuswide sustainability initiative, the college has renovated two residence halls, Campbell and Rebekah Scott, earning them LEED Gold and Platinum certifications, respectively.

"In every course, there is a cross-curricular approach."

In addition to outstanding instruction in the sciences, Agnes Scott provides students with solid grounding in the liberal arts, leadership, global learning, and professional success through an approach called SUMMIT. As part of SUMMIT, all first-year students participate in a two-day leadership immersion experience following orientation in the fall, and then in the spring semester, during a week known as Peak Week, embark on a faculty-led, global study tour to places like Ghana, Iceland, and Peru. All sophomores are required to take an interdisciplinary SCALE course focused on leadership development, which includes spending Peak Week shadowing leaders of local business and nonprofit organizations, such as AT&T, Decatur Housing Authority, and Zoo Atlanta. Juniors and seniors select an Applied Career Experience during Peak Week to learn about topics and skills like data analysis,

Website: www.agnesscott.edu
Location: Small City
Private
Total Enrollment: 1,023
Undergraduates: 1,008
Male/Female: 0/100
Financial Aid: 100%
Pell Grant: 47%
Expense: Pr $
Student Loans: 63%
Average Debt: N/A
Applicants: 1,625
Accepted: 70%
Enrolled: 27%
Grad in 6 Years: 75%
Returning Freshmen: 84%
Academics: ✍ ✍ ✍
Social: ☎ ☎
Q of L: ★ ★ ★ ★
Admissions: (404) 471-6285
Email Address: admission@ agnesscott.edu

Strong Programs:
Biology
Mathematics
Astrophysics
Neuroscience
English Literature

graphic design, or digital literacy. Each student also assembles her own board of advisors with faculty and staff members, a peer advisor, and a career mentor, and documents her progress throughout her four years with a digital portfolio. A junior praises SUMMIT for connecting students with "a group of people totally committed to making sure you get where you want to be."

Academically, Agnes Scott delivers strong programs in biology, math, astrophysics, neuroscience, English literature, and creative writing. The school also offers a top-notch German program, a rarity these days in U.S. higher education. Popular majors include public health, psychology, biology, and business management. Aspiring engineers may complete their degrees through a 3–2 program with Georgia Tech, while nurses benefit from a dual-degree program with Emory.

The overall academic climate at ASC is rigorous but collaborative, and students are focused on learning first. "We are encouraged to find our own paths instead of competing for the same one," says a public health major. Adds a senior, "In every course, there is a cross-curricular approach. You will, at the end of your four years, be an excellent writer, speaker, and critical thinker." An honor system, enforced by a student judiciary, allows for self-scheduled and unproctored exams. Sixty-three percent of classes have fewer than 20 students, which encourages close student/faculty interactions in the classroom. A sophomore says, "I cannot emphasize enough how invested Agnes Scott professors are in their students."

As part of SUMMIT, all first-year students embark on a weeklong global study tour in the spring.

For those students wishing to leave Agnes Scott's idyllic campus behind for a time, there are study abroad options available at more than 150 universities in more than 50 countries. The Hubert Scholars Program combines experiential learning with humanitarian service either at home or abroad. Past Hubert scholars have mentored refugee girls in the local community and developed gender-equality education programs in Bangladesh. About two-thirds of students participate in research, and many present their results at an annual conference held in the spring.

Agnes Scott students "recognize the value of two very simple things: the value of diversity and the value of women's education," says a sophomore. Sixty-one percent of students are Georgia natives, 2 percent are international, and most of the rest hail from the Southeast. Despite the school's small size, its student body is hugely diverse; 33 percent of ASC denizens are Black, 15 percent are Hispanic/Latina, 6 percent are Asian American, and 7 percent are multiracial. The school has made socioeconomic diversity a priority as well—an impressive 47 percent of current freshmen are eligible for Pell Grants. Ample support is available for students of diverse backgrounds, and the school has implemented initiatives like the Transgender 101 Workshop and Diversity and Racial Justice programs to educate the campus community. A business management major comments, "I am challenged every day to think about the world from perspectives that I could never think about myself." Most Scotties are liberal-leaning, and national issues of equal rights and immigration have attracted attention on campus recently. Under the new Agnes Assurance Scholarship program, all admitted undergraduates receive guaranteed, renewable merit-based scholarships of at least $23,000 per year.

"I cannot emphasize enough how invested Agnes Scott professors are in their students."

All admitted undergraduates receive guaranteed, renewable merit-based scholarships of at least $23,000 per year.

Seventy-seven percent of students live in Agnes Scott's six dorms, which are linked by tree-lined brick walks. "The residence halls are pretty nice. They have walk-in closets, lots of storage, and all but one of them have air-conditioning," says a student. Juniors and seniors can live in Avery Glen, the college-owned apartment complex, while incoming students are assigned to one of two first-year dorms. Students say that dining services staff is friendly and receptive to student feedback, and while the food is usually decent, options can be limited. They report feeling safe on campus, and one student says, "Campus security is very tight. There are always officers around keeping watch."

As for the ASC social scene, there are no sororities, but the college itself is a close-knit sisterhood. During the week, socializing tends to revolve around study groups, student club activities, and events planned by the campus programming board ("ProBo"), but when the weekend comes, social life moves off campus. "Parties at other colleges, nightclubs, bars, and off-campus restaurants are common places to find Agnes Scott students," says a senior. Enforcement of drinking policies falls under the honor code; students of legal age can enjoy alcohol in their dorms and at certain functions. Every October, students celebrate Black Cat week, a tradition since 1915 that marks the end of orientation and recognition of each new class and ends with a formal dance. Other quaint traditions survive, too, such as the ring ceremony where sophomores receive the black onyx class rings that make them part of the ASC "Black Ring Mafia." Seniors who get into grad school or find jobs ascend to the top of the college bell tower, ringing the bell to share the good news.

At the annual ring ceremony, sophomores receive the black onyx class rings that make them part of the ASC "Black Ring Mafia."

Decatur (population 25,000) itself is not really a college town, but there are some attractions for Agnes Scott students. "There are nice little venues and coffee shops; very hip and fun," a student says. Convenient public transportation serves cultural landmarks and provides access to the social scene in nearby Atlanta. Many ASC students get involved with community service both on and off campus, with organizations like the DeKalb Rape Crisis Center, Hands Across Atlanta, and Best Buddies. Popular road trips include Stone Mountain and Six Flags, or New Orleans for Mardi Gras.

"[ASC students recognize] the value of diversity and the value of women's education."

Agnes Scott competes in the Division III USA South Athletic Conference. Scottie tennis has been the most successful of the school's six varsity teams, winning multiple conference championships, and softball and soccer are also competitive. Students stay active with a variety of recreational and intramural activities, such as Zumba, dodgeball, and club lacrosse.

Small but mighty, ASC stands out for the little touches that make students feel they're part of an intimate community, starting with pine-scented brochures sent to accepted applicants. One Scottie Sister reflects, "Agnes Scott builds women who are fearless, who change the world, who question things and inspire others."

Overlaps

Georgia State, Spelman, Kennesaw State, University of Georgia, Mercer, Emory, Mount Holyoke, Smith

If You Apply To ›

Agnes Scott: Early decision, early action I and II, regular decision. SATs or ACTs: optional. Accepts the Common Application. Accepts applications from students who were assigned female at birth as well as students who were assigned male or female at birth but identify as female, transgender, agender, gender fluid, or nonbinary.

University of Alabama

Box 870132, Tuscaloosa, AL 35487

"Roll, tide, roll" still says a lot—but not everything—about Alabama, which is one of the fastest-growing public flagships in the country. Passion for the Crimson Tide is as strong as ever, but also look for strong honors programs, emphasis on undergraduate research, and pockets of professional excellence. Though its football team is among the nation's elite, 'Bama still lacks the academic luster of rivals University of Georgia and University of Florida.

Website: www.ua.edu
Location: City Center
Public
Total Enrollment: 31,845
Undergraduates: 28,074
Male/Female: 44/56
Financial Aid: 41%
Pell Grant: 17%
Expense: Pub $ $
Student Loans: 48%
Average Debt: $ $ $ $
Applicants: 42,421
Accepted: 79%
Enrolled: 23%
Grad in 6 Years: 72%
Returning Freshmen: 89%
Academics: ✍ ✍ ✍
Social: ☎ ☎ ☎
Q of L: ★ ★ ★
Admissions: (205) 348-5666
Email Address: admissions@ua.edu

Strong Programs:
Marketing
Management Information
    Systems
Communication Studies
Journalism
Food and Nutrition
Athletic Training
Metallurgical and Materials
    Engineering
Studio Art

The Honors College serves 7,300 students and houses UA's three university-wide honors programs.

Although the University of Alabama first earned its national reputation on the gridiron, the state's first university (with roots all the way back to 1820) is committed to making an academic name for itself as well. In an effort to attract the South's best and brightest, UA has increased its emphasis on global perspectives, computer-based technologies, freshman learning communities, and undergraduate research and adopted a generous policy of merit scholarships, including for out-of-state students.

'Bama's thousand-acre campus combines pristine brick, classical, revival-style buildings (a few of which survived the Civil War) with modern structures. One of the most stunning in the South, the campus boasts an expansive lawn and majestic trees and wraps around a shaded quadrangle, the home of the main library and "Denny Chimes," a campanile carillon that rings the Westminster Chimes on the quarter hour. Hewson Hall, a $60 million building housing business programs, opened in 2021.

The only course Alabama requires students to take during their first year on campus is a two-term English composition sequence. Before graduation, students must also complete courses in natural sciences, math, humanities, and social sciences, and either two semesters of a foreign language or one of computer science. Optional Freshman Learning Communities allow students to take two or three academic courses together and a one-credit seminar taught by a full professor that ties the other courses together. All students may also enroll in the two-credit Academic Potential Seminar, which covers skills like personal responsibility, time management, and test preparation. Incoming freshmen who are at the low end of UA's admissions spectrum may participate in the Crimson Edge Program, which requires an academic support class and includes specialized academic advising.

"I have always felt that my professors cared about me academically and as a person."

The university is organized into eight undergraduate colleges and schools, which together offer more than 80 undergraduate degree programs. The Culverhouse College of Business offers strong programs in marketing and management information systems. The College of Communication and Information Sciences is one of the country's top communication schools, while respected programs in the College of Human Environmental Sciences include food and nutrition and athletic training. Among STEM fields, metallurgical and materials engineering is noteworthy. The School of Music is a regional standout, drawing guest artists such as Itzhak Perlman and Wynton Marsalis, and the studio art and art history programs are well regarded. New College allows students to work with faculty to design their own interdisciplinary major. The most popular majors include business, engineering, communication studies, journalism, and health-related programs. Full professors occasionally teach freshman courses, and a mechanical engineering major says, "I have always felt that my professors cared about me academically and as a person."

The Honors College serves 7,300 students and houses UA's three university-wide honors programs: computer-based honors, international honors, and university honors. "Honors classes can include a Habitat for Humanity course, Theory and Practice of Mentoring, or the one that takes the cake: the chocolate-tasting class," explains one participant. Honors students also get early registration privileges and the opportunity to write a senior thesis. The University Scholars Program provides gifted undergraduates whose objectives include master's or doctoral degrees an opportunity to begin graduate work during their senior year and become eligible for graduate fellowships and scholarships. More than 2,000 undergraduates conduct research each year, and other offerings include the May interim term, when students spend three weeks focusing on one course in depth. Fourteen percent of students study abroad through more than 40 faculty-led programs, as well as reciprocal exchanges and third-party affiliate options around the world.

Just 43 percent of 'Bama's undergraduates are Alabama residents, and 1 percent are international students representing nearly 60 countries. UA students are "warm and welcoming," says a marketing major. Eleven percent of UA undergrads are Black, 1 percent are Asian American, 5 percent are Hispanic/Latino, and 4 percent are multiracial. The biggest social and political issues on campus include free speech and race relations, and although UA traditionally leans right, a senior points out that "the influx of out-of-state students has brought a lot more political attention and representation to our school." 'Bama awards nearly 275 athletic scholarships in 21 sports and has expanded the number of merit scholarships, which now average $15,800. Consistent with its efforts to attract strong students from outside of Alabama, the school spends over $157 million on merit aid—more than double what it allocates to need-based scholarships and grants.

The annual Auburn–Alabama game, the Iron Bowl, is one of the most intense rivalries in the nation.

Although UA requires freshmen to reside on campus, most Alabama students live in off-campus apartments in the Tuscaloosa area; only 29 percent remain in campus residence halls. "UA has the best dorms around!" cheers a public relations major. "Seventy-five percent of the dorms are suite-style, which means students get their own bedroom." A freshman gives high marks to the living/learning communities for their tight-knit atmosphere. Students report that some campus dining halls are better than others, and one recommends the made-to-order fare at Bryant Dining, adding, "I would gladly eat at Bryant for the rest of my life." A senior notes that sexual assault awareness is "not something that's swept under the rug."

Much of 'Bama's social life revolves around the Greek system and athletic events. Twenty-eight percent of men pledge fraternities and 43 percent of women join sororities, and a sophomore says, "Something is always going on in the mansions we call Greek houses." Partying has remained a staple of the social scene in recent years, despite administrators' efforts to weaken it by prohibiting fraternities and sororities from having parties on campus, but students say alcohol policies are well enforced.

"If you pass someone on the quad and say 'Roll Tide,' you've pretty much made a friend for life."

Those looking for alternatives will find everything from dance crews to Bible study groups among the school's 600-plus student clubs. A modern trolley service connects the 'Bama campus to the city's thriving downtown. Tuscaloosa is described as "an awesome college town," that is "mostly centered around the university." Road trips to New Orleans (for Mardi Gras and Greek weekend formals), Atlanta, Nashville, and the Gulf Coast and Florida beaches are popular, but "many people never leave UA!" says a sophomore.

'Bama football—whose coach, Nick Saban, is the highest-paid public employee in the country—is a perennial Division I powerhouse, having won six national championship titles since 2009. The annual Auburn–Alabama game—the Iron Bowl, one of the most intense rivalries in the nation—is the highlight of the school year. "Any Alabama football game is a festival," a sophomore says. Men's basketball, women's gymnastics, and softball have brought home recent Southeastern Conference titles. 'Bama sports a number of solid nonathletic teams as well, including the Alabama Forensic Council, which consistently places in the top 10 in national competition. Intramural and club sports draw about 12 percent of students.

Although sports are still an integral part of the UA experience, the university's declared emphasis is now on technology, merit scholarships, global perspectives, and undergraduate research. It's an approach that's bringing in more serious, cosmopolitan students. Best of all, says one finance and marketing major, "The students are so friendly, if you pass someone on the quad and say 'Roll Tide,' you've pretty much made a friend for life."

Overlaps

University of Alabama at Birmingham, Auburn, University of Mississippi, University of Georgia, University of Tennessee Knoxville, Florida State, University of Florida

Albion College

Albion, MI 49224

Nestled between evangelical Hope and Calvin and out-there Kalamazoo, Albion is Michigan's middle-of-the-road liberal arts college. Think Gerald Ford, the moderate Republican president who is the namesake of Albion's signature institute for public service. Serious emphasis on hands-on learning. Future doctors, lawyers, and businesspeople are well served.

Website: www.albion.edu
Location: Small Town
Private
Total Enrollment: 1,498
Undergraduates: 1,498
Male/Female: 46/54
Financial Aid: 100%
Pell Grant: 47%
Expense: Pr $ $
Student Loans: 76%
Average Debt: $ $ $ $
Applicants: 6,864
Accepted: 73%
Enrolled: 9%
Grad in 6 Years: 64%
Returning Freshmen: 73%
Academics: ✍ ✍ ✍
Social: ☎ ☎
Q of L: ★ ★ ★
Admissions: (517) 629-0321
Email Address: admission@albion.edu

Strong Programs:
Public Policy
Economics and Management
Psychology
Exercise Science
Biology
Communication Studies
Environmental Studies
Premed

Albion College is a small, private college in Michigan that emphasizes the importance of mixing learning with hands-on experience, particularly when it comes to community engagement and service. Albion helps students achieve their goals through personal attention from professors, internships, and a devoted alumni network, and despite its small-town setting, the college has managed to attract an increasingly diverse student body. In the words of a mathematics major, "The culture of Albion College is centered around inclusion and helping people find out who they are."

Founded in 1835 by the Methodist Church, Albion is located near the banks of the Kalamazoo River, about 90 miles west of Detroit. In addition to its newer Georgian-style architecture, the college has retained and restored several of its 19th-century buildings. The campus is spacious, with statuesque oaks and a beautiful nature center. Robinson Hall, the campus centerpiece, houses myriad departments, including the Shaw Center for Gender Equity. The college's equestrian center is home to one of the largest indoor riding arenas in the United States.

Albion has a rich academic history and was the first private college in Michigan to have a Phi Beta Kappa chapter (1940). Students are required to take core courses distributed among humanities, natural sciences, social sciences, fine arts, and math. They must also satisfy requirements in environmental science and gender and ethnicity studies. Freshmen take a first-year seminar designed to provide a "stimulating learning environment" in a small-class setting; recent offerings include Ancient Aliens and Lost Civilizations, Fly Me to the Moon, and To Sleep or Not to Sleep. The academic climate is described as competitive in certain departments but generally supportive and positive. Sixty percent of classes have fewer than 20 students, and professors are said to be interested in students' academic performance and their emotional well-being. According to a senior, "The professors at Albion put the students first in every situation."

> **"Albion College is centered around inclusion and helping people find out who they are."**

Consistent with Albion's interest in developing civic leaders, the Gerald R. Ford Institute for Leadership in Public Policy and Service takes an innovative approach: students participate in a simulation of city government in which they play the roles of community leaders. Visiting speakers include senators and congresspeople, governors and state legislators, and interest-group representatives. Albion's Wilson Institute for Medicine supports the popular premed program. Three other established centers and institutes, dedicated to business and management, sustainability and the environment, and teacher development, offer courses, specialized academic advising, field trips, speakers, and other immersive opportunities that enhance the learning experience. "Take advantage of the academic institutes on campus!" urges a biology major. Albion's economics and management, psychology, and exercise science majors are well respected, as is the prelaw program. Other popular majors include biology and communication studies. A major in data science and a minor in data analytics are the newest offerings.

Launched in 2021, Albion's School for Public Purpose and Professional Advancement houses the college's various institutes and centers, including the recently created Institute on Race and Belonging. In addition, the school sponsors an "experiential certificate" that combines coursework with hands-on learning opportunities (internships, volunteer work, etc.) and professional training in areas such as project management and human resources. The school also provides real-world learning environments, including a student-run consulting firm and a social innovation incubator. Albion's Foundation for Undergraduate Research, Scholarship, and Creative Activity, which pairs students from all disciplines with faculty mentors, is highly commended by students. One participant, a biochemistry major, says, "My professor walked me through new and old techniques individually, so I feel much more independent in the lab than most." An honors program is available for highly motivated students. For those looking to take their educational experience to more distant shores, Albion offers more than 100 study abroad programs in 30 countries; 8 percent of students go abroad.

An "experiential certificate" combines coursework with hands-on learning opportunities and professional training in areas such as project management.

Albion attracts an ambitious, involved group of students. Michigan residents make up 72 percent of the student population, and just 2 percent hail from abroad. "Since my first semester here, the school has evolved in a big way in terms of diversity," says a junior; currently, 18 percent of students are Black, 12 percent are Hispanic/Latino, 2 percent are Asian American, and 4 percent are multiracial. Politically, the student body is a relatively moderate mix of liberals and conservatives concerned with issues like racial and social injustice. There are a number of merit scholarships available, averaging $34,700, but no athletic scholarships. The Albion College Promise covers full tuition and fees for in-state students from families that make less than $65,000 per year. Forty-seven percent of freshmen are now Pell-eligible.

"Take advantage of the academic institutes on campus!"

Since Albion is a residential college, 95 percent of students call the co-ed residence halls home, and the general consensus is that the accommodations "could use some updating to make them appear more modern and comfortable," reports a senior. The majority of the freshman class inhabits Wesley Hall. During their sophomore year, many students move to the suite-style rooms in Whitehouse Hall or Mitchell Towers; seniors occupy apartment-style housing called The Mae. Meals are served in the centrally located dining hall and are said to be "pretty good" but lacking variety. Students rate campus security staff and counseling services—including efforts to prevent sexual assault—highly.

Forty-seven percent of Albion freshmen are now Pell-eligible.

Thirty-five percent of Albion men and 29 percent of the women belong to one of the school's six national fraternities and six sororities. Greek parties draw large crowds, composed of Greeks and non-Greeks, making them a primary part of many students' social lives. "Campus Safety monitors every party and there is a curfew in place," notes a sophomore. Students 21 and older may consume alcohol in certain campus residence areas. A well-run union board organizes all sorts of activities—films, lectures, plays, comedians, and concerts—to keep students occupied in their spare time. On the weekends, Ann Arbor, East Lansing, and Chicago are frequent road-trip destinations.

Students report that the town of Albion's annual Festival of the Forks is always highly anticipated, and the movie theater is free for students with a valid school ID. "Downtown Albion may be quaint, but it is growing and thriving with support from both the college and the community," comments a psychology major. Newer developments include a brewpub, a bakery, a bookstore/coffeehouse, a community center, and a community theater. Students focus some of their energy by working for groups supported by the Student Volunteer Bureau; in fact, half of the students volunteer in the community on a regular basis, participating in "city clean-up day, Habitat for Humanity, and volunteering at nursing homes and schools." Some traditional events that offer a nice break from academics are the Big Show, which brings a major artist or comedian to campus, and the Day of Woden, which is a picnic held in the spring on the last day of class.

> **"Downtown Albion may be quaint, but it is growing and thriving."**

The Britons football team competes in the Division III Michigan Intercollegiate Athletic Association and has won 38 conference championships—the most in MIAA history. Other strong teams include men's and women's lacrosse and track and field, as well as co-ed equestrian. Men's and women's wrestling and co-ed eSports were recently added to the varsity roster. Hope College is a bitter rival, as is Alma College. Intramural and club sports attract 17 percent of students, and some of the most popular include basketball, sand volleyball, soccer, and canoeing.

At Albion College, professors are accessible and interested, academics are challenging without being overwhelming, and students feel supported and motivated. At the same time, increasing efforts to connect students with real-world learning and service opportunities are garnering more applications from more diverse groups of students. In the words of one senior, "Even though Albion is a small school in a rural town in Michigan, we want to make a big impact on the world and make our school known."

Overlaps

Alma, Hope, Kalamazoo, Adrian, Trine, Lawrence, Ursinus, Washington & Jefferson

If You Apply To ›

Albion: Early action, rolling admissions. Accepts the Common Application with supplement. Please consult Albion's website for the most up-to-date information regarding standardized test requirements.

Alfred University

Alumni Hall, 1 Saxon Drive, Alfred, NY 14802

Talk about an unusual combination: Alfred combines a nationally renowned and state-supported college of ceramics, a school of art and design, an engineering program, and a business school wrapped up in a university of 1,400 undergraduates. The Finger Lakes is a region full of natural beauty, but it takes elbow grease to pry coastal types to the hinterlands of western New York.

Website: www.alfred.edu
Location: Rural
Private
Total Enrollment: 1,588
Undergraduates: 1,421
Male/Female: 48/52

With about 1,400 undergraduate students, Alfred University isn't a bustling academic factory; it's a quiet, cloistered, self-described "educational village" in a tiny town wholly dedicated to the "industry of learning." The university, founded in 1836, boasts highly respected programs in art and design, as well as ceramic engineering. Innovation not only shapes the curriculum but also has a profound effect on campus life. Small classes and friendly competition support this diversity while encouraging individuals to succeed. Along with being able to handle the academic rigors of the college, students also have to weather brutal winters that dump snow by the foot on the region.

Alfred's campus consists of a charming, close-knit group of modern and Georgian brick buildings, accompanied by a stone castle. The Kanakadea Creek runs right through campus, and the town of Alfred (population 4,900) consists of two colleges (the other is Alfred State College) and a main street with one stoplight. (College students make up 85 percent of the town's population.) There are a few shops and restaurants, but certainly no malls, parking lots, or tall buildings. Notable campus facilities include the 36 kilns in Harder Hall and the five telescopes at the Stull Observatory.

The university and its students share a no-nonsense approach to education. Although prospective students apply directly to one of four colleges and declare a tentative major, half of all requirements for a bachelor's degree are earned in the liberal arts college. Requirements are quite different in each school. However, the mix usually includes coursework in oral and written communication, quantitative reasoning, humanities, social and natural sciences, global perspectives, and health and wellness. All new students fulfill the one-credit Common Ground requirement, a series of discussions on diversity and inclusion.

Alfred, though private, is actually the "host" school for the New York State College of Ceramics, which is a unit of the state university system and comes with a modest public university price tag. Ceramic engineering (the development and refinement of ceramic materials) is the academic cornerstone and the program that brings Alfred international recognition. All engineering pro-

"[Students are] creative and like to be challenged."

grams are found within the Inamori School of Engineering, including uncommon majors in materials science and engineering, renewable energy engineering, and glass engineering science. The School of Art and Design's art department, with its programs in ceramics, glass, printmaking, sculpture, video, interactive media, and teacher certification, is also highly regarded. The College of Business gets good reviews from students and provides undergraduates with work experience through a small business institute where students have real clients. Art and design majors are the most popular, followed by mechanical engineering, business administration, and psychology. Newer degrees include a B.A. in computer science and a B.S. in biochemistry. The Track II program enables students to design their own interdisciplinary majors with personal guidance from top faculty members.

"I would say that Alfred is pretty competitive," says a junior. "The studio courses are challenging," adds a sophomore. Whatever their major, all students enjoy small classes, and the quality of teaching is reported as high. Most classes are taught by full professors, with graduate students and teaching assistants helping out only in lab sessions. "Most teachers have high expectations, resulting in greater student performance," says one junior. Alfred's academic advising and career planning services stress the university's commitment to helping undergrads plan their future. Through the APEX (Applied and Experiential Learning) program, juniors and seniors can apply for up to $1,000 in funding to help offset costs associated with pursuing hands-on experiences like internships, apprenticeships, study abroad, and research positions. Faculty-led study abroad programs are offered during the May term and spring break, in addition to hundreds of exchange and affiliate programs, but only 3 percent of students study internationally. Forty-six percent do research, often as senior capstone projects.

Alfred students are "creative and like to be challenged," says a business administration major. Seventy-three percent of the students at Alfred are from New York State, and 6 percent are international. Black students make up 12 percent of the student body, Hispanics/Latinos 9 percent, Asian Americans 2 percent, and multiracial

(continued)

Financial Aid: 98%
Pell Grant: 41%
Expense: Pr $
Student Loans: 77%
Average Debt: $ $
Applicants: 6,243
Accepted: 67%
Enrolled: 9%
Grad in 6 Years: 60%
Returning Freshmen: 70%
Academics: ✍ ✍ ✍
Social: ☎ ☎ ☎
Q of L: ★ ★ ★
Admissions: (607) 871-2115
Email Address: admissions@ alfred.edu

Strong Programs:
Ceramic Engineering
Materials Science and
    Engineering
Renewable Energy Engineering
Glass Engineering Science
Art and Design
Mechanical Engineering
Business Administration
Psychology

Ceramic engineering is the academic cornerstone and the program that brings Alfred international recognition.

students 2 percent. Forty-one percent of freshmen are Pell-eligible, a notable number for a school of Alfred's size. Outstanding students can apply for many merit scholarships, averaging $20,300. There are no athletic scholarships.

Seventy-three percent of students live on campus, and no one seems to mind the three-year residency requirement because the rooms in the co-ed dorms are large and comfortable. Upperclassmen have a choice of single rooms, suites, or apartments. Special-interest housing, such as Modern Language House and Unity House, is another option. The school has two dining halls, and students say the offerings include plenty of selections for vegetarians and vegans. "The dining facilities are very nice and well equipped, and the food is both diverse and edible," says a junior. Campus security is good, according to most students. "AU security will provide rides or walking escorts if you feel unsafe walking alone," a biology major says.

Alfred's location in the Finger Lakes region, almost two hours from Buffalo and an hour and a half from Rochester, is isolated. The other chief complaint is the chilly, snowy weather. Social life is a challenge due to the rural atmosphere and lack of Greek organizations, but the Student Activities Board brings many diversions to campus, including musicians, comedians,

> **"Alfred University will prepare you to go into the real world."**

lecturers, and movies. Alfred is a dry campus, and students say the alcohol policy is largely respected and enforced in the dorms. "Alfred doesn't have too many problems with drinking that I have heard of," a student says. Because the university shares the town with Alfred State College, the dominant student population makes Alfred a good college town and "a very close community," observes a biology major. The downtown scene provides students with an adequate number of movie theaters and eateries, and many students volunteer in the community. Every spring brings the annual Hot Dog Weekend, a big carnival-like event that fills Main Street with game booths, bands, and lots of hot dog stands.

Alfred's Division III Saxons are ominous opponents on the football, soccer, and lacrosse fields, and the softball team is a recent Empire 8 Conference champion. The equestrian team is competitive too. Many Alfred students are skiing, hunting, camping, and rock-climbing enthusiasts, and favorite road trips include Letchworth and Stony Brook state parks, as well as Ithaca, Rochester, Buffalo, and Toronto. Intramurals and club sports draw nearly half of the students, with soccer, basketball, and handball being most popular.

"Alfred University will prepare you to go into the real world," says a freshman. Although small and somewhat secluded, Alfred University is a good choice for those students who want to concentrate on the ABCs of arts, business, and ceramic engineering—just be sure to bundle up for the long, snowy winters.

Every spring brings Hot Dog Weekend, a big carnival-like event that fills Main Street with lots of hot dog stands.

Overlaps

St. John Fisher, Clarkson, Rochester Institute of Technology, SUNY–Buffalo, Stevens Institute of Technology, SUNY–Albany, Alfred State, Ithaca

---

If You Apply To ›

Alfred: Early action, rolling admissions. Accepts the Common Application with supplement. Applicants to School of Art and Design must submit portfolio. Please consult Alfred's website for the most up-to-date information regarding standardized test requirements.

Allegheny College

520 North Main Street, Meadville, PA 16335

An unpretentious cousin to more well-heeled places like Dickinson and Bucknell. Draws heavily from the Buffalo-Cleveland-Pittsburgh area. The college's powerhouse athletic teams feast on Division III competition. Fraternities and sororities give Allegheny a robust traditional college life. If you've ever wondered what lake-effect snow is, you'll find out here.

Allegheny College is a down-to-earth Eastern liberal arts school boasting a rich history of academic excellence in an intimate setting. Administrators here understand the importance of providing students with real-world experience to complement their classroom work, and the school places a special emphasis on the development of oral communication skills. A May term offers time for internships or other off-campus work and study, and a commitment to civic responsibility has spurred several programs. Allegheny's small size means students get plenty of personal attention, and despite the heavy workload, anyone struggling academically will get help before the situation becomes dire.

Allegheny's 80-acre campus is tucked away in Meadville, Pennsylvania, 90 miles north of Pittsburgh. Founded in 1815 to bring New England–style education to what was then the frontier, the school is nestled in the Norman Rockwell–esque rolling hills of northwestern Pennsylvania. The campus is home to traditional architecture and redbrick walkways, as well as newer additions such as apartment-style housing for upperclassmen. A

> **"[Courses] challenge students to think independently and develop complex ideas."**

nationally acclaimed science complex supports already strong programs, and the college also owns a 283-acre research reserve and an 80-acre protected forest. Recent campus projects include the Innovation and Creativity Lab, which houses high-tech fabrication and computer labs, and a total renovation of the school's oldest building, Bentley Hall.

Allegheny operates on two 15-week semesters each year, and each features an Academic Programming Day: classes do not meet and students participate in a variety of college-sponsored programs, including open houses and advising and career counseling workshops. Allegheny's curriculum requires all students to complete at least one minor in addition to their major. Students also take at least one course in each of eight distribution areas: civic learning; human experience; international and intercultural perspectives; modes of expression; power, privilege, and difference; quantitative reasoning; scientific process and knowledge; and social behavior and institutions. Freshmen enroll in two first-year seminars that help them transition to college-level work and develop writing and speaking skills. Sophomores complete a communication-focused seminar, juniors take a seminar in their major field, and seniors pursue an intensive capstone project in their major, where they are required to orally defend a work of independent research.

The school's strongest programs include environmental science and sustainability, economics, physical and biological sciences, computer science, and international studies (which offers a track in Middle Eastern and North African studies). Biology, psychology, environmental science, and economics enroll the most students. Accelerated and dual-degree programs include 3–2, 3–3, and 3–4 options leading to degrees in engineering, public policy and management, psychology, and several health professions, from nursing to pharmacy.

"The courses offered at Allegheny challenge students to think independently and develop complex ideas through integration of the course topics," says a biology

Website: www.allegheny.edu
Location: Small City
Private
Total Enrollment: 1,525
Undergraduates: 1,525
Male/Female: 46/54
Financial Aid: 90%
Pell Grant: 25%
Expense: Pr $ $
Student Loans: 76%
Average Debt: $ $ $ $
Applicants: 4,667
Accepted: 75%
Enrolled: 12%
Grad in 6 Years: 75%
Returning Freshmen: 83%
Academics: ✎ ✎ ✎
Social: ☎ ☎ ☎
Q of L: ★ ★ ★
Admissions: (800) 521-5293
Email Address: admissions@ allegheny.edu

Strong Programs:
Environmental Science and Sustainability
Economics
Physical Sciences
Computer Science
International Studies
Biology
Psychology

major. Students praise the faculty for their passion, knowledge, and accessibility. "All the professors I've had take my success very seriously and understand that my learning is different from other students'," comments an economics major. You won't find a teaching assistant at the lectern in any Allegheny classroom, and 80 percent of courses have fewer than 20 students. The college's honor code allows students to take unproctored exams.

The Maytum Center for Student Success works with students to coordinate internships, study abroad, community service, and undergraduate research, and the school encourages students to have multiple experiences in these areas. "The people working in the [Student Success] offices are helpful and have a great network established," says a junior. Off campus, the college offers sponsored study-away programs in several U.S. cities and 15 countries, as well as semester internships and field-based research opportunities. Twenty-one percent of students partake in some type of international experience. There's also an on-campus independent study option, and a three- or four-week Experiential Learning term in May that allows students to pursue short-term study abroad programs and internships that aren't available during the year. Allegheny boasts an award-winning undergraduate research program, and more than 100 students receive funding each summer to participate in faculty-guided research.

"[Professors] understand that my learning is different from other students'."

Forty-seven percent of Allegheny's students hail from Pennsylvania, and sizable contingents come from Ohio, New York, and California. Four percent of students are international. "I would describe the general student body as curious, hardworking, and tolerant," says a global health studies major. Black students make up 9 percent of the student population, Hispanics/Latinos 9 percent, Asian Americans 4 percent, and multiracial students 4 percent. Politically, a sophomore reports, the school "veers heavily left," and students cite environmental sustainability as a top concern; in 2020, Allegheny became the first college in the state to achieve carbon neutrality. Merit scholarships averaging $32,300 are available, but there are no athletic awards.

Allegheny students live on campus for all four years, a requirement that a senior says "helps build community but also means that people live in a dorm room longer than they may want to." Options include all-freshman dorms, co-ed and single-sex halls, small special-interest houses, and apartment-style housing for juniors and seniors. Students are mostly satisfied with their on-campus food choices and note that the dining staff encourages suggestions. A student organization called Why Not Us? actively promotes sexual assault awareness and advocacy.

According to a senior, "People stay on campus on the weekends to hang out, since we all live here"—and because school policies allow alcohol on campus for those of age. Fraternities and sororities draw 17 percent of the men and 22 percent of the women and provide a great deal of nightlife, but no one describes Allegheny as a party school. The Office of Student Leadership and Involvement offers a campus theater series, free movies in the quad, and comedians, hypnotists, slam poets, and live bands. Homecoming, Wingfest in the fall (featuring free chicken wings), and Springfest (a day full of bands, activities, and food) break up the monotony of studying, and midnight breakfasts help ease end-of-semester stress. When you're crossing the campus's Rustic Bridge at the start of the year, remember to look down—it's a long-standing Allegheny tradition for students to steal the 13th plank.

"People stay on campus on the weekends to hang out, since we all live here."

Downtown Meadville is a 10-minute walk from campus and worlds away from a college town, although a junior points out that "there are some hidden gems, including great restaurants, a movie theater, and a bowling alley." It also has several community playhouses, as well as schools, hospitals, children's homes, animal shelters, and other organizations that benefit from the more than 60,000 hours of service that students contribute each year. "We've really gotten to know the local businesses and take pride in supporting our local community," says an English major. Large-scale philanthropic events like Make a Difference Day and Service Saturdays are particularly popular. When students hit the road, they usually venture to factory outlets in nearby Grove City, Pennsylvania, or toward the bright lights of Pittsburgh, Erie, or Cleveland. Nearby state parks, Conneaut Lake, and Lake Erie offer hiking, waterskiing, and boating in warm weather and cross-country skiing in the winter.

Athletics play a big role in Allegheny life, and the Wise Sport and Fitness Center gives students looking to break a sweat reason to cheer. About a third of Allegheny students compete in Division III athletics, and the Gators field 23 varsity teams, most of which compete in the Presidents' Athletic Conference. Baseball, men's and women's cross-country, and women's track and field, volleyball, and golf are the most competitive teams. Ten percent of students participate in club and intramural sports, with ice hockey, ultimate Frisbee, basketball, and equestrian sports drawing the most interest.

In anticipation of future enrollment declines, Allegheny has embarked on a three-year plan to reduce the size of its faculty and eliminate majors in geology, religious studies, and film and digital storytelling. Nevertheless, the college continues to augment its rich history of academic excellence with a growing emphasis on extracurricular experiences designed to produce well-rounded alumni. The campus's natural beauty and the genuine affection students feel for it and for each other remain unchanged. What's more, students appreciate the value placed on individuality and involvement. "Students are encouraged to explore their unusual combinations of interests, skills, and talents," says one junior. "The word 'no' is not often used here."

It's a long-standing Allegheny tradition for students to steal the 13th plank of the campus's Rustic Bridge.

Overlaps

Gettysburg, Dickinson, Denison, College of Wooster, Kenyon, Bucknell, Washington and Jefferson, Franklin & Marshall

If You Apply To ›

Allegheny: Early decision I and II, early action, regular decision. SATs or ACTs: optional. Accepts the Common Application with supplement.

Alma College

Alma, MI 48801-1599

The college that put the "Alma" back in "alma mater." As friendly a campus as you'll find, Alma savors its Scottish heritage and combines the liberal arts with strengths in health and preprofessional fields. Students are fairly diverse socioeconomically, but few out-of-staters enroll. If central Michigan eventually gives you cabin fever, join the hordes who go abroad. Bring your bagpipes.

A tiny gem on Michigan's lower peninsula, Alma College was founded in 1886 by Presbyterians with an ambitious fourfold mission: "To prepare graduates who think critically, serve generously, lead purposefully, and live responsibly as stewards of the world they bequeath to future generations." Located in the city dubbed "Scotland, USA," the college puts its strong Scottish Presbyterian heritage on display. "Every spring, the city of Alma holds an annual Highland Festival that draws participants from all over the world," explains an environmental health major. "Our marching

Website: www.alma.edu
Location: Small City
Private
Total Enrollment: 1,311
Undergraduates: 1,298
Male/Female: 42/58

(continued)

Financial Aid: 81%

Pell Grant: 26%

Expense: Pr $

Student Loans: 79%

Average Debt: $ $ $ $

Applicants: 2,908

Accepted: 69%

Enrolled: 16%

Grad in 6 Years: 63%

Returning Freshmen: 79%

Academics: ✍ ✍ ✍

Social: ☎ ☎ ☎

Q of L: ★ ★ ★

Admissions: (800) 321-2562

Email Address: admissions@
   alma.edu

Strong Programs:

Integrative Physiology and
   Health Science

Biology

Business Administration

New Media Studies

Political Science

Education

Nursing

Psychology

Students interested in experiences like internships, research fellowships, or study abroad can receive up to $2,500 in Alma Venture funding.

band also wears traditional Scottish kilts to every football game." Alma offers a wide array of choices for its undergraduates, including distinctive programs in health and preprofessional fields, as well as plenty of opportunities to learn abroad.

Alma's campus, located an hour north of the state capital of Lansing, features 27 Prairie-style buildings of red brick and limestone surrounding a scenic central mall. Although Alma was founded 137 years ago, most of the buildings have been built or renovated in recent years. There are lots of trees and open places to sit, at least in the warmer months. A major renovation of the college's library was completed in early 2023.

Alma's recently updated general education requirements include a First-Year Seminar to help ease the transition into college and coursework in writing, math, and a foreign language. During their first two years, students take four Explore courses, one in each of the following categories: making and understanding the arts,

"Your professors double as your advisors, which allows you to build great relationships."

self and society, applying scientific thinking, and engaging in equity and justice. An interdisciplinary seminar is required in the junior or senior year. A peer mentoring program places successful upper-class students in contact with new students to help them adapt to the opportunities and expectations of the Alma community. Students accepted to the four-year Presidential Honors Program complete a two-credit honors seminar for each of their first two years, followed by an honors thesis or research project their junior and senior years.

The college offers nearly 50 majors, of which integrative physiology and health science, biology, business administration, new media studies, and political science are some of the strongest. Alma's most popular majors, by student enrollment, are business administration, integrative physiology and health science, education, nursing, and psychology. A number of health-related preprofessional tracks are available, ranging from dentistry and optometry to physical therapy and sports medicine, in addition to preprofessional programs for engineering and law. Students interested in the Scottish arts find a range of opportunities to work with nationally known instructors of bagpipe and Highland dance.

According to a psychology major, the academic atmosphere is "relaxed, but the workload is busy." Fifty-one percent of classes have fewer than 20 students, and many of them incorporate service-learning opportunities. Undergraduate research is big at Alma, too, with 39 percent of students pursuing an independent project under a professor's guidance or joining faculty projects. "Your professors double as your advisors, which allows you to build great relationships with them," explains a communication major.

Alma's student-centered philosophy is exemplified by the Alma Commitment, which offers a promise that students will graduate on time (within four or four and a half years, depending on the major) and a pledge that each interested student can undertake an experiential learning opportunity, such as an internship, research fellowship, or study abroad. Participating students receive up to $2,500 in Alma Venture funding. Despite Alma's small size and rural surroundings, the terms "provincial" and "insular" just don't apply here. International study is highly encour-

"I've been on five continents in the past four years thanks to [the Posey Global Leadership] program."

aged, and 36 percent of students go abroad. Fittingly, Alma has a study abroad partnership with the University of Aberdeen in Scotland, along with programs in 14 other countries. During the one-month spring term in May, students enroll in a single intensive course; about a third of the courses offered involve off-campus travel, such as studying social change in China, rainforest ecology in Costa Rica, and backpack filmmaking in Italy. Additionally, the Posey Global

Leadership Initiative funds more than 30 fellowships each year for students to participate in international internship, research, and leadership experiences. "I've been on five continents in the past four years thanks to this program, and each time I was able to give back to the community I went to," enthuses an environmental science major.

"Most students are really friendly and willing to help other people out, even if they do not know them well," says a senior. The campus is largely homogeneous, with 89 percent of the student population coming from Michigan and 2 percent from abroad. Black students account for 4 percent, Asian Americans 1 percent, Hispanics/Latinos 5 percent, and multiracial students 4 percent of the student population. Alma is generally not an overly political campus. Brainy types can vie for merit scholarships worth an average of $27,600; there are no athletic scholarships.

Ninety percent of Alma's students reside on campus, and the college has invested $24 million in remodeling and modernizing the residence halls. Freshmen are assigned rooms in co-ed halls, while upperclassmen play the lottery and usually get suites. Other options include an international house, a Model UN house, and college-owned apartments in a historic, converted opera house downtown. For meals, students go to the all-you-can-eat Hamilton Commons or Joe's Place, a snack bar, and most students describe the food as adequate. Students say they feel safe on campus, and a senior comments, "When there is a report filed with the Title IX office, it is handled promptly, discreetly, and respectfully."

When it comes time to socialize, the Alma College Union Board provides plenty of on-campus fun. "We offer music performances, movie nights, speakers, student panels, and tons of events in the dorms," says a senior. Fourteen percent of the men and 19 percent of the women go Greek. Parties at Greek houses are registered and monitored by security officers who scan IDs and distribute wristbands; students say these policies help keep underage drinking in check.

Town/gown relations at Alma are strong, with the vast majority of students volunteering, taking part-time jobs, and otherwise getting involved in the community. When it comes to nightlife, though, one student says the small city of Alma (population 9,000) "does not offer too much to do," other than a movie theater and a few restaurants. The annual Highland Festival features traditional Scottish games, bagpipers, and dancing; for members of the Alma marching band, who strut in kilts

> "The Alma community loves supporting athletics."

stitched from the school's own registered Alma College tartan, every performance might as well be a festival. Students with wheels will find diversions within easy reach, as Mount Pleasant, Saginaw, and the East Lansing campus of Michigan State are less than an hour away, and ski slopes are just a bit farther. In the warmer months, the beaches of two Great Lakes, Huron and Michigan, are two hours away.

The Alma Scots compete in Division III as a member of the Michigan Intercollegiate Athletic Association. Alma offers 26 varsity sports—including an eSports program—and some of the strongest include wrestling, men's lacrosse, and women's volleyball. "The Alma community loves supporting athletics, and you can always expect a large student section at home events," cheers a sophomore. For non-varsity types, there is an active intramural program—about 30 percent of the students participate. Alma's Model United Nations team has received top recognition at the National Model UN Conference in New York City for a record 26 consecutive years (1997 through 2022), the longest streak of any college or university.

Alma challenges students to take their learning beyond the classroom and around the globe, and with caring faculty—and ample funding for off-campus experiences—students feel supported every step of the way. While students enjoy their school's warm, inviting atmosphere, they're also eager to venture out, explore, and pursue their goals. But no matter where their futures take them, for Alma alumni, bagpipes will always sound like home.

Members of the Alma marching band strut in kilts stitched from the school's own registered Alma College tartan.

Overlaps
Albion, Adrian, Trine, Olivet, Hope, Kalamazoo, Augustana (IL), College of Wooster

Alverno College

3400 South 43rd Street, P.O. Box 343922, Milwaukee, WI 53234

At last, a college that evaluates students on what they can do rather than how well they can memorize. Forget oval-blackening; students here show mastery in their chosen fields. Practical and hands-on, Alverno gives its all-female and economically diverse students the real-life experience necessary to succeed beyond graduation.

Website: www.alverno.edu
Location: City Outskirts
Private
Total Enrollment: 1,322
Undergraduates: 692
Male/Female: 0/100
Financial Aid: 99%
Pell Grant: 63%
Expense: Pr $
Student Loans: 82%
Average Debt: $ $ $ $
Applicants: 666
Accepted: 91%
Enrolled: 19%
Grad in 6 Years: 48%
Returning Freshmen: 69%
Academics: ✍ ✍ ✍
Social: ☎
Q of L: ★ ★ ★ ★
Admissions: (414) 382-6100
Email Address: admissions@
  alverno.edu

Strong Programs:
Nursing
Education
Business
Communication
Social Work
Music Therapy
Psychology
Biology

If you're the type of student who obsesses over your GPA, take heed: at Alverno College, you can forget about earning an A. That's because this Roman Catholic, women's liberal arts college emphasizes ability-based learning instead of letter grades. While its roots go back to 1887, Alverno came into its own in the 1970s with its distinctive approach to learning and, unlike other educational innovations of that era, has found a continuing niche. The student body is diverse—in age, background, and religion—and while the ability-based method centers on individual growth, the learning environment is highly collaborative. "Alverno is empowering," says a music therapy major, because it's all about "finding each student's gifts and celebrating them."

Alverno is located in a quiet residential area of Milwaukee. The parklike 46-acre campus is just 15 minutes from downtown and a 10-minute walk from shops and restaurants. The Sister Joel Read Center houses 73,000 square feet of science labs, multimedia production space, and computer facilities. Alexia Hall features a high-tech nursing simulation center, art and dance studios, classrooms, private study rooms, and a student commons area.

Alverno students are required to show mastery in eight key abilities: communication, analysis, problem-solving, valuing in decision-making, social interaction, developing a global perspective, effective citizenship, and aesthetic engagement.

"The level of professionalism that Alverno students have…is amazing."

Students move through interdisciplinary progressive levels toward a degree by being "validated" in these areas. For example, a course in sociology might contribute to validation in communication and social interaction, as well as in making independent value judgments. The college offers detailed feedback rather than traditional letter grades, and faculty find innovative, "real-life" ways to assess students' mastery of subject matter and specific abilities. First-year students take a First-Semester Seminar and introductory courses in the arts and humanities, science, psychology and social science, communication, and math. Religious studies aren't required, but for those who seek it, a Catholic liturgy is available. Students are also required to participate in off-campus, credit-bearing internships through Alverno's highly acclaimed internship program—one of the longest-standing programs of its type in the country.

"The level of professionalism that Alverno students have compared to those at other colleges or universities is amazing," one junior says. Alverno's nursing, education, and business programs are well established and among the most popular majors, along with psychology and biology. Students praise the communication, social work, and music therapy programs as well. Many professors at Alverno teach all levels of classes, so the quality of teaching is consistent throughout a student's college career, and regular academic advising keeps students on track. With 95 percent of classes enrolling fewer than 20 students and a low student/faculty ratio, students have easy access to faculty. "The faculty and staff really care whether you are successful," says a student. "They want to see you achieve and are willing to go [above] and beyond to make sure you do." Alverno also boasts a dedicated Career Studio that provides career planning and job search assistance to students and alumnae, including frequent networking and on-campus recruiting events with employers. "We couldn't have more help," one junior says. Fifteen percent of Alverno students study abroad, often heading out on short, 10- to 14-day trips that complement a semester-long course. Twenty-five percent of students undertake faculty-guided research projects.

"Students are extraordinarily driven, and they know what it takes to succeed in the real world," says a junior. Ninety-two percent of Alverno undergraduates hail from Wisconsin, and a quarter are above the age of 24; there are few international students. Alverno is one of the most inclusive and diverse colleges in the state, particularly socioeconomically: 63 percent of freshmen are eligible for Pell Grants. Black students account for 16 percent of the

"My school is the most uplifting place that I've ever encountered."

student body, Hispanics/Latinas 36 percent, Asian Americans 6 percent, and multi-racial students 4 percent. Thirty-two percent of students are Catholic. According to a sophomore, the political climate is "fairly liberal, especially in relation to immigration, prison reform, and women's and LGBTQ rights." Merit scholarships are awarded based on a personal evaluation of each incoming student.

A two-day orientation program serves freshmen, transfer, resident, and commuter students. The majority of students are commuters, though dorm rooms house 14 percent of students, who say the residence halls offer clean, spacious rooms with fully equipped lounges, laundry, and cooking facilities available on each floor. Male visitors are allowed, but they must sign in and be out by midnight on weekdays. Dining services draw complaints for offering limited options (especially for those with dietary restrictions), inconvenient hours, and overpriced meals. Events like Love Your Body Week and Denim Day promote student wellness and prevention of sexual violence.

Dozens of cultural, dance, theater, and other student groups are active on campus, and the school has an on-site childcare center and a fitness center. But most of the social life takes place off campus at local clubs, bars, restaurants, coffee shops, and nearby colleges. "Milwaukee is a thriving city of the arts—visual, theatrical, and performance—not to mention the festivals that go on every year," says one art education major. In addition to a Performing Arts Center, free outdoor concerts, and multicultural festivals, the city also offers professional sports teams, parks, and shopping centers. Students look forward to Alverno's annual homecoming festivities and Community Day, which allows students and faculty to participate in an annual day of service. "Many of our programs are family friendly and inviting for students with children to attend," explains a sophomore.

Alverno competes in Division III athletics, including basketball, cross-country, golf, soccer, softball, tennis, and volleyball. The Inferno tennis and basketball teams have been the most successful programs, having recently set school records for wins. An informal intramural program occasionally offers activities like kickball and board-game tournaments. One-credit wellness courses on skills ranging from yoga and meditation to self-defense and crochet are offered every semester.

Attending a school like Alverno promises an experience far afield in some ways from the traditional college world. The emphasis on real-world applications builds

Overlaps

UW–Milwaukee, Mount Mary University, Carroll University, Cardinal Stritch

confidence in one's actual ability to perform, rather than the ability to score an A. Diverse students and faculty are often on a first-name basis from the start and build relationships that help students cultivate their personal strengths. The result? In the words of one biology major, "My school is the most uplifting place that I've ever encountered."

If You Apply To ›

Alverno: Rolling admissions. Does not accept the Common Application. Admits students who consistently live and identify as women, regardless of biological sex, and female students who identify as nonbinary or gender nonconforming. Please consult Alverno's website for the most up-to-date information regarding standardized test requirements.

American University

4400 Massachusetts Avenue NW, Washington, D.C. 20016-8001

If the odds are stacked against you at Georgetown and you can't see yourself on GW's ultra-urban campus, welcome to American University. The allure of AU is simple: Washington, D.C. American has a nice campus in a nice neighborhood with easy access to the Metro and endless internship opportunities. American is smaller and less selective than GW.

Website: www.american.edu
Location: City Outskirts
Private
Total Enrollment: 10,968
Undergraduates: 7,882
Male/Female: 36/64
Financial Aid: 68%
Pell Grant: 11%
Expense: Pr $ $
Student Loans: 62%
Average Debt: $ $ $ $
Applicants: 19,650
Accepted: 64%
Enrolled: 19%
Grad in 6 Years: 79%
Returning Freshmen: 91%
Academics: ✍ ✍ ✍ ½
Social: ☎ ☎ ☎
Q of L: ★ ★ ★
Admissions: (202) 885-6000
Email Address: admissions@american.edu

Strong Programs:
Political Science
International Studies
Business Administration

Located just a few miles from our country's seat of power, American University has been a breeding ground for the next generation of reporters, diplomats, lobbyists, political leaders, and policy makers since it opened its doors in 1914. Alongside these eager buzzhounds is a host of students who take advantage of AU's strong programs in the arts, sciences, and business, and who recognize that Boston and New York City are not the only tempting urban destinations for college students. "American University is a diverse, pulsing, and dynamic school driven by some of the best faculty, staff, scholars, and students in the world," a senior says. Thanks to phenomenal internships, a comfortable location, and a strong international focus, AU continues to attract students from around the world.

AU's 84-acre residential campus is located in the northwest corner of Washington, D.C., in an upscale (and safe) area that's just minutes from downtown; free shuttle buses transport students to the nearby Metro (subway) station. There's a mix of classical and modern architecture. Flower gardens line the parking lots, and the quad has numerous sitting areas for reflection and study. The 70,000-square-foot, environmentally friendly School of International Service building is LEED Gold–certified. In 2018 AU became the first university in the United States to achieve carbon neutrality. AU has been boosting research efforts in the sciences and recently opened the 125,000-square-foot Hall of Science, housing four life sciences departments.

"AU is more of an academic community, rather than a pressure cooker."

AU's core curriculum aims to develop students into "effective citizens" and lifelong learners. First-years begin by taking Complex Problems, a small-group seminar focused on analyzing a special topic, and a yearlong AU Experience sequence that acclimates them to university life. In addition to coursework in writing, math or statistics, and diversity, students fulfill Habits of Mind requirements that cover five areas, ranging from ethical reasoning to creativity and aesthetics. Finally, all students complete a capstone course or project in their major. The core still leaves plenty of time for students to study abroad—choosing from more than 100 programs in roughly 40 nations—or participate in an internship or co-op facilitated by the school's relationships with hundreds of private, nonprofit, and government institutions. The school also uses these connections in its Washington Semester, which is open to students at other colleges; the program combines academic seminars with internships and career guidance, attracting a wide range of majors. Fifty-two percent of AU students study abroad and 89 percent complete internships.

(continued)

Communication Studies
Journalism
Public Relations
Environmental Science
Politics, Policy, and Law

In the classroom, says a public health major, the atmosphere is supportive: "AU is more of an academic community, rather than a pressure cooker." AU has outstanding programs in political science, international studies, business, communication studies, journalism, public relations, and environmental science. A popular interdisciplinary major in communication, legal institutions, economics, and government combines many of AU's traditional strengths, and students also have the option to design their own interdisciplinary major. In all, students may choose from more than 70 programs. Three-year bachelor's degree programs are available in international studies; public health; and politics, policy, and law. Fifty-eight percent of all classes taken by undergraduates have fewer than 20 students, and teaching assistants do not teach classes. "Almost every professor I've interacted with has previous experience in the field," notes a communication studies and computer science major. A four-year honors program offers a select group of about 25 entering students small seminars, special sections of many courses, and designated floors in the residence halls, plus specialized research or creative work in their major.

The Washington Semester program combines academic seminars with internships and career guidance, attracting a wide range of majors.

"Students at AU are smart, compassionate, politically aware, and driven to make the world a better place," a senior says. AU prides itself on drawing students from every state and more than 120 foreign countries; just 14 percent of undergrads come from the D.C. metro region, and 10 percent hail from outside the U.S. "AU is a very international campus," observes one senior. Eight percent of undergraduates are Black, 12 percent are Hispanic/Latino, 7 percent are Asian American, and 5 percent are

"AU is a very international campus."

multiracial. A relatively high proportion—nearly two-thirds—are women. Not surprisingly, AU is politically active—remember, this is Washington, D.C. "If you aren't into politics in the slightest, it can be a bit frustrating to navigate the school socially," cautions a senior. The university offers hundreds of merit scholarships, averaging $13,500, and athletic scholarships.

More than two-thirds of AU students live in campus housing, which is guaranteed for the first two years. AU offers traditional, suite-style, and apartment-style options; students report that the quality varies. Living/learning options are available for first-years and come highly recommended, including the two-year Community-Based Research Scholars program, which involves opportunities for service-oriented research. Campus dining receives mixed reviews. A junior says, "AU is an open campus and feels very safe," and educational programming on personal wellness and preventing sexual assault is extensive.

Founder's Week features the Founder's Day Ball, a formal dance held at a museum or other location in downtown D.C.

On-campus social life can be limited, students report, and tends to revolve around club activities and functions organized by the student government. Nine percent of the men and 11 percent of the women go Greek, and a psychology major says, "Greek organizations are the only source of parties." The AU campus is officially dry, and with no on-campus Greek housing, parties take place off campus. The immediate area around AU has restaurants and shops, but you need to get a bit farther away for true nightlife over in Dupont Circle or Georgetown. D.C. offers ample entertainment, much of it free—the art house movie theaters, gallery openings, pro soccer games, museums and monuments, and funky live music. "You just jump on the Metro to get anywhere in the city," says a communication studies major. Each year, Family Weekend brings games, rides, and popular bands to campus, along with a carnival on the quad. Another annual favorite is Founder's Week, featuring late-night drag queen bingo and the Founder's Day Ball, a formal dance held at a museum or other location in downtown D.C. Popular road trips include Baltimore, Williamsburg, Richmond, and the Ocean City shore.

The American University Eagles compete in the Division I Patriot League. Without a football team, students are most enthusiastic about men's basketball, which has been among the most successful teams, along with men's soccer, women's volleyball, and field hockey. Games against Bucknell, Holy Cross, and the Naval Academy highlight the schedule. Students also take part in 22 intramural and 24 club sports, ranging from beach volleyball and badminton to sailing and eSports, which are divided into different levels of competitiveness.

AU is heaven on earth for C-SPAN junkies. But even if you are not addicted to following cable news 24/7, AU and Washington, D.C., are still a top combo for a rich college life. The opportunities for real-world experience—in fields ranging from business to international studies to political science—are outstanding. But AU is small enough to keep students from feeling lost in the fast-paced world inside the Beltway. As a junior explains, "We are a small campus, which gives the feeling of being out of the city, yet the city is at our fingertips."

If You Apply To ›

American: Early decision I and II, regular decision. SATs or ACTs: optional. Accepts the Common Application with supplement.

Amherst College

Amherst, MA 01002

Original home to the well-rounded, superachieving, gentle-person jock. Compare to Williams, Middlebury, and Colby. Not Swarthmore, not Wesleyan. Amherst has always been a standout in part because there are four other local institutions in easy reach to add diversity and depth. Among the few liberal arts colleges with nearly as many men as women. Leader among elite privates in seeking socioeconomic diversity.

Amherst was founded in 1821 when the president of Williams College decided that Williamstown was too remote. With a handful of Williams professors and students in tow, he relocated 50 miles closer to Boston and set in motion centuries of fierce rivalry. Amherst has traditionally been a bastion of New England's elite, but over the last several decades, it has done an about-face. It has used its $3.3 billion endowment to become a national leader in extending high-quality liberal arts education to a racially and socioeconomically diverse student body. Indeed, about half of those admitted in the fall of 2022 were domestic students of color. The president has formally apologized to Black students and alumni for past inequities and published a detailed anti-racism plan. Emphasizing "freedom to explore," Amherst puts the spotlight on learning and allows students to focus not on racking up high grade point averages, but rather on becoming people who base their thinking on a strong foundation in the liberal arts. "If your education is really your first priority," says a sophomore, "then I don't think there's a better school."

"If your education is really your first priority, then I don't think there's a better school."

Amherst's 1,000 acres overlook the picturesque town of Amherst and the Connecticut River Valley and offer a panoramic view of the Holyoke Range and the Pelham Hills. On campus, a plot of open land housing a wildlife sanctuary and a forest shares space with academic and residential buildings, athletic fields, and facilities. Amherst looks like a college is supposed to look, with trees and paths winding through the buildings to offer long, contemplative walks. While Amherst's predominant architectural style remains 19th-century academia—red brick is key— everything from a "pale yellow octagonal structure to a garish, modern dorm" can be found here. A $242 million makeover of the east side of campus included the construction of four new residence halls and the 255,000-square-foot, inter-disciplinary Science Center.

Amherst offers a dynamic curriculum in the traditional academic disciplines and in numerous interdisciplinary fields. There are no core curriculum or distribu-tion requirements, so students choose their program based on their own individual interests and plans for the future. To graduate, students must take a first-year semi-nar, declare a major at the end of sophomore year, and satisfy all major program requirements. First-year seminars, limited to 15 students and occasionally taught by two or more professors, help foster interdisciplinary approaches across topics and are offered in several subject areas. About 45 percent of students choose to under-take a yearlong senior honors thesis in their major.

The most popular of Amherst's 41 majors include mathematics, economics, psy-chology, computer science, and English. About half of the students typically pursue double majors, and a few overachievers even triple major. Students may create their own courses of study from Special Topics classes if the subject of their interest is not available. Amherst's unique Law, Jurisprudence, and Social Thought program is not a prelaw major; instead, it's an interdisciplinary study of the law, drawing on fields as diverse as psychology, history, philosophy, and literature, with a strong theoretical focus. New offerings include a major in educational

"Amherst professors are what gives this place its life."

studies. Amherst's membership in the Five College Consortium means that students can also take courses from partner schools Mount Holyoke, UMass Amherst, Smith, and Hampshire, a benefit that significantly expands students' options.

The academic climate at Amherst is intense, but on such a small campus, the classroom environment is supportive and interaction with faculty is encouraged. Through the Take Your Professor Out program, students receive funding to invite their professors out for dinner off campus once per semester. "Amherst professors are what gives this place its life," says a computer science and environmental studies major. "They will play a huge part in your time here." Students also praise the col-lege's robust career services.

Amherst's commitment to academic flexibility extends beyond traditional coursework. Students report that, with no graduate students around, it's easy to get involved with faculty research as early as your first semester. The Meiklejohn Fellows program provides summer internships and research opportunities for low-income and first-generation students. About half of the students spend a semester or year abroad, choosing from more than 150 programs in dozens of countries; partici-pants are able to apply their financial aid packages to approved programs. Amherst also has a sister university in Göttingen, Germany, and another in Kyoto, Japan, where one of the college's colonial-style buildings has been duplicated.

"Students at Amherst are self-driven and independent," says a neuroscience major. Only 12 percent of Amherst students hail from Massachusetts, and 10 per-cent are international. A linguistics major comments, "Amherst is a politically active campus with the loudest voices being liberals. While other views are not silenced, they are sometimes drowned out." The student body is notably diverse; 15 percent

(continued)

Returning Freshmen: 98%
Academics: ✎ ✎ ✎ ✎ ✎
Social: ☎ ☎ ☎
Q of L: ★ ★ ★ ★
Admissions: (413) 542-2328
Email Address: admission@ amherst.edu

Strong Programs:
Mathematics
Economics
Psychology
Computer Science
English
Law, Jurisprudence, and Social Thought

About half of the students typically pursue double majors, and a few overachievers even triple major.

are Asian American, 15 percent are Hispanic/Latino, 10 percent are Black, and 7 percent are multiracial. As part of its ongoing efforts to increase racial and socioeconomic diversity, Amherst announced in 2021 that it would no longer consider legacy status in admissions—a practice that gives preference to the children of alumni. Furthermore, admissions is need-blind for all students, and all financial aid is awarded based on need, meaning no merit or athletic scholarships. Amherst guarantees to meet 100 percent of admitted students' demonstrated financial need with loan-free financial aid packages, which has helped attract a substantial number of low-income and Pell-eligible students.

Amherst no longer considers legacy status in admissions and is need-blind for all students.

Housing at Amherst is guaranteed for four years, and 98 percent of students live on campus. "First-year students live together in seven dorms on the First-Year Quad, which is really good for community-building," says a sophomore. Those who don't want to take their chances with the room draw can participate in a lip-synch competition; the winner receives the top room pick for his or her class. Everyone who lives on campus, and anyone else who wants to, eats in Valentine Hall, which includes a buffet-style central serving station and five dining rooms. Much of the produce comes from Book and Plow, the on-campus farm, but students give the meals lukewarm reviews. Students agree that the campus feels safe, and a Black studies major comments, "There is definitely a culture here of sexual respect, and in instances where that culture is breached, the college takes swift action."

Although frats are nothing more than a faint memory, social activities are conducted almost entirely on campus. They range from dorm study breaks to club events to low-key gatherings. Sports teams host most of the parties, which are generally open to all students, and a history and computer science major reports, "The college takes a realistic approach to handling student alcohol use." The Powerhouse, a building that originally served as a campus steam plant at the turn of the 20th century, has been converted into a nightlife venue for live performances, dances, movie screenings, art exhibits, pub nights, and other special events. Although some students bemoan a lack of campus traditions, seasonal festivals in the fall, winter, and spring and Farm Fest are popular. Students also take advantage of the Five Colleges membership for social life and cultural events.

"Students at Amherst are self-driven and independent."

The town of Amherst is "small but charming," says a sophomore, with a few coffee shops, bars, and late-night dining options. The nearby city of Northampton offers more in the way of restaurants, concerts, and nightlife. Many students take part in community service projects, such as Big Brothers Big Sisters and Habitat for Humanity, and the college funds roughly 150 summer public service internships every year. For the many outdoorsy types, good skiing in Vermont is not far, and Boston (an hour and a half) and New York (a little over three hours) are close enough to be convenient road-trip destinations.

Many students take part in community service projects, and the college funds roughly 150 summer public service internships every year.

Sports are taken seriously, both varsity and intramurals, and "impact" athletes are said to get favored treatment from the admissions office. The school has removed its century-old unofficial mascot, "Lord Jeff" (Lord Jeffery Amherst was a British general who sought to exterminate indigenous people), and introduced a new mascot, the Mammoth. Amherst competes in Division III, but the strong baseball team takes on Division I opponents as well. Women's basketball has won two national championships in recent years, while men's basketball, baseball, and cross-country and women's ice hockey and soccer have brought home recent New England Small College Athletic Conference titles. Any showdowns with "Little Three" archrivals Williams and Wesleyan are the biggest games of the season, drawing fans from all corners of campus. Amherst students pioneered the development of ultimate Frisbee in the mid-1960s, when players were still using metal cake pan lids, and the college's intramural and club programs continue to be well supported.

In recent years Amherst has become an outspoken proponent—and model— of the value of diversity and inclusivity for the liberal arts, and these institutional values are not lost on its students. "People carry themselves very seriously here, and that in itself creates a culture of pressure to succeed and achieve," remarks one sophomore. Yet the lack of restrictive requirements, a cadre of professors who are focused on teaching, and a devoted alumni network make it clear why most students love their institution. Says a junior, "The Amherst community goes far beyond your years on campus."

If You Apply To ›

Amherst: Early decision, regular decision. Accepts the Common Application. Please consult Amherst's website for the most up-to-date information regarding standardized test requirements.

Antioch College

Yellow Springs, OH 45387

Part social activist, part granola, and part anarchist with plenty of none-of-the-above mixed in, Antioch is a haven for square pegs. After shutting its doors for three years, Antioch is back in business and offering its signature co-op program: academic study interspersed with 11-week work experiences. March and protest to change the world, then get a job. Cool.

Antioch has long been the poster child for the funky diversity that characterizes U.S. higher education. Since its founding in 1852 by abolitionist and social reformer Horace Mann, this small liberal arts college in the Ohio boondocks has nurtured outspoken and socially aware students who thrive under the rigors of refreshingly nontraditional education. In 1902 Antioch pioneered the concept of co-op education, in which students alternate time in the classroom with jobs in the "real world."

The college was forced to shut its doors in 2008 because of inept management, but in 2011 it reopened, phoenix-like, thanks to loyal alumni and others unwilling to allow Antioch's signature approach to education to become a footnote to history. As it grapples with inevitable enrollment and financial challenges, Antioch is relying on a new generation of pioneers—students included—to reinvent the college for the 21st century.

Antioch is located in the progressive village of Yellow Springs (population 3,700), which has grown up around the college and become a popular destination for weekend tourists, thanks to its restaurants, art, and music. The campus is a mixture of traditional and eco-friendly buildings in various states of repair, including the giant Main Hall that looks like Hogwarts. The campus includes a working farm and dozens of geothermal wells, and it abuts the 1,000-acre Glen Helen Nature Preserve that serves both hikers and science students looking for field experience.

> "[In eleven weeks] we do the same amount of work that most people do in a semester."

The academic climate is informal and collaborative, with most everyone called by their first name, but the overall atmosphere is hardly laid-back. "Because we are on an 11-week quarter system, we do the same amount of work that most people do

Website: www.antiochcollege.edu
Location: Small Town
Private
Total Enrollment: 133
Undergraduates: 133
Male/Female: 31/69
Financial Aid: 100%
Pell Grant: 77%
Expense: Pr $
Student Loans: 88%
Average Debt: $
Applicants: 210
Accepted: 72%
Enrolled: 21%
Grad in 6 Years: 82%
Returning Freshmen: 73%
Academics: ✍ ✍ ✍
Social: ☎ ☎ ☎
Q of L: ★ ★ ★
Admissions: (937) 319-6082
Email Address: admission@antiochcollege.edu

in a semester," explains a psychology major. "Then there's the workload of helping to run a new college. That can be very mentally taxing."

Classes tend to be discussion-based, and take-home tests are common. The faculty is highly regarded but small, which means that turnover can be a problem. "A department can go from rock solid to extremely fragile in a matter of weeks," says a junior. Antioch's general education program includes a core curriculum with distribution requirements, as well as mandatory courses on dialogues across difference, race/ethnic studies, gender/sexuality studies, and a class that prepares students for cooperative education. In addition, students complete two capstone experiences, starting with an original research project or some sort of creative work or performance. Seniors also write a Senior Reflection Paper integrating their educational experiences in and out of the classroom over the previous four years.

Rather than selecting preset majors, all Antioch students design their own degree plans, picking and choosing courses from broad areas that suit their academic interests and needs. Environmental science is Antioch's strongest academic area, and students also praise the biomedical and other sciences. "We have well-equipped labs and do a lot of sustainability projects, such as learning about climate change, recycling, composting, and other things that would help save our planet," says a sophomore. Everyone agrees that political economy is both strong and demanding. Media arts, psychology, literature, and visual arts are also popular. A peer mentoring program supports first-year and first-generation students, while Early Alert and First Watch programs ensure that students do not fall through the cracks. Career and other counseling services are said to be caring but understaffed. Antioch, which views itself as a laboratory for democracy, is governed by a Community Council. "Students, staff, and faculty get elected and make important decisions for our school. Our shared governance is pivotal to Antioch," says one denizen.

Antioch, which views itself as a laboratory for democracy, is governed by a Community Council of students, staff, and faculty.

Under Antioch's flagship co-op program, students engage in full-time cooperative education experiences, generally off campus, for three or four quarters throughout their time at the college. "By the time you graduate, you have four amazing jobs on your résumé," gushes a sophomore. Each student is assigned a co-op advisor to help with the nearly continuous job hunt, which is eased by Antioch's extensive network of alumni. The downside: with students constantly coming and going, it is sometimes hard to maintain friendships and engage in extracurricular activities. Antioch has no study abroad program, but about 10 percent of students do co-ops in foreign countries.

"We're all self-motivated and driven. We're weirdos and proud."

Antioch students tend to be independent spirits. "We're all self-motivated and driven," says a freshman. "We're weirdos and proud." The student body is fairly diverse geographically, with 38 percent coming from out of state, but rural Ohio is an unlikely destination of choice for many students of color, and there are no international students. "It's an adjustment, especially if you're coming from a diverse area," says a junior. Black students currently make up 17 percent of the student body, Hispanics/Latinos 14 percent, American Indians 2 percent, Asian Americans 1 percent, and multiracial students 4 percent—but with such a small student body, these figures can shift significantly with each incoming class. "Our campus is almost entirely 'liberal' with a mixture of Marxists, Democrats, and Socialists," claims a student. "There are maybe two Republicans in the student body." A huge 77 percent of freshmen are eligible for Pell Grants. The college offers a handful of merit scholarships, but most financial aid is need-based.

Under the flagship co-op program, students engage in full-time cooperative education experiences, generally off campus, for three or four quarters.

Antioch operates a single dining facility with an all-or-nothing meal plan—19 meals a week or cook for yourself—and much of the food is supplied by local farmers and the student-staffed campus farm. That means, as a junior points out, that "Students can work on the farm and later eat their work." Students are required to live on campus in one of two residence halls or apartments until they are within a year of graduation. "There is no trouble finding housing," says a freshman. "Everything is very comfortable." Antioch was the first college to have a Sexual Offense Prevention Policy (SOPP) mandating verbal consent at every step of a sexual encounter, and entering students receive SOPP training during orientation. "We were famously mocked for it on SNL, but the rest of the country has slowly been following along," notes a political economy major.

In the absence of Greek organizations, social life tends to be rather low-key. "There's hiking, movies, two bars, and plenty of art and music events to attend both on campus and off," says a history major. Other diversions include the Camelot bike ride and quarterly dances before students head off on their co-ops. Dayton is 30 minutes away, Columbus and Cincinnati one hour. All sports at Antioch are intramural.

Antioch College is happily back on its feet but showing some growing pains. "We lose a lot of students due to the stressful environment," says a junior. "I think once we understand our institutional personality and promote it, we will have better retention rates." For many students, however, Antioch's search for an updated identity for the 21st century is part of what makes the place exciting. "Almost every person here has a different idea of what Antioch needs to be," observes a psychology major. "A perk of coming here is that you get to lend your hand in deciding what that will be."

If You Apply To ›

Antioch: Early decision I and II, rolling admissions. SATs or ACTs: optional. Accepts the Common Application. Application includes option to indicate gender identity and preferred pronouns. Art applicants must submit portfolios.

University of Arizona

1200 East University Boulevard, Tucson, AZ 85721

Tucson is an increasingly popular academic destination, and not just because of the scenic mountain views. A large and highly regarded honors college attracts top students, as do excellent programs in the sciences, arts, engineering, and business. Generally viewed as a cut above ASU in academic quality. Offers generous merit scholarships to eligible out-of-staters. Bring plenty of shorts and sunscreen.

With a campus that's encircled by mountain ranges and the beautiful Sonoran Desert, lined with palm trees and cacti, and set against a backdrop of stunning Tucson sunsets, it's no surprise that students at the University of Arizona love to hang out at the Mall. Not the shopping center, mind you—but a huge grassy area in the middle of campus where 36,000 Wildcats gather between classes. Judging by numbers alone, that's enough people to fill a medium-sized town. But students are quick to point out that Arizona has a strong sense of community. "I always see familiar and friendly faces around the Mall," says a senior. With all the natural beauty that surrounds them, many Wildcats simply purr through four satisfying years.

Architecturally, Arizona's campus distinguishes itself from the city's regiment of adobe buildings with a design that seems a study in the versatility of red brick. Old Main, the university's first building, is into its second century, but it has plenty of modern neighbors, including high-tech science facilities. A $28 million aerospace and mechanical engineering building has a state-of-the-art subsonic wind tunnel and rocket-combustion test facility. Eager shutterbugs can pore through

Website: www.arizona.edu
Location: City Center
Public
Total Enrollment: 36,430
Undergraduates: 29,570
Male/Female: 43/57
Financial Aid: 87%
Pell Grant: 30%
Expense: Pub $ $ $
Student Loans: 44%
Average Debt: $ $
Applicants: 48,202
Accepted: 87%
Enrolled: 21%

(continued)

Grad in 6 Years: 64%
Returning Freshmen: 84%
Academics: ✎ ✎ ✎ ½
Social: ☎ ☎ ☎ ☎
Q of L: ★ ★ ★ ★
Admissions: (520) 621-3237
Email Address: admissions@
   arizona.edu

Strong Programs:
Astronomy
Architecture
Biomedical Engineering
Optical Sciences
Nursing
Entrepreneurship
Business Management
Retailing and Consumer
   Science

Arizona's new gen-ed curriculum requires students to engage in interdisciplinary learning and showcase their work in e-portfolios.

photographer Ansel Adams's personal collection at the first-rate Center for Creative Photography. The Student Recreation Center is LEED Certified, and the recently completed Student Success District centralizes health and wellness, tutoring, and academic advising services, in addition to providing access to library and technology resources like 3-D printers.

Launched in spring 2022, Arizona's new general education curriculum incorporates opportunities for students to engage in interdisciplinary learning, showcase their work in e-portfolios, and reflect on their experiences. In addition to a first-year writing requirement and a one-credit general education capstone course, students complete coursework that focuses on different Perspectives (Artist, Humanist, Natural Scientist, and Social Scientist) and Attributes (Diversity and Equity, Quantitative Reasoning, World Cultures and Societies, and Writing).

> **"The academic climate is challenging but rewards student initiative and hard work."**

Arizona, whose origins date to 1885, has 20 colleges and more than 300 undergraduate majors. Sciences are unquestionably the school's forte—the astronomy department is among the nation's best, helped by those clear night skies. Students have access not only to leading astronomers, but also to the most up-to-date equipment, including a huge 256-inch telescope operated jointly by the university and the Smithsonian. The small but rigorous College of Architecture, Planning, and Landscape Architecture is a national leader in sustainable planning for arid regions. Programs in biomedical engineering, optical sciences, nursing, entrepreneurship, business management, and retailing and consumer science are particularly well regarded, and the English and history departments are also standouts. The university also offers the first B.A. degree in law in the country.

"The academic climate is challenging but rewards student initiative and hard work," comments a history major. Some first-year courses are taught by graduate students, and 35 percent of all classes enroll fewer than 20 students. "Most of my professors are very well versed in their fields and continue to do research," says one student. Students also praise the THINK TANK tutoring program that operates out of several academic buildings and residence halls for academic support.

Arizona's Student Engagement and Career Development office connects students with real-world learning experiences, whether through courses that involve experiential learning components or through out-of-classroom opportunities like internships, fieldwork, and research or service projects. Career educators in the LifeLab assist students with career planning. The Franke Honors College offers one of the nation's largest and most selective honors programs, serving more than 3,700 students. In addition to offering a variety of honors courses, the college features smaller classes, personalized advising, research opportunities, and the Honors Village living/learning community. The Undergraduate Biology Research Program also has a national reputation. For those seeking new vistas, there are study abroad programs available in more than 60 countries; 6 percent of undergrads take part.

"Arizona students are often driven, fun, energetic, and innovative," says a business management major. Out-of-staters constitute 33 percent of the undergraduate

> **"Tucson is a hippie town and offers a different local vibe and a fun atmosphere."**

student body; another 4 percent hail from foreign countries. Hispanics/Latinos account for 28 percent, Black students 4 percent, Asian Americans 5 percent, and multiracial students 5 percent. A diversity action council, a student minority advisory committee, and cultural resource centers help promote positive race relations. There is a mix of political views on campus, and a senior reports, "Gender, race, and immigration seem to be the hottest political topics." Merit scholarships averaging $11,300 and hundreds of athletic scholarships are available to eligible students; out-of-staters with decent

GPAs enjoy more generous merit scholarships here than at some of Arizona's biggest competitors. Arizona guarantees that incoming students' tuition and fees won't increase for four years. In addition, the university now provides full-tuition grants to in-state, Pell-eligible students at the main Tucson campus.

Arizona offers the first B.A. degree in law in the country.

A junior says the quality of Arizona's 23 residence halls is "all over the board," but all are generally well maintained: "Dorms range from brand new with every amenity to a 1920s women-only dorm with sleeping porches that's a historical landmark." Only 22 percent of undergraduates live in the dorms; some first-years and most older students flock to the abundant and less expensive apartments near the school. Several restaurants are located in the student union food court and sprinkled around campus, but many students express a desire for more traditional dining

"Professors and advisors urge us to get…as many experiences as we possibly can under our belts."

halls and healthy choices. In regards to the national issue of campus sexual assault, a sophomore says that the university "emphasizes consent" and that "students seem to take the issue seriously."

Despite the high percentage of off-campus residents, students stream back to campus on weekends for parties, sports, cultural events, and other activities organized by more than 600 student clubs and organizations. Four percent of the men belong to fraternities, and 10 percent of the women join sororities; students say Greek groups have an outsize influence on the social scene. The campus is technically alcohol-free, though some question whether the frats have realized that yet. Homecoming, with its Homecoming Olympics competition between student orgs on the Mall and its massive bonfire, is always a crowd-pleaser. One of Arizona's most time-honored traditions is Spring Fling, said to be the largest student-run carnival in the country. On Reading Day, the day before final exams begin, the university offers free snacks and stress-relieving activities like yoga, meditation, and coloring. "Tucson is a hippie town and offers a different local vibe and a fun atmosphere for a college town," says a junior. Students enjoy Tucson's shops, restaurants, bars, and various dance clubs, not to mention easy access to hiking and other outdoor activities. Phoenix is less than two hours away.

One of Arizona's most time-honored traditions is Spring Fling, said to be the largest student-run carnival in the country.

The university is home to 500 athletes who compete in 17 sports as a member of the Division I Pac-12 Conference. The Wildcats men's basketball, baseball, and golf teams have won conference titles in the last few years, and women's golf, basketball, and softball are competitive too. Football and basketball enjoy national prominence and provide great weekend entertainment, especially when the opposing team is big-time rival Arizona State. As one Wildcat points out, "Every time we play against ASU in any sport, there are T-shirts, stickers, and people asking, 'A-S-who?'" Arizona's battle cry, "Bear Down!"—frequently heard at sporting events—dates back to 1926, when a campus football hero, fatally injured in a car crash, whispered his last message to his teammates: "Tell them, tell the team to bear down." Nearly 100 years later, the enigmatic slogan still appears all over campus.

The University of Arizona offers a wide variety of academic opportunities along with spectacular weather. Prospective students are warned to honestly evaluate how that will affect their ability to concentrate. "Professors and advisors urge us to get involved in any way possible and get as many experiences as we possibly can under our belts before we finish our four years," says a marketing major. Indeed, Arizona is a place to go in pursuit of knowledge, experience, and a good tan.

Overlaps

CU Boulder, UCLA, Michigan State, U of I at Urbana–Champaign, University of Washington, Arizona State, Northern Arizona, University of Oregon

If You Apply To ›

Arizona: Rolling admissions. SATs or ACTs: optional. Accepts the Common Application with supplement.

Arizona State University

Box 870112, Tempe, AZ 85287

ASU is the largest university in the nation—with ambitions to grow even larger, enhance interdisciplinary applied research, and increase socioeconomic diversity. Location in the Valley of the Sun attracts plenty of out-of-staters who like the idea of seeing the sun every day. Administration's relentless emphasis on growth makes the professional schools and Barrett, The Honors College, the best bets. Strong student support services.

Website: www.asu.edu
Location: City Center
Public
Total Enrollment: 69,236
Undergraduates: 58,993
Male/Female: 50/50
Financial Aid: 90%
Pell Grant: 30%
Expense: Pub $ $
Student Loans: 43%
Average Debt: $ $
Applicants: 61,603
Accepted: 88%
Enrolled: 26%
Grad in 6 Years: 68%
Returning Freshmen: 86%
Academics: ✐ ✐ ✐
Social: ☎ ☎ ☎ ☎
Q of L: ★ ★ ★ ★ ★
Admissions: (480) 965-7788
Email Address: admissions@ asu.edu

Strong Programs:
Journalism
Architecture
Art
Design
Performing Arts
Education
Engineering
Business

With a history that dates to 1885, Arizona State University has transformed itself over the last decade into the nation's largest public university. With no pretense of modesty, this mega-university, situated in a desert oasis that is one of the nation's fastest-growing metro areas, describes itself as the model for a New American University—one where "massive innovation" is the norm and where an interdisciplinary culture is seen as the best means of developing "world-changing ideas."

> **"Sun Devils buckle down and focus on what needs to get done."**

ASU's stated goal is to serve any Arizona student qualified for college-level work and, in the process, it has become a national model of how to navigate the emerging demographics of U.S. higher education. Research spending is up, as are student retention and graduation rates. Not surprisingly, ASU can seem overcrowded and overwhelming at times, but it provides motivated students who can find a manageable niche with countless opportunities for work and play.

The most populous of ASU's four locations, the Tempe campus offers a beautiful blend of palm-lined walkways and contemporary urban architecture. It is home to The College of Liberal Arts and Sciences, business, art and design, and engineering programs. Fifteen minutes by light rail brings you to the Downtown Phoenix campus, which looks like it sounds. It houses journalism, nursing, public service, and law programs and has a young professionals feel. The Polytechnic campus, a converted Air Force base, specializes in science and technology and boasts a desert arboretum, while West campus has the feel of a liberal arts learning community, with a large central lawn and a focus on interdisciplinary, collaborative studies. Each of the four campuses has a Pat Tillman Veterans Center, which brings together academic and student support services that serve the university's continually growing enrollment of veterans and their dependents—currently 3,000 undergraduate and graduate students. In addition, the ASU Local program allows students to pursue hybrid degrees, taking online courses and participating in hands-on learning experiences two days a week at satellite locations in Los Angeles and Washington, D.C.

The academic star at ASU is Barrett, The Honors College, a selective school-within-a-school that serves more than 7,000 students from every school and college across all four campuses. Most of these denizens reside in a cloistered complex on the Tempe campus that was designed by students, faculty, and staff working with

> **"ASU has an incredible amount of school spirit."**

nationally renowned architects. It features multiuse classrooms and meeting spaces, a dining hall, a fitness center, numerous outdoor courtyards, and a central amphitheater. The nation's first four-year residential honors college within a major public university, Barrett has more than 40 dedicated faculty members who oversee students' ambitious honors projects.

ASU has 14 undergraduate schools and more than 400 undergraduate degree programs. Regardless of major, all students must fulfill distribution requirements that include courses in three awareness areas: global, historical, and U.S. cultural diversity. The most popular majors are in business and management, engineering, and biological and biomedical sciences. The School of Sustainability, part of the College of Global Futures, emphasizes the study of land use and planning models that minimize environmental harm. The Walter Cronkite School of Journalism and Mass Communication enjoys state-of-the-art facilities and a strong national reputation, while the Herberger Institute for Design and the Arts features nationally recognized majors in architecture, art, design, film, music, and dance. The sciences (including biochemistry, chemistry, geology, and biology) and social sciences boast first-class facilities, notably the largest university-owned meteorite collection in the world. The School of Earth and Space Exploration is a leading center for research in astronomy and astrophysics. Anthropology benefits from its association with the Institute of Human Origins' Donald Johanson, who discovered the 3.2-million-year-old fossil skeleton named Lucy. ASU also offers the largest teacher preparation program of any university in the nation.

Barrett, The Honors College serves more than 7,000 students from every school and college across all four campuses.

Engineering programs, especially microelectronics, robotics, and computer-assisted manufacturing, are sure bets; the facility for high-resolution microscopy allows students to get a uniquely close-up view of atomic structures. The Fulton Schools of Engineering, composed of seven discipline-specific schools, offers a traditional engineering education with an emphasis on designing and creating innovative and entrepreneurial solutions. Future engineers can opt for a B.S. degree or, for those with broader interests, a B.A. The Fulton Undergraduate Research Initiative provides engineering students with hands-on lab experience, independent and thesis-based research guided by faculty mentors, and travel to national conferences.

"Classes embrace political discussion in a healthy manner."

Faculty members are expected to do both teaching and research, preferably with a practical emphasis. As one administrator explains, "We don't do 30-year longitudinal studies." And while, according to a geological sciences major, many professors are "excited and passionate about what they do," students say the university's emphasis on research can have a negative impact on the classroom experience when professors put their research first. Thirty-nine percent of undergraduate classes have fewer than 20 students, and one senior says the academic climate is "mostly relaxed, but focused." The university has made serious efforts to provide students with strong support services. The First-Year Success Center connects new students with upperclassmen and graduate students for weekly coaching sessions on topics like time management, finances, and health and wellness. Incoming freshmen who are undecided on a major participate in the Major and Career Exploration program, which involves seven-week courses offering opportunities for hands-on career exploration. ASU has drawn national attention for its innovative and patented eAdvisor system that keeps students on track to meet degree requirements and is backed up by a corps of full-time professional advisors. It also guarantees that students will find a place in any required course. The 7 percent of students who study abroad have access to more than 250 programs in some 65 countries worldwide.

The School of Sustainability, part of the College of Global Futures, studies land use and planning models that minimize environmental harm.

"Sun Devils buckle down and focus on what needs to get done," says a senior. "We love to have fun, but we also love to succeed." Sixty-seven percent of ASU students are Arizona residents, while 6 percent come from abroad. Twenty-six percent of the undergraduate student body is Hispanic/Latino; Black students contribute 4 percent, Asian Americans 8 percent, and multiracial students 5 percent. Students here can be divided in their politics, but a sophomore says that "classes embrace political discussion in a healthy manner." ASU offers merit scholarships averaging $9,500 to qualified students and awards more than 420 athletic scholarships annually to athletes in 24 sports. It also guarantees to meet the demonstrated need of any student from Arizona and now covers the full tuition costs for Pell-eligible students.

Twenty-four percent of ASU students live in the co-ed dorms. "It is mostly freshmen who choose to live on campus, but our dorms are so nice! I've visited several other schools, and ASU has some of the largest rooms," says one junior. Students don't have to buy a meal plan, no matter where they live, which many say is a good thing. Some complain about the campus's "walk-only zones" that prevent students from using bikes (of which there are thousands), skateboards, or other modes of transportation in certain high-traffic areas. Students say campus security is sufficient, and the Devils in the Bedroom student group helps promote awareness regarding sexual assault prevention.

"Sometimes I feel there is so much stuff going on that I have to pick between two or three things on a day or night or weekend," says one junior. "But, hey, that's a good problem to have!" ASU's Greek system, concentrated in the lavish Greek Leadership Village, attracts 8 percent of the men and 10 percent of the women, and "small kick-backs in dorms are just as common as huge house parties," says a sophomore. The campus is officially dry, so many students head off campus on weekends—often far off campus. Those with cars have easy access to the mountains of Northern Arizona, the lakes on the outskirts of town, and the natural beauty of the Grand Canyon. Tempe gets generally positive reviews from students. "It has great restaurants nearby,

"Small kick-backs in dorms are just as common as huge house parties."

different shopping centers, and a street called Mill Ave that has stores, food, and bars/nightclubs for the 21-and-over set," says a communication major. Devils in Disguise, an annual, student-run day of service, sends students out to complete various volunteer projects in the community.

"ASU has an incredible amount of school spirit," says a junior. Arizona State's Division I athletics department—supported by a fee required of all students—is consistently ranked among the nation's best. Women's triathlon has won multiple national championships in recent years. Softball is a recent Pac-12 Conference winner, and football, men's wrestling, men's swimming and diving, and women's golf are also highly competitive. Teams are known as the Sun Devils after a meteorological phenomenon, and the biggest rival is the University of Arizona, normally referred to simply as "that school down south." The first-rate Sun Devil Fitness Complex hosts dozens of intramurals and the huge club sports program, which boasts more than 50 club teams.

Arizona State may seem like an overwhelmingly big school with a reputation for rowdiness, but that's not the full story. "ASU has gotten away from its party school reputation in recent years," says a senior. To its credit, ASU likes to pride itself on how many students it accepts, not how many it turns away, and on its strong student support services. Despite common college complaints ("Parking, parking, parking!"), the university gives students much to appreciate. For those not intimidated by its sheer immensity, ASU may be a good place to earn a degree while enjoying a four-year relationship with the sun.

Overlaps

UCLA, Michigan State, University of Minnesota, Ohio State, UT Austin, University of Arizona, Northern Arizona, San Diego State

If You Apply To ›

Arizona State: Rolling admissions. SATs or ACTs: optional. Accepts the Common Application with supplement.

University of Arkansas

200 Hunt Hall, Fayetteville, AR 72701

University of Arkansas occupies the second tier of Southern public universities alongside Alabama, LSU, and Ole Miss. Though somewhat conservative by national standards, Fayetteville is a relatively progressive Arkansas city. With traditional roots in agriculture, U of A has also developed strong programs in business, engineering, architecture, and other professional fields. Its most popular program takes the field on Saturday afternoons in the fall.

The flagship public institution for the state of Arkansas, the University of Arkansas is a nationally competitive, student-centered research institution. Freshman class enrollment has increased by more than 36 percent in the last 10 years, and the university has grown to keep pace. A $300 million cash gift from the family of Walmart founder Sam Walton created the undergraduate Honors College and endowed the graduate school. More recently, contributions from the Walton Family Charitable Support Foundation have funded the School of Art and the Institute for Integrative and Innovative Research.

The Arkansas campus is nestled among the mountains, lakes, and streams of the Ozarks, in the northwest corner of the state. "Come to a Razorback game in the fall when the leaves are changing," says one student, "and you will be totally won over." The community is friendly and safe, and the moderate climate means recreational opportunities abound in all seasons. Architectural styles range from modern concrete to collegiate

> **"We have lots of accessible resources and engaging and involved faculty and staff."**

Gothic buildings constructed during the Depression. The center of campus is the stately brick Old Main, dating to 1875, which once housed the entire university. The $14 million Harvell Civil Engineering Research and Education Center opened in 2021.

Established as a land grant institution in 1871, with agricultural and mechanical roots, U of A serves 21,500 undergraduates and includes 10 colleges, as well as more than 50 research and outreach centers. U of A's core requirements include credits in English, history, math, humanities, fine arts, science, and social sciences. The more than 3,800 undergrads who join the Honors College complete research or creative work culminating in an honors thesis; the College awards up to 90 freshman fellowships and more than $1 million in research and study abroad grants each year. The Sam M. Walton College of Business offers three of the strongest and most popular majors on campus: marketing, finance, and supply chain management. The college's recently formed strategy, entrepreneurship, and venture innovation department launched its first major in 2021. Other popular disciplines include nursing, industrial engineering, communication sciences and disorders, English (particularly creative writing), and studio art. The Bumpers College of Agricultural, Food, and Life Sciences is home to the Center of Excellence for Poultry Science, a national leader in research on poultry epidemiology. The Jones School of Architecture and Design's architecture program is also notable.

U of A's academic climate is "laid-back, but still demanding a high standard of excellence," says a senior. To help ease into the college transition, students recommend ROCK Camp, an optional summer orientation weekend, as well as the tutoring services of the Harrington Center for Success. "We have lots of accessible resources and engaging and involved faculty and staff," cheers a communication major. While there is a healthy portion of large lecture classes taught by teaching assistants, 38 percent of classes enroll fewer than 20 students. Undergraduates in all

Website: www.uark.edu
Location: Small City
Public
Total Enrollment: 23,225
Undergraduates: 21,454
Male/Female: 44/56
Financial Aid: 48%
Pell Grant: 18%
Expense: Pub $
Student Loans: 48%
Average Debt: $ $
Applicants: 21,462
Accepted: 83%
Enrolled: 34%
Grad in 6 Years: 70%
Returning Freshmen: 87%
Academics: ✐ ✐ ✐
Social: 🕿 🕿 🕿 🕿
Q of L: ★ ★ ★
Admissions: (479) 575-5346
Email Address: uofa@uark.edu

Strong Programs:
Marketing
Finance
Supply Chain Management
Architecture
Nursing
Industrial Engineering
Communication Sciences and
   Disorders
Creative Writing

disciplines are encouraged to conduct research, and 35 percent do so, often with generous funding. "Getting involved in campus research is very easy and often just requires talking to an enthusiastic professor with room in their lab," says a biology major. The university sponsors study abroad programs in nearly 30 countries across six continents, including its flagship Rome Center and roughly 40 short-term, faculty-led programs; 12 percent of students participate.

Forty-nine percent of undergraduates are Arkansas residents, with Texans representing the next largest contingent at 29 percent; 2 percent are international. Black students make up just 4 percent of the student body, Hispanics/Latinos 10 percent, Asian Americans 3 percent, and multiracial students 5 percent. The student body tends to lean right, although a variety of political views are visible on campus. "There are women's marches and people asking you to sign petitions to legalize weed, and there are also Republican rallies," observes a biology major. Arkansas awards thousands of merit scholarships each year, averaging $5,300, as well as roughly 400 athletic scholarships in 19 varsity sports. Additionally, the New Arkansan Non-Resident Tuition Award gives scholarships to incoming students from neighboring states who meet certain academic requirements.

Twenty-three percent of all undergrads at Arkansas live in the residence halls; most move to Greek houses or other off-campus digs after their first year. About 150 students participate in six living/learning community options. A unique "Adopt-a-Prof" program places designated faculty members in residence halls to spend time interacting informally with students. Campus dining is described as adequate. Campus police are said to be effective, and they have a presence at Greek parties. A senior reports, "The Title IX office has stepped up and improved procedures and outreach" related to the issue of campus sexual assault.

"We're surrounded by mountains and rivers, [and] weekends are filled with hiking and camping."

Arkansas's Greek chapters attract 25 percent of the men and 38 percent of the women, and Greek parties are the most visible outlet for weekend social life, aside from the revelry that accompanies Razorback athletics. "Even if you aren't in a Greek organization, chances are you're attending something put on by one," notes a sophomore. School-sponsored Cardinal Nights offer alternative programming on Fridays, and students look forward to the annual Springtime of Youth music festival. Dickson Street, the core entertainment district in the town of Fayetteville (population 95,000), is full of restaurants and bars that are popular with upperclassmen; the town also offers live music at local clubs and touring Broadway shows at the Walton Arts Center. "We have a very outdoorsy culture because we're surrounded by mountains and rivers," explains a horticulture major. "So weekends are filled with hiking and camping." Students are also big on community service, especially through programs like Gearhart Full Circle Food Pantry, Make a Difference Day, and Hogs Care Week. Those with cars will find Dallas, Tulsa, Oklahoma City, Memphis, and St. Louis all within a six-hour drive.

The Razorbacks (wild hogs) compete in the Southeastern Conference, and the beloved Hog Call "Wooo! Pig sooie!" rings out during football and basketball weekends, although according to one senior, "No matter the time, place, or situation, it is always considered appropriate to call the hogs." Red Razorback logos are all over town—on T-shirts, napkins, book covers, license plates, and on game day, the cheeks of ecstatic fans. Other powerhouse teams include baseball, men's and women's track and field and golf, and women's gymnastics. Recreational sports are hugely popular and include everything from flag football and sand volleyball to ballroom dance and bass fishing.

At the University of Arkansas, Southern hospitality means poultry science students aren't the only ones flocking to the state for a solid education at a bargain

Overlaps

University of Oklahoma, Louisiana State, University of Missouri, University of Nebraska–Lincoln, Iowa State, University of Alabama, Texas A&M, Texas Tech

price. Northerners may feel outnumbered, and those who frown on football should keep their feelings to themselves. But all students here look forward to graduation day, when their names will join forever those of more than 200,000 other alumni, engraved into the nearly four-mile network of sidewalks on campus.

If You Apply To ›

Arkansas: Early action, rolling admissions. Accepts the Common Application with supplement. Please consult Arkansas's website for the most up-to-date information regarding standardized test requirements.

Atlanta University Center

Atlanta is viewed as the preeminent city in the country for bright, talented, and successful Black people. It became the capital of the civil rights movement in the 1960s—a town described by its leaders as "too busy to hate." Atlanta evolved in the 1970s to become known as the "Black mecca of the South," it economically burgeoned to "Olympic City" in the 1990s, and it currently reigns as the hub of Black Hollywood.

At the heart of this storied culture is the Atlanta University Center (AUC), the largest African American educational complex in the world. The center consists of two undergraduate colleges (Morehouse and Spelman) as well as two that offer graduate degrees (Clark Atlanta University and the Morehouse School of Medicine) on adjoining campuses in the center of Atlanta, three miles from downtown. Two other institutions, Morris Brown College and the Interdenominational Theological Center, are no longer members. Students at the affiliated schools can enjoy the quiet pace of their beautiful magnolia-studded campuses or plunge into all the culture and excitement of this most dynamic of Deep South cities.

AUC, serving 8,000 students, is home to a myriad of unique offerings, including Spelman's Innovation Lab; Morehouse's cinema, television, and emerging media studies major; Clark Atlanta University's Center for Innovation and Entrepreneurial Development; and Morehouse School of Medicine's Satcher Health Leadership Institute. The four component institutions have educated numerous generations of Black leaders. The Reverend Martin Luther King Jr. graduated from Morehouse, while his grandmother, mother, sister, and daughter all attended Spelman. Both schools gained national reputations at a time when they were among the best of the few colleges to which talented Black students could aspire. Even now, when the options are almost limitless, alumni continue to send their children back for more.

The six original schools—all but the medical school—became affiliated in 1929 using the model of California's Claremont Colleges, but the remaining members are fiercely independent. Each has its own administration, board of trustees, and academic specialties, and each maintains its own dorms, cafeterias, and other facilities. There is cross-registration among the institutions (Morehouse students, for example, go to Spelman for drama and art courses) as well as with Georgia State and Emory University. The governing body of the consortium, the Atlanta University Center, Inc., administers a centerwide dual-degree program in engineering in conjunction with Georgia Tech, and it runs campus security, a student crisis center, and a joint institute of science research. There is also a centerwide service of career planning and placement, where recruiters may come and interview students from all four institutions.

Dating and social life at the coeducational institutions tend to take place within the individual schools, though Morehouse, a men's college, and Spelman, a women's college, maintain a close academic and social relationship. The Morehouse–Spelman Glee Club takes its abundance of talent around the nation, and its annual Christmas concert on the Spelman campus is a standing-room-only event.

Morehouse and Spelman (see full write-ups) constitute the Ivy League of historically Black colleges and universities (HBCUs). The following is a sketch of the other institution within the AUC system offering undergraduate degrees, Clark Atlanta University.

CLARK ATLANTA UNIVERSITY (WWW.CAU.EDU)

Formed by the consolidation of Clark College, a four-year liberal arts institution, and Atlanta University, which offered only graduate degrees, CAU is a comprehensive coeducational institution that offers undergraduate, graduate, and professional degrees as well as nondegree certificate programs. The university draws on the former strengths of both schools, offering quality programs in the health professions, public policy, and mass communications (including print journalism, radio and television production, and filmmaking). Graduate and professional programs include education, business, library information studies, social work, and arts and sciences. CAU is the only private, independent graduate research institution in the HBCU community, and the only HBCU member of the Georgia Research Alliance. The university enrolls 3,200 full-time undergraduates; about two-thirds come from out of state, and 76 percent are women.

Morehouse College

830 Westview Drive SW, Atlanta, GA 30314

Along with sister school Spelman, Morehouse is the most prestigious of the historically Black schools. Alumni list reads like a *Who's Who* of Black leaders. Best known for business and popular 3–2 engineering program with Georgia Tech. Built on a Civil War battlefield, Morehouse epitomizes the new South. "Morehouse Men" share a special bond.

Website: www.morehouse.edu
Location: City Center
Private
Total Enrollment: 2,196
Undergraduates: 2,196
Male/Female: 100/0
Financial Aid: 83%
Pell Grant: 56%
Expense: Pr $
Student Loans: 80%
Average Debt: $ $ $
Applicants: 3,777
Accepted: 65%
Enrolled: 26%
Grad in 6 Years: 47%
Returning Freshmen: 86%
Academics: ✍ ✍ ✍
Social: 🐿 🐿 🐿
Q of L: ★ ★ ★ ★
Admissions: (844) 512-6672
Email Address: admissions@
   morehouse.edu

Strong Programs:
Business Administration
Economics
Biology
English

Founded in 1867, Morehouse College has the distinction of being the nation's only historically Black, four-year liberal arts college for men. Top students come to Morehouse because they want an institution with a strong academic program and a culture that focuses equally on developing global leaders and fostering a sense of brotherhood among students. Notable alumni include the Reverend Martin Luther King Jr., Senator Raphael Warnock, Samuel L. Jackson, and Spike Lee. Says a psychology major, "Morehouse is a college of young, assertive, ambitious Black men."

Located near downtown Atlanta, the Morehouse campus was built on 66 acres that were once a Civil War battlefield. The campus is home to 42 buildings, many of them historic, including the Martin Luther King Jr. International Chapel. The college has continued to evolve over the last decade, as it has enriched its academic program, conducted a successful national fund-raising campaign, increased student scholarships and faculty salaries, and improved its physical plant.

Morehouse's general education program includes not only coursework in four major disciplines (humanities, natural sciences, math, and social sciences), but also the study of "the unique African and African American heritage on which so much of our modern American culture is built." A cornerstone of that study is a scheduled series of campuswide assemblies called the Crown Forum, which brings in community leaders and national figures from an array of industries for special presentations, artistic performances, and dialogues on topical issues. Students must attend at least six Crown Forum events per semester for six semesters to graduate. The academic climate at the House can get intense: "Morehouse offers an academic structure that is both competitive and rigorous," states a freshman. Forty-five percent of the classes have fewer than 20 students, and students say their classmates strive to be the best in the classroom but take time to support each other too. A sense of mentorship pervades the campus, and students consider the school's full breadth of counseling services to be quite strong.

> **"Morehouse is a college of young, assertive, ambitious Black men."**

Undergraduate programs include the traditional liberal arts majors in the humanities and social and natural sciences, but as a rule of thumb, the more pre-professional your plan, the better Morehouse fits. While STEM fields have been traditionally strong at Morehouse, business and economics have risen in prominence, and business administration is now the most popular major. Engineering, another popular choice, is actually a 3–2 program in conjunction with Georgia Tech and other larger universities. Many students major in economics, biology, English, and political science. The cinema, television, and emerging media studies major is growing, and a major in Chinese studies is available. Notable minors include journalism and sports, sustainability, and neuroscience. Programs that receive less favorable reviews from students are art and drama, and the administration admits that some of the humanities offerings could use strengthening. A four-year honors program is available for the highly motivated, and research opportunities in the sciences abound, including a research partnership with NASA. Thirty-one percent of students study abroad in more than 200 programs worldwide.

Seventy-two percent of Morehouse students come from outside the state, with the majority hailing from Southeast and Mid-Atlantic states; about 1 percent come from other nations. Ninety-eight percent are Black, and one student attests, "Many students are here to get a greater understanding of their heritage and to promote it." Fifty-six percent of incoming freshmen are eligible for Pell Grants. Merit scholarships averaging $16,600 are available, in addition to 126 scholarships for athletes. Morehouse now accepts transgender students who self-identify as male; however, enrolled students who transition to self-identifying as females would be asked to leave because, as administrators explain, being a men's college is central to Morehouse's identity. Morehouse has come under fire in recent years over how it has handled allegations of sexual misconduct and accusations of a "hypermasculine" culture.

Students are required to live on campus for their first three years; seniors find their own off-campus accommodations. Some students grumble that campus housing is "too small" and "not well maintained." For freshmen, students recommend Graves Hall, the college's oldest building, constructed in 1889. Themed residential academic programs are available for students interested in the arts, business, global

"Morehouse offers an academic structure that is both competitive and rigorous."

learning, and STEM. The meal plan at Morehouse is mandatory for students living on campus and draws its share of complaints as well, although dining services have expanded recently to include fast-food options and a coffee shop.

Morehouse's membership in the Atlanta University Center expands students' academic, social, and extracurricular options, particularly with neighboring Spelman College. Homecoming week, for instance, is a joint effort with Spelman and is one of the nation's largest at a historically Black college or university (HBCU), with events like pep rallies, hip-hop and R&B concerts, step shows, and a jazz brunch drawing thousands of alumni and community members. Spelman women have been known to quip, "You can always tell a Morehouse man, but you can't tell him much." Morehouse's four fraternities, which sign up just 3 percent of the students, hold parties, though most students concur that "drinking is not a big deal here." Community service is an important emphasis, through student organizations as well as service-learning courses. Going out on the town in Atlanta is a popular evening activity, and on-campus football games, concerts, movies, and religious programs all draw crowds.

In its early years, Morehouse left much to be desired in the area of varsity sports, but the Maroon Tigers now compete well in the Division II Southern Intercollegiate Athletic Conference. The basketball and track and field teams have

(continued)

Political Science
Cinema, Television, and
  Emerging Media Studies
Chinese Studies
Pre-engineering

The Crown Forum brings in community leaders and national figures for special presentations and dialogues on topical issues.

Homecoming week is a joint effort with Spelman and is one of the nation's largest at an HBCU.

enjoyed the most success, but it is the intramural program that allows students a chance to become the superstars they know are lurking within them. During football season, students road-trip to follow the games at Howard, Hampton, and Tuskegee universities.

Benefiting as it is from the recent surge of interest in HBCUs, Morehouse is well equipped to serve the contemporary heirs of a distinguished tradition. Morehouse students don't just attend Morehouse. They become part of a prominent and proud network of Morehouse Men who share the bonds of having had the Morehouse experience. Graduates find that alumni stand ready and willing to help them with jobs and other opportunities as they work to effect positive change in their communities and the world.

Overlaps

Spelman, Howard, Davidson, Furman, Millsaps, Rhodes, Georgia State, Florida A&M

If You Apply To ›

Morehouse: Early decision, early action, regular decision. SATs or ACTs: required. Accepts the Common Application. Accepts applications from students who live and self-identify as male.

Spelman College

350 Spelman Lane SW, Atlanta, GA 30314

With a strong tradition of academic excellence, Spelman is a historically Black women's college that draws students from all corners of the country. Particularly strong in the sciences with noteworthy emphasis on undergraduate research. Wooded 42-acre Atlanta campus adjacent to brother school Morehouse offers easy access to urban attractions. Has dropped varsity sports to emphasize lifelong physical fitness.

As one of only two surviving Black women's colleges in the United States (the other is Bennett), Spelman College holds a special appeal for Black women seeking to become leaders in fields ranging from science to the arts. Students flock here for that something special that predominantly white institutions lack: a supportive environment with first-rate academics and a tight-knit sisterhood where Black women can develop self-confidence and leadership skills before venturing out into the wider world—exactly the reasons for the current national resurgence of interest in historically Black colleges and universities (HBCUs). "It's a true sisterhood," enthuses a psychology major. "The bonds are everlasting. There is no one on this planet who will know what you're going through except for your Spelman sisters."

Spelman was founded in 1881 by Sophia B. Packard and Harriet E. Giles, two pioneers in women's education from New England who were concerned with the lack of educational opportunities for Black women. John D. Rockefeller was an early funder, and the school was named in honor of his wife, Laura Spelman Rockefeller, and her parents, who were longtime activists in the antislavery movement. Spelman was traditionally the starting point for teachers, nurses, and other Black female leaders. Today's emphasis is on getting Spelman grads into boardrooms, courtrooms, and engineering labs. Honing women for leadership is the main mission, and that nurturing takes place on a classic collegiate-green campus with a $463 million endowment.

"There is no one on this planet who will know what you're going through except for your Spelman sisters."

Website: www.spelman.edu
Location: City Center
Private
Total Enrollment: 2,363
Undergraduates: 2,363
Male/Female: 0/100
Financial Aid: 85%
Pell Grant: 43%
Expense: Pr $
Student Loans: 67%
Average Debt: $ $
Applicants: 11,176
Accepted: 51%
Enrolled: 14%
Grad in 6 Years: 76%
Returning Freshmen: 91%
Academics: ✐ ✐ ✐ ✐
Social: ☎ ☎ ☎ ☎
Q of L: ★ ★ ★ ★ ★
Admissions: (800) 982-2411

These are heady times for Spelman. Although it finds itself competing head-on with the Seven Sisters and other prestigious and predominantly white institutions that are eager to recruit talented Black women, the college is holding its own. Spelman offers a well-rounded liberal arts curriculum that emphasizes the importance of critical and analytical thinking and problem-solving. Usually, by the end of sophomore year, students are expected to complete 40 credit hours of core requirements, including English composition, foreign language, mathematics, African diaspora and the world, international or comparative women's studies, wellness and health, and computer literacy. In addition, freshmen are required to take a First-Year Experience course, and sophomores must take Sophomore Seminar.

Spelman's established strengths lie in the natural sciences (especially biology) and the humanities, both of which have outstanding faculty. Biology is among the most popular majors, as are psychology, political science, and economics. An interdisciplinary major in health sciences is one of the fastest-growing offerings, along with a minor in food studies. Over the last decade, the college has greatly strengthened its math and science offerings; extensive undergraduate research programs in these areas provide students with publishing opportunities, and many end up attending grad school. In fact, Spelman leads the nation in the number of Black women who go on to earn Ph.D.s in STEM fields. Premed and prelaw programs are strong, and the 3–2 dual-degree program in engineering in cooperation with Georgia Tech is also a standout. The Women's Research and Resource Center specializes in women's studies and community outreach.

"The academic climate is very competitive," says an English major. "The school is made up of the top students from around the country, and the courses are designed to be a challenge for the best of the best." Individual attention is the hallmark of a Spelman education. Many faculty members are Black and/or female—and thus, excellent role models, ones the students find very accessible. "The professors here genuinely love what they do," says a sociology major. Except for some of the required introductory courses, classes are small; 59 percent have fewer than 20 students. Through the Spelman MILE (My Integrated Learning Experience), all students complete internships or undergraduate research projects

"Spelman's personality is definitely 'Black Girl Magic.'"

in their majors. Students who want to spread their wings can venture abroad, as 19 percent do, through a variety of programs in 40 countries, or try one of the domestic exchange arrangements with Wellesley, Mount Holyoke, or Vassar.

"Spelman's personality is definitely 'Black Girl Magic,'" cheers a biology major. "We exude positivity, happiness, and success." Spelman's reputation continues to attract high-achieving, goal-oriented Black women from all over the country, including a high proportion of alumnae children, and the school has become increasingly selective. Twenty-six percent of students come from Georgia, and less than 1 percent come from abroad. Ninety-seven percent are Black; American Indian, Hispanic/Latina, Asian American, and white students combine to make up 2 percent of the student body. The political atmosphere is liberal, and according to a history major, "Hot topics on campus include the gentrification of the city of Atlanta (particularly the West End neighborhood that the campus is located in), women's rights, and issues related to the preservation of Black lives." Spelman offers a limited number of merit scholarships, and 43 percent of freshmen receive Pell Grants. There are no athletic scholarships.

Fifty-eight percent of students live on campus in Spelman's 11 residence halls. Older halls add to the school's historical charm; students recommend that freshmen check out Howard-Harreld Hall. Students report that there are more juniors and seniors who would like to live on campus than there are beds to accommodate them. The meal plan is mandatory for campus-dwellers, and the food gets average

(continued)

Email Address: admiss@ spelman.edu

Strong Programs:
Biology
Psychology
Political Science
Economics
Health Sciences
Mathematics
Premed
African Diaspora Studies

All students complete internships or undergraduate research projects in their majors.

Spelman attracts a high proportion of alumnae children, though 43 percent of freshmen receive Pell Grants.

reviews. A psychology major says the school's security efforts, gated campus, and Title IX procedures help students "feel protected" on campus.

In part because of the Atlanta University Center, students have plenty of chances for social interaction with other nearby colleges, especially Morehouse. "Students mingle in the student centers of all four schools all the time, especially on Fridays," one denizen explains. Spelmanites also take advantage of the big-city nightlife; they attend plays, symphonies, and the hot Atlanta nightclubs. Lenox Square is popular for shopping. "Atlanta is a great college town!" gushes one junior. "If there is any place that a student can be academically enriched, it is here." About half of the students get involved with service opportunities in the city. Sororities are present but only in small numbers—roughly 5 percent of the students go Greek. The attitude on drinking leans toward the conservative. Says one student, "No alcohol on campus—period." The most anticipated annual events include sisterhood initiation ceremonies, homecoming, and the Founders Day celebration. Varsity sports, never all that important, have been replaced with a general fitness and nutrition program that features an extensive list of physical activities such as running and yoga. The college has also introduced an intramural program that includes basketball, flag football, soccer, and volleyball.

Spelman College has spent more than 140 years furthering the education and opportunities of Black women. It has adapted its curriculum to meet the career aspirations of today's youth, built up its bankroll, and successfully met the recruitment challenge posed by affirmative action at other universities. As elite an institution as ever, Spelman is staking its future on its ability to provide a unique kind of education that gives its graduates a competitive edge in the 21st century.

If You Apply To ›

Spelman: Early decision, early action, regular decision. Accepts the Common Application. Accepts applications from students who consistently live and self-identify as women, regardless of their gender assignment at birth. Please consult Spelman's website for the most up-to-date information regarding standardized test requirements.

College of the Atlantic

105 Eden Street, Bar Harbor, ME 04609

In today's status-driven world, COA is as out-there as it gets—a haven for community-minded, environmentally conscious students who would rather save the world than make a buck. Lacks many of the usual trappings of college life, such as sports teams and Greek life. But with roughly 350 undergrads, it makes its distinctive blend of smallness and diversity an academic and social virtue. Students get lots of hands-on experience and have a big voice in running the school.

Website: www.coa.edu
Location: Rural
Private
Total Enrollment: 361
Undergraduates: 357
Male/Female: 30/70
Financial Aid: 99%
Pell Grant: 30%

The College of the Atlantic attracts rugged individualists concerned with the world's most pressing issues, notably climate change, social justice, and food systems. The college's curriculum and sole major is focused on human ecology—the study of the relationship between humans and their natural, social, and built environments. COA bucks the national obsession with growth—seeing smallness as the key to education that cuts across disciplines—while eschewing academic conventions and taking a personalized approach to teaching and learning. "I chose COA because I found no other school that gave me as much freedom to create my own educational path," says one sophomore.

The 35-acre campus, covered in lush flowers, vegetable gardens, and lawns, sits on Mount Desert Island (pronounced like "dessert"), along the shoreline of Frenchman Bay and adjacent to the magnificent Acadia National Park. In addition, the college maintains two offshore island research centers, two agricultural properties, a 100-acre wooded protectorate, wood-pellet-heated "green" dorms, and an oceanside campus center. Founded by local residents in 1969, COA is serious about its mission, and this is reflected in the facilities: sustainability is prized, and the college uses environmentally responsible materials as much as possible. "We believe the most sustainable building is that which isn't built," says an administrator. COA's organic vegetable operation, Beech Hill Farm, includes housing where student workers live during the summer season. The $13 million Davis Center for Human Ecology, featuring classrooms, science labs, art studios, and a teaching greenhouse, opened in 2021.

Instead of traditional academic departments, COA has three broad resource areas: environmental sciences, arts and design, and human studies. Many students choose to concentrate on more narrowly defined topics within human ecology, such as climate change and energy, environmental law and politics, educational studies, farming and food systems, or sustainable business. With advisors and resource specialists, each student designs an individual course of study. The natural sciences are

> **"I found no other school that gave me as much freedom to create my own educational path."**

stellar, with excellent instruction in marine science, field ecology and natural history, and zoology. Allied Whale, the school's marine mammal laboratory founded in 1972, offers excellent opportunities for hands-on field research. For the entrepreneurially minded, the Hatchery is COA's sustainable business incubator, offering eligible students academic credit, a variety of resources, and 10 weeks to develop a business venture and build a prototype. The emphasis is on interdisciplinary exploration, and the most compelling ideas get a $5,000 grant from the college along with a year of professional services.

Student life at COA is intense and semicommunal, beginning with an optional, rugged five-day wilderness orientation preceding the first trimester, in which 80 percent of incoming students take part. Before graduating, students must complete 40 hours of community service, a 10-week off-campus internship, and a 10-week senior project. Other requirements are few: first-years must take the human ecology core course, and two courses are required in environmental sciences, human studies, and arts and design. Sophomores must submit a writing portfolio for evaluation. All students incorporate research into their studies, whether it is a development impact study for the local government or a study on the aggression of fire ants for Acadia National Park.

"The classes at COA are unique, innovative, and tailored to the students," explains a senior. Some areas only have a professor or two, and 95 percent of all classes have fewer than 20 students. Since the student body is so small, students can become close to faculty members. "We get one-on-one time with our professors and individualized support," says a junior. In addition to traditional grades, students receive in-depth written evaluations of their work. They must reciprocate with a self-evaluation of their performance.

COA offers regular study abroad programs in Mexico's Yucatán Peninsula and in Vichy, France. In the Yucatán, students do ethnographic, agricultural, or scientific research of their own choosing. In France, they take literature, philosophy, politics, and/or art classes. Both programs include a strong language immersion component. COA also supports student participation in other study abroad programs through partner institutions such as the EcoLeague. Fifty-one percent of students go abroad during their time at COA.

(continued)

Expense: Pr $
Student Loans: 56%
Average Debt: $ $ $
Applicants: 525
Accepted: 61%
Enrolled: 29%
Grad in 6 Years: 67%
Returning Freshmen: 81%
Academics: ✐ ✐ ✐
Social: ☎ ☎
Q of L: ★ ★ ★
Admissions: (800) 528-0025
Email Address: inquiry@coa.edu

Strong Programs:
Human Ecology
Environmental Science
Climate Change and Energy
Environmental Law and Politics
Farming and Food Systems
Marine Science
Field Ecology and Natural History
Zoology

The college's sole major is human ecology—the study of the relationship between humans and their natural, social, and built environments.

"Students at COA are open-minded, hardworking, adventurous, flexible, self-motivated, and curious to explore passions other than their main area of study," says one contented sophomore. Fifteen percent of students are native to Maine, but another 61 percent hail from nearly 40 other states. The student population also has a strong international flavor—24 percent of students come from nearly 50 countries—driven by the school's affiliation with the Davis United World College Scholars Program, an international scholarship program. Many students traveled the world before beginning school and move on to the Peace Corps or AmeriCorps after. The student body is less than 1 percent Black, 2 percent Asian American, 5 percent Hispanic/Latino, and 4 percent multiracial, and women outnumber men more than 2 to 1. The college's governance system gives students and administrators almost equal voices in how it's run; anyone may raise concerns or vote on policy-change proposals or the hiring of new faculty at the All College Meeting. The overtly liberal student body isn't shy about speaking out on global issues either, including "climate change, food justice, biodiversity, and gender rights," says a junior. A limited number of merit scholarships, worth an average of $14,600, are available to top achievers.

"COA open-mics are a culture all their own, and they are an absolute blast!"

With the opening of two new residential buildings in 2022 and 2023 and the purchase of multiple off-campus townhouses, COA has been working to address a housing crunch created by an expanding tourism season that has driven up prices and limited the availability of rental housing in and around Bar Harbor. Roughly 75 percent of students now live in college-owned housing. Dining fare in the TAB ("Take-a-Break") Dining Hall and the Sea Urchin Café is "like home-cooked meals but with more options," according to one student. Another says COA "is a safe campus situated in a safe town in one of the safest states in the U.S." All students are required to take bystander intervention training once a year to learn strategies for preventing sexual assault.

Bar Harbor is a tourist community that "nearly shuts down in the winter," according to one student, although students do enjoy the coffee shops, bakeries, restaurants, and movie theaters that stay open. Students get to know the towns-people through community service. On-campus activities include open-mic nights, talent shows, concerts, dances, and, during the winter, "weekly Fireside Fridays with free cookies, hot chocolate, and coffee," says a sophomore. A senior adds, "COA open-mics are a culture all their own, and they are an absolute blast!" There are no fraternities or sororities, so students kick back at small off-campus house parties, which often revolve around potluck meals, since campus dining services are closed on weekends. Drinking is permitted on campus for those of legal age, only in private student rooms, but students agree that alcohol has little influence on the social scene. There are no varsity sports (not even ice hockey), but many students sign up for programs at the local YMCA, which offers sports such as soccer and volleyball. Outdoor programs, which take students hiking, sailing, cross-country skiing, and rock climbing in the wilds of Maine, are very active.

"You can't just play it safe. This community, the professors, your fellow students, won't allow it."

College of the Atlantic is a place where Earth Day really is cause for celebration, where students have been known to cut class to march on Washington, and where everyone who wants to, from students to trustees, jumps into frigid Frenchman Bay on the first Friday of the fall term to swim the stretch of water between the school's pier and the neighboring island. At COA, "You can't escape good conversations, or controversies, or being challenged, or learning something you never thought you'd learn or try," observes a senior. "You can't just play it safe. This community, the professors, your fellow students, won't allow it."

Overlaps

Bennington, Warren Wilson, Hampshire, Eckerd, Lewis & Clark, Prescott, University of Vermont, University of Maine

If You Apply To ›

COA: Early decision I and II, regular decision. SATs or ACTs: optional. Accepts the Common Application with supplement. Application includes space for applicants to describe their gender identity.

Auburn University

202 Mary Martin Hall, Auburn, AL 36849

Sweet Home Alabama, where the skies are so blue and the spirit of football lasts year-round. Auburn was once called Alabama Polytechnic Institute, and today AU's programs in engineering, agriculture, and the health fields are still among its best. AU's down-home, small-town atmosphere may feel claustrophobic to those from outside the Deep South. As for the role of football, the $14 million scoreboard says it all.

Founded in 1856, Auburn University is a public land grant university that excels in professional and technical fields such as architecture, engineering, and agriculture. But the school also welcomes students with frenzied athletics, warm and cozy hospitality, and Southern charm. "It truly is a family atmosphere. We are here to learn and help each other," says one happy Tiger.

The town of Auburn, which grew up amid miles of forest and farmland largely to serve the university, is called the "loveliest village of the plain," a moniker taken from a line in an Oliver Goldsmith poem. The campus stretches for nearly 2,000 acres, graced by mossy trees, lush lawns, and majestic colonnades. Most buildings are redbrick and Georgian in style, with some more modern facilities grouped in a compact central location. Newer facilities include the $44 million Engineering Student Achievement Center and the $70 million Gogue Performing Arts Center.

Auburn's core curriculum includes courses in the humanities and fine arts, science and mathematics, and social sciences. A writing-in-the-disciplines program bolsters every major with significant writing instruction. To ease the transition into college life, freshmen undergo the two-day Camp War Eagle orientation. Auburn's SKILL Program provides academic coaching and support to students with learning differences and ADHD. The academic climate varies by department, and a senior says, "I have found that rather than students competing with each other for higher grades, they are more willing to help their classmates through tutoring or group study sessions." Regardless of the rigor, students say professors generally go the extra mile for them. "Although I have not liked every teacher I've had, every teacher has taught me something new and useful," reasons a junior.

> **"We are here to learn and help each other."**

The engineering, architecture, agriculture, and pharmacy programs are stellar. Auburn boasts a first-of-its-kind program in wireless engineering for students who want to design network hardware or software for cell phones and other mobile devices. The Ginn College of Engineering also offers aerospace engineering, and Auburn has produced six NASA astronauts. The most popular majors include marketing, mechanical engineering, accounting, and finance, and the environmental science, human development and family studies, and interior architecture programs also draw attention. Accelerated degree programs in numerous fields allow eligible students to count approved graduate hours toward both a bachelor's and a master's degree, with the goal of completing both in as little as five years.

Website: www.auburn.edu
Location: Small City
Public
Total Enrollment: 26,227
Undergraduates: 22,674
Male/Female: 50/50
Financial Aid: 54%
Pell Grant: 11%
Expense: Pub $ $
Student Loans: 40%
Average Debt: $ $ $
Applicants: 27,619
Accepted: 71%
Enrolled: 27%
Grad in 6 Years: 81%
Returning Freshmen: 93%
Academics: ✍ ✍
Social: ☎ ☎ ☎
Q of L: ★ ★ ★
Admissions: (334) 844-6425
Email Address: admissions@auburn.edu

Strong Programs:
Engineering
Architecture
Agriculture
Prepharmacy
Environmental Science
Human Development and Family Studies
Interior Architecture
Marketing

Many Auburn students are eager to get started on their careers, so the co-op program, which provides pay and credit in several professional fields, is increasingly popular. Five interdisciplinary areas identified as "strategic research clusters" compete for millions of dollars in special funding, which means more opportunities for undergrads to assist faculty with research in areas including health disparities, pharmaceutical engineering, climate and earth systems science, omics and informatics, and scalable energy conversion science and technology. Twenty-nine percent of undergrads have worked with faculty on research by the time they graduate. Eleven percent of students join the Honors College, which culminates in a six-credit Senior Year Experience that may involve a traditional thesis, enhanced study abroad, service learning, or other capstone project. Through the Auburn Abroad Experience, 19 percent of all students study abroad in programs that include more than 50 faculty-led expeditions. Closer to home, the Rural Studio program sends students in the College of Architecture, Design, and Construction to live in economically underserved Hale County, Alabama, to design and build innovative community buildings and homes for local residents.

Auburn boasts a first-of-its-kind program in wireless engineering for students who want to design network hardware or software for mobile devices.

Auburn students are "mostly Southern people who are from Alabama and who have family that went to Auburn," says a junior. Indeed, 57 percent of Auburn undergraduates are Alabama natives, and many are second- or third-generation legacies. Black students account for a mere 5 percent of the largely homogeneous student body, Hispanics/Latinos represent 4 percent, Asian Americans make up 2 percent, and multiracial students add 3 percent; 4 percent hail from foreign countries. The conservative tone of this public Bible Belt campus makes it hospitable for more than 30 Christian student groups. "Half of Auburn students love politics and enjoy the political process, while the other half wouldn't know where their polling place was if you gave them a map," quips one senior. In an effort to increase diversity and address racial disparities on campus, Auburn has tripled the amount of money that it allocates to need-based financial aid for incoming freshmen. The university also awards merit scholarships averaging $8,100 and more than 400 athletic scholarships in 21 sports.

"Social life is great whether you are Greek or not."

The majority of Auburn's 32 residence halls are co-ed by floor, but there are several single-sex halls; 18 percent of undergrads live on campus. First-year students compete for rooms on a first-come, first-served basis with returning students, and the dorms fill up fast. "Get on a waiting list ASAP," advises a junior. The university helps those moving off campus find apartments and roommates. Twenty-five percent of Auburn men join fraternities, and 47 percent of women join sororities, perhaps because chapters get space in the best dorms. Students grumble about the mandatory—and pricey—meal plan, but say the dining has improved considerably in recent years. "The food continues to diversify and get healthier," confirms a student.

The Rural Studio program sends students to live in economically underserved Hale County, Alabama, to design and build homes.

Aside from varsity sporting events and off-campus fraternity and apartment parties, students enjoy school-sponsored concerts, free movies, and plenty of intramural leagues. "Social life is great whether you are Greek or not," says a freshman. The campus is officially dry, except on game days, and students say the alcohol policy is enforced. Long-standing traditions include Hey Day, when everyone wears a name tag and walks around saying, "Hey!" Seventy percent of students participate in a variety of community service programs, frequently as part of service-learning courses.

Auburn is a football powerhouse with pockets as deep as its location in the South and values to match. The school's $14 million video scoreboard was hailed by the athletic director as "a great asset, not only for our fans but also our students and our prospective student-athletes." Okay! On fall Saturdays, nearly 90,000 screaming fans turn the campus into Alabama's fifth-largest city, and the rallying cry "Warrrrr Eagle!" rocks the place each time an Auburn back runs to daylight. The annual Iron Bowl pits Auburn against Southeastern Conference archrival Alabama. Other solid Tigers teams include men's basketball, baseball, softball, and women's equestrian. Aubie, the official tiger mascot, has won a record 10 titles (yes, mascots compete in national championships too) at the UCA Cheer and Dance competition. The Auburn Recreation and Wellness Center is a 240,000-square-foot facility containing everything from weight-training areas to a virtual golf simulator and an outdoor leisure pool.

The Auburn Creed, a beloved tradition, states a belief in the value of "work, hard work," and Auburn is working hard to increase the caliber of its students and academic programs. "Auburn has become more focused on the future," one senior says. But students agree that certain key characteristics have stayed the same—and that's a good thing. Says one student, "We just keep getting cooler."

If You Apply To ›

Auburn: Early action I and II, regular decision. Accepts the Common Application with supplement. Portfolio required for art applicants. Audition required for music, dance, and theater applicants. Out-of-state enrollment is capped on a year-to-year basis; there are no set limits. Please consult Auburn's website for the most up-to-date information regarding standardized test requirements.

Austin College

900 North Grand Avenue, Sherman, TX 75090

The second most famous institution in Texas with Austin in its name. Half the size of Trinity (TX), runs neck and neck with Southwestern to be the leading small liberal arts college in Texas—and supports a more diverse student body. Combines the liberal arts with strong programs in business, education, science, and health, including premed. Don't look for the 'Roos on a map of the city of Austin. The college is just north of Dallas.

For historical reasons over which reasonable persons can and do disagree, the Kangaroo has become the symbol of all things Austin College. All freshmen receive #RooNation T-shirts at orientation, and students hold a trick-or-treat alternative known as 'Roo Boo for local children. The college was founded by a Presbyterian missionary in 1849, and its continuous ties to the Presbyterian Church (USA) are evident in the emphasis on values in core courses and high participation in service activities. Professors here even serve students breakfast at 10 p.m. the night before finals. It's just another example of the personal style that is typical of this charming Southern institution, which also boasts preprofessional programs, most notably premed, that are among the strongest in the state.

Austin College's 100-acre campus is in a residential area in the city of Sherman (population 45,000), an hour's drive from Dallas. The campus is designed in the traditional quadrangle style and comprises beige brick buildings, tree-lined plazas, decorative fountains, and an impressive 70-ton sculptured solstice calendar. Residence halls are conveniently located about 200 yards from most classrooms, which eases the pain of early morning classes. The IDEA Center for hands-on learning in the sciences features laboratory classrooms as well as a

Website: www.austincollege.edu
Location: Small City
Private
Total Enrollment: 1,220
Undergraduates: 1,204
Male/Female: 47/53
Financial Aid: 99%
Pell Grant: 32%
Expense: Pr $
Student Loans: 60%
Average Debt: $ $ $
Applicants: 4,130
Accepted: 43%
Enrolled: 16%
Grad in 6 Years: 68%
Returning Freshmen: 76%

(continued)

Academics: ✍ ✍ ✍
Social: ☎ ☎ ☎
Q of L: ★ ★ ★
Admissions: (903) 813-3000
Email Address: admission@
    austincollege.edu

Strong Programs:
Business Administration
Education
Neuroscience
Public Health
Biochemistry
Health Care Administration
Psychology
Biology

$1 million, 24-inch telescope and astronomical image camera in the building's domed observatory.

The core curriculum begins with a first-year seminar. Each professor who teaches the course becomes the mentor for the 20 freshmen in his or her class. Then students select from courses in humanities, social sciences, and natural sciences, as well as classes that focus on writing skills, quantitative literacy, and diversity. Students must complete one major and a minor or a double major to graduate. Additionally, all students satisfy an applied learning requirement by completing an internship, practicum, or similar experience. "I never imagined myself completing independent economics research while taking premed classes, but at Austin College, I was not only able to do so but was also encouraged by professors to pursue all my interests," enthuses a senior. During the January term, students focus on just one course, and many use that time to study abroad or undertake off-campus internships.

> "[I was] encouraged by professors to pursue all my interests."

When it comes time to apply to grad school, premed, predentistry, and prelaw students at this little college have some of the highest acceptance rates of any Texas school. Those interested in the healing arts benefit from strong programs in neuroscience, public health, biochemistry, and health care administration. The noteworthy Austin Teacher Program allows students to earn both a bachelor's and a master's degree in five years. Business administration, psychology, biology, and business finance are the most popular majors. The Jordan Family Language House is home to students who want an immersive experience in French or Spanish; native speakers of each language live in the house, and students speak the language in all common areas. New offerings include minors in social justice and nonprofit organizations and public affairs. A cooperative engineering program links the college with other schools. Students with eclectic interests can combine three of AC's majors into an interdisciplinary degree.

Of the academic climate, a psychology and theater major says, "Students are competitive with each other in a way that fosters creativity and growth rather than rivalry." Sixty-six percent of all classes have fewer than 20 students. "Teachers always make time for students, they're approachable, and the mentor program really helps when it comes to registering for classes and looking for summer research programs or internships," says a student. The college also offers independent study and departmental honors programs. The Posey Leadership Institute offers seminars and courses, and a minor in leadership studies is available. AC provides five research areas in Grayson County, including the Sneed Prairie Restoration Project. Forty-two percent of students conduct faculty-mentored undergraduate research, and 55 percent study abroad in programs offered in more than 60 countries. The Global Outreach fellowship program gives 10 to 15 students the chance to volunteer in educational programs around the world.

> "If you need help, often before you need it, people are reaching out to provide it to you."

New offerings include minors in social justice and nonprofit organizations and public affairs.

According to an international relations major, students at AC are "tight-knit like a family. Everybody knows everybody." Ninety-two percent of AC students hail from the Lone Star State, with 1 percent from abroad. Hispanics/Latinos comprise 25 percent of the student body, Black students 8 percent, Asian Americans 14 percent, and multiracial students 3 percent. Politically, students say the campus leans liberal. AC offers merit scholarships worth an average of $27,800 but no athletic scholarships.

Eighty-four percent of undergraduates live on campus, and all are required to do so for their first three years. "All of the housing on campus is extremely comfortable," a biology major says. Residence halls are co-ed, except for one all-female and one all-male dorm. Juniors and seniors choose from suites, flats, and cottages. Dean Hall is a popular choice for freshmen, despite (or perhaps because of) its reputation as being loud and social. As for campus dining, "The staff here is amazing," cheers one student. "They always have smiles on their faces and aren't afraid to save you an extra cookie." The Pouch Club, an on-campus joint, serves pizza and burgers, as well as beer and wine for those of legal age. Students report feeling safe on campus thanks to thorough campus security and sexual assault prevention programs.

Most of the social life is either on or near campus. "There is always something to do on campus, from smaller activities and club meetings to big dinners and guest speakers," a junior says. Twenty-six percent of the men and 29 percent of the women belong to local fraternities and sororities, respectively, but Greek groups are not allowed to advertise off-campus parties without the college's permission. Students can have alcohol in their rooms if they are 21 or older. Mega Texas is a campus carnival in the fall, and Kangapalooza brings a big-name musician to campus in the spring. Popular weekend excursions are a drive to Dallas or to the college's 28-acre recreational spot on Lake Texoma (a half hour north). Sherman is "quaint" and "historic," students say, but not a vibrant college town. "There are lots of restaurants," a junior says, "but for the most part there is nothing to do late at night."

The Kangaroos compete in Division III, and the women's water polo team captured back-to-back Collegiate Water Polo Association national championships in 2021 and 2022. Other solid teams include women's basketball, men's soccer, and men's and women's swimming and diving. The recreational sports program draws a third of the students, with flag football, volleyball, and soccer proving popular.

At this college with roots in the Presbyterian Church, students praise the preprofessional programs and the intimate, supportive environment. "Austin College cares for each student, and no one falls through the cracks," says a senior. "If you need help, often before you need it, people are reaching out to provide it to you." And while Sherman may seem to be a sleepy little place, Austin College is definitely hoppin'.

Popular weekend excursions include a drive to the college's 28-acre recreational spot on Lake Texoma (a half hour north).

Overlaps

Southwestern, Hendrix, St. Mary's University (TX), Trinity University (TX), Rhodes, Baylor, UT Austin, Texas A&M

If You Apply To ›

Austin: Early action I and II, regular decision. SATs or ACTs: optional (test-optional applicants must submit graded expository writing paper). Accepts the Common Application with supplement.

Babson College

Babson Park, MA 02457-0310

The only college in the *Fiske Guide* devoted entirely to business. Babson is the birthplace of entrepreneurial studies—which continue to define the campus ethos. Only 10 miles from college student mecca Boston and tougher to get into than ever. About two-thirds the size of Bentley, its closest competitor, and 28 percent of students are international. The one college in Massachusetts where it is possible to be a Republican with head held high.

Babson is a preeminent training ground for budding entrepreneurs and corporate bigwigs. The college is a pioneer in the study of entrepreneurship, dating to the 1970s—a time when people thought it couldn't be taught. Here, hands-on experience is the norm; students get school funding to start businesses during their first year and may hone their stock-picking skills by managing part of the college's endowment. Always the foremost business college in the Boston area, Babson attracts budding tycoons and entrepreneurs from around the globe.

Website: www.babson.edu
Location: Suburban
Private
Total Enrollment: 3,089
Undergraduates: 2,532
Male/Female: 57/43

Founded in 1919 by financier Roger Babson, the college sits on 370 acres near the sedate Boston suburb of Wellesley. The campus features open green spaces, gently rolling hills, and heavily wooded areas. Buildings are gently shaded and parking lots (filled with expensive foreign cars) are discretely hidden. Architecturally, the campus is mainly neo-Georgian and modern. Park Manor West doubles as a first-year residence hall and the home of the Schlesinger Innovation Center, offering an amphitheater, classrooms, and collaboration spaces.

Although Babson is a business school, students take business classes blended with coursework in the liberal arts and sciences. Babson's revised core curriculum, launched in fall 2021, emphasizes three major components. In the first, the year-long Foundations of Management and Entrepreneurship course, first-year students split into groups to develop start-up business plans; each group gets up to $3,000 in seed money from the college to get their concept up and running. At the end of the year, the business is liquidated and profits go to charity. Former FME groups have developed Babsonopoly (a Babson-themed version of Monopoly), published children's books, and sold solar-powered smartphone chargers. Second, sophomores take Socio-Ecological Systems, a cotaught course where they imagine sustainable solutions to real-world challenges. Finally, the Advanced Experiential course pairs juniors and seniors with an outside company or nonprofit organization for a semester-long, business-oriented project.

> **"No one blinks an eye when a student is walking around campus in a suit."**

All Babson students major in business and may select a concentration, such as business analytics, operations management, or real estate—or even identity and diversity studies or literary and visual arts—to further refine their studies. (The Sorenson Visual Arts Center has painting, ceramics, and sculpture studios; labs for photography and digital art; a student art gallery; and workspace for artists-in-residence.) Finance, economics, marketing, and entrepreneurship are the most popular concentrations, and the entrepreneurship program is one of Babson's strongest, bringing in venture capitalists and executives from such companies as Dunkin' and Jiffy Lube for how-to lectures.

In the classroom, Babson relies on the case-study approach more typically employed by M.B.A. programs. Students break into groups or act as officers of pseudo-corporations to address specific business situations and solve marketplace problems. "Even though most of our classes are group project–based, there is still a very intense, competitive atmosphere," says a student. Just

> **"Students with financial constraints would definitely find a challenging time fitting in."**

10 percent of classes have fewer than 20 students, but others rarely exceed 50. "The professors at Babson are the real deal, and the care for students is immeasurable," enthuses a senior. Accounting students may take graduate classes at Babson in the summer and fall after finishing their bachelor's degrees, letting them sit for the CPA exam about one year earlier than most other programs. The Center for Women's Entrepreneurial Leadership promotes women in business and offers scholarships, special events, and networking opportunities. Babson offers more than 100 global study programs around the world, in which 63 percent of students participate; students in the Honors Program are required to do so. Not all programs are business oriented; the London Theatre Program, for example, focuses on arts appreciation.

Babson students are go-getters. "We enjoy comparing how full our Google calendars are," says one senior, and another student adds, "No one blinks an eye when a student is walking around campus in a suit." Black students make up 5 percent of the undergraduate student body, Hispanics/Latinos 14 percent,

In Foundations of Management and Entrepreneurship, first-year students get up to $3,000 in seed money to get their start-up businesses up and running.

Asian Americans 13 percent, and multiracial students 2 percent. Massachusetts residents comprise 23 percent, while 28 percent are international. No one seems to care much about politics, or at least most prefer to avoid political discussions. "Students with financial constraints would definitely find a challenging time fitting in," cautions an accounting student, because "there is a lot of wealth on this campus," and socializing with friends often involves pricey nights out in Boston. Merit scholarships averaging $33,500 are available; there are no athletic scholarships.

Babson guarantees housing for four years, and 76 percent of undergraduates live on campus, resulting in high demand for singles and suites. "The suite-style living is awesome," says a freshman. "It allows you to live with a bunch of your best friends but still have separate singles to sleep in." After the first year, rooms are assigned by lottery, with standing based on credits earned. At the main dining hall, you'll find sushi, make-your-own stir-fry, vegan stations, and other options, and the food receives average reviews. Security gets high marks, and the student-led Alliance for Sexual Assault Prevention organization is active in raising awareness about campus sexual assault.

The entrepreneurship program brings in venture capitalists and executives from such companies as Dunkin' for how-to lectures.

Social life is centered on campus during the first two years through participation in more than 100 student organizations; after that, most students are 21 and have cars, so they head to the clubs and bars of Boston proper, about 20 minutes away. "Boston offers a very vibrant social scene for upperclassmen," confirms a senior. The Campus Activities Board brings in comedians, organizes bingo nights, and throws parties, as do Greek organizations, which attract 10 percent of the men and 17 percent of the women. "We never have any Friday classes, so Thursday and Saturday are the big party nights," explains a sophomore. Underage drinking on campus is treated with a three-strike policy, and the third offense gets violators kicked out of the dorms. Favorite campus festivals include alumni week-

"Boston offers a very vibrant social scene for upperclassmen."

end (great networking opportunities) and Spring Concert, when bands come to play and parties are thrown. Students also contribute more than 30,000 volunteer hours annually through the Office of Faith and Service.

The "very affluent" town of Wellesley has shops and restaurants, and there is a subway stop. Students can take the T's Green Line into the city to explore Quincy Market or the campuses of Harvard, Northeastern, Emerson, and Boston universities. The school sponsors trips to Celtics and Red Sox games. Wellesley is also home to Wellesley College, and it's not unheard of for Babson students to socialize with Wellesley women; Babson also offers cross-registration at Wellesley and neighboring Olin College of Engineering. Popular road trips include the beaches of Cape Cod and Martha's Vineyard, the ski slopes of Vermont and New Hampshire, and the bright lights of New York City and Montreal.

While making money may be the most popular form of competition at Babson, students recognize the importance of keeping their bodies in competitive condition too. Popular intramural and club sports include volleyball, rugby, and ice hockey, and on the varsity level, the Beavers play in Division III. Any match against archrival Bentley and soccer games against Brandeis and Colby draw crowds. The men's ice hockey team is formidable, and men's and women's basketball and alpine skiing are frequent title contenders.

At Babson, students embrace entrepreneurship as an ethos and are willing to work hard for what they want. After all, learning how to balance work with everything else that's important in life is a prerequisite to climbing the corporate ladder or becoming the next Elon Musk. And thanks to small classes, strong faculty connections, a laser-like focus on entrepreneurial leadership, and plenty of hands-on experience, students leave Babson well equipped to begin scampering up those rungs.

Overlaps

Bentley, Northeastern, Boston University, Boston College, NYU, Cornell, UC Berkeley, University of Pennsylvania

Bard College

Annandale-on-Hudson, NY 12504

A dominant presence in the world of nontraditional liberal arts colleges, Bard offers what is arguably the most innovative range of academic programs anywhere. Like Reed on the West Coast, combines unabashed individuality with rigorous traditional academics. Long-standing president Leon Botstein, a polymath known by all simply as "Leon," is an iconic educator who has championed the liberal arts in countries around the world.

Website: www.bard.edu
Location: Rural
Private
Total Enrollment: 2,019
Undergraduates: 1,727
Male/Female: 38/62
Financial Aid: 79%
Pell Grant: 26%
Expense: Pr $ $ $
Student Loans: 63%
Average Debt: $ $
Applicants: 5,161
Accepted: 60%
Enrolled: 15%
Grad in 6 Years: 72%
Returning Freshmen: 87%
Academics: ✍ ✍ ✍ ✍
Social: ☎ ☎ ☎
Q of L: ★ ★ ★ ★
Admissions: (845) 758-7472
Email Address: admission@bard.edu

Strong Programs:
Literature
Written Arts
Studio Arts
Photography
Film and Electronic Arts
Human Rights
Environmental and Urban Studies
Music

Bard College has come a long way since its 1860 founding by 12 men studying to enter the seminaries of the Episcopal Church. Those pioneers would no doubt be surprised at the eclectic mix of students now running around Annandale-on-Hudson in an ethos once described by the *New Yorker* as one of "quixotic unworldliness." But the idea that Bard is strictly a school for artists and social science majors has largely disappeared, and the result is a school with lots of intellectual depth. Having expanded its mission beyond undergraduate and graduate education to also encompass support for the arts, secondary education reform, and the development of partnerships that bring education to underserved areas around the globe, Bard has earned a well-deserved national, even international, profile. To succeed in such a dynamic environment, one student advises, "You don't need perfect grades. You just need an adventurous spirit, an ambitious attitude toward self-improvement, and an ability to evaluate your experiences and capabilities."

Bard's campus occupies 1,000 well-landscaped acres in New York's Washington Irving country, on the shores of the Hudson River. Consistent with everything else at Bard, there's no prevailing architectural theme, so each ivy-covered brick building stands out—especially the dorms, which range from cottages in the woods to Russian Colonial in style. Renowned architect Frank Gehry designed the stunning, $62 million Fisher Center for the Performing Arts, which provides teaching and performance space for everything from opera to improvisation. The Center for Science and Computation, designed by Rafael Vinoly, promotes collaborative, hands-on science. Montgomery Place, a 380-acre estate and National Historic Landmark adjacent to the main campus, provides additional facilities for programs in the arts, humanities, and environmental sciences.

> **"There are plenty of pseudo jocks and intellectuals in good shape."**

Despite Bard's reputation for nonconformity, the list of requirements is extensive, including nine distribution requirements. Classes are small and seminar style, and freshmen show up three weeks before classes start for the Workshop in Language and Thinking, where they read extensively in several genres and meet in small groups to discuss reading and writing. (A literature major calls L&T "the best three weeks of my life.") The First-Year Seminar introduces the intellectual, artistic, and cultural ideas at the core of a liberal arts education. Citizen Science, another three-week workshop in January, examines topics not normally covered in the traditional science curriculum, such as infectious disease; organized into teams, the entire first-year class then teaches science lessons in the local public schools. In the spring of the second year, students declare a major through Moderation, a midway review of performance and proposed study plans discussed with a board of professors in the relevant area. In junior year, preparation for the Senior Project begins. Students create original work as evidence of mastery in their field or fields, and their Senior Project is reviewed by a faculty board.

With authors such as Neil Gaiman, Francine Prose, and Dinaw Mengestu teaching at Bard, literature and written arts are among the school's best programs. Bard was one of the first to grant a B.A. in visual and performing arts and boasts one of the finest studio programs in the country; photography is one of the toughest majors to get into, and the film and electronic arts program is well regarded. Bard established what administrators believe is the first collegiate program in human rights. Environmental and urban studies is also strong. There is a five-year, dual-degree conservatory program for music students, and although Bard is far from preprofessional, it does offer combined programs of its own and with other schools in finance, engineering, public health, and a number of other fields.

Bard's academic climate is "intellectual and consistently challenging," says a senior, but students agree that the atmosphere is collaborative. "Students are more eager to engage in discussions about what they just learned in class than they are likely to discuss what grades they received on the most recent exam," says a sociology and human rights major. Eighty-nine percent of classes have fewer than 20 students, and if students want more

"If you like the woods, it's amazing. If you like the city, you'll go stir-crazy."

individual attention, they can devise a syllabus for their own tutorial and find a professor to sponsor it. There are no teaching assistants here, and professors receive outstanding reviews, for both their expertise and their personal approach. "Professors value the students as individuals first," says a senior.

A semester-long program in New York City lets students study biology and medicine at Rockefeller University, and spots are reserved for Bard students as Summer Undergraduate Research Fellows. Also located in New York City, Bard's Globalization and International Affairs program merges advanced coursework in global affairs with internships at leading public, private, and nonprofit agencies. Study abroad is available in nearly 50 countries around the globe; more than half of the students take part. The Trustee Leader Scholar program provides grants and support for student-run community service projects. In an effort to expand liberal arts instruction overseas and to help nurture emerging democratic societies, Bard has developed partnerships with educational institutions in locations as diverse as Lithuania, Kyrgyzstan, South Africa, and the West Bank, as well as among prison inmates in the U.S.

Bard students tended to march to their own drummer in high school. "Many struggle their first year, when they realize everyone is just as unique as they are," says one senior. While the school has its share of extremely wealthy children of media moguls and Hollywood actors, Bardians take pride in diversity, whether socioeconomic, racial, geographical (66 percent are from out of state, with 12 percent from foreign countries), or ideological, though they admit the latter can be lacking. "If you're a Republican or conservative, please come and add some dimension to our conversation," implores one student. "I'm sick of agreeing with everyone." Black students make up 6 percent of the student body, Asian Americans 3 percent, Hispanics/Latinos 13 percent, and multiracial students 6 percent. Academic scholarships based on financial need are available, but there are no athletic awards. Bard offers a unique early-decision application option in which students can take the Bard Entrance Examination, demonstrating their academic ability by submitting four 2,500-word essays on a range of scholarly topics that are graded by professors.

Students declare a major through Moderation, a midway review of performance and proposed study plans discussed with a board of professors.

With authors such as Neil Gaiman, Francine Prose, and Dinaw Mengestu teaching at Bard, literature and written arts are among the best programs.

Three-quarters of Bard students live on campus; freshmen and sophomores are required to do so. Residence halls vary in style, explains one student: "Some are old Victorian mansions, some are new modern buildings that are eco-friendly, one looks like a castle, and others are big cement monsters from the 1950s." Many upperclassmen move off campus; to help ease their commute, Bard runs a shuttle to the nearby small towns of Red Hook and Tivoli (cumulative population 11,000), which are home to a variety of restaurants, bars, and other conveniences. Campus dining is described as "decent, but not amazing," but students appreciate that much of the fresh produce comes from Bard's own student-operated farm. Students say they feel safe on their rural campus, but administrative handling of sexual assault has been a point of student activism.

All Bard students are automatically made members of the student government, and cocurricular life is run by students; there are more than 150 different clubs. The school offers cultural shows and performances, concerts, and movies, with indie films and alternative rock and hip-hop particularly popular. The Student Activities Board plans Urban Cowboy Night, Welcome Back Weekend, Midnight Breakfast complete with karaoke, the ever-popular Thursday Night Live, and Spring Fling. There are no fraternities or sororities, and when it comes to alcohol, policies are focused on safety and respect, although underage drinking in the dorms is taken seriously. Bard's hometown of Annandale-on-Hudson is 20 miles from the crafts and antiques meccas of Woodstock and Rhinebeck, and not much farther from the ski slopes of the Catskills and the Berkshires. Having a car helps to prevent occasional attacks of claustrophobia, and New York City is just 100 minutes away by train.

"The one real thing that unites Bard is an ability to be self-driven and independent."

The Raptors compete in 18 Division III sports and are members of a number of conferences, including the Eastern College Athletic Conference, the Liberty League, and the College Squash Association. Bard is virtually devoid of dedicated athletes, but one student notes, "There are plenty of pseudo jocks and intellectuals in good shape." Thirty-five percent of the students get involved in intramurals, such as basketball, floor hockey, and bowling, which emphasize participation and fun. Across campus, miles of trails stretch through the woods along the Hudson, perfect for everything from raspberry picking to jogging and hiking. "If you like the woods, it's amazing," muses an anthropology major. "If you like the city, you'll go stir-crazy."

Thanks to the iconoclastic vision of President Leon Botstein (who also conducts the American Symphony Orchestra) and a $500 million challenge grant from George Soros, Bard is looking forward to continuing to offer strong programs that reach far beyond the arts. Come prepared to work hard and have your mind opened. "The Bard culture is a weird mixture of apathy and activism, arts and sciences, quirkiness and coolness," says a senior. "However, the one real thing that unites Bard is an ability to be self-driven and independent. Bard students are not followers, but establish their own paths."

Overlaps

NYU, Oberlin, Reed, Vassar, Wesleyan, Skidmore, Macalester, Sarah Lawrence

If You Apply To ›

Bard: Early decision, early action, regular decision. SATs or ACTs: optional. Accepts the Common Application.

Barnard College

New York, NY 10027

The most selective women's college in the country, Barnard is academically right up there with Wellesley, and the workload is on par with the Ivies. Step outside and you're on Broadway; across the street lies Columbia University, whose academic riches are yours for the taking. Barnard women are a little more artsy, outspoken, and city-ish than their counterparts at Columbia.

Barnard students get the best of both worlds—the small, close-knit atmosphere of a liberal arts school along with the limitless opportunities of Columbia College, the undergraduate division of the Ivy League research institution just across Broadway. Whether they are passionate about art, urban studies, or computer science, women seeking a high-energy, empowering environment with top-notch academics are likely to find a niche here.

Barnard was founded in 1889 by suffragists in response to Columbia's refusal to admit women and was strategically named after a recently deceased Columbia president. Its campus is on the Upper West Side of Manhattan, in the Morningside Heights neighborhood, just blocks from Riverside Drive, with its lovely path parallel to the Hudson River for running or biking. Trees and other greenery shade grand prewar apartment buildings, and grassy medians break up the wide expanse of Broadway itself. Barnard's architecturally diverse buildings are more modern than Columbia's, and in recent years, the college has invested to upgrade labs, classrooms, and the residence halls. The 128,000-square-foot Milstein Center includes a state-of-the-art library featuring interactive technologies and learning spaces.

Barnard competes head-to-head with Columbia in admissions, an interesting dilemma because Barnard is an affiliate college of Columbia University, along with the engineering school, the medical school, the business school, and, of course, Columbia College. In general, women looking for a more traditional "rah-rah" experience may prefer Columbia. Some students apply to Barnard as a back door to Columbia, which is harder for women to get into, but Barnard's admissions officers have become adept at sniffing out Columbia wannabes. Those who opt for Barnard like the fact that advising and housing are better on their side of Broadway and value its distinctive approach to educating women. Once enrolled, Barnard students share a first-year orientation program with Columbia, where they mix together in small groups and take tours of the campus and city. Students can also take part in a preorientation urban volunteer program.

> **"From research in labs to internships at the Met, there is no shortage of amazing opportunities."**

Barnard's Foundations curriculum is designed to enable students to gain general knowledge in a range of academic disciplines, develop critical-thinking and communication skills, and spend more of their time exploring other areas of interest or pursuing cocurricular opportunities that enhance their major. First-year students must take a writing course, a first-year seminar, and a physical education class. In addition to standard distribution requirements, students must fulfill Modes of Thinking requirements in six areas, such as Thinking Technologically and Digitally, Thinking Locally, and Thinking about Social Difference. A senior project or thesis ensures academic depth within the major.

Barnard's most popular majors are economics, psychology, history, political science, English, biology, and neuroscience (there's a healthy contingent of premeds). Architecture, computer science, and the visual and performing arts, especially

Website: www.barnard.edu
Location: City Center
Private
Total Enrollment: 2,958
Undergraduates: 2,958
Male/Female: 0/100
Financial Aid: 47%
Pell Grant: 20%
Expense: Pr $ $ $ $
Student Loans: 35%
Average Debt: $
Applicants: 10,395
Accepted: 12%
Enrolled: 64%
Grad in 6 Years: 93%
Returning Freshmen: 97%
Academics: ✍ ✍ ✍ ✍ ✍
Social: ☎ ☎ ☎
Q of L: ★ ★ ★
Admissions: (212) 854-2014
Email Address: admissions@ barnard.edu

Strong Programs:
Architecture
Computer Science
Visual and Performing Arts
English
Women's, Gender, and
    Sexuality Studies
Economics
Psychology
History

dance, are also well regarded. Barnard boasts strong support for budding writers and is a hotbed of new talent. Women's, gender, and sexuality studies draws praise as well. New options include a major in educational studies. The Athena Center for Leadership Studies offers workshops, mentoring programs, internships, guest speakers, and other special features. Several 4–1 pathways allow students to earn a bachelor's degree from Barnard and a master's degree from Columbia in public health, engineering, international and public affairs, and other areas in just five years. A dual-degree program is available with the nearby Jewish Theological Seminary, and music students may apply to take classes at Juilliard and the Manhattan School of Music. About a third of the students study abroad in their choice of more than 35 countries, including Argentina, Australia, China, Morocco, and Spain.

Several 4–1 pathways allow students to earn a bachelor's degree from Barnard and a master's degree from Columbia in just five years.

Barnard students may cross-register for courses at Columbia, and vice versa; in certain majors, some required classes are only offered at Columbia, where the academic climate can be more competitive, with a stronger "stress culture," says a physics major. "Compared to Columbia, the atmosphere in Barnard classes tends to be warmer and more collaborative—almost family-like—without loss of rigor." Many students come to Barnard because of its low student/faculty ratio. Seventy-two percent of classes have fewer than 20 students. Another plus: Barnard has no graduate teaching assistants. In fact, Barnard professors enjoy Columbia's proximity almost as much as undergraduates, and each year one-third of the full-time faculty teaches in graduate departments throughout the university. Still, faculty members focus on their teaching responsibilities to undergraduates first, and a chemistry major calls the quality of instruction "impeccable." Undergraduate research is also a priority at Barnard, especially in the sciences, and often occurs within guided internships, colloquia, and seminar courses. "From research in labs to internships at the Met, there is no shortage of amazing opportunities outside of the classroom for Barnard students in New York City," cheers a junior. Three-quarters of students complete internships before they graduate. Beyond Barnard, which connects students with internship, career, and other postgraduate opportunities, receives positive reviews.

"Barnard students are smart, driven, strong go-getters who are going to change the world one day."

Three-quarters of students complete internships before they graduate.

"Barnard students are smart, driven, strong go-getters who are going to change the world one day," asserts a senior. Twenty-six percent of Barnard students are New York natives, and 13 percent are international. Asian Americans make up 19 percent of the student body, Black students 6 percent, Hispanics/Latinas 13 percent, and multiracial students 7 percent. Students are mostly liberal and politically active. Barnard does not offer merit or athletic scholarships, but it does commit to a need-blind admissions process for domestic first-year applicants and to meet admitted students' full demonstrated financial need.

Ninety-one percent of Barnard students live in the dorms, which have come a long way in recent years: there's an 18-story Barnard dormitory tower, plus one dorm complex and eight off-campus apartment buildings. Nonresidents must be signed in by a resident, and entries are always guarded, so students say they feel safe. "The dorms are clean, comfortable, spacious (mostly!), and very well maintained," reports a senior. Barnard guarantees four years of housing to enrolling first-years, which one student says is "a relief considering how difficult and expensive it can be to find an apartment in New York City." Seniors get the best rooms through a lottery system. All students must buy a meal plan, which may also be used at Columbia. "The college has created a Being Barnard program that teaches students how to recognize sexual assault and how to handle it both as a potential victim and as a passerby," explains a junior.

"[You have] the infinite opportunities of New York City right outside the gates."

When it comes to social life, students tend to divide their time between the campus and the city. "Most of the social life takes place around campus," a junior says, "but you obviously have all of New York City to explore." Traditions include Big Sub in the fall, when a 700-foot-long sub sandwich is assembled throughout campus and everyone grabs a piece, and Midnight Breakfast the night before finals begin, when deans and administrators serve up eggs and waffles in the student center. Barnard women interested in Greek life are allowed to join sororities at Columbia, and about 10 percent do so. Alcohol is permitted in residential spaces for those of legal age, and students seeking parties head next door to Columbia or bars in Morningside Heights, but an English major notes, "This is not a school where students go out every night. Maybe once a weekend, or every other weekend." Many of the city's cultural offerings are free to students with their school ID. Road trips are infrequent, as not many students have cars, but when they happen, destinations range from Washington, D.C., to Boston, easily reached by train and plane.

Barnard athletes compete in the Division I Ivy League conference alongside their peers enrolled at Columbia, and basketball, softball, tennis, track and field, and crew are popular and competitive. The fencing team is also strong. Columbia's marvelous gym, co-ed intramurals, and club sports are also available; the women's ultimate Frisbee and rugby clubs are particularly popular with Barnard students.

Students see Barnard as having "the supportive community of a small liberal arts women's college, the resources of a large research institution through Columbia, and the infinite opportunities of New York City right outside the gates," in the words of one proud Barnard woman. It's a winning combination that turns out well-rounded students ready to leap toward the future.

Traditions include Big Sub, when a 700-foot-long sub sandwich is assembled throughout campus and everyone grabs a piece.

Overlaps
Brown, Columbia, Pomona, Swarthmore, Wellesley, University of Chicago, Smith, NYU

If You Apply To ›

Barnard: Early decision, regular decision. Accepts the Common Application with supplement. Accepts applications from students who consistently live and identify as women. Please consult Barnard's website for the most up-to-date information regarding standardized test requirements.

Bates College

23 Campus Avenue, Lewiston, ME 04240

Bowdoin got rid of its frats; Bates never had them, and therein hangs a tale. With its long-held tradition of egalitarianism and sense of community, Bates is a kindred spirit to Quaker institutions such as Haverford and Swarthmore. A four-week spring term helps make Bates a leader in studying abroad. Boasts a pioneering debate team. Blue-collar Lewiston is not a draw, but New England countryside is within arm's reach.

Founded by abolitionists in 1855, Bates College takes pride in its heritage as a haven for seekers of guidance, freedom, and justice, and it aims to help students find a broader purpose for their lives. The college's 4–4–1 calendar offers ample opportunity for study abroad, even for just four weeks at year's end. Its small size also means student/faculty interaction is plentiful, and close friendships are easily formed.

The Bates campus features a mix of Georgian and Federal buildings and Victorian homes spread out over the grassy lawns of Lewiston. Over the last two decades, Bates has transformed its campus core: the college has converted two former student

Website: www.bates.edu
Location: Small City
Private
Total Enrollment: 1,821
Undergraduates: 1,821
Male/Female: 49/51
Financial Aid: 40%

(continued)

Pell Grant: 9%
Expense: Pr $ $ $ $
Student Loans: 29%
Average Debt: $ $
Applicants: 7,319
Accepted: 17%
Enrolled: 44%
Grad in 6 Years: 92%
Returning Freshmen: 92%
Academics: ✍ ✍ ✍ ✍ ½
Social: ☎ ☎ ☎
Q of L: ★ ★ ★
Admissions: (855) 228-3755
Email Address: admission@
   bates.edu

Strong Programs:
Psychology
Politics
Economics
History
Environmental Studies
Music
Art

residence halls into key academic buildings, renovated historic Victorian homes into student residences, turned one of the country's earliest college football fields into a multisport turf field, and opened a state-of-the-art science center for the biology, chemistry, and neuroscience departments.

Bates emphasizes a broad-based education in the liberal arts. In addition to a writing-intensive first-year seminar, students take at least one class in each of five Modes of Inquiry: analysis and critique, creative process and production, historical and social inquiry, scientific reasoning, and quantitative and formal reasoning. All students select a major and a second area of study, which may be a minor, a second major, or a general education concentration (GEC). Bates's GECs consist of four interrelated courses structured around a central theme, such as Class, Inequity, Poverty, and Justice; Globalization; and Queer Studies. More than 75 concentrations are available, and they may fall within one department or program or may be designed by faculty from different disciplines. "One unique part of Bates is that just about all seniors write a thesis," says a chemistry major. "Some are semester-long, while others are yearlong, depending on the department and what you want to do." The Ladd Library is often crowded with students who choose to write a thesis or produce an equivalent research, service, performance, or studio project.

> "One unique part of Bates is that just about all seniors write a thesis."

While Bates was a pioneer in not requiring standardized tests for admission, that doesn't mean its standards are lax. "The academic standard for an institution such as Bates is high, and students are held to that standard in all aspects across all major and minor disciplines," says a junior. The most popular majors include psychology, politics, economics, history, and environmental studies, and these are also among Bates's best. The music and art departments benefit from the Olin Arts Center, which houses a performance hall, gallery, recording studio, art studios, and practice rooms. Interdisciplinary programs at Bates include rhetoric, film, and screen studies; Earth and climate sciences; and gender and sexuality studies. Professors teach all courses, including lab and discussion sections, and 70 percent of classes enroll fewer than 20 students. "The professors are always so accessible and make a real effort to get to know their students on a personal basis," one senior states.

For those whose horizons extend beyond the charms of Lewiston, Bates offers study abroad opportunities in more than 80 foreign locations, and 65 percent of students take advantage of them. Bates's 4–4–1 calendar allows for a four-week short term at the end of the academic year, and students may use this term to focus on a single subject of interest, frequently off campus. Recent examples include geological fieldwork in the Northern Rockies; marine biological studies at stations on the coast of Maine; and art, theater, and music studies in New York City and Europe. A "purposeful work" initiative includes practitioner-taught courses that, in an effort to blend philosophical and pragmatic themes, apply classroom lessons to real-world problems, such as finding mentors and reflecting on career paths that promote personal satisfaction.

> "The professors are always so accessible."

A "purposeful work" initiative includes practitioner-taught courses that apply classroom lessons to real-world problems, such as finding mentors and career paths.

Nine percent of Bates students come from Maine, 9 percent arrive from foreign countries, and many others hail from Massachusetts, California, and New York. "Students at Bates are intelligent, quirky, and eager to try new things," a student says. The administration has slowly been making Bates more diverse, and Black students currently account for 6 percent of the student body, Hispanics/Latinos 8 percent, Asian Americans 6 percent, and multiracial students 7 percent. With just 9 percent of first-year students qualifying for Pell Grants, socioeconomic diversity is low as well. Students are drawn to social and political causes, and a French major reports, "Diversity is the biggest social issue on campus." There are no merit or athletic scholarships available, although the college does guarantee to meet 100 percent of the demonstrated financial need of all students.

Ninety-one percent of Bates students live on campus, as housing is guaranteed for four years, and singles, doubles, triples, quads, and suites are available. "Housing is great here," a student cheers. Students report that the campus dining hall offers tasty fare, with several stations ranging from brick-oven pizza and pasta to a vegan bar. Students say campus security is visible and more than adequate. "Given the nature of a small campus, students know a majority of the officers' names and do not feel intimidated to approach them about a problem," explains a history major.

Since there's not much to do in Lewiston (population 37,000), weekend diversions mostly occur on campus. "Whether it is parties, comedians, movies, or bands, there is always something to do for everyone on campus," a first-year student says. The Chase Hall Programming Board, run by students, plans many of the social events, including an annual gala. Without a Greek system, college alcohol policies are fairly loose, a student says, and a ban on hard liquor is often ignored. Barbecues and clambakes are big when the weather is nice, and the annual Winter Carnival includes a ski shredding competition, ice skating, and the Puddle Jump, where a hole is cut in the ice on Lake Andrews and students plunge in. Students with cars can easily

"Students at Bates are intelligent, quirky, and eager to try new things."

road-trip to the outlet stores in Freeport and Kittery, Maine. Other popular destinations include Bar Harbor in Acadia National Park, or "Portland, for great food," says a senior. Montreal and Boston are not far, and neither are the ski slopes of Vermont and New Hampshire. The Outing Club hosts weekend trips into the great Maine outdoors.

Bates's 31 varsity Bobcat teams compete in Division III, except for the ski team, which is Division I. Everyone gets excited for matches against Bowdoin and Colby, especially when it comes to basketball, football, and lacrosse. The women's rowing team has won five national championships in the last eight years. The intramural program, organized by students, is "strong and spirited" and attracts a large number of participants, with ice hockey, ultimate Frisbee, soccer, and rugby being some of the favorites. Bates is home of the famed undergraduate debate organization the Brooks Quimby Debate Council. Founded in 1855 when completing a public debate was a graduation requirement, the team was one of the first in the nation to go co-ed and to include Black students. Bates was also the first American institution to debate with foreign universities, and the team continues to achieve national success today.

If you can stand the cold and the silent, starry nights, Bates may be a good choice. With caring professors, a small student body, a focus on the liberal arts, and a free-spirited culture, students quickly become big fans. "I came to Bates for the people," says a sophomore. "The friends you make here will remain your friends well beyond your final days at Bates."

Overlaps

Colby, Bowdoin, Hamilton, Wesleyan, Connecticut College, Middlebury, Haverford, Swarthmore

If You Apply To ›

Bates: Early decision I and II, regular decision. SATs or ACTs: optional. Accepts the Common Application.

Baylor University

Waco, TX 76798

The largest and best-endowed Baptist university anywhere, Baylor has set its sights on becoming a leading research university. Atmosphere is avowedly Christian, but religious image has been tarnished by continuing controversies over how administrators have dealt with allegations of sexual assault. Strong sense of community, especially at Saturday afternoon home football games.

Baylor University offers students a solid Christian-influenced education at a bargain price. The university was founded in 1845, 10 months before Texas became a state, and its Baptist tradition fosters a strong sense of community among students and faculty. The school's strategic plan, Illuminate, promises a slew of changes, such as lowering the student/teacher ratio, building new residence halls while renovating old ones, and investing in resources to become a top-tier research university while enhancing its Christian identity. "Baylor's commitment to academic excellence and an incredible alumni network ensures a great education and a chance to get a job," says a junior.

The 1,000-acre Baylor campus abuts the historic Brazos River near downtown Waco, Texas (population 140,000). The Georgian architectural style emphasizes the gracious tradition of the Old South, and the central part of campus, the quadrangle, was built when Baylor moved from Independence, Texas, in 1886. The campus has been witness to a number of renovations and new construction, including the Foster Campus for Business and Innovation and the $185 million Foster Basketball Pavilion, scheduled to open in 2024.

Core requirements in the College of Arts and Sciences include a standard distribution of coursework in several liberal arts areas as well as two religion courses and two semesters of Chapel, a series of lectures and meetings on various aspects of faith and Christian service. All new students take a New Student Experience course in the fall, and everyone completes a Cultural Events Experience. The Honors College oversees the honors program (which offers opportunities for course integration and independent research) and the University Scholars Program (which waives most distribution requirements).

"While a lot is expected of us, professors are willing to help."

Of Baylor's 126 undergraduate degrees, some of the most popular include nursing, biology, health science studies, communication, and accounting. Computer science, communication sciences and disorders, business, psychology, and neuroscience programs are well regarded. More unusual options include institutes focusing on environmental studies and childhood learning disorders, a minor in military studies, and a major and minor in Great Texts, an interdisciplinary program exploring "the richness and diversity of the Western intellectual heritage." The archaeology and geosciences departments benefit from fossil- and mineral-rich Texas prairies. Fourteen percent of students travel on study abroad programs, which send them packing to dozens of countries.

Students say that one of Baylor's greatest strengths is its sense of campus community, fostered by the university's emphasis on Christianity and the faculty's focus on teaching, along with research. Baylor's hefty $2 billion endowment is the largest among the nation's Baptist-affiliated schools. Administrators strive to keep classes small—46 percent have fewer than 20 students. Full professors often teach freshman courses, and opportunities for mentored research abound. "While a lot is expected of us, professors are willing to help and students work

---

Website: www.baylor.edu
Location: Small City
Private
Total Enrollment: 18,463
Undergraduates: 14,841
Male/Female: 40/60
Financial Aid: 94%
Pell Grant: 16%
Expense: Pr $ $
Student Loans: 48%
Average Debt: $ $ $ $
Applicants: 36,588
Accepted: 57%
Enrolled: 21%
Grad in 6 Years: 82%
Returning Freshmen: 88%
Academics: ✏️ ✏️ ✏️
Social: ☎ ☎ ☎
Q of L: ★ ★ ★
Admissions: (254) 710-3435
Email Address: admissions@baylor.edu

Strong Programs:
Computer Science
Communication Sciences and
   Disorders
Business
Psychology
Neuroscience
Geosciences
Nursing
Biology

together to help one another excel academically," says an environmental health science major.

"The students at Baylor tend to be kind, involved, and driven," says a finance and economics major. "They differ from some of our closest rivals mainly because of the spiritual influence that many students tend to have and seek out." Sixty percent of undergraduates are Texans and 21 percent are Baptist; 3 percent are international. Black students account for 5 percent of the student body, Hispanics/Latinos 16 percent, Asian Americans 9 percent, and multiracial students 5 percent. The university has launched several initiatives to increase and support diversity on campus, including cultural competence training for students, faculty, and staff and programs supporting first-generation students. Students vie for numerous academic scholarships, averaging $18,100, and more than 400 athletic scholarships in 19 varsity sports.

All students take two semesters of Chapel, a series of lectures and meetings on various aspects of faith and Christian service.

As might be expected on such a conservative, religious campus, dorms are single sex and have limited visitation privileges, which draws complaints from many of the 35 percent of students who call them home. The Faculty-in-Residence program houses one faculty member in each residence hall who plans special events and supports "learning and faith development." Upperclassmen look off campus for cheaper housing with private rooms and fewer rules, but there has been a push for more students to stay on campus with the recent construction of three residence halls with apartment-style rooms. Students say they feel safe on campus with frequent police patrols. Allegations in 2016 that Baylor failed

"Greek organizations are a big part of the culture at Baylor."

to comply with gender-equity laws or to respond properly to incidents of sexual violence led to the resignation of the president and football coach. Under new leadership, the university says that it has implemented "more than 100 improvements to infrastructure, policies, and procedures," including sexual assault training and prevention programs. "I have watched Baylor learn to address its shortcomings and challenges instead of ignoring them," remarks a senior.

Twenty percent of Baylor's men and 34 percent of the women belong to a fraternity or sorority, and frats dominate the strong off-campus party scene. "Greek organizations are a big part of the culture at Baylor," reports a student. "Many students go to parties and violate the drug and alcohol policies." Alcohol is not served on campus or at campus-sponsored events. Students may also join more than 350 other student organizations, most of which involve a community service requirement. "Common Grounds, an on-campus coffee shop, hosts concerts most weekends," says one student. "The movies are popular (a ticket costs $5 with a student ID)." Easy road trips include Dallas, Austin, San Antonio, Bryan/College Station, and beaches at Galveston, South Padre Island, and Corpus Christi. Most destinations are within a two-and-a-half-hour drive, students say, making a set of wheels a big help, if not a necessity.

On Diadeloso (Day of the Bear), classes are canceled for a day in April in favor of a campuswide celebration.

Highlights of Baylor's social calendar include the weekly Dr Pepper Hour with free ice cream floats and Diadeloso (Day of the Bear), when classes are canceled for a day in April in favor of a campuswide celebration. Christmas on 5th Street, organized by Student Life, gives students an opportunity to enjoy the annual Christmas tree lighting, concert, and other holiday festivities. The school claims to have the largest collegiate homecoming parade in the nation.

When it comes to football, remember: you're in Texas. The Division I Baylor Bears play in the $266 million McLane Stadium. Freshmen wear special custom jerseys to games and take the field before the players, then sit together as a pack. "It's a very awesome part of the freshman experience," one student says. But recently it's the basketball teams that are generating the most excitement. The women's team won the national championship in 2019, and the men did likewise in 2021. Acrobatics and tumbling have claimed several national titles in recent years. Big

12 Conference winners include football, men's tennis, and men's and women's basketball. For weekend warriors, the McLane Student Life Center offers one of the tallest rock-climbing walls in Texas. The university maintains a small marina for kayaking and paddleboating, and several lakes with good beaches, fishing, and watersports are nearby. Popular intramurals include flag football, volleyball, and the country's largest collegiate dodgeball tournament; 29 club sports are another big draw.

"Baylor is a Baptist institution that has been 100 percent commissioned to do God's work in education," states one student. As the university struggles to put its sexual assault scandals in the rearview mirror, students looking to focus on strong academics, community involvement, and discovering their vocational calling may find a good fit here.

Overlaps

Southern Methodist, Texas A&M, UT Austin, Texas Tech, Texas Christian, University of Houston, Texas State, Rice

If You Apply To ›

Baylor: Early decision, early action, regular decision. Accepts the Common Application with supplement. Please consult Baylor's website for the most up-to-date information regarding standardized test requirements.

Beloit College

700 College Street, Beloit, WI 53511

A small Midwestern college known for freethinking students, international focus, and ever-growing emphasis on practical, hands-on experiences. Wisconsin location makes Beloit easier to get into than comparable schools in sexier places. Well-known anthropology program is among the best in the nation.

Website: www.beloit.edu
Location: Small City
Private
Total Enrollment: 956
Undergraduates: 956
Male/Female: 48/52
Financial Aid: 98%
Pell Grant: 36%
Expense: Pr $ $ $
Student Loans: 56%
Average Debt: $
Applicants: 3,277
Accepted: 67%
Enrolled: 13%
Grad in 6 Years: 74%
Returning Freshmen: 90%
Academics: ✍ ✍ ✍
Social: ☎ ☎ ☎
Q of L: ★ ★ ★ ★
Admissions: (608) 363-2500
Email Address: admiss@beloit.edu

Beloit College remains dedicated to the liberal arts and sciences but is increasingly focused on connecting its brand of liberal education to career preparation and professional success, encouraging students to pursue diverse hands-on learning experiences. Known for attracting liberal freethinkers in the 1960s and '70s, the school has steered back toward the mainstream. What hasn't changed is its emphasis on inclusion, understanding, and the world beyond the United States. "To really enjoy Beloit, you should be open to new ideas, concepts, and people," advises an education and youth studies major. "You will learn how to think critically about your positions and beliefs and work to have a deeper understanding of the world as a whole."

Beloit was founded by transplanted New Englanders in 1846 when Wisconsin was still a territory. Its 40-acre campus is a Northeastern-style oasis an hour's drive from Madison and Milwaukee and less than two hours from Chicago. Academic and

> **"Students are expected to do significant work…but there is also an atmosphere of meaningful collaboration."**

administrative buildings sit on one side, with residence halls on the other. Nineteenth-century Federal and Romanesque architecture dominates, with a few modern facilities mixed in, like the LEED Platinum–certified Sanger Center for the Sciences. The college's newest facility is a 120,000-square-foot student union and recreation center called the Powerhouse; the $38 million project repurposed a defunct power plant on the Rock River, adjacent to campus.

In the absence of core requirements, students complete three writing-intensive courses, a quantitative reasoning class, one intercultural literacy course, a service-learning experience, and a capstone experience. In addition, Beloiters tackle classes across five domains that focus on systems, arts, behavior, the universe, and texts. To satisfy an "Experience" requirement, students may undertake an internship, an entrepreneurial or research project, or a designated course with a similar component, such as field work or travel.

Anthropology is a signature program at Beloit, and the geology, international relations, creative writing, theater, and dance programs are also popular and well regarded. Biology, psychology, and business economics enroll high numbers too. Among the more distinctive options are a museum studies minor, enhanced by hands-on experience in the college's Wright Museum of Art and Logan Museum of Anthropology, which was established in 1894 and emphasizes social justice in museum practices. Notable interdisciplinary offerings include majors in health and society and critical identity studies. A 3–2 engineering dual degree is available with WashU in St. Louis and Rensselaer Polytechnic Institute.

The academic milieu is described as challenging but not competitive. "Students are expected to do significant work—papers, research, symposiums—but there is also an atmosphere of meaningful collaboration," says one student. Teaching is the faculty's first priority, and 76 percent of classes have fewer than 20 students. "The professors at Beloit are superb," says a political science and psychology double major. "They help students develop critical skills such as communication, creative problem-solving, teamwork, etc." Beloit has bolstered academic advising and career services with the Advanced Mentoring Program, which matches each incoming student with a faculty mentor as soon as they enroll, so that guidance can begin before they arrive on campus in the fall. In addition, students may join any of eight broad Career Channels—ranging from Business & Entrepreneurship to Health & Healing, Justice & Rights, and Curating & Communicating—to explore potential career options through interactions with faculty, peers, and alumni working in their fields of interest as well as on- and off-campus experiences.

Thanks to Beloit's emphasis on hands-on learning, opportunities for practical cocurricular experiences abound. Budding scientists may conduct biological and biomedical research at Northwestern and Rush Universities in Chicago. The Center for Entrepreneurship in Liberal Education at Beloit, located a few blocks away in downtown Beloit, enables students from any major to plan and execute original entrepreneurial projects. Thirty-five percent of students study or do research abroad, choosing from programs in 60 countries.

> "Beloiters like to be different. We like to think of ourselves as iconoclasts."

"Beloiters like to be different," observes a creative writing major. "We like to think of ourselves as iconoclasts." While Beloit may not be as far-out as it once was, the student body is still decidedly liberal. Just 7 percent of students hail from Wisconsin, and 14 percent come from abroad. Hispanics/Latinos represent 16 percent of the total, Black students 10 percent, Asian Americans 3 percent, and multiracial students 4 percent. The Sustained Dialogue program encourages conversations about diversity and identity. Merit scholarships averaging $38,700 are available, although there are no athletic scholarships. Thirty-six percent of freshmen are Pell-eligible. Through its Midwest Flagship Match program, Beloit guarantees academically qualified residents of several states that it will match the in-state tuition rate of the flagship public university in their home state.

Eighty-five percent of Beloit students live in the 38 on-campus housing facilities, where they're required to remain for three years. "The dorms at Beloit will never win an award for beauty, but the rooms are large and comfortable," according to one student. Fraternities attract 11 percent of the men, and sororities draw 13 percent of the women; members may live in their chapter houses. Numerous

(continued)

Strong Programs:
Anthropology
Geology
International Relations
Creative Writing
Theater
Dance
Health and Society
Critical Identity Studies

The Logan Museum of Anthropology, which was established in 1894, emphasizes social justice in museum practices.

The Advanced Mentoring Program matches each incoming student with a faculty mentor as soon as they enroll.

special-interest houses cater to those interested in world languages, the arts, anthropology, and other disciplines, as well as to student organizations. Food in the Commons dining hall is said to be average college fare, but options in Grace's Place and Hamilton's are better received; co-ops where students cook for each other are another option. "Beloit offers strong support by way of mental health services," reports a junior. "They offer unlimited free sessions at the Health & Wellness Center as well as free online therapy services." Campus safety gets good ratings too.

Social life is almost entirely campus-based. "On the weekends there are always events going on such as lectures, music groups, movie showings, theater productions, dance shows, and parties," says one junior. Highly anticipated annual events include the Folk and Blues Fall Music Festival, which brings jazz, reggae, folk, and blues bands to campus, and Spring Day, when classes give way to a carnival and everyone kicks back to enjoy the (finally!) warmer weather. Traditional Bell Runs involve running from the quad to a bell and back, disencumbered of

> **"Beloit offers strong support by way of mental health services."**

clothing. Students describe the party scene as very low-key, and Greek organizations often team up with special-interest houses and other student clubs to throw parties. And while the school enforces state drinking laws, students say the attitude toward alcohol on campus is relaxed. "We have an alcohol philosophy," says a sociology major. "Beloit would never go so far as to say 'policy.'"

Beloit (population 37,000) is a small, historically industrial city that has undergone a revitalization in recent years. A river walk connects the campus to downtown, and several restaurants, bars, shops, and a record store have popped up, as has a popular Saturday farmers market. The city also offers a bowling alley, a movie theater, and a Walmart. "Groups such as Habitat for Humanity, Beloit Interaction Committee, and the Outreach Center work hard to integrate students into the community," says a sophomore. When in need of a change of scenery, Beloiters take off for Chicago or the college town of Madison, easily reached through a cheap regional bus service. For the outdoors-minded, nearby Wisconsin Dells offers camping and water parks.

Sports at Beloit are played more for fun than glory, unless, of course, it's a football game against rival Ripon College. Among the school's 18 Division III Buccaneers squads, standouts in the Midwest Conference include women's soccer, women's track and field, and baseball. Intramural ultimate Frisbee draws around a hundred players and spectators, and intramural basketball, volleyball, and soccer are also popular.

Beloit is a bundle of contradictions: a small liberal arts college in the heart of Big Ten state university country, and an academic program that has an East Coast rigor but a laid-back classroom vibe reflective of the friendly spirit of the Midwest. Although the school continues to evolve, "the essential core of Beloit has stayed the same," says a senior. "It is still a campus full of artistic creators, unabashed activists, and people who love making dorm-room forts. We're still weird, and we like it that way."

Overlaps

**Macalester,
Grinnell,
Reed, Oberlin,
Bennington, Knox,
Lake Forest,
St. Olaf**

If You Apply To ›

Beloit: Early decision, early action I and II, regular decision. SATs or ACTs: optional. Accepts the Common Application with supplement. Applicants are invited to submit nonbinary gender identity and pronouns.

Bennington College

Bennington, VT 05201-6003

Known for top-notch performing arts and lavish attention on every student. Arts programs rely heavily on faculty who are practitioners in their field. Slightly less competitive than Bard and Sarah Lawrence, comparable to Hampshire. With just under 700 undergraduates, Bennington is one-third the size of most liberal arts colleges.

Bennington College is a school where architects are teachers, biologists sculpt, and a sociologist might work on Wall Street or in graphic design. The college's focus is on learning by doing. Since its founding in 1932, Bennington has pioneered in self-directed education and emphasized fieldwork and personal relationships with professors—an approach that sets it apart even from other liberal arts colleges of similar (read: small) size. Says one junior, "If you want an education you can shape yourself and you want that education to transcend your homework and the classroom, this is a great place to go to school."

Bennington sits on 470 acres at the foot of Vermont's Green Mountains. The campus was once an active dairy farm, and a converted barn houses many classrooms and administrative spaces. But don't let the quaint New England setting fool you. The Dickinson Science Building boasts high-tech equipment for aspiring chemists, biologists, environmental scientists, and geneticists. A recent renovation of the central Commons building added new student social spaces, larger dining facilities, and ADA-accessible classrooms.

> **"If you want an education you can shape yourself...this is a great place to go to school."**

Thanks to its focus on John Dewey–style experiential learning, Bennington's academic structure differs from that of a typical college or university. Rather than selecting from preset majors, students design their own cross-disciplinary course of study (known as their "Plan"). There are some academic requirements, including the Field Work Term, in which students spend seven weeks each January and February conducting an internship or other work experience in a field of interest and a location of their choice—meaning that all students graduate with at least four internships under their belts. Students receive narrative evaluations instead of grades (although they do have the option to request grades in addition to the evaluations). Even Bennington's application process is nontraditional. In lieu of a standard application, prospective students may choose to submit a "dimensional application"—an open-form application that allows them to choose any materials, in any format, that they believe best convey why they are well suited to attend Bennington.

The most popular areas of study include visual and performing arts, especially drama and music; society, culture, and thought; cultural studies and languages; literature; and psychology. Computer science and mathematics are strong, too, although they attract a smaller number of students than many of the college's programs. A notable offering in architecture is heavily arts-oriented. "Half of the students here do work in the arts, whether it's theater or dance or studio art. Those are obviously well regarded," says a sophomore. Consistent with Bennington's judgment that traditional academics have become "insular and self-perpetuating," the Center for the Advancement of Public Action invites students to put the world's

> **"Bennington prides itself on being a place for the weird, independent kid to find a community."**

most pressing problems at the center of their education via classwork and hands-on workshops. Closely related are the "pop-up mini-courses" that faculty offer in

Website: www.bennington.edu
Location: Small Town
Private
Total Enrollment: 808
Undergraduates: 695
Male/Female: 33/67
Financial Aid: 99%
Pell Grant: 23%
Expense: Pr $ $ $ $
Student Loans: 50%
Average Debt: $ $
Applicants: 1,726
Accepted: 67%
Enrolled: 21%
Grad in 6 Years: 68%
Returning Freshmen: 84%
Academics: ✐ ✐ ✐
Social: ☎ ☎ ☎
Q of L: ★ ★ ★ ★
Admissions: (800) 833-6845
Email Address: admissions@
   bennington.edu

Strong Programs:
Visual and Performing Arts
Society, Culture, and Thought
Cultural Studies and
   Languages
Literature
Psychology
Computer Science
Mathematics
Architecture

response to unfolding events or current cultural phenomena. Recent topics of these three-week courses, often suggested by students, have included The War in Ukraine and Confronting Fascism in the Wake of an Insurrection. Cross-registration options at nearby Williams College expand students' access to course offerings, and 17 percent of Bennington students study abroad.

"Students here are encouraged to study the things that keep them up at night, that are important to them personally," explains a literature, music, and drama student. As a result, students tend to bring a certain level of intensity to their classes. Eighty-seven percent of courses enroll fewer than 20 students. Without academic departments, the faculty works to provide students with a well-rounded academic foundation. "Professors work independently with students on their personal trajectory of progress," says a student studying conflict resolution. The First-Year Forum is a yearlong advising program that acclimates students to Bennington's approach to academics.

"Bennington prides itself on being a place for the weird, independent kid to find a community," remarks a literature and anthropology student. Curiosity and excitement about exploration and experimentation will take you far here, and if you lean liberal in the voting booth, so much the better. Just 5 percent of undergrads are from Vermont, and a surprising 19 percent are international. Racial and ethnic diversity are a challenge: Black students account for only 2 percent of the student body, Hispanics/Latinos 10 percent, Asian Americans 1 percent, and multiracial students 4 percent. Women outnumber men 2 to 1, but students report that the campus is diverse in terms of gender identity and sexual orientation. Merit scholarships worth an average of $32,400 are awarded to qualified students; no athletic scholarships are available.

> "All students are invited to the big house parties that happen on Fridays and Saturdays."

As Bennington lacks traditional departments, requirements, and even faculty tenure, it's probably not surprising that the school also eschews traditional dorms. Virtually all students live in one of the college's co-ed houses; a dozen are white New England clapboard, and six are more modern. Each house holds 30 to 40 people with two appointed chairs to govern house affairs. "Each house has a distinct history and personality," says a student. The college dining hall is "reasonably accommodating" of food allergies and special diets, according to a junior, and the meals are usually tasty. While students say the campus is generally safe, most agree that student support services, from public safety to health and counseling services to academic services, are suffering from understaffing.

With no Greek system, social life happens in the residential houses. "All students are invited to the big house parties that happen on Fridays and Saturdays. The themes are fun and creative, and everyone gets dressed up," explains a creative writing student. "There's no pressure to drink or smoke, but many do." Students say campus alcohol policies focus on keeping students safe rather than punishing them. Twice each year, the college turns part of its huge Visual and Performing Arts complex into an indoor roller rink for a Rollerama party. For 12 hours one day each May, the campus celebrates spring with Sunfest, which features music, games, and other events. And during the last week of each term, when (in lieu of final exams) students present their work to faculty, the ringing of the Commons bell at midnight calls weary students to the dining hall, where professors, staff, and the college president serve up French toast and other breakfast favorites.

Although the vibe on Bennington's campus is liberal and cosmopolitan, the neighboring town of the same name—four miles away, with a population of 15,000—is far more conservative, typical of rural New England. For that reason, one student says, students often avoid it, and "when you combine the hilltop isolation of the campus, the result is a sense of an enclave." Still, the area offers some good

For the Field Work Term, students spend seven weeks each January and February conducting an internship or other work experience.

Faculty sometimes offer "pop-up mini-courses," such as The War in Ukraine, in response to unfolding events or current cultural phenomena.

Twice each year, the college turns part of its Visual and Performing Arts complex into an indoor roller rink for a Rollerama party.

restaurants, coffee shops, galleries, and a lake with a public beach. Students also find their way into the community through volunteer work in local schools and homeless shelters, though committing to long-term programs can be tough because of the mandatory midyear internship term, which takes most students away from campus.

Sports aren't a big focus, and Bennington has no varsity teams. Even so, 15 percent of students compete in intramural and club sports, with soccer, dodgeball, basketball, and badminton proving the most popular. Bennington's rugged location is ideal for outdoor adventures, and an active outdoor collective takes students hiking, rock climbing, white-water rafting, and camping. Ski slopes beckon in the colder months.

As the first school in the nation to grant the arts equal status with other disciplines, Bennington offers a novel, participatory, and hands-on approach. Whether they're painters or writers, musicians or scientists, sculptors, dancers, or some combination thereof, what Bennington students have in common is self-motivation and a real thirst for knowledge. "There is a level of independence necessary to thrive in this very free environment," advises a junior. "Many Bennington students are very self-driven, and this type of personality tends to do best here."

Overlaps

Bard, Sarah Lawrence, Oberlin, Emerson, Skidmore, Mount Holyoke, Hampshire, Reed

If You Apply To ›

Bennington: Early decision I and II, early action, regular decision. SATs or ACTs: optional. Accepts the Common Application with supplement. Applicants may submit an alternative "dimensional application" consisting of any materials they choose; under this option, transcripts are preferred but not required.

Bentley University

175 Forest Street, Waltham, MA 02452

Bentley means business—studying it, that is, in the context of strong liberal arts. Now competes on even footing with archrival Babson. Offers both B.S. and B.A. degrees and provides career-oriented internships to 95 percent of its students. Boasts a scenic colonial-style campus with easy access to Boston and Harvard Square.

Bentley University is a midsized New England university that excels at turning out students who are committed to taking their place among the ranks of future business leaders. "Bentley prepares its students for the workplace by giving them comparable experiences socially, academically, and—most importantly—professionally," says a sophomore. With the university's solid courses in business, state-of-the-art facilities, dedication to the liberal arts, and growing emphasis on service learning, students find much to admire.

Bentley, which was founded in 1917 by Harry Clark Bentley, a prominent accountant, is situated on 163 acres in suburban Waltham, Massachusetts, just minutes west of the hustle and bustle of Boston. The dominant architectural style is Georgian, and the majority of campus buildings are classically built in red brick. The Bentley campus has three tiers. The north campus revolves around academics and features a library, "smart" classrooms, and high-tech labs and academic centers. The main campus centers on student life and is anchored by the 70,000-square-foot student center. Finally, the south campus focuses on recreation and includes the Dana Athletic Center and Bentley Arena. Residential housing is spread throughout each tier of the campus.

Website: www.bentley.edu
Location: Suburban
Private
Total Enrollment: 4,413
Undergraduates: 3,996
Male/Female: 61/39
Financial Aid: 74%
Pell Grant: 14%
Expense: Pr $ $ $
Student Loans: 55%
Average Debt: $ $ $ $
Applicants: 9,311
Accepted: 61%
Enrolled: 18%
Grad in 6 Years: 88%
Returning Freshmen: 91%

(continued)

Academics: ✏ ✏ ✏
Social: ☎ ☎ ☎
Q of L: ★ ★ ★
Admissions: (800) 523-2354
Email Address:
  ugadmission@bentley.edu

Strong Programs:
Finance
Marketing
Economics-Finance
Management
Accountancy
Professional Sales
Computer Information Systems
Data Analytics

First-years take a six-week Career Development Introduction Seminar to get on track early for internships and jobs.

Bentley has long been committed to producing well-rounded business students, and this is reflected in the curriculum, which offers both B.S. and B.A. tracks. Although certain requirements vary based on which track a student is on, every student must complete both a general business core (Business Dynamics) to develop an understanding of how successful businesses operate and an arts and sciences core (Context and Perspectives) covering categories such as Scientific Inquiry, Institutions and Power, and Globalization. All first-year students take the Falcon Discovery Seminar that is designed to help them with their overall adjustment to college. Their seminar instructor also serves as their academic advisor for the first three semesters. In addition, first-years take a six-week Career Development Introduction Seminar to get on track early for internships and jobs.

> **"Bentley is competitive in a sense…but there is also a great sense of camaraderie."**

Not surprisingly, Bentley's most popular majors are finance, marketing, economics-finance, management, and accountancy. Students seeking a B.S. degree have their pick of more than a dozen disciplines, including majors in professional sales, computer information systems, and data analytics, while those interested in B.A. degrees can select from such fields as English, international affairs, sustainability science, and health studies. In 2021 Bentley launched a new major in diversity, equity, and inclusion, available both as a B.S. that emphasizes organizational strategy and as a B.A. that emphasizes social justice. Motivated students may choose the liberal studies major (LSM), a highly integrated second major that is paired with a B.S. degree and requires a final project in the senior year. Current LSM concentrations range from American studies to earth, environment, and global sustainability to political economy and development. Those pursuing B.A. degrees may opt to add a business studies major or minor to enhance their business knowledge.

"Bentley is competitive in a sense because we are all career-driven and want to do well in similar fields, but there is also a great sense of camaraderie," says a sophomore. Twenty-one percent of classes have fewer than 20 students, but none have more than 50, and group work is routine. Adjunct professors and senior lecturers with professional expertise teach many of the courses, and a finance major says this is beneficial because they can "bring in real-world examples from their current work and projects." Students rave about Bentley's career services. "It really does take stress away when you have that extra helping hand sourcing interviews/opportunities, teaching you the basic skills, checking in, etc.," says a senior.

As befits the university's focus on the corporate world, 95 percent of undergraduates complete at least one internship, and 74 percent complete two or more. In keeping with the university's mission to educate students to be active leaders in

> **"[Adjunct professors] bring in real-world examples from their current work and projects."**

a global economy, the Cronin Office of International Education offers semester, summer, or weeklong faculty-led programs in more than 25 countries; many programs include internship and service-learning opportunities. Forty-eight percent of students go abroad before they graduate. The top 10 percent of students in each entering class are invited to participate in the honors program, which tackles a variety of topics—from the ethics of genetic research to analyzing complex financial crises—all in a seminar setting that is designed to promote discussion and debate.

Forty-eight percent of students go abroad before they graduate.

"Bentley students are wealthy and privileged on average. Most share a common drive and business savviness," says a marketing major. Although half again as large as rival Babson College, Bentley's undergraduate student body is less diverse. Thirty percent of Bentley undergrads are from Massachusetts, and 13 percent are international. Black students account for 4 percent of the student body, Asian Americans 9 percent, Hispanics/Latinos 10 percent, and multiracial students 3 percent. Bentley has a conservative tenor, but for students, social and political issues generally take a back seat to classes and internships. Merit scholarships averaging $19,700 are doled out annually, and talented athletes vie for 210 athletic scholarships in 18 sports. Through the BentleyFirst program, Massachusetts residents who are the first in their families to go to college and whose family incomes are less than $125,000 per year can attend Bentley for the same tuition rate as the state's flagship public university, UMass Amherst.

> *Massachusetts residents who are the first in their families to go to college can attend Bentley for the same tuition rate as UMass Amherst.*

The university's student residences include apartments, suites, and traditional dormitories and house 74 percent of the student body. Ten percent of students participate in living/learning communities, in which service learning is a big emphasis. The dining hall food is not a selling point, but a junior says, "Meals at Bentley have improved over time." Students report feeling safe on campus, thanks to an active police patrol, 24/7 safety escorts, and "Title IX staff who are in constant contact with students and put on various events throughout the year," says a junior.

Students say the social scene begins on campus and spills out into the surrounding areas. "There is so much involvement in Bentley's 100-plus organizations," says one student. "A group is bound to have an event on any given day." Sponsored events include the annual Back to Bentley and Spring Day festivals and activities put on by various cultural groups, like Latin dance night. Practically the entire student body shows up for Super Bingo, "which is like normal bingo, but with awesome prizes like TVs and iPhones," explains a sophomore. The Greek system attracts 8 percent of the men and 17 percent of the women, and

> **"Bentley students are wealthy and privileged on average."**

Greeks and sports teams host frequent off-campus parties, but neither group dominates the social scene. Students of legal age may have alcohol, but "peer pressure is not an issue" for those who prefer not to imbibe, according to an accounting major.

Waltham (population 64,000) may not have the cachet of nearby Boston, but students say it has the basic amenities every college student craves: restaurants, bars, shops, and salons. "Overall, Waltham does not play a huge role in a Bentley student's daily way of life," comments one student. Those seeking a bit more action take the campus shuttle to Harvard Square or the T (subway) to the city, where students can mix and mingle with peers from other local colleges and universities. Jaunts to the beaches of New Hampshire, the ski resorts of Vermont, and weekend trips to the Cape make for popular diversions as well.

Competition at Bentley is not confined to the classroom; the university also fields 21 men's and women's varsity teams at the Division II level and a competitive Division I men's ice hockey team. The powerhouse women's basketball team makes regular appearances in the NCAA tournament. Other solid Falcon teams include men's basketball, women's field hockey, and men's golf. Students get fired up anytime rivals Babson and Bryant take the field, and there is the predictable T-shirt reading, "Friends don't let friends go to Babson." Popular intramural and club sports include flag football, soccer, volleyball, and ultimate Frisbee.

"Bentley is a school that will simulate the real world as much as possible so that its students graduate prepared!" cheers one enthusiastic junior. Like the university itself, Bentley students have a keen sense of who they are and where they're headed. For those students charting a course into the upper echelons of corporate America, Bentley may be the first step to a long and fruitful career.

Overlaps

Babson, Boston College, Bryant, Boston University, Northeastern, UMass Amherst, UConn, Fordham

If You Apply To ›

Bentley: Early decision I and II, regular decision. Accepts the Common Application. Please consult Bentley's website for the most up-to-date information regarding standardized test requirements.

Birmingham–Southern College

Box 549008, 900 Arkakelphia Road, Birmingham, AL 35254

One of the Deep South's better liberal arts colleges, BSC is smaller than Rhodes (Tennessee), larger than Millsaps (Mississippi). Strong emphasis on service, and the Greek system is a throwback to the way college used to be. "Tuition reset" aims to mitigate the problem of sticker shock by significantly lowering the school's published sticker price. But financial problems persist.

Website: www.bsc.edu
Location: City Outskirts
Private
Total Enrollment: 1,039
Undergraduates: 1,039
Male/Female: 49/51
Financial Aid: 93%
Pell Grant: 27%
Expense: Pr $
Student Loans: 51%
Average Debt: $ $
Applicants: 2,461
Accepted: 66%
Enrolled: 15%
Grad in 6 Years: 70%
Returning Freshmen: 78%
Academics: ✐ ✐ ✐
Social: ☎ ☎ ☎
Q of L: ★ ★ ★
Admissions: (205) 226-4696
Email Address: admiss@
bsc.edu

Strong Programs:
Art
Theater
Music
Musical Theater
Media and Film Studies
Applied Computer Science
Biology
Business Administration

Once an old-school conservative Southern institution, BSC is now striving to prepare students for all aspects of the modern world, with high-tech facilities and a curriculum that prioritizes critical thinking, teamwork, and global awareness. Affiliated with the United Methodist Church, the college continues to emphasize the value of service: more than half the student body volunteers through the Bunting Center for Engaged Study and Community Action. Attentive faculty add to a sense of commitment to both personal and community growth. But BSC has struggled to recover from a major financial crisis in 2010, a problem exacerbated in recent years by declining enrollment, a drained endowment, and accounting errors. The college announced in December 2022 that it is working to raise $200 million by 2026 through private donors as well as government funding in order to keep its doors open.

Known as the Hilltop for readily discernable topographical reasons, BSC is the product of the 1918 merger of two smaller colleges: Birmingham College and Southern University. The 190-acre campus, a green and shady oasis in an urban neighborhood, contains a pleasing hodgepodge of traditional and modern architecture, all surrounded by a security fence for added safety.

The Explorations general education curriculum focuses on effective communication and problem-solving skills, local and global citizenship, and hands-on learning experiences. All students must complete at least two Exploration Term projects, which can range from innovative on-campus courses and research projects to off-campus internships and faculty-led travel projects, during the four-week E-Term in January. Seniors complete a capstone experience and a public presentation of their work.

Biology, business administration, psychology, and mathematics are the most popular majors. Students interested in medical or law school can participate in special advising programs, and majors in health sciences and architectural studies are now available. The art, theater, and music programs are all among the best in the South, and the college offers a major in musical theater as well. Students stage several major productions each year, often including American and world premieres. Other notable majors include media and film studies and applied computer science. Dual-degree programs in engineering, nursing, and environmental studies are offered in partnership with such institutions as Auburn, WashU in St. Louis, and Duke.

> **"[Professors] love to challenge our beliefs and ideas by making us defend what we think."**

Each student at BSC is assigned a faculty member who serves as their academic advisor from freshman convocation to graduation, an arrangement that students praise for its effectiveness. Equal praise goes out to faculty in the classrooms, where 77 percent of classes have fewer than 20 students. An education major says professors "love to challenge our beliefs and ideas by making us defend what we think." The honors program allows 35 exceptional first-year students to take small seminars with one or more professors. The Krulak Institute coordinates opportunities for experiential learning, such as service-learning projects, study abroad programs, and an entrepreneurial scholars program. Fifteen percent of BSC students study internationally, and 25 percent collaborate with faculty on research projects. "Undergraduate research opportunities and internships are easy to come by for those who are looking," says a biology major.

Sixty-two percent of the students are homegrown Alabamians, and practically all the rest hail from Deep South states; many have family ties to BSC, and 18 percent are Methodist. Just 1 percent are international. Sixteen percent of students are Black, 6 percent are Hispanic/Latino, 3 percent are Asian American, and 1 percent are multiracial, but, "The college is taking steps to diversify," a student says. The student-run Cross-Cultural Committee sponsors cultural events to promote awareness of diversity on campus. Politically, the student body leans conservative, and issues like racial justice and abortion have been divisive on campus, students report. Birmingham–Southern has reset its sticker price in an effort to avoid the sticker shock caused by high published prices that can deter applicants. Merit- and need-based financial aid is still awarded to eligible students, although in smaller amounts.

Seventy-two percent of the students live on campus, including many whose families reside in Birmingham. Dorms are described as comfortable and convenient. First-years all live together in three traditional halls that have recently been renovated. "The housing selection process after freshman year depends on year and class rank, so there is definitely an incentive to do your best in the classroom," advises a senior.

> **"Undergraduate research opportunities and internships are easy to come by."**

Students dine at three locations on campus. "BSC's food provider covers a wide range of special tastes and always offers variety and tasty options," says a biology major. Campus security officials are said to be visible and effective.

At BSC, 40 percent of the men and 50 percent of the women join Greek life. "Unlike other schools, Greek organizations do not limit or turn away anyone from parties; so although they set the tone, they are very inclusive," explains a senior. As for alcohol, it's not allowed on the quad, and elsewhere it must be in an opaque container, a policy most students find reasonable, described by one senior as a "'don't see it, ignore it' policy." The biggest social event of the year is SoCo, a two-day music festival. Freshmen take part in a square dance during orientation. Other popular events include the E-Fest concert and Halloween on the Hilltop, where students "dress up in costumes and the neighborhood kids go trick-or-treating." When social opportunities on campus dry up, many students head to downtown Birmingham for the city's restaurants and nightlife. Road trips to Auburn, Nashville, and Atlanta are popular, and beaches and mountains are less than five hours away.

BSC currently fields 22 varsity teams for men and women. The Panthers compete in the Division III Southern Athletic Association, and the baseball, softball, and men's and women's swimming and diving and track and field teams have performed well in recent years. Forty-two percent of students take part in the intramural program. Basketball, flag football, and soccer are popular, but less traditional sports, such as dodgeball and inner-tube water polo, are also offered.

Students at BSC continue to focus on academics while balancing community service and an active social scene. Small classes, a caring faculty, and an expanding menu of academic offerings continue to draw attention to this close-knit liberal arts school. A junior says BSC is a good choice for those students who "want to spend four years preparing, maturing, and challenging their minds so that they can make a difference in the world."

Exploration Term projects range from innovative on-campus courses and research projects to off-campus internships and faculty-led travel projects.

The biggest social event of the year is SoCo, a two-day music festival.

Overlaps

Rhodes, Berry, Sewanee, Centre, Millsaps, Belmont University, University of Alabama, Auburn

If You Apply To ›

Birmingham–Southern: Early decision, early action, regular decision. SATs or ACTs: optional (test-optional applicants must interview and submit academic portfolio). Accepts the Common Application with supplement.

Boston College

140 Commonwealth Avenue, Devlin Hall, Room 208, Chestnut Hill, MA 02467

One of the main reasons that Boston is the ultimate college town. Set on a quiet hilltop at the end of a T (subway) line, BC is a close second to Notre Dame in the pecking order among true-blue Roman Catholics (though many students clamoring for a spot are not aware of its religious ties). About 70 percent of students identify as Catholic, compared to 50 percent at Georgetown and 80 percent at Notre Dame.

Website: www.bc.edu

Location: Suburban

Private

Total Enrollment: 13,370

Undergraduates: 9,532

Male/Female: 47/53

Financial Aid: 69%

Pell Grant: 12%

Expense: Pr $ $ $ $

Student Loans: 45%

Average Debt: $

Applicants: 39,846

Accepted: 19%

Enrolled: 33%

Grad in 6 Years: 94%

Returning Freshmen: 93%

Academics: ✐ ✐ ✐ ✐

Social: ☎ ☎ ☎ ☎

Q of L: ★ ★ ★

Admissions: (617) 552-3100

Email Address: admission@bc.edu

Strong Programs:
Management
Nursing
International Studies
Film Studies
Theology
Finance
Economics
Biology

Boston College, one of the largest Roman Catholic schools in the country, is a study in contrasts. The academics and the athletic teams are both well respected. The environment is safely suburban, yet barely 20 minutes from Boston, the hub of the Eastern seaboard's college scene. The influence of the Society of Jesus (Jesuits) on the college provides a guiding spirit for campus life, but the social opportunities still seem endless. Despite the paradoxes (or perhaps because of them), students at BC enjoy a rich college experience.

Don't let the modest name fool you. Boston College is actually a research university with nine schools and colleges. It has three campuses: the main campus at Chestnut Hill, the Brighton campus across the street, and the Newton campus a mile and a half away. The dominant architecture of the main campus (known as "the Heights") is Gothic Revival, with modern additions over the past several years. There's lots of grass and trees, not to mention a large, peaceful reservoir (perfect to jog around) right in the front yard. The university recently completed a multiyear master plan that doubled the size of the main campus with a new dorm, a field house, a recreation center, and other facilities. A $150 million science facility housing the Schiller Institute for Integrated Science and Society was completed in 2021.

> "I have certainly been challenged by my professors but also supported."

Boston College was founded by the Jesuits in 1863 to teach the offspring of Irish immigrants. These days, the college's mission is to "educate skilled, knowledgeable, and responsible leaders within each new generation." To accomplish this goal, the Core Curriculum requires courses not only in literature, natural science, history, philosophy, social science, and theology, but also in writing, mathematics, the arts, and cultural diversity, in addition to specific requirements set by each undergraduate school. Students in arts and sciences must also show proficiency in a modern foreign language or classical language before graduation. Freshmen are required to take a writing workshop in which each student develops a portfolio of personal and academic writing and reads a wide range of texts. About a quarter of students participate in the Capstone Program, choosing one of several seminars that aim to give a "big picture" perspective to the college experience and students' personal development.

The schools of arts and sciences, management, education and human development, and nursing award bachelor's degrees. Finance, economics, biology, and political science are the most popular majors. Programs in management, nursing, international studies, film studies, and theology are particularly well regarded. BC recently launched a new undergraduate major in human-centered engineering, the university's only engineering program at any level. Outside the traditional classroom at the McMullen Museum of Art, students find exhibitions, lectures, and gallery tours. The Music Guild sponsors professional concerts throughout the year, and

> "There is a pervasive spirit of compassion that runs through the student body here."

music students emphasizing performance can take advantage of facilities equipped with Steinways and Yamahas. Theater majors find a home in the 600-seat Robsham Theater Arts Center, which produces eight student-directed productions each year.

BC students are serious about their work, but not excessively so, helping to create a collaborative atmosphere. "If you are better at science than your roommate, you will help her out," states one senior, "and perhaps when it comes time to fulfill your philosophy core requirement, her love of Plato will get you through the class." Sixty-five percent of classes have fewer than 20 students, and professors are praised for their passion and knowledge, as well as their accessibility. "I have certainly been challenged by my professors but also supported, since they consistently make themselves available outside of the classroom," says one history major. The Jesuits on BC's faculty (about 25 out of 880) exert an influence out of proportion to their numbers. "The philosophy, theology, and ethics departments are the most important in setting the tone of the campus, because they encourage the students to be open-minded," says a freshman.

Students searching for out-of-the-ordinary offerings will be happy at BC. The PULSE program provides participants with the opportunity to fulfill their philosophy and theology requirements while engaging in social-service fieldwork at any of about 35 Boston organizations. The program reinforces the Jesuit emphasis on community service and sometimes inspires students to major in those areas. Forty-four percent of Boston College undergraduates study internationally by the time they graduate. BC offers nearly 60 academic programs in more than 30 countries around the world, as well as three-week summer study abroad programs. Students participating in the Undergraduate Faculty Research Fellows Program spend an average of 100 hours per semester assisting faculty with serious research, for which they are paid an hourly wage.

Students in the Undergraduate Faculty Research Fellows Program spend an average of 100 hours per semester assisting faculty with serious research.

Twenty-six percent of BC undergraduates come from Massachusetts and 7 percent from abroad. Catholics comprise about 70 percent of the student body. Black students constitute 4 percent, while Asian Americans make up 11 percent, Hispanics/Latinos 11 percent, and multiracial students 4 percent. "The student body is a socially conscious, environmentally responsible, academically oriented group on the whole," offers one student. "There is a pervasive spirit of compassion that runs through the student body here." Indeed, the Jesuit appeal for tolerance means that students can find support and interaction even when approaching hot-button issues that orthodox Catholicism frowns upon, such as homosexuality. Nearly 300 athletic awards are doled out annually; merit scholarships are worth an average of $23,000. Additionally, BC observes need-blind admissions and meets the full demonstrated need of accepted students.

Spiritual retreats occur throughout the year at BC's own retreat center on the Charles River, 30 minutes from campus.

"[With no Greek system] the social life is much more inclusive."

Eighty-two percent of BC students live on campus. When students are admitted, they are notified whether they will get on-campus housing for three or four years; most juniors with three-year guarantees live off campus or study abroad, then return to campus for their final year. The city of Boston has a fairly reliable bus and subway system to bring distant residents to campus; the few students who drive to school are required to show that they need to park on campus. "The dorms are comfortable and spacious," says an international studies major. Students pay in advance for a certain number of dining hall meals, served à la carte. "The food is expensive," a student says, "but it is great quality." The Stand Up BC program is intended to combat the issue of campus sexual assault.

The traditional Eagles football contest with the Fighting Irish of Notre Dame is jokingly referred to as the "Holy War."

BC's campus is replete with sporting events, movies, festivals, concerts, and plays. As at other Jesuit institutions, there is no Greek system at BC, and "the social life is much more inclusive" as a result, according to a senior. Those of legal age can drink on campus but are only allowed to carry in enough beer or wine for personal consumption. Spiritual retreats occur throughout the year at BC's own retreat center on the Charles River, 30 minutes from campus, and one student says, "Volunteer work is huge." Bars and clubs in Boston ("the college town of all college towns," cheers a junior) are another big draw, along with Fenway Park. On weekends, especially in the winter, the mountains of Vermont and New Hampshire beckon outdoorsy types.

Division I athletic events, especially football games, become social events, too, with frequent tailgate and victory parties. The traditional Eagles football contest with the Fighting Irish of Notre Dame is jokingly referred to as the "Holy War" and makes for a popular road trip. BC meets fierce competition from Atlantic Coast Conference rivals Duke, Miami, Virginia Tech, and others, and Boston University is the archrival when it comes to ice hockey. Solid teams include men's and women's ice hockey, soccer, basketball, lacrosse, fencing, and golf. Intramural sports are huge here. Nearly half of BC undergrads participate in 40 intramural and club sports, from basketball and volleyball to skiing and rugby. Students even get the day off from classes to line the edge of campus and cheer Boston Marathon runners up "Heartbreak Hill."

Since its founding as a Jesuit institution, Boston College has been committed to "educating students who will use their knowledge, talents, and abilities in the service of others." BC students spend four years fine-tuning the art of the delicate balance, finding ways to make old-fashioned morals relevant to life in the 21st century, and finding time for fun while still tending to their academic performance.

If You Apply To ›

BC: Early decision I and II, regular decision. Accepts the Common Application with supplement. Apply to particular school or program. Please consult BC's website for the most up-to-date information regarding standardized test requirements.

Boston University

121 Bay State Road, Boston, MA 02215

One of the nation's largest private universities and namesake to a city that boasts more than 40 four-year colleges. Location adjacent to the Fenway is the promised land for hordes of students from all over the world seeking a funky, artsy, youth-oriented urban setting that is less in-your-face than New York City. More selective than in the past and comparable to NYU.

Like NYU and USC, Boston University, founded by Methodists in 1839, is an integral part of the city it calls home (although it actually started in Vermont). The school's ample collection of nondescript high-rises stretches along bustling, six-lane Commonwealth Avenue—and so do thousands upon thousands of students. From aspiring actors, musicians, journalists, and filmmakers, to future scientists, doctors, dentists, and entrepreneurs, BU seems to offer something for everyone. A junior says, "You definitely walk away from BU with a sense of accomplishment and individuality."

The BU campus is practically indistinguishable from the rest of the urban landscape that surrounds it. A measure of relief is available on the tree-lined side streets, which feature quaint Victorian brownstones. New facilities include the 19-story, eco-friendly Center for Computing & Data Sciences, notable for being heated and cooled via geothermal wells rather than fossil fuels. BU's recently established Center for Antiracist Research, led by author and activist Ibram X. Kendi, aims to develop research-based policies, advocacy campaigns, and educational programs to address the problems of racial inequity and injustice in the U.S.

BU's university-wide general education curriculum, the BU Hub, requires students to complete coursework focusing on diversity, civic engagement, global citizenship, digital communication, and innovation, among other areas. The BU Cross-College Challenge, the BU Hub's signature feature, gives juniors and seniors the chance to collaborate with a small team of classmates and faculty from across the university on an interdisciplinary project.

BU's 10 undergraduate schools and colleges offer more than 300 majors and minors; business administration, communication, biology, economics, engineering, international relations, and psychology are the most popular. "All of the academic programs I've encountered have an accomplished faculty that brings real-world experiences into the classroom," says a political science major. The College of Communication combines theory with hands-on training—some of it

> **"[BU has] an accomplished faculty that brings real-world experiences into the classroom."**

by adjunct professors with day jobs at major newspapers and TV networks. It also houses the nation's first center for the study of political disinformation. The well-regarded School of Theatre benefits from the 250-seat, flexibly designed Booth Theatre, which adjoins production and costume shops, design labs, and classrooms. The College of Arts and Sciences offers some 90 majors and special advising for premed and prelaw students. A highly competitive seven-year program admits qualified students simultaneously to the undergraduate program and the university's medical school. Many students in the College of Health and Rehabilitation Sciences: Sargent College go on to earn graduate degrees from the college's highly ranked physical and occupational therapy programs.

The Questrom School of Business, one of BU's top programs, offers an honors program for sophomores and concentrations in such areas as law, innovation and entrepreneurship, and business analytics. Future employers of students in the School of Hospitality Administration offer internships in exotic locales such as Sydney and Shanghai. The College of Engineering, known for its biomedical engineering program, boasts a high-tech robotics lab. Students in the Wheelock College of Education and Human Development can test their ideas for curricular reform in the public schools of nearby Chelsea, while those in the School of Visual Arts may show their work in one of three campus galleries. The cross-disciplinary Faculty of Computing & Data Sciences offers a B.S. degree in data science. Fifty-eight percent of classes have fewer than 20 students, and students say the academic climate encourages both cooperation and competition. "While I am consistently challenged, I do not feel overwhelmed by the workload," says one senior.

Students rave about the First-Year Student Outreach Project, which brings freshmen to campus a week early to do community service. For a break from brutal Boston winters, BU offers more than 70 study abroad programs, including internships, field work, research, language study, and liberal arts programs, in 17 countries; 37 percent of students typically participate. The Kilachand Honors College is a four-year undergraduate living/learning community that offers students

> **"For being in an urban area, I feel extremely safe on campus."**

the small classes, close interaction with faculty, and communal atmosphere of a small liberal arts college along with the resources of a major urban research university.

According to a biology major, BU students are "really cool nerds: smart, but also fun." Fifty-seven percent of BU undergrads are from out of state, and another 22 percent come from foreign countries. Asian Americans make up 20 percent of

(continued)

Average Debt: $ $ $ $
Applicants: 75,778
Accepted: 19%
Enrolled: 28%
Grad in 6 Years: 89%
Returning Freshmen: 94%
Academics: ✍ ✍ ✍ ✍
Social: ☎ ☎ ☎ ☎
Q of L: ★ ★ ★
Admissions: (617) 353-2300
Email Address: admissions@bu.edu

Strong Programs:
Business Administration
Communication
Theatre
Hospitality Administration
Biomedical Engineering
Biology
Economics
International Relations

The new 19-story, eco-friendly Center for Computing & Data Sciences is heated and cooled via geothermal wells rather than fossil fuels.

the population, Hispanics/Latinos 11 percent, Black students 4 percent, and multiracial students 5 percent. Students report that low socioeconomic diversity is one of the biggest social issues on campus. "Many students come from high-income backgrounds and lack a perspective on what it's like to live on a small budget," comments a senior. BU has introduced a number of initiatives to address affordability: the university now guarantees to meet 100 percent of domestic students' demonstrated financial need and promises that if tuition increases, need-based scholarships will also increase by the same percentage. Loans are not included in financial aid packages for incoming freshmen who are eligible for Pell Grants. In addition to need-based aid, BU offers merit scholarships averaging $23,900 each year as well as 382 athletic scholarships in 19 sports.

Typically, 70 percent of BU students live in campus housing, which is guaranteed for four years and selected via a lottery system. "Freshman/sophomore dorms are fairly typical, but housing gets better as you get to be a senior," explains a psychology major, and some of the newest facilities are like "luxury apartments." Meal plans are flexible, and one of the six dining halls on campus is kosher. There's also a farmers market and a food court with national chains like Starbucks and Panda Express. "For being in an urban area, I feel extremely safe on campus," reports one senior. The Sexual Assault Response and Prevention Center provides prevention-based programming and support and advocacy for survivors.

"We can just hop on our Boston trains and be anywhere in the city within minutes."

"The social scene at BU has a lot to offer," a student says. "We always have on-campus events every day of the week, including the weekends. If we don't feel like staying on campus, we can just hop on our Boston trains and be anywhere in the city within minutes." With less than 1 percent of the men and just 3 percent of the women joining fraternities and sororities, Greek life has little influence on the social scene. Parties happen off campus, including at neighboring schools, and policies regarding underage drinking on BU's campus are reportedly strict. Owing to Boston's pervasive Irish heritage, St. Patrick's Day is an occasion for revelry. The Splash student activity fair and homecoming in the fall are favorite annual events, along with comedy nights that bring big-name comedians like Colin Jost, Vanessa Bayer, and Hasan Minhaj to campus once a semester. Lobster Night, where the dining halls serve up whole lobsters, is always a big hit. Road trip options include Cape Cod, Cape Ann, and Providence, Rhode Island. Even better, "Fenway Park, downtown, Lansdowne Street, and Boston Common are all within walking distance," says a marine biology major.

BU doesn't field a football team, so hockey season is the athletic high point of the school year. Most Terrier teams compete in the Division I Patriot League, and solid teams include men's basketball and women's softball, soccer, field hockey, and rowing. BU has won 31 of 70 titles in the annual Beanpot men's ice hockey tournament, which pits BU against Harvard, Northeastern, and archrival Boston College. The Head of the Charles regatta, which starts at BU's crew house each fall, draws college crew teams from across the country. Of the dozen or so intramural sports offered, by far the most popular is broomball, which is like ice hockey on sneakers, with a ball instead of a puck and a broom instead of a stick; students may also compete in 34 club sports.

Boston University shamelessly urges students to just "Be You" (ahem) and most are happy to do so, but they warn that being successful here requires a certain degree of initiative. The school is "a great place, with lots of academic and social opportunities, but it's not for the timid student," remarks a geophysics and planetary sciences major. "You have to be proactive about finding out what's going on around campus, so that you can find your niche."

Overlaps

UCLA, NYU, University of Southern California, Northeastern, UC Berkeley, Boston College, Tufts, Johns Hopkins

Bowdoin College

Brunswick, ME 04011

Rates with Amherst, Williams, and Wesleyan for liberal arts excellence and pioneered in not requiring the SAT. Slightly more selective than Bates and on par with Colby. Bowdoin's science programs are especially strong, and outdoor enthusiasts benefit from proximity to the Atlantic Coast. Not as large as some of its peers, with less overt competition among students.

Since 1794, Bowdoin College has sought to make nature, art, and friendship as integral to the student experience as the world of books. This is, after all, the alma mater of the great American authors Longfellow and Hawthorne. In fact, when they matriculate, new students sign their names in a book on Hawthorne's very desk. Though the New England winter can be frigid, students are quick to point out that good food and friendships that "transcend labels" help make the campus a warm and friendly place.

Bowdoin's 215-acre campus sits in Brunswick, a coastal town in southern Maine. Hidden amid the pine groves and athletic fields are 120 buildings, in styles from German Romanesque, colonial, medieval, and neoclassical to neo-Georgian, modern, and postmodern. The historic Harriet Beecher Stowe House, in which the famed author wrote *Uncle Tom's Cabin*, has been carefully renovated and now houses faculty offices. Bowdoin has opened seven new eco-friendly, apartment-style residential buildings for upperclassmen since 2019.

To graduate, Bowdoin students must complete courses in five distribution areas that emphasize interdisciplinary study and issues vital to a liberal education in the 21st century: mathematical, computational, or statistical reasoning; inquiry in the natural sciences; difference, power, and inequity; international perspectives; and visual and performing arts. First-years also have their choice of seminars, capped at

> **"[Students] can often be found assisting each other, sharing notes, and studying together."**

16 students each, which emphasize reading and writing; recent topics have included The Supreme Court and Social Change, Deconstructing Racism, and The Science of Solving Crime. "Freshman Seminars are immensely valuable," says one senior. "They can give you a good sense of what you really need to work on to succeed at Bowdoin." In an effort to level the playing field when it comes to access to digital tools and technology, all incoming first-years receive a MacBook Pro, an iPad, an Apple Pencil, and access to a range of course-specific software. As sophomores, all students participate in a five-day career "boot camp" during winter break, featuring workshops that focus on skill development and industry-specific advice.

Academic strengths include the sciences, particularly environmental studies, earth and oceanographic science, neuroscience, chemistry, and biology. Making a virtue out of climatic necessity, Bowdoin also offers a concentration in Arctic studies (its mascot is the polar bear), as well as opportunities for Arctic archaeological

Website: www.bowdoin.edu
Location: Small Town
Private
Total Enrollment: 1,948
Undergraduates: 1,948
Male/Female: 49/51
Financial Aid: 51%
Pell Grant: 16%
Expense: Pr $ $ $ $
Student Loans: 26%
Average Debt: $
Applicants: 9,325
Accepted: 9%
Enrolled: 63%
Grad in 6 Years: 94%
Returning Freshmen: 97%
Academics: ✑ ✑ ✑ ✑ ✑
Social: ☎ ☎ ☎
Q of L: ★ ★ ★
Admissions: (207) 725-3100
Email Address: admissions@bowdoin.edu

Strong Programs:
Environmental Studies
Earth and Oceanographic
   Science
Neuroscience
Mathematics
Computer Science
English
Government
Economics

research in Labrador, Canada, or ecological research at the Bowdoin Scientific Station on Kent Island in the Bay of Fundy. The Schiller Coastal Studies Center, located just 15 minutes away on a 118-acre plot on Orr's Island, provides additional opportunities for multidisciplinary, field- and lab-based research on critical coastal and climate issues. Mathematics, computer science, and English are also well regarded, and students say the popularity of government and economics—the majors with the highest enrollment—is well deserved. Dual-degree programs in engineering are available through Caltech, Columbia, Dartmouth, and the University of Maine.

In an effort to level the technology playing field, all incoming first-years receive a MacBook Pro, an iPad, and an Apple Pencil.

"Students take their schoolwork seriously, and the work is difficult," says a government and economics double major, adding that students "can often be found assisting each other, sharing notes, and studying together." About 70 percent of classes have fewer than 20 students. Professors teach all Bowdoin classes—there are no graduate students here, and thus no teaching assistants—and their skills in the classroom are highly praised. "Professors make an effort to teach in many different ways in order to reach all types of learners," says a senior.

Before school begins, the entire entering class takes preorientation hiking, canoeing, kayaking, or community service trips that teach them about the people and landscape of Maine. Service learning, coordinated by the McKeen Center for the Common Good, is increasingly an emphasis at Bowdoin; 53 percent of students apply their classroom work to real-world problems faced by local community groups. Undergraduate research is a priority, too, and it's common for juniors and seniors to conduct independent studies with faculty members, then publish their results in professional journals. Nineteen percent of seniors complete yearlong honors projects culminating in a written thesis, oral defense, or original creative piece. Sixty percent of students study abroad through more than 100 programs offered in more than 50 countries.

"Everyone has an interest and a passion that might surprise you."

Bowdoin offers a concentration in Arctic studies (its mascot is the polar bear), as well as opportunities for Arctic research in Labrador, Canada.

Just 9 percent of students hail from Maine, and 7 percent are international. Black students make up 6 percent of the student body, Hispanics/Latinos 11 percent, Asian Americans 9 percent, and multiracial students 9 percent. On this liberal campus, "Many students are outdoorsy, athletic, a little preppy—but everyone has an interest and a passion that might surprise you," a mathematics major says, "and most people have friends from all different social groups on campus." In 1970 Bowdoin became the first leading college to make SAT I scores an optional part of the admissions process, shifting the emphasis to a student's whole body of work. Additionally, Bowdoin employs a need-blind admissions policy, meets the full demonstrated financial need of admitted students, and has eliminated loans from its financial aid packages, replacing them with scholarships.

Ninety-three percent of Bowdoin students live on campus, where first-years start off in quads, with two double bedrooms and a shared common room, in renovated historic residence halls. After that, students may apply to live in "College Houses," many of which used to be fraternity houses before Bowdoin phased out Greek groups more than 20 years ago. Students give rave reviews to dining services, especially the lobster bake that kicks off each school year and the offerings for vegans and vegetarians. "Bowdoin's food is restaurant quality, and the menu is different every day," cheers a senior. Several student groups are active in raising awareness around issues of sexual violence, and a senior says, "Campus security protects students effectively."

"We have a system of nine College Houses that host all types of events—academic, cultural, and parties."

Social life at Bowdoin centers around two groups: sports teams and College Houses. "We have a system of nine College Houses that host all types of events—academic, cultural, and parties—that are open to all students at the college," explains a junior. "This sense of inclusivity ensures that people do not feel the pressure to drink." Hard liquor is prohibited on campus. "The party culture is fun and celebratory but overall safe and controlled," says a senior. Students look forward to homecoming in the fall and Ivies, a last blast of fun before spring finals that brings major performers like Childish Gambino and Jamila Woods to Whittier Field for an outdoor concert.

One student says Brunswick (population 22,000) is "a great, quiet college town." Habitat for Humanity and various mentoring programs help build bridges between students and local residents. A car comes in handy for the 15-minute drive to the shopping outlets of Freeport (including L.L. Bean's flagship 24/7 factory store) or the 30-minute trip to Portland for a "real" night out. Students can also opt to take a school shuttle, the inexpensive Metro Breez bus, or the nearby Amtrak train to these destinations or to Boston, a little more than two hours away. Ski bums will find several resorts within easy reach.

Students give rave reviews to dining services, especially the lobster bake that kicks off each school year.

While the long winters can be grueling, they do bring out school spirit, especially when Bowdoin's ice hockey teams take the ice. The Polar Bears compete in the Division III New England Small College Athletic Conference. Any sporting event against Colby is exciting, and the annual hockey matchup draws crowds of alumni and Brunswick locals alike. The women's rugby team won its third consecutive national title in 2022, and conference champs include women's volleyball and men's tennis. Also popular are club sports, intramurals, and recreational activities, including those organized by the student-run Bowdoin Outing Club, whose weekend jaunts range from rock climbing, skiing, and white-water rafting to fireside knitting and sledding.

Students who love the outdoors, even when it's cold, will find warm and inviting academics at Bowdoin, where close friendships with peers and professors are easily forged. As a sociology major puts it, "Life at Bowdoin involves little anonymity, and most students enjoy that fact and play active roles in the campus community."

Overlaps

Amherst, Brown, Dartmouth, Middlebury, Williams, Wesleyan, Swarthmore, Colby

If You Apply To ›

Bowdoin: Early decision I and II, regular decision. SATs or ACTs: optional. Accepts the Common Application with supplement.

Brandeis University

Waltham, MA 02453

Founded in 1948 by members of the American Jewish community who sought to expand access to higher education, Brandeis is an elite institution seeking top students of all faiths and backgrounds. Academic specialties range from the natural sciences to music and Near Eastern and Judaic studies. Has one of the top programs in neuroscience at a midsized research university. Competes with Tufts in the Boston area.

Brandeis University, founded to provide educational opportunities to those facing discrimination, has always had a reputation for intense progressive thought. Now it's being recognized as a rising star among research institutions, hosting more than 30 on-campus research centers, and is expanding its experiential- and service-learning offerings. The only nonsectarian Jewish-sponsored college in the nation, Brandeis was named for Louis Brandeis, the first Jewish justice on the U.S. Supreme

Website: www.brandeis.edu
Location: Suburban
Private
Total Enrollment: 5,120
Undergraduates: 3,568

Brandeis is virtually unrivaled in Near Eastern and Judaic studies, and Hebrew is a specialty.

Court. In recent years the university appears to be focusing less on maintaining its Jewish identity and more on attracting a well-rounded, eclectic group of students from all backgrounds.

Set on a hilltop in a pleasant residential neighborhood nine miles west of Boston, Brandeis's attractively landscaped 235-acre campus boasts many distinctive buildings. The music building, for example, is shaped like a grand piano; the theater looks like a top hat. The 24-hour Shapiro Campus Center includes a student theater, offices for student clubs, and bookstore. The Shapiro Academic Complex houses the International Center for Ethics, Justice, and Public Life; the Mandel Center for Studies in Jewish Education; conference rooms; and faculty offices.

Undergraduates enter the School of Arts and Sciences, which offers more than 40 majors and 50 minors through its departments and interdepartmental programs. About half of the students graduate with double majors. The Brandeis core curriculum is rooted in a commitment to developing strong communication, digital literacy, foreign language, and quantitative-reasoning skills and an interdisciplinary and cross-cultural perspective. First-year students must take a writing seminar and attend at least one of several Critical Conversation events held throughout the year, in which professors from different disciplines discuss major issues in a moderated setting, in an effort to "model civil discourse." Other Brandeis Core requirements include credits in health and wellness; life skills; diversity, equity, and inclusion in the U.S.; and difference and justice in the world.

> "Peer advisors are super cool because they have lived through the Brandeis experience."

Neuroscience, biochemistry, chemistry, and physics are top-notch programs; economics, biology, business, and psychology enroll the most students. The university caters to premed students with special advisors and access to internships and research opportunities. With the largest faculty in the field outside of Israel, Brandeis is virtually unrivaled in Near Eastern and Judaic studies; Hebrew is a specialty. The program in Islamic and Middle Eastern studies is strong too. A growing number of interdisciplinary programs are becoming increasingly popular, particularly the international and global studies major and the health: science, society, and policy major. Brandeis also maintains a commitment to the creative arts, with strong theater offerings and a theory-based music program founded by Leonard Bernstein. A new major in science engineering is under development.

"Brandeis takes its academic integrity seriously," says a creative writing and English major, and the climate can be intense. Sixty-one percent of classes at Brandeis have fewer than 20 students, and a junior says, "Professors are very accommodating and are good lecturers and discussion leaders." All incoming first-years are assigned a student advisor, an academic advisor, and a faculty advisor. "Peer advisors are super cool because they have lived through the Brandeis experience and are truly a wealth of information," explains an American studies major. The Kraft Transitional Year Program is a one-year academic program for promising students from educationally underserved populations that guarantees small classes, rigorous academics, and strong academic support.

Rising sophomores and juniors have the opportunity to earn credit through study abroad related to their majors. Forty percent of undergrads take advantage of more than 200 off-campus programs offered in more than 50 countries, including two university-run programs: an economics program in Copenhagen and a studio art and art history program in Siena, Italy. Undergraduates have numerous opportunities to conduct original research with faculty, and some even publish their work in academic journals. The Justice Brandeis Semester allows groups of 10 to 15 students to earn credits while focusing on topics of personal interest, such as bio-inspired design, ethnographic fieldwork, or mobile app and game development. The linked courses feature fieldwork, internships, or research under faculty supervision.

"Brandeisians are friendly!" cheers a sophomore. "Everyone here is very warm and always willing to meet new people." Thirty percent of Brandeis undergraduates are from Massachusetts, and the population is heavily bicoastal otherwise, with sizable numbers of New York, New Jersey, and California residents. Twenty percent hail from foreign nations. Three chapels on campus—Roman Catholic, Jewish, and Protestant—are situated so that the shadow of one never crosses the shadow of another. It's an architectural symbol that students say reflects the realities of their diverse campus community. Less than half of undergraduates are Jewish. Muslim students, with an enrollment of more than 200, have their own dedicated prayer space, as do followers of Dharmic religions. Black students make up 6 percent of the student body, Hispanics/Latinos 8 percent, Asian Americans 17 percent, and multiracial students 3 percent. Social justice is a big emphasis on this liberal campus.

"Students care a lot about women's rights, LGBTQ+ rights, intersectionality, race relations, and a number of other issues," explains

"Brandeisians are friendly! Everyone here is very warm."

a theater arts major. With one of the highest tuition rates in the country, Brandeis now meets the full demonstrated financial need of all undergraduates. It also offers merit scholarships averaging $14,900 to qualified students, although there are no athletic awards.

Housing options include traditional quadrangle dormitories, where first-years and sophomores live in singles, doubles, or triples. Juniors and seniors can opt for singles, suites, or apartment-style housing. "Housing on campus improves as you get older," one student observes. First-years and sophomores are guaranteed housing, while upperclassmen play the lottery each spring. Seventy-six percent of students live on campus, and the rest find affordable off-campus housing nearby. As for campus dining, a business major says, "Some days the dining halls have pretty good food, and other days it is terrible." The food court in the Usdan Student Center provides decent alternatives, and there are always kosher, vegan, gluten-free, and allergensafe options. The university has opened a prevention, advocacy, and resource center on campus aimed at addressing sexual harassment and violence.

"The social life is lively, with on-campus productions, events, and activities predominantly occupying students' free time," says an anthropology major. Brandeis hosts more than 250 student clubs; some of the largest include the Waltham Group (a community service organization), the Campus Activities Board, and Triskelion (an LGBTQ+ social group). The unofficial fraternities and sororities that have colonized at Brandeis are clamoring for recognition from the school but hardly dominate the social scene. Weekends often feature live entertainment at the on-campus Stein pub or Cholmondeley's Coffee House (a.k.a. Chum's) and small dorm parties. Annual events include 'DEIS Impact, a weeklong social justice festival; the Springfest outdoor concert; and the 24-Hour Musical, in which students

"Brandeis is a haven for students who are seeking… an environment where social justice is revered."

learn and produce an entire musical in just 24 hours ("It's a total disaster, but it's hysterical," says a sophomore). Also well attended are the homecoming soccer match and carnival and the Leonard Bernstein Festival of the Creative Arts.

The possibilities for off-campus diversion are nearly infinite, thanks to the proximity of Boston and Cambridge, which are accessible by the free Brandeis shuttle bus or a nearby commuter train. (A car is more trouble than it's worth.) Brandeis's host town, Waltham, has a diverse selection of restaurants and a cheap movie theater but otherwise receives lukewarm reviews from students. One global studies major asks, "Who needs Waltham for excitement when Boston is a short shuttle ride away?"

Though the school does not field a football team, the Judges (remember Louis?) athletic program gets a boost from its membership in the Division III University Athletic Association, a neo–Ivy League for high-powered academic institutions such as the University of Chicago, Emory, and NYU. The men's and women's soccer teams make regular NCAA tournament appearances, and men's tennis, women's cross-country, and softball are also strong. An extensive intramural and club sports program draws 42 percent of students, and contests run nearly every day of the year.

Few private universities have come as far as Brandeis so quickly, evolving from the bare 235-acre site of a failed veterinary/medical school to a modern research university of more than 100 buildings, a $1.2 billion endowment, and ever-growing academic opportunities. At the same time, it has cultivated a highly supportive atmosphere. One student sums it up this way: "Brandeis is a haven for students who are seeking academic challenge and an environment where social justice is revered, where they can hold leadership roles and collaborate with professors."

If You Apply To ›

Brandeis: Early decision I and II, regular decision. SATs or ACTs or three exams from approved list: optional (applicants who choose not to submit test scores must submit a graded analytical paper and an additional letter of recommendation). Accepts the Common Application with supplement.

Brigham Young University

Provo, UT 84602

From the time they are knee high, Mormons all around the world dream about coming to BYU. Most men and some women do a two-year stint as a missionary. Strongest academic programs are all preprofessional. The atmosphere is generally mild-mannered and conservative, but BYU goes bonkers for its sports teams.

Website: www.byu.edu
Location: Small City
Private
Total Enrollment: 30,293
Undergraduates: 28,290
Male/Female: 49/51
Financial Aid: 68%
Pell Grant: 12%
Expense: Pr $
Student Loans: 21%
Average Debt: $
Applicants: 11,608
Accepted: 59%
Enrolled: 77%
Grad in 6 Years: 77%
Returning Freshmen: 89%
Academics: ✍ ✍ ✍
Social: ☎ ☎ ☎
Q of L: ★ ★ ★ ★

Brigham Young succeeded the martyred prophet Joseph Smith in 1844 as head of the much-persecuted Church of Jesus Christ of Latter-day Saints and subsequently led his fellow Mormon pioneers on their treacherous trek from Illinois to the "Promised Land" of Utah. Three decades later, in 1875, church fathers established an eponymous institution to fulfill Young's vision of "a good education unmixed with the pernicious atheistic influences that are found in so many of the higher schools of the country." It is a vision that lives on at Brigham Young University, where a sense of spirituality pervades most everything, where faith and academia are intertwined, and where life is governed by a demanding code of ethics that has even led to the suspension of star athletes in mid-season.

The church's values of prosperity, chastity, and obedience are strongly evident on BYU's 557-acre campus, where the utilitarian buildings, like everything else, are "clean, modern, and orderly." The campus lies on the western edge of the Rocky Mountains, 4,600 feet above sea level, between the shores of Utah Lake and Mount Timpanogos, offering breathtaking sunsets and easy access to magnificent skiing, camping, and hiking areas. Days begin early; church bells rouse students at 8 a.m. with the first four bars of the hymn "Come, Come Ye Saints." (The same bells also peal every hour throughout the day.)

The strict Honor Code covers everything from dating practices to academic honesty; no-no's include men wearing beards; the consuming of drugs, alcohol, and caffeinated tea and coffee (although caffeine in soda is allowed); and entering the bedroom of a member of the opposite sex. While students elsewhere might find the code burdensome, at BYU it is a point of pride. Indeed, the school's commitment to church values is the reason most students choose it. "The students who attend BYU are unique," says a communications major. "Everyone is clean-cut, shaven, modestly dressed, and proper in their etiquette."

The church's influence continues when students set their schedules; students must take one religion course per term to graduate, and subjects include, of course, the Book of Mormon. In addition to an extensive liberal arts core, BYU requires students to demonstrate proficiency in math, writing (first-year and advanced), and advanced languages, a catch-all category that can be satisfied with coursework in a foreign language or in statistics, advanced math, or advanced music.

BYU's academic offerings run the gamut, from liberal arts and sciences to solid preprofessional programs in engineering, nursing, business, and law. Students say the strongest offerings include education, exercise science, the Clark Law School, and most departments in the Marriott School of Business, especially accounting. There are also degrees in public health promotion and ancient Near Eastern studies. Brigham Young boasts campuses in Idaho and Hawaii, a center in Jerusalem, and a large study abroad program— nearly 200 programs in more than 50 countries. Approximately 90 percent of the men and 40 percent of the women interrupt their studies—typically after the freshman year—to serve two years as a missionary.

> "Most professors have a passion for their subject and for teaching."

Students agree that the academic climate is demanding. "It is competitive," a senior reports, and "some courses are known for being extremely difficult to pass, such as American Heritage or Econ 110." Freshmen are often taught by full-time professors, who generally get good marks. "Most professors have a passion for their subject and for teaching," says a student. General education courses can be quite large, although 46 percent of all undergraduate classes enroll fewer than 20 students, and registration can be a chore. The honors program, open to highly motivated students, offers small seminars with more faculty interaction and is "an excellent way to get more out of your college experience," one participant says. The strength of the faculty is one reason BYU has more full-time students than any other church-sponsored university in the United States, almost all of them undergraduates.

> *The strict Honor Code covers everything from dating practices to academic honesty.*

Not surprisingly, the typical BYU student is socially conservative. "The students are very academically and spiritually minded," confides a junior, who further describes students as "intelligent, friendly, and honest." Thirty-three percent of BYU undergraduates are from Utah. Many others hail from California and Idaho, and 5 percent come from more than 100 other countries. Hispanic/Latino students contribute 7 percent to the student body, Asian Americans 2 percent, Black students less than 1 percent, and multiracial students 4 percent. Tuition for church members is lower than for nonmembers, because Latter-day Saint families contribute to BYU through their tithes. Academic scholarships averaging $4,500 are available, as are hundreds of athletic scholarships in 21 sports.

> "BYU's dedicated faculty, devout atmosphere, and beautiful, clean campus set it apart."

Just 17 percent of BYU undergrads—primarily freshmen—live in the single-sex residence halls. "The dorms are small but comfortable and very clean," says a student. Upperclassmen typically opt for cheaper off-campus apartments, which are also single-sex (remember the Honor Code?). When it comes to food, the student dining outlets on campus are described as adequate. "The school provides decent, affordable on-campus meal plans," says a senior. Although it is widely assumed that,

(continued)

Admissions: (801) 422-4104
Email Address: admissions@ byu.edu

Strong Programs:
Engineering
Nursing
Business
Prelaw
Education
Exercise Science
Accounting
Public Health Promotion

because of the Honor Code and the religious tone on campus, sexual violence is not much of a problem, BYU drew national attention after female students and alumni spoke out against the school's practice of opening Honor Code investigations of students who report being assaulted. The protests resulted in a new policy of immunity for survivors.

Whether it's work with the homeless or disabled, dances, firesides, concerts, plays, sporting events, or special activities within the campus religious wards (small groups of about 100 students), most of BYU's social life is organized through or linked to the church. Community service is big, with students visiting patients at hospitals and care centers, performing at local festivals, and building and refurbishing houses. Social life is carried out within the church's bounds of propriety and is given a lighthearted feeling with groups that encourage "creative dating and lots of dating, period," says a senior. There are no fraternities or sororities to provide housing or parties, which is just fine with most students, since alcoholic drinks are banned. Road trips include Vegas or southern Utah and, with the mountains being so close, you'll find plenty of skiing and camping. Provo itself has plenty of places to eat and shop. "Provo wouldn't really exist without BYU," says a student, and "it's a good college town for people who don't like bustling metropolises."

Physical fitness is big here, and the intramural facilities are some of the country's best, with indoor and outdoor jogging tracks; courts for tennis, racquetball, and handball; and a pool. Also important are Division I varsity sports. The church philosophy of discipline and obedience has worked wonders for Cougar teams, and the football rivalry against the University of Utah provides some serious end-of-season intensity—ESPN has dubbed the BYU–Utah rivalry the "Holy War." One of the most popular courses offered at BYU is ballroom dancing, partly because many participants aspire to join BYU's award-winning dance team.

To most Americans, BYU probably seems old-fashioned or like a step back in time. But for young members of the Church of Jesus Christ of Latter-day Saints, that may be just what the elder ordered. "BYU's dedicated faculty, devout atmosphere, and beautiful, clean campus set it apart from all other universities," a satisfied senior says.

The football rivalry against the University of Utah—dubbed the "Holy War"—provides some serious end-of-season intensity.

Overlaps

BYU–Hawaii, BYU–Idaho, University of Utah, Utah State, Utah Valley State

If You Apply To ›

BYU: Regular decision. Does not accept the Common Application. Ecclesiastical endorsement required. Please consult BYU's website for the most up-to-date information regarding standardized test requirements.

University of British Columbia: See page 358.

Brown University

45 Prospect Street, Providence, RI 02912

To today's stressed-out students, the fantasy of taking every course pass/fail seems like a dream come true. Nobody at Brown actually does this, but the pass/fail option, combined with the school's notable lack of distribution requirements, gives it the freewheeling image that students love. In reality, doing well at Brown is just as tough as at other Ivies. Scorned by conservatives as a hotbed of political correctness.

Brown University is a perennial "hot college," with an overwhelming number of happy students and many more clamoring to join their ranks. Once here, students receive not only a prestigious and quality education, but also a chance to explore their creative sides at a liberal arts and sciences college that does not idolize grades or preprofessionalism and shuns GPAs, required courses, and competitive attitudes among its undergraduates. Brown's environment and policies have drawn both praise and criticism over the years, but its students thrive on this discussion and lively debate. "Brown's open curriculum, though not for everyone, is incredibly liberating," says one student.

Founded in 1764 as the College in the English Colony of Rhode Island and Providence Plantations, Brown was renamed in 1804 after Nicholas Brown Jr., a major benefactor whose father—one of the school's founders—was a businessman with controversial ties to the slave trade. The school has established a memorial to slaves at Brown and a Center for the Study of Slavery and Justice. The university sits atop College Hill on the east side of Providence, and its 140-acre campus affords an excellent view of downtown Providence. Campus architecture is a composite of old and new—plenty of grassy lawns surrounded by historic buildings that offer students refuge from the city streets beyond. The neighborhoods that surround the campus lie within a national historic district and boast beautiful tree-lined streets full of ethnic charm.

> "Brown's open curriculum, though not for everyone, is incredibly liberating."

Brown's faculty has successfully resisted the notion that somewhere in their collective wisdom and experience lies a core of knowledge that every educated person should possess. As a result, aside from completing courses in a major and a minimum of 30 courses total, the only university-wide requirement for graduation is "the ability to write well." All students must demonstrate that they have worked at least twice on developing their writing (once during their first two years and again as upperclassmen) by taking approved English or writing-across-the-curriculum classes or by documenting their writing work in any other Brown course. Students can take their classes one of two ways: for traditional marks of A, B, C, or No Credit; or for Satisfactory/No Credit. The NC is not recorded on the transcript, while the letter grade or Satisfactory can be supplemented by a written evaluation from the professor. A habit of NCs, however, lands students in academic hot water.

The most popular majors (or concentrations, as they are called here) are computer science, economics, English, and biology. Neuroscience, computer science, computational biology, applied mathematics, classics, and environmental studies are some of the university's best concentrations, and students also praise political science, engineering, religious studies, and history—although one says, "As far as I know, all our academic departments are super strong (like oxen or Heracles)." Other top-notch programs include comparative literature, modern languages, and the writing program in the English department. Future doctors can try for a competitive eight-year liberal medical education program where students can earn an M.D. without having to sacrifice their humanity. Fields related to scientific technology have very good facilities, including an instructional technology center, while minority issues are the focus of the Center for the Study of Race and Ethnicity in America.

> "As far as I know, all our academic departments are super strong (like oxen or Heracles)."

Those with interests in interdisciplinary fields will enjoy Brown's wide range of concentrations that cross departmental lines and cover everything from cognitive science to public policy to a program in business, entrepreneurship, and organizations. Students can create their own concentration from the array of goodies

Website: www.brown.edu
Location: Small City
Private
Total Enrollment: 10,250
Undergraduates: 7,076
Male/Female: 49/51
Financial Aid: 43%
Pell Grant: 14%
Expense: Pr $ $ $ $
Student Loans: 31%
Average Debt: $ $
Applicants: 46,568
Accepted: 6%
Enrolled: 66%
Grad in 6 Years: 96%
Returning Freshmen: 98%
Academics: ✍ ✍ ✍ ✍ ✍
Social: ☎ ☎ ☎ ☎
Q of L: ★ ★ ★ ★ ★
Admissions: (401) 863-2378
Email Address: admission@ brown.edu

Strong Programs:
Neuroscience
Computer Science
Computational Biology
Applied Mathematics
Classics
Environmental Studies
Political Science
Engineering

offered. Brown also offers group independent study projects, a popular alternative for students with the gumption to take a course they have to construct primarily by themselves, and a five-year dual-degree program with the Rhode Island School of Design (RISD), also located on College Hill. Students can cross-register for individual courses at RISD as well. "Brown provides amazing financial support for research opportunities through our UTRAs (Undergraduate Teaching and Research Awards)," says a junior. Adventurous students can choose to spend time in study abroad programs in 75 countries. Roughly 30 percent of undergrads study abroad, and others go overseas to complete independent research or internships during the summer. Brown leads U.S. research universities in the number of graduates who win Fulbrights.

Brown offers a five-year dual-degree program with the Rhode Island School of Design (RISD), also located on College Hill.

"Although the coursework is definitely rigorous, students are mostly only in classes that they really want to be in, and therefore it leads to an enjoyable, relaxed climate," explains a computer science major. Brown prides itself on undergraduate teaching and considers skill in the classroom as much as the usual scholarly credentials when making tenure decisions. An applied math and biology double major says, "Professors come to Brown interested in engaging with undergrads and being part of our experience, so they're really accessible." The advising system reflects the administration's commitment to treating students as adults. It pairs each freshman with a professor and a peer advisor, and a computer science major says, "This duo is great," especially because peer advisors offer "informal advising, social advice, and class advice." Resident counselors in the dorms are also available to lend an ear. "CareerLAB and BrownConnect are super helpful resources for finding jobs and internships," cheers a junior.

"Brown provides amazing financial support for research opportunities."

Brown offers nearly 90 special freshman seminars annually, capped at 20 students each and taught by faculty in all disciplines. "First-year seminars enable you to experience niche, in-depth seminar classes right away, along with your larger, introductory lecture courses," explains a sophomore. Overall, 69 percent of undergraduate classes have fewer than 20 students. Even so, particularly popular courses are usually jammed with students, and often there aren't enough teaching assistants to staff them effectively. Some, especially writing courses in the English department and studio art courses, can be nearly impossible to get into, although the administration claims that perseverance makes perfect—in other words, show up the first day and beg shamelessly.

Brown offers nearly 90 special freshman seminars annually, capped at 20 students each and taught by faculty in all disciplines.

"Brown students are very independent, which is an important quality for navigating our unique curriculum," says a sophomore. With a mere 6 percent of undergraduates hailing from tiny Rhode Island and 11 percent coming from foreign countries, geographical diversity is one of Brown's hallmarks. Consistent with the spirit of openness that defined Roger Williams's Rhode Island from the outset, Brown was the first Ivy League school to accept students from all religious affiliations. Today, Brown is a hot spot of student activism; nary a semester has passed without at least one demonstration about the issue of the day. Black students account for 8 percent of the student body, Hispanics/Latinos 11 percent, Asian Americans 18 percent, and multiracial students 7 percent. The LGBTQ community is also prominent. "Brown is one of the most conscious schools when it comes to identities, and students take the initiative to create spaces for people of all identities," observes a cognitive science major. Although Brown doesn't offer athletic or academic merit scholarships, it does practice need-blind admissions and guarantees to meet the full demonstrated need of everyone admitted with loan-free financial aid packages. The university also covers the cost of books for students on financial aid.

"Brown is one of the most conscious schools when it comes to identities."

About half of the freshmen are assigned to one of eight co-ed Keeney Quad dorms, in "loud and rambunctious" units of 40 to 60 with several sophomore or junior dorm counselors. The other half live in the quieter Pembroke campus dorms or in a few other scattered locations. According to a sophomore, "Freshman accommodations are by and large quite plush." Options for upperclassmen include apartment-like suites with kitchens, special-interest houses, two social dorms, and Greek housing. Brown guarantees housing for all four years and requires students to live on campus through sophomore year; 70 percent of undergrads reside in university housing. Nearby off-campus apartments are becoming more plentiful—and more expensive—as the area gentrifies. Students appreciate the variety of accommodations offered at the two main dining halls and various smaller locations, one of which is vegetarian only, although the food gets middling reviews. "The larger the eatery is, the less flavorful food you can expect to get," observes a senior. Students say the campus feels safe, and one notes, "Brown emphasizes consent education and makes sexual health resources widely available."

A favorite tradition involves a beloved music professor performing lively midnight organ concerts in a stately campus hall.

"Much of the social life is on campus. I love that! You always feel part of the community," says an American studies major. More than a dozen a cappella groups, daily and weekly newspapers, political organizations, and "even a Scrabble club and a successful croquet team" represent just a few of the ways Brown students manage to keep themselves entertained. The university also sponsors frequent campuswide parties, dances, plays, concerts, and special events. The few residential Greek organizations tend to be considered much too un-mellow for Brown's taste—just 6 percent of the men and 7 percent of the women sign up. The nonresidential multi-

"It's cool to be excited about anything here."

cultural fraternities and sororities serve a more comprehensive student-life function, and parties are more likely to be held off campus by sports teams. Students report that alcohol policies focus on safety more than punishment. The biggest annual bash of the year is Spring Weekend, which features plenty of parties and a big-name band on the Main Green. A favorite tradition involves a beloved music professor performing lively midnight organ concerts in a stately campus hall "on the four scariest nights of the year: the night before freshman classes start, Halloween, and the night before finals each semester," explains a denizen.

Providence, an old industrial city that has undergone a renaissance of sorts, is Rhode Island's capital, so many internship opportunities in state government are available, as are a few good music joints, lively bars, and several fine, inexpensive restaurants, especially along Thayer Street. The city is also home to a number of other colleges, which helps to liven up the social scene. "Providence is a great place to see a concert or attend a festival," says a junior. For those interested in community service—and many at Brown are—the university's nationally recognized Swearer Center for Public Service helps place students in a variety of volunteer positions. Brown Community Outreach is, in fact, the largest student organization on campus. For a change of scenery, many students head to Boston or the beaches of Newport, each an hour away.

For those interested in volunteer work, Brown Community Outreach is the largest student organization on campus.

Brown does not have a reputation as an especially sports-minded school, and it recently cut several sports from its roster in a controversial move to focus its efforts on making its remaining 34 varsity teams more competitive. The Bears women's crew team has won multiple Division I championships, and men's soccer, lacrosse, and water polo have been competitive in the Ivy League Conference. Athletic facilities include an Olympic-sized swimming pool and an indoor athletic complex with everything from tennis courts to weight rooms. Thirty-three club sports, plus intramurals ranging from softball and kickball to cornhole tournaments, offer a good mix of competitiveness and fun.

Ever since the days of Roger Williams, Rhode Island has been known as a land of tolerance, and Brown certainly is a 21st-century embodiment of this tradition. "Brown students build themselves up by building others up," says a physics and philosophy double major. "It's cool to be excited about anything here, and Brown students celebrate the talents of all of their peers." The education offered at this university is decidedly different from that provided by the rest of the Ivy League, or for that matter, by other top universities. Brown is content to gather a talented bunch of students, offer a diverse and imaginative array of courses, and then let the undergraduates, with a little help, make sense of it all. It takes an enormous amount of initiative, maturity, and self-confidence to thrive at Brown, but most students feel they are up to the challenge.

If You Apply To ›

Brown: Early decision, regular decision. Accepts the Common Application with supplement. Please consult Brown's website for the most up-to-date information regarding standardized test requirements.

Bryn Mawr College

101 North Merion Avenue, Bryn Mawr, PA 19010-2899

Bryn Mawr has the most brainpower per capita of the elite women's colleges. Politics range from liberal to radical, and the honor code shapes the campus culture. Mawrters may take themselves a bit too seriously. The college still benefits from ties to nearby Haverford, though the relationship may not be as tight-knit as in the days when Haverford was all-male. A train station just off campus offers easy access to Philadelphia.

Website: www.brynmawr.edu
Location: Suburban
Private
Total Enrollment: 1,652
Undergraduates: 1,420
Male/Female: 0/100
Financial Aid: 78%
Pell Grant: 12%
Expense: Pr $ $ $
Student Loans: 48%
Average Debt: $ $
Applicants: 3,391
Accepted: 39%
Enrolled: 32%
Grad in 6 Years: 87%
Returning Freshmen: 89%
Academics: ✍ ✍ ✍ ✍ ✍
Social: ☎ ☎ ☎
Q of L: ★ ★ ★
Admissions: (610) 526-5152

Leafy suburban enclaves are a dime a dozen around Philadelphia, but only one is home to Bryn Mawr College, a top-notch liberal arts school that happens to be for women. On this campus, students find a range of academic pursuits from archaeology to film studies to physics, and a diverse yet community-oriented student body. Founded in 1885, Bryn Mawr has evolved into a hotbed of intellectualism that prepares students for life and work in a global environment. Although students here abide by a strict honor code and participate in a host of long-standing campus traditions, they remain doggedly individualistic. "We are social-justice minded, fiercely independent trailblazers who do not take no for an answer," asserts one sophomore. "I am absolutely certain that we will run the world someday."

Bryn Mawr's lovely campus is a path-laced oasis set among trees (many carefully labeled with Latin and English names) and lush green hills, perfect for an afternoon walk, bike ride, or jog. Just a 20-minute train ride from downtown

"I am absolutely certain that we will run the world someday."

Philadelphia, Bryn Mawr provides a suburban setting with a vital and exciting city nearby. The architecture is predominantly the collegiate Gothic style, a combination of the Gothic architecture of Oxford and Cambridge Universities and the local material, that Bryn Mawr was instrumental in establishing in the United States. Ten of Bryn Mawr's buildings are listed in the National Register of Historic Places. Variations on the collegiate Gothic theme include a sprinkling of modern buildings, such as Louis Kahn's slate-and-concrete residence hall.

The general education requirements include one semester of "quantitative" work; one semester in each of four "approaches to inquiry" (scientific investigation, critical interpretation, cross-cultural analysis, and inquiry into the past); two semesters of a foreign language; and the requirements of a major. Students are also required to take eight half-semesters of physical education, pass a swimming test, and complete the 10-week THRIVE program, which introduces freshmen to the Bryn Mawr community and teaches life skills. In addition, all freshmen take a Balch Seminar (named for alumna and Nobel Peace Prize laureate Emily Balch) to develop their critical-thinking, writing, and discussion skills.

Most departments are strong, especially the sciences, classics, archaeology, history of art, museum studies, and the foreign languages, including Russian and French. The growth and structure of cities major is a unique interdisciplinary program that blends coursework in urban studies, architecture, history, economics, and sociology, among other subjects. Combined degree programs, in which students earn both a bachelor's and a master's degree from Bryn Mawr, are available in a number of fields, ranging from chemistry and physics to classical and Near Eastern archaeology. The most popular majors are psychology, mathematics, literatures in English, biology, and sociology. Doing major work in music, fine arts, linguistics, religion, or astronomy requires a hike over to nearby Haverford College, Bryn Mawr's partner in the bicollege system, which allows students at each institution to take courses or even major or minor in programs offered by the other. Bryn Mawr and Haverford students cooperate on a weekly newspaper, radio station, orchestra, and other clubs and sports, and they may use facilities at each school, including dining halls and even dormitories. A free shuttle bus connects the campuses. Students may also cross-register with Swarthmore and the University of Pennsylvania; 95 percent of Mawrters take courses at these institutions or at Haverford at some point during their four years. Five-year dual-degree programs in engineering are offered in conjunction with Caltech, Columbia, and Penn.

Out of respect for their honor code, Mawrters refrain from discussing their grades, but they freely admit that they work hard to keep up with their rigorous courses. Freshmen and transfer students are initiated to the Bryn Mawr experience during Customs Week, which includes a variety of seminars and workshops, and Customs peer advisors support their transition throughout their first year. The quality of teaching at Bryn Mawr is unquestionably high, and faculty members are accessible, thanks to small class sizes and flexible office hours. "The professors here trust and respect the students and treat them as equals," comments a psychology major.

For those looking ahead to see what Bryn Mawr's steep tuition will buy in the long term, there is no lack of special academic programs with which to fill their résumés. The 360° Course Cluster program is an interdisciplinary experience that brings students from a variety of majors together to examine a central theme, like Europe from the Margins or Struggles for Global Health Equity, from multiple perspectives. Students take a cluster of two or three courses in a single semester and also complete a hands-on component, such as travel, fieldwork, or lab research. Thirty-three percent of students study overseas during their time at Bryn Mawr, choosing from about 70 programs in 30 countries. With easy access to a diverse variety of organizations in Philadelphia, 78 percent of Mawrters complete internships before they graduate. The Career and Civic Engagement Office connects students with internship and community service opportunities and offers guidance on networking, interviewing, and other professional skills.

"Bryn Mawr tends to attract passionate, intelligent, kind, supportive, and involved individuals," says one student. The campus has a strong international

(continued)

Email Address: admissions@ brynmawr.edu

Strong Programs:
Natural Sciences
Classics
Archaeology
History of Art
Museum Studies
Foreign Languages
Growth and Structure of Cities
Psychology

Ninety-five percent of Mawrters take courses at Swarthmore, Penn, or Haverford at some point during their four years.

"A lot of people are talking about race at Bryn Mawr, and also transgender issues."

Freshmen and transfer students are initiated to the Bryn Mawr experience during Customs Week, which includes a variety of seminars and workshops.

flavor, with an impressive 15 percent of undergraduates hailing from abroad; only 15 percent are Pennsylvania residents. Black students make up 5 percent of the student body, Hispanics/Latinas 10 percent, Asian Americans 12 percent, and multiracial students 5 percent. "A lot of people are talking about race at Bryn Mawr, and also transgender issues," says one student. There are no athletic scholarships, but merit scholarships averaging $18,000 are available, and the school does guarantee to meet the demonstrated financial need of everyone admitted, including international students.

More than 90 percent of undergrads typically reside on campus, and housing is guaranteed for four years. "Each dorm is unique and has a character of its own," says a senior. "Many people liken the architecture to that of Hogwarts." Dorm features include hardwood floors, window seats, and fireplaces. Dining services, which receive rave reviews, offer plentiful, tasty choices as well as a nutritionist to assist students with dietary restrictions. A classical culture and society major says, "Public Safety are there to help and keep students safe."

Traditions are an important part of the campus social scene: "They play a big role in uniting all four classes and give students a role in the greater history of the college," says a student. The Elizabethan-style May Day festivities are held the Sunday after classes end in May. Everyone wears white, eats strawberries and ice cream, watches student plays, and dances around maypoles. Mawrters have been known to skinny-dip in the fountains and drink champagne on the lawn. The presentation of lanterns and class colors to incoming freshmen on Lantern Night—and regal pageants, such as Parade Night and Step-Sing—fill life with a Gothic sense of wonder and school spirit. Bryn Mawr is located on suburban Philly's wealthy Main Line (named after a railroad), and the campus is two blocks from the train station, which provides students with convenient access to cultural attractions, as well as social and academic events at the nearby University of Pennsylvania and elsewhere in the city. "I consider our social life to be hanging out with friends, poetry slams, and watching plays and cultural shows," muses a junior.

> **"Many people liken the architecture to that of Hogwarts."**

As for athletics, most Bryn Mawr Owls teams compete in the Division III Centennial Conference; field hockey, track and field, and crew are among the stronger teams. Club sports range from all-female teams to co-ed teams shared with Haverford, such as ultimate Frisbee and fencing, and intramurals are an option too.

Bryn Mawr is a symphony of contrasts: the campus is in suburbia but steps from a major city. Humanities programs are very strong, but science majors are also strong and enormously popular. The students are seriously intellectual and independent but revel in college traditions. The result is overwhelmingly positive. Says a student, "The Bryn Mawr experience is one of complete freedom to explore one's interests and individuality without the fear of being ostracized."

Overlaps

Barnard, Mount Holyoke, Smith, Wellesley, Haverford, Swarthmore, Wesleyan, NYU

If You Apply To ›

Bryn Mawr: Early decision I and II, regular decision. SATs or ACTs: optional. Accepts the Common Application with supplement. Accepts applications from all individuals who identify as women, intersex individuals who do not identify as male, and individuals assigned female at birth who do not identify within the gender binary.

Bucknell University

Lewisburg, PA 17837

Bucknell, Colgate, Hamilton, Lafayette—all a little more conservative than the Ivy schools, and all a little less selective. Bucknell is the biggest of this bunch and, like Lehigh, offers engineering with a global touch. Bucknell's Greek system is strong, but students don't join until they are sophomores. The central Pennsylvania campus is remote but one of the most beautiful anywhere.

The students at Bucknell University strike a healthy balance between hitting the books and hitting the lively social scene on their pastoral central Pennsylvania campus. Yes, they tend to be preppy: "Bucknell students are mostly upper-middle-class, relatively conservative, and materially conscious. However, they are also highly motivated and eager to succeed," says one student. With small classes, engaging faculty, and not a subpar dorm to be found, it's no wonder that students like this junior complain, "Four years at Bucknell go by way too fast."

In addition to being comfortable and friendly, Bucknell, founded in 1846 and named after an early benefactor, is physically beautiful. Located on a hill just south of quaint Lewisburg, the campus overlooks the scenic Susquehanna River valley. Playing fields, shaded by leafy trees, are sprinkled among the Georgian-style buildings. While some structures date from the 19th century, lending a fairy-tale quality, others are far more modern. The $38 million Academic East building houses laboratory space for engineering and scientific research, as well as the education department. Holmes Hall, a 79,500-square-foot facility featuring high-tech labs and studios for Bucknell's business and art programs, opened in 2021.

Students in Bucknell's College of Arts & Sciences and Freeman College of Management must complete general education courses in three areas—Intellectual Skills (including a writing-intensive Foundation Seminar), Tools for Critical Engagement, and Disciplinary Perspectives—and must complete a culminating experience their senior year. In the College of Engineering, students take a common course their first semester that introduces them to all eight of the engineering degree programs, and they undertake a capstone senior design experience as part of their curriculum. All freshmen, regardless of discipline, participate in the First-Year Integration Series, workshops designed to help them transition to college, featuring topics such as university resources, diverse perspectives, and lifelong learning. In addition to faculty advisors, first-year students are assigned peer mentors who answer questions and connect them with campus resources and opportunities. Along with major-related requirements, each student must demonstrate competence in writing in order to graduate.

While Bucknell is known for engineering, management, and the natural sciences, students say academics are strong across the curriculum, with weaker programs hard to find. The most popular majors are economics, political science, psychology, accounting, and finance. Other highlights include biomedical engineering; the animal behavior program, which benefits from an outdoor naturalistic primate facility for teaching and research; and environmental studies, which includes not only science courses but also classes in the humanities, social policy, and civil engineering. Management 101 is a favorite course among business students, who work together to create and sell a product and use the profits to fund community service projects.

> **"[Research] has really helped shape what I want to do in the future."**

Website: www.bucknell.edu
Location: Small Town
Private
Total Enrollment: 3,729
Undergraduates: 3,713
Male/Female: 47/53
Financial Aid: 61%
Pell Grant: 10%
Expense: Pr $ $ $ $
Student Loans: 39%
Average Debt: $ $ $ $
Applicants: 11,263
Accepted: 35%
Enrolled: 26%
Grad in 6 Years: 88%
Returning Freshmen: 91%
Academics: ✍ ✍ ✍ ✍
Social: ☎ ☎ ☎ ☎
Q of L: ★ ★ ★
Admissions: (570) 577-3000
Email Address: admissions@bucknell.edu

Strong Programs:
Engineering
Management
Animal Behavior
Environmental Studies
Economics
Political Science
Psychology
Accounting

In the classroom, the emphasis is on discussion and group work; 54 percent of Bucknell's courses enroll fewer than 20 students. Professors facilitate the cooperative atmosphere and receive praise for always putting students first. "The professors care as much about their professional relationship with the students as they do about the courses they teach," says a senior.

Forty-two percent of all Bucknell undergrads study abroad. Semester-long, faculty-led programs take them to England, France, Ghana, Greece, and Spain. Relationships with other colleges and universities enable students to choose from more than 400 other programs worldwide. The College of Engineering has one of the highest study abroad participation rates for students in an engineering program, and it also offers a specialized three-week, faculty-taught study abroad course that places engineering concepts into a real-world, global context. Department-specific honors programs attract top scholars, and twenty percent of all undergraduates—in all disciplines—participate in undergraduate research. A cell biology/biochemistry major points to research as a defining experience at Bucknell: "I knew nothing about research coming into college, but it has really helped shape what I want to do in the future."

Twenty-two percent of students are Pennsylvanians, and 58 percent went to public high school. Racial and cultural diversity have been slow in coming, an issue cited by many students, although "efforts to create more inclusion and equity have become more pronounced," comments a managing for sustainability major. Black students account for 4 percent of the student body, Hispanics/Latinos 7 percent, Asian Americans 5 percent, and multiracial students 4 percent, while international students represent 5 percent. "Bucknell tends to be more conservative than most schools," says a chemical engineering major, but social and political issues generally take a back seat here. Each year, Bucknell awards merit scholarships averaging $21,100, as well as 210 athletic scholarships in 14 sports.

> **"Bucknell tends to be more conservative than most schools."**

Most undergrads—89 percent—live on campus, as the university limits the number of seniors allowed to move off campus. Thirty-seven percent of each entering class join the Residential Colleges (which a biomedical engineering major calls "fantastic for first-years"), choosing from among eight themed living/learning communities: Arts, Discovery, Food, Global, Humanities, Languages and Cultures, Social Justice, and Society and Technology. Dining facilities offer an adequate variety, and a junior notes, "I am a vegetarian and have a lot of good options." A recently created food pantry aims to alleviate food insecurity on campus. Speak UP, a peer education group, holds mandatory workshops on sexual assault prevention and holds sessions throughout the year. Even so, some students express concerns about the prevalence of sexual misconduct incidents within the Greek system.

"Greek life runs the social scene—there is no other way to put it," a senior reports. Indeed, Bucknell's robust Greek system draws 34 percent of the men and 42 percent of the women, though rush is delayed until the start of sophomore year. Drinking at frat parties and a few bars close to campus is a weekly pastime for many students of age, but the university offers plenty of on-campus alternatives. Two student organizations arrange everything from carnivals and hypnotists to religious retreats, while the school-run Uptown nightclub offers bands, karaoke, pub nights, and other social events. "Friday nights are generally not a time to be in the library," confirms one student. Favorite traditions include the Fall Fest carnival that features a nationally known musical act, the Bison Sound concert with student performers, Greek Week, and the formal Chrysalis Ball in the spring. Also special are the Candlelighting and Convocation ceremonies. "Convocation is an important tradition to Bucknell because you only pass through the Christy Mathewson Gates twice in your life: on your first and last days as a student here," explains a senior.

Lewisburg is small and rural, but Market Street has boutiques, restaurants, and an Art Deco movie theater that serves up first-run flicks as well as student-produced films. "Market Street is a great way to get off campus without having to get in a car to do so," says a senior. Through the Office of Civic Engagement, students have opportunities to volunteer and participate in service learning. When students get claustrophobic, New York, Philadelphia, and Washington/Baltimore are less than three hours away; the main campus of Penn State, in State College, Pennsylvania, is even closer. Bucknell sponsors road trips to these communities for students who lack wheels.

> **"Greek life runs the social scene—there is no other way to put it."**

The Division I Bucknell Bison have captured the Patriot League Presidents' Cup, for the league's all-sports champion, 18 times in 31 years. Men's and women's cross-country and track and field are perennially competitive, having combined for dozens of Patriot League championships. Other strong teams include field hockey and men's and women's basketball and water polo. Basketball is a fan favorite, and Bucknell's biggest rivalries are with Lafayette and Lehigh, though these aren't a tremendous focus. Intramural and club sports draw 41 percent of the students.

In the absence of diversity, Bucknell students get the best of several other worlds: excellence in engineering, management, and the liberal arts; abundant research opportunities; and a healthy social life. Another perk: "Both students and alumni have a serious amount of pride for their school," says a senior, "and you find that alumni want to give back." The school's rural Pennsylvania location and the preponderance of preppies may seem stifling at times, but if you're seeking small classes and a supportive environment, Bucknell may be a good fit.

If You Apply To ›

Bucknell: Early decision I and II, regular decision. Accepts the Common Application. Audition required for applicants to music program. Please consult Bucknell's website for the most up-to-date information regarding standardized test requirements

Butler University

4600 Sunset Avenue, Indianapolis, IN 46208

Small, private university with an attractive campus near downtown Indianapolis and a relaxed Midwestern feel. Butler combines a strong liberal arts emphasis with hands-on learning. Strong in business, dance, and prepharmacy. Students are a homogeneous lot who share Indiana's trademark passion for basketball. Larger than DePauw, smaller than Northwestern.

College hoops fans may recognize Butler University as the unheralded outsider that fought its way to the final game of the men's Division I Basketball Championships not once but twice in the last 13 years. But those who attend this midsized Midwestern university explain that Bulldogs basketball is representative of the Butler way of life, which emphasizes teamwork, tenacity, and sound fundamentals. Indeed, students here find their school's cozy campus and solid academics to be a slam dunk.

Butler was founded in 1855 as a "nonsectarian institution free from the taint of slavery" on property donated by Ovid Butler, a lawyer and abolitionist. Located five miles north of downtown Indianapolis in the city's historic Butler-Tarkington

Website: www.butler.edu
Location: City Outskirts
Private
Total Enrollment: 4,796
Undergraduates: 4,323
Male/Female: 40/60
Financial Aid: 99%
Pell Grant: 18%

(continued)

Expense: Pr $
Student Loans: 55%
Average Debt: $ $ $ $
Applicants: 15,340
Accepted: 81%
Enrolled: 9%
Grad in 6 Years: 84%
Returning Freshmen: 87%
Academics: ✍ ✍ ✍
Social: ☎ ☎ ☎
Q of L: ★ ★ ★ ★
Admissions: (888) 940-8100
Email Address: admission@
   butler.edu

Strong Programs:
Business
Dance
Prepharmacy
English
Marketing
Communication/Journalism
Education
Health Sciences

Students in the Butler Summer Institute produce an original research or creative project with the support of a $4,500 stipend.

neighborhood, Butler's 300-acre campus is hailed as one of the most attractive in the Midwest for its parklike setting, which includes centuries-old trees, open landscaped lawns, curving sidewalks, fountains, a nature preserve, a prairie, a historical canal, a formal botanical garden, an observatory, and jogging paths. The first building, Jordan Hall, features Gothic architecture and has set the tone for subsequent buildings. Butler's Hinkle Fieldhouse, which opened in 1928, has reigned as one of the nation's great sports arenas for nine decades. Opened in 2021, the $100 million Sciences Complex boasts state-of-the-art labs, high-tech classrooms, and the Science Innovation Center.

As part of Butler's core curriculum, students enroll in two common elements: First-Year Seminar, a two-semester sequence in their first year, and Global and Historical Studies, a sophomore-year sequence of courses. In addition to a standard distribution of liberal arts and science classes, students must take a social justice and diversity course. They also complete the Butler Cultural Requirement, which involves attending eight campus events over four years, and the Indianapolis Community Requirement, which connects students to the local area through off-campus community service. Incoming freshmen looking to make friends before the start of their first semester can sign up for one of several optional preorientation programs that range from volunteering in Indianapolis to learning how major sporting events like the Indianapolis 500 and Super Bowl are organized.

> **"Professors have a tendency to deviate from the normal lectures, notes, papers, and exams."**

"Butler students are extremely competitive," says a strategic communication major. "Whether that be for who has the best presentation in a class, the highest grade on a test, and even for internships in the Indianapolis area—Butler students want to be the best and be recognized for that." The university's most popular programs include marketing, finance, communication/journalism, education, health sciences, and preprofessional tracks in pharmacy and physician assistant studies. Other solid offerings include dance (especially classical ballet), international business, and English, especially the creative writing track. Students in the risk management and insurance major learn how to mitigate and manage risks and can get hands-on experience through the school's student-run insurance company. New options include an art history major and an eSports communication minor. Butler now offers three-year degree tracks for more than 30 academic majors. The university also sponsors a five-year engineering dual degree in partnership with Purdue. Half of all undergraduate classes enroll fewer than 20 students, and the majority of classes taken by freshmen are taught by full professors. "Professors have a tendency to deviate from the normal lectures, notes, papers, and exams and allow us to take a more hands-on approach," comments a psychology and Spanish double major.

The University Honors Program is designed to foster a diverse and challenging intellectual climate; students take four honors courses, participate in special honors events, and research and write a thesis. About 30 students are selected each year for the Butler Summer Institute, where they produce an original research or creative project under the guidance of a faculty mentor and with the support of a $4,500 stipend. For those who wish to travel to far-flung locales around the globe, Butler offers more than 200 study abroad options in 60 countries, including Australia, Ireland, Germany, Ghana, and India. Roughly a third of Butler students participate.

"School spirit is really big at Butler," explains an elementary education major. "We love to take part in school activities and support our teams." Forty-four percent of Butler students come from Indiana. Black students account for 4 percent of the student body, Hispanics/Latinos 6 percent, Asian Americans 4 percent, and multiracial students 4 percent; another 1 percent are international. Most students come from middle- to upper-class families. While there is not usually much overt political activism on campus, the lack of diversity and the cost to attend are common student complaints. Merit scholarships averaging $19,300 are available to qualified students, as are numerous athletic awards.

Butler's varsity and club-level esports teams compete in the swanky new Butler Esports Park.

Sixty-six percent of students live in university-sponsored housing, with all but seniors and commuters required to do so. Options include dorms, university-owned houses and apartments, and Greek houses. Eating in Butler's two campus dining halls is becoming more palatable, students say, after renovations and changing the food service provider. And while Butler is "not in the best part of town," students report feeling safe on campus: "Butler is a very tight-knit community, and we all look out for each other," says a junior, "but it feels good to know that our campus security is always there."

"Greek organizations and sports teams set the tone for social life," says a student; 25 percent of the men and 36 percent of the women go Greek. Although the university allows alcohol on campus, students say the social scene doesn't revolve around booze. "Butler students think they know how to party, but compared to state schools like IU and Purdue, that's laughable," remarks one senior. More

"School spirit is really big at Butler."

than 140 student organizations coordinate social activities throughout the week, and favorite annual traditions include homecoming in the fall. Students seeking a change of pace head off campus and into the Broad Ripple neighborhood or downtown Indianapolis, where bars, restaurants, museums, cultural events, and professional sports are plentiful.

Butler fields 20 Division I teams (the Bulldogs), and all but one compete in the Big East—the football team is a member of the Pioneer Football League. Aside from basketball, the men's and women's soccer, cross-country, and track and field teams are strong. Intramurals are popular, especially five-on-five basketball, soccer, volleyball, and flag football, and more serious students may also compete in 21 club sports. Butler's varsity and club-level esports teams compete in the swanky new Butler Esports Park, which opened in 2022.

Butler University strives to provide students with a strong undergraduate liberal arts experience and access to professional programs of "local impact and global reach." Students have taken note of the school's revamped programs, improved facilities, and focus on personal attention. "Butler truly becomes a community for our students," says a sophomore. "The students and faculty all work to make Butler life an enjoyable experience for all."

Overlaps

Creighton, Providence, Valparaiso, Xavier (OH), Gonzaga, DePauw, Drake, Bradley

If You Apply To ›

Butler: Early action, regular decision. SATs or ACTs: optional. Accepts the Common Application with supplement. Art applicants must submit portfolio.

California Colleges and Universities

California's three-pronged system of universities, colleges, and community colleges has long been viewed as a model of excellence by other public higher education institutions nationwide and even around the world. The system offers a wealth of educational riches, including world-class research universities, enough Nobel Prize winners to fill a couple of classrooms, and colleges on the cutting edge of everything from film to viticulture. Underlying the creation of this remarkable system was a commitment to the notion that all qualified Californians, whatever their economic status, are entitled to the benefits of a college education.

The California system is composed of the 10 combined research and teaching units of the University of California (UC) and 23 California State University (CSU) campuses that focus primarily on undergraduate teaching. It also includes more than 100 two-year community colleges that offer both associate's degrees and the pathway of transferring into four-year institutions. Like other state systems, California public colleges and universities have been hit with budget cuts in recent years that have, among other things, led to greater proportions of out-of-state and international students, who pay much higher tuition rates. But it seems that the tide is turning. Governor Gavin Newsom has substantially increased funding for all three systems and vowed to limit the proportion of nonresident students on all campuses to no more than 18 percent of the student population. The new Tuition Stability Plan essentially locks in the tuition rate and student services fee for new first-year and transfer students at UC universities for up to six years for California residents and nonresidents alike. The UC system also has a Native American Opportunity Plan that covers tuition and student services fees for residents who belong to federally recognized Native American, American Indian, and Alaska Native tribes.

ADMISSIONS REQUIREMENTS

Admissions requirements for the three systems and the institutions within them vary widely. Community colleges are open to virtually anyone with a high school diploma or equivalent. To be considered for admission to a CSU or UC campus, applicants must complete a minimum of 15 yearlong college-preparatory courses in seven subject areas (referred to as "a-g courses"), including two semesters in the fine or performing arts. Applicants will be eligible for admission to the CSU system with a 2.5 or higher "a-g" GPA (3.0 for nonresidents). Applicants to a UC university must earn a 3.0 "a-g" GPA (3.4 for nonresidents) or better. GPA for eligibility is calculated using only 10th- and 11th-grade results. Choice of major continues to be an important factor for some campuses, and students interested in popular majors such as engineering and computer science are wise to take advantage of the opportunity to list an alternate major.

In May 2021, amid the COVID-19 pandemic and after settling a lawsuit brought by students claiming that standardized tests create inequities in assessing a student's chances of success in college, the UC system announced that it would no longer consider SAT or ACT scores in the admissions process, becoming test-free. In fact, there is no place in the testing section of the UC application to report these scores. The CSU system's board of trustees followed suit in March 2022, announcing that CSU schools will no longer consider SAT or ACT scores, even if they are submitted.

UNIVERSITY OF CALIFORNIA (UC)

The UC system boasts more than 280,000 students, 227,000 faculty and staff, and 2 million living alumni. Although one university system, each of the nine undergraduate UC campuses (UC San Francisco only offers graduate and professional degrees) offers a full range of academic programs, and each has its own distinctive character. The newest member, Merced, opened in 2005 as the first American research university to be founded in the 21st century. In response to record-breaking numbers of applications, the UC system has announced plans to increase enrollment by 23,000 students by the end of the decade, the equivalent of adding an entire new campus.

In making admissions decisions, UC employs a "comprehensive review" process that takes into consideration not only curriculum and grades but also leadership, special talents, and the educational opportunities available to each student. To apply for admission to the University of California, students complete an application available at admission.universityofcalifornia.edu. The application is standardized across all UC campuses, making it easy for an applicant to apply to multiple campuses. For each campus selected, students must choose a major and, in some cases, an alternate major. There is a $70 application fee for each campus. In order to enhance their chances of gaining admission to at least one campus, prospective students are encouraged to use this application to apply to more than one school. They should understand that each campus to which they apply reviews their application using its own methodology and criteria. Decisions are thus campus-unique, and each university's admissions office is not aware of an individual applicant's other options. Applicants who rank in the top 9 percent of California high school students or the top 9 percent of their own California high school, but who are not accepted to any UC campus, will be offered a place at another campus if space is available.

UC Merced is described below. Full profiles of the other eight undergraduate UC universities follow this overview.

UC Merced (full-time enrollment 9,000) is the newest addition to the UC system. Opened in 2005 with a mission of bringing public higher education to one of the state's underserved areas, Merced is expanding rapidly and has established itself as a promising school for those seeking to avoid the competitiveness of more selective UC universities. The campus, which sits on the shore of Lake Yosemite surrounded by green fields and considerable land set aside for conservation, boasts an environmentally friendly design and has a small-town feel. Merced offers 26 undergraduate majors through its three schools: engineering; natural sciences; and social sciences, humanities, and arts. It has a diverse student body, with students of color making up 85 percent of the undergraduate population, and a higher proportion of students from low-income and first-generation backgrounds than any other campus. It boasts a strong counseling and support system. Merced has the highest acceptance rate of any UC university (87 percent) and draws relatively few students from out of state. Faculty are bringing in substantial research funding, especially in the biological sciences.

CALIFORNIA STATE UNIVERSITY (CSU)

The California State University system is separate from the University of California and constitutes the largest system of comprehensive four-year public institutions in the U.S. Unlike UC, where the mandate to publish or perish is alive and well, teachers in the state system are there to teach.

The 23-campus system caters to more than 475,000 students a year. And while many of the campuses serve mainly commuters, Chico, Humboldt, Monterey Bay, Cal Poly–San Luis Obispo, Cal Maritime, and Sonoma stand out as residential campuses. While a solid liberal arts education is offered in CSU institutions, the emphasis is often on career-oriented professional training; the system produces large numbers of engineers, nurses, and teachers for California's workforce. Size varies dramatically, from more than 30,000 full-time students at Northridge and Long Beach to fewer than 7,000 at several other campuses, like Channel Islands and Monterey Bay. Each campus has its strengths, although in most cases, a student's choice of school is dictated by location rather than by academic specialties. For those with a wider choice, some of the more distinctive campuses are profiled below.

Chico (full-time enrollment 13,300), situated in the beautiful Sacramento Valley, draws a large majority of its students from outside a 100-mile radius and continues to become more selective in its admissions. The on-campus undergraduate life is strong and the social life is great. **California Polytechnic at San Luis Obispo** (20,400), colloquially known as Cal Poly–San Luis Obispo or Cal Poly SLO, is the toughest Cal State university to get into. It provides excellent training in the applied branches of such fields as agriculture, architecture, business, and engineering. **Fresno** (20,400), located in the verdant Central Valley, has the only viticulture school in the state outside of UC Davis, and undergraduates can work in the school winery. Yosemite, Kings Canyon, and Sequoia national parks are nearby.

San Diego State (30,700) is the balmiest of the campuses, with a more residential, outdoorsy, and campus-oriented social scene. "You could go for the weather alone—some do," says one former student. Contrasted with most other state schools, athletics are very important, and the academic offerings are almost as oriented to the liberal arts as at its neighbor, UC San Diego. San Diego State is highly selective for students from out of the area.

San José State (26,400), located in the heart of Silicon Valley, boasts strong programs in computer science and engineering (including aerospace) as well as amazing internship opportunities for students right in its backyard. **Sonoma State** (6,100), situated just north of San Francisco in the wine-growing capital of the state, has become increasingly popular, with strong programs in computer science, creative writing, and electrical engineering, as well as a concentration in wine business strategies within the business school. The Hutchins School of Liberal Studies allows students to complete their lower-division general education requirements in small (15 students) seminar-style classes that emphasize critical examination and excellence in written communication. Housing and the new student life building are gorgeous.

California Polytechnic at Humboldt (5,000), colloquially known as Cal Poly–Humboldt, is perched at the top of the state near the Oregon border in the heart of the redwoods. Humboldt's forestry and wildlife departments have national reputations, and the natural science departments are strong. Students have the run of excellent laboratory facilities and Redwood National Park, and the university added nine new majors in fall 2022. Many in-staters come here to enjoy the rugged coastline north of San Francisco. **California Maritime Academy** (900), located 30 miles northeast of San Francisco, specializes in marine transportation, engineering, and maritime technology. It boasts the 500-foot training ship *Golden Bear*, which serves as a classroom. **Monterey Bay** (6,300) is one mile from the beach, and 52 percent of students live on campus. It offers an interdisciplinary focus with a global perspective, opportunities for internships, and a unique Capstone Festival featuring the culminating projects of graduating seniors, credential candidates, and master's students.

The California State University application system features a single application for all 23 campuses that is available at www2.calstate.edu/apply. Applicants must indicate the term they are applying for and their preferred campuses and majors.

Admissions criteria are influenced by the student's location, with priority often given to students coming from local high schools or community colleges. Due to increasing demand, all campuses are becoming increasingly selective, especially for popular majors. As with UC universities, there is a $70 application fee for each campus.

UC Berkeley

110 Sproul Hall #5800, Berkeley, CA 94720-5800

Like everything else at Berkeley, the academic offerings at this flagship of flagship universities can be overwhelming. With 30,000 full-time undergraduate overachievers crammed into such a small space, it is no wonder that the academic climate is about as intense as you can get at a world-class public university. Don't expect to be on a first-name basis with your professor in Intro Bio.

Website: www.berkeley.edu
Location: Small City
Public
Total Enrollment: 40,535
Undergraduates: 29,952
Male/Female: 45/55
Financial Aid: 65%
Pell Grant: 25%
Expense: Pub $ $ $
Student Loans: 28%
Average Debt: $
Applicants: 109,597
Accepted: 14%
Enrolled: 43%
Grad in 6 Years: 93%
Returning Freshmen: 96%
Academics: ✍ ✍ ✍ ✍ ✍
Social: 🍺 🍺 🍺 🍺
Q of L: ★ ★ ★
Admissions: (510) 642-3175
Email Address: N/A

Berkeley. Mention the name, and even down-to-earth students get stars in their eyes. Students who come here want the biggest and best of everything, though sometimes that idealism runs headlong into budget cuts, tuition increases, and housing shortages. Never mind. Berkeley is where the action is. If you want a quick indicator of Berkeley's academic prowess, look no farther than the parking lot. The campus is dotted with spots marked "NL"—spots reserved for resident Nobel laureates. The last time anyone counted, Berkeley boasted 10 of them on the current faculty. Then there are the hundreds of Guggenheim fellows, Pulitzer Prize recipients, MacArthur fellows, and Fulbright scholars. Is it any wonder that this radical institution of the '60s still maintains the kind of reputation that makes the top private universities take note? The social climate at this mother of UC schools, founded back in 1868 as the state's land grant university, is not as explosive as it once seemed to be, but don't expect anything tame on today's campus. It has often been at the epicenter of the Free Speech movement. Flower children and granola chompers still abound, as do fledgling Marxists, young Republicans, and body-pierced activists.

"Expect very little sleep."

Spread across more than 1,200 scenic acres on a hill overlooking San Francisco Bay, the Berkeley campus is a parklike oasis in a small city. The startlingly wide variety of architectural styles ranges from the stunning classical amphitheater to the modern Berkeley Art Museum and Pacific Film Archive sheathed in stainless steel. Large expanses of grass dot the campus and are just "perfect for playing Frisbee or lying in the sun." The oaks along Strawberry Creek and the eucalyptus grove date back to Berkeley's beginnings more than 150 years ago. Sproul Plaza, in the heart of the campus, is one of the great people-watching sites of the world.

Of course, Berkeley is not only gorgeous; it's also academically intense. "Everyone was the top student in his or her high school class, so they can't settle for anything less than number one," says one student. Another says bluntly, "Expect very little sleep." Although half of all undergraduate classes have fewer than 20 students, a handful of introductory courses, particularly in the sciences, enroll as many as 1,000, and professors, who must publish or disengage from the university's highly competitive teaching ranks, devote a great deal of time to research. After all, Berkeley has made a large part of its reputation on its research and graduate programs, many of which rank among the best in the nation.

While the undergraduate education is excellent, students take a gamble with the trickle-down theory, which holds out the promise that the intellectual might of those in the ivory towers will drip down to them eventually. As a political science major explains, "This system has allowed me to hear outstanding lectures from amazing professors who write the books we read, while allowing far more personal attention from the graduate-student instructors." Another student opines, "It's better to stand 50 feet from brilliance than five feet from mediocrity." Evidence of such gravitational pull is seen in the promising curricula designed specifically for freshmen and sophomores that include interdisciplinary courses in writing, public speaking, and the history of civilization and an offering of small student seminars (with enrollment limited to 18) taught by regular faculty. Despite these attempts at catering to undergraduates, the sheer number of students at Berkeley makes it difficult to treat each student as an individual. As a result, such things as academic counseling can suffer. "Advising? You mean to tell me they have advising here?" asks one student.

> **"[Berkeley allows] me to hear outstanding lectures from amazing professors who write the books we read."**

Each of Berkeley's six undergraduate colleges or schools has its own set of general education requirements, which are generally not extensive, and a set of breadth requirements, which expose students to disciplines outside of their major. All students, however, must take English composition and literature and one term each of American history and American institutions, as well as fulfill an American cultures requirement—an original approach (via courses offered in several departments) to comparative study of ethnic groups in the United States.

Most of the departments at Berkeley are noteworthy, and some are about the best anywhere (like engineering and architecture). Business, economics, political science, sociology, mathematics, physics, chemistry, history, and English are just a handful of the truly dazzling programs. Berkeley offers eight departments and eight interdisciplinary programs in engineering; electrical engineering and computer science is the most popular. Interdisciplinary study and research are common across the sciences, such as the biological sciences division's programs in integrative biology and molecular and cell biology.

Special programs abound at Berkeley, though it's up to the student to find out about them. Students may study abroad on fellowships at one of 50 centers around the world, or spend time in various internships around the country. If all you want to do is study, the library system, with more than 13 million volumes and more than 20 branches, is one of the largest in the nation and maintains open stacks. The DARE (Diversifying Access to Research in Engineering) program helps connect undergraduates with research opportunities in engineering and computer science, focusing particularly on supporting women and students from underrepresented groups.

Although most Berkeley students are California residents, 14 percent come from out of state, and 13 percent come from foreign nations. Thirty-five percent are Asian

(continued)

Strong Programs:
Engineering
Architecture
Business
Economics
Political Science
Sociology
Mathematics
Molecular and Cell Biology

Professors, who must publish or disengage from the university's highly competitive teaching ranks, devote a great deal of time to research.

American, 2 percent are Black, 20 percent are Hispanic/Latino, and 6 percent are multiracial. The university provides a variety of programs to promote diversity and inclusion, including the Center for Race and Gender and a peer education program for preventing sexual violence. Despite Berkeley's liberal reputation, recent trends have inched toward conservatism. Business majors and fraternity members outnumber young Communists and peaceniks these days, though the school does produce a large number of Peace Corps volunteers. Merit scholarships averaging $7,600 are awarded to qualified students, and athletic scholarships are available.

Berkeley's highly prized residence halls have room for only 26 percent of the students, and new students receive housing priority. After that, the Cal Rentals is a good resource for finding an apartment in town. Many students live a couple of miles off campus, and a number of student-housing projects have opened in recent years, offering a variety of rooms in low-rise and high-rise settings. In the absence of a mandatory meal plan, everybody eats "wherever and whenever they wish," including in the residence halls.

"Social life at UC Berkeley is killer!"

If the housing shortage gets you down, the beautiful California weather will probably take your mind off it, as will the never-ending social opportunities. "Social life at UC Berkeley is killer!" exclaims one geography major. More than 1,400 student clubs and groups are registered on campus, which ensures that there is an outlet for just about any interest and that no one group will ever dominate campus life. Only 2 percent of the men and 6 percent of the women join fraternities or sororities. Weekends are generally spent in Berkeley, hanging out at the many bookstores, coffeehouses, and sidewalk cafés, heading to a fraternity or sorority party, or taking advantage of the many events right on campus. Berkeley is a quintessential college town ("kind of a crazy little town," says one anthropology major), and of course, there's always the people-watching; where else can an individual meet people trying to convert pedestrians to strange New Age religions or revolutionary political causes on every street corner? Nearby Telegraph Avenue is famous (notorious?) for such antics every weekend.

Many students use the weekend to catch up on studying, but when they want to get away, the BART public transportation system provides easy access to San Francisco, by far one of the most pleasant cities in the world and a cultural and countercultural mecca. The Bay Area boasts myriad professional sports teams as well, including the Golden State Warriors, the Oakland A's, the San Francisco 49ers, and the San Francisco Giants. Get access to a car, and you can hike in Yosemite National Park, ski and gamble in Nevada, taste wine in the Napa Valley, or visit the aquarium at Monterey. But be advised that a car is only an asset when you want to go out of town—students warn that parking in Berkeley is difficult, to say the least.

"At Berkeley, it is worse to be dull than odd."

Division I varsity athletics have always been important here, and the university is a top producer of Olympic athletes. Men's gymnastics, men's crew, and men's and women's swimming are strong performers in the Pac-12. The Golden Bears basketball team has surged in popularity, and just about everyone turns out for the football team's "Big Game," where the favorite activity on the home side of the bleachers is bad-mouthing the rival school to the south: Stanford. Intramurals and fitness programs are enhanced by an extensive recreational facility and gorgeous weather year-round.

The common denominator in the Berkeley community is academic motivation, along with the self-reliance that emerges from trying to make your mark among 30,000 talented peers. Beyond that, the diversity of town and campus makes an extraordinarily free and exciting college environment for almost anyone. "It makes one feel free to dress, say, think, or do anything and not be chastised for being unorthodox," explains a student. "At Berkeley, it is worse to be dull than odd."

Overlaps

UCLA, University of Southern California, Stanford, University of Washington, Harvard, UC San Diego, UC Santa Barbara, UC Davis

UC Davis

178 Mrak Hall, Davis, CA 95616

The closest thing to a cow college in the UC system, but with cultured, pedigree cows. Described by the *New Yorker* as "the MIT of American fermentation." Premed, prevet, food science—you name it. If the subject lives and breathes, you can study it here. A small-town alternative to the bright lights of UC Berkeley and UCLA. As is often true at science-oriented schools, the work is hard.

At the University of California Davis, environmental science and most everything that has to do with animals, agriculture, winemaking, or biological science is noteworthy. The Aggies' cup truly runneth over. Originally established in 1905 as the University Farm, the campus maintains its sprawling, verdant beauty, replete with native and imported forestry, charming bike paths, and mooing cows. But lest you assume this environmentally oriented university is full of quaint country folk right out of *American Gothic*, think again. UC Davis is a major research university and has become an international leader in the agricultural, biological, biotechnical, and veterinary sciences.

Located 20 miles west of Sacramento and 73 miles north of San Francisco, the 5,300-acre campus is located along the Capitol Corridor, skirting the Sacramento–San Joaquin Delta watershed. It features a 100-acre arboretum and hundreds of buildings with a blend of architectural styles, from traditional dairy barn to the modern Sciences Laboratory building with its rooftop greenhouse. The hub of the university is a central area known as the Quad, one of many grassy open spaces on campus outfitted with hammocks, perfect for soaking up the abundant California sunshine. The 75,000-square-foot Shrem Museum of Art devotes one-third of its space to education.

> "Everyone is extremely helpful, and it doesn't seem impossible to do your best here."

General education requirements aim to equip students with a breadth of knowledge to complement the expertise they develop in their chosen fields of study. UC Davis students are expected to address four core literacies: quantitative, scientific, and civic and cultural literacy, as well as literacy with words and images.

Biological sciences, economics, managerial economics, psychology, and an interdisciplinary program in neurobiology, physiology, and behavior are among the campus's most popular majors. Animal science, engineering, and biotechnology are strong, and the agriculture program is one of the best anywhere. The school is "the number 1 choice for any prevet," according to one student, and it's great for premeds too. The food science major is also stellar and not for the faint of heart or those afraid of chemistry. It was Davis scientists who discovered how to optimize grape growing for California's wine industry and devised the method for creating orange juice concentrate. UC Davis's World Food Center is dedicated to innovating food production methods for improved human health and environmental sustainability. Studio art, boasting several internationally known artists, is also among the top in the nation.

Website: www.ucdavis.edu
Location: Small City
Public
Total Enrollment: 38,345
Undergraduates: 30,707
Male/Female: 40/60
Financial Aid: 73%
Pell Grant: 30%
Expense: Pub $ $ $
Student Loans: 45%
Average Debt: $
Applicants: 87,120
Accepted: 49%
Enrolled: 18%
Grad in 6 Years: 87%
Returning Freshmen: 91%
Academics: ✐ ✐ ✐ ✐
Social: ☎ ☎ ☎
Q of L: ★ ★ ★ ★
Admissions: (530) 752-2971
Email Address: undergraduate admissions@ucdavis.edu

Strong Programs:
Environmental Science
Biological Sciences
Animal Science
Engineering
Biotechnology
Agriculture
Food Science
Studio Art

Academically, "Davis can be challenging, but it challenges students in the right way," comments a biopsychology major. "Everyone is extremely helpful, and it doesn't seem impossible to do your best here." Many introductory courses are quite large, and students complain that the average class size is on the rise, but UC Davis also offers more than 200 small freshman seminars taught by the best instructors. The quality of teaching can vary considerably, according to students, although "most professors are willing to hold extra office hours and make time for the students," says a psychology major.

Faculty members here are expected to do top-level research as well as teach, giving 41 percent of undergraduates the chance to work directly with professors and grad students as assistants in first-class research groups. The University Honors Program is for academically talented first-year and transfer students who want to enhance their education through special courses. Roughly 15 percent of students study internationally, frequently through the 50-plus programs designed and led by faculty in more than 30 countries. "You can study abroad essentially wherever your heart desires for as short as one month or upwards of a year," cheers one senior. The innovative UC Center Sacramento and the Washington Program give undergraduates academic credits for courses and internships in state and federal governments, respectively.

The campus's beauty is replete with native and imported forestry, charming bike paths, and mooing cows.

"Students at Davis are friendly, and you really feel a sense of community when you're here," observes one senior. Eighty-three percent of undergraduates hail from California, and 15 percent come from abroad. Black students account for 2 percent of undergrads, Asian Americans 30 percent, Hispanics/Latinos 24 percent, and multiracial students 6 percent. The university's Office of Campus Diversity, Cross-Cultural Center, and academic success centers for students of various ethnicities help support diverse populations. Campus hot topics include social justice and sustainability. Davis awards merit scholarships averaging $6,600, and there are more than 280 athletic awards.

"You have to put in the effort to find places and events you like."

Only a quarter of undergraduates live on campus, although 92 percent of freshmen choose to do so. Campus housing is secure, well maintained, and includes a number of living/learning community options. "Dorms are really nice and new and air-conditioned," a student says. Three meal plans for the three dining halls offer a wide range of options, including vegan and kosher items at every meal. Food trucks are positioned around campus at lunchtime, and a weekly on-campus farmers market provides ready access to fresh produce. A senior notes, "Our fraternities, sororities, and student government have taken steps to address sexual assault and promote a stance against it."

UC Davis offers more than 200 small freshman seminars taught by the best instructors.

"Davis has a good social scene, but you have to put in the effort to find places and events you like," says a design major. Active drama and music departments provide frequent entertainment, and the 1,800-seat Mondavi Center for the Performing Arts features international and local groups. There are more than 800 student clubs, and fraternities and sororities attract 5 percent of the men and 7 percent of the women. While alcohol is allowed in the dorms for those of age, a senior says the party scene "can get dull, so a lot of students like to go out of town" for more vigorous nightlife. Major annual social events include Lawntopia, a student-run music festival; Picnic Day, in which alumni join current students in a massive outdoor shindig; nearly three months of cultural celebrations every spring; and the Whole Earth Festival, "an earthy, tie-dyed sort of event." Health and environmental consciousness run high here, and bicycles are the main form of transportation across the incredible 100 miles of bike paths that crisscross the campus and environs. "Bicycles are the norm at Davis. Don't come without

"Bicycles are the norm at Davis. Don't come without one."

one," advises one psych major. The university also sponsors sustainability projects and promotes such novelties as contests between residence halls for the lowest heating and electric bills.

In between quizzes and cram sessions, the surrounding communities offer a welcome change of pace. With its tree-lined streets and quiet nights, the city of Davis itself is small but has enough restaurants, activities, and entertainment to keep those who want to stay close to campus happy. The relationship between the college and town is one of unusual cooperation (partly because the students, who make up half the population, like to vote in local elections). A car can come in handy if you are looking for an urban night out in Sacramento (20 minutes) or a big-name show in San Francisco (a little more than an hour). Undergrads who lack wheels of their own can get around town for free on the student-run Unitrans bus system or head to UC Berkeley via an intercampus shuttle. Beaches are a two-hour drive from the campus, and the ski slopes and hiking trails of Lake Tahoe and the Sierra Nevada mountains are a little closer.

Most of UC Davis's 25 Division I varsity teams (the Aggies) compete in the Big West Conference. Men's basketball is a fan favorite, and women's basketball and cross-country are recent conference champions. The annual Causeway Classic football game against rival Sacramento State stirs passions, as do recreational sports: students are active in nearly 40 club sports and more than 25 intramurals. Given the Mediterranean climate, outdoor activities are popular, and almost everyone does something athletic—jogging, softball, tennis, swimming, or Frisbee—if only to break up their studies with a different kind of competition.

Proud of its small-town atmosphere, UC Davis is not for the lazy or faint of heart. As one student says, "There's no free ride. You are going to have to work for everything you get." And most students get a lot out of their four or more years at UC Davis. It's the ideal spot to combine high-powered work in science and agriculture with that famous easygoing California lifestyle.

> *The university promotes such novelties as contests between residence halls for the lowest heating and electric bills.*

If You Apply To ›

Davis: Regular decision. SATs or ACTs: not considered. Does not accept the Common Application. Apply to a particular college, school, or program. Application includes optional question about gender/sexual identity.

UC Irvine

260 Aldrich Hall, Irvine, CA 92697

Irvine sits in the midst of one of the nation's biggest suburbs, combining funky, modern architecture with a studious, preprofessional student body. Premed is the featured attraction, along with computer science and engineering. Not quite as close to the beach as Santa Barbara—but close enough for students to enjoy it regularly.

On the surface, UC Irvine's clean, contemporary campus appears to be home to students who study diligently in the busy library, wear sensible shoes to class, and at least try to resist that double shot of espresso at the busy coffee shops around campus. But that image starts to dissipate as soon as you hear that bizarre noise: "Zot! Zot! Zot!" Then a UCI student explains that "it's the sound that an anteater supposedly makes when it swipes an ant with its tongue." Hey, any school that has a marauding anteater as a mascot can't be completely straitlaced. The university is,

Any school that has a marauding anteater as a mascot can't be completely straitlaced.

however, serious about its reputation as a school with stellar programs in science, technology, and the arts.

Located in the heart of Orange County and founded in 1965, UCI is among the newest of the UC campuses. While enrollment is up and the administration anticipates further expansion, according to one English major, "It is the perfect size." UCI is liberally supplied with trees and shrubs from all over the world. Futuristic buildings are arranged in a circle around 21-acre Aldrich Park, "giving it the appearance of a relaxed art school," says one observer. Undergraduates have long quipped that UCI stood for "Under Construction Indefinitely." Newer campus additions include residential towers housing nearly 500 first-year students at the Middle Earth community (named after the Lord of the Rings trilogy).

> **"UCI is fairly competitive, and the courses are moderately rigorous."**

UCI's general education requirements involve three courses each in writing, science and technology, social and behavioral sciences, and arts and humanities. Students also fulfill requirements in foreign language; quantitative, symbolic, and computational reasoning; multicultural studies; and international/global issues. Optional first-year seminars, limited to 15 students each, create a more intimate environment in which to adjust to academic life at a research university. Students may choose from more than 80 majors, and the Campuswide Honors Program is available for top students; several individual departments offer honors programs as well.

A "premed mentality" reigns at Irvine, and the School of Biological Sciences is the best and most competitive academic division; undergraduate degrees in nursing science and pharmaceutical sciences are also notable. The university houses multiple medical research centers focusing on areas like aging and dementia, neurological disorders, and spinal cord trauma. After biology, the most popular majors are computer science, psychology, business economics, and political science. The computer science department is bolstered by a fast-growing major in computer game science, and the engineering school is highly competitive. The Claire Trevor School of Arts offers nationally ranked programs in dance, drama, music, studio art, and music theater, and the school's Beall Center for Art and Technology enables students to explore the relationship between digital technology and the arts and sciences. An interdisciplinary major in social ecology combines criminology, environmental and legal studies, and psychology and social behavior, and strongly emphasizes faculty/student relationships. Languages are solid at UCI, and a creative writing program is gaining national recognition.

Like most of the other UC campuses, UCI is on a 10-week quarter system, so the pace is fast and furious. "UCI is fairly competitive, and the courses are moderately rigorous," says a junior, but students are also said to be "surprisingly cooperative." Getting into required classes can be difficult at times, and "Graduate students teach lower-division writing courses," says one student, adding that "many classes are overcrowded, leaving little room for personal attention." Even so, 55 percent of undergraduate classes enroll fewer than 20 students.

Eighty percent of undergraduates are in-staters, the majority from Southern California and many of those from wealthy Orange County—although an impressive 51 percent of incoming freshmen are first-generation college students and 39 percent qualify for Pell Grants. Fifteen percent hail from foreign countries. The campus leans liberal, but students are generally not as active in political or social causes as their peers at some other UC campuses. Students of color account for more than two-thirds of the student body, with Asian Americans representing 37 percent, Hispanics/Latinos 26 percent, Black students just 2 percent, and multiracial students 5 percent. One senior

> **"You have to find the social life on this campus. It won't find you."**

notes, "Cultural groups seem to segregate from each other," although several initiatives and events, including the Cross-Cultural Center, the Community Roots Festival, and the Deconstruction Zone Series, are designed to educate and engage the campus community in diversity, social justice, and cultural wellness. Merit scholarships averaging $8,900 are awarded annually, as are more than 130 athletic awards.

Forty-two percent of undergraduates live on campus. Condominium-style dorms, both single sex and co-ed, are "exceptional compared to the high-rise dormitories of other institutions," says one senior. Others agree that the homey campus dwellings provide a good experience for freshmen. Although freshmen are guaranteed on-campus housing for two years, 23 percent of them choose to live off campus, which can create a slight commuter-school atmosphere. Most upperclassmen opt for themed housing, fraternity and sorority houses, or off-campus dwellings, often on the beach.

One student remarks, "You have to find the social life on this campus. It won't find you." The 18 fraternities and 18 sororities attract 4 percent of the men and 7 percent of the women, and each has something going on every weekend. Students of legal age can unwind at the campus pub. The one event that brings everybody out is Celebrate UCI, a daylong, student-run festival featuring live performances, free food, carnival games and rides, and a car show.

If life on campus is slow, beyond it is not. That's because UCI is located just 50 miles from L.A., five miles from the beach, and a little more than an hour from the ski slopes. Catalina Island, with beaches and hiking trails, is a quick boat trip off Newport Harbor; Mexico is two hours away. While some students treasure the city of Irvine's quiet setting, others lament its "lackluster, homogeneous communities" and conservative feel.

UCI fields 20 Division I Anteater athletic teams. Tennis and cross-country are perennial Big West powerhouses, and men's basketball is a recent conference champion. Men's volleyball and water polo are nationally ranked. There is no football team, but intramurals are extremely popular, as is the state-of-the-art campus recreation center. UCI's varsity eSports program for organized, multiplayer video game competitions is the first of its kind at a public research university.

What lures students to UCI is its top-name professors, innovative academic programs, and the chance to be a part of its cutting-edge research. For those who come here prepared to keep their heads buried in a book for a few years, the reward can be an exceptional education. Where else can you study anteaters in the lab and then cheer them on in the gym?

The computer science department is bolstered by a fast-growing major in computer game science.

Overlaps

UCLA, UC San Diego, UC Santa Barbara, UC Davis, UC Berkeley, UC Riverside, UC Santa Cruz, UC Merced

If You Apply To ›

Irvine: Regular decision. SATs or ACTs: not considered. Does not accept the Common Application. Apply to a particular college, school, or program. Application includes optional question about gender/sexual identity.

UC Los Angeles

1147 Murphy Hall, Box 951436, Los Angeles, CA 90095

Tucked into exclusive Bel Air with the beach, the mountains, and chic Hollywood hangouts all within easy reach. The adjacent town of Westwood is an ideal student hangout. Practically everything is offered here, but—no surprise, given its location in La La Land—the programs in arts and media are some of the best in the world. Less politically active than Berkeley but just as difficult to get into.

In Fall Quarter, freshmen can begin a yearlong cluster of interdisciplinary courses or enroll in small-group seminars.

With four Nobel Prizes awarded to alumni and faculty in the past decade, you might think UCLA is an intellectual brain trust. Or with a long list of well-known and highly accomplished alumni in the arts, film, and sports, maybe UCLA is some sort of incubator for truly talented and gifted people. Well, UCLA is all that and more. A superb faculty, a reputation for outstanding academics, and a powerful athletics program make this university an ultimate place to study.

UCLA's prime location—sandwiched between two glamorous neighborhoods (Beverly Hills and Bel Air) and a short drive from the beach, Hollywood, the Sunset Strip, and downtown Los Angeles—makes it appealing for students who want more from their college experience than going to class. The beautifully landscaped, 419-acre campus features a range of architectural styles, with Romanesque/Italian Renaissance as the dominant motif, providing only one of a number of reasons students enjoy staying on campus. A wealth of gardens— botanical, Japanese, and sculpture—add a touch of quiet elegance. The campus is philosophically divided into North and South. North attracts more liberal arts aficionados, while those in math and science tend to favor South.

> **"We are spoiled by incredible faculty at UCLA."**

First-year students are encouraged to participate in a three-day summer orientation that provides workshops, counseling, an introduction to the campus and community, and a chance to register for classes. In Fall Quarter, freshmen can begin a yearlong cluster of interdisciplinary courses on topics such as Environment and Sustainability or enroll in small-group seminars such as Student Activism from the Sixties to Present. To graduate, first-year students are required to take (or test out of) quantitative reasoning and English composition courses. Lab science and a language requirement are necessary for a liberal arts degree, and all students must take a course on diversity. Concerned that too many majors have been asking too little of students, the university is now encouraging departments to require capstone projects in which students must use the methodological training of their discipline and integrate what they have learned across topics and fields.

Strong programs abound at UCLA, which joined the UC system in 1919, and many are considered among the best in the nation. UCLA is well established in the STEM fields; the Samueli School of Engineering and Applied Science is highly regarded and sets the tone on campus, and biological sciences, mathematics, and chemistry are also strong. The School of Theater, Film, and Television is first-rate, and its students have the opportunity to study in Verona, Italy, with the Theater Overseas program.

> **"[Students are] very invested in building up their peers and the community around them."**

The popular Alpert School of Music offers an institute of jazz performance and boasts legend Herbie Hancock among its distinguished faculty. Dance and design/media arts are standouts in the School of the Arts and Architecture. Sociology, psychology, political science, and economics enroll the most students.

UCLA gets more applications than any other college in the country—nearly 140,000 per year—and the academic environment is intense, especially in STEM fields. Although 48 percent of all undergraduate classes have fewer than 20 students, required core classes, usually taken in the first two years, can be as large as 300 to 400 people, with smaller sections. Students warn that some profs are mainly interested in their research, but a political science major says, "We are spoiled by incredible faculty at UCLA—top researchers in their field and amazing lecturers." Two undergraduate research centers, one for the sciences and one for the arts, humanities, and social sciences, help students develop research skills and connect them with opportunities. The university regularly ranks in the top 10 in the nation in federal funding for research. Faculty-led study abroad programs are popular, and "financial aid travels with you," according to a junior.

"UCLA students love a challenge," says a computer science major. "They are also very invested in building up their peers and the community around them." Seventy-six percent of undergraduates are California residents, and 10 percent are international. Asian Americans account for 29 percent of UCLA's student population, Hispanics/Latinos 22 percent, Black students 3 percent, and multiracial students 7 percent. The political atmosphere is liberal; UCLA is one of the few universities in the nation with a gay fraternity and a lesbian sorority, and students often advocate for social justice issues. Merit scholarships are available, averaging $5,900 each, as well as more than 360 athletic scholarships in 23 sports.

Forty-eight percent of undergraduates, including almost all freshmen, live on campus in the residential area known as "the Hill"; freshmen are guaranteed three consecutive years of university housing, and the dorms get great reviews. Residential learning communities with a faculty member in residence are an option for those who wish to bond with classmates over shared interests. Fifteen dining halls, restaurants, and snack bars serve meals that students rave about. "I have friends who attend other universities who will visit me just so they can eat UCLA's food," says a senior. UCLA has its own police department that keeps the campus safe, and a junior says, "Our Title IX officer is actively working to spread awareness [of sexual assault] and connect those affected with the right resources."

Consistent with UCLA's huge enrollment, there is no shortage of social options on campus. "Social life is bustling," cheers a junior. "What I love about UCLA is that a lot of social things happen on campus—you always feel like you are a part of something greater because so many students participate in activities going on." Eleven percent of men and 13 percent of women join one of UCLA's nearly 60 fraternities and sororities, and a senior says Greek life "is a fun way to get involved and meet people, but it does not monopolize social life." The university's alcohol policy is similar to that of other UC schools—open consumption is a no-no. Top-name entertainers, political figures, and speakers of all kinds come to the campus; film and theater presentations are frequent, and the air is thick with live music. Spring Sing, a campuswide student talent show presided over by celebrity judges, is a favorite tradition. Volunteer Day is a big deal here, too, and attracts more than 8,000 student volunteers annually.

> "You always feel like you are a part of something greater."

With all the attractions of the City of Angels at UCLA's doorstep, social life is hardly confined to campus. "There is constantly a variety of different concerts, plays, art shows, comedy shows, and festivals in L.A. that students can take advantage of," says a junior. The hopping Westwood neighborhood, which borders the university, has at least 15 movie theaters and scores of coffee shops and affordable restaurants, although the shops tend to cater to the upper class. The beach is five miles away, and the mountains are only a short drive. Although public transportation is cheap, it's also relatively inconvenient (although new bus routes have eased this somewhat). The easiest solution is to live close to campus and ride a bike.

The UCLA Bruins have won a staggering number of collegiate titles, including 120 Division I team national championships. Some of the most recent include women's soccer in 2022, men's water polo, softball, and women's beach volleyball. UCLA athletes have won 270 Olympic medals and have won a gold medal in every Olympics in which the U.S. has competed since 1932. Along with crosstown rival USC, UCLA will move to the Big Ten Conference in 2024, but until then it competes in the Pac-12. The men's football and basketball teams are the undeniable crowd-pleasers, although beating USC is the name of the game in any sport. UCLA fans regard their intra-city rivalry with enthusiasm. Beat USC Week, the week leading up to the football game between the two, is an event in itself, featuring a bonfire, concert, and blood drive. About a third of students compete in club and intramural sports.

Students in the School of Theater, Film, and Television have the opportunity to study in Verona, Italy, with the Theater Overseas program.

Spring Sing, a campuswide student talent show presided over by celebrity judges, is a favorite tradition.

Overlaps

UC Berkeley, UC San Diego, Stanford, University of Southern California, UC Irvine, UC Davis, UC Santa Barbara, Harvard

"Although everyone is striving for excellence, UCLA allows everyone to experience *life*," muses a junior. "That means taking time to prepare for exams and do it well, while also making time to play beach volleyball at Sunset Rec with all of your friends." A leading research center, 200 fields of study, distinguished faculty members, and outstanding athletics make UCLA one of the most prestigious universities in the nation. And despite the huge size, students still feel they are part of a tight-knit community bubbling with Bruin pride.

If You Apply To ›

UCLA: Regular decision. SATs or ACTs: not considered. Does not accept the Common Application. Apply to a particular college, school, or program. Application includes optional question about gender/sexual identity.

UC Riverside

Riverside, CA 92521

Most diverse UC school, one of the least difficult to get into, and offers a more personal touch. UCR's traditional strengths in the sciences are bolstered by expanding opportunities for undergraduate research. Since many students commute, social life is relatively tame. While some complain of a lack of nightlife in Riverside, they readily agree that activities on campus make up for it.

Website: www.ucr.edu
Location: Small City
Public
Total Enrollment: 25,706
Undergraduates: 22,069
Male/Female: 46/54
Financial Aid: 85%
Pell Grant: 45%
Expense: Pub $ $ $
Student Loans: 59%
Average Debt: $
Applicants: 52,675
Accepted: 66%
Enrolled: 15%
Grad in 6 Years: 77%
Returning Freshmen: 88%
Academics: ✎ ✎ ✎ ½
Social: ☎ ☎
Q of L: ★ ★ ★
Admissions: (951) 827-3411
Email Address: admissions@ucr.edu

Strong Programs:
Plant Biology
Entomology

Lacking the big-name reputation and booming athletic programs of many other UC schools, UC Riverside has chosen to place its emphasis on something that not all universities consider to be an important priority: the student. Riverside offers one of the lowest student/faculty ratios in the UC system, strong academic and cocurricular programs, and a richly diverse community. "Students are well taken care of and get personal attention," says one satisfied senior. Though part of the UC system, UC Riverside is a breed apart.

Located 60 miles east of Los Angeles, UCR is surrounded by mountains on the outskirts of the city of Riverside. The beautifully landscaped, 1,200-acre campus consists of mainly modern architecture, with a 160-foot bell tower (with a 48-bell carillon) marking its center. Wide lawns, clusters of oaks, and a botanical garden make ideal spots for relaxing between classes. Acres of citrus groves form a half-circle on the outer edges of campus and perfume the air. Recent campus additions include the 800-bed Dundee Residence Hall, the Glasgow Dining Hall, and the 62,000-square-foot Student Success Center.

> **"Students are well taken care of and get personal attention."**

All students are required to meet extensive "breadth requirements" that include courses in English composition, natural sciences and math, humanities, and social sciences. Some majors include a foreign language requirement. The campus libraries have an impressive 4 million volumes, an interlibrary loan system within the UC system, and hundreds of electronic databases. A specialized research collection in science fiction is world-class. UCR's California Museum of Photography, located in downtown Riverside and accessible online, has grown in stature.

Decades ago, researchers at the Citrus Experiment Station in Riverside perfected the growing methods for the imported navel orange, making discoveries to protect the fruit from disease and pests and saving California's citrus industry. Riverside continues to excel in plant biology and entomology. But the campus has grown since its founding in 1954 to include excellent programs spanning a number of disciplines. The biological sciences program is UCR's most prestigious and demanding, especially the medical biology track. The Bourns College of Engineering, which has strong majors in computer science, computer engineering, and environmental engineering, is also quite selective, more so than the campus as a whole. Creative writing is notable, and Riverside is the only UC school that offers an undergraduate major in public policy. Business administration, biology, psychology, and sociology are the most popular majors.

(continued)
Biological Sciences
Computer Science
Computer Engineering
Environmental Engineering
Creative Writing
Public Policy

Students say the academic climate is cooperative. "Instead of being super competitive," says a student, "I see more students working together to get the job done." Currently, 34 percent of undergraduate classes have more than 50 students. Research is an institutional priority for faculty, and the quality of instruction can vary. Still, UCR has a tradition of undergraduate and faculty interaction; 31 percent of undergrads conduct research, and a wide range of research grants are available during the academic year. "The professors are usually happy to help students, as are the teaching assistants," says a psychology and education major. The University Honors Program offers exceptional students further academic challenges, in addition to extracurricular activities and special seminars for freshmen. Talented student singers, dancers, and actors can earn stipends for performing in the community through an arts outreach program. Faculty-led, five-week summer study abroad options are expanding, and through the UC system, students have access to 120 international programs; 4 percent of students go abroad.

Riverside is the only UC school that offers an undergraduate major in public policy.

Ninety-six percent of UCR undergraduates are from California, mainly L.A., Riverside, San Bernardino, and Orange County; 3 percent are international. "UCR is one of the most diverse universities in the nation," a political science major says, which creates "a blended environment of different cultures, nationalities, and social statuses." Indeed, Asian Americans account for 35 percent of the students, Hispanics/Latinos 41 percent, Black students 3 percent, and multiracial students 6 percent. A hefty 45 percent of first-time freshmen receive Pell Grants. As part of the UC commitment to diversity, UCR's Costo Hall

"UCR is one of the most diverse universities in the nation."

houses centers for various ethnicities, for women, and for LGBTQ students. The political atmosphere is liberal, and a junior comments, "The student body is pretty chill and open-minded." Numerous merit scholarships averaging $6,400 are doled out every year, as well as more than 200 athletic scholarships.

Housing is relatively easy to obtain, but the quality varies greatly. "While West Lothian looks like a prison, Pentland Hills is like a resort," says one student. Thirty-four percent of undergrads live in the dorms. Construction is ongoing on the massive North District development, which will eventually add about 6,500 beds, new dining and athletic facilities, and other mixed-use spaces to accommodate the university's growing student population. The district's first apartment community, North District Apartments, opened in 2021 with beds for 1,500 students. Five academically oriented living/learning communities are popular with freshmen, who are guaranteed housing for their first year. Campus dining is generally described as adequate. Students say they feel safe on campus; security measures include an escort service, patrolling security officers, and regular training on sexual assault prevention and intervention.

Construction is ongoing on the massive North District development, which will eventually add 6,500 beds and new dining and athletic facilities.

Fraternities and sororities attract 3 percent of the men and 5 percent of the women. "There is always something going on, whether it be a concert, lecture, or sorority/fraternity party," one sophomore says. Campus hangouts, including the recently renovated and expanded Barn, have live bands and comedy nights, and a cultural arts program brings professional shows to campus. Every Wednesday the campus can enjoy a "nooner," where the music department puts on free concerts and lectures during lunch. Returning students are welcomed back every year with a campuswide block party, and the Spring Splash concert brings in hot bands. University Village is a commercial center offering a movie theater, restaurants, and an arcade right on the edge of campus. Riverside weather is temperate except during the summer months, when the heat and haze combine to make a trip to the ocean look really inviting. The coast is only about 45 minutes by freeway and the desert is an hour east. Big Bear and numerous ski resorts are also within an hour's drive.

The Riverside Highlanders compete in the Division I Big West Conference in 17 sports, and the men's soccer and women's golf teams have been successful in recent years. A recreational program in men's and women's karate has turned out national champions. A student recreation center offers a health-club atmosphere with sand volleyball, weight and workout machines, and intramural sports, including perennially popular basketball and soccer leagues.

All in all, Riverside is expanding and improving, albeit not without some growing pains, including tuition and living costs. But it still offers more personal attention to its students than many of its larger, sister UC campuses. "UCR has grown immensely over the past few years," one sophomore says. "The emphasis for the future is to establish a name for UCR, to let the nation know what a wonderful university this is."

Overlaps

UC Santa Barbara, UC Irvine, UC Davis, University of Oregon, UC Santa Cruz, UC San Diego, UCLA, Cal State Fullerton

If You Apply To ›

Riverside: Regular decision. SATs or ACTs: not considered. Does not accept the Common Application. Apply to a particular college, school, or program. Application includes optional question about gender/sexual identity.

UC San Diego

9500 Gilman Drive, MC 0021, La Jolla, CA 92093

Applications have doubled in the past 10 years at this seaside paradise. UC San Diego now rivals better-known Berkeley and UCLA as the Cal campus of choice for top students. Six undergraduate colleges break the university down to a more manageable size. Best known for science, engineering, and the famed Scripps Institution of Oceanography.

Website: www.ucsd.edu
Location: City Outskirts
Public
Total Enrollment: 39,928
Undergraduates: 32,371
Male/Female: 49/51
Financial Aid: 60%
Pell Grant: 24%
Expense: Pub $ $ $
Student Loans: 43%
Average Debt: $
Applicants: 118,410
Accepted: 34%
Enrolled: 18%

Some say that looking good is better than feeling good, but at UC San Diego, they're doing a lot of both. Set against the serene beauty of La Jolla's beaches, students catch as much relaxation time as they do study time. But it's not all fun and games around this campus. Established in 1960, San Diego is now the research star of the UC system, and its faculty rates high nationally among public institutions in science productivity. And within each of the six undergraduate colleges, a system that offers undergraduates more intimate settings, students are honing their minds with the classics and the cutting edge in academics. Sure, San Diegans tend to be more mellow than the average Southern Californian, and the students here follow suit. But beneath the tanned foreheads and bright smiles, UC San Diego is bubbling with intellectual energy and the healthy desire to be at the top of the UC system.

San Diego's tree-lined campus sits high on a bluff overlooking the Pacific in the seaside resort of La Jolla. The predominant architectural theme is contemporary, with a few out-of-the-ordinary structures, including a library that looks like an inverted pyramid. Another tinge of the postmodern is the nation's largest neon sculpture, which wraps around one of the high-rise academic buildings and consists of seven-foot-tall letters that spell out the seven virtues superimposed over the seven vices. Work is underway on a significant campus expansion that will add several new academic and residential facilities, including the $67 million Design and Innovation Building, which opened in 2021.

UC San Diego's six undergraduate colleges have their own sets of general education requirements, their own personalities, and differing ideals on which they are based. Revelle College, the oldest, is the most rigorous and mandates that students become equally acquainted with a certain level of coursework in the humanities, sciences, and social sciences, as well as fulfill a language requirement. Muir allows more flexibility in the distribution of requirements.

"You end up teaching a lot of the material to yourself."

Thurgood Marshall College was founded to emphasize and encourage social awareness. Like Revelle, it places equal weight on sciences, social sciences, and humanities, but it also stresses a liberal arts education based on "an examination of the human condition in a multicultural society." Warren has developed a highly organized internship program that gives its undergraduates more practical experience than the others do. Eleanor Roosevelt College devotes its curriculum to international and cross-cultural studies. Sixth College focuses on art, culture, and technology, with the aim of preparing students to work collaboratively and enjoy working in their communities. Prospective freshmen apply to the university but must indicate their preferred college.

UC San Diego's programs in science, engineering, and computer science have global reputations and are "not for the faint of heart," says one student. The engineering school, notable for offerings like structural engineering and nanoengineering, is particularly competitive, and a limit to the number of students who can declare these majors means acceptance usually requires an A average and top test scores in entry-level courses. The nearby Scripps Institution of Oceanography is also excellent. Biology (the most popular major) and chemistry are also strengths, but you really can't go wrong in any of the hard sciences. Although the humanities and social sciences are not as solid in comparison, international studies, psychology, and cognitive science are popular majors. Students may also devise their own majors. Twenty-one percent of students study abroad; San Diego's five-week, faculty-led Global Seminars in the summer are especially popular.

San Diego operates on the quarter system, which means students cram 3 or 4 courses into 10 weeks. Science students in particular find the workload intense. The quality of research done by the faculty, half a dozen of whom are Nobel laureates, is extremely high, and students have ample opportunities to assist with research, sometimes as early as freshman year. Students say the typical scenario of research over teaching seen at most large research universities is not as common at UC San Diego. Even so, given the large class sizes—24 percent of undergraduate courses enroll more than 50 students—"you end up teaching a lot of the material to yourself," according to an anthropology major.

A theater major notes that the university's academic intensity "does not mean that all the students here are nerdy. We enjoy athletics and extracurricular activities, but academic excellence is our priority." A short walk to the beach, however, reveals the student body's wild and crazy half-surfers and their fans, who celebrate the "kick back." Students jumping curbs on skateboards are common on this campus.

"We enjoy athletics and extracurricular activities, but academic excellence is our priority."

Yet these beach babies are no scholastic slouches. San Diego ranks highly among public colleges and universities in the percentage of graduates who go on to earn a Ph.D. and in the percentage of students accepted to medical school. Seven percent

(continued)

Grad in 6 Years: 89%
Returning Freshmen: 95%
Academics: ✐ ✐ ✐ ✐ ✐
Social: ☎ ☎ ☎
Q of L: ★ ★ ★ ★
Admissions: (858) 534-4831
Email Address: admissions reply@ucsd.edu

Strong Programs:
Engineering
Computer Science
Oceanography
Biology
Chemistry
International Studies
Psychology
Cognitive Science

The engineering school, notable for offerings like structural engineering and nanoengineering, is particularly competitive.

of undergraduates are from states outside of California, and 16 percent are international. Representation of students of color is high, with 38 percent of the student body being Asian American, 21 percent Hispanic/Latino, and 3 percent Black. Diversity education includes a Cross-Cultural Center for students, faculty, and staff that provides activities, brown-bag luncheons, and programs on race relations. Merit scholarships averaging $11,000 are doled out to eligible undergraduates, and the university has begun to offer athletic scholarships in some sports as it transitions to Division I status.

Each of the university's colleges has its own housing complex, with either dorms or apartments. Most freshmen live on campus and are guaranteed housing for their first two years. "The residence halls are very nice, with all the amenities," says an animal physiology major. Dorm residents are required to buy a meal plan, and their Dining Dollars are good at any of the campus's 13 eateries. Overall, 37 percent of undergraduates live on campus; by junior year, students usually decide to take up residence in La Jolla proper or nearby Del Mar, often in beachside apartments. But that can be costly. If you are willing to relinquish the luxury of a five-minute walk to the beach, a short commute will bring you relatively affordable housing.

> "[We have] a beautiful beachfront environment that eases a life of academic rigor."

"La Jolla is a rich, conservative, retired, white, snobbish community," one sophomore says. "Not a college town!" Cars are, of course, an inescapable part of Southern California life, and owning one—many people do—makes off-campus living even more pleasant. "No car equals no fun," one international studies major says. Unfortunately, trying to park on campus can be difficult. Mexico is a half-hour drive (even nearer than the desert, where many students go hiking), and the two-hour trip to Los Angeles makes for a nice weekend jaunt.

For those looking to stay closer to campus, the Pacific Beach and downtown San Diego, with its zoo, Sea World, and Balboa Park, are all only 12 miles away. Torrey Pines State Natural Reserve is great for outdoor enthusiasts. "Most students hang out at the dance clubs, jazz bars, and great restaurants in the Gaslamp Quarter," says a senior. The university offers nearly 600 student-run groups, and 14 percent of the men and 14 percent of the women join a fraternity or sorority. The campus is dry, but some students claim that lax RAs and good fake IDs make for easy underage drinking. Although campus life is relatively tame, everyone looks forward to university-sponsored festivals, including the Open House, UnOlympics, and the Reggae Festival. The biggest annual event pays tribute to a hideously loud and colorful statue of the Sun God, which is the unofficial mascot for this sun-streaked student body. The Sun God Festival draws such big-name performers as Drake and Wiz Khalifa.

Although San Diego will never be mistaken for a sports-crazed school (à la USC), the university is in the process of transitioning from Division II to the Division I Big West Conference. Triton volleyball, water polo, soccer, basketball, and tennis teams have traditionally been the strongest. The school's club surfing team has won seven national championships. For weekend warriors, classes are available in windsurfing, sailing, scuba diving, and kayaking at the nearby Mission Bay Aquatic Center. Most students participate in one intramural league or another, and according to one, if you're not on a team, "you're not a true UC San Diego student."

The students at UC San Diego are exceptionally serious and out for an excellent education. But the pace (study, party, relax, study more) and the props (sun, sand, Frisbees, and flip-flops) give the rigorous curriculum an inimitable flavor that undergraduates would not change. Indeed, many believe they have the best setup in higher education: "a beautiful beachfront environment that eases a life of academic rigor."

Overlaps

University of Michigan, U of I at Urbana–Champaign, University of Virginia, University of Washington, UW–Madison, UCLA, UC Berkeley, UC Santa Barbara

If You Apply To ›

San Diego: Regular decision. SATs or ACTs: not considered. Does not accept the Common Application. Apply to a particular college, school, or program. Application includes optional question about gender/sexual identity.

UC Santa Barbara

Santa Barbara, CA 93106

Willpower is the watchword at UC Santa Barbara. On a beautiful day with the sound of waves crashing in the distance, that's what it takes to hang in there with pen, paper, laptop, or book. Fairly or not, Santa Barbara is known as the party animal of the UC system. In the classroom, science is the best bet. Free spirits should check out the unusual College for Creative Studies.

For students at UC Santa Barbara, California's famed beaches serve as both classroom and playground. On weekends, sun-worshipping students grab surfboards and don bikinis and head to the water for some serious fun. During the week, those same students can likely be found studying technology rather than tan lines. "On a nice sunny day, the beaches and grassy areas will be flooded with students," says a freshman, "but most of them are there with a book."

UCSB provides a comfortable mixture of work and play that is unique even in the UC system. Located just a stone's throw from the beach, UC Santa Barbara's 1,000-acre campus is bordered on two sides by the Pacific Ocean, with a clear view of the Channel Islands. On the landward side are a nature preserve and the predominantly student community of Isla Vista, and five miles to the north lie the Santa Ynez Mountains. The campus, which joined the UC system in 1944, features mainly 1950s Southern California architecture with a Southern California atmosphere to match.

UCSB's general education program features the usual distribution requirements and coursework in writing, non-Western cultures, quantitative relationships, and ethnicity. Not surprisingly, the marine biology department stands out among the university's best, capitalizing on the school's aquatic resources; chemical engineering, physics, and chemistry are also well regarded. The Bren School of Environmental Science and Management is home to world-renowned faculty, boasting six Nobel Prize winners in economics, chemistry, and physics. The most popular majors include sociology, psychological and brain sciences, communication, and global studies. The economics and accounting program is strong, and the courses are geared toward taking and passing the CPA exam, so graduation is usually followed by a mass recruitment by California's big accounting firms. The College of Creative Studies offers an unstructured curriculum to about 400 self-starters ready for advanced and independent work in the arts, math, or the sciences. The interdisciplinary global studies major, another noteworthy option, combines language study with global history, culture, economics, and politics.

> "UC Santa Barbara is very collaborative, [but] the workload is definitely strenuous at times."

"The academic climate of UC Santa Barbara is very collaborative," says one sophomore, but "the workload is definitely strenuous at times." Fifty-six percent of all undergraduate classes have fewer than 20 students, but teaching is a hit-or-miss affair, according to one junior: "Many of the professors are more interested in their research than teaching a class." On the flip side, many opportunities

Website: www.ucsb.edu
Location: Suburban
Public
Total Enrollment: 25,204
Undergraduates: 22,244
Male/Female: 44/56
Financial Aid: 67%
Pell Grant: 28%
Expense: Pub $ $ $
Student Loans: 43%
Average Debt: $
Applicants: 103,174
Accepted: 29%
Enrolled: 16%
Grad in 6 Years: 89%
Returning Freshmen: 91%
Academics: ✐ ✐ ✐ ✐
Social: ☎ ☎ ☎ ☎
Q of L: ★ ★ ★ ★
Admissions: (805) 893-2881
Email Address: admissions@sa.ucsb.edu

Strong Programs:
Marine Biology
Chemical Engineering
Physics
Chemistry
Environmental Science
Economics and Accounting
Global Studies
Sociology

are available for undergrads to assist professors, and 60 percent of students get involved in undergraduate research. For those who seek time away, Santa Barbara is the headquarters of the UC system's Education Abroad Program, which sends students to any of 120 host universities worldwide; 17 percent of UCSB students study abroad.

UCSB students, 84 percent of whom are California residents, are traditionally public-spirited and laid-back. "There are some who aren't the most academically focused, but for the most part I'd say the students are great at balancing their academic and social lives while getting involved in helping the community," says one mechanical engineering major. Asian Americans contribute 20 percent of the student body, Black students make up 2 percent, Hispanics/Latinos account for 26 percent, and multiracial students add 7 percent; 11 percent are international. The campus vibe is decidedly liberal. "Some of the biggest political issues on campus have to do with the environment. As a coastal area, UCSB is very susceptible to pollution," explains one student. Merit scholarships averaging $8,100 and more than 200 athletic scholarships are available for those who qualify.

University housing, which includes both dorms and privately run residence halls, is comfortable, well maintained, and much sought after. "Our on-campus housing is amazing, right in front of the beach," a junior says. "They come fully furnished, with high-speed Internet, cable, telephone lines, and a great atmosphere." Thirty-nine percent of students, most of whom are freshmen, snag on-campus housing. Meals in the dorms are available to residents and nonresidents alike, and are, according to most students, more than simply edible. "Great food and tons of it!" cheers one student. While students say they feel safe on campus, one oft used motto is "four years, four bikes," because of the frequency of bicycle thefts. Regarding campus sexual assault, "The school has provided as many resources as it can, really," says a chemical engineering major, and it "does its best to prevent it."

> **"Our on-campus housing is amazing, right in front of the beach."**

"It is really easy to get involved and make friends through campus activities," says a sophomore. "Additionally, the social scene off campus is really thriving in the community of Isla Vista." Neighboring Isla Vista has welcomed its student population—after all, most of its population is UCSB students. Students in turn are very active in the community. The fraternities and sororities, which attract 7 percent of men and 13 percent of women, are known for their philanthropy. The campus is dry, and one student says, "Drinking alcohol on campus is pretty well regulated and not easy to do." Movies and concerts are also available, and the mountains, Los Padres National Forest, and L.A. are all an easy drive away. The annual Extravaganza is an all-day free concert, and students are known to go wild on Halloween and dress up for the entire weekend. "Halloween is our claim to fame," boasts one student.

All of UCSB's varsity teams (the Gauchos) compete in Division I, and the most successful include soccer, water polo, baseball, volleyball, swimming, and basketball. A never-ending rotation of intramurals is available on and off the beach, and about a quarter of the students participate. Ultimate Frisbee is also quite popular, as well as nationally competitive.

Sure, UCSB students love to play, but that's not why most come to this coastal institution. "If there was anything that I would like to improve, it would be the lingering reputation UCSB has as a party school," observes one student. "This reputation is more of a relic from times past." Students sometimes gripe about their professors and the academic challenges they face. But they also know a good thing when they see it: not everyone gets to spend four years on the beach and come away with a degree.

The College of Creative Studies offers an unstructured curriculum to about 400 self-starters ready for advanced, independent work.

Sixty percent of students get involved in undergraduate research.

Overlaps

UCLA, UC Berkeley, UC San Diego, UC Irvine, UC Davis

UC Santa Cruz

1156 High Street, Santa Cruz, CA 95064

From its flower-child beginnings, UC Santa Cruz has wandered back toward the mainstream. The yoga mats and surfboards still abound and Sammy the banana slug is still the mascot, but the students are a lot more conventional than their predecessors. The emphasis here continues to be on environmental stewardship, community engagement, and teaching students how to think, not what to think. Relatively small size and residential college system give it a homey feel.

UC Santa Cruz, still a baby in the UC system, was born during the radical '60s when it reigned as the ultimate alternative school, a place that consciously rebelled against the stodginess of educational institutions. The founding vision of an integrated learning environment remains to this day, and every undergraduate affiliates with one of the residential colleges. Progressive thought continues to flourish, as does a strong academic program that strives to focus on undergraduate education. Students still come to UC Santa Cruz to do their own thing.

The campus, among the most beautiful in the nation, is set on a 2,000-acre expanse of meadowland and redwood forest overlooking Monterey Bay. Bike paths and hiking trails wind throughout the redwood-tree-filled campus, and the beach is a quick drive away—or a spectacular bike ride or scenic hike. The buildings range from 1860 Cowell Ranch farm structures to the award-winning, modern residential colleges, whose styles range from Mediterranean to Japanese to sleek concrete block. Thanks to a unique building code, nothing may be built taller than two-thirds the height of the nearest redwood tree. The

"I've been very impressed with how accessible professors are."

26,000-square-foot Digital Arts Research Center serves as a social and intellectual hub for UC Santa Cruz's Arts Division. Newer additions to campus include the LEED Gold–certified Coastal Biology Building, supporting research and teaching on coastal conservation, ecology, climate change impacts, and similar concerns.

UC Santa Cruz's academic offerings range as widely as its architecture and feature both traditional and innovative programs, but overall, the emphasis is on the liberal arts and sciences, and a majority of the students eventually go on to graduate study. To graduate, students must fulfill a standard set of distribution requirements, in addition to taking one of three "perspectives" courses focused on environmental awareness, human behavior, or technology and society, and a course on creative process, collaborative endeavor, or service learning. A disciplinary communication requirement helps students develop writing skills specific to their chosen field of study. All seniors complete a capstone experience.

Led by marine biology and biology, the sciences are UC Santa Cruz's strongest suit. Science facilities include state-of-the-art laboratories; the Institute of Marine Sciences, which boasts one of the largest groups of experts on marine mammals in the nation; and the nearby Lick Observatory for budding stargazers. UCSC's Baskin School of Engineering offers strong programs in robotics engineering and computer

Website: www.ucsc.edu
Location: Small Town
Public
Total Enrollment: 19,004
Undergraduates: 17,087
Male/Female: 52/48
Financial Aid: 55%
Pell Grant: 33%
Expense: Pub $ $ $
Student Loans: 49%
Average Debt: $
Applicants: 61,822
Accepted: 59%
Enrolled: 12%
Grad in 6 Years: 76%
Returning Freshmen: 89%
Academics: ✍ ✍ ✍ ✍
Social: ☎ ☎ ☎
Q of L: ★ ★ ★ ★ ★
Admissions: (831) 459-4008
Email Address: admissions@ucsc.edu

Strong Programs:
Marine Biology
Biology
Robotics Engineering
Computer Engineering
Computer Game Design
Linguistics
Environmental Studies
Community Studies

engineering. The computer game design B.S. is noteworthy as the first such major in the UC system, and linguistics is strong. Students in STEM fields may benefit from research or internship opportunities coordinated through the university's satellite campus in Silicon Valley. UCSC boasts more than the average number of interdisciplinary programs, including feminist, Latin American/Latino, and critical race and ethnic studies; environmental studies and community studies are standouts. The most popular majors are computer science, psychology, business management economics, and sociology. While most students pursue traditional majors, the possibility is still there for eclectically minded students to pursue "history of consciousness" or just about anything else they can get a faculty member to OK. Thirty-four percent of students engage in faculty-guided undergraduate research, and 9 percent study abroad; field study and internships are also encouraged.

The LEED Gold–certified Coastal Biology Building supports research and teaching on coastal conservation, ecology, and climate change impacts.

"Courses are very rigorous, in my experience," warns one undergrad. Though the curriculum is demanding and the quarter system keeps the academic pace fast, the atmosphere is emphatically noncompetitive. Classes can be large, with 26 percent enrolling more than 50 students. All UC campuses insist on faculty research, but most professors at UC Santa Cruz are there to teach. "I've been very impressed with how accessible professors are," says a sophomore. "Whether it's via email or regular office hours, I feel very comfortable approaching and talking to all of my professors."

"Before I came here I was told that UCSC was a 'hippie-dippie' college," says one student, "but it's not true at all." Even so, UC Santa Cruz remains the most liberal of the UC campuses and, according to one student, is "still a school with a social con-

> **"I was told that UCSC was a 'hippie-dippie' college, but it's not true at all."**

science." Ninety-two percent of undergraduates are Californians, though the university always manages to lure a few Easterners; 6 percent are international. Asian Americans account for 23 percent, Hispanics/Latinos 28 percent, Black students 2 percent, and multiracial students 8 percent. "Racial, ethnic, and cultural diversity is celebrated and strongly encouraged by the majority of the students here," reports a politics major. One-third of incoming freshmen qualify for Pell Grants. Merit scholarships, which average $7,800 each, are available, but there are no athletic scholarships.

In an effort to become what one official calls a "near-perfect hybrid" between the large university and the small college, campus life revolves around the residential colleges, each of which has dedicated faculty fellows and support staff. About half of the undergraduate population lives in university-sponsored housing. Freshmen and transfer students are guaranteed on-campus housing for two years. Some dorms have their own dining halls with reasonably good food; students may also opt to join a food co-op. The CARE (Campus Advocacy, Resources, and Education) office provides education on issues of sexual assault and support to survivors.

The McHenry Cup College Challenge is a yearlong scavenger hunt that pits the residential colleges against each other.

A dozen fraternities and sororities attract 2 percent of the men and 5 percent of the women, respectively. Students 21 and over are allowed to drink alcohol on campus, although not in public areas, and parties must be registered. More than 150 student organizations on campus—including major-focused clubs, ethnic and cultural groups, hobby clubs, volunteer groups, and honor societies—cover a wide range of interests. The beach and resort town of Santa Cruz, with its boardwalk and amusement park, are only 10 minutes away from campus by bike, although pedaling back up the hill takes much longer. Those looking for city lights can take the windy, mountainous highway to San Jose (35 miles away) or the slow, scenic coastal highway to San Francisco (75 miles), or ride a bus to either city. If you have a car, destinations such as Monterey, Big Sur, the Napa Valley, and the Sierras are easily accessible.

Although UC Santa Cruz fields only a handful of varsity teams, which slug it out in Division III, students love their school mascot, Sammy the banana slug (who sports a brand-new logo!). Men's and women's volleyball, men's swimming and diving, and women's soccer and golf have performed well in recent years. Participation in intramurals ("Friendship through Competition" is the motto) and club sports is widespread, with rugby in particular growing in popularity. Sailing and scuba diving are among the many physical education classes offered, and the student recreation department sponsors the McHenry Cup College Challenge, a yearlong scavenger hunt that pits the residential colleges against each other.

UC Santa Cruz is a progressive school with a gorgeous campus and innovative academic programs, where the main priority is the education of undergraduates. Many students are concerned that it is growing too fast, and an ambitious proposal for future expansion has threatened its heretofore cozy relationship with local citizens. Still, as long as the university retains its belief in "to each his or her own," it will remain uniquely UC Santa Cruz. Where else do you get to rally around a banana slug?

If You Apply To ›

Santa Cruz: Regular decision. SATs or ACTs: not considered. Does not accept the Common Application. Apply to a particular college, school, or program. Application includes optional question about gender/sexual identity.

California Institute of Technology

1200 East California Boulevard, Pasadena, CA 91125

If you're a Caltech student looking for tips on how to win a Nobel Prize, just ask a professor who already has one. The small, West Coast counterpart to MIT among bastions of STEM research and teaching, Caltech looks for hardworking students with grit, wide-ranging intellectual curiosity, and a propensity for jaw-dropping pranks.

The California Institute of Technology counts 46 Nobel Prize winners among its faculty and alumni, and students' demanding courseload means plenty of opportunities to tap into that brilliance. Expectations are high; "Techers" are fond of saying that "the admissions office doesn't make mistakes," and it's not unheard of to take time off to deal with stress and avoid burnout. "The atmosphere promotes a love of science, learning, and discovery that is truly exhilarating," says a biology major. No doubt about it—if you prefer particle physics to partying, Caltech is a good place to be.

Caltech's 124-acre campus is located in Pasadena, a wealthy suburban city less than 15 miles from downtown Los Angeles. "It's not a college town at all," says a senior. The distance means the school is relatively isolated from the glitz, glamour, and good times that many people associate with La La Land. Outside the classroom, at least, tranquility prevails, with olive trees, lily ponds, and plenty of flowers breaking up clusters of older Spanish mission-style buildings. Leafy courtyards and arcades link these with what one student describes as more modern, "block institutional" structures. The Beckman Auditorium (affectionately dubbed "The Wedding Cake" due to its round shape and conical roof) features spaces for performing arts, lectures, films, classes, and entertainment events. Newer additions include the $64 million, 211-bed Bechtel Residence.

> **"The atmosphere promotes a love of science, learning, and discovery."**

Caltech's mission, one official says, is "to train the creative type of scientist or engineer urgently needed in our educational, governmental, and industrial development." After all, it was here that Albert Einstein abandoned his concept of a static cosmos in favor of the expanding-universe model. This is also where physicist Carl

Website: www.caltech.edu
Location: Small City
Private
Total Enrollment: 2,397
Undergraduates: 987
Male/Female: 55/45
Financial Aid: 50%
Pell Grant: 10%
Expense: Pr $ $ $
Student Loans: 29%
Average Debt: $
Applicants: 13,026
Accepted: 4%
Enrolled: 53%
Grad in 6 Years: 93%
Returning Freshmen: 99%
Academics: ✍ ✍ ✍ ✍ ✍
Social: ☎
Q of L: ★ ★ ★
Admissions: (626) 395-2645
Email Address:
ugadmissions@caltech.edu

Anderson discovered the positron. With these luminaries as their models, students plunge right into the extensive core institute requirements, which include math, physics, chemistry, biology, science communication, two introductory lab terms, and 12 terms in the humanities and social sciences to round things out. Students complain about the latter, and "usually take no more than absolutely required," says a biology major. Still, they can be tough to get into come registration time, says a computer science major, since enrollment is limited "to allow for discussion among a small group." The pass/fail grading system in the freshman year goes a long way toward easing the acclimation period for new arrivals. And the honor system, which mandates that "no one member of the Caltech community shall take unfair advantage of any other member," helps discourage unfair tactics to get better grades. Professors give take-home exams, and if violations of the honor code are suspected, "students decide if a violation was indeed made," one student explains.

"GPS majors are some of the happiest at Caltech."

Founded in 1891, Caltech made its name in physics, and students say that program remains strong; it's also one of the most popular majors, along with computer science, mechanical engineering, electrical engineering, chemistry, bioengineering, and math. Students praise the geological and planetary sciences department for being "flexible with students and having excellent field trips," says a freshman. "GPS majors are some of the happiest at Caltech." Caltech's endowment is one of the largest among the nation's tech schools, and regardless of major, students benefit from state-of-the-art STEM facilities, including the Beckman Institute, a center for fundamental research in biology and chemistry. Ninety percent of undergraduates participate in research, including 80 percent who receive Summer Undergraduate Research Fellowships, which offer the chance to get a head start on their own discoveries, with help from a faculty sponsor. Many summer fellows publish results from their endeavors in scientific journals. Eighteen percent of students also find time to study abroad.

Eighty percent of students receive Summer Undergraduate Research Fellowships.

Despite Caltech's reputation for pervasive brilliance, "The quality of instruction is variable, since Caltech is a research institution," says a sophomore. "But even the professors who are not stellar lecturers still provide a breadth of knowledge." Another student notes that professors in the humanities and social sciences really shine, since they actually want to teach, rather than hole up in a lab with mass spectrometers and computer simulations of atomic fission. Coursework tends to be heavily theory-based, and one student describes the academic climate as "collaborative, intense, and busy." While teaching assistants do lead some recitation sections affiliated with large lectures, it's not uncommon for professors to lead them too—even for freshmen—and 71 percent of all classes have fewer than 20 students.

"[The academic climate is] collaborative, intense, and busy."

"Caltech students are quirky, awkward, extremely passionate, and supportive," says a mechanical engineering major. Thirty-two percent of Techers come from California, and 8 percent hail from foreign nations. Thirty-five percent of undergrads are Asian American; other minorities are less well represented, with Hispanics/Latinos making up 22 percent of the student body, Black students just 3 percent, and multiracial students 9 percent. Men outnumber women, which has inspired the bittersweet observation among distaff Techers that "the odds are good, but the goods are odd." Students describe their classmates as mostly apathetic when it comes to politics, but a physics major says, "The LGBTQ community is well supported and very present on campus." All financial aid is awarded based on need—meaning no merit or athletic scholarships—and Caltech guarantees to meet the full demonstrated need of all admitted students.

Caltech's eight co-ed "houses" inspire a loyalty worthy of the Greeks and offer social and emotional support.

Caltech undergrads are required to live on campus for all four years in housing that one students calls "comfortable and convenient." There are no fraternities or sororities, but the campus's eight co-ed "houses" inspire a loyalty worthy of the Greeks and offer social and emotional support in an academically intense environment. "Housing is the most special thing about Caltech: we are sorted into houses in a fashion similar to rushing, except that everyone gets into a house," explains a computer science major. During Rotation Week, freshmen spend an evening visiting each house, indicating at week's end the four they like the most; the Office of Residential Experience then sorts them into houses. The four older houses, which have been renovated, offer single, double, and triple rooms, while the newer ones have doubles. Each dorm has a dining hall, and those who live on campus must buy a meal plan, which a junior calls "quite expensive for the quality of food." Special plates are prepared daily for those with specific dietary needs. During an annual, student-led Title IX Summit, students plan solutions and strategies to prevent sexual violence.

The houses are the social center of Caltech life, and since each one takes a turn hosting a themed "interhouse" party, students can count on at least eight school-wide parties throughout the year. Caltech requires any house or organization hosting a party to hire a professional bartender, who checks IDs, and to have students trained in safety and emergency procedures in attendance. Other than house parties, students say, social life is pretty tame, since everyone is so busy with their schoolwork.

"Ask any local bartender for a Caltech Cocktail and you will get three ounces of straight water."

"Ask any local bartender for a Caltech Cocktail and you will get three ounces of straight water," quips a sophomore. Some students head off campus—to Old Pasadena, nearby schools like USC, Occidental, and the Claremont Colleges, or to downtown L.A., easily reachable on the Metro's gold line. Disneyland and Hollywood are always options, and road trips to the beach, mountains, or desert—or south of the border, to Mexico—are possible for those with cars.

Even with ample off-campus diversions, many Caltech students still prefer to make their own fun. The annual Pumpkin Drop (on Halloween, of course) involves immersing a gourd in liquid nitrogen and then dropping it from the library roof, so that it shatters into a zillion frozen shards. On Ditch Day, underclassmen solve complex puzzles, defeat obstacles, and engage in "wild adventures" that have been planned by seniors, who disappear from campus, and then claim a prize at the end of the day. "All classes are canceled, all deadlines are extended, and it's just a day of nerdiness," says a sophomore. During finals week, stereos blast "The Ride of the Valkyries" at seven o'clock each morning, just the thing to get you going after that all-nighter. Caltech also has a storied history of practical jokes. The most fabled student prank occurred during the 1984 Rose Bowl game, when UCLA played Illinois. A group of Caltech whiz kids spent months devising a radio-control device that would allow them to take control of the scoreboard in the second half, to gain national exposure for Caltech by flashing pictures of their school's mascot, the beaver, and a revised score that had Caltech trouncing MIT.

As for Caltech's actual athletic exploits, some of the most successful of the school's 16 Division III teams include men's and women's tennis, swimming and diving, and cross-country. The Beavers' men's basketball team became campus heroes in 2011 when they ended a conference losing streak that dated back to 1985. Perhaps more popular than varsity competition, though, are the intramural matches between the houses, in nine sports every year. Another favorite is the annual design competition that is the culmination of Mechanical Engineering 72, in which student-built robots must complete tasks while traversing an obstacle course.

Caltech students must learn to thrive under intense pressure, thanks to the school's tremendous workload and somewhat lackluster social life. But students say they appreciate the freedom to think and explore—and the trust administrators

Overlaps

MIT, Harvey Mudd, Stanford, Harvard, Princeton, Yale, UC Berkeley, University of Chicago

place in them through the honor code. "The unique student body, how available professors are (I call almost all of them by their first names), and how much we learn make Caltech a special place," says a sophomore.

If You Apply To ›

Caltech: Early action, regular decision. Accepts the Common Application with supplement. Students have the option of submitting published scientific research papers and letters from research mentors. Please consult Caltech's website for the most up-to-date information regarding standardized test requirements.

Calvin University

3201 Burton Street SE, Grand Rapids, MI 49546

An evangelical Christian institution that ranks high on the private college affordability list. More than a quarter of the students are members of the Christian Reformed Church. Archrival of Michigan neighbor Hope and Illinois cousin Wheaton. Best known in the humanities and as one of the few Christian universities with engineering. Big emphasis on study abroad.

Website: www.calvin.edu
Location: Small City
Private
Total Enrollment: 2,887
Undergraduates: 2,785
Male/Female: 46/54
Financial Aid: 100%
Pell Grant: 17%
Expense: Pr $
Student Loans: 56%
Average Debt: $ $ $
Applicants: 3,267
Accepted: 92%
Enrolled: 25%
Grad in 6 Years: 77%
Returning Freshmen: 86%
Academics: ✍ ✍ ✍
Social: ☎ ☎ ☎
Q of L: ★ ★ ★ ★
Admissions: (800) 688-0122
Email Address: admissions@calvin.edu

Strong Programs:
Business Administration
Engineering
Education
Nursing
Philosophy

Calvin University takes seriously its mission to equip students to "think deeply, to act justly, and to live wholeheartedly as Christ's agents of renewal in the world." Along with Wheaton College in Illinois, it is regarded as one of the country's top evangelical colleges. Though no one is required to attend the school's daily chapel services, classes stop when worship starts, and most students view Christian values as central to the academic experience. "Students at Calvin will go out of their way to get to know you, have a meal with you, and invite you to play spikeball on the lawn," says a secondary education major. "Although not every student at Calvin is religious, Christian ideals and morals are very prevalent on campus."

Calvin was founded in 1876 as the educational wing of the Christian Reformed Church in North America. After outgrowing one of its first homes, the school bought a tract of land on the edge of Grand Rapids and built its present campus. Calvin, which changed its name from "college" to "university" in 2019, spreads out over 400 beautifully landscaped acres that include three ponds and a 100-acre woodland and wetland ecosystem preserve used for classes, research, and recreation. Most facilities are less than 50 years old and were designed by a student of famed architect Frank Lloyd Wright. The east campus includes the DeVos Communication Center, the Gainey Athletic Facility, and a new $11 million School of Business building that opened in 2022.

> "Students at Calvin will go out of their way to get to know you."

Launched in fall 2021, the Calvin Core consists of four components: Foundations (Christian thought and engagement); Competencies and Skills (writing, health, and world languages); Knowledge and Understanding (coursework in a broad range of liberal arts and science disciplines); and Cross-Disciplinary Integration (coursework that helps equip students to be global citizens). In addition, Calvin LifeWork is an optional program that teaches skills like financial literacy and career readiness, to prepare students for success after college.

Preprofessional programs, such as business, engineering, education, and nursing, tend to be Calvin's best bets, students say, and those programs are among the most popular majors. Philosophy, English, and religion are also regarded as strong. Calvin is the only Christian college in the U.S. to offer a comprehensive Asian studies program, which includes courses in Chinese, Japanese, and Korean language, history, and culture. New majors in operations and supply chain management, strategic communication, and criminology are available, and five-year bachelor-to-master's programs are offered in accounting and in speech pathology and audiology.

Calvin is founded on the belief that every subject—even the sciences or mass media and popular culture—can be approached from a Christian perspective, and faculty members work hard to integrate faith and learning. "Topics like ethics or the synthesis of religion and science are addressed in my classes," explains an engineering major. In the absence of teaching assistants, professors are expected to reserve about 10 hours per week for advising and assisting students outside of class. Thirty-seven percent of the classes at Calvin have fewer than 20 students and only a few have more than 50. "The academic climate is appropriately challenging," says an elementary education major, and "the professors are very understanding." Students give high ratings to peer tutoring and mental health counseling services.

> **"Topics like ethics or the synthesis of religion and science are addressed in my [engineering] classes."**

Learning also takes place outside of the classroom through internships and practicums, and 89 percent of students complete at least one internship before they graduate. About 15 percent collaborate with faculty on research projects. Calvin offers 15 to 20 faculty-led off-campus programs in such locales as Britain, Peru, Nepal, and Washington, D.C., in addition to programs offered in conjunction with partner institutions. Fifty-five percent of students study abroad.

A new $11 million School of Business building opened in 2022.

Though Calvin still has a strongly Dutch heritage, students who are members of the Christian Reformed Church now account for just 29 percent of the student body. "Calvin has evolved in regards to the way it tries to deal with conversations on diverse thinking and faiths," remarks a student. Fifty-four percent of students are Michigan natives, and 12 percent are international. Black students constitute 4 percent of the total, Hispanics/Latinos 4 percent, Asian Americans 5 percent, and multiracial students 3 percent. "Political views are not a defining characteristic of campus, even if they are discussed and argued in various settings," says a junior. Eligible Calvin students receive scholarships based on academic merit, worth an average of $17,000 annually; there are no athletic awards.

Calvin requires undergraduates to live on campus for three years. For their first two years, students bunk in residence halls—each of which has separate wings for men and women—in four-person suites with two bedrooms connected by a shared bathroom. "The suites are typically set up with two freshmen on one side and two sophomores on the other," explains a nursing major. "It's nice to have an older individual who knows the ropes to guide you in your first year." Juniors can choose between residence halls and on-campus apartments, and many seniors opt to move off campus. Calvin offers three intentional living/learning floors—Creation Care (recreational pursuits/environmental stewardship and sustainability), Justice and Equity (diversity and inequality in the U.S.), and Honors. Students report that campus dining facilities could use "more options for variety" and "extended hours." Safety is highly rated. "The Sexual Assault Prevention Team is active on campus, and Campus Safety is patrolling 24/7, even during school breaks," notes a sophomore.

> **"The academic climate is appropriately challenging [and] the professors are very understanding."**

Chaos Night brings the dorms together for an evening of wacky games and athletic contests.

"Calvin is a dry campus, and there is no Greek life, but the students aren't uptight—meaning that those who are of legal age take advantage of going to bars and breweries in Grand Rapids for a drink with friends on the weekends," says a senior. The downtown area also offers restaurants, coffee shops, minor-league sports, galleries, and the annual ArtPrize festival and competition. On campus, students find a wealth of entertainment, including movies, speakers, concerts, and dances. Popular annual traditions include Chaos Night, which brings the dorms together for an evening of wacky games and athletic contests, and the Rangeela cultural show. Hardy souls look forward to the Cold Knight Plunge, where hundreds of students voluntarily jump into the frozen Seminary Pond each winter, led by the college president and chaplain. Road trips include the beaches of Lake Michigan (a 45-minute drive) or Chicago (three hours distant). Spring break trips see a number of students traveling to places like Mississippi and Louisiana to complete service projects.

Calvin fields a robust Division III athletic program that competes in the Michigan Intercollegiate Athletic Association (MIAA). Particularly competitive Knights teams include women's volleyball, men's and women's cross-country, and men's soccer. The men's ice hockey program has also seen consistent success. Calvin's competition with Hope College is one of the great rivalries in Division III athletics and "makes any sporting event fun," says a sophomore; current students and alumni alike rally together for the annual basketball game. The intramural program offers leagues and tournaments in sports ranging from dodgeball to ultimate Frisbee and flag football; half of all undergraduates participate.

Those who come to Calvin University are looking to build community with friends and faculty members who share their already strong Christian faith. Says one senior, Calvin is a place where "people are intentionally seeking connection with one another, in pursuit of a community where people are welcomed and embraced."

> ## Overlaps
>
> **Hope, Wheaton (IL), Taylor, St. Olaf, Cedarville, Cornerstone University, Dordt, Messiah**

If You Apply To ›

Calvin: Rolling admissions. SATs or ACTs: optional. Accepts the Common Application with supplement.

Carleton College

Northfield, MN 55057

Less selective than Amherst, Williams, and Swarthmore, if only because of its out-of-the-way Minnesota location. Carleton retains its position as the premier liberal arts college in the upper Midwest. Predominantly liberal, but not to the extremes of its more antiestablishment cousins, and turns out lots of students who go on to get Ph.D.s. Students at Carleton excel at making their own fun.

> **Website:** www.carleton.edu
> **Location:** Small Town
> **Private**
> **Total Enrollment:** 2,008
> **Undergraduates:** 2,008
> **Male/Female:** 49/51
> **Financial Aid:** 82%
> **Pell Grant:** 13%
> **Expense:** Pr $ $ $ $
> **Student Loans:** 36%
> **Average Debt:** $
> **Applicants:** 7,915
> **Accepted:** 18%

Minnesota is many things: the land of 10,000 lakes, home to the massive Mall of America, birthplace of lore from Hiawatha to Paul Bunyan, and proud parent of the Mississippi River. Beyond all that history-book stuff, tucked into a small town in the southeastern corner of the state is Carleton College, arguably the best liberal arts school in the expansive Midwest. Add to this badminton competitions that raise money to fight cancer, an expulsion of Coca-Cola from campus for human rights violations, and an all-day spring music festival known as "Sproncert," and you have the makings of an engaged, unique institution. "Carleton is quirky, and we're not afraid to embrace our quirk. In fact, we revel in it," says a biology major.

Carleton was founded in 1866 and named for an early benefactor. Surrounded by rolling farmland, Carleton's 1,040-acre campus is in the small town of Northfield, whose one-time status as the center of the Holstein cattle industry brought it the motto "Cows, Colleges, and Contentment." The campus boasts of fragrant lilacs in spring, rich summer greens, red maples in the fall, and a glistening blanket of white in winter. Lakes, woods, and streams abound, and you can traverse them on 15 miles of hiking and cross-country skiing trails. There's even an 880-acre arboretum. Carleton's architectural style is somewhat eclectic, with everything from Victorian to contemporary, but mostly red brick. Recent additions include the Integrated Science Center, which consists of two renovated facilities and Anderson Hall, housing science labs and classrooms.

Carleton's top-notch academic programs are no less varied. The sciences—biology, physics, astronomy, chemistry, geology, and computer science—are among the best anywhere, and scores of Carleton graduates go on to earn Ph.D.s in these areas. Political science/international relations is a traditional strength; mathematics and psychology are popular too. Engineers can opt for a 3–2 program with Washington University in St. Louis, and for geologists seeking fieldwork—and maybe wanting to thaw out after a long Minnesota winter—Carleton sponsors a program in Death Valley. Closer to home at the "arb," as the arboretum is affectionately known, students in the well-regarded

> **"Carleton is quirky, and we're not afraid to embrace our quirk."**

environmental studies program have their own wilderness field station, which includes a prairie-restoration site. At the opposite end of the academic spectrum, the arts also flourish. Music and studio art majors routinely get into top graduate programs, and the college has expanded offerings in dance and theater. Carleton offers interdisciplinary programs in Asian, Jewish, urban, African and African American, and women's studies. A minor in cross-cultural studies brings in international students to discuss global issues and dynamics with their American counterparts. Seventy percent of Carleton students spend at least one term abroad; offerings include 18 to 20 faculty-led programs every year. Seventy-seven percent of students conduct undergraduate research.

Distribution requirements ensure that a Carleton education exposes students not only to rigor and depth in their chosen field, but also to "a wide range of subjects and methods of studying them," administrators say. All students must show proficiency in writing and a second language while fulfilling requirements in the areas of humanistic and social inquiry, literary/artistic analysis, the arts, science, and quantitative reasoning. There's also a Global Citizenship requirement, under which students must take one course on international studies and one course on intercultural domestic studies, and a first-year Argument and Inquiry Seminar. In their final year, all students complete a senior comprehensive project (known around campus as "Comps").

With highly motivated students and a heavy workload, Carleton isn't your typical mellow Midwestern liberal arts college. The trimester calendar means finals may be just three months apart, and almost everyone feels the pressure. "I often joke that the hottest social spot at our school is the library," says a linguistics major, and a junior adds, "Everyone is really working diligently, but this breeds a climate of solidarity." The five-week Christmas vacation is Carleton's way of dealing with the cold winters. Seventy-three percent of classes have fewer than 20 students, so Carls are expected to participate actively. Carleton's faculty members are accessible and committed. "My professors are

> **"Everyone is really working diligently, but this breeds a climate of solidarity."**

personal mentors as much as they are formal educators," says a physics major. As part of its extensive advising program, Carleton assigns a "liberal arts advisor" to work with entering students for their first two years.

"Students here have a sense of adventure and curiosity," says a senior. Not to be confused with the quintessentially Midwestern students across town at St. Olaf, just 8 percent of Carleton students are Minnesota residents, and 10 percent are international. More than half of the out-of-staters are from outside the Midwest, with

(continued)

Enrolled: 40%
Grad in 6 Years: 94%
Returning Freshmen: 94%
Academics: ✍ ✍ ✍ ✍ ✍
Social: ☎ ☎ ☎
Q of L: ★ ★ ★
Admissions: (800) 995-2275
Email Address: admissions@ carleton.edu

Strong Programs:
Biology
Physics
Computer Science
Political Science/International Relations
Environmental Studies
Music
Studio Art
Mathematics

Lakes, woods, and streams abound, and you can traverse them on the campus's 15 miles of hiking and cross-country skiing trails.

both coasts heavily represented. Black students account for 6 percent of the student body, Hispanics/Latinos 9 percent, Asian Americans 10 percent, and multiracial students 8 percent. "As a person of color, it's easy to find other people of color, and we form a tight-knit community," says a sophomore. The Carleton campus is decidedly liberal ("I have watched the conservative minority at this school vanish," remarks a senior), concerned with issues including diversity, racial justice, political correctness, and LGBTQ rights, and students are active in the local community. Carleton meets the full demonstrated financial need of all enrolled students, and all financial aid is need-based—there are no merit or athletic scholarships.

Ninety-six percent of Carleton students live on campus, and housing is guaranteed for all four years; those who wish to live off campus must receive approval to do so. On-campus options range from comfortable old houses to modern hotel-like residence halls. "Even the worst dorms are totally livable and spacious compared to those of friends that I have from other colleges," says a junior. Dorms are co-ed by room, but there are two halls with single-sex floors. Several college-owned "theme" houses, situated in an attractive residential section of town close to campus, focus on special interests such as social activism and the outdoors; the Farm House is an environmental studies house located on the edge of the arb. All campus residents must submit to a meal plan, to the chagrin of many. "The meals are usually the same, and bland," gripes a freshman. Fortunately, students can also use their meal plans at neighboring St. Olaf, where the food gets rave reviews. Students say the campus is safe, especially given its small-town location.

> "My professors are personal mentors as much as they are formal educators."

Absent a Greek system, Carleton's social life tends to be relaxed and informal, as well as campus-based. "Carleton students have fun and let loose in their own ways," says a freshman. "Parties vary a lot, ranging from packed dorm dancing to bonfires in the woods. I have been to parties with themes such as Limes, Fire, and Illinois." A group called Co-op sponsors dances and Wednesday socials every two weeks, free movies, and special events like Comedy Night. Students say there is no pressure to drink on campus. Popular annual events include the Midwinter Ball, the Spring Concert, and Mai Fete, a gala celebrated on an island in one of the two lakes on campus. Traditions include the weeklong freshman orientation program, where, during opening convocation, students bombard professors with bubbles as the faculty members process. Another distinctive Carleton tradition is the regular liberation and dramatic reappearance of a plaster bust of Friedrich Schiller, the Romantic philosopher and buddy of Goethe—such as dangling from a helicopter over homecoming football games.

Northfield itself is a history-filled town with a population of about 21,000. A favorite town event is the annual reenactment of Jesse James's failed bank robbery in 1876. "Northfield is quaint," a sophomore says, with old-style shops, a beautiful old hotel, cafés, and a handful of bars and breweries. Students often frequent St. Olaf's campus and a popular coffee shop called Goodbye Blue Monday. Minneapolis-St. Paul, 35 miles to the north, is a popular road-trip destination. Students aren't allowed to have cars on campus, but daily bus service is available.

> "I have been to parties with themes such as Limes, Fire, and Illinois."

The Knights compete in Division III athletics. Men's and women's cross-country have won multiple Minnesota Intercollegiate Athletic Conference titles in recent years, and men's soccer and men's and women's tennis and track and field are also competitive. The school's ultimate Frisbee club teams have won several national championships. About half of the students compete in 24 club and 14 intramural sports, including broomball in the winter and Rotblatt, which is "the world's longest intramural sport," according to one junior. "Played once each spring, this marathon

Overlaps

Bowdoin, Williams, Amherst, Pomona, Swarthmore, Grinnell, Middlebury, University of Chicago

softball game begins at sunrise and lasts one inning for each year of Carleton's existence. It is Rotblatt tradition for players to both bat and field with a beverage of their choice in one hand."

It can be cold in Minnesota, in a face-stinging, bone-chilling kind of way. And the classes are far from easy. But Carleton is a warm campus where students toe the line between individuality and community. At Carleton, says one student, "It isn't about getting the degree; it's about having an impactful experience where students learn more about themselves and the world they live in."

If You Apply To ›

Carleton: Early decision I and II, regular decision. Accepts the Common Application with supplement. Please consult Carleton's website for the most up-to-date information regarding standardized test requirements.

Carnegie Mellon University

5000 Forbes Avenue, Pittsburgh, PA 15213-3890

The only premier university equally strong in technology and the arts, Carnegie Mellon is a national leader in blending interdisciplinary and practical education. Applications continue to increase, so it must be doing something right. Shares its urban neighborhood with a variety of cultural and academic institutions, including the University of Pittsburgh. Working hard to reduce student stress levels.

Students at Carnegie Mellon don't have to choose between soaking up the high drama of Shakespeare and plunging into the fast-paced tech world. The university is known for both its science offerings and strong drama and music programs. But scholars can't just focus on their own course of study—Carnegie Mellon continues to strive to offer both its technical and liberal arts students a well-rounded education that requires a lot of hard work but promises great results.

Tracing its origins to 1900, when industrialist Andrew Carnegie founded a technical school for the children of Pittsburgh's blue-collar workers, Carnegie Mellon was formed by the merger of Carnegie Institute of Technology and the Mellon Institute in 1967. Its self-contained, 157-acre campus is attractively situated in Pittsburgh's affluent Oakland section. Next door is the city's second-largest park and its major museum, named after—you guessed it—Andrew Carnegie. Henry Hornbostel, who attended the École des

> **"There is absolutely no stigma against tutoring or outside resources."**

Beaux-Arts in the 1890s, designed the campus using a plan that is a modification of the Jefferson plan for the University of Virginia, with the Beaux-Arts device of creating primary and secondary axes and grouping buildings around significant open spaces. Buildings are designed in a Renaissance style, with buff-colored brick arches and piers, tile roofs, and terra cotta and granite details. The $75 million Scaife Hall of Engineering, completed in 2023, is part of an ongoing revitalization and expansion of the university's engineering facilities.

Carnegie Mellon has seven constituent colleges that offer undergraduate and graduate degrees: the College of Fine Arts, the Dietrich College of Humanities and Social Sciences, the College of Engineering, the Mellon College of Science, the School of Computer Science, the Tepper School of Business, and the Heinz College of Information Systems and Public Policy. Each college has its own distinct character

Website: www.cmu.edu
Location: City Center
Private
Total Enrollment: 14,756
Undergraduates: 7,164
Male/Female: 49/51
Financial Aid: 51%
Pell Grant: 15%
Expense: Pr $ $ $
Student Loans: 40%
Average Debt: $ $ $
Applicants: 32,896
Accepted: 14%
Enrolled: 43%
Grad in 6 Years: 93%
Returning Freshmen: 97%
Academics: ✐ ✐ ✐ ✐
Social: ☎ ☎ ☎
Q of L: ★ ★ ★
Admissions: (412) 268-2082
Email Address: admission@andrew.cmu.edu

Strong Programs:
Engineering

and admissions requirements. All the colleges, however, share the university's commitment to interdisciplinary and practical education, which shows the relevance of the liberal arts while stressing courses that develop technical skills and good job prospects. Students interested in humanities and social science can major in applied history, professional writing, or information systems, for example, instead of traditional disciplinary concentrations.

Most departments at Carnegie Mellon are strong, but exceptional ones include engineering, computer science, architecture, and drama. The undergraduate business program focuses on the technical aspects of management and quantitative decision-making. The most popular majors are computer science, business administration, electrical and computer engineering, and mechanical engineering. Initiatives aimed at connecting art and technology include the Integrative Design, Arts, and Technology network, which offers interdisciplinary minors like game design, animation and special effects, and innovation and entrepreneurship.

Courses are "extremely rigorous with many hours expected outside of the classroom," says one student. Students at Carnegie Mellon work hard, no doubt about it, and many complain that the academic environment encourages a serious culture of stress,

> **"Most CMU students own up to their identities as nerds."**

but the university has taken steps to try to counteract that. Every day includes a designated "meeting-free" time for students, allowing them time to study or participate in student activities. A mechanical and biomedical engineering double major notes that there is a "mindfulness room" that serves as "a space for students to relax and take a break from schoolwork" (and get weekly visits from trained therapy dogs), and that students are encouraged to use campus counseling services "even if it is just to discuss stress and how to manage a new environment." Students also recommend the Academic Development Office, and one says, "There is absolutely no stigma against tutoring or outside resources." Sixty-nine percent of classes have fewer than 20 students, and professors rate highly with most students. "Some professors are better than others at lecturing, but I have not encountered a professor that doesn't care about the course," says an electrical and computer engineering major.

Students looking to hone their professional skills will find ample opportunities, including five-year dual-degree options, co-op programs, and advising and other resources within the Career and Professional Development Center. Research opportunities are available across the curriculum, as are several types of grants and fellowships to fund them. Those interested in service learning can get involved with the university's extensive outreach efforts to improve youth STEM education in the local area. Study abroad options are plentiful and include the university's established undergraduate campus in the Arabian Gulf nation of Qatar, but many students have difficulty fitting study abroad into their rigorous schedules.

"CMU is for people who know what they want to do," asserts one student. Despite the university's core emphasis on interdisciplinary, well-rounded education, Carnegie Mellon remains one of the most fragmented campuses in the nation. Students divide themselves between actors, designers, and

> **"Financial aid is not the most generous in comparison to peer institutions."**

other artsy types and engineers, scientists, and architects. "Most CMU students own up to their identities as nerds, whether they be of the drama, history, or science variety," says a math major. In any case, students here are all high achievers and are united in their quest for a good job after graduation.

Once a largely regional institution, drawing mostly Pennsylvania residents, Carnegie Mellon now counts 90 percent of its full-time undergraduate students from out of state, including 23 percent from foreign countries. Half are students of color, including 32 percent Asian American, 4 percent Black, 9 percent Hispanic/Latino,

Carnegie Mellon shows the relevance of the liberal arts while stressing courses that develop technical skills and good job prospects.

and 5 percent multiracial. Students report that campus politics lean liberal, but most students don't get actively involved in social or political matters. The university says it remains committed to need-blind admissions and guarantees to meet the full demonstrated financial need of domestic students, including permanent residents and DACA students. Most financial aid is need-based, and there are no merit- or athletic-based awards. "Financial aid is not the most generous in comparison to peer institutions," remarks a student, in part because Carnegie Mellon's endowment is smaller.

Housing is guaranteed for undergraduates all four years if they stay in the university housing system, and 48 percent do so. Upperclassmen get first pick, so the popular university-owned apartments fill up fast, but there are a number of residence halls specifically for first-year students. The quality of each dorm varies, says a junior, but "the facilities are all very livable." The best dorms for freshmen are Stever House—the first LEED-certified residence hall in the U.S.—Donner, Resnik, and Morewood Gardens. "Instead of buffet-style dining halls, we have several themed eateries that you can pick from," explains a sophomore,

"Whatever type of evening you're looking for, Pittsburgh has it."

and meals are described as satisfying. Students report feeling safe on campus, thanks to a comprehensive security program, but one comments, "There is not enough campus conversation or emphasis on the issue of sexual assault."

With all the academic pressure at Carnegie Mellon, it's a good thing there are so many opportunities to unwind, especially with the entire city of Pittsburgh close at hand. "Pittsburgh is a great place to go to college," cheers a junior. "Whatever type of evening you're looking for, Pittsburgh has it." Nearby Oakland has coffeehouses, inexpensive films, dances, and concerts, and the downtown area (just 20 minutes away by bus) offers a rich social scene, with opera, ballet, symphony, concerts, and sporting events.

The Greek system provides the most visible form of on-campus social life, with 14 percent of men and 12 percent of women joining fraternities and sororities, and the school offers late-night events and concerts too. Those of legal age are allowed to have alcohol in their rooms, but according to one student, "Drinking takes place mostly off campus." One event that brings everyone together is the Spring Carnival, a four-day weekend festival. Student groups build themed booths and design, build, and race buggies made of lightweight alloys. Members of the student-run "Scotch 'n' Soda" theater organization also present a show.

As for sports, the Carnegie Mellon Tartans compete in the Division III University Athletic Association. The Kiltie Band, clad in kilts honoring Andrew Carnegie's Scottish heritage, rallies the crowd during home football and basketball games. In recent years, men's and women's golf and cross-country, men's indoor track and field, and women's soccer have performed well in their respective national championship tournaments. Students also participate in 47 intramural and club sports.

Carnegie Mellon appeals just as much to those yearning for the bright lights of Broadway as it does to those pursuing the glowing computer screens of the scientific and business worlds. And with a broad range of liberal arts and technical courses available to explore, there's no doubt students leave with a well-rounded education—and an impressive diploma. Students more interested in specializing in one field than being exposed to many may fare better elsewhere, but most who opt for Carnegie Mellon agree that the demanding environment is well worth it.

Overlaps

UC Berkeley, Northwestern, University of Southern California, Boston University, Princeton, Cornell, MIT, UCLA

If You Apply To ›

Carnegie Mellon: Early decision, regular decision. Accepts the Common Application. Apply to particular school or college. Please consult Carnegie Mellon's website for the most up-to-date information regarding standardized test requirements.

Case Western Reserve

103 Tomlinson Hall, 10900 Euclid Avenue, Cleveland, OH 44106

CWRU has most of the offerings available at Carnegie Mellon or WashU in St. Louis, but somehow it hasn't quite found its deserved niche in the national consciousness. Students in the know sing its praises, especially since CWRU is less difficult to get into than other institutions of comparable quality. Students get an outstanding technical education with solid offerings in other areas.

Website: www.case.edu
Location: City Center
Private
Total Enrollment: 10,930
Undergraduates: 5,646
Male/Female: 53/47
Financial Aid: 98%
Pell Grant: 18%
Expense: Pr $ $ $ $
Student Loans: 51%
Average Debt: $ $
Applicants: 33,232
Accepted: 30%
Enrolled: 16%
Grad in 6 Years: 84%
Returning Freshmen: 94%
Academics: ✍ ✍ ✍ ✍
Social: ☎ ☎
Q of L: ★ ★ ★
Admissions: (216) 368-4450
Email Address: admission@case.edu

Strong Programs:
Biomedical Engineering
Mechanical Engineering
Nursing
Business Management
Computer Science
Pre-Architecture
Polymer Science
Music

Cleveland's Case Western Reserve has much in common with Pittsburgh's Carnegie Mellon. Both are the product of mergers between a technical college, known for excellence in engineering, and a more traditional university, focused on the arts and sciences. Both are located in erstwhile Rust Belt cities that have long since reinvented themselves through technology, medicine, education, and advanced manufacturing. And both tend to attract brainy students more concerned with studying than socializing. While CWRU has received less national attention than Carnegie Mellon and WashU, a senior calls it "a university on the rise": applications have nearly doubled since 2013, and the school has become more selective. CWRU has also increased its investment in the arts, humanities, and social sciences, with an aim toward helping students connect these disciplines with their technical studies.

> **"CWRU is a collaborative environment that allows students to excel in their own way."**

CWRU is located on the eastern edge of Cleveland, at University Circle. This 550-acre area of parks and gardens is home to more than 50 cultural, educational, medical, and research institutions, including the city's museums of art and natural history, its botanical gardens, and Severance Hall, home of the Cleveland Orchestra. Campus buildings are an eclectic mix of architectural styles, and several are listed on the National Register of Historic Places. The Peter B. Lewis Building (or "PBL," as it's known around campus), designed by Frank Gehry, is home to the Weatherhead School of Management and features undulating walls similar to those of Gehry's Guggenheim Museum in Bilbao, Spain. The Tinkham Veale University Center ("the Tink") meets LEED Silver standards and serves as a hub for campus dining, special events, and more than 200 student organizations, while the Sears think[box] is a fabrication lab designed to support cross-disciplinary entrepreneurial innovation.

The product of the 1967 marriage between Case Institute of Technology and Western Reserve University, CWRU has four undergraduate schools: the College of Arts and Sciences, the Case School of Engineering, the Bolton School of Nursing, and the aforementioned Weatherhead School; all also offer graduate programs. All CWRU students participate in a general education program known as SAGES—the Seminar Approach to General Education and Scholarship. Emphasizing small seminars, critical thinking, and writing, the program requires four seminars, a writing portfolio, and a senior capstone experience that can be an individual or group effort. According to a biomedical engineering major, "CWRU is a collaborative environment that allows students to excel in their own way."

> **"A navigator is a great resource for nonmajor-specific questions."**

CWRU's strongest programs include engineering—especially the biomedical and mechanical kind—nursing, business management, computer science, and pre-architecture. The school's polymer science major is one of the few such undergraduate programs in the country. Strengths in the College of Arts and Sciences include music (a joint program with the nearby Cleveland Institute of Music), psychology, anthropology (especially medical anthropology), and biology. Combined bachelor's and master's programs are popular, as is the Preprofessional Scholars program, which gives top freshmen conditional acceptance to CWRU's medical or dental schools, assuming satisfactory progress through prerequisite courses. Fifty-nine percent of all undergraduate classes enroll fewer than 20 students. "The quality of instruction is variable," says a biology major, "but the majority of instructors are very good and willing to help at any time."

Undergraduate research is highly encouraged, and 80 percent of students conduct research as part of senior capstone projects or independent studies. Thirty-one percent of students take part in study abroad, often in faculty-led programs during winter, spring, or summer breaks. For help with academic and career planning, every undergraduate is assigned a faculty advisor as well as a "navigator," a staff member who assists them throughout their four years. "A navigator is a great resource for nonmajor-specific questions relating to campus resources, academic resources, club suggestions, etc.," explains a freshman.

All students participate in a gen-ed program known as SAGES—the Seminar Approach to General Education and Scholarship.

A senior says CWRU students are "driven, high achievers" who often "feel the need to prove themselves." Nineteen percent of CWRU's students are Ohio natives, and international students represent a strong contingent at 13 percent. Black students make up 5 percent of the student body, Asian Americans 24 percent, Hispanics/Latinos 11 percent, and multiracial students 6 percent. Diversity 360 is a campuswide training program designed to increase knowledge and awareness about diversity issues. Students describe the political climate as low-key, with liberals and conservatives both well represented on campus. Eligible students receive scholarships based on academic merit that average $24,500, but there are no athletic awards. The university has adopted a need-aware admissions policy that includes a commitment to meet the full demonstrated financial need of incoming freshmen.

"We're surrounded by museums and cultural institutions."

Students are required to live on campus for their first two years, and 70 percent of all undergrads stay on campus. Each first-year student participates in one of four residential colleges. "First-year rooms are adequate but nothing special," says one student, but upperclassmen rave about the amenities in the university's apartment-style suites. Dining-hall fare is "not Mom's cooking every night, but it's not bad," reasons one student. Some upperclassmen opt for off-campus apartments within walking distance of campus. "As it is an urban campus, crime does occasionally happen in the surrounding area or (rarely) on campus," reports a psychology major. "The school takes many strong measures to keep students safe, including many security officers and free rides across campus at night."

As for social life, says a junior, "Case is not ideal for anyone who prioritizes a vibrant social scene, but students who enjoy being social and going to parties/bars are able to find enough opportunities." On campus, there are dances, concerts, and movies. Fraternities and sororities draw 20 percent of the men and 29 percent of the women, but students report that Greek groups here are more focused on philanthropy than partying. Popular campus traditions include the Springfest carnival to celebrate the end of classes and "Study Overs," where students gather during finals week for free food, massages, study groups, and more. The annual sci-fi movie marathon is a rite of passage, while Engineering Week features a fuel-cell-powered car competition.

"Study Overs," where students gather during finals week for free food, massages, study groups, and more, are popular.

CWRU is located five miles from downtown Cleveland, which provides ample opportunities for internships, volunteer work, dining, and entertainment. "We're surrounded by museums and cultural institutions, which become a part of our education," enthuses a history major. "It's very budget-friendly," adds a senior. The city features the Rock and Roll Hall of Fame, and—in the warmer months—major league baseball games at Progressive Field. Convenient RTA train passes are included in student charges for a reasonable price, but having a car can be helpful, especially for road trips to nearby cities in Ohio or for longer jaunts to Chicago.

Although sports are not a major focus on campus, the Spartans field 17 Division III teams, and the annual football game against Carnegie Mellon is big. Baseball and softball are recent University Athletic Association champions, and men's and women's cross-country, men's basketball, and women's soccer are nationally competitive. Twenty-four percent of students participate in at least one of the 25 intramural and 16 club sports available, ranging from flag football and pickleball to ice hockey, badminton, and fencing. The 26-mile Hudson Relay, held the last week of the spring semester to commemorate CWRU's relocation from Hudson to Cleveland, pits teams of runners from the four classes against one another, with each person running a half mile.

A rigorous, science- and engineering-oriented research university, CWRU also devotes noteworthy attention to the student experience. "CWRU's personality is friendly and spirited," says a senior. "People can be self-deprecating and make a lot of jokes about Cleveland's bad weather, but the campus community itself is warm and inviting." With challenging academics, preprofessional programs, and research opportunities across all disciplines, students here are well-equipped to excel in their future careers.

Overlaps

Carnegie Mellon, Johns Hopkins, Vanderbilt, University of Rochester, Emory, WashU in St. Louis, Ohio State, University of Michigan

If You Apply To ›

CWRU: Early decision I and II, early action, regular decision. Accepts the Common Application with supplement. Audition required for artists and musicians. Please consult CWRU's website for the most up-to-date information regarding standardized test requirements.

The Catholic University of America

Washington, D.C. 20064

There are other Roman Catholic–affiliated universities, but this is THE Catholic University. Catholics make up 72 percent of the undergraduate student body here (versus roughly half at nearby Georgetown). If you can't be in Rome, there is no better place than D.C. to work and play. CUA even has a Metrorail stop right next to campus. Academic freedom is the norm except in theology.

Founded in 1887 under a charter from Pope Leo XIII—making it a "pontifical" university—The Catholic University of America was the brainchild of U.S. bishops who wanted to provide an American educational institution where the curriculum was guided by the tenets of Roman Catholic thought. Over time, the university has garnered a reputation as a research-oriented school that also provides a strong undergraduate, preprofessional education and an appreciation for the arts. Faced in recent years with the challenges of declining enrollment and changing demographics and social attitudes, top administrators have nonetheless doubled down on the university's image of "cultivating Catholic minds," sparking renewed debate on campus about whether CUA is marketing itself as "too Catholic" and making itself less welcoming to prospective students in the process. "Our authentic Catholic background rules our academics, campus activities, and institutional offices all over campus," says a senior.

Catholic University's campus comprises 176 tree-lined acres, an impressive layout for an urban university, and houses 34 research facilities. Buildings range from ivy-covered limestone and brick to ultramodern, giving the place a true collegiate

Website: www.catholic.edu
Location: City Center
Private
Total Enrollment: 3,670
Undergraduates: 2,801
Male/Female: 44/56
Financial Aid: 96%
Pell Grant: 13%
Expense: Pr $ $
Student Loans: 63%
Average Debt: $ $ $ $
Applicants: 5,895
Accepted: 86%
Enrolled: 14%
Grad in 6 Years: 74%

feel. A new 500-seat dining facility opened in 2022, and a new nursing and sciences building will open in 2024.

CUA is one of the few schools in the country that began as a graduate institution (others are Clark University and The Johns Hopkins University), and grad students still account for a respectable portion of the student population. Ten of its 12 schools admit undergrads. Specific graduation requirements vary by program, but all undergraduates participate in the First-Year Experience, an introduction to CUA's brand of liberal arts guided by the Catholic intellectual tradition. Assigned to Learning Communities of about 18 classmates, students

> **"Our authentic Catholic background rules our academics, campus activities, and institutional offices."**

take core classes in philosophy, theology, and English, and they receive one-on-one academic advising throughout the year. First-years also join their Learning Communities for out-of-class activities and group excursions into the city.

Students have excellent options in almost any department at CUA. In addition to politics, which is the most popular major and sets the tone on campus, psychology, business, and physics are strong. The physics department enjoys a modern vitreous-state lab, a boon for both research and hands-on undergraduate instruction. The School of Nursing is one of the best in the nation. Engineering and architecture are highly regarded and have outstanding facilities; environmental engineering is the university's newest major. The Benjamin T. Rome School of Music, Drama, and Art is best known for its music offerings, including a joint degree that combines music with business. The National Catholic School of Social Service offers a bachelor of social work degree.

In the classroom, says a politics major, "CUA is not necessarily tough, but there are moments where you may be intellectually or academically challenged." Sixty-three percent of classes have fewer than 20 students, which means individual attention from faculty members is common. According to a sophomore, professors "teach with passion, and it is apparent that they love what they do." About 60 percent of faculty members are Catholic (the Vatican requires that figure to be at least 50 percent). Clergy are at the helm of the School of Theology and Religious Studies and the graduate School of Canon Law. CUA's chancellor is the archbishop of Washington, mass is held on campus daily, and Catholic churches across the country donate a fraction of their annual collections to the university. One corollary of being the only Catholic school with a papal charter is that officials in Rome, who do not always warm up to American traditions of academic freedom, keep a sharp eye on who teaches in the theology school and what they write and say.

Top students are invited to enroll in the University Honors Program, which features challenging seminar-style classes and the option of living in a dedicated honors community. The university offers a wide variety of education abroad programs in more than 75 locations around the globe; 31 percent of students participate. The flagship Rome Center, jointly operated by CUA and an Australian counterpart, sponsors programs for liberal arts and architecture students,

> **"[CUA students have] a healthy sense of ambition."**

as well as a three-week summer program for the First-Year Experience. Eighty percent of students complete at least one internship at organizations ranging from NASA and the National Institutes of Health to the Smithsonian Institution. For the politically minded, international internships are available with the British, Irish, and European Union parliaments. Students give mixed reviews to career and counseling services.

CUA students are "very open to friendship," comments a philosophy major, and they tend to have "a healthy sense of ambition." Catholicism is clearly the tie that binds the student body, with 72 percent of students identifying as Catholic.

(continued)

Returning Freshmen: 88%
Academics: ✍ ✍ ✍
Social: ☎ ☎ ☎
Q of L: ★ ★ ★
Admissions: (202) 319-5305
Email Address: cua-admissions@cua.edu

Strong Programs:
Politics
Psychology
Business
Physics
Nursing
Engineering
Architecture
Music

About 60 percent of faculty members are Catholic (the Vatican requires that figure to be at least 50 percent).

Most students are also conservative, although some socially liberal causes are slowly gaining traction on campus; students report that the administration's insistence on single-sex dorms, refusal to recognize LGBTQ student groups, and ban on speakers who have expressed pro-choice views have been controversial among the student body. "It is hard for a lot of students to reconcile their own personal set of beliefs with the Catholic identity of the school, which can be said even for many of the students who are Catholic themselves," remarks a politics major. Ninety-seven percent of undergraduates are from outside D.C.; 3 percent arrive from foreign countries and most of the rest hail from the Northeast. Four percent are Black, 15 percent are Hispanic/Latino, 3 percent are Asian American, and 4 percent are multiracial. Catholic University maintains a need-blind admissions policy, and all applicants are considered for merit scholarships, which average $25,700. No athletic scholarships are available.

The flagship Rome Center sponsors programs for liberal arts and architecture students, as well as a summer program for the First-Year Experience.

Fifty-five percent of undergraduates live in the 16 single-sex residence halls, which are intended to foster an environment of virtuous living. On-campus housing offers a variety of options ranging from the traditional to suites and apartments. "Most of the residence halls are nice and comfortable enough to make your own impermanent home," says a politics major.

"Most of the residence halls are nice and comfortable enough to make your own impermanent home."

Campus fare is a mixed blessing: "The dining is unlimited, which is awesome for big appetites," says one student. "The problem is that it's overpriced and bland." Shuttle buses and safety escort services are provided as part of campus security, and students agree that they feel safe on campus, as long as they are careful. The Peer Educators Empowering Respectful Students (PEERS) group helps to raise awareness about sexual assault prevention.

When students want to explore the city, they need only walk to the Brookland-CUA Metrorail stop adjacent to campus and then enjoy the ride. Capitol Hill is 15 minutes away and the stylish Georgetown area, with its chic restaurants and nightspots, a half hour. "Because we're in the city, most students would rather get dressed up to go out to a bar than to a house party," observes a senior. CUA does not have a Greek system, and most students agree that school policies are effective in curbing underage drinking. On campus, students have their choice of more than 100 clubs and organizations. Campus Ministry offers numerous opportunities to engage in faith and service through frequent community service events, student retreats, summer mission trips, and other programs. Forty-six percent of students regularly participate in community service. Annual activities on campus include Fall Festival, the Capital Fest concert featuring a well-known band, Mistletoe Ball, Founders Day Ball, and Cardinalpalooza, a popular celebration of the end of the academic year.

Capitol Hill is 15 minutes away and the stylish Georgetown area, with its chic restaurants and nightspots, a half hour.

CUA's Cardinals compete in Division III. Women's lacrosse has won 13 Landmark Conference championships in the last 15 years, and other recent winners include women's field hockey and men's soccer, swimming and diving, and lacrosse. Intramural and club-level programs attract plenty of interest, too, especially basketball, indoor soccer, and ultimate Frisbee.

When the idea of a Catholic university was first raised, the man who would become the university's first rector, Bishop John Joseph Keane, argued for an institution that would "exercise a dominant influence in the world's future" with a superior intellectual foundation. Now, 136 years later, CUA offers students a wealth of preprofessional courses spanning the arts and sciences. Even as it grapples with how best to express and uphold its Catholic identity, the university remains dedicated to its mission of providing "scholarly research, education, and service in the light of the Catholic intellectual tradition."

Overlaps

Notre Dame, Villanova, Fordham, Loyola University Maryland, Saint Joseph's University, Georgetown, American University, Fairfield

Centre College

600 West Walnut, Danville, KY 40422

Centre may not be the most famous institution of higher learning in Kentucky, but it is certainly the best, and it offers college the way it used to be—football games, Greek row, and a decades-old tradition of streaking through campus and circling a statue of a flame (nude). There is also the closeness between students and faculty that comes with a student body of 1,300. Compare to Sewanee, Rhodes, and Davidson.

Centre College, the only independent school in Kentucky with a Phi Beta Kappa chapter, has produced two-thirds of the state's Rhodes scholars over the last 40 years. But the school is not all work and no play. It's also a retro throwback to the way college used to be, with Friday night parties on Greek row and Saturday afternoon football games. Centre's small size offers an intimate classroom environment. And its liberal arts focus means that despite Centre's southern location, students are progressive, intellectual, and perhaps more well-rounded than their peers at neighboring schools.

Located in the heart of Kentucky Bluegrass country, Centre's campus is a mix of old Greek Revival and attractive modern buildings. More than 14 of them are listed on the National Registry of Historic Places, a fact that's less surprising when you know that Centre, which dates to 1819, is the 48th oldest college in the United States. The college is home to four LEED-certified buildings, including two at the Gold level. New facilities include a 135,000-square-foot athletics complex featuring an aquatic center, an indoor track and turf field, a strength and conditioning center, and a nutrition and wellness center.

Centre's general education curriculum requires coursework in each of the college's three academic divisions: arts and humanities, social studies, and science and mathematics. Students take three Doctrina Lux Mentis courses (named after the school's motto, Latin for "Learning is the light of the mind"), beginning with a two-course sequence in the first year that emphasizes written communication in the fall and oral communication in the spring. The third course, taken junior or senior year, focuses on interdisciplinary thinking and serves as a capstone experience. Additionally, all students complete an experiential learning component, such as independent research or community-based learning.

> **"Our small class sizes allow professors to really feed off of the energy and needs of the class."**

Centre's most popular majors are economics and finance, international studies, mathematics, and psychology. Other strong programs include politics, behavioral neuroscience, and English. Art is solid, too, and glassblowing enthusiasts will find one of the few fully equipped undergraduate facilities for their pursuit in the nation. Centre launched a new business major in 2021. A 3–2 program sends aspiring engineers on to one of four major universities, including the University of Kentucky and Vanderbilt. Sixty-six percent of classes have fewer than 20 students. "My professors took the time to really get to know me and my learning style," says a politics major.

Website: www.centre.edu
Location: Small Town
Private
Total Enrollment: 1,320
Undergraduates: 1,320
Male/Female: 48/52
Financial Aid: 96%
Pell Grant: 22%
Expense: Pr $ $
Student Loans: 51%
Average Debt: $ $
Applicants: 2,567
Accepted: 68%
Enrolled: 22%
Grad in 6 Years: 86%
Returning Freshmen: 89%
Academics: ✐ ✐ ✐ ½
Social: ☎ ☎ ☎
Q of L: ★ ★ ★
Admissions: (800) 423-6236
Email Address: admission@ centre.edu

Strong Programs:
Politics
Behavioral Neuroscience
English
Art
Economics and Finance
International Studies
Mathematics
Psychology

"Our small class sizes allow professors to really feed off of the energy and needs of the class and make it a more personal environment."

The Centre Commitment guarantees students an internship or research experience, a study abroad opportunity, and a degree in four years—or the college will cover the cost of a fifth year of study. Approximately 65 percent of students choose to engage in an internship, 37 percent perform collaborative research with faculty, and 85 percent take advantage of Centre's extensive study abroad programs. Centre runs 13 regular semester-long programs for students in all majors in 10 countries, including a new program in Bhutan, in addition to several shorter options offered during the January term. A study-away semester in Washington, D.C., combines coursework with internships. A psychology major highly recommends the college's career services: "They have monthly programs on 'adulting' and provide constant assistance and support in the job-search process."

Fifty-three percent of Centre students hail from Kentucky, and 4 percent arrive from foreign nations. Black students represent 6 percent of the student body, Asian Americans 4 percent, Hispanics/Latinos 7 percent, and multiracial students 4 percent. Politically, the atmosphere is mostly liberal and "not hugely charged," says an international studies major. Increasing diversity among faculty and staff has been a particular focus of late. Centre offers merit-based awards averaging $26,500, but no athletic scholarships. Through the Grissom Scholars Program, 10 incoming first-generation students per year are awarded full-tuition scholarships plus $5,000 to support study abroad, research, or an internship.

> **New facilities include a 135,000-square-foot athletics complex featuring an aquatic center, an indoor track, and a nutrition and wellness center.**

> **"[By senior year] I felt cultivated as a public speaker, a problem solver, and a leader."**

Virtually all students live on campus, thanks to a four-year residential requirement that students say makes for a strong sense of community. "As you gain seniority, your housing options get nicer and nicer," explains a sophomore. Suite- and townhouse-style accommodations are available for upperclassmen, and small Greek houses are an option for some, but most members of Greek life live in the residence halls. Students dine in one main dining hall, Cowan, and three café-style eateries, including Einstein Bros. Bagels, which recently opened in the library. "Cowan offers many selections, except on weekends," notes a senior. Students give high ratings to campus safety.

Greek life is the center of the social scene, with 37 percent of men and 42 percent of women joining up, and their parties are open to all. "Alcohol is a large part of the weekend social life here for many students," says a senior. The Student Activity Council sponsors a variety of alternatives, such as free midnight movies at the local theater and events like comedians, karaoke, and laser tag. Students also get free admission to Centre's separately endowed Norton Center for the Arts, a palatial, 1,500-seat auditorium that brings major musicals, concerts, and other performances to campus. Homecoming in the fall and Carnival in the spring are big annual events. Campus superstitions involve placing pennies on the toe of the Abraham Lincoln statue for good luck on exams, and avoiding stepping on the Centre Seal so as not to fail them. But Centre's most hallowed (unofficial) tradition is "Running the Flame" (remember the school motto?), which has students dashing from their residence halls to a large sculpture of a flame in the center of campus, circling it three times, and running back—"naked, of course." Community service through the Greek system, Habitat for Humanity, or other organizations is another popular activity. Danville (population 17,000) offers some small-town charm, but there is more to do in Lexington and Louisville, both within an hour's drive, and it's easy to get to the countryside for camping, fishing, and other outdoor pursuits.

Centre's football team has been around for more than a century, and while it now competes against regional opponents in Division III, that wasn't always the

> **The Centre Commitment guarantees students an internship or research experience, a study abroad opportunity, and a degree in four years.**

case. In 1921 the Colonels beat then-powerhouse Harvard, six to zero, a triumph that has been called the greatest sports upset in the first half of the 20th century. Nowadays, Rhodes College and nearby Transylvania University are Centre's key rivals. Men's and women's soccer, track and field, and cross-country are particularly competitive. A majority of the student body regularly participates in the intramural program, with flag football, soccer, and basketball drawing the most players.

Centre College often takes visitors by surprise. Although situated in a quaint, historic setting, much of the campus has a fresh, modern feel. Students come here for a well-rounded liberal arts education yet receive plenty of real-world preparation along the way. "By the time I reached my senior year," recalls a math major, "I felt cultivated as a public speaker, a problem solver, and a leader." With faculty who care about forming lasting friendships with students and a commitment to providing hands-on learning opportunities, this undiscovered gem may be worth a look.

> ## Overlaps
>
> **Rhodes, Sewanee, Furman, Wofford, Davidson, Kenyon, University of Kentucky, Transylvania**

If You Apply To ›

Centre: Early decision, early action, regular decision. Accepts the Common Application. Please consult Centre's website for the most up-to-date information regarding standardized test requirements.

Champlain College

251 South Willard Street, Burlington, VT 05401

A small college with a unique "upside-down" approach to blending professional education and the liberal arts. Champlain's major academic strengths are game design, whose students tend to shape the campus culture, as well as business and information technology. A good fit for students eager to get started in a career but not a great place to explore options and find yourself. Social life revolves around student-friendly Burlington, and nearby ski slopes beckon. Low graduation rate is a challenge.

Champlain is an up-and-coming small college, situated on a hill overlooking Vermont's scenic Lake Champlain, that has set out to reinvent the relationship between professional studies and the liberal arts through its so-called upside-down curriculum. Instead of following the traditional academic path—two years of general education courses followed by two years of in-depth study in a major—students at Champlain immediately pursue both their major and a highly structured liberal arts curriculum and then continue this pattern simultaneously for all four years. This approach appeals to career-minded students who still appreciate the value of a strong dose of the liberal arts.

The college, whose roots date to 1878, sits on 22 acres in the historic Hill Section of Burlington, adjacent to the University of Vermont. The core academic campus consists of a mix of lovely restored Victorian mansions and complementary modern structures of brick with slate roofs and green trim. The adjacent "lakeside" campus houses the Leahy Center for Digital Investigation and a variety of administrative facilities, while a "downtown" campus, connected to the academic core by shuttle buses, provides housing and dining for 300 upperclassmen. The Center for Communication and Creative Media, a 75,000-square-foot facility, offers game and audio labs, studio spaces, and a traditional and digital photo lab.

> **"[Professors bring] experience that the students can tap into to expand their own knowledge."**

> **Website**: www.champlain.edu
> **Location**: Small City
> **Private**
> **Total Enrollment**: 2,256
> **Undergraduates**: 2,220
> **Male/Female**: 60/40
> **Financial Aid**: 89%
> **Pell Grant**: 23%
> **Expense**: Pr $
> **Student Loans**: 72%
> **Average Debt**: $ $ $ $
> **Applicants**: 6,444
> **Accepted**: 62%
> **Enrolled**: 11%
> **Grad in 6 Years**: 68%
> **Returning Freshmen**: 69%
> **Academics**: ✍ ✍ ✍
> **Social**: ☎ ☎ ☎
> **Q of L**: ★ ★ ★

(continued)

Admissions: (802) 625-0201
Email Address: admission@
champlain.edu

Strong Programs:
Computer and Digital Forensics
Graphic Design and Visual
  Communication
Game Design
Business
Law
Computer Networking and
  Cybersecurity
Computer Science and
  Innovation
Game Programming

Students at Champlain pursue both their major and a highly structured liberal arts curriculum simultaneously for all four years.

Champlain's distinctive curriculum is built around three legs ("Education in 3-D," to use the local lingo). The first leg is professional programs. Students apply to one of four academic divisions—Stiller School of Business; Communication and Creative Media (CCM); Education and Human Studies; or Information Technology and Sciences—and then select a major in that division. For example, CCM, the largest division, offers 11 choices, with broadcast media production, filmmaking, and professional writing among them. Students disillusioned by their initial choices can easily transfer to another major within their division, but switching to another division is harder. The second leg, the liberal arts component, is a highly structured set of Core courses

> **"You will be engaged in discussions and group projects almost every day."**

taught on an interdisciplinary basis by professors from all departments. Students pursue a series of courses over three years that focus in progressive fashion on the nature of the self, concepts of a just and sustainable community in the West, and global themes, such as human rights. Seniors complete a capstone experience that integrates learning from their professional, liberal arts, and out-of-classroom experiences. The school argues that four years of working simultaneously in a professional field and the liberal arts gives students the broad thinking and learning skills that will serve them well beyond their first jobs. The third and final curricular leg is the InSight career and personal finance program, an array of workshops, company visits, and other activities that teach such real-world skills as developing a résumé and cover letter, setting a budget, and earning a good credit score. "Champlain puts in extra effort to make sure its students are prepared for their career field of interest," remarks a senior.

Professors bring "a great deal of passion, dedication, and experience that the students can tap into to expand their own knowledge," says one student. Eighty-three percent of classes at Champlain have fewer than 20 students, and all are taught by professors (who are not awarded tenure) or adjuncts, with no teaching assistants. A senior says, "From your Core classes to your major-specific classes, you will be engaged in discussions and group projects almost every day." Computer and digital forensics, graphic design and visual communication, and game design are highly regarded fields, and the well-established business school offers seven majors, from accounting to game production management. Seniors in game-development-related majors often compete against one another to complete projects for school-sponsored events. Students interested in legal concerns like contracts and intellectual property can prepare for law school by pursuing Champlain's unusual B.A. degree in law. The majors with the highest enrollment are computer networking and cybersecurity, game design, computer science and innovation, and game programming. Many students also take minors in areas such as global studies and social justice. Newer options include majors in app development, applied sustainability, and marketing communication.

Virtually all students participate in some sort of internship at some point. Study abroad, which draws roughly half of the students, plays an important role at Champlain, and the college offers free passports to students who do not already

> **"Most of the campus is comprised of geeks and gamers."**

have them. The college maintains international satellite campuses in Dublin, from which students have easy access to the rest of Europe, and Montreal, a major global center for the game industry. Dozens of other students go abroad through the school's internship sites in Shanghai or through Champlain's service-learning program. There are no honors programs, and most graduates head for the job market rather than graduate or professional schools.

Twenty-four percent of students are native Vermonters, with the rest hailing mainly from the East Coast and Midwest. Champlain students are a fairly homogeneous crowd, with Black students accounting for 6 percent of the total, Hispanics/Latinos 8 percent, Asian Americans 4 percent, multiracial students 4 percent, and international students less than 1 percent. Largely because of the nature of the curriculum, men outnumber women by a ratio of three to two. "Most of the campus is comprised of geeks and gamers," says a student. "There are many skiers and snowboarders, of course, and a great deal of people who care about the environment or social issues." The school awards merit scholarships averaging $18,900.

The college maintains international satellite campuses in Dublin and Montreal, a major global center for the game industry.

"Champlain's first-year residence halls are renovated Victorian mansions that have modern technology and safety features with the old charm preserved," explains a senior. Sophomores and upperclassmen can choose among well-maintained traditional dorms, some quite new, that feature tuning and repair facilities for bikes, skis, and skateboards, or they can live in an off-campus apartment hall or find their own off-campus digs. Overall, 72 percent of undergrads reside in college-owned housing. Students take their meals at a single dining hall where, this being Vermont, the emphasis is on fresh, local, and healthy foods and sustainable practices: there are no trays, and paper plates or plastic utensils are definite no-nos. One

"Hard-core party folks go to our neighbors, UVM."

student reports, "Our school's Public Safety department is incredibly friendly and always shows up quickly (even if you just locked yourself out of your room)."

"Because our campus is so small, most of the social life is off campus," says a marketing major, "whether it's downtown on Church Street, by the lake, a friend's apartment, or a concert." The campus is dry and policies are enforced; in the absence of fraternities and sororities, says a sophomore, "hard-core party folks go to our neighbors, UVM." The college sponsors roughly 50 student clubs and organizes a range of activities on and off campus. A small city of 45,000 residents, Burlington is near the top of everyone's list of best college towns. The Church Street pedestrian mall, just below the campus, offers an array of cafés and shops for all tastes, as well as a vibrant music scene and abundant nightlife, and there is a park and bike path that runs along the lake's waterfront.

No one seems to mind that Champlain has no varsity sports (except for a new varsity eSports team).

No one seems to mind that Champlain has no varsity sports (except for a new varsity eSports team). But it does have a mascot named Chauncey T. Beaver as well as plenty of intramural options for all skill levels, including soccer, basketball, and dodgeball, and a rugby club that competes against other schools; nearly a third of Champlain students participate. Not surprisingly for a school full of gamers, Humans vs. Zombies and Quadball (formerly known as Quidditch) are popular. Annual traditions include the Rail Jam skiing and snowboarding competition in the fall and the Spring Meltdown carnival just before final exams. The end of the year brings the Game Development Senior Show, where graduating seniors show off their projects to the college community, family members, and company recruiters.

Administrators at Champlain are sensitive about the fact that only 68 percent of entering students graduate within six years. One contributing factor, students suggest, is the need to plunge immediately into a professional field that may not be a good fit. "Students end up switching out of the program or out of the school, especially if they have trouble deciding what major they want," says a sophomore. Other students point to the heavy workload in some majors and the lack of cultural diversity as possible factors. "The gaming culture might be a deterrent to those who aren't interested in video games," says a game art and animation major. Administrators are working hard to mitigate these stressors, emphasizing well-being—including making Wednesdays free of daytime classes to give students time during the week to "recharge and rejuvenate the mind, body, and spirit"—and bolstering student support services.

For gaming enthusiasts, techies, creatives, and other career-oriented students, Champlain is a small school with a big vision of how to refashion the relationship

Overlaps

Saint Michael's, Wentworth Institute of Technology, Worcester Polytechnic, Salve Regina, Roger Williams, University of Vermont, Rochester Institute of Technology, Southern New Hampshire

between professional training and the liberal arts. It offers a unique option for students who have a strong, focused interest in its professional majors and who are eager to "press start" on their careers.

If You Apply To ›

Champlain: Early decision, regular decision. SATs or ACTs: optional. Accepts the Common Application with supplement. Apply to particular academic division. Some majors require portfolio submission.

Chapman University

One University Drive, Orange, CA 92866

Chapman sits at the hub of Orange County and a stone's throw from L.A. Has parlayed its O.C. location into burgeoning popularity in film, television, and the performing arts. Those without showbiz aspirations can opt for strong programs in business, communication studies, or biology. Disneyland is in the neighborhood, but you need a car or a ride to get there.

Website: www.chapman.edu
Location: Suburban
Private
Total Enrollment: 8,919
Undergraduates: 7,148
Male/Female: 39/61
Financial Aid: 87%
Pell Grant: 18%
Expense: Pr $ $ $ $
Student Loans: 47%
Average Debt: $ $
Applicants: 15,098
Accepted: 60%
Enrolled: 18%
Grad in 6 Years: 80%
Returning Freshmen: 92%
Academics: ✐ ✐ ✐
Social: ☎ ☎ ☎
Q of L: ★ ★ ★
Admissions: (714) 997-6711
Email Address: admit@
 chapman.edu

Strong Programs:
Film and Television Production
Writing for Film and Television
Performing Arts
Business Administration
Communication Studies
Biology

Although best known as a Southern Californian mecca for budding filmmakers to hone their craft, Chapman University continues to stake its claim as a comprehensive institution that happens to offer one of the nation's best film programs—rather than a film school that also happens to offer other majors. Chapman boasts stellar programs in business and has increased its emphasis on health sciences and technology. It also facilitates countless internships to send its students out into the workforce with real-world experience.

Founded in 1861, Chapman is one of the oldest private universities in California. Originally called Hesperian College, the school was renamed in 1934 in honor of C. C. Chapman, an Orange County entrepreneur and benefactor of the school. The beautiful residential campus, situated on 80 tree-lined acres, features a mixture of landmark historic buildings and state-of-the-art facilities. It is located in the historic Old Towne district of Orange, near outstanding beaches, Disneyland, and the world-class cultural offerings of Orange County and Los Angeles. Recent construction includes the Swenson Hall of Engineering, which opened in 2021 as part of the Keck Center for Science and Engineering, and the Simon Center for Dance.

Regardless of major, all students complete a four-part general education program: a First-Year Foundations Course taken in the fall; six inquiry categories (natural science, quantitative reasoning, writing, social sciences, values and ethics, and artistic studies); a Global Citizen cluster (two courses in global studies, one in civic issues, and a language course); and a mini-minor, minor, or second major. Chapman's first-year experience program, Fenestra (Latin for "window"), encourages students to approach their first year as a "window of opportunity"; the program involves a weeklong orientation and special workshops, field trips, and social activities held throughout the year.

> **"At Chapman, you are going to have an in-depth and personalized education."**

The most popular majors are business administration, psychology, strategic and corporate communication, communication studies, and film and television production. Dodge College of Film and Media Arts is a comprehensive, production-based school that offers such majors as news/broadcast journalism and documentary, writing for film and television, public relations and advertising, and creative producing, as well as internships and other active learning opportunities. Emerging entrepreneurs can take advantage of a well-stocked portfolio of business programs through the Argyros School of Business and Economics. The Economic Science Institute allows for the study of experimental economics under the direction of Nobel laureate Dr. Vernon Smith and encompasses fields as diverse as finance, engineering, neuroscience, computer science, and philosophy, among others. Notable programs in music, theatre, and dance involve frequent national and international performance components. Among the sciences, biology and health sciences are solid. The fledgling Fowler School of Engineering offers undergraduate degrees in computer engineering, computer science, data analytics, electrical engineering, and software engineering. Accelerated degree programs allow students to earn a bachelor's and a master's in five years in several disciplines, including pharmaceutical sciences.

(continued)
Health Sciences
Psychology

"Regardless of the course of study you are taking at Chapman, you are going to have an in-depth and personalized education," says a creative producing major. Forty-six percent of classes have fewer than 20 students. Freshmen are taught by professors—there are no teaching assistants—and a sophomore says, "My professors have been supportive, understanding, intellectual, friendly, and innovative." Students interested in conducting faculty-mentored research can apply to the SURF (Summer Undergraduate Research Fellowship) program, which awards up to $4,000 in funding to selected fellows. An English and sociology major highly recommends the Honors Program, which allows students to "dive deeply into very niche topics" as well as "build and teach their own classes to their peers." Those seeking a global learning experience can choose from semester-long study abroad programs, in addition to short-term, faculty-led travel courses and international summer internships; 42 percent of students avail themselves of these opportunities. As for career services, a junior says, "I have had over five internships in two years, and most of that can be attributed to the responsiveness and knowledge of the Office of Career and Professional Development."

Dodge College of Film and Media Arts is a comprehensive, production-based school that offers such majors as writing for film and television.

"Students are active, social, and friendly," says a data analytics major, "and they certainly enjoy the warm weather." Sixty-three percent of Chapman's largely affluent student body hail from California, and 3 percent are international. Black students constitute 2 percent of the population, Asian Americans 16 percent, Hispanics/Latinos 18 percent, and multiracial students 8 percent. Chapman recently opened a

"Students are active, social, and friendly, and they certainly enjoy the warm weather."

Cross-Cultural Center, and a senior says, "Discussions of diversity, tolerance, inclusion, and safety are common on campus." Eligible undergraduates receive merit scholarships worth an average of $20,400, but since Chapman is a Division III school, there are no athletic scholarships.

Thirty-eight percent of Chapman students reside on campus. First-years are housed in residence halls based on their chosen academic program; one student explains, "This allows for students to know their peers on day one of classes and always have a study partner throughout the semester." Meals at the Randall Dining Commons are described as tasty and diverse. Campus safety receives positive reviews, and the CARES (Creating a Rape-Free Environment for Students) student organization is active in raising awareness about campus sexual assault.

Students flock to the homecoming celebration's chili cook-off and fireworks and WinterFest, complete with fake snow and a visit from Santa.

Twenty-two percent of the men join fraternities, and sororities attract 35 percent of the women; all members of the Greek community are required to perform community service, and Greek life doesn't dominate the social scene. A junior describes Chapman's off-campus party culture as "intimate," adding, "Students prefer to keep it to a lower scale, mostly due to the lack of a Greek row." Students also enjoy a plenitude of school-sponsored events, including movies, dances, museum visits, hiking trips, and, of course, sunny beach excursions. Every year, students flock to the homecoming celebration's chili cook-off and fireworks, WinterFest (complete with fake snow and a visit from Santa), the Spring Sizzle festival, and Midnight Breakfast during finals week.

The city of Orange (population 140,000) is a college town only in the technical sense of the term. "It's actually a very quiet city," says a junior. The Old Towne district is well known as "the Antique Capital of California," although several trendy restaurants, brew pubs, and boutiques have opened their doors in the last few years. When students grow weary of the area, they take advantage of the pristine Southern California weather to explore the great outdoors or take trips to Disneyland, L.A., or San Diego.

The Chapman Panthers compete in the Division III Southern California Intercollegiate Athletic Conference. Football, baseball, and men's and women's basketball are among the most competitive teams. The Chapman Dance Team has brought home several national championships in the last decade. Intramurals and club sports draw a quarter of the student body; intramural basketball and soccer are the most popular, and the men's club lacrosse team is nationally competitive.

Students at Chapman are expected not only to hit the books but also to actively express their creativity through hands-on learning, on-campus involvement, and forays into the real world. In return, they are rewarded with a supportive environment that both nurtures and challenges them every step of the way.

Overlaps

Loyola Marymount, Santa Clara, University of San Diego, Elon, Pepperdine, University of Southern California, UCLA, NYU

If You Apply To ›

Chapman: Early decision, early action, regular decision. SATs or ACTs: optional. Accepts the Common Application. Art and talent-based programs require submission of a creative supplement.

College of Charleston

Charleston, SC 29424

A public school one-third the size of the University of South Carolina that blends a small-college feel with the advantages of a midsized, urban university. College of Charleston compares to William & Mary in both scale and historic surroundings but is far less rigorous academically. Offers business, education, and the liberal arts and sciences. Location a feast for history and culinary buffs.

Website: www.cofc.edu
Location: Small City
Public
Total Enrollment: 9,490
Undergraduates: 9,184
Male/Female: 33/67
Financial Aid: 77%
Pell Grant: 20%
Expense: Pub $ $
Student Loans: 54%
Average Debt: $ $ $
Applicants: 20,484
Accepted: 76%

Whether sampling the traditional Lowcountry cuisine or delving into the wide range of courses offered at this strong liberal arts and sciences institution, students at the College of Charleston know they are getting a solid education based on creative expression, intellectual freedom, and hands-on learning experiences. Founded in 1770 as Colonial South Carolina's first college, CofC's original commitment to the liberal arts and sciences and to the citizens of the region has helped it become a well-respected institution throughout the Southeast. And the location only adds to the experience, providing opportunities for research and internships, and a robust social scene.

The 13th oldest college in the country, CofC was founded as a private college and, after a number of identity changes, became a state university exactly 200 years later. Located in Charleston's famous Historic District, the campus features many of the city's most venerable buildings. More than 80 of its buildings are former private residences, ranging from the typical Charleston "single" house to the Victorian, and the clap-clap of horse-drawn carriages bearing tourists is a routine sight. The campus is within easy walking distance of the city's shopping and restaurant district and offers proximity to beaches. Cistern Yard, the area in front of Randolph Hall lined with moss-draped live oaks, is a student gathering point and the site of May graduation ceremonies. The campus has received countless awards for its design and has been designated a national arboretum and a National Historic Landmark.

The college's core curriculum is rooted in the liberal arts, sciences, and professional programs. The focus is on the development of problem-solving and critical-thinking skills, as well as taking an entrepreneurial approach to addressing global issues like climate change, social injustice, and economic inequality. Each student is required to satisfy credits in English, history, mathematics or logic, social science, natural sciences, humanities, and foreign language. All new students attend Convocation, where they are introduced to the college's academic traditions, and freshmen from underrepresented groups can participate in several support programs designed to ensure their successful transition to college. All freshmen take part in the First-Year Experience and choose between seminar and learning community options; sample seminars include Charleston Writers, Black Lives, and Paddling Toward Sustainability.

"The city is a social playground for college students."

Biology, chemistry, and psychology are some of the strongest programs; many graduates go on to the Medical University of South Carolina, a few blocks down the street. Marine biology, German, and arts management are also strengths. The most popular majors are psychology, business administration, communication, biology, and public health. New majors in electrical engineering and environmental geosciences have been added. "Courses are challenging but always engaging," says a senior. Thirty-two percent of all classes enroll fewer than 20 students, and while students say the quality of instruction can be hit-or-miss, a communication major comments, "The majority of my professors have been unforgettable mentors to me and have played a critical role in my learning."

About 850 students enroll in the Honors College, where they are given a more demanding workload, including a culminating Bachelor's Essay that is undertaken with the support of a faculty mentor. The Undergraduate Research and Creative Activities program awards competitive grants to fund student/faculty research projects. Roughly a quarter of undergrads study internationally; the college sponsors more than 30 faculty-led study abroad programs, as well as several weeklong spring break trips that are tied to First-Year Seminar courses. Students may also choose from hundreds of additional options through preapproved providers. Many performing arts majors take advantage of internships with Spoleto Festival USA, Charleston's annual international arts festival. The city's growing biomedicine, tech, and aerospace industries also provide opportunities for research and internships.

All freshmen take part in the First-Year Experience and choose between seminar and learning community options.

According to an English major, CofC's student body is "pretty accepting, artistic, and fun." Forty-two percent of students hail from out of state, and another 1 percent from foreign countries. The administration has been pushing to increase the proportion of students of color; currently, Black students account for 6 percent of the student body, Asian Americans 2 percent, Hispanics/Latinos 7 percent, and multiracial students 4 percent. Racial tension in the city of Charleston, known for its history as a major slave-trading port, has sparked "some protests and disagreements" on campus, says a junior, but overall, the political climate is left-leaning and usually relatively calm. The Race and Social Justice Initiative and the Center for the Study of

"There's so much history here that you can't help but feel like you're making some yourself."

(continued)

Enrolled: 16%
Grad in 6 Years: 67%
Returning Freshmen: 83%
Academics: ✍ ✍ ✍
Social: ☎ ☎ ☎ ☎
Q of L: ★ ★ ★ ★
Admissions: (843) 953-5670
Email Address: admissions@cofc.edu

Strong Programs:
Biology
Chemistry
Psychology
Marine Biology
German
Arts Management
Business Administration
Communication

Slavery raise awareness of racial injustice and the legacies of slavery through research, public events, exhibitions, and other projects. The college offers merit scholarships averaging $13,300 and more than 100 athletic scholarships.

"On-campus housing at CofC is very nice, with choices between dormitories, apartments, or historic houses," says a student. Thirty-two percent of students live on campus, and students say more would stay if there were space to accommodate them. Off-campus housing can get quite expensive, although the college has acquired multiple housing buildings within walking distance of campus in order to help ease the strain. Dining services provide options for all types of eaters, including vegetarian, vegan, and kosher fare. "The omelets at Liberty are what I live for!" cheers a junior. As for security, "Being in the heart of a city can sometimes be overwhelming, but generally, campus feels safe," says one student.

Charleston's growing biomedicine, tech, and aerospace industries provide opportunities for research and internships.

Sixteen percent of the men and 19 percent of the women belong to fraternities and sororities, respectively. A junior says, "Greek groups are the gatekeepers of party culture at CofC." More than 240 student organizations help provide alternatives, and students enjoy Charleston's sporting events, concerts, and numerous festivals. As one student puts it, "The city is a social playground for college students. There are tons of restaurants, events to attend, and beautiful architecture to enjoy." On weekends, students can head to beaches such as Folly Beach, Sullivan's Island, and Isle of Palms, which are merely minutes away. For those who don't mind a drive, there's "the Grand Strand," Myrtle Beach, 90 miles north, Savannah and Hilton Head to the south, and Atlanta to the west.

The absence of a football team is a common gripe among students, but other athletic teams are popular, none more so than basketball. The College of Charleston is a Division I school, and several Cougar teams are competitive in the Colonial Athletic Association conference, including men's basketball and men's and women's golf. The sailing team is a top performer nationally. The intramural program offers eight team sports throughout the year, and basketball and soccer are the most popular, both in terms of participation and competitive fervor; more than 25 club sports are also available.

Overlaps

Appalachian State, James Madison, University of Mary Washington, UNC Wilmington, Elon, University of South Carolina, Clemson, Coastal Carolina

The College of Charleston has become the finest public liberal arts and sciences institution in South Carolina, propelled by its historic setting, an honors college, opportunities for internships and study abroad, and a healthy social life. "There's so much history here that you can't help but feel like you're making some yourself," muses an anthropology and biology major. "There's no pressure to be some world-moving individual, but there's all the support in the world to be different, to be you, and to be the best you possible."

If You Apply To ›

Charleston: Early decision, early action, regular decision. Accepts the Common Application with supplement. Application includes optional questions regarding preferred first name, birth sex, and gender identity. Please consult Charleston's website for the most up-to-date information regarding standardized test requirements.

University of Chicago

Rosenwald Hall 105, 1101 East 58th Street, Chicago, IL 60637

Traditionally known as a haven for true intellectuals who enjoy nothing more than the chance to debate a fresh idea. The Common Core remains the intellectual heart of the school, but Chicago has worked hard to shed its reputation as the place "where fun comes to die." Recent investments in dormitory life, the arts, and athletic facilities—coupled with more aggressive recruiting—have helped cement UChicago's status alongside the top Ivies and Stanford. Quarter system can be stressful.

The University of Chicago attracts students eager to move beyond the cliquishness of high school and the superficial trappings of Ivy League résumé building—the kids more concerned about learning for learning's sake than about getting a job after graduation, though they're certainly capable of the latter. "'Life of the Mind' is taken very seriously," says a student. "The academic atmosphere extends beyond the classroom, and most people like it that way." Still, administrators have realized that in the 21st century, even the best schools cannot survive on intellectual might alone. To make UChicago more attractive, they've broadened the offerings in the core curriculum, expanded study abroad programs and career advising, and completed a bevy of new facilities. The result? Applications have doubled in the last decade and enrollment is surging. Says a freshman, "The fact that college here is a good time just makes us that much happier."

The university's 217-acre, tree-lined campus sits in Hyde Park, an eclectic community on Chicago's South Side, surrounded by neighborhoods on three sides and Lake Michigan on the other. One of 77 city neighborhoods, Hyde Park "is pretty intellectual," says one student, noting that "two-thirds of our faculty live here." Streets are lined with brownstones, rowhouses, and townhouses, giving way to luxury high-rises with beautiful views as you get closer to the lake; the city's

> **"The academic atmosphere extends beyond the classroom, and most people like it that way."**

Museum of Science and Industry is within spitting distance. The campus itself is self-contained and architecturally magnificent. The main quads are steel-gray Gothic—gargoyles and all—and other buildings were designed by the likes of Frank Lloyd Wright, Eero Saarinen, and Mies van der Rohe. The Regenstein Library (known as "the Reg") is a national treasure, symbolically located in the heart of the campus. Next to the Reg is the Mansueto Library, a geodesic dome.

Founded in 1890 thanks to John D. Rockefeller and Marshall Field largesse, UChicago has historically drawn praise for its graduate programs, but in recent years the undergraduate college has flourished, competing successfully with the likes of Stanford, Harvard, and Princeton. To that end, the university remains unequivocally committed to the view that a solid foundation in the liberal arts is the best preparation for future study or work and, moreover, that theory is better than practice. Thus, music students study musicology, but also learn calculus, along with everyone else. Regardless of major, 15 to 18 of a student's 42 courses fall under general education requirements called the Common Core, which is one of the most comprehensive sets of distribution requirements anywhere. (The precise number of courses in the Core depends on how much foreign language instruction a student needs to reach proficiency.)

Other Core requirements include courses in the sciences and math, humanities, arts, social sciences, and a sequence of study in a specific civilization. There is a required writing tutorial as well. Sound intense? Well, yes, students say it is, especially because UChicago pioneered the quarter system, whereby class material

Website: www.uchicago.edu
Location: City Outskirts
Private
Total Enrollment: 12,918
Undergraduates: 7,511
Male/Female: 52/48
Financial Aid: 57%
Pell Grant: 14%
Expense: Pr $ $ $ $
Student Loans: 15%
Average Debt: $ $
Applicants: 37,958
Accepted: 6%
Enrolled: 83%
Grad in 6 Years: 96%
Returning Freshmen: 99%
Academics: ✏️ ✏️ ✏️ ✏️ ✏️
Social: ☎ ☎ ☎
Q of L: ★ ★ ★ ★
Admissions: (773) 702-8650
Email Address: college
   admissions@uchicago.edu

Strong Programs:
Economics
Environmental and Urban
   Studies
Global Studies
Area Studies
Biological Sciences
Mathematics
Public Policy Studies
English

is presented over 10-week periods, with the first term starting in late September and ending in mid-December. In practice, this means that students take more classes over four years than they would on a semester-based system, with virtually uninterrupted work through the year, punctuated by a long summer vacation and three exam weeks. A senior says, "With an intense workload, it is important to practice time management in order to succeed. Once you get into the swing of things, however, everything is manageable (though still intense)." Seniors are also encouraged to do final-year projects. Classes are intimate, with 78 percent enrolling fewer than 20 students, and led by brilliant and distinguished faculty members who've won Nobel Prizes, Guggenheims, and other prestigious awards. Professors "expect your work to be completed at a very high level, which causes some assignments to take longer than they would somewhere else," says one mathematics major.

The economics department, which has produced numerous Nobel laureates, is known as a bastion of free market economics and is UChicago's main academic claim to fame. Popular majors include economics, biological sciences, mathematics, public policy studies, and English. Interdisciplinary majors in environmental and urban studies and global studies are notable. The university also prides itself on area studies programs, such as those focusing on East Asia, South Asia, the Middle East, and the Slavic countries. The Accelerated Medical Scholars Program allows exceptional undergrads to begin medical school during their fourth year, and similar joint-degree and professional options allow undergrads to engage with any of the university's other graduate and professional schools. The cross-subject molecular engineering major—the university's only undergraduate degree in engineering—focuses on "solving societal problems at the molecular level"; students delve into such topics as water conservation, quantum computing, and advances in biological immuno-engineering.

> "With an intense workload, it is important to practice time management."

> The university remains unequivocally committed to the view that theory is better than practice.

Students enjoy an abundance of research assistantships and opportunities for publication, even before they graduate. Through the Metcalf Internship Program, students have access to 3,000 fully funded internships that are offered exclusively to UChicago students. Established internships are available at the Argonne National Laboratory and Fermilab, both located in nearby suburbs, and at the UChicago-affiliated Marine Biological Laboratory in Woods Hole, Massachusetts. When Chicago gets too cold and snowy, students may take advantage of more than 60 study abroad programs, which reach most corners of the globe and include study at the university's centers in Hong Kong, Beijing, Delhi, and Paris. Financial aid applies to study abroad programs, and 40 percent of students take part. All students are assigned both an academic and a career advisor, and UChicago has one of the best career advising systems of any school, aimed at assuring that its graduating intellectuals can still get a job.

At UChicago, says a junior, "What brings together the student body is a love for learning and maybe just a bit of geekiness, whether that comes from a love of Plato or an obsession with big bang theory." Sixty-nine percent of undergraduates come from out of state, including many East Coasters with academic parents; another 16 percent are international. Just 6 percent of freshman applicants are accepted here, in part because the admissions office is wary of admitting students whom it thinks might not come. Asian Americans represent 20 percent of the total, Hispanics/Latinos 15 percent, Black students 6 percent, and multiracial students 7 percent. Students are quick to give voice to opinions and political allegiances. "It would be nice if there was a less hostile political climate on campus," laments one student. In a sign of UChicago's educational philosophy that attracted national attention

> "What brings together the student body is a love for learning and maybe just a bit of geekiness."

several years ago, incoming freshmen received a letter reiterating the university's commitment to freedom of speech and thought, rejecting "safe spaces" for the hypersensitive and cancelations of invitations to controversial speakers.

Admissions at UChicago are need-blind, and the university meets 100 percent of students' demonstrated need with financial aid packages that include grants instead of loans. The Odyssey Scholarship program offers generous financial aid packages, funding to support internships or study abroad, and other benefits to first-generation and lower-income students. Socioeconomic diversity is slowly inching upward—still, just 14 percent of incoming freshmen qualify for Pell Grants. The university has made a major effort in recent years to serve veterans, investing in dedicated housing facilities, academic advising, and career counseling for its veteran population.

UChicago guarantees on-campus housing for four years, and 59 percent of all undergrads live in the dorms. "Every incoming first-year has to live in a house," explains a student. "Houses here are like Hogwarts in the sense that students form very intense loyalty toward their house and therefore there is competition between houses." All halls are co-ed, though some offer single-sex floors, and each dorm is different—some house fewer than 100 people in traditional, shared double rooms without kitchens, while another has 700 beds organized into colorful suites. The recently built Woodlawn Residential Commons offers a dining facility and 11 college houses accommodating 1,200 undergrads. It is part of a long-term campaign to provide more on-campus housing. Still, "Hyde Park has tons of really cute, cheap apartments," reports one student, so many of the more "independent-minded" students move off campus. "The campus feels very safe," says one student. "Not only does UChicago employ its own police force, but security guards are stationed around the neighborhood to help increase the safety." Through the Sexual Assault Dean-on-Call program, students who have experienced assault can reach a trained campus official 24/7 for crisis assistance and continued support.

> **"The city of Chicago is the backyard for UChicago, and students are always exploring it."**

The UChicago social scene is varied, according to a senior. "There is always some sort of event going on around campus, be it a theater performance or an a cappella show, but the city of Chicago is the backyard for UChicago, and students are always exploring it." Indeed, the university's a cappella scene is one of the tops in the country, and the city offers museums galore; world-class symphony, opera, and dance; the Second City comedy improv troupe (invented by University of Chicago undergrads); professional spectator sports; and plenty of clubs and bars. The university provides students with free, unlimited access to all parts of the city via public transportation, and Arts Pass offers free or discounted student admission to city art, theater, and cultural events. Cars are a nice luxury (if you can find a parking place). Road trips are infrequent, but one popular destination is Ann Arbor, about five hours away, for concerts and more traditional collegiate fun at the University of Michigan. Greek life has a small presence on campus, with 8 percent of the men and 12 percent of the women joining local fraternities and sororities.

> **"[Scavenger Hunt is] a pumped-up version of a regular scavenger hunt, with a list of 300 bizarre items."**

Tradition is a hallmark at UChicago. Students have fond memories of freshman orientation, known as O-Week, an event administrators claim was invented at the university in 1934. In the winter, students head for the outdoor skating rink on the Midway, site of the 1893 World's Fair, for broomball. Students also celebrate the festival of Kuviasungnerk/Kangeiko ("Kuvia" for short), a week of early morning calisthenics and other activities, culminating in a Friday morning yoga session by Lake Michigan and a Polar Bear Run, where naked or seminaked Maroons dash across the academic quad. Each spring, students look forward to the four-day

Joint-degree and professional options allow undergrads to engage with any of the university's other graduate and professional schools.

The Metcalf Internship Program gives students access to 3,000 fully funded internships that are offered exclusively to UChicago students.

Scavenger Hunt ("Scav"), "a pumped-up version of a regular scavenger hunt, with a list of 300 bizarre items," says a sociology major. Campuswide games of Humans vs. Zombies are played once every quarter.

UChicago's Maroons compete in Division III, and the school belongs to the University Athletic Association, where rivals include Emory and Washington University in St. Louis. Aside from hitting the gridiron or the basketball court, "even the varsity athletes are Phi Beta Kappa (that is, very smart) and involved with university theater," a junior marvels. In fact, athletes here have a higher overall GPA than the student body as a whole. To everyone's surprise, the football team has had a couple of winning seasons. Consistently solid programs include women's basketball and men's and women's tennis, soccer, cross-country, and track and field. Intramurals draw heavy participation, with students competing on their house teams in sports ranging from the traditional (flag football, soccer, and volleyball) to the offbeat (inner-tube water polo, broomball, and archery). Thirty-nine club sports are available as well.

Although T-shirts lovingly mock the university's rigor ("Where Fun Comes to Die"), the University of Chicago has moved well beyond the Spartan attitudes of former president Robert Maynard Hutchins, who led UChicago from 1929 to 1951 and once told members of the football team that was about to be abolished, "When I feel like exercising, I just lie down until the feeling goes away." A major national force for the liberal arts, he also once declared, "My idea of education is to unsettle the minds of the young and inflame their intellects." UChicago undergraduates today are certainly more social and more heavily involved in extracurricular activities than their predecessors, but the university still occupies its distinctive historical academic niche. The prevailing culture remains highly academic, and the university draws strength from its role as a high-powered haven for superbright students, including those who lack the polished nonacademic credentials favored by admissions committees in places like Cambridge and New Haven. Students at UChicago continue to relish a different kind of fun.

Students have fond memories of freshman orientation, known as O-Week, an event administrators claim was invented at the university in 1934.

Overlaps

Columbia, Harvard, Yale, Stanford, University of Pennsylvania, Northwestern, Princeton, Cornell University

If You Apply To ›

UChicago: Early decision I and II, early action, regular decision. SATs or ACTs: optional. Accepts the Common Application with essay supplement. In lieu of essays, applicants may submit an Alternative Project (such as videos, artwork, photo essays, or poetry) as supplemental material.

University of Cincinnati

P.O. Box 210091, Cincinnati, OH 45221

In most states, UC would be a big enchilada. But with Ohio State two hours up the road and Miami of Ohio even closer, Cincinnati has to hustle to get its name out there. A pioneer along with Antioch in co-op education, it offers quality programs in everything from engineering to art—and a competitive men's basketball team to boot.

Website: www.uc.edu
Location: Small City
Public
Total Enrollment: 30,158
Undergraduates: 24,214

Many first-time visitors to Cincinnati are surprised to find an attractive and very livable city. As they traverse the city's hilly roads, they are in for another surprise—its university. Not only has the University of Cincinnati made its mark with its extensive research programs, but its signature cooperative education program, first established in 1906, is also the largest of any public college or university in the country.

The compact campus is a mile uphill from Cincinnati's downtown area. Ultramodern buildings rise up next to traditional ivy-covered Georgian halls. A major $233 million university construction project created a "Main Street" in the center of campus and consolidated all student activities. Recent additions include a $120 million facility housing UC's business programs and a $65 million building for the College of Allied Health Sciences.

Research has been a longtime forte. Campus scientists have given the world anti-knock gasoline, the electronic organ, antihistamines, and the U.S. Weather Bureau. But the university is perhaps best known for cooperative education, which allows students to earn while they learn. More than 40 programs across the Cincinnati curriculum offer the popular five-year professional-practice option, and about 3,500 students participate in co-ops each year. UC has taken steps to improve the quality of undergraduate education by strengthening its general education requirements to focus on critical thinking and expression, by creating more than 100 learning communities for freshmen, and by expanding its honors program. Freshmen must take English, math, and a contemporary issues class, and all students are required to complete a capstone experience. Other requirements vary by college.

"We are your traditional hardworking college students."

The colleges of engineering; business administration; and design, architecture, art, and planning (the schools with the most co-op students) are the best bets at UC. The university's music conservatory, one of the top programs in the field, also offers electronic media and broadcasting training. The colleges of nursing and pharmacy are well known and benefit from UC's health center and graduate medical school. The most popular majors fall under the fields of business administration, health professions, engineering, and biological sciences. Education students earn two bachelor's degrees: one in education and one in a liberal arts subject. Additional initiatives include a culinary arts and science degree program offered jointly with Cincinnati State, and the state's first baccalaureate program in facilities and hospitality management. UC also sponsors a language-immersion house, a freestanding residence where students are required to live, work, study, and play 24/7 in another language. About a quarter of undergrads choose to study abroad or work in international co-ops offered in more than 50 countries.

At UC, the academic rigor is largely a function of one's major; fields such as engineering and nursing require a substantially larger academic commitment. "I would say that the most rigorous courses are those that are nontraditional," offers one student, citing "study abroad, capstones, projects with corporate partners, and advanced topics classes." Some courses end up being quite large (in popular design courses, two people to a desk is not unusual); 34 percent of all classes have fewer than 20 students. A third of the faculty members hold outside jobs, bringing fresh, practical experience to the classroom. "Most of my professors are accessible because they offer office hours; however, I have run into difficulty from time to time receiving answers to my emails," reports one student.

"We are your traditional hardworking college students," says a sophomore of UC's largely homogeneous student body. Eighty-three percent of undergraduates are native Ohioans, and 5 percent come from abroad. Black students make up a mere 7 percent of the student body, Asian Americans 5 percent, and Hispanic/Latino and multiracial students each add

"There is a party culture present…but it is by no means dominant."

4 percent. Diversity, feminist issues, campus construction, and rising tuition are the hot topics on campus. The school offers merit scholarships averaging $6,100 and nearly 250 athletic scholarships.

Twenty-two percent of UC students live on campus. Many upperclassmen consider off-campus living far better than dorm life, and apartments can usually be found

(continued)

Male/Female: 51/49
Financial Aid: 60%
Pell Grant: 17%
Expense: Pub $ $ $
Student Loans: 57%
Average Debt: $ $
Applicants: 25,949
Accepted: 85%
Enrolled: 24%
Grad in 6 Years: 73%
Returning Freshmen: 87%
Academics: ✍ ✍
Social: ☎ ☎ ☎
Q of L: ★ ★ ★
Admissions: (513) 556-1100
Email Address: admissions@uc.edu

Strong Programs:
Engineering
Business Administration
Architecture
Art and Design
Music
Nursing
Prepharmacy
Biological Sciences

UC's signature cooperative education program is the largest of any public college or university in the country.

nearby. For meals, "Campus has three dining facilities, multiple fast food restaurants in the university center, and a few cafés located in certain buildings," explains a senior. A marketing major adds, "Living in an urban environment means there are extra safety precautions that keep students safe. Never have I felt unsafe on campus."

Merchants have turned the area surrounding UC, called Clifton, into a mini college town with plenty to do. Although not a major metropolis like Chicago or Boston, the "Queen City" of Cincinnati (as in "Queen of the West") does offer an urban feel. Nine nearby bus lines take undergraduates into the heart of the city in minutes; there, they find museums, ballet, professional sports teams, parks, rivers, hills, and as many large and small shops as anyone could want. On-campus activities include 550 student clubs, with everything from mountaineering to clubs in various majors. Fraternities and sororities attract just 4 percent of the men and 4 percent of the women but are still the most active places to party on campus, usually opening their functions to everyone. "There is a party culture present at the university, but it is by no means dominant," says one senior. The university sponsors some events, such as WorldFest and Greek Week. Cleveland and Columbus make for good road trips.

Seventeen Bearcat teams compete in the Division I American Athletic Conference. The men's basketball team is highly competitive, as are football, women's basketball, and women's volleyball. Everyone mentions the football rivalry with Miami of Ohio as a game you won't want to miss, and the same holds true when the men's basketball squad takes on Xavier University. Weekend athletes take advantage of UC's first-rate recreation center, and more than 50 club sports and 15 intramurals are an option too.

UC offers students a lively social scene, both on campus and minutes away in downtown Cincinnati. But cooperative education is the name of the game at this Ohio school, where the co-op program allows students to take their degrees out for a test drive before graduation and have a head start on their peers after it.

Overlaps

Ohio State, Miami University (OH), Ohio University, Bowling Green State, Wright State, Xavier (OH)

If You Apply To ›

UC: Early action, rolling admissions. Accepts the Common Application with supplement. Apply to particular program. Please consult UC's website for the most up-to-date information regarding standardized test requirements.

Claremont Colleges

In 1925, theologian and educator James A. Blaisdell had the vision to create a group of colleges patterned after Oxford and Cambridge in England—an "Oxford of the Orange Groves," as he elegantly put it. Nearly a century later, the five schools that comprise the Claremont Colleges thrive as a consortium of separate and distinct undergraduate colleges with two adjoining graduate institutions, a theological seminary, and botanical gardens. Like families, the colleges coexist, interact, and experience their share of both cooperation and tension. Ultimately, however, the Claremont Colleges consortium forms a mutually beneficial partnership that offers its students the vast resources and facilities one might only expect to find at a large university.

The colleges are located 35 miles east of Los Angeles on 546 acres in the suburb of Claremont (population 36,000), a peaceful, tree-lined neighborhood at the foot of the San Gabriel Mountains. The picture-perfect California weather has sometimes been marred by smog, courtesy of the neighbors in nearby L.A., but the smog level has declined dramatically in the past few years.

Of the five undergraduate colleges that make up the Claremont Colleges—Claremont McKenna, Harvey Mudd, Pitzer, Pomona, and Scripps—Pomona is the largest, with about 1,700 students. Each school retains its own institutional identity, with its own faculty, administration, admissions, and curriculum, although the boundaries of both academic work and extracurricular activities are somewhat flexible. Each of the schools also tends to specialize in a particular area that complements the offerings of all the others. Claremont McKenna, which caters mainly to students planning careers in economics, business, law, or government, has 11 research institutes located on its campus while Harvey Mudd is a liberal arts college specializing in engineering, science, and math. Pitzer, a classical liberal arts institution and the most socially progressive of the five, excels in environmental and sustainability studies, and at the all-women Scripps, the top majors include the social sciences, biology, and visual and performing arts. The oldest of the five colleges, Pomona ranks as one of the top liberal arts colleges anywhere and is strong across the board.

Collectively, the colleges share many services and facilities, including a student newspaper, a biological field station, a student health center, auditoriums, a 2,500-seat concert hall, a 350-seat theater, bookstores, a maintenance department, a business office, and a shared campus safety force. The Queer Resource Center, housed at Pomona but serving the whole community, is a model of collaboration between schools, and the EmPOWER Center provides the community with comprehensive support and educational resources on sexual assault, dating and domestic violence, and stalking. The Claremont library system makes 2 million volumes available to all students. Faculties and administrations are free to arrange joint programs or classes between all or just some of the schools. Courses are open to students from the other colleges (approximately 2,700 courses in all), but each college sets limits on the number of classes that can be taken elsewhere. Perhaps the best example of academic cooperation is the team-taught interdisciplinary courses, which are organized by instructors from the different schools and appeal to a mix of different academic interests.

The Claremont Colleges draw large numbers of students from within California, although their national reputation is growing. These days, about half the students hail from other Western and non-Western states, with a sizable contingent from the East Coast. The tone at the Claremont Colleges is decidedly intellectual, and graduate programs in the arts and sciences are more common goals than business or law school. Anyone who is bright and hardworking can find a niche at one of the five schools.

One student describes the town of Claremont as "a wonderful place if you're married or about to die." Indeed, the quiet local community ("the Village") has its share of senior citizens, but it also offers a flavor reminiscent of Ann Arbor (home to the University of Michigan), with quirky boutiques, coffee shops, truly remarkable candy stores, a Sunday farmers market, and eateries ranging from fine dining to diners and specialty bagel shops. There are even ice cream shops that freeze your ice cream with liquid nitrogen before your eyes—and it's all an easy walk or bike ride from any campus. Students report that the endless list of social activities offered at the colleges makes up for anything Claremont might lack. For hot times, Hollywood's glamour and downtown L.A. are within sniffing distance. The availability of shared Zipcars, rideshare services, and a nearby Metro line make these and other locations easy to access. Nearby mountains and the fabled surfing beaches make this collegiate paradise's backyard complete. Mount Baldy ski lifts, for instance, are only 15 miles away, and you'll reach Laguna Beach before the end of your favorite album. For spring break, Mexico is cheap and a great change of pace.

On campus, extracurricular life maintains a balance between cooperation and independence. Claremont McKenna, Harvey Mudd, and Scripps field joint athletic teams, and the men's teams especially are Division III powers, due to the exploits of CMC athletes. Pomona and Pitzer also compete together with particular strength in water polo, track and field, and soccer. The popular Claremont Colleges Ballroom Dance Company has won multiple national collegiate championships, as has the perennially successful Claremont Colleges Debate Union.

Each of the five colleges has its own dorms, and since off-campus housing is limited in Claremont proper, the social life of students revolves around their dorms. Large five-school parties are regular Thursday, Friday, and Saturday night fare. "In my opinion, Mudd's parties are the best because they always have themes," says a physics major. Claremont McKenna is said to have the most raucous party scene, while Pitzer hosts multiple music festivals throughout the year. There are no fraternities, except for three local ones at Pomona, where joining is far from de rigueur. All cafeterias are open to all students, and most big events—films, concerts, etc.—are advertised throughout each campus. Day-to-day social interaction among students at different schools, be it for meals or dates, is not what it might be. Occasional political squabbles break out between liberal faculty and students at Pitzer and their conservative counterparts at Claremont McKenna. For the most part, students benefit not only from the nurturing and support within their own schools, each of which has its own academic or extracurricular emphasis, but also from the abundant resources that the Claremont Colleges consortium offers as a whole.

Claremont McKenna College

890 Columbia Avenue, Claremont, CA 91711

Make way, Pomona—this rising star is no longer content with being a social sciences specialty school. CMC is half the size of a typical liberal arts college and smaller than Pomona by about 300 students. Most conservative of Claremont schools. CMC continues to develop its national and global reputation, and Californians now make up less than half the student body.

Website: www.cmc.edu
Location: Suburban
Private
Total Enrollment: 1,414
Undergraduates: 1,409
Male/Female: 49/51
Financial Aid: 47%
Pell Grant: 22%
Expense: Pr $ $ $ $
Student Loans: 33%
Average Debt: $
Applicants: 5,632
Accepted: 11%
Enrolled: 57%
Grad in 6 Years: 93%
Returning Freshmen: 98%
Academics: ✍ ✍ ✍ ✍ ½
Social: ☎ ☎ ☎
Q of L: ★ ★ ★
Admissions: (909) 621-8088
Email Address: admission@ cmc.edu

Strong Programs:
Economics
Government
International Relations
Psychology
History
Environment, Economics, and Politics

Claremont McKenna College's special niche in the Claremont College pantheon is top programs in government, economics, and international relations. In addition, CMC has 11 research institutes located on campus, which offer its undergraduates ample opportunities to study everything from political demographics to the environment. The arts and humanities are also available, but Claremont McKenna is better suited to those with high ambitions in business leadership and public affairs. "CMC provides students with a pragmatic liberal arts education that will prepare them for grad school and a career," a senior says. "It is a great place to spend four years."

The 69-acre campus is mostly "California modern" in its architecture, with lots of Spanish tile roofs and picture windows that look out on the San Gabriel Mountains. Described by one student as "more functional than aesthetic," the physical layout fits right in with the school's practical attitude. Kravis Center is a state-of-the-art academic center that houses classrooms, seminar rooms, a computer laboratory, and faculty offices. Roberts Pavilion serves as an athletic, fitness, and events center.

CMC's extensive general education requirements include two semesters in the humanities; three in the social sciences; one each in the natural sciences and mathematics; and a senior thesis. All first-years take a Freshman Writing Seminar and a Freshman Humanities Seminar. Claremont McKenna offers top programs in economics and government, but the international relations, psychology, and history programs are also considered strong. A few programs combine these strengths into interdisciplinary majors, such as the environment, economics, and politics major.

"[Professors] are both brilliant and devoted to their students."

The biology, chemistry, and physics departments are greatly enhanced through the use of Keck Science Center, an outstanding facility providing students with hands-on access to a variety of equipment. In addition, the 85-acre Bernard Biological Field Station is located just north of the CMC campus and is available to students for field work. Newer majors include public policy and data science. The college also offers a popular 3–2 program in economics and engineering, a four-year B.A./M.A. program, and a 4–1 M.B.A. program in conjunction with the Claremont Graduate University.

The academic climate is fairly strenuous at Claremont McKenna, but not overwhelming. "There are very difficult courses that will push you to the brink of your comfort zone in every major," a junior says. Seventy-four percent of classes have fewer than 20 students ("one of the perks of a small college," says a neuroscience major), and professors are praised for their accessibility. "I have met some of the most incredible teachers at CMC who are both brilliant and devoted to their students," an economics major says. All freshmen take part in a five-day orientation program that includes a Welcome Orientation Adventure (WOA!) trip and a reception with the president and department chairs. Thirty-three percent of Claremont McKenna students take advantage of study abroad programs offered in more than 55 countries, including Australia, Brazil, Costa Rica, and Japan. Participants in the Washington Semester can intern with the State Department, the White House, and lobbying groups, and a semester-long Silicon Valley internship program places liberal arts students in technology firms. The college provides stipends to low-income and first-generation students in order to allow them to take unpaid internships.

A senior describes CMC students as "career-oriented, ambitious, and serious about their classes." The CMC student body is 39 percent Californian, with many other domestic students coming from the East Coast, and 15 percent of students coming from other countries. Asian Americans account for 14 percent of the student body, Hispanics/Latinos 16 percent, Black students 5 percent, and multiracial students 7 percent. Although CMC is the most conservative of the five Claremont schools, one student notes, "There is a good mix of liberals, conservatives, and libertarians," and different viewpoints are welcomed. The school accepts domestic applicants on a need-blind basis and guarantees to meet the demonstrated need of all admitted students. It also awards a limited number of merit scholarships to eligible students.

Participants in the Washington Semester can intern with the State Department, the White House, and lobbying groups.

Ninety-three percent of CMC students live on campus, "because of the social life," according to one. All the residence halls are co-ed, and Stark Hall, a substance-free dorm, gives students more living options. A cluster of on-campus apartments equipped with kitchen facilities is a popular option for upperclassmen. Dorm food is said to be quite good, and students can eat in dining halls at any of the other four colleges, though the best bet may be CMC's Collins Dining Hall. "They have a large spread with lots of different options," says one student, including vegetarian, vegan, and organic fare. CMC has expanded its staff dedicated to assisting the campus community with issues related to discrimination, harassment, and sexual misconduct.

"Leadership pervades almost everything that goes on here."

Most students agree that the social life at CMC is more than adequate, thanks to the five-college system. "There are always parties, club events, barbecues, movie screenings, and other events," says a junior. Perhaps consistent with its origins in 1946 as an all-male college (it became co-ed in 1976), CMC has a reputation for raucous partying, at least in comparison to its other Claremont counterparts; CMC is said to have something of a "bro culture" around drinking—an atmosphere that appeals to some students but keeps others away. Aside from that party scene, Monte Carlo Night is a favorite annual bash, and Club Claremont plans on-campus events as well as outings for everything from surfing and skiing nearby to day trips to Disneyland and L.A. Ponding, another unusual CMC tradition, involves being thrown into one of the two campus fountains on one's birthday. The college sponsors an outstanding lecture series at the Athenaeum (a.k.a. "the Ath") on Monday through Thursday nights each week. Before each lecture, students and faculty can enjoy a gourmet dinner together and engage in intellectual debates. Students also highly recommend road trips to Joshua Tree, Coachella, San Francisco, and Las Vegas.

Ponding, an unusual CMC tradition, involves being thrown into one of the two campus fountains on one's birthday.

Division III athletics are an important part of life at Claremont McKenna, and the school has an overstuffed trophy case to prove it. The women's tennis team brought home the national title in 2018 and 2022. Recent Stag (men's) and Athena (women's) conference champions include cross-country, swimming and diving, track and field, golf, and volleyball. A third of the students play varsity sports, and CMC students tend to dominate the teams jointly fielded with Harvey Mudd and Scripps. Top rivalries include Pomona–Pitzer, both in athletics and academics, one student claims.

CMC has embraced its mission to produce great leaders by providing students with ample opportunities for research and study abroad, as well as top-notch programs in government and economics. "Leadership pervades almost everything that goes on here," says a junior. "Claremont McKenna builds character, fosters a sense of ambition among its students, and drives them to set their sights high."

Overlaps

UC Berkeley, UCLA, Pomona, University of Southern California, Stanford

Harvey Mudd College

301 Platt Boulevard, Claremont, CA 91711

Harvey Mudd may rank as the finest institution that few people outside of STEM fields have ever heard of. Future Ph.D.s graduate from here in greater percentages than at any other school in the nation. Renowned for encouraging women to go into engineering and other STEM areas, HMC rivals larger neighbor Caltech for sheer brainpower and tops it in access to outstanding faculty. Offers more exposure to the liberal arts than most science- and technology-oriented schools, and a tight-knit community.

Website: www.hmc.edu
Location: Suburban
Private
Total Enrollment: 902
Undergraduates: 902
Male/Female: 50/50
Financial Aid: 68%
Pell Grant: 13%
Expense: Pr $ $ $ $
Student Loans: 42%
Average Debt: $ $
Applicants: 4,737
Accepted: 10%
Enrolled: 48%
Grad in 6 Years: 94%
Returning Freshmen: 98%
Academics: ✍ ✍ ✍ ✍ ½
Social: ☎ ☎ ☎
Q of L: ★ ★ ★
Admissions: (909) 621-8011
Email Address: admission@ hmc.edu

Strong Programs:
Engineering
Computer Science
Physics
Mathematics
Computer Science and
    Mathematics

A top-ranked liberal arts college with a technical bent, Harvey Mudd College, established in 1955 and named for a founder, strives to give its students a sense of academic balance. Although it's a leading provider of high-quality programs in science and engineering (Where else can you take an introductory engineering class where you build your own underwater robot?), it also emphasizes a well-rounded education with knowledge in the humanities, social sciences, and arts. "Harvey Mudd is a nerdy, organic, stressful, and academically engaging college," says a first-year student. A senior adds, "I really think the culture and community at Harvey Mudd is my favorite part about this school."

HMC's mid-'50s vintage campus of cinder-block buildings, in the words of one student, "looks like an engineering college; it's very symmetrical and there's no romance." In addition, most buildings have small, square prism bricks, intended to accentuate architectural lines, that students have dubbed "warts"—not a very attractive picture. As part of a massive building campaign, however, the college has added a modern residence hall, the Shanahan Center for Teaching and Learning, and the $30 million McGregor Computer Science Center, which boasts a cutting-edge makerspace.

While most STEM-oriented schools tend to have a narrow focus, HMC has come up with the novel idea that even scientists and engineers "need to know and appreciate poetry, philosophy, and non-Western thought," says an administrator. The Common Core includes coursework in mathematics, computer science, and engineering; physics, chemistry, and biology (each with an associated laboratory); college writing (taught by faculty from all departments); humanities, social sciences, and the arts; and an Impact course that explores the intersection of STEM and society. Students report that classes are formidable, and the heavy workload is a common complaint. Concerned that the core curriculum has indeed become too onerous and even "soul crushing," the administration has taken steps to relieve student stress without sacrificing rigor, including reducing the number of courses students are required to take in their first four semesters and setting up a multidisciplinary care team to help students struggling with academic or personal issues. "There is a huge focus on getting help if you need it," says a chemistry major. The faculty has also set a goal for the Common Core of nurturing "the joy of

> **"In research positions, students are working one-on-one with the professors—they aren't washing beakers."**

learning." The small class sizes and absence of graduate programs means that under-graduates get uncommon amounts of attention, even from top faculty. A physics major says, "Instruction here is excellent, and professors have a really wonderful open-door policy," in addition to regular office hours.

Of the school's 10 majors, engineering enrolls the most students; computer science, mathematics, and physics are other top choices. HMC has one of the nation's best computer science programs and an award-winning math department, and a combined major in computer science and mathematics is also very popular. Students rave about the Clinic Program, which plops real-life math, science, and engineering tasks (sponsored by major corporations and government agencies) into the laps of students. Recent sponsors have included NASA Jet Propulsion Laboratory, Google, Microsoft, and Toyota. All students must either participate in the Clinic Program or complete original thesis-driven research in order to graduate. About 200 students stay on campus in the summer for 10-week research experiences, and a sophomore says, "In research positions, students are working one-on-one with the professors—they aren't washing beakers." Twenty-two percent of students pack their bags for study abroad programs in their choice of more than 20 countries, usually during their junior year.

"To the surprise of no one, Harvey Mudd attracts 'nerds,' but more specifically, people who have a lot of passion for technical things, are overachievers, and like to have fun with that," explains a physics major. For a technically oriented school, Mudd boasts a relatively high proportion of female students, at 50 percent, and it is also one of the few colleges strong in engineering

"To the surprise of no one, Harvey Mudd attracts 'nerds.'"

and science that has a female president. Forty-three percent of the students are homegrown Californians, and 9 percent are international. Black students represent 5 percent of the student body, Hispanics/Latinos 21 percent, Asian Americans 24 percent, and multiracial students 10 percent. A senior notes that while students are often too "wrapped up in schoolwork" to get involved in social and political issues, student groups like FEM Union (Female Empowerment at Mudd) and BLAM (Black Lives and Allies at Mudd) "have created spaces for discussions about issues of diversity and privilege." Merit scholarships averaging $14,000 help some with the hefty tuition bill, but as a Division III college, Mudd offers no athletic scholarships. It does, however, honor policies of need-blind admissions and covering 100 percent of students' demonstrated need with its financial aid packages.

Ninety-eight percent of undergrads live on campus, and students speak of a strong "dorm culture" on campus. "Each dorm has a proctor (think: the 'mom' or 'dad' of the dorm, usually a senior) as well as several mentors (the 'older siblings' of the dorm, who are mostly there for freshmen)," explains a computer science major. "The proctor-mentor team helps keep the dorm community strong and safe." Mudd's dining options are said to be satisfying, and students appreciate their access to dining facilities at the other Claremont Colleges, which vastly expands their options.

Despite their heavy workload, most HMC students find abundant social outlets, even if it's just joining the parade of unicycles that has overrun the campus—not to mention skateboards, longboards, scooters, and freeline skates. Dorms host parties almost every weekend, a favorite being the Wild Wild West party, "where we fill a dorm courtyard with peanut shells and get a mechanical bull," says a physics major.

"Pranking the president's house is one of the first things you do as a first-year student."

Students describe the party scene as a pressure-free one where classmates look out for each other. While students do frequent the other Claremont campuses to socialize, it's Mudd's many traditions that really get them going. When finals roll around each semester, Noisy Minutes provide breaks from long hours of studying with loud music, snacks, and activities like a bouncy ball drop, non-Newtonian fluid racing, and battle tie-dye. Engineering pranks are popular but must be reversible within 24 hours, as established by the honor code. "Pranking the president's house is one of the first things you do as a first-year student at Harvey Mudd!" enthuses a senior.

Mudd fields varsity sports teams together with Claremont McKenna and Scripps, and the teams do extremely well. Women's tennis (recent national champions), women's volleyball and golf, and men's and women's cross-country, swimming and diving, and track and field are some of the strongest teams. Intramurals, also in conjunction with Claremont McKenna and Scripps, are even more popular. King among these is inner-tube water polo, which draws huge cheering crowds and, most importantly, removes the most difficult aspect of the sport—treading water.

HMC is right on the heels of Caltech as the best technically oriented school in the West. The college offers a gem of a technical education blended with a worthwhile amount of humanities and social sciences, and the administration seems serious about addressing the common student refrain that the heavy workload comes at the expense of time to reflect on what they are learning. HMC offers a welcoming attitude toward women and other groups traditionally underrepresented in STEM fields. As one student asserts, "Mudd is the college for students to be challenged like they never have been before and have the support to go through it."

Overlaps

MIT, Olin College of Engineering, Caltech, Stanford, Carnegie Mellon, UC Berkeley, UCLA, Harvard

If You Apply To ›

Harvey Mudd: Early decision I and II, regular decision. Accepts the Common Application. Please consult Harvey Mudd's website for the most up-to-date information regarding standardized test requirements.

Pitzer College

1050 North Mills Avenue, Claremont, CA 91711

Offers a haven for the otherwise-minded without the hard edge of nonconformity at places like Bard and Evergreen. Traditional strengths lie in the social and behavioral sciences, including innovative options such as secular studies. Students play a role in college governance. Far more selective than it was 15 years ago. A national leader in turning out Fulbright Scholars.

Website: www.pitzer.edu
Location: Suburban
Private
Total Enrollment: 1,132
Undergraduates: 1,132
Male/Female: 41/59
Financial Aid: 36%
Pell Grant: 10%
Expense: Pr $ $ $ $
Student Loans: 38%
Average Debt: $
Applicants: 3,676
Accepted: 18%
Enrolled: 53%

As the most socially aware of the Claremont Colleges, Pitzer College offers students a creative milieu, abundant opportunities for intellectual exploration, and a sense of fierce individualism. Founded in 1963 and named for a benefactor, this small liberal arts and sciences school has changed with the times but continues to emphasize progressive thought, social responsibility, environmental sustainability, and an open social attitude. In the last 25 years, Pitzer students and alumni have been awarded more than 240 Fulbright fellowships, and the school continues to attract top talent from around the world.

Even Pitzer's campus is, well, different. The classroom buildings are modernistic octagons, and the grass-covered "mounds" that distinguish the grounds "are perfect for sunbathing and Frisbee," says one student, and for lounging in Adirondack chairs beneath the palm trees. Drought-tolerant landscaping pervades the campus, and there is an organic garden. One interesting campus curiosity is the Grove House, a California craftsman-style house students saved from the wrecking ball decades ago and moved to campus. It houses a dining room, study areas, and art exhibits.

Additional facilities include eight LEED-certified residence halls, Benson Auditorium, and the Gold Student Health and Wellness Center.

In keeping with Pitzer's philosophy of student autonomy, each student has the maximum freedom to choose which classes to take. Instead of traditional academic departments, Pitzer has "field groups," which, as a political studies and Spanish double major explains, "allow for students to major in one subject area, yet receive a holistic education." All students take a sequence of courses on social justice and intercultural exploration, and a lively first-year seminar program sharpens students' learning skills, especially writing. Students select from 37 majors, and they're also encouraged to design their own. Almost anything in the social and behavioral sciences is a sure bet, especially psychology. Environmental analysis, economics, political studies, media studies, biology, and English and world literature are other strong and popular programs. Pitzer is the first college in the country to offer a program in secular studies, with courses such as God, Darwin, and Design in America. Most courses in Pitzer's weaker areas can be picked up at one of the other Claremont schools; on average, Pitzer students take 30 percent of their courses at the other colleges.

> "[Field groups] allow for students to major in one subject area, yet receive a holistic education."

The academic climate is "relaxed, interdisciplinary, collaborative, and very discussion-based," according to a sociology major. Class size is generally small, with 69 percent of classes enrolling fewer than 20 students, which promotes close interaction between students and faculty. "The professors I have had are very down-to-earth and incredibly knowledgeable in their fields," says a sociology and gender/feminist studies major. Students play a large role in Pitzer's community government and sit on all policy committees, including those on curriculum and faculty promotion. The environment is a big focus here, and the college boasts the Robert Redford Conservancy for Southern California Sustainability. The Firestone Center for Restoration Ecology in Costa Rica is home to programs in science, language, and international studies and provides opportunities for research. Pitzer also runs its own study abroad programs in Brazil, Ecuador, Italy, Nepal, Vietnam, and Southern Africa and offers students access to 38 international and five domestic exchange programs; in all, 54 percent of Pitzer students go abroad. Forty-six percent conduct undergraduate research.

> Students sit on all policy committees, including those on curriculum and faculty promotion.

Individualism is a prized characteristic among Pitzer students, but one junior says the oft-bandied "hippie" label is unfair: "Pitzer people are genuinely socially conscious and academically adventurous, but do go on to good jobs." Thirty-nine percent of students are from California, and 7 percent are from foreign nations. Many come from wealthy backgrounds. Black students represent 5 percent of the student body, Hispanics/Latinos 13 percent, Asian Americans 12 percent, and multiracial students 9 percent. Students are heavily involved in volunteer work and cite "racism on campus, labor rights, immigration reform, environmental issues, and police brutality" as hot-button social and political issues. The school is committed to meeting 100 percent of enrolled students' demonstrated need, but it is not need-blind in its admissions. A limited number of merit scholarships are awarded to top achievers.

> "[Pitzer is] a place that values the silly and the weird parts of yourself."

Eighty-two percent of students live on campus, and many find themselves in the newer, environmentally friendly dorms; the remainder hang their hats in "old but spacious" rooms. Boarders can choose from a variety of meal plans, and the food gets rave reviews, especially the fresh salad, sandwich, and fruit juice bars in the main dining hall. "The food is awesome: locally sourced, excellent variety, easy to be vegetarian," says a senior. Students say the Pitzer Advocates for Survivors of Sexual Assault student group has been a helpful campus resource.

> Kohoutek, an alternative music festival, is the big annual event, featuring bands, food, and "hoopla."

(continued)

Grad in 6 Years: 88%
Returning Freshmen: 93%
Academics: ✑ ✑ ✑
Social: ☎ ☎ ☎
Q of L: ★ ★ ★
Admissions: (909) 621-8129
Email Address: admission@pitzer.edu

Strong Programs:
Psychology
Environmental Analysis
Economics
Political Studies
Media Studies
Biology
English and World Literature
Secular Studies

As for the social scene, "Most students stay on campus to attend events or go to parties," says a senior. Pitzer has no Greek organizations, nor does it want any, and social life tends to be fairly low-key. Kohoutek, an alternative music festival, is the big annual event, featuring bands, food, and a "whole week of hoopla"; there is a rockabilly festival as well. "There is very heavy alcohol and weed usage on campus," says a junior. All parties that serve alcohol must be registered. As much as students enjoy the campus scene, some warn that without a car, things can get claustrophobic.

The Pomona–Pitzer football team has had winning seasons, and the school fields a variety of competitive Sagehens teams within the Southern California Intercollegiate Athletic Conference. Men's and women's water polo and men's cross-country have won national championships recently. Recreational sports thrive, with more than 25 club sports, about a dozen intramurals, and a hugely popular annual Humans vs. Zombies game that draws 500 participants across campus.

Pitzer College attracts open-minded students looking for the freedom to go their own ways. "Pitzer people are really caring and often fight for what they believe in. It is a really loving place," muses one student, "a place that values the silly and the weird parts of yourself."

Overlaps

Kenyon, Bates, Franklin & Marshall, Occidental, Dickinson, Pomona, Scripps, Colorado College

If You Apply To ›

Pitzer: Early decision I and II, regular decision. SATs or ACTs: not considered (test-free pilot policy in effect through fall 2025). Accepts the Common Application. Application includes optional fields for gender identity and gender pronouns.

Pomona College

333 North College Way, Claremont, CA 91711

The finest liberal arts college in the West, and one of the few that Ivy-oriented Easterners will travel across the country to attend. Offers twice the resources of stand-alone competitors with access to the other Claremonts. A haven for the otherwise-minded, though not to the same extent as nonconformist neighbor Pitzer. Strong across the academic spectrum.

Website: www.pomona.edu
Location: Suburban
Private
Total Enrollment: 1,747
Undergraduates: 1,747
Male/Female: 45/55
Financial Aid: 58%
Pell Grant: 21%
Expense: Pr $ $ $
Student Loans: 32%
Average Debt: $
Applicants: 11,620
Accepted: 7%
Enrolled: 58%
Grad in 6 Years: 93%
Returning Freshmen: 96%

Pomona College, located just 35 miles east of the glitz and glamour of Hollywood, is the undisputed star of the Claremont Colleges and one of the top small liberal arts colleges anywhere. This small, elite institution is the top liberal arts college in the West. But the school's prestigious reputation doesn't go to the heads of Pomona's friendly students. "Students here are very open about different types of people—Pomona prides itself on its diverse community," chirps one Sagehen (the school's mascot).

The architecture is variously described as Spanish Mediterranean, pseudo-Italian, or, as a sophomore puts it, "a perfect mix of Northeastern Ivy and Southern California modern." One certainly notices more than one stucco building topped with a red tile roof on campus, as well as eucalyptus trees, canyon live oaks, and an occasional "secretive courtyard lined with flowers." The numerous open courtyards and gardens are popular study spots. By virtue of its location and beauty, Pomona's campus has served as the quintessential collegiate milieu in various Hollywood movies. Recent campus projects include Andrew Science Hall, which features a host of cutting-edge spaces and equipment, including a digital planetarium and electron microscope, and the Pomona College Museum of Art.

Pomona was founded in 1887 by Congregationalists who wanted to import "New England–type" education to Southern California. In order to graduate, students must take at least one course in each of six Breadth of Study areas: criticism, analysis, and contextual study of works of the human imagination; social institutions and human behavior; history, values, ethics, and cultural studies; physical and biological sciences; mathematical and formal reasoning; and creation and performance of works of art and literature. The required Critical Inquiry seminar emphasizes thoughtful reading, logical reasoning, and graceful writing; students choose from more than two dozen offerings, with subjects such as Pomona Goes Green and Molecules and the Mind. Students must also complete a senior exercise in their final year. A five-day freshman orientation program divides the new arrivals into groups of six to 12 students headed by a sophomore. "We provide a great deal of support in acclimating students to a college environment," says a senior. Economics, mathematics, computer science, neuroscience, and public policy analysis are the most popular majors; international relations is well regarded.

> **"Students are laid-back in a very Southern California kind of way."**

"Although classes can be difficult, students help each other out, and the classroom environment is an enjoyable one," offers one economics major. Students often form study groups in an effort to help one another through the demanding curriculum. One undergrad estimates the average student spends 20 to 30 hours a week studying outside the classroom. Classes are small—74 percent have fewer than 20 students—and the faculty makes a point of being accessible. An ever-popular take-a-professor-to-lunch program gives students free meals when they arrive with a faculty member in tow. Better still, "We do not have graduate students or TAs teaching class," says a senior.

Educational enrichment opportunities abound at Pomona. Students can spend a semester at Colby or Swarthmore, pursue a 3–2 engineering plan with the California Institute of Technology or Dartmouth College, or spend a semester in Washington, D.C., working for a congressperson. Half of the students take advantage of 60 study abroad programs offered in 35 countries. Fifty-three percent conduct research mentored by a faculty member, and the Summer Undergraduate Research Program provides funding to more than 200 students to pursue such opportunities each summer.

Pomona students "tend to be high-achieving, confident, verbal students with a fairly liberal political ideology," says a senior. "Students are laid-back in a very Southern California kind of way," adds another. Twenty-seven percent are Californians, and a growing number venture from the East Coast; 11 percent come from abroad. Nine percent are Black, 16 percent are Hispanic/Latino, 17 percent are Asian American, and 8 percent are multiracial. There is a healthy mix of liberals and conservatives on campus, though the leftists, especially the feminist wing, are much more vocal. The student government is active, and the administration is credited with respecting students' opinions. One interesting way students voice their concerns is by painting the Walker Wall. Anyone is allowed to paint any message they want

> **"We provide a great deal of support in acclimating students to a college environment."**

on the wall, and the school will even provide groups with the paint. Pomona is need-blind in admissions and meets the full demonstrated financial need of all those who attend. Although there are no merit or athletic awards, the college has replaced loans with grants in an effort to reduce the debt burden for families. The college also participates in the QuestBridge and Posse programs.

Virtually all Pomona students (98 percent) live on campus all four years. The dorms are co-ed, student-governed, and divided into two distinct groups. Those on South campus are family-like and fairly quiet, offer spacious rooms, and house

(continued)

Academics: ✍ ✍ ✍ ✍ ✍
Social: ☎ ☎ ☎
Q of L: ★ ★ ★ ★
Admissions: (909) 621-8134
Email Address: admissions@pomona.edu

Strong Programs:
Economics
Mathematics
Computer Science
Neuroscience
Public Policy Analysis
International Relations

An ever-popular take-a-professor-to-lunch program gives students free meals when they arrive with a faculty member in tow.

freshmen and sophomores, while those on the North end have smaller rooms with a livelier social scene and house juniors and seniors. "Pomona's dorms are like palaces," says a student. The two newest residence halls, Dialynas and Sontag, are LEED Platinum–certified and feature suite-style apartments for upperclassmen. Oldenborg Center is a language dorm with wings for speakers of Mandarin Chinese, French, German, Japanese, Spanish, and Russian, and Pomona also has established language tables at lunch. Boarders must buy at least partial meal plans. The food is good, with seafood certified by the Marine Stewardship Council, humanely raised beef and cage-free eggs, and ice cream for dessert every day. Students generally feel safe on campus. "The worst that usually happens are bike thefts," says a junior.

Social life begins in the dorms, where study breaks, barbecues, and parties are organized. There are movies several nights a week, and students also enjoy just tossing a Frisbee on the lawn. One student wanted to be sure that incoming freshmen and transfers knew of the Coop's (student union) "best milkshakes west of the Mississippi," pool tables, and large-screen TV and gaming system. Students often spend Friday afternoons relaxing with friends over a brew at the Greek Theater. Pomona is unique among the Claremont Colleges in that it has three nonnational fraternities (two co-ed; there are no sororities). As for booze, "I haven't noticed any pressure to drink here," reports one student, but "alcohol is definitely present in the social scene."

> **"You are guaranteed to meet new and interesting people whenever you step off campus."**

"I appreciate the diversity and depth that the five-college community brings to the social life," says a student. "You are guaranteed to meet new and interesting people whenever you step off campus." Five-college parties happen nearly every weekend. During midterms and finals, however, the campus is a "social ghost town." Harwood dorm throws the five-college costume party every Halloween. Freshman orientation gets interesting too. "First-years have to run through the gates of Pomona with blue and white carnations while upperclassmen throw water balloons and shoot water at them," says a student. It helps to have a set of wheels here, although Zipcar and rideshare services are readily available. Every February or March, hundreds of students spend the morning at a nearby ski resort, then head to a local beach to swim, and end the day with an oceanside cookout.

There once was a time when the Pomona Sagehens were an athletic powerhouse; the football team even knocked off mighty USC on Thanksgiving Day back in 1899. In the last few years, the men's and women's water polo and men's cross-country teams have brought home national titles. Intense rivalry exists between the Claremont Colleges; basketball games between Pomona–Pitzer and CMS (Claremont–Mudd–Scripps) are "particularly heated." Pomona–Pitzer enjoys a lively rivalry with Occidental College as well. Intramurals, including hotly contested inner-tube water polo matches, attract many participants, and the Outdoor Education Center facilitates numerous outdoor adventures.

Overlaps

Brown, Stanford, UC Berkeley, Williams, Yale, Pitzer, Harvard, Dartmouth

"Pomona offers a unique and desirable juxtaposition of rigorous academics and a comfortable social atmosphere," says a student. The strongest link in an extremely attractive chain, Pomona continues to symbolize the rising status of the Claremont Colleges—and the West in general—in the world of higher education. There are few regrets about coming to Pomona. Says a senior, "We're in California. The sun is always shining. What's the problem?"

If You Apply To ›

Pomona: Early decision I and II, regular decision. Accepts the Common Application with supplement. Please consult Pomona's website for the most up-to-date information regarding standardized test requirements.

Scripps College

1030 Columbia Avenue, Claremont, CA 91711

Scripps is easily the premier women's college on the West Coast, offering a commitment to women's education while interacting with co-ed institutions that are literally next door. Boasts strengths in social sciences, biological sciences, and the arts. Innovative Core Curriculum takes an interdisciplinary approach to learning.

Scripps College offers the best of both worlds—a close-knit women's college, where traditions include weekly tea and fresh-baked cookies, and the diversity of a major research institution, thanks to its membership in the Claremont Colleges. Founded in 1926 by newspaper publisher Ellen Browning Scripps, the college continues to pursue her vision through its mission: "To educate women by developing their intellects and talents through active participation in a community of scholars." Students tend to be outgoing, articulate, and serious about their studies, though they still know how to have fun.

Scripps's scenic 32-acre campus, listed on the National Register of Historic Places, offers a tranquil, safe, and comfortable environment. The architecture is Spanish and Mediterranean, with tiled roofs and elegant landscaping. A performing arts center provides permanent space for the Claremont Concert Orchestra and Concert Choir. In addition to a 700-seat theater, the center offers a music library, recital hall, practice rooms, faculty offices, and classrooms. The Lincoln Ceramic Art Building offers more than 5,000 square feet of work area and kiln yards.

The required Core Curriculum in Interdisciplinary Humanities is a sequence of three courses focusing on ideas about the world and the methods used to generate them. In addition to Core, everyone takes courses in fine arts, letters, natural sciences, and social sciences—one of these classes must focus on gender and women's studies and one must cover race and ethnic studies. All students also complete a senior thesis or project.

Popular and well-regarded majors at Scripps include biology/life sciences, social sciences, psychology, environmental analysis, media studies, English, and visual and performing arts, especially studio art and music. The Williamson Gallery offers a state-of-the-art studio and freestanding museum-quality gallery for aspiring painters and sculptors. Premeds benefit from the Keck Science Department, a joint program for students at Scripps, Claremont McKenna, and Pitzer. Programs in area and ethnic studies, such as Middle East and North Africa studies and Chicanx/Latinx studies, are strong, and the feminist, gender, and sexuality studies department is also popular. The Scripps Humanities Institute offers seminars and lectures open to the general public, along with fellowships for juniors; recently, the institute explored immigration policy and nationalism in the U.S. and abroad. The Scripps Presents event series also brings prominent writers, performers, visual artists, and activists to campus for public lectures as well as student-only discussions and workshops.

> **"My professors are always up for a discussion, always willing to answer questions."**

The academic experience at Scripps emphasizes cooperation. "Scripps is a very supportive community," a junior says. "It is a place where professors encourage you to work in groups because more brains [are] always better." Seventy-seven percent of classes have fewer than 20 students. "My professors are always up for a discussion, always willing to answer questions (even difficult ones), and always up to chat about how their day is going," says one student. When they're ready to branch out, typically in the junior year, more than 60 percent of Scripps students study abroad, choosing from more than 115 program options in 47 countries.

Website: www.scrippscollege.edu
Location: Suburban
Private
Total Enrollment: 1,087
Undergraduates: 1,087
Male/Female: 0/100
Financial Aid: 72%
Pell Grant: 9%
Expense: Pr $ $ $ $
Student Loans: 35%
Average Debt: $
Applicants: 2,952
Accepted: 30%
Enrolled: 38%
Grad in 6 Years: 82%
Returning Freshmen: 97%
Academics: ✐ ✐ ✐ ½
Social: ☎ ☎ ☎
Q of L: ★ ★ ★ ★
Admissions: (909) 621-8149
Email Address: admission@scrippscollege.edu

Strong Programs:
Biology/Life Sciences
Social Sciences
Psychology
Environmental Analysis
Media Studies
English
Visual and Performing Arts
Area and Ethnic Studies

Forty-three percent of Scripps undergraduates are from California, and 4 percent come from other countries. Black students account for 4 percent of the student body, Hispanics/Latinas 13 percent, Asian Americans 14 percent, and multiracial students 10 percent. "The students here are diligent, thoughtful, and really down-to-earth," observes one politics major. "They are usually privileged and have had the opportunity to have really impressive experiences." Just 9 percent of incoming first-year students are Pell-eligible. Student organizations supporting Jewish, Asian American, Black, Latina, international, and LGBTQ students are available. Scripps Communities of Resources and Empowerment provides support and funding to student organizations that promote inclusion and social justice. Scripps meets 100 percent of admitted students' demonstrated financial need and has made more grant money available for students with the most need. The college also awards merit scholarships averaging $18,400 to top achievers but no athletic scholarships.

Virtually all of Scripps students live in one of the 14 "spectacular" residence halls, where options include singles, suites, and apartment-style living arrangements. A student says, "The dorms are gorgeous. They are well maintained and have lots of charm with French doors, balconies, or the occasional fireplace." First-years live in the same halls as sophomores, juniors, and seniors. The dining hall garners rave reviews as well: "The salad bar is gourmet, the bread comes from a local bakery, and the pizza is made in a wood-fired brick oven," cheers a bioethics major. "Don't get me started about the hot cookies!"

"Don't get me started about the hot cookies!"

Social life at Scripps centers on the residence halls, which take turns throwing parties. "Our social life is very much based on campus," explains a chemistry major. "With five undergraduate colleges literally across the street from each other, it is challenging not to have something to do—from movie screenings, art exhibits, concerts, special events like a carnival or the International Festival, and parties." Alcohol doesn't play a major role in Scripps social life, but the school does have a medical amnesty policy for underage students in need of emergency medical assistance. Traditions are important here, including the Matriculation Ceremony at the start of each year and the signing of Graffiti Wall by each class before graduation. For students with cars, popular road trips include Pasadena, Mount Baldy, San Diego, and even Las Vegas and Mexico; students without wheels can hop on the Metrolink commuter train to get to and from downtown Los Angeles.

Athletic rivalries aren't the focus here, but Scripps does field joint teams with Claremont McKenna and Harvey Mudd, and when those teams face off against Pomona and Pitzer, students pay attention. All of the Stag (men's) and Athena (women's) teams compete in Division III, and the women's volleyball, tennis, and cross-country teams are especially strong. Intramural and club sports are also played jointly, and popular options include inner-tube water polo, soccer, flag football, and volleyball.

With a winning combination of outstanding academics and personal attention, not to mention a cooperative, noncompetitive feel, Scripps offers the best of both worlds. Scripps students want to achieve great things, but not if that requires stepping on their classmates' toes. And just beyond campus, the other Claremont Colleges beckon, with parties, student clubs, intramural sports, and cross-registration privileges for a comprehensive college experience.

If You Apply To ›

Scripps: Early decision I and II, regular decision. SATs or ACTs: optional. Accepts the Common Application.

Clark University

950 Main Street, Worcester, MA 01610-1477

Clark has a distinguished history that dates to the late 19th century, and had it been established an hour to the east, it probably would have become a household name. Worcester is no Boston, but Clarkies bring a sense of mission and partnership to their relationship with this historic industrial town. Clark is liberal, tolerant, and world-renowned in psychology, geography, and game design. Has a higher proportion of in-state students than some institutions of comparable quality.

Founded in 1887 as an all-graduate school on a German model, excelling in the social sciences, Clark University today welcomes undergraduates of all backgrounds and interests with small classes and no shortage of faculty attention. Clark's Liberal Education and Effective Practice (LEEP) educational model is designed to prepare students for success after college by combining a liberal arts curriculum with "intensive world, workplace, and personal experiences." As a junior explains, "LEEP serves to push students to bring their college education into the real world."

Clark's compact, 50-acre campus has "enough ivy, tall maples, and collegiate brick buildings to make a traditionalist happy," even though it's located in the rather gritty Main South section of Worcester. Buildings range from remodeled Victorian-era residences—former homes of prosperous merchants—to the award-winning Robert Hutchings Goddard Library. Careful restoration has brought a renewed sense of history to the area. Clark is the only American university where pioneering psychoanalyst Sigmund Freud lectured, and his statue adorns the center of campus. The 70,000-square-foot Center for Media Arts, Computing, and Design, slated to open in fall 2023, will host classrooms, a multimedia gallery, virtual reality and robotics labs, a data science lab, and a video game library.

> **"Professors are keen to let their students explore the lab and do actual hands-on research."**

While Clark now serves primarily undergraduates, its history of graduate education is evident in its classrooms. Most courses are seminars, and 60 percent have fewer than 20 students. First-Year Intensives, required of all students, are limited to a small number of students (usually no more than 16) to help introduce them to the intellectual, social, and emotional growth they will experience in college. In most cases, the faculty member teaching the course acts as an academic advisor until students declare a major.

Clark's Program of Liberal Studies promotes the habits, skills, and perspectives essential to lifelong learning. In addition to fulfilling requirements for their major, each student must complete eight courses: one in verbal expression, one in formal analysis, and six in perspectives—aesthetic, global comparative, historical, language, scientific, and values. One class must also satisfy a diversity and inclusion requirement. Many of Clark's course offerings, such as Problems of Practice courses, are practice-based, incorporating hands-on experiences outside the classroom. Before graduating, all students must complete a culminating capstone demonstrating the knowledge and capabilities they have honed during their four years.

Clark's historically strong psychology and geography departments continue to burnish their national reputations. Clark is the birthplace of the American Psychological Association and the concept of adolescence as being distinct from childhood. International development and social change is another traditional strength, as is environmental science, and the most popular majors include psychology, political science, economics, biology, and management. Established in 2021 in

Website: www.clarku.edu
Location: Small City
Private
Total Enrollment: 3,161
Undergraduates: 2,280
Male/Female: 42/58
Financial Aid: 95%
Pell Grant: 19%
Expense: Pr $ $
Student Loans: 62%
Average Debt: $ $ $ $
Applicants: 8,151
Accepted: 48%
Enrolled: 13%
Grad in 6 Years: 79%
Returning Freshmen: 87%
Academics: ✐ ✐ ✐ ✐
Social: ☎ ☎ ☎
Q of L: ★ ★ ★
Admissions: (508) 793-7431
Email Address: admissions@ clarku.edu

Strong Programs:
Psychology
Geography
Interactive Media/Game Design
International Development and Social Change
Environmental Science
Political Science
Economics
Biology

the wake of the closure of nearby Becker College, Clark's Becker School of Design & Technology offers majors in interactive media design (with several concentrations in game development), integrated graphic design, and eSports management. About 30 percent of graduating seniors take advantage of an accelerated B.A./M.A. program that allows them to take a fifth year of courses, with the help of a full- or partial-tuition scholarship, to obtain a master's degree, providing they meet the requirements.

The Center for Media Arts, Computing, and Design will host a multimedia gallery, virtual reality and robotics labs, and a video game library.

While courses at Clark are challenging and professors expect regular participation, students say the small class sizes mean that collaboration and support are the norm. "It's not hard to find study-buddies-turned-friends in your classes," says a senior. Thirty percent of Clark students spend at least one semester studying abroad, usually during their junior year, at one of more than 50 available programs in more than 20 countries. Sixty-four percent of students participate in undergraduate research, often assisting faculty with projects or pursuing their own as an independent study. "Professors are keen to let their students explore the lab and do actual hands-on research," says a physics and mathematics major.

"Clark students really dig into their niche and make it their own, both in their academic and social circles," says a senior. Forty-two percent of Clarkies hail from Massachusetts, and international students make up another 8 percent. Black students account for 5 percent of the student body, Hispanics/Latinos 9 percent, Asian Americans 7 percent, and multiracial students 3 percent. The political climate on campus is decidedly liberal, and a psychology and management major comments that "it is difficult to foster debate" because "most people agree with each other to begin with." Merit-based scholarships average $19,300, but athletic scholarships are not available. The Presidential Scholarship, awarded to highly motivated students with exceptional academic records, includes full tuition, room, and board for four years. Clark commits to meeting the full demonstrated financial need of students admitted through early decision plans.

"Clark students really dig into their niche and make it their own."

Clark is the birthplace of the American Psychological Association, and psychology is one of the most popular majors.

First-year students and sophomores at Clark are required to live in the residence halls. In all, 63 percent of undergrads live on campus in accommodations that are described as clean, comfortable, and "surprisingly big." Some upperclassmen looking to save money find apartments and group houses nearby. Campus dining gets average reviews for quality and diversity; "The secret is to use the spice and sauce rack as much as possible," confides an economics major. The school's urban location means that students must be "a little more open-minded and realistic about living in a city," says an environmental science major, but students agree that the campus feels safe.

Clark has no Greek life, and as a psychology and screen studies major explains, "The energy that might go into fraternities or sororities is instead redirected into a really vibrant club life on campus." More than 130 student-run organizations offer endless concerts, improv and theater shows, game nights, and other programs. First-year dorms are dry, but alcohol may be consumed in other dorms by those who are of age, and students say that alcohol policies emphasize safety over punishment. "Most parties happen in the off-campus apartments near Clark and never get too rowdy or crazy," notes a senior. Coping with the frigid New England winters includes quaffing cups of hot chocolate and dreaming about Spree Day in April, when classes are canceled and students enjoy live music, food trucks, face-painting, rock-climbing walls, mechanical bulls, and other festivities. Students also look forward to the annual International Gala, where students choreograph and perform dances representing 20 to 30 different countries.

"[Main South Worcester has] flavor and spice, and you'll either love it or hate it."

Worcester hosts several colleges, and Worcester itself is described as "a city of hidden gems," according to one student, offering movie theaters, restaurants with every conceivable type of cuisine, small clubs with live music, and the DCU Center, a 13,000-seat arena. "Main South Worcester is not the prettiest, quietest locale for a college, but it's got flavor and spice, and you'll either love it or hate it," a biology major says. Students mix with neighborhood residents through extensive volunteer programs coordinated by the Office of Community Engagement and Volunteering. To get away, Clarkies head to Boston and Providence (both about an hour away), New York (three hours), or the rural wilds of Vermont, New Hampshire, and Maine.

The Clark Cougars compete in the Division III New England Women's and Men's Athletic Conference (NEWMAC), and the university fields 17 intercollegiate teams. Men's and women's soccer, women's rowing and volleyball, and men's lacrosse are among the most competitive teams. About half of the students participate in intramural and club sports; ultimate Frisbee, ice hockey, and basketball are popular options. In addition, the Office of Wellness Education offers weekly stretching and meditation sessions and a Wednesday walking group to help students practice healthy habits.

Like Johns Hopkins and the Catholic University of America, Clark started out serving only graduate students but now offers a dynamic, undergraduate-focused educational environment. Clark continues to challenge convention, pioneering new teaching methods, pursuing new fields of knowledge, and finding new ways to connect thinking and doing. Through all this, community has remained a constant. Says a junior, "Clark is a warm and accepting place with students who hold the door open for others for just a little too long."

The Office of Wellness Education offers weekly stretching and meditation sessions and a Wednesday walking group.

Overlaps

Brandeis, Northeastern, Mount Holyoke, Skidmore, American University, Tufts, Vassar, Union

If You Apply To ›

Clark: Early decision I and II, early action, regular decision. SATs or ACTs: optional. Accepts the Common Application. Application includes optional field for gender identity.

Clarkson University

Holcroft House, Box 5605, Potsdam, NY 13699

You know you're in the North Country when the nearest major city is Ottawa. Clarkson lies over the river and through the woods. With an informal and close-knit atmosphere, Clarkson is one of the few small, undergraduate-oriented technological universities in the nation. Compare to Lehigh, Bucknell, and Union. Out-of-the-way location makes Clarkson easier to get into, but doing well is another matter.

At Clarkson University, engineering and ice hockey reign supreme. About half of the student body is enrolled in the engineering program, and the hockey teams are perennial contenders for top honors. Students here get a quality technical education with an emphasis on teamwork and professional preparation in a small-town environment that offers plenty to do, especially during the sled-dog days of winter. At Clarkson, says a junior, "We value academic integrity and success, but we also value failure, because it is in failure that we learn to grow."

The village of Potsdam, New York, is cloistered away between the Adirondacks and the St. Lawrence River. The campus relies mainly on modern architecture and lots of woods and wildlife. Academic buildings are connected by covered walkways that help take the sting out of getting around campus in the cold, snowy

Website: www.clarkson.edu
Location: Small Town
Private
Total Enrollment: 3,403
Undergraduates: 2,778
Male/Female: 69/31
Financial Aid: 99%
Pell Grant: 19%
Expense: Pr $ $
Student Loans: 78%

winters. Renovations across campus are ongoing, including the Schuler Educational Resources Center's Innovation Hub, which features labs, makerspaces, and group meeting rooms.

The university's general education program (Clarkson Common Experience) emphasizes four components: learning to communicate effectively; developing an appreciation for diversity; recognizing the importance of personal, societal, and professional ethics; and understanding how technology can be used to serve humanity. Freshmen (except those in the honors program) take a first-year seminar that helps develop critical-thinking, reading, and writing skills. All students are required to complete a capstone professional experience, like a co-op, internship, research project, or thesis.

Engineering isn't the only academic offering at Clarkson, but it certainly gets top billing, and it represents the three most popular majors: mechanical engineering, engineering and management, and civil engineering. In the natural sciences, biology and biomolecular science are among the strongest offerings, along with environmental science and policy and environmental health science, which are bolstered by the extensive research and outreach activities of the Institute for a Sustainable Environment. The Reh School of Business is highly praised,

> **"I would give the professors top marks for their lectures as well as…labs, office hours, and approachability."**

too, and offers several majors, including distinctive programs in global supply chain management and innovation and entrepreneurship. All business students must have an international study experience and an internship in order to graduate, and first-year students actually start and run a business. Clarkson does offer a few liberal arts majors, like history, literature, and political science, but even these programs incorporate a focus on technology.

Clarkson, which was founded in 1896 to honor a local entrepreneur, prides itself on intimacy and personalized instruction; 58 percent of classes have fewer than 20 students, and 27 percent of students conduct research with a faculty mentor. "I would give the professors top marks for their lectures as well as other aspects such as labs, office hours, and approachability," says a mechanical engineering major. Some students say Clarkson isn't the academic pressure cooker that many technical institutes can be. "The heavy and sometimes daunting workload is counteracted by the supportive nature of the students and faculty," says an environmental engineering major. "We are encouraged to work together to solve problems." Students recommend taking advantage of the private, small-group, and drop-in tutoring services offered by the Student Success Center, and they uniformly praise the school's career services for contributing to the university's high job-placement rate. "The Career Center is there to help you from day one and will provide assistance on *anything* related to preparing you for your career," enthuses a senior.

Environmental programs are bolstered by the extensive research and outreach activities of the Institute for a Sustainable Environment.

Study abroad opportunities are available in nearly 30 countries, although just 8 percent of students participate. The honors program accepts about 50 first-year students, who undertake an intensive four-year curriculum. Several hundred students from all majors join teams in Clarkson's Student Projects for Engineering Experience and Design program, such as Formula SAE, concrete canoe, and robotics competition teams. For women interested in STEM fields on this male-dominated campus, the Women in Science and Engineering program enrolls about 25 first-year students into a residential living/learning program.

> **"We are encouraged to work together to solve problems."**

"Most students here like to have fun on the weekends and grind during the week," says an engineering and management major. Sixty-five percent of the student body is native to New York. Clarkson has trouble luring minorities to its remote locale, although efforts to change that are underway; Black students currently make up 3 percent of the undergraduate population, Hispanics/Latinos 6 percent, Asian Americans 4 percent, and multiracial students 4 percent. International students add another 3 percent. Students agree that the campus doesn't usually get too vocal about national political issues. Clarkson awards merit scholarships each year averaging $32,200. Forty-one athletic scholarships are offered, but only men's and women's ice hockey players need apply (it's Clarkson's only Division I sport).

Eighty-four percent of students live in campus housing. Students are required to reside on campus all four years, unless exempted to live in an off-campus Greek house. All freshmen are housed in living/learning communities with students in their major or department, giving them the chance to study and learn together. Students say the quality of the dorms varies considerably, but the on-campus apartments offer more gracious living. The dining facilities generally get average marks. "The food is very edible," says a student. "Even professors eat it."

In keeping with Clarkson's "come-as-you-are" atmosphere, the social scene is low-key. Residence halls and student clubs organize plentiful on-campus entertainment, and 14 percent of the men and 9 percent of the women join the Greek system. Drinking is permitted on campus for those of age, who also head to the handful of bars in downtown Potsdam, which one student describes as having "small-town charm with an Adirondack twist." With three other colleges nearby, the town caters to students. The extended snowy winters are great for snowboarders and ice climbers, and many students join the popular Outing Club to enjoy such outdoor adventures year-round. "In the fall and spring students can be found working toward their '46,' or summiting all 46 high peaks in the Adirondack State Park," according to a senior. For those who crave the bustle of city nightlife, Ottawa and Montreal are each about an hour and a half away by car.

> **"The food is very edible. Even professors eat it."**

When it comes to sports, Golden Knights ice hockey is first and foremost in the hearts of Clarkson students. The men's and women's teams are perennially competitive in the Eastern College Athletic Conference and nationally, contending for the Division I championship with other blue-chip teams like St. Lawrence and Cornell. The annual game against archrival St. Lawrence has evolved into a popular two-day festival called Cold Out Gold Out, featuring live music, ice skating, horse-drawn carriage rides, and an alumni hockey match preceding the big game. Clarkson also offers 18 Division III sports. Women's volleyball has won nine of the last 10 Liberty League championships, and the men's Alpine and women's Nordic ski teams have brought home recent USCSA national titles. Most students take advantage of club sports and intramurals, with soccer, broomball, crew, and volleyball proving to be favorites.

"At Clarkson, we pride ourselves on being hardworking, innovative, creative, and very ambitious," comments a biology major. "We even hold friendly competitions each year to showcase and reward student innovation." While other majors are offered, Clarkson's bread and butter is its technological programs, particularly its slew of engineering majors. Students here gain ample exposure to the ever-growing variety of specialties in the field, and they also remember to have some fun along the way.

The annual ice hockey game against archrival St. Lawrence has evolved into a popular two-day festival called Cold Out Gold Out.

Overlaps

Rochester Institute of Technology, Rensselaer, Worcester Polytechnic, Wentworth Institute of Technology, Stevens Institute of Technology, Lehigh, Bucknell, Union

If You Apply To ›

Clarkson: Early decision, regular decision. Accepts the Common Application with supplement. Application includes optional field for gender identity. Please consult Clarkson's website for the most up-to-date information regarding standardized test requirements.

Clemson University

Clemson, SC 29634

Clemson is a technically oriented public university in the mold of Georgia Tech, North Carolina State, and Virginia Tech. Smaller than the latter two and more focused on undergraduates than Georgia Tech, Clemson serves up its education with ample helpings of school spirit and orange paint. Small-town location makes for a tight-knit campus, though also something of a hayseed image next to more sophisticated Carolina locales such as Columbia and Chapel Hill. Big on undergraduate research.

Nestled in the foothills of the Blue Ridge Mountains, Clemson University is a place where traditional Southern spirit continues to flourish alongside modern academics, big-time athletics, and state-of-the-art facilities. This public university, founded in 1889 as an agricultural college, has the ring of a private institution and features quality academics in technical and scientific areas such as engineering and biology. Tiger spirit is as strong as ever, as evidenced by the ubiquitous orange tiger paws that decorate the campus, and students here are happy to make tracks of their own.

CU's 1,400-acre campus is situated on what was once Fort Hill Plantation, the homestead of Thomas Green Clemson. The campus is surrounded by 17,000 acres of university farms and woodlands and offers a spectacular view of the nearby lake and mountains. Architectural styles are an eclectic mix of modern and 19th-century collegiate. Clemson Bottoms, half a mile down the road from the 80,000-seat football stadium, is home to the Calhoun Field Laboratory, a pastoral site dedicated to agricultural research that features a large, student-run organic garden. A fantastic resource for science enthusiasts and history buffs is the library's collection of first editions of the scientific works of Galileo and Newton. Douthit Hills is a $212 million residential village complete with dining and fitness facilities.

General education requirements include courses in advanced writing; oral communications; mathematical, scientific, and technological literacy; social sciences; arts and humanities; cross-cultural awareness; and science and technology in society. Biological sciences is Clemson's largest department, and computer engineering is among the nation's best in research on large-scale integrated computer circuitry and robotics. The School of Architecture offers intensive semesters at the Overseas Center for Building Research and Urban Study in Genoa, Italy. The accounting, animal and veterinary sciences, and agriculture programs are also well regarded. Management, biological sciences, psychology, marketing, and mechanical engineering are the most popular majors. Undergraduate teaching has always been one of Clemson's strong points, and for students interested in pursuing a liberal arts curriculum, the school has degrees in fine arts, philosophy, and languages and enjoys a strong regional reputation for its history program. Because of its prevailing technical emphasis, however, most students interested in the liberal arts head "down country" to the University of South Carolina.

> **"While challenging at times, the coursework is stimulating and applicable."**

Academically, the level of difficulty varies. "Classes are very competitive," says one junior. "While challenging at times, the coursework is stimulating and applicable." Professors run the gamut, but most receive high marks from students. "Professors not only teach the classes but also make themselves available for tons of extra hours outside of the classroom," says a psychology major. Thirty-two percent of the classes have fewer than 20 students. Fifty-four percent of undergrads take

Website: www.clemson.edu
Location: Small Town
Public
Total Enrollment: 23,910
Undergraduates: 20,834
Male/Female: 48/52
Financial Aid: 87%
Pell Grant: 13%
Expense: Pub $ $ $ $
Student Loans: 48%
Average Debt: $ $ $
Applicants: 47,001
Accepted: 49%
Enrolled: 20%
Grad in 6 Years: 85%
Returning Freshmen: 94%
Academics: ✍ ✍ ✍
Social: ☎ ☎ ☎ ☎
Q of L: ★ ★ ★ ★
Admissions: (864) 656-2287
Email Address: admissions@clemson.edu

Strong Programs:
Biological Sciences
Engineering
Architecture
Accounting
Animal and Veterinary Sciences
Agriculture
Management
Psychology

advantage of research opportunities during their time at Clemson. Ambitious students should consider applying to the Calhoun Honors College—the oldest honors program in South Carolina. Clemson also offers exchange programs in venues from Mexico to Australia, and 29 percent of students study abroad.

Clemson's student body has a decidedly Southern air, as 69 percent of undergrads hail from South Carolina, with most of the rest from neighboring states; less than 1 percent come from foreign countries. The university has accepted large numbers of community college graduates in recent years. "Students are approachable and willing to help on any given day," says a marketing major. Black students make up only 6 percent of the student body, Hispanics/Latinos 7 percent, Asian Americans 3 percent, and multiracial students 4 percent. The average Clemson student is friendly and conservative, and though, as a public institution, the school isn't affiliated with any church, there is a strong Southern Baptist presence on campus. The university offers thousands of merit scholarships averaging $4,700 and more than 350 athletic scholarships.

The computer engineering program is among the nation's best in research on large-scale integrated computer circuitry and robotics.

Housing gets positive reviews, with several new residence halls opening in the last few years, and one-third of the students live on campus, usually during their first two years. Options include single-sex, co-ed, traditional, and apartment-style housing. Meals in Clemson's three main dining halls are satisfactory, according to students. "They have specials and even ask students to contribute recipes," explains one student. Students say they feel safe on campus, thanks to diligent security officers. To address the issue of sexual assault, a senior reports, Clemson has implemented "awareness initiatives, events, and instructions on how to take action."

"At Clemson, the fun is mostly right outside our windows."

"At Clemson, the fun is mostly right outside our windows," says one student. "Whether it's a football game, a pep rally, a Residence Hall Association program, or one of our U-Nites Friday night activities, students always find something to do." Fraternities and sororities provide much of the social life, with 8 percent of Clemson men and 17 percent of women going Greek. The administration has introduced measures such as limiting fraternity members to bringing just one six-pack of beer to events, in an effort to curb hazing, alcohol abuse, and other problems related to the Greek scene. The town of Clemson is small, with a handful of restaurants, bars, and shops, but many students love it. After class, many students hop on their bikes and head to nearby Lake Hartwell. The beautiful Blue Ridge mountain range is also close by for hiking and camping, and beaches and ski slopes are both within driving distance. Atlanta and Charlotte are only two hours away by car, and Charleston is four hours away on the coast.

Tiger fans are especially rowdy when the reviled University of South Carolina Gamecocks are in town.

Clemson has a high-powered sports scene and fields a number of competitive teams in the Division I Atlantic Coast Conference. The football team has won two national championships since 2016, and the men's soccer team captured the national title in 2021. Football fever starts with the annual First Friday Parade, held before the first home game, and on game days the campus dissolves into a sea of Tiger orange, with pep rallies, cookouts, dances, and parties for the mobs of excited fans. The roads leading to campus are painted with large orange pawprints. So, too, are half the fans, making the stands in "Death Valley" look like an orange grove. Tiger fans are especially rowdy when the reviled University of South Carolina Gamecocks are in town; witness the traditional pregame pep rally known as Cocky's Funeral, during which "a giant cardboard 'chicken' is burned to the ground and free chicken sandwiches are given out to students," explains a senior. Known as the Palmetto Bowl, the annual South Carolina game has been played for more than a century. Baseball, men's and women's golf, and women's soccer are also very competitive. A plethora of intramural and club sports are available too.

Clemson is best at serving those whose interests lie in technical fields. School spirit is contagious, fueled by a love of big-time college sports, and becomes life-long for many Clemson students. Everyone can become part of the Clemson family, from Southern belle to Northern Yankee, as long as they're friendly, easygoing, and enthusiastic about life in general and the Tigers in particular.

If You Apply To ›

Clemson: Early action, regular decision. Accepts the Common Application. Music and theater applicants must audition. Please consult Clemson's website for the most up-to-date information regarding standardized test requirements.

Colby College

Waterville, ME 04901

The northernmost venue for high-quality, private higher education in New England. Colby's picturesque setting is a short hop from the eastern sea coast or Maine's western lakes and mountains. No Greek life since the college abolished it nearly 40 years ago. An active, outdoorsy, community-minded student body in the mold of Middlebury and Dartmouth, and more buttoned-up than Bates or Bowdoin. Invented the monthlong January term.

Website: www.colby.edu
Location: Rural
Private
Total Enrollment: 2,262
Undergraduates: 2,262
Male/Female: 47/53
Financial Aid: 46%
Pell Grant: 16%
Expense: Pr $ $ $ $
Student Loans: 24%
Average Debt: $ $
Applicants: 15,857
Accepted: 9%
Enrolled: 47%
Grad in 6 Years: 87%
Returning Freshmen: 95%
Academics: ✎ ✎ ✎ ✎ ½
Social: ☎ ☎ ☎
Q of L: ★ ★ ★ ★
Admissions: (800) 723-3032
Email Address: admissions@ colby.edu

Strong Programs:
Biology
Economics
Environmental Studies

Colby College draws students who like to push themselves, whether in the class-room, in creative pursuits, in volunteer work, or on skis. The city of Waterville, Maine (population 16,000), offers few distractions, and close friendships with peers and professors help ward off the long winter chill. Colby's top study abroad program offers students an opportunity to explore the world, and even those who don't spend a semester or year away can get a taste during the month of January, when Jan Plan trips send Colby students far and wide.

Colby sits high on Mayflower Hill, with beautiful views of the surrounding city and countryside. Its 714 acres include a wildlife management area, miles of cross-country trails, and a pond used in winter as an ice-skating rink. Georgian architecture predominates, and the oldest buildings are redbrick with white trim and brass nameplates above their hunter green doors. The more contemporary buildings lend a touch of modernity, and the Colby Museum of Art is renowned. One of the most iconic Colby buildings is the library tower, which is topped with a blue light proudly showing off the primary school color. The Schupf Art Center, an $18 million community arts center in downtown Waterville, opened in 2022, and the $85 million Gordon Center for Creative and Performing Arts is slated for completion in 2023. Colby has also acquired two islands in the Gulf of Maine previously owned by the painter Andrew Wyeth and his wife Betsy to use as centers for teaching, research, and artistic inspiration related to biodiversity and other current issues.

> "Professors are challenging and provoke students to think critically."

As a small college with a history of innovation and educational excellence dating to 1813, Colby encourages students to learn for learning's sake rather than for a good grade. Students must complete distribution requirements in English composition, foreign language, "areas" (courses in arts, historical studies, literature, quantitative reasoning, social sciences, and natural sciences), diversity, and wellness (five supper seminars over the first two semesters). Colby was the first men's college in New England to admit women and the first college anywhere to establish a 4–1–4 academic calendar with a four-week January term—known on campus as Jan Plan—between semesters. Students must take three Jan Plan terms for credit to graduate, but almost all take four, using the month to pursue one intensive academic or career experience, such as a research project, internship, or study abroad. The COOT program (Colby Outdoor Orientation Trips), required of all first-years, involves three-day excursions by bicycle, canoe, or foot that introduce newcomers to the beauty of the Maine wilderness or to service or theater experiences.

(continued)
Government
Global Studies
Psychology
Computer Science
Computational Biology

Colby offers 57 majors. Popular and well-regarded programs include biology, economics, environmental studies, government, global studies, psychology, computer science, and computational biology. In 2021 Colby established the cross-disciplinary Davis Institute for Artificial Intelligence, the first such institute at a liberal arts college, offering significant new opportunities for faculty and student research. Students study oceanography through Colby's partnership with the Bigelow Laboratory for Ocean Sciences in East Boothbay, Maine. For would-be engineers, there is a joint 3–2 program with Dartmouth and 3–2 and 4–2 programs with Columbia; others may opt for exchange programs with the Claremont Colleges and Howard. Classes are small and academics are demanding, but it helps that Colby's faculty is unusually devoted to undergraduate teaching and easily accessible. "Professors are challenging and provoke students to think critically, but not at the expense of helping you find your passions," muses an education and French major.

Almost all students take four Jan Plan terms, using the month to pursue a research project, internship, or study abroad.

Study abroad is a serious emphasis at Colby, and the opportunities to do so begin early. First-year students can apply to the Global Entry Semester program, whisking off to France or Spain with 20 or so classmates for the fall semester. Half of the school's majors have an international component, and nearly 70 percent of Colby students spend some time abroad, taking advantage of roughly 200 approved international programs, including Colby-sponsored Jan Plan trips.

"Lots of Colby students are outdoorsy."

About 40 percent of students conduct undergraduate research, and those who stay on campus during the summer as research assistants for faculty are rewarded with a two-day Summer Research Retreat in Forks, Maine, dedicated to short talks, presentations, and white-water rafting or hiking adventures. DavisConnects provides career advising and guarantees every student access to at least one internship, research, and global experience, regardless of their ability to pay.

Colby's student body, in the words of a junior, has a "preppy crunchy" vibe. "Lots of Colby students are outdoorsy," says a student, and although the proportion of Pell-eligible students (16 percent of current first-years) has been rising in recent years, a sophomore reports that "students are mostly from affluent backgrounds." The college has been working to increase other types of diversity as well: Black students account for 5 percent of the student body, Hispanics/Latinos 8 percent, Asian Americans 10 percent, and multiracial students 6 percent. Just 7 percent of Colby students are Mainers, and 10 percent are international. Politically, "Mayflower Hill is a very liberal space," says a sophomore; environmental issues are of top concern. All financial aid at Colby is need-based, the college meets 100 percent of students' demonstrated need, and it has replaced student loans with grants in all its financial aid packages.

A residential complex in downtown Waterville offers a living/learning community focused on civic engagement for 200 juniors and seniors.

Students are required to live in college housing for all four years. On-campus residence halls, which students describe as "very average," have live-in faculty members. A residential complex in downtown Waterville offers a living/learning community focused on civic engagement for 200 juniors and seniors. "Colby has three good dining halls, each with their own flair, and makes an effort to source locally and sustainably," says a senior; a grab-and-go spot in the student union and a student-run coffee shop offer more options. First-years and sophomores take training workshops on sexual violence prevention, and one student remarks, "Colby makes its standards very clear to students."

Colby may eschew fraternities and sororities, but parties in the senior apartments are a weekend staple and tend to be driven by sports teams. "Campus policies around alcohol are about creating a healthy drinking culture," says a junior, and a sophomore adds, "There are school-sponsored events every weekend with no alcohol." Fall Concert and Spring Concert bring well-known musical acts to campus once per semester. Another favorite—but not school-sanctioned—tradition is Doghead, "where students party and stay up the whole night on St. Patrick's Day weekend and watch the sunrise from the library steps together," explains a senior. Downtown Waterville offers some good restaurants and bars, but otherwise it's "not the most active town for young people," says a computer science major. Popular Maine road trips include Portland, Freeport (home to the L.L. Bean factory and store), Mount Desert Island, and Sugarloaf Mountain (for skiing). Also easy to reach are the bright lights of Boston and Montreal.

> "Campus policies around alcohol are about creating a healthy drinking culture."

The Colby Mules have come a long way since the first intercollegiate croquet game, played at Colby in 1860. Sports are Division III, except for squash and skiing, which are Division I, and solid programs include women's lacrosse, women's Nordic skiing, and men's ice hockey, cross-country, and track and field. Games against Bates and Bowdoin draw crowds, especially the annual Bowdoin hockey match. A majority of the students participate in club and intramural sports; rugby, ultimate Frisbee, basketball, and badminton are some of the most popular.

Colby's traditional New England liberal arts college feel and increasingly global focus extend far beyond its small-city setting and historic buildings. They permeate the air, punctuated by the long-standing traditions, abundant school spirit, and caring faculty members who focus on developing their students' minds.

Overlaps

Bowdoin, Amherst, Williams, Middlebury, Hamilton, Dartmouth, Bates, Carleton

If You Apply To ›

Colby: Early decision I and II, regular decision. SATs or ACTs: optional. Accepts the Common Application.

Colgate University

13 Oak Drive, Hamilton, NY 13346

With just over 3,100 students, Colgate is smaller than Bucknell and Dartmouth but bigger than Hamilton and Williams. Like the other four, it offers small-town living and close interaction between students and faculty. Greek organizations and jocks are still well entrenched despite perennial administrative efforts to neutralize their influence.

Website: www.colgate.edu
Location: Rural
Private
Total Enrollment: 3,147
Undergraduates: 3,142

While you may see the same Canada Goose jackets coming and going (and coming and going) as you stroll across Colgate University's campus, the students in them aren't all spun from the same cloth. "Most students at Colgate are freethinkers and open to new ideas," says a sophomore. From the herbarium to the Devonian fossils to the abundance of interdisciplinary courses, it's clear that Colgate has more to offer than just its picture-postcard setting. "I think Colgate draws students who want a high level of academic rigor and a top-tier liberal arts education," says one student, "without the competitive air that usually accompanies these."

Colgate's 13 founders started the school in 1817 with 13 prayers and 13 dollars. Their prayers were answered by soapmaking mogul William Colgate and his sons (think: toothpaste), whose decades of philanthropic gift-giving to the fledgling university were enough to get the name changed in 1890 from Madison to Colgate. Today, the 575-acre campus sits on a hillside in rural New York, overlooking the village of Hamilton. Stately bluestone buildings peek out from tree-lined drives; lush green spaces are perfect for rugby, Frisbee, or other outdoor diversions, at least in the warmer months. Rolling hills and farmland surround the campus, making for stunning vistas during the snowy season, which stretches from mid-October to mid-March.

Aside from blazing a trail to rural New York, Colgate has led its peers in emphasizing interdisciplinary study. The faculty first established an interdisciplinary core program in 1928, and it's been a foundation of the curriculum ever since. Even now, all freshmen take a first-year seminar, capped at 18 students each, that introduces liberal arts topics, skills, resources, and ways of learning. Students choose from more than 40 topics, and seminar instructors double as academic advisors until students declare majors their sophomore year.

> "The academic climate is rigorous, inquisitive, and personalized."

Everyone completes four liberal arts core courses—Legacies of the Ancient World, Challenges of Modernity, Sciences, and Communities. Students also take classes in a range of disciplines that cover three broad areas: Human Thought and Expression; Social Relations, Institutions, and Agents; and Natural Sciences and Mathematics.

"The academic climate is rigorous, inquisitive, and personalized," muses a political science major. Students give high marks to Colgate's natural and social sciences programs, and economics, political science, English, psychology, and computer science are the most popular majors. Befitting Colgate's rugged location, there are five interdisciplinary environmental majors: environmental studies, environmental biology, environmental geography, environmental geology, and environmental economics. Seventy percent of classes have fewer than 20 students, and an English major says, "Colgate professors do an excellent job of breaking down the professor/student hierarchy that can sometimes make students—especially underclassmen—nervous."

Classrooms and labs devoted to foreign language study help students gain comfort with another tongue—a good thing, since 62 percent of students study abroad. In addition to about 20 semester-long, faculty-led off-campus study programs (called "study groups"), Colgate offers five to eight "extended-study" travel programs that serve as two- or three-week extensions of regular on-campus courses. More than 100 other preapproved study abroad programs offer additional options. The Sophomore Residential Seminars program enables selected students to live together in the same residence hall and take a semester-long course that is capped off with a weeklong trip; recent participants have traveled to the U.S.–Mexico border to study the economics of immigration and to Colombia for a course on the geography of global beverages. Eighty percent of students get involved with undergraduate research, many of them working under faculty members as paid summer research assistants. Students rave about Colgate's Career Services office. "We have a big network of a lot of big-shot alumni that they are good at connecting students with," explains a senior. "They can even get kind of annoying, honestly, because they are always in your inbox trying to help you plan out your next steps."

A senior says, "Students at Colgate are ambitious, driven, and intellectually curious," and according to a junior, they are "often preppy." Twenty-four percent of students are New Yorkers, while 9 percent are international. Black students account for 4 percent of the population, Hispanics/Latinos 9 percent, Asian Americans 5

(continued)

Male/Female: 45/55
Financial Aid: 52%
Pell Grant: 13%
Expense: Pr $ $ $ $
Student Loans: 30%
Average Debt: $ $
Applicants: 17,540
Accepted: 17%
Enrolled: 29%
Grad in 6 Years: 90%
Returning Freshmen: 93%
Academics: ✍ ✍ ✍ ✍ ½
Social: ☎ ☎ ☎
Q of L: ★ ★ ★
Admissions: (315) 228-7401
Email Address: admission@ colgate.edu

Strong Programs:
Natural Sciences
Social Sciences
Environmental Studies
Economics
Political Science
English
Psychology
Computer Science

Befitting Colgate's rugged location, there are five interdisciplinary environmental majors.

percent, and multiracial students 5 percent. Students credit the ALANA Cultural Center with "fostering a comfortable and friendly environment" and describe a left-leaning political climate. "Several discussion points on campus have been about general inclusivity, the influence of Greek life on campus, and gender and safety issues," notes a physics major. Colgate does not award merit scholarships, but about 200 athletic scholarships are available in 13 sports. The university meets 100 percent of enrolled students' demonstrated financial need. In addition, Colgate has removed loans from aid packages for students whose annual family income is less than $150,000, and students whose annual family income is less than $80,000 attend tuition-free.

Ninety-three percent of Colgate students live in the residence halls, which range from traditional buildings with fireplaces to newer facilities that seem more like hotels. Students are housed in residential communities called Commons for their first two years and remain affiliated with their Commons throughout their four years. About 250 upperclassmen are allowed to live off campus each year. The main dining hall, Frank, serves up plenty of all-you-can-eat options, but the quality is said to be "hit or miss." A junior reports that the school's support center for survivors of sexual assault is "making students more aware of the issue and how they can help." A psychology major adds, "There is a large focus on mental health within the Colgate community, creating an open and encouraging space for students to discuss it honestly."

"[Career Services] can even get kind of annoying, honestly, because they are always in your inbox."

Twenty percent of the men and 33 percent of the women join fraternities and sororities. "Colgate students party hard," says a senior. "I think the administration is trying to limit excessive partying and drinking, but students will always find a way to party." The university owns and manages all Greek housing, and recruitment is delayed until sophomore year. While the Greek system may dominate the party scene, most students agree that there is little pressure to participate, and with more than 200 campus clubs and organizations, there are plenty of alternatives. "Colgate is a place where people want to be doing something social even in the dead of winter," says an economics major. Students enjoy free "Take Two" movies on Friday and Saturday nights and open-mic nights at the campus pub, Donovan's. Everyone looks forward to ALANApalooza, Dancefest, and Springfest, a last blast before finals that celebrates the thaw with a big concert, barbecues, and fireworks. Given the significance of the number 13 to the school's founding, every Friday the 13th is dubbed Colgate Day, a time to show off school spirit and pride. On the eve of graduation, seniors don their graduation robes for the Torchlight Ceremony.

In addition to a required four-day orientation, freshmen may participate in one of several preorientation programs, such as Wilderness Adventure, where groups of 8 to 12 canoe and hike in the Adirondacks. Hamilton is within walking distance of campus, but there's also a free bus that cycles through every half hour, especially nice in the depths of winter. The Old Stone Jug is a favorite hangout, and the Palace Theater draws crowds with music, dancing, and a bar, but students say the quiet village doesn't have much else to offer. For those with wheels, skiing is 45 minutes away at Labrador Mountain, and the malls and city lights of Syracuse and Utica are roughly the same distance.

"Colgate is a place where people want to be doing something social even in the dead of winter."

About a third of Colgate students enjoy facing off in 12 intramural competitions and 40 club sports, but students' most fervent cheers are reserved for Division I men's ice hockey against Cornell. "When Cornell comes to our rink, we throw Big Red gum on the ice, and they throw Colgate toothpaste on the ice," explains a junior. Women's ice hockey is a powerhouse, and the Raiders men's basketball and women's volleyball teams are recent Patriot League conference champions. Even weekend warriors may take advantage of facilities like the Sanford Field House, the Lineberry natatorium, and the Seven Oaks golf course, which is ranked among the top five collegiate courses nationally.

Colgate led the way in interdisciplinary work and continues to do so now. What else has remained constant? A senior offers this assessment: "I think Colgate has embraced its identity as different from other liberal arts colleges in that we are not a crunchy granola hippie school, and we are not a socially progressive bastion of forward thinking. Colgate is what it is: a hidden gem in the Chenango Valley."

If You Apply To ›

Colgate: Early decision I and II, regular decision. Accepts the Common Application with supplement. Please consult Colgate's website for the most up-to-date information regarding standardized test requirements.

University of Colorado Boulder

Regent Administrative Center 125, 552 UCB, Boulder, CO 80309

Boulder is a legendary place that draws everyone from East Coast ski bums to California transplants. The scenery is breathtaking and the science programs are first-rate. The University of Arizona is the only public university of similar stature in the Mountain West. Check out the residential academic programs.

Wild buffalo may be all but extinct on America's Great Plains, but they're in boisterous residence, proudly wearing gold and black, at the University of Colorado Boulder. A bevy of scholars' programs and residential academic programs give the campus a community feel, and students choose from a solid menu of academic offerings, including research experience, study abroad, and service learning. "There are so many ways to be active and engaged in your learning at Boulder," cheers a sophomore. And with more than 300 days of sunshine a year, it's no surprise that CU Boulder Buffaloes are a happy herd.

Tree-shaded walkways, winding bike paths, open spaces, and an incredible view of the dramatic Flatirons rock formation make CU's 600-acre Boulder campus a haven for students from both coasts and for Colorado residents eager to pursue knowledge in a snowy paradise. The university was founded in 1876 as Colorado was becoming a state, and the campus includes about 200 classic rural Italian-style buildings and complexes built of Colorado sandstone with red tile roofs. City bus passes are included in the cost of tuition and fees, the campus Environmental Center facilitates sustainable culture and practices, and ongoing renovations and construction projects embody the university's commitment to sustainability and energy efficiency. Recent campus projects include an addition that physically connects the main engineering and business buildings and features an innovation and entrepreneurship hub as well as a 200-seat auditorium.

> **"There are so many ways to be active and engaged in your learning at Boulder."**

Entering freshmen and transfer students at CU Boulder choose from the following colleges, schools, and programs: the College of Arts and Sciences (which enrolls 70 percent of the students); the College of Music; the College of Engineering

Website: www.colorado.edu
Location: Small City
Public
Total Enrollment: 31,240
Undergraduates: 28,344
Male/Female: 54/46
Financial Aid: 62%
Pell Grant: 14%
Expense: Pub $ $ $
Student Loans: 38%
Average Debt: $ $
Applicants: 54,756
Accepted: 80%
Enrolled: 15%
Grad in 6 Years: 74%
Returning Freshmen: 87%
Academics: ✐ ✐ ✐ ✐
Social: ☎ ☎ ☎ ☎ ☎
Q of L: ★ ★ ★
Admissions: (303) 492-6301
Email Address: admissions@ colorado.edu

and Applied Science (the hardest to enter, students say); the College of Media, Communication, and Information; the Program in Environmental Design; the Leeds School of Business; the School of Education; and the Program in Exploratory Studies (which allows students to explore options before selecting a major). General education requirements cover three skills acquisition areas—written communication, quantitative reasoning and math, and foreign language—and three distribution categories: arts and humanities, natural sciences, and social sciences.

"Unlike other highly competitive universities, there is a high level of collaboration," says an applied mathematics major. "Your classmates won't refuse to work with you, and you are always comfortable asking questions and asking for help." CU Boulder offers more than 4,500 courses each year in approximately 160 areas of study; psychology, finance, strategic communication, and integrative physiology are among the most popular majors. Outstanding programs include aerospace engineering sciences, physics, astronomy, chemical and biological engineering, computer science, music, business administration, and environmental studies. CU

> **"Unlike other highly competitive universities, there is a high level of collaboration."**

Boulder consistently ranks among the top universities in the country to receive NASA funding, leading to lots of opportunities for the design, construction, and flight of model spacecraft—and to 18 CU Boulder alumni having worked as astronauts. A space minor is open to qualified students in any major. Established in 2021, the Center for African and African American Studies supports teaching and research focused on the history and culture of people of African descent. The university also offers 44 bachelor's-accelerated master's degree programs, which allow students to earn two degrees in a shorter period of time. Forty-five percent of all undergraduate classes enroll fewer than 20 students, and a freshman says, "In my experience, professors and graduate student instructors alike have taken a keen interest in students' progress, success, and learning."

CU Boulder has tried to make its large campus seem smaller through its 12 residential academic programs (small, specialized living/learning environments) focusing on topics such as global studies, natural sciences and the environment, the arts, and engineering. Participants take one or two courses, each limited to 25 students, in their residence halls. "The Residential Academic Program for freshmen is essential for gaining a well-rounded experience at CU," advises a senior. The Presidents Leadership Class is a four-year scholarship program that provides super promising students with leadership training, internships, volunteer opportunities, and visits with influential political, business, and community leaders. The top 10 percent of each incoming class in the College of Arts and Sciences is invited to join the Honors Program, which offers more than 80 honors courses per year. About a third of students undertake undergraduate research, and just as many pack their bags for the 350 university-sponsored study abroad programs available in 65 countries around the world.

CU Boulder ranks among the top universities in the country to receive NASA funding, and a space minor is open to students in any major.

"Students are relaxed and explorative, curious and inquisitive, fun-loving and good-natured, focused and committed," says one Buffalo. Fifty-seven percent of CU Boulder's undergraduates come from Colorado, and 4 percent come from abroad. Hispanics/Latinos account for 13 percent of the undergraduate population, Asian Americans 6 percent, Black students 2 percent, and multiracial students 6 percent. Social and political issues on campus include "wealth, liberalism, and inequality," according to one student. Qualified undergrads receive merit scholarships worth an average of $9,600, and about 250 athletes receive scholarships as well. Additional programs provide debt-free financial incentives for qualified in-state students whose family income is at or below the federal poverty line. The university also guarantees incoming freshmen that tuition and fees will not increase over their four years.

First-year students are required to live on campus, and 26 percent of all undergrads stay in university housing. "The older dorms are still in pretty good shape but aren't as nice as the newer dorms," a sophomore reports. Most sophomores, juniors, and seniors find off-campus digs in Boulder. An alternative to the main Center for Community dining center and 16 smaller dining locations is the Alferd Packer Restaurant & Grill, which takes its name from a controversial 19th-century folk figure known as the "Colorado Cannibal." *Bon appétit.* Generally, students say the campus is safe. CU Boulder offers nighttime transportation via a service called CU NightRide.

For the culturally minded, the university and the city of Boulder offer films and plays, the renowned Colorado Shakespeare Festival, art galleries and museums, and concerts by top bands. Denver is only 30 miles southeast, reachable by a free bus service. Most students get involved in community service, and the CU Engage center coordinates service-learning courses and community-based research opportunities. Thirteen percent of CU Boulder men and 22 percent of women go Greek, though fraternity and sorority parties have changed dramatically since CU Boulder's sorority chapters became the first in the nation to voluntarily make their houses dry. On campus, the ban

Ralphie, the live buffalo who acts as CU Boulder's mascot, doesn't miss a game—and neither do many students.

"The party scene is fairly large and has a lot going on most weekends."

on alcohol is taken seriously, and dorms are officially substance-free. Still, "The party scene is fairly large and has a lot going on most weekends," says a political science major. Day trips to ski resorts like Breckenridge and Vail largely replace weekend getaways here, but for those who've got to get out of the cold, Las Vegas isn't so far, says one student.

Physical exercise is a popular extracurricular activity at CU Boulder, especially the sort that involves sliding down snow-covered mountains. The massive Student Recreation Center features indoor and outdoor pools, a multipurpose turf gym, an ice rink, a climbing gym, and several multipurpose courts, among other facilities. Varsity teams compete in the Division I Pac-12 Conference, and the Buffaloes men's and women's basketball, cross-country, and skiing teams are some of the strongest, along with women's soccer and lacrosse. Ralphie, the live buffalo who acts as CU Boulder's mascot, doesn't miss a game—and neither do many students. Each year, football fans flock to Denver to watch the Rocky Mountain Showdown game against Colorado State. The club sports program, which boasts 30 options, is highly competitive, regularly bringing home national titles in sports ranging from ice hockey and snowboarding to cycling and triathlon. Intramurals sign up about a third of the students each year.

If you want to flex your muscles as well as your mind, look beyond the ivy-covered bricks and gray city skies endemic to so many Eastern institutions, and consider all the West has to offer instead. "The amount of resources students can utilize to further their education or gain experience in their field at CU and in the city of Boulder is immense and overwhelming," says one student.

Overlaps

University of Arizona, Colorado State, UW–Madison, Cal Poly–San Luis Obispo, University of Oregon, University of Washington, Indiana University, Arizona State

If You Apply To ›

CU Boulder: Early action, regular decision. SATs or ACTs: optional. Accepts the Common Application. Music applicants must audition.

Colorado College

14 East Cache La Poudre Street, Colorado Springs, CO 80903

The Block Plan, a one-course-at-a-time academic schedule, is CC's claim to fame. It is great for in-depth study and short-term study abroad but less suited to academic projects that take an extended period of time. Colorado Springs is an ideal location at the base of the Rockies, which draw outdoor enthusiasts and East Coasters who want to ski. CC is the only top liberal arts college between Iowa and the Pacific.

Website: www.coloradocollege
.edu
Location: City Center
Private
Total Enrollment: 2,197
Undergraduates: 2,187
Male/Female: 43/57
Financial Aid: 48%
Pell Grant: 15%
Expense: Pr $ $ $ $
Student Loans: 29%
Average Debt: $
Applicants: 10,975
Accepted: 14%
Enrolled: 40%
Grad in 6 Years: 86%
Returning Freshmen: 96%
Academics: ✍ ✍ ✍ ✍
Social: ☎ ☎ ☎ ☎
Q of L: ★ ★ ★ ★
Admissions: (800) 542-7214
Email Address: admission@
coloradocollege.edu

Strong Programs:
Geology
Environmental Science
Southwest Studies
Economics
Political Science
Organismal Biology and
Ecology
Computer Science
Molecular Biology

Colorado College is one of the few U.S. schools offering one-course-at-a-time block scheduling. For more than a century, CC's focus on creative approaches to academics and its breathtaking location at the edge of the Rocky Mountains have drawn bright, independent liberal arts enthusiasts who also like to go out and play. "People don't come to CC because they want to make a ton of money or maintain the status quo," asserts a senior. "They come because they want to change the world, help others, and have a little fun."

Colorado's campus lies at the foot of Pike's Peak, in the town of Colorado Springs. Many homes in the surrounding neighborhood are on the National Register of Historic Places, as are many CC buildings, including its first, Cutler Hall, and Palmer Hall, named after town founder William J. Palmer, a major force behind the establishment of the college in 1874. The prevailing architectural styles are Romanesque and English Gothic, with some more modern structures thrown in. The $52 million, 3,400-seat Robson Arena, hosting CC's Division I men's ice hockey team, opened in 2021.

CC requires students to take courses focused on global cultures, issues of inequality (with respect to nationality, race, ethnicity, gender, class, and/or sexuality), natural sciences, and quantitative reasoning. Foreign language proficiency is also required. What really defines the academic climate, though, is the Block Plan (see also Cornell College in Iowa). Students take eight courses between early September and mid-May but focus on each one, in turn, for three and a half weeks. Some courses, such as those involving longer-term projects, are two blocks long. Four-and-a-half-day breaks separate the blocks. The plan helps students stay focused, eliminating the temptation to let one course slide so that they can catch up in another. But there are trade-offs. Students say it can be hard to integrate material from courses taken one at a time. There's also the danger of burnout, because so much material on a single subject is crammed into such a short span. An optional "half block" in January gives students a chance to explore niche academic interests or learn professional skills to become more competitive in the job market. In addition, an optional summer session offers three blocks.

> **"CC is extremely collaborative. However, it's extremely intense."**

The First-Year Program, consisting of a two-block sequence of courses with a student mentor and two advisors, helps students adjust to college-level academics, research, and the fast pace of the Block Plan. "CC is extremely collaborative," notes an environmental policy major. "However, it's extremely intense." Two-thirds of the classes have fewer than 20 students, and required courses aren't hard to get into, since spots are secured with an auction system. At the beginning of each year, students get 80 points to "bid" on the classes they want. Those who bid the most for a particular class get a seat. If you're going to take only one class at a time, it helps to like the teacher, and students say that's usually no problem here. "The professors are very accessible, and it is easy to have a good working relationship," says a history and political science major.

The most popular majors at Colorado include economics, political science, organismal biology and ecology, computer science, and molecular biology. Students say that the sciences in general, and particularly geology and environmental science, are strengths. The block schedule permits some classes at unique times and in unique places—for instance, astronomy at midnight, or coral biology work in the Caribbean. The college's popular major in Southwest studies includes time at its Baca campus, 175 miles away in the historic San Luis Valley. Other interesting inter-disciplinary programs include race, ethnicity, and migration studies and a new major in business, economics, and society. In addition to giving students the option to pick semester- and yearlong abroad programs in more than 60 countries, Colorado College faculty also teach about 25 off-campus blocks, both domestically and inter-nationally, throughout the school year and summer session. Roughly three-quarters of the students study off campus at least once during their time at Colorado.

Just 20 percent of Colorado College students are in-staters, 7 percent are inter-national, and the rest are from all over the United States. "The students are laid-back, nature-loving hippies," says a student. CC is more selective but less socioeconomically diverse than its closest peer, Cornell College—just 15 percent of Colorado freshmen qualify for Pell Grants. Three percent of undergrads are Black, 11 percent are Hispanic/Latino, 5 percent are Asian American, and 7 percent are multiracial—and the school is trying to attract more diversity. Groups like the Queer Straight Alliance, the Feminist Collective, the Jewish Chaverim, and the Black Student Union provide support to students of varied backgrounds and viewpoints. "The general political orientation is extremely liberal," says a senior. The college meets 100 percent of admitted students' demonstrated financial need, and a limited number of merit scholarships, averaging $8,700, and athletic scholarships are available.

> **"It is easy to have a good working relationship [with professors]."**

> *The $52 million, 3,400-seat Robson Arena, hosting CC's Division I men's ice hockey team, opened in 2021.*

Seventy-nine percent of students call campus housing home, and only seniors are permitted to live off campus. "The underclassmen dorms range from brand-new, almost luxury suites, to pretty old but full of character," says a senior. The "excep-tional" dining facilities include a traditional, all-you-can-eat dining hall; a grill with American, Mexican, and sushi options; and an all-natural café and convenience store. The Student Organization for Sexual Safety raises awareness and addresses campus culture around issues like consent and sexual assault.

When the weekend comes, students unwind at parties in friends' rooms or seniors' off-campus houses. "There is a very large drug and alcohol presence on campus," reports a senior, "though it absolutely is not mandatory," socially speak-ing. The "low-key" Greek system attracts 12 percent of the men and 8 percent of the women. Favorite traditions include the annual Llamapalooza and Blues & Shoes (bluegrass and horseshoes) music festivals, and the monthly Full Moon Cruisers, where "students gather at 10 p.m. decked out in crazy outfits to ride their bikes downtown and party under the full moon," explains a student. For those seeking a bit of urban culture, Denver and Boulder are a short drive away. Most CC students love heading off campus to ski or hike, either at nearby resorts or in Utah, New Mexico, or the Grand Canyon. Freshman outdoor orientation trips help newcomers sort out the options, from backpacking and hiking to rafting, bicycling, and windsurfing. Students can even reserve a college-owned mountainside cabin. Service trips are sponsored during block breaks, and the major-ity of students do some type of community service during their time at CC, often through community-based learning courses.

> *The college's popular major in Southwest studies includes time at its Baca campus, 175 miles away in the historic San Luis Valley.*

> **"The students are laid-back, nature-loving hippies."**

The Colorado College Tigers compete in two Division I sports—men's ice hockey and women's soccer—as well as 15 Division III sports. Men's and women's soccer, lacrosse, swimming, and cross-country and women's volleyball have made national tournament appearances in recent years. The hockey rivalry with the University of Denver is huge. Students are also active in a dozen intramurals and 16 club sports.

> ## Overlaps
> **Cornell College, University of Denver, Middlebury, Colby, Whitman, Carleton, Wesleyan, University of Colorado Boulder**

The Block Plan made Colorado College what it is today, and the school continues to build on this reputation. As one senior underscores, "The intensive and demanding nature of the Block Plan calls for deep but quick thinkers [and] hard but patient workers." For those who are up to the challenge, CC offers a supportive environment, with a healthy dose of fun, where they can thrive.

If You Apply To ›

Colorado College: Early decision I and II, early action, regular decision. SATs or ACTs: optional. Accepts the Common Application with supplement.

Colorado School of Mines

1812 Illinois Street, Golden, CO 80401

Mines is the preeminent technical institute in the Mountain West. Getting in is not all that hard; getting through is another story. One-sixth the size of Texas Tech and best known for mining-related fields but strong in many areas of engineering. Men outnumber women by more than 2 to 1. Golden provides easy access to the mountains and Denver. Graduates are heavily recruited.

Website: www.mines.edu
Location: Small City
Public
Total Enrollment: 6,439
Undergraduates: 5,176
Male/Female: 68/32
Financial Aid: 77%
Pell Grant: 13%
Expense: Pub $ $ $ $
Student Loans: 48%
Average Debt: $ $ $
Applicants: 12,022
Accepted: 57%
Enrolled: 21%
Grad in 6 Years: 83%
Returning Freshmen: 91%
Academics: ✍ ✍ ✍ ½
Social: ☎ ☎ ☎
Q of L: ★ ★
Admissions: (888) 446-9489
Email Address: admissions@
mines.edu

Strong Programs:
Geophysical Engineering
Metallurgical and Materials
Engineering
Petroleum Engineering

If you're a bit of a geek whose only dilemma is what type of engineer to become, and you want to spend your scarce free time hiking, biking, and skiing with friends, then Colorado School of Mines may be the place for you. This public school's small size and rugged location endear it to the students who shoulder heavy workloads to earn their degrees. "There are often fun and entertaining conversations that could only be possible with the types of students here," says a mechanical engineering major. Just down the road from Coors Brewing Co., which taps the Rockies for its legendary brews, students at Mines learn to tap the same mountains for coal, oil, and other natural resources.

The school's 373-acre campus sits in the shadow of the spectacular Rocky Mountains in tiny Golden (as in gold mining), Colorado. Architectural styles range from turn-of-the-century gold dome to present-day modern, and native trees and greenery punctuate lush lawns. The $50 million CoorsTek Center for Applied Science and Engineering is among the recent additions to campus.

At Mines, the academics are rigorous. Core requirements include coursework in humanities, social sciences, physical education, and, of course, science and engineering, with extra doses of physics, chemistry, calculus, and differential equations. In the first year, everyone takes the Freshman Success Seminar, an advising and mentoring course. The required two-semester EPIC program—the acronym stands for Engineering Practices Introductory Course—helps develop communication, teamwork, and problem-solving skills with weekly presentations and written reports. Because of Mines's narrow focus, the undergraduate majors—or "options," as they're called—are quite strong. There's plenty of variety, as long as you are into engineering; programs range from geophysical, metallurgical, and petroleum to chemical, electrical, and mechanical. Computer science, another popular choice, is the school's fastest-growing program. Mines offers the only B.S. degree in economics in Colorado and has been investing more in humanities and social sciences, offering several minors

> **"Most of the teachers have industry experience and bring that into the classroom."**

in these areas. Courses in a student's option start in the second semester of sophomore year, and as seniors, all students complete a capstone requirement.

Pass/fail grading is unheard of at Mines, but failing grades are not. "The courses are hard," says a junior, "but good time management and friends" help ease the angst. "We are all working together," another adds. Professors are qualified and helpful, and adjunct professors, who work in the fields they teach, draw raves for their practical knowledge. "Most of the teachers have industry experience and bring that into the classroom," a chemistry major says. Twenty-seven percent of undergraduate classes have fewer than 20 students.

Mines supplements coursework with a required six-week summer field session, enabling students to gain hands-on experience. About 100 undergraduates participate in the McBride Honors Program, which includes seminars and off-campus activities that encourage them to think differently about the implications of technology. The WISEM program provides training, mentoring, and other support for women in science, engineering, and math. The school also offers exchange programs with 25 universities worldwide, but typically only 7 to 10 percent of students study abroad. Each year, 100 to 120 undergraduates participate in research with faculty members or on their own.

Established in 1874 to serve the emerging mining industry in the West, Mines is a state school, making it an especially good deal for homegrown students, who comprise 55 percent of the undergraduate student body. Four percent hail from foreign nations. "Most of the students would be considered nerds or geeks at other schools," a civil engineering major explains, "but almost everyone fits in here." Hispanics/Latinos represent 12 percent of the student body, Asian Americans 5 percent, Black students just 1 percent, and multiracial students 6 percent. Students are generally too wrapped up in academics to pay attention to political issues, according to a physics major. Merit scholarships averaging $8,400 are available to qualified students, and athletes may vie for more than 200 athletic scholarships.

Freshmen are required to live in the residence halls; most students move off campus after the first year. Most buildings are co-ed, though the preponderance of men results in a few single-sex dorms. "All the residence halls have been refurbished and are looking better than ever," a sophomore says. Options for upperclassmen include fraternity or sorority housing, college-owned apartments, and off-campus condos and houses. There's only one cafeteria, Mines Market, and a junior says, "The vegetarian options are not very good unless you really like cereal and salad" (presumably not during the same meal).

"When you leave here, you're prepared for anything."

There is life outside of the computer labs here. On campus, a junior says, "There is always a club putting together an event or just students throwing parties." Mines has an active Greek system, with fraternities and sororities attracting 12 percent of the men and 21 percent of the women. Rush is dry, and underage drinking is met with consequences. CU Boulder offers livelier partying 20 minutes away. The social scene also includes comedy shows, homecoming, and Engineering Days (E-Days)—a three-day party with lawn games, a carnival, cardboard boat races, comedians, concerts, fireworks, and cheap beers. New student orientation features the traditional "M Climb," in which freshmen hike up Mount Zion lugging a 10-pound rock from their hometown, then "whitewash it, and each other," says one participant. The rock is added to an M formation atop the mountain, and at the end of the year, "seniors return to take down a rock, completing the cycle."

The school's location at the base of the Rockies means gorgeous Colorado weather (make sure to bring sunscreen) and easy access to skiing, hiking, mountain climbing, and biking. Denver is also nearby, and aside from its museums, concerts, and sports teams, the city is home to many government agencies and businesses

(continued)

Chemical and Biological
  Engineering
Electrical Engineering
Mechanical Engineering
Computer Science

Mines supplements coursework with a required six-week summer field session, enabling students to gain hands-on experience.

During the traditional "M Climb," freshmen hike up Mount Zion lugging a 10-pound rock from their hometown and add it to an M formation.

involved in natural resources, computers, and technology, including the regional offices of the U.S. Geological Survey and Bureau of Mines. Golden hosts the National Earthquake Center, the National Renewable Energy Laboratory, and, of course, the Coors Brewery. Road trips to Las Vegas or Texas provide occasional respite from the school's heavy workload.

Mines's 18 Division II varsity teams compete in the Rocky Mountain Athletic Conference. The men's cross-country team is a recent national champion. Other competitive Oredigger teams include men's and women's soccer and basketball, women's cross-country, and women's volleyball. The intramural and club sports programs have grown dramatically, with the majority of students now participating.

While time spent in the classroom at Mines may be intense, for those who are focused on engineering, educational options don't get much better than those offered here. "Lots of companies recruit our students," says one senior, thanks to a stellar reputation in the fields of mining and engineering. A junior adds, "When you leave here, you're prepared for anything." Especially if you are an engineer.

Overlaps

Texas Tech, Rice, Carnegie Mellon, Worcester Polytechnic, Rensselaer Polytechnic, MIT, CU Boulder, Texas A&M

If You Apply To ›

Mines: Early action, regular decision. SATs or ACTs: optional. Accepts the Common Application.

Colorado State University

Fort Collins, CO 80523

It lacks Boulder's glitz and glamour, but Colorado State offers a more complete slice of the Rocky Mountain West. Known throughout the region for its prevet program, CSU turns out more STEM (science, technology, engineering, and math) graduates than any other Colorado campus. Has a traditional college feel with a first-rate student center and strong ties to the local community.

Website: www.colostate.edu
Location: Small City
Public
Total Enrollment: 24,945
Undergraduates: 22,002
Male/Female: 46/54
Financial Aid: 52%
Pell Grant: 19%
Expense: Pub $ $
Student Loans: 52%
Average Debt: $ $
Applicants: 31,586
Accepted: 90%
Enrolled: 18%
Grad in 6 Years: 69%
Returning Freshmen: 86%
Academics: ✍ ✍ ✍
Social: ☎ ☎ ☎ ☎
Q of L: ★ ★ ★ ★

Founded in 1870 as the Colorado Agricultural College, Colorado State University began with five students, two faculty members, and a mission "to serve society through teaching, research, and outreach." Today, the university boasts approximately 1,900 faculty across eight colleges, as well as more than 240,000 living alumni, including state governors, corporate CEOs, Olympic gold medalists, teachers, researchers, and artists. Students here enjoy ample research opportunities, a slew of solid academic programs, and an unbeatable location, so it's little wonder they take pride in calling CSU home.

Situated at the foot of the spectacular Rocky Mountains, CSU gives students easy access to abundant natural resources. The open space on the main campus reflects the university's heritage as a land-grant institution. The Oval, a wide expanse of lawn encircled by towering elm trees, anchors the northeast corner of campus. Architectural styles range from Beaux-Arts to Renaissance Revival, and the campus features a spacious outdoor plaza, 32 acres of recreation fields, and stunning views of Long's Peak. The university also boasts a 1,400-acre foothills campus, a 1,600-acre agricultural campus, and the 1,200-acre mountain campus, which provide opportunities for hands-on learning and research.

"[Fort Collins is] a fun city that revolves around the school."

All CSU undergrads complete a university-wide core curriculum that includes coursework in writing, quantitative reasoning, biological/physical sciences, arts/

humanities, social/behavioral sciences, historical perspectives, and diversity/ global awareness. CSU offers more than 75 undergraduate majors, the most popular of which include business administration (especially the finance concentration), psychology, human development and family studies, health and exercise sciences, and communication studies. Science and engineering are the university's main strengths, and the prevet program is distinguished. Computer science, ecosystem science and sustainability, and international studies are notable, and fermentation science and technology is a unique specialty. The performing arts have received a boost thanks to improved facilities, but the humanities are not as solid as other departments.

The academic climate can be competitive—especially in the preprofessional programs. "The courses are hard but manageable," a junior says. Thirty-eight percent of classes have fewer than 20 students, and one student says, "If you express an interest in their area of study, [professors] may invite you to do research in their lab, write a paper and be published in a major journal, or help you with graduate school applications—who knows!" Freshmen may participate in a midsummer orientation and a variety of first-year seminars designed to ease the transition from high school to college. A sophomore highly recommends the Key Communities living/learning program for first-years: "As a Key student you take three classes with a cluster of 19 people whom you meet before classes start. This is so nice because you immediately have friends and people you know who also live in [the same hall] and can help you study." Qualified students can opt for the Honors Program to take honors seminars, receive specialized advising, and complete a senior thesis. Undergraduate research academies allow students to join a faculty-mentored, interdisciplinary team investigating a common problem or theme from different disciplinary perspectives. Overall, more than 5,000 undergraduates participate in faculty research each year. Twenty-two percent of undergrads study abroad via hundreds of programs worldwide, and 56 percent complete at least one internship.

"The students at CSU are friendly and accepting," says a junior. Sixty-six percent of CSU students are from Colorado, and 3 percent are international. Black students account for only 2 percent of undergrads, Asian Americans 3 percent, Hispanics/ Latinos 15 percent, and multiracial students 5 percent. CSU is a politically active campus, with liberal and conservative viewpoints both well represented. "The biggest issues on campus are probably environmental issues," explains a student, "due mainly to our proximity to the Rocky Mountains." Thousands of merit scholarships averaging $5,900 are handed out each year, and athletes vie for nearly 200 scholarships in 15 men's and women's sports. The CSU Tuition Assistance Grant provides financial support for in-state, low-income students.

"The Rocky Mountain Showdown is probably the biggest event of the year."

Twenty-four percent of CSU students live on campus in residence halls and campus apartments; students may move off campus after their first year. "Residence halls are in great condition and more like a resort than the dorms we all picture from movies," says a student. Campus residents may choose from among six meal plans, and the residence hall dining center provides an all-you-can-eat option. "The food is awesome," a student says. "I think it is as good as any restaurant in town." Students also report feeling safe on campus; security measures include a "safe walk" escort program and an active security staff.

The Greek scene attracts just 5 percent of the men and 6 percent of the women, so it's not a major force in campus social life. "Campus activities, such as free movies or concerts, draw a large crowd," says one student, "while parties and other gatherings off campus do the same." The Lory Student Center hosts events on a regular basis, and more than 470 active student clubs serve as a social outlet too. The CSU

(continued)

Admissions: (970) 491-6909
Email Address: admissions@ colostate.edu

Strong Programs:
Engineering
Computer Science
Ecosystem Science and
 Sustainability
International Studies
Fermentation Science and
 Technology
Business Administration
Psychology
Human Development and
 Family Studies

CSU boasts a 1,400-acre foothills campus, a 1,600-acre agricultural campus, and the 1,200-acre mountain campus.

Undergraduate research academies allow students to join a faculty-mentored, interdisciplinary team investigating a common problem or theme.

campus is dry and "there is no tolerance for alcohol in the residence halls," a biochemistry major notes. "The policies are enforced."

Fort Collins (population 170,000) is "a fun city that revolves around the school," says one junior. "There is a definite sense of community and support for CSU in the town," a senior adds. Students not only frequent the downtown bars, shops, and eateries but also can be found performing volunteer work or community service alongside the locals. Popular road trips include quick getaways to nearby ski resorts and hiking trails, and longer treks to Utah and Nevada. Back on campus, students enjoy a number of traditions: "We have a huge homecoming," says one student, "with a bonfire, lighting of the 'A,' parade, and football game."

The CSU Rams compete in Division I as members of the Mountain West Conference, and the most competitive teams include women's volleyball and men's and women's track and field. The University of Colorado is the hated rival—especially in football—and "the Rocky Mountain Showdown is probably the biggest event of the year," says a family and consumer sciences major. Intramurals and club sports attract 17 percent of the student body; baseball, ice hockey, ultimate Frisbee, and eSports garner the most interest. The Student Recreation Center features an indoor track, a climbing wall, basketball and volleyball courts, cardio machines and free weights, and a host of other facilities for students who want to stay in shape.

Despite ubiquitous complaints about limited parking, rising tuition, and the need for more bike racks, students at Colorado State are quick to say why they appreciate their alma mater: "Because CSU rocks! It is an awesome school to go to and has lots to offer students of all ages and backgrounds," cheers a student. What's more, it's a "fun and beautiful place to be," says a junior, "and you know that your degree will mean something."

Overlaps

Iowa State, Kansas State, Michigan State, Oregon State, Washington State, CU Boulder, Arizona State, University of Arizona

If You Apply To ›

CSU: Early action, regular decision. SATs or ACTs: optional. Accepts the Common Application.

Columbia University

212 Hamilton Hall, New York, NY 10027

Once a high-powered Ivy League afterthought, Columbia now rivals the Ivy League's big three in selectivity. Applications have nearly doubled in the past 10 years for one simple reason: Manhattan trumps New Haven, Providence, Ithaca, and every other Ivy League city, with the possible exception of Boston. The often overlooked engineering program is among the best in the nation for undergraduates. The heart of Columbia is still its Core Curriculum.

Website: www.columbia.edu
Location: City Center
Private
Total Enrollment: 27,457
Undergraduates: 6,696
Male/Female: 49/51
Financial Aid: 53%

Students entering Columbia will, of course, expect the rigorous academic program they'll encounter at this Ivy League school, but they must also be streetwise, urbane, and together enough to handle one of the most cosmopolitan cities in the world. Columbia lets its students experience life in the Big Apple but serves as a refuge when it becomes necessary to escape from New York, allowing students to immerse themselves in the best academia has to offer, starting with the Core Curriculum. "Students here want a classical liberal arts education but do not want to live in a college bubble," says a freshman. Famous alums can be found in the highest echelons of their chosen professions, whether it be politics, literature, sports, or entertainment. Think Barack Obama.

The fifth-oldest university in the country, Columbia was founded under Anglican auspices in 1754 as King's College and renamed in 1784, after the American Revolution. With a total university-wide enrollment of more than 27,000 full-time students, says one of them, "It's easy to feel lost." Columbia's 6,700 traditional undergraduates are split into two divisions: the flagship Columbia College and The Fu Foundation School of Engineering and Applied Science. (The School of General Studies offers undergraduate education to part-time and nontraditional students. Sister school Barnard College, affiliated with Columbia University but governed by its own board of trustees, has an additional 3,000 students.) Columbia's campus has a large central quadrangle in front of Butler Library and at the foot of the steps leading past the statue of Alma Mater to Low Library, which is now the administration building. The redbrick, copper-roofed neoclassical buildings are "stunning," and the layout, says an undergrad, "is well thought out and manages to provide a beautiful setting with an economy of space."

> "Students here want a classical liberal arts education but do not want to live in a college bubble."

The undergraduate experience at Columbia centers on its renowned Core Curriculum. While these courses occupy up to a third of the first two years and can become laborious, students generally praise them as worthwhile and enriching. "The Core truly unifies the school in a way that transcends most social limitations," says a freshman. As it has since World War I, the college remains committed to the Core while at the same time expanding the diversity of the canon and requiring Core classes on non-Western cultures. According to a junior, some students find that the Core can "spark some interest in a subject they had never thought of before."

Two of the most demanding introductory courses in the Ivy League—Contemporary Civilization (CC) and Literature Humanities (LitHum)—form the basis of the Core. Both are yearlong and taught in small sections, generally by full professors. CC examines political and moral philosophy from Plato to Camus, though professors have some leeway in choosing 20th-century selections. LitHum covers about 26 masterpieces of literature from Homer to Dostoyevsky, usually with some Sappho, Jane Austen, and Toni Morrison thrown in for alternative perspectives. One semester each of art and music history is required and, while they are not given the same reverence as their literary counterparts, they are eye-opening all the same. Foreign language proficiency is required, as are two semesters of science, two semesters of "global Core" classes dealing in cultures not covered in the other Core requirements, two semesters of phys ed, and University Writing. Students at the School of Engineering and Applied Science complete approximately half of the Core Curriculum.

Columbia is an intellectual school, not a preprofessional one, and even though a large percentage of students aspire to law or medical school, "we are mostly content to be liberal artists for as long as possible," says an English major. Even students in the School of Engineering and Applied Science pursue "technical education" with a liberal arts base. Almost all departments that offer undergraduate majors are strong, notably English, history, political science, economics, neuroscience, and computer science. Chemistry and biology are among the best of Columbia's high-quality science offerings. The earth and environmental science department owns 200 acres in Rockland County, home to many rocks and

> "We are mostly content to be liberal artists for as long as possible."

much seismographic equipment. The fine arts are improving, thanks to newer facilities and joint programs with schools such as the Juilliard School of Music. Many challenging combined majors are available, such as philosophy/economics and biology/psychology. There are 50 offerings in foreign languages, ranging from Czech to

(continued)

Pell Grant: 19%
Expense: Pr $ $ $ $
Student Loans: 19%
Average Debt: $ $
Applicants: 60,551
Accepted: 4%
Enrolled: 66%
Grad in 6 Years: 97%
Returning Freshmen: 99%
Academics: ✍ ✍ ✍ ✍ ✍
Social: ☎ ☎ ☎
Q of L: ★ ★ ★ ★
Admissions: (212) 854-2522
Email Address: ugrad-ask@ columbia.edu

Strong Programs:
Engineering
English
History
Political Science
Economics
Neuroscience
Computer Science
Chemistry

Contemporary Civilization (CC) and Literature Humanities (LitHum) are yearlong introductory courses that form the basis of the Core Curriculum.

Persian to Urdu, and the East Asian languages and cultures department is one of the best anywhere. There is also an African American and African diaspora studies major and a women's and gender studies major taught in cooperation with Barnard. Students can take classes in any department at Barnard and graduate-level courses in several Columbia departments. A notable five-year bachelor's/master's program gives students access to the resources of the highly regarded School of International and Public Affairs and its multitude of regional institutes.

There are 50 offerings in foreign languages, ranging from Czech to Persian to Urdu.

Columbia is tough; the workload is often stressful, and since most students are used to being top achievers, classmates can be intimidating to the faint of heart. A financial economics major offers this advice: "Prepare to be average and to be happy that you are an average student at Columbia." Student/faculty interaction is supported by one of the smallest student-to-faculty ratios in the country, and 57 percent of classes have fewer than 20 students. "Some of the professors are real leaders in their fields," says a philosophy major, who also cautions, "Many Core classes are taught by grad students, which has led to some less than ideal experiences for me." Additional interaction stems from professorial involvement in campus politics and forums and from the faculty-in-residence program, which houses professors and their families in spruced-up apartments in several of the residence halls. First-year students are assigned an academic advisor with whom they work for all four years, and they receive a departmental faculty advisor when they declare a major at the end of sophomore year. For students wishing to spend time away from New York, Columbia offers credit through more than 150 programs in more than 100 cities around the world; about a third of students go abroad. Research is big here, too, and the university conducts nearly $1 billion of research annually in the sciences, humanities, and social sciences; hundreds of undergraduates participate.

"I love that no one activity dominates the social scene."

"In general, Columbia students are eager to learn, engaged with the world around them, and happy to explore New York City," says a sociology major. Twenty-one percent of undergraduates come from New York, and 16 percent come from abroad. Students of color make up more than half of the undergraduate population: 8 percent are Black, 16 percent are Hispanic/Latino, 21 percent are Asian American, and 7 percent are multiracial. Columbia remains one of the nation's most liberal campuses, and an economics major notes, "Students take an active approach to solving the problems that face marginalized groups." The university awards financial aid based on need, meeting the full demonstrated need of all students, domestic and international, with grants instead of loans. Students coming from families with annual incomes below $150,000 and typical assets attend Columbia tuition-free.

The faculty-in-residence program houses professors and their families in spruced-up apartments in several of the residence halls.

Given the exorbitant nature of the New York housing market, 87 percent of Columbia students live in university housing, which is guaranteed for four years. Many rooms are singles, and it is possible to go all four years without a roommate. Carman Hall, one of three exclusively first-year dorms, is a popular choice for its private bathrooms. "Going into sophomore year, my roommate and I had a very bad lottery number," recalls one student, "but we were still able to get a room in an air-conditioned building with a view of the Empire State Building." First-year students are automatically placed on a 19-meal-a-week plan and take most of those meals at John Jay. Dining options receive positive reviews, but for students who prefer to do their own cooking, several dorms have kitchens. The university has introduced a number of Title IX initiatives, including a comprehensive gender-based misconduct policy and the addition of a second sexual violence support center on campus. "Columbia has a robust Title IX

"This is not a school that rallies together at football games."

investigation team," reports a senior. "I've never felt unsafe as a young woman walking around campus at night. We have guards in every dorm, a blue-light system, and campus patrols."

The social scene starts on the Columbia campus and spills over into the bustling streets of New York City. "We have the best of both worlds, because Columbia students can be a part of the vibrant on-campus community but also take part in New York's eclectic environment!" cheers one student. The challenge, others say, is finding time to relax and enjoy all the city has to offer. Rarely are there big all-inclusive bashes, the exceptions being the Tree Lighting celebration in December and spring's Bacchanal concert. "My favorite tradition is the Varsity Show, a more than 125-year-old tradition of a student-written musical that satirizes Columbia, the Ivy League, and current campus and world events," says a sophomore. Eleven percent of the men and 12 percent of the women go Greek; the advent of co-ed houses has raised interest in Greek life, as has the arrival of sororities open to both Columbia and Barnard women. But Columbia is hardly a Hellenocentric campus. "I love that no one activity dominates the social scene," says a freshman. The Community Impact organization coordinates 27 local community service programs, in which nearly 1,000 students participate.

Columbia athletics don't inspire rabid loyalty. "Columbia students are individualists," according to one sophomore. "This is not a school that rallies together at football games." Still, the Lions field 31 Division I teams. Men's and women's fencing are recent national champions, while baseball, men's squash, and women's cross-country have claimed Ivy League conference titles. As an urban school, Columbia lacks team field facilities on campus; however, 100 blocks to the north is the modern Baker Field, home of the football stadium, the soccer fields, an Olympic track, and the crew boathouse. On campus, the Dodge Gymnasium, an underground facility, houses four levels of basketball courts, swimming pools, weight rooms, and exercise equipment. Dozens of intramural and club sports are available; men's and women's ultimate Frisbee are both nationally competitive.

"Columbia is definitely not a stress-free, friendly community, but it has its own charm," explains a senior. "The university is quintessentially New York: as a student, there are so many experiences to be had, but you really have to engage in the community and seek them out." Columbians are proud to attend college in New York City, and most would have it no other way.

Students coming from families with annual incomes below $150,000 and typical assets attend Columbia tuition-free.

Overlaps

Harvard, Yale, Stanford, MIT, Princeton, University of Pennsylvania, Brown, UC Berkeley

If You Apply To ›

Columbia: Early decision, regular decision. SATs or ACTs: optional. Accepts the Common Application with supplement.

University of Connecticut

2131 Hillside Road, Unit 3088, Storrs, CT 06269

Squeezed in among the likes of Brown, UMass, Trinity, Wesleyan, and Yale—all within a two-hour drive—UConn could be forgiven for having an identity problem. But applications have been soaring, with championship basketball teams helping to ignite Husky pride and boost selectivity. One of the highest retention and graduation rates among public universities. Storrs is nobody's idea of an exciting destination, but it does offer easy access to beautiful countryside.

Website: www.uconn.edu

Location: Rural

Public

Total Enrollment: 23,538

Undergraduates: 17,883

Male/Female: 47/53

Financial Aid: 80%

Pell Grant: 22%

Expense: Pub $ $ $ $

Student Loans: 52%

Average Debt: $ $

Applicants: 36,753

Accepted: 56%

Enrolled: 18%

Grad in 6 Years: 83%

Returning Freshmen: 92%

Academics: ✎ ✎ ✎ ✎

Social: ☎ ☎ ☎

Q of L: ★ ★ ★

Admissions: (860) 486-3137

Email Address: beahusky@
uconn.edu

Strong Programs:

Business

Engineering

Education

Pharmacy

Nursing

Physical Therapy

Agriculture

Coastal Studies

*Three-quarters
of freshmen take
at least one First-
Year Experience
course that guides
them through the
transition to college.*

The top public university in New England and highly regarded nationally, the University of Connecticut has recently seen billions of dollars poured into new facilities and into expanding educational opportunities and research in STEM disciplines. UConn is the only public university in New England with its own law school, medical school, dental school, and school of social work—and undergraduates benefit indirectly from these resources. What's more, it's one of the few major public universities that continues to significantly expand its faculty ranks, adding nearly 300 tenure-track positions in recent years. Couple these initiatives with the glow of two nationally competitive basketball teams, a wealth of research opportunities, and more than 600 clubs and organizations, and it's clear why UConn has moved well beyond its erstwhile "cow college" image. "I'm incredibly proud to be a UConn student," says a senior.

UConn's 4,000-acre campus is about 23 miles northeast of Hartford. Building styles range from collegiate Gothic and neoclassical to half-century-old red brick. Dense woods surround the campus, which also boasts two lakes, Swan and Mirror. Ongoing renovations are the norm, sparking jokes about the "University of Construction," but the results are impressive. The 212,000-square-foot NextGen residence hall houses more than 700 students in several living/learning communities and features an innovative makerspace. The five-story, $95 million Engineering and Science Building and the $75 million Student Recreation Center are among the newest additions to campus.

Students say UConn's strongest offerings are preprofessional—business, engineering, education, pharmacy, and allied health, including nursing and physical therapy. The school's historic focus on agriculture is giving way to an emphasis on environment and ecology, including a strong program in coastal studies. Also notable are neuroscience, linguistics, history, human rights, and, of course, agriculture. (UConn was founded more than 140 years ago as a farm school; it's where America learned to get more eggs per chicken by leaving the lights on in the coops.) Engineering is demanding, and, as at many schools, it has a relatively high attrition rate, with many students switching to the less rigorous major in management information systems. A special program in medicine and dentistry allows students to earn bachelor's degrees in any of UConn's more than 100 disciplines, and guarantees admission to the School of Medicine or Dental Medicine if they meet all criteria.

"As you get involved, you will be wicked busy!"

UConn's academic atmosphere is described as moderately competitive and challenging, depending on a student's course of study. Core requirements include courses in four basic areas: arts and humanities, social sciences, diversity/multiculturalism, and science and technology. Students must also achieve competency in writing, quantitative skills, information literacy, a second language, and environmental literacy. Seminar-style writing classes are available to all freshmen, and three-quarters also take at least one First-Year Experience course that guides them through the transition to college. The Academic Center for Exploratory Students helps freshmen and sophomores who still need to decide on a major. Students generally applaud the enthusiasm of their professors—and the graduate teaching assistants who administer tests, collect assignments, and run labs and discussion groups—but a senior grumbles, "Some lack the ability to connect with students and the skills to teach students effectively."

UConn's engineering, business, pharmacy, and honors students are required to undertake research projects, and each year two teams of finance majors run their own $1 million portfolios for the student-managed investment fund. Students who aspire to graduate school in academic fields, rather than professional certification, may win grants to work independently under faculty members through the undergraduate summer research program. The 8 percent of students who qualify for the honors program gain access to special floors and dorms; several programs for disadvantaged students are also available. In addition, 15 percent of students participate in the study abroad program, which offers 275 options in more than 60 countries.

UConn students are "hardworking, responsible, intelligent, passionate, and inspirational," according to one psychology major. Seventy percent of UConn undergraduates are from Connecticut, and 8 percent are international. Many students choose to transfer to the Storrs campus after beginning coursework in their chosen major and earning 54 credits at one of UConn's four regional campuses. Seven percent of undergrads are Black,

> "It is good luck to rub the nose of the bronze statue of our mascot, Jonathan."

14 percent are Hispanic/Latino, 13 percent are Asian American, and 4 percent are multiracial. There are cultural centers for Black, Asian American, Latin American, and Puerto Rican students, as well as the Rainbow Center, a resource for LGBTQ students. "Students are very much concerned with what is going on today in our world," a student says. Eligible UConn students receive merit scholarships averaging $10,800, and hundreds of athletic scholarships are available in 18 sports. Persistence rates are notably high for a public flagship university, with 92 percent of freshmen returning for their sophomore year and a six-year graduation rate of 83 percent.

Fifty-seven percent of the students live in university housing, which is available to all undergraduates. "All the dorms are very well maintained," says a senior. Dorms are all co-ed, and the entire campus, including outdoor areas, is equipped with Wi-Fi. Eight dining halls offer plenty of choices, even for vegetarians and vegans, though many students would just as soon visit the snack bar for some ice cream, freshly made with help from the cows grazing nearby. "The food at UConn each night is diverse, and a student can always find something he or she wants," one student says. A group of students are selected to live on a sustainable farm just off campus where they raise foods that are served in the dining halls. Students report feeling safe on campus. "Crime is so low we think it doesn't exist, the police don't bother anyone unless they have to, and we have a great system of security alerts," says a junior.

UConn's engineering, business, pharmacy, and honors students are required to undertake research projects.

"Social life is the best part of college life and includes clubs, frats, sports, and so much more," says one student. "As you get involved, you will be wicked busy!" Students 21 and over are allowed to possess no more than a six-pack of beer, one bottle of wine, or a small bottle of liquor. Underage students caught with booze may be evicted from campus housing. Late-night activities at the student union and other campus events provide a lot

> "We are a well-rounded campus with students from every background."

of alternatives to alcohol use. Fraternities attract 10 percent of the men, and sororities claim 13 percent of the women; members can live in chapter housing at the Husky Village. On weekends, there are buses to Hartford (only 30 minutes away), Boston, New Haven, New York, and Providence. Cape Cod and the Vermont ski slopes are within weekend driving distance. Favorite annual campus events include the mud volleyball tournament, carnival-style UConn Late Nights, midnight breakfasts during finals, homecoming, Winter Weekend, and Midnight Madness—the first official day of basketball practice. In addition to cheering for the Huskies, "it is good luck to rub the nose of the bronze statue of our mascot, Jonathan," says a sophomore.

The men's basketball team won the national Division I title in 2023, and the women were runners-up in 2022.

The town of Storrs "is basically UConn," says one student. A recent downtown Storrs initiative offers shops, restaurants, and a town green, as well as additional living options available to students. The university provides transportation for students who volunteer in area schools and hospitals. Legend holds that UConn also offers one diversion most other colleges can't: cow tipping—that is, sneaking up on unsuspecting cows, which sleep standing up, and tipping them over. The administration contends that this is a myth, though students always claim to "know someone who did it."

UConn's teams are known as the Huskies (UConn. Yukon. Get it?), and in a state without any major league professional sports teams, UConn basketball routinely sells out the XL Center. The men's team won the national Division I title in 2023, and the women were runners-up in 2022. (It's headline news when the women's team *loses*!) Women's field hockey and men's soccer are also strong. Intramurals are offered at three levels, from recreational to competitive. Popular options range from underwater hockey and inner-tube water polo to basketball, volleyball, and flag football.

UConn continues to build on its agricultural roots and adapt them to the 21st century. Those seeking greener pastures will be hard-pressed to find a more dynamic public institution. "We are a well-rounded campus with students from every background," a junior pharmacy student says. And with the campus undergoing a complete face-lift, it's a good time to be at UConn.

If You Apply To ›

UConn: Regular decision. Please consult UConn's website for the most up-to-date information regarding standardized test requirements. Accepts the Common Application. Most fine arts programs require a portfolio, audition, or interview.

Connecticut College

270 Mohegan Avenue, New London, CT 06320

Like Skidmore and Vassar, Connecticut College long ago made a successful transition from women's college to co-ed. That means a slightly more progressive campus tenor than at, say, Hamilton or Trinity. The college is strong in the humanities, dance, and drama, and notable for its study abroad programs and funded internships. New London does not offer much, but at least it is on the water.

Website: www.conncoll.edu
Location: Small City
Private
Total Enrollment: 1,810
Undergraduates: 1,810
Male/Female: 41/59
Financial Aid: 95%
Pell Grant: 15%
Expense: Pr $ $ $ $
Student Loans: 54%
Average Debt: $ $ $ $
Applicants: 7,682
Accepted: 41%
Enrolled: 16%
Grad in 6 Years: 81%
Returning Freshmen: 86%
Academics: ✐ ✐ ✐ ✐

Students at Connecticut College follow the example of their mascot, the camel—they take pride in drinking up and storing knowledge. The student-run honor code means finals are not proctored; they're even self-scheduled, whenever students prefer, during a five-day window. "The honor code gives the freedom for the student to be responsible for their actions academically and socially," says an economics major. "It creates a respectful and trustful relationship between professors and students."

Placed majestically atop a hill, the Conn College campus sits within a 750-acre arboretum with a pond, wetlands, wooded areas, and hiking trails. It offers beautiful views of the Thames River (pronounced the way it looks, not like the "Temz"

"[The academic climate is] rigorous and intense, but supportive all the same."

that Wordsworth so dearly loved) on one side and Long Island Sound on the other. The granite campus buildings are a mixture of modern and collegiate Gothic in style, with some neo-Gothic and neoclassical architecture thrown in for good measure. A $24 million renovation of Palmer Auditorium, the college's main performing arts building, was completed in 2021.

Conn was founded in 1911 as a women's college and went co-ed in 1969. The general education program, cleverly called Connections (get it?), spans all four years of a student's undergraduate experience. Coursework includes two semesters of foundational courses, including a first-year seminar, an interdisciplinary ConnCourse, and two Social Difference and Power courses, followed by a series of thematically linked classes called an "Integrative Pathway." The senior year culminates with an integrative project that is presented at an All-College Symposium. Academics are definitely the focus here. "I'd consider the academic climate at Conn to be rigorous and intense, but supportive all the same," says a film studies major. Much of that support comes from professors, who are lauded for their accessibility and thoughtfulness. "I've found that a majority of professors at Conn take great personal responsibility in their teaching styles and try to cater to students' needs as much as possible," observes a psychology major.

Conn's dance and drama departments are superb, and it's not uncommon for dancers to take time off to study with professional companies. Aspiring actors, directors, and stagehands may work on numerous on-campus productions and with the Eugene O'Neill Theater Institute, named for New London's best-known literary son. Chemistry majors may use high-tech gas chromatograms and mass spectrometers from their very first day. Conn also offers strong programs in biology, environmental studies, and international relations. Five interdisciplinary centers offer courses, certificates, and special programming in international studies, arts and technology, public policy and community action, the environment, and the study of race and ethnicity. The most popular majors are economics, psychology, government, biology, and sociology. New minors have been added in applied statistics, geosciences, linguistics, and Jewish studies.

To escape Conn's small size and occasionally claustrophobic feel, the Study Away/Teach Away (SATA) initiative allows groups of about a dozen Conn students and a faculty member to spend a semester living and working together at an overseas university, in locations as far-flung as Italy, South Africa, Peru, and Vietnam. In fact, about half of Connecticut College students study abroad through SATA and other college-approved programs offered in 40 countries. All students who participate in a set of career workshops are guaranteed an internship opportunity and may receive up to $3,000 in flexible funds to help cover housing or other costs. Opportunities for funded summer research with professors are also available.

"The a cappella groups are the closest thing Conn has to Greek life."

"Connecticut College has a reputation for being a 'preppy' school; many of the students are very well-off," says a computer science major. Only 17 percent of students come from Connecticut, and 9 percent come from abroad. Black students make up 5 percent of the student body, Asian Americans account for 4 percent, Hispanic/Latino students add 11 percent, and multiracial students represent 3 percent. Freshmen must attend a session on issues of race, class, and gender, run by a panel of diverse peers. Students say there is a growing interest in activism on campus, and the political atmosphere is largely liberal. There are no athletic scholarships, but merit scholarships average $19,100 annually, and the college meets all admitted students' full demonstrated financial need. Loan reduction is available for students of highest need.

Ninety-six percent of students live on campus. Options include first-year-only and mixed-class housing, and dorms are run by seniors who apply to be "house fellows." Several specialty houses are dedicated to interests such as environmental awareness, substance-free living, quiet lifestyles, and international languages. "There is a great sense of house pride on campus," says one student. The campus boasts two dining halls that receive generally good reviews. "Students can make requests to dining staff by writing their thoughts on a 'napkin note' and pinning it to a provided bulletin board," reports a senior. A junior says that life on campus feels

(continued)

Social: ☎ ☎ ☎
Q of L: ★ ★ ★ ★
Admissions: (860) 439-2200
Email Address: admission@
   conncoll.edu

Strong Programs:
Dance
Drama
Chemistry
Biology
Environmental Studies
International Relations
Economics
Psychology

The senior year culminates with an integrative project that is presented at an All-College Symposium.

safe: "Campus safety officers patrol campus constantly." Another adds, "Conn has a local Green Dot program, which is really successful in educating the community about consent and destigmatizing discussions about sexual assault."

Students keep busy with parties, movie nights, comedy shows, student productions, and dances—sometimes with out-of-town bands and DJs. "The a cappella groups are the closest thing Conn has to Greek life, the only major difference being their preference for practicing complex vocal arrangements over playing mindless drinking games," quips a sophomore. Students say the absence of Greek groups creates a more inclusive community. The alcohol policy falls under the honor code, and students take prohibitions seriously. Students anticipate the annual Floralia festival in the spring, when "students camp out in tents, eat lots of free food, and dance to music," says a junior.

Many students volunteer at the local schools, aquarium, youth community center, and women's center; a college van makes it easy to get to and from work sites. When students get the urge to roam, the beaches of New London and other shore towns are 20 minutes from campus, and the Mohegan Sun casino is also very close. Trains go to Providence (Rhode Island), New York City, or Boston, while Vermont and upstate New York offer camping, hiking, and skiing.

The Conn Camels compete in 28 Division III sports, and men's ice hockey games against NESCAC rival Wesleyan draw crowds. Men's soccer won its first national championship in 2021; women's soccer and men's swimming are also among the stronger teams. Intramural and club sports range from floor hockey and squash to ultimate Frisbee and skiing. Between classes or at the end of the day, all students may use the natatorium's pool and fitness center and the rowing tanks and climbing walls at the field house.

On its friendly campus, Conn College encourages strong student/faculty bonds and takes pride in its ability to challenge—and trust—students, both in and out of the classroom. "Connecticut College promotes a sense of self-awareness and being able to be yourself in an environment that fosters creativity, acceptance, and community," reasons one junior. A classmate asks, "Who else has a dromedary camel as the mascot?!"

The Study Away/ Teach Away initiative allows groups of Conn students and a faculty member to spend a semester at an overseas university.

Overlaps

Skidmore, Bates, Trinity College (CT), Northeastern, Hamilton, Union, Colby, Boston College

If You Apply To ›

Conn College: Early decision I and II, regular decision. SATs or ACTs: optional. Accepts the Common Application.

The Cooper Union

30 Cooper Square, New York, NY 10003

As college costs skyrocket, so does the popularity of The Cooper Union's low-cost education in art, architecture, and engineering. Expect competition approaching Ivy level for a place in the class here. Instead of a conventional campus, The Cooper Union has the cool and funky East Village. But be prepared to spend your nights hitting the books rather than the cafés.

Website: www.cooper.edu
Location: City Center
Private
Total Enrollment: 898
Undergraduates: 869

Tuition is no longer free at The Cooper Union for the Advancement of Science and Art, but if you manage to get accepted into this technical institute, you get a half-tuition scholarship (with additional aid to those who demonstrate need) and some of the nation's finest academic offerings in architecture, engineering, and art. With the always vibrant East Village in the background and rigorous studying in the forefront, college life at The Cooper Union may seem to be faster than a New York minute. Whatever the pace, though, no one can deny that a CU education is one of the best bargains around—arguably the best anywhere. The only complication is that the number of applicants is booming, and the competition is stiff.

The school was founded in 1859 by entrepreneur Peter Cooper, who believed that education should be "as free as water and air." With hefty contributions from Andrew Carnegie, J. P. Morgan, and various other fellow robber barons, the school was able to maintain its tuition-free policy and stay afloat in order to recruit poor students of "strong moral character." Trustees ended the famous policy in 2013, citing dire financial straits—although the school has announced aspirations to reinstate full-tuition scholarships for all undergraduates by 2029.

In place of a traditional collegiate campus, Cooper offers two academic buildings and one dorm wedged between two busy avenues in the East Village, one of New York's most eclectic and exciting neighborhoods. The stately brick Foundation Building, home to architecture and art programs, is a beautiful historic landmark. The building's Great Hall was the site of Lincoln's "Right Makes Might" speech that turned him into a national political figure and the birthplace of the NAACP,

> "Cooper Union has a performance-oriented culture. You are expected to produce great work."

the American Red Cross, and the national women's suffrage movement. The school also boasts the first academic building in New York City to achieve LEED Platinum status, the highest and most rigorous level of certification; known as 41 Cooper Square, the modern, nine-story building houses the engineering program and some art facilities. Built of brick and topped by a classic water tower, Cooper's dorm blends right in with the neighborhood. Opened in 2021, the high-tech IDC Foundation Art, Architecture, Construction, and Engineering Lab offers students access to advanced digital tools and fabrication equipment.

CU's curriculum is highly structured, and all students must take a sequence of required courses in their programs of study as well as in the humanities and social sciences. The first year is devoted to language and literature and the second to the making of the modern world; students can then choose from a range of electives after that. The nationally renowned engineering school offers both bachelor's and master's degrees in chemical, electrical, mechanical, and civil engineering and a bachelor of science in general engineering studies, as well as minors in computer science, math, and bioengineering. The architecture school is "phenomenal—even unparalleled," in the words of one pleased participant. The art school, rather than offering individual majors, awards a bachelor of fine arts degree that encompasses a broad-based generalist curriculum in graphic design, drawing, painting, sculpture, photography, printmaking, film, and video. Students in any school can choose to pursue one of the few minors offered in the humanities and social sciences. All students must fulfill a capstone requirement: engineers complete a senior design project and presentation, architects a yearlong senior thesis and presentation, and artists a senior exhibition.

The academic climate is intense and the workload heavy across all programs, but collaborative group projects and study groups are common. "Cooper Union has a performance-oriented culture. You are expected to produce great work, and you are in an environment that is conducive to that," explains a senior. Academic advising and counseling is available—as are peer mentors—but the school's rigorously structured academic programs largely determine the core set of courses that students take, eliminating a

> "[Apartment] leases are passed down from Cooper student to Cooper student."

lot of confusion or decision-making. Classes are small—61 percent enroll fewer than 20 students—and, with a little persistence, not too difficult to get into. "The full-time faculty at Cooper is known to be really great, but the adjunct professors can be

The school's rigorously structured academic programs largely determine the core set of courses that students take.

hit or miss," reports a freshman. Even so, students say it's usually easy to build personal relationships with professors.

Students interested in long-term, interdisciplinary research can join a Vertically Integrated Project team, earning academic credit over multiple semesters while participating in faculty-led research on topics as diverse as smart cities, motorsports, and drones. Engineers can participate in the popular Invention Factory summer program to build their own use-inspired inventions; prizes are awarded to the top projects, and all participants file provisional applications for U.S. patents. Roughly 10 percent of students find time to take their education global through a variety of study abroad programs.

Students interested in long-term, interdisciplinary research can join a Vertically Integrated Project team on topics such as smart cities, motorsports, and drones.

Strong moral character is no longer a prerequisite for admission, but an outstanding high school academic record most certainly is. CU students "range from being complete geeks who love math, science, and gaming to artsy and out-of-this-world," one student says, and another adds that "most students stick to their own school." Fifty-one percent of undergraduates are from New York State, and most of them grew up in the city; 14 percent are international. Asian Americans account for 29 percent of the student population, Black students 5 percent, Hispanics/Latinos 12 percent, and multiracial students 4 percent. Many are the first in their family to attend college. The political climate depends on whom you ask; most students are liberal, but you'll probably find more activism in the art school than elsewhere on campus.

Students love the dorm, a 15-story residence hall that saves its occupants from commuting into the Village or cramming themselves into expensive apartments.

"The Cooper Union is absolutely not a party school."

The downside is that housing here is not guaranteed, and only 20 percent of the student body (mostly freshmen) reside on campus. The facility is composed of furnished apartments with kitchens and bathrooms and is "in great condition and well maintained," says one resident, even if space can be tight. For those seeking off-campus housing, a freshman assures, "Few students have trouble finding an apartment, as leases are passed down from Cooper student to Cooper student." With no meal plan available, students cook for themselves, eat at the unexciting but affordable school cafeteria, or head for one of the myriad nearby delis and coffee shops. Students are mindful of potential safety concerns, given the urban campus, and Cooper has expanded its education and training programs aimed at preventing sexual assault.

The heart of Greenwich Village, with its abundance of theaters, art galleries, and cafés, is just a few blocks to the west.

Many students belong to professional societies, such as the American Society of Civil Engineers, and cultural groups are active on campus. Students have their choice of more than 75 clubs for everything from table tennis and jazz band to religion and drama. Drinking on campus is allowed during some school-sponsored events for students 21 and over—otherwise, no alcohol on campus. "The Cooper Union is absolutely not a party school," states an architecture major; the few parties that do occur are typically small, inclusive affairs at off-campus apartments. Annual events include the Fall Festival at the beginning of the year and the Culture Show, featuring multicultural music and dance. Nightlife and other social options are not far: McSorley's bar is right around the corner, and nearby Chinatown and Little Italy are also popular destinations. The heart of Greenwich Village, with its abundance of theaters, art galleries, and cafés, is just a few blocks to the west. The Bowery and SoHo's galleries and restaurants are due south; all of midtown Manhattan spreads to the northern horizon.

Cooper Union has no varsity sports, but it does sponsor a co-ed soccer team, which plays on nearby Randall's Island, as well as co-ed basketball and men's and women's volleyball teams that compete against other area schools. Students stay fit and participate in recreational activities in several different facilities in the city.

Overlaps

Carnegie Mellon, Cornell University, RISD, Olin College of Engineering, Harvey Mudd, NYU, Pratt Institute, Georgia Tech

The Cooper Union offers an environment for survivors. Getting in is tough, and once admitted, students find that dealing with the onslaught of city and school is plenty tough as well. "Your first year at Cooper is sink or swim," cautions a civil engineering major. "You either develop a work ethic (whatever you had before isn't enough) or you drop/transfer out." But most students like the challenge and the rewards of Cooper's academic rigors. Thriving here requires talent, self-sufficiency, and a clear sense of one's career objectives. Students who don't have it all can be sure that there are six or seven people in line ready to take their places. That's quite an incentive to succeed.

If You Apply To ›

The Cooper Union: Early decision, regular decision. Accepts the Common Application with supplement. Apply to particular program. Art applicants must complete take-home test, architecture applicants must complete studio test, and engineering applicants must complete writing supplement. Please consult Cooper's website for the most up-to-date information regarding standardized test requirements.

Cornell College

600 First Street Southwest, Mount Vernon, IA 52314-1098

The One Course At A Time model is Cornell's calling card. The main challenge: trying to lure top students to rural Iowa. Encourages students to do off-campus study in distant corners of the world. More accessible than Colorado College, which follows a similar academic model. Though primarily a liberal arts institution, Cornell has programs in business, engineering, and education.

Cornell College attracts the type of student who seeks an intense yet flexible, self-designed program and a liberal, progressive atmosphere. It suits those who aren't satisfied with easy answers, don't mind heading to the rural Midwest, and thrive on loads of personal attention while focusing on one class and exercising disciplined study habits. "If you want a normal college experience, don't pick Cornell," warns one student, but "if you want to pour yourself into a class for three and a half straight weeks and feel exhausted but accomplished," Cornell may be just the right fit.

Aside from its distinctive schedule (shared only by Colorado College among major colleges), Cornell has one of only two U.S. college or university campuses listed in its entirety on the National Register of Historic Places. Cornell was founded in 1853, 12 years before the better known, similarly named Ivy League university. A pedestrian mall runs through campus, and the majestic clock tower of King Chapel has ticked continuously since 1882. The school's Cole Library is also the town of Mount Vernon's public library, one of few such libraries in the country. Cornell's student center, Thomas Commons, features an indoor-outdoor fireplace, classrooms and meeting spaces, and a glass-enclosed dining room with panoramic views of campus. Recent projects include an expansion and renovation of the Small Sport Center.

"If you want a normal college experience, don't pick Cornell."

Cornell's core curriculum, called Ingenuity, combines distribution requirements in several liberal arts areas with opportunities for learning outside the classroom. In their first two years, all students take three discussion-oriented Foundations seminars, one of which is writing-intensive. The Ingenuity in Action component requires

Website: www.cornellcollege.edu
Location: Small Town
Private
Total Enrollment: 1,045
Undergraduates: 1,039
Male/Female: 52/48
Financial Aid: 100%
Pell Grant: 29%
Expense: Pr $ $
Student Loans: 64%
Average Debt: $ $ $ $
Applicants: 2,836
Accepted: 81%
Enrolled: 13%
Grad in 6 Years: 64%
Returning Freshmen: 78%
Academics: ✎ ✎ ✎
Social: ☎ ☎ ☎
Q of L: ★ ★ ★
Admissions: (800) 747-1112

(continued)

Email Address: admission@
cornellcollege.edu

Strong Programs:
Education
Creative Writing
Business
Theater
Geology
Kinesiology/Exercise Science
Biochemistry and Molecular
   Biology
Computer Science

students to participate in at least two out-of-class experiences, such as internships, research or service projects, or study abroad—with funding provided by the college as needed. All students track and reflect on their progress over four years in an electronic portfolio, and most complete a capstone experience in their major.

A sophomore explains block scheduling this way: "At Cornell, a semester's worth of work is completed in a month. This makes for a fast-paced class that is normally composed of a couple of papers, maybe some annotations, a midterm, a final, and a final project." A biology and Spanish double major adds, "Each class is pretty intense." If that sounds intimidating, it can be. But administrators say it also improves the quality of Cornell's liberal arts education by helping students acclimate to the business world, where "what needs to be done needs to be done quickly and done well." The One Course method also helps in academic advising—with grades every four weeks, signs of trouble are quickly apparent.

> **"'Beat Coe' and 'Coe Sucks' have been emblazoned on Cornell fanwear since the 1920s."**

Cornell awards degrees in more than 50 academic majors, as well as an extensive group of preprofessional programs. The bachelor of special studies, pursued by 2 percent of students, allows students to broaden or deepen their studies by combining courses in an individualized fashion. Among the most popular majors are kinesiology/exercise science, biochemistry and molecular biology, computer science, and psychology; other strong options include education, creative writing, business, theater, and geology. The college also offers preprofessional centers for health sciences, law and society, and literary arts. Classes are taught by full professors and are intimate, with 68 percent enrolling fewer than 20 students. Says a sophomore, "Professors spend all of their time teaching and improving their courses to provide the best education possible."

The school's Cole Library is also the town of Mount Vernon's public library, one of few such libraries in the country.

Fifty-three percent of Cornell students typically study off campus. Cornell faculty teach 15 to 20 courses off campus each year; recent international courses have included Holocaust and Human Rights in Europe, Gender and Development in India, and Macroeconomics in Shanghai. Programs are also available in nearly 40 countries through partner providers. During the short breaks between courses, students can take advantage of symposia and athletic events. The Cornell Summer Research Institute offers an eight-week stipend for faculty-directed summer research projects. Career coaches at the Berry Career Institute help each student identify an individual path for their professional development.

"'Cornell weird' is a phrase that gets thrown around a lot, and it's accurate," says one student. "There is no singular way to describe a Cornellian other than *unique*." Twenty-nine percent of students are homegrown Iowans, and 3 percent hail from other nations. Black students represent 7 percent of the student population, Hispanics/Latinos 8 percent, Asian Americans 3 percent, and multiracial students 2 percent. "Cornell starts with one huge disadvantage in terms of diversity: it's in the middle of a relatively small town in Iowa," admits one student. Politically, Cornell leans liberal. Merit scholarships averaging $29,300 are offered to qualified students, although there are no athletic awards.

> **"Every block [students] have to remap their schedules to succeed in an entirely new course."**

Seventy-nine percent of students live on campus. First-years enjoy completely renovated residence halls, while upperclassmen prefer the suite-style halls. Everyone eats together in Thomas Commons, where the food is "usually good," a junior says. Vegetarian options are always available. Student safety is taken seriously, students say, and, "Campus Security is very accessible, with an officer on call and on campus 24/7."

"Most of the social life happens on campus," says a psychology major. "Because everyone lives on campus, there is a lot of effort to make sure that there is always a lot to do and nobody has time to be bored." Local fraternities and sororities draw 8 percent of the men and 18 percent of the women; membership in a couple of fraternities is open to all genders, and in most sororities, any female-identifying student can join. "Some are completely dry or emphasize their commitment to service," reports one student, "while others are notorious for parties and jungle juice (never, *ever* drink jungle juice)." The Performing Arts and Activities Council is in charge of bringing entertainment to campus, which includes comedians, speakers, musicians, and hypnotists. Mount Vernon (population 4,500) is "small, but very welcoming," says a student. Students either love the town's idyllic pace—a few local bars; an acclaimed restaurant; some funky shops; and a lot of peace, quiet, and safety—or long for more excitement. The latter is available in Cedar Rapids (home of archrival Coe College) or Iowa City (home to the University of Iowa), each less than half an hour away. Chicago is about four hours away.

On the field or on the court, Cornell's competition with Coe is always heated, especially when it comes to Rams football and basketball. "'Beat Coe' and 'Coe Sucks' have been emblazoned on Cornell fanwear since the 1920s," says one student of institutional history. "We have the archival records to back that up." Women's basketball, baseball, and softball are competitive in the Division III Midwest Conference, and women's volleyball has won several conference titles in recent years. Thirty-four percent of students participate in intramural sports.

Cornell offers a top-notch education, plenty of opportunities, and a supportive community. Flexibility and a sense of adventure are key to thriving in Cornell's One Course At A Time system. "Students must be able to adapt to a new environment very quickly—every block they have to remap their schedules to succeed in an entirely new course," explains a psychology major. "The block plan is not easy. Students who succeed on this plan are not afraid of the failures that are nearly inevitable, and they're excited for the opportunity to grow as a learner."

> *Cornell requires students to participate in at least two out-of-class experiences, such as internships—with funding provided by the college.*

Overlaps

Coe, Augustana (IL), Luther, St. Olaf, Knox, Lawrence, Loras, Colorado College

If You Apply To ›

Cornell College: Rolling admissions. SATs or ACTs: optional (test-optional applicants must respond to two short-answer questions and may submit an optional personal portfolio). Accepts the Common Application with supplement.

Cornell University

Ithaca, NY 14850

Cornell University's reputation as a pressure cooker comes from its preprofessional attitude and a "we try harder" mentality. Spans seven undergraduate colleges—four private and three public—and tuition varies accordingly. Strong in engineering, architecture, and sustainability, world famous in hotel administration. Least difficult Ivy to get into, and also the farthest from an urban center. Once you're there, Ithaca is a great college town.

Cornell University has a long tradition of being the lone wolf among the Ivy League universities—not least for its stated ambition to become the finest research university for undergraduate education in the nation. The mixture within one institution of private and state-funded colleges and schools, preprofessional programs, and liberal arts results in, as one student says, "a diversity of opportunities in and outside of the classroom."

Website: www.cornell.edu
Location: Rural
Private
Total Enrollment: 25,008
Undergraduates: 15,450

Perched atop a hill that commands a view of both the city of Ithaca and Cayuga Lake, Cornell is breathtakingly scenic, with ravines, waterfalls, and parks bordering all sides of the campus. (As the saying goes, "Ithaca is gorges.") The Cornell Botanic Gardens, more than 3,500 acres of woodlands, natural trails, streams, and gorges, provide space for walking, picnicking, or contemplation. Cornell's superb library system consists of 20 libraries, including the beautiful underground Carl A. Kroch Library, featuring sky-lit atriums and renowned collections of Icelandic and Southeast Asian materials. The Johnson Museum of Art, designed by I. M. Pei, is one of the best university museums in the nation. The state-of-the-art Bill and Melinda Gates Hall houses high-tech research and teaching labs for computer and information sciences, while the LEED Platinum–certified Klarman Hall is dedicated to teaching, research, and education in the humanities.

Cornell was founded in 1865 and named for cofounder and telegraph mogul Ezra Cornell. At the undergraduate level, the university has four privately endowed colleges: architecture, art, and planning; arts and sciences; business; and engineering. Cornell is also New York State's land grant university, and as such operates three other colleges under contract with the state: agriculture and life sciences, human ecology, and the school of industrial and labor relations. New York residents at these "contract colleges" pick up their Ivy League degrees at an almost-public price (as in-state tuition at these schools is slightly steeper than SUNY rates). The Cornell College of Business houses two undergraduate schools (the privately endowed School of Hotel Administration and the Dyson School of Applied Economics, which it shares with the agriculture college) and one graduate school. Prospective students apply to one of the seven colleges or schools through the central admissions office, and admissions standards vary by school. Each college sets its own general education requirements, but all Cornell undergrads take at least one First-Year Writing Seminar.

> "There are many office hours held by teaching assistants, and professors make additional help extremely accessible."

Cornell offers over 4,000 courses in more than 100 fields of study. The most popular majors lie in the areas of engineering, business, biological sciences, and agriculture. The College of Architecture, Art, and Planning's offerings in architecture and fine arts are standouts. The College of Arts and Sciences boasts considerable strength in history, government, environment and sustainability, and just about all the natural and physical sciences. The English program has turned out a gaggle of celebrated writers, including the late Toni Morrison, Thomas Pynchon, and Kurt Vonnegut. Foreign languages, required for all arts and sciences students, are strong (try taking Tamil, Zulu, or Nepali), and the performing arts, mathematics, and social science departments are considered good. Cornell was early among universities to add women's studies to the curriculum and continues to be an innovator, with programs like China and Asia-Pacific studies, which requires a semester in China and another in Washington, D.C. The College of Agriculture and Life Sciences is highly ranked and a good bet for anyone hoping to make it into veterinary school (Cornell's graduate College of Veterinary Medicine is among the best), while the School of Industrial and Labor Relations is the preeminent school of its kind. The College of Business offers more than a dozen noteworthy concentrations, including agribusiness management; finance, accounting, and real estate; and business analytics.

Cornell is also New York State's land grant university, and as such operates three of its undergraduate colleges under contract with the state.

"The quality of teaching is top-notch because the majority of professors are regarded as experts in their respective fields," says one student, who also cautions, "Some of the educators struggle to communicate their knowledge." First-year courses in the sciences and social sciences are generally large lectures, but overall, 55 percent of classes have fewer than 20 students. "There are many office hours held by teaching assistants, and professors make additional help extremely accessible," reports a computer science major.

Cornell academics are demanding and foster an intensity found on few campuses. "There is a competitive atmosphere, as students who attend Cornell are ambitious and passionate. However, this is a positive and motivating force," says one sophomore. Those who were the class genius in high school should be prepared for a struggle to rise to the top. After a series of well-publicized suicide incidents in 2009, Cornell greatly strengthened its mental health support program. To cope with the anxieties that the high-powered atmosphere can create, the university has one of the best psychological counseling networks in the nation, including an alcohol-awareness program, peer sex counselors, personal-growth workshops, and EARS (Empathy, Assistance, and Referral Service).

"The number of quality study abroad programs seems inexhaustible."

A co-op program is available to engineering students, and Cornell-in-Washington is popular among students from all seven undergraduate colleges. Students looking to study abroad can choose from hundreds of programs in 80 countries, including Indonesia, Belgium, Ireland, and Nepal; 31 percent of students participate. "The number of quality study abroad programs seems inexhaustible," says a sophomore. Roughly half of all undergraduates participate in a faculty-guided research experience during their four years. The Presidential Research Scholars program, open to undergraduates in all disciplines, provides as many as 200 selected students with up to $8,000 in funding to carry out individually designed research programs with the support of faculty mentors. Seventy-eight percent of students engage in community service opportunities coordinated by the Public Service Center and the Office of Engagement Initiatives.

The innovative China and Asia-Pacific studies program requires a semester in China and another in Washington, D.C.

What do Cornell students have in common? "We are cooler than the nerdy kids, and nerdier than the cool kids," quips one senior. "We don't quite fit in anywhere else. We by and large didn't get into other Ivies, so compared to those students we feel a need to validate and distinguish ourselves through hard work and a more robust social life." Thirty-three percent of Cornell's undergraduates hail from New York; another 10 percent are international. Black students constitute 7 percent of the student body, Hispanics/Latinos account for 15 percent, Asian Americans comprise 22 percent, and multiracial students add 5 percent. All freshmen participate in discussion-based diversity workshops aimed at increasing dialogue and engagement. Upon graduation, nearly one-third of Cornell students attend graduate and professional schools.

"We feel a need to validate and distinguish ourselves through hard work and a more robust social life."

Cornell is need-blind in admissions and meets the demonstrated need of all accepted applicants, but the proportion of outright grants—as opposed to loans that must be repaid—in the financial aid package varies based on income. Cornell eliminates loans and the parental contribution for students from families with incomes below $60,000 and assets below $100,000, and caps need-based student loans at varying amounts based on family incomes above $60,000. The Cornell Installment Plan allows students or their parents to pay a year's or semester's tuition in monthly interest-free installments. The university does not award merit or athletic scholarships.

The Collegetown neighborhood abutting campus is packed with student-oriented apartment buildings, restaurants, bars, and shops.

Fifty-five percent of Cornell's undergrads live in university housing; others try their luck off campus in Collegetown, a neighborhood abutting the southwest end of campus that is packed with student-oriented apartment buildings, restaurants, bars, and shops. Demand has kept the housing market tight and rents high, although options are increasing. "Housing was one of the main reasons I chose Cornell," says one junior. "I was able to essentially guarantee myself a single room even freshman year. My room was huge, and my dorm was quiet." North Campus residence halls, including four newly built halls, are the home of all first-years and sophomores. Upperclassmen live in the West Campus house system, in five living/learning "houses" with professors in residence, house chefs, and creative programming. Students on both campuses can opt to take one-credit Learning Where You Live courses taught in the residential communities. There are dorms devoted to everything from ecology to music, and cultural houses include the International Living Center, Latino Living Center, Ujamaa Residential College, and Akwe:kon, a program house focusing on American Indian culture (the only facility of its kind in the U.S.). Cornell's food service is reputedly among the best in the nation, with eight residential dining halls that function independently; one student enthuses, "The food is very diverse and super tasty!"

Despite the intense academic atmosphere—or maybe because of it—Cornell social life beats most of the other Ivies hands down. Once the weekend arrives, local parties, state parks, and ski slopes fill with Cornell students seeking to redress the balance between study and play. With 28 percent of men and 25 percent of women pledging fraternities and sororities, these groups play a significant role in the social scene. "Social life at Cornell is really built around Greek life, especially for those under 21. Students who go Greek tend to have busy social schedules, and those who

"Social life at Cornell is really built around Greek life, especially for those under 21."

don't really need to find an organization they are passionate about," advises one student. Alcohol is part of the social scene, but one student says the university is "cracking down" on underage and high-risk drinking. Freshmen are not allowed to attend fraternity parties during the fall semester, and alcohol is banned from recruitment and new-member events in the spring. Students have their pick of roughly 1,000 student organizations—including clubs for Japanese drumming and Bhangra dancing—and there are innumerable concerts and sporting events throughout the year. Big events include Dragon Day (architecture students build a dragon and parade it through campus) and Springfest (a gathering on Ho Plaza). Students celebrate the last day of classes—Slope Day—with a concert on Libe Slope.

Cornell athletes have won their share of Ivy League team titles over the last decade and make regular Division I national championship appearances. Men's ice hockey is unquestionably the dominant sport on campus (its chief raison d'être being to defeat Harvard), and camping out for season tickets is an annual ritual. Women's ice hockey, men's lacrosse, wrestling, and women's sailing are nationally competitive, and women's lightweight rowing has brought home a number of Intercollegiate Rowing Association titles. Cornell boasts the largest intramural program in the Ivy League, with more than a dozen sports, including nearly 100 basketball teams. The "four seasons of Ithaca" (rain, snow, slush, and drizzle) can make walking to class across the vast and hilly campus challenging, but with the first snow of the winter, "traying" down Libe Slope becomes the sport of choice for hordes of fun-loving Cornellians. Students head to Greek Peak Mountain for skiing, Cayuga Lake for boating and swimming, and countless places for hiking and watching the clouds roll by.

Like most other Ivy League universities, Cornell is a premier research institution with a distinguished faculty and outstanding academics. What sets it apart is its focus on preprofessional preparation for undergraduates and a student body that strives for high academic achievement and at the same time a vigorous social life. One junior sums up the Cornell experience like this: "The people are passionate, the academics are rigorous, and the extracurricular activities are empowering."

University of Dallas

Irving, TX 75062

Bulwark of academic traditionalism in the Big D, with a Core Curriculum focused exclusively on Western civilization. Despite being a "university," UD has just 1,500 undergraduates, making small classes and personal attention a priority. The only outpost of Roman Catholic education between Loyola of New Orleans and University of San Diego. A compelling drawing card is the university's program in Rome, embraced by most sophomores.

While many universities around the nation have reexamined their Eurocentric core curriculums, the University of Dallas—the best Roman Catholic university south of Washington, D.C.—remains proudly dedicated to a classic liberal arts education that fosters the study of "the great deeds and words of Western civilization." The campus tenor is conservative, but students say there are plenty of lively happenings to be found. Whether it's discussing Homer and Dante on the campus mall or cutting loose for the school's quirkiest event, a massive Groundhog Day party, one student says, "UD cherishes tradition."

UD's 744-acre campus occupies a pastoral home in a Dallas suburb on top of what one student calls "the closest thing this region has to a hill." A major portion of the campus is situated around the Braniff Mall, a landscaped and lighted gathering place near the Braniff Memorial Tower, the school's landmark. Many campus buildings, including the tower, were designed by the midcentury modern architect O'Neil Ford. The primary tone of the buildings is, like the surrounding North Texas landscape, brown, and the dominant style, as described by one student, is "post-1950s, done in brick, typical Catholic—institutional." Even so, the campus boasts a beautiful chapel and a state-of-the-art science building.

Appropriately for a Catholic school, most eyes at UD look to Rome, where about 80 percent of undergraduates trek for the unique, semester-long Rome Program, usually during sophomore year. "It sounds cliché to say that a semester could change your life, but the Rome semester does precisely that," enthuses a politics major. The program involves intense coursework, as well as trips to northern Italy and Greece

> **"The average student at UD is enthusiastically Catholic [and] loves debate and discussion."**

(not to mention long weekends for individual travel). It is part of UD's four-semester Western civilization Core Curriculum, which includes philosophy, English, math, fine arts, science, American civilization, Western civilization, politics, economics, a serious foreign language requirement, and two theology courses (Understanding the Bible and The Western Theological Tradition). All students also complete a senior thesis or project, a comprehensive exam, and/or a senior seminar, depending on their major.

Students at UD, which was established in 1956, choose from more than 30 majors and 38 concentrations, including a few preprofessional options. Business,

Website: www.udallas.edu
Location: Suburban
Private
Total Enrollment: 1,775
Undergraduates: 1,465
Male/Female: 43/57
Financial Aid: 99%
Pell Grant: 36%
Expense: Pr $
Student Loans: 55%
Average Debt: $ $ $
Applicants: 4,990
Accepted: 58%
Enrolled: 16%
Grad in 6 Years: 72%
Returning Freshmen: 81%
Academics: 🖋 🖋 🖋
Social: ☎ ☎
Q of L: ★ ★ ★
Admissions: (800) 628-6999
Email Address: crusader@udallas.edu

Strong Programs:
Business
Biology
English
Politics
Psychology
Classics
Human and Social Sciences
Chemistry

biology, English, politics, and psychology are some of the strongest and most popular majors. The business program draws on abundant internship opportunities in the Dallas/Fort Worth Metroplex. The politics major offers a concentration in political philosophy. Classics is, no surprise, a traditional strength, and a concentration in human and social sciences tackles 21st-century issues through theory and practical research in areas like anthropology, sociology, and social psychology. Premed students are well served by the biology and chemistry programs. Other students take advantage of 3–2 dual-degree programs in nursing and electrical engineering, as well as 4 + 1 bachelor's/master's programs in a number of fields. The O'Hara Chemical Science Institute offers a hands-on, eight-week summer program to prepare new students for independent research.

"The University of Dallas is very much like a coffeehouse," muses one junior. "It is laid-back, but intellectual, it is fun, and all your friends are there with you." The university uses no teaching assistants, and professors are easy to get to know, especially since 61 percent of classes enroll fewer than 20 students. "The professors are very devoted to their jobs," says a politics major. "They truly care about the success of their students."

"The average student at UD is enthusiastically Catholic, loves debate and discussion, and loves to think about big questions," says an English major. Seventy-two percent of UD students are Catholic, and many of them choose this school because of its religious affiliation. Fifty-eight percent of undergraduates are Texan, and 2 percent are international. Twenty-six percent are Hispanic/Latino, 7 percent are Asian American, 3 percent are Black, and 2 percent are multiracial. Most students are conservative and "think similarly about social issues such as gender and abortion," says one student, and there is not much political activism on campus. Thirty-six percent of freshmen are Pell-eligible. UD offers various merit scholarships averaging $22,700 but no athletic awards, as it is a Division III school.

> "[You] graduate with a deep sense of your place in the Western cultural tradition."

Sixty-one percent of students live on campus, where tradition and religious principle govern conduct. Students under 21 who don't reside at home with their parents must live on campus in single-sex dorms with strict visitation regulations. "The freshman dorms are a little old, but there is a great feeling of community there," says a junior. The sole dining hall is spacious and boasts a wonderful view of north Dallas, but the food draws complaints for being too expensive for the quality. The fast food and snacks at the Rathskeller are said to be better. "UD is a small and pretty safe campus, so we have few cases of sexual assault," reports a junior.

With no fraternities or sororities at UD, the Campus Activities Board sponsors most on-campus entertainment. Free movies, dances, and visiting speakers are usually on the agenda. Church-related and religious activities provide fulfilling social outlets for a good number of students. During Charity Week in the fall, the junior class organizes a variety of fund-raising events. The biggest event of the year is Groundhog, a whole week of events celebrating Groundhog Day and culminating in a huge party at Groundhog Park, featuring "live bands, free food, beer for students over 21, and sports games throughout the day," explains an English major. Smaller off-campus parties happen frequently; on campus, a student warns, "The Office of Student Life runs a tight ship regarding alcohol." Students describe Irving (population 255,000) as "a suburb just like any other," but Dallas offers almost unlimited possibilities, including a full agenda for barhopping on Lower Greenville Avenue and food, craft breweries, and culture in the Bishop Arts District, both about 15 minutes away. The West End and Deep Ellum offer a taste of shopping and Dallas's alternative music scene. And for the more adventurous, Austin and San Antonio aren't too far away.

The University of Dallas is unusual for a Texas school in that its entire population does not salivate at the sight of a football. But the Crusaders men's soccer and men's and women's basketball and golf teams are competitive in the Division III Southern Collegiate Athletic Conference. Club and intramural sports are well organized and sign up about a quarter of the students. The club rugby team (known as the Hoggies, after the school's favorite Groundhog tradition) is particularly popular.

Although some students complain that UD's focus on Western liberal arts and its Catholic emphasis can feel academically limiting, most say they appreciate the sense of shared experience and strong tradition that defines their school. In the words of one senior, "Come here to have fun, build sincere friendships, work hard, and graduate with a deep sense of your place in the Western cultural tradition."

If You Apply To ›

Dallas: Early action I and II, regular decision. Accepts the Common Application with supplement. Please consult Dallas's website for the most up-to-date information regarding standardized test requirements.

Dartmouth College

6016 McNutt Hall, Hanover, NH 03755

The smallest Ivy and the one with the strongest emphasis on undergraduates. Traditionally the most conservative member of the Ivy League, it has steered toward more student diversity and more serious scholars, but long-standing party culture persists. Ivy ties notwithstanding, Dartmouth has much of the feel of places like Colgate, Middlebury, and Williams. Great for those who like the outdoors.

Unlike the other seven members of the Ivy League, which trace their roots to Puritan New Englanders or progressive Quaker colonists, Dartmouth College was founded in 1769 to educate Native Americans. The student body has always been the smallest in the Ancient Eight, and the school's focus on undergraduate education differentiates Dartmouth from its peers, though it does offer graduate programs in a range of academic subjects and professional areas. The college attracts plenty of hiking and skiing enthusiasts, and the Dartmouth Outing Club, the oldest in the country, is the most popular extracurricular organization. In recent years, Dartmouth has increasingly emphasized the importance of developing a global presence in its traditionally warm and inclusive community. According to one freshman, "We strongly value traditions, we like to have fun in our woodsy New Hampshire home, and at the same time, everyone is incredibly academically involved."

Dartmouth's picturesque campus is the most rural of the Ivies, and its winters may be the coldest (with the possible exception of those at Cornell). Set in the small town of Hanover, New Hampshire, which is bisected by the Appalachian Trail, the campus is arranged around a traditional New England green, bounded by the impressive library at one end and by the college-owned Hanover Inn at the other. Architectural styles range from Romanesque to postmodern, but the dominant theme is copper-topped colonial frame. The nearest big city, Boston, is two hours away, but major artists like Yo-Yo Ma routinely visit Dartmouth's Hopkins Center for the Arts, adding to the growing arts culture on campus. The $200 million Engineering and Computer Science Center opened in 2022.

Website: www.dartmouth.edu
Location: Rural
Private
Total Enrollment: 6,713
Undergraduates: 4,533
Male/Female: 51/49
Financial Aid: 50%
Pell Grant: 16%
Expense: Pr $ $ $ $
Student Loans: 34%
Average Debt: $
Applicants: 28,356
Accepted: 6%
Enrolled: 70%
Grad in 6 Years: 95%
Returning Freshmen: 98%
Academics: 🎓 🎓 🎓 🎓 🎓
Social: 🍷 🍷 🍷 🍷 🍷
Q of L: ★ ★ ★
Admissions: (603) 646-2875

(continued)

Email Address: admissions
.reply@dartmouth.edu

Strong Programs:
Engineering
Biological Sciences
Environmental Studies
Foreign Languages
Computer Science
Economics
Government
English

Ninety percent of incoming students opt to go on five-day preorientation trips with the Outing Club, exploring the great outdoors.

Dartmouth's status as a member of the Ivy League means academic excellence is a given. First-years must take a writing-intensive seminar that involves both independent research and small-group discussion; about 75 are offered each year across different departments. Students must also demonstrate proficiency in at least one foreign language and take three world culture courses (one non-Western, one Western, and one Culture and Identity), and 10 courses from several distribution areas spanning the liberal arts and sciences. In addition, Dartmouth has a senior culminating activity—a thesis, public report, exhibition, seminar, production, or demonstration—that allows students to pull together work done in their major with a creative and intellectual twist of their own. Before arriving on campus for their first year, 90 percent of incoming students opt to go on five-day preorientation trips with the Outing Club, getting to know their classmates while exploring the great outdoors.

"We like to have fun in our woodsy New Hampshire home."

Though Dartmouth students work hard, a history major remarks, "I think that students are pleasantly surprised by our noncompetitive academic climate." Popular majors include economics, government, engineering sciences, computer science, English, and history. Programs in engineering, biological sciences, and environmental studies are particularly strong, and the languages are also well regarded. Computer science offerings are among the best in the nation, thanks in no small part to the late John Kemeny, the former Dartmouth president who coinvented time-sharing and the BASIC language. Unique programs include quantitative social science and human-centered design.

Professors get high marks at Dartmouth, perhaps because of the school's focus on undergraduates. The rural location also helps; faculty make a conscious choice to teach here, leaving behind some of the distractions afflicting their peers at more urban schools. "If you come to Dartmouth for only one thing, it would be the faculty," says an economics major. "The professors are truly the best out there for undergraduates." Sixty-two percent of undergraduate classes have fewer than 20 students, and 48 percent of undergrads take advantage of abundant research opportunities. The Presidential Scholars Program provides one-on-one paid research assistantships with faculty. The Rockefeller Center's Policy Research Shop helps undergraduate public policy students write policy briefs for state legislators and government agencies in New Hampshire and Vermont. Female students interested in STEM fields can participate in the Women in Science Project, which offers mentors, speakers, and even research positions for first-years. Montgomery Fellowships bring well-known politicians, writers, and others to campus for periods ranging from a few days to several months.

The school's most notable eccentricity is the Dartmouth Plan, or "D-Plan"—four 10-week terms a year, including one during the summer. Students must be on campus for three terms during the freshman and senior years, and also during the summer after the sophomore year, but otherwise, as long as they're on track to graduate, they can take off whenever they wish. About half of Dartmouth undergrads take advantage of their "leave term" to study abroad, usually signing up for one of the college's more than 30 faculty-led programs, selecting from options ranging from theater in London to environmental studies in South Africa to biology in Costa Rica.

"If you come to Dartmouth for only one thing, it would be the faculty."

Ninety-seven percent of undergraduates hail from outside of New Hampshire, including 12 percent from other countries. Dartmouth went co-ed in 1972, and it subsequently became the first major university to award more bachelor's degrees in engineering to women than to men. Black students represent 5 percent of the student population, Asian Americans 14 percent, Hispanics/Latinos 10 percent, and multiracial students 6 percent. Consistent with its historical roots, Dartmouth continues to have a strong interest in recruiting and supporting Native American students, who currently represent 1 percent of the undergraduate student body. Students here have a "true, true love for this school and a passion for learning not simply for the grade but for the experience," says a senior. Students retain that passion after graduation, as Dartmouth has the most elaborate network of alumni organizations of any college in the country. Politically, an economics major says, "Most students are either liberal or quietly conservative." Admissions are need-blind, even for students admitted from the waitlist, and the school meets the full demonstrated need of all admits. Dartmouth has eliminated student loans from all financial aid packages, and the college covers the cost of tuition for students from families with incomes below $125,000 a year. No merit or athletic scholarships are awarded; the Ivy League prohibits the latter.

The school's most notable eccentricity is the Dartmouth Plan, or "D-Plan"—four 10-week terms a year, including one during the summer.

Eighty-four percent of Dartmouth students live on campus in one of more than 30 dorms, which, in an effort to create a greater sense of community among undergraduates, have been organized into six House Communities, each led by a House Professor. "From suites to singles to apartment-style housing, it's easy to find housing on campus that will suit you," says an engineering physics major. Beginning in their freshman year, students can apply to live in one of several living/learning communities, from the Sustainable Living Center to Global Village to various identity-based communities. Housing is guaranteed for freshmen and sophomores. Because of

"[Students have] a passion for learning not simply for the grade but for the experience."

the D-Plan, people are always coming and going, so it may be easier to find a new room or roommate than at schools on the semester system. Seniors may move off campus, where there are plenty of readily available options. Dining facilities stay open until 2:30 a.m. for those needing sustenance during late-night study sessions. Students say their rural campus generally feels safe but report that sexual assault has been a hot-button issue. "Dartmouth has taken a lot of steps to constantly address the issue of sexual assault, but sometimes it feels like it's more a result of trying to combat scandals than to actually take steps to address the problem," comments a junior.

"Social life primarily occurs on campus," says a senior. "There is college programming every Friday and Saturday night, including everything from roller-skating to pottery nights and comedy shows." Dartmouth's Greek system attracts 29 percent of the men and 38 percent of the women, who rush during the fall of their sophomore year. Although still the center of the school's party scene, fraternity parties are inclusive: "What's really unique about our Greek system is that it's open to the entire campus—if you have a Dartmouth ID card, you cannot be denied entry," explains a student. Dartmouth was one of the first schools to develop a counseling and educational program to combat alcohol abuse. More recently, the Moving Dartmouth Forward plan has focused on bolstering behavioral standards and offering more options for social life. As part of its continuing efforts to reduce binge drinking and other alcohol-soaked misbehavior, the college has banned hard liquor on campus. "While it can be annoying at times, I really do think the ban has been effective in controlling excessive drinking on campus,"

Admissions are need-blind, and Dartmouth has eliminated student loans from all financial aid packages.

"What's really unique about our Greek system is that it's open to the entire campus."

reasons a senior. Parties and kegs must be registered, and the houses where they're being held are subject to walk-throughs by college safety and security personnel. Good road trips, although relatively infrequent, include Montreal or Boston, for a dose of bright lights and the big city, or the White Mountains for camping. Dartmouth has a 27,000-acre land grant in the northeast corner of New Hampshire where cabins may be rented for five dollars a night.

"I was sold on Dartmouth because it is steeped in tradition," says one senior. Major traditions include homecoming, which boasts a 75-foot-tall bonfire, and Winter Carnival, which involves ski racing at the college's skiway located 20 minutes away, as well as snow-sculpture contests, a polar plunge, and partiers from all over the Eastern seaboard. Spring brings mud as the snow slowly melts, and also Green Key weekend, an annual rite of spring featuring live music and parties. Community service is popular, and the Center for Social Impact sponsors immersion trips to places like New Orleans, Puerto Rico, and the Dominican Republic.

Dartmouth offers 35 Division I varsity sports. Big Green football and women's basketball teams have each won the most championships in Ivy League history. The women's rugby team has captured three national titles in the last five years. The school also offers 36 club sports, including nationally competitive teams in sailing, skiing, figure skating, and ultimate Frisbee, and 24 intramural sports. Nonathletes beware: Dartmouth does have a nontimed swimming test and a physical education requirement for graduation; you can fulfill the latter with classes such as fencing or ballet, or with participation in a club or intramural sport.

Dartmouth attracts outdoorsy, inquisitive, down-to-earth students who develop extremely strong ties to the school—and each other—during four years together in this quintessential rural New England setting. It seems as if every other grad has a title like deputy assistant class secretary, and many return to Hanover when they retire, further cementing their bonds with the college and driving local real estate prices beyond the reach of most faculty members. You'll have to be made of hardy stock to survive the harsh New Hampshire winters. But once you defrost, you'll be rewarded with lifelong friends and a solid grounding in the liberal arts, sciences, and technology.

Overlaps

Colgate, Middlebury, Williams, Harvard, Princeton, Yale, Brown, University of Pennsylvania

If You Apply To ›

Dartmouth: Early decision, regular decision. Accepts the Common Application. Submission of a peer recommendation is strongly recommended. Application includes an optional question on gender identity. Please consult Dartmouth's website for the most up-to-date information regarding standardized test requirements.

Davidson College

P.O. Box 7156, Davidson, NC 28035

Traditionally styled as the "Dartmouth of the South." Goes head-to-head with Washington and Lee (VA) as the top liberal arts college below the Mason-Dixon Line, and Division I sports are an advantage. An early leader in the trend to replace loans with grants, it boasts a strong honor system that sets the campus tone. Small-town location is close to Charlotte and prime vacation spots.

Website: www.davidson.edu
Location: Small Town
Private
Total Enrollment: 1,970
Undergraduates: 1,970
Male/Female: 47/53
Financial Aid: 70%

Davidson College combines the Southern tradition and gentility of neighbors like Rhodes and Sewanee with the academic prowess more common to Northern liberal arts powerhouses such as Dartmouth and Williams. It turns out more than its share of the region's political, education, legal, and other leaders. Often overlooked because of its small size and Carolina location, Davidson offers students strong interdisciplinary, international, and preprofessional programs, as well as a thriving social scene. As a senior economics major boasts, "Davidson is *the* liberal arts school of the South."

Located in a beautiful stretch of the North Carolina Piedmont, Davidson's wooded campus features Georgian and Greek Revival architecture. The central campus is designated as a national arboretum, and college staff lovingly maintain a collection of the woody plants that thrive in the area. Davidson retains its original quadrangle, which dates from its founding in 1837, plus literary society halls built in the 1850s.

In addition to classes in a range of liberal arts areas, core requirements at Davidson include coursework in a foreign language; cultural diversity; justice, equality, and community; first-year writing; and physical education. The most popular majors are economics, political science, biology, psychology, and English. Those whose academic interests lie outside the mainstream can work closely with select faculty members to pursue one of several majors established by the Center for Interdisciplinary Studies, such as Arab studies, bioinformatics, or global literary theory, or to design a major of their own. The interdisciplinary health and human values minor explores the role ethical values play in defining problems as "medical" and worthy of scientific study. A 3–2 engineering program is available with Columbia University and Washington University in St. Louis.

> **"Davidson is *the* liberal arts school of the South."**

Davidson's academic climate is "challenging and rigorous, but you're surrounded by a community of support," says a political science major. Sixty-one percent of classes have fewer than 20 students. Davidson's Honor Code allows students to take exams independently and to feel comfortable leaving doors unlocked. "The Honor Code is a cornerstone not just for academics, but for all aspects of life at Davidson," says a student. Every entering freshman agrees to abide by the code, and all work submitted to professors is signed with the word "pledged." Professors are highly lauded for being friendly and accessible, and with no graduate students around, opportunities to work with faculty members on research projects are plentiful.

The Sustainability Scholars Summer Program provides students with real-world projects that emphasize sustainability issues; students can be found in locations ranging from skyscrapers to community gardens. Students looking to sharpen their business or technical skills may take advantage of hands-on learning opportunities provided by the Hurt Hub for Innovation and Entrepreneurship. Study abroad programs, including 8 faculty-led and more than 125 partner programs, are available in countries

> **"The Honor Code is a cornerstone not just for academics, but for all aspects of life."**

from France, Germany, and England to Cyprus and Zambia. About 80 percent of students graduate with some international experience, whether it's coursework, service learning, research, or an internship.

"Davidson students are people who learn because they love to learn, not to perform intellectual ability but because of a genuine interest," comments an English major. While the school embraces its Presbyterian heritage, an Africana studies major says there is "a good amount of religious diversity" on campus. Twenty-one percent of Davidson students come from North Carolina and 8 percent from abroad. Black students represent 6 percent of the student body, Hispanics/Latinos 9 percent, Asian Americans 6 percent, and multiracial students 5 percent. "Politically, there's a left lean, but it's not significant compared to other liberal arts schools," observes a senior. The college practices need-blind admissions and, thanks to its highly touted Davidson Trust, guarantees to meet 100 percent of admitted students' demonstrated need through grants and student employment—eliminating loans from all need-based financial aid packages. Additionally, a limited number of merit scholarships and 175 athletic scholarships are available.

Ninety percent of Davidson's students live on campus in co-ed or single-sex dorms. Freshmen are housed together and eat in Vail Commons, where the food

(continued)

Pell Grant: 15%
Expense: Pr $ $ $
Student Loans: 26%
Average Debt: $
Applicants: 6,434
Accepted: 18%
Enrolled: 48%
Grad in 6 Years: 90%
Returning Freshmen: 95%
Academics: ✍ ✍ ✍ ✍ ½
Social: ☎ ☎ ☎
Q of L: ★ ★ ★ ★ ★
Admissions: (800) 768-0380
Email Address: admission@davidson.edu

Strong Programs:
Economics
Political Science
Biology
Psychology
English
Interdisciplinary Studies
Health and Human Values
Environmental Studies

The Sustainability Scholars Summer Program provides students with real-world projects in locations ranging from skyscrapers to community gardens.

is "average" but "accommodating to any dietary restrictions or needs, including religious needs," says a political science major. Seniors get apartment-style housing with private bedrooms. Many upperclassmen take meals at one of the fraternity or eating houses, which have their own cooks and serve meals family style. A limited number of upperclassmen receive permission to live off campus. Regarding campus safety and sexual assault, a senior reports, "I've seen more spaces emerge for conversation and support of sexual assault victims/survivors."

The Alvarez College Union provides a main gathering place, and students have around 200 clubs and organizations at their disposal, but Davidson's eight fraternities, three sororities, and four all-female eating houses are the real center of social life on campus. These nonresidential groups, which are housed in Patterson Court, charge dues that cover meals, parties, and other campuswide events. Fraternities claim 26 percent of the men, and sororities attract 49 percent of the women. The eating houses, each of which supports a different philanthropic cause, such as cancer and autism research, are not much different from Greek life. Freshmen women simply sign up for the eating house they want to join on Self-Selection Night, with no "rushing" allowed. And even if you don't join up, don't despair: "Greek life isn't elitist or exclusive. You can go to their open events and you'll be encouraged to as

"**Greek life isn't elitist or exclusive. You can go to their open events.**"

well," explains a senior. The party scene is said to be low-pressure, and one student points out that "[alcohol] policies are tied into the Honor Code, so they are enforced." Davidson's first-year orientation includes the Cake Race, a tradition since 1930 that provides each runner with a cake they select based on the order in which they finish a (voluntary) 1.7-mile race. Another favorite tradition is Spring Frolics, a weekend of games, concerts, and plenty of free food.

The cozy town of Davidson (population 15,000) and the equally quaint neighboring town of Cornelius are common destinations for a relaxed night out, with coffee shops, cafés, beer gardens, miniature golf, and movie theaters. "For a college town, the town of Davidson shuts down pretty early," notes a junior. The college's 110-acre Lake Norman campus is ideal for sailing, swimming, and rowing. When those diversions grow old, North Carolina's largest city, Charlotte, is just 20 miles away, offering nightlife and other attractions. A car definitely helps here, as beaches and skiing are a few hours away, in different directions. Public transit is an option, too, as is the college's shuttle service.

Davidson fields 21 varsity teams (the Wildcats), 19 of which compete in the Division I Atlantic 10 Conference. The nonscholarship football team plays in the Division I Pioneer Football League, and the wrestling team competes in the Southern Conference. About a quarter of students are varsity athletes. Basketball (one of whose alumni is Stephen Curry), soccer, and wrestling are the most competitive programs. Intramural and club sports are varied and popular.

Despite its North Carolina location, Davidson has the look and feel of a New England liberal arts college and continues to attract top students to its charming neck of the woods. From study abroad and independent research to a reception with the college president for graduating seniors, students here combine Southern tradition with forward thinking to make great memories, friends, and intellectual strides.

If You Apply To ›

Davidson: Early decision I and II, regular decision. SATs or ACTs: optional. Accepts the Common Application with supplement.

Part of a cohort of Roman Catholic institutions in the Midwest that includes DePaul, Duquesne, Loyola of Chicago, Saint Louis University, and Xavier (OH). Drawing cards include engineering, entrepreneurship, education, and health sciences, as well as a pioneering program in human rights. Medium–size school with larger feel. The city of Dayton, home to the Wright Brothers, is enjoying a resurgence. UD's appeal is largely regional.

Anyone who thinks college students of today subscribe to postmodern cynicism ought to take a peek at Dayton, where optimism and Roman Catholic charity are alive and well. Although its name suggests that it is a public university, Dayton was founded in 1850 by the Society of Mary (Marianists) and continues to emphasize that order's devotion to service. "If you used one word to describe UD students, it would be 'friendly,'" explains a senior. "We smile and say hi to people we don't know and hold the doors open for each other." There's good reason for the cheery disposition: Dayton continues to innovate new academic programs and has increased student funding for hands-on experiences like research and study abroad.

Located two miles from downtown Dayton, the 398-acre parklike campus with a riverfront vista is bordered by a quiet suburban neighborhood. The more historic buildings make up the central core of the campus and blend architectural charm with modern technological conveniences. The historic UD Arena, which was recently updated, has hosted more Division I basketball tournament games than any other venue. The $51 million EPISCenter boasts labs where UD

> "Students work hard but support each other."

researchers and students work side by side with GE Aviation scientists and engineers to create advanced electrical power technologies. "New initiatives are being put in place all the time to do our part in regards to sustainability," says a junior, including a large food-composting program. A 95,000-square-foot innovation hub opened in 2021, offering learning labs, classrooms, and opportunities for students to interact with local entrepreneurs.

The undergraduate curriculum, the Common Academic Program, is designed to equip students with the skills and experience to participate in a complex global society. The first-year experience course helps incoming students prepare for their academic careers and explore various majors, and all students complete a capstone experience and public presentation their senior year. UD students take full advantage of the strong offerings found in engineering (especially mechanical), entrepreneurship, biology, nursing, and early childhood education; marketing, communication, and finance are among the most popular majors. Consistent with its religious mission, Dayton offers a major in human rights studies, the first of its kind, and a Human Rights Center. The school has also developed the first undergraduate certificate in Applied Creativity for Transformation, focusing on creative competencies like complex problem-solving and collaboration with others. The entrepreneurship program dispenses $5,000 loans to participating sophomores to start their own businesses, with any profits going to charity; local entrepreneurs act as mentors. Through the Davis Center for Portfolio Management, finance students manage one of the largest student-run investment funds in the country, worth more than $60 million. Motivated students can earn two degrees at an accelerated pace through the Bachelor's Plus Master's program, choosing from two dozen available degrees.

Website: www.udayton.edu
Location: Small City
Private
Total Enrollment: 10,738
Undergraduates: 8,265
Male/Female: 52/48
Financial Aid: 98%
Pell Grant: 19%
Expense: Pr $
Student Loans: 59%
Average Debt: $ $ $
Applicants: 17,262
Accepted: 81%
Enrolled: 16%
Grad in 6 Years: 80%
Returning Freshmen: 88%
Academics: ✍ ✍ ✍
Social: ☎ ☎ ☎ ☎
Q of L: ★ ★ ★
Admissions: (937) 229-4411
Email Address: admission@udayton.edu

Strong Programs:
Engineering
Entrepreneurship
Biology
Nursing
Early Childhood Education
Human Rights Studies
Marketing
Communication

In the classroom, an education major says, "Students work hard but support each other." Thirty-eight percent of classes have fewer than 20 students. Students speak highly of professors' enthusiasm about their courses and the quality of their teaching. Career services get good ratings for making sure students are well networked and for continuing to offer assistance to alumni at any stage of their careers. "Career services does an outstanding job of coordinating events with employers and prepping students for internships," says a senior.

Qualified freshmen and transfer students may join the University Honors Program, which features special activities and opportunities for fellowships and research. The University of Dayton Research Institute also offers students a chance to gain hands-on experience. Study abroad options include academic and internship programs in such locations as Ireland, Spain, China, and Cameroon; 47 percent of students study internationally. "Campus ministry provides opportunities for retreats, service-learning trips, cultural immersion, and outreach," adds a senior.

Fifty-one percent of Dayton's undergraduates are from Ohio, while 4 percent come from abroad. A junior comments, "Although diversity and inclusion are very important on campus, it is still an area that is lacking." Currently, 5 percent of students are Black, 7 percent are Hispanic/Latino, 2 percent are Asian American, and 3 percent are multiracial. Fifty-two percent of the students are Catholic. A marketing and economics major describes the political atmosphere as "fairly moderate," and overt political activism is not common on campus. Dayton doles out about 100 athletic scholarships each year, and merit-based academic awards average $24,600. High school applicants who visit campus and file the FAFSA are eligible for a textbook scholarship of up to $4,000 ($500 per semester) if they choose to enroll.

> **"Campus ministry provides opportunities for retreats [and] service-learning trips."**

Seventy-three percent of undergraduates live in university housing; those who live off campus generally live adjacent to it. First-year students live in traditional residence halls, and about 20 percent of them opt to join living/learning communities with their classmates. Sophomores select suites or apartments, while upperclassmen take up quarters in the 400 university-owned houses, apartments, and townhouses that comprise the much-loved student neighborhood. The PATH points system determines the order in which returning students select housing; students accumulate points by attending eligible enrichment events like lectures, film screenings, and performances. A sophomore warns, "If you don't have a lot of PATH points, you're screwed." Dining facilities offer full-service, casual restaurant-style menu selections, along with a variety of cafés, delis, and convenience stores spread throughout the campus. Students report that campus safety is adequate and the Green Dot bystander intervention program has improved awareness of the issue of campus sexual assault.

"Students love to stay on campus for the weekends or even for some of our shorter breaks," says a student. The student neighborhood serves as a sort of continuous social center. A lit porch light beckons party-seeking students to join the weekend festivities, and one student says the party scene has "a very communal, open-door kind of feel." St. Patrick's Day has traditionally been a major event, although students warn

> **"Don't tell my mom this, but there is no place I feel more at home than UD."**

that university administrators and police have been cracking down on this and other parties. Greek organizations draw 12 percent of UD men and 25 percent of the women. More than 30 student groups are devoted entirely to service, and Christmas on Campus, when UD students host about 1,000 local elementary students for a night of crafts, games, and a visit with Santa, is one of the most student-involved activities.

The university is part of Dayton's bike share program, which has five stations on campus, and a free city bus service called The Flyer links the campus with downtown Dayton. Just a short ride away are attractions like the Dayton Dragons minor-league baseball team, the Dayton Art Institute, the U.S. Air Force's museums, and a symphony or opera in the Schuster Performing Arts Center. Weekend excursions take aim at cities ranging from Louisville to Chicago to Indianapolis, as well as the restaurants, shops, and sports arenas of Cincinnati.

The Dayton Flyers field 17 Division I men's and women's teams, and sports play a big role in campus life. Football competes in the Pioneer League, women's golf plays in the Metro Atlantic Athletic Conference, and all other teams are in the Atlantic 10 Conference. Both the men's and women's basketball teams have reached the Elite 8 in recent years, and the Red Scare student cheering section loves to intimidate opponents. Men's soccer and women's volleyball are recent conference champions. About half of the students participate in 27 club sports and the many intramural offerings.

As a midsized university where the undergraduates come first, Dayton has managed to maintain an exciting balance of personal attention, academic challenge, and all-American fun. The success of Dayton's attempts to provide its students with a high quality of life and a sense of cohesiveness is reflected in the strong social life and family-like atmosphere among both students and faculty. "The word that I use most when describing UD is 'community,'" says a mechanical engineering major. "Don't tell my mom this, but there is no place I feel more at home than UD."

> ## Overlaps
>
> **Marquette, Ohio University, Saint Louis University, Ohio State, Xavier (OH), University of Cincinnati, Miami (OH), Indiana University**

If You Apply To ›

Dayton: Early action, regular decision. SATs or ACTs: optional. Accepts the Common Application with supplement.

Deep Springs College

Deep Springs Ranch Road, Highway 168, Big Pine, CA 93513

Picture 27 Ivy League–caliber individuals living and learning on a working ranch in a remote desert outpost—that's Deep Springs. DS is the most elite two-year institution in the nation, and also the most unusual—and not just because of its free tuition. Occupies a handful of ranch-style buildings set on 50,000 acres on the arid border of Nevada and California. Students transfer to highly selective colleges after two years. After a century as an all-male school, Deep Springs has gone co-ed.

If the thought of spending countless hours under the fluorescent lights of the classroom makes you grimace, you may consider getting your hands dirty at Deep Springs College. This two-year—and now co-ed—institution doubles as a working ranch. Students enjoy a demanding and individualized education supplemented by the challenges and lessons of ranch life. Both, it seems, demand the same things: hard work, commitment, and pride in a job well done. Deep Springs students are also rewarded for their efforts in other ways: tuition is free, as is room and board. Most Deep Springers have wide-ranging interests and have shunned acceptance at Ivy League schools to embrace the rigors of a truly unique approach to learning.

California's White Mountains provide a stunning backdrop for the Deep Springs campus, set on a barren plain in Deep Springs Valley 5,200 feet above sea level,

Website: www.deepsprings.edu
Location: Rural
Private
Total Enrollment: 27
Undergraduates: 27
Male/Female: 41/59
Financial Aid: 100%
Pell Grant: N/A
Expense: Pr $
Student Loans: N/A
Average Debt: N/A

(continued)

Applicants: 225
Accepted: 6%
Enrolled: 86%
Grad in 6 Years: 100%
Returning Freshmen: 100%
Academics: ✑ ✑ ✑ ✑ ½
Social: ☎
Q of L: ★ ★ ★
Admissions: (760) 872-2000
Email Address: apcom@
   deepsprings.edu

Strong Programs:
Humanities
Literature
Philosophy

The college has 170 acres under cultivation, mostly with alfalfa, and an assortment of barnyard animals.

near the only water supply for miles around and 28 miles from the nearest town, a thriving metropolis known as Big Pine, population 1,875. The campus is an oasis-like cluster of trees and a lawn with eight ranch-style buildings that were built from scratch by the school's first class of students in 1917. The focal point is the Main Building, a venerable ranch-style structure with wide eaves that houses classrooms, offices, and the library. Faculty houses and the dining hall are grouped around the circular lawn a few yards away from the sole dorm, and the trappings of farm life surround the tiny settlement. The college has 170 acres under cultivation, mostly with alfalfa, and an assortment of barnyard animals. A solar array produces twice as much energy as the college requires—except during peak summer times when the alfalfa needs irrigating.

Founded in 1917 by industrialist L. L. Nunn, who made a fortune in the electric-power industry, Deep Springs today remains true to its charter to combine taxing

"As long as [faculty's] porch lights are on, students can stop by to talk."

practical work, rigorous academics, and genuine self-government—the three pillars of the school. In addition to coursework, students are required to perform 20 to 25 hours per week of labor, which can include everything from harvesting alfalfa to branding and herding cattle to cooking dinner. Applicants must be committed to the ideals of self-government, reflectiveness, frugality, and community activity. Those who are admitted can truly boast of being handpicked to attend: of the roughly 200 to 350 applications received each year, only a handful of students are accepted. The two-round admissions process is intense, spanning months and involving several essays, letters of recommendation, and an on-campus admissions interview. Admits typically have near-perfect academic records. More importantly, administrators say, applicants must be able to demonstrate a serious interest in "pursuing a life of service to humanity." Deep Springs now accepts applications from students of all gender identities and admitted its first co-ed class in 2018. To accommodate all members of its student body, the college added two private bathrooms in the dorm, as well as an outhouse in one of the vegetable fields.

Student input carries a lot of weight at Deep Springs. Four student-body committees are an essential part of the school's self-governance pillar: the Applications Committee, the Curriculum Committee, the Review and Reinvitations Committee, and the Communications Committee. These groups play a determining role in admissions and curricular decisions, help choose the college's faculty, and even elect two of their own to be full-voting members on the board of trustees. And they abide by a Spartan community code that bans all drugs, including alcohol, and forbids

"Vegetarians are usually provided for, but we are a cattle ranch."

students from leaving Deep Springs Valley (the 50 square miles of desert surrounding the campus) while classes are in session, except for medical visits and college business. There are no phones and no Internet in the dorm, although there is limited Wi-Fi in all the other buildings on campus, including classrooms and the library. Lest these rules sound unnecessarily strict, keep in mind that these are all decided on and enforced by the student body, not the administration.

Like almost everything else about it, Deep Springs has an unorthodox academic schedule: two summer terms of seven weeks each, and a fall and spring semester of 14 weeks each. Between 7 and 10 classes are offered every term. All new students arrive in July to complete an intensive summer seminar with some of their older peers. The seminar, often taught by an interdisciplinary team of professors, focuses on issues of ethics and governance and prepares students to read and write effectively for the fall. Currently, the only required courses are public speaking and composition. The students control the academic program and quickly replace courses—and faculty—that do not work out. The humanities, especially literature and philosophy, tend to set the academic tone.

The faculty consists of three "permanent" professors—the humanities chair, the social sciences chair, and the natural sciences chair—who sign on for two years but can stay for up to six. Other courses are taught by the dean, the president, and visiting professors who stay for a single semester or summer term. The quality of particular academic areas varies as professors come and go. With class sizes ranging from two to 14, there is ample opportunity for close student/faculty interaction—and students must be prepared to discuss their ideas. Close living arrangements have fostered a kind of kinship between faculty and students, who routinely continue class discussions over meals. "Faculty are generally accessible most hours of the day or night—as long as their porch lights are on, students can stop by to talk about papers, books they are reading outside of class, or life advice," says a student.

Deep Springs combines taxing practical work, rigorous academics, and genuine self-government—the three pillars of the school.

"Students at Deep Springs are hardworking, intellectually motivated, and eager to grow," says a sophomore. With only 26 to 30 students enrolled in a given year, demographics can fluctuate from year to year. Many Deep Springers are transplanted urbanites; the rest hail from points scattered across the nation or across the seas. Political leanings run the gamut, and there is diversity even among this small population, although that may only translate to a handful of students of color here. Since everyone's tuition, room, and board is covered by a scholarship, students pay only for indirect costs (books, travel, health insurance, and personal items); the average cost of one year at Deep Springs is about $3,500. While most students come from upper-middle-class families, an increasing number qualify for additional, need-based financial aid to help cover these indirect costs. Almost all students transfer to prestigious universities after their two-year program, and 70 percent eventually earn a Ph.D. or law degree.

"Movies, board games, dance parties, and hangouts are the regular staples of student life."

Rooms in the dorm are said to be spacious and comfortable, and a student explains, "The dorm includes a lovely common room with a library and a fireplace (the 'rumpus room'), as well as a gym, meditation room, multiple porches, and a backyard (with a treehouse!)." Room selection and dorm maintenance is entirely the responsibility of the students, who also pitch in with preparing the meals, from butchering the meat to milking the cows to washing the dishes. "The food is usually five stars," boasts a student. "Vegetarians are usually provided for, but we are a cattle ranch." A committee of trained students, faculty, and staff runs workshops to educate the student body on preventing sexual assault and creating a safe, healthy climate on campus. For those seeking mental health services, Deep Springs provides access to two off-site counselors who conduct sessions with students remotely. And what about security? "Unless a tractor runs over you, you're fine," says a freshman. But a classmate warns, "Sometimes the bulls get loose."

The Spartan community code forbids students from leaving Deep Springs Valley (50 square miles of desert) while classes are in session.

Social life can be a challenge, and loneliness can be an issue. Still, one student says, "Movies, board games, dance parties, and hangouts are the regular staples of student life and are integral in keeping the community close." Perhaps the most popular social activity on campus is conversation over a cup of coffee in the Boarding House (Deep Springs's dining hall), where the chatter is usually lively until the wee hours of the morning. Other common activities include pick-up soccer games, hikes in the nearby mountains, horseback riding, and competitive gopher-trapping in the winter months. Every Thanksgiving,

"The level of responsibility and independence that students are required to have…is mind-blowing."

students host their families and friends for an on-campus feast and football game. End-of-term dinners, summer garden parties, and Sludgefest (an annual event involving cleaning out the reservoir) are only some of the time-honored Deep Springs traditions.

Critics of Deep Springs charge that DS cultivates arrogance and social backwardness among students who were too intellectual to be in the social mainstream during high school. While that charge is debatable, even supporters of Deep Springs confess to a love-hate relationship with the college. Although the interpretations may vary, one common thread winds through the DS mission from application to graduation: training for a life of service to humanity.

Perhaps more than any other school in the nation, Deep Springs is a community where students and faculty interact day-to-day on an intensely personal level. Though the financial commitment is small, the personal commitment is serious—all must quickly learn how to get along in a community where the actions of each person affect everyone. "The level of responsibility and independence that students are required to have, and the ownership that they have over this educational project, is mind-blowing," remarks a sophomore. Time will tell what kind of influence coeducation will have on the atmosphere of the place, but one thing is certain: urban cowboys and cowgirls who dream of riding into the sunset are in for a rude awakening. For a select few, however, the camaraderie and soul-searching fostered in this tight-knit community can be mighty tempting.

Overlaps

Columbia, Yale, St. John's College, Cornell University, Harvard, UC Berkeley, Reed, Bard

If You Apply To ›

Deep Springs: Regular decision. SATs or ACTs: optional. Does not accept the Common Application. Accepts applications from students of all genders and gender identities.

University of Delaware

116 Hullihen Hall, Newark, DE 19716

Plenty of students dream of someday becoming Nittany Lions or Cavaliers—even Terrapins—but fewer aspire to be Blue Hens. The challenge for UD is how to win its share of students without the name recognition that comes from big-time sports. The state of Delaware is tiny, and only about a third of the students are in-staters. Check out the variety of residential learning options.

Website: www.udel.edu
Location: Small City
Public
Total Enrollment: 20,786
Undergraduates: 17,288
Male/Female: 41/59
Financial Aid: 49%
Pell Grant: 17%
Expense: Pub $ $ $ $
Student Loans: 61%
Average Debt: $ $ $ $
Applicants: 33,965

The University of Delaware is a public gem that boasts solid academic programs, from engineering to nursing. Though lacking the national reputation of a big-time sports program, UD has been gradually attracting more and more out-of-state students who are looking for strong academics and hands-on experiences. "UD is a big school with a small-school feel," explains a freshman. "There are limitless opportunities here, but it does not feel overwhelming. You see familiar faces everywhere, and the experience is very personalized."

Founded in 1743 as a private college that turned out three signers of the Declaration of Independence, Delaware became a public land grant university in 1869. Its 970-acre Newark campus has an attractive mix of colonial and modern geometric buildings, set among flowering and native plantings. The hub of the campus is a grassy green mall, flanked by classic Georgian buildings. The Mechanical Hall art gallery is home to the Paul R. Jones collection of African American Art. Hotel and restaurant management students benefit from classes in a fine dining restaurant and a Courtyard by Marriott right on campus, which doubles as a learning and research facility. The Wellbeing Center at Warner Hall, opened in 2021 after an $18.7 million renovation, consolidates UD's counseling, health, and wellness services.

As UD has grown in popularity, academic standards have become more rigorous. To graduate, students must pass freshman English (critical reading and writing) and earn at least three credits of discovery-based or experiential learning, such as an internship, research, or study abroad. All incoming freshmen begin with a First-Year Seminar course, usually limited to 30 students, that emphasizes class discussion, and a capstone experience is required during the senior year; other requirements vary by college.

Delaware's academic menu includes more than 150 undergraduate majors, ranging from the liberal arts and sciences to more professional programs like fashion merchandising and human relations administration. Finance, marketing, psychology, nursing, and biological sciences are the most popular majors. Engineering, especially chemical engineering, is one of UD's specialties, and the school benefits from the close proximity

"You see familiar faces everywhere, and the experience is very personalized."

of DuPont, the chemical giant that has been a major benefactor of the university. The music department is another attraction, with a 300-member marching band and several faculty members holding impressive professional performance credits. New offerings include majors in game studies and eSports, human physiology, and business analytics.

Classes tend to be on the large side, but 35 percent enroll fewer than 20 students. A senior calls the academic atmosphere "low pressure" and collaborative. The quality of teaching varies, but, for the most part, "Professors take time out of their busy schedules to make sure that the needs of students are met," says a biological sciences major. Students describe career preparation here as hands-on and useful. "I love how Career Services really wants us as students to experience everything that we might encounter in the real world before we get there," opines a biochemistry major.

UD created the nation's first study abroad program in 1923, and today 25 percent of students take part in programs offered in more than 40 countries, mostly for short-term, faculty-led courses during the monthlong winter session or summer break. Each year, more than 500 UD undergrads receive stipends to do summer research with faculty members. Those wishing to spend their summers serving the local community may apply for the Service Learning Scholars Program, a 10-week immersion program. Overall, 65 percent of students get involved in some form of community service during their time at UD. About 500 new students enter the Honors College each year, which offers interdisciplinary colloquia, priority seating in honors sections of regular courses, personal attention, and extracurricular and residence hall programming.

UD created the nation's first study abroad program in 1923, and today 25 percent of students take part.

"Students here are positive, friendly, and have a strong social life but also strong career goals," says a senior. Only 36 percent of undergraduates at Delaware hail from the First State; many of the rest are from the Northeast, and 5 percent come from abroad. Racial diversity continues to increase; 6 percent of students are Black, 9 percent are Hispanic/Latino, 5 percent are Asian American, and 4 percent are multiracial. "UD is a

"[Students] have a strong social life but also strong career goals."

politically apathetic campus that leans liberal," states a political science major. Merit and athletic scholarships are offered, with merit awards averaging $9,400. The Commitment to Delawareans initiative is designed to meet the full demonstrated need of state residents.

Thirty-eight percent of students live on campus, including all freshmen not commuting from home. After that, dorm housing is guaranteed and awarded by

(continued)

Accepted: 70%
Enrolled: 18%
Grad in 6 Years: 84%
Returning Freshmen: 92%
Academics: ✐ ✐ ✐
Social: ☎ ☎ ☎ ☎ ☎
Q of L: ★ ★ ★
Admissions: (302) 831-8123
Email Address: admissions@udel.edu

Strong Programs:
Engineering
Chemical Engineering
Music
Finance
Marketing
Psychology
Nursing
Biological Sciences

lottery, though many juniors and seniors move into off-campus apartments. Honors students live together in designated residence halls, and certain academic departments require first-year students to reside in living/learning communities. Students in traditional residence halls must buy the meal plan; the food receives average reviews. "Caesar Rodney has 13 different dining stations and serves food all day," reports a student. Campus safety is said to be good, and a senior says, "Our kNOw MORE campaign reaches out to all students on a group and individual level about sexual assault awareness."

"Social life happens equally on and off campus," says a junior. Fraternities attract 15 percent of the men and sororities 22 percent of the women; while the party scene is lively, there is no Greek row and most parties occur off campus. As an international business studies major puts it, "Greek organizations do not drive all social life on campus and are an available choice, rather than a social necessity." More than 400 student organizations coordinate regular on-campus events, and UD's two student centers, Perkins and Trabant, sponsor plenty of alternative pro-

> **"[Main Street] practically runs right through campus. It's easy walking distance from anywhere."**

gramming, such as live entertainment, weekly trivia, and late-night events on Friday and Saturday nights. A favorite tradition is the candlelight ceremony that welcomes freshmen to campus each fall, and popular annual events include homecoming celebrations on the central campus green, the Senior Fling concert in the spring, and Ag Day, when the agriculture college hosts a large festival with vendors, music, animals, and hayride farm tours.

Main Street, the heart of downtown Newark (pronounced "New-ark"), "practically runs right through campus," one student says. "It's easy walking distance from anywhere, and there are tons of coffee shops, pizza places, restaurants, a movie theater, bookstores, and shops—anything you could possibly want." For those seeking further excitement, New York, the Washington/Baltimore area, and Philadelphia are all within a two-hour drive. When the weather is warm, the beaches of Rehoboth and Dewey beckon, and in chilly months, the Pennsylvania ski slopes aren't too far.

"We are not a very athletics-oriented school, but we have a lot of school spirit," says a senior. Delaware's Division I Blue Hens are becoming more competitive. The men's lacrosse, women's field hockey, and men's and women's basketball teams have brought home recent Colonial Athletic Association conference titles, and the basketball teams enjoy a lively rivalry with Drexel. UD's varsity eSports team competes in the Perkins Student Center's sleek new Esports Arena, which can also be enjoyed by casual gamers. Recreational sports are popular; students have their pick of more than 35 club sports and 30 intramural programs.

UD is a public flagship university that is large enough to offer something for everyone, yet at a more manageable size than many of its closest competitors. With UD's traditional emphasis on out-of-classroom experiences, stimulating academic environment, and up-and-coming athletic teams, Blue Hens need never put all their eggs in one basket.

Overlaps

Penn State, Rutgers, SUNY–Binghamton, University of Maryland, University of Pittsburgh, UConn, Temple, Villanova

If You Apply To ›

Delaware: Regular decision. Accepts the Common Application with supplement. Please consult Delaware's website for the most up-to-date information regarding standardized test requirements.

Denison University

Granville, OH 43023

Denison draws more Easterners than Wooster and Ohio Wesleyan, and it fashions itself as a sort of Midwestern Haverford. Denison has a middle-of-the-road to liberal student body, fewer preppies than in years past, and one of the most beautiful campuses anywhere. Increasing popularity fueled by some distinctive majors and an innovative summer program have helped create a more academically serious student body.

Denison University, tucked into the "quaint, small, and beautiful" village of Granville, draws "curious, down-to-earth" students from diverse backgrounds, according to one matriculant. Thanks to Denison's small size, there's ample opportunity to interact (and do research) with professors and to form close relationships with peers, as everyone focuses on the liberal arts. "Denison is a special place because it helps students figure out how their diverse interests intersect," says a politics and public affairs major. "This campus is a place where you are encouraged to keep doing everything you love."

> **"[Denison] helps students figure out how their diverse interests intersect."**

Founded in 1831 to bring higher education to what was then the Northwest Territory, Denison was named after an early benefactor. The campus is set atop rolling hills in central Ohio. Huge maples shade the sloping walkways, which offer a panoramic view of the surrounding valley. Denison retained park architect Frederick Law Olmsted (designer of New York City's Central Park) for its first master plan back in the early 1900s. The Georgian style of many buildings—redbrick with white columns—also evokes shades of New England and its private liberal arts colleges. Recent campus additions include the 108,000-square-foot Michael Eisner Center for Performing Arts (named for the former Disney CEO and Denison alum) and the Hoaglin Wellness Center, which opened in 2022.

Denison's general education requirements are comprehensive. In addition to a spate of coursework spanning the liberal arts and sciences, students take two first-year seminars and complete an "interdivisional requirement" by selecting a course from one of seven interdisciplinary programs, such as international studies or queer studies. The Power and Justice requirement seeks to give students the ability to question their own place in the structures of power and privilege that constitute human societies. For help navigating the transition to college, most freshmen sign up for optional Advising Circles, meeting weekly with a faculty advisor in groups of around 10 students.

> **"Professors excel at facilitating rich discussions."**

Although biology, psychology, economics, and communication have the highest enrollment, students say some of the best majors are distinctive to Denison. The PPE major is effectively a triple major in philosophy, politics, and economics. The music department features a concentration in bluegrass designed by a faculty member who is an accomplished fiddler, while Denison's 350-acre biological reserve is a boon for biology and environmental studies majors. The global commerce; financial economics; computer science; data analytics; health, exercise, and sport studies; and theater programs are strong as well. Courses are rigorous, but an English major says, "Classes are organized to be very hands-on, and professors excel at facilitating rich discussions." Classes are small—74 percent have fewer than 20 students—and individual attention is the norm. Students rave about the school's Denison Seminars, small, interdisciplinary classes that are team-taught by two professors and involve a travel

Website: www.denison.edu
Location: Small Town
Private
Total Enrollment: 2,258
Undergraduates: 2,258
Male/Female: 48/52
Financial Aid: 95%
Pell Grant: 11%
Expense: Pr $ $ $
Student Loans: 51%
Average Debt: $ $ $
Applicants: 9,513
Accepted: 28%
Enrolled: 24%
Grad in 6 Years: 82%
Returning Freshmen: 87%
Academics: ✍ ✍ ✍ ½
Social: ☎ ☎ ☎ ☎ ☎
Q of L: ★ ★ ★
Admissions: (740) 587-6276
Email Address: admission@denison.edu

Strong Programs:
Philosophy, Politics, and Economics
Music
Global Commerce
Financial Economics
Computer Science
Data Analytics
Health, Exercise, and Sport Studies
Theater

component. "I've taken two Denison Seminars," says a history major, "and they were defining classes of my time at Denison."

Denison's award-winning undergraduate research program includes the signature Summer Scholar Program, which provides scholarships for about 120 students to stay on campus during the summer to complete 10 weeks of full-time research in collaboration with faculty members. Typically, more than half of the summer scholars are science students. Those with wanderlust can choose from more than 180 programs in 70 countries; overall, 60 percent of the students go abroad, about a third of them in short-term, faculty-led programs. The school has invested $50 million in the Knowlton Center for Career Exploration, which one senior says "has become an incredible asset for students, helping them easily adapt to the ever-changing career landscape." Those considering a run for office may be interested in the Richard Lugar Program in Politics and Public Service, which includes courses on campus and culminates in a House or Senate internship in Washington. (The late former senator happened to be a Denison grad.)

Denison Seminars are small, interdisciplinary classes that are team-taught by two professors and involve a travel component.

Twenty percent of Denison's population is homegrown, and 15 percent come from abroad. Black students constitute 6 percent of the student body, Hispanics/Latinos 8 percent, Asian Americans 3 percent, and multiracial students 4 percent. Denison is left-leaning, but a communication major explains, "The political climate is not prominent unless you're actively involved in it." Denison now commits to meeting the full demonstrated need of all incoming freshmen. The average merit-based financial aid award is $17,600, and there are no athletic scholarships.

Virtually all Denison students live on campus; the only ones allowed to live elsewhere are those commuting from home. (Another exception is the dozen Homesteaders, who live in three student-built, solar-paneled cabins on a sustainable farm less than a mile away and grow much of their own food.) Students generally live in dorms for the first three years and campus apartments their senior year, and they report that recent renovations have vastly improved the accommodations. Dining hall meals are "generally good," and a freshman notes, "The provisions for special needs are excellent." A psychology major says the university has been "extremely diligent in confronting the issue of sexual assault on campus" by increasing educational programming and holding campuswide dialogues on sexual respect.

"I wish I could experience it all over again!"

Given the residential nature of the campus, social life at Denison tends to revolve around student housing and clubs more than anything else. Twenty-five percent of the men and 44 percent of the women join the Greek system. Greek organizations and other student groups host open parties in the senior apartments (a.k.a. the Sunnies) and in Moon Hall's social spaces (a.k.a. the Moonies) every weekend. Students report that regulations aimed at curtailing excessive drinking have improved the party scene: parties must be registered, have a sober host trained in safety, and offer food. School-sponsored events like guest speakers, plays, and concerts offer an alternative, and everyone looks forward to three all-campus festivals each year: D-Day, Gala, and Aestavalia. Naked Week, held during National Eating Disorders Awareness Week in February, is another notable event. "Each night of the week, students streak at different areas of campus to promote self-acceptance and body positivity," explains a sophomore. "This is a favorite Denison tradition, and some nights over 70 students will run!"

Greek groups host open parties in the senior apartments (a.k.a. the Sunnies) and in Moon Hall's social spaces (a.k.a. the Moonies) every weekend.

Granville is a small, quiet town with four churches on the corners of the town's main intersection, and town-gown relations are said to be good. "Granville has great places to eat and hosts things for students, such as a farmers market and a holiday celebration," says a psychology major. The Denison Community Association frequently sends students into Granville and nearby Newark to provide tutoring, mentoring, and other volunteer services. Columbus, the state capital, is only 30 miles away, and the school runs trips to the city's Easton Town Center, an outdoor shopping and dining mecca. Pittsburgh, Cleveland, Cincinnati, and Dayton are also close by.

Denison students are enthusiastic supporters of the Big Red, especially when rival Kenyon is in town, and Division III lacrosse games against Ohio Wesleyan always draw large crowds. The men's swimming team is a powerhouse, claiming five national championships in the last 12 years, and the women's team is a top performer too. Men's and women's lacrosse, golf, and tennis are recent North Coast Athletic Conference champions, along with baseball and women's soccer. Intramurals and club sports remain hugely popular, with basketball, soccer, flag football, rugby, and ice hockey drawing the most interest.

Denison University aims to graduate independent thinkers who become active citizens of a democratic society. The school continues to value tradition—woe to the students who step on the school seal in front of the chapel, for doing so will definitely cause them to fail all their finals—while growing and evolving to emphasize academics and the life of the mind. "Denison has grown more diverse, new programs have been introduced, and much of campus has been renovated," says a graduating senior. "I wish I could experience it all over again!"

> **Overlaps**
>
> **Miami (OH), Wake Forest, Colgate, Bucknell, Colby, Haverford, Elon, Ohio Wesleyan**

If You Apply To ›

Denison: Early decision I and II, regular decision. SATs or ACTs: optional. Accepts the Common Application.

University of Denver

2199 South University Boulevard, Denver, CO 80208

The only major midsized private university between Tulsa and the West Coast. DU's campus in residential Denver is pleasant, and admissions brochures shamelessly tout Rocky Mountain landscapes and healthy lifestyles. Senior faculty teach all core courses. A haven for skiing enthusiasts, business majors, and future diplomats, DU has become much more selective in recent years.

The oldest private university in the Rocky Mountain region, dating to 1864, the University of Denver is where former secretary of state Condoleezza Rice earned her B.A. in political science at age 19 and later returned for a Ph.D. in international studies. Her mentor was Soviet specialist Josef Korbel, father of the late secretary of state Madeleine Albright. Thus, it's not surprising that DU boasts strong programs in political science, international studies, and public affairs. Many students, however, opt for DU's business program, and the campus location offers ample opportunities for networking, skiing, and taking in the beautiful Colorado landscape. A freshman says, "DU students share a sense of adventure, risk-taking, and spending time doing what one values."

DU's 125-acre main campus is located in a comfortable residential neighborhood only eight miles from downtown Denver and an hour east of major ski areas. Architectural styles vary and materials include brick, limestone, Colorado sandstone, and copper. Nearby Mount Evans (14,265 feet) is home to the world's loftiest observatory, a DU facility available to both professors and students. Recent campus projects include the 500-bed, LEED Gold–certified Dimond Family Residential

Website: www.du.edu
Location: City Center
Private
Total Enrollment: 8,871
Undergraduates: 5,431
Male/Female: 45/55
Financial Aid: 92%
Pell Grant: 15%
Expense: Pr $ $ $
Student Loans: 45%
Average Debt: $ $ $
Applicants: 22,694
Accepted: 64%
Enrolled: 11%
Grad in 6 Years: 75%

(continued)

Returning Freshmen: 84%

Academics: ✍ ✍ ✍

Social: ☎ ☎ ☎ ☎

Q of L: ★ ★ ★ ★

Admissions: (303) 871-2036

Email Address: admission@
du.edu

Strong Programs:
Political Science
International Studies
Business
Hospitality Management
Music
Biology
Engineering
Computer Science

Village for first-year students. The $64 million, 132,000-square-foot Community Commons, housing the campus's main dining hub, spaces for student organizations and special events, indoor and rooftop lounges, and academic advising services, opened in 2021.

Under the general education requirements, undergraduate students choose from a series of courses from the Common Curriculum that emphasize writing, quantitative reasoning, experiential learning, and cross-disciplinary inquiry. University rules stipulate that all core courses must be taught by senior faculty. Core courses are supplemented by a First-Year Seminar (limited to 15 students) that introduces students to college-level work and an advanced seminar that serves as a capstone to the curriculum model.

DU is known for business; the Daniels College of Business is home to the Knoebel School of Hospitality Management, one of the top hospitality programs in the country. Music, biology, engineering, and computer science have solid reputations. Finance, psychology, marketing, and international studies are among the most popular majors. The university has added a new major in physiology and two new minors in critical race and ethnic studies and kinesiology and sport studies. Several dual-degree programs allow undergraduates to earn a bachelor's degree and an advanced degree from Denver's graduate schools in business, education, the arts, international studies, social work, and law.

Since DU operates on a quarter system, classes move quickly and the workload can get intense. "I personally enjoy how rigorous the quarter system can be, because you are constantly learning something new," says an art history major. Students say small class sizes—57 percent have fewer than 20 students—make for a collaborative environment with plenty of support from faculty. "Even over Zoom or in-person masked classes, professors are still engaging teachers," comments an environmental science major. DU is also recognized for its strong academic support services. A psychology major says, "The Learning Effectiveness Program has been amazing and given me the accommodations and resources I need to succeed."

> **"Even over Zoom or in-person masked classes, professors are still engaging teachers."**

DU's selective Honors Program accepts about 100 students each year who take a sequence of honors courses and complete a thesis or final project. Funded undergraduate research opportunities are widely available. Juniors and seniors have the chance to study abroad at no additional cost through the Cherrington Global Scholars program; 73 percent of Pioneers go abroad, and they say the 150 available programs are an integral part of the DU experience. "DU fosters a global perspective in which students understand their role in and responsibility to the global community," says a psychology major.

"We have a funky mix of really preppy East Coasters and Midwesterners mixed in with all the laid-back outdoorsy people," says one student. Twenty-seven percent of undergraduates come from Colorado, and 4 percent arrive from other countries. Black students account for 2 percent of the student body, Asian Americans 4 percent, Hispanics/Latinos 13 percent, and multiracial students 6 percent. The campus leans liberal, and students cite the environment and social justice as issues of particular concern. As one of the few private colleges in the West, DU is also among the most expensive in the region. But more than half of undergrads receive merit scholarships, which average $20,500, and more than 200 athletic scholarships are also available. "Students have relatively expensive hobbies like skiing, backpacking, and traveling," observes a senior. "I think individuals from low-income backgrounds have a hard time fitting in."

About half of all undergrads reside on campus; students are required to spend their first two years in the residence halls. Students praise the five living/learning

The $64 million Community Commons, housing the main dining hub, spaces for student organizations, and rooftop lounges, opened in 2021.

communities open to first-years: "Being able to come onto campus and already have a structured and supportive group of people who shared a similar interest was incredibly helpful," a senior recalls. Most juniors and seniors opt for the decent off-campus quarters found within walking distance. Dining options in the new Community Commons get rave reviews, and students report that dietary restrictions are easily accommodated. The university has increased staffing of its mental health counseling services, and a junior comments, "All leaders of student organizations receive training to reduce instances of sexual assault on campus and become better supporters of survivors."

Seventy-three percent of Pioneers go abroad, and they say the 150 available programs are an integral part of the DU experience.

More than 100 student organizations offer on-campus activities for every interest. Fraternities and sororities draw 20 percent of the men and 24 percent of the women, but students agree that Greek groups don't set the tone for social life. "The campus is pretty quiet on the weekends because everyone is either in the mountains, downtown, or enjoying the sun at a neighboring park," explains a media studies major. "There is a lot to do aside from parties." Indeed, free access to the nearby light rail makes it easy to get downtown, where students enjoy "great shopping, festivals,

"The campus is pretty quiet on the weekends because everyone is either in the mountains [or] downtown."

events, concerts, phenomenal restaurants, and, for students over 21, one of the best microbrewery scenes," cheers a student. With consistently beautiful, sunny weather and great skiing, hiking, and camping less than an hour away in the Rockies, many DU students head for the hills on weekends, often on low-cost trips organized by the Alpine Club. Students also explore Estes Park, Mount Evans, and Echo Lake.

Students unite when the powerhouse DU hockey team—national champions in 2022—skates out onto the ice, especially against archrival Colorado College. Other competitive Division I Pioneers programs include co-ed skiing, men's lacrosse, men's golf, and men's and women's soccer. Intramural and club sports are varied and popular; more than a quarter of students take part. Each February, academics are put aside for the three-day Winter Carnival. Top administrators, professors, and students all pack off to Keystone, Winter Park, or another ski area to catch some fresh powder and see who can ski the fastest, skate the best, or build the most artistic ice sculptures.

Students like the University of Denver for its modest size, its friendly atmosphere, and the flexibility afforded by the albeit sometimes stressful quarter system. As the school pushes for a more ethnically diverse student body and improves its curriculum and facilities, the University of Denver is striving to become better known for its intellectual rigor than for its gorgeous setting in the Rocky Mountains.

Overlaps

American University, Syracuse, Southern Methodist, University of San Diego, Santa Clara, Tulane, Northeastern, CU Boulder

If You Apply To ›

DU: Early decision I and II, early action, regular decision. SATs or ACTs: optional. Accepts the Common Application.

DePaul University

Chicago, IL 60604

Few universities have come so far, so fast. DePaul gets the nod over Loyola as the top Roman Catholic university in Chicago. Its Lincoln Park setting is like a Midwestern version of New York's Greenwich Village or Upper West Side. One in five undergraduates who report a religion are Catholic. Especially strong in business, public relations, film, and the arts.

*The Pathways
Honors Program
provides top students
with specialized
prehealth advising
and summer research
opportunities.*

The largest Roman Catholic university in the nation, DePaul University pursues the Vincentian mission of service and contributing to the "common good." Students claim the university's diversity and politically liberal leanings set it apart from rival institutions. Based in the heart of the city, DePaul is a feeder to Chicago's business community. A spate of campus construction has transformed it from the "little school under the El" to Chicago's version of NYU.

DePaul, which was founded by Vincentian fathers in 1898 and is named after the 17th-century French priest Vincent de Paul, has two residential campuses. The Lincoln Park campus, with its state-of-the-art library and student center, is home to the colleges of liberal arts and social sciences, education, and science and health; the theatre and music schools; and residence halls and recreational facilities. Lincoln Park itself is a fashionable Chicago neighborhood with century-old brownstone homes, theaters, cafés, parks, and shops. The Loop (or "vertical") campus is 20 minutes away by elevated train (a.k.a. the El or "L," depending on whom you ask) in downtown Chicago and houses the colleges of business, communication, computing and digital media, and law, as well as the School of Continuing and Professional Studies. The DePaul Center, a $70 million teaching, learning, and research complex, is the cornerstone of this campus.

> **"[The Discover Chicago] class is one of the best things about DePaul."**

All freshmen take a course called Discover Chicago or its alternative, Explore Chicago, which introduces them to the city. "This class is one of the best things about DePaul. It's really fun and valuable," says a senior. Other common core courses include composition and quantitative reasoning for freshmen, a sophomore seminar on multiculturalism in the United States, and an experiential learning program that requires an internship, research, study abroad, or service-learning experience. In their senior year, students create a final project.

DePaul's name is closely associated with Midwestern business and law, and undergraduates can find internships year-round with local legal and commercial institutions. The School of Accountancy and MIS is reported to be the most challenging department in the Driehaus College of Business. The College of Science and Health offers a health sciences program that prepares students for a variety of health care professions, and the Pathways Honors Program provides top students with specialized prehealth advising and summer research opportunities. The School of Cinematic Arts has teamed up with Cinespace Chicago, the city's premier movie studio, to create a learning environment that provides students with film and television production experience in the midst of a working studio. Other notable programs include theatre, game design, and animation. Combined, six-year bachelor's/law degree options are available in several fields, ranging from economics to Islamic world studies, and a number of five-year bachelor's/master's degree programs are also offered. The most popular majors include finance, accounting, psychology, and film and television.

Classes are often small, with 43 percent enrolling fewer than 20 students, and professors teach at all levels. The administration appoints student representatives from each school and college to faculty promotion and tenure committees. "DePaul professors are respectful, intelligent, and don't put up with nonsense," says one senior. Clerics teach some courses and celebrate (voluntary) mass every day. In addition, the University Ministry hosts other religious services and leads programs to teach students about other faiths. The highly selective honors program includes interdisciplinary courses and a senior thesis. Thirteen percent of students participate in study abroad programs that take them to their choice of more than 40 countries around the world, including India, Ireland, Peru, and Switzerland.

"DePaul is both a city school and a commuter school," observes a psychology major, and as such, its student body is more self-sufficient and independent than most. Seventy-four percent of undergraduates hail from Illinois, while 3 percent come from foreign countries. Hispanics/Latinos represent 22 percent of the student body, Black students 8 percent, Asian Americans 12 percent, and multiracial students 5 percent. DePaul has a reputation for being politically liberal, and according to a senior, "Students are actively working to improve both DePaul and Chicago." In addition to academic merit scholarships, DePaul also awards scholarships to students who have artistic talent or strong leadership skills or those who participate in community service; such awards average $17,200 per year. Scholarships for athletes are available too.

With such a large commuter population, just 17 percent of undergraduates live in university housing. One student complains, "Weekends can be boring because many students go home." Those who stay find the dorms comfortable and well maintained, but they recommend applying early to secure a bed, especially after freshman year. "Housing is in high demand around here," says a junior. The Lincoln Park campus includes six modern co-ed dorms and six townhouse and apartment buildings. At the Loop campus, a 1,700-bed residence hall includes a rooftop garden, fitness center, and music, art, and study rooms. Campus dining receives lackluster reviews; many find the food overpriced and the options limited. Students say they feel reasonably safe

"DePaul professors are respectful, intelligent, and don't put up with nonsense."

on campus but report that the Loop campus has experienced issues with crime in recent years. Campus safety officers regularly patrol the area and provide late-night rides home, and dorms require students to swipe ID cards at multiple points before allowing entrance. Nevertheless, "It's good to be wary near either campus at nighttime," advises a senior.

Fraternities and sororities draw just 4 percent of DePaul men and 6 percent of the women, respectively, and parties aren't a big part of campus life. Not surprisingly, with the school's proximity to Chicago's concert and comedy venues, restaurants, bars, clubs (especially on Rush Street), and sporting events, most social life occurs off campus. A music major says of the city, "There is everything to do here." In the warmer months, the beaches of Lake Michigan beckon students, while the university's huge annual outdoor Fest concert attracts large crowds from both campuses. On Vincentian Service Day in May, a tradition for more than 20 years, about 1,000 students, staff, faculty, and alumni participate in community service.

DePaul competes in the Division I Big East Conference in 15 sports. Men's basketball is the headline story, beginning with the Blue Madness of each fall's first practice in October. The game against Notre Dame always draws a capacity crowd, though Loyola is DePaul's oldest rival. The men's tennis team recently won a Big East championship, and women's basketball and softball are also competitive. Intramurals and club sports are big draws, as is the 123,000-square-foot Meyer Fitness and Recreation Center.

Expanding academic programs, a diverse student body, and all the opportunity of the city of Chicago make DePaul a dynamic university, but students say its popularity is due as much to the special bonds they feel with fellow Blue Demons. "DePaul University provides students a unique atmosphere in which to learn and grow," says a sophomore. "The campus and its students are friendly, open, and always inviting."

Overlaps

Loyola University Chicago, Marquette, Saint Louis University, Seattle University, U of I at Chicago, U of I at Urbana–Champaign, Columbia College Chicago, Northwestern

If You Apply To ›

DePaul: Early action, regular decision. SATs or ACTs: optional (test-optional applicants are encouraged to submit optional personal essay). Accepts the Common Application.

DePauw University

204 East Seminary Street, Greencastle, IN 46135

DePauw is a small Midwestern liberal arts institution in the mold of Denison, Dickinson, Knox, and Ohio Wesleyan. Its Greek system is among the strongest in the nation. DePauw's Fellows and Honors Scholar programs are a major draw for career-oriented students looking to take their liberal arts experience to the next level. Almost all students study abroad.

Website: www.depauw.edu
Location: Small Town
Private
Total Enrollment: 1,700
Undergraduates: 1,700
Male/Female: 50/50
Financial Aid: 99%
Pell Grant: 14%
Expense: Pr $ $
Student Loans: 77%
Average Debt: $ $
Applicants: 5,695
Accepted: 65%
Enrolled: 14%
Grad in 6 Years: 82%
Returning Freshmen: 88%
Academics: ✍ ✍ ✍ ½
Social: ☎ ☎ ☎
Q of L: ★ ★
Admissions: (765) 658-4006
Email Address: admission@depauw.edu

Strong Programs:
Economics and Management
Communication
Natural Sciences
Music
Computer Science
Psychology
English

DePauw University offers a liberal arts education with an orientation toward experiential learning. The economics and management, communication, and natural sciences programs are strong, and the university produces a high number of Fulbright Scholars. Students here are career-oriented and eager to take advantage of the rigorous classwork and ample real-world experiences. With an undergraduate population of 1,700 students, close ties to classmates and faculty are a given.

Founded in 1837 by the Methodist Church to bring New England–style liberal education to what was then the frontier, DePauw is set amid the gently rolling hills of west-central Indiana. The lush green campus has a mix of older buildings and more modern redbrick structures. The DePauw Nature Park, about a mile away, is a well-kept, 520-acre park featuring nature trails and the LEED Gold–certified Prindle Institute for Ethics. DePauw has significantly upgraded its main campus in recent years, completing a major renovation of its main library, opening a new first-year residence hall and a state-of-the-art dining hall, and improving its energy efficiency.

DePauw's first-year program helps students transition into college by combining academically challenging coursework with cocurricular activities and programs. Before arriving on campus, each student is assigned to a mentor group with 10 to 12 peers, an upperclassman advisor, and a faculty member who will teach their first-year seminar and serve as their academic advisor until they declare a major. By graduation, students must demonstrate competence in writing, quantitative reasoning, and oral communication and pass a course on power, privilege, and diversity. They must also complete at least two extended study experiences, which may include courses taken during the monthlong Winter or May terms, off-campus study (a very popular choice), independent study or research, service-learning projects, or internships.

> **"Students here constantly push themselves to do their best possible work."**

Academically, the DePauw student body is as career-oriented as they come in a liberal arts college. The most popular majors include economics and management, communication, computer science, psychology, and English, and students may also design their own majors. Launching in fall 2023, DePauw's new School of Business and Leadership is a rarity among liberal arts colleges. A new school focusing on creative and performing arts is expected to open in 2024. The School of Music, one of the oldest in the country, offers a five-year dual-degree program in music performance/liberal arts. Students may supplement their coursework through eight academic centers offering cocurricular learning and professional development opportunities. Future reporters, editors, anchors, and producers will find a home in the Pulliam Center for Contemporary Media, which supplements DePauw's strong student-run newspaper, TV station, and radio stations. Seven other centers focus on management and entrepreneurship, ethics, technology, diversity and inclusion, civic engagement, student engagement, and 21st-century musicianship.

Students say classes are challenging but well supported, with high-quality instruction from professors. "Students here constantly push themselves to do their best possible work, but we all work together to achieve our goals," says a global French studies and political science double major. For exceptionally motivated students, Fellows programs in media, management, the environment, and science research offer a semester-long internship or research experience and opportunities to interact with top scholars and industry leaders on and off campus. Additionally, the Honor Scholars Program allows high-achieving students to embark on interdisciplinary study and complete a capstone thesis. About 97 percent of DePauw students study off campus, mostly through short, faculty-led programs during the Winter and May terms; semester and yearlong options are also available.

One student describes her peers at DePauw as "intellectually curious, philanthropically minded, and socially active." Thirty-seven percent of students are from Indiana, and 17 percent are international. Campus diversity has grown, thanks in part to recruitment of Posse Foundation students from New York and Chicago. Black students now account for 6 percent of the student body, Hispanics/Latinos 9 percent, Asian Americans 3 percent, and multiracial students 3 percent. During the annual DePauw Dialogue event, classes are canceled so students, faculty, and staff can gather to explore issues like bias, privilege, and identity. Merit scholarships averaging $31,400 are available, although there are no athletic scholarships.

DePauw is a totally residential college, meaning all students live on campus for all four years, with few exceptions. Options include homey residence halls, suites, apartments, and college-owned houses, as well as Greek chapter houses. Meals are served in Hoover Dining Hall and a few small cafés and grab-and-go options around campus. A whopping 66 percent of DePauw's men and 59 percent of the women go Greek. That's not surprising, given that the first modern-day sorority, Kappa Alpha Theta, began here in 1870, and the university is home to the two longest continually running fraternities anywhere: Beta Theta Pi and Phi Gamma Delta.

"Students love being at DePauw on the weekends."

"Students love being at DePauw on the weekends," says a student. Perhaps because of the prevalence of Greeks on campus, Greek groups have worked hard to change the negative stereotypes of fraternities and sororities. A community council reviews allegations of misconduct, and rush is delayed until the spring semester so freshmen can first get their feet on the ground academically. Still, students say it's relatively easy for underage drinkers to imbibe, especially at fraternity parties. More than 100 student organizations offer ample alternatives, and students are active in about 20 volunteer programs.

The town of Greencastle (population 10,000) has a movie theater, a bowling alley, and several pizza places and restaurants. "The first Friday of every month, part of the town shuts down and they have food trucks, live music, and fun games going on," explains a sophomore. In good weather, the DePauw Nature Park and several state parks offer hiking trails and lakes. Indianapolis is only a 45-minute drive, and St. Louis, Chicago, and Cincinnati make for good road trips. A cherished tradition is a takeoff on Indiana University's famed Little 500 bike race, itself a takeoff on the Indianapolis 500 auto race—teams of cyclists compete on a course that circles the heart of the DePauw campus.

Everyone gets excited about Division III varsity athletics, especially the annual football game against Wabash College, which is the oldest small-college rivalry west of the Alleghenies. The winner of each year's contest claims possession of the much-cherished, 300-pound Monon Bell, an artifact from the defunct Monon Railroad line. The Tigers football, field hockey, men's cross-country, women's basketball, and softball teams have all brought home recent North Coast Athletic Conference titles. Club sports and intramurals are growing in popularity, and students stay fit in the two-story Welch Fitness Center.

Launching in fall 2023, DePauw's new School of Business and Leadership is a rarity among liberal arts colleges.

A whopping 66 percent of DePauw's men and 59 percent of the women go Greek.

Overlaps

Denison, Ohio Wesleyan, College of Wooster, St. Olaf, Wabash, Butler, Miami (OH), Knox

For a small school, DePauw offers a multitude of opportunities, balancing strong academics with a healthy dose of school spirit and a wealth of opportunities to lead—whether in one of the abundant extracurricular activities or by blazing a trail through study abroad.

If You Apply To ›

DePauw: Early decision I and II, early action, regular decision. SATs or ACTs: optional (required for students applying to Honor Scholars and Fellows programs). Accepts the Common Application.

Dickinson College

P.O. Box 1773, Carlisle, PA 17013

With traditions dating to the 18th century, Dickinson occupies a historic setting in the foothills of central Pennsylvania. Curriculum blends traditional liberal arts values with attention to international studies, foreign languages, study abroad, and sustainable development. With students of color, international students, and free spirits now more numerous, Dickinson is shedding its image as a preppy haven. Competes head-to-head with nearby Gettysburg.

Website: www.dickinson.edu
Location: Small Town
Private
Total Enrollment: 2,127
Undergraduates: 2,124
Male/Female: 42/58
Financial Aid: 86%
Pell Grant: 14%
Expense: Pr $ $ $ $
Student Loans: 55%
Average Debt: $ $
Applicants: 6,366
Accepted: 48%
Enrolled: 22%
Grad in 6 Years: 82%
Returning Freshmen: 92%
Academics: ✎ ✎ ✎ ✎
Social: ☎ ☎ ☎
Q of L: ★ ★ ★
Admissions: (717) 245-1231
Email Address: admissions@ dickinson.edu

Strong Programs:
Workshop Physics
Foreign Languages
Environmental Science

Dickinson College won its charter just six days after the Treaty of Paris recognized the United States as a sovereign nation in 1783, and this small liberal arts school has been blazing trails ever since. The moving force behind it was Dr. Benjamin Rush, the famous physician and signer of the Declaration of Independence who convinced John Dickinson, the then governor of Pennsylvania, to lend his name to the new school. Rush's founding mission was "to provide a useful education in the liberal arts and sciences." Now, administrators are also focused on global education, civic engagement, and attracting the best and brightest academic talent.

Almost all of Dickinson's Georgian buildings are crafted from local gray limestone, which lends pleasing architectural consistency. The 144-acre campus is part of the historic district of Carlisle, an economically prosperous central Pennsylvania county seat nestled in a fertile valley. Newer additions to campus include a $19 million, LEED Platinum–certified residence hall housing 130 upperclassmen in single and double rooms. Dickinson has been a leader in sustainability education, and the college achieved carbon neutrality in 2020.

To help students understand how the liberal arts fit into the broader world, Dickinson supplements standard distribution requirements with courses in multidisciplinary and cross-cultural studies, such as sustainability and U.S. and global diversity. The required First-Year Seminar introduces new students to college-level writing and critical thinking through interdisciplinary courses such as Ideas That Have Shaped the World, Storytelling with Food in France, and Natural Disasters and You. Sophomores choose from 46 majors, and 85 percent of seniors complete a capstone program.

"Peers help each other become the best students they can be, instead of trying to compete."

Dickinson is best known for its workshop approach to science education, for its outstanding and comprehensive international education program, and for the depth of its foreign language program, with more than a dozen languages offered, including Arabic, Chinese, Japanese, Hebrew, Italian, and Portuguese. The college's environmental studies and environmental science department is well respected. International business and management, one of Dickinson's most popular majors, involves coursework in economics, history, and financial analysis, as well as internships and overseas education. Other popular majors include political science, psychology, quantitative economics, and international studies.

(continued)

International Business and
    Management
Political Science
Psychology
Quantitative Economics
International Studies

In addition, Dickinson offers certificates in food studies, social innovation and entrepreneurship, security studies, health studies, global preparedness (with the Army ROTC), and ballet (with the Central Pennsylvania Youth Ballet). Students can gain a hands-on understanding of human culture and behavior by studying archaeology in far-flung locations like Greece and Bolivia. Interdisciplinary programs such as neuroscience and workshop physics offer chances to carry out research with faculty members. Dual-degree programs in engineering and law are available with partner institutions, and students interested in pursuing graduate studies in areas like business management and public health may partake in special advising programs.

Academics are demanding, but the environment is supportive. "Peers help each other become the best students they can be, instead of trying to compete for the best grades," explains a sophomore. Seventy-seven percent of classes have fewer than 20 students, allowing freshmen easy access to their professors, who are highly rated by students. "I have had some of the most caring and intelligent professors," says a junior. The Advising, Internships, & Career Center receives positive reviews as well: "After each appointment, I feel enthusiastic and hopeful about my professional interests," cheers a neuroscience major.

The foreign language program offers more than a dozen languages, including Arabic, Chinese, Japanese, Hebrew, Italian, and Portuguese.

Dickinson sponsors faculty-directed study abroad programs in 15 countries around the world and offers more than 30 partner programs on six continents; 60 percent of students participate. Options include academic year, semester, and summer programs; globally integrated courses that include a short-term international field experience; and specialized programs such as Mosaics, which combine domestic study with international study. Most students complete internships, and the college guarantees one for every student. Undergraduate research in the sciences and humanities involves 16 percent of students.

At Dickinson, says a sociology major, "There are a lot of determined, passionate students who are committed to the concept of making these four years mean something." Twenty-eight percent of the student body hails from the Keystone State. Black students account for 5 percent of the student population, Asian Americans 4 percent, Hispanics/ Latinos 9 percent, and multiracial students 4 percent; international students represent 11 percent. Dickinson

"I have had some of the most caring and intelligent professors."

has been enrolling a growing number of students of color and international students, especially through partnerships with the Posse Foundation, the Philadelphia Futures Foundation, and schools and foundations abroad, but some students note that the atmosphere on campus does not feel as much like an integrated, inclusive community as they would like. Dickinson awards five levels of merit scholarships but no athletic scholarships.

Dickinson students live in college housing throughout their four years. A senior reports that "freshman and sophomore housing is not typically as nice" as the accommodations for upperclassmen, which include small houses and apartments. Twenty-three percent of freshmen choose to participate in living/learning communities, as extensions of the First-Year Seminar program. The college farm manages 80 acres and supplies produce to the dining hall and a local food bank. It also serves as a living laboratory and work-study opportunity for students interested in sustainable development. Aside from the main cafeteria, there are café and snack-bar options, and "several provisions are met (e.g., kosher, vegan, nut-free, organic, gluten-free)," says a senior. In response to student protests in

Most students complete internships, and the college guarantees one for every student.

2020 over inadequate handling of sexual assault cases, Dickinson's administration has made several amendments to its sexual misconduct policies, procedures, and reporting process.

"Whether it is a club, a sport, or a floor in your dorm, you must get involved in something to have a good social life," advises a political science major. Fraternities and sororities attract 4 percent of the men and 25 percent of the women, and they throw parties in houses that are owned and maintained by the college. Kegs aren't permitted in any college housing, and four underage drinking incidents will get you suspended. "Drinking and parties are a large part of the social culture on campus, especially on the weekends," says a student. At the Quarry, a former frat house turned social space, you can gather with friends, play some video games, or show your moves on the dance floor. Each fall brings an arts festival and a well-attended drag show, and Springfest gives students one last blast before finals with a carnival and concert.

Carlisle is 20 miles from the Pennsylvania state capital of Harrisburg and has plenty of eclectic cafés, restaurants, shops, and festivals. "The town is very cute and fun to eat out and walk around in," says an English major. Big Brothers Big Sisters, the Alpha Phi Omega community service fraternity, and other programs help bring the school and community together. In the

"The town is very cute and fun to eat out and walk around in."

spring and early fall, beaches in Maryland, Delaware, and New Jersey beckon; they're just a two- to three-hour drive. Come winter, good skiing is half an hour away. Nature lovers will enjoy hiking the nearby Appalachian Trail. For those craving urban stimulation, the best road trips are to Philadelphia, New York, and Washington, D.C. All are accessible by bus or train—a good thing, since first-years can't have cars.

Dickinson students get riled up for any Division III Red Devils match against top rival Franklin & Marshall, and two annual football battles—the Conestoga Wagon game against Franklin & Marshall and the Little Brown Bucket match against Gettysburg—are popular traditions. The softball and men's lacrosse teams recently won Centennial Conference championships; men's and women's soccer and track and field are also strong. About 42 percent of students take part in club sports; equestrian, ultimate Frisbee, and the Outing Club are the most popular. Recreational events like trivia nights and dodgeball tournaments are an option too.

Although Dickinson has been growing and evolving for more than two centuries, some things remain the same. Seniors still share a champagne toast before graduation. And the steps of Old West, the first college building, are still used only twice a year—in the fall, at the convocation ceremony that welcomes new students, and in the spring, for commencement. Dickinson continues to honor Rush's global vision, with its wealth of study abroad options and its demand that students cross the traditional borders of academic disciplines to grasp the interrelated nature of knowledge.

Overlaps

Franklin & Marshall, Bucknell, Gettysburg, Lafayette, Skidmore, Connecticut College, American University, Hamilton

If You Apply To ›

Dickinson: Early decision I and II, regular decision. SATs or ACTs: not considered. Accepts the Common Application with supplement.

Drew University

Madison, NJ 07940

From Drew's wooded perch in suburban New Jersey, Manhattan is only a 30-minute train ride away, and Wall Street, the UN, and Broadway are common destinations for Drew interns. Drew is the state's only prominent liberal arts college and one of the few in the greater New York City area. About two-thirds of the students are from Jersey, and Drew is still struggling to develop a national identity.

Founded more than 155 years ago as a Methodist university by Daniel Drew, a financier and railroad tycoon, Drew University has grown into a place where an emphasis on hands-on learning, research, and internships is just as important as performance in the classroom. The university encourages theater and the arts to thrive, promotes internships in New York City, and sends its students abroad for monthlong educational ventures. As part of its reinforced commitment to global education, Drew has heavily recruited international students in recent years. As a junior explains, students here benefit from "both a traditional college experience and professional excellence, due to our proximity to New York City."

The school occupies 186 acres of peaceful woodland in the upscale suburb of Madison and is known as the "University in the Forest." Fifty-six campus buildings peek through splendid oak trees and boast classic and contemporary styles, a physical reflection of Drew's respect for both scholarly traditions and progressive education. Recent campus renovation projects have included the Commons Dining Hall and the International Student Center.

In addition to an array of distribution requirements, Drew's general education program includes a first-year experience dubbed the Drew Seminar, the highlight of which is a daylong, faculty-led, course-related field trip to Manhattan. As part of an initiative known as Launch, first-years also take a workshop on career development and academic success in the spring. Launch requires all Drew students **"Everyone bonds with a mentor on campus."** to complete two hands-on learning experiences, such as internships, lab research, creative projects, and study abroad; students select their own mentorship team of faculty, counselors, and alumni to guide them through their four years. As seniors, students complete a capstone experience.

Political science is among Drew's strongest undergraduate departments, and future politicos can take advantage of off-campus opportunities in New York City, Washington, D.C., and London. Other popular majors include business, psychology, media and communication, and biology; programs in theatre arts, international relations, neuroscience, and biochemistry are well regarded. The theatre arts department works closely with the Tectonic Theater Project in New York City and other theaters to produce plays that are written, directed, and designed by students. Several dual-degree programs allow students to earn a bachelor's from Drew and a graduate degree in areas like engineering, law, nursing, and medicine from Rutgers, Duke, Columbia, and other universities. Intent on using New York City as a classroom whenever possible, Drew offers seven intensive semesters—Wall Street, the United Nations, Social Entrepreneurship, Communications and Media, New York Theatre, Contemporary Art, and Museums and Cultural Management—that take students into the city each week for real-world learning experiences.

Students take their academics seriously and rate their professors highly. Small class sizes and extensive enrichment opportunities allow students to develop personal relationships with faculty. "No student goes unnoticed; everyone bonds with a mentor

Website: www.drew.edu
Location: Suburban
Private
Total Enrollment: 1,880
Undergraduates: 1,507
Male/Female: 43/57
Financial Aid: 95%
Pell Grant: 28%
Expense: Pr $
Student Loans: 61%
Average Debt: $ $
Applicants: 3,793
Accepted: 74%
Enrolled: 9%
Grad in 6 Years: 69%
Returning Freshmen: 88%
Academics: ✍ ✍ ✍
Social: ☎ ☎ ☎
Q of L: ★ ★ ★
Admissions: (973) 408-3739
Email Address: cadm@drew.edu

Strong Programs:
Political Science
Theatre Arts
International Relations
Neuroscience
Biochemistry
Business
Psychology
Media and Communication

on campus," says a sociology major. The Research Institute for Scientists Emeriti offers opportunities for students to do research with distinguished retired industrial scientists. Participants in the Baldwin Honors program take specialized classes, attend receptions with guest speakers, and complete an honors thesis. Drew's Center for Civic Engagement supports teaching, research, scholarship, art, and other university-based activities that benefit communities. Drew has long been a proponent of study abroad programs and offers eight to 12 faculty-led TREC (Travel, Rethink, Explore, Connect) courses during winter, spring, and summer breaks each year, in addition to lengthier options through partner programs. Forty-nine percent of undergrads go abroad.

Drew offers seven intensive semesters that take students into New York City each week for real-world learning experiences.

"Drew students are a welcoming bunch; we like new people, we like new ideas, and we like new ideals," observes a junior. About two-thirds of undergraduates are from New Jersey and most attended public high schools; 11 percent are international. The school is relatively diverse: 9 percent of students are Black, 12 percent are Hispanic/Latino, 4 percent are Asian American, and 3 percent are multiracial. "My favorite thing about Drew is that although people are politically and socially active, they are more interested in listening to what others have to say than in projecting their own opinions," says a senior. Merit awards average $17,320, but there are no athletic scholarships. Drew decreased its sticker price by 20 percent in fall 2018 and has since kept rates relatively low.

Eighty-three percent of the students live in university housing, which is guaranteed for four years and includes both single-sex and co-ed dorms, theme houses, and, for upperclassmen, townhouses. A lottery gives housing preference to seniors and juniors, making room selection "an easy process," according to a sophomore. Most first-years reside in dorms situated at the back of campus, and 40 percent choose to take part in living/learning communities. Students report that a "massive renovation" to the Commons dining hall has vastly improved the quality of meals; "There's always something that I can look forward to eating," says a junior. As for safety, a senior says, "Campus is very safe, but Drew could be better at acknowledging sexual assault and teaching students to take it seriously."

> "[Madison] is a nice college town according to my parents."

With no Greek life, a sophomore explains, "The athletic teams and theatre groups hold the most vibrant parties on campus," and for those who don't care to party, "Our Office of Student Activities supplements student-run programming by bringing in comedians, musicians, slam poets, and other performers every Thursday to engage the community." There is a 21-and-over pub on campus, as well as two coffeehouses. The Shakespeare Theatre of New Jersey is in residence on campus part of every year and offers both performances and internships. The long-standing First Annual Picnic, held on the last day of classes and numbered like Super Bowls (spring 2022 marked FAP XLIX), provides an opportunity to enjoy free food, carnival games, and music. Other traditions include the Holiday Ball, 99 Nights for seniors, and Fern Fest, where students plant native ferns and wildflowers during Earth Week.

The Shakespeare Theatre of New Jersey is in residence on campus part of every year and offers both performances and internships.

Approximately 50 percent of students volunteer in local and international activities such as Mentors at Drew and working with children in the Dominican Republic.

> "I think Drew is like the coffeehouse of colleges. There's always intellectual stuff going on, but it's very cozy."

The commuter town of Madison doesn't have the amenities of larger metropolitan areas, of course, but there are several unique shops and restaurants within walking distance of campus. One student says the town "is a nice college town according to my parents, but not to students. Everything closes up pretty early." Nearby Morristown is more of a college place. New York City's Pennsylvania Station is less than an hour away by commuter train, and Philadelphia, the Jersey Shore, and the Delaware River are close by.

Interest in Drew's 22 Division III varsity teams has grown as the Rangers have become more successful. Men's and women's tennis and golf, men's basketball, and women's swimming are recent Landmark Conference winners. The competitive men's and women's fencing teams beat and parry with the likes of Duke and Cornell. Intramural and club sports range from basketball and floor hockey to rugby and eSports, and special recreation events like Hunger Games Dodgeball and the Rock Paper Scissors Tournament are student favorites.

Drew offers its small body of students a wide range of opportunities, excellent access to the riches of New York City, and plenty of personal attention in a classic liberal arts structure. "I think Drew is like the coffeehouse of colleges," a theatre major muses. "There's always intellectual stuff going on, but it's very cozy." Not too bad for a school in the forest.

If You Apply To ›

Drew: Early decision I and II, early action, regular decision. SATs or ACTs: optional. Accepts the Common Application with supplement.

Drexel University

3141 Chestnut Street, Philadelphia, PA 19104

Drexel is a streetwise, no-nonsense technical university in the heart of Philadelphia. Like Lehigh, Drexel also offers programs in business and arts and sciences, and its most distinctive offering is the Westphal College of Media Arts and Design. A financial bargain compared to other leading technical schools, Drexel has abandoned its aggressive expansion plans and in-your-face recruitment style of recent years in a successful effort to increase yield and graduation rates. Check out the co-op program.

For career-minded students who want to bypass the soul-searching of their liberal arts counterparts, Drexel University offers both solid academics and an innovative co-op program that combines high-tech academics with paying job opportunities—a mix that's particularly appealing in today's economic climate. The school dates to 1891, when Anthony J. Drexel, a Philadelphia financier and philanthropist, set up the Drexel Institute of Art, Science, and Industry in order to prepare young men and women to work in the emerging industrial society. Drexel began offering co-op education in 1919. "If you want a good job, you go to Drexel and you do co-op," asserts a student.

"Drexel's campus is impressive for its downtown Philadelphia location, with gardens and greenery on every block," says a student, "but the campus is woven tightly into the fabric of the city." Drexel's 123-acre campus, which is adjacent to the University of Pennsylvania, is condensed into about a 20-block radius. It lies in a formerly crime-ridden neighborhood that is now

> **"The campus is woven tightly into the fabric of the city."**

one of the most desirable parts of Philadelphia, with plenty of restaurants and stores. A long-term, multiphase neighborhood remake will include a $3.5 billion "Innovation Neighborhood" along the Schuylkill River rail yards that will house new research facilities and incubator space. The campus's older buildings are simple and fashioned of brick; most are modern and in good condition. Additional facilities include the Center City Campus for the College of Nursing and Health Professions.

Website: www.drexel.edu
Location: City Center
Private
Total Enrollment: 17,329
Undergraduates: 13,094
Male/Female: 52/48
Financial Aid: 96%
Pell Grant: 27%
Expense: Pr $
Student Loans: 67%
Average Debt: $ $ $ $
Applicants: 34,519
Accepted: 83%
Enrolled: 10%
Grad in 6 Years: 78%
Returning Freshmen: 90%
Academics: ✑ ✑ ✑
Social: ☎ ☎
Q of L: ★ ★ ★
Admissions: (800) 2-DREXEL

(continued)

Email Address: enroll@ drexel.edu

Strong Programs:
Engineering
Nursing
Business
Architecture
Game Design and Production
Film and Television
Physics
Computer Science

Cooperative education is the hallmark of Drexel's curriculum, which alternates periods of full-time study and full-time employment for four or five years, providing students with six to 18 months of job experience before they graduate. The co-op possibilities, which 95 percent of undergraduates take advantage of, are unlimited: students can pursue co-ops virtually anywhere in the U.S. or in 28 other countries. Students in five-year programs spend their freshman and senior years on campus; the three intervening years (sophomore, prejunior, and junior) usually consist of six months of work and six months of school. A 10-week preparatory course, Co-op 101, covers such topics as skills assessment, ethics in the workplace, résumé writing, interviewing skills, and stress management. Most co-ops are paid, and the median six-month salary for co-op students is more than $19,000. And although some students complain that jobs can turn out to be six months of busywork, most enjoy making important contacts in their potential fields and learning while earning.

To accommodate the co-op students, Drexel operates year-round. "I would describe the climate as intense but manageable," says one senior. "Being on a quarter system is rigorous at times." Flexibility in requirements varies by college, but in the first year everyone must take English composition, mathematics, and two one-credit courses: one that introduces students to university resources and one on civic engagement in the local community. Engineering majors must also complete the Drexel Engineering Curriculum, which integrates math, physics, chemistry, and engineering to make sure that even techies enter the workforce well-rounded and able to write as well as they can compute and design. Students enjoy the Hagerty Library, which offers a 24-hour study space and plenty of room for group work. What's more, each entering freshman is assigned a "personal librarian" charged with helping them make the best use of library facilities. Professors receive high praise from most and are noted for their accessibility and warmth. Says one student, "The only things that teaching assistants run are labs and study sessions." Fifty-five percent of classes have fewer than 20 students.

> *Cooperative education is the hallmark of Drexel's curriculum, providing students with six to 18 months of job experience before they graduate.*

The most popular majors are mechanical engineering, computer science, finance, and biological sciences. Drexel's greatest strength is its engineering college, where the materials science, electrical, and architectural engineering programs are particular standouts. Other noteworthy programs include nursing, business, and the Westphal College of Media Arts and Design's majors in architecture, game design and production, and film and television; the College of Arts and Sciences is well recognized for theoretical and atmospheric physics. An honors college is available for those who seek an even more challenging experience, and about 8 percent of undergrads study abroad.

Drexel has long shed its reputation as an easy-admission commuter college. According to one sophomore, Drexel students are "not afraid of hard work because we do it all the time, even when we're exhausted." About half of the undergraduate student body is Pennsylvanian, with another large chunk of students from adjacent New Jersey, and the campus tends to lean right politically. The international student population is 9 percent. Asian Americans account for 23 percent, Black students 8 percent, Hispanics/Latinos 8 percent, and multiracial students 4 percent. In addition to need-based financial aid, merit scholarships averaging $19,500 and more than 200 athletic scholarships are awarded to qualified students. Starting in 2023, community college graduates from Pennsylvania and New Jersey receive a 50 percent discount on tuition.

> **"It's hard to get people involved because of the amount of schoolwork and co-ops."**

Freshmen live in one of nine co-ed residence halls, including a luxurious high-rise, but most upperclassmen reside in nearby apartments or fraternity houses.

Overall, just 20 percent of the students live in the dorms. Students say the two main dining centers offer a variety of "adequate" food. If all else fails, nomadic food trucks park around campus, providing quick lunches. Students are encouraged to use a shuttle bus between the library and dorms at night, and access to dorms, the library, and the physical education center is restricted to students with IDs, so most say they feel safe on campus.

With so many students living off campus and the city of Philadelphia at their disposal, Drexel tends to be a bit deserted on weekends. Friday-night flicks on campus are cheap and popular with those who stay around, and dorms sponsor floor parties. The dozen or so fraternities, which recruit 12 percent of the men, also contribute to the party scene, especially freshman year; the handful of smaller sororities attract 10 percent of the women. "Greek life is relatively small, so there are plenty of other ways to be involved socially," a senior says. "There's no pressure to drink," adds a communication major, and campus policies are strict; dorms require those of age to sign in alcohol and limit the quantities they may bring in.

Drexel's co-op program often undermines any sense of class unity and can strain personal relationships. Activities that depend on some continuity of enrollment for success—music, drama, student government, athletics—suffer most. "It's hard to get people involved because of the amount of school-work and co-ops," says one student. Even so, the university sponsors 18 Division I

"When I graduate, I will be prepared and proud of it."

teams, competing in the Colonial Athletic Association. There is no football team, but the Dragons men's and women's basketball, crew, and squash teams are strong. "Our biggest rivalry is our feud with Delaware," admits one frenzied student. "We delight in sacrificing blue plastic chickens!"—Delaware's mascot. An extensive intramural program serves all students, and joggers can head for the steps of the Philadelphia Art Museum, just as Rocky did in the movies. Students take full advantage of their urban location by frequenting clubs, restaurants, cultural attractions, and shops in Philadelphia, easily accessible by public transportation.

Aspiring poets, musicians, and historians may find Drexel a bit disorienting. But future computer scientists, engineers, and other technical minds could get a fantastic jump-start on their careers, thanks to the university's unique approach to learning inside and outside the classroom. As one satisfied student explains, "The terms are intense, the activities unlimited, but Drexel graduates are surely among the most capable and motivated individuals I have ever met. When I graduate, I will be prepared and proud of it."

Starting in 2023, community college graduates from Pennsylvania and New Jersey receive a 50 percent discount on tuition.

Overlaps

Penn State, Syracuse, University of Pittsburgh, George Washington, Temple, Rochester Institute of Technology, Lehigh, Ursinus

If You Apply To ›

Drexel: Early decision, early action, regular decision. Please consult Drexel's website for the most up-to-date information regarding standardized test requirements. Accepts the Common Application. Apply to particular school or program.

Duke University

2138 Campus Drive, Durham, NC 27708

What fun to be at Duke—face painted blue, rocking Cameron Indoor Stadium as the Blue Devils win again. The most prestigious private university in the South, Duke is academically competitive with the Ivies and Stanford. Strong in engineering as well as the humanities, it offers public policy and economics rather than business. Study across disciplines, international perspectives, and civic engagement define its brand. DukeEngage service program is special. Generous in financial aid to neediest students.

Website: www.duke.edu
Location: Small City
Private
Total Enrollment: 16,780
Undergraduates: 6,789
Male/Female: 48/52
Financial Aid: 42%
Pell Grant: 13%
Expense: Pr $ $ $ $
Student Loans: 30%
Average Debt: $ $
Applicants: 49,523
Accepted: 6%
Enrolled: 60%
Grad in 6 Years: 96%
Returning Freshmen: 98%
Academics: ✐ ✐ ✐ ✐ ✐
Social: ☎ ☎ ☎ ☎
Q of L: ★ ★ ★ ★
Admissions: (919) 684-3214
Email Address: undergrad
-admissions@duke.edu

Strong Programs:
Engineering
Ecology
Biology
Neuroscience
Global Health
Public Policy Studies
English
Dance

Duke University is one of the handful of elite U.S. colleges where strong academics and championship-caliber sports teams manage to coexist. It might be south of the Mason-Dixon Line, and may seem a bit wet behind the ears compared to those ancient and prestigious Northeastern schools known for the erstwhile foliage on their walls, but Duke wins its fair share of intellectually serious superachievers, as well as lots of top athletes. One senior says Duke offers plenty to cheer about, including "a diverse student body, challenging academics, world-renowned professors, research opportunities, and an immense amount of school spirit."

Founded in 1838 as the Union Institute (later Trinity College), Duke University is young for a school of its stature. It sprouted up in 1924, thanks to a stack of tobacco-stained dollars known as the Duke Endowment. Duke's campus in the North Carolina Piedmont is divided into two main sections, West and East, and with 8,300 acres of adjacent forest, offers enough open space to satisfy even the most diehard outdoors enthusiast. West Campus, the hub of the university, is laid out in spacious quadrangles and dominated by the impressive Gothic chapel, a symbol of the university's Methodist tradition. Constructed in the 1930s, West includes collegiate Gothic residential and classroom quads, the administration building, the huge Perkins Library, and the recently renovated student union. East Campus, built in the 1920s, consists primarily of Georgian redbrick buildings. East and West are connected by shuttle buses, though many students enjoy the mile or so walk or bike ride between them along wooded Campus Drive.

> **"[Duke has] a diverse student body, challenging academics, [and] world-renowned professors."**

Students opt for one of two undergraduate schools: the Pratt School of Engineering and Trinity College of Arts & Sciences. The school's engineering programs—particularly electrical and biomedical—are national standouts. Natural sciences, most notably ecology, biology, and neuroscience, are also first-rate. The proximity of the Medical Center enhances study in biochemistry and global health. Duke's Sanford School of Public Policy offers an interdisciplinary major—unusual at the undergraduate level—that trains aspiring public servants and future leaders of nonprofit organizations, government agencies, and other bodies that shape public life. Internships and apprenticeships are a big part of the program. Duke's English and dance programs are notable, but students say the language offerings can be weak. Duke has more than 60 interdisciplinary centers, including the Duke Global Health Institute, the Nicholas Institute for Environmental Policy Solutions, and the John Hope Franklin Humanities Institute. Computer science attracts the most majors, followed by public policy studies, biology, and economics.

Trinity College's curriculum, part of the traditional undergraduate coursework known as Program I, requires courses in five general areas of knowledge: arts, literature, and performance; civilizations; social sciences; natural sciences; and quantitative studies. Students must also fulfill requirements in six modes of inquiry, including foreign language; writing; research; ethical inquiry; science, technology, and society; and cross-cultural inquiry. All students complete three Small Group Learning Experiences: one seminar course during the freshman year, on topics such as Politics on Camera and How Hospitals Work, and two more as upperclassmen. Those who wish to explore subjects outside and between usual majors and minors may choose Program II, to which they are admitted after proposing a topic, question, or theme for which they plan an individualized curriculum with faculty advisors and deans.

When college counselors say Duke is hot, they're not referring to the boiling temperatures in the South. "The workload is heavy, but, because of the highly collaborative environment, it is manageable," says a public policy major. Seventy percent of classes have fewer than 20 students, and the university focuses resources on undergraduate education and having senior professors teach more classes. A senior says, "Faculty members are accessible, especially through a program called FLUNCH, where you are able to have a meal with a faculty member on Duke's dime." Interdisciplinary work, long part of the Duke culture, is a priority for faculty and students alike. The highly regarded FOCUS program offers first-year students two linked seminars with no more than 18 students clustered around

Duke has more than 60 interdisciplinary centers, including the Duke Global Health Institute.

"The workload is heavy, but, because of the highly collaborative environment, it is manageable."

a single broad, interdisciplinary theme, such as geopolitics and culture or science and the public; participants also live together in the same residence hall and attend weekly dinners with faculty. It is "an incredible opportunity to engage with the university's top professors," a senior reports. The Bass Connections program gives undergraduates a chance to work with faculty and graduate students in interdisciplinary, research-based project teams in thematic areas such as global health and energy and environment.

Those who wish to see the world before embarking on their undergraduate career may apply to the Duke Gap Year Program; accepted students receive between $5,000 and $15,000 toward the cost of their chosen gap year program. Fifty-seven percent of Duke's undergrads study abroad in their choice of more than 50 university-administered programs and 130 other partner programs, and there are ample opportunities for those who want a break from campus life without leaving the country. DukeEngage, an ambitious and innovative program backed by a $30 million endowment, supports students willing to spend summers working on projects ranging from building schools in Kenya to working with Gulf Coast flood victims. About a quarter of all undergrads participate in the program, which has become a centerpiece of the school's commitment to "knowledge in service to society."

First-year students in the highly regarded FOCUS program live together in the same residence hall and attend weekly dinners with faculty.

"Students tend to be extremely driven, upper middle class, and focused on succeeding far after college," says one public policy major. Eighteen percent of Duke students are from North Carolina, and the Northeastern corridor sends a fair-sized contingent, as does California. Nine percent of undergraduates hail from overseas. Duke's Southern gentility is reflected in campus attire, which is generally neatly pressed on guys and maybe a bit outfit-y on women, in contrast to the thrown-together antistatus uniform of jeans and sweats that dominates on many other campuses. Undergraduate women sometimes complain about the pressure they feel to demonstrate, in the words of a former president, "effortless perfection" in all respects. Despite the unmistakable air of wealth on campus, about two-thirds of the students come from public high schools. Eight percent are Black, 11 percent are Hispanic/Latino, 21 percent are Asian American, and 6 percent are multiracial. Students of different

"The dorms look like castles on the outside and feel like Harry Potter."

ethnicities and races tend to "self-segregate," students say, producing little tension but also little interaction. The Center for Race Relations works to improve the way Duke educates its students about diversity and conflict resolution. Also noteworthy: Duke was among the first universities to include in their admissions application an optional short essay question in which applicants can discuss their sexual, gender, or other identities.

Duke admits students without regard to financial need and meets 100 percent of their demonstrated need.

Duke admits students without regard to financial need and meets 100 percent of their demonstrated need. The university has eliminated loans from financial aid packages for families with incomes below $40,000 a year, and families with incomes below $60,000 a year are not expected to contribute to the cost of tuition. Like other Division I universities, Duke hands out lots of athletic scholarships. The university also offers a small number of merit scholarships, including those offered through the Rubenstein Scholars Program for high-achieving, first-generation students from low-income backgrounds. Incoming Rubenstein Scholars participate in a six-week summer academic program, receive personal mentoring from top faculty, and take special seminars during the academic year.

Duke undergrads are required to live on campus for three years; overall, 81 percent stay in university-owned housing. Students live in residence halls or quads that house both independent students and members of selective living groups such as fraternities. Freshmen all reside in dorms on the East Campus led by a faculty member and his or her family. "The dorms look like castles on the outside and feel like Harry Potter," says a junior, who adds that the new dorms "are like five-star hotels." Sophomores move to West Campus, where there are also special-interest dorms focused on themes such as women's studies, the arts, languages, and community service. Seniors can move off campus. Students give good ratings to campus security.

"There is a strong drinking and party culture on campus."

Duke has been engaged in a massive physical expansion over the last few years aimed at enhancing students' creature comforts, including a 72,000-square-foot, state-of-the-art Student Wellness Center. The glass-fronted Brodhead Center for Campus Life, which recently underwent an $80 million renovation, is host to an over-the-top collection of dining options operated by local chefs and restaurateurs that, consistent with Durham's reputation as a foodie haven, the university trumpets as offering the most lavish (and, students say, costly) dining on any college campus. Off-campus restaurants are linked to the Duke meal plan.

Durham includes most of the Research Triangle Park, the largest research center of its kind in the world.

"Duke students are the type who will start a club if they are interested in something that nobody else is doing, work hard on a paper late into the night, and then go out Thursday, Friday, and Saturday," says a public policy major. Students agree that most social life takes place on campus or in surrounding houses and apartments. Although it has been pushed away from the center of campus, "the Greek scene dominates," says a history major. Fraternities and sororities attract 29 percent of the men and 42 percent of the women, respectively. Fraternity parties are open to everyone, and the free shuttle bus service that connects the school's various dorm and apartment complexes runs until 4 a.m. "There is a strong drinking and party culture on campus, though students are not pressured to participate," one sophomore reports.

Duke is also a culturally active campus; theater groups thrive, and the Nasher Museum of Art, with its world-class exhibits by Picasso, Calder, and El Greco, among others, has become a popular social hub. The Springternational festival brings in live bands and vendors peddling local crafts and exotic foods each spring, and the traditional Joe College Day has been revived as a daylong fall affair filled with food, arts and crafts, and music. In warm weather, the broad beaches on North Carolina's outer banks beckon from two to three hours away, while winter ski slopes are three to four hours distant.

Durham is a small, working-class city that has had its share of racial tensions but also boasts a vibrant Black middle class and good political leadership. Duke as an institution has been active in the community, especially in public schools, and hundreds of undergrads are involved in service learning, tutoring, and related activities. "Everyone is involved in volunteer work," says one student. Downtown Durham has undergone a revival, with old tobacco warehouses being converted into restaurants, stores, offices, and apartments. The town is proud of its Durham Bulls, the local minor-league baseball team, which coined the term "bullpen." No one misses the irony of the fact that Durham, once known as the "City of Tobacco," now bills itself as the "City of Medicine." (In another irony, the Duke campus went smoke-free in 2020.) Durham includes most of the Research Triangle Park, the largest research center of its kind in the world. Duke, North Carolina State, and the University of North Carolina at Chapel Hill created the park for nonprofit, scientific, and sociological research. Many Silicon Valley technology companies have East Coast outposts in the park, which has helped give the area the highest percentage of Ph.D.s per capita in the United States.

At basketball games, students transform into the legendary Cameron Crazies and make life miserable for the visiting team.

Duke's official motto is *Eruditio et Religio* only to a few straitlaced administrators; everyone else knows it as *Eruditio et Basketballio*, which translates more or less as "Go to hell, Carolina"—meaning UNC at Chapel Hill, Duke's archrival in the rough-and-tough Atlantic Coast Conference. At games, students transform into the legendary Cameron Crazies and get the best courtside seats, where

"There is something magical about Duke basketball."

they make life miserable for the visiting team. The Blue Devils won the national Division I men's basketball championship five times under fabled coach Mike Krzyzewski, who retired in 2022. Sports-crazed Blue Devils erect a temporary tent city—dubbed "Krzyzewskiville"—to vie for the best seats. This is far from roughing it—students form groups to hold their places so that some fraction can go to class and keep their peers who hold down the fort on track academically. "There is something magical about Duke basketball, and the feeling of being in the student section with the Cameron Crazies during the Duke–UNC game is something that can't be captured in words," gushes one fan. Men's lacrosse and women's golf are national powerhouses as well. Previously hapless football has undergone something of a renaissance. The team now plays in a renovated stadium complete with luxury boxes for Iron Duke supporters and earns occasional bowl bids. Duke's stellar debate team brought home the national title recently. Intramurals are big, with roughly 950 teams, and operate on two levels of competitiveness; more than 40 club sports are available as well.

Meandering around Duke's up-to-date campus, you can see the latest technology, but you can also hear the whisper of the Old South through those big old trees and stunning architecture. In addition to a sophisticated blending of old and new, Duke also does an impressive job combining sports and academia, producing students who almost define the term "well-rounded." With its distinctive blend of interdisciplinarity, internationalization, and civic engagement, Duke has put any lingering "Ivy envy" in the rearview mirror.

Overlaps

Brown, Columbia, Dartmouth, University of Pennsylvania, University of Chicago, Stanford, Harvard, Yale

If You Apply To ›

Duke: Early decision, regular decision. Please consult Duke's website for the most up-to-date information regarding standardized test requirements. Accepts the Common Application with supplement. Additional optional essay invites applicants to share a perspective or experience related to community, family, culture, sexual orientation, or gender identity.

Earlham is a member of the proud circle of solid liberal arts colleges that includes Beloit, Grinnell, Kenyon, and Oberlin, to name just a few. Smallest of the group, but manages to attract a highly diverse student body despite its conservative southern Indiana location. Earlham is distinctive for its Quaker orientation, welcoming environment, and international perspective.

Website: www.earlham.edu
Location: Small City
Private
Total Enrollment: 689
Undergraduates: 653
Male/Female: 46/54
Financial Aid: 96%
Pell Grant: 40%
Expense: Pr $ $
Student Loans: 71%
Average Debt: $ $
Applicants: 1,659
Accepted: 69%
Enrolled: 15%
Grad in 6 Years: 73%
Returning Freshmen: 73%
Academics: ✍ ✍ ✍ ✍
Social: ☎ ☎ ☎
Q of L: ★ ★ ★ ★ ★
Admissions: (765) 983-1600
Email Address: admissions@
earlham.edu

Strong Programs:
Psychology
Biology
Biochemistry
Global Management
International Studies
Peace and Global Studies
Japanese Studies
Computer Science

Earlham is a study in contradictions—a top-notch liberal arts college in a relatively conservative city that few could place on a map, and an institution that in the 21st century remains true to the traditions of community, peace, and justice that are hallmarks of its Religious Society of Friends (Quaker) heritage. Earlham's curriculum and programs engage students with the world by exposing them to classmates from more than 50 nations and offering some 200 academic courses that incorporate an international perspective. Varied study abroad programs provide close faculty involvement and a thoughtful focus on cross-cultural perspectives.

Earlham was established in 1859 in the wake of the Great Migration of Quakers from Eastern states that took place in the first half of the 19th century. The college's 800-acre campus sits in the small, quintessentially Midwestern city of Richmond, just a short distance from Cincinnati and Indianapolis. Georgian-style buildings dominate, surrounded by mature trees and plantings, while the Japanese gardens symbolize the college's long friendship and closeness with Japan.

To graduate, students must complete general education requirements in the arts, analytical reasoning, wellness, scientific inquiry, foreign language, and, not surprisingly, diversity. All students take a reading- and writing-focused first-year seminar and complete a capstone experience. Psychology, biology, biochemistry, global management, and international studies are some of the strongest and most popular majors, and computer science also garners high enrollment. As of fall 2023, engineering is now available as a major, with a curriculum that administrators say is designed to prepare students to approach engineering problems "with a sense of compassion and justice." A wide range of interdisciplinary offerings includes such programs as peace and global studies, environmental sustainability, and Japanese studies, a field in which Earlham is a national leader. "The Japanese program has high national standing," says one student, "and the sciences have high placement for graduate studies and jobs post-graduation." Preprofessional preparation and integrated learning programs are available in such areas as health sciences, education, business and entrepreneurship, and law and social justice.

> **"Richmond has great opportunities for volunteering or interning with NGOs."**

An international studies major says the academic climate is "very collaborative, but still leaves room for individual critical thinking." Discussion rather than lecture is the predominant learning style here, facilitated by small classes—87 percent have fewer than 20 students. Earlham faculty members are selected for their excellence in teaching and their ability to cross disciplinary lines. "Professors at Earlham are clear in what they expect from students and help as much as they can," says a sophomore. Another student explains that, as a matter of Quaker principle, faculty, staff, and students are never addressed by honorifics or social titles like Dr. or Ms., but by their first names: "It's an equality thing."

The EPIC Advantage program provides every Earlham student with the opportunity to pursue a fully funded internship or faculty-guided research experience, on or off campus, typically during the summer before their junior or senior year. Seventy percent of students participate in at least one off-campus study experience. Earlham offers study abroad programs in more than two dozen countries, including Ecuador, Germany, India, Japan, and New Zealand, most of which are managed by the college. In a Border Studies program, students live with families in Tucson, Arizona, and take courses focusing on United States–Mexico border issues. Popular May Term classes send students off campus with faculty for one-month intensive courses in various locations around the world. "One of my friends, only a rising sophomore, is spending several weeks in Germany with a professor studying ancient fossils in one of the most advanced DNA analysis labs in the world," says one sophomore. "His story is not an uncommon one for freshmen, and this speaks to the unique availability of great opportunities here." About half of students eventually pursue postgraduate study, often after taking some time off for a job or to participate in volunteer or service programs.

As of fall 2023, engineering is now available as a major designed to prepare students to approach problems with a sense of compassion and justice.

Only 20 percent of the students are Hoosiers; impressively, another 20 percent hail from abroad. Eight percent are Black, with Hispanics/Latinos adding 9 percent, Asian Americans 2 percent, and multiracial students 5 percent. These days, just 3 percent of students are Friends, but traditional Quaker values still permeate this liberal campus. "Earlhamites come at all of their endeavors with their whole hearts," says a senior. "Many students walk around barefoot (weather permitting), and

"Earlham is crunchy and a bit of an underdog but definitely punches above its weight class."

peace and justice are an Earlhamite's deepest love." Merit scholarships averaging $25,000 are available for qualified students; there are no athletic scholarships. Forty percent of incoming first-year students qualify for Pell Grants.

Ninety-four percent of Earlham students live on campus, with first-years occupying eight traditional residence halls. The newest, Mills Hall, offers suite-style accommodations. Upperclassmen can opt to live in the dorms, the Campus Village Apartments, or one of 20 themed college houses. Dining facilities receive average reviews. Some say the administration has been slow and ineffective in its response to the issue of campus sexual assault. "Information around reporting is sparse," says a junior, "and reporting rates are scary low."

There are no fraternities or sororities at Earlham, but on-campus activities abound. "Most everything happens on campus, which is great because everything is more open and accessible," a student says. Students enjoy improv comedy, a cappella music, equestrian programs, a lip-synch competition, fall and spring festivals, concerts, and sports. Student groups include numerous religious, ethnic, and cultural organizations, some of which also take the lead on throwing campus parties. Students 21 and over can consume alcohol, although only in their residence hall rooms, and a senior expresses the opinion that "Earlham parties are usually regarded as lame." Day trips to Cincinnati, Indianapolis, or Columbus and weekend visits to other nearby universities are popular diversions.

As a matter of Quaker principle, faculty, staff, and students are never addressed by titles like Dr. or Ms., but by their first names.

Though not a college town, the city of Richmond offers standard American and a variety of ethnic restaurants, as well as movie theaters, bowling alleys, golf, and a popular biking and running trail. "Richmond has great opportunities for volunteering or interning with NGOs, but is less exciting if you are looking for a happening night life," reports a politics major. Students fan out into the city, racking up more than 23,000 hours of volunteer service a year.

Earlham's 19 varsity teams (the Quakers) attract nearly a third of the student body and compete in Division III sports. Men's and women's soccer, men's tennis and baseball, and women's track and field are strong. About half of the students play club and intramural sports, and soccer, basketball, and kickball are the most popular.

Overlaps

Oberlin, College of Wooster, Kalamazoo, Hanover, Knox, St. Olaf, Kenyon, Beloit

Earlham students graduate ready to take on the world, thanks to the school's cooperative, can-do spirit, international perspective, and caring student/faculty community—and its commitment to a values-oriented education. "Earlham is crunchy and a bit of an underdog but definitely punches above its weight class," opines a junior. "At Earlham, everyone is rooting for you and working with you to dream bigger and then achieve those dreams."

If You Apply To ›

Earlham: Early action, regular decision. SATs or ACTs: optional (recommended for applicants who wish to be considered for merit scholarships). Accepts the Common Application with supplement.

Eckerd College

4200 54th Avenue South, St. Petersburg, FL 33711

There are few places more tempting to attend than a college with its own stretch of beach on the shores near Tampa Bay. Eckerd's only direct competitor in Florida is Rollins, which has a business school but is otherwise similar. Marine science, environmental studies, and international studies are among Eckerd's biggest draws. The student body is mainly from out of state, with an abundance of Yankee accents.

Website: www.eckerd.edu
Location: Suburban
Private
Total Enrollment: 1,981
Undergraduates: 1,981
Male/Female: 30/70
Financial Aid: 99%
Pell Grant: 21%
Expense: Pr $ $
Student Loans: 59%
Average Debt: $ $ $ $
Applicants: 5,581
Accepted: 70%
Enrolled: 17%
Grad in 6 Years: 69%
Returning Freshmen: 80%
Academics: ✎ ✎ ✎
Social: ☎ ☎ ☎
Q of L: ★ ★ ★ ★ ★
Admissions: (727) 864-8331
Email Address: admissions@
eckerd.edu

Strong Programs:
Marine Science
Environmental Studies

Attending Eckerd College demands a special sort of willpower. As an international business major explains, "We are right on the water, and it is like going to college in a resort." With free paddleboards, canoes, kayaks, boats, coolers, and tents always available for student use, it's a wonder anyone finds time to study. But study they do, as administrators continue to lure adventurous students to Eckerd with small classes, skilled professors, and a thriving social scene. "It's Eckerd's paradise-like setting that seals the deal for most prospective students," says a sophomore.

Founded in 1958 as Florida Presbyterian College and renamed 14 years later after a generous benefactor (of drugstore fame), Eckerd considers itself nonsectarian. Still, the school maintains a formal "covenant" with the major Presbyterian

> **"We are right on the water, and it is like going to college in a resort."**

denomination, from which it receives some funds. The lush, grassy campus is on the tip of a peninsula bounded by the Gulf of Mexico and Tampa Bay, with plenty of flowering bushes, trees, and small ponds—it's not unusual to spot dolphins frolicking in the adjacent waters. Campus buildings are modern, and none are taller than three stories. Highlights include the $25 million, LEED Platinum–rated James Center for Molecular and Life Sciences and the state-of-the-art studios in the Nielsen Center for Visual Arts.

Autumn Term, Eckerd's version of freshman orientation, is a three-week term before the regular fall semester that introduces new students to the academic expectations and social responsibilities of the Eckerd community. First-years also take a Human Experience course in the fall, focusing on topics like justice, power, freedom, and global citizenship, and a First-Year Experience Seminar in the spring. In addition to standard distribution requirements, all students take one course each in environmental and global perspectives and complete at least 40 hours of community service before graduation; service opportunities are built into reflective service-learning courses that are offered in every major. Imagining Justice, the required senior capstone seminar, asks students to draw on what they've learned during college to find solutions to important issues. Seniors present their capstone work at a festival in the spring.

Eckerd students take their coursework seriously, but on the whole, a human development major says, "The atmosphere is relaxed. How could it not be when you can study and sunbathe at the beach?" Popular majors include environmental studies, marine science, animal studies, biology, psychology, chemistry, business administration, international studies, and creative writing. Wet subjects are especially strong. "The close proximity to the ocean gives [marine science] majors a great amount of hands-on, close-up experience," a student says. The Eckerd College Search and Rescue team, for instance, performs more than 500 marine rescues annually. Eckerd was a pioneer of the 4–1–4 term schedule, in which students work on a single project for credit each January. Every stu-

(continued)
International Studies
Animal Studies
Biology
Psychology
Chemistry
Business Administration

"[Students are] friendly, liberal, free-spirited, and intelligent."

dent has a faculty mentor, and there are no graduate assistants; 47 percent of all classes have fewer than 20 students. "The professors are genuinely interested in what they're teaching, and you can see that passion through their willingness to work with students," says a marine science major.

Each year, 20 to 25 top incoming students are selected to participate in First-Year Research Associateships, receiving stipends of up to $1,000 to work side by side with leading professors on active research projects. A four-year honors program is also available. While St. Petersburg isn't exactly a college town, a side benefit to the school's location is the Academy of Senior Professionals at Eckerd College, a group of senior citizens who mentor undergrads, work with professors on curriculum development, and lead workshops in their areas of expertise. Fifty-four percent of students study abroad, mostly during three-week terms in January and May. Programs are available in more than 300 destinations, including the school's study center in London.

A former Eckerd president once referred to the school's quirky students as "intellectuals in sandals," reports a junior. "I like the quote, and it really works." Another student says Eckerd attracts "friendly, liberal, free-spirited, and intelligent" students who enjoy the great outdoors and care about protecting the environment. Seventy-nine percent of the student body hails from out of state, with a large contingent coming from the Northeast; another 4 percent come from other countries. Hispanics/Latinos account for 9 percent of the student body, Black students 3 percent, Asian Americans 3 percent, and multiracial students 6 percent. Merit scholarships averaging $17,200 and athletic awards are available to qualified students.

Imagining Justice, the required senior capstone seminar, asks students to draw on what they've learned to find solutions to important issues.

Eighty-three percent of students live in the housing quads. First-years usually live in doubles or triples, while suite- and apartment-style residence halls are available for upper-class students. Most campus housing is gender neutral. Waterfront views and beach access are a given, and a sophomore notes, "We have many different types of themed housing, including pet-friendly, all-female, and health and wellness housing options." Vegan and vegetarian options in Eckerd's dining

"We have dogs, we have beaches, we have intense science labs, and tons of research opportunities."

facilities are plentiful; the food generally gets average reviews. A management major explains that, given the school's location near a tourist destination, "a security post at the entrance of the school provides a safer environment for students."

"Eckerd is a primarily student-run campus," says a junior, "and there are usually fun and interactive events that happen every Thursday, Friday, and Saturday." Students can partake in concerts, lectures, shows, and games arranged by the student activity board. There are no Greek organizations (a sophomore comments, "We have residence halls named after Greek letters, making fun of the tradition of having frats and sororities"), and weekend parties are usually held in the Kappa, Nu, and Omega dorms. Kegs and glass bottles are prohibited on campus, and students 21 and over must wear wristbands at campus parties. Students and professors gather regularly for Fridays with Faculty and Friends to enjoy good conversation, food, and root beer floats in the campus pub. The last few weeks of the school year bring Springtopia, featuring major events like the Spring Ball and the Kappa Karnival, with rides, games, and cotton candy galore.

Off campus, students enjoy downtown St. Petersburg's First Friday block parties and Saturday Morning Market. Tampa and St. Pete also offer a Salvador Dalí museum—free for Eckerd students—and professional baseball, football, hockey, and soccer teams. The nightclubs and bars of Latin-flavored Ybor City are about 30 minutes away, and tempting road trips include Orlando's Walt Disney World and Universal Studios theme parks, Miami's South Beach, and that hub of debauchery on the delta, New Orleans.

Varsity teams (the Tritons—after a Greek sea god) compete in the Division II Sunshine State Conference. "Men's basketball is the only sport that attracts lots of fans and spectators," a senior says, and for good reasons—the men's and women's teams are both frequent conference winners. The Triton Tip-Off pep rally helps kick off the season. Baseball and women's volleyball (both indoor and beach) are competitive, too, and the co-ed sailing team has claimed several recent divisional and regional titles. Eckerd doesn't have a football team, but popular club sports include rugby, lacrosse, soccer, and ultimate Frisbee.

Eckerd is committed to offering "experiential, service, and international learning" alongside the traditional classroom experience. That mission, combined with a focus on social justice and, of course, all the fun to be had in the Florida sun, gives Eckerd its distinctive flavor. As a sophomore puts it, "We have dogs, we have beaches, we have intense science labs, and tons of research opportunities. If you are serious about working hard and studying, and getting tan while doing it, Eckerd is the right place to do it!"

Each year, 20 to 25 top incoming students receive stipends of up to $1,000 to work with leading professors on active research projects.

Overlaps

Allegheny, Goucher, Saint Anselm, Lewis & Clark, Rollins, Cornell College, University of Puget Sound, Roger Williams

If You Apply To ›

Eckerd: Early action, rolling admissions. Accepts the Common Application with supplement. Please consult Eckerd's website for the most up-to-date information regarding standardized test requirements.

University of Edinburgh: See page 372.

Elon University

Elon, NC 27244

With tough in-state competition from the likes of Duke, Wake Forest, and the UNCs, Elon has put itself on the map with aggressive marketing and a classic colonial-style campus. Strong emphasis on global perspectives and active, experiential learning. A counterpart to University of Richmond with medium size, strong preprofessional programs, well-heeled student body, and popularity among Northerners.

Elon University derives its name from the Hebrew word for "oak," and at each year's opening convocation, entering students are given an acorn. Four years later, they are presented with an oak sapling at commencement. It's a charming tradition and a reminder of how things grow and change. With an emphasis on undergraduate research, internships, service learning, study abroad, and leadership—the five Elon Experiences—the university also provides its students with plenty of opportunities to mature, intellectually and socially. "Elon encourages students to not only ask questions but also find complicated and nuanced answers," explains a strategic communications major.

> **"My professors have supported my goals and endeavors and connected me with resources."**

Elon was founded in 1889 and occupies a 656-acre campus in North Carolina's Piedmont region. With apologies to Colby and Miami (OH), it is arguably the most architecturally consistent campus in the nation. Buildings are Georgian-style brick with white trim, and newer buildings have been adapted to modern architectural lines while maintaining this classic collegiate feel. On the north end of campus is Lake Mary Nell, home to an abundance of geese and ducks. Academic buildings are organized in five clusters: a historic quad near a fountain in the older section of the campus; the Lambert Academic Village; the School of Communications, a three-building quad; a business center; and a newly constructed Innovation Quad, home to engineering and other STEM programs. Other recent construction includes a 5,100-seat athletics arena, three residence halls, and a learning center for academic advising and support services.

To graduate, students must complete a core curriculum that includes a broad range of liberal arts and science subjects, as well as an interdisciplinary capstone seminar. All students must fulfill an Experiential Learning Requirement (ELR) by completing at least two of the five Elon Experiences. "I've found the critical thinking and reflection that comes from ELRs to be extremely beneficial for discussing my experiences and strengths in job interviews," says a journalism major. The university offers more than 70 undergraduate degrees. Business majors—especially finance, marketing, and accounting—are some of the strongest and most popular; students also flock to strategic communications and psychology. Programs in drama, education, and biology are strong. The School of Communications is nationally recognized, and its cinema and television arts program benefits from two ultramodern digital television studios. Aspiring engineers may enroll in Elon's fledgling four-year engineering degree program or pursue a 3–2 dual degree with partner institutions like Virginia Tech, Georgia Tech, Penn State, and others.

> **"Greek life and club sports support a robust off-campus social life."**

Elon has an elaborate faculty-managed support system designed to ensure that first-year students don't fall through the cracks. Students begin general studies with a first-year course called The Global Experience, a seminar-style interdisciplinary class that investigates challenges facing the world. Elon 1010 serves as an academic orientation for all first-years; students meet weekly in small groups with an academic advisor and an upper-level student. Undergraduate courses are capped at 33 students, to encourage discussion-based classes and close student/faculty interaction. "My professors have supported my goals and endeavors and connected me with resources to help me succeed both as a student and as a young professional," says an English major.

"We don't have the same level of academic rigor as other private liberal arts schools in the region," remarks an anthropology major, "but we make up for it with our focus on experiential learning." Twenty-four percent of undergrads engage in research with faculty and present their work at a research forum in the

Website: www.elon.edu
Location: Suburban
Private
Total Enrollment: 6,876
Undergraduates: 6,125
Male/Female: 40/60
Financial Aid: 76%
Pell Grant: 13%
Expense: Pr $
Student Loans: 37%
Average Debt: $ $ $
Applicants: 17,834
Accepted: 78%
Enrolled: 12%
Grad in 6 Years: 83%
Returning Freshmen: 88%
Academics: ✐ ✐ ✐
Social: ☎ ☎ ☎ ☎
Q of L: ★ ★ ★ ★ ★
Admissions: (800) 334-8448
Email Address: admissions@elon.edu

Strong Programs:
Finance
Marketing
Accounting
Drama
Education
Biology
Communications
Cinema and Television Arts

A newly constructed Innovation Quad is home to engineering and other STEM programs.

spring. Seventy-three percent study abroad, thanks to the 4–1–4 academic calendar and more than 100 study abroad programs. For career preparation, 84 percent of students complete internships. Elon's eight Fellows Programs, to which prospective students can apply alongside their admissions applications, are designed for exceptionally motivated students. They offer faculty support, scholarships, and peer networks, and current participants highly recommend them as being "profoundly impactful."

All students must fulfill two of the five Elon Experiences—undergraduate research, internships, service learning, study abroad, and leadership.

Given Elon's emphasis on out-of-classroom endeavors, students here tend to have a lot going on. Nineteen percent of undergrads come from North Carolina, with most of the rest hailing from the Northeast, and women outnumber men 3 to 2. Six percent of students are Black, 6 percent Hispanic/Latino, 2 percent Asian American, 3 percent multiracial, and 2 percent international. Somewhat surprisingly for a school that was once a top choice for first-generation college students, only 13 percent of undergraduates qualify for Pell Grants. Lack of racial and socioeconomic diversity is a common complaint, but students say the administration is making efforts to diversify the "fairly rich, white, and preppy campus." Politically, says a senior, the campus "certainly does lean liberal, but there are more conservatives here than you think." The top 15 percent of admitted applicants are automatically awarded the Presidential Scholarship. Overall, merit scholarships average $7,300 per year, and the university awards more than 280 athletic scholarships.

Sixty-two percent of students reside on campus; they are required to do so for their first two years, and many choose to say on campus for all four years. "The new dorms and apartments are gorgeous and nicer than where I'll be living after graduation," says a senior. Options include traditional residence halls, university-owned apartments, and the Global and Colonnades neighborhoods, which feature two dozen living/learning communities, such as Creative Arts, Gender and Sexuality, and Innovation. Designed to bridge classroom learning with social experiences, these communities also serve to bring together diverse groups of students with common interests in a safe space; many participants in the Gender and Sexuality community, for instance, identify as LGBTQIA. Those who move off campus find plenty of options within walking distance. Campus dining, which consists of three dining halls and almost 20 retail locations, receives rave reviews for taste, variety, and accommodations for allergies and special diets. Campus security programs are said to be effective and include escort services, Safe Rides, and the Live Safe app to help students get home safely.

"Elon's best asset is honestly its commitment to engaged learning."

When it's time to let off steam, students generally turn to the active Greek scene—which attracts 20 percent of the men and 39 percent of the women. "Greek life and club sports support a robust off-campus social life for all students to partake in," says a senior, and students report that alcohol policies are loosely enforced. The Student Union Board hosts events every weekend, like bingo and trivia nights, a cappella concerts, and comedy shows. Favorite campus traditions include a weekly College Coffee, where students and faculty mingle over free breakfast and coffee—a tradition since 1984. An exercise science major says, "We have a Festival of Lights before winter break, and a holiday party at our president's house is a hallmark of the holiday season."

A weekly College Coffee where students and faculty mingle over free breakfast and coffee has been a tradition since 1984.

The tiny town of Elon is virtually indistinguishable from the university. "There are three bars in the town of Elon, with little else to do," gripes a junior. Students do take an active role in the community through volunteer projects. Eighty-four percent of students participate in community service, both domestically and abroad, and one student confirms, "Service is one of the bigger components of life as an Elon student." The nationally known Elon University Poll, which the school runs as a public service, tracks political and public policy issues. Road trips to the beach (three hours), the mountains (one hour), and Chapel Hill or Raleigh-Durham (less than an hour) are popular diversions.

Elon competes in the Division I Colonial Athletic Association and offers 17 Phoenix teams. Women's basketball, women's cross-country, men's tennis, and baseball are recent conference champs. Men's soccer, men's basketball, and softball are also strong. The intramural program covers more than 20 sports, and a successful club sports program lets students compete with other schools.

"Elon's best asset is honestly its commitment to engaged learning," says one student. By steadily ramping up its educational offerings, increasing and improving its facilities, and becoming more selective, this supportive liberal arts university is quickly outgrowing its local reputation. "Elon is not just a place," says a senior, "it's an experience and a community."

> ## Overlaps
>
> **University of Richmond, American University, Bucknell, Chapman, Furman, James Madison, William & Mary, Wake Forest**

If You Apply To ›

Elon: Early decision, early action, regular decision. Accepts the Common Application with supplement. Application includes optional field for students who identify as part of the LGBTQIA community. Please consult Elon's website for the most up-to-date information regarding standardized test scores.

Emerson College

120 Boylston Street, Boston, MA 02116

Emerson is strategically located on Boston Common in the heart of Boston's Theater District and within walking distance of many of the city's major attractions. Specializes in communication and the arts. With roughly 4,000 undergraduates, Emerson is a smaller alternative to neighboring giants Boston U and Northeastern. Like most Beantown institutions, it is far more selective than it once was.

Those who aspire to a career in film, television, or marketing may want to start with a four-year stint in Boston. There they will find Emerson College, a small liberal arts school that offers strong programs in communication and the arts, as well as top-notch performance and production facilities. At Emerson, students take notes from professors who also happen to be working directors, producers, actors, editors, and writers. It's an approach that helps talented, city-savvy students find their voices. Emerson has turned out such notable alumni as actors and comedians Denis Leary, Jennifer Coolidge, Jen Kirkman, and Jay Leno. "If you are serious about surrounding yourself with creative people during your college years," says a journalism major, "this is the school for you." Prospective students take note: getting into Emerson requires more than dreams. You'll need a solid academic record as well as plenty of talent.

"The classes at Emerson are more challenging creatively than academically."

Founded in 1880, Emerson is located on Boston Common in the middle of the city's Theater District, and much of the surrounding city is accessible by foot. The campus features a mix of traditional and modern high-rise buildings. The historic Cutler Majestic and Emerson Colonial theaters, the anchors of Emerson's urban campus, have been restored to their original grandeur. The 11-story Tufte Performance and Production Center features rehearsal spaces, a costume shop, a makeup lab, and television studios. Students here also have access to professional-grade equipment

Website: www.emerson.edu
Location: City Center
Private
Total Enrollment: 5,319
Undergraduates: 4,035
Male/Female: 36/64
Financial Aid: 75%
Pell Grant: 14%
Expense: Pr $ $
Student Loans: 59%
Average Debt: $
Applicants: 11,568
Accepted: 45%
Enrolled: 20%
Grad in 6 Years: 79%
Returning Freshmen: 87%
Academics: ✍ ✍ ✍
Social: ☎ ☎
Q of L: ★ ★ ★

(continued)

Admissions: (617) 824-8600
Email Address: admission@
emerson.edu

Strong Programs:
Communication Studies
Performing Arts
Film Art
Visual and Media Arts
Writing, Literature, and
Publishing
Journalism
Marketing Communication
Business of Creative
Enterprises

and digital labs, audio postproduction suites, radio stations (Emerson is home to the oldest noncommercial radio station in Boston), a multimedia newsroom, and a marketing research suite featuring eye-tracking technology and a two-way mirror for conducting focus groups.

Core requirements at Emerson consist of a combination of traditional courses and interdisciplinary seminars. All students must take courses in two areas: Foundations, which includes writing and oral communication, and Perspectives, which includes courses in aesthetics; ethics and values; history; literature; quantitative reasoning; diversity; world languages; and scientific, social, and psychological perspectives. Honors students take intensive seminars in their first three years and complete a senior thesis.

Undergraduates may choose from 25 majors in communication and the arts, ranging from stage and screen design technology and business of creative enterprises to communication disorders and journalism. Performance-related majors, such as acting and musical theatre, tend to be the most popular, along with visual and media arts; writing, literature, and publishing; journalism; and marketing communication. An entrepreneurship minor features a business plan competition known as the Entrepreneurship Exposition; students vie for thousands of dollars in start-up funds.

In 2020 Emerson completed an agreement with Marlboro College under which Marlboro closed its campus in Southern Vermont and transferred its academic programs to Emerson. Tenure-track faculty at Marlboro were offered teaching positions at the renamed Marlboro Institute for Liberal Arts and Interdisciplinary Studies at Emerson College. The partnership perpetuates Marlboro's innovative approach to liberal arts education, which emphasizes independent study and close student/faculty relationships. Students in the Marlboro Institute design their own interdisciplinary studies major tailored to their unique academic interests and complete a yearlong senior capstone project.

> **"[Professors] always have an ear to the ground for those of us looking for internships."**

"The classes at Emerson are more challenging creatively than academically," says a junior. A media arts production major agrees: "Students are encouraged to try new things and explore new mediums and apply for weird, wacky opportunities." Eighty percent of all classes have fewer than 20 students, and a political communication major says professors "give us real-world perspective and also always have an ear to the ground for those of us looking for internships."

For those seeking a spotlight and stage in a different setting, Emerson offers several global study options, including a semester-long program at Kasteel Well (in the Netherlands), where students are housed in a restored, college-owned, 14th-century castle complete with moats, gardens, and a gatehouse. Each semester about 200 students live at Emerson's Los Angeles Center on Sunset Boulevard in Hollywood, where they participate in internships with companies such as HBO, Warner Bros., Dreamworks, and the *Los Angeles Times*. Another semester-long program sends participants to Washington, D.C., for classes and internships. "Above all, cocurriculars are the backbone of an Emerson education," a film production major says. "Classes are thought-provoking, but nothing prepares you for the real world better than actually getting out into the field to practice as much as possible." In an effort to establish a global presence, Emerson's Global Portals initiative allows international students without U.S. passports to earn select Emerson degrees at partner universities in France, Switzerland, and Australia.

Performance-related majors, such as acting and musical theatre, tend to be the most popular.

"The students at Emerson are artistic, passionate, and career-focused," says a student. Adds another, "We have a very large 'hipster' presence at our school." Seventeen percent of undergraduates hail from Massachusetts, and most come from public high schools. Fifteen percent are international. Black students account for

4 percent of the student body, Hispanics/Latinos 12 percent, Asian Americans 6 percent, and multiracial students 4 percent. Despite a noticeable lack of socioeconomic and ethnic diversity, "Emerson is known for being extremely LGBTQ-friendly," says one senior. "Students are always championing liberal social causes." Emerson offers merit scholarships averaging $13,600 to qualified applicants, as well as scholarships to support underrepresented students. There are no athletic awards.

A majority of undergrads reside on campus, since they are required to live in college housing for their first three years. After that, says a junior, "A lot of students take it as a rite of passage to move off campus." Several living/learning communities are available, such as Community Outreach, Digital Culture, and Writers' Block. A senior says campus fare passes muster: "The food is fine, but definitely not a highlight." Each building requires an ID to enter, and public safety officers regularly patrol the streets outside the buildings. "Emerson has had a rocky history with handling sexual assault," reports a junior. Although the college has taken steps to address concerns, another student explains, "The student body believes that there is still more to be done."

"While there is no shortage of on-campus events like comedy shows, performances, and club meetings, a lot of the traditional college nightlife tends to happen in the city or at someone's off-campus apartment," says a sophomore. More than 100 student organizations offer ample opportunity for involvement, including two radio stations, six humor and literary journals, 10

"Emerson is known for being extremely LGBTQ-friendly."

performance troupes, and six production organizations. "Each student is involved in a million different things," claims a student. Popular annual festivities include the EVVY Awards, the largest student-run awards show in the country. Greek life, which attracts a mere 2 percent of Emerson men and 3 percent of the women, is a negligible influence at Emerson. Those seeking a more active party scene head to larger Boston universities on weekends. Students need only step off campus or hop on the T (Boston's subway system) to enjoy other diversions, including theater, museums, the Franklin Park Zoo, the Boston Public Garden, the Freedom Trail, the Boston Symphony Orchestra, and major league baseball at Fenway Park. A student says, "Emerson students live, study, work, and volunteer in almost every major neighborhood and area of the city."

Emerson fields 14 Division III athletic teams, and the Lions compete as a member of the Eastern College Athletic Conference and the New England Women's and Men's Athletic Conference. Solid teams include baseball, softball, basketball, cross-country, lacrosse, and soccer. Students also enjoy an active intramural program and take advantage of the 10,000-square-foot fitness center featuring state-of-the-art equipment, classes, and wellness workshops.

"Emerson prepares creative thinkers to get out into the workforce and make a difference," says one senior. While you are not guaranteed to become the next Oscar-winning director, the possibility is not out of the question at Emerson. And even if a lifestyle of fame is not for you, the excellent education, small classes, and attentive professors may teach you how to be the "star" of your own life story.

Overlaps

Bentley, Chapman, Butler, Rollins, Elon, Boston University, Northeastern, NYU

If You Apply To ›

Emerson: Early decision I and II, early action, regular decision. SATs or ACTs: optional (test-optional applicants are encouraged to submit an optional creative sample or portfolio). Accepts the Common Application with supplement. Additional materials required for applicants to performing arts, media production, comedic arts, and honors programs.

200 Boisfeuillet Jones Center, Atlanta, GA 30322

Often compared to Duke and Vanderbilt, Emory may be most similar to Washington University in St. Louis. Both are in major cities and both tout business and premeds as major draws. Emory's suburban Atlanta location is tough to beat. Attracts a larger contingent from the Northeast than more Southern competitors such as Vanderbilt. Also consider Oxford College, Emory's two-year, small-town liberal arts campus.

Website: www.emory.edu
Location: Suburban
Private
Total Enrollment: 13,310
Undergraduates: 6,974
Male/Female: 42/58
Financial Aid: 60%
Pell Grant: 20%
Expense: Pr $ $ $
Student Loans: 37%
Average Debt: $ $
Applicants: 33,435
Accepted: 13%
Enrolled: 34%
Grad in 6 Years: 90%
Returning Freshmen: 95%
Academics: ✏ ✏ ✏ ✏
Social: ☎ ☎ ☎
Q of L: ★ ★ ★ ★
Admissions: (404) 727-6036
Email Address: admiss@
emory.edu

Strong Programs:
Business Administration
Biology
Chemistry
Quantitative Sciences
Political Science
English and Creative Writing
Nursing
Neuroscience

Emory University may lack the liberal arts prowess of the Northeastern schools with which it competes, but it's a favorite of preprofessional students from both U.S. coasts and around the globe. They come for its size (big, but not too big), location, national reputation, and, increasingly, for its diversity. One sophomore says, "Probably the best part of Emory [is] meeting people from all over the world and all different kinds of backgrounds." Despite the university's academic rigor, students say they feel supported in the classroom, and an atmosphere of Southern friendliness enhances the vibrant campus life.

Founded in 1836 and named in honor of a Methodist bishop, Emory is set on 631 acres of woods and rolling hills in the Druid Hills suburb of Atlanta. The campus spreads out from an academic quad of marble-covered, red-roofed buildings. Contemporary structures dot the periphery of the lush, green grounds. Emory has expanded science and math research facilities, added a performing arts center, and updated freshman housing in recent years. The three-story Emory Student Center houses the campus's main dining facilities, student organizations, and various multipurpose spaces.

> "[Faculty] set aside a significant amount of time for mentoring and helping students."

Emory University offers applicants the choice between two different undergraduate experiences at two distinct campuses: Emory College in Atlanta, Georgia, and Oxford College, 45 minutes away in Oxford, Georgia. Emory College may be best for students who seek a standard four-year undergraduate experience at a research institution that values academic independence and intellectual engagement. Oxford College, which enrolls about 1,000 students, is suited for those who seek a small liberal arts college experience and early opportunities for leadership. Following two years of study at Oxford, all students continue as juniors at the Atlanta campus. Emory's distribution requirements span the liberal arts and sciences, aiming to develop competence in writing, quantitative methods, a second language, and physical education. All freshmen take a first-year seminar that is limited to 15 students each and introduces them to college-level work.

Fifty-seven percent of classes have fewer than 20 students. Just as Emory has invested in its physical plant, the school has spent lavishly in the past to add star faculty members to key departments, such as the late Archbishop Desmond Tutu in the school of theology, the Dalai Lama, Salman Rushdie, and, more recently, Tayari Jones in the creative writing program. "Faculty members make teaching a priority and set aside a significant amount of time for mentoring and helping students with both the course material and with life in general," says one student. Opportunities for mentored research are available in all fields, and a chemistry major says, "Many students find research opportunities through professors they had during their freshman year."

> "We are so close to Atlanta nightlife that many students choose to explore the area."

Business administration is a traditional strength and one of the most popular majors, along with nursing, biology, neuroscience, and economics. Notable offerings

244 EMORY UNIVERSITY

Fiske Guide to Colleges 2024

in biology and chemistry benefit from physical proximity to the federal Centers for Disease Control, while a major in quantitative sciences allows students to combine the study of data science with one of 18 liberal arts tracks, ranging from art history to psychology. Many political science professors have ties to the Carter Center (named for the former president, who for nearly 40 years participated in an annual town hall meeting on campus) and serve as regular guests on nearby CNN. The English and creative writing program is nationally recognized. Emory has received a significant portion of Nobel laureate Seamus Heaney's archive, and its unique Irish studies program is said to rival those of Notre Dame and Boston College. A 3–2 dual-degree program allows students to earn a bachelor's degree at Emory and a bachelor's degree in engineering at Georgia Tech. The Center for International Programs Abroad offers more than 100 study programs on six continents. The 26 percent of students who participate earn Emory credit and Emory grades, and they can receive Emory financial aid, scholarships, and grants.

Emory has spent lavishly in the past to add star faculty members to key departments, such as Tayari Jones in the creative writing program.

"Though Emory is definitely not an easy school, and you have to work hard to earn your grades, overall, everyone manages to find a good balance between class-work, extracurriculars, and socializing," says a senior. Fourteen percent of Emory undergraduates are from Georgia, and 17 percent are international, coming from more than 100 countries. New York, New Jersey, California, and Florida are also well represented. Black students make up 8 percent of the student body, Asian Americans 23 percent, Hispanics/Latinos 11 percent, and multiracial students 5 percent. Politically, the campus is left-leaning, but according to one sophomore, political activism "is not a huge part of campus life." That's not to say students aren't concerned about social issues; in fact, many do service work through Volunteer Emory. Emory meets the full demonstrated need of all admitted students; merit scholarships worth an average of $28,600 are awarded annually, but there are no athletic scholarships. Furthermore, university financial aid packages eliminate or cap loans for students from families who meet certain income requirements.

Notable offerings in biology and chemistry benefit from physical proximity to the federal Centers for Disease Control.

Sixty-two percent of Emory students live on campus; freshmen and sophomores are required to do so. Each first-year dorm has a special living theme, such as social innovation and global cultures, and a theater studies major reports, "The accommodations for first-years are really nice because all of the rooms have been renovated recently, but the sophomore residence halls aren't as nice." Lucky juniors and seniors may hang their hats in the one- to four-bedroom Clairmont Campus apartments, which boast such luxuries as private bedrooms, a washer-dryer in each unit, a rec center, and a heated, outdoor, Olympic-sized pool. In addition to the dining halls, there are small cafés, grills, and food courts on campus. Meals get fair reviews, but a nursing major cautions that "a disproportionate amount of tofu and catfish is served." When it comes to combating sexual violence, one student says, "Emory is very big on education and prevention."

"[Emory] still has the hospitality and charm of a Southern school."

"Most social life takes place on campus, but we are so close to Atlanta nightlife that many students choose to explore the area," says a student. Fraternities and sororities attract 19 percent of Emory's men and 21 percent of the women so, of course, Greek parties are abundant. Other options include concerts, Theater Emory shows, and other events organized by the Student Programming Committee. Alcohol isn't allowed in the freshman dorms, and "anyone caught will definitely suffer consequences," a freshman warns. A very popular highlight of the social calendar is Dooley's Week, a spring festival in honor of the "Spirit of Emory" (the school's unofficial mascot), Dooley, a skeleton who reportedly escaped from the biology lab more than 100 years ago. If Dooley walks into your class, the class is dismissed, and the week culminates with a costume ball in his honor. Freshman halls also have Songfest, a competition where residents make up spirit-filled song-and-dance routines.

The school's unofficial mascot, Dooley, is a skeleton who reportedly escaped from the biology lab more than 100 years ago.

Just 20 minutes away, downtown Atlanta offers a multitude of diversions, from major league sports to plays at the Fox Theatre, exhibits at the High Museum of Art, marine wildlife at the Georgia Aquarium, and shopping at the Lenox Square. Upperclassmen enjoy the Atlanta bar scene, and some local dance clubs host college nights. The Emory Experience Shuttle provides free transportation to popular neighborhoods and festivals. Road trips include Stone Mountain, Athens, Savannah, and the beaches of Florida and the Carolinas.

Emory doesn't field a varsity football team, but the Eagles have produced a number of Division III national champs in recent years, including men's swimming and diving and men's and women's tennis. Emory competes against academic powerhouses such as the University of Chicago and Carnegie Mellon in the University Athletic Association conference. Many students join at least one intramural or club sports team at either a competitive or a recreational level. Popular options include basketball, flag football, soccer, crew, and lacrosse.

While many Southern schools suffer from a regional provincialism, that isn't true at Emory, which blends a focus on teaching and research to nurture creativity and turn out leaders who are highly sought after in the working world—and by postgraduate law, medical, and business programs. As one satisfied student concludes, Emory offers "high academic quality and rigor," yet "still has the hospitality and charm of a Southern school."

Overlaps

Duke, Georgetown, University of Pennsylvania, Vanderbilt, WashU in St. Louis, Johns Hopkins

If You Apply To ›

Emory: Early decision I and II, regular decision. Accepts the Common Application with supplement. Please consult Emory's website for the most up-to-date information regarding standardized test requirements.

Eugene Lang College of Liberal Arts

65 West 11th Street, New York, NY 10011

Home to nearly 1,700 street-savvy, freethinking urbanites, Eugene Lang College is becoming increasingly popular as an alternative to much larger neighbor NYU in Manhattan's chic Greenwich Village. Emphasis on progressive critical inquiry pursued in seminar settings. With the city as its campus, Lang offers a less cohesive sense of community than traditional small liberal arts schools. Long-standing international perspective and strength in arts and humanities still predominate.

Website: www.newschool.edu /lang
Location: City Center
Private
Total Enrollment: 1,663
Undergraduates: 1,663
Male/Female: 20/80
Financial Aid: 92%
Pell Grant: 20%
Expense: Pr $ $
Student Loans: 55%
Average Debt: $ $ $

Students seeking a typical college experience—large lectures, rowdy football games, and rigid academic requirements—would do well to steer clear of Eugene Lang College of Liberal Arts, The New School's undergraduate liberal arts college. That's because Lang offers small seminars instead of traditional lectures, individualized academic programs with minimal required coursework, and not a single varsity sport—not to mention an urban campus that reflects the quirky and kinetic atmosphere of Greenwich Village. "We don't want to become business leaders, but instead teachers, community organizers, thinkers, professors, and writers," a junior says. "Students here want to change the world."

Lang fits right in amid the brownstones and trendy boutiques of one of New York's most vibrant neighborhoods. Lang's main hub is a single five-story building between Fifth and Sixth avenues on West 11th Street, although students make use of all 16 of the buildings that The New School occupies along lower Fifth Avenue.

The New School's library is small, but students have access to the massive Bobst Library at NYU, which is just a few blocks away, as is the excitement of Greenwich Village and Washington Square Park. The 16-story University Center offers state-of-the-art facilities, including "smart" classrooms, design studios, a residence hall, and an auditorium. The 301 Residence Hall, a 24-story building housing primarily first-year students, opened in 2021.

The New School was founded in 1919 by a band of progressive scholars that included John Dewey, Charles Beard, and Thorstein Veblen. A decade and a half later, it became a haven for European intellectuals fleeing Nazi persecution, and over the years it has been the teaching home of many notable thinkers, including Buckminster Fuller and Hannah Arendt. Created in 1975, the undergraduate college was renamed 10 years later for Eugene Lang, a progressive philanthropist who made a significant donation to the school. In addition to Lang, today's New School includes a graduate program in social research, a school of management, and various arts and music programs, most notably Parsons School of Design. At night, the Schools of Public Engagement are host to a huge assortment of public lectures and performances, as well as continuing education courses.

> "[We want to become] teachers, community organizers, thinkers, professors, and writers."

The two most distinctive features of Lang are the small classes—89 percent have fewer than 20 students—and undergraduates pursuing their own path of study with minimal general education requirements. As freshmen, students take one year of writing and choose one required first-year seminar from a broad-based menu; the seminar also incorporates workshops on nonacademic concerns and study skills and is taught by a professor who serves as students' faculty advisor. Additionally, all students take two University Lecture courses, choosing from three categories: Tools for Social Change, Introductions to Social Research, and Interdisciplinary Approaches to the Arts and Humanities. In their final year, students take on a senior capstone through a seminar or project that synthesizes their educational experience.

Lang's most popular majors include literary studies, journalism + design, culture and media, psychology, and the arts; economics, theater, and politics are other strengths. Its city location enhances the urban studies program, and the writing minor is highly praised. While introductory language courses are plentiful, upper-level language offerings are limited. The college has, however, beefed up its offerings in global studies and added a minor called "code as a liberal art," which focuses on coding and computational systems in a liberal arts context. Thirty percent of undergrads take advantage of more than 40 joint B.A./M.A. and B.S./M.S. programs, including public and urban policy, international affairs, and arts management and entrepreneurship. "The coursework and expectations are demanding," a senior says, but the focus is on "communal and collaborative learning." A large portion of the faculty consists of part-time adjuncts who hold other jobs in their respective fields. "For the most part, professors here are compassionate and listen intently to student voices," opines a politics major.

The main academic complaint is the limited range of seminars, but outside programs and partnerships offer more variety. Students may enroll in approved classes in other divisions of The New School, including Parsons, and nearly 60 minors offered across the university provide opportunities to study topics like law and social change, sustainable cities, creative entrepreneurship, and capitalism studies. Lang's popular Civic Liberal

> "Professors here are compassionate and listen intently to student voices."

Arts program offers courses that incorporate visiting fellows from community partners, the likes of which have included the *New York Times*, the Center for Traditional Music and Dance, and Brooklyn Grange. Seventeen percent of students study

(continued)

Applicants: 2,643
Accepted: 88%
Enrolled: 18%
Grad in 6 Years: 60%
Returning Freshmen: 78%
Academics: ✐ ✐ ✐
Social: ☎
Q of L: ★ ★ ★
Admissions: (800) 292-3040
Email Address: lang@newschool.edu

Strong Programs:
Economics
Theater
Politics
Urban Studies
Literary Studies
Journalism + Design
Culture and Media
Psychology

Nearly 60 minors offered across the university provide opportunities to study topics like law and social change, sustainable cities, and capitalism studies.

abroad, and semester-long exchange programs are available with the University of Amsterdam, John Cabot University in Rome, and Sophia University in Tokyo, among others.

Lang attracts a disparate group of undergraduates, but most of them can be described as idealistic, independent, and politically progressive. "Students are curious, hipster, artistic, queer-friendly, 'woke,' and involved in their field," observes a senior. Some are slightly older than conventional college age and are used to looking after themselves; 80 percent are female. Twenty percent of Lang's students are from New York, and 8 percent come from abroad. Five percent are Black, 15 percent are Hispanic/Latino, 7 percent are Asian American, and 8 percent are multiracial. Lang admits students regardless of their finances. Merit scholarships averaging $16,700 are offered, but no varsity teams means no athletic awards.

The New School's residence halls accommodate roughly one-third of Lang students. A gender-inclusive housing policy assigns housing based on students' preferred gender pronouns. Off-campus dwellers live in apartments in the Village (if they can afford it) or in Brooklyn (if they can afford it), or elsewhere in the New York City area. Students complain that food in the

"Students are curious, hipster, artistic, queer-friendly, [and] 'woke.'"

Dining Commons, while tasty and healthy, is too expensive, so most opt for the hundreds of delis, coffee shops, and restaurants that line Fifth and Sixth Avenues. Students also report that counseling and other support services need to be made more accessible. "Eugene Lang and The New School do not take sexual assault reporting as seriously as they should," comments a politics major.

Many students cite the school's location as one of its best features. "Whatever is desired can be found somewhere in New York City," says a junior. "It's a nice place to be if you want to party or be a stone-cold intellectual." The social network at Lang is quite small and, like many things, is left up to the student. "Our lack of campus kind of makes all activity 'off campus,' though we do have dances and club activities within the school facilities themselves," a junior says. On-campus activities tend to involve intellectual pursuits, such as poetry readings, open-mic nights, and working on the student newspaper and the literary magazine. A multitude of cultural events, like Bollywood Night and Gospel Night, enhance campus diversity. Students generally avoid drinking on campus. Fifty-seven percent of students get involved in community service. Athletics barely register here, although the school does field a few club teams: men's and women's basketball and co-ed cross-country.

Despite the seeming lack of tradition and typical sense of college community, Lang's stock continues to rise. Students relish the freedom and independence they have here. For a student who yearns for four years of "traditional" college experiences, Lang would likely be a disappointment. But for those desiring an intimate education in America's cultural capital, Lang offers all the stimulation of the city it calls home.

Overlaps

NYU, Fordham, Emerson, Sarah Lawrence, CUNY–Hunter, Pratt Institute, RISD, Columbia

If You Apply To ›

Eugene Lang: Early action, regular decision. SATs or ACTs: optional. Accepts the Common Application.

The Evergreen State College

Olympia, WA 98505

There's no mistaking Evergreen for a typical public college. Never mind its unconventional students; Evergreen's interdisciplinary, team-taught curriculum is unique. To find anything remotely like Evergreen, you'll need to go private and travel east to places like Hampshire or Sarah Lawrence. Accepts just about anyone who applies, and graduation rate is underwhelming. Traditions show a sense of humor.

In "La Vie Bohème," the anthem of Jonathan Larson's rock opera *Rent*, one of the characters asks, "Anyone out of the mainstream / Is anyone in the mainstream?" At The Evergreen State College, the answer has always been a vehement "No!" The school's unofficial motto is *Omnia Extares*, Latin for "Let it all hang out." Founded in 1967 as Washington State's experimental college, Evergreen has narrative evaluations instead of grades and lacks formal majors, and even departments. This system may sound strange, but it works for those seeking the freedom to chart their own course. Where else will you find a criminologist and a theater professor teaching a class together?

Evergreen lies in a fir forest at the edge of the 90-mile-long Puget Sound. The peaceful, 1,000-acre campus includes an organic plant and animal farm as well as 3,300 feet of saltwater beach. Most of Evergreen's buildings are boxy concrete-and-steel creations, though the Longhouse Education and Cultural Center is designed in the Native American style typical of the Pacific Northwest. The college has also built an Indigenous Arts Campus featuring a fiber arts studio and a carving studio. In keeping with Evergreen's progressive nature, all new building projects strive to comply with LEED standards.

> **"If you are someone who doesn't like high-energy debate, you may find yourself struggling."**

At first glance, Evergreen's wide-open curriculum might look like Easy Street. The college operates on 10-week quarters, but the structure of learning is different. Instead of signing up for unrelated classes to fulfill distribution requirements, students enroll in a single coordinated, 12- to 16-credit "program" spanning several disciplines that are often team-taught by multiple professors. Recent program offerings include Advanced Computing and Machine Learning, Psychology and Popular Music, and Business Start-Ups. In addition to professor and self-evaluations, students must write an annual Academic Statement, reflecting on their academic experiences and goals. Upperclassmen may fulfill an Individual Learning Contract developed in partnership with a faculty sponsor, and many complete some form of capstone experience, such as a senior thesis.

Students praise Evergreen's environmental and sustainability studies offerings, which span agriculture, ornithology, and marine science, among others. To supplement their coursework, environmental scientists may also study marine animals while sailing in Puget Sound, spend seven weeks at a bird sanctuary in Oregon, or trek to the Grand Canyon or the tropical rainforests of Costa Rica. The Native American and indigenous studies program is notable, and computer science and various arts programs—dance, writing, visual arts, and media arts—also get high marks. Regardless of what they study, stu-

> **"We have the amazing student-run café, the Flaming Eggplant."**

dents warn that while the integrated approach to learning may improve comprehension and deepen understanding, it likewise means a lot of work. "The academic climate at Evergreen is robust, collaborative, and engaging," says a junior. "It gives

Website: www.evergreen.edu
Location: Small City
Public
Total Enrollment: 1,795
Undergraduates: 1,621
Male/Female: 39/61
Financial Aid: 62%
Pell Grant: 38%
Expense: Pub $
Student Loans: 58%
Average Debt: $ $ $
Applicants: 1,108
Accepted: 99%
Enrolled: 20%
Grad in 6 Years: 43%
Returning Freshmen: 67%
Academics: ✍ ✍ ✍
Social: ☎ ☎ ☎
Q of L: ★ ★ ★ ★
Admissions: (360) 867-6170
Email Address: admissions@ evergreen.edu

Strong Programs:
Environmental Studies
Sustainability Studies
Native American and
    Indigenous Studies
Computer Science
Dance
Writing
Visual Arts
Media Arts

space for both self-directed learning and small learning communities." Many academic programs include a service-learning component, and several faculty-led study abroad programs are available; 8 percent of undergrads study abroad.

Because Evergreen attracts many nontraditional students and students who are older than the typical college freshman, administrators take advising and career counseling seriously. In hopes of improving notoriously low retention and graduation rates, they've also asked faculty members to do more to help students adjust to life on campus. First-Year Experience programs focus on developing skills for college success, such as study skills, health and wellness education, and academic planning. "A goal of the faculty here is to get to know each student personally and to understand their interests and goals," explains a political economy student. Another bonus: because Evergreen doesn't award formal tenure, there's less pressure for professors to conduct research and publish their findings—and less to distract them from teaching undergraduates. Professors who do engage in research often involve students in their work, and students may apply for competitive Summer Undergraduate Research Fellowship stipends.

Evergreen has narrative evaluations instead of grades and lacks formal majors, and even departments.

"Greeners want to be open-minded, intelligent, and actually meaningful to the world in which they live," says a student. Eighty-two percent of Evergreen's students are Washington residents, and less than 1 percent come from foreign countries. Black students account for 5 percent of the student body, Hispanics/Latinos 12 percent, Asian Americans 3 percent, American Indians 5 percent, and multiracial students 6 percent. Thirty-three percent of students identify as LGBTQ, and 42 percent are of a nontraditional age. Liberal views and student activism dominate the campus; "If you are someone who doesn't like high-energy debate, you may find yourself struggling to connect with the school," says a media studies major. Feminists in Solidarity Together, Food Not Bombs, T-Rex (a transgender group), and Black Cottonwood Collective (an anarchist group) represent just a small sampling of the student activist groups on campus. A recently hired vice provost for equity and inclusion is working to address campus culture and climate. Thirty-eight percent of incoming freshmen are eligible for Pell Grants, and the proportion of first-generation students has risen to 30 percent. A limited number of merit and athletic scholarships are available for qualified students. The statewide Washington College Grant provides free or reduced tuition for in-state students from low- and middle-income families who meet certain requirements.

"[Olympia is] a rad little town with its own personality."

Twenty-two percent of Evergreen students, mostly freshmen, live on campus. Students appreciate the amenities in the school's apartment complexes but say the dorms need sprucing up. There's an efficient bus system to get nonresidents to class on time, though it helps to have a car. Evergreen's food service offers a wide variety of dishes. "We have the amazing student-run café, the Flaming Eggplant. They serve delicious, locally sourced food that caters to special diets," cheers one student. Students say campus security is good and although instances of sexual assault are uncommon, one student says, "Evergreen needs to work on reconciling its progressive, liberal image with the way that assaults are actually handled."

Evergreen's mascot is an eight-foot clam named "Speedy" (a nod to the large geoduck clams found in Puget Sound).

Given the pervasive individualism that flavors Evergreen, it's little surprise that the college lacks a Greek system. Still, the housing and student activities offices organize plenty of events—including open-mic nights, soccer and other field games, and parties. Student musicians are often at the center of the social scene, hosting on-campus performances or playing popular "house shows" off campus. "We are in a marijuana-legal state, but you cannot have pot on campus. As you can imagine, this is the most violated rule on campus," quips a religious studies student. The fall Harvest Festival on the college's organic farm is a favorite annual event.

Olympia (population 56,000), the state capital, hardly qualifies as a college town, but it is progressive and open-minded, with art walks through local galleries, coffee shops, clothing stores, co-ops, and a thriving music scene. "It's a rad little town with its own personality," says a junior. The college's outdoor program organizes mountaineering, backpacking, and rock-climbing trips and offers a wide range of gear for rent. Seattle (just over an hour away) and Portland and the rugged Oregon coast (two to three hours away) provide changes of scenery; everything is kept green and lush by the (interminable) rain, which stops in time for summer break and resumes by November.

You may chuckle at Evergreen's mascot, an eight-foot clam named "Speedy" (a nod to the large geoduck clams found in Puget Sound), but the school has an active intercollegiate athletics program. Geoduck teams compete in seven sports in the NAIA Division II Cascade Conference, and men's soccer, men's track and field, and women's volleyball have enjoyed recent success. About a quarter of students choose to participate in recreational or intramural sports.

Evergreen remains one of the best choices for students who see traditional academic structures as too restrictive. Freed from requirements and grades, Greeners delight in exploring the connections between disparate disciplines at their own pace. It's a challenging task that requires an ability to focus, but for Greeners, the rewards lie in an education that is personally meaningful and that allows them to develop and express their own identities. "Here you can truly be whoever you want to be," says a junior. "There's really nothing to fit into. There is no box at Evergreen; there's just the experience of being here."

If You Apply To ›

Evergreen: Rolling admissions. SATs or ACTs: optional (test-optional applicants must submit essay). Accepts the Common Application with supplement.

Fairfield University

Fairfield, CT 06824

Strategically located on Long Island Sound near New York City, Fairfield offers a classic Jesuit-style Roman Catholic education. Nursing and business are the biggest academic draws. Lack of big-time sports keeps Fairfield from enjoying the visibility of Boston College or Holy Cross. Minimal diversity, socioeconomic and otherwise, is both a problem and an issue on campus. Lively party scene.

Fairfield University is still trying to move into the same class as older, more revered East Coast institutions founded by the Society of Jesus (Jesuits), such as Boston College to the north and Georgetown to the south. It offers a dynamic living/learning environment that combines solid academics, real-world opportunities in and outside the classroom, and an abundance of community service projects. Priests and lay faculty alike promote traditional Jesuit religious and humanistic values to the largely preprofessional student body, and the absence of Greek organizations is never an obstacle to organizing a good party.

The physical beauty of the university's scenic, tree-lined campus just 60 minutes from Manhattan is a source of pride. Fairfield was founded in 1942 on two adjoining private estates, and the administration takes pains to preserve a lush atmosphere of

Website: www.fairfield.edu
Location: Suburban
Private
Total Enrollment: 5,052
Undergraduates: 4,485
Male/Female: 42/58
Financial Aid: 81%
Pell Grant: 8%
Expense: Pr $ $
Student Loans: 61%

(continued)

Average Debt: $ $ $ $
Applicants: 12,674
Accepted: 56%
Enrolled: 18%
Grad in 6 Years: 84%
Returning Freshmen: 89%
Academics: ✐ ✐ ✐
Social: ☎ ☎ ☎ ☎
Q of L: ★ ★ ★ ★
Admissions: (203) 254-4100
Email Address: admis@
fairfield.edu

Strong Programs:
Nursing
Finance
Marketing
Accounting
Communication
Psychology
Irish Studies
Humanitarian Action

sprawling lawns, ponds, and natural woodlands. Buildings are a blend of collegiate Gothic, Norman château, English manor, and modern. The newest addition is the $51 million Mahoney Arena in the center of campus. Students enjoy a 24-hour computer lab and a Geographic Information Systems lab along with a new building for the business school that includes a big data analytics lab, an entrepreneurship center, a gaming lab, and other high-tech tools.

Students may have difficulty finding time to savor the beautiful facilities. Everyone completes the Magis Core, a classic Jesuit-style liberal arts core curriculum that constitutes about a third of a student's total courseload over four years. The core requires coursework in math, natural sciences, history, social and behavioral sciences, philosophy and religious studies, literature, writing, visual and performing arts, modern and classical languages, and social justice. Freshmen are introduced to Fairfield with a thorough orientation program that includes a series of seminars and events throughout the fall term. A formal academic convocation in the first week of classes features a speaker chosen to reflect the school's Jesuit values.

> "Fairfield's faculty are not only well-versed in their fields but also eager to engage with students."

Fairfield's main academic strengths—and most popular majors—are nursing, business (finance, marketing, accounting, and management), communication, and psychology. Students enrolled in the Dolan School of Business have access to the state-of-the-art Business Experiential, Simulation, and Trading Floor classroom. Irish studies has strong ties to the University of Galway, and Italian studies features links to the Florence University of the Arts. A minor in humanitarian action is an outgrowth of Fairfield's involvement as a founding member, along with Fordham and Georgetown, of the Jesuit Universities Humanitarian Action Network (JUHAN). Students can also join the JUHAN club to organize campus events raising awareness for humanitarian issues, participate in alternative spring breaks, and serve as delegates to the UN Youth Assembly.

In the classroom, says an international studies major, "We are challenged and encouraged to challenge ourselves." There are no teaching assistants at Fairfield, and 40 percent of classes have fewer than 20 students. "Fairfield's faculty are not only well-versed in their fields but also eager to engage with students," says an accounting and finance double major.

Thirty-nine percent of students study abroad through their choice of more than 60 programs. Fairfield administers its own programs in Australia, France, Ireland, Italy, and Spain, and several professors lead short educational tours for credit during the winter intercession, spring break, and the summer. Eleven percent of students join the four-year honors program, and while participants give it mixed reviews, most agree that its best feature is the team-teaching from professors across departments, which lends an interdisciplinary perspective that "challenges you to think critically," according to a senior. Twenty-three percent of students carry out undergraduate research projects, and qualified students in biology, chemistry, and physics are guaranteed the opportunity to do so.

A minor in humanitarian action is an outgrowth of Fairfield's involvement in the Jesuit Universities Humanitarian Action Network.

Twenty-one percent of Fairfield undergraduates are from Connecticut, and most of the rest hail from elsewhere in the Northeast; 3 percent come from abroad. Sixty-three percent are Catholic. The student body leans conservative, but a politics major observes, "Students are not very politically active and do not usually display their opinions on campus." Hispanic/Latino students constitute 7 percent of the student body, Black students 2 percent, Asian Americans 3 percent, and multiracial students 2 percent. Noting that only 7.5 percent of Fairfield freshmen are eligible for Pell Grants, the *New York Times* recently reported that Fairfield has "the lowest percentage of Pell Grant recipients of any college in the United States." A senior comments, "Our university lacks diversity in almost every category"—a nearly universal complaint among the student body. "Anyone who is not white, wealthy, or heterosexual may have a hard time fitting in," cautions a junior. Others report that the student body can be "cliquey." To help students with Fairfield's price tag, the school offers merit scholarships, averaging $18,400 annually, as well as more than 100 athletic scholarships in 20 sports.

Fairfield's residence halls house 78 percent of the student body, and housing is guaranteed for all four years. Several living/learning communities are available for undergrads of all levels and come highly recommended. "Living/learning communities are a great way to meet new people who have similar interests as you," explains a junior. Seniors can apply to live off campus, and the most popular options are the privately owned beach houses and apartments on Long Island Sound made available to students off-season. Meals in the main dining hall get good reviews for taste and variety.

In an effort to enhance the residential nature of the school and at the same time curb the number of rowdy beach parties along the Sound, the university has added more on-campus townhouses and apartments for upperclassmen. The former Jesuit residence has been overhauled and reopened as student housing. Nevertheless, students say their school still parties hard. "The level of alcohol consumption is just a culture at this point and is almost expected," says a sophomore. A medical amnesty policy protects violators from punishment when reporting emergency situations. Counseling services and campus safety receive positive reviews. "Fairfield is proactive from day one about educating students about the issue of sexual assault," reports a junior.

> The Clam Jam beach party with live music, kegs, and food trucks is a favorite annual event.

> "Our university lacks diversity in almost every category."

Party culture notwithstanding, students find plenty of on-campus activities to keep them busy, including a growing number of student organizations to meet just about any interest. Sponsored events range from dances to hanging out at the campus coffeehouse to concerts. The Presidential Ball in the fall is a favorite annual event, along with the Clam Jam beach party with live music, kegs, and food trucks. The Campus Ministry draws a large following, with daily masses, annual retreats, and regular community service work, including many service immersion trips, both domestic and international.

> Boisterous home-court fans, who come to basketball games in full Fairfield regalia, have been dubbed the "Red Sea."

As for the surrounding area, some students say the quaint, wealthy town of Fairfield can feel a bit "snobby," and though they enjoy frequenting the many shopping centers, boutiques, and restaurants, relations with local residents are sometimes strained. Even so, the campus bookstore moved downtown and is becoming a community meeting place. In keeping with Jesuit values, volunteerism abounds, with 56 percent of the student body performing community service. "Fairfield on Fire is a day devoted to service in neighboring towns that is such a huge, inspiring initiative," enthuses a junior. Road trips to New York (an hour by train) and Boston (two hours away) are popular.

> "Fairfield on Fire is a day devoted to service in neighboring towns that is such a huge, inspiring initiative."

The Stags compete in Division I, and women's lacrosse, basketball, and volleyball are recent Metro Atlantic Athletic Conference champions; field hockey and baseball are competitive too. Men's and women's basketball both draw crowds, and the boisterous home-court fans, who come to games in full Fairfield regalia, have been dubbed the "Red Sea." Living up to the Jesuit commitment to sound mind and body, 45 percent of students compete in one of 28 intramural and 26 club sports.

"Fairfield focuses on self-improvement and really allows students to make mistakes and learn from their experiences, both good and bad," comments a junior. Although Fairfield is reflecting seriously on issues of diversity and how to create an inclusive social atmosphere on campus, it remains committed to its Jesuit ideals and to offering an undergraduate experience defined by close bonds with faculty, challenging academics, an emphasis on community involvement, and the holistic development of each student.

Overlaps

Providence, Bentley, Fordham, Elon, Santa Clara, Quinnipiac, Boston College, Villanova

University of Florida

Gainesville, FL 32611

It should come as no surprise that UF is a world leader in citrus science. But add accounting, engineering, and Latin American studies to the list of renowned programs. Among Deep South public universities, only the University of Georgia rivals UF in overall quality. Top-shelf varsity sports teams are a year-round draw, and UF's party-school reputation remains intact. Economic and racial diversity not a strong priority.

Website: www.ufl.edu
Location: Small City
Public
Total Enrollment: 44,091
Undergraduates: 31,023
Male/Female: 43/57
Financial Aid: 89%
Pell Grant: 22%
Expense: Pub $
Student Loans: 27%
Average Debt: $
Applicants: 51,207
Accepted: 30%
Enrolled: 44%
Grad in 6 Years: 91%
Returning Freshmen: 97%
Academics: ✍ ✍ ✍ ✍
Social: 🐦 🐦 🐦 🐦 🐦
Q of L: ★ ★ ★ ★
Admissions: (352) 392-1365
Email Address: webrequests@
  admissions.ufl.edu

Strong Programs:
Engineering
Accounting
Prepharmacy
Entomology
Latin American Studies
Journalism
Communications
Business

Set on 2,000 acres of rolling, heavily forested terrain in north-central Florida, the University of Florida is an athletic powerhouse, and administrators are working hard to gain the same level of national recognition for their academic offerings as well. With roughly 31,000 full-time undergraduates, the school is already massive and continues to become more so as it adds scores of new faculty in areas such as artificial intelligence, food security, big data, and drug discovery. While some students certainly get lost in the shuffle, those who can navigate the bureaucratic red tape will find ample resources at their fingertips. The state's flagship university, founded in 1853, has become more selective in its admissions—especially for out-of-staters—and continues to wage an aggressive campaign against its long-standing tradition of free-flowing alcohol.

UF's campus has more than 20 buildings on the National Register of Historic Places. Most are collegiate Gothic in style—redbrick with white trim. They're augmented by more modern facilities, such as Hernandez Hall, a 110,000-square-foot chemistry building. UF's research capabilities and equipment are likewise impressive and a boon to aspiring physicians and scientists. Cypress Hall is one of only a few residence halls in the nation designed specifically to accommodate students with severe physical impairments. The $150 million Malachowsky Hall for Data Science and Information Technology, a high-tech hub for the university's expanding initiatives in artificial intelligence, data science, and cyber systems, opened in 2023.

> **"[The quality of instruction] ramps up significantly in more specialized courses."**

Academically, UF's strongest programs are those with a preprofessional bent, including engineering, accounting, and prepharmacy. To balance students' preprofessional coursework, the UF Quest general education program requires students to take a Quest Humanities course and a Quest Natural or Social Science course, along with engaging in experience-based learning. Popular majors include biology, computer science, psychology, and finance; entomology and Latin American studies are specialties. Students also give high marks to the College of Journalism and Communications, which boasts the lavish Innovation News Center that houses the college's news, weather, and sports operations. The Graham Center for Public Service trains students in languages, culture, and other skills vital to careers in public service.

Top incoming freshmen are invited into the Honors Program, where they live together in a residential college and take honors sections of standard academic subjects and special interdisciplinary courses, most of which are limited to 25 students. The Innovation Academy offers another distinct living/learning opportunity for undergraduates with a spring-summer schedule, offering options for internships and research in the fall. It draws students from more than 30 majors with one common minor: innovation. Overall, 69 percent of UF's undergraduates conduct research, while 14 percent study abroad through university-sponsored, exchange, and affiliate programs all over the world.

UF's academic climate is intense and collaborative. "Closer to midterms and final exams, campus feels constricted and very tense, with everyone huddled in libraries. However, around football season, campus tends to be more relaxed," says one political science major. Despite the university's huge size, 55 percent of all undergraduate classes have fewer than 20 students. Some students say they have to climb a mountain of bureaucracy if a course they need is full, but the administration reports that UF has hired 500 new faculty to further reduce class sizes and improve undergraduate student/faculty ratios. Professors often have deep professional experience and bring enthusiasm to their work, though students often find teaching assistants behind lecterns. A junior says, "The quality of instruction is somewhat low in introductory classes but ramps up significantly in more specialized courses."

> "[Getting involved is] a surefire way to find a mini-community in a university that can be dauntingly massive."

Students describe their classmates as "very outgoing and friendly" and "leadership-oriented." UF is Florida's flagship university, and 88 percent of undergraduates hail from the Sunshine State, while 2 percent come from overseas. Black students represent 5 percent of the student body, Asian Americans 10 percent, Hispanics/Latinos 24 percent, and multiracial students 5 percent. Students say there is a mix of political views on campus, and racial tensions can occasionally flare up. One first-generation student of color remarks, "It's great to be a Gator, but it's hard to not be represented on this campus." UF offers more than 250 athletic scholarships as well as thousands of merit scholarships averaging $4,300. The university has also raised special funds for financial aid for students from low-income families.

Undergrads typically live on campus during their freshman year but then move out after that, for the sake of more space and privacy; overall, 22 percent of students stay on campus. Dorms are described as comfortable, and a senior advises, "It is great to live on campus for at least one year to really immerse oneself in the UF experience and for simple convenience." Dining halls get mixed reviews, but students agree that suitable provisions are made for vegetarians and vegans. Campus security draws praise, thanks to a robust police presence and a late-night "Later Gator" transportation system. "The STRIVE center works to educate the student body against sexual assault and other sexual violence on campus," notes a sociology and women's studies major.

Students at UF have more than 900 student organizations to choose from, and a psychology major says, "Getting involved on campus takes time, but it's a surefire way to find a mini-community in a university that can be dauntingly massive." Sixteen percent of UF's men and 23 percent of the women go Greek; rush is held before classes start in the fall and again in the spring. Students report that "elitism" of Greek groups and the

> "Gainesville is an awesome, young town that is perfectly suited for college students."

outsize influence they have on campus life, especially student government, are common complaints. UF students have a well-deserved national reputation for knowing how to party, but the binge-drinking rate has fallen sharply as a result of tough enforcement of zero-tolerance campus policies, including a ban on drinking games. A senior points out that "off-campus parties are certainly a fixture" of the social scene, especially in the Midtown area across from the football stadium.

The $150 million Malachowsky Hall is a high-tech hub for the university's expanding initiatives in artificial intelligence, data science, and cyber systems.

The annual homecoming extravaganza, known as "Gator Growl," is billed as the biggest student-run pep rally in the country.

Gainesville, a city of about 140,000 between the Atlantic Ocean and the Gulf of Mexico, largely revolves around the university. "Gainesville is an awesome, young town that is perfectly suited for college students who wish to relax and unwind," a student says. There are plenty of stores, restaurants, and bars, as well as a sports arena and the Center for Performing Arts, which brings in world-class symphony orchestras, Broadway plays, opera, and large-scale ballet productions. The university owns a nearby lake, which is "great for lazy Sundays" and more vigorous water sports, and there's a plethora of parks, forests, rivers, and streams for backpacking, camping, and canoeing. Orlando and the beaches of St. Augustine and Jacksonville are also popular destinations.

Sports are a year-round obsession here, and the students go wild anytime the Division I Gators take to the court, field, or gridiron, especially when they're squaring off against rivals Florida State or the University of Georgia. The annual homecoming extravaganza, known as "Gator Growl," is billed as the biggest student-run pep rally in the country. The university fields 19 varsity teams, most of which compete in the ferocious Southeastern Conference. Men's tennis and women's indoor track and field recently won national titles. Men's swimming and diving and women's gymnastics, softball, and lacrosse are recent conference champions. More than 40 intramural leagues and tournaments are offered, as well as nearly 50 club sports, and for those who don't want to join a team, the 60,000-square-foot fitness park offers aerobics classes, martial arts, strength training equipment, and squash and racquetball courts.

For some students, Florida's sheer size is overwhelming. For others, it's a drawing card that means plenty of opportunities to pursue their interests or find new ones. Combine great weather with nationally recognized programs in engineering and business and nationally ranked athletic teams, and it's easy to see why Sunshine State natives like to study here.

If You Apply To ›

Florida: Regular decision. SATs or ACTs: required. Accepts the Common Application. Apply to particular school within UF.

Florida Institute of Technology

Melbourne, FL 32901

Florida Tech is practically a branch of the nearby Kennedy Space Center, so aeronautical science, aviation, and aerospace engineering are popular specialties. The Atlantic Ocean is close at hand, making the school an ideal spot for marine biology and ocean engineering. The only geographical drawback is the occasional early-fall hurricane evacuation. Florida Tech is the smallest of the major technical institutions in the Southeast. Strong international flavor.

Students at the Florida Institute of Technology can explore the endless depths of the ocean or shoot for the stars. Located just 40 minutes from one of NASA's primary launch pads, Florida Tech is a child of the nation's space program and the only independent technological university in the Southeast. The school's subtropical setting is perfect for scientific research and study in oceanography, meteorology, marine biology, and environmental science. It comes as no surprise that some of the most cutting-edge work in space and water-related sciences happens here.

The combination of academic excellence and a convenient central Florida location draws students to this high-flying and innovative school.

Founded in 1958 to meet the academic needs of engineers and scientists working at what is now the Kennedy Space Center, Florida Tech's 130-acre contemporary campus features a botanical garden and an aquatic center. Campus architecture ranges from traditional redbrick to modern. The L3Harris Student Design Center is a high-tech space that serves seniors working on capstone projects in engineering and science. Opened in 2022, the $18 million Nelson Health Sciences building has expanded opportunities for undergraduate education and research in biomedical engineering and biomedical sciences.

If you're considering Florida Tech, make sure you have a strong background in math and science, especially chemistry and physics. Everyone must take courses in communication, physical or life science, mathematics, humanities, and social sciences and demonstrate proficiency in the technologies pertinent to their chosen major. All majors include hands-on projects and capstone requirements. Almost all freshmen take part in the University Experience course, which helps them adapt to college life. Popular majors include aerospace engineering, mechanical engineering, computer science, biomedical engineering, and electrical engineering. Sustainability studies is one of Florida Tech's fastest-growing majors, and astrobiology is the first undergraduate program of its kind. Prospective aviation students can major in aviation management, aviation meteorology, aviation human factors and safety, and aeronautical science—all of which are offered with or without a flight option. The flight school has a modern fleet of more than 40 airplanes and 11 flight-training simulators.

"Students here want to spend extra time in the library."

The academic climate is rigorous, but Florida Tech students enjoy rising to the challenge. "Students here want to spend extra time in the library or take those unpaid undergrad research positions," asserts a senior. Half of the classes have fewer than 20 students, and the majority are taught by full professors. "The professors here are always open to getting to know students personally, and they encourage questions and interaction in class," says a software engineering major. In a move designed to elevate its national standing, Florida Tech now offers faculty tenure. Students in the Honors College work to achieve one of three tiers of recognition, depending on GPA and the number of honors credits completed: Mercury (honors), Gemini (high honors), and Apollo (highest honors). Research opportunities are available at the Indian River Lagoon or on the RV *Delphinus*, a 60-foot research boat owned by the school. Established in collaboration with Apollo 11 astronaut Buzz Aldrin, the Aldrin Space Institute conducts research and development intended to support an eventual human settlement on Mars. The ProTrack cooperative education program allows students in the College of Engineering and Science to complete three semester-long paid work experiences. Study abroad options are available in Oxford, England, and other locales, although only 6 percent of undergrads take advantage of them.

"We are a space school," comments a psychology major. "Everyone knows about and follows advances in space technology in some way." Forty-two percent of Florida Tech students are Florida natives, and at 19 percent, the school's international population is huge. "It is a microcosm of intelligent people representing 100 countries," says a sophomore. "It's like traveling the world in four years." Black students represent 5 percent of the student body, Asian Americans 2 percent, Hispanics/Latinos 12 percent, and multiracial students 3 percent. The proportion of women is low even by techie school standards. Florida Tech offers merit scholarships averaging $15,800 and nearly 90 athletic scholarships.

Forty-seven percent of students make their home in Florida Tech's modern dorms, which an aviation management major calls "very comfortable." Freshmen

(continued)

Financial Aid: 83%
Pell Grant: 23%
Expense: Pr $
Student Loans: 47%
Average Debt: $ $ $ $
Applicants: 10,650
Accepted: 66%
Enrolled: 11%
Grad in 6 Years: 66%
Returning Freshmen: 82%
Academics: ✑ ✑ ✑
Social: ☎ ☎ ☎
Q of L: ★ ★ ★
Admissions: (800) 888-4348
Email Address: admission@ fit.edu

Strong Programs:
Aviation
Aerospace Engineering
Marine Biology
Ocean Engineering
Astrobiology
Mechanical Engineering
Computer Science
Biomedical Engineering

The flight school has a modern fleet of more than 40 airplanes and 11 flight-training simulators.

are required to live on campus in large double rooms or suite-style accommodations. Four-student apartments are available to a small percentage of qualifying upperclassmen by lottery. The meal plan is an open, unlimited arrangement, and students give the food positive reviews for variety and diversity. The Stop It Before It Starts campaign, developed by students as a senior design project, aims to prevent sexual assault on campus.

Watching rocket launches from campus with a trained eye and a cold brew is a treasured pastime. The Rat, a campus eatery with pool tables and big-screen TVs, is a popular hangout, and there are more than 120 active clubs and organizations on campus; gaming, sci-fi, and performance-oriented groups such as Pep Band are student favorites. Fraternities and sororities claim 3 percent of the men and 2 percent of the women, respectively, and students describe the party scene as moderate. "This is a smaller STEM school, so there aren't parties everywhere you turn, but they are there if you look for them," reports a construction management major. Homecoming and the annual International Festival are much-anticipated events.

> "Everyone knows about and follows advances in space technology in some way."

Melbourne is "a nice little beach town," says a senior, and students spend much of their downtime surfing, fishing, sailing, and hanging out at the beach. "Everybody goes to the beach whenever they can, even just to do homework," explains a sophomore. Bikes and skateboards are popular modes of transportation around campus; dining halls and other common areas are equipped with skateboard racks. Public transportation in the area is limited, so students recommend having a car on campus. More diversions can be found in the abundant theme parks of Orlando or at the Kennedy Space Center, each within an hour's drive. Students also hit the road for other Sunshine State cities, including Tampa, Key West, Miami, Daytona, and St. Augustine.

The Florida Tech Panthers field 18 varsity teams that compete in Division II. Men's and women's rowing are highly competitive nationally, and the women's team has claimed four of the last five Sunshine State Conference championships. Men's and women's soccer and swimming, men's basketball, and men's lacrosse are also strong. The university's Precision Flight Team, the Falcons, regularly wins awards from the National Intercollegiate Flying Association. The expanding intramural and club sports programs offer sports like soccer, flag football, and cricket.

Whether it's surveying the sky 30,000 feet above or marine coral 50 feet below the surface of the sea, students at Florida Tech get hands-on experience that serves to sharpen the school's already specialized, high-quality academics—all in a small, more personal setting. The administration continues to focus on capital improvements, sponsor cutting-edge research, and embrace global diversity. And with beaches and amusements close at hand, students can have some real fun in the sun while they prepare for high-flying or low-lying careers.

Overlaps

Embry-Riddle Aeronautical, Worcester Polytechnic, Illinois Institute of Technology, Caltech, Stevens Institute of Technology, Rochester Institute of Technology, University of Central Florida, University of Florida

If You Apply To ›

Florida Tech: Rolling admissions. SATs or ACTs: required. Accepts the Common Application with supplement.

Florida Southern College

111 Lake Hollingsworth Drive, Lakeland, FL 33801

FSC combines top-ranked Division II athletics, strong career-oriented programs, an active Greek system, and a picturesque campus that doubles as a Frank Lloyd Wright museum. Centrally located between Tampa and Orlando. Competes with Rollins and Eckerd among leading liberal arts schools in the Southeast.

Since its founding in 1883, Florida Southern College has been committed to providing students with a solid liberal arts foundation and exceptional signature programs. Students enjoy a bevy of academic choices, including outstanding preprofessional programs, extensive internship opportunities, and a vigorous study abroad program. They also appreciate the college's attractive setting and its mission to develop well-rounded graduates. The college is affiliated with the United Methodist Church, to which 5 percent of students belong.

Situated on 113 acres overlooking pristine Lake Hollingsworth, Florida Southern is home to the world's largest single-site collection of structures designed by iconic architect Frank Lloyd Wright. The campus features 12 original Wright structures, as well as the Usonian Faculty House, which the college constructed in 2013 based on Wright's 1939 design for single-family faculty housing and which serves as a museum and welcome center for the college's architectural tourism. Wright's Annie Pfeiffer Chapel is a popular meeting and performance venue. The campus also houses several buildings designed by Robert A. M. Stern, former dean of the Yale School of Architecture, including the Becker Business Building. The recently opened Weinstein Computer Sciences Center features high-tech classrooms, workshops, and study spaces.

> **"FSC is a huge advocate for engaged learning."**

Florida Southern's core curriculum is based on student learning outcomes in eight areas, ranging from critical and creative thinking to effective communication to personal and social responsibility. Most classes meet for four hours a week, with at least one of those hours fully devoted to engaged learning techniques such as debate, small-group discussions, case studies, and research. As part of the required Passport Program for student involvement, students attend a minimum of six events every year, choosing from more than 300 options across six Passport categories: school pride, learning beyond the classroom, fine arts, service and diversity, health and wellness, and pathways to profession.

FSC students may choose from more than 70 undergraduate programs. The most popular majors include business administration, psychology, nursing, biology, elementary education, computer science, and accounting; all are among the college's strongest programs. The premed program boasts an exceptional placement rate in medical, dental, and pharmacy schools nationwide. Unique at the undergraduate level, a major in citrus and horticultural science involves plenty of hands-on experience thanks to FSC's on-campus collection of citrus trees. In addition to seven majors, the Barnett School of Business and Free Enterprise offers minors in entrepreneurship, eSports management, and healthcare management.

> **"The school sponsors various bimonthly wellness trips that vary from paintball to snorkeling with manatees."**

Dual-degree programs are available in engineering with Washington University in St. Louis and in pharmacy with Lake Erie College of Osteopathic Medicine.

"We have a very relaxed academic climate," says a senior. "FSC is a huge advocate for engaged learning, so we always end up working in groups, creating

Website: www.flsouthern.edu
Location: Small City
Private
Total Enrollment: 3,004
Undergraduates: 2,646
Male/Female: 36/64
Financial Aid: 99%
Pell Grant: 32%
Expense: Pr $
Student Loans: 87%
Average Debt: $ $
Applicants: 10,759
Accepted: 61%
Enrolled: 12%
Grad in 6 Years: 68%
Returning Freshmen: 79%
Academics: ✐ ✐ ✐
Social: ☎ ☎ ☎
Q of L: ★ ★ ★
Admissions: (863) 680-4131
Email Address: fscadm@ flsouthern.edu

Strong Programs:
Business Administration
Psychology
Nursing
Biology
Elementary Education
Computer Science
Accounting
Citrus and Horticultural Science

a very collaborative culture." Fifty-seven percent of classes enroll fewer than 20 students, and students praise professors for their accessibility. "The faculty take time to get to know the students," comments a criminology major. Students are bullish about FSC's career services. Says an interpersonal and organizational communication major, "The Career Center is the *best* resource on campus. They offer résumé building, [mock] interviews, and many more things to help you with your future career."

The premed program boasts an exceptional placement rate in medical, dental, and pharmacy schools nationwide.

All FSC students are guaranteed an internship, and 60 percent avail themselves of this opportunity. Students have interned with Charles Schwab, the Kennedy Center, OPEC, Fox News, the Walt Disney Company, NASA, and scores of other organizations. Sixty-eight percent of students go abroad, mostly through the Junior Journey program, which guarantees all full-time undergraduates a short-term travel-study experience, often at no additional cost. Students may embark on faculty-led trips in May or during academic breaks to domestic and international locales such as Alaska, the Bahamas, Spain, and Japan. Traditional study abroad options are available as well. Qualified students may enroll in the highly selective Honors Program, which offers specialized gen-ed courses. Thirty-seven percent of students carry out undergraduate research projects during their time at FSC, usually as part of a senior capstone course. More than 100 students present their research and creative projects every year at Fiat Lux (Latin for "Let there be light"), the college's annual celebration of undergraduate work.

Florida Southern students are "very down-to-earth and easy to get along with," says one denizen. Sixty-one percent of students hail from Florida; 3 percent are international. Black students account for 6 percent of the population, Asian Americans 3 percent, Hispanics/Latinos 16 percent, and multiracial students 2 percent. "While the school is mostly conservative (as one might expect of a school in central Florida), students are generally tolerant of their peers' political opinions," reports an environmental studies major. The college awards merit scholarships averaging $26,200, as well as talent awards and 267 athletic scholarships.

"Parties are often very inclusive."

Seventy-eight percent of FSC undergrads reside in student housing. First-year students live together in dedicated residence halls, while upperclassmen may choose from a variety of living arrangements, including college-owned apartments within walking distance of the campus. According to one student, some residential buildings "could be updated to be more modern." The cafeteria serves up "average" fare, including special options for vegetarians and vegans. Students report feeling safe on campus, and the "Just Ask" initiative aims to educate the community on preventing sexual assault and gender-based discrimination.

The Junior Journey program guarantees all full-time undergraduates a short-term travel-study experience, often at no additional cost.

The social scene is active on campus, with frequent cookouts, concerts, sporting events, a farmers market, and activities organized by more than 100 student clubs. "The school sponsors various bimonthly wellness trips that vary from paintball to snorkeling with manatees," adds a student. Twenty-three percent of the men and 26 percent of the women go Greek, and a junior says, "Greek life definitely defines the party culture, but parties are often very inclusive." Alcohol is prohibited on campus, and a senior notes that alcohol policies "are not always obeyed but are enforced." FSC offers a number of traditions, including Southern's Got Talent, Cram Jam during finals week, the Winter Wonderland festival (complete with a Christmas tree lighting and temporary Florida-style snow), and the end-of-year Fair-Well Festival.

Lakeland (population 115,000) offers eateries, malls, movie theaters, and a historic downtown district with unique shops and attractions. "Lakeland is a great college town!" cheers a junior. "There are plenty of hip stores and restaurants." Many students venture out into the local community to volunteer, often through Greek life programs, or to take part in off-campus church services. For those with access to wheels, popular road trips include excursions to the Gulf Coast's sandy beaches, Orlando's famed theme parks, or the Florida Keys.

The Florida Southern Moccasins (the snake, not the footwear) field 22 varsity teams, most of which compete in Division II as a member of the Sunshine State Conference. In addition, three club sports compete at the varsity level: equestrian, eSports, and men's ice hockey. Men's swimming and women's lacrosse have claimed recent conference titles. Other competitive "Mocs" teams include men's and women's basketball, men's cross-country, baseball, and women's volleyball. "Our athletes dominate Division II sports every year," boasts one student, and Rollins and the University of Tampa are the Mocs' chief rivals. Intramural sports and activities sign up 23 percent of undergraduates; the most popular activities include flag football, volleyball, basketball, floor hockey, and Wiffle ball.

Florida Southern has a lot going for it. Despite the ubiquitous college student laments of limited parking and so-so food, most are quick to point out that they have access to strong academic programs, championship athletics, and all the sun and fun a person could want. "Florida Southern College is a great community where students can grow academically, socially, and emotionally," says one senior.

Overlaps

University of Tampa, Rollins, High Point, Stetson, Elon, Eckerd, Florida State, University of Florida

If You Apply To ›

Florida Southern: Early decision, early action, regular decision. Accepts the Common Application with supplement. Please consult Florida Southern's website for the most up-to-date information regarding standardized test requirements.

Florida State University

A2500 University Center, Tallahassee, FL 32306

Located in Florida's down-home panhandle, FSU is far from the glitz of South Beach. The College of Motion Picture Arts is among the best around, and business and the arts are also strong. Big emphasis on undergraduate research. Location in the state's capital is an asset. Notable programs include several living/learning options for freshmen.

At Florida State University, you could have a Nobel laureate for a professor, study in one of the finest science facilities in the Southeast, or network at the state capitol. While the choices are plentiful here, the pace of life makes it possible to taste a little of everything: a wide array of solid academic options, blistering Florida sunshine, and plenty to do, from football to Tallahassee hangouts. "There is a relaxed feel to campus that makes FSU the cool, laid-back friend of the Florida university system," says a junior.

FSU is located in the "Other Florida": the one with rolling hills, flowering azaleas and dogwoods, and a canopy of moss-draped oaks. Glistening Gulf of Mexico waters are only half an hour away. Situated on 485 compact acres, the main campus features collegiate Jacobean structures surrounded by plenty of shade trees, with some modern facilities sprinkled in. A massive, $125 million expansion and renovation of the Oglesby Student Union was completed in 2022, offering new and improved dining facilities, spaces for student clubs, the campus bookstore, a nightclub/music venue, a 12-lane bowling alley, and more.

Website: www.fsu.edu
Location: Small City
Public
Total Enrollment: 36,683
Undergraduates: 30,065
Male/Female: 42/58
Financial Aid: 62%
Pell Grant: 25%
Expense: Pub $
Student Loans: 39%
Average Debt: $
Applicants: 65,256
Accepted: 37%
Enrolled: 32%

(continued)

Grad in 6 Years: 83%
Returning Freshmen: 94%
Academics: ✍ ✍ ✍
Social: ☎ ☎ ☎
Q of L: ★ ★ ★ ★ ★
Admissions: (850) 644-6200
Email Address: admissions@
   fsu.edu

Strong Programs:
Motion Picture Arts
Business
Fine and Performing Arts
Life Sciences
Computer Science
Communication
Statistics
English

FSU's newest major is human rights and social justice, an interdisciplinary program based in the religion department.

Study abroad options include time at FSU's branch campuses in England, Italy, Spain, and Panama.

FSU offers nearly 200 undergraduate degrees, the most popular of which are psychology, business-related majors (especially finance and marketing), criminology, and biological sciences. Outstanding programs include music, drama, art, and dance. The sciences are solid, particularly health sciences, physics, ecology and evolutionary biology, and computer science. Communication, statistics, and business have strong reputations in the Southeast, and FSU boasts the nation's first stand-alone college of entrepreneurship at a public university. The English department and the College of Motion Picture Arts have consistently won national and international awards. Engineering programs are a joint effort with neighboring Florida A&M; the FAMU-FSU College of Engineering holds the distinction of being the country's only shared college of engineering. FSU's newest major is human rights and social justice, an interdisciplinary program based in the religion department.

> **"FSU [is] the cool, laid-back friend of the Florida university system."**

Students report that the academic climate varies by department and depends on how much students choose to challenge themselves. As part of FSU's liberal studies curriculum, students must fulfill diversity and civic literacy requirements and take two Scholarship in Practice courses, in which they apply their learning to produce an original project. Sixty-three percent of undergraduate classes have fewer than 20 students, and a psychology major says, "Professors and graduate instructors are amicable, welcoming, and express genuine interest in the success of their students." Freshmen can take advantage of living/learning communities (where students with similar interests or majors live together in the same residence hall) and freshman interest groups (clusters of high-demand freshman courses that have been linked by a theme or academic program).

Honors courses, usually limited to 20 students, offer gifted students the opportunity to rub shoulders with top faculty. Certain students can even earn their degrees in three years. About a quarter of undergrads conduct some sort of out-of-class research, and students highly praise the nationally acclaimed Undergraduate Research Opportunity Program, which connects freshmen and sophomores to faculty research projects for two semesters. Internships and political jobs abound for tomorrow's politicians, since the state capitol and Supreme Court are nearby. For those with wanderlust, FSU offers extensive study abroad programs, in which 15 percent of students take part. Options include time at branch campuses in England, Italy, Spain, and Panama and faculty-led programs in several other countries.

Perhaps not surprisingly, FSU's student body has a distinctly Floridian flavor: in-staters comprise 81 percent of the group and international students just 2 percent. Eight percent of undergraduates are Black, 3 percent are Asian American, 23 percent are Hispanic/Latino, and 5 percent are multiracial. Seminoles are a mixture of friendly small towners and city dwellers, and students say political tastes tend to be somewhat conservative compared to other universities but more liberal than the surrounding town. "Politically minded students have many opportunities to join marches, protests, and campaigns," says a sophomore. Merit scholarships averaging $3,300 are available to qualified scholars, and athletes vie for more than 350 scholarships in 20 sports.

> **"[Professors] express genuine interest in the success of their students."**

Twenty percent of FSU's undergrads live in the university residence halls, some of which have just been built in the last few years. The halls get mixed reviews from students, but a junior says that on-campus living makes for "a fun, smooth first-year experience." After freshman year, students generally move into the ample apartments and houses located within walking distance of campus; the city and campus bus systems are useful for those who live farther away. Students enjoy meals in the

Suwannee Room, a grand Gothic dining hall built in 1913, and they can choose from nearly 30 other dining locations around campus as well. Students cite FSU's student-driven "kNOw MORE" campaign as helping to educate the community about preventing sexual assault.

When they're not studying, FSU students keep busy with films, concerts, and parties in the dorms or off campus. Fifteen percent of the men and 22 percent of the women belong to Greek life; Greek social activities have been somewhat curtailed with the implementation of safety measures intended to reduce the hazards of under-age and binge drinking. With roughly 800 student organizations, there are plenty of other activities for students to get involved in. Many head out to Tallahassee's "beautiful bar patios, art parks, and cafés," says one junior, or to its hopping club scene for nightlife.

The Seminoles compete in the Division I Atlantic Coast Conference. School spirit runs high during football season, and each game is heralded by the beating of the campus spirit drum. The women's soccer team brought home the national title in 2021, and the softball team was national runner-up. Men's and women's track and field and women's beach volleyball have claimed conference championships. Thirty percent of students participate in the school's more than 40 intramural sports and 40 sports clubs.

Florida State remains a solid choice for those seeking knowledge under the blazing Florida sun. The school's laid-back, cheery atmosphere is appealing to many, but make no mistake: students here take their learning and their futures seriously. As one freshman comments, "At FSU, the only limiting factor to your success will almost always be your own motivation."

Overlaps

Indiana University, Michigan State, Iowa State, Kansas State, Missouri State, University of Florida, University of Central Florida, University of South Florida

If You Apply To ›

Florida State: Early action, regular decision. SATs or ACTs: required. Accepts the Common Application with supplement.

Fordham University

Rose Hill Campus: 441 East Fordham Road, Bronx, NY 10458
Lincoln Center Campus: 113 West 60th Street, New York, NY 10023

New York City's Fordham is riding the wave of euphoria for colleges in New York. Though still operating in the shadows of urban icons like NYU and Boston College, Fordham is coming on strong. There is no better location than Lincoln Center in Manhattan, where the performing arts programs are housed. The Bronx campus is less appealing but home to larger programs and adjacent to the New York Botanical Garden and Bronx Zoo.

At Fordham University, the tradition of the Society of Jesus (Jesuits) pervades all aspects of life, from the quality of teaching to the emphasis on personal relationships to the pursuit of both "wisdom and learning," which also happens to be the school's motto. Students benefit from two campuses: the gated Bronx community of Rose Hill and the Lincoln Center facility, just a short subway ride away from the heart of midtown Manhattan. Though 48 percent of the student population is Roman Catholic, there's plenty of variation in ethnic background and in students' political, social, and religious views. Fordham, which dates to 1841, is "more diverse than Boston College, less funky than NYU," says a German and English double major.

Website: www.fordham.edu
Location: City Center
Private
Total Enrollment: 13,375
Undergraduates: 9,409
Male/Female: 41/59
Financial Aid: 82%
Pell Grant: 21%

(continued)

Expense: Pr $ $ $
Student Loans: 57%
Average Debt: $ $ $ $
Applicants: 46,275
Accepted: 58%
Enrolled: 11%
Grad in 6 Years: 83%
Returning Freshmen: 88%
Academics: ✐ ✐ ✐
Social: ☎ ☎ ☎
Q of L: ★ ★ ★
Admissions: (718) 817-4000
Email Address: enroll@
    fordham.edu

Strong Programs:
Business
Performing Arts
History
Biological Sciences
Psychology
Economics
Film and Television
Communication

Students complete four distinctly Jesuit Eloquentia Perfecta (or "perfect eloquence") seminars, including a senior seminar on values.

The 85-acre Rose Hill campus is an oasis of trees, grass, and Gothic architecture; it's close to the New York Botanical Garden and Yankee Stadium and had cameo appearances in films such as *A Beautiful Mind*. Rose Hill is home to Fordham College at Rose Hill, the largest liberal arts school at the university, as well as the primary programs of the Gabelli School of Business. Multiphase construction is ongoing on a $200 million campus center at Rose Hill that combines fitness and dining facilities, student services, and event spaces, to be completed by 2025. The Lincoln Center campus benefits from its proximity to the Juilliard School, the CBS and ABC television studios between 10th and 11th Avenues, and Lincoln Center itself, Manhattan's performing arts hub. In addition to its own liberal arts college, the campus also houses some business programs, Fordham's law school, and three other graduate schools. Shuttles run between the two campuses.

"[Fordham is] more diverse than Boston College, less funky than NYU."

Undergraduate requirements include coursework in English, social and natural sciences, philosophy, theology, history, math/computer science, fine arts, and foreign languages. Students also complete four distinctly Jesuit Eloquentia Perfecta (or "perfect eloquence") seminars, including a capstone senior seminar on values. Freshmen can opt to participate in Urban Plunge, three days of exploring the city's diverse neighborhoods and working on a team service project before the start of the fall semester.

No matter where at Fordham you study, humanities are a good choice. Strengths at Rose Hill include history, philosophy, biological sciences, psychology, economics, and film and television, while at Lincoln Center, theatre, English, and communication shine. The most popular majors across the university are business administration, economics, finance, and psychology. The B.F.A. in dance is offered in partnership with the Alvin Ailey American Dance Theater; students must be accepted both by Fordham and by the Ailey audition panel. Fordham's public radio station, WFUV, offers hands-on experience for aspiring deejays and radio journalists, and there is a TV production studio at Rose Hill. The notable global business program at Lincoln Center engages students in courses about the global dimensions of business and requires a study abroad experience. Rose Hill offers 3–2 engineering programs with Columbia and Case Western Reserve, and both colleges have a 3–3 program with Fordham Law School and a teacher-certification program.

"Fordham offers a good balance between academic rigor and a relaxed atmosphere," says a business administration major, especially since students frequently work together on homework and projects. Fifty-two percent of all undergraduate classes have fewer than 20 students, and professors are praised for bringing much-appreciated professional experience and real-world perspective to the lectern. Helped by alumni connections, business students often obtain internships on Wall Street or elsewhere in the Manhattan financial community. Half of all undergrads study abroad, choosing from 110 programs in 52 countries, including those offered by the university's London Centre.

A political science major says Fordham students are "open-minded and eager to learn about different cultures and perspectives" but are also "opinionated, assertive, and outspoken." This is, after all, New York City. The atmosphere is less intellectual than at nearby Columbia and NYU. Forty-two percent of undergraduates hail from New York State, and many of the rest are from elsewhere on the East Coast; 7 percent come from abroad.

"[Students are] open-minded…opinionated, assertive, and outspoken."

Black students make up 5 percent of the student body, Asian Americans 13 percent, Hispanics/Latinos 17 percent, and multiracial students 5 percent. The university supports a vibrant LGBTQ community, and while it leans left, there is a healthy variety of political views. Hundreds of merit and audition-based scholarships averaging $20,100 are available to eligible students, as well as athletic scholarships in 19 sports.

About half of Fordham undergrads live in the dorms, and all are guaranteed university housing for four years. Those who snag rooms in the two high-rise residence halls near Lincoln Center are saved from the borough's greedy brokers and unconscionable rents. Both campuses offer living/learning communities; all Lincoln Center freshmen participate in the first-year experience integrated learning community, while first-years at Rose Hill can apply for the Manresa Scholars Program, which offers access to academic live-in tutors and a Jesuit priest in residence. Students across the university complain about strict guest policies that require sign-ins and restrict overnight passes to visitors of the same sex. Campus dining is said to need "more dietary options and extended hours," according to a marketing major. Both campuses are safe, students say. "The constant presence of Public Safety and guards at each gate has made me feel very safe and comfortable at Fordham," reports a film and television major.

Students look forward to Spring Weekend, which features a major concert and the Under the Tent dance on Martyrs' Lawn at Rose Hill.

Fordham's Campus Activities Board sponsors events like movies, concerts, and dances on both campuses; there is no Greek system. Says one student, "Parties with alcohol are practically unheard of on campus." Students are far more likely to head to nearby bars, clubs, performances, festivals, and cultural events. "We are in the center of NYC, so there are more than enough options to have a good social scene," enthuses a Lincoln Center student. The Rose Hill campus backs up against the Bronx Zoo and

"Students graduate as experts of the city and have their Jesuit ideals to guide them."

is around the corner from Arthur Avenue, the Little Italy of the Bronx. Both provide welcome weekend diversions. Students look forward to homecoming and Spring Weekend, which features a major concert and the Under the Tent dance on Martyrs' Lawn at Rose Hill. Fordham's Center for Community Engaged Learning helps connect students with local community service opportunities.

The Fordham Rams compete in Division I and the Atlantic 10 Conference (and the Patriot League for football), and its location near the Hudson River has helped to produce the women's rowing Metropolitan champs. Women's softball has brought home several conference titles, and baseball and women's basketball are also competitive. The Lombardi Memorial Athletic Center (named for football legend Vince, an alumnus) supports club sports and intramurals. Perhaps Fordham's most unusual athletic endeavor is Riding the Ram. "Students are expected to climb on the granite blocks and sit on the bronze statue of the Fordham Ram at least once in their time here," explains a computer science major. "However, ride the Ram at your own risk, as you will be reprimanded if caught in the act."

Consistent with its Jesuit tradition, Fordham fancies itself a family. Some things are changing—including its admissions and academic standards, which are inching up, and its national profile, which is also far higher than in years past. What hasn't changed is the idea that diversity and community can coexist, instilling confidence and pride in Fordham students and loyalty in the expanding alumni base. "Fordham University is the Jesuit university of New York," asserts one student. "The bustle of New York City is unlike anywhere else on the planet, and our students graduate as experts of the city and have their Jesuit ideals to guide them for the rest of their lives."

Overlaps

George Washington, Boston University, Syracuse, Northeastern, Villanova, NYU, Boston College, SUNY–Binghamton

If You Apply To ›

Fordham: Early decision, early action, regular decision. Accepts the Common Application. Apply to particular school or program. Theatre and dance applicants must audition. Portfolio recommended for visual arts applicants. Please consult Fordham's website for the most up-to-date information regarding standardized test requirements.

Franklin & Marshall College

637 College Avenue, Lancaster, PA 17604

F&M is known for churning out hardworking preprofessional students. Faces tough competition from the likes of Bucknell, Dickinson, Gettysburg, and Lafayette for Pennsylvania-bound students. Known for natural sciences, business, government, and emphasis on civic engagement. Bases all financial aid on need and meets the demonstrated need of every student. Strong contingent of international students.

Website: www.fandm.edu
Location: Small City
Private
Total Enrollment: 2,127
Undergraduates: 2,127
Male/Female: 44/56
Financial Aid: 59%
Pell Grant: 16%
Expense: Pr $ $ $ $
Student Loans: 54%
Average Debt: $ $
Applicants: 7,720
Accepted: 38%
Enrolled: 18%
Grad in 6 Years: 83%
Returning Freshmen: 91%
Academics: ✍ ✍ ✍ ✍
Social: ☎ ☎ ☎
Q of L: ★ ★ ★
Admissions: (877) 678-9111
Email Address: admission@ fandm.edu

Strong Programs:
Natural Sciences
Business, Organizations, and Society
Government
Computer Science
Creative Writing
Economics
Psychology
Biology

Franklin & Marshall College is set in one of the country's 50 largest metro areas, but you can still enjoy the serene hills of Pennsylvania's Amish country, and you might come nose-to-nose with a horse and buggy. While the city of Lancaster has modernized beautifully, parts of this historic town look much the same as they did when two acclaimed but struggling colleges decided to pool their resources. In 1853, Marshall College (named for Chief Justice John Marshall) merged with Franklin College (started with a donation of 200 English pounds from Ben himself). These days, F&M is trying to modernize, too, particularly by bringing a more international and service-oriented bent to the curriculum.

F&M's 220-acre campus is surrounded by a quiet residential neighborhood shaded by majestic maple and oak trees. The campus itself is an arboretum and boasts 65 buildings of mainly Gothic and colonial architecture. The Blue Line Café and nearby Hartman Green appeal to students seeking a study respite. Other notable facilities include the Life Sciences and Philosophy Building and Martin Library of the Sciences. As part of a decade-long urban renewal project, the college has developed 28 acres of land, once home to aged industrial buildings and rail yards, into a North Campus for athletic fields and facilities. Other recent additions include the $29 million Winter Visual Arts Center.

First-year students are introduced to F&M's academic community through a required Connections seminar, an intimate course that teaches the skills of critical analysis, research, writing, and civil debate. First-years also live together in seminar-based living/learning communities. Additional general education components include writing and language requirements and distribution requirements in the arts, humanities, social sciences, natural sciences, and world perspectives. F&M has long been known for being strong in the natural sciences, its computer science and creative writing programs are on the rise, and the school is now placing more emphasis on service-learning courses in many disciplines. A preprofessional college in line with Lafayette and Bucknell, F&M has an excellent reputation for preparing undergrads for medical school, law school, and other careers. Business, organizations, and society is the most popular major, followed by government, economics, psychology, and biology. F&M also offers several cooperative-degree and domestic-exchange programs.

> **"[The College House system] provides a strong academic and social structure within living spaces."**

Students uniformly describe the coursework as demanding, but a biology major says, "Despite the intensity of the academics, there is not a strong sense of competition." The relatively small student body and intimate class sizes help create a feeling of community between students and professors. A business major says the professors are caring and "make Franklin & Marshall an exciting and comfortable place to learn." More than 40 percent of F&M students engage in directed research under the guidance of faculty, including students in the Hackman Summer Research Scholars program. In the summer, faculty-led study abroad programs head to countries such as China, Italy, Russia, and South Africa, and 43 percent of students study in locations around the world during their time at F&M.

A government major says her classmates are hardworking and "stressed out about academics" but also intellectually curious and welcoming. Thirty-one percent of students hail from Pennsylvania, and 18 percent come from foreign nations. Black students comprise 6 percent of the student body, Hispanics/Latinos 10 percent, Asian Americans 4 percent, and multiracial students 3 percent. Perhaps because most of the community shares a liberal point of view, "intense political debate is uncommon," according to a senior. Fummers do, however, take an interest when it comes to extracurricular activities and social opportunities. The 100-plus clubs on campus attest to that, as does a notably high level of participation in community service activities (70 percent). There are no athletic scholarships, and the school offers financial aid based solely on need, guaranteeing to meet 100 percent of admitted students' demonstrated need.

More than 40 percent of F&M students engage in directed research under the guidance of faculty.

The college requires students to live in college-affiliated housing all four years, and housing options include residence halls organized into five College Houses, apartments, lofts, townhouses, and special-interest housing. The faculty-led College House system "provides a strong academic and social structure within living spaces," says a music and math double major. Boarders eat most of their meals

"We have a stellar reputation and the best faculty."

in the campus dining hall under a flexible meal plan, but students are issued debit cards that they may use at a number of different food stops on campus. A first-year reports, "We have been very informed about the need for consent and respect," but students express dissatisfaction with how the administration has handled sexual assault cases.

Three fraternities attract 12 percent of the men, and seven sororities attract 29 percent of the women. They are integral to much of the nightlife, although the residence halls and student organizations such as the College Entertainment Committee offer a range of alternatives, including concerts and comedians. "Off-campus parties dominate the lives of students on the weekends," one student says. Ben's Underground, a popular student-run nightclub, and Hildy's, a tiny local bar, are also favorite meeting places. The biggest annual event is the Spring Arts Festival, held the weekend before finals, which includes live concerts, student air-band contests, art exhibits, games, booths, and barbecues. Another highlight is Flapjack Fest, when professors serve pancakes to students.

A social highlight of the year is Flapjack Fest, when professors serve pancakes to students.

Lancaster is a historical and well-to-do city located in a larger metro area of more than 500,000. Lancaster offers a 16-screen cinema, scores of shops and art galleries, a historic farmers market, brick-and-cobblestone streets, and a plethora of quaint restaurants and cafés. Students have a measured, realistic appreciation of its urban amenities and rural ambiance. "Downtown is always a fun place to go if you can spend money," says a senior. The Amish culture, although not as visible as some newcomers might expect, draws the interest of some students too. Those with a hankering for contemporary action take road trips to Philly, Baltimore, Washington, D.C., and New York City.

With the exception of wrestling, which is Division I, F&M teams compete in Division III. The college boasts recent Centennial Conference championships in men's and women's lacrosse and men's golf. Varsity squads are called the Diplomats, a moniker that gained currency in 1935 when the football team nearly upset national powerhouse Fordham. The annual football game against Dickinson for the Conestoga Wagon trophy is always a crowd-pleaser. The college also offers a selection of five co-ed intramural sports and 13 club sports, such as cycling, rugby, and ultimate Frisbee, which sign up about a quarter of the students.

At Franklin & Marshall, a happy senior says, "We have a stellar reputation and the best faculty. An F&M education will prep you for any job, and alumni jump at the chance to help." The college's illustrious namesakes would no doubt be proud of the quality academics and ever-evolving opportunities at the institution that bears their names.

Overlaps

Dickinson, Lafayette, Gettysburg, Bucknell, Skidmore, Lehigh, Union College, American University

Furman University

3300 Poinsett Highway, Greenville, SC 29613

Furman's campus is one of the most gorgeous anywhere, with the swans being a particularly elegant touch. With roughly 2,300 undergraduates, Furman is larger than Davidson and half the size of Wake Forest. Academic life includes a strong emphasis on off-campus experiences as well as undergrad research. Furman is relatively conservative, and the student body is predominantly Christian and regional.

Website: www.furman.edu

Location: Suburban

Private

Total Enrollment: 2,370

Undergraduates: 2,278

Male/Female: 40/60

Financial Aid: 83%

Pell Grant: 11%

Expense: Pr $ $ $

Student Loans: 38%

Average Debt: $ $ $

Applicants: 7,174

Accepted: 71%

Enrolled: 13%

Grad in 6 Years: 82%

Returning Freshmen: 91%

Academics: ✍ ✍ ✍ ½

Social: ☎ ☎ ☎

Q of L: ★ ★ ★

Admissions: (864) 294-2034

Email Address: admissions@
furman.edu

Strong Programs:

Business Administration

Chemistry

Biology

Health Sciences

Communication Studies

Politics and International
Affairs

Psychology

History

While deeply rooted in Southern culture and academic traditions, Furman University is seeking to be known as a place where strong liberal arts and sciences, not big-time athletic rivalries or a boisterous Greek scene, set the campus tone. Student diversity is still a work in progress, but a strong sense of community is well established. As one denizen puts it, "I love how Furman builds a community with such a homey feel."

Furman's 750-acre campus is one of the country's most beautiful, with tree-lined malls, fountains, a formal rose garden and Japanese garden, and a 30-acre lake replete with swans and ducks. Flowering shrubs dot the well-kept lawns, which surround buildings in the classical revival, Colonial Williamsburg, and modern architectural styles. Many have porches, pediments, and other Southern touches, such as handmade Virginia brick. Recent campus projects include a renovation of the Clark Murphy Housing Complex.

Founded by Southern Baptists in 1826 and named for a denominational leader, Furman operates under the "semester-plus" system. The school year begins in late August, and the first semester ends prior to the December holiday break. Students begin the second semester in January and then have the option of attending a three-week May Experience in (guess when). General education requirements include a first-year writing seminar and a series of

"Only a handful of labs are taught by teachers' assistants."

core requirements that fulfill the following "ways of knowing": empirical studies; human cultures; mathematical and formal reasoning; foreign language; ultimate questions; and body and mind. Finally, students must fulfill global awareness requirements. The most popular majors include health sciences, communication studies, politics and international affairs, psychology, and history. Business administration is among the stronger programs, along with chemistry and biology. Students in the health sciences program have access to the innovative international health and nutrition program as well as a human performance laboratory. Internships and research opportunities are available through the Institute for the Advancement of Community Health.

Furman's academic climate is challenging. "Furman students all understand that the courses are difficult and seem to commiserate with one another," says one junior. Seventy-three percent of classes have fewer than 20 students, helping students get to know faculty members well, and the Pathways advising program helps freshmen and sophomores stay on track. "All classes are taught by professors, and only a handful of labs are taught by teachers' assistants," says one senior.

The Furman Advantage ensures that every undergraduate will have the opportunity to participate in research, an internship, or study abroad. "I have participated in all three of these areas," explains an elementary education major, "and these opportunities, funded by the Furman Advantage, have added immensely to my holistic learning and development as an individual." Forty-two percent of undergrads conduct research, many assisting professors through paid Furman Summer Research Fellowships. Furman typically sends one of the largest student delegations to the annual National Conference on Undergraduate Research. Internships are popular, with 66 percent of students taking part. Sixty percent of students study abroad through one of two dozen Furman-sponsored programs on five continents, including programs in Iceland, Japan, Belize, and Botswana. Entering freshmen have the opportunity to travel in small groups to an island off the coast of Charleston, the mountains of North Carolina, or even China during the summer before they enroll.

Furman typically sends one of the largest student delegations to the annual National Conference on Undergraduate Research.

Furman broke with the South Carolina Baptist Convention in 1992, but it remains in South Carolina, where religion ranks second only to football as a cultural institution; 79 percent of freshmen identify as Christian. Three-quarters of undergrads hail from Southeastern states, including 27 percent from South Carolina; 3 percent are international. A political science major says, "Students here tend to be sheltered" and "image-conscious." The administration has committed to erasing Furman's traditional image as the "Country Club of the South" and diversifying the school, and the Student Diversity Council promotes such efforts, but they have been slow to bear fruit. "Socioeconomically, Furman generally draws from a more upper-middle-class to upper-class background," reports a senior. Despite the school's location in the South, Black students make up only 7 percent of the student body, Hispanics/Latinos 6 percent, Asian Americans 3 percent, and multiracial students 3 percent. The Task Force on Slavery and Justice seeks to examine and help the community understand Furman's historic ties to slavery. Every year, Furman awards hundreds of merit scholarships averaging $23,100, plus more than 175 athletic scholarships in 18 sports.

"Greek life does tend to dominate life on Furman's campus."

Furman is a residential campus, with 97 percent of students living in university housing, and students enjoy the resulting camaraderie. "The residence halls undergo cyclical renovations such that no one dorm is in disrepair," says a junior. Furman is no longer a dry campus, although the alcohol policy is strictly enforced in freshman and sophomore dorms, where most students shouldn't be imbibing anyway. The atmosphere is more relaxed for students of legal drinking age, who may consume alcohol in North Village, a university-owned apartment complex of 10 buildings for juniors and seniors. Meal plan credits can be used in the dining hall or food court, and, overall, students say campus fare is tasty and diverse. Campus police help provide a relatively safe environment and "are transparent about all sexual assault issues that happen on campus," says a student.

Sixty-seven percent of Furman's students devote spare time to the Heller Service Corps.

When the weekend comes, Furman's Student Activities Board sponsors "free movies, weekend trips, restaurant deals, and huge concerts," says a communication studies major. Fraternities claim 30 percent of the men and sororities 58 percent of the women, and off-campus Greek parties draw crowds. "Greek life does tend to dominate life on Furman's campus," reports one student. "As someone who is not a part of Greek life, I've had to seek out activities on my own. There are a lot of interesting cultural and religious programs on campus, and great outdoor/sporting facilities."

"Downtown [Greenville] is booming and is a really fun place to visit."

"Greenville is a great city that is seeing a large amount of growth," says a senior. "The downtown is booming and is a really fun place to visit." The Peace Center for the Performing Arts, located downtown, brings in touring casts of Broadway shows and other top-rated acts. Sixty-seven percent of Furman's students devote spare time to the Heller Service Corps, which provides volunteers to more than 50 community agencies and organizes the annual Exceptional Adults Valentine's Day Dance for adults with special needs. The best road trips are to the mountains of Asheville (only 45 minutes away), Atlanta (for the big city and shopping, about two hours), and Charleston or Myrtle Beach (four hours).

Furman's athletic teams are the Paladins (after the toughest warrior in Charlemagne's court), and they compete in the Division I Southern Conference. Recent conference champs include men's and women's cross-country and women's tennis. Students happily yell out the school's tongue-in-cheek cheer ("F.U. one time, F.U. two times, F.U. three times, F.U. all the time!") during football games against archrivals Wofford and the Citadel. Two-thirds of the student body plays intramural and club sports, and Greek groups compete annually for the coveted All Sports Trophy. Furman's debate and mock trial teams are both nationally ranked and regularly compete in intercollegiate tournaments.

Three decades after severing its religious ties, Furman is still a largely homogeneous institution, although it continues to evolve. It may call itself a university, but its educational approach is closer to that of a traditional college of liberal arts and sciences, emphasizing broad exposure to many fields, problem-solving, and experience-based learning.

Overlaps

Davidson, Rhodes, Wake Forest, Elon, University of Richmond, Sewanee, Washington and Lee, Wofford

If You Apply To ›

Furman: Early decision I and II, early action, regular decision. SATs or ACTs: optional. Accepts the Common Application with supplement.

George Mason University

4400 University Drive, Fairfax, VA 22030

The largest public research university in Virginia, George Mason offers an alternative to UVA—traditions may still be in their infancy here, but the student body is more diverse, inclusive growth is a dominant value, and the Northern Virginia location is a boon for job and internship seekers. Mason is a bastion of conservative political and economic thought. Big focus on overall student well-being. Nearly half of students start out in community colleges.

Website: www.gmu.edu
Location: Suburban
Public
Total Enrollment: 25,710
Undergraduates: 21,014
Male/Female: 50/50
Financial Aid: 68%
Pell Grant: 28%
Expense: Pub $ $ $
Student Loans: 59%
Average Debt: $ $ $
Applicants: 20,527

Located in the middle of the budding high-tech corridor of greater Washington, D.C., George Mason University features a suburban campus and symbiotic relationship with the surrounding region that contrasts starkly with Virginia's two other major universities, which have operated for many years in the relative isolation of Charlottesville and Blacksburg. Well-established as a center of conservative thinking on social issues, Mason has grown by leaps and bounds for most of the past two decades, largely because of its commitment to extend the benefits of higher education to as many Virginians as possible.

Founded in 1957 as a sleepy outpost of the University of Virginia, Mason became independent in 1972. It sits on a 677-acre wooded campus 20 miles southwest of Washington, D.C., in suburban Fairfax, Virginia. Campus architecture is modern and homogeneous, with lots of brick, glass, and metal, and just about everything is within a 15-minute walk. The campus observatory is second in the area only to that of NASA. The 100,000-seat Eagle Bank Arena hosts both sporting and entertainment events. Although Mason's campus doesn't have the colonial ambiance or tradition of William & Mary or UVA, its namesake does have the same Old Virginia credentials. George Mason drafted Virginia's influential Declaration of Rights in 1776, and he later opposed ratification of the federal Constitution because there was no Bill of Rights attached.

Though it is growing up fast, Mason shows its youth in a number of ways. Programs taken for granted at more established universities are just hitting their stride here. Its physical plant is expanding, thanks largely to a small but growing endowment, funding from the State of Virginia, and some public-private partnerships. Horizon Hall, a six-story, $108 million building housing the College of Humanities and Social Sciences, opened in 2021, part of a spate of construction.

> **"GMU does a particularly good job of providing support and resources for off-campus, transfer, and adult students."**

Through the university libraries, which are also growing, students have access to nearly two million electronic resources and borrowing privileges of the Washington Research Library Consortium.

Mason has standard general education requirements, but students who prefer to find their own way can design a major under the bachelor's in integrative studies, which teams small groups of faculty and undergraduates on projects that can be easily connected to the world outside the campus. Nontraditional students who enter Mason have the option of creating their own degree in the bachelor of individualized studies program. All students must complete a capstone or synthesis course in their major.

Mason has had two Nobel laureates in its libertarian-friendly economics department, which is probably its strongest. Not surprisingly, given the school's location, the Schar School of Policy and Government also receives accolades. Business-related majors are popular, along with information systems; computer science; accounting; criminology, law, and society; and biology. Other notable majors include the nation's first conflict analysis and resolution major, fast-growing computer game design and cybersecurity engineering majors, and forensic science. The Mercatus Center, which has been supported with tens of millions of dollars from billionaire Charles Koch and his late brother David, is nationally recognized for its espousal of free market economic principles.

The academic climate varies by program, students say, and classes are often fairly large, but 44 percent have fewer than 20 students. All faculty members are required to teach, and according to a global affairs major, the majority are "flexible, accommodating, and helpful." Mason's Center for the Advancement of Well-Being is a national leader in encouraging students, faculty, and staff members to live more mindful and meaningful lives. "GMU does a particularly good job of providing support and resources for off-campus, transfer, and adult students," notes a computer science major.

Students here are decidedly career focused: 83 percent enter the working world directly after graduation. A computer science major comments, "A lot of people here see their degree as a means to an end, and they care more about getting a good job after graduation than they do about getting perfect grades." Mason does offer its undergrads nearly 70 accelerated master's degree programs for those interested in graduate study.

> **"Our student life offices are very active."**

The Smithsonian-Mason School of Conservation allows students to live on-site at the Smithsonian Conservation Biology Institute of the Smithsonian's National Zoo and study global conservation issues and civic concerns. About half of students participate in Mason's strong undergraduate research program, and an Honors College is available to top achievers. For those seeking

(continued)

Accepted: 91%
Enrolled: 21%
Grad in 6 Years: 70%
Returning Freshmen: 84%
Academics: ✍ ✍ ✍
Social: ☎ ☎
Q of L: ★ ★
Admissions: (703) 993-2400
Email Address: admissions@gmu.edu

Strong Programs:
Economics
Government
Business
Information Systems
Computer Science
Accounting
Criminology, Law, and Society
Biology

Mason offers its undergrads nearly 70 accelerated master's degree programs for those interested in graduate study.

adventure in faraway places—as about 10 percent of undergraduates do—the Global Education Office offers more than 140 different study abroad programs in more than 50 sites around the world, including Mason's own campus in South Korea.

Nearly half of incoming students start out at Northern Virginia Community College or other two-year institutions, and 18 percent of undergraduates are over the age of 24. As such, many commute. Eighty-three percent are from Virginia, and 5 percent are international; the university boasts students from 49 states and more than 130 countries. Black students account for 11 percent of the undergraduate population, Hispanics/Latinos 17 percent, Asian Americans 22 percent, and multi-racial students 5 percent. Students point to the campus's diversity as a highlight of the Mason experience. "I've learned about many different cultures here, and I don't ever feel singled out," reflects a senior. Students are politically aware and, being so close to D.C., have plenty of opportunities to get involved. Merit scholarships averaging $6,400 are available to those who qualify, as are 260 athletic scholarships in 22 sports.

George Mason's traditional status as a commuter school is changing. On-campus housing is guaranteed for the first year; 26 percent of students live on or around campus in university-sponsored housing, including 54 percent of first-time fresh-men. "Housing is competitive but the residence halls are generally nice," says a global affairs major. Those who want an active campus social life should definitely consider a stint in the dorms, but freshmen dorms are dry, and you can get the boot if you're caught having a party with alcohol. All freshmen living on campus reside in Presidents Park and are assigned to one of 25-plus academic, identity, and lifestyle-focused living/learning communities, which offer tighter-knit relationships with classmates. Sophomores and upperclassmen get rooms on a first-come, first-served basis prioritized by class status. Campus dining facilities are plentiful and operate around the clock but receive mixed reviews. Students report that the campus generally feels safe. "We have apps that can alert others of your location and when you expect to arrive home, and police escorts if students ever feel unsafe walking around campus," explains a junior.

Mason's Johnson Center, with its food court, movie theater, library, classrooms, computer labs, student support offices, and study areas, is the center of on-campus social life. Two student unions, the Student Union Building and the HUB, offer additional options for socializing and studying. "Our student life offices are very active, and there are events happening every day on campus," says a junior. Just 5 percent of the men and 6 percent of the women go Greek. With barely three generations of history under its belt, Mason is still developing traditions and annual events: "Come here and invent one!" a student urges. Patriots Day, Gold Rush, and Mason Day are major bashes, in addition to homecoming and International Week. On the weekends, students find a predictable assortment of malls and shopping centers in Fairfax, but off-campus parties and the sights and sounds of downtown D.C., Georgetown, and Old Town Alexandria beckon when the sun goes down. Best of all, these are only a short commute away via a free shuttle bus to the Metro. Those searching for alternative collegiate scenes take road trips to James Madison and UVA.

Mason competes in the Division I Atlantic 10 conference, and the basketball team is the marquee program. Any game against Virginia Commonwealth University draws a big crowd, and the budding Revolutionary Rivalry with George Washington is gaining momentum. Students are proud of the colorful pep band, known as the Green Machine and directed by a beloved tuba professor known as Doc Nix. Patriots teams that have recently brought home conference titles include men's and women's track and field and men's swimming and diving. Club sports and intramurals are growing in popularity, with 14 percent of students participating.

All freshmen living on campus are assigned to one of 25-plus academic, identity, and lifestyle-focused living/learning communities.

Downtown D.C., Georgetown, and Old Town Alexandria are only a short commute away via a free shuttle bus to the Metro.

"Nearly every aspect of Mason is developing at breakneck speed."

Overlaps

Virginia Commonwealth, Arizona State, Temple, UMBC, Virginia Tech, James Madison, Christopher Newport, University of Maryland

"Nearly every aspect of Mason is developing at breakneck speed. We haven't hit our best yet," says one student. The name of George Mason may not have the cachet of George Washington, James Madison, or the other luminaries of Virginia history who have had universities named for them, but with improving academics, an ever-expanding physical campus, and the rich cultural and economic resources of Washington, D.C., Mason's namesake may be set to follow in their footsteps.

If You Apply To ›

Mason: Early action, regular decision. SATs or ACTs: optional. Accepts the Common Application with supplement. Additional materials required for applicants to dance, music, art and visual technology, computer game design, and theater programs.

The George Washington University

Washington, D.C. 20052

Not so long ago, GW was a backup school maligned for its lack of identity. But the allure of Washington, D.C., coupled with ambitious leadership and an intellectually stimulating educational environment, has made it increasingly selective. Located steps away from the State Department. Among the most expensive private schools in the country, it is also a national leader in internships per capita.

Like Washington, D.C., itself, the George Washington University draws students from all over America—and from 130 countries around the world. Upon arrival, they find a bustling campus in the heart of D.C., enriched with cultural and intellectual opportunities, including internships with the Smithsonian Institution, the U.S. Capitol, the Library of Congress, NASA, and other national treasures. GW offers a front-row seat to history as top political officials and influential leaders serve as frequent guest speakers and visiting professors—and it is the only school in the country to hold its commencement on the National Mall. "We are the students who will make change in the world and we are at the center of the important things that are going on right now," says one confident junior.

GW was established in 1821 by an act of Congress as a testament to George Washington's dream of a national institution of higher learning in D.C. Today, as GW enters its third century, undergraduates experience life on primarily two campuses— the Foggy Bottom campus on Pennsylvania Avenue near the State Department and the Mount Vernon campus, three miles away in the Foxhall neighborhood. (A few other satellite campuses in the area serve mostly graduate students.) The Foggy Bottom campus has a mix of renovated federal row houses and modern buildings and is virtually indistinguishable from the rest of the neighborhood, while the wooded Mount Vernon campus spans 23 bucolic acres near Georgetown and includes athletic fields, tennis courts, and an outdoor pool. Students live and take classes on both campuses and travel between the two on the "Vern Express," a shuttle that runs 24/7 during the academic year. The 500,000-square-foot Science and Engineering Hall is the largest academic building in D.C. dedicated to STEM fields.

Incoming students may enroll in the School of Engineering and Applied Science, the School of Business, the Elliott School of International Affairs, the Milken Institute School of Public Health, and the largest undergraduate division, the Columbian

> **"GW offers a challenging curriculum without the pressure to outperform your peers."**

Website: www.gwu.edu
Location: City Center
Private
Total Enrollment: 17,659
Undergraduates: 10,196
Male/Female: 37/63
Financial Aid: 69%
Pell Grant: 15%
Expense: Pr $ $ $ $
Student Loans: 47%
Average Debt: $ $ $
Applicants: 27,236
Accepted: 50%
Enrolled: 19%
Grad in 6 Years: 84%
Returning Freshmen: 91%
Academics: ✑ ✑ ✑ ½
Social: ☎ ☎ ☎
Q of L: ★ ★ ★
Admissions: (202) 994-6040
Email Address: gwadm@ gwu.edu

Strong Programs:
International Affairs
Political Science
Finance

College of Arts and Sciences (which also houses the School of Media and Public Affairs and the Corcoran School of the Arts and Design). All undergraduates are required to complete a 19-credit core curriculum in the following areas: writing, natural or physical science, mathematics or statistics, social science, and the humanities, plus two writing-in-the-disciplines courses. During their first year, all undergraduates take a University Writing course. Some of the strongest and most popular majors are international affairs, political science, finance, and biology. GW's political communication major, which combines political science, journalism, and communication technologies, is one of the few undergraduate programs of its kind and benefits from its Washington location. Programs in public health, geography, biomedical engineering, interaction design, and archaeology are also well regarded. A number of accelerated undergraduate/graduate degree programs are available. Students warn that recent budget cuts have impacted several humanities and arts programs, including women's studies, music, and dance.

> **"Students intern at Capitol Hill (we call it hill-terning because of how common it is)."**

Academically, "GW offers a challenging curriculum without the pressure to outperform your peers," says a systems engineering major. Forty-one percent of the classes taken by undergraduates have fewer than 20 students; professors handle lectures and seminars, and teaching assistants facilitate discussions or labs. Almost half of GW's faculty members divide their time between the halls of academia and real-world positions, many of them governmental, but the quality of teaching is said to be "hit or miss."

GW is the only school in the country to hold its commencement on the National Mall.

For about 500 highly motivated and capable students in all majors, the University Honors Program offers special seminars, dedicated advising, independent study, and a university symposium on both campuses. Thirty-one percent of students study abroad via 300 programs available in more than 60 countries, including GW-run programs in England, France, Spain, and Chile. The Center for Career Services hosts job fairs, offers career coaching, and connects students with more than 12,000 internship opportunities. "Students intern at Capitol Hill (we call it hill-terning because of how common it is), the Kennedy Center, the Smithsonian, and many other local organizations," reports a junior. Volunteering is big, too, and more than 80 GW courses combine academics with service work in the D.C. community.

"Students who go to GW are driven by success," says an economics major. "They know what they want and they will go after it." Ninety-six percent of undergraduates come from outside D.C., including 9 percent who hail from foreign countries. Eight percent are Black, 13 percent are Hispanic/Latino, 12 percent are Asian American, and 5 percent are multiracial. Many students come from wealthy backgrounds (and pricey nights out on the town are a common diversion), and a senior comments that the campus "remains fairly segregated according to race and cultural background." Diversity training is now mandatory for all incoming students. As you might expect, political issues of all sorts are important here. Merit scholarships are available, averaging $23,100, and athletes vie for 165 awards. GW is need-aware, not need-blind, in its admissions.

> **"Students who go to GW are driven by success."**

GW's political communication major, which combines political science, journalism, and communication, is one of the few undergrad programs of its kind.

Fifty-seven percent of GW undergrads live in campus housing, which is required for the first three years, although rising juniors interested in living off campus can enter a lottery that grants a limited number of exemptions. "Most dorms are converted apartment buildings that are old and in need of renovation," reports a senior. Those who move off campus typically find group houses in Foggy Bottom or go to fashionable nearby neighborhoods like Dupont Circle and Georgetown, just a short walk from campus. GW's meal plans allow students to dine at on-campus cafés or at more than 100 off-campus vendors, which means there are a "variety of options ranging from fast food, to food trucks, to nice sit-down dinners at fancier restaurants," according to one sophomore. Given GW's open, urban campus, safety can be a concern, but one student says, "There are many services to ensure security," including the university's police department. A junior adds, "Student organizations like Students Against Sexual Assault (SASA), Allied in Pride, the Feminist Student Union, and others work very diligently to increase awareness of sexual assault and provide students with the tools to protect themselves and others."

"If you're bored at GW, you're doing something wrong," states one business administration major. "Whether it's on campus or off campus, there's always something to do." Nine percent of GW men and 15 percent of the women go Greek, and there are more than 475 student organizations on campus. Alcohol consumption is allowed on campus for those of legal age. Major annual events include the Fall Fest and Spring Fling carnivals, with free food and nationally known musical performers. And every four years, GW celebrates the beginning of the new U.S. presidential term with a formal Inaugural Ball of its own in January. Popular weekend trips include the Blue Ridge Mountains and the beaches of

Every four years, GW celebrates the beginning of the new U.S. presidential term with a formal Inaugural Ball of its own in January.

"If you're bored at GW, you're doing something wrong."

Ocean City, Maryland, and Virginia Beach, Virginia. Philadelphia and New York City are easily accessible by bus or train, a boon because most GW students don't have cars.

While GW's official mascot resembles a certain Founding Father, its quirky, unofficial one is the hippopotamus. The university has dropped its longtime Colonials moniker following student protests over its association with colonialism. GW doesn't field a football team, but its 20 varsity teams are competitive in Division I Atlantic 10 Conference play. Men's and women's basketball make regular NCAA tournament appearances, and recent conference champions include men's and women's swimming and diving, women's cross-country, and softball. Fourteen percent of undergraduates participate in 41 club sports and 14 intramural activities throughout the year.

Perhaps it's fitting that a university located in the nation's seat of government would generate complaints about red tape: "Stop with the bureaucracy," grumbles one student. "The simplest of problems for students could be fixed if we didn't have to go through so many hoops to just get an answer." Still, despite the bureaucratic annoyances, GW continues to build its reputation by putting its location to good use. "The opportunities are endless," says a student. "Picking and choosing what you want to do is the hardest part." For students interested in urban living in the heart of the nation's political establishment, GW may fit the bill. But that bill will be hefty.

Overlaps

Boston University, NYU, Northeastern, University of Miami (FL), University of Southern California, American University, Georgetown, University of Maryland

If You Apply To ›

GW: Early decision I and II, regular decision. SATs or ACTs: optional. Accepts the Common Application. Art and design applicants must submit portfolio.

Georgetown University

37th and O Streets NW, Washington, D.C. 20057

For anyone who wants to be a master of the political universe, this is the place. Strong international and multicultural environment. Georgetown is the most academically prestigious of the Jesuit schools in the U.S. and one of the most tolerant of religious diversity. A national leader in actively confronting its historical links to slavery. Occupies a tree-lined neighborhood that is home to many of the nation's most powerful people.

Website: www.georgetown.edu

Location: City Center

Private

Total Enrollment: 15,252

Undergraduates: 7,178

Male/Female: 43/57

Financial Aid: 56%

Pell Grant: 14%

Expense: Pr $ $ $ $

Student Loans: 34%

Average Debt: $ $

Applicants: 27,629

Accepted: 12%

Enrolled: 48%

Grad in 6 Years: 95%

Returning Freshmen: 98%

Academics: ✍ ✍ ✍ ✍ ½

Social: ☎ ☎ ☎ ☎

Q of L: ★ ★ ★ ★

Admissions: (202) 687-3600

Email Address: guadmiss@
georgetown.edu

Strong Programs:

International Affairs

International History

International Economics

Regional and Comparative
    Studies

Theology

International Business

Government

Nursing

The religious atmosphere is by no means heavy-handed, and the student body tends to be liberal.

As the oldest and most selective of the nation's Roman Catholic schools, Georgetown University offers students unparalleled access to the corridors of power of Washington, D.C. Aspiring politicos benefit from the university's emphasis on public policy, international business, and foreign service. The national spotlight shines brightly on this elite institution, drawing dynamic students and athletes from around the world. A senior says, "Georgetown balances academics, social life, and faith in an all-encompassing college experience based on 'care of the whole person.'"

From its scenic location just blocks from the Potomac River, Georgetown affords its students an excellent vantage point from which to survey the world. Established in 1789, the 104-acre campus reflects the history and growth of the first university in the nation to be founded by the Society of Jesus (Jesuits). The Federal style of Old North, which once housed guests such as George Washington and Lafayette and is now home to the McCourt School of Public Policy, contrasts with the towers of the Flemish Romanesque-style Healy Hall, a post-Civil War landmark on the National Register of Historic Places.

> **"Georgetown balances academics, social life, and faith in an all-encompassing college experience."**

Although Georgetown is a Catholic university, the religious atmosphere is by no means heavy-handed, and the student body tends to be liberal. Roughly half of the undergraduates are Catholic, but all major faiths are respected and practiced on campus. That's partially due to the pronounced international influence here. The school's hefty endowment is the largest among the nation's Jesuit colleges and universities. Georgetown has worked to confront its historical ties to slavery by offering preferential admissions status to descendants of 272 slaves who were sold in 1838 to keep its doors open. In addition to offering a formal apology, it has created an African American studies department and in 2021 formally established the Institute for Racial Justice to understand and address systemic racial inequities. But critics say fund-raising has lagged on a pledge to raise $100 million to atone for the university's participation in the slave trade.

Through its broad liberal arts curriculum, GU focuses on developing the intellectual prowess and moral rigor its students will need in future national and international leadership roles. All students must complete requirements in humanities, philosophy, theology, engaging diversity, and writing; other requirements are specific to each school. Optional Ignatius Seminars, which focus on educating the "mind, body, and spirit," give first-years the chance to form close relationships with professors and reflect on their work. Would-be Hoyas may apply to one of four undergraduate schools: Georgetown College for liberal arts, the School of Nursing and Health Studies, McDonough School of Business, and the Walsh School of Foreign Service. Prospective freshmen must declare intended majors on their applications, and their secondary school records are judged accordingly. This means, among other things, intense competition within the college for the limited number of spaces in Georgetown's popular premed program.

> **"Students take their coursework very seriously."**

International affairs, international history, international economics, and regional and comparative studies are among the hottest programs, as evidenced by the late secretary of state Madeleine Albright's nearly 40-year tenure at the Walsh School of Foreign Service (SFS). For future diplomats, journalists, and others, SFS offers several five-year undergraduate and graduate degree programs in conjunction with the Graduate School of Arts and Sciences. Georgetown's most popular majors include international affairs, government, international politics, finance, and nursing. Of course, the theology department is also strong. The business school balances liberal arts with professional training, which translates into strong offerings in international business as well as an emphasis on ethical and public policy issues.

Curiously, given its location in D.C., Georgetown does not offer an undergraduate public policy major. The School of Nursing and Health Studies runs an integrated program combining the liberal arts and humanities with professional nursing theory and practice. The Faculty of Languages and Linguistics, the only undergraduate program of its kind nationwide, grants degrees in nine languages, as well as degrees in linguistics and comparative literature.

"Students take their coursework very seriously," says a senior. "The courses are challenging, but it certainly isn't impossible to do well." Fifty-five percent of classes have fewer than 20 students. Georgetown likes to boast about its faculty, and it should. "The professors are outstanding and the teaching is first-rate," says an American studies major, and TAs are used only to lead discussion sections and recitations. That GU views most subjects through an international lens is evidenced by the fact that 58 percent of the school's undergraduates study abroad. The Office of Global Education offers more than 210 programs in 57 countries.

International affairs, international history, international economics, and regional and comparative studies are among the hottest programs.

A senior says GU students are not the stereotypical "pastel polo and pearl-clad preppies from Long Island." Eighty-four percent come from states outside D.C., and another 14 percent are international. Black students make up 6 percent of undergrads, Hispanics/Latinos 8 percent, Asian Americans 13 percent, and multiracial students 6 percent. A student committee works with the vice president for student affairs to improve race relations and develop strategies for improving inclusiveness and sensitivity to issues of multiculturalism. Georgetown offers no academic merit scholarships, but it does guarantee to meet the full demonstrated need of every admit, and more than 400 athletic scholarships draw athletes of all stripes. The Georgetown Scholarship Program offers financial and academic support to eligible low-income students.

"The professors are outstanding and the teaching is first-rate."

University-owned dorms, townhouses, and apartments accommodate 79 percent of undergrads, and "housing is extremely nice," says a senior. All dorms are co-ed, and some have more activities and a stronger community feel than others. Two dining halls serve "steadily improving" but expensive fare. GU students feel relatively safe on campus, thanks to the school's ever-present Department of Public Safety and its walking and riding after-dark escort services.

Should you notice the hills begin to tremble with a chant—"Hoya Saxa Hoya Saxa"—don't worry; it's probably just another Georgetown basketball game.

Jesuits know something about secret societies and thus frown on fraternities and sororities at their colleges. The lack of a Greek system and the university's strict enforcement of the 21-year-old drinking age has led to a somewhat decentralized social life, which is not necessarily a bad thing. Alcohol is forbidden in undergrad dorms, and all parties must be registered. The dozens of bars, nightclubs, and restaurants in Georgetown—Martin's Tavern and the Tombs are always popular—are a big draw, but they can get pricey. Bulldog Tavern, a campus pub in the spectacular student activity center, is a more affordable alternative. Popular annual formals such as the Diplomatic and the Blue/Gray Ball inspire students to dress up and pair off. "Social life is a major part of campus," says a student. "Kids can easily find their niche." Georgetown has a reputation as a gay-friendly campus, and regular events include OUTober, a month of LGBTQ pride and awareness events held in October.

"Washington is an ideal place to spend your college years."

Washington offers unsurpassed cultural resources, ranging from the museums of the Smithsonian to the Kennedy Center. "Washington is an ideal place to spend your college years," says a student. "The city has everything students could want, including culture, shopping, museums, monuments, social life, and the clean and convenient Metro for transportation." Given the absence of on-campus parking, a car is probably more trouble than it's worth. Road trips are said to be infrequent.

Should you notice the hills begin to tremble with a deep, resounding, primitive chant—"Hoya Saxa Hoya Saxa"—don't worry; it's probably just another Georgetown basketball game. Hoya is derived from the Greek and Latin phrase *hoya saxa*, which means "What rocks!" Some say it originated in a cheer referring to the stones that formed the school's outer walls. The Hoya men's basketball team has a long history of prominence. Recent Division I Big East champions include men's and women's soccer, men's lacrosse, and women's cross-country. The thrill of victory in intramural competition at the superb underground Yates Memorial Field House is not to be missed either.

For anyone interested in discovering the world, Georgetown offers an outstanding menu of choices in one of the nation's most dynamic cities. Professors truly pay attention to their undergrads and the diverse students, who are "hardworking, diligent, caring individuals," says one sophomore. "Georgetown is a place where students of all backgrounds, all traditions, and all faiths come together for a common purpose of educating each other and making an impact on the world."

Overlaps

Boston College, Notre Dame, University of Virginia, George Washington, UC Berkeley, University of Pennsylvania, UCLA, Cornell University

If You Apply To ›

Georgetown: Early action, regular decision. SATs or ACTs: required. Does not accept the Common Application. Apply to particular schools or programs.

University of Georgia

212 Terrell Hall, Athens, GA 30602-1633

What a difference (nearly) free tuition makes. Thanks to the HOPE Scholarship program, top Georgia students now choose UGA over highly selective private institutions. Business, journalism, social and natural sciences, and engineering head the list of strong and sought–after programs. The college town of Athens boasts a great nightlife and is within easy reach of Atlanta. Undergraduates also have access to rich research opportunities.

Website: www.uga.edu
Location: Small City
Public
Total Enrollment: 35,574
Undergraduates: 28,160
Male/Female: 42/58
Financial Aid: 42%
Pell Grant: 16%
Expense: Pub $ $
Student Loans: 40%
Average Debt: $
Applicants: 39,090
Accepted: 40%
Enrolled: 37%
Grad in 6 Years: 87%
Returning Freshmen: 95%
Academics: ✎ ✎ ✎

Three decades ago, the state of Georgia began using lottery receipts to fund the HOPE Scholarship program. The program covers 73 percent of tuition at the University of Georgia for all four years for students who finish high school in the state with a B average and maintain that average in college. The impact of the scholarship has been huge. Top Georgia students who in the past would have looked to more prestigious out-of-state universities are opting instead to set their sights on UGA, which is now much tougher to get into. The program has been widely criticized as a somewhat cynical middle-class assistance program, but there is no doubt that it has helped transform a school that was previously known primarily for its dynamite football team and raucous parties into a widely respected research university. Today, "Georgia offers the most complete 'Southern college experience' in the South," opines a senior.

> "Georgia offers the most complete 'Southern college experience' in the South."

Founded in 1785 with the help of three Yale graduates, Georgia was the nation's first state-chartered university (UNC was chartered later but wins bragging rights as the first public university to open its doors). Its attractive 762-acre campus is dotted with greenery and wooded walks. The older north campus houses the Morehead

Honors College, the Business Learning Community complex, the School of Public and International Affairs, administrative offices, and the law school and features 19th-century architecture and landscaping. The southern end of campus has more modern buildings, STEM facilities, and residence halls. The Delta Innovation Hub is the latest addition to UGA's Innovation District, designed to support entrepreneurialism among students, faculty, and community members.

UGA's core curriculum includes courses in world languages and culture, humanities, the arts, life sciences, and physical sciences. First-Year Odyssey Seminars allow new students to study under a senior faculty member in a small, personalized setting while earning an hour of academic credit. All students must take part in a hands-on learning opportunity, such as research, study abroad, service learning, and internships, before they graduate. "The experiential learning requirement has made me explore things outside of what I am predisposed to and has expanded my horizons to more professional opportunities," enthuses a psychology major. UGA's Grady College of Journalism and Mass Communication is home to the prestigious Peabody Awards for broadcasting excellence, and the Terry College of Business is also noteworthy. Ecology, agricultural sciences, public relations, international affairs, engineering, and computer science are also strengths, and the university's health-related programs are rapidly expanding. The most popular majors are biology, finance, psychology, and marketing. The Double Dawgs program enables students to earn both a bachelor's and a master's degree in five years or less; students may choose from some 265 combinations of degrees.

A junior describes UGA's academics as "a mixture of individual and collaborative work that encourages both teamwork and competition." Large lecture classes are common, but the university recently hired more than 50 faculty members and added roughly 320 new course sections in an effort to reduce class sizes. "Professors strive to make their lessons not just about grades, but also about developing and growing our minds," says an international affairs major. Students find ample assistance with securing internships and jobs from the counselors in the Career Center.

"Professors strive to make their lessons…about developing and growing our minds."

The 2,500 students in UGA's highly regarded honors college enjoy small classes taught by top professors, as well as special opportunities like Lunchbox Lectures and summer internships in Savannah, Washington, D.C., and New York City. The Center for Undergraduate Research Opportunities allows students to conduct a research or service project, write a thesis, or develop a creative work with close faculty supervision, awarding 500 stipends per semester of up to $1,000 each. The University of Georgia is highly ranked among research universities for the proportion of students who study abroad each year (34 percent). In addition to courses at its campuses in Cortona, Italy; Oxford, England; and Washington, D.C., UGA offers more than 100 faculty-led study abroad trips to dozens of countries, exchange programs with partner universities, and independent research and internship opportunities.

Eighty-five percent of UGA undergrads are Georgians, and 2 percent are international. A political science and psychology double major calls UGA students "driven, charismatic, and a lot of fun." Black students account for 7 percent of the student body, Asian Americans 12 percent, Hispanics/Latinos 7 percent, and multiracial students 4 percent. A junior points out that "Athens is a liberal town located in a conservative state," and both sides of the political aisle are said to be well represented on campus. Merit scholarships are available, and UGA also doles out 436 athletic scholarships in 21 sports. As many as 100 top undergraduates are named Foundation Fellows, netting a full scholarship plus stipends for international travel and research.

(continued)

Social: ☎ ☎ ☎ ☎ ☎
Q of L: ★ ★ ★
Admissions: (706) 542-8776
Email Address: adm-info@ uga.edu

Strong Programs:
Journalism
Business
Engineering
Ecology
Agricultural Sciences
Public Relations
International Affairs
Computer Science

First-Year Odyssey Seminars allow new students to study under a senior faculty member in a small, personalized setting.

Thirty-four percent of Bulldogs live in the 28 residence halls, and freshmen are required to do so. "Each dorm caters to different personality types, bathroom preferences, and social environments," explains a public relations major. There are five campus dining halls—each with its own specialty cuisine—and students drool over the delicious options; many choose to keep their meal plans even after moving off campus. "You don't feel like you're in a dining hall—it's that good," insists a junior. A psychology major reports, "Campus safety is pretty strong. We have a great campus police department and various safety measures in place for students."

When the weekend comes, students know how to have a good time. "The party scene is alive and well with house parties, frat parties, and downtown Athens," says a senior. Fraternities and sororities attract 21 percent of the men and 34 percent of the women, respectively. Alcohol is prohibited in the dorms, but as at most schools, the determined manage to imbibe anyway. There are also more than 700 student organizations for students to choose from. A favorite campus tradition is ringing the Chapel bell for athletic victories as well as personal accomplishments. "Hearing the Chapel bell ring is a heartwarming sound because you know that regardless of what's going on in your day, there's a Bulldog out there who has something worth celebrating," cheers one happy Dawg.

A favorite campus tradition is ringing the Chapel bell for athletic victories as well as personal accomplishments.

The funky mix of shops, restaurants, clubs, and various music and cultural events found in downtown Athens is only a 10-minute walk from most residence halls. A senior explains that Athens is "far enough away from Atlanta to maintain the college community, yet close enough to provide an escape." Students enjoy getting involved in mentorship and volunteer programs in the Athens community, and philanthropic organizations like UGA Miracle, UGA HEROs, and CURE are some of the largest student groups on campus. Popular road trips include the Florida and Carolina beaches and anywhere the Bulldogs are playing on a fall Saturday.

"Games at Sanford Stadium have to be seen to be believed."

It's no stretch to claim that Athens residents worship UGA's perennially fierce football team. The team won back-to-back national championships for the 2021 and 2022 seasons, defeating Alabama and Texas Christian, respectively. "Georgia football is a huge part of the school," says a biology major. "Games at Sanford Stadium have to be seen to be believed." The Georgia–Florida rivalry is the stuff of lore. The Bulldogs (remember that early Yale connection?) compete in the tough Southeastern Conference, and men's and women's tennis, men's track and field, and women's swimming and diving, basketball, gymnastics, and equestrian are especially competitive. Georgia's Debate Union enjoys consistent national success as well. Recreational sports are taken seriously, too, with more than 40 clubs and 40 intramural sports available for students to compete in.

UGA's sheer size means you could coast through four years here as nothing more than a number. But with a little effort, that doesn't have to happen. Freshmen seminars, research projects, study abroad, and honors courses offer the opportunity to graduate with a solid background in any number of areas and fond memories of Saturdays spent cheering on the Bulldogs—along with 92,000 of your closest friends.

Overlaps

UNC at Chapel Hill, UW–Madison, University of Florida, University of Minnesota, UC Davis, Georgia Tech, Clemson, Florida State

If You Apply To ›

Georgia: Early action, regular decision. SATs or ACTs: required. Accepts the Common Application with supplement.

Atlanta, GA 30332

As the South's premier technically oriented university, Ma Tech does not coddle her young. Students must contend with the sometimes mean streets of downtown Atlanta and fight through a wall of graduate students to talk with their professors. Big-time sports offer respite from the engineering focus. Tech's 60/40 male/female ratio is tempered by women from all-female Agnes Scott.

If you're looking for lazy days on the college green and hard-partying weekends, look elsewhere. You won't find those at Georgia Institute of Technology, the South's premier tech university. What you will find are challenging courses that prepare you for a high-paying job as an engineer, architect, or computer scientist. "Tech is tough," reasons one student. "You have to want to be here." Even those who want to be there are happy to finally arrive at graduation day. What makes Tech a special place? "The fact that I survived it and got out with a degree," says a computer science major, only partially joking (we think). As part of its efforts to become a top technological research university globally, Tech has developed an extensive offering of Massive Open Online Courses (MOOCs), available for free to the general public.

Georgia Tech was founded in 1885 to promote industry in the post–Civil War South. Located just off the interstate in Georgia's capital city, Tech's 450-acre campus embraces 40 undergraduate residence halls, an aquatic center, a sports performance complex, and an amphitheater. Taking in the campus architecture is like traveling through time: building styles include the Georgian Revival and collegiate Gothic of the historic Hill District (listed on the National Register of Historic Places) and surrounding area, the International Style buildings constructed from the 1940s into the 1960s, the modernist structures of the 1970s and '80s, the postmodern facilities of the '90s, and the newly built high-tech facilities. All these styles coexist comfortably on a tree-filled, landscaped campus that serves as a green oasis in the midst of a dense urban environment.

Regardless of major, students must complete credit hours in social sciences, science, English and humanities, math, U.S. or Georgia history, U.S. and global perspectives, and wellness. Strong programs include math and computer science, as well as most types of engineering, especially industrial, biomedical, aerospace, civil, and mechanical. The school of architecture has done pioneering work in historic preservation and energy conservation. The architecture program's alumni include Michael Arad, designer of the September 11 memorial in lower Manhattan. Students in several disciplines complete a Capstone Design course, in which they work in teams to design, build, and test prototypes of products with real-world applications. Aside from the technical fare, Tech's business college is increasingly popular. The prelaw certificate is a boon to aspiring patent attorneys, as is the minor in law, science, and technology. Tech has plenty of liberal arts courses, but students say history, philosophy, and literature aren't the reasons why most students enroll.

> **"There are a lot of left-brain types here—high on the introspection and thinking, low on the social skills."**

Courses at Tech are "extremely rigorous," says a senior, at least in the sciences and engineering. "Grading on a curve creates hypercompetitive situations because your absolute grade is largely irrelevant—you just have to do better than most of the others." Classes tend to be big; 31 percent enroll more than 50 students. A computer science major warns that Tech is "absolutely horrible for things like freshman math

Website: www.gatech.edu
Location: City Center
Public
Total Enrollment: 22,504
Undergraduates: 15,178
Male/Female: 60/40
Financial Aid: 82%
Pell Grant: 12%
Expense: Pub $ $
Student Loans: 35%
Average Debt: $ $
Applicants: 45,388
Accepted: 18%
Enrolled: 42%
Grad in 6 Years: 92%
Returning Freshmen: 97%
Academics: ✏️ ✏️ ✏️ ✏️ ✏️
Social: ☎ ☎
Q of L: ★ ★
Admissions: (404) 894-4154
Email Address: admission@gatech.edu

Strong Programs:
Industrial Engineering
Biomedical Engineering
Aerospace Engineering
Civil Engineering
Mechanical Engineering
Computer Science
Mathematics
Architecture

classes. You're typically taught by TAs. Things get better as you progress and get to know professors." Faculty members have real-world experience; some are Nobel Prize winners and former NASA astronauts.

The school of architecture has done pioneering work in historic preservation and energy conservation.

Tech's demanding workload means it's common to spend five years getting your degree. Students say the course selection process can be frustrating, and getting into required courses can be an issue. One positive factor contributing to delayed graduation dates is the popular co-op program, through which more than 3,000 students earn money for their education while gaining on-the-job experience with more than 700 organizations worldwide. The university offers more than 90 exchange programs and 30 faculty-led study abroad programs; 56 percent of students have some sort of international study or internship experience by the time they graduate.

"Tech is tough. You have to want to be here." Georgia Tech's innovative Vertically Integrated Projects program allows students to join student/faculty teams to work on large-scale, long-term, multidisciplinary research projects, earning academic credit over the course of multiple semesters. An honors program is available for the super motivated, and the Center for the Study of Women, Science, and Technology offers a living/learning community and research opportunities for women in STEM fields.

Most Georgia Tech students are too focused on school or their co-op jobs to care much about politics or social issues, although improving campus resources for mental health and the LGBTQ community has been a hot topic of late. According to a senior, "There are a lot of left-brain types here—high on the introspection and thinking, low on the social skills." And though they may be united in their pursuit of technical expertise, the campus is hardly homogeneous: Black students account for 8 percent of the student body, Hispanics/Latinos 8 percent, Asian Americans 27 percent, and multiracial students 4 percent. Fifty-seven percent of undergraduates hail from Georgia, and there are large contingents from California, Florida, and Texas; 11 percent come from abroad. To limit burgeoning enrollment, out-of-state applicants must meet somewhat higher criteria than their Georgia counterparts. Georgia residents who graduated high school with a B average benefit from the state's HOPE Scholarship, which covers about 94 percent of their tuition over four years, assuming they keep their grades up in college. In addition, Tech has eliminated loans for Georgia residents with family incomes below $33,300 a year. Merit scholarships are available, as are more than 300 athletic scholarships.

The Vertically Integrated Projects program allows students to join student/faculty teams to work on long-term, multidisciplinary research projects.

Forty-seven percent of undergrads live in the dorms, where freshmen are guaranteed a room. A senior says the quality of residence halls varies widely: "Some dorms are new, apartment-style, and nice. Others are foul dungeons." The campus dining halls offer "little variety and less quality," according to another student. Off-campus housing is generally comfortable, but parts of the surrounding neighborhood are sketchy. "Far too many cars are broken into or stolen," says one student. "There's usually a couple of armed robberies (at least) per semester." Campus police are said to be quick to respond to incidents. VOICE is a campuswide initiative working to address the issue of campus sexual assault.

Traditions include "stealing the T," in which students try to remove the huge yellow letter T from the tower on the administration building.

Being located smack-dab in the middle of "Hot-Lanta" does have its upside: an endless supply of clubs, bars, movie theaters, restaurants, shopping, and museums, both in midtown Atlanta and the Buckhead district. "Atlanta is not a college town," reasons a computer science major. "However, it is the best thing going in Georgia," with friendly, young residents, good cultural activities, beautiful green spaces, and a booming economy. The city also offers plenty of community service opportunities. Fraternities draw 23 percent of Tech's men, sororities attract 26 percent of the women, and members may live in their chapter houses. Alcohol flows freely at frat parties, but otherwise, students say, Tech's policies against open containers and underage drinking are strictly enforced. "There's not much in the way of social life here outside of the frats," says a senior. "You have your group of friends and you do your own thing." The best road trips include Florida's beaches, which are a half day's drive, and Athens, Georgia, for basketball or football games against the University of Georgia.

Tech's Division I varsity sports teams (the Yellowjackets) have become as big-time as any in the South, and when the weekend comes, students throw off their lab coats and become wild members of the "Rambling Wreck from Georgia Tech." The men's golf team has won multiple Atlantic Coast Conference championships in recent years; men's and wom-

> **"Some dorms are new, apartment-style, and nice. Others are foul dungeons."**

en's track and field and women's basketball are also competitive. About 40 percent of students participate in the university's 43 club and 20 intramural sports. Among Tech's many other traditions is "stealing the T," in which students try to remove the huge yellow letter T from the tower on the administration building and return it to the school by presenting it to a member of the faculty or administration. The addition of alarms, motion sensors, and heat sensors on the T has made the task more difficult but "certainly not impossible for a Georgia Tech engineer," says an electrical engineering major. And then there's the Mini 500, a 15-lap tricycle race around a parking garage with three pit stops, a tire change, and a driver rotation.

Forget fitting the mold; the engineers of Georgia Tech are proud to say they make it. Self-direction, ambition, and motivation will take you far here, as will a fondness for highly complex software algorithms. And despite their complaints about the workload, the social life (or lack thereof), and the safety of their surrounding neighborhood, Tech students do have a soft spot for their school. Says one student, "I love a good challenge, and Tech is perfect for that."

> ## Overlaps
> **Carnegie Mellon, MIT, Purdue, UC Berkeley, UT Austin, University of Georgia, U of I at Urbana–Champaign, University of Florida**

If You Apply To ›

Georgia Tech: Early action, regular decision. SATs or ACTs: required. Accepts the Common Application.

Gettysburg College

300 North Washington Street, Gettysburg, PA 17325

The "college by the battlefield" is strong in U.S. history—that's a given. The natural sciences and English are also noteworthy, and political science majors enjoy good connections in D.C. and Baltimore. Participation in undergraduate research and study abroad is notably high.

Whether the reference is to the Pennsylvania town steeped in Civil War history or the small, high-caliber college located in the famed battlefield's backyard, a certain pride and reverence are immediately evident when the name "Gettysburg" is uttered. This feeling is not lost on students at Gettysburg College, who come to southeastern Pennsylvania to acquaint themselves with American history while gearing up for the future. "Gettysburg is rooted in fun and exciting traditions that make our campus special and our time here that much more meaningful," says a junior.

Gettysburg was founded in 1832 on land donated by famed abolitionist Thaddeus Stevens. Situated in the midst of gently rolling hills, the college's 200-acre campus is "a historical treasure," an eclectic assemblage of Georgian, Greek, Romanesque, Gothic Revival, and modern architecture, plus several styles not easily categorized. One campus building—Penn Hall—was used as a hospital during the

Website: www.gettysburg.edu	
Location: Small Town	
Private	
Total Enrollment: 2,397	
Undergraduates: 2,397	
Male/Female: 48/52	
Financial Aid: 65%	
Pell Grant: 20%	
Expense: Pr $ $ $ $	
Student Loans: 63%	
Average Debt: $ $ $ $	

(continued)

Applicants: 6,206
Accepted: 56%
Enrolled: 18%
Grad in 6 Years: 82%
Returning Freshmen: 91%
Academics: ✍ ✍ ✍ ½
Social: ☎ ☎ ☎
Q of L: ★ ★ ★
Admissions: (717) 337-6100
Email Address: admiss@
gettysburg.edu

Strong Programs:
English
History
Biology
Health Sciences
Political Science
Organization and Management
Studies
Economics
Civil War Era Studies

Battle of Gettysburg. Rumor has it that ghostly Civil War soldiers can still be seen walking the grounds. Major renovations to the College Union Building and an addition to the Dining Center are among the latest construction projects.

Curricular requirements cover typical liberal arts and sciences disciplines and goals, and students in all majors must complete a capstone requirement, such as a research project or senior seminar course. The English department is among the school's strongest; the college's acclaimed literary journal, the *Gettysburg Review*, offers internships to a few lucky students. The excellent history department is bolstered by the school's nationally recognized and prestigious Civil War Institute and its minor in Civil War era studies. Also strong are the natural sciences, especially biology and health sciences, which are well endowed with state-of-the-art equipment. Political science, organization and management studies, health sciences, and economics are among the most popular majors. Students may choose from three degrees within the Sunderman Conservatory of Music, and a cooperative dual-degree program in engineering is available.

"The academic climate is competitive and rigorous, but there are still opportunities for students to branch out and explore things outside of their major," explains a sophomore. Seventy percent of classes enroll fewer than 20 students, and the small class sizes make for close student/faculty relationships; the academic honor code contributes to the atmosphere of community and mutual trust as well. Popular first-year seminars explore topics such as Death and the Meaning of Life and Shop Class as Soulcraft; participants live in the same residence hall and belong to the same first-year residential college program.

Undergraduate research is taken seriously at Gettysburg, with 56 percent of students participating across all disciplines. The annual Celebration colloquium in the spring allows students to present and showcase their work. For students in the natural sciences, the Cross-Disciplinary Science Institute offers a seminar series and opportunities for hands-on research in the lab. About 80 percent of students complete at least one internship before they graduate. Participation in study abroad programs is also high, with 57 percent of students choosing from more than 100 programs worldwide for the same price they pay for regular tuition back home. Gettysburg sponsors a United Nations semester through Drew University and a Washington semester.

> **"[Gettysburg students] branch out and explore things outside of their major."**

Gettysburg students are "kindhearted, passionate, respectful, and open-minded," according to a health sciences major. Just 25 percent are native Pennsylvanians, and 5 percent are international. Black students represent 5 percent of the student body, Asian Americans 4 percent, Hispanics/Latinos 11 percent, and multiracial students 1 percent. Both sides of the political aisle are well represented, and while tensions occasionally arise, a public policy major reports that "most members of the campus community can engage in productive, civil debate." No athletic scholarships are available, but merit-based academic scholarships average $22,700.

All Gettysburg students are required to live on campus, with limited exceptions for those who live at home with their parents or guardians. First-years reside in traditional dorms; after that, options include suite- and apartment-style housing, fraternity houses, and theme houses. "Housing selection is a very messy process," complains a junior, and others agree that the lottery system is stressful. Dining options in the Dining Center (a.k.a. Servo), Bullet Hole, and Dive receive enthusiastic reviews. Concerning safety, a senior says, "Campus security is very good and very visible."

Most social life happens on campus, and it largely involves the Greek system and 120 other student groups. Twenty-eight percent of the men and 34 percent

Fifty-seven percent of students study abroad for the same price they pay for regular tuition back home.

of the women go Greek; rush does not occur until sophomore year. Students 21 and older are allowed to have alcohol on campus, and Greek parties are open to all students. "Fraternity parties are a massive part of the social life and nightlife," comments a senior, although students insist they're not the only source of fun on campus. The Campus Activities Board provides alternative social events, including concerts, comedians, movies, and campus coffeehouses, as well as bus trips to destinations like Washington, D.C., and New York City.

The orchards and rolling countryside surrounding the campus are peaceful and scenic, and there is a small ski slope nearby. "The Center for Public Service provides a lot of opportunities to make positive change in our community through volunteer work, immersion trips, and social projects," says an economics major; 82 percent of students actively volunteer. A prominent campus tradition is the First-Year Walk during orientation, where all first-year students walk through town to the National Cemetery following the same route that students took in 1863 to hear Abraham Lincoln deliver the Gettysburg Address. Today, an honored guest delivers the Gettysburg Address with remarks to the incoming class. Servo Thanksgiving, where faculty and staff serve students a holiday feast, the International Food Festival, and Springfest are other treasured traditions. Students, who get free passes to the historic attractions in town, sometimes grumble about the profusion of tourists. But those who want to escape can do so—the campus is within an hour and a half of both Washington, D.C., and Baltimore, where students enjoy the scenic Inner Harbor area.

> "Fraternity parties are a massive part of the social life and nightlife."

Gettysburg sponsors 24 varsity sports—12 for men and 12 for women—that compete at the Division III level as the Bullets. The women's lacrosse team is nationally competitive, and women's basketball, softball, men's lacrosse, and men's soccer have performed well in the Centennial Conference. The annual football game against Dickinson draws a good turnout, and the Little Brown Bucket, mahogany with silver handles, is passed to the team that wins. Intramural leagues and one-day tournaments are hugely popular, and Gettysburg also offers nine club sports.

At Gettysburg, students stay true to their slogan: "Do Great Work." A junior says, "Gettysburg students have a network of friends and faculty supporting their every decision." Students wanting personal attention from professors, solid academics, and an area rich with history might consider getting their education with a Gettysburg address.

> A prominent tradition is the First-Year Walk, where all first-years walk through town to the National Cemetery to hear the Gettysburg Address.

Overlaps

Dickinson, Franklin & Marshall, Lafayette, Bucknell, Muhlenberg, American University, University of Richmond, Colgate

If You Apply To ›

Gettysburg: Early decision I and II, early action, regular decision. SATs or ACTs: optional. Accepts the Common Application.

University of Glasgow: See page 375.

Gonzaga University

502 East Boone Avenue, Spokane, WA 99258-0102

Best known outside the Northwest for holding its own with big-time opponents on the basketball court, Gonzaga is a medium-sized private university with a picturesque residential campus in an urban setting. Offers classic Jesuit education with rigorous core and emphasis on service, though less than half of undergrads are Roman Catholic. Spokane is not as cosmopolitan as Seattle or San Francisco. Less selective than Santa Clara or USD, comparable to USF. Good bet for those who relish school spirit.

Gonzaga University ("Gone-ZAG-uh") burst into the nation's frontal lobes in 1999 when its men's basketball team fought its way to the quarterfinals of the Division I tournament. Consistent success in the tournament since then has softened the Zag's image as a midsized David doing battle with Goliaths like UNC at Chapel Hill. What has lingered, though, is the image of a solid regional liberal arts university committed to the Jesuit ideal of educating the whole person: mind, body, and spirit. According to a senior, Gonzaga supports an "empathetic, service-oriented, basketball-loving, adventure-seeking culture."

Founded in 1887 by the Society of Jesus (Jesuits) as a mission, the school takes its name from St. Aloysius Gonzaga, a 16th-century Italian aristocrat who joined the Jesuits and died while serving victims of an epidemic. The campus occupies 152 picturesque acres along the Spokane River, only a 15-minute walk from downtown Spokane. The Centennial Trail, a 37-mile paved bike path, borders the campus and river. Architectural styles range from the Romanesque College Hall to the sleek PACCAR Center for Applied Science. The university's Crosby Collection contains recordings, photographs, and other memorabilia pertaining to Gonzaga's most famous alumnus, crooner Bing. The LEED Gold–certified Hemmingson Center boasts ample space for the student body association, student clubs and organizations, and the main dining hall. The Integrated Science & Engineering facility opened in 2021, and the $60 million Health Sciences Center was completed in 2022.

> **"[Gonzaga supports an] empathetic, service-oriented, basketball-loving, adventure-seeking culture."**

Consistent with its Jesuit liberal arts tradition, Gonzaga requires undergraduates to complete an extensive core curriculum, beginning with a First-Year Seminar and ending with a Core Integration Seminar. Centered around the question of how students may "educate themselves to become people for a more just and humane global community," the core includes courses in English composition, communication and speech, and critical reasoning, with doses of philosophy and religious studies, literature, scientific inquiry, and mathematics. Writing, social justice, and global studies are emphasized throughout the core. Although Gonzaga is a Jesuit school and sponsors 16 spiritual retreats annually, there are no requirements to attend mass or chapel.

Gonzaga offers more than 50 undergraduate majors through the College of Arts and Sciences and the Schools of Business Administration, Education, Engineering and Applied Science, and Nursing and Human Physiology. Students say some of the strongest programs are engineering, nursing, accounting, integrated media studies, special education, and business. Biology majors have the option of adding a research concentration to their degree, while psych students may focus on specialized areas of interest such as child psychology and clinical research. Recently established programs include a minor in health equity.

While the workload can get challenging, students are supportive and "study groups are abundant and helpful," says a mechanical engineering major. Students say professors are knowledgeable and ready to help, and most "practically beg their students to get to know them through visiting office hours," comments a senior. Forty-one percent of undergraduate courses have fewer than 20 students. Students praise the school's academic support resources, including strong support for students with learning disabilities. A criminal justice and philosophy major says the Career and Professional Development staff has "helped me clean up my résumé, research internships, and given me the tips I needed to attend a career fair and not make a total fool of myself."

Writing, social justice, and global studies are emphasized throughout Gonzaga's extensive core curriculum.

Top students may apply for the four-year Honors Program, and many of them show off their research projects during Undergraduate Research Week. Other special offerings include the three-year Hogan Entrepreneurial Leadership Program, open to high-achieving first-year students seeking an entrepreneurial leadership minor in addition to their major, and the Comprehensive Leadership Program, which provides a minor in leadership studies. Gonzaga's Army ROTC program (Bulldog Battalion) ranks as one of the best anywhere. The centerpiece program for study abroad is Gonzaga-in-Florence, which allows students of any major, including engineering, to study at Gonzaga's campus in Florence, Italy, without delaying their four-year path to graduation. A junior calls Gonzaga-in-Florence "one of the most transformative and influential experiences of my college career." Overall, the university offers more than 60 international programs, in which 63 percent of students participate.

"[Professors] practically beg their students to get to know them through visiting office hours."

"Gonzaga students are excited, passionate, service-driven, and open-minded," according to one history major. Two percent of Zags are from other countries, with the rest almost equally divided between Washingtonians and out-of-staters. Black students make up just 1 percent of the student body, while Hispanics/Latinos represent 12 percent, Asian Americans 6 percent, and multiracial students 7 percent. "There are a lot of white and affluent students here, which can be a bit of an adjustment if you are not both white and affluent," remarks a junior. Thirty-eight percent of students identify as Catholic. Social activism on this left-leaning campus tends to revolve around issues of race, sexual orientation, and religion. The school awards merit scholarships averaging $19,800 and 120 athletic scholarships.

The Gonzaga-in-Florence program allows students of any major, including engineering, to study at Gonzaga's campus in Florence, Italy.

Fifty-three percent of undergraduates reside in campus housing. First- and second-year students are required to live on campus and purchase a meal plan, but space for upperclassman is limited, so most juniors and seniors find their own housing in the surrounding neighborhood. On-campus residence halls offer a variety of living styles, including both co-ed and single-gender corridors and floors and several living/learning communities. A senior explains that residence halls "range in how old they are and how nice some of the facilities are. Regardless of this, you will find devout fans of each residence hall." Campus

"The downtown Spokane area is full of spunk and character."

meals are primarily served in the COG dining hall, and a secondary education major says, "The dining facilities are amazing and the meals are occasionally great as well." Students report feeling safe on campus, and a senior says, "Campus security is helpful and quick to respond."

There are no fraternities or sororities at Gonzaga, but students say their absence has hardly put a damper on social life, either on or off campus. Students agree that while "there is a noticeable party scene off campus in the houses of upperclassmen," they don't feel pressured to drink. Underage students found in possession of drugs or alcohol may be required to take an awareness and safety program. The Hemmingson Center hosts a variety of social activities, including late-night programming on the weekends and the Coffeehouse Concert Series. With 230,000 residents, Spokane is the second-largest city in Washington but has the feel of a much smaller city. "The downtown Spokane area is full of spunk and character," says a public relations major, and it provides plenty of restaurants, outdoor recreation, and community activities.

The culture of Gonzaga places strong emphasis on issues of social justice and service. The school offers more than 50 community engagement courses, and roughly half of all undergraduates participate in some form of community service. "Being involved in the community is a specific Jesuit trait that we all try to live out," says one student. During winter, spring, and summer breaks, nearly 200 students travel to sites across the nation to participate in community service projects, and the university produces a large number of Peace Corps volunteers.

GU's 14 intercollegiate teams, known as the Zags or Bulldogs, compete in the Division I West Coast Conference. In the absence of football (shut down in 1941 and never resurrected), basketball is both king and queen. The men's team was the national runner-up in 2017 and 2021. Men's and women's basketball, baseball, and women's rowing are recent conference champs. Intramurals and 30-plus club sports, which range from flag football and pickleball to climbing and soccer, sign up students in droves. Outdoorsy types can take advantage of five ski areas within a 90-mile radius, and GU Outdoors sponsors adventures like rafting, hiking, and skiing excursions.

School spirit is a big deal at Gonzaga—mainly when it comes to sports and especially when the opponent is St. Mary's College of California. Since Gonzaga's mascot is the Bulldog, the student cheering section is naturally known as the Kennel. Students go through an elaborate process for tickets to big home basketball games that involves strategic tweeting and camping out in tents days before the opening tip. "It's insanity," confesses one sophomore, "but it's so much fun." A junior adds, "Every Zag should experience this at least once."

At Gonzaga, "spirit" takes on multiple meanings. Basketball may inspire the most vocal outpourings of school spirit, but students say the religious and humanistic values to which the university has long been committed run deep. "Community is a word tossed around quite frequently at all college campuses," says a psychology major, "but at GU, community is almost a belief."

Since Gonzaga's mascot is the Bulldog, the student cheering section at basketball games is naturally known as the Kennel.

Overlaps

Santa Clara, Loyola Marymount, Seattle University, University of San Diego, University of Portland, University of Washington, Washington State, Cal Poly–San Luis Obispo

If You Apply To ›

Gonzaga: Regular decision. SATs or ACTs: optional. Accepts the Common Application.

Gordon College

255 Grapevine Road, Wenham, MA 01984

Gordon is the most prominent Christian college in New England and competes nationally with Wheaton (IL) and Messiah, though it lacks the prestige of the former. Not quite in Boston but close enough to be within easy reach. Extensive core curriculum shapes the undergraduate experience. Emphasis on integrating faith and learning.

Evangelical Christian values are at the heart of almost all aspects of life at this New England college, where faith sets the tone for campus life inside and outside the classroom. Gordon College is unique in that it is the only Christian college of its type that has no formal denominational ties. Founded in 1889 as a missionary training school "to prepare the people of God to do the work of God," the college now sees its mission as promoting intellectual maturity and Christian character. Always evolving, Gordon is sharpening its offerings across the board, from international education to accelerated learning and leadership programs, and looking to increase its diversity. "Gordon is a place where asking genuine questions is encouraged and the goal is to stretch your mind and learn the material well," says a social welfare major.

Gordon is located on Massachusetts's scenic North Shore, three miles from the Atlantic Coast and 25 miles from Boston. The campus sits on more than 480 forested acres, landscaped with flowers and boasting four large ponds. Most campus structures are Georgian-influenced traditional red-brick, except for the administration building, Frost Hall, an old stone structure modeled after a European castle that provides an eye-catching contrast. The Olsen Science Center, an 83,500-square-foot science and technology center at the heart of the campus, is home to a fabrication lab, a vivarium, an aquarium, a human cadaver lab, and a biology greenhouse space.

"Gordon is a place where asking genuine questions is encouraged."

Religious commitment at Gordon is seen as the foundation of serious academic learning rather than a threat to free inquiry. Gordon's core curriculum includes distribution requirements in biblical studies and theology, the fine arts, humanities, social sciences, historical perspectives, natural sciences, math, and computer science. Freshmen complete an outdoor education requirement, choosing between a 12-day expedition in the Adirondacks and a seven-week, campus-based course. They also take the Great Conversation, a writing-intensive first-year seminar that helps them learn how to integrate faith into their academic experience.

Gordon's most popular majors are economics, business administration, psychology, biology, and communication arts. Biblical studies, music, education, kinesiology, and visual arts are also strong programs, although they may draw fewer students. Finance is available as a major—a rarity at small Christian colleges—as are a 3–2 engineering program and a dual-degree nursing program. Sixty-three percent of classes have fewer than 20 students, and students say professors have high expectations but are helpful. "The personal attention I've gotten from my professors is remarkable—even among institutions of our size," says a sophomore.

The Global Honors Institute encompasses three distinct four-year scholars programs, each providing hefty tuition support for high-achieving students: Global Honors Scholars, which offers honors seminars and travel experiences; A. J. Gordon Scholars, a personalized program culminating in a senior thesis or project; and Clarendon Scholars, which focuses on urban leadership development. Additional honors opportunities include a yearlong great books seminar known as the Jerusalem and Athens Forum and the Pike Honors Program, which allows students to design their own majors. The college operates signature study abroad programs in Orvieto, Italy, and the Balkans. Gordon also partners with other programs to offer nearly 40 approved study locations; 25 percent of students participate. The Career and Connection Institute is working to expand opportunities for internships, mentorship, and preparation for graduate school and the workplace, while the Center for Entrepreneurial Leadership helps students launch their own start-ups.

Gordon is one of two top evangelical schools that require undergraduate applicants to describe how their faith impacts their lives and to affirm that they recognize the Bible as "the Word of God and hence fully authoritative in matters of faith and

---

Website: www.gordon.edu
Location: Suburban
Private
Total Enrollment: 1,333
Undergraduates: 1,291
Male/Female: 40/60
Financial Aid: 98%
Pell Grant: 22%
Expense: Pr $
Student Loans: 67%
Average Debt: $ $ $ $
Applicants: 1,466
Accepted: 77%
Enrolled: 28%
Grad in 6 Years: 72%
Returning Freshmen: 79%
Academics: ✎ ✎ ✎
Social: ☎ ☎
Q of L: ★ ★ ★ ★
Admissions: (866) 464-6736
Email Address: admissions@gordon.edu

Strong Programs:
Biblical Studies
Music
Education
Kinesiology
Visual Arts
Economics
Business Administration
Psychology

Freshmen complete an outdoor education requirement, choosing between a 12-day expedition in the Adirondacks and a campus-based course.

conduct" (see also Wheaton College in Illinois). Gordon's trustees have reaffirmed the college's policy forbidding "homosexual practice." While observation of the Sabbath is expected, Gordon gives students a bit more latitude than some Christian colleges in determining how they will "separate themselves from worldliness."

Gordon students are interested in "outdoor adventure, spiritual discovery, and overcommitment to both academics and extracurricular activities," says a psychology major. Thirty-five percent of students are Massachusetts residents, and 8 percent are international. Up to 6 percent of students are Roman Catholic. Asian Americans account for 4 percent of the student body, Black students 6 percent, Hispanics/Latinos 12 percent, and multiracial students 3 percent. Racial affinity groups on campus, including ALANA, ASIA, Afro Hamwe, and La Raza, are expanding, and a biology major says, "The events that they put on are huge learning opportunities." Students report that LGBTQ rights are a hot-button issue, although one student notes, "Because it's a Christian school, even the liberals aren't too liberal." Beginning in fall 2021, Gordon reduced its sticker price by 33 percent in an effort to make its brand of Christian liberal arts education more affordable. Merit scholarships are offered to qualified undergrads, but athletic scholarships are not.

Eighty-five percent of Gordon students live in the residence halls, which are clustered either around the central quad or on an area of campus known as the Hill.

"Because it's a Christian school, even the liberals aren't too liberal."

Men and women live in separate wings of the same buildings—separated by a lobby, a lounge, and a laundry room. Persons of the opposite sex may traverse these barriers only at specified times. Permission to move off campus may be granted by petition, but the requirements for doing so are stringent. Students report that meals in the main dining hall, which overlooks a pond and doubles as a study area at night, are usually satisfying. Campus safety receives good ratings, and a junior adds that, with respect to campus sexual assault, Gordon is "taking the issue much more seriously."

Gordon's student-led Campus Events Council organizes activities like movie showings, dances, and coffeehouses held in Chester's Place, a student-run coffee shop with a pub atmosphere, named after a cat. But campus social life can be lacking, since social events are not held every week and the school doesn't have, in the words of one senior, "a pure student center with activities or other things to help students congregate and enjoy each other's company." There is also no Greek system. Still, students highly anticipate annual events like Christmas Gala and the Gordon Globes student film festival, during which students dress up and walk a red carpet. The "always hilarious" Golden Goose talent show, which pits all four classes against each other, is another favorite tradition. Drinking and smoking are forbidden on campus (and may result in suspension or expulsion); those who are 21 or older may drink off campus but are expected to do so responsibly. The town of Wenham offers "cute shops and restaurants along with other oddities—like used bookstores, jewelry shops, and fresh markets."

For those who love the outdoors, Gordon's setting on rugged Cape Ann, a local tourist attraction, is ideal. The campus has cross-country ski trails and ponds for swimming, canoeing, and skating. The ocean is a quick bike ride away, nice beaches

"Gordon doesn't feel like a cookie-cutter conservative Christian school."

are available on Cape Cod and in Maine, and students frequently ski New Hampshire's nearby White Mountains. Volunteering through a prison ministry and in soup kitchens and local churches is popular, and domestic and international mission trips take students all over, including West Virginia, Northern Ireland, and India. Boston is 25 miles away by a five-minute drive to the T, the city's public transit system, so access to weekend diversions (and excellent internship opportunities) is relatively easy. Gordon students enjoy free entry to the city's Museum of Fine Arts and can also attend Harvard lectures for free.

Gordon's Fighting Scots compete in Division III athletics, and "a good portion of the student body comes out to the games" when the opponent is rival Endicott College, says a history major. Men's and women's soccer and women's track and field are recent Commonwealth Coast Conference champions, and men's and women's basketball are also competitive. Forty percent of the student body participates in club and intramural sports. Everyone looks forward to the annual Highland Games, a day of games and traditional Scottish competitions between dorms.

For many students, Gordon's combination of Christian values, strong academics, and a relatively relaxed atmosphere is a winning one. "Gordon doesn't feel like a cookie-cutter conservative Christian school that's out of touch with the wider world," says a sociology major. "Spirituality partnered with the liberal setting of New England makes Gordon a cool place where faith intersects with real-life issues."

If You Apply To ›

Gordon: Early action I and II, regular decision I and II. SATs or ACTs: optional. Accepts the Common Application with supplement. Applicants to music or art programs must audition or submit portfolio.

Goucher College

Baltimore, MD 21204

Strategically located near Baltimore and not far from D.C., Goucher offers an excellent internship program, a diverse student body, and plenty of personal attention. Strong in the sciences and communication. Distinctive requirement that all students spend time studying or working abroad makes for a globally oriented community.

Goucher is the kind of place where quirky students take part in stellar programs ranging from dance to chemistry. The school's mission is to prepare students for a life of inquiry, creativity, and critical and analytical thinking. There's a decidedly international bent to the Goucher experience, including a robust study abroad program that sends students packing for far-flung locales around the globe. Says a senior, "Individuals who truly want to expand their mind and perspective through immersion in different cultures should seriously consider Goucher."

Formerly a staid women's college that was founded in 1885 and went co-ed in 1987, Goucher has a long-standing history of excellence. (The name comes from donors of its original campus in downtown Baltimore.) Phi Beta Kappa established a chapter on campus only 20 years after the college was founded, and Goucher ranks high among liberal arts colleges in turning out students destined for Ph.D.s in the sciences. Set on 287 landscaped acres in the suburbs of Baltimore, Goucher's wooded campus features lush lawns, stately fieldstone buildings (the fieldstone is mined from local quarries), and an equestrian field. The Athenaeum is the central gathering place, housing the library, an open forum for performances, exercise spaces, a café, and other vital college facilities. Recent campus additions include the First-Year Village, featuring three new residence halls.

The Goucher Commons curriculum is designed to expose students to complex problem-solving through a multidisciplinary lens. All students must demonstrate proficiency in writing, data analytics, and a foreign language and take coursework

Website: www.goucher.edu
Location: Suburban
Private
Total Enrollment: 1,113
Undergraduates: 1,046
Male/Female: 34/66
Financial Aid: 85%
Pell Grant: 26%
Expense: Pr $ $
Student Loans: 64%
Average Debt: $ $ $
Applicants: 2,723
Accepted: 82%
Enrolled: 12%
Grad in 6 Years: 68%
Returning Freshmen: 80%
Academics: ✐ ✐ ✐
Social: ☎ ☎ ☎
Q of L: ★ ★ ★
Admissions: (410) 337-6100

(continued)

Email Address: admissions@
goucher.edu

Strong Programs:
Biology
Chemistry
Communication and Media
    Studies
Computer Science
Dance
Psychology
Environmental Science
Business Management

Goucher was the first college in the nation to require all of its undergraduates to study abroad at least once before graduation.

focusing on environmental sustainability and race, power, and perspective. First-year students begin with a First-Year Seminar course, juniors study abroad, and seniors synthesize and reflect on their educational experiences by completing a capstone experience or research project.

Of Goucher's offerings, the science departments (especially biology and chemistry) are arguably the strongest, bolstered by resources like a nuclear magnetic resonance spectrometer and an observatory with a six-inch refractor telescope. Communication and media studies and computer science are other traditional strengths, and the dance department is recognized as one of the best at a liberal arts school. The psychology, communication and media studies, environmental science, and business management majors draw the highest enrollment. Newer majors include integrative data analytics, professional and creative writing, and engineering science. Unique minors include Arabic studies, historic preservation, and equine studies.

> **"Everyone receives individualized suggestions and attention specific to [their] strengths and improvement points."**

According to a psychology major, Goucher academics focus on "growth, meaning that everyone receives individualized suggestions and attention specific to [their] strengths and improvement points." Faculty members here devote most of their time and energy to undergraduate teaching and have a good rapport with students. "Professors are exceptionally accessible to students, whether for homework help, understanding key concepts, or just getting to know one another," explains a political science major. Each first-year has a dedicated student success team to assist with academic advising, career skills, and the overall adjustment to college life, which is made easier by Goucher's trademark small classes and individual instruction. Students roundly praise the Academic Center for Excellence (ACE), which offers academic support services like study-skills workshops and supplemental instruction. Says a senior, "ACE contains some of the most calming, enlightened souls you'll encounter."

Goucher was the first college in the nation to require all of its undergraduates to study abroad at least once before graduation; more than 60 programs are available in more than 30 countries. Most students head for foreign lands during their junior year, and the experience is expected to complement their major field of study. About half of students embark on semester-long programs, while the other half engage in three-week intensive courses offered during January term or summer. Students may apply their Goucher financial aid packages to study abroad. Many students opt to complete an internship or off-campus experience related to their major. Popular choices include congressional offices, museums, law firms, and media companies.

Forty-three percent of Goucher's students are homegrown and 2 percent are international; most of the rest hail from Pennsylvania, New York, New Jersey, and California. Women still outnumber men 2 to 1. Black students make up 26 percent of the student body, Hispanics/Latinos 8 percent, Asian Americans 4 percent, and multiracial students 2 percent. The Center for Race, Equity, and Identity supports marginalized populations on campus and creates programming that encourages cross-cultural understanding. Students agree that progressive social activism is prevalent on campus. "People are consistently tabling, signing petitions, voicing their opinions, and getting involved," confirms a women, gender, and sexuality studies major. Goucher offers merit scholarships averaging $24,200 for those who qualify but no athletic scholarships.

> **"We are dining pretty lavishly here."**

Seventy-three percent of students live on campus. Options range from new, hotel-like residences for first-years to senior apartments. Upperclassmen select housing through lotteries, and a sophomore says, "Housekeeping is friendly, and most students get the rooms that they want. It's a very family-like atmosphere." Campus dining options, which include vegan and vegetarian fare, receive enthusiastic reviews. Says a senior, "We are dining pretty lavishly here." One student notes, "Sexual assault is not a taboo topic at Goucher, and many people feel comfortable talking about it," which helps bring attention to "opportunities for improvement."

Goucher has no sororities or fraternities, but the housing units hold periodic events, and the college hosts concerts, lectures, weekend movies, and more than 60 student clubs. Parties tend to be low-key affairs ("small gatherings with less than 15 people," says a psych major); neighboring Towson University offers a more traditional party scene. Alcohol is ever-present but not the hub of Goucher's social life. Major annual events include Gala, Winter Carnival, and Get into Goucher Day, which is "a huge festival held every spring that students look forward to. There are inflatables, great food, live music, and all kinds of other cool stuff," explains a senior. Students frequent the restaurants and bars in Towson, the small but bustling college town a five-minute walk away, and a car is useful for visiting Baltimore's Inner Harbor for entertainment. Roughly two-thirds of students volunteer, many through community-based learning programs that tie hands-on service experience in the local area with academic coursework. Students get involved in local politics, too, says a senior: "The Goucher Poll is a pretty unique activity that monitors public perception of social issues and decisions via telephone poll."

The Gophers field 20 varsity teams that compete in the Division III Landmark Conference. The co-ed equestrian team is nationally competitive, and men's tennis, men's golf, and women's field hockey are perennial conference playoff contenders. Twenty percent of students play on club and intramural teams, with ultimate Frisbee and eSports being the most active. Students here can get creative with their recreational pursuits: the Humans vs. Zombies game originated at Goucher in 2005.

Far from a stagnant place, Goucher is constantly rethinking its mission and redirecting its resources to broaden student experiences in a hands-on, global way. "Goucher will force you to engage with challenging topics like sexism, racism, and classism," says a senior, but in a close-knit, supportive environment focused on personal growth for all kinds of learners.

Goucher's co-ed equestrian team is nationally competitive.

Overlaps

Connecticut College, Kalamazoo, Kenyon, Bard, Muhlenberg, American University, Wheaton (MA), Lewis & Clark

If You Apply To ›

Goucher: Early action, regular decision. SATs or ACTs: optional. Accepts the Common Application.

Grinnell College

Grinnell, IA 50112

Iowa cornfields provide a surreal backdrop for Grinnell's funky, progressive, and talented student body. With just over 1,700 students, Grinnell is two-thirds the size of Oberlin. That translates into tiny classes and tutorials. Second only to Carleton as the best liberal arts college in the Midwest. Grinnell's biggest challenge is simply getting prospective students to the campus. The cornfields make for a tight-knit campus community with lots of future Ph.D.s.

Website: www.grinnell.edu

Location: Rural

Private

Total Enrollment: 1,709

Undergraduates: 1,709

Male/Female: 47/53

Financial Aid: 89%

Pell Grant: 17%

Expense: Pr $ $ $ $

Student Loans: 57%

Average Debt: $

Applicants: 10,513

Accepted: 11%

Enrolled: 43%

Grad in 6 Years: 78%

Returning Freshmen: 93%

Academics: ✑ ✑ ✑ ✑ ½

Social: ☎ ☎

Q of L: ★ ★ ★

Admissions: (641) 269-3600

Email Address: admission@ grinnell.edu

Strong Programs:

Economics

Political Science

Computer Science

Theater and Dance

Foreign Languages

Biology

Psychology

The first-semester writing tutorial, modeled after Oxford University's program, allows first-years to work individually with professors.

"Go West, young man, go West," Horace Greeley said to Josiah B. Grinnell in 1846. The result of Grinnell's wanderings into the rural cornfields, about an hour from Des Moines and Iowa City, is the remarkable college that bears his name. Despite its physical isolation, Grinnell is an academic powerhouse on the national scene. Its $2.9 billion endowment, largely built on the stock-picking advice of erstwhile trustee Warren Buffett, is one of the largest of any liberal arts college.

Ever progressive, Grinnell was the first college west of the Mississippi to admit Black students and women and the first in the country to establish an undergraduate political science department. It was once a stop on the Underground Railroad, and its graduates include Harry Hopkins, architect of the New Deal, and Robert Noyce, inventor of the integrated circuit, two people who did as much as anyone to change the face of American society in the 20th century. The school's 120-acre campus is an attractive blend of collegiate Gothic and modern Bauhaus academic buildings and Prairie-style houses. (Architecture buffs should take note of the dazzling Louis Sullivan bank facade just off campus.) Recent additions include the $112 million Humanities and Social Studies Complex, which facilitates multidisciplinary collaboration and research.

True to its liberal arts focus, Grinnell mandates a first-semester writing tutorial, modeled after Oxford University's program, but doesn't require anything else. The roughly 35 tutorials, limited to about 12 students each, help enhance critical thinking, research, writing, and discussion skills and allow first-year students to work individually with professors. Recent offerings include Pandemics and Society, The Empire Writes Back, and Go the F**k to Sleep. "Tutorials are fun, interesting, and a great introduction to the academic possibilities that Grinnell has to offer," one student says. When it comes to declaring a major, students determine their own course of study with help from faculty. In an effort to show the practical relevance of the liberal arts, Grinnell assigns an "explanatory advisor" to every first-year student to help them develop a sense of direction. They can then join any of seven "career communities," such as Education Professions and Business and Finance.

"Due to the college's enormous endowment, the sciences are top-notch."

Departments in the social and natural sciences are strong, the latter bolstered by an influx of research grants. "Due to the college's enormous endowment, the sciences are top-notch, with the best equipment and graduate-level research at the undergraduate level," offers one student. Economics, political science, computer science, theater and dance, and foreign languages (including German and Russian) are among the strongest majors; computer science, economics, biology, political science, and psychology enroll the most students. Grinnell's admissions standards are high, and nearly one-third of graduates move on directly to graduate and professional schools. Students who don't mind studying, even on weekends, will be happiest here. Although the workload can be intense, a political science major says, "Virtually no one has the cutthroat attitude I've heard about at other schools." Sixty-three percent of classes have fewer than 20 students. Teaching is the top priority for Grinnell faculty members, and because the college awards no graduate degrees, there are no teaching assistants hanging around. "In general, profs are here to teach and have generous office hours," a sophomore says.

When the urge to travel arises, students may study abroad in the Grinnell-in-London program or in more than 100 other approved programs. Fifty-five percent of students spend some time away from campus, and financial aid extends to study abroad. The Grinnell-in-Washington program combines coursework with an internship in the nation's capital. Forty-five percent of students participate in undergraduate research, including the Mentored Advanced Project program, which enables them to work closely with a faculty member on scholarly research or the creation of a work of art. Co-ops in architecture, business, law, medicine, and 3–2 engineering programs are also available.

Grinnell is a bit of Greenwich Village in corn country. Despite the rural environment, the college attracts an urban clientele, especially from the Chicago area. Only 7 percent of Grinnellians are from Iowa, while 20 percent are international. "We're quirky, often hippie and liberal, though increasingly diverse," a student observes. The student body is 8 percent Hispanic/Latino, 8 percent Asian American, 5 percent Black, and 6 percent multiracial. Student groups such as the Intersectional Feminism Alliance, Social Entrepreneurs of Grinnell, and Grinnell Advocates (offering support for survivors of gender-based violence) help set the tone on campus. Admissions are need-blind, and the college meets 100 percent of admitted students' demonstrated need with loan-free financial aid packages. Merit awards averaging $19,200 are handed out annually, but there are no athletic awards. Grinnell policy dictates that at least 15 percent of every first-year class will be students whose parents did not go to college.

Admissions are need-blind, and the college meets 100 percent of students' demonstrated need with loan-free financial aid packages.

Grinnell guarantees four years of campus housing, and 88 percent of students take advantage of the residence halls, which are clustered into three areas: "East Campus is lovely but can be isolated and quiet, while South Campus is a sprawling warren usually known for being the hub of campus nightlife, and North Campus is a bit of a happy medium," explains a sophomore. All but two residence halls are co-ed, and after their first year, students participate in a sometimes stressful room draw. Meals in the dining hall are usually satisfactory, students say, although the options and hours can be limited. Safety on this rural campus is reported to be strong.

"We're quirky, often hippie and liberal, though increasingly diverse."

With no fraternities or sororities, all-campus parties revolve mainly around sports teams and the residence halls. "I liken the experience to that of a cruise ship," says one student, "in that the students all stay in one place and entertainment is brought to campus." Each dorm periodically sponsors a party using wordplay from its name in the title. For instance, James Hall puts on the Mary-Be-James party, for which everyone comes in drag. As for alcohol, a senior reports, "Grinnell is not a dry campus, but there are no bars on campus and there is no peer pressure to drink or culture of problematic drinking." Grinnell's social groups and activities range from the SciFi Association and the Queer Rainbow Super Team to improvisational workshops, poetry readings, symposia, concerts, and movies. Highlights of the campus calendar include semiformal Winter and Spring Waltzes, where "most people wear formals and look very nice, not a common occurrence at a school where comfort is the usual standard and women rarely wear makeup," notes one student. Titular Head is a festival of five-minute student films. During finals week, the library sponsors study breaks that have been known to feature free milk and cookies, choir sing-alongs, librarians reading their favorite picture books aloud, bubble-wrap-popping sessions, and other stress-relieving activities.

During finals week, the library sponsors study breaks that have been known to feature choir sing-alongs and bubble-wrap-popping sessions.

Grinnell (population 9,500) is "a small farming community with a nice downtown." The college's Service and Social Innovation Program works to bridge the town-gown gap by connecting students with more than 80 area nonprofit and community partners for service opportunities. Nearby Rock Creek State Park lends itself to biking, running, camping, kayaking, and cross-country skiing, and the Grinnell Outdoor Recreation Program sponsors a variety of pursuits, including off-campus trips and open rock-climbing sessions. There are a few bars and pizza joints downtown, but for those craving bright lights, Iowa City and Des Moines are within an hour's drive, and the college runs a shuttle service to them. Chicago and Minneapolis are each about four hours distant.

"We love that you won't come here because you want a big name."

The Grinnell Pioneers compete in Division III athletics, and the men's basketball team has won national attention for an unusual run-and-gun offense that uses waves of five players like hockey shifts in an effort to wear down opponents. Recent conference champions include women's tennis and men's and women's swimming and diving. About a third of students play intramural sports, which offer competitive and noncompetitive options.

Grinnell wouldn't put a grin on every prospective college student's face. "Most of us don't apologize for what at first turns people off about Grinnell," explains a senior. "We like being in the middle of Iowa, we like that you've probably never heard of us, we love that you won't come here because you want a big name." But there's no denying that Grinnell—a first-rate liberal arts college in an unlikely location—is a real gem of a school, and one that is still relatively accessible.

Overlaps

Macalester, St. Olaf, Kenyon, Carleton, Colorado College, Beloit, Oberlin, Vassar

If You Apply To ›

Grinnell: Early decision I and II, regular decision. SATs or ACTs: optional. Accepts the Common Application.

Guilford College

5800 West Friendly Avenue, Greensboro, NC 27410

One of the few schools of Quaker heritage in the South, Guilford emphasizes a collaborative approach and is among the most liberal institutions below the Mason-Dixon line. A kindred spirit to Earlham in Indiana. With a notably high Black population and strong socioeconomic diversity, Guilford's signature program is community and justice studies. Presence of a cluster of older students enriches the campus culture.

Website: www.guilford.edu
Location: Small City
Private
Total Enrollment: 981
Undergraduates: 981
Male/Female: 50/50
Financial Aid: 100%
Pell Grant: 56%
Expense: Pr $
Student Loans: 70%
Average Debt: $
Applicants: 2,584
Accepted: 96%
Enrolled: 10%
Grad in 6 Years: 55%
Returning Freshmen: 58%
Academics: ✐ ✐ ✐
Social: ☎ ☎
Q of L: ★ ★ ★ ★
Admissions: (336) 316-2100
Email Address: admission@ guilford.edu

If your idea of a rousing road trip is protesting in Washington, D.C., you'll likely find plenty of like-minded compatriots at Guilford College. Founded in 1837 by the Religious Society of Friends (Quakers), this left-leaning campus loves to debate just about any issue and get involved in the world around it. The student body is becoming more diverse in every respect, and campus inclusiveness is enhanced by a long-standing adult education program. "I'm proud to be part of a school that is very accepting and open," comments a sports management and marketing major.

Located on 350 wooded acres in northwest Greensboro, Guilford's redbrick buildings are mainly in the Georgian style. The school is the only liberal arts college in the Southeast with Quaker roots; it's the oldest coeducational institution in the South and the third oldest in the nation. During the Civil War, Guilford was one of a few Southern colleges that remained open—perhaps because it was also an embarkation point on the Underground Railroad. All of the first-year residence halls have recently been renovated, and 200 solar panels have made the campus more environmentally friendly.

> **"[Students] will be forming strong student and professor relationships."**

Guilford's general education program for traditional students, the Guilford Edge, emphasizes team-based, interdisciplinary projects. Guilford follows a 12–3 academic calendar, in which every semester includes a 12-week session as well as a three-week intensive course or off-campus experience. In addition to selecting a traditional, primary major, students identify a passion or issue that they explore in-depth, in the spirit of Quaker queries or questions. Guilford Edge also builds in comprehensive academic and career advising, campuswide events aimed at enhancing community spirit, and training in ethical leadership development that the college hopes will, among other things, boost applications and retention rates.

"The college is centered on the Quaker values of community, diversity, equality, excellence, integrity, justice, and stewardship," explains a senior. Students say Guilford's most popular programs are also some of its best: business administration, psychology, exercise and sport sciences, biology, and sport management. Forensic biology and religious studies are notable as well. Business analytics is Guilford's newest major. The signature justice and policy studies department offers majors in community and justice studies and criminal justice. A unique, issues-based minor in principled problem-solving experience (PPSE) combines interdisciplinary coursework with hands-on learning that addresses a complex social issue. The PPSE topic changes regularly; one recent topic, Every Campus a Refuge, focused on how to mobilize college campuses to provide housing and other support to refugees during their initial resettlement. Classes at Guilford are small, with 73 percent enrolling fewer than 20 students, helping to create a more personal environment. A student says, "As long as students are willing to be challenged, they will be forming strong student and professor relationships."

> **"In most classes, you will be doing some kind of hands-on learning."**

(continued)

Strong Programs:
Community and Justice Studies
Criminal Justice
Business Administration
Psychology
Exercise and Sport Sciences
Biology
Sport Management
Religious Studies

Guilford believes that experiential learning adds immeasurably to classroom work, so faculty-mentored research and travel are important emphases. "In most classes, you will be doing some kind of hands-on learning, applying the knowledge you're learning to real-life situations," says a health sciences and chemistry double major. In addition to standard laboratory equipment, science students have access to a lake, an organic farm, and 220 acres of woodland property on campus, which provide a rich resource for fieldwork in environmental and sustainability studies. Guilford has several endowed funds that support student scientific research and travel, including an award for Women in Physical Science. The college offers study abroad in 75 nations; 12 percent of students participate. The Brunnenberg Semester gives students a chance to live and learn in a 13th-century castle in the Italian Alps.

In addition to selecting a traditional, primary major, students identify a passion or issue that they explore in-depth.

In the words of a sophomore, Guilford students are "hardworking, brave, smart, and outgoing." They come from across the globe and a range of socioeconomic backgrounds; most are liberal and about 2 percent identify with the Quaker religious tradition. Seventy-six percent of students are in-staters, and 1 percent are international. Black students represent 28 percent of the student body, Hispanics/Latinos 15 percent, Asian Americans 3 percent, and multiracial students 5 percent; 56 percent of freshmen are eligible for Pell Grants. Guilford has made a point of enriching its student body by enrolling a sizable number of older students. About 10 percent of full-time undergraduates are 23 or older and benefit from a large selection of evening classes and their own adult education orientation and counseling services. A junior says the population of adult students "adds a lot to classes because of their different life experiences." In an effort to promote affordability, Guilford now promises to award every first-time applicant an automatic scholarship of at least $15,000 (and up to $30,000, depending on high school GPA) and guarantees that tuition will not increase over a student's four years. In addition, every student who lives on campus receives a $4,000 housing grant. As a Division III school, Guilford does not offer athletic scholarships.

> **"It is easy to find people just lounging in the grass or down by the lake."**

All traditional students under the age of 23 are required to live on campus; Guilford's many older students are generally commuters and less involved in campus social life. On-campus apartments for juniors and seniors are comparable in price to off-campus digs. Bryan is the party dorm, while Mary Hobbs is all-female and Shore is gender-inclusive. "The dining options on campus are fantastic," cheers a student. Campus safety gets good ratings too.

Guilford's social life revolves around student clubs and organizations, of which there are more than 50. "When the weather is nice, a lot of events happen outside, and it is easy to find people just lounging in the grass or down by the lake," says one student. Greek life is nonexistent, and alcohol is not allowed at college functions; nonetheless, there is a moderate party scene that students describe as "not toxic" and "very safe." Serendipity, a weeklong celebration of spring with student performances, games, lots of free food, big-name musicians, and a formal dance, is a beloved tradition. Beyond the campus gates, students find all of the essentials—Target, Starbucks, some clubs in downtown Greensboro (only 10 minutes away), the ethnic restaurants of Tate Street, and the college's Quaker Village. About a third of the students regularly volunteer in the community. Popular road trips include UNC at Chapel Hill (one hour), Asheville and the mountains (three and a half hours), and the famous Outer Banks beaches (four and a half hours).

Guilford's Division III athletic teams compete as the Fighting Quakers, and students cherish the oxymoron, as in their cheer: "Fight, fight, inner light! Kill, Quakers, kill!" Students root for the football team in the annual Soup Bowl against Greensboro College, while the men's golf team has brought home a slew of conference titles in recent years. The men's basketball, women's volleyball, baseball, and softball teams have also been successful. Intramural and club sports draw 20 percent of the students. Because of Guilford's emphasis on developing the whole person, physically, mentally, and spiritually, students are encouraged to participate in school-sponsored outdoor adventures, such as a ropes course, sailing, and white-water rafting.

A popular Guilford mantra is: "How are you going to change the world?" And with students who'd rather get involved than sit back and watch, you can expect some pretty passionate answers to that question. It all goes back to Guilford's traditional Quaker goal of "educating individuals not only to live, but to live well." As one student explains it, "You will be pushed outside of your comfort zone in a lot of ways, but Guilford is also a place for growth."

Overlaps

Bridgewater, Eckerd, Roanoke, Centre, Wofford, Earlham, Albright, Elmhurst

If You Apply To ›

Guilford: Early decision, early action, rolling admissions. SATs or ACTs: optional (test-optional applicants must submit an additional essay). Accepts the Common Application with supplement.

Gustavus Adolphus College

800 West College Avenue, St. Peter, MN 56082

A touch of Scandinavia in southern Minnesota, GA is a guardian of the tried and true in Lutheran education. With Minnesotans comprising 83 percent of the students, GA is less national than cross-state rival St. Olaf. Extensive distribution requirements include exploring values and moral reasoning. Minnesota location makes for a friendly and homogeneous student body. And where else can you find a Hello Walk?

Website: www.gustavus.edu
Location: Small Town
Private
Total Enrollment: 2,215
Undergraduates: 2,215

Gustavus Adolphus College is named for Sweden's King Gustav II Adolph (1594–1632), who is credited with making Sweden a major European power and defending Lutheranism against the Roman Catholics. While the king's military victories earned him the title Lion of the North, he was also an advocate of education and culture. Save for the women now attending classes, King Gustav would probably feel at home at the college that bears his name, where a not-so-subtle

Swedish influence pervades everything from the buildings to the curriculum. The college, founded in 1862, is the "epitome of Minnesota nice," says one sophomore admiringly.

The 340-acre GA campus is about 65 miles southwest of the Twin Cities. Not surprisingly, the prevailing architectural theme is Scandinavian, with mostly modern and semimodern brown brick buildings. Highlights include the 147-year-old Old Main and the centrally located Christ Chapel, with spires and shafts resembling a crown. Thirty bronze works by sculptor and alumnus Paul Granlund are strategically placed, and the 135-acre Linnaeus Arboretum and Interpretive Center offers plant study and retreats. The sidewalk running through the middle of campus is nicknamed the Hello Walk, because it's a tradition for students to greet one another as they pass—whether they know each other or not. A $70 million renovation and expansion of the Nobel Hall of Science has nearly doubled the size of the school's natural sciences facilities.

> "[Gusties are] friendly, easy to talk to, energetic, and hardworking."

To fulfill core requirements, Gustavus students have two options. The first, the Liberal Arts Perspective Curriculum, involves fulfilling standard distribution requirements in nine liberal arts areas, plus the First-Term Seminar, which covers critical thinking, writing, speaking, and recognizing and exploring values. The second option, known as the Three Crowns Curriculum, is an integrated 12-course sequence focused on classic works and ideas of the Western tradition, emphasizing connections between different disciplines. Three Crowns is limited to 60 students per entering class, filled on a first-come, first-served basis. In addition to the core courses, students must satisfy a writing-across-the-curriculum requirement, with three courses that have a substantial amount of writing.

In the classroom, students find an academic smorgasbord, as GA aims to offer an education both "interdisciplinary and international in perspective." There are interdisciplinary programs in Scandinavian studies; gender, women, and sexuality studies; and environmental studies, to name a few, and if neither those nor traditional departments suffice, students may design their own courses of study. While biology, psychology, economics, and communication studies are among the most popular majors, nursing, physics, and classics are also strengths, and students give high marks to GA's premed advising program and its offerings in music. For the professionally minded, Gustavus offers 3–2 engineering programs with the University of Minnesota and Minnesota State in Mankato. Overall, academics at Gustavus are rigorous, but students say small classes make it easy to form dependable study groups, and classmates don't compete for grades. "The courses require a lot of work both inside and outside the classroom," says one junior. "Professors expect you to give your best every day, and in return they give you their best." Students find faculty members not just knowledgeable but also friendly, especially when they're serving up a free meal for students during Midnight Express, which precedes final exams.

During the January term, when winter winds force almost everyone indoors, Gustavus students (appropriately known as Gusties) may take concentrated courses on campus or pursue travel and co-op opportunities. The school sponsors study abroad programs at five colleges and universities in—surprise, surprise—Sweden, as well as others in non-Scandinavian haunts such as India, Malaysia, Australia, Russia, and Scotland, and 46 percent of students participate. Learning opportunities also come from several internationally renowned meetings, such as the Nobel Conference, which brings Nobel laureates and other experts to campus for two days each October. Undergraduate research is a hallmark, and Gustavus Adolphus consistently ranks in the top 10 for papers presented at the National Conference on Undergraduate Research.

(continued)

Male/Female: 43/57
Financial Aid: 96%
Pell Grant: 25%
Expense: Pr $ $
Student Loans: 83%
Average Debt: $ $ $ $
Applicants: 3,799
Accepted: 73%
Enrolled: 20%
Grad in 6 Years: 78%
Returning Freshmen: 84%
Academics: ✎ ✎ ✎
Social: ☎ ☎ ☎
Q of L: ★ ★ ★
Admissions:
   1-800-GUSTAVUS
Email Address: admission@ gustavus.edu

Strong Programs:
Nursing
Physics
Classics
Music
Biology
Psychology
Economics
Communication Studies

During the January term, Gustavus students may take concentrated courses on campus or pursue travel and co-op opportunities.

An elementary education major describes Gusties as "friendly, easy to talk to, energetic, and hardworking." For all its good points, though, this liberal arts college is hardly a model of diversity: 79 percent of students are white, 83 percent are Minnesotan, and 52 percent are Lutheran. The school is working hard to increase diversity, but that continues to be a challenge in its region. Black students currently account for 3 percent of the student body, Hispanics/Latinos 5 percent, Asian Americans 4 percent, and multiracial students 4 percent; international students add another 4 percent. Politically, the campus leans liberal but has its fair share of conservatives, and students report that environmental issues and women's and LGBTQ rights are frequent topics of discussion. The merit-based President's Scholarship program offers top students awards of up to $32,000 annually, while Dean's Scholarships range from $15,000 to $27,500. There are no athletic scholarships.

> **"Saturday Night Lights puts on events like poker night, dances, game nights, etc."**

On-campus living is required for all four years, and only about 9 percent of students receive permission to live off campus as seniors, which can be a source of frustration for upperclassmen. One student says the dorms "stay full on the weekends and are well maintained." Single rooms and apartment-style suites, and some college-owned houses, are reserved for upperclassmen. The Crossroads International House is an option for students interested in languages and contemporary global issues. Students rave about the à la carte meal plan and especially about the Marketplace dining hall. In response to recommendations from a student task force, the administration has updated its sexual misconduct policies.

Eleven percent of the men and 15 percent of the women go Greek, but GA's social life does not revolve around fraternities and sororities. "Saturday Night Lights puts on events like poker night, dances, game nights, etc., which always seem to be really fun and always include free food," says a junior. Because students 21 and older may drink in their rooms—with the door closed—underage students can get alcohol if they want it, but students say drinking isn't a popular pastime here. GA's many musical ensembles all perform together at the Christmas in Christ Chapel concert. The chapel holds

> **"Any time, any sport—if St. Olaf is in town, the event is packed."**

1,500 people and performances usually sell out. Sixty-eight percent of students participate in service projects, volunteering 15,000 hours each semester. Projects include working with children, the elderly, and the local animal shelter, as well as with Habitat for Humanity. The town of St. Peter has coffee shops and bowling, and the college offers periodic trips to Mankato, 10 miles away, and to the Twin Cities, for "real" shopping at the Mall of America or for a professional baseball, basketball, or hockey game.

When it comes to athletics, "Any time, any sport—if St. Olaf is in town, the event is packed," says a lusty Gustie fan. GA competes in Division III, and the men's and women's tennis teams are perennial contenders for the national championship title. Men's and women's golf and swimming and women's ice hockey and volleyball have also been successful in Minnesota Intercollegiate Athletic Conference play. The college's forensics team is nationally competitive. A majority of Gusties participate in intramural and club sports, including rugby and cross-country skiing.

The Gustavus Adolphus campus may be gorgeous in the spring and fall and too cold in the winter, but it's warmhearted all year long. Small classes, one-on-one academic attention, a plethora of research opportunities, and an active campus social life go a long way toward making St. Peter, Minnesota, seem a lot less isolated. Says one senior, "Our core values of community, service, faith, justice, and excellence prevail both in and out of the classroom, and students commit themselves and their time here to such values."

The Nobel Conference brings Nobel laureates and other experts to campus for two days each October.

Overlaps

Augustana (IL), Luther, Illinois Wesleyan, College of St. Benedict and St. John's University, St. Olaf, University of St. Thomas, Hamline, College of Wooster

Hamilton College

198 College Hill Road, Clinton, NY 13323

Hamilton is part of the network of elite, rural, Northeastern liberal arts colleges that extends from Colby in Maine through Middlebury and Williams to Colgate, about half an hour's drive to Hamilton's south. Hamilton is on the small side of this group and emphasizes collaboration with faculty. Need-blind admissions with no merit scholarships. Strong commitment to diversity and inclusion.

Founded in 1793, Hamilton College took its name from Alexander Hamilton, who was an early trustee, and for much of its early life offered its male students a staunchly traditional education rooted in a classical curriculum. In 1978, Hamilton merged with adjacent Kirkland College, the artsy, experimental women's college founded under its auspices a decade before. Hamilton is marked by its close sense of community and its commitment to the liberal arts. Particularly dedicated to transforming students into excellent communicators, the college has also increased opportunities for experiential learning and internships and is adding programs to develop students' digital fluency. "Come to Hamilton because you will learn much more than simple facts and data," says an economics major. "You will learn how to think critically, communicate clearly, and lead effectively."

The original Hamilton campus features collegiate Victorian architecture rendered in rich, warm brownstone. In fact, the only facility interrupting the rhythmic beauty of the campus is the eyesore that houses the library. By contrast, the original Kirkland campus consists mostly of boxy concrete structures of a 1960s "brutalist" vintage, otherwise described as "faux I. M. Pei." Straddling the ravine that divides the campuses and joining them literally and figuratively is a student activities building with a diner, lounges, and areas for student and faculty relaxation. Surrounding the campuses are more than 1,000 college-owned acres of woodlands, open fields, and glens, with trails for hiking or cross-country skiing. The college has invested nearly $340 million over the past 15 years in new and renovated facilities, including a studio art building, a theater, and the Johnson Center for Health and Wellness.

> **"You will learn how to think critically, communicate clearly, and lead effectively."**

In the classroom, Hamilton is pure liberal arts. The open general education curriculum has no distribution requirements, but all students must pass at least three writing-intensive courses and a quantitative and symbolic reasoning course. The development of writing skills is a key area of focus in all majors, and more than 100 courses each year require oral presentations. In an effort to reinforce its commitment to inclusion, the college requires that all majors feature relevant, mandatory coursework on diversity. First-year orientation combines on-campus programming with adventure and service trips; more than 65 options are typically available, from participating in local arts events to working with refugee communities to kayaking Lake Champlain. First-year students may also participate in an optional series of proseminars—classes of no more than 16 that require intensive interaction through writing, speaking, and

Website: www.hamilton.edu
Location: Rural
Private
Total Enrollment: 2,048
Undergraduates: 2,048
Male/Female: 46/54
Financial Aid: 51%
Pell Grant: 22%
Expense: Pr $ $ $ $
Student Loans: 47%
Average Debt: $
Applicants: 9,380
Accepted: 14%
Enrolled: 40%
Grad in 6 Years: 92%
Returning Freshmen: 94%
Academics: ✍ ✍ ✍ ✍ ½
Social: ☎ ☎ ☎ ☎
Q of L: ★ ★ ★
Admissions: (800) 843-2655
Email Address: admission@ hamilton.edu

Strong Programs:
Public Policy
Natural Sciences
Economics
Mathematics
Psychology
Government
World Politics
Literature

discussion. Hamilton requires all students to undertake a senior project in their area of concentration, which may take the form of a research project, a seminar with a presentation and research paper component, or a comprehensive exam.

Public policy and the natural sciences are among the strongest programs. Hamilton's Arthur Levitt Public Affairs Center, named for the former New York State comptroller, is a working think tank where undergraduates focus on leadership and social innovation. Economics, mathematics, psychology, and government enroll the most students; world politics, literature, sociology, biology, neuroscience, and creative writing are also popular. New offerings include a major in Japanese and minors in statistics and data science. Courses are rigorous, but "the environment is not viciously competitive," explains a literature major. "People are willing to share notes, sources, research, and even internship openings." Most classes are intimate in size—74 percent enroll fewer than 20 students—and students say professors are dedicated to helping them succeed.

> "People are willing to share notes, sources, research, and even internship openings."

Every incoming student is assigned a faculty advisor, a career advisor, and an ALEX (Advise, Learn, and EXperience) advisor who can assist them with course planning, off-campus learning opportunities, career exploration, and personal growth. Hamilton awards stipends to 130 students each year for summer research, and another 200 students receive stipends to pursue unpaid summer internships. When the village of Clinton (population 2,000) gets claustrophobic, about 60 percent of students spend a semester or a year abroad through more than 100 approved programs or through Hamilton's programs in France, China, and Spain. Students can also study off campus for a term in Washington, D.C., or New York City.

"It's cool to be passionate about things here," says a psychology major. "Students are so involved in a range of different activities; it's kind of lame if you only go to class and don't have a whole bunch of extracurriculars." Twenty-six percent of Hamilton students are New York residents, and 7 percent are international. Black students constitute 3 percent of the student body, Hispanics/Latinos 10 percent, Asian Americans 8 percent, and multiracial students 5 percent. Although the campus is no political hotbed, students report that current issues (both local and global) receive ample attention from student activists. Consistent with Hamilton's commitment to socioeconomic diversity and its Division III status, there are no merit or athletic scholarships, but the college has a need-blind admissions policy and guarantees to meet 100 percent of admitted domestic students' demonstrated financial need.

> "[The professors] picked Hamilton because they wanted to be closer to students."

All students reside on campus. Options range from stately old mansions and former fraternity houses converted into dorms to newer apartments that accommodate three to four students each. Thanks to the lottery system, explains a student, "It's possible to get decent housing even as a rising sophomore." The two sides of campus, Hamilton and Kirkland, feature distinct student cultures and a rivalry that students call "playful" and "endearing." Hamilton (nicknamed "the Light Side") is known for partying and is said to house many "preppy, sporty" students, while Kirkland (nicknamed "the Dark Side") has a more mellow reputation and tends to attract artsy free spirits. Campus dining options receive average reviews. Students say campus security is effective: "The campus is very safe, and we have an amazing Campus Safety team," reports a senior.

Social life at Hamilton ranges from the campus pub, which occupies an old barn, to programming arranged by the campus activities board, such as comedy shows, a casino night, and concerts. There's also the Greek system, which draws 19 percent of the men and 14 percent of the women. Much of the social life does revolve

The development of writing skills is a key area of focus, and more than 100 courses each year require oral presentations.

The two sides of campus, Hamilton and Kirkland, feature distinct student cultures and a rivalry that students call "playful" and "endearing."

around alcohol, students say, although stiff punishments are meted out to underage imbibers. "Campus parties tend to be dominated by underclassmen. Upperclassmen generally make their own parties in the suites or the quads or they go downtown to the two bars," one student says.

Clinton is "a picturesque village good for pizza and coffee," says a sophomore. The nearest small city, Utica, is only 10 minutes away by car. The college maintains a jitney service for student transportation; Uber and Lyft are also options. "On the weekend, people will sometimes go to the Adirondacks because they are so close and beautiful," a student says. "This can be a great way to get back in touch with nature and also have a fun weekend excursion." Given the long, snowy winters, such outings are often best enjoyed by skiers and other winter-sports enthusiasts. Other popular road trips include Syracuse and New York City, while Boston, Toronto, and Montreal are each less than five hours away.

In athletics, Hamilton offers 29 varsity sports teams (the Continentals) and is a member of the highbrow New England Small College Athletic Conference. Women's rowing, women's lacrosse, and men's basketball have been competitive in recent years. The extensive intramural and club sports programs draw high participation, especially in soccer, basketball, and dodgeball. Even some school traditions are athletically minded. Feb Fest features snowshoeing, an ice-sculpture contest, and other winter activities, while Class & Charter Day marks the last day of classes in the spring with ceremonies, a picnic, a concert, and a triathlon the week before.

Feb Fest features snowshoeing, an ice-sculpture contest, and other winter activities.

Hamilton students are, by necessity, hearty. They're used to the cold and the snow—and some may say that's what leads to the strong sense of community evident on campus. But for most, it's the dedicated faculty who foster community spirit as they teach students how to think critically and express themselves effectively. Says a senior, "The professors at Hamilton, from my experience at least, picked Hamilton because they wanted to be closer to students—to watch them grow and to help them grow both inside of the classroom and outside of it."

Overlaps

Amherst, Bates, Bowdoin, Carleton, Colby, Colgate, Middlebury, Williams

If You Apply To ›

Hamilton: Early decision I and II, regular decision. Accepts the Common Application. Please consult Hamilton's website for the most up-to-date information regarding standardized test scores.

Hampden–Sydney College

P.O. Box 667, Hampden–Sydney, VA 23943

The last bastion of the Southern gentleman and one of three all-male colleges in the nation. Feeder school to the economic establishment in Richmond. Picturesque rural setting evokes the old South. While some would argue that it is out of step with today's world, H–SC holds to its mission of asking what it means to be a "good man" in today's society.

Hampden–Sydney College was founded by Scotch-Irish Presbyterians in 1775 with the University of Edinburgh as its model and took its name from two 17th-century English patriots (John Hampden and Algernon Sydney). Seemingly a bit of an anachronism in a society increasingly focused on diversity, the all-male school still aims to expose its small student body to a broad liberal arts education, which is entirely focused on undergraduates. H–SC is one of only three all-male colleges in the nation

Website: www.hsc.edu
Location: Rural
Private
Total Enrollment: 851
Undergraduates: 851

(continued)

Male/Female: 100/0
Financial Aid: 98%
Pell Grant: 19%
Expense: Pr $ $
Student Loans: 66%
Average Debt: $ $ $ $
Applicants: 2,911
Accepted: 37%
Enrolled: 21%
Grad in 6 Years: 65%
Returning Freshmen: 90%
Academics: ✎ ✎ ✎
Social: ☎ ☎ ☎ ☎
Q of L: ★ ★ ★ ★
Admissions: (434) 223-6120
Email Address: admissions@
    hsc.edu

Strong Programs:
Rhetoric
Economics and Business
Economics
Mathematical Economics
History
Biology
Government
Physics

The Wilson Center for Leadership in the Public Interest puts a public service focus on the study of political science.

and one of only two without a coordinate women's college (see also Wabash). The environment supports "a special sense of brotherhood and community," says one student. Tradition reigns here and students like to call themselves "Southern gentlemen." Of course, says another, there's plenty of not-always-gentlemanly fun to be had when you have 850 guys together.

Hampden–Sydney's 1,340-acre campus, surrounded by farmland and woods, features mainly redbrick buildings in the Federal style. The Pannill Center for Rhetoric and Communication houses the college's Rhetoric Program, writing and speaking centers, and student publications. Completed in 2022, the $40 million Pauley Science Center features state-of-the-art labs, classrooms, and interactive spaces. The nearby town of Farmville, population 7,500 and home to Longwood University, offers restaurants, stores, and a movie theater; it's just five miles from H–SC, but one student describes the town as "a black hole inside a time warp."

> **"Most students are willing to put in that work in order to become better writers and thinkers."**

To graduate, students must demonstrate proficiency in rhetoric and a foreign language, complete coursework in a range of liberal arts areas, and take at least three experiential learning courses, one of which must have a significant off-campus component, such as fieldwork, an internship, or travel abroad. All freshmen participate in a special advising program, and 30 percent take freshman seminars linked to living/learning communities. Most majors require a capstone course involving a 20-page research paper. The most popular department is economics and business, which may help explain why more than half of the school's alumni have pursued business careers. The department offers three majors: economics and business, general economics, and mathematical economics. History, biology, and government are also popular, and physics is strong. The Wilson Center for Leadership in the Public Interest puts a public service focus on the study of political science, preparing students for government work and garnering high marks in return. The school's small size offers many opportunities to work closely with professors, but has some academic drawbacks, including limited resources in some departments and fewer than 30 majors.

Students at Hampden–Sydney say there are no free passes when it comes to classwork, and the atmosphere can get competitive. "You really have to work hard," says a junior, "but most students are willing to put in that work in order to become better writers and thinkers." Classes are small; 79 percent have fewer than 20 students and none exceed 50. Most H–SC professors live on campus and make themselves very available to students. Some even make house calls to find out why a student missed class. "Professors encourage us to contact them whenever we have a question, even if that means at nine o'clock on a Wednesday night," says a junior.

Additional educational opportunities include the honors program, the summer research program (which is particularly popular among students in the sciences), and the Tigerfund, which allows students to manage an equity fund. More than 100 study abroad options are available in 30 countries and revered institutions around the world, including Oxford, Cambridge, and the London School of Economics; 20 percent of students spread their wings in this way. Career services are said to be effective, particularly when it comes to connecting students with alumni for job opportunities.

"The prototypical Hampden–Sydney student is a Southern, white, Christian gentleman with conservative political values," says a junior. Seventy percent of students are state residents, and less than 1 percent come from foreign countries. Black students make up 7 percent of the student body, Hispanics/Latinos constitute 5 percent, Asian Americans add 1 percent, and multiracial students represent 4 percent. The Office of Inclusion and Intercultural Affairs works to increase tolerance for diversity, which students say is among the hot-button political issues on campus. As a Division III school, Hampden–Sydney offers no athletic scholarships. There are, however, academic awards averaging $22,400 for qualified students.

Ninety-eight percent of students live on campus in traditional and apartment-style residence halls, and housing is guaranteed for four years. "Freshmen are usually grouped in the larger housing areas in order for them to get the college roommate experience," says one student, and a dozen living/learning communities are available to choose from as well. The spacious dining facilities supply hungry students with "decent," all-you-can-eat fare. Student support services receive good reviews, although one religion major notes, "There is a bit of a stigma [against] using the counseling service, as we all aim to be macho at this boys' school."

> "[Farmville is] a black hole inside a time warp."

Students praise the close-knit atmosphere fostered by Hampden–Sydney's all-male status. "Our code of etiquette requires that we acknowledge people we pass on the sidewalk and reserve our phone calls and headphones for less populated areas, so we get to know each other on a personal level," explains a junior. Hampden–Sydney's social nexus is the Circle, the site of the school's fraternities, which claim 30 percent of the students. "The party culture is huge. Greek organizations absolutely set the tone for the vast majority of our social environment," says one student, who adds, "Alcohol policies are not effective." The annual spring Greek Week brings out the *Animal House* instincts of Hampden–Sydney's budding gentlemen—but students warn that campus security will crack down on underage drinkers if parties get too wild. Student clubs offer another important outlet for socializing, and homecoming and various music festivals are also eagerly anticipated. Nearby women's colleges—Hollins, Sweet Briar, and Mary Baldwin—help mix up the social scene.

More than 100 study abroad options are available, including programs at Oxford, Cambridge, and the London School of Economics.

Despite its lack of bright lights ("You come here for the school, not the town," one student points out), nearby Farmville does provide numerous community service and outreach opportunities. A campus volunteer group called Good Men, Good Citizens spearheads projects such as tutoring, highway cleanup, and Habitat for Humanity home building; 75 percent of students perform community service. When rural Virginia gets too insular, H–SC students can be found on road trips to the University of Virginia and James Madison University, Virginia's beaches, or Washington, D.C. The ski slopes of Wintergreen are within a two-hour drive.

> "The party culture is huge. Greek organizations absolutely set the tone."

Perhaps because of all that testosterone on campus, Hampden–Sydney men are competitive, and that spells excellence in athletics. Tiger football is big; students attend games in coat and tie, and alumni come out in droves for tailgating. H–SC's football rivalry with Randolph–Macon (not the former women's college!) is one of the oldest in the South. At the annual pregame bonfire, the college rallies to sing songs and hear student and faculty leaders vilify the enemy and extol "the garnet and gray." The golf and lacrosse teams are nationally ranked. Sixty percent of students participate in intramural and recreational sports ranging from basketball and flag football to clay-target club and rugby.

Hampden–Sydney likes to tell new students that when they enter the campus gates, they're "joining a brotherhood older than America itself." The school's legacy as the 10th-oldest college in the United States may make it largely conservative and rather homogeneous. But 248 years of tradition, an unwavering commitment to the liberal arts, and a tight-knit student body also make for a rich—and unique—undergraduate experience.

Overlaps

Wabash, Augustana (IL), Austin College, Randolph–Macon, Roanoke, Transylvania, James Madison, Sewanee

Hampshire College

P.O. Box 5001, Amherst, MA 01002

Long a leader in progressive and student-focused higher education, Hampshire is on the rebound from a bruising financial and enrollment crisis that forced administrators to pause freshman enrollment in 2019. After a period of regrouping and bolstered by a $60 million fund-raising campaign led by filmmaker and alumnus Ken Burns, Hampshire has increased its total enrollment to 465 undergraduates and plans to restore full enrollment by 2025. This nonconformist college has been marching to its own academic drummer for more than 50 years.

Website: www.hampshire.edu
Location: Small Town
Private
Total Enrollment: 465
Undergraduates: 465
Male/Female: 38/62
Financial Aid: 73%
Pell Grant: 48%
Expense: Pr $ $
Student Loans: 68%
Average Debt: $ $ $
Applicants: 1,337
Accepted: 75%
Enrolled: 13%
Grad in 6 Years: 62%
Returning Freshmen: 72%
Academics: ✍ ✍ ✍ ✍
Social: 🐦 🐦 🐦
Q of L: ★ ★ ★
Admissions: (413) 559-5471
Email Address: admissions@
hampshire.edu

Strong Programs:
Film, Video, and Photography
Communications
Creative Writing
Psychology
Social Sciences
Environmental Studies
Cognitive Science

Passion reigns at Hampshire College. It's found in just about everything students do—from devising their own courses to starting new clubs to debating the most current social issues. There's no one way to do things at Hampshire, and the students revel in the freedom they have to direct the path of their education. "We love what we are studying because we get to choose what we are studying," says a junior focusing on sustainable agricultural methods. Without the yoke of traditional majors and the nail-biting stress of regular grades, Hampshire offers a virtually boundary-free exercise in intellectual nirvana.

Located in the Connecticut River Valley of western Massachusetts, Hampshire's 800-acre campus sits amid former orchards, farmland, and forest. Buildings are eclectic and contemporary, and the school is proud of its bioshelter, arts village, and multi-sports and multimedia centers. Two nationally known museums—the Yiddish Book Center and the Eric Carle Museum of Picture Book Art—are located right on campus. The innovative Kern Center is the campus's "living building." Constructed entirely with local and regional nontoxic materials, the 17,000-square-foot building generates its own electricity and collects its own water. It's the latest in a series of sustainability efforts that also include converting the campus to 100 percent solar electricity.

> "The academic climate is not competitive because no two students study the exact same thing."

Hampshire was created in 1965 by four nearby colleges—Amherst, UMass Amherst, Mount Holyoke, and Smith—that now make up the Five College Consortium. The goal was to reimagine liberal arts education. Instead of grades, Hampshire professors hand out "narrative evaluations," which consist of written evaluations and critiques. The Community-Engaged Learning program requires all students to commit to 40 hours of service or a semester-long equivalent. Degrees are obtained by passing a series of examinations—not tests but portfolios of academic work, evaluations, and students' self-reflections on their academic development.

The first milestone, known as Division I, begins with transdisciplinary seminars in two of four "learning collaboratives"—communities of faculty, staff, and students—centered on the themes of environments and change, justice and injustice, media and technology, and time and narrative. The second milestone, Division II, is each student's "concentration." Unlike a major elsewhere, the requirements of a concentration are unique to each student, emerging from regular discussions with two faculty members, and include courses, independent study, and fieldwork or internships. Division III, or "advanced study," begins in the fourth year, when students complete a sizable independent study project centered on a specific topic, question, or idea, much like a master's thesis. In recent years, students have created smartphone software to monitor blood sugar and examined U.S. military interventions in global conflicts.

Because of the division system, there are as many curricula at Hampshire as there are students. The common denominators are a rigorous workload, an emphasis on self-initiated study, close contact with faculty advisors, and the assumption that students will eventually function as graduate students do at other institutions. "The academic climate is not competitive because no two students study the exact same thing," explains a student. The importance of qualified, attentive faculty is not to be underestimated in an environment like this, and students heap praise on their professors. One says, "Professors at Hampshire are truly invested in their students."

Hampshire's flexibility is ideal for artists, and programs in film, video, and photography are dazzling, which is also the reason they are overcrowded. Communications, creative writing, psychology, social sciences, and environmental studies are also good bets, and Hampshire was the first college in the nation to offer an undergraduate program in cognitive science. The Integrated Sciences first-year program gives new students a chance to work together on innovative projects in an interdisciplinary science environment. The college's Farm Center serves as a living laboratory for learning about sustainability, social justice, and community building. Students also have access to selected courses at sister schools in the Five College Consortium, which are connected by a free bus service; Hampshire students take 1,200 classes per year at the other schools. Internships and other real-world experiences are highly encouraged. Hampshire offers its own study abroad programs in China, Cuba, and Germany, and students may also participate in programs through more than 150 institutions in nearly 50 countries. Thirty-five percent of students typically study abroad. Befitting Hampshire's entrepreneurial nature, when it comes time for "Div Free" (as students call life after Hampshire), one in four students begin their own businesses, and a large percentage go on to graduate school.

> **"[Hampshire] is deliberately unique and experimental."**

"We are not cookie-cutter students," says a sophomore. "We are students who passionately teach ourselves in a school that is deliberately unique and experimental." Just as Hampshire eschews letter grades, it also refuses to consider SAT or ACT scores in the admissions process. Only 23 percent of students come from Massachusetts, and 6 percent come from abroad. Enrollment of students of color is growing—8 percent are Black, 11 percent are Hispanic/Latino, 3 percent are Asian American, and 7 percent are multiracial—and most students would like to see these numbers continue to rise. A hefty 48 percent of incoming students qualify for Pell Grants. Hampshire's LGBTQ community is visible and vocal. According to a philosophy student, "Political correctness doesn't even begin to describe" the social atmosphere. Take as examples the school's gender-neutral bathrooms and identity-based housing, which allows members of historically marginalized groups to live together. Aside from need-based aid, merit scholarships worth an average of $20,000 are available to qualified students.

Ninety percent of undergraduates live on campus. First-year students live in dorms, while older students may move to one of more than 100 "mods"—apartments in which groups of four to 10 students share the responsibility for cleaning, cooking, and maintaining their space. Campus meals are diverse and include "many great vegan and vegetarian options," says one nanotechnology student, not to mention great ice cream from local cows. Students can also get healthy options from Mixed Nuts, a student-run food co-op that is Hampshire's longest-running student group. Campus safety is good, students say, and sexual assault is addressed up front. "We have a loud and well-known consent culture on campus," says a student

Degrees are obtained via portfolios of academic work, evaluations, and students' self-reflections on their academic development.

Hampshire's flexibility is ideal for artists, and programs in film, video, and photography are dazzling.

concentrating in geology and sustainability. "Students learn about appropriate consent during orientation and it is reinforced consistently throughout all four years."

Not surprisingly, Hampshire has no fraternities or sororities, and on weekends, some students head for Boston, New York, Hartford, or, in season, the ski trails of Vermont and New Hampshire. But there are plenty of cultural resources within the Five College area, and the free buses to Amherst, Northampton, and South Hadley (all within 10 miles) are always crowded. From edgy record stores to ethnic restaurants and boutiques, the area abounds with diversions. The annual Spring Jam brings live bands to campus, and throughout the year, there's almost always a party going on, including the drag ball and the much-anticipated Halloween bash—an intense, all-campus blowout complete with fireworks. A tradition called "Div Free Bell" celebrates the completion of Division III requirements—and graduation—with soon-to-be alumni ringing a bell outside the library, surrounded by friends.

Hampshire is no place for competitive jocks, since many sports are co-ed and primarily for entertainment (there never was a football team here). Division III Hampshire

> **"We have a loud and well-known consent culture on campus."**

is affiliated with the United States Collegiate Athletic Association and is also a member of the Yankee Small College Conference. Students organize their own intramural teams and sports clubs (men's and women's soccer, basketball, and fencing are the biggies, and there's also the competitive Red Scare Ultimate Frisbee Team). The outdoors program offers mountain biking, cross-country skiing, and kayaking; equipment may be borrowed for free. The school also has its own climbing wall and cave, a gym with a solar-heated pool, and a co-ed sauna.

Hampshire's six-year graduation rate is low in comparison to other pricey, private liberal arts colleges, though not necessarily for bad reasons. Some students find the culture of individual study unnerving, if not stressful, or miss traditional college life more than they thought they would. Others, however, having taken full advantage of Hampshire's freedom to explore, discover a passion that might be their life's work and move on to pursue it at a larger school with more resources. Hampshire considers the latter situation a success story.

"If you're an independent student and like to think outside the box, then Hampshire is for you," says a student focusing on animal behavior. With the power to make up their own education and the support of devoted faculty members, there's little Hampshire students can't accomplish.

Mixed Nuts, a student-run food co-op, is Hampshire's longest-running student group.

Overlaps

Bennington, Bard, Sarah Lawrence, College of the Atlantic, Evergreen State, Pitzer, Antioch, Mount Holyoke

If You Apply To ›

Hampshire: Early decision I and II, early action, regular decision. SATs or ACTs: not considered. Accepts the Common Application with supplement.

Hartwick College

Oneonta, NY 13820

Hartwick is known for its cozy atmosphere and ability to take good care of students. Combines liberal arts education with experiential learning opportunities. A general education program emphasizes hands-on learning, and a Three-Year Bachelor's Degree Program is an option. Offers deep tuition discounts to students who attended high school in neighboring counties of upstate New York. Bring your mountain climbing shoes.

Hartwick College emphasizes community-centered learning, crystallizing the school's philosophy that learning isn't about memorization, it's about creating experiential knowledge and developing skills. In recent years, Hartwick has focused on expanding its liberal arts offerings and making itself more affordable for its mostly homegrown student body. Students say they enjoy the comfortable atmosphere on this close-knit campus. "You will feel like you instantly become an active and important member of the community," assures one denizen.

Hartwick was founded way back in 1797 under the will of Lutheran pastor John Christopher Hartwick, and its campus has a New England feel with its ivy-covered, redbrick buildings and white cupolas, gables, and trim. The campus setting on Oyaron Hill, overlooking the city of Oneonta and the Susquehanna Valley, provides a breathtaking view, though the steepness of the campus may have some students wishing for the legs of a mountain goat. Facilities include a greenhouse, an herbarium, a cold room, a biotechnology "clean lab," and a graphics imaging lab. The Wright Observatory, LEED-certified Golisano Hall, and the state-of-the-art Campbell Fitness Center are other notable campus features.

Hartwick operates on a 4–1–4 academic calendar, with two 14-week semesters and a four-week January term, or J term, in between. The Promise Core Curriculum features an extensive first-year experience program that includes a seven-day summer orientation, a first-year seminar, a college writing course, an off-campus First-Year Discovery trip during J term, and three 21st Century Modules—four-week mini courses in the spring focused on developing skills in political and cultural fluency, applying data, and understanding the importance and limitations of science and technology. Sophomores attend a mandatory Success Summit to learn skills like networking and interviewing, and all Hartwick students are guaranteed a career-related work experience, such as an internship, research project, or fellowship. The culminating Promise Capstone requires students to reflect on their experiences and create a personal statement in both written and oral or video format.

> "[Hartwick] makes one feel like everyone is on the same team working toward the same goal."

The most popular majors are business administration, nursing, biology, psychology, and sociology. The English, music, and art programs receive high marks too. The course catalog is necessarily limited by Hartwick's small size, but the Individual Student Program enables students to create their own major dealing with a particular interest, and several majors have recently been introduced, including criminal justice, global studies, and public health. Students may also broaden their options by taking courses at nearby SUNY Oneonta. The Three-Year Bachelor's Degree Program allows students in nearly 30 majors to take on a larger courseload in order to earn a B.A. or B.S. within three years—and save significantly on the cost of earning a degree.

Hartwick's academic environment is described as collaborative and relaxed. "Not only are students encouraged to discuss ideas among each other and work together to learn, but students are also welcomed to work alongside their professors," explains a political science major. "It makes one feel like everyone is on the same team working toward the same goal." Small class sizes are the norm, and a business administration major says, "The professors here are kind and spend a lot of time with students who really need them." Individual tutoring and help sessions are offered, along with an innovative freshman early-warning program that identifies struggling students early and offers counseling.

Hartwick's emphasis on learning through real-world experiences is evident in the wide-ranging activities its students have pursued, often during J term, such as working in a Jamaican hospital and interning with the Metropolitan Museum of Art. Seventy percent of students take community-based service-learning classes, which combine academic coursework with service opportunities in the Oneonta area. Participants in

Website: www.hartwick.edu
Location: Small Town
Private
Total Enrollment: 1,135
Undergraduates: 1,135
Male/Female: 42/58
Financial Aid: 95%
Pell Grant: 39%
Expense: Pr $ $
Student Loans: 85%
Average Debt: $ $ $ $
Applicants: 3,394
Accepted: 96%
Enrolled: 11%
Grad in 6 Years: 57%
Returning Freshmen: 63%
Academics: ✍ ✍ ✍
Social: ☎ ☎ ☎ ☎
Q of L: ★ ★ ★
Admissions: (888)-HARTWICK
Email Address: admissions@ hartwick.edu

Strong Programs:
English
Music
Art
Business Administration
Nursing
Biology
Psychology
Sociology

the Honors Program carry out four self-selected academic challenges, such as honors seminars, a second major, or independent research. Fifty-two percent of students take part in study abroad courses available in 25 nations around the globe.

Hartwick has traditionally attracted a somewhat less academically oriented student body than most of the colleges with which it competes, but it has improved its academic rigor in recent years, thanks to a focused recruitment program. "The students here are hardworking, well-rounded, driven, and accepting," says a junior. Seventy-six percent are from New York State, especially upstate, and most of the rest come from New England or the Mid-Atlantic states; 2 percent are international. Black students make up 11 percent of the student body, Hispanics/Latinos 8 percent, Asian Americans 3 percent, and multiracial students 3 percent. Thirty-nine percent of first-year students are eligible for Pell Grants. Students tend to be liberal but not particularly politically engaged; a senior says, "We try not to let outside issues affect our studies." Hartwick awards merit scholarships averaging $17,800 but no athletic scholarships. Under the HartLand Promise program, incoming students who attended high school in one of eight counties surrounding the college are charged a significantly lower tuition rate that is comparable to the cost of most public four-year institutions in New York State.

All students except commuters reside on campus, most in traditional dorms, although suite-style options are available. Says a sophomore, "The dorms are all a comfortable size and are maintained properly." Upperclassmen may move into one of the fraternity or special-interest houses or into the coveted apartment community or townhouses. Hartwick's 256-acre Pine Lake Environmental Campus, located eight miles from the main campus, has cabins that are heated by pellet stoves and a lodge where environmentally conscious students can live in rustic style. Students give on-campus dining fair marks but praise campus safety officers; says one student, "It's obvious through their actions that they really care about the well-being of the students at this college."

> **"The students here are hardworking, well-rounded, driven, and accepting."**

Hartwick's social scene is found both on and off campus, according to students, and tends to be as mellow or rowdy as one chooses. From campus, it's only a short walk, bike ride, or bus ride downhill into the small city of Oneonta, with its tantalizing profusion of bars. Students say the administration is tough about enforcing alcohol policies on campus. Four fraternities and four sororities attract 7 percent of the men and 12 percent of the women. The school sponsors events like movies, comedians, and lectures every Friday and Saturday night. Popular campuswide traditions include Wicktoberfest, Pine Lake Winterfest, the Last Day of Classes Bash, and the notorious "Wick Wars," a schoolwide sports competition held every spring. There's also the Breakfast of Champions before final exams, when professors and administrators serve students breakfast between 11 p.m. and 2 a.m. Walking to class each day provides great hill workouts for your ski legs, and skiing is popular throughout the region. Oneonta is a "quaint, peaceful town," according to one student. "There aren't very many things to do, but my friends and I haven't gotten bored yet."

As for sports, the Hartwick Hawks deliver plenty of excitement. The school's 19 varsity teams compete in the Division III Empire 8 Conference; women's basketball and field hockey are among the more successful teams. Intramurals are popular as well, especially soccer, basketball, and flag football—20 percent of students take part.

Change is good, the sages say, and the folks at Hartwick would definitely agree. By focusing its efforts on recruiting strong students and emphasizing top-notch experiential learning, Hartwick is bolstering its image as a solid liberal arts college. Even some of the T-shirts sold on campus broadcast the students' attitudes about their education: one simply says "Smartwick."

Hartwick's extensive first-year experience program includes an off-campus First-Year Discovery trip during January term.

Hartwick's 256-acre Pine Lake Environmental Campus, located eight miles from the main campus, has cabins where students can live in rustic style.

Overlaps
Ithaca, Juniata, Hobart and William Smith, Alfred, SUNY–Oneonta, Elmira, Moravian, Lycoming

Harvard University

86 Brattle Street, Cambridge, MA 02138

An acceptance here is the gold standard of American education. Gets periodic slings and arrows for not paying enough attention to undergraduates, some of which is carping from people who didn't get in. It takes moxie to keep your self-image under control in the midst of all those overachievers, but most Harvard students can do it. ("I go to school in Boston.")

For nearly four centuries, the name Harvard has been synonymous with academic excellence, prestige, and achievement. The nation's first institution of higher learning (founded in 1636), Harvard University was named for clergyman John Harvard in gratitude for his bequest of 400 books and half his estate. Harvard is still the benchmark against which all other colleges are compared. Seeking to "educate citizens and citizen leaders," it attracts the best students, the most academically accomplished faculty, and the most lavish donors of any institution of higher education nationwide. Sure, some academic departments at "Hah-vahd" may be smaller than others, but all have faculty members who have made a name for themselves and have written the standard works in their fields. Olympic athletes, concert pianists, and Rhodes scholars blend in easily here, ready to embrace the challenges and rewards only Harvard's quintessential Ivy League milieu can offer.

Spiritually as well as geographically, the campus centers on the famed Harvard Yard, a classic quadrangle of Georgian brick buildings whose walls seem to echo with the voices of William James, Henry Adams, Alain Locke, and other intellectual greats who trod its shaded paths in centuries past. Beyond the yard's wrought-iron gates, the campus is an architectural mix, ranging from the modern ziggurat of the science center to the white towers of college-owned houses along the Charles River. The Loker Commons student center provides a place for students to meet and philosophize over gourmet coffee or burritos of epic proportions. The massive, $1 billion Science and Engineering Complex across the river in Allston opened in 2021.

> **"You can have unlimited contact with professors, but it must be on your initiative."**

Harvard's state-of-the-art physical facilities are surpassed only by the unparalleled brilliance of its faculty. Under its "star" system, Harvard grants tenure only to scholars who have already made it—usually somewhere else—and then gives them free rein for research. It seems like every time you turn around, a Harvard professor is winning a Nobel Prize or being interviewed on CNN or moving to Washington to hash out national policy. But one of Harvard's finest qualities is also one of its biggest problems. "You can have unlimited contact with professors, but it must be on your initiative," notes a biology major. "This is not a small liberal arts college where people will reach out to you." That's not to say profs are uncaring. Most teach at least one undergraduate course per year, and even the luminaries occasionally conduct small undergraduate seminars (including those reserved for freshmen, which can be taken pass/fail). Harvard also sponsors faculty dining programs, such

Website: www.college.harvard.edu

Location: City Center

Private

Total Enrollment: 20,309

Undergraduates: 7,095

Male/Female: 50/50

Financial Aid: 55%

Pell Grant: 22%

Expense: Pr $ $

Student Loans: 21%

Average Debt: $

Applicants: 57,786

Accepted: 4%

Enrolled: 84%

Grad in 6 Years: 97%

Returning Freshmen: 96%

Academics: ✍ ✍ ✍ ✍ ✍

Social: ☎ ☎ ☎

Q of L: ★ ★ ★ ★

Admissions: (617) 495-1551

Email Address: college@fas.harvard.edu

Strong Programs:
Economics
Government
Computer Science
Applied Mathematics
History
Biological Sciences
East Asian Studies
African and African American Studies

as Professors & Pastries and Classroom to Table, encouraging professors to chew on ideas and éclairs with students at residential houses and local eateries.

Back in the mid-1970s, Harvard helped launch a major curriculum reform movement. Although it was revised in 2018, the core curriculum that emerged was for decades regarded as perhaps the most exciting collection of academic offerings in all of American higher education. Current general education requirements include one

"The courses are difficult, particularly in the beginning."

course from each of four perspectives: aesthetics and culture; ethics and civics; histories, societies, and individuals; and science and technology in society. Additionally, students take one quantitative reasoning course and one departmental course from each of the three main divisions of the Faculty of Arts and Sciences: Arts and Humanities; Social Sciences; and Natural Sciences and the School of Engineering and Applied Science. The revised gen-ed program is intended to give students more freedom in the courses they choose and to prepare them to succeed in a diverse, inclusive, and interconnected world.

The African and African American studies department has assembled the most high-powered group of Black intellectuals in American higher education.

Harvard's best-known departments tend to be its largest; economics, government, computer science, applied mathematics, history, biological sciences, and psychology account for a large chunk of majors. But many smaller departments are gems as well: East Asian studies is easily top in the nation. And under the leadership of Henry Louis Gates Jr., the African and African American studies department has assembled the most high-powered group of Black intellectuals in American higher education. Smaller, interdisciplinary honors majors, to which students apply for admission, boast solid instruction and happy undergraduates too. These programs—social studies, history and science, history and literature, and folklore and mythology—are the only majors that require a senior thesis, although many students in other departments elect to do one. Harvard's visual and environmental studies department serves filmmakers, studio artists, and urban planners, and a major in theater, dance, and media is quickly growing in popularity. Students can also petition for individualized majors, typically during the sophomore year. And should you not find a class you are looking for, Harvard offers cross-registration with several of its graduate schools and MIT.

Freshmen are encouraged to explore a range of disciplines during their first year on campus. Seventy-one percent of classes have fewer than 20 students, but students uniformly complain about the overuse of teaching fellows (graduate students) for introductory courses in mathematics and the languages. TFs aren't all bad, though,

"It's certainly normal to spend Friday and Saturday nights studying."

says a junior: "They can give good advice, having just been in our position." Besides, it's easier to ask "dumb questions" of mere mortals than of the demigod professors. For many students, the most rewarding form of instruction is the sophomore and junior tutorial, a small-group directed study in a student's field of concentration that is required in most departments within the humanities and social sciences. Teaching of the tutorials is split between professors and graduate students, and the weight of each party's responsibility varies with the subject and the professor. With more than 200 study abroad programs available to choose from, more than half of Harvard undergrads indulge in some sort of international experience before they graduate.

The oft-made claim that "the hardest thing about Harvard is getting in" is right on target. Flunking out takes serious and sustained effort. Then again, Harvard can feel indifferent and antisocial. While its resources—including fellow students—are unparalleled, brilliant overachievers who desire the occasional ego stroke might be better off at a top-notch small liberal arts college. But for those who are motivated, the possibilities are endless. All incoming freshmen participate in a weeklong orientation, and optional preorientation groups, such as the urban, outdoor, and arts programs, help students acquaint themselves with one another and the Boston area. Although most students feel little competition, the academic climate is still intense. "The courses are difficult, particularly in the beginning as students make the transition from high school to college," says one student. Stressed-out students can count on help from a variety of quarters, including the various deans' offices, the Bureau of Study Counsel, the Office of Career Services ("dedicated to working with Harvard students and alums for the rest of their lives," claims a senior), and counselors associated with each residential house. The Radcliffe Institute for Advanced Study, which has evolved from the former Radcliffe women's college, affords undergrads access to a network of professional women, alumnae, and research fellows (both female and male). Sooner or later, all roads lead to Widener Library, where incredible facilities lie in wait (and where snow-covered steps make prime sledding runs in the winter).

Harvard does have one thing its $51 billion endowment can't buy: a diverse, high-powered, ambitious, and exciting student body. You will meet smooth-talking government majors who appear to have begun their senatorial campaigns in kindergarten. You will meet flamboyant fine arts majors who have cultivated an affected accent all their own. You will sample the intensity of Harvard's extracurricular scene, where 7,100 of the world's sharpest undergrads compete for leadership positions in a luminous galaxy of extracurricular opportunities.

No one can tell you exactly what it takes to gain admission to Harvard (and if anyone tries, apply a large grain of sodium chloride), but here's a hint: superachiever academic records are the norm. And, of course, there are old-money types who probably spit up their baby food on a Harvard sweatshirt. (Many enter as sophomores when no one is looking.) Undergraduates come from all 50 states—73 percent are out-of-staters—although the student body is weighted toward the Northeast. Twelve percent are international, representing 70 different countries.

"Cambridge's Harvard Square is the perfect college town. There are tons of shops, restaurants, and bars."

Fifty-eight percent went to public high school. Just over half of Harvard undergrads identify as students of color: Black students account for 9 percent, Hispanics/Latinos 12 percent, Asian Americans 22 percent, and multiracial students 8 percent. There are no merit or athletic scholarships to ease the pain of Harvard's hefty tuition, but the university does practice need-blind admissions and it meets the full demonstrated need of accepted students. For students from low-income families who can get in, Harvard is the ultimate bargain in U.S. higher education. Families with annual household incomes below $75,000 are not expected to contribute to the cost of tuition; students from these families also receive a $2,000 "start-up" grant to help cover initial expenses, like dorm-room supplies. Harvard also limits the family contribution for families with incomes between $75,000 and $150,000 to fixed percentages of their incomes, ranging between 0 and 10 percent.

Virtually all undergraduates reside on campus, and every first-year class lives as a single unit in Harvard Yard, dining together at the beautifully renovated Annenberg Hall. The older dorms provide spacious wood-paneled rooms, working fireplaces, and gentle reminders of Harvard's rich traditions. For their last three years, students live in one of 12 co-ed residential houses, built around their own courtyards with their own dining halls, libraries, and special facilities—from art studios to squash courts. Designed as learning communities, each house holds between 300 and 500 students, plus resident tutors and affiliated faculty members. Each house has a student council that plans social activities. Students are randomly assigned (with up to 15 friends) to a house, but some houses still retain a personality from the days of old when each stood for a particular ideology or interest. "The housing is one of the best parts of Harvard!" raves one student. Nine houses lie along the Charles River, while the other three sit a half mile away at the Radcliffe Quad. Some students consider the latter equivalent to a Siberian exile, especially during harsh Cambridge winters—although a shuttle does run regularly to the main campus.

Socializing at Harvard tends to occur on campus and in small groups. "It's certainly normal to spend Friday and Saturday nights studying," says a philosophy major. With the exception of the annual all-school Freshman Mixer and the annual theme festivals each house throws, parties tend to be private affairs in individual dorm rooms. Students report that the legal drinking age is well enforced on campus.

Harvard's distinctive and increasingly controversial "final clubs" are exclusive and upscale social clubs.

The most distinctive and increasingly controversial aspect of social life at Harvard is the role of the so-called final clubs. These are exclusive and upscale social clubs that, while occupying their own buildings and in other ways completely separate from the university, play a significant role in the campus social life for the small minority of students who are "punched" for membership. In recent years, the clubs have been engaged in a recurring struggle with Harvard's administration, which has condemned the exclusive values of final clubs as being out of place on the university's increasingly diverse campus. For many, the key to happiness in Harvard's high-powered environment is finding a niche, a comfortable academic or extracurricular circle around which to build your life. Outside activities include about 80 plays performed annually, two newspapers and several journals, and plenty of community service projects coordinated through the Phillips Brooks House Association student group.

"I gauge myself by how many allusions in the *New Yorker* I understand."

The possibilities of Harvard's social life are increased exponentially by Cambridge and Boston, where there are many places to have fun. Harvard Square itself is a legendary gathering place for tourists, shoppers, bearded intellectuals, and coffeehouse denizens. "Cambridge's Harvard Square is the perfect college town," a student cheers. "There are tons of shops, restaurants, and bars." The American Repertory Theater, transplanted from Yale in the mid-1980s, offers a season of professional productions and nearly as many professional student shows. Cambridge also enjoys an exceptional selection of new and used bookstores, including, of course, the Harvard Bookstore and the mammoth Harvard Co-op, known universally as "the Coop." Boston boasts Faneuil Hall, the Red Sox, the Bruins, and more than 40 other colleges.

Intramural sports teams are divided up by house, and each fall, league champs play teams from Yale.

Harvard has 41 varsity sports (21 men's, 20 women's), which is the most of any Division I school and the most women's sports. The athletic facilities are across the river from the campus, and their incredible offerings often go unnoticed by students buried in their books. Both the men's and women's squash and crew teams are perennial national powers, and men's ice hockey and women's lacrosse are also strong. Men's basketball has prospered in recent years under coach Tommy Amaker, a former Duke star. As for football, the team has been doing better in recent years, but the season always boils down to the Yale game, memorable as much for the antics of the spectators and marching band as for the fumbles of the players. Intramural sports teams are divided up by house, and each fall, league champs play teams from Yale the weekend of the game. Another fall highlight is the annual Head of the Charles crew race, the largest event of its kind in the world, where as many as 200,000 people gather to watch the racing shells glide by.

Nowhere but Harvard does the identity of a school—its history, its presence, its pretense—intrude so much into the details of undergraduate life. Admission here opens the door to a world of intellectual wonder, academic challenges, and faculty minds unmatched in the United States—but then drops students on the threshold. "I have quickly gained exposure to major theories in literature, psychology, anthropology, social sciences, and evolutionary biology," says a junior. "I gauge myself by how many allusions in the *New Yorker* I understand." That's the way Harvard is; what other kind of place could produce statesmen John Quincy Adams and John F. Kennedy, pioneers W. E. B. DuBois and Helen Keller, and artists T. S. Eliot and Leonard Bernstein? Even its dropouts are movers and shakers (witness Bill Gates and Mark Zuckerberg). But caveat emptor: It is only the most motivated and dedicated student who can take full advantage of the Harvard experience.

If You Apply To ›

Harvard: Single choice early action, regular decision. Accepts the Common Application with supplement. Please consult Harvard's website for the most up-to-date information regarding standardized test requirements.

Harvey Mudd College: See page 150.

Haverford College

Haverford, PA 19041

Quietly prestigious college of Quaker heritage. With an enrollment of about 1,400, Haverford is half the size of some competitors but benefits from its relationship with neighbor Bryn Mawr. Close cousin to nearby Swarthmore but not as far left politically. Exceptionally strong sense of community, with parklike campus amid the bustle of suburban Philadelphia. Honor code drives campus culture. A great option if you want to play varsity cricket.

An overarching honor code covering everything from the classroom to the dorm room defines student life at Haverford College. Students schedule their own final exams, take unproctored tests, and police underage drinking on their own. "The honor code, in some respects, is a self-selecting system which draws many students to Haverford. For this reason, nearly all students who come here share common values of trust, concern, and respect for others as well as academic integrity," says a junior econ major. Haverford may be smaller and less well-known than some of its peers, but it holds its own against the finest liberal arts colleges in the country.

Founded under the auspices of the Religious Society of Friends (Quakers) in 1833, Haverford functions much like a family. The campus consists of 216 acres just off Philadelphia's Main Line, an affluent area named after a former railroad, and resembles a peaceful, well-ordered summer camp. The densely wooded campus has an arboretum, duck pond, nature trails, and more than 400 species of shrubs and trees. Architectural styles range from 19th- and early 20th-century stone buildings to a sprinkling of modern structures here and there. The combination enhances the sense of a balanced community, bringing together two traditional Quaker philosophies: development of the intellect and appreciation of nature. Completed in 2021, a new addition to Roberts Hall houses the music program and a 100-seat recital hall.

Haverford's curriculum reflects commitment to the liberal arts. General education requirements call for passing a freshman writing seminar and taking three

> "The professors are only here for us. They really enjoy teaching."

Website: www.haverford.edu
Location: Suburban
Private
Total Enrollment: 1,419
Undergraduates: 1,419
Male/Female: 46/54
Financial Aid: 44%
Pell Grant: 13%
Expense: Pr $ $ $ $
Student Loans: 23%
Average Debt: $
Applicants: 5,332
Accepted: 18%
Enrolled: 43%
Grad in 6 Years: 90%
Returning Freshmen: 94%
Academics: ✐ ✐ ✐ ✐ ✐
Social: ☎ ☎ ☎
Q of L: ★ ★ ★ ★ ★
Admissions: (610) 896-1350

(continued)

Email Address: admission@ haverford.edu

Strong Programs:
Physics
Mathematics
Biology
Psychology
Political Science
Computer Science
Peace, Justice, and Human Rights

Under the bicollege system, Haverford and Bryn Mawr students cooperate on a weekly newspaper, radio station, orchestra, and other clubs and sports.

courses in each of three divisions: social sciences, natural sciences, and humanities. Every Haverford student completes a senior thesis, project, or performance, partnering with a faculty mentor to do what amounts to graduate-level research in their major. Biology, psychology, political science, and computer science are among the most popular majors, and the physics and mathematics programs are also strong. There are more than a dozen areas of concentration—which are different from minors—that are attached to certain majors, including peace, justice, and human rights; biophysics; and Middle Eastern and Islamic studies.

The bicollege system with Bryn Mawr College, the nearby women's school, allows Haverford students to major in subjects such as art history, growth and structure of cities, and environmental studies. The unique relationship between Bryn Mawr and Haverford dates to the days when Haverford was all-male, and it enables students at each institution to take courses, use facilities, eat, and even live in the dormitories of the other. Haverford and Bryn Mawr students cooperate on a weekly newspaper, radio station, orchestra, and other clubs and sports, and a free shuttle bus connects the campuses. About half of Haverford students take at least one course at Bryn Mawr. Cross-registration is also available at Swarthmore and the University of Pennsylvania, and joint-degree programs are available with a number of institutions, including Penn, Caltech, Claremont McKenna, and Georgetown.

"We don't have a dean's list or any sort of academic honors program."

The academic workload at Haverford may be sizable, but students say the atmosphere is supportive. "We do not talk about grades on campus, and we don't have a dean's list or any sort of academic honors program," explains a history major. "All of this helps to foster an academic environment that isn't competitive." Classes are small and advising is ever-present: freshmen are matched with professors who work with them from their arrival until they declare majors two years later, while upper-class "Customs people" are resources and mentors for living/learning groups of eight to 16 first-year students. Haverford's biggest strength may be its faculty members, who are unusually accessible—40 percent of them live on campus. "The professors are only here for us. They really enjoy teaching as well as involving us in research." Haverford's Center for Peace and Global Citizenship—appropriate for a Quaker school—offers summer internships that emphasize the study and promotion of social justice and global issues. Nearly 70 study abroad programs around the globe attract 49 percent of the students.

Haverford's distinctive honor code governs all aspects of campus life. "I can take my final exam at 3 a.m. on Founder's Green," says a junior as an example. The code, administered by students and debated and reratified each year at a meeting called Plenary, helps instill the values of "integrity, honesty, and concern for others." In good Quaker tradition, decisions are made by consensus rather than formal voting, and students play a large role in shaping college policy. While the social honor code encourages students to "voice virtually any opinion so long as it is expressed rationally," this can also mean self-censorship, says a philosophy major. "Sometimes you feel like you are walking on eggshells to avoid offending anyone."

"I can take my final exam at 3 a.m. on Founder's Green."

Only 13 percent of Haverford's students hail from Pennsylvania, but many are East Coasters nonetheless; 11 percent are international. Eleven percent of students are Asian American, 13 percent are Hispanic/Latino, 5 percent are Black, and 7 percent are multiracial. Though the college is nonsectarian, the Quaker influence lives on in the form of an optional silent meeting each week. Students tend to be interested in progressive political and social ideas, and a senior says, "There are not very many conservative voices on campus." Haverford meets the full demonstrated financial need of every admitted student and, for students from families with annual incomes below $60,000, has replaced loans with grants in its financial aid packages. Merit-based academic and athletic scholarships are not available.

Haverford's residence halls are spacious and well maintained, and most rooms are singles—even for freshmen—so it's no surprise that 98 percent of all students live on campus. "Some of the dorms are incredible. The apartments are the best freshman housing anywhere," cheers an economics major. All dorms are co-ed, but students may request single-sex floors. The school-owned Haverford College Apartments sit on the edge of campus and feature coveted one- and two-bedroom units, each with a living room, kitchen, and bathroom. "Under the Quaker ethos, we all eat under the same roof in the Dining Center," says a senior; special diets are easily accommodated, and meals receive average reviews. Campus security is good, owing in part to the school's location in the upscale Philadelphia suburbs, but the school is working to educate the campus community about gender-based violence and safe relationships. "I think the most effective resource is the Women*s Center, which creates programming to make the issue of sexual assault and survivors' experiences more visible," comments a senior.

Social life is mainly campus-based, although students do find opportunities to explore the surrounding area. "We have a group on campus called Fords Against Boredom (FAB) that does trivia nights, bingo games, and other events on campus, but they also take students to the museums in Philly, to apple orchards in the fall, and to the King of Prussia Mall," explains a sopho-

"The apartments are the best freshman housing anywhere."

more. The alcohol policy is connected to the honor code, and without fraternities and sororities, students describe the party scene as "super chill" and pressure-free. Haverford and Bryn Mawr occasionally hold joint campus parties. Traditional events include the weekend-long, pre-exams Haverfest—a carnival-like, themed festival with music, food, and games. Life in the close-knit, introspective environment that is Haverford can get stifling at times, but there are easy escapes. Downtown Philadelphia is just 20 minutes away by train. New York City, Washington, D.C., the New Jersey beaches, Pocono ski areas, and Atlantic City are only a couple hours away by car or train. About half of the students participate in volunteer projects coordinated by the Allen Office of Service and Community Collaboration.

Haverford's rich athletic history dates back more than a century to 1905, when the school played Harvard in the first ever intercollegiate soccer game in the United States; Haverford has since racked up more soccer wins than any other school. A popular T-shirt brags that the football team has been "Undefeated Since 1972"—a reference to the year the sport was abolished. The men's cross-country team is a perennial Division III national contender, and women's cross-country, volleyball, and lacrosse are competitive in the Centennial Conference. Back in the 1850s, Haverford became one of the first colleges in the country to play cricket, and the school still boasts one of the top collegiate teams. Despite a lively rivalry with Swarthmore, these Quakers have struggled to reconcile their peace-loving heritage with the desire to bash opponents' frontal lobes out on the court or the field. For now, students root for their Black Squirrels and chant, "Fight, fight, inner light— kill, Quakers, kill!" Intramural and club sports are popular, too, especially because participation counts toward the required six quarters of athletic credit.

Haverford students may be committed to the college's honor code and founding values, but the downside, according to one student, is that "students are challenged to meet an ideal set before them of creating the best community possible. For this reason, students are constantly criticizing themselves and the community as a whole to find ways of solving the problems facing them." See? Mom was right. With freedom comes responsibility.

Overlaps

Carleton, Wesleyan, Hamilton, Swarthmore, Davidson, Williams, Bowdoin, Bryn Mawr

University of Hawai'i at Mānoa

2600 Campus Road, Room 001, Honolulu, HI 96822

One of the most accessible of the public flagships in the U.S.—at least when it comes to admissions—the University of Hawai'i at Mānoa pursues research and teaching in a uniquely cosmopolitan setting. A majority of undergrads are Asian Americans, Native Hawaiians, or other Pacific Islanders, and two-thirds are in-staters. Astronomy, marine biology, and environmental studies are strong. Proximity to some of the world's best surfing an obvious plus.

Website: www.manoa.hawaii .edu

Location: City Outskirts

Public

Total Enrollment: 13,788

Undergraduates: 11,140

Male/Female: 39/61

Financial Aid: 56%

Pell Grant: 27%

Expense: Pub $ $

Student Loans: 40%

Average Debt: $

Applicants: 16,244

Accepted: 58%

Enrolled: 21%

Grad in 6 Years: 59%

Returning Freshmen: 80%

Academics: ✍ ✍

Social: ☎ ☎ ☎

Q of L: ★ ★ ★

Admissions: (808) 956-8975

Email Address: manoa .admissions@hawaii.edu

Strong Programs:

Astronomy

Pacific and Asian Studies

Ethnomusicology

Tropical Agriculture

Environmental Studies

Engineering

Geology

Marine Biology

One of the goals of the University of Hawai'i at Mānoa, which was founded in 1907, is to "serve as a bridge between East and West." Despite—or perhaps because of—the fact that a high percentage of students are in-staters, UH Mānoa is one of the most ethnically diverse institutions in the country. Budget cuts triggered by the state's economic troubles have been an issue in recent years, and students complain of bulging classrooms and outdated facilities in need of upgrades and repairs. Despite these challenges, a plant and environmental protection science major says, "Students, faculty, and community members are friendly and give off the Aloha Spirit."

The UH Mānoa campus occupies 320 acres in the Mānoa Valley, a residential Honolulu neighborhood. The architecture is regionally eclectic, mirroring historical and modern Pacific-Asian motifs, and is enhanced by extensive subtropical landscaping. The campus doubles as an arboretum with more than 4,000 trees and 500 species from all over the world. Situated within a few miles of the state capital and the city's major business district, the university provides excellent opportunities for students to interact with thought leaders, including mentorships and internships.

Core requirements are extensive: all students must take courses in math, humanities, social sciences, natural sciences, world civilization, and a foreign language or 'ōlelo Hawai'i (Hawaiian). The First-Year program supports freshmen in their transition to the university by gathering diverse groups with similar interests to work and study together in Access to College Excellence academic learning communities made up of no more than 15 students. The Mānoa Writing Program, founded in 1987, is one of the oldest writing-across-the-curriculum programs in the country. Faculty from 82 departments teach writing-intensive (W) courses that use a variety of discipline-specific writing-to-learn techniques, with an emphasis on student/faculty interaction during the writing process. Students are required to take five W courses in order to graduate, but many take more.

> **"Students, faculty, and community members are friendly and give off the Aloha Spirit."**

UH Mānoa offers nearly 100 bachelor's degrees; among the best are astronomy, Pacific and Asian area studies, languages and the arts, ethnomusicology, and tropical agriculture. Astronomy and astrophysics benefit from the clear Hawaiian skies. It should come as no surprise that ocean-, climate-, and environment-related programs are also first-rate, with world-class facilities. The university takes pride in its programs in engineering, geology and geophysics, marine biology, international business, political science, travel industry management, and the School of Hawaiian Knowledge—the only college of indigenous knowledge at a major research university in the United States. The most popular majors, by enrollment, are biology, marine biology, kinesiology and rehabilitation science, computer science, and psychology. "The courses can be challenging based on what you take and the major you declare," says a senior. Forty-five percent of undergraduate classes have fewer than 20 students. Desirable classes and times are said to be difficult for freshmen and sophomores to get into, although departmental academic advisors keep close tabs on whether students are on schedule to complete their degrees in four years. The Student Success Center offers academic advising, tutoring, and other support services. Professors receive generally favorable reviews. "Each professor has their own style and priorities, but every professor that I have had is knowledgeable," says a biology and music double major. "Most of them are thoughtful and interested in the success of their students."

The two-tier Honors Program offers qualified freshmen and sophomores the opportunity for general education courses in small, intensive classes, along with personalized academic advising and peer mentorship. Upper-class honors students are guided by faculty through independent, sustained research or creative work and must complete a final Honors thesis. The Undergraduate Research Opportunities Program connects students in all disciplines with opportunities to engage in faculty-mentored research or creative projects. Participants present their work at a semester-end symposium. Students who tire of Hawai'i's endless beaches and beautiful sunsets can study abroad in locations around the world, including Asia, Australia, Europe, and South America.

> *The School of Hawaiian Knowledge is the only college of indigenous knowledge at a major research university in the United States.*

> **"The climate and diversity in Hawai'i allow for...more open dialogue about race and culture."**

"Many students are very driven, but others are here to appreciate the island life," says a student. Fifty-eight percent of undergraduates are in-staters, and 4 percent are from other countries. Hawai'i stands out among major American universities in that 35 percent of its undergraduates are Asian American and another 17 percent are of Native Hawaiian or other Pacific Islander descent. Black and Hispanic/Latino students each represent 2 percent of the student body, and 16 percent identify as multiracial. "The climate and diversity in Hawai'i allow for a greater and more open dialogue about race and culture," observes an English and history major. Political and social issues often take a back seat to academics and play, but among the more prominent concerns are the environment and Native Hawaiian rights. Especially promising students can compete for merit scholarships, which average $13,100 annually. The university also disburses roughly 250 athletic scholarships in 21 sports. The Mānoa Service Award offers $1,000 scholarships to current full-time students who complete 50 hours of volunteer work each semester.

Eighteen percent of students live in campus housing, and those who apply by the May deadline are guaranteed a spot. Students recommend the Hale Aloha residence hall, consisting of four towers, 'Ilima, Lehua, Lokelani, and Mokihana; the rooms are compact but the hallways are happening. If you're thinking about off-campus housing, take note: housing in Honolulu is scarce and expensive. Residential dining is located throughout the campus and serves diverse and adequate fare. "The Department of Public Safety has advertised more campus apps to help with safety so students can avoid getting into vulnerable situations," reports a history and economics double major.

> *Athletic teams are the Rainbow Warriors and the Rainbow Wahine, and legend has it that if a rainbow appears during a game, UH Mānoa will win.*

Because many students are commuters, UH Mānoa is pretty sedate after dark, especially on weekends. Most social activity revolves around student clubs and, as one student explains, "simply being around the Campus Center, where you can find many students studying, socializing, or hitting the gym." Only 1 percent of the men and 1 percent of the women join the tiny Greek system. Drinking is not allowed in the residence halls. A couple of local hangouts provide an escape, and Mānoa Gardens, an on-campus bar, is also an option. Many students head off campus to enjoy "more beaches and hikes than one can handle," according to a

"[There are] more beaches and hikes than one can handle."

sophomore. Lest anyone forget, some of the world's most beautiful resorts are less than a 20-minute drive away. Waikīkī Beach? Within two miles' reach. And round-trip airfare to the neighboring islands—including Maui, Kaua'i, and the Hawai'i Island—is reasonable. Favorite annual traditions include the homecoming fair and football game as well as the Aloha Bash, a big concert held every April featuring popular local bands.

UH Mānoa's athletic teams compete in Division I. The men's teams are known as the Rainbow Warriors, while the women's teams are the Rainbow Wahine, and legend has it that if a rainbow appears during a game, UH Mānoa will win. Twenty minutes before kickoff at every home football game, the team performs the Warrior Ha'a—their version of a traditional Māori dance. Men's and women's volleyball, men's basketball, baseball, and swimming, and eSports are among the other top draws. Intramural and recreational activities range from soccer and basketball to tai chi and snorkeling.

Students seeking warm weather and great surfing won't be disappointed, and those pursuing UH Mānoa's strong specialized programs undoubtedly benefit from the university's one-of-a-kind setting. But it's up to you, one student says, to get the best out of UH Mānoa. "The location allows mainland students to get a different cultural experience," adds another. "You're only young once—might as well be 20 in Hawai'i."

Overlaps

UCLA, Hawaii Pacific, University of Hawai'i at Hilo, University of Southern California, University of Washington

If You Apply To ›

UH Mānoa: Rolling admissions. Does not accept the Common Application. Please consult UH Mānoa's website for the most up-to-date information regarding standardized test requirements.

Hendrix College

1600 Washington Avenue, Conway, AR 72032

Hendrix is in the same class of Southern liberal arts colleges as Millsaps and Rhodes. The most progressive of the three, Hendrix places a strong emphasis on international awareness and boasts colorful campus traditions. Arkansas is a tough sell, and the college accepts seven of every 10 students who apply. About 60 percent of Hendrix students are from Arkansas, and most of the rest are Southerners.

Website: www.hendrix.edu
Location: Suburban
Private
Total Enrollment: 1,120
Undergraduates: 1,089
Male/Female: 49/51
Financial Aid: 100%

For a school in the heart of the Bible Belt and Walton-land, Hendrix College, whose roots date to 1876, is surprisingly liberal. In fact, it's among the South's most progressive liberal arts colleges. Academics are demanding but the atmosphere is laid-back. Students tend to be liberal—even radical—in their political and social views. Ironically, healthy dialogue about tough issues such as LGBTQ rights, the environment, and racial equity draws students together. "People here are passionate, intelligent, and fun," says a freshman. "They really want to change the world."

Hendrix's compact and comfortable campus stretches for 180 acres between the Ouachita and Ozark mountains. College land boasts more than 80 varieties of trees and shrubs and more than 10,000 budding flowers each spring. The main campus—with its own lily pool, fountain, and gazebo—occupies about one-fourth of the total acreage. The redbrick buildings are a mix of old and new, and a pedestrian overpass connects the main campus to the college's athletic facilities and a wooded fitness trail. The recently built Miller Creative Quad combines arts facilities, including music practice rooms, a screening auditorium for the film studies program, and an art museum, with residential space on the upper floors housing 106 students.

Under Hendrix's general education program, known as the Collegiate Center, freshmen take two required courses, The Engaged Citizen and Explorations: Liberal Arts for Life. The Capacities component involves requirements in writing, foreign language, quantitative skills, and physical activity, while the Learning Domains component requires coursework in seven broad liberal arts areas. The Odyssey Program requires students to complete three experiences—which may be coursework, internships, or independent projects—selected from six categories: artistic creativity, global awareness, professional and leadership development, service to the world, special projects, and undergraduate research. "The Odyssey Program has helped me to be well-rounded and explore random interests," reflects a biology major. All seniors must complete a capstone experience. Hendrix freshmen also participate in a weeklong orientation program, which includes a two-day, off-campus trip featuring outdoor experiences, urban exposure, or volunteer service.

> **"The Odyssey Program has helped me to be well-rounded and explore random interests."**

Hendrix is strong in many areas, but natural and social sciences are definitely the school's forte. Popular majors include psychology, health science, economics and business, biochemistry and molecular biology, and English. The neuroscience and politics programs are also notable. The Murphy Scholars Program draws participants from a broad range of majors, including the sciences, who are interested in deeper study of literature and language, awarding funding to support independent projects. Doing well at Hendrix means keeping up with the intense workload. Thankfully, students are usually willing to work together, and with 68 percent of classes enrolling fewer than 20 students, personal attention from faculty is the norm. "The professors at Hendrix stand out because they are not only experts in conveying information about their field, but they are also able to ignite a sense of curiosity and excitement for learning," says a biochemistry and molecular biology major. The school also offers dual-degree programs with Columbia and Washington University in St. Louis for aspiring engineers.

> *The Murphy Scholars Program awards funding to support independent projects in literature and language.*

At Hendrix, undergraduate research is a priority, especially within the sciences, with nearly two-thirds of all students taking part; many get the chance to present original papers at regional and national symposia. Students also earn course credit for internships at U.S. embassies and organizations such as the National Institutes of Health and the U.S. Agency for International Development. Thirty-five percent of students participate in a wide variety of opportunities to work, study, and serve abroad. Accademia dell'Arte in Arezzo, Italy, exposes participants to the world of European theater, vocal arts, and dance, while the Heilongjiang program in China focuses on Mandarin Chinese. Hendrix also sponsors programs in Austria, England, Costa Rica, Spain, France, Germany, and Cyprus, and students have access to more than 150 partner exchange programs as well. For career preparation, Hendrix requires all sophomores to participate in a three-day Career Term during winter break, in which students learn practical skills like interviewing and networking.

> **"[Professors are] able to ignite a sense of curiosity and excitement for learning."**

(continued)

Pell Grant: 29%
Expense: Pr $
Student Loans: 65%
Average Debt: $ $
Applicants: 2,385
Accepted: 68%
Enrolled: 19%
Grad in 6 Years: 66%
Returning Freshmen: 80%
Academics: ✐ ✐ ✐
Social: ☎ ☎ ☎ ☎
Q of L: ★ ★ ★ ★
Admissions: (501) 450-1362
Email Address:
   adm@hendrix.edu

Strong Programs:
Neuroscience
Politics
Psychology
Health Science
Economics and Business
Biochemistry and Molecular
   Biology
English

"Most students are liberal and eclectic, but all are respectful of political and social beliefs," says one student. Fifty-nine percent of Hendrix students are from Arkansas, and just 2 percent come from abroad. Black students represent 8 percent of the student body, Hispanics/Latinos 9 percent, Asian Americans 4 percent, and multiracial students 5 percent. The Office for Diversity and Inclusion seeks to enhance campus diversity. Hendrix offers a variety of merit scholarships, averaging $33,400, to academically qualified students, but there are no athletic scholarships. Through the Arkansas Advantage Program, the college guarantees to meet the full demonstrated financial need of Arkansas residents who meet certain academic requirements.

All students are required to live on campus, and only a few are granted exceptions each year, which students say adds to the sense of community. Residence halls offer "a classic dorm experience," says a senior, but the quality is "very hit or miss"; the college is in the process of gradually renovating older dorms. Most upperclassmen take up quarters in on-campus apartments. As for dining, an English major asserts, "Hendrix has the best cafeteria food in the state," and students report that plenty of choices are available for those with special dietary needs. Students also report feeling safe on campus, due in part to a visible security program and the close-knit nature of the campus.

"Hendrix has such a vibrant social life," says a junior. Greek life—a staple of most Southern schools—is conspicuously absent at Hendrix, and students are proud of their independence. The student-run Social Committee (SoCo) organizes campus-wide events like concerts, dances, and parties, including the annual SoCo 54 disco-inspired party. Parties are governed by a wristband system that "keeps outsiders from crashing our events and making them unsafe," explains a senior, and the

"Hendrix has the best cafeteria food in the state."

school has an amnesty policy for reporting emergency situations involving alcohol. Ample alternative programming is offered for those who don't wish to party. The annual Campus Kitty charity fund-raiser is highlighted by the always memorable Miss Hendrix drag competition. Last but not least is the Shirttail Serenade, a 100-year-old tradition that has evolved into a friendly dance-off held early in the fall semester. Donning white button-down shirts and dorm-specific paraphernalia (different colored shorts, crazy socks, glitter, etc.), teams of freshmen from each residence hall perform dance routines while upperclassmen cheer them on. The winning team jumps in the fountain.

Home to three colleges, Conway (population 65,000) is undergoing a revitalization and offers a growing number of shops and restaurants, as well as Toad Suck Daze, a rollicking annual carnival downtown featuring bluegrass music. Little Rock, a 30-minute drive, provides more options. Popular road trips are Memphis (two hours by car) and Dallas and Oklahoma City (each a five-hour drive) for concerts and the like. For those who stay in town, the Volunteer Action Center coordinates participation in projects on Service Saturdays.

The Division III Hendrix Warriors field a number of competitive teams in the Southern Athletic Association; football, men's basketball, and women's volleyball have been successful in recent years. Rhodes College is the chief rival. For outdoor buffs, the college sponsors trips around Arkansas for canoeing, biking, rock climbing, and spelunking. Thirty-seven percent of students also compete in intramural or club sports, with ultimate Frisbee, indoor soccer, and basketball proving popular.

"Hendrix is tight-knit with a place for everyone," says one student. Musician Jimi Hendrix—whose mug inevitably adorns a new campus T-shirt each year—once asked listeners, "Are you experienced?" After four years at Hendrix College, with small classes, an emphasis on research, and a laid-back atmosphere in which to test their beliefs and boundaries, students here can likely answer, "Yes!"

Overlaps

Austin College, Kalamazoo, Millsaps, Southwestern, Ursinus, Rhodes, Trinity University (TX), Centre

Hiram College

P.O. Box 96, Hiram, OH 44234

One of the smaller prominent liberal arts colleges in Ohio. Less known nationally than Denison or Wooster, Hiram draws the vast majority of its students from in state—and then sends them around the globe. Lots of classes are taught in seminar format, with ample undergraduate research opportunities. Unique academic calendar allows for off-campus learning.

Hiram College offers students a solid liberal arts education and plenty of opportunities to dive into a research lab, test out the corporate life, or travel the globe. In fact, all students are required to have a hands-on learning experience before they graduate. No matter where they hang their hats, students here enjoy a close-knit environment. "Most students know one another, word spreads fast, and small class sizes make for a very personalized academic experience," says a political science and international studies major.

Set on a charming hilltop campus that occupies the second-highest spot in Ohio, Hiram is blessed with an abundance of flowers and trees as well as a nice view of the valley below. Hiram was founded in 1850 by the Disciples of Christ in a frontier area seen as "healthful and free of distractions." The prevailing architectural motif is New England brick, and many Hiram buildings are restored 19th-century homes. Science majors frequently work, study, and conduct research at the college-owned, 550-acre Barrow Biological Field Station a few miles away.

The Hiram Plan organizes the academic year into two longer 12-week sessions, each of which is followed by a shorter three-week term. Hiram's core curriculum is extensive. Freshmen take a First-Year Enduring Questions seminar in the fall and a more advanced First-Year Urgent Questions seminar in the spring. Juniors complete an interdisciplinary, team-taught Urgent Challenges course. Students are also required to take courses in eight Ways of Knowing, such as experimental scientific methods, social and cultural analysis, and understanding diversity. In addition, students satisfy an experiential learning component by studying off campus, conducting research, or working in an internship, and in the senior

> **"Students have time to breathe between classes and an opportunity to thrive without overstressing."**

year, they complete and present a capstone project. Hiram also requires students to reflect on their career and other goals and on their progress at four points, starting in the spring of their first year. Thanks to the college's Tech and Trek mobile education program, every full-time, traditional student is outfitted with an iPad, an Apple Pencil, a keyboard, and a pair of hiking boots.

Financial difficulties in recent years have forced Hiram to shrink the size of its faculty as well as trim the number of majors. At the same time, it has launched new programs in areas like integrative exercise science, public health, and digital marketing, as well as opportunities to focus on societal challenges like climate change. The sciences, especially biology and chemistry, are strong, as is the creative writing program. Hiram has the longest-standing biomedical humanities major in the country,

---

Website: www.hiram.edu
Location: Rural
Private
Total Enrollment: 800
Undergraduates: 780
Male/Female: 48/52
Financial Aid: 87%
Pell Grant: 43%
Expense: Pr $
Student Loans: 89%
Average Debt: $ $ $ $
Applicants: 1,856
Accepted: 93%
Enrolled: 14%
Grad in 6 Years: 53%
Returning Freshmen: 72%
Academics: ✐ ✐ ✐
Social: ☎ ☎ ☎
Q of L: ★ ★ ★
Admissions: (800) 362-5280
Email Address: admission@
   hiram.edu

Strong Programs:
Biology
Chemistry
Creative Writing
Biomedical Humanities
Public Leadership
Accounting and Financial
   Management
Education
Neuroscience

and the Garfield Institute, named after the Hiram educator who went on to become the 20th U.S. president, offers a notable minor in public leadership. The most popular majors include accounting and financial management, education, biology, neuroscience, business management, and nursing. Dual-degree engineering programs are available with nearby Case Western Reserve as well as WashU in St. Louis. Fifteen three-year degree programs are available, enabling participants to graduate faster and save tens of thousands of dollars. For most students, however, "the academic climate is relaxed," muses a communication major. "Students have time to breathe between classes and an opportunity to thrive without overstressing." Academic resources abound, including tutors, the writing center, and help from peers or profs. Classes are small, with 81 percent enrolling fewer than 20 students, and students enjoy an impressive degree of faculty accessibility. "Professors are involved and are fun to talk with," says a freshman.

Science majors frequently study and conduct research at the college-owned, 550-acre Barrow Biological Field Station a few miles away.

Hiram's unique academic calendar allows ample time for off-campus endeavors of all types. Professors lead three to five study abroad programs each year in all corners of the globe. Hiram offers several unusual summer opportunities as well, most notably the Northwoods Field Station in the wilds of Michigan's Upper Peninsula, where students choose courses ranging from botany and photography to geology and writing. Political internships are available in Washington, D.C. A four-year honors program offers further opportunities for networking, independent study, and advanced coursework.

"Hiram students are willing to go out and explore," opines a junior. "Trying new things and being trailblazers is what Hiram is all about." Seventy-four percent of Hiram students are in-staters, though the administration is working aggressively to recruit more students from other states. International students represent less than 1 percent of the student body. Black students constitute 13 percent, Asian Americans 1 percent, Hispanics/Latinos 9 percent, and multiracial students 3 percent. Hiram's Intercultural Forum club is one of the largest and most active on campus, and the Office for Diversity and Inclusion offers peer mentoring and tutoring programs for first-generation students, among other services. A hefty 43 percent of freshmen qualify for Pell Grants. In addition to need-based financial aid, Hiram awards merit-based aid, luring good students with irresistible scholarships. Hiram also reduced its sticker price by 35 percent in hopes of avoiding the problem of sticker shock that can discourage students from applying to private colleges.

"Trying new things and being trailblazers is what Hiram is all about."

Most Hiram students—76 percent—live on campus, and everyone who wants a room gets one. "Ours are much better than some I have seen at other schools," says a junior. Most halls are co-ed, and upperclassmen who like their location can stay in the same room year after year. Most students live in two-person suites; the popular (and larger) triple and quad suites and the townhouse apartments are scarcer and usually claimed by upper-class students. Dining services receive good reviews, and expanded educational programming on sexual assault has been well received.

Hiram reduced its sticker price by 35 percent in hopes of avoiding the problem of sticker shock.

When the weekend rolls around, don't expect to find most Hiram students gathered around a keg; the college has cracked down on underage drinking, and participation in the school's two sororities and one fraternity is minimal. Parties thrown in suites and townhouses tend to be low-key. "The school does a pretty good job of providing activities to do on campus (most of the events involve free food!), but in the surrounding village there isn't much to do," says a senior. Homecoming and Springfest are weeklong celebrations with diversions like "dive-in" movies at the pool and campuswide barbecues. Every spring brings Sugar Day, which is "a day dedicated to service and giving back to the community and also highlights graduating seniors, who present their capstone projects," explains a junior. Neighboring Garrettsville offers a few restaurants and bars, but those in search of a more active social scene make the 45-minute drive to Cleveland for concerts, professional sports, and the Rock and Roll Hall of Fame, which can get students rockin' all year-round.

Hiram is hardly a mecca for budding athletic superstars, but it does have a decent Division III sports program. Most of its 17 varsity Terriers teams compete in the North Coast Athletic Conference; softball, men's and women's volleyball, and cheer and STUNT have been the most successful. About half of the students play intramural and club sports, including volleyball, kickball, and disc golf, and many enjoy the on-campus disc golf course as well. An excellent golf course lies three miles away, and good downhill slopes are about an hour distant.

Those looking for a school where anonymity is ensured need not apply. People here are so close that they share an equivalent of a not-so-secret handshake. "Hiram is known for the 'Hiram Hi' because everyone is always greeting one another as they pass," says a senior. Indeed, those seeking a friendly, all-American institution with a touch of internationalism might want to give Hiram a look.

If You Apply To ›

Hiram: Rolling admissions. SATs or ACTs: optional. Accepts the Common Application with supplement. Submission of a graded writing sample or essay is recommended.

Hobart and William Smith Colleges

Geneva, NY 14456

With a campus overlooking one of New York's picturesque Finger Lakes, HWS builds on its heritage as two separate, single-sex colleges to create a unified academic environment that gives new meaning to gender and inclusion. Takes pride in personal attention from full professors and a culture of community service. Much of the social life takes place on campus, but skiing and other outdoor activities beckon.

Founded as two separate, single-sex colleges—Hobart for men and William Smith for women—HWS operates under a distinctive "coordinate system." All students share the same campus, faculty, and curriculum, but each college has its own dean and maintains some of its own traditions, including student government and athletics. Students thus enjoy a close-knit, co-ed community while experiencing the sort of deep brotherly and sisterly bonds that are typically associated with single-sex institutions. If you can tolerate the frigid winters of upstate New York, you'll be rewarded with small classes, caring faculty, and a place where tradition still matters.

Hobart College was founded in 1822 by Episcopal Bishop John Henry Hobart, who conceived it to be an outpost for civilized and learned behavior. William Smith College opened in 1908 and bears the name of a wealthy businessman and philanthropist who wanted to introduce women to opportunities that were largely unrecognized at the time. The HWS campus stretches for 325 tree-lined acres and includes a forest and a wildlife preserve. Architectural styles range from colonial to postmodern, with stately Greek Revival mansions and ivy-clad brick residences and classrooms. The nationally ranked sailing team enjoys a boathouse on the shores of Seneca Lake. Newer campus additions include a $3.5 million sports dome, featuring a massive multisport turf field.

Website: www.hws.edu
Location: Small City
Private
Total Enrollment: 1,645
Undergraduates: 1,621
Male/Female: 48/52
Financial Aid: 96%
Pell Grant: 28%
Expense: Pr $ $ $ $
Student Loans: 72%
Average Debt: $ $ $ $
Applicants: 3,771
Accepted: 68%
Enrolled: 14%
Grad in 6 Years: 77%
Returning Freshmen: 88%
Academics: ✐ ✐ ✐

(continued)

Social: ☎ ☎ ☎
Q of L: ★ ★ ★
Admissions: (800) 852-2256
Email Address: admissions@
  hws.edu

Strong Programs:
Women's Studies
Queer Studies
Architectural Studies
Biology
Geoscience
Environmental Studies
Economics
Media and Society

The Colleges were among the first in the nation to offer full-fledged undergraduate programs in women's studies and queer studies.

The HWS curriculum has no distribution requirements. Instead, students start by taking an interdisciplinary seminar in the first year, constructed around a different interest; recent seminar offerings include Britpop, Podcasting America, and Earth vs. Humans. First-years in each seminar are assigned to the same orientation group, "so they are well acquainted before they start their first class together," explains an economics major. Students must also complete a major and a minor or second major, and all students conduct a senior capstone experience.

Under the coordinate system, students are free to identify with either college (or with HWS as one entity). One student cites "many benefits, like more student voices being heard, more individualized attention from deans, and more opportunities from alums." Administrators say that HWS

> **"[The coordinate system means] more individualized attention from deans and more opportunities from alums."**

is intentional about embracing all forms of gender identity and nonconformity and that its coordinate heritage offers students a springboard to engage with issues of gender and justice in an era when such issues are in flux. Indeed, the Colleges were among the first in the nation to offer full-fledged undergraduate programs in women's studies and queer studies in addition to a first-of-its-kind minor in men's studies. The most popular majors include economics, media and society, psychology, and English, and the long list of minors includes aquatic sciences, data analytics, social justice studies, and aesthetics. Other solid programs include architectural studies, biology, geoscience, and environmental studies. A new major in management and entrepreneurship is now available. The Finger Lakes Institute gives students wide opportunities to work in various fields of scientific inquiry, as well as public policy. "I would not describe the academic climate as competitive at all, but that's not to say the workload is not intense," says one student. Small classes are the norm here: 72 percent have fewer than 20 students. Professors are praised for being accessible and engaging. "Professors treat students like peers and are open to any and all questions and challenges that students may introduce in class," says an environmental studies and geoscience major.

HWS students may take a term away from campus, and 68 percent do so, choosing from more than 50 study abroad programs, many of which are faculty led. Each year, about 40 seniors elect to complete an honors project involving research, a critical paper, or an equivalent creative work in addition to written and oral exams on their projects. At the Senior Symposium each spring, seniors present research findings, discuss theory, display creative works, or present other significant scholarly activities. Students who complete the Pathways Program, a series of workshops and career counseling activities, are guaranteed an opportunity for a paid internship or research experience.

According to an international relations major, HWS students are "welcoming, friendly, and excited to try new things." New Yorkers make up 42 percent of the HWS student body and international students 7 percent. Black students account for

> **"Professors treat students like peers and are open to any and all questions and challenges."**

7 percent of undergraduates, Hispanics/Latinos 9 percent, Asian Americans 3 percent, and multiracial students 3 percent. "Preppy students from up north who come from wealthy families" make up the majority, explains one student, and a junior remarks, "The most diverse part about HWS is the range of political opinions." Merit scholarships averaging $27,800 are awarded to qualified students; athletic scholarships are available for Hobart's lacrosse team.

At HWS, all students are required to live on campus and buy a meal plan. Housing includes lakefront residences, theme houses, and townhouses. Single-sex, co-ed, and gender-neutral options are available. Thirty percent of first-years opt to participate in living/learning communities. While no one raves about the dining hall fare, most agree that "the meals get the job done," says one pragmatic student. When it comes to safety, a sophomore comments that campus security officers are "very efficient and helpful at all times." Sexual assault has been a high-profile issue at HWS, but a senior reports, "HWS has taken several steps to address sexual assault, such as extensive bystander training, student-led initiatives, Title IX workshops, and more."

Six Hobart fraternities claim 18 percent of the men, who aren't permitted to pledge until sophomore year, and William Smith's sole sorority signs up 2 percent of the women. Much of the social life involves Greek parties and bashes at off-campus houses, although a junior notes that the bar scene downtown is also popular. Underage students caught with booze must attend alcohol awareness classes and may face social probation. The Campus Activities Board plans movies, concerts, plays, and other events each weekend. "The lake is a hot spot for socialization at the beginning and end of the school year," adds a junior. Annual traditions, which are open to all members of the HWS community, remain important. Hobart, for instance, celebrates Charter Day in April. William Smith, meanwhile, holds Founder's Day festivities in the fall, and at the end of the year, on Moving Up Day, seniors symbolically hand over their leadership role to juniors. Other favorite events include the annual Quad-a-Palooza bash during homecoming and lacrosse matches against rivals Syracuse and Cornell.

> *The Finger Lakes Institute gives students wide opportunities to work in various fields of scientific inquiry as well as public policy.*

> **"The lake is a hot spot for socialization."**

The old industrial city of Geneva has been revitalized in recent years and offers many amenities for students out on the town, including restaurants, bars, shops, concerts, and the Smith Opera House. Students are active in the community: collectively, HWS students contribute more than 80,000 hours of service each year, often through service-learning courses, one-day opportunities like Days of Service, and extended volunteering with groups like the Boys and Girls Club. Rochester, Ithaca, and Syracuse, all about 45 minutes away, make for popular road trips. Seneca Falls, birthplace of the suffrage movement, is also nearby. More adventurous excursions include "skiing with friends or going into New York City or Boston," according to an art history major.

> *HWS has announced plans to significantly expand its varsity athletics program, adding 12 new sports by 2026.*

Varsity sports teams' mascots and colors reflect HWS's coordinate heritage: the Hobart Statesmen wear purple, while the William Smith Herons sport green. Teams compete in Division III, except for Hobart lacrosse, which is Division I. Hobart rowing and William Smith soccer and lacrosse are recent conference champions. The Colleges' co-ed sailing team is also perennially competitive. HWS has announced plans to significantly expand its varsity athletics program, adding 12 new sports by 2026, including men's and women's Alpine skiing, track and field, baseball, softball, and more. The HWS Debate Team has had national success recently. Twenty percent of students participate in intramural and club sports.

While some students may see little value in HWS's unusual coordinate college system, others feel that the blending of two traditions "plays into the personality that differentiates HWS from other schools," says a senior, adding, "The school takes in mind these differences and traditions, but ultimately, HWS is still one school."

Overlaps

Dickinson, Franklin & Marshall, Gettysburg, St. Lawrence, Union, SUNY–College at Geneseo, Ithaca, Colgate

If You Apply To ›

HWS: Early decision I and II, early action, regular decision. SATs or ACTs: optional. Accepts the Common Application. Applicants' gender identity is considered in the admissions process.

Hofstra University

Hempstead, NY 11549

Boasts a combination of suburban setting with ready access to the Big Apple. Hofstra has outgrown its commuter-school origins and offers a broad range of preprofessional and other academic programs. Well known as a lacrosse powerhouse. Has become more selective in recent years, but for many, it is still a backup to urban schools like BU and Northeastern.

Website: www.hofstra.edu
Location: Suburban
Private
Total Enrollment: 8,727
Undergraduates: 5,730
Male/Female: 43/57
Financial Aid: 64%
Pell Grant: 24%
Expense: Pr $ $
Student Loans: 59%
Average Debt: N/A
Applicants: 24,886
Accepted: 68%
Enrolled: 10%
Grad in 6 Years: 70%
Returning Freshmen: 80%
Academics: ✐ ✐ ✐
Social: ☎ ☎ ☎
Q of L: ★ ★ ★
Admissions: (516) 463-6700
Email Address: admission@
  hofstra.edu

Strong Programs:
Business
Communication
Engineering
Health Sciences
Accounting
Journalism
Television and Film
Radio Production

Although it sits within easy striking distance of Manhattan concrete, Hofstra University occupies one of the loveliest campuses you'll find anywhere. Its bucolic setting is home not only to an accredited art museum and a nationally recognized arboretum but also to the school's blossoming preprofessional offerings. Whatever their field, Hofstra students enjoy special learning communities, research and internship opportunities, and first-year programs that help harried freshmen get off to a good start. "It's a friendly environment that allows you to find your special niches, without forcing anything upon you," reflects an accounting and political science major.

Founded in 1935 with one building—the Dutch colonial mansion left in trust by Kate and William Hofstra on their 15-acre estate—the campus is now home to 117 buildings on 244 acres. The suburban campus offers a parklike environment

> **"[Hofstra] allows you to find your special niches, without forcing anything upon you."**

with a variety of architecture, from ivy-covered stone buildings to modern facilities with sleek angles and electronic signage, which surround open green quads. The campus is especially beautiful in the spring, when its 100,000 tulips, a tribute to the Dutch heritage of Hofstra's founders, are in bloom. Several buildings have undergone major renovations, and the Zarb School of Business has a 52,500-square-foot building boasting an incubator lab, a market research and behavioral science lab, and other amenities.

With more than 160 academic programs for undergraduates, Hofstra offers students plenty of career paths. Regardless of what major they choose, all undergrad students must complete distribution requirements, including coursework in humanities; natural sciences, mathematics, and computer science; social sciences; cross-cultural studies; and interdisciplinary studies. Students must also demonstrate their competence as writers, usually by taking the Writing Proficiency Exam in their first year.

With the recent establishment of the DeMatteis School of Engineering and Applied Science and the Kalikow School of Government, Public Policy, and International Affairs, as well as joint undergraduate programs with its medical school, Hofstra seeks to model itself on much larger and better-known Northeastern universities like NYU and Syracuse. Traditional areas of strength include business, communication, engineering, and health sciences; marketing, accounting, journalism, television and film, radio production, and community health are particularly notable. Business students benefit from one of the largest simulated trading rooms in the New York area. Several dual-degree programs have recently been introduced (bringing the overall count to 16), pairing undergraduate degrees with corresponding master's degrees in such areas as physician assistant studies, labor studies, sustainability studies, and others. Nursing is now available as an undergraduate major from the Hofstra Northwell School of Nursing and Physician Assistant Studies.

"Most majors focus on ensuring that students are learning how to be a professional in their field, as opposed to being able to simply regurgitate the information," explains a junior. Fifty-one percent of undergraduate classes have fewer than 20 students, allowing for plenty of access to faculty. "The professors really care about your successes and often celebrate them with you," says a journalism major. Support services for students with learning disabilities are particularly strong and include accommodations as well as skill-development and coaching programs.

The First-Year Connections program offers new students a combined social and academic experience centered on small seminars (limited to 19 students) taught by senior faculty; recent seminars include Macro Freakonomics, Art in the Information Age, and The Mathematics of Elections. Freshmen may also enroll in clusters of thematically related courses, and several seminars and clusters also have living/learning community options associated with them. The Honors College offers about 250 qualified entering students a multidisciplinary program with a special housing option. The university's 17 research centers facilitate opportunities for students to work with professors on scholarly projects, and internships in New York City are another popular pursuit. Students with wanderlust can take advantage of study abroad options around the world, including programs in Cuba, India, Italy, and Japan, and about 15 percent of undergrads do so.

The university's 17 research centers facilitate opportunities for students to work with professors on scholarly projects.

"I wanted to make sure I wound up at a school where everyone loved different things and brought something different to the table, and I definitely found it here," says a journalism major. Sixty-one percent of undergraduates hail from New York, and 4 percent come from abroad. Black students account for 9 percent of the student body, Hispanics/Latinos 16 percent, Asian Americans 13 percent, and multiracial students 4 percent. Hofstra has hosted a trio of U.S. presidential debates, and a senior describes the political climate as "semi-intense" but "respectful." The university offers merit scholarships worth an average of $22,000 and 120 athletic scholarships in 23 men's and women's sports.

"The professors really care about your successes and often celebrate them with you."

Thirty-nine percent of undergraduates, including 57 percent of first-year students, live in university housing, which is guaranteed for all four years. Many dorms have been renovated in the last few years. Students have nearly 20 different dining options to choose from, and a health science major says, "Most meals are made to order, which ensures freshness and deliciousness." A junior reports, "The school takes safety very seriously, which is why we have five shuttle systems, including a night shuttle."

As for social life, "This is where Hofstra excels," boasts a sophomore, "offering an incredible number of clubs, in-dorm activities, and departmental organizations." Six percent of the men and 11 percent of the women go Greek, but they don't dominate the social landscape. Students of legal age are allowed to consume alcohol in their rooms; "parties are there if you're looking for them," says a junior. Hofstra is big on festivals, which include Fall Fest; a spring music festival; Irish, Italian, and Dutch festivals; and a long-running Shakespeare Festival that features performances on a stage that is purported to be the most authentic replica in the U.S. of the original Globe Theatre.

Hofstra is big on festivals: Fall Fest; a spring music festival; Irish, Italian, and Dutch festivals; and a long-running Shakespeare Festival.

Hofstra's location 40 minutes east of New York City makes it easy to enjoy day trips and nights on the town, and the school organizes Explore Next Door events that take students to various neighborhoods, museums, shows, and sporting events. The two largest community service activities at Hofstra are Shake-a-Rake and Snow Angels, which send students out to do yard work and shoveling for elderly and disabled neighbors.

The Hofstra Pride compete in Division I and play an important role in shaping campus culture—especially the perennially powerful lacrosse and men's basketball teams. Women's soccer, volleyball, and men's basketball have won Colonial Athletic Association championships recently. The dance team is nationally ranked, and the forensics, or debate, team has achieved national success as well. Roughly one-quarter of undergrads participate in the university's 25 club sports and 6 intramural leagues.

Opportunities abound at Hofstra, and the university continues to add resources—both curricular and extracurricular—to serve its diverse, career-oriented student body. As one junior puts it, "Many schools feel like buffets, where students are offered services and told to forge their own way to where they hope to be, while Hofstra caters directly to the individual student and asks what they can do to get a student from point A to point B." By connecting solid academics with hands-on learning experiences, the university seeks to put its students in a New York state of mind.

If You Apply To ›

Hofstra: Early action I and II, rolling admissions. SATs or ACTs: optional. Accepts the Common Application with supplement.

Hollins University

P.O. Box 9707, Roanoke, VA 24020

One of the South's leading women's colleges, Hollins sits on the edge of Roanoke, the biggest city in southwest Virginia, where it has long been noted for creative writing, the performing arts, and its equestrian program. Social life often involves road trips to Virginia Tech and Washington and Lee, both about an hour's drive, or venturing into the great outdoors.

Traditions rule at Hollins University, Virginia's first women's college, founded in 1842 (and named after local donors) on a lush, 475-acre campus in the mountains. Each fall, students and staff hike up Tinker Mountain for skits, a picnic lunch, and a bird's-eye view of the changing foliage. During the holiday season, faculty and administrators sing carols outside students' residence halls. And after graduation, juniors inherit seniors' decorated gowns during Passing of the Robes. A few dozen male students can be found on campus, since Hollins offers 18 co-ed degree and certificate programs for graduate students. "A student should only attend Hollins if they want to be a part of a close-knit community that fosters creative minds and ambitious spirits," says a senior.

Described by the *New York Times* as "achingly picturesque," the neoclassical redbrick buildings at Hollins date back to the mid-19th century. There are some modern structures too, such as the Wetherill Visual Arts Center. Several buildings have been renovated in recent years, including Hollins Theatre and Dana Science Building. Construction is ongoing on a new student apartment village that will add a total of 96 beds; seven of the village's 10 planned buildings have been completed.

> **"We get lots of individual attention and extra help."**

Hollins's general education program (known as Education through Skills and Perspectives) teaches real-world skills, including writing, oral communication, applied quantitative reasoning, and applied research techniques, while examining seven perspectives from which people view and understand the world: aesthetic

Website: www.hollins.edu
Location: Suburban
Private
Total Enrollment: 746
Undergraduates: 707
Male/Female: 0/100
Financial Aid: 100%
Pell Grant: 38%
Expense: Pr $
Student Loans: 73%
Average Debt: $ $ $ $
Applicants: 3,093
Accepted: 75%
Enrolled: 10%
Grad in 6 Years: 59%
Returning Freshmen: 74%
Academics: ✍ ✍ ✍
Social: ☎ ☎ ☎
Q of L: ★ ★ ★ ★
Admissions: (800) 456-9595

analysis, creative expression, ancient and medieval worlds, modern and contemporary worlds, social and cultural diversities, scientific inquiry, and global systems and languages. Two terms of physical education are mandatory, and those looking to take advantage of Hollins's acclaimed equestrian program can earn PE credits with riding lessons. All freshmen take a required first-year seminar and participate in Orientation Week, which includes academic programming, a day of community service, and plenty of time to form friendships with new classmates. All seniors complete a capstone course or project.

Academics are the priority at Hollins. "I have been challenged by most of my classes here, but the workload has been manageable enough that I have been able to do a bunch of extracurriculars too," says one senior. Of the school's 29 undergraduate majors, psychology, English, biology, business, and creative writing are the most popular. Public health is the newest. Students majoring or minoring in creative writing benefit from the nationally recognized Jackson Center for Creative Writing. Environmental studies and the visual and performing arts, especially film, theatre, and dance, have good reputations too. Serious dance students have the opportunity to attend the American Dance Festival at Duke University to study intensively during the summer. Motivated students are encouraged to design their own majors. Classes are small, with 88 percent enrolling fewer than 20 students and none exceeding 50, and professors are well regarded. "We get lots of individual attention and extra help," says an art history and international studies major.

The Rutherfoord Center for Experiential Learning helps coordinate hands-on learning opportunities like study abroad, research projects, and internships, which students often pursue during the monthlong January Short Term. Around 20 percent of undergrads undertake independent research projects. The Signature Internship Program places upperclassmen in for-credit internships, offered by loyal alumnae across the country, that come with a $300 stipend. The Batten Leadership Institute, open to students of all majors, offers a certificate in leadership studies and opportunities for students to develop skills like effective conflict management, negotiation, and team building. The Entrepreneurial Learning Institute coordinates courses in applied entrepreneurship and other opportunities for students in all disciplines. In addition to a Hollins Abroad program in London, students may study through more than 20 affiliated programs around the world; 35 percent of students study internationally before they graduate.

> "[We have] an active women's studies department that puts together a lot of rallies and events."

At Hollins, says a sophomore, "students are opinionated, passionate, and driven" but also supportive of each other. Forty-eight percent of undergrads are Virginians, and 9 percent hail from foreign countries. Black students make up 14 percent of the total, Asian Americans 2 percent, Hispanics/Latinas 8 percent, and multiracial students 8 percent. "We have a very active gay and lesbian club called OUTloud, and also an active women's studies department that puts together a lot of rallies and events," says a first-year student. "Our campus has a definite liberal leaning, although there is a small, committed Republican group." Hollins also hands out merit scholarships averaging $33,400 to qualified students, but no athletic scholarships. Thirty-eight percent of incoming freshmen qualify for Pell Grants.

Eighty-eight percent of Hollins students live in the dorms; they have to, unless they're married, older than 23, or living at home in Roanoke with their parents. Options include traditional residence halls, several special interest houses, and the new apartment village. "Most of the dorms are beautiful historic buildings full of character and comfort," says a student. First-years live in Randolph and Tinker. Upperclassmen make their homes in Main, West, and East, which have 10-foot ceilings and hardwood floors, and some rooms also boast brass doorknobs, walk-in

(continued)

Email Address: huadm@
 hollins.edu

Strong Programs:
Creative Writing
Environmental Studies
Film
Theatre
Dance
Psychology
English
Biology

Those looking to take advantage of Hollins's acclaimed equestrian program can earn PE credits with riding lessons.

The Signature Internship Program places upperclassmen in for-credit internships, offered by loyal alumnae, that come with a $300 stipend.

closets, and even fireplaces. Students chow down at Moody Dining Hall, Greenberry's Coffee, or the Hub. While the adjacent Roanoke neighborhood has its rough spots, "the campus is very safe," says one student.

"Most social gatherings take place on campus," says a student. "People meet at dinner to talk about their day or hang out until midnight watching movies and talking in their dorm rooms." Hollins shuns sororities, and sporadic student efforts to bring them to campus draw lively debate. To fill the gap, the school organizes mixers, concerts, dances, and second-run movies each weekend. There's also a free shuttle to help students get around Roanoke (population 100,000). "Roanoke is a quaint city, not tall and towering but not small, either," says an English major. "There are local markets, a few clubs, a mall, and curious little local shops." As a result, road-tripping remains the preferred social option—to all-male Hampden–Sydney College, Virginia Tech, the University of Virginia, or Washington and Lee.

Hollins's on-campus stable, where students can board their own horses, complements the school's top-notch equestrian program, which has brought home the Old Dominion Athletic Conference championship 21 times. The university also sponsors eight other Division III sports. Although there are no intramural sports, the popular Hollins Outdoor Program offers hiking, spelunking, and other activities for all skill levels in the beautiful Shenandoah Valley and Blue Ridge Mountains.

As the number of women's colleges continues to dwindle, Hollins remains committed to the virtues of single-sex education. Students leave with confidence, critical-thinking skills, and intellectual depth, thanks to a solid grounding in the liberal arts. And the school's Southern heritage doesn't hurt, either. "Hollins is a great school that empowers women," says one senior. "It has made me independent."

If You Apply To ›

Hollins: Early decision, early action, regular decision. SATs or ACTs: optional. Accepts the Common Application with supplement. Accepts applications from students who consistently live and identify as women, regardless of the gender assigned to them at birth.

College of the Holy Cross

Worcester, MA 01610

A tight-knit Roman Catholic community steeped in church and tradition, much more so than relatively secularized Boston College. Many students are the second or third generation to attend. Set high on a hill above an evolving Worcester, an hour from Boston. Sports teams compete (and hold their own) with schools 10 times HC's size.

Students at Holy Cross, a Roman Catholic college in the heart of New England, are devoted to the Society of Jesus (Jesuit) tradition of becoming "men and women for and with others." Students on "the hill" are driven to do something for their college or community, whether it's a football player becoming a Big Brother or an upperclassman interning at city hall. Peers and professors alike offer support and spiritual guidance, and more than 90 community-based learning courses incorporate service opportunities. The classroom focus is critical thinking and writing, but the school's proximity to several other colleges in the Worcester area means Crusaders can cultivate their social lives as well.

Located on one of the seven hills overlooking the industrial city of Worcester, the 174-acre Holy Cross campus is a registered arboretum. The school's landscaping has won national awards, including two first-place prizes as the best-designed and best-planted campus in the nation. Architectural styles range from classical to modern. The college opened a new recreation and wellness center in 2021, and the $107 million Prior Performing Arts Center was completed in 2022.

General education requirements at Holy Cross, which was founded in 1843, comprise 12 courses in nine areas spanning the liberal arts and sciences. Ideas and thinking are the focus, rather than preparation for a specific vocation. All first-year students participate in Montserrat, a comprehensive living/learning program named for the Spanish mountain where St. Ignatius began his spiritual journey. It centers on a small, yearlong seminar that students select from one of six clusters, each devoted to a specific theme: contemporary challenges, the divine, the self, the natural world, global society, and core human questions. Students live with other members of their cluster in the same residence hall and participate in cocurricular activities like special lectures, workshops, and field trips. "It was an eye-opening experience for me, and the friendships I made in my Montserrat class lasted throughout my entire four years," reflects a psychology major.

> **"The friendships I made in my Montserrat class lasted throughout my entire four years."**

HC's health professions advising program boasts a particularly high success rate for getting students accepted to medical school. The economics, political science, psychology, and English programs are both strong and popular, and students give high marks to chemistry, physics, and sociology. One student opines that the classics department is one of the best-kept secrets on campus. As might be expected, philosophy and religious studies are strong, and concentrations in Latin American studies and peace and conflict studies are popular, as these are disciplines central to Jesuit missionary work.

Classes are small—59 percent have fewer than 20 students—which helps faculty members keep in touch with undergraduates. Courses are demanding and intense, but professors are praised for being willing to help. "There really is a partnership between professors and students here at HC," says a political science and Spanish double major. And students say the support they receive from each other is exceptional. One senior shares, "I have found notes in the Dinand Library with a positive quote or an encouraging message for the next student who sits there."

HC's popular community-based learning courses require weekly service with local volunteer, education, or health organizations in addition to time in the classroom; some courses focus on research that benefits local organizations. The honors program enables a small number of juniors and seniors to enroll in exclusive courses and thesis-writing seminars, while the Fenwick Scholar program helps students design and carry out independent projects. Each April, approximately 300 Holy Cross students participate in a four-day conference and present the results of their independent work. Forty-one percent of students pack their bags for a range of study abroad programs around the world, and the college strongly encourages yearlong programs. Two intensive study away programs, the Washington Semester and the New York Semester, combine an internship with a seminar course and an independent, research-based thesis or capstone project. Students praise the Center for Career Development, especially for its strong relationships with alumni.

> **"Pancakes taste infinitely better when served by a Jesuit."**

The religious influence at Holy Cross is somewhat greater than at other Jesuit schools—69 percent of students are Catholic—but students of all faiths are

HC's popular community-based learning courses require weekly service with local volunteer, education, or health organizations.

(continued)

Expense: Pr $ $ $
Student Loans: 63%
Average Debt: $ $
Applicants: 6,498
Accepted: 42%
Enrolled: 29%
Grad in 6 Years: 93%
Returning Freshmen: 96%
Academics: ✍ ✍ ✍ ✍
Social: ☎ ☎ ☎ ☎
Q of L: ★ ★ ★ ★
Admissions: (508) 793-2443
Email Address: admissions@ holycross.edu

Strong Programs:
Economics
Political Science
Psychology
English
Chemistry
Physics
Sociology
Religious Studies

welcomed, and daily mass is not required. The chaplain's office runs numerous types of retreats for all faiths and reflective practices, including an optional five-day silent retreat. Thirty-nine percent of students are in-staters, and 3 percent are international. Black students make up 4 percent of the student body, Asian Americans represent 4 percent, Hispanics/Latinos account for 11 percent, and multiracial students add 3 percent. Social justice issues are a constant focus on campus, and the college sponsors many campuswide forums and panel discussions. "Healthy debate is encouraged, and I do not feel that the college is too biased one way or the other," comments a psychology major. HC dropped its need-blind admissions policy in 2019, citing concerns over an unsustainably high financial aid budget, but still guarantees to meet admitted students' full demonstrated financial need. Students from families with annual incomes of $75,000 or less and typical assets receive full-tuition grants. Limited merit-based scholarships are available to top students, and athletes may vie for roughly 300 athletic awards in 14 sports.

Dorms compete against each other for prizes in athletic and other contests.

Eighty-seven percent of Holy Cross students live in the residence halls, where freshmen and sophomores have double rooms, and juniors and seniors may opt for suites or apartment-style accommodations. Floors are single-sex; buildings are co-ed. First-years live on "Easy Street," in Hanselman, Clark, and Brooks-Mulledy (on the college's central hill next to the Hogan Campus Center). Dorms receive decent reviews, especially for their size and storage space. Dining options include several campus eateries and the main dining hall; students rate the food as tasty and plentiful. Students say they feel safe thanks to regular campus security patrols and a safe-ride program. Although campus sexual assault has been a hot-button issue, a junior reports, "Holy Cross has made a concerted effort in the past few years to be more transparent on issues of sexual assault and to foster a culture of sexual respect."

"Volunteering is one way students live out the Holy Cross mission."

Because, consistent with Jesuit tradition, there are no Greek organizations, dorm life takes center stage. Each dorm has its own T-shirt, and they compete against each other for prizes in athletic and other contests. The Campus Activities Board hosts a variety of events, including karaoke, comedians, casino nights, and movie nights. Underage students caught with alcohol are put on probation. Still, "On the weekends there are always loads of parties going on, which are generally very accessible to all students from all classes," a student says. Tradition is big at Holy Cross, from Reunion to Purple Pride Day to the 100 Days weekend, which begins the senior class countdown to graduation. Spring Weekend brings well-known performers and a carnival. Midnight breakfasts, which provide sustenance as students cram for finals, are always highly anticipated: "Pancakes taste infinitely better when served by a Jesuit, especially one who happens to be your philosophy professor," observes a history major.

Holy Cross's moot court team, which simulates Supreme Court arguments, is a top performer nationally.

"Volunteering is one way students live out the Holy Cross mission," a student says; 45 percent of students get involved in community service. The SPUD (Student Programs for Urban Development) student organization is particularly popular and active in underserved areas of Worcester, which is an underrated college town gradually making a comeback from tough economic times. A school shuttle service takes students to the orchestra, the DCU Center for athletic events and concerts, and the Worcester Art Museum. "Shrewsbury Street is an entire street devoted to incredible restaurants where I spend all of my money," says a sophomore. Students are discouraged from having cars, but the college organizes trips to Boston, Providence, and New York City.

Holy Cross's Crusaders (as in those who fight for social justice) compete in Division I athletics. The football and women's basketball teams have taken home

Patriot League championships in recent years, and men's basketball, baseball, and women's ice hockey have also been successful. About half of HC students participate in recreational sports. Holy Cross's moot court team, which simulates Supreme Court arguments, is a top performer nationally.

Holy Cross is keeping the faith—its emphasis on Catholicism and the Jesuit tradition, that is—even as administrators place a renewed focus on academics and small classes. "Holy Cross has prepared me to think critically, challenge the status quo, ask questions, and step outside my comfort zone to make changes in our world," cheers one senior. Indeed, the close-knit atmosphere offers students a multitude of opportunities to grow, serve others, and create lasting friendships.

If You Apply To ›

Holy Cross: Early decision I and II, regular decision. SATs or ACTs: optional. Accepts the Common Application.

Hood College

401 Rosemont Avenue, Frederick, MD 21701

Strategically located within striking distance of both D.C. and Baltimore, Hood offers an innovative mix of liberal arts and specialized career preparation. Big on technology, including a state-of-the-art trading room, and distinctive core curriculum stresses thematic study. Diverse student body.

Founded as a women's college way back in 1893, Hood College reinvented itself as a co-ed institution in 2003, and men now account for nearly 40 percent of undergraduates. Situated in historic Frederick, Maryland, Hood maintains a rich set of traditions, historical and otherwise, while taking full advantage of its location near two major cities. Students see their school's biggest strength in its people: students, staff, and faculty. "There are so many cultures and ethnicities and traditions to be shared," says one junior. "I love living here. I'm having the time of my life."

Hood's strikingly beautiful 50-acre campus features redbrick buildings and lush, tree-shaded lawns. Located at a major crossroads, the town of Frederick saw considerable action during the Civil War. Today, Hood is within an hour and a half of nearly 30 colleges and within minutes of a major National Cancer Institute research complex, high-tech firms, and small and large businesses. On campus, technology programs, which are already important, get a further boost thanks to the Hodson Science and Technology Center. A state-of-the-art trading room allows students to practice using technology and analytical tools similar to what is used on Wall Street. Newer additions include a 200-bed residence hall accommodating upperclassmen in suites and semi-suites.

> "[Professors] are very accessible when students need help."

Hood's core curriculum, designed to expose students to different modes of thinking and critical reflection on global issues, is comprised of two parts, Foundations and Methods of Inquiry. Foundation courses include English composition, quantitative literacy, foreign language, and health and wellness. Methods of Inquiry requires coursework in six traditional liberal arts areas, plus global perspectives. Entering students participate in a writing-intensive First-Year Seminar program designed to help build academic skills, confidence, and a sense of belonging.

Website: www.hood.edu
Location: Small City
Private
Total Enrollment: 1,876
Undergraduates: 1,156
Male/Female: 36/64
Financial Aid: 99%
Pell Grant: 32%
Expense: Pr $
Student Loans: 80%
Average Debt: $ $ $ $
Applicants: 3,192
Accepted: 77%
Enrolled: 13%
Grad in 6 Years: 66%
Returning Freshmen: 72%
Academics: ✑ ✑ ✑
Social: ☎ ☎ ☎
Q of L: ★ ★ ★
Admissions: (800) 922-1599
Email Address: admission@hood.edu

Strong Programs:
Chemistry

In the classroom, says a sophomore, "hard work is required to do well." Hood's major strength lies in the sciences, especially the chemistry department and the biology department, with its special emphases on molecular biology, marine biology, and environmental science and policy. A semester-long coastal studies program takes students along the East Coast on a biological educational mission. Education, especially early childhood, and English are programs of note, as is a B.A. degree in law and criminal justice. The most popular majors are business administration, nursing, biology, psychology, and elementary/special education. Five-year bachelor's/master's programs are available in business, environmental biology, biomedical science, psychology and counseling, and information technology. Only labs are taught by graduate assistants, and 74 percent of classes have fewer than 20 students. "The teachers want their students to succeed and are very accessible when students need help," cheers a math major.

A semester-long coastal studies program takes students along the East Coast on a biological educational mission.

If you really want to stimulate the brain cells, the four-year Honors Program features team-taught courses, a sophomore-year seminar on global issues that involves a community service project, and a senior seminar for which students choose both the topic and the professor. All students admitted to the Honors Program receive an automatic $2,000 scholarship. Internship opportunities include overseas jobs for language and business majors and legislative and cultural positions in Washington, D.C. Study abroad destinations, to which 8 percent of students take flight, include Ireland, Cyprus, Costa Rica, Morocco, and South Korea. The school's strong career resources give students a leg up on their next step in life, whether it be a job or graduate school.

In general, Hood students are "interested in their education and are serious and hardworking," says a sophomore. Nearly three-quarters of undergraduates call Maryland home, while 2 percent come to Hood from other countries. Eighteen percent of students are Black, 12 percent are Hispanic/Latino, 3 percent are Asian American, and 6 percent are multiracial. Students say the campus leans slightly left, politically speaking, and key issues include the environment and fiscal concerns. Hood provides merit scholarships worth an average of $20,300.

"Downtown Frederick is a very up-and-coming, artsy town."

Hood's co-ed residence halls are well liked, with good-sized, air-conditioned rooms. The lottery system is based on seniority, and just over half of the students live on campus. First-year students live in dedicated freshman residence halls and can expect to be assigned to doubles (juniors and seniors can compete for singles and suites), and Spanish and French majors may apply to live in the language houses. In the college's two dining facilities, a senior says, "the meals are OK if you are not picky." Campus security receives praise: "I feel very safe on our small, homey campus with lots of lights at night and plenty of officers walking or driving around at all times," says one student.

The four-year Honors Program features team-taught courses and a senior seminar for which students choose both the topic and the professor.

Social life among the students is centered on the dorms, as each has its own personality as well as its own house council, rules, and social activities. Students report that although there is no Greek life, there are parties every weekend, along with movies, dances, and other forms of entertainment. The Whitaker Campus Center, with its table tennis and pool tables, grill and sandwich shop, bookstore, and meeting rooms, offers a great gathering place for residents and commuters 24 hours a day. Campus alcohol policies have been tightened, but drinking is generally not a huge part of the social life at Hood. "At parties and events, you have to show ID to get alcohol," one senior says. "If you don't like to stay on campus, there are restaurants, bars, clubs, malls, and coffeehouses within 10 minutes of the college by car," explains an English major. Scenic Frederick is described as small, safe, and beautiful. "Downtown Frederick is a very up-and-coming, artsy town," says one student. A one-hour car ride delivers students to the multiple diversions in Baltimore or Washington, D.C.

With over a century of history, Hood is rife with traditions. Some of the most important ones include the junior class ring dinner and formal, the May Madness festival and crab feast, a strawberries-and-ice-cream breakfast for seniors the morning of commencement, and the Hood "Hello"—the custom of greeting people you pass on campus. The Blazers compete in 22 Division III sports. Baseball and men's and women's basketball, track and field, and golf are among the stronger teams. Recreational and intramural sports attract 20 percent of undergraduates; popular activities include soccer, touch football, basketball, and the equestrian club.

Hood's mission statement seeks to prepare graduates to "lead purposeful lives of responsibility, leadership, service, and civic engagement." It does so with an eye to its past as well as the demands of a fast-changing social and professional environment. "The traditions are amazing," boasts a sophomore, "topped only by professors who care and friends you'll have forever."

Overlaps

McDaniel, Mount St. Mary's, Loyola University Maryland, Manhattanville, Otterbein, Towson, UMBC, Frostburg

If You Apply To ›

Hood: Rolling admissions. SATs or ACTs: optional. Accepts the Common Application with supplement.

Hope College

P.O. Box 9000, Holland, MI 49422

Hope has an in-between size—bigger than most small colleges but smaller than a university. It is evangelical in orientation, but less than 10 percent of the students are members of the founding Reformed Church in America. In addition to the liberal arts, Hope offers education, engineering, and nursing and makes undergraduate research a priority.

Each fall since 1898, Hope College freshmen have spent three grueling hours engaged in "the Pull," an epic tug-of-war against the sophomores, who stand assembled on the opposite end of a 650-pound rope across the 250-foot-wide Black River. This well-known annual tradition evokes the daily struggle Hope students face: maintaining their faith in a world eager to challenge it at every turn. The heritage of Hope's Dutch founders remains strong and visible on campus. "The academic programs, particularly the research and collaboration opportunities, far surpass those of Hope's rivals," opines a sophomore.

Hope was founded in 1866 with support from the Reformed Church in America and the biblical (Book of Hebrews) mission of becoming an "anchor of hope" for Dutch Calvinism in the West. It is situated on six blocks near downtown Holland, the tulip capital of the nation, and a short bike ride from the shores of Lake Michigan. There's a lush pine grove in the center of campus, which features an eclectic array of buildings in architectural styles ranging from 19th-century Flemish to modern. A $6 million campus ministries building sits in the heart of campus as a reminder of the role of Christianity in the student experience.

> **"The research and collaboration opportunities far surpass those of Hope's rivals."**

Hope's general education program, designed around the themes "knowing how" and "knowing about," includes a first-year seminar that provides "an intellectual transition into Hope." Courses in expository writing, health dynamics, math and natural science, foreign language, religious studies, social sciences, the arts, and

Website: www.hope.edu
Location: Small City
Private
Total Enrollment: 2,964
Undergraduates: 2,964
Male/Female: 38/62
Financial Aid: 51%
Pell Grant: 17%
Expense: Pr $
Student Loans: 60%
Average Debt: $ $ $
Applicants: 4,172
Accepted: 92%
Enrolled: 21%
Grad in 6 Years: 84%
Returning Freshmen: 88%
Academics: ✍ ✍ ✍
Social: ☎ ☎ ☎
Q of L: ★ ★ ★
Admissions: (616) 395-7850

(continued)

Email Address: admissions@
hope.edu

Strong Programs:
Biology
Chemistry
Psychology
Communication
English
Business
Education
Engineering

cultural heritage are also required; one class must have a focus on cultural diversity and one on international perspectives. All students take an interdisciplinary senior seminar in which they explore their beliefs, values, worldviews, and life goals in relation to the Christian faith. The FACES mentoring program helps underrepresented first-year students make the transition to college.

Among Hope's academic offerings, the sciences (especially biology and chemistry) stand out, with excellent laboratory facilities and faculty who are eager to involve students in their funded research. During the school year, undergraduates often conduct advanced experiments and even publish papers; come summer, more than 200 students receive stipends to participate in research full-time. Overall, 49 percent of undergrads get involved with research. Not surprisingly, a large portion of science majors go on to medical and engineering schools and Ph.D. programs. For those otherwise inclined, Hope's offerings in business and education are popular, and psychology, communication, and English are solid too. The Visiting Writers Series gives students an opportunity to interact with noteworthy authors. New offerings include majors in environmental science and neuroscience.

"I would describe the academic climate as competitive in the sense that I feel pushed to work hard and study to perform at my best," says a psychology major. Classes are usually small, and a business major says, "Professors are dedicated to ensuring that each student has a great understanding of the material." Students may study abroad in programs offered in more than 60 countries, and about half do so; options include semester-long exchanges and programs that combine classes with internships. The Boerigter Center for Calling and Career helps students explore the concept of vocation and find career and leadership opportunities through mentorship and networking events.

"This is a place where people are involved and love to build community."

Students at Hope are "very outgoing, social, and friendly," says a business major. "This is a place where people are involved and love to build community with one another." The student body is a rather homogeneous lot, with 67 percent hailing from Michigan and 2 percent coming from overseas. Black students account for 3 percent of the student body, Hispanics/Latinos 8 percent, Asian Americans 2 percent, and multiracial students 4 percent. Politically, according to a senior, Hope is "a liberal arts school trying to toe the line between liberal and Christian politics," and LGBTQ rights, abortion, and gun control can be hot-button issues. Merit scholarships averaging $12,800 are available to qualified students, but there are no athletic scholarships.

All students take a senior seminar in which they explore their beliefs, values, worldviews, and life goals in relation to the Christian faith.

Virtually all Hope students live in university-sponsored housing. Traditional dorms are arranged in freshman clusters by gender or co-ed by suite. "Dorms are fine, and I enjoyed them as a freshman, but most students opt for the college-owned apartment complexes and cottages surrounding the campus area," explains a student. On-campus students eat in one of two large dining halls where the fare—especially homemade bread and desserts—is tasty. "The STEP (Students Teaching and Empowering Peers) program focuses on peer education regarding sexual assault," says a senior. "They do a good job, but the school could always do more."

"The weekends are full and busy. The Student Activities Committee is the organization that makes the social life at Hope College thrive," says one student. The committee brings in comedians, bands, and hypnotists; shows movies in campus auditoriums; and plans the Spring Fling carnival, held on the last Friday of the academic year. A favorite annual tradition is the Nykerk Cup, which pits freshmen against sophomores in singing, acting, and orating competitions. Seven fraternities and eight sororities, all local organizations, claim 13 percent of the men and 19 percent of the women, respectively. Some parties do happen off campus, but those caught drinking on Hope's dry campus must atone by performing community service. Among the 60 student organizations are a variety of active religious life and service organizations, including Emmaus Scholars, Hope Way (campus ministry), InterVarsity Christian Fellowship, and Silent Praise, a student group that seeks to praise God through American Sign Language (ASL) and worship music.

Holland (population 34,000) is the site of spring's Tulip Time, one of the largest U.S. flower festivals. When Hope's cozy campus and the quaint town of Holland get too close for comfort, students find relief at the beaches of Lake Michigan ("definitely one of the highlights," says a junior) or drive 30 minutes to Grand Rapids, which offers some large-city amenities and good weekend rental deals at the ski slopes. Chicago and Detroit are other typical destinations for those trying to hit the road.

On the field and on the court, Hope's Flying Dutch and Flying Dutchmen are talented Division III competitors. Men's and women's basketball, men's soccer, and women's volleyball are strong, and the college has won a record number of Michigan Intercollegiate Athletic Association Commissioner's Cups, recognizing the conference's best overall sports program. Especially important are any competitions against Calvin (a century-old rivalry) and football versus Albion and Kalamazoo for the Wooden Shoes trophy. Hope's men's ice hockey team claimed its second-straight American Collegiate Hockey Association national championship in 2022. Fifty-three percent of students take part in roughly two dozen intramural and club sports, which range from soccer and badminton to inner-tube water polo.

Hope's Flying Dutchmen football team competes against Albion and Kalamazoo for the Wooden Shoes trophy.

Hope's mission is "to educate students for lives of leadership and service in a global society." For those seeking an institution with traditional Christian roots and an emphasis on undergraduates, Hope may be worth a look. "Hope is a place where students are challenged to become better students," says one senior, "but, more important, better people."

Overlaps

Calvin, Wheaton (IL), DePauw, College of Wooster, St. Olaf, Albion, Alma, Butler

If You Apply To ›

Hope: Early action, rolling admissions. SATs or ACTs: optional. Accepts the Common Application with supplement.

Houghton College

Houghton, NY 14744

The Mid-Atlantic's leading evangelical Christian college. All students are required to take Biblical Literature and Introduction to Christianity, and most go to chapel three times a week. Perks include two honors programs and expansive indoor and outdoor equestrian facilities. Rural New York setting fosters an intimate sense of community, but when things gets claustrophobic, students have ample possibilities for a semester away.

Located in the bucolic New York town that shares its name, Houghton College offers a solid, growing academic program and strong athletic teams while remaining committed to its core mission as a Christian liberal arts school. Sponsored by the Wesleyan Church and dating to 1883, Houghton celebrates its Christian heritage and encourages students to do the same. Applicants must explain in their essays why they desire to be a part of a Christian academic community, and current students are

Website: www.houghton.edu
Location: Rural
Private
Total Enrollment: 764
Undergraduates: 748

The music and theology programs are strong, and a new major has been added in worship arts.

expected to attend a set amount of chapel services throughout the semester. These expectations help create true community on campus. One junior says, "Houghton combines academic rigor, athletic excellence, and intentional spiritual formation in a fun-loving and Christ-centered community."

Houghton's scenic hilltop campus covers 1,300 acres of rural beauty, surrounded by vast expanses of western New York countryside. In addition to a 386-acre horseback-riding facility, the college has its own ski trails. The academic buildings are a mix of area "creekstone" (to use the local lingo) and brick. Recent construction includes a 115,000-square-foot athletic complex and a 36,000-square-foot indoor equestrian arena.

Houghton students complete general education requirements designed to provide a context and framework for the entire educational program. Freshmen must take Biblical Literature, Writing in the Liberal Arts, and a course titled Transitions, which helps students adjust to college and includes diversity training. Seniors complete a capstone seminar, project, or performance, depending on their major. Houghton is known for its equestrian studies program, and the music, education, and theology programs are also strong. The school's most popular majors include business, biology, psychology, and communication. New majors have been added in biomedical sciences, neuroscience, and worship arts. Electrical engineering is the school's only four-year engineering program. Other options include a 3+4 Pharm.D. program with the University of Buffalo, a 3+1 nursing program with Indiana Wesleyan, and a medical early-acceptance program with the Lake Erie College of Osteopathic Medicine.

"At Houghton I have coffee with my professors and real conversations."

Houghton's academic climate is "rigorous and in-depth," according to a senior, but not overwhelmingly so. Eighty-four percent of classes have fewer than 20 students, and most courses are taught by senior faculty, who students say do an outstanding job of fostering a sense of community. "At Houghton I have coffee with my professors and real conversations. I see them at church and in the dining hall, and I've gotten to know their kids," says an intercultural studies major.

Houghton offers two honors programs for incoming freshmen. The London Honors program provides qualified students an intensive, hands-on experience in the humanities, along with study abroad experiences in the United Kingdom. The Science Honors program allows select students to engage with significant scientific problems in a hands-on, research-oriented environment. Houghton's Summer Research Institute, designed for students in math and the sciences, is also well regarded. Fifty-five percent of all students take advantage of off-campus study in a variety of programs throughout the year, including four-week Mayterm programs in New York City, Alaska, Costa Rica, Europe, and Sierra Leone.

Sixty-two percent of students are from New York, and 4 percent are international, coming from 19 countries. A senior describes Houghton students as "thoughtful and excited about going out and influencing the world in a positive way." Racial and ethnic diversity is limited: Black students account for 7 percent of the student body, Hispanics/Latinos 1 percent, Asian Americans 2 percent, and multiracial students 5 percent. "Politically, Houghton is very diverse," comments a political science major. "It is a religiously conservative school with many progressive students, so there is tension" over certain issues, particularly LGBTQ rights. Beginning in fall 2021, Houghton cut its sticker price by more than half, a "reset" aimed at making college costs more transparent. Merit scholarships are available, and 42 percent of incoming freshmen are eligible for Pell Grants.

Houghton's campus houses 71 percent of students. "Housing is fairly limited in terms of options, but all students are guaranteed a spot on campus," says one student. Freshmen and sophomores live in traditional residence halls, while juniors and seniors can apply for campus townhouses and apartments; all accommodations are single-sex. Dining options get good reviews for taste and variety. "Special dishes can be ordered at some stations, and bagged lunches are customizable," says a senior. Students report feeling safe on their rural campus. Houghton's Community Covenant prohibits "premarital sex, adultery, and homosexual behavior," but as one student points out, "Students are able to report sexual assault without facing consequences regarding our Community Covenant."

Houghton cut its sticker price by more than half, a "reset" aimed at making college costs more transparent.

"Most of the social life takes place on campus," explains an art major. "The surrounding area offers much to do in regards to nature and the outdoors, but not necessarily socially." The Campus Activities Board plans regular happenings, and dorm-identity events, film festivals, and concerts are popular. Seventy percent of students are involved in service projects such as Big Brothers Big Sisters, nursing home visitation, and local church outreach; the area surrounding the college is one of the poorest in New York State. Both the campus and the town of Houghton are dry, and the college's Community Covenant forbids

"Houghton is not a party campus, unless you count a group with tea and board games as a party."

alcohol. As a senior puts it, "Houghton is not a party campus, unless you count a group with tea and board games as a party." Students eagerly anticipate annual celebrations for homecoming, Christian Life Emphasis Week, the Christmas Prism concerts, the SPOT talent show, and Hall Brawl, a week of friendly competitions between dorms.

Houghton competes in Division III, and the men's tennis team recently claimed the Empire 8 Conference title. Other competitive Highlanders teams (so named because of the campus topography) include women's cross-country and men's and women's track and field. Intramurals draw steady interest, with basketball and co-ed volleyball being the most popular. The college also offers two club sports: cheerleading and disc golf.

Students don't come to Houghton for the surrounding town of 1,700 souls, which is 30 minutes by car from the nearest mall, or for the weather, which can be tough once winter sets in. But they do come, and for good reason: there's little to distract them from their studies, their campus's natural beauty, and their spiritual growth. As one junior observes, "There are few schools that will work so closely with their students, through setting academic goals, [helping them pursue] internships, listening to their passions, and equipping them to work where their deep gladness and the world's deep hunger meet."

Overlaps
Roberts Wesleyan, Grove City, Messiah, Gordon, Wheaton (IL), Taylor, Nazareth, Alfred

If You Apply To ›

Houghton: Rolling admissions. SATs or ACTs: optional. Accepts the Common Application with supplement. Music majors apply directly to music program.

Howard University

2400 Sixth Street NW, Washington, D.C. 20059

The flagship university of Black America and the first to integrate the Black experience into all areas of study. Strategically located in D.C., Howard depends on Congress for much of its funding. Preprofessional programs such as nursing, business, and architecture are strong. Sixty-seven percent of students identify as Black.

Website: www.howard.edu
Location: City Center
Private
Total Enrollment: 11,055
Undergraduates: 8,418
Male/Female: 27/73
Financial Aid: 85%
Pell Grant: 43%
Expense: Pr $
Student Loans: 73%
Average Debt: $ $ $
Applicants: 29,396
Accepted: 35%
Enrolled: 27%
Grad in 6 Years: 64%
Returning Freshmen: 91%
Academics: ✍ ✍ ✍
Social: ☎ ☎ ☎
Q of L: ★ ★ ★
Admissions: (202) 806-2755
Email Address: admission@howard.edu

Strong Programs:
Business
Political Science
Nursing
Journalism
Architecture
Computer Science
Psychology
Afro American Studies

Contrary to the advice of early Black leaders such as Booker T. Washington, who argued in favor of technical training, Howard has promoted the liberal arts since its inception. This focus has served the school well; Howard's law school counts the late Supreme Court Justice Thurgood Marshall among its alumni, and Vice President Kamala Harris, the late Nobel Prize–winning author Toni Morrison, and actors Taraji P. Henson and the late Chadwick Boseman are graduates too. In recent years, Howard has strengthened its financial position and has been implementing a strategic plan structured around "Leadership for America and the Global Community." The four-part plan focuses on strengthening academic programs and services, promoting excellence in teaching and research, increasing private support, and enhancing national and community services.

Founded in 1867 by Union General Oliver Howard primarily to educate freed slaves, the university now operates five campuses and serves roughly 11,000 full-time students. Interestingly, Howard is one of a handful of universities in the nation supported partly by federal subsidies; these days, the school gets about 55 percent of its budget from Congress. The 89-acre main campus houses most classrooms, dorms, and administrative offices, as well as the university center, the Founders, and undergraduate, medical, and dental libraries. The Howard Law Center is on the west campus near Rock Creek Park, the Divinity School is on a 22-acre site in northeast Washington, and there's also a 108-acre campus in suburban Beltsville, Maryland, and a campus in Silver Spring. Architecturally, the main campus is a blend of old and new, with numerous sculptures and murals created by Jacob Lawrence, Richard Hunt, Elizabeth Catlett, and Romare Bearden. Newer facilities include the state-of-the-art, 82,000-square-foot Interdisciplinary Research Building.

> **"Some courses are more rigorous than others. But overall this school is tough."**

All students must complete general education requirements, which vary by school or college but uniformly encompass 18 credits in science, social sciences, humanities, computer literacy, math, languages, and one Afro American studies course. Freshman seminars and various other special programs for first-year students are available in the undergraduate schools, such as communication, engineering, and arts and sciences. Seniors in arts and sciences must weather a comprehensive exam to graduate.

The school has excellent programs in business, political science, nursing, journalism, architecture, computer science, and psychology, and it has intensified offerings in Africana and diaspora studies. Other intriguing academic options are jazz studies, engineering (especially electrical engineering), and accelerated programs for a B.S. on the way to a medical or dental degree. The most popular majors are in the areas of business, communication, physical sciences, and biology. The Howard University Science, Engineering, and Mathematics Program, a multidisciplinary program involving nine departments, is designed to support underrepresented students pursuing degrees in STEM disciplines. The classics department, unique among historically Black colleges and universities (HBCUs), has been dissolved as part of a "prioritization" effort. Howard students can cross-register for courses at 13 other area schools, including American University, Georgetown, and GWU's Corcoran School of the Arts and Design.

In general, students say that the workload at Howard is demanding. "Some courses are more rigorous than others. But overall this school is tough," says a junior. Another student adds, "Come to Howard ready to study." Forty-seven percent of classes have fewer than 20 students. Most students agree that professors are ready and willing to help when asked, though academic advising is not Howard's strength. "Sometimes you may get professors who do not know how to break down anything," explains a psychology major. "Then it is your job to speak up and ask questions. You must ask questions because a closed mouth does not get fed!" Howard's prime D.C. location means that internship, co-op, and service-learning opportunities with all manner of government organizations, nonprofits, and corporations are practically limitless. Qualified students can apply for the Junior Experiential Learning Program, which helps them secure internships and other practical work experiences. The program also assigns each participant an alumni career mentor with experience in their field of interest who can assist with networking and career advice. A modest 1 percent of students study abroad at one of the more than 200 institutions in 36 countries where Howard grants credit.

The Junior Experiential Learning Program assigns each participant an alumni career mentor who can assist with networking and career advice.

Ninety-four percent of Howard undergraduates hail from states outside of the District of Columbia, and another 3 percent are international. Black students represent 67 percent of the student body, Hispanics/Latinos 7 percent, Asian Americans 4 percent, and American Indians 2 percent; 4 percent identify as multiracial. Many come from decidedly middle-class backgrounds,

"[Greek groups are] an integral part of the university."

although 43 percent of freshmen qualify for Pell Grants. Howard seems to be a very cohesive community, but career-minded and highly motivated students fit in best, students say, and most are politically liberal. "It's a very competitive school, from grades to fashion," says a junior. A range of renewable merit scholarships are available on a first-come, first-served basis to freshman applicants, and these awards average $12,300 per year. Transfer students are eligible for a separate pool of merit scholarships, and Howard also awards athletic scholarships. A deferred-payment plan allows families to pay each semester's tuition in three installments.

Fifty-six percent of Howard's students are accommodated on campus, and facilities receive lukewarm reviews. "Housing at Howard is average in regards to availability, maintenance, and comfort," says one student. Freshmen get room assignments, while upperclassmen take their chances in a lottery. Many students live off campus purely to avoid the mandatory meal plan.

Weekends bring an assortment of social happenings to campus, many of which take place in the student center. On-campus parties and sports events are always big draws, but the restaurants and clubs in the nearby U Street corridor, the bars of Georgetown and Adams Morgan, and the Capital One Arena (home to the NBA's Wizards and the NHL's Capitals) also beckon and are easily accessible by public transit. Fraternities and sororities do not have their own housing or dining facilities, and only 8 percent of the men and 6 percent of the women go Greek. Though small in numbers, one student says the Greeks are "an integral part of the university."

Howard's scholarship and collections of artwork, rare books, manuscripts, and photographs are a repository of the Black experience.

Athletics are also an important presence on campus, particularly Division I Bison basketball, soccer, and football. Howard boasts the only all-Black collegiate swim team in the country (Northeast Conference champions in 2023), and thanks to the largesse of basketball star Stephen Curry, it has developed one of only a few Division I men's and women's golf programs at HBCUs. The highlight of the season is always the grudge match with Hampton University to decide which school is the "true HU." Howard's homecoming is one of the best annual events, along with various Greekfests, concerts, and talent shows that current students, alumni, and community members enjoy together. Intramurals and club sports attract plenty of students, especially flag football, soccer, basketball, and baseball.

Among America's HBCUs, Howard stands out as the standard-bearer, a long-time center of excellence and leadership. Its scholarship and collections of artwork, rare books, manuscripts, and photographs are a repository of the Black experience, informing students' intellectual and personal growth. And with an increased focus on providing opportunities for real-world experience and service, Howard is sure to continue its long tradition of turning out Black leaders in all areas of society.

If You Apply To ›

Howard: Early decision, early action, regular decision. Accepts the Common Application with supplement. Please consult Howard's website for the most up-to-date information regarding standardized test requirements.

The College of Idaho

Caldwell, ID 83605

Got a map? You'll need a sharp eye to spot C of I, the *Fiske Guide*'s only liberal arts school between the Rocky Mountains and the West Coast. Innovative PEAK curriculum allows students to specialize in multiple fields. Just over half of the students are from Idaho.

Website: www.collegeofidaho.edu
Location: Small Town
Private
Total Enrollment: 1,118
Undergraduates: 1,104
Male/Female: 49/51
Financial Aid: 100%
Pell Grant: 28%
Expense: Pr $
Student Loans: 95%
Average Debt: $ $ $
Applicants: 3,464
Accepted: 56%
Enrolled: 15%
Grad in 6 Years: 56%
Returning Freshmen: 79%
Academics: ✍ ✍ ✍
Social: ☎ ☎ ☎
Q of L: ★ ★ ★
Admissions: (208) 459-5305
Email Address: admission@collegeofidaho.edu

With an emphasis on education and experiential learning, the College of Idaho, the state's oldest four-year university, offers students an opportunity to earn a solid liberal arts education through small classes in a small town. Outside class, the school's scenic environment allows sports and nature enthusiasts to explore freely before heading back into the classroom. At C of I, you'll be exposed to "hard work, great opportunities, and a healthy amount of fun," says a freshman.

The college is in the small town of Caldwell, where the atmosphere is calm and serene. For those looking for a little excitement, the state capital of Boise is a short drive from campus. Also nearby are some of Idaho's most scenic locations, such as beautiful mountains, deserts, and white-water rivers. The school, originally a Presbyterian college, first planted roots in downtown Caldwell in 1891 and then moved to its present site in 1910, where its nearly 30 buildings now occupy 43 acres. Newer campus additions include a 60,000-square-foot, state-of-the-art library.

The school's academic schedule is composed of 12-week semesters, spring and fall, separated by a four-week winter session, during which students can assist professors with research, take an internship, volunteer, or travel abroad. The college's distinctive PEAK program combines a liberal arts education with specialization in multiple fields. Over four years, students earn a major and three minors spread across four knowledge "peaks"—the humanities, social sciences, natural sciences, and a professional field. Students choose among 33 majors and 29 minors. Freshmen sign an honor code and go through a first-year program that involves a first-year seminar, a premodern civilization course, a junior or senior mentor, a team of advisors, and a weeklong orientation that includes an off-campus overnight stay at a lakeside camp.

"**The professors are masters of their craft.**"

"The workload can be relaxed or intense depending upon a student's desire for success," says one senior. Business, psychology, biology, health sciences, and environmental studies are among the majors recommended by students, and pre-professional programs, such as premed, prenursing, and prelaw, are also popular and strong. Sixty percent of all classes at C of I have fewer than 20 students, and faculty are praised for their knowledge and accessibility. "The professors are masters of their craft," a senior says. The college cooperates with the University of Idaho to offer a five-year course of study in engineering. Undergraduate research opportunities are available in all fields, and students present their findings at state and regional conferences. The Center for Experiential Learning coordinates out-of-classroom experiences, such as international education and service learning. For those who want to venture abroad, the college offers options for attending a foreign university or traveling overseas during the summer and winter breaks. Travel has really taken off, with study abroad opportunities in nearly 60 countries around the world.

"Everyone seems like some kind of repressed genius trying to figure out their own existence, pursue stability, and create something meaningful," muses one student, adding, "There are also those who are more career-minded." Fifty-six percent of the students are from Idaho and an impressive 19 percent come from foreign countries. Thirteen percent are Hispanic/Latino, 1 percent are Black, 2 percent are Asian American, and 6 percent are multiracial. Political issues receive plenty of attention on campus, and debates about the school's honor code are not uncommon among students. The college offers merit scholarships averaging $24,300 as well as more than 120 athletic scholarships. Not surprisingly, some of those dollars are set aside for skiers.

Over four years, students earn a major and three minors spread across four knowledge "peaks."

Sixty-five percent of students live on campus. "Residences are great, easy to decorate, and relatively big," says one student. Options include five traditional residence halls, two suite-style apartment buildings, and more than 20 rental houses. For meals, C of I provides "a grill, deli, salad bar, pizza, and vegetarian options" that are "to die for," according to one student. "Campus safety gets a 10 out of 10," says a junior. "There is an officer on duty 24/7 even over breaks and summer vacation."

Thirteen percent of men and 11 percent of women participate in the Greek system, which dominates campus social life. Students 21 and over are permitted to have alcohol on campus, in moderation (i.e., no kegs). Annual social highlights include Winterfest, Spring Fling, and homecoming week. Games against rival

"Intramurals are huge at our school."

Northwest Nazarene also attract attention. "We have a fantastic social scene. We host events almost nightly," a student reports. Undergraduates can choose among more than 50 student clubs, and the arts are strong. Students of all majors participate in a wide range of instrumental and choral music, theater, visual arts, and other activities, and the choir has performed at Carnegie Hall and other venues around the country. "Finals breakfasts" offer something for bleary-eyed students to look forward to during finals week; at midnight on Tuesday, faculty and staff cook breakfast for students.

The student-run Outdoor Program offers hiking, fishing, rock climbing, and white-water rafting trips and classes.

Caldwell, with about 60,000 people, is not a great spot for college students, but students get involved by helping out the local school district. Nearby Boise is a popular destination for shopping, dining, and cultural events, including a symphony orchestra, art museum, zoo, professional baseball and hockey, and the must-see World Center for Birds of Prey. Outdoor enthusiasts relish the fact that the C of I campus is just minutes away from world-class opportunities for skiing, hiking, camping, fishing, rock climbing, and white-water rafting. The student-run Outdoor Program offers trips, classes, and equipment rentals.

More than a third of students play for one of the college's 20 varsity teams, which compete in NAIA Division II. The Yotes (translation: "We are the Coyotes") have earned team national championships in baseball, basketball, and skiing. For those who enjoy the game but might not make the team, there is an active intramurals program and the large Albertson Activities Center. "Intramurals are huge at our school," says a sophomore, drawing nearly half the students.

C of I has much to offer its Yotes. They enjoy a well-designed liberal arts education and personal academic attention on a campus striving to keep its offerings on the cutting edge. What's more, students here are encouraged to take an active role in the school's future. From creating traditions to upholding the honor code, a sophomore says, "We are involved in all aspects of campus life."

If You Apply To ›

Idaho: Early action I and II, regular decision. SATs or ACTs: optional. (Test-optional applicants must complete additional short-answer essay questions.) Accepts the Common Application with supplement.

University of Illinois at Urbana–Champaign

901 West Illinois Street, Urbana, IL 61801

Half a step behind Michigan and neck and neck with Wisconsin among top Midwestern public universities. U of I's strengths include business, communication, engineering, architecture, and the natural sciences. More than three-quarters of the undergraduates hail from in state. Huge Greek system.

Website: www.illinois.edu
Location: Small City
Public
Total Enrollment: 46,177
Undergraduates: 33,113
Male/Female: 54/46
Financial Aid: 56%
Pell Grant: 26%
Expense: Pub $ $ $ $
Student Loans: 44%
Average Debt: $
Applicants: 47,527
Accepted: 60%
Enrolled: 29%
Grad in 6 Years: 85%
Returning Freshmen: 94%
Academics: ✑ ✑ ✑ ✑ ✑
Social: ☎ ☎ ☎
Q of L: ★ ★ ★
Admissions: (217) 333-0302
Email Address: admissions@
    illinois.edu

Like many of its Midwestern neighbors, the University of Illinois, which dates to 1867, has its roots in agriculture. The Morrow Plots, the oldest experimental fields in the nation, still rest symbolically in the middle of campus—and when the wind blows the wrong way, students are not-so-subtly reminded of their heritage as a farm school. Like most big, public universities, U of I has a barn full of choices, and with a strong Greek system and 1,000 clubs, social activities are more than plentiful. Homecoming weekend was invented at the University of Illinois, and whether cheering for the Illini, pledging a Greek organization, or celebrating Moms', Dads', or Siblings' Weekends, students here stir up a vibrant mix of school spirit and good times. This may look and feel like a laid-back Midwestern campus, but make no mistake: Illinois's stellar academics and learning communities are up there with any of the country's public flagships.

Befitting one of the earliest land grant institutions, the Illinois campus was built in farm country between the twin cities of Champaign and Urbana. The flat, park-like campus was designed along a mile-long axis where trees and walkways separate stately white-columned Georgian structures made of brick. The impressive Illinois library system, one of the largest public university collections worldwide with 14 million physical volumes, makes it easier to keep up with classwork. A 225,000-square-foot computer science center and the physical education center are notable. Newer facilities include the $48 million Siebel Center for Design.

> "The quality of teaching is high with few exceptions."

Illinois has eight undergraduate colleges and one school that together offer more than 150 undergraduate programs; if none of these strike your fancy, you may design your own. The general education program includes standard distribution requirements across a range of subjects; students may fulfill some requirements by taking Grand Challenge Learning courses, interdisciplinary classes that explore three main "pathways," or real-world challenges facing today's society: Inequality and Cultural Understanding; Health and Wellness; and Sustainability, Energy, and the Environment.

Partially because of its size, Illinois can afford to support excellent programs across the university, including the expansion of undergraduate minors campuswide. Engineering, business, communication, social sciences, architecture, education, industrial design, and the sciences—especially biological sciences, agriculture, and veterinary medicine—get high marks from students and lots of resources from administrators. A "CS + X" degree program allows students to combine the study of computer science with one of 12 other liberal arts fields, ranging from anthropology and advertising to chemistry and crop sciences, without having to go so far as double majoring. The initiative is a way for students to demonstrate both technical competence and career-related expertise to future employers. The interdisciplinary Beckman Institute for Advanced Science and Technology offers opportunities for undergraduate research in areas like intelligent systems and molecular science and engineering. Thirty-two percent of undergrads conduct research during their four years.

A "CS + X" degree program allows students to combine the study of computer science with one of 12 other liberal arts fields.

"Overall, classes are demanding," says a senior. Freshmen and sophomores, who register last, may have trouble getting into necessary courses, but professors and academic advisors can usually help if needed classes are full, and students appreciate their dedication. Illinois has its share of stellar faculty, including Nobel laureates, National Medal of Science winners, and dozens of members of the National Academy of Sciences. "The quality of teaching is high with few exceptions," says a psychology major. "They are truly invested in our success," adds a senior. Even freshmen stuck in large lectures (750 seats) will find some personal attention in the associated discussion sections, led by graduate teaching assistants. Freshman Discovery Courses, seminars limited to 19 students, enable first-year students

"The school is continuously getting more diverse."

to interact closely with full professors. The Campus Honors Program includes faculty mentoring, intensive seminars, advanced sections of regular courses, and access to special resources. Twenty-four percent of undergraduates travel and study abroad, roaming 50 countries around the globe.

Seventy-seven percent of Illinois undergrads are homegrown, and "the school is continuously getting more diverse," a sophomore says. Since Illinois stretches from the wealthy north suburbs of urbane Chicago to the unspoiled rural hills bordering Kentucky and encompasses classic farm towns as well as factory towns, students do come from multiple backgrounds and fit less into the stereotypical "Midwest" mold than one might think. Black students make up 6 percent of the student body, Hispanics/Latinos 14 percent, Asian Americans 22 percent, and multiracial students 4 percent, while international students account for 13 percent. Merit scholarships averaging $6,000 and more than 200 athletic awards are doled out annually. The Illinois Commitment program provides free tuition and fees for four years for qualified in-state freshmen or transfer students whose family income is $67,100 or less.

Illinois has a strong athletic program for students with disabilities, including wheelchair basketball, which was invented at the university.

Half of all undergrads live in U of I's co-ed and single-sex residence halls, which range in size from 51 to 660 beds and are arranged in quadrangle-like groups. Some dorms are quite a hike from classrooms, veterans warn. The university offers 11 themed living/learning communities, such as WIMSE (Women in Math, Science, and Engineering) and Innovation LLC (entrepreneurship and creativity), that combine in-hall courses with specialized cocurricular activities. Each residence hall is a mini neighborhood, with dining halls, darkrooms, libraries, music practice rooms, computers, and lounges creating a sense of community. Chefs keep the food interesting, and campus security maintains a visible presence.

Illinois claims to have one of the largest Greek systems anywhere, with 87 chapters drawing 21 percent of the men and 27 percent of the women. Illinois attracts many socially oriented students who love parties and intramural sports, which may be why the Greek influence is particularly strong. Independents don't have to suffer boredom, though, as there are also roughly 1,000 registered student clubs and organizations, ranging from the ice hockey team to cultural affinity groups. "It is a big campus that likes to have a lot of fun," a student says. Though drinking is prohibited in the dorms, many regard campus alcohol policies as a "token gesture," a business major says. The Illini Union hosts bands, comedians, movies, trivia, karaoke, and other activities every week. The impressive Krannert Center for the Performing Arts, with four theaters and more than 350 annual performances, serves as the area's cultural center, while Assembly Hall hosts national touring acts. Students get a discount at both facilities. For those who itch for the stimulation of a big city, the campus is just about equidistant from Chicago, Indianapolis, and St. Louis, and Mardi Gras makes for a good road trip in the dead of winter.

The Division I Illini compete in the Big Ten, and men's basketball and baseball have winning traditions. Men's golf and basketball are recent conference champs, and women's gymnastics, soccer, and softball are solid too. The intramural program is extensive, with available facilities that include 16 full-length basketball courts, five pools, 19 handball/racquetball courts, a skating rink, a baseball stadium, and the Atkins Tennis Center. The majority of the student body participates in recreational sports. Illinois has a strong athletic program for students with disabilities, including wheelchair basketball, which was invented at the university.

While the University of Illinois may seem mammoth to some students, don't be scared off by this giant institution. Academic and social opportunities are incredibly diverse, and classroom sizes, while growing, are supplemented by smaller group discussions. The breadth of the programs offered combined with an active campus life makes for a well-rounded college experience, students say. "We have a great reputation, and it only grows stronger and stronger."

Overlaps

University of Iowa, University of Michigan, Northwestern, Purdue, UW–Madison, WashU in St. Louis, University of Kansas, Indiana University

If You Apply To ›

Illinois: Early action, regular decision. SATs or ACTs: optional. Accepts the Common Application. Apply to particular schools or programs. Music, dance, and theater applicants must audition.

Illinois Institute of Technology

10 West 33rd Street, Chicago, IL 60616

Forget about cheerleaders, homecoming games, and other traditional trappings of college life. Illinois Tech is all about learning about technology, getting a degree, and landing a job. Academic focus is on engineering, computer science, and a bit of architecture thrown in for good measure. If your goal is a technical career in the Chicago area, this is your place.

Website: www.iit.edu
Location: City Center
Private
Total Enrollment: 5,081

At the Illinois Institute of Technology, classwork and real-world experience promise to propel future engineers, architects, and computer scientists to the top of their fields. Students here engage in undergraduate research in state-of-the-art labs and gain practical work experience through abundant internship opportunities. The coursework may be hard, says a junior, but the effort "will pay off in the end" as students enter the workforce in high-paying technical jobs. And although students here tend to burn the midnight oil, they frequently escape to downtown Chicago for culture and much-deserved fun.

Illinois Tech's home is an urban, 120-acre campus designed by Ludwig Mies van der Rohe, the influential 20th-century architect who directed the architecture school for 20 years. Founded by a merger in 1940 but with roots dating to the 1890s, the school is just three miles south of Chicago's Loop and one mile west of Lake Michigan. Guaranteed Rate Field, home of the White Sox, is located directly across from the campus. Miesian-style buildings reflecting his rectangular "less is more" style are adorned by trees and grassy open parks. Crown Hall, which houses the College of Architecture, is a National Historic Landmark. The recently opened Kaplan Institute boasts high-tech labs, collaborative hubs, and makerspaces that allow students to work on cross-disciplinary projects and develop entrepreneurial ideas.

> **"Biomedical engineering is very new and well funded."**

Along with humanities and social science courses, students must fulfill general education requirements that include mathematics, computer science, natural science, and engineering; writing is emphasized across the curriculum. All freshmen take an introduction to the professions seminar, which includes discussion of innovation, ethics, teamwork, communication, and leadership. Multidisciplinary, group-based learning is big here. Every student must complete two semester-long interprofessional projects that sharpen real-world skills.

Engineering and computer science are the most popular majors, and they set the tone at Illinois Tech. Every engineering department is first-rate. Architecture is also popular and highly regarded; the curriculum emphasizes a team approach that mixes third- through fifth-year students under the supervision of a master professor. "Architecture has a strong faculty," says one student, "and biomedical engineering is very new and well funded." Business rounds out the most popular majors, and the sciences, physics in particular, are strong. Guided by an academic reorganization, the physical sciences have been bolstered, grouped together with career-oriented fields such as psychology and computer information systems. Illinois Tech is the first university to offer a B.S. in bioanalytical chemistry, and it recently added majors in artificial intelligence, food science and nutrition, and environmental chemistry. Accelerated master's programs enable students to earn both a bachelor's and a master's in five years. Dual admissions programs are available in pharmacy, optometry, and osteopathic medicine.

The academic climate is pretty unforgiving, students say. Both the workload and the competition are fierce. "The courses are very difficult," says a junior. Forty-five percent of classes have fewer than 20 students, and professors always teach their own classes, while teaching assistants are available for labs and extra help. "Professors take an active role in their students' education," states a biochemistry major.

In addition to meeting outside of class to go over problem sets or for career direction, Illinois Tech students and professors often work side by side on research projects. The Lewis College of Science and Letters awards several $5,000 scholarships to undergrads to perform research work under the supervision of faculty during the summer. Engineering students make use of sophisticated labs and have access to independent research labs in Chicago. Two dozen on-campus

> **"Students at Illinois Tech are nerds, in a good way."**

research centers, such as the Pritzker Institute of Biomedical Science and Engineering and the Wanger Institute for Sustainable Energy Research, provide additional opportunities. The five-year co-op program—another possibility for hands-on experience—helps lead Illinois Tech students directly into high-paying jobs after graduation.

(continued)

Undergraduates: 2,675
Male/Female: 67/33
Financial Aid: 100%
Pell Grant: 32%
Expense: Pr $ $
Student Loans: 54%
Average Debt: $ $ $
Applicants: 6,520
Accepted: 66%
Enrolled: 12%
Grad in 6 Years: 71%
Returning Freshmen: 87%
Academics: ✍ ✍ ✍ ½
Social: ☎ ☎
Q of L: ★ ★
Admissions: (800) 448-2329
Email Address: admission@iit.edu

Strong Programs:
Engineering
Architecture
Computer Science
Business
Physics
Bioanalytical Chemistry

The architecture curriculum emphasizes a team approach that mixes third- through fifth-year students under the supervision of a master professor.

Study abroad programs send students to more than 50 nations around the globe, including France, Greece, Chile, and Singapore; 10 percent of students—mostly architecture majors—participate.

"Students at Illinois Tech are nerds," reports a communication major, but "in a good way." In-state students account for 61 percent of the undergraduate population, and 15 percent hail from foreign countries. Black students constitute 4 percent of the student body, Hispanics/Latinos 19 percent, Asian Americans 17 percent, and multiracial students 4 percent. Students say International Fest is one of the year's most popular events, and the school sponsors a multitude of cultural awareness workshops and events on different diversity-related topics. Merit scholarships averaging $27,800 are available to qualified students.

First-years and sophomores are required to live on campus, although those who live with their families within a 20-mile radius of campus are allowed to commute. Several residence halls have been renovated in the last few years. The Women in Social Engagement learning community attracts female students who are interested in leadership, civic engagement, and social change. Some students live in apartments in the area; others inhabit one of the eight fraternity houses. The dining hall has several meal plans and a special vegetarian menu. Engineers and architects—notorious late-night studiers—have to hit the library early, since it closes at 10 p.m.

Illinois Tech's six-block campus sits in Bronzeville, a historically Black neighborhood on Chicago's South Side famous for nurturing the likes of Gwendolyn Brooks, Mahalia Jackson, and Herbie Hancock. The area is undergoing a revitalization, and the university connects students with local community organizations for volunteer work. Most students love exploring Chicago; the city skyline is beautiful and a veritable museum, with buildings designed by the likes of Frank Lloyd Wright, Louis Sullivan, and, of course, Mies van der Rohe. "Chicago provides educational opportunities, internship opportunities, and countless things to do," says one biomedical engineering major. Lake Michigan is within jogging distance, Chinatown is a walk away for lunch or dinner, and the school provides free shuttle bus service to downtown on weekends.

"The social life at Illinois Tech has improved over my four years."

Although students who stick around campus on weekends must work hard to find social events, "the social life at Illinois Tech has improved over my four years," says a senior. Fraternities claim 7 percent of the men and sororities attract 3 percent of the women, and many students say the social aspect of Greek life is a welcome addition to campus. The Union Board offers movies, concerts, and comedians, and the Bog brings in bands on Thursdays and Saturdays. The annual boat cruise and casino night on the *Odyssey* sightseeing boat is a favorite event, and students can also take advantage of the city's ample nightlife or plan outings to museums, plays, or the Chicago Symphony.

In sports-crazy Chicago, Illinois Tech's Division III athletic teams (the Scarlet Hawks) are not much of a draw. Still, students praise the men's baseball and basketball teams, and the men's tennis team recently won the Northern Athletics Collegiate Conference title. Men's and women's soccer and women's volleyball are also competitive. Several recreational sports are available for more casual athletes.

Shipping off to Chi-town to take on the mammoth workload at Illinois Tech means hitting the books for hours upon hours and a fair share of all-nighters. But the payoff is undeniable. One student says bluntly, "This school is for people who want to make a lot of money after college." Indeed, students who take advantage of this small school's ever-improving engineering departments are likely to have their pick of careers after graduation. And with the innumerable diversions offered in the Windy City, students at Illinois Tech revel in the best of two worlds: a challenging academic climate and a great city in which to let off all that steam.

Overlaps

Carnegie Mellon, Loyola University Chicago, Marquette, Rensselaer Polytechnic, U of I at Urbana–Champaign, DePaul, Purdue, U of I at Chicago

Illinois Wesleyan University

Bloomington, IL 61701

IWU is a small Midwestern university with a penchant for creativity and the spirit of inquiry. The curriculum is basic liberal arts with additional divisions devoted to fine arts and nursing. An optional three-week term in May allows students to travel or explore an interest. IWU's reputation is limited outside Illinois and surrounding states.

Illinois Wesleyan University has its sights set on a special breed of student—the kind who isn't afraid to be many things at once. Students here are encouraged to pursue diverse passions, and IWU is a mecca for students who have preprofessional interests, especially those with unusual pairings like management and music. "What makes Wesleyan really stand out is its care and attention for each student as an individual," says a junior.

Founded in 1850, IWU occupies an 83-acre campus site in a north-side residential district of Bloomington. The heart of campus is the central quadrangle, and tree-lined walkways connect buildings that range in style from gray stone Gothic to ultramodern steel and glass. IWU's main classroom building, State Farm Hall, includes state-of-the-art classrooms and research spaces. An expansion of the Shirk Center doubled the size of the university's fitness facilities.

Illinois Wesleyan's general education requirements expose students to a broad array of liberal arts disciplines and are intended to help them develop critical-thinking and writing skills, imagination, intellectual independence, social awareness, and sensitivity to others. All first-year students must take a Gateway Colloquium, a topic-based, seminar-style class of 15 that stresses critical reading, writing, discussion, and analytical skills. Recent topics include Issues in Public Health, Mathematics of Computer Security, and Can I Cite TikTok? First-years register for classes and begin to reflect on their college experience during the Rising Titan summer orientation. They also attend the four-day Turning Titan orientation program, which involves an opening convocation, a common reading program, a day of community service, the Titan Carnival, and other events before classes begin in the fall.

> **"[Professors] love pursuing new ideas with students outside of the classroom."**

Among the top-notch programs in the College of Liberal Arts are biology, English, chemistry, and math, and some of the most popular majors include business administration, nursing, accounting, and biology. The business administration department offers a Portfolio Management course in which students buy and sell orders overseen by a client board composed of university trustees. IWU's School of Nursing is another big draw. The interdisciplinary health promotion and fitness management major prepares students for careers in exercise science, physical therapy, cardiac rehabilitation, sports nutrition, and similar fields. The College of Fine Arts houses three separate schools of music, art, and theater; music and theater are the standouts, offering eight distinct majors between the two. New offerings include majors in data science, neuroscience, and public health.

Website: www.iwu.edu
Location: Small City
Private
Total Enrollment: 1,645
Undergraduates: 1,645
Male/Female: 49/51
Financial Aid: 99%
Pell Grant: 26%
Expense: Pr $ $
Student Loans: 77%
Average Debt: $ $ $ $
Applicants: 4,543
Accepted: 45%
Enrolled: 10%
Grad in 6 Years: 81%
Returning Freshmen: 85%
Academics: ✍ ✍ ✍ ½
Social: ☎ ☎ ☎
Q of L: ★ ★ ★ ★
Admissions: (800) 332-2498
Email Address: iwuadmit@ iwu.edu

Strong Programs:
Biology
English
Chemistry
Math
Business Administration
Nursing
Music
Theater

"IWU's academic climate is collaborative and explorative," says an accounting major. "Professors are always available for extra support and love pursuing new ideas with students outside of the classroom." Sixty-three percent of courses have fewer than 20 students. In addition to the usual fall and spring semesters, IWU has an optional three-week May term that gives students a chance to focus on a single intensive course or undertake research, a service project, or an internship. Faculty-led May term travel courses are a particularly popular option. About 40 percent of students take advantage of the university's study abroad program, which sends them packing to their choice of more than 70 countries. Research opportunities are also plentiful, with 54 percent of students taking part, and IWU hosts an annual student research conference that attracts scholars from all disciplines. Students praise advising and career services: "My advisor is my biggest cheerleader at IWU," enthuses an accounting major.

About 40 percent of students study abroad; faculty-led May term travel courses are a particularly popular option.

At IWU, a finance major says, "Everyone has a sense of Titan pride that comes out in our mantra 'Titan Green Over Everything.'" Undergraduates here are largely the homegrown variety, with 78 percent hailing from Illinois and 3 percent from outside the country. Although IWU began admitting Black students in 1867, they still account for only 7 percent of the student body. Hispanics/Latinos represent 10 percent, Asian Americans 7 percent, and multiracial students 3 percent. In response to student concerns about inclusion on campus, the university has implemented mandatory diversity training for students, faculty, and staff. Students here are generally liberal, socially conscious, and active in groups like Circle K, the Alpha Phi Omega service fraternity, and Habitat for Humanity. Merit scholarships averaging $27,200 are available to qualified students; there are no athletic scholarships.

"Everyone has a sense of Titan pride that comes out in our mantra 'Titan Green Over Everything.'"

IWU requires students to live on campus for three years, and students say the housing is not a highlight. "The dorms are very outdated," reports a business administration major, but a junior adds, "Upperclassman dorms are a lot nicer, newer, and more spacious." Campus food is described as "nothing to rave about," although offerings for those with dietary restrictions have been improving. Most students say campus security is good, and the university's Consent Is Sexy campaign is helping push awareness of and discussions about sexual violence on campus.

Twenty-one percent of the men and 29 percent of the women go Greek, and fraternities and sororities are the focus of IWU's social life. A student explains, "Most parties occur at frat houses, but the campus is so small that they are open to everyone." Alcohol policies allow drinking on campus for those of legal age. For alternatives, the Office of Student Activities sponsors free events in the student center almost every weekend, and academic departments and the Student Senate regularly bring guest speakers to campus. Each fall during homecoming, Greeks and dorm dwellers compete in the Titan Games to get appropriately psyched, and the Big Show brings major performers to campus in the spring.

Each fall during homecoming, Greeks and dorm dwellers compete in the Titan Games to get appropriately psyched.

Thanks to the proximity of Illinois State University—less than a mile away in neighboring Normal—IWU offers more than the typical small college town atmosphere. The area's total student population of about 25,000 provides students at tiny IWU with "the best of both worlds," says a senior. A freshman adds, "Some kids from big cities say there is nothing to do in Bloomington-Normal, but in my opinion, they are exaggerating." Options include nearby theaters, concert venues, coffee shops, bars, and a farmers market in warmer months. The best road trips are to Peoria or Urbana–Champaign (home of the University of Illinois) or to Chicago or St. Louis, each two and a half hours away.

The IWU Titans compete in the Division III College Conference of Illinois and Wisconsin. Football is well and good, but Titans basketball really gets students going. The men's golf team won the national championship in 2019 and 2021, and women's golf, women's swimming, and men's and women's basketball are also strong. IWU's varsity eSports team is nationally competitive. The Fort Natatorium houses an impressive 14-lane swimming pool, and the swim team has had its share of stars. The small but active recreational sports program offers about a dozen club and intramural sports.

One of the Midwest's better-kept secrets, Illinois Wesleyan is at once cozy and diverse, loaded with opportunities for ambitious students with traditional or offbeat interests. As one junior advises, "The school provides a multitude of paths down which one can travel, and it is up to the student to decide which path to take. IWU allows you to become who you want to be, but only if you let it."

If You Apply To ›

Illinois Wesleyan: Early action, rolling admissions. SATs or ACTs: optional. Accepts the Common Application with supplement. Music and theater applicants must audition or interview. Art applicants are encouraged to submit portfolio.

Indiana University

300 North Jordan Avenue, Bloomington, IN 47405

Though men's basketball has traditionally been IU's most famous program, it may not be its best. That distinction could easily go to the world-renowned music school or to the distinguished foreign language and business offerings. IU enrolls more out-of-staters than the University of Illinois. Bloomington is a great college town, and most students live off campus after freshman year.

With just over 33,000 undergraduates on its enormous campus, Indiana University is the prototype of the large Midwestern school. (And it is emphatically "Indiana University," not "the University of Indiana"—a common mistake.) With strong academics, a thriving social scene, and some of the best sports teams around, this top-notch public institution is a testament to Hoosier determination.

Located in southern Indiana's gently rolling hills, the 1,953-acre campus boasts architecture from Italianate brick to collegiate Gothic limestone to the distinctive style of world-famous architect I. M. Pei. Other unique campus features include fountains, gargoyles, an arboretum of more than 450 trees and shrubs surrounding two reflecting pools, a limestone gazebo, and the Campus River, a pretty creek that runs along-

> "With 4,000 different courses per semester, a variety of intensity levels exists."

side a shaded path. The $10 million, modernist Mies Building for the Eskenazi School of Art, Architecture, + Design, based on a 1952 design by renowned architect Ludwig Mies van der Rohe, opened in 2021.

Founded in 1820, Indiana prides itself on its liberal arts education—most freshmen are admitted not to preprofessional schools but to the "University Division," and students are encouraged to explore their interests. General education coursework includes math, science, arts and humanities, social and historical studies, English composition, world languages and cultures, and additional requirements that vary by school.

IU's schools and colleges offer more than 200 undergraduate majors, interdisciplinary study, a design-your-own-major option, and intense honors and research programs. The highly touted Kelley School of Business, with its respected global studies component, is among the most popular on campus, and the School of Education is also strong. Overall, the management, marketing, biological sciences, and computer and information technology majors enroll the most students. When it comes to the performing arts, the Jacobs School of Music is top in its field, setting the, ahem, tone for much of the campus, and the dance program is solid. The notable Media School gives students the language, communication, research, and technological skills they need to excel in media-related careers, while the O'Neill School of Public and Environmental Affairs is a top choice for those interested in public policy. The Hamilton Lugar School of Global and International Studies brings together language, area studies, and international studies programs to prepare students in the global competencies of the 21st century. The internationally known Kinsey Institute, which studies critical issues in sexuality, gender, and reproduction, is housed on IU's campus as well. Recently added academic offerings include majors in organizational and business psychology, environmental geoscience, and counseling and student services.

Students describe the academic climate as rigorous but not cutthroat. "With 4,000 different courses per semester, a variety of intensity levels exists," says a marketing major. "There is a balance with room for both competitive overachievers and laid-back, carefree individuals." Students say they regularly share ideas with each other, and group projects are commonplace. Faculty members bring their research results directly to students, and some profs, especially in math and the sciences, bring undergrads into their labs to assist with ongoing projects. "The professors here are remarkable," says an art history major. As for advising, many students seem surprised by the personal attention they receive at such a large university, and they soon learn that many available resources are helpful to those students who seek them out. For those seeking study abroad opportunities, the university offers more than 380 programs in 70 countries and 17 languages for students in nearly every field of study; about 20 percent of students take part.

> **"The professors here are remarkable."**

Fifty-nine percent of IU undergraduates are from in state, and 5 percent are international. Black students account for 4 percent of the student body, Hispanics/Latinos 8 percent, Asian Americans 8 percent, and multiracial students 5 percent. By and large, students do not seem to dwell on political or social issues. And while IU does not guarantee that it will meet the full demonstrated financial need of every student, it does admit on a need-blind basis. Merit scholarships are awarded to qualified students and average $7,900 annually, and more than 300 athletic scholarships are available for qualified jocks.

> *The O'Neill School of Public and Environmental Affairs is a top choice for those interested in public policy.*

Housing is guaranteed to all incoming freshmen and ranges from Gothic quads (co-ed by building) to 13-floor high-rises (co-ed by floor or unit). One student explains the housing situation this way: "All dorms have laundry facilities, cafeterias, computer clusters, and undergraduate advisors, and some even have special amenities like language-speaking floors." Living/learning communities are popular with students who wish to explore common interests like civic leadership, public health, and the arts. Dining options range from buffet-style to food courts with outlets offering international and healthful menus sprinkled among the fast food. Alcohol is prohibited in the dorms, which may help explain why 65 percent of the student body lives off campus. Most off-campus residents choose apartments or small houses with big front porches within walking distance of the campus or the IU bus system. A number of student-driven initiatives, including Culture of Care, Step UP! IU, and It's on Us, are working to promote student wellness and safety on campus.

> **"Some [dorms] have special amenities like language-speaking floors."**

Although IU's more than 800 campus organizations host numerous events, the most active on-campus groups, in terms of social life, seem to be the Greeks, which attract 18 percent of the men and 20 percent of the women. Some complain of a polarized atmosphere. "There is a large separation between the Greek community and the rest of the student body," says a senior. With concerts, ballets, recitals, and festivals right on campus, students are not lacking for things to keep them busy. Indiana Memorial Union is one of the largest student unions in the nation, and the range of extracurricular organizations is also impressive. Modeled after the Indianapolis 500, the Little 500 bike race in the spring, in which teams of IU undergrads race around a quarter-mile track, is one of the most highly attended events of the year; 2023 marked the 72nd running of the race. The 36-hour Dance Marathon in the fall raises money for Riley Children's Hospital in Indianapolis. Various cultural centers and community partnerships provide plenty of opportunities for students to make a difference on campus and in the community.

Modeled after the Indianapolis 500, the Little 500 bike race is highly attended; 2023 marked the 72nd running of the race.

Students say Bloomington (population 80,000) is a great college town. There are many excellent bars, shops, art venues, and ethnic restaurants, including one of the few Tibetan restaurants in the country. Locally, the area offers some impressive limestone quarries, miles of public forests, and three nearby lakes. Spelunkers will find heaven down below in the many nearby caves. Chicago, Cincinnati, Indianapolis, St. Louis, and even New Orleans are popular road trips.

Although dozens of intramural and club sports are available, recreational sports pale in comparison with Division I varsity athletics here; basketball is an established religion in the state of Indiana. Students and faculty are all eligible for men's basketball tickets, but they've got to get requests in early. In recent years, the Hoosiers men's basketball, baseball, and soccer teams and men's and women's swimming and diving teams have claimed Big Ten championships; the women's basketball team has been a contender for the national title. Even the football team draws cream-and-crimson crowds. Purdue has been IU's main athletic rival since 1891, and their football teams battle annually for the Old Oaken Bucket, found on a farm in southern Indiana in 1925 and alleged to have been used during the Civil War. The winner of the game with Michigan State takes home the Old Brass Spittoon.

Along with IU's reputation as a basketball powerhouse, it also provides committed students with stellar academics spanning a wide range of disciplines and a lively social scene. Those who don't mind its large size will find a welcoming atmosphere and ample opportunities for more intimate learning experiences, not to mention plenty of Hoosier pride.

Overlaps

UT Austin, UC Berkeley, CU Boulder, University of Iowa, University of Kansas, Purdue, U of I at Urbana–Champaign, UW–Madison

If You Apply To ›

Indiana: Early action, regular decision. SATs or ACTs: optional. Accepts the Common Application with supplement.

International Universities

Do you thrive on new experiences? Like to meet new people? Want to learn about different cultures? You can do all that at a college or university in the United States, but if you really want to jump in with both feet, think about attending a school in a foreign country. This section highlights the opportunities available in Canada, Great Britain, and Ireland, by far the most common destinations outside the United States for degree-seeking undergraduates.

The absence of a language barrier is the most obvious reason why these three countries are the preferred destinations for study abroad. Plenty of students do a junior year abroad where the language is Spanish or Swahili, but only a handful can realistically expect to earn an entire degree in a foreign tongue. A growing number of European universities are offering instruction in English, not only to Americans but to students from throughout the world. A smattering of American universities do exist in places ranging from Paris to Cairo, but most are small and the majority of their enrollment is students from other countries seeking an American-style education. If you're willing to venture halfway around the world, Australia is an English-speaking destination that might be worth a look for its combination of beautiful scenery, quality universities, and, at least by American standards, reasonable tuition.

Look for coverage of Australian institutions in a future edition of the *Fiske Guide*. The following sections examine Canada, Britain, and Ireland in more detail, followed by full-length articles on selected institutions.

Canadian Universities

Horace Greeley told ambitious young men of his generation to "go West." Today his admonition to young men and women seeking a quality college education at a relatively modest cost would probably be to "go North"—to Canada. A growing number of American students are discovering the educational riches that lie just above their northern border in this huge land of 38 million people that is known for its rugged mountains, bicultural politics, spirited ice hockey, and cold ale. What's drawing them is easy to discern.

The top Canadian universities are the academic equals of most flagship public universities and many leading privates in the United States. Canadian campuses and the cities in which they are located are safe places, and unless one opts for a French course of study, there are no language and few cultural barriers. Canadian schools are strong on international exchange programs, and their degrees carry weight with U.S. graduate schools.

Canada has 90 institutions of higher learning, ranging from internationally recognized research universities to the small undergraduate teaching institutions in the country's more rural areas. Most of the larger universities are located in highly urban centers, but some are situated in smaller towns where they dominate the life of the community. Most are almost literally next door to the United States, within 100 miles of the Canada–U.S. border. In this guide, we feature four of Canada's strongest universities: the University of British Columbia, McGill University, Queen's University, and the University of Toronto.

Institutions of higher learning in Canada were established from the earliest days of French settlement in the mid-17th century, making them some of the oldest in North America. The precursors to the public universities in Canada were the small, elite, denominational colleges that sprang up in Quebec, in the Maritimes, and later in Ontario. A few private denominational colleges and universities still exist in Canada, but most have been subsumed into affiliations or associations with the larger universities. Education in Canada, including university education, became the exclusive jurisdiction of provincial governments.

One of the key differences between Canadian and U.S. universities is that Canadian universities (and this is what they are, not "colleges") are primarily funded from public monies. Calculating the cost for an American to attend a Canadian university can be tricky. For one thing, the exchange rate between the U.S. and Canadian dollar fluctuates (at this writing, it significantly favors the U.S. dollar). Moreover, tuition and fee rates vary by field of study. The cost of pricey majors such as medicine and other hard sciences can easily be double or triple that of less expensive ones such as social work or theology. Canadian citizens, of course, pay far less than visitors from south of the border. Depending on the factors just described, tuition and fees at the four universities included in the *Fiske Guide* range from less than US $15,000 to more than US $70,000. For many U.S. students, education at one of the top Canadian universities is comparable to out-of-state rates at a flagship public university in the States.

Federal and provincial loans and grants that are readily available to Canadian students are generally not available to students from the United States and other countries. However, the majority of universities with competitive admissions, particularly those featured in the *Fiske Guide*, offer merit-based awards and scholarships to students of all nationalities. American students who attend leading Canadian schools can apply their U.S. student assistance funds, including Federal Direct Loans and Pell Grants.

The criteria for obtaining a degree are set by each institution, as are the admissions requirements and prerequisites. Unlike the United States, Canada does not offer nor require its own students to take a Canadian college entrance test. Some Canadian universities admitting students from the United States will ask for SAT or ACT scores along with high school marks from academic subjects in the last two or three years of high school. In general, top universities are about as selective as their American counterparts.

Application fees vary by institution, as do deadlines. Canadian universities are aware of the May 1 deadline operative in the United States, and they try to accommodate. Applications to the University of Toronto and Queen's University in Ontario are handled centrally through the Ontario Universities' Application Service, although Queen's also accepts the Common Application as an alternative for students applying from the U.S. McGill and British Columbia handle their own applications directly. Canadian universities differ widely in the amount of credit and/or advanced standing they offer for Advanced Placement examinations or International Baccalaureate Higher Level examinations.

The following admissions requirements apply to applicants from an American school system. In response to the COVID-19 pandemic, many Canadian schools have relaxed their SAT and ACT testing requirements for applicants from the United States. Prospective students are advised to consult universities' websites or contact admissions officers directly for the most up-to-date information regarding testing requirements. Aside from SAT and ACT scores, the University of British Columbia bases admissions decisions on the average of eight full-year academic courses over the last two years of high school. McGill bases its assessment of American high school graduates on the overall record of marks in academic subjects during the final three years of high school and their class standing. Queen's looks at class rank. Toronto's Arts and Science faculties want a high grade point average. These universities generally have additional program-specific requirements for STEM fields that may be more stringent. ACT and CEEB Advanced Placement Examination scores are also considered.

It is hard to beat Canadian universities for the quality of student life. Although many students commute, most of the universities in Canada offer on-campus housing; some even guarantee campus housing for first-year students. Universities offer active intramural and intercollegiate sports programs for both men and women, and the usual student clubs, newspapers, and radio stations provide students with opportunities to get involved and develop friendships. As in the United States, student-run organizations are active participants in university life, with leaders serving on university committees and lobbying on issues ranging from creating more bicycle paths to keeping tuition low. Few Canadian campuses are troubled by issues of student safety or rowdiness. In the larger urban centers, Canadian campuses reflect the rich diversity of Canada's cultural mosaic, and most encourage their students to gain international experience by spending a term or a full year abroad.

Americans wondering about the currency of a Canadian degree in the United States should be reassured that top American and multinational companies—the likes of Chase, IBM, and Microsoft—actively recruit on Canadian campuses, as do American graduate schools. According to the Institute of International Education in New York, more than 10,000 Canadians are currently enrolled in graduate schools in the United States.

The one thing that is different for U.S. and other international students intending to study in Canada is that they will have to obtain a Student Authorization, equivalent to a visa, from Canadian immigration authorities as well as a passport. Getting a Student Authorization is fairly straightforward for American citizens, but this slight bureaucratic hurdle is a reminder that Canada, for all of its similarities in language and culture with the United States, is still a separate country.

Universities Canada, a nonprofit organization representing Canada's colleges and universities, has more information at www.univcan.ca.

Canadian universities are currently playing host to about 1,600 American students on their campuses, and as a result of funding cutbacks and internationalization policies in the early 1990s, they have become increasingly active in recruiting students from south of the border. This is but one more reason why it makes sense for more young Americans to check out the "Canadian option." Canada, eh?

University of British Columbia

Vancouver, British Columbia V6T 1Z1 CAN

Natural beauty is the first thing that draws Americans to Vancouver—and Canada's premier western university. A similar scale to places like University of Washington but with two major differences—no big-time sports to unite the campus and limited dorm life. The university is active in recruiting overseas, which creates an international ambience.

Website: www.you.ubc.ca
Location: City Outskirts
Public
Total Enrollment: 52,944
Undergraduates: 42,330
Male/Female: 44/56
Financial Aid: 25%
Pell Grant: N/A
Expense: Pub $
Student Loans: N/A
Average Debt: N/A
Applicants: 38,197
Accepted: 57%
Enrolled: 51%
Grad in 6 Years: 81%
Returning Freshmen: 95%
Academics: ✍ ✍ ✍ ✍ ½
Social: ☎ ☎
Q of L: ★ ★ ★ ★
Admissions: (604) 822-8999
Email Address:
international@askme.ubc.ca

Strong Programs:
Anthropology
First Nations and Indigenous Studies
Asian Studies
Economics
Geography
International Relations
Microbiology
Commerce

What do three prime ministers of Canada, three provincial premiers, an astronaut, a world-renowned opera singer, and two Nobel Prize winners have in common? They are all graduates of the University of British Columbia. Founded in 1908, UBC offers students hundreds of solid programs, such as business, science, engineering, the social sciences, and fine arts, as well as ready access to beaches and mountains and a diploma with instant name recognition. Though the massive campus can sometimes feel isolating, students are nevertheless happy to be here in such illustrious company.

Located just 25 minutes from downtown Vancouver, UBC's striking Point Grey campus covers a peninsula that borders the Pacific Ocean and is bounded by an old-growth forest. Mountains—perfect for skiing—loom in the distance. Architectural styles are a mix of Gothic and modern, and students can enjoy a leisurely stroll through the university's botanical gardens. Notable campus facilities include the Kaiser Building (the central hub of engineering), the Barber Learning Centre, the Mitchell Thunderbird Sports Arena, and the Nest (a $106 million student union building). The university also has a smaller campus—UBC Okanagan—located in Kelowna, in the Okanagan Valley.

"There is a huge diversity here that many smaller schools may lack."

UBC offers more than 260 undergraduate degree options, and popular majors include psychology, biology, English, and political science. Programs in anthropology, First Nations and indigenous studies, and Asian studies are highly regarded and enhanced by the university's excellent Museum of Anthropology, which features one of the world's best collections of Northwest Coast First Nations art. Music majors benefit from the Chan Centre for the Performing Arts. Economics, geography, international relations, microbiology, and commerce are strong too. Additional programs include majors in applied animal biology, applied plant and soil sciences, geographical biogeosciences, and zoology.

Freshmen benefit from a wide array of first-year programs, including Imagine UBC and Create UBC Okanagan, a first-day orientation. Arts One and the Coordinated Arts programs offer enriched, integrated approaches to broad interdisciplinary themes in arts and humanities. Qualified students can take advantage of Science One, featuring team-taught courses in biology, chemistry, math, and physics. The UBC study abroad program has more than 200 institutional partners in 40 countries, and co-op programs in engineering, science, arts, commerce, and forestry give students an opportunity to earn while they learn. In addition, honors and double-honors programs are available to superbrains and budding geniuses.

The academic climate is exactly what you would expect from a university of UBC's international stature. "Courses can be hard," says one student, "but success is based on your interest and willingness to learn." One student grumbles about his 8 a.m. philosophy lecture: "Who can focus on the big questions at that time of the morning?" Most classes have fewer than 50 students, while larger lectures are supplemented with smaller labs and discussion groups. Overall, the faculty receives good marks. "The professors are extremely intelligent people who are truly dedicated to their disciplines," says a junior. Academic advising is a mixed bag, with some students complaining that finding a knowledgeable advisor can be time-consuming.

With more than 40,000 undergraduates attending the Vancouver campus, it's no surprise that UBC's student population is a melting pot—26 percent come from outside Canada. "There is a huge diversity here that many smaller schools may lack," says a sophomore. The typical UBC student is bright, hardworking, and gregarious. Students of color are well represented (Asians make up the largest contingency), and the university encourages diversity through a series of special programs and active recruiting. Hot political issues include LGBTQ, women's, and human rights. The International Scholars program offers financial support, as well as special service projects, workshops, and other opportunities to top international students.

The anthropology program is highly regarded and enhanced by the university's excellent Museum of Anthropology.

Roughly one-third of the students currently live on campus. A major expansion of on-campus housing, estimated at US $650 million, was completed in 2022, and UBC now guarantees a spot to all incoming first-time, first-year students. On-campus options include co-ed complexes (primarily for freshmen), theme houses, university apartments, and family units for upperclassmen.

"Vancouver is one of the most livable cities in the world."

A history major says on-campus living is worth it to "enjoy the community spirit." Those seeking off-campus accommodations must contend with Vancouver's pricey rental market. Hungry students will find an endless variety of meal options at the school's 45 dining locations, including "Japanese, Lebanese, Italian, and vegetarian" plates, according to one student. The Sexual Assault Support Centre provides support services and educational programming related to sexual violence.

On such a large campus, isolation is a real threat. "You need to get in touch with other students quickly when you get here or you could feel lost on such a big campus," says a freshman. Social life happens mostly on campus but largely "depends on the crowd you hang with," according to one student. For partying types, there are the requisite bashes, courtesy of UBC's small but active Greek scene—one of the few places where underage drinkers may sneak a sip of booze. Alternatives include university-sponsored events, such as movies and guest speakers. Popular campus events include Storm the Wall, long-boat racing, and the Arts County Fair.

Thanks to a major expansion of on-campus housing, UBC now guarantees a spot to all incoming first-time, first-year students.

Vancouver, with its population of 675,000, offers students countless opportunities, though one health science major says, "It isn't a college town. It is a well-developed semicosmopolitan city." Another adds, "Vancouver is one of the most livable cities in the world and UBC is located in the nicest, most beautiful part—it's not too hard to imagine what a pleasure it is to go to school here." Beautiful weather draws students outdoors and to nearby beaches and mountains for in-line skating, snowboarding, and swimming. Eleven recreational sports leagues and 16 intramural events are a huge draw for students at the Vancouver campus; popular sports include sailing, skiing, and cycling. UBC has 31 varsity teams (the Thunderbirds), which have brought home more than 120 national championships—the most of any institution in Canada. Men's and women's volleyball and swimming, along with women's ice hockey and field hockey, have been particularly competitive in recent years.

Overlaps

University of Washington, UCLA, University of Colorado Boulder, NYU, UC Berkeley, University of Victoria, University of Toronto, Simon Fraser

Spending four years at this mammoth university can be intimidating for the shy student. But for those willing to take control of their social lives, UBC offers an impressive academic milieu. A history major offers this point of view: "I think that the school's biggest strength is its size; there are so many opportunities here."

If You Apply To ›

British Columbia: Rolling admissions. Does not accept the Common Application. Apply to specific program. Please consult British Columbia's website for the most up-to-date information regarding standardized test requirements.

McGill University

Montreal, Quebec H3A 0C8 CAN

The Canadian university best known south of the border. Though instruction is in English, McGill is located in French-speaking Montreal, a world-class city that has it all. Individualism is encouraged, and there's a strong international flavor. Just over 10 percent of students live in university housing, and anyone coming here will be on their own for housing after freshman year.

Website: www.mcgill.ca
Location: City Center
Public
Total Enrollment: 31,876
Undergraduates: 23,811
Male/Female: 40/60
Financial Aid: 24%
Pell Grant: N/A
Expense: Pub $
Student Loans: N/A
Average Debt: N/A
Applicants: 44,534
Accepted: 38%
Enrolled: 37%
Grad in 6 Years: 84%
Returning Freshmen: 92%
Academics: ✍ ✍ ✍ ✍ ½
Social: 🐾 🐾 🐾 🐾
Q of L: ★ ★ ★ ★
Admissions: (514) 398-7878
Email Address: N/A

Strong Programs:
Medicine
Law
Engineering
Environmental Studies
Psychology
Political Science
Commerce
Education

With such strong preprofessional programs and a diverse student body, it's easy to see why enterprising men and women from around the world flock to McGill University, which was founded in 1821 by a bequest from Scottish merchant James McGill. But beware: this is not a cookie-cutter school, and fitting in actually seems to be discouraged. "McGill is a university where people are allowed to become individuals," a senior says. "Difference and creativity are celebrated here."

Montreal's climate alternates between hot summers and freezing winters. A junior describes McGill's 80-acre main campus as "an oasis in the heart of the city." Located in downtown Montreal amid the hustle and bustle, the campus provides students with ample green space and a welcome respite from the decidedly urban atmosphere of the city. A free outdoor skating rink adds charm in the frigid winter months. Campus buildings range from "Gothic-like" structures with vines growing up the sides to more modern structures. Trees and greenery dot the campus landscape, and the sprawling recreation trails of Mount Royal rise to its immediate north. Notable facilities include a $71 million life sciences research complex. The Schulich School of Music offers an ultramodern symphony and multimedia hall that functions as a recording studio, performance venue, and research studio. A short drive west of downtown, the Macdonald Campus occupies 1,600 acres of woods and fields on the shores of Lac St-Louis, providing unique opportunities for fieldwork and research.

> **"There are always free concerts and festivals all over the city throughout the year."**

To fulfill the university's general education requirements, students must first choose which discipline (or faculty) to enter. A senior says, "It is important to consider the university on the basis of which faculty you would be interested in, because they vary greatly and operate almost as independent units." Freshmen must accumulate six to 12 credits in three of four disciplines, including languages, math and science, social sciences, and humanities, and declare a major before their sophomore year. Upon entering their major, students have a menu of course options that includes honors programs and double majors.

Though the most popular majors are psychology, political science, commerce, and education, there is no denying that the university's strengths lie in preprofessional programs such as medicine, law, and engineering. The sciences receive uniform praise, as does the School of Environment. A double-degree interdisciplinary program allows students to combine a bachelor of arts program with one in the sciences. Several programs help freshmen with the transition to college, and some are tailored to international students, which includes those from the United States. For those who want to escape Montreal's brutal winters, there are internships; field studies in Barbados, Africa, and the Smithsonian Tropical Research Institute in Panama; and exchange programs with more than 150 partner universities around the world.

Regardless of major, students can expect classes to be demanding. "McGill has a very stressful and competitive atmosphere," a finance major says. Classes tend to be large—some introductory courses enroll up to 1,000 students—and students must be willing to seek out professors and advisors. "The quality of teaching is generally above average," a student says. "Many of the professors are kind, intelligent, and devoted to their students." Students grumble that academic advising is a bureaucratic tangle. "There is way too much red tape and dealing with the administration can be horrible," says one senior.

Forty-four percent of undergraduates are Quebecers (or Québécois, as Francophones would say), and 30 percent are international, representing more than 135 countries. Indeed, McGill students are a diverse lot, and the only common thread among them seems to be their fierce independence. A geography major says McGill students are "hardworking, driven, very intellectual, and research-oriented." Environmental issues are a big concern, and students report that political and social issues receive ample attention on campus. Qualified students are eligible for merit scholarships and a limited number of awards for athletes. There is also a work-study program for those in need of financial assistance.

The university's traditional and alternative residence halls house about 13 percent of undergrads in dorms, apartments, and shared facilities houses. Dorms run the gamut, but one recent acquisition is, according to a senior, a "four-star hotel, turned into a six-star dorm." Party animals will feel free to crank up the stereo in Molson or McConnell, while bookworms might be better suited for Gardner. Off-campus apartments are a popular alternative for upperclassmen, who take advantage of Montreal's clean, affordable housing. "The dining facilities are good," says a sophomore. Despite its urban location, the McGill campus is safe and security receives positive reviews. "There are student organizations like 'Walksafe' and 'Drivesafe' that will walk or drive students to their residences at night regardless of where they are or where they are going," reports one student.

> "The McGill–Harvard rugby match is a must-watch."

"McGill students are very sociable and love to party!" says one student. Though there are "considerable on-campus social activities, with many clubs and associations," many students venture off campus into Montreal for fun and adventure. "A cultural epicenter, Montreal is home to some of the world's best museums, galleries, restaurants, shops, and music," a senior says. "There are always free concerts and festivals all over the city throughout the year." Drinking is a popular pastime, but underage drinkers are few and far between since the legal age in Quebec is 18 and, a senior says, "McGill treats its students as mature, educated adults." Greek organizations sign up about 2 percent of the students, and McGill boasts Canada's first social fraternity for gay, bisexual, transgender, and progressive men. Well-attended campus events include homecoming, Winter Carnival, and Frosh activities during orientation week. New York City, Ottawa, and Toronto are popular road-trip destinations, and ski slopes are less than an hour away.

Men's and women's basketball and ice hockey, men's rugby, and women's soccer are among the most popular varsity sports; men's baseball and women's basketball and synchronized swimming have captured recent national championships. According to one student, "The McGill–Harvard rugby match is a must-watch." Intramurals offer would-be jocks an opportunity to blow off steam after classes and on weekends, with soccer and ice hockey attracting the most interest.

In recent years the government of Quebec has been less than enthusiastic about funding its English-speaking academic gem, and large classes and mountains of red tape are undeniably part of the McGill experience. Nevertheless, most denizens seem happy. "The students who go to McGill are very invested in their academic life and are proud of their school," a student says.

A double-degree interdisciplinary program allows students to combine a bachelor of arts program with one in the sciences.

Some introductory courses enroll up to 1,000 students— and students must be willing to seek out professors and advisors.

Overlaps

University of British Columbia, Concordia, University of Montreal, NYU, Queen's University, University of Toronto

Queen's University

Kingston, Ontario K7L 3N6 CAN

With about 18,000 undergraduates, Queen's is the smallest of the major Canadian universities. It is also the only one set in a metropolitan area of modest size. Engineering and business are the strongest areas of study, followed by nursing. Toronto and Montreal are both about three hours away. With 90 percent of its first-year students in the dorms, Queen's has a more active residential life than other Canadian universities.

Website: www.queensu.ca
Location: Small City
Public
Total Enrollment: 25,757
Undergraduates: 20,996
Male/Female: 40/60
Financial Aid: 58%
Pell Grant: N/A
Expense: Pub $
Student Loans: 34%
Average Debt: N/A
Applicants: 46,061
Accepted: 49%
Enrolled: 28%
Grad in 6 Years: 87%
Returning Freshmen: 95%
Academics: ✐ ✐ ✐ ✐ ½
Social: ☎ ☎ ☎ ☎
Q of L: ★ ★ ★ ★
Admissions: (613) 533-2218
Email Address: admission@ queensu.ca

Strong Programs:
Engineering
Commerce
Nursing
Biomedical Computing
Cognitive Science
Software Design
Education
Creative Arts

Students at Queen's University approach work and play with equal zeal and enjoy a potent mix of school spirit and intellectual drive. Success requires energy and a willingness to get into the thick of things. "People who aren't interested in being a part of the school community are better off at a school that isn't such a big family," warns a sophomore. Solid academics, a pervasive school spirit, and long-standing traditions make life at this storied university unique—and demanding. "Getting into Queen's is just the first challenge," says a senior. "Succeeding at Queen's is another battle."

The 161-acre Queen's campus is located on the north shore of Lake Ontario, just minutes from the heart of Kingston, Ontario ("the limestone city"), and directly between Montreal and Toronto. "Almost all buildings are constructed using lime-stone," explains a senior. Historically significant buildings have been maintained, and "there are some modern buildings with a lot of glass to provide a bright and welcoming atmosphere." Ample greenery and open spaces provide students a place to stretch out under the sky and hit the books. The 80,000-square-foot Isabel Bader Centre for the Performing Arts features common teaching rooms and shared public spaces designed to encourage interactivity.

> "The courses are often theory-driven and require a substantial amount of work."

Established by the Church of Scotland in 1841 under a Royal Charter of Queen Victoria, Queen's University offers undergraduate degrees in a variety of faculties, including science, engineering, commerce, education, music, nursing, and creative arts. Academics are unilaterally solid, but the most demanding are engineering and commerce, and nursing is popular. The bachelor of commerce program was the first of its kind in Canada and provides students with an internationally focused liberal business education, enhanced by leadership modules and the integration of technology. The School of Computing offers bachelor of computing degrees in biomedical computing, cognitive science, and software design, as well as B.A. and B.S. degrees. Computing and the Creative Arts is a multidisciplinary program that allows students to use cutting-edge software programs for music, drama, art, and film production. General education requirements vary by program, but all students can expect to confront a rigorous series of core and elective courses. Students participating in programs at the Queen's Bader International Study Centre are whisked away to the university's campus in East Sussex, England, where they enjoy small classes and integrated field studies while residing in a 15th-century castle. In addition, there are exchange programs with 180 universities in 45 countries around the world. Queen's is considered a leader in study abroad; 20 percent of students participate. Opportunities for undergraduate research are abundant as well.

"The academic climate is quite competitive, and the courses are often theory-driven and require a substantial amount of work to prepare for class and complete assignments," says one senior. The general consensus among struggling students is that As are hard to come by. "After working your butt off and reading stacks of textbooks, your grades pale in comparison to the marks of students at other universities," gripes a biology major. The QSuccess program helps orient first-year students academically and socially, and Bounce Back is an opt-in academic support program for first-year students who earn low GPAs in their first term. Participating students are paired with Bounce Back Facilitators, peer mentors who help them set goals and identify strategies for academic success.

The Computing and the Creative Arts program allows students to use cutting-edge software programs for music, drama, art, and film production.

Classes tend to be large for freshmen and sophomores but dwindle in size as one approaches graduation. The majority of classes are taught by full professors, who receive praise for their accessibility and intelligence. "The teachers I have had have been thorough, challenging, and concerned about my success," says a junior. Office hours and special "wine and cheese" functions give students ample opportunity to mingle with faculty. Students report that there is little trouble getting into desired classes, and "there is lots of counseling available for students who need it."

Queen's students are an industrious, intelligent group, and most are used to academic success. School spirit runs high and campus issues include rising tuition fees—and determining just who is responsible for the cost. Undergraduates come from every Canadian province and 79 countries; 78 percent are from Ontario and 11 percent are international. A sociology major says that "Queen's is very PC and inclusive, regardless of gender, race, religion, or sexual orientation." Though there are no athletic scholarships, hundreds of merit awards averaging $2,000 are handed out annually. "I have had great help through scholarships and financial aid," relates a senior. "There is quite a lot of money for you. You just have to go after it." International students are automatically considered for available merit awards.

"Queen's is very PC and inclusive."

Ninety percent of undergraduates live in 17 residence halls, and all freshmen are guaranteed a place to hang their hats. Co-ed and single-sex dorms are available, and students say all accommodations are well maintained. A mandatory meal plan gives freshmen a wide variety of foods to choose from, and the surrounding city also offers a plethora of dining options. After freshman year, most students pack their bags and head off campus to the "student village," where comfortable apartments are available. Most Queen's students live within a reasonable walk of campus. Safety is practically a nonissue on campus; students report that they feel quite safe and that security is more than adequate.

The annual "kill McGill" football game against rival McGill draws pigskin-crazed students from every corner of campus.

Make no mistake about it, Queen's students know how to have a good time. One says, "Campus pubs and city pubs have both found their niche." On Thursday nights, students flock to the campus pub, the Underground, for a drink or two, while Saturday nights are reserved for city bars and nightclubs. The legal drinking age is 19, and kiddies will have a tough time skirting the law. "The bouncers in Kingston actually have a couple of brain cells and can spot a fake ID from 90 kilometers away," says a senior. Nonalcoholic alternatives include school-sponsored movies and extracurricular clubs (there are more than 220). "Extracurricular activities are a must, not an option!" says one student. Frosh Week is a favorite event, with "cheers that even the most blasé of students will be shouting out with pride by the end of the week." The school is steeped in Scottish tradition

"Campus pubs and city pubs have both found their niche."

and modeled on counterparts in Edinburgh and Glasgow, and it's normal to see kilt-wearing bandsmen at important campus events.

Once the capital of Canada, Kingston is described as "very much a university town." There are several universities in the area (including the Royal Military College), and downtown provides students with shops, clubs, museums, and movie theaters. The city's relative isolation makes it the favored stomping ground for students without wheels. Town/gown relations are good, and students are very active in the community. Toronto and Montreal (less than three hours away) are popular road trips.

With 13 varsity teams, 35 varsity clubs, and 30 recreational clubs, Queen's athletic program is not only the largest in Canada but also ranks with Harvard and MIT for the largest programs in North America. Competitive Gaels teams include men's and women's rugby, ice hockey, soccer, and volleyball. The annual "kill McGill" football game against rival McGill draws pigskin-crazed students from every corner of campus; homecoming is a lively affair. Intramural competition is fierce too, and nearly half of the students are involved on some level. A student says, "There is so much school spirit, sometimes it makes you sick."

Life at Queen's University is one of extremes. Though the academic climate can be tough and the winters long, students here find much to celebrate. "One of the great things about Queen's is that it's constantly growing and expanding to meet the needs of its students," says one senior, "but at the same time, it never loses sight of where it came from or what it stands for."

Overlaps

Western University of Ontario, University of Toronto, McMaster, McGill, University of Alberta, University of British Columbia, Dalhousie

If You Apply To ›

Queen's: Rolling admissions. Accepts the Common Application. Apply to particular program. Please consult Queen's website for the most up-to-date information regarding standardized test requirements.

University of Toronto

Toronto, Ontario M5S 1A1 CAN

U of T is one of the largest institutions in the *Fiske Guide* and one of the biggest in the world. If ever there were a place where go-getterism is a necessity, this is it. In the absence of American-style school spirit, U of T students cut loose to find their fun in the city. Toronto is one of the most diverse and cosmopolitan cities in the world, with nearly half of its 3 million denizens born outside of Canada.

Website: www.utoronto.ca
Location: City Center
Public
Total Enrollment: 85,747
Undergraduates: 69,085
Male/Female: 44/56
Financial Aid: 20%
Pell Grant: N/A
Expense: Pub $
Student Loans: N/A
Average Debt: N/A
Applicants: 66,476

Students at the University of Toronto avoid getting lost in the shuffle by taking part in a unique residential college system that allows them to model their educational experience after their own personalities. Each college has a distinct character and appeal yet blends seamlessly into the university's overall academic milieu. And when it comes to academics, the U of T delivers, says a senior: "The students were likely at the top of their class in high school and are very competitive—more so than at Queen's or York universities."

The University of Toronto, founded by royal charter in 1827, is so large that it spans three campuses. The St. George campus in downtown Toronto features Gothic architecture and historic buildings. The suburban campuses in Mississauga and Scarborough feature more modern structures. A spate of new research buildings, athletic facilities, and student residences have opened in the last few years, and construction is underway on a 23-story, 508-bed residence hall on the St. George campus, scheduled for completion in 2024. As befitting such a gargantuan institution, the university's endowment is the largest of any Canadian college or university.

Students apply directly to one of Toronto's nine colleges—seven of which are on the St. George campus—and choose from more than 700 undergraduate degree programs. The most popular programs include physical sciences, computer science, engineering, commerce, and management; majors in international relations, biochemistry, and forensic science and a minor in food studies are notable as well. The Faculty of Arts and Science offers a wide array of disciplines that span the arts, science, and business, while the Faculty of Music is the oldest in Canada and offers bachelor's, master's, and doctoral degrees in all of their programs. The concurrent education program allows undergraduates to complete the requirements for a bachelor of education, professional teacher certification,

"U of T is very diverse and the student body is generally intelligent, progressive, and open-minded."

and a second undergraduate degree simultaneously. Distinctive learning options include First-Year Learning Communities and a wide range of research opportunities. Optional first-year seminars (called First-Year Foundations: The One Programs) are "a good transition from high school to university," says a senior, and give incoming freshmen the chance to learn from leading faculty members in a less intimidating environment of around 25 to 50 students. Topics range from public policy to urban environments to geological fieldwork.

Courses require a great deal of reading outside the classroom and are typically demanding. "During exam periods and the final weeks of each semester, the academic climate can understandably become quite intense," says one senior. Large lecture classes are accompanied by smaller tutorials, facilitating personal attention, and professors get high marks for their teaching skills and their smarts. "Even in classes of 1,500 students, professors have been consistently engaging and well-versed," says a student. Faculty-led Summer Abroad courses are an option for students who wish to venture farther afield.

"Students are from all over the world and represent the full spectrum of values and backgrounds," says an anthropology major. "U of T is very diverse and the student body is generally intelligent, progressive, and open-minded." Twenty-seven percent of undergraduates are international—from outside Canada, that is—including more than 500 Americans. The most significant issues on campus include "tuition fees, unequal pay, the environment, and critical social justice," according to one student. The Ontario Public Interest Research Group and Amnesty International attract sizable followings. A limited number of competitive academic scholarships are available for the most high-achieving international students.

Roughly 11 percent of students live in campus housing, and first-years are guaranteed rooms. "There are new buildings and historic old buildings that are beautiful," says an anthropology major. "They are cozy and comfortable and pretty well maintained." All of the dorms are affiliated with one of the nine undergraduate colleges, which act as "local neighborhoods" and center on specialties, such as Buddhism, Celtic studies, and criminology. "Every cafeteria always has a vegetarian, vegan, halal,

"Social life here revolves around the very energetic city in which the school is located."

kosher, gluten-free, or dairy-free option," a junior reports. "Security is pretty good on campus, and our campus is in a good part of Toronto," a bioethics major says.

"Social life here revolves around the very energetic city in which the school is located," says a sociology and English major. Another student adds, "Social events are balanced between off-campus pubs, clubs, skating rinks, banquet halls, and stadiums to on-campus pubs, event spaces in Hart House, and student lounges." Toronto boasts great culture, super shopping, a clean and safe nightlife district—and the picturesque

(continued)

Accepted: 45%
Enrolled: 31%
Grad in 6 Years: 77%
Returning Freshmen: 91%
Academics: ✏️ ✏️ ✏️ ✏️ ½
Social: ☎ ☎ ☎
Q of L: ★ ★ ★
Admissions: (416) 978-2190
Email Address: future.students @utoronto.ca

Strong Programs:
International Relations
Biochemistry
Forensic Science
Music
Physical Sciences
Computer Science
Engineering
Commerce

Students apply directly to one of Toronto's nine colleges and choose from more than 700 undergraduate degree programs.

shores of Lake Ontario, lovely in warmer weather. The legal drinking age here is 19; students who are of age may have alcohol in their rooms but not in common spaces, and anyone caught violating local laws or the open-container policy is reported to the dean of the residence. But according to one student, "There isn't much of a party culture at U of T, because we are much more focused on studying." Students looking to unwind on campus will find plenty of school-sponsored events, such as movies and guest speakers, and while there are no fraternities or sororities, there is a club for nearly every interest. Students turn out in droves to celebrate PRIDE, reputedly the largest gay pride event in North America, along with Frosh Week, which includes wacky fun such as bed races between the colleges, and the annual Fireball formal dance.

Varsity sports are not a focus of campus life at Toronto, though ice hockey, volleyball, and basketball draw something of a following, especially when the opponent is Queen's University or the University of Western Ontario. The Varsity Blues women's swimming team is a recent national champion, and the men's and women's water polo and fencing teams are also competitive. The intramural program, however, is another story. It's one of the largest in Canada, involving more than 10,000 students in 26 sports, with 57 leagues and 20 tournaments each year. Residence halls and groups of friends compete in everything from badminton to indoor cricket, karate, dodgeball, squash, broomball, and eSports. Students can also be found cheering the city's many professional teams, including the Blue Jays (baseball), the Raptors (basketball), and the Maple Leafs (hockey).

Toronto's biggest liability, its sheer and sometimes overwhelming size, may also be its biggest asset, students say—as long as they learn to speak up and proactively take advantage of all of the school's resources. Says a senior, "A prospective student should choose the University of Toronto due to its outstanding academic reputation and convenient location in the social hub of Toronto's downtown core."

If You Apply To ›

University of Toronto: Regular decision. Does not accept the Common Application. Apply to specific program. Please consult University of Toronto's website for the most up-to-date information regarding standardized test requirements.

British and Irish Universities

If going to college in Canada sounds adventuresome, you'll need even more moxie to venture overseas. But give it some thought. As the most popular overseas destination, Great Britain currently has about 4,500 Americans enrolled in undergraduate degree programs, and another 40,000 per year are pursuing shorter study abroad stints. Hundreds more have found their way to the Republic of Ireland. Depending on your course of study, studying in Britain or Ireland may or may not turn out to be less expensive than a flagship public university in the U.S., but the top British and Irish universities offer a richer international experience, infused with historical and cultural perspectives, than you will find on this side of the Atlantic.

Before we go further, here's a word to parents and guardians: you may get queasy at the thought of sending your little cherub across a 3,000-mile ocean, but a flight to Dublin or London is quicker than driving 10 hours to get to First Choice U. Once you're there, the cities are at least as safe as those in the U.S., and the small towns have a crime rate roughly equivalent to that of the town of Mayberry on *The Andy Griffith Show*. The best part for parents: you'll need to visit at least once—and preferably more.

For those who are hazy on their geography, England, Scotland, and Wales make up Great Britain; throw in Northern Ireland and the moniker changes to the United Kingdom. The Republic of Ireland, occupying the southern part of the Emerald Isle across the Irish Sea, used to be part of Great Britain but won its independence in 1921. Ireland is the closest European nation to the East Coast of the U.S. and the only English-speaking country in the eurozone. Britain and Ireland make the most sense for American students interested in studying English literature, history, foreign languages, and anything related to international studies. If medieval history is your passion, why not go to school where the remains of that long-ago world still dot the landscape? If you're looking for a career in international business, perhaps consider a country where the global village has been a way of life and you can make lifelong friends from around the world. Though Britain is an English-speaking country, it offers far better instruction in European and other languages than you can get in the U.S., and Ireland's favorable corporate tax rates have led U.S. companies such as Google, Microsoft, and Meta to make it their European headquarters (think internships). No matter what your academic interests, your classmates will include a cross section of nationalities that would be the envy of any North American institution. Most importantly, study in Britain and Ireland has the potential to be a life-changing experience that will broaden your horizons and deepen your understanding of our increasingly interconnected world. With cheap flights and trains readily available, travel to Continental Europe and beyond becomes second nature.

With all of these benefits come some challenges. American students in Britain need to adjust to a different tenor of academic life than is found at U.S. colleges and universities. Students are treated as adults and expected to behave accordingly. The legal drinking age is 18, which obviates the need for fake IDs but puts the onus on students to behave responsibly. Dorms are generally the domain of first-year students; expect to find a "flat" (apartment) for subsequent years. "Sport" means playing, not watching. The student body will not come out on a Saturday afternoon for the big game for a simple reason: there are no big games. Most faculty members (a.k.a. tutors) are ready to help you if you are struggling with your studies, but only if you take the initiative. There is no Dean of Student Hand-Holding in British universities (nor do they offer landing pads for helicopter parents).

Americans thinking about studying in Britain and Ireland should also be aware of differences in the academic system "across the Pond." Most important: whereas American universities generally require students to sample a variety of fields for two years before choosing a major, British and Irish institutions expect students to identify a field of concentration before they set foot on campus. That's because students take their general education courses in high school. Thus students in Britain and Ireland take only two or three courses at a time, mostly related to their major. American-style distribution requirements are all but unheard of—good news for students who want to get out of those nasty math or foreign language requirements. But keep in mind that since British and Irish students tend to take courses only in subjects that seriously interest them, all classes are taught at a high level, even introductory ones. Moreover, although students get fewer hours in class, they are expected to put in more hours of study per course outside of class. Anyone who wants to change majors after a year or two may encounter difficulty.

Another important academic difference is that British and Irish universities evaluate applicants almost entirely on the basis of academic credentials, with emphasis on demonstrated ability in their field of study. (Only St Andrews does holistic reviews.) No essays about page 236 of your autobiography or need to present yourself as a well-rounded overachiever who will enrich the campus environment. As one administrator put it, "We don't do social engineering." Along with Trinity College Dublin, the top British universities, especially the four "ancient" Scottish universities, are thus a good bet for U.S. students who may have the smarts to do Ivy League work but whose résumés do not include an Olympic medal or building a school in Belize during spring vacation. Standards are high. In response to the COVID-19 pandemic, however, some British and Irish schools have relaxed their SAT and ACT testing requirements for applicants from the United States. Prospective students are advised to consult universities' websites or contact admissions officers directly for the most up-to-date information regarding testing requirements. Aside from SAT and ACT scores, some schools may require scores from AP exams. For the application essay, the British usually ask about commitment to your intended major and why you want to study it. They view American-style personal essays as fluff.

As with Canadian universities, the cost for an American studying at one of the leading Scottish and Irish universities will vary with fluctuating exchange rates, which currently reflect a strong dollar. To complicate matters, tuition and fee levels vary not only across universities but also according to the course of study and academic level within each institution. Total tuition and fees among the five universities described in the *Fiske Guide* range from US $22,000 to more than US $50,000 per year—roughly equivalent to the costs for out-of-state students at flagship public universities in the U.S. but less than the sticker price of many highly selective privates. The downside is that the sticker price is also the final price; academic scholarships are scarce and institutional financial aid all but nonexistent. British and Irish students, along with those from the European Union, generally receive government funding. Federal aid such as Federal Direct Loans and Pell Grants can be transported, but many, if not most, families will find themselves paying the full freight. For a searchable database of the few scholarships available for study in Great Britain, visit the British Council at www.britishcouncil.org/usa. One reason that financially strapped British universities have recently begun showing a greater interest in recruiting U.S. students is that they are a source of much-needed revenue. By and large, the academic bars for U.S. students are slightly lower than for native Brits.

If you are considering a British university, you may be picturing yourself in England, the most populous region of Great Britain that includes London as well as fabled universities Oxford and Cambridge. But here's the rub: the English have a system of higher education that makes degree study impractical in many cases. In England, undergraduate degrees are completed in three years, not four, and students are generally assumed to have completed 13 years of schooling rather than 12. As a result, the most selective English universities are reluctant to admit American high school graduates—some refuse to admit any—and the students who do get in will find themselves navigating a world more appropriate for juniors and seniors in college. One note on terminology: in Britain and Ireland, a program of study is called a "course." The British word for what we call a course is "module."

The University of Cambridge (www.cam.ac.uk) is particularly blunt about "the possible mismatch between the broad liberal arts curriculum of the North American high school and the specialist emphasis of British degree courses." The University of Oxford (www.ox.ac.uk) does offer a glimmer of hope for a select few superachievers arriving with American dollars; Oxford will consider American students who graduate in the top 2 percent of their class, and it has recently stepped up its recruiting efforts in U.S. high schools. In a recent year, it enrolled about 70 U.S. students. Even so, the odds of admission to Oxford are lower than at any college in the U.S., including Harvard. The vast majority of American undergraduates at both Oxford and Cambridge are there for a second bachelor's degree after earning one from an American institution. Students with their hearts set on the Oxbridge institutions should consider them for graduate school, where both welcome Americans (and their dollars) in significant numbers.

Students will hear a similar story at the third-most recognized name in English higher education, the London School of Economics (www.lse.ac.uk), which enrolls about 5,000 undergraduates. The LSE says it will not normally consider U.S. students until they have a year of higher education under their belts. Less selective English institutions are more receptive to Americans, but once again, only those who feel certain of what they would like to study should apply. If you are in this category, there is one potential benefit to an English degree: the three-year degree program will save you a year of tuition bills.

So what to do? One answer is to cast your gaze on Scotland, England's less populous neighbor, where universities offer four-year degrees that are much better suited to the needs of American high school graduates. Scotland, which lies north of England, was an independent nation until 1706 and has its own parliament that exercises considerable power when it comes to domestic policy. It has an illustrious intellectual history and has produced the likes of David Hume, Adam Smith, Rudyard Kipling, Robert Louis Stevenson, J. K. Rowling, and the world's most famous ogre, Shrek. Scotland is more egalitarian in feel than England—less hung up on social class.

The Scots take great pride in their universities, which are central to their national identity and have deep historical ties with American higher education. The American-style liberal arts institution was imported directly from Scotland in the person of John Witherspoon, a graduate of the University of Edinburgh who was lured to the U.S. in 1768 to head Princeton University. With the model of his alma mater in mind, Witherspoon transformed Princeton from a small-time school for ministers into a broad-based institution that taught philosophy, history, geography, science, mathematics, and theology. Like their U.S. counterparts, Scottish universities offer four-year programs; thus, they represent something of a middle ground between the American system and that of Oxford and Cambridge with their three-year, entirely specialized programs. Scottish universities expect early specialization, but there is some room to explore fields outside your major during the first two years. One downside of studying in Scotland is its northern location, which makes for long winter nights. Scotland has also been historically regarded as a "dreich" corner of Britain—a Highland term referring to weather variously described as dull, overcast, drizzly, cold, misty, and miserable, or a combination thereof. Scottish higher education is noted for its four "ancient" universities—Aberdeen, Edinburgh, Glasgow, and St Andrews—each of which is profiled in the pages that follow.

There are seven universities in Ireland, but Trinity College Dublin is by far the most distinguished, and it is the only one that operates on a four-year system for undergraduates. TCD was founded in 1592 by Queen Elizabeth as an Irish counterpart to Oxford and Cambridge to train Anglican clergymen. While TCD follows the Scottish system, its cultural ties remain distinctly English, and graduates who subsequently enroll in Oxford or Cambridge are automatically entitled to an "ad eundem" courtesy degree from the English university. TCD was founded as the

University of Dublin with the expectation that it would serve as "the mother of a university" and other colleges would grow up around it à la Oxbridge. Alas, this never happened, so for all practical purposes, Trinity College Dublin is the University of Dublin. Roman Catholics make up the overwhelming majority of students despite the fact that up until 1972, they needed special permission from church authorities to attend this bastion of Anglican scholarship.

Students applying to UK institutions should generally use the Universities and Colleges Admissions Service (UCAS, www.ucas.com), which functions like the Common Application group in the U.S. The UCAS form asks you to list all your courses and the grades you received in them, as well as your SAT and/or ACT scores. It also requires an essay and a letter of recommendation. Most institutions will accept applications through the spring, though we recommend that you apply by the deadline for British students, January 15. The deadline for applying to Oxford and Cambridge, or to apply to any program in medicine, is October 15 for entrance the following fall. Many institutions have rolling admissions, another reason to apply early. A few institutions—Aberdeen, Glasgow, and St Andrews—now accept the Common Application as an alternative for American students. Applicants to Trinity College Dublin apply directly to the university, which has rolling admissions.

A high proportion of U.S. students currently enrolled in British universities come from families with international connections, such as close relatives living in other countries or diplomat parents, but prior international experience is by no means required. College in Britain is not for the faint of heart, but it can be richly rewarding for those with the initiative to take the plunge. After college in Britain, students will have the skills and savvy to succeed almost anywhere in the world.

University of Aberdeen

Aberdeen, Scotland AB24 3FX UK

Located in Scotland's third largest city, Aberdeen is the most accessible—and least competitive—of the four "ancient" universities. Notable for the flexibility of its curriculum and emphasis on independent learning. Major attractions include engineering, life and health sciences, and anything related to Europe. City of Aberdeen combines charm with the bustle of a small city. Outdoor enthusiasts will love the Scottish Highlands.

The University of Aberdeen was founded in 1495, three years after a certain well-known explorer sailed from Spain to the New (to him) World. Students seeking the flavor of old Europe will not be disappointed. With plenty of cobblestone streets and buildings made of ancient stone (it's the Granite City), the university has a distinctly medieval aura. It offers top-notch academics, a curriculum that is unusually flexible by UK standards, and a slice of life far richer than any U.S. institution can muster. "It's great fun and has a lot of opportunities," says a senior, "both academically and socially."

With a population of 230,000, the port city of Aberdeen is Scotland's third largest city. Once a hub for fishing, shipbuilding, and textiles, it is now a center for the thriving oil extraction business in the North Sea. With two universities—the other is Robert Gordon—it is the educational capital of Northeastern Scotland. Aberdeen is perched at a latitude roughly the same as Juneau, Alaska, but because of the Gulf Stream, winter temperatures are generally milder than those on the East Coast of the United States. December days are short in winter, but sky-gazers are often treated to glimpses of the fabled northern lights.

"We do a lot of group work, and student interaction is really key."

Most university buildings are concentrated in a quiet enclave known as "Old Aberdeen." The campus is crowned, literally, by a 16th-century tower in the shape of an imperial crown. Lightly traveled streets pass through the campus, and the multitude of green lawns and picturesque courtyards are ideal for lounging on

Website: www.abdn.ac.uk
Location: Small City
Public
Total Enrollment: 14,500
Undergraduates: 12,000
Male/Female: 49/51
Financial Aid: N/A
Pell Grant: N/A
Expense: Pub $
Student Loans: N/A
Average Debt: N/A
Applicants: 13,000
Accepted: 27%
Enrolled: N/A
Grad in 6 Years: N/A
Returning Freshmen: N/A
Academics: ✐ ✐ ✐ ✐ ½
Social: ☎ ☎ ☎ ☎
Q of L: ★ ★ ★ ★

(continued)

Admissions: (+44) 1224
272000

Email Address:
ugadmissions@abdn.ac.uk

Strong Programs:
Engineering
Health Sciences
English Literature
Biology
Religious Studies
Environmental Science
International Relations
Politics

sunny days. The university has invested $450 million in infrastructure and facilities in recent years, including the Sir Duncan Rice Library, the Sports Village, and the Aquatics Centre. A $47 million Science Teaching Hub opened in 2021.

Academics at Aberdeen are organized across 12 schools that encompass disciplines in the arts and social sciences, life sciences and medicine, physical sciences, and business. The relative broadness and flexibility of the university's curriculum is more in line with the academic systems of Harvard, Melbourne, Hong Kong, and other top universities around the world than it is with Aberdeen's three "ancient" counterparts in the UK. Students are expected to sample a series of interdisciplinary Sixth Century Courses, such as Science and the Media or Oceans and Society, during their first two years. Other curriculum innovations are designed to encourage students to pursue interests outside their core disciplines—what might be called "electives" in an American context. Popular majors include English literature, biology, religious studies, environmental science, and a joint international relations/politics concentration. Engineering is also strong, especially for programs related to the oil industry. The Centre for Learning and Teaching helps faculty members find ways to enhance the learning experience, while the Student Learning Service helps students develop their academic skills.

With approximately 14,500 undergraduate and graduate students, Aberdeen is a medium-sized university by U.S. standards. "The academic climate at Aberdeen is largely collaborative. We do a lot of group work, and student interaction is really key," says a business major. Courses in the first two years generally consist of lectures supplemented by smaller weekly discussion sections. "In my first year I was taught by a mixture of Ph.D. students and lecturers (professors). In my honours years, my lecturers were leading experts in their fields and widely published," says

> **"In my honours years, my lecturers were leading experts in their fields and widely published."**

a student. Professors typically team-teach introductory "modules," with each covering the topics that are his or her specialty. As in other Scottish universities, students generally take only three subjects at a time in the first two years, with extensive reading and research outside of class generally taken for granted. "Often we are expected to come to class prepared to discuss certain topics, but given no minimum reading assignment. The professor gives out a list of selected readings from which we can choose," explains a history major. Grades are typically determined by end-of-the-term evaluations with few intermediate assignments. At the end of their second year, students must typically pass exams in order to advance to "honors level," the equivalent of the junior and senior years of college in the States. Upper-level science students typically spend long hours in the lab. One nice feature: there is generally no limit to the number of students who can enroll in a particular course, thereby giving students the freedom to sign up for anything that strikes their fancy.

Students are expected to sample a series of interdisciplinary Sixth Century Courses, such as Science and the Media, during their first two years.

Overall, about 56 percent of undergraduates hail from Scotland, 13 percent come from the rest of the UK, and 30 percent arrive from more than 100 different countries. "We have a very international student body," says one senior. The political climate on campus is described as conservative and relatively subdued. Upon their arrival at the university, students partake of Freshers Week, when student organizations sponsor informational meetings. Aberdeen is a selective institution for U.S. students, though less so than the other "ancient" universities.

On-campus housing at Aberdeen is varied and guaranteed to all first-year students who apply before the deadline. A majority of the international students live in single rooms in the recently refurbished Hillhead Student Village, a complex of houses and flats that is about a 20-minute walk from the campus. Students may elect catered rooms (two meals per day) or self-catering, wherein they cook their own food with kitchen facilities generally located down the hall from the rooms. Many students choose to move off campus after their first year, and a variety of housing options are available near the campus. Only a few students own cars, as the university is within easy walking distance of the city center and the North Sea and is on a regular bus route.

"Social life is great," raves one student. "There's always something going on." Another adds, "We have around 200 societies and sports clubs, and most students are involved in at least one." Since the drinking age in Britain is 18, social life at Aberdeen entails relaxed, legal consumption. You may find yourself doing what Britons call "the pub crawl," which means sampling the refreshment of several pubs before heading home in the wee hours. Popular campus social events include periodic formal balls, to which the men wear kilts and the women wear evening gowns. Perhaps the biggest event of the year is the Torcher's Parade, which is held every spring and features floats made by various student organizations. Sports are mainly for playing, rather than watching, with more than 50 sports clubs at students' disposal. Individual sports rather than team intramurals are the staple of weekend warriors, and students can purchase passes for various athletic facilities, depending on their interests.

Upon their arrival at the university, students partake of Freshers Week, when student organizations sponsor informational meetings.

Aberdeen is described by one student as "a fantastic college town!" The city center offers a variety of pubs and clubs to suit all tastes, as well as inexpensive cinemas, music, and theater. The city has plenty of old-world charm, and outdoorsy types will love the dramatic scenery that is everywhere in northeast Scotland. Picturesque cliffs overlooking the North Sea are within an

"We have around 200 societies and sports clubs."

easy bus or train ride. Fifteen miles south of Aberdeen is breathtaking Dunnottar Castle, a 14th-century ruin set high on a rocky outcrop that was the set for Mel Gibson's film rendition of *Hamlet*. Within a half-hour ride inland is the edge of the legendary Scottish Highlands. Famous castles abound in all directions, including the royal family's summer hideaway, Balmoral. For the Scottish version of the big city, Glasgow and Edinburgh are close by, and two hours on a plane will get you to most places in Western Europe.

Though Aberdeen may lack some of the conveniences of home, most Americans are happy they came. "Between classes on a sunny day, students will buy something from the bakery and sit on the grass in the midst of 500-year-old buildings and cobblestone streets. It is such a carefree atmosphere with that special touch of Scottish tradition," says a satisfied history major. If you're the kind of person who likes to meet new people and learn about different cultures, you might thrive on the Aberdeen air.

Overlaps

Dundee, University of Edinburgh, University of Glasgow, University of St Andrews, Harvard

If You Apply To ›

Aberdeen: Rolling admissions. Accepts the Common Application with supplement. Apply to particular program. Please consult Aberdeen's website for the most up-to-date information regarding standardized test requirements.

University of Edinburgh

Old College, South Bridge, Edinburgh, Scotland EH8 9JS UK

With close ties to the city that created it in the 16th century, Edinburgh is the most prestigious of Scotland's major research universities. Combines deep roots in Scottish culture and history with the cosmopolitan flavor and cultural riches of a sophisticated capital city. Competitive admissions for top British students but better odds for Americans with Ivy-level academic credentials. More diverse student body than St Andrews.

Website: www.ed.ac.uk
Location: City Center
Public
Total Enrollment: 33,090
Undergraduates: 22,950
Male/Female: 38/62
Financial Aid: N/A
Pell Grant: N/A
Expense: Pub $
Student Loans: N/A
Average Debt: N/A
Applicants: 60,983
Accepted: 46%
Enrolled: 23%
Grad in 6 Years: 96%
Returning Freshmen: 95%
Academics: ✑ ✑ ✑
Social: ☎ ☎ ☎
Q of L: ★ ★ ★
Admissions: (+44) 131 650 4296
Email Address: international .enquiries@ed.ac.uk

Strong Programs:
Economics
Philosophy
English Literature
International Relations
Veterinary Medicine
International Business
Law
Computer Science

The largest and best-known of the "ancient" Scottish universities, the University of Edinburgh is part and parcel of Scotland's most vibrant urban center. The city of Edinburgh is home to the Scottish Parliament, the national museum, abundant historical sites, winding streets, and countless restaurants and pubs. The university, like the city, has an unmistakable international feel, including long-standing connections across the pond. In addition to the likes of Charles Darwin and J. K. Rowling, eminent graduates include two signatories of the U.S. Declaration of Independence, Benjamin Rush and John Witherspoon.

Edinburgh is unique among the major Scottish universities in that it was founded (in 1583) by a municipality rather than under religious auspices. Its buildings are spread throughout the city, which, despite having about 525,000 residents, is really an overgrown town. The two main campus areas are known as the Central Area, home to George Square, the main library, and humanities courses, and King's Buildings, housing science and engineering courses. Public transport is good, but just about everything is within walking distance. The older university buildings are Georgian and tend to bear names from the Scottish Enlightenment (David Hume and Dugald Stewart), while more modern ones date to the '60s and '70s. The recently expanded and renovated Health and Wellbeing Centre operates as a hub for student health, counseling, residential life, and other services.

The university is organized around three colleges: Arts, Humanities, and Social Sciences; Science and Engineering; and Medicine and Veterinary. Edinburgh has traditionally been strong in the sciences, and historical ties to economists like Adam Smith and philosophers like John Locke have contributed to strong programs in those fields. English literature, international relations, veterinary medicine, international business, and law attract a lot of U.S. students, and computer science, linguistics, sociology, and history (Scottish and otherwise) are strong. Unlike in the U.S., the programs in veterinary medicine and medicine are five- and six-year programs, respectively, for undergraduates. Veterinary graduates can go on to practice immediately in the U.S. Research opportunities are available for undergraduates, including summer placements in animal biology through the Roslin Institute. Edinburgh also offers some 200 study abroad programs at leading universities around the world.

> **"All the work is independent even from the beginning of your first year."**

Applicants apply to study a particular subject, such as physics or English literature, but unlike the situation in the leading English universities, it is possible to make changes once enrolled. There is no core curriculum, and no one has to endure a class on science or any other subject in which they have little interest. Students normally take three courses for each of their first two years in a variety of fields and then concentrate on one or two subjects the last two years. Most courses involve a combination of lectures, which are taught by full professors, and weekly tutorials, or groups of 10 to 20 students led by tutors. Professors and tutors alike get generally high ratings from students. One student notes, "The faculty is very international."

Coursework throughout the year mostly involves essays, with final exams in late April or May accounting for most of the final grade. In their final year, all undergraduates complete a research project or thesis. The academic system is built around self-study. "As an American student, I find the academics very rigorous in comparison to my friends' at American universities, because all the work is independent even from the beginning of your first year," explains an English literature major. The academic pressure at Edinburgh is said to be intense, with little grade inflation, and although faculty members do not view their role as seeking out students who may need help, "professors and tutors are more than happy to help out when you ask," says one American denizen.

> "Professors and tutors are more than happy to help out when you ask."

Edinburgh is the leading destination for top-performing Scottish students, who face tighter admissions standards than North Americans. Twenty-nine percent of undergraduates hail from Scotland, 26 percent from elsewhere in the United Kingdom, 13 percent from the European Union, and 32 percent from other foreign countries. There are roughly 650 regular American undergrads and 600 postgrads, as well as more than 800 study abroad students. Edinburgh students tend to be more middle class than their counterparts at St Andrews, which is more upper class. Edinburgh is slightly more expensive than the other "ancient" Scottish universities but a bargain compared to the Ivies in the U.S. The university makes scholarships available to international students, and American students can use their U.S. student loans to attend. Given the nature of the student body, there is plenty of discussion of global issues. "Scotland is inherently left-leaning as a country," reports a language student, and recent student activism has focused on diversity, inclusion, and climate action.

Unlike in the U.S., the programs in veterinary medicine and medicine are five- and six-year programs, respectively, for undergraduates.

About a quarter of undergraduates live in university housing, and Edinburgh guarantees housing to all international first-year students. Many American and international students live in Pollock Halls, a collection of houses with mostly single rooms that are centered around a common cafeteria. Accommodations at Pollack are catered, meaning that residents get 14 meals per week in the cafeteria—breakfast and dinner during the week and brunch on the weekends. Students can also choose self-catered options in which they make their own cooking arrangements. Self-catered flats (apartments) generally consist of three to five students, each with an individual room, sharing a large common living and kitchen area. All university accommodations are described as clean and well maintained. Most students move off campus after their first year; the Student Union Advice Place will help you find a flat. "Edinburgh is a very competitive city when it comes to flat pricing," cautions a second-year American student, "and sometimes the cost of living for international students can be expensive." Cafeteria food is described as "fine but not that diverse," although several cheap cafés nearby offer alternatives. Students report that both the university and the city are safe: "Edinburgh has always made me feel secure," says one.

> "First-years tend to explore club life in the city center."

Since the university is so closely tied to the city, it's no surprise that social life takes place both on and off campus. "First-years tend to explore club life in the city center," explains an American student, "and as they get into their second and third years, the partying transfers homeward into flat parties." Two student unions, Teviot and Potterrow, offer cafés, coffee shops, and bars; on weekend nights, a large, open study area in Potterrow is converted into a nightclub for dancing. Frequent comedy nights, student productions, and pub crawls are other options. Since the drinking age is 18, the university has no school policy on the

Most courses involve a combination of lectures and weekly tutorials, or groups of 10 to 20 students led by tutors.

Various societies sponsor weekly or monthly ceilidhs (pronounced "kaylees") or traditional Scottish Dance Nights.

serving of alcohol. The city of Edinburgh offers its own menu of ancient and contemporary traditions. The Beltane Fire Festival, with roots in pagan times, celebrates the arrival of spring, and every August, the city is host to the huge Fringe Festival, which draws artists and spectators from all over the world. Thanks to affordable trains and low-cost airlines like Ryanair and easyJet, trips throughout Britain and all over Europe are easy to arrange. "You get good at traveling," says one American undergrad.

The Edinburgh University Student Association and the Edinburgh University Sports Union combine to offer what one American describes as "just about every sport, charity, or special interest society/club conceivable." A fair is held during Welcome Week to give first-year students a sense of the options. Does the Chocolate Lovers Society sound tasty? Edinburgh's sports clubs, which compete against other Scottish and European universities in sports like rugby, soccer, and rowing, do well, but compared to varsity sports in the U.S., one student says, "the competition is laid-back." Most attention goes to the "very strong and popular intramural sports program, which, depending on the sport, has quite a high caliber of play." Many of the teams are co-ed, and there are eight levels of rugby. The Centre for Sport and Exercise boasts sports equipment, studios, weight rooms, a climbing wall, and archery ranges. In all, Edinburgh hosts more than 280 societies and 64 sports clubs.

> **"The ethereal castle and the wee pubs constantly remind me where I am."**

Much of the fun of going to college in Scotland comes from taking part in centuries-old traditions, of which Edinburgh has an abundance. Various societies and degree programs sponsor weekly or monthly ceilidhs (pronounced "kaylees") or traditional Scottish Dance Nights. Robert Burns Night is a big deal, as is Guy Fawkes Night on November 5, when students set off fireworks throughout the city. Whereas American commencements feature students moving the tassel of their mortarboards from one side to the other, Edinburgh places a common cap on the head of each student in turn that contains a piece of the trousers of John Knox and a NASA emblem that accompanied an Edinburgh graduate on a space mission.

American students, especially those who are self-motivated, tend to do well at Edinburgh. "They are smart and well-traveled and tend to be independent thinkers," observes a faculty member. A philosophy and English literature major comments, "The university's culture is progressive, engaged, academic, and open." Another American transplant hails the fact that Edinburgh is "incredibly international but still Scottish," adding that "the bagpipes playing in the city streets, the ethereal castle, and the wee pubs constantly remind me where I am."

Overlaps

University of Glasgow, University of St Andrews, King's College London, Oxford, Cambridge, UC Berkeley, Columbia, UCLA

If You Apply To ›

Edinburgh: Rolling admissions. Does not accept the Common Application. Apply to particular program. Please consult Edinburgh's website for the most up-to-date information regarding standardized test requirements.

University of Glasgow

University Gardens, Glasgow, Lanarkshire, Scotland G12 8QQ UK

A major urban research university located in the bohemian section of a friendly working-class city. U of Glasgow is slightly smaller than U of Edinburgh and its atmosphere somewhat more laid-back. The West End is student-friendly, with lots of cafés and shops. Glasgow is a financial, cultural, and shopping center also known for its nightlife. Locals claim "you can have more fun at a Glasgow funeral than at an Edinburgh wedding." Glasgow students get the point.

The second oldest of Scotland's major universities (after St Andrews), the University of Glasgow shares the history and culture of Scotland's largest city. Glasgow (population 635,000) was a major center of the 18th-century Scottish Enlightenment and the 19th-century Industrial Revolution, and it now ranks as Britain's largest financial center after London. The University of Glasgow was founded in 1451 with quarters in Glasgow Cathedral before moving to its own main campus in Gilmorehill in the city's West End in 1870. In contrast to the elitist traditions of the other "ancient" British universities, Glasgow pioneered in serving the educational needs of the growing urban and commercial classes and in 1894 became the first Scottish university to grant degrees to women.

Not surprisingly for a place with more than five centuries of history, the dominant architectural style on campus is brownish neo-Gothic, with a healthy mix of Victorian thrown in. While other sections of Glasgow retain the feel of a hardscrabble industrial area, the West End is a bohemian residential area with an abundance of restaurants, cafés, and shops catering to the college crowd. "The area is very student-oriented, with plenty of venues offering student discounts," reports one student. The city center, a 15-minute walk from the university, offers a multitude of historical sites and world-class museums as

> **"There is an air of camaraderie between students."**

well as the best shopping in Britain outside London. Kelvingrove Park and the Botanical Gardens are down the street from the university's main gate. The university has embarked on a $1.2 billion development plan that will double the 15-acre campus footprint by 2026. The first phase of the ambitious plan is underway; the $115 million Smith Learning Hub opened in 2019. New business and engineering schools and science facilities are on the way.

Students describe the academic climate as balanced and supportive. "There is an air of camaraderie between students," comments an archaeology major. "Some courses are more competitive than others, but overall it's not nearly as intense as I perceive some U.S. schools to be." But another warns, "Specific assignments aren't given. You're told which books go with the course, and you'd better read them on your own!" The workload is said to increase noticeably in later years, but because students apply to study in a particular field, they "rarely find themselves in courses they would prefer to avoid." All undergraduates complete a dissertation or research project based on independent research. First-year students go through a Fresher's Week, with tours of the university, concerts, and other events, and special orientation is also provided for international students.

Glasgow is the only Scottish university with the full range of both professional and academic offerings. The university is divided into four colleges: Arts; Social Sciences; Science and Engineering; and Medical, Veterinary, & Life Sciences. Befitting the alma mater of physicist Lord Kelvin (of absolute temperature fame), the sciences are strong, notably veterinary medicine, nursing, and geography. The economics department is proud that it turned out Adam Smith, and history is well regarded. English language and literature is a traditional strength, and Glasgow maintains the only department of Scottish literature anywhere. Eastern European languages like Czech and Polish are specialties. Newer offerings include an international relations program and an undergraduate degree in common law for students who intend to practice law outside Scotland. About half of the 450 full-time U.S. undergraduates major in veterinary medicine; a five-year undergraduate degree is accredited by the Veterinary Medical Association. Other popular majors tend to be psychology, business (especially accounting and finance), politics, history, and English literature.

Students describe faculty members as respected and knowledgeable. "Many professors practice in their fields daily, so they teach us not only the theory but also the practical application," explains a veterinary medicine major. Lectures are offered by full professors, and tutorials of about 15 students are occasionally handled by graduate students. Twenty-five percent of Glasgow undergraduates take advantage of semester-long or yearlong study abroad programs, especially through the Erasmus program, which allows students to take courses at European universities. A year of study abroad is mandatory for foreign language students during their third year.

"You're told which books go with the course, and you'd better read them on your own!"

According to a sociology major, Glasgow students are "hip, hardworking, welcoming, and fun-loving." Consistent with the university's cosmopolitan setting and traditions, the student body is a diverse lot with regard to nationality, race, religion, and socioeconomic backgrounds. Twenty-three percent of undergraduates are international, hailing from the U.S., the European Union, and dozens of other countries; 63 percent are native to Scotland, and the balance come from elsewhere in the UK. Support services for international students are strong. "You don't have an exclusive student body," reports a sophomore. "Dealing and working with people from different backgrounds is the norm." The university offers a fourth-year tuition waiver as a merit scholarship for qualified international students, including those from the U.S., and it also accepts U.S. federal loans, as determined by the FAFSA.

Freshmen usually live in university housing, which is not on campus but spread throughout the northwest sections of the city, and then move into readily available independent housing in later years. Overall, 17 percent of undergraduates live in the dorms, which are generally comfortable and well maintained; international students are guaranteed housing. As for dining, only one of the seven residence halls offers catered food, and it is located away from the main campus.

"It's easy to get to visit Europe while studying in Glasgow with cheap flights and accommodations."

The others are self-catered, which means that students cook for themselves (and save money) or savor the offerings of dining facilities sprinkled throughout the campus. "The on-campus dining is very good, and they have a range of foods from Indian to Scottish on various days," reports one denizen. Students describe campus security as good. "I always feel safe on campus," says an archaeology major. The university's Let's Talk campaign aims to educate the community on issues of sexual assault and provide resources to survivors.

Social life is equally divided between on- and off-campus activities. Glasgow offers an abundance of quality restaurants, clubs, and pubs. There are plenty of ceilidhs (pronounced "kaylees") or Gaelic social gatherings, and the city sponsors an International Comedy Festival each March. Glasgow has a vigorous music scene that hosts an average of 130 music events every week. Much of the on-campus social life revolves around the two student-run university unions, the Glasgow University Union (GUU) and the Queen Margaret Union (QMU), which host student organizations, provide dining and social activities, and, of course, have their own bars. Since most students are above the drinking age of 18, underage imbibing is a nonissue. GUU favors sports, debates, and formal dances, while QMU is big on live music. One popular event is GUU's Daft Friday, a black-tie affair at the end of the first term where the entire building is elaborately decorated around a secret theme.

The Student Representative Council sponsors an annual Raising and Giving week to aid volunteer organizations and raise awareness of volunteer opportunities. Social activism tends to be most vigorous when the issue involves cuts to the university budget and increases in tuition levels, but there are plenty of student groups organized around issues such as the environment, gender equality, and LGBTQ rights. Travel is a major attraction of studying in Scotland. "It's easy to get to visit Europe while studying in Glasgow with cheap flights and accommodations," reports one student. Loch Lomond, a 45-minute drive, offers watersports, hiking, and camping.

Intercollegiate debating is taken seriously, and the university has won the world championship several times. A majority of students belong to the Glasgow University Sports Association, and more than 4,000 students play in 50 sports clubs. Competitive team sports include field hockey, rugby, soccer, basketball, American football, cricket, and many others, and recreational clubs are available for everything from cycling to skydiving to surfing. The only athletic rivalry of any consequence in town is the impassioned (to put it mildly) off-campus competition between the two Glasgow soccer clubs, Celtic (Roman Catholic) and the Rangers (Protestant). A student warns, "It's better not to get involved, as the games are just staging grounds for sectarian hatred. Much of the city's police funding goes to monitoring these violent affairs."

The city of Glasgow is shedding its rough reputation, and undergrads describe their experience living and studying in the West End as rewarding. One American sums up her experience as follows: "Glasgow offers a good mix of academics and fun. It's a highly rated school with many good departments, not too competitive, and has all types of students. And other than the weather, Glasgow is a great city to live in."

Overlaps

University of Edinburgh, University of Dundee, University of Aberdeen, University of St Andrews, University of Manchester, King's College London, Boston University, NYU

If You Apply To ›

Glasgow: Rolling admissions. Accepts the Common Application with supplement. Please consult Glasgow's website for the most up-to-date information regarding standardized test requirements.

University of St Andrews

St Andrews, Scotland KY16 9AX UK

The most international of Scotland's four "ancient" universities and the most popular overseas degree destination in the world for U.S. students. Small by British standards and comparable in feel and stature to Brown, St Andrews has pulled even with Oxford and Cambridge in UK university rankings. Major drawing cards range across English literature, international relations, history, the sciences, and modern languages. St Andrews is inseparable from the town, which boasts the famed "Old Course." With more than 600 years to gestate, traditions reign supreme.

Harvard likes to brag about the fact that it was founded way back in 1636. Think that's old? Try 1413, the date Pope Benedict XIII issued a Papal Bull recognizing the University of St Andrews as Scotland's first university and the third in the English-speaking world. Set in an ancient town on the North Sea opposite Norway, St Andrews is an ideal spot for adventuresome Americans who want a world-class

Website: www.st-andrews.ac.uk
Location: Small Town
Public
Total Enrollment: 10,120

More so than in the United States, the onus is on the students to keep current with their rigorous workload.

education and an introduction to life outside North America. It now numbers roughly 1,600 Americans (16 percent of the student body), with the number on the rise. Success here requires a go-getter mentality. Support services are available, but students on this side of the Atlantic are accustomed to being treated like adults. "They don't hold your hand," says one U.S. student.

St Andrews is the only institution in the *Fiske Guide* whose most prominent landmark is the spot where a student was burned at the stake. In 1528, a Protestant reformer named Patrick Hamilton fell victim to a prolonged burning imposed by the local archbishop. Tradition deems that if you step on the stones that mark the spot where he was martyred, you will fail your final exams, unless you submerge yourself in the North Sea just before dawn the first day of May as part of a tradition called the May Dip. Academic buildings are interspersed through the town's narrow medieval streets, and for all practical purposes, says one student, "The university *is* the town." Buildings are constructed of ancient stone and include the ruins of a 13th-century castle and a cathedral. Narrow alleys, called "wynds" by the Scots, lead to secluded gardens and courtyards that add to the old-world charm. A number of academic buildings are perched on cliffs overlooking the North Sea, and white beaches are a two-minute walk from some of the dorms.

"The university *is* the town."

Though more flexible than most British universities, St Andrews offers less latitude to explore a variety of subjects than U.S. institutions and so is best suited to those who arrive with clear academic goals in mind. Students typically take three courses, or "modules," per semester in each of their first two years and then opt for a single or double honors program in the final two years. (The course structure and/or number of class hours varies for students in the sciences, medicine, and arts and divinity.) "Pick your courses carefully," counsels one U.S. student. "You can't major in something you haven't taken the first year." Modules generally consist of three lectures per week with 100 or more students and a tutorial with 10 to 20, while honors-level courses are generally taught in seminar format. Fewer courses means less time in class but also significant outside reading and individual work. Modules typically end with papers or exams that account for most of the grade.

More so than in the United States, the onus is on the students to keep current with their rigorous workload and seek help from faculty when necessary. Nevertheless, the faculty gets high marks, and a modern history and Russian major says, "You are being taught by academics leading in their fields, and thus they place high expectations on their students." Academic and personal support is also available from Student Services, wardens (RAs) in the residence halls, and ramped-up career services that are, according to a school official, working with American companies to ensure that "U.S. students are returning to the States as competitive in the job market as their peers who studied in the U.S. are."

"You are being taught by academics leading in their fields."

Signature offerings at St Andrews include international relations, classics, art history, geography, economics, and physics. Psychology (especially neuroscience), English literature, history, and modern languages are strong, and the university is a world leader in the study of international terrorism. The most popular majors include medicine, international relations, English, history, and economics and finance. Americans at St Andrews tend to cluster in a few departments, notably psychology and international relations. Standards in foreign language are higher than in the United States, an opportunity but also a challenge. A new joint degree in Chinese studies allows students to study Chinese culture and language in combination with a second major in one of 14 fields, ranging from modern history to film studies. Students in the International Honours joint-degree program spend two years at William & Mary in Virginia and two years at St Andrews and earn degrees in classical studies, economics, English, film studies, history, or international relations from both institutions. Fifteen percent of undergraduates study abroad during their time at St Andrews.

"In general, students at St Andrews are very open-minded and happy to share ideas," says a history major. St Andrews is one of the world's most international universities, with roughly 31 percent of its students from Scotland, 28 percent from elsewhere in the UK, and 41 percent from the rest of the world, including sizable contingents from Scandinavia, Eastern Europe, Asia, the Middle East, and, of course, the U.S. In fact, Americans represent the largest international group and are typically given a warm welcome, students say. The international melting pot seems to work, although the upper-middle-class background of many English students lends a more conservative tenor to the campus than some Americans might expect—as is generally true of top universities in the UK. "St Andrews feels preppy but inclusive," muses an American third-year student, "and the endless string of social events tends to include things like formal balls, sailing races, and charity polo matches."

St Andrews is inviting enough to have attracted the likes of Prince William and Catherine, Princess of Wales (a.k.a. Kate Middleton), who met there. While it is competitive for European students, who must be in the top 10th academically, it is more accessible for U.S. students who have the brains to make it into the Ivies but can't also throw a football or play a Liszt concerto. Many of the Americans at St Andrews arrive with an international orientation, including "diplobrats" whose parents have worked in international organizations such as the World Bank or the State Department. Tuition varies depending on the course, but the bill for a year at St Andrews is likely to be roughly $36,000, depending on the exchange rate. The university now fixes rates for each incoming class so that tuition won't increase over a student's four years.

> **"Social events [tend] to include things like formal balls, sailing races, and charity polo matches."**

Housing is guaranteed for first-year students only, and students can request a single or shared room. Forty-one percent of students reside in university housing; those who do choose between the university meal plan or self-catering, in which they use kitchens in the dorms to prepare their own food. Catered halls are the most central and ancient, and students give the food generally positive reviews. Meals are served at specified times with standard portions, so don't expect the glitzy food courts or all-you-can-eat service typical in the States. After their first year, students generally move to one of the many flats (apartments) in town, which can be expensive. "There is a bit of a scramble for flats in February, but most students are able to find good accommodations," reports an international relations and French major.

Given the symbiosis of town and gown, gathering with friends in local pubs is a favorite activity on weekends. "Parties are thrown by halls of residence and the student union," adds a computer science major. A peek inside the student union reveals something never seen on a U.S. campus: a fully equipped bar with, of course, an ample array of scotch. The drinking age is 18 in Britain, and St Andrews boasts 18 pubs. Though there may not be more alcohol than at an American institution, it is certainly more out in the open and thus less of an issue. Black-tie balls and fashion shows are also staples, as are ceilidhs (pronounced "kaylees"), which feature traditional Scottish dancing akin to square dancing. Like other Scottish universities, St Andrews offers "a society for everything you can think of," says a student. Interested in philosophical debate? A cappella singing? Belly dancing? Harry Potter? Stargazing from the university observatory? Then there's a society just waiting for

Americans at St Andrews tend to cluster in a few departments, notably psychology and international relations.

St Andrews is inviting enough to have attracted the likes of Prince William and Catherine, Princess of Wales (a.k.a. Kate Middleton).

you. The St Andrews debating society was founded in 1793 and continues to do well in international competitions. Political activism is muted, but the annual Charities Campaign raises £100,000 a year for local charities.

As befitting a 600-year-old institution, St Andrews is rife with traditions. Red gowns, once the student uniform, are only worn on special occasions, but pubs are still forbidden to serve anyone wearing one. The aforementioned May Dip, aimed at purging oneself of academic bad luck, has roots in pagan times. One student explains that during Raisin Weekend in October, first-year students "equipped with multiple cans of shaving foam and dressed up in costume are taken by their adopted academic parents (older students who will take the first-years under their wing) to a massive shaving foam fight in one of the school squares." Students emerging from their last exam are greeted by their friends and doused with buckets of cold water.

During Raisin Weekend in October, first-year students have a massive shaving foam fight in one of the school squares.

The nearest road-trip destination is the medium-sized city of Dundee, about 20 minutes away, which offers shops, nightclubs, and movie theaters. "The public transport links in town are really good for students to get around and visit different places in Scotland," notes an English major. Scotland's two largest cities, Edinburgh and Glasgow, are about an hour away, and for outdoorsy types, the legendary Scottish Highlands are within easy reach. The Student Association helps with overseas travel.

Soccer, a.k.a. football, is the national sport, and students congregate to watch pro teams in the pubs or on the big-screen TV at the union. Rugby, tennis, golf, soccer, rowing, and water polo are among the school's most competitive sports teams, although these draw fewer spectators than do varsity sports in the U.S.— "you don't have 40,000 screaming fans," notes one

"St Andrews is a modern institution set in a medieval past."

student. Students tend to be much more enthusiastic about their "hall sport" competitions (the equivalent of intramurals in the U.S.), in sports ranging from rugby and ultimate Frisbee to shinty, a violent Scottish mix of field hockey and lacrosse. Students can also join the sports center, which has recently been renovated and upgraded with top-of-the-line facilities and equipment. The fabled Old Course, where golf was invented in the 1500s, offers student discounts, but the sport is not as popular among students here as one might assume.

"St Andrews is a modern institution set in a medieval past," comments an ancient history major. "Students still embrace their gowns, walk the cathedral, and hang out on the beach below the castle." Although St Andrews comes the closest of any of the Scottish universities to having the feel of a liberal arts college, this is not the United States. Those who come here must be ready to adjust to a different way of life, and the tight identification of the university and the town can eventually make for a bit of claustrophobia. But these are small prices to pay for the richness of living abroad among the best and brightest from all corners of the globe—and St Andrews delivers it all against a hauntingly beautiful backdrop that will remain forever etched in the minds of all who come here.

Overlaps

University of Edinburgh, Brown, University College London, Durham University, Oxford, University of Glasgow, University of Warwick, Cambridge

If You Apply To ›

St Andrews: Rolling admissions. Accepts the Common Application with supplement. Please consult St Andrews's website for the most up-to-date information regarding standardized test requirements.

Trinity College Dublin

College Green, Dublin 2, Ireland

The oldest four-year university in Ireland, Trinity College Dublin belongs to a peer group consisting of Oxbridge and the four "ancient" Scottish universities—albeit with a more European feel. Trinity combines rich academic offerings across the curriculum with life in one of the world's most vibrant capital cities. Traditions abound, academic and otherwise. Where else do honors students reportedly get the right to graze their sheep on the college green?

Founded in 1592 by Queen Elizabeth as an Irish Protestant counterpart to Oxford and Cambridge, Trinity College Dublin, the University of Dublin is the largest and most distinguished of the seven universities in Ireland and one of the strongest anywhere. Although best known for its offerings in the humanities and social sciences, Trinity is strong across the curriculum, including in new specialties such as nanoscience. The university has produced enough distinguished alumni to fill an encyclopedia (Jonathan Swift, Oscar Wilde, Edmund Burke, Samuel Beckett, Ernest Walton, Mary Robinson, and Sally Rooney for starters), and its students bathe in centuries-old academic traditions while enjoying life in one of Europe's most vibrant capital cities.

Trinity College Dublin occupies a 47-acre oasis in the heart of Dublin, within easy walking distance of the national museums, government buildings, and other major cultural attractions. "When you pass under the archway you move from the bustle of the city to a traditional liberal arts setting, complete with rugby and cricket pitches," explains a sophomore. Most of the central buildings are built of light gray Georgian stone, including its iconic Campanile. The college's Old Library, with its oak-ceilinged Long Room, is home to the Book of Kells, an illuminated Latin manuscript of the Gospels that draws a steady stream of tourists onto the campus. The library, which has

> **"[Trinity] invests some of its best faculty toward teaching undergraduate freshmen."**

been in constant use since 1732, will temporarily close in fall 2023 for a three-year, $95 million restoration. Another library bears the name of James Ussher, the university's first student, who went on to make a name for himself by devising a Biblically based calculation that the world started at 6:00 p.m. on October 22, 4004 BC. A freshman describes Dublin as "a fantastic city in all regards," but cautions, "Let's not go overboard. There is also a lot of rain."

Trinity is organized around three schools in each of the traditional areas: arts, humanities, and social sciences; engineering, math, and science; and health sciences. Unlike other universities in Ireland, Trinity offers a four-year undergraduate program parallel to the four "ancient" universities in Scotland. There are no "core" courses that everyone is required to take, although all students must complete an undergraduate research project in their final year in order to graduate. The college has traditionally been best known for its English and literature courses, along with history, political science, European studies, and international studies. Mathematics and the sciences are also strong, especially molecular biology, genetics, immunology, nanoscience, and chemistry. The Trinity Biomedical Sciences Institute is a state-of-the-art research facility, while the Trinity Long Room Hub accommodates research in the arts and humanities. The BESS program (Business, Economics, and Social Studies) and global business are particularly popular among American students, who are also beginning to pursue the sciences in greater numbers. Trinity has a strong interdisciplinary culture, and the Trinity Elective option encourages students to exercise their curiosity in a module (course) outside their specialty, such

Website: www.tcd.ie
Location: City Center
Public
Total Enrollment: 19,075
Undergraduates: 13,274
Male/Female: 40/60
Financial Aid: N/A
Pell Grant: N/A
Expense: Pub $
Student Loans: N/A
Average Debt: N/A
Applicants: 22,564
Accepted: 14%
Enrolled: 74%
Grad in 6 Years: 95%
Returning Freshmen: 90%
Academics: ✍ ✍ ✍ ✍ ✍
Social: 🐿 🐿 🐿 🐿
Q of L: ★ ★ ★ ★
Admissions: (+353) 1 896 4500
Email Address: academic .registry@tcd.ie

Strong Programs:
English Literature
History
Political Science
European Studies
International Studies
Mathematics
Molecular Biology
Global Business

as film studies or globalization. An incubation program for student-run companies encourages an entrepreneurial spirit.

Trinity's academic climate is described as relaxed, and a history and economics double major says, "The vast majority of students are open to collaborative learning and prove helpful to each other outside of the lectures and seminars." The academic year runs for 11 weeks each in the fall and spring, followed by three to four weeks of exams. Students accumulate 60 credits per year through modules offering various numbers of credits, with strong weight given to final exams, although the balance of continuous and final assessment varies by module. A final-year capstone project brings 20 credits. "The major difference between Trinity and American universities is that the onus falls much more on the students," says a junior. Lectures coupled with weekly tutorials are common the first two years but then give way to small seminars the last two years. A junior observes that Trinity "invests some of its best faculty toward teaching undergraduate freshmen." Each entering student is assigned a peer mentor and a personal academic tutor, not one of his or her professors, who will be available for personal, academic, and professional advice over four years and, if necessary, become an advocate. American students can also sign up for the weeklong Trinity Smart-Start Program to help them get the hang of the university and its setting.

The BESS program (Business, Economics, and Social Studies) and global business are particularly popular among American students.

Trinity students are encouraged to take advantage of the nearly 300 foreign study options, including those with leading institutions in Australia, Canada, India, China, and Singapore; 30 percent take part. Trinity participates in the Erasmus Program with other European universities and has special relationships in the U.S. with such prestigious institutions as Brown, Chicago, and Columbia. Dublin serves as the European headquarters for several major companies, such as Google, Airbnb, Microsoft, and Meta, which frequently recruit students for internships, summer jobs, and postgraduation careers.

"[Students are] very academic, well-read, and very inclusive, especially toward the LGBTQ community."

As the top university in Ireland, Trinity is highly competitive academically. Twenty-six percent of undergraduates are international students from more than 120 nations, with the U.S. and Canada making up the largest group. Many U.S. students hail from elite public high schools and prep schools, and have traveled abroad. Trinity is an ideal option for top students who are strong enough academically to qualify for Ivy League schools but who neglected to star on the soccer team or do community service in Bujumbura. Trinity draws heavily from New York and New England, but it is attracting an increasing number of Texans and Californians who find access to the University of California frustrating. A neuroscience major describes Trinity students as "very academic, well-read, and very inclusive, especially toward the LGBTQ community."

Dublin serves as the European headquarters for several major companies, such as Google and Microsoft, which frequently recruit students.

Trinity participates in the U.S. federal student loan program and offers a number of scholarships, including one for U.S. students. All students can try their luck in a series of competitive tests that sophomores can take just after Christmas known as the Foundation Scholarship Exams. More than 400 students typically sit for the exams, with about 90 becoming either "scholars" or "foundation scholars." Scholars become members of the university's governing board. Other benefits include five years of free or heavily discounted tuition, free accommodations and evening meals, and, best of all, the rumor goes, the privileges of carrying a sword into an exam and grazing their sheep on the campus green.

"All of Dublin's nightclubs, bars, and pubs are pretty much a stone's throw away."

One drawback of Trinity's self-contained campus is the limited space for housing—only 33 percent of undergrads reside in university-owned facilities. Most first-year students live in Trinity Hall, a modern apartment building about 20 minutes away by bus. After that, preference for on-campus rooms goes to students in their final year. As in any big city, housing in Dublin is pricey. But strong public transportation makes access to affordable accommodations feasible, and the college's Global Room stands ready to help out. Given that residences include communal kitchens, Trinity offers no university-wide meal plan. Students learn to cook for themselves or head to the two main restaurants or smaller cafés on campus, which provide simple meals. And as a senior points out, given the school's prime location, "Trinity students are spoiled for choice in terms of eating establishments extremely close to the university." Despite its urban setting, the campus is said to be safe, and an engineering major comments, "Trinity has started to introduce sexual consent workshops to incoming students."

Extracurricular activities may not help you get into Trinity, but they play an important role in campus culture once you get there. There are more than 170 student societies devoted to activities from yoga to traditional Irish music to entrepreneurialism. The most famous are the Philosophical Society ("the Phil"), which is the oldest debating club in the English-speaking world (1684), and its rival, the Historical Society ("the Hist"). The two groups share a building, sponsor weekly public debates, and award medals to notable visiting speakers. The Metaphysical Society ("the Metafizz") also gives students a chance to show off how much they know about Plato or Bertrand Russell. The Student Union is active in campaigning for a variety of political and social causes; divestment from fossil fuels has been a hot topic of late.

> **"You get a top-tier degree that costs less than most private colleges in the U.S."**

Social life takes place both on and off campus. Student societies are mandated to throw events once a month, so there is plenty to choose from every day of the week. The drinking age is 18, and most students attend "Pav Fridays," where the lively on-campus Pavilion Bar offers cheap beer and cider. Later in the evening, socializing usually spills out into the surrounding city and its vibrant music and cultural scene. As a senior puts it, "All of Dublin's nightclubs, bars, and pubs are pretty much a stone's throw away." (Where else can you go pub crawling in the footsteps of Bram Stoker, of *Dracula* fame, and James Joyce?) St. Patrick's Day is always a time to celebrate, but unquestionably the biggest event is Trinity Week. It starts on Monday, when the new Scholars are announced, given black robes, and invited to take on current Scholars in a game of marbles on the steps of the chapel. Festivities culminate on Friday with the Trinity Ball, "a massive music festival where many popular Irish and European bands perform," says a recent graduate. "It draws 8,000 students, staff, and alumni in formal dress and takes over the city." Recent headliners have included Bastille and Ellie Goulding. Trinity is ideally located for travel to European and other destinations. "There are cheap buses from Dublin to any corner of Ireland," reports a senior. "It is also possible to fly to continental Europe or the UK for well under 50 euros."

Sports here are for playing, not watching, at the local, national, or intercollegiate level. Says a history major, "There is no school mascot or particular set of colors that students wear. People tend to do sport mainly as an extracurricular activity. It's not really a status symbol." Nevertheless, there are at least 50 club and intramural sports; men's rugby and women's field hockey are the most competitive club teams. Although the English invented rugby, students at Trinity started the first club, and the boat (rowing) club is also one of the oldest. The university does hire coaches for some intercollegiate sports, such as rugby and soccer, and team leaders are eligible for scholarships. The annual dodgeball tournament is also a highlight.

Trinity College Dublin combines strong academics with the benefits of a beautiful campus in the midst of a thriving capital city that is also a gateway to the rest

Most first-year students live in Trinity Hall, a modern apartment building about 20 minutes away by bus.

The Philosophical Society ("the Phil") is the oldest debating club in the English-speaking world (1684).

Overlaps
University of St Andrews, University of Edinburgh, Columbia, King's College London, University College Dublin, Brown, NYU

of Europe. "You get a top-tier degree that costs less than most private colleges in the U.S. and gives you the international experience of a lifetime," comments one American denizen. "And I met the nicest, most interesting, and hilarious people—the Irish."

If You Apply To ›

Trinity: Rolling admissions. Does not accept the Common Application. Please consult Trinity's website for the most up-to-date information regarding standardized test requirements.

University of Iowa

108 Calvin Hall, Iowa City, IA 52242

A bargain compared with other Big Ten schools such as Michigan and Illinois. Iowa is world-famous for its creative writing program and Writers' Workshop. Other areas of strength include health sciences, social and behavioral sciences, and business. Future scientists should check out the Research Fellows Program. The university is a regional draw, although more students are arriving from outside the Midwest.

Website: www.uiowa.edu
Location: Small City
Public
Total Enrollment: 24,706
Undergraduates: 19,644
Male/Female: 44/56
Financial Aid: 87%
Pell Grant: 18%
Expense: Pub $
Student Loans: 50%
Average Debt: $ $ $
Applicants: 22,434
Accepted: 86%
Enrolled: 23%
Grad in 6 Years: 74%
Returning Freshmen: 88%
Academics: ✍ ✍ ✍ ✍
Social: 🍷 🍷 🍷
Q of L: ★ ★ ★
Admissions: (319) 335-3847
Email Address: admissions@uiowa.edu

Strong Programs:
Creative Writing
Performing Arts
Business
Education
Sustainability Science

At first glance, one might dismiss Iowa as a standard-issue Midwestern State U. But look beyond the state's endless miles of fields and corn and you'll find one of the most dynamic schools in the country—and one of the best values to boot. Iowa is known for producing stellar nurses, future doctors, and, of course, wrestlers. Founded in 1847, Iowa was the first public university in the 19th century to admit men and women on an equal basis and the first to accept theater, music, and the other arts as equal to more traditional areas of academic research. The university has long been a major player in the creative fields, particularly writing, and its small-town atmosphere is just one of many reasons students nationwide flock to this "budget Ivy."

The 1,770-acre campus is located in the rolling hills of the Iowa River valley. Among the 300 major buildings is Old Capitol, the first capitol of Iowa, a national historic landmark and the symbol of the university. The primary architectural styles of the campus buildings are Greek Revival and modern. Notable newer facilities include a 216,000-square-foot, state-of-the-art recreation and wellness center, the Voxman Music Building, Hancher Auditorium, and the Visual Arts Building.

Seven of Iowa's 11 colleges offer either direct or delayed admission to undergraduates, with requirements varying by college. Liberal arts students must fulfill comprehensive requirements that include general education courses in the areas of communication and literacy; natural, quantitative, and social sciences; and culture, society, and the arts. The three-day On Iowa! program immerses incoming freshmen in the campus culture and introduces them to popular activities and traditions. Optional First-Year Seminar courses help students hone their discussion skills in a small-group setting.

> **"The English department is…possibly the best in the country—at least for creative writing."**

Iowa has a long tradition in creative arts and is the home of the famed Writers' Workshop, a two-year graduate program for emerging authors whose graduates have included Jane Smiley, John Irving, and Yaa Gyasi. The school also prides itself on its International Writing Program. "The English department is stellar," raves one English major. "It's possibly the best in the country—at least for creative writing."

Iowa's programs in dance, music, and theater arts are also well respected. The university's on-campus hospital is one of the largest teaching hospitals in the United States. Undergraduates benefit from strong programs in the health professions, such as nursing, physician's assistant, and medical technician. The most popular majors are finance, enterprise leadership, health and human physiology, and psychology. Iowa is also strong in business, education, and sustainability science. Combined degree programs permit students to earn degrees in liberal arts and their choice of business, engineering, nursing, or medicine. Agriculture, veterinary medicine, forestry, architecture, and animal science are only taught at Iowa's sister institution, Iowa State.

(continued)

Finance
Enterprise Leadership
Health and Human Physiology

Fifty-one percent of the classes have fewer than 20 students, and "freshmen do tend to spend a majority of their time in large lectures," says a senior. The level of academic rigor tends to depend on the program, and professors are a mixed bag, students report. "I have had a few really amazing teachers become mentors, and I've had more than a few terrible teachers who don't care," a journalism major says. The university's Four-Year Graduation Plan guarantees that stu-

"[Iowa City] is built with the college student in mind."

dents who fulfill certain requirements will not have their graduation delayed by unavailability of a needed course. The University Honors Program provides special academic, cultural, and social opportunities to students who maintain a cumulative grade point average of 3.3 or higher. About 150 undergraduates—across all disciplines—are chosen each year to be ICRU Research Fellows, earning scholarships of up to $2,500 to engage in faculty-mentored research. Roughly 18 percent of undergrads take advantage of study abroad programs offered in nearly 50 countries worldwide, mostly in UI-sponsored programs.

The university's on-campus hospital is one of the largest teaching hospitals in the United States.

"Generally, students are very open-minded and kind," says an English major. Sixty-one percent of undergraduates hail from Iowa, with most of the rest coming from contiguous states, especially Illinois; 3 percent are international. Black students account for 3 percent, Hispanics/Latinos 9 percent, Asian Americans 5 percent, and multiracial students 4 percent. Students describe the left-leaning campus as tolerant and supportive of a community atmosphere in and out of the classroom. In addition to more than 400 athletic scholarships, there are academic scholarships averaging $6,300 for eligible students. Twenty Carver Scholarships are awarded each year to juniors who have "overcome unusual or debilitating circumstances in life."

"The residence halls range from hotel-like (Catlett and Petersen) to antiquated but charming (Currier and Hillcrest) to slightly gross (Burge, a.k.a. 'Dirty Burge,' and Mayflower)," explains a sophomore. All are co-ed by floor or wing, and first-years can opt to live in one of nearly 20 living/learning communities, such as Global Mosaic, Living Literature, and Justice for All. Twenty-five percent of undergrads live in uni-

"No one has to be 'just an engineer,' or 'just an artist.' There's crossover everywhere on campus."

versity housing; most students move off campus after their first year, often to apartments or houses adjacent to the campus. The "very nice" dining halls are "set up like food courts, with numerous options for varying ethnic and special tastes," says a senior. The student union includes a coffee shop, two cafeterias, and the State Room Restaurant. Regarding safety, a student notes, "The university talks a lot about preventing sexual assault and other forms of violence/intimidation."

Students often venture to Iowa City's lively downtown area, across the street from campus, which "is built with the college student in mind," a student says. "There are two university theaters right on campus and many affordable cultural events take place at Hancher Auditorium. Mickey's, Sports Column, and George's are all popular hangouts with students." Thirteen percent of the men and 17 percent of the women belong to fraternities and sororities, respectively. Policies against underage drinking are strictly enforced, and alcohol is only permitted at Greek events if

A state-of-the-art, $31 million wrestling facility is slated for completion in 2024.

there is a licensed, third-party vendor checking IDs, serving drinks, and providing security. "Students disobey the policy," says a student, "but there are fines and academic ramifications." Students look forward to the annual Iowa City Jazz Festival, homecoming, Dance Marathon, and Big Ten football, especially the game against Iowa State. For a change of scene, Chicago, Kansas City, or St. Louis are all within four to six hours by car, a short road trip by Midwestern standards.

Iowa's Hawkeyes compete in the Division I Big Ten Conference. The football team is a national powerhouse and regularly appears in New Year's Day bowl games. Hawkeye fans are serious about their team: "The whole town is basked in black and gold," a freshman says. The wrestling program also enjoys a national reputation, bolstered by a national championship in 2021, the addition of a varsity women's wrestling team for the 2023–24 season, and a state-of-the-art, $31 million wrestling facility slated for completion in 2024. Women's basketball was the national runner-up in 2023, and the men's team claimed the Big Ten title in 2022. Students are active in 38 club sports and the extensive intramural program, which offers more than 40 individual, dual, or team sports; basketball, sand volleyball, and indoor soccer are some of the most popular intramural leagues.

Much more than a campus among the cornfields, Iowa is an ever-evolving university where scientific innovation thrives alongside artistic creativity in a relatively progressive college town. "No one has to be 'just an engineer,' or 'just an artist,'" remarks an English major. "There's crossover everywhere on campus, and it leads to a culture of inclusiveness and respect that is hard to find elsewhere." The scope of Iowa's academic programs is broad and social activities abound—especially when it comes to rooting for their Hawkeyes.

Overlaps

U of I at Urbana–Champaign, Indiana University, Michigan State, University of Minnesota, UW–Madison, Iowa State, University of Michigan, University of Arizona

If You Apply To ›

Iowa: Rolling admissions. SATs or ACTs: optional. Accepts the Common Application with supplement. Applicants have the option of selecting preferred gender pronouns, preferred name, and sexual orientation.

Iowa State University

100 Alumni Hall, Ames, IA 50011

Agriculture and engineering are the twin pillars of Iowa State's curriculum, and the university is a magnet for preveterinary medicine students. Ames is a small city, and ISU must still endure barbs from certain snobby people in Iowa City. In truth, ISU is relatively cosmopolitan, with students hailing from more than 100 countries all over the world. While others retrench, ISU continues to expand.

Website: www.iastate.edu
Location: Small City
Public
Total Enrollment: 27,508
Undergraduates: 24,416
Male/Female: 56/44
Financial Aid: 86%
Pell Grant: 20%
Expense: Pub $

Love for Iowa State University runs as deep as its Midwestern roots. Strong programs in engineering, technology, and agriculture attract students from around the globe. The close-knit, small-town atmosphere fostered at this school of more than 24,000 full-time undergraduates keeps them here. At a time when many state universities are tightening the purse strings and retrenching, Iowa State has expanded major research initiatives focused on areas like bioeconomics, food safety and security, human/computer interaction, and animal health.

The university has lavished attention on its parklike setting, located on a 1,984-acre tract in the middle of Ames, population 66,000. The campus, which boasts a combination of dignified old buildings and award-winning new ones, is a model of landscape design with numerous shady quadrangles with floral plantings and artwork that create a garden-like quality. History and tradition prevail, from the campanile, which serenades the campus with its carillon bells, to the huge public art collection, including murals by native Iowan Grant Wood (think *American Gothic*) and sculptures by Danish artist Christian Petersen. Much of the campus is closed to cars, largely for the benefit of walking and bicycling, as well as the swans (Sir Lancelot and Lady Elaine) and ducks that reside on Lake LaVerne. The free-to-students CyRide bus system delivers students around campus and the city. Recent additions include an $84 million Student Innovation Center.

All undergraduates must take two semesters of foundational courses covering written, oral, visual, and electronic communication and demonstrate proficiency in English prior to graduation, in addition to taking a half-credit course on the use of the library and satisfying a three-credit requirement in diversity. Other general education requirements vary by college. When Iowa State opened its doors in 1869 as a land grant university, agriculture and engineering ruled the academic roost, and these colleges still field out-

"We have some world-class profs here who are doing important research."

standing programs in animal science, agribusiness, agronomy, and agricultural engineering. These days, though, the liberal arts are nearly as popular, and the College of Liberal Arts and Sciences is the largest of ISU's seven undergraduate colleges. Other colleges include business, design, veterinary medicine, and human sciences. Among the university's 100-plus majors, mechanical engineering is the most popular, followed by marketing, kinesiology and health, and finance. Programs in supply chain management; industrial, civil, aerospace, and software engineering; and elementary education are also strong.

Thirty-two percent of all undergraduate classes have fewer than 20 students, and students report that academic intensity varies by program. Despite the university's size, professors teach most classes, with the exception of some English gen-eds. "We have some world-class profs here who are doing important research," one senior says. Academic and career counseling draw praise, too, and advisors are "always readily available" to help students. Seventy-nine percent of first-year students join ISU's 90 highly touted learning communities, taking a common set of classes or living together on the same residence hall floor with other newcomers who share similar academic interests. The Honors Program enrolls about 1,400 outstanding students, who take special seminars, complete an independent honors research project or creative work, and have the option of living in honors housing. Roughly 5 percent of undergrads study overseas in programs offered in more than 50 countries; popular destinations include Italy, the United Kingdom, China, Australia, and the Netherlands. Fourteen percent take advantage of undergraduate research opportunities with faculty members.

Sixty-one percent of ISU's undergraduates are Iowans, though all 50 states and more than 100 countries are represented here. According to an animal science major, the atmosphere on campus is inclusive and respectful, and "people tend to keep their political ideas to themselves." International students make up 3 percent of the student body. Iowa State was the first co-ed land grant institution, but attracting students of color has proven more difficult: Hispanics/Latinos account for 7 percent, Asian Americans 4 percent, Black students 3 percent, and multiracial students 3 percent. "We have a lot of farmers and small-town Iowans," says a senior. "This is a pretty white campus." To help remedy this situation, ISU launched a $25 million campaign aimed at increasing the number of scholarships available for students of color, athletes, and student leaders. In addition to need-based financial aid and more than 400 athletic scholarships, thousands of merit awards, which average $4,300 annually, are available.

(continued)

Student Loans: 57%
Average Debt: $ $ $
Applicants: 20,357
Accepted: 91%
Enrolled: 29%
Grad in 6 Years: 75%
Returning Freshmen: 88%
Academics: ✍ ✍ ✍
Social: ☎ ☎ ☎ ☎
Q of L: ★ ★ ★
Admissions: (515) 294-5836
Email Address: admissions@ iastate.edu

Strong Programs:
Agriculture
Engineering
Animal Science
Agribusiness
Supply Chain Management
Elementary Education
Marketing
Kinesiology and Health

Seventy-nine percent of first-year students join ISU's 90 highly touted learning communities, taking a common set of classes or living together.

Twenty-nine percent of students live in on-campus residence halls and apartments; most others find their own apartments near campus. Single-sex, co-ed, and suite-style dorms are available, as are special floors for international students, teetotalers, and particularly studious undergraduates, and rooms are said to be well maintained. "The dorms are sterile to begin with but the traditions are very strong here and students transform them into home with their own personal touch," explains a junior. Students dine at 26 campus locations, including four main dining centers. Campus safety receives good ratings, and students say educational and training efforts, including the Green Dot initiative, have been effective in raising awareness about campus sexual assault and violence.

Iowa State is not simply located in Ames—in many respects it *is* Ames, but whether it qualifies as a college town depends on whom you ask. Des Moines, the state capital, is about 30 minutes away, and Iowa City, Minneapolis, and Chicago are other easy and enjoyable road trips. Socializing tends to stay on campus, though, with big-name bands playing at Hilton Coliseum and parties always rocking. More than 800 student organizations cater to just about any interest.

"We have a lot of farmers and small-town Iowans."

Fourteen percent of the men and 17 percent of the women go Greek. Students of legal age are allowed to have alcohol on campus, and students report that alcohol policies are well enforced. Across the street from campus, Campustown offers several bars as well as a variety of cafés and international restaurants. One long-held tradition is campaniling, where students kiss under the campanile at the stroke of midnight. And students have learned not to walk over the zodiac sign in the Memorial Union—it brings bad luck.

In sports, Cyclone basketball is king; the men's and women's teams are usual invitees to the NCAA Division I tournament, and the men's team has won the Big 12 title four times in the last nine years. Football, wrestling, and men's and women's track and field and cross-country are also competitive. ISU's football stadium bears the name of Jack Trice, ISU's first Black athlete, who was fatally injured in a 1923 football game. The Cyclones' rivalry with the University of Iowa's Hawkeyes is one of the strongest in the nation. "Everyone dresses in red and gold in support of our teams," cheers a first-year, and "Beat Iowa" paraphernalia is ubiquitous. Thirty-six percent of students participate in nonvarsity sports; the intramural program, which is one of the largest in the country, offers 47 sports—and if that's not enough, students have their pick of 53 club sports too.

From its first class of 28 men and two women in 1869, Iowa State has taken to heart Abraham Lincoln's land grant ideal: to open higher education to all, to teach practical courses, and to share that knowledge beyond the borders of the school. According to one junior, it's this dynamic combination that draws "hardworking, kind students" from near and far.

If You Apply To ›

Iowa State: Rolling admissions. SATs or ACTs: optional. Accepts the Common Application with supplement.

Ithaca College

953 Danby Road, Ithaca, NY 14850

Ithaca offers an unusually wide array of programs for a smallish university. The common thread: solid preprofessional programs rooted in the liberal arts. Communications and music are traditional strengths, along with physical therapy and other health sciences. Struggling to deal with recent enrollment declines, downsizing of faculty, and reduction in course offerings. Crosstown neighbor Cornell adds curricular and social opportunities.

Located in the picturesque center of the beautiful upstate New York Finger Lakes region, Ithaca College was founded in 1892 as a music conservatory. Since then, it has led the way in showing how to combine hands-on preprofessional training in a wide range of fields, from communications and theatre to health sciences, with a solid grounding in the liberal arts. Recent enrollment declines have led to reductions in the size of the faculty and the elimination of 10 majors and the honors program. Nevertheless, Ithaca's size continues to allow for easy friendships with peers and professors alike. Ithaca's special approach to hands-on learning helps prepare students for life outside institutional walls.

Ithaca's campus, midway between Syracuse and Binghamton, lies on the city's southern hill overlooking Cayuga Lake. The college did not move to its present location, a sprawling 757-acre property, until the 1960s. The surrounding area is dotted with forests, rolling hills, some 150 waterfalls,.and, of course, those ever-present gorges. Author Tom Wolfe dubbed the college "the emerald eminence at the fingertip of Cayuga Lake." Campus facilities afford students access to more than 100 labs, smart classrooms, studios, practice rooms, and performance spaces.

Ithaca has five schools—business; communications; health sciences and human performance; humanities and sciences; and music, theatre, and dance. Together, they offer 90 undergraduate majors and 70 minors. All students complete the Integrative Core Curriculum (ICC), which is designed to help them connect concepts across disciplines. All first-year students take a four-credit Ithaca Seminar during their first semester; recent examples of the nearly 100 offerings include Inquiring Minds Want to Know and Hello China: Preparing for the Future. These classes are limited to about 15 students each, and professors and students decide together how to use the fourth hour of instruction each week, covering topics related to the transition to college life, such as personal, social, and academic responsibility.

> "Students don't learn from simply reading and listening, we learn from applying course material."

Ithaca is best known for its preprofessional programs—especially music, which dates to the college's founding. "The music school has always been lauded and maintained an excellent academic program," a freshman says. The school, which now encompasses theatre and dance programs in addition to music, requires an audition, making it a destination for already-accomplished performing artists. Professional programs in the School of Health Sciences and Human Performance range from speech-language pathology and public and community health to the highly regarded physical and occupational therapy programs. The Park School of Communications houses two of the college's most popular programs: television and digital media production and integrated marketing communications. The business school offers undergraduate programs in business administration and accounting. The School of Humanities and Sciences recently added a major in race, power, and resistance. Students who are undecided on a major enroll in the Exploratory Program, which

Website: www.ithaca.edu
Location: Small City
Private
Total Enrollment: 5,084
Undergraduates: 4,716
Male/Female: 45/55
Financial Aid: 96%
Pell Grant: 23%
Expense: Pr $ $
Student Loans: 69%
Average Debt: $ $ $ $
Applicants: 13,445
Accepted: 78%
Enrolled: 11%
Grad in 6 Years: 77%
Returning Freshmen: 84%
Academics: ✍ ✍ ✍
Social: 🐵 🐵 🐵 🐵 🐵
Q of L: ★ ★ ★
Admissions: (800) 429-4274
Email Address: admission@ithaca.edu

Strong Programs:
Music
Music Education
Theatre
Communications
Physical Therapy
Business Administration
Television-Radio
Integrated Marketing
  Communications

helps them find an academic path through advising, workshops, and courses in a variety of fields. Cross-registration is available at nearby Cornell University and Wells College, and Ithaca also offers a 3–2 physics and engineering program.

Ithaca is best known for its preprofessional programs—especially music, which dates to the college's founding.

"The teaching approach here is discussion-based and hands-on. Students don't learn from simply reading and listening, we learn from applying course material," says a junior. Sixty-eight percent of classes have fewer than 20 students, and professors are praised for their knowledge and enthusiasm. A sophomore says, "If you do struggle, as I have, there are lifelines in the form of TAs, free tutoring (in most cases), and persistent professor interaction." Research opportunities in the sciences and psychology are plentiful; students in other departments generally do research as part of an independent study course. Those seeking immersive real-world experience may apply for a semester-long program in Los Angeles that combines an internship with industry-related courses. Ithaca offers study abroad programs at the Ithaca College London Center and in more than 50 countries; 29 percent of students typically study off campus.

What defines a typical Ithaca student? A senior says, "Students are passionate, creative, eclectic, and determined." Forty-four percent of Ithaca students hail from New York State; many of the rest come from elsewhere in New England, and 2 percent come from other nations. Black students represent 6 percent of undergraduates, Asian

"Ithaca is the best college town in the whole state!"

Americans 4 percent, Hispanics/Latinos 10 percent, and multiracial students 4 percent. Politically, the campus is liberal, and according to one student, "Hot-button issues include LGBTQ+ rights, the Black Lives Matter movement, climate change, and fighting antisemitism." Merit scholarships averaging $17,600 are available to top-performing applicants; there are no athletic awards. In-state residents with annual family incomes of $125,000 or less are eligible to receive an Ithaca College New York State Tuition Award of up to $6,000 per year for four years.

Each fall brings Applefest, a local downtown festival that celebrates the harvest, and in the winter, Chilifest helps students warm up.

Seventy-six percent of Ithaca's students live on campus, thanks in part to the college's Circle and Garden Apartments, which have full kitchens and space for 630 upperclassmen in units that house two to six students each. First-year students participate in the First-Year Residential Experience, living in communities focusing on themes like multiculturalism and sustainability. A junior recommends learning communities as a way to "meet new people and become more involved in the Ithaca area." Campus residents can eat in any of the dining halls, each with a different daily menu and options for those with special dietary needs; the meals get mixed reviews. An integrated marketing communications major reports, "Campus is overall very safe—Public Safety has a noticeable presence on campus."

Ithaca recognizes only academic fraternities and sororities, not social ones, but that doesn't slow down the campus social scene. "Between music school concerts, theatre performances, Student Activities Board movies, club events, open-mic nights, comedy shows, or athletic events, it is impossible to be bored on campus," one sociology major says. Nearly 200 student organizations also keep students busy. Students agree that the party scene is low-key; those looking for livelier bashes check out

"Come mid–February or so, we hate the snow!"

Greek life at neighboring Cornell. The city of Ithaca caters well to college students, with a variety of coffee shops, bars and clubs, live music venues, a mall, a bowling alley, and movie theaters. "Ithaca is the best college town in the whole state!" cheers a junior. Each fall brings Applefest, a local downtown festival that celebrates the harvest, and in the winter, Chilifest helps students warm up. The area's hilly terrain provides abundant opportunities for hiking, biking, sledding, and skiing. Popular road trips include Syracuse and Binghamton, each an hour away, and New York City, Philadelphia, Boston, Washington, D.C., and Toronto, each between a four- and six-hour drive.

Ithaca fields 27 competitive Division III varsity athletics programs. The Bombers (a nickname of obscure origin) have claimed recent Liberty League conference championships in men's and women's track and field, baseball, and women's basketball, swimming and diving, and crew. The wrestling team, which competes in the Empire Collegiate Wrestling Conference, also brought home a conference title. The biggest annual athletic tradition is the "Cortaca Jug" football game that pits the Ithaca Bombers against rival SUNY–Cortland. (The winner gets the jug-shaped stoneware trophy, and the game is "the only Division III football game you can bet on in Vegas," boasts a sophomore.) More than 20 percent of students sign up for club and intramural sports; popular options include rugby, ultimate Frisbee, swimming, flag football, basketball, and volleyball.

If you can endure the harsh winters ("Come mid-February or so, we hate the snow!" gripes one senior), you'll appreciate the small size and personal attention characteristic of Ithaca College. "Everybody who is part of the Ithaca College community knows that they are part of something special," observes one student. "At other schools, you're a number. At Ithaca, we know your name."

Overlaps

Elon, Emerson, Gettysburg, Marist, St. Lawrence, Muhlenberg, Syracuse, Quinnipiac

If You Apply To ›

Ithaca: Early decision, early action, regular decision. SATs or ACTs: optional. Accepts the Common Application with supplement.

James Madison University

Harrisonburg, VA 22807

JMU has carved out a comfortable niche among Virginia's superb system of public universities. More undergrads than UVA and three times as many as William & Mary. Strong in preprofessional fields such as business, health professions, and education. Undergraduates rule the roost.

No doubt about it: students at James Madison University get down to business. In fact, the school's business programs continue to garner national attention and attract top-notch students from coast to coast. The university has been growing at a steady rate, causing growth pains. But an emphasis on undergraduate teaching, close student/faculty interaction, and a warm and welcoming climate are still business as usual here. "JMU is comfortable—everyone has a place, you just have to find it," says a senior.

Founded as a teachers' college in 1908, JMU sits in the heart of the Shenandoah Valley, two hours from both Washington, D.C., and Richmond, Virginia. The university straddles Interstate 81, an outlet to several major East Coast cities. Three types of architecture make up the campus. The buildings on front campus have red-tile roofs and are constructed of a distinctive limestone block known as bluestone. Back campus has more modern, redbrick structures. The College of Integrated Science and Technology campus features modern beige buildings. Newer facilities include a three-story west campus dining hall and a 500-bed residence hall.

The General Education Program requires each student to take courses in several clusters, including Skills for the 21st Century, Arts and Humanities, The Natural World, Social and Cultural Processes, and Individuals in the Human Community. The idea is to give students a basis for lifelong learning by challenging them to

Website: www.jmu.edu
Location: Small City
Public
Total Enrollment: 19,802
Undergraduates: 18,696
Male/Female: 42/58
Financial Aid: 63%
Pell Grant: 14%
Expense: Pub $ $ $
Student Loans: 50%
Average Debt: $ $ $
Applicants: 21,176
Accepted: 86%
Enrolled: 26%
Grad in 6 Years: 82%
Returning Freshmen: 91%
Academics: ✎ ✎ ✎
Social: ☎ ☎ ☎ ☎

(continued)

Q of L: ★ ★ ★ ★

Admissions: (540) 568-5681

Email Address: admissions@ jmu.edu

Strong Programs:

Business

Health Sciences

Education

Health Services Administration

Sport and Recreation Management

Biology

Nursing

Psychology

Outdoor Adventures, held before classes begin, give first-year students an opportunity to meet while hiking and climbing in the mountains.

become active in their own education and to explore the foundations of knowledge. Freshmen are offered a variety of programs to help smooth their transition into the university. Outdoor Adventures, held before classes begin, give first-year students an opportunity to meet while hiking and climbing in the mountains.

JMU is recognized nationally for its College of Business, while education is also strong. In addition to health sciences, some of the most popular majors include health services administration, sport and recreation management, biology, nursing, and psychology. Undergraduates in the biology department have employed recombinant DNA technology to help develop organisms that produce biodegradable plastics, while a mathematical modeling laboratory helps undergrads solve real-world applied math problems. Also worth noting is the geology department's undergraduate summer geology field course in Ireland.

"You feel like you can ask questions [and] get to know your professors one-on-one."

With undergrads far outnumbering grad students, JMU's main mission is undergraduate teaching, and students say the classroom atmosphere is usually relaxed and supportive. Forty percent of classes have fewer than 20 students, and a political science major reports that even in larger classes, "You feel like you can ask questions, get to know your professors one-on-one, and make connections." Student support services get high ratings. "The counseling center offers a student oasis and arts center where anyone can go free of charge to do yoga, rest, play relaxing games, make crafts, etc.," notes a senior.

Those looking for a more intense intellectual experience can apply for admission to the Honors College, which offers small classes and opportunities for independent study. Many upper-level programs encourage undergraduate participation with faculty research. Thirty percent of students study internationally; JMU runs its own semester abroad programs in Belgium, England, Italy, Scotland, and Spain, as well as dozens of short-term, faculty-led programs in more than 40 countries.

Students describe their classmates as cheerful folks who hold doors open for each other, and a junior says JMU students are interested in "finding lifestyles that they love instead of just jobs." Most undergrads attended public high schools, and 77 percent are from Virginia. In fact, there's a conscious effort to keep out-of-state enrollment below 30 percent; international students represent just 1 percent. Racial and ethnic diversity, although low, has been slowly on the rise; Black students currently account for 5 percent of JMU's student body, Hispanics/Latinos 7 percent, Asian Americans 5 percent, and multiracial students 5 percent. As for political inclinations, both sides of the aisle are represented, but an economics major says most students are "rather apathetic." JMU offers limited merit scholarships averaging $6,300 and more than 350 athletic scholarships.

"You're supposed to miss your mom's cooking…but I end up missing my college's food when I'm home."

Thirty-one percent of students live on campus, which is a requirement for freshmen. On-campus housing runs the gamut from the old high-ceiling variety to newer, air-conditioned dorms with fitness centers and apartments for sophomores. For upperclassmen, "Off-campus housing is extremely easy to find," reports a senior, "and there is a wide range of prices and amenities available." With 27 dining options on campus serving all sorts of dietary needs and preferences, students rave about the meal plan. "You're supposed to miss your mom's cooking when you go away, but I end up missing my college's food when I'm home," says one student. (We won't tell Mom.) According to a math major, JMU's Title IX office is "working hard to advance services" and the Campus Assault Response student group "is a great nonreporting resource for students" coping with sexual violence.

Favorite traditions include taking graduation photos with the various campus statues of James Madison (or "JMaddy").

"Social life is really fun for a rural area," observes one student. "The students mostly gather at off-campus apartments via a bus system that runs into the late hours." Greek life attracts only 4 percent of the men and 6 percent of the women. The school cracks down on underage drinking on campus, and after three strikes, "students are asked to leave," says a student. Favorite traditions include the holiday tree-lighting ceremony, Spring Concert, the Madipalooza music festival, and taking graduation photos with the various campus statues of James Madison (or "JMaddy," as he's been dubbed by students). Most students find Harrisonburg a friendly, if not always lively, Southern town. As for road trips, the University of Virginia, almost an hour's drive to the south, is a top destination, but equally enticing are the many nearby natural delights of the Shenandoah Valley, including hiking, camping, and even skiing.

Sports fans here are known as the JMU Nation, and to say they are enthusiastic about their Division I Dukes (named after a popular university president) would be an understatement, especially when it comes to football. Women's lacrosse, tennis, golf, swimming and diving, and softball and men's soccer are recent Colonial Athletic Association champions. About half of the students participate in intramurals and club sports. JMU's debate team ranks as one of the top public debate programs in the nation.

Though JMU still has a ways to go before establishing itself as a front-rank national university, it is making progress. The school is growing, but not outgrowing its Southern charm. "The school spirit is really what sets us apart," says an elementary education major. "No matter where you go on campus, you are always going to find someone wearing purple and gold."

Overlaps

Appalachian State, Clemson, College of Charleston, Grand Valley State, Illinois State, George Mason, University of Virginia, Virginia Tech

If You Apply To ›

James Madison: Early action, regular decision. SATs or ACTs: optional. Accepts the Common Application.

The Johns Hopkins University

3400 North Charles Street, Baltimore, MD 21218

Hopkins's reputation as a top-notch premed factory can be misleading. It's true, of course, but Hopkins also has fine programs in international studies (with D.C. close at hand) as well as in the humanities and social sciences. Hopkins is smaller than most people think. Major effort underway to diversify the student body, aided in part by long-standing elimination of legacy preferences in admissions.

One of the few U.S. universities initially founded (in 1876) as a graduate school, The Johns Hopkins University has garnered widespread acclaim for its exceptional professors, extensive resources, and abundant research opportunities. Though the university has a reputation for churning out premed students, the administration has been working for a number of years to make it clear that this midsized Baltimore university has plenty to offer undergrads whose interests are decidedly nonmedical or nonscience based. Students who attend this elite university burn the midnight oil, but a first-year student insists that they also "let loose every once in a while."

The arts and sciences and engineering schools are on the main Homewood campus, 140 picturesque acres in Baltimore's Charles Village neighborhood, just three miles north of the vibrant Inner Harbor. Tree-lined quadrangles, open lawns, and playing fields make for an idyllic setting on the edge of a major urban center.

Website: www.jhu.edu
Location: City Outskirts
Private
Total Enrollment: 8,235
Undergraduates: 5,318
Male/Female: 46/54
Financial Aid: 48%
Pell Grant: 20%
Expense: Pr $ $ $
Student Loans: 41%
Average Debt: $

(continued)

Applicants: 39,515
Accepted: 8%
Enrolled: 48%
Grad in 6 Years: 95%
Returning Freshmen: 96%
Academics: ✍ ✍ ✍ ✍ ✍
Social: ☎ ☎ ☎
Q of L: ★ ★ ★
Admissions: (410) 516-8171
Email Address: gotojhu@
  jhu.edu

Strong Programs:
Public Health Studies
Engineering
Creative Writing
Film and Media Studies
Music
International Studies
Neuroscience
Molecular and Cellular Biology

As much as some try to deny it, students bound for medical school dominate the campus.

Undergraduate research is a Hopkins hallmark, with 80 percent of students having at least one research experience.

The architecture on this urban campus is mainly Georgian redbrick, with several recently built, more modern structures scattered throughout. Malone Hall is a state-of-the-art building that houses several collaborative research institutions. Construction is underway on the Hopkins Student Center—the university's first space dedicated solely to student socialization and relaxation—slated for completion in 2024. Hopkins's School of Medicine and Peabody Conservatory are easily accessible from the Homewood campus via a crosstown shuttle.

Although Hopkins is a firm supporter of traditional and interdisciplinary scholarship, there are no university-wide requirements other than a four-course writing component. Each major has its own distribution requirements; students entering the Krieger School of Arts and Sciences are required to take a first-year seminar. First-years buckle down to a Herculean workload right from the get-go, but the university has developed and strengthened several student support resources in recent years to help ease the transition to college. First-years are assigned a premajor advisor, and arts and sciences students are encouraged to wait until at least their sophomore year to declare a major. During the optional January intersession, students can take courses or pursue independent study for one or two credits. "Intersession is one of the best times of the year," cheers an international studies major. "The classes are pass/fail and so much fun: everything from profiling mass murderers to a Harry Potter literature class to a chocolate lab!"

> **"Intersession is one of the best times of the year. The classes are pass/fail and so much fun."**

As much as some try to deny it, students bound for medical school dominate the campus. Public health studies is among the most popular majors, along with biomedical engineering, neuroscience, and molecular and cellular biology. The Johns Hopkins Hospital and School of Medicine play such a major role in the identity of Hopkins that students sometimes fear they "overshadow the vibrant undergrad life that exists at Homewood." But administrators say the university is paying more attention to undergraduate programs and emphasizing interdisciplinary, cooperative approaches to the coursework, and students seem to agree. "Hopkins is a rigorous institution, but with its collaborative academic culture, learning is very manageable and enjoyable," says a behavioral biology major.

Engineering majors enjoy strong departments, such as mechanical engineering, chemical and biomedical engineering, electrical and computer engineering, and computer science. New offerings include a major in systems engineering and a minor in energy that is administered in conjunction with the earth and planetary sciences department. Students can receive a B.A. in creative writing through the Writing Seminars program, where they study with the likes of novelist Alice McDermott and poet Andrew Motion. The film and media studies program is notable, bolstered by the JHU-MICA Film Centre and the annual Maryland Film Festival. Musicians can pursue a dual degree in music performance with the university's Peabody Conservatory. There also are broad "area majors," such as natural sciences and romance languages, and students can choose from a cluster of related disciplines to design their own program. Students are generally happy with the quality of teaching, which is enhanced by small class sizes—79 percent of undergraduate classes enroll fewer than 20 students. "The professors here are *awesome*," enthuses a neuroscience and music double major. "I feel like I'm part of a conversation, engaged, and enjoying my time in class."

> **"I feel like I'm part of a conversation, engaged, and enjoying my time in class."**

The well-developed graduate side of Hopkins proves to be a boon to undergraduates as well. The international studies program, for example, is enriched by its offerings at the university's Bologna Center in Italy, its Nanjing Center in China, and its Nitze School of Advanced International Studies in nearby Washington, D.C. About 40 percent of all undergraduates study abroad in these and other locations across the globe. Undergraduate research is a Hopkins hallmark, with 80 percent of students having at least one research experience. "Without any prior experience, any student can get a meaningful research job," says a political science major. "I was able to secure a research position within my first month as a freshman at JHU." The Provost's Undergraduate Research Awards offer funding and faculty support for research projects. The Clark Scholars Program provides special academic and networking opportunities to top engineering students. Those interested in service can apply for one of 50 paid summer internships with Baltimore area nonprofits and government agencies through the Community Impact Internships program.

The university guarantees to meet 100 percent of admitted students' demonstrated need with loan-free financial aid packages.

"JHU students are driven and motivated to succeed," muses a neuroscience major. "We have a special culture of genuine intellectual curiosity." Geographically, most students come from the Mid-Atlantic region and New England; only 10 percent are Maryland natives, and 13 percent are international. Twenty-eight percent of undergrads are Asian American, 9 percent are Black, 19 percent are Hispanic/Latino, and 7 percent are multiracial. The proportion of first-generation students (about 15 percent) has more than doubled over the last decade, in part because of the elimination of legacy preferences in admissions. Politically, the campus leans liberal. At more than $8 billion, Hopkins's endowment is among the top 15 in the

"I was able to secure a research position within my first month as a freshman at JHU."

country. In addition to moving to a need-blind admissions process for domestic students, the university guarantees to meet 100 percent of admitted students' demonstrated need with loan-free financial aid packages. Hopkins rewards the extraordinarily talented with hefty Hodson Trust scholarships worth about two-thirds of tuition annually, regardless of need. Forty-five athletic scholarships are also awarded in women's and men's lacrosse, where Hopkins is a perennial national powerhouse.

Fifty-one percent of undergrads live in student housing; first-years and sophomores are required to do so. "The freshman-year dorms are classic and encourage social interactions," explains a student. "The sophomore-year dorms are spacious, new, and have excellent amenities." Most upperclassmen choose to scope out the row houses and apartment buildings that surround Hopkins, but some stay on campus in the Charles Commons or university-owned "luxury" apartments. Campus dining gets positive reviews, as does security, thanks to the consistent presence of security personnel. The Sexual Assault Resource Unit student organization is active in raising awareness about sexual violence.

The biggest and most popular undergraduate social event of the year is the student-organized Spring Fair.

The image Hopkins students once had as antisocial bookworms is giving way to a more balanced social life. Rowdy dorm parties and all-campus festivities may be few and far between, but fraternity parties can be found on the weekends; 18 percent of the men and 26 percent of the women belong to the Greek system. There are also more than 400 clubs and student organizations to pick from. Students speak fondly of the Lighting of the Quads celebration each

"We have a special culture of genuine intellectual curiosity."

winter, but the biggest and most popular undergraduate social event of the year is the student-organized Spring Fair. "Tons of Baltimore food vendors and shops come and line up on the quads, there is a concert, and the campus is generally full of merriment," says an international studies major.

In addition to on-campus events like guest lectures and performances, says a senior, "You have the whole city of Baltimore and its social scene to explore." Downtown and the famed Inner Harbor are not too distant, and some of the city's best attractions, such as the Baltimore Museum of Art, Wyman Park, and the funky

Hampden neighborhood, are right near campus. Trendy Baltimore hot spots—like Canton, Fells Point, and Little Italy—are favorites. Students also head downtown for plays, the symphony, films, clubs, restaurants, the zoo, and major league sports; Camden Yards, home of MLB's Orioles, is the most commodious park in the country. Annapolis is less than an hour away by car, while Washington, D.C., only an hour's train ride, beckons with tourist activities and ample nightlife. In the warmer months, a trek out to the Delaware and Maryland beaches takes the mind off the books.

When the nationally acclaimed Division I men's lacrosse team hits the road, students often take advantage of the opportunity to road-trip with them and cheer them on. Women's lacrosse is Division I as well, but the rest of the Blue Jays athletic program competes in Division III. The women's cross-country team has won eight national titles in the last 11 years, and Centennial Conference champs include men's cross-country, women's volleyball, and field hockey. The Johns Hopkins Undergraduate Debate Council has also had national success. Twenty percent of undergraduates compete in intramurals and club sports.

With one of the world's premier medical schools, top science programs, and first-rate programs in areas as diverse as writing, international studies, environmental engineering, and philosophy, Hopkins is clearly among the best schools in the country. Students here take pride in the fact that they belong to the cream of the academic crop. "Hopkins is a place of discovery and exploration, and it really embodies creating new knowledge and expanding your horizons," says a junior. "It's a place for people who like to go the extra mile and find out something new."

If You Apply To ›

Johns Hopkins: Early decision I and II, regular decision. Accepts the Common Application with supplement. Biomedical engineering students must apply to that program. Please consult Johns Hopkins's website for the most up-to-date information regarding standardized test requirements.

Juniata College

1700 Moore Street, Huntingdon, PA 16652

Located in the middle of rural Pennsylvania and named after a nearby river, Juniata boasts one of the best undergraduate science programs among liberal arts colleges. Students are encouraged to customize their own education and to think globally. Peace and conflict studies is a specialty. Lots of merit scholarships, but not much diversity among students.

Website: www.juniata.edu
Location: Small Town
Private
Total Enrollment: 1,198
Undergraduates: 1,190
Male/Female: 45/55
Financial Aid: 89%
Pell Grant: 24%
Expense: Pr $ $

Set amid the ridges and valleys of central Pennsylvania, Juniata College offers students a tantalizing mix of academic flexibility, small classes, and surprisingly solid programs in the natural sciences. Students here chart their own course of study, partner with faculty on research projects, and pack their bags for study abroad opportunities around the world. "The types of students who are attracted to Juniata are those who have a motivation to learn but are not interested in learning in the conventional way," says a psychology major.

Juniata's quiet 110-acre campus features a central stand of structures reflecting three architectural styles. The college was founded in 1876, and its landmark building, Founders Hall, is a colonial Revival structure, built of brick atop a stone foundation. Halbritter Center for the Performing Arts, Ellis Hall, and the von Liebig Center for Science are all Classical Revival buildings, the prominent pillars on each visible all over campus. The college also boasts a Beaux-Arts building, Carnegie Hall, originally built as a Carnegie library in 1907 and redesigned on the interior to house the college's art museum. Newer facilities include the Integrated Media and Studio Arts building.

Under Juniata's general education curriculum, all students complete coursework in five "Ways of Knowing" (creative expression, formal reasoning, humanistic thought, social inquiry, and scientific process), as well as a first-year composition class and a first-year seminar. As juniors or seniors, students take four Connections courses, which are team-taught by faculty from different departments, on the U.S. experience, ethical responsibility, local engagement, and global engagement. Every student creates a personal portfolio demonstrating their knowledge, skills, and personal reflections throughout their four years, and seniors complete a capstone project.

> **"[Juniata students] are not interested in learning in the conventional way."**

In lieu of preset majors, Juniata has flexible Programs of Emphasis (POEs). Each student works with two advisors to either shape an existing POE to fit their academic interests or to create an entirely new program. Approximately one-third of students take the latter path, designing their own customized POE. Of the more than 60 established POEs, some of the most popular are biology, psychology, computer science, environmental science, and social work. The physics and chemistry programs are well regarded, and strong offerings in environmental science and wildlife conservation are enhanced by the college's field station at nearby Raystown Lake. "Juniata has long been known as a school for the natural sciences," confirms a senior. In addition, peace and conflict studies, which is one of the oldest and most comprehensive programs of its kind in the United States, includes study abroad opportunities and internships. Museum studies teaches students how to curate art (and provides internships at prestigious galleries around the nation), while the Center for Entrepreneurial Leadership bestows up to $15,000 in seed capital to budding business leaders. New offerings include criminal justice, neuroscience, and public health.

A psychology major describes the academic atmosphere as "flexible but challenging." Sixty-three percent of classes have fewer than 20 students, which allows for plenty of interaction between professors and students. The Inbound program allows new students to spend a week on campus as part of a particular club or activity in order to "make their first few days of immersion into college life easier," says a student. Juniata has international exchange/study abroad agreements with colleges and universities in 24 countries, and 37 percent of students participate. "Juniata makes it super affordable and possible for every student to go abroad, no matter what they're majoring in," cheers a sophomore. About 55 percent of students get involved in faculty-guided research projects. The annual Liberal Arts Symposium features student research presentations, art exhibitions, and a Multicultural Storyfest, where international students share stories from their home cultures.

Sixty-three percent of Juniata students hail from Pennsylvania, and 7 percent come from foreign nations. Black students account for 4 percent of the student body, Asian Americans 3 percent, Hispanics/Latinos 8 percent, and multiracial students 4 percent. A junior comments that while the school is still working to increase racial diversity, it has also "put a lot more effort into making people of color feel welcome." Although the campus leans left, students report that all viewpoints are represented and respected. "Compared to schools in New England, we're Bible-thumpers, whereas compared to schools in the South, we're

(continued)

Student Loans: 73%
Average Debt: $ $ $ $
Applicants: 2,753
Accepted: 74%
Enrolled: 16%
Grad in 6 Years: 76%
Returning Freshmen: 83%
Academics: ✐ ✐ ✐
Social: ☎ ☎ ☎
Q of L: ★ ★ ★
Admissions: (877) 586-4282
Email Address: admissions@ juniata.edu

Strong Programs:
Physics
Chemistry
Environmental Science
Wildlife Conservation
Peace and Conflict Studies
Museum Studies
Biology
Psychology

Environmental science and wildlife conservation are enhanced by the college's field station at nearby Raystown Lake.

socialists," quips one student. Hundreds of merit scholarships are available, averaging $27,400, but there are no athletic scholarships. All full-time, degree-seeking international students receive an automatic International Friendship Award worth $2,000 per year.

Juniata requires students to live on campus for four years. "Student housing isn't glorious," reasons a freshman, "but dorms are adequate." Two living/learning communities, Global Village and Eco House, are options for those interested in intercultural exchange and sustainable living. For grub, Juniata provides two main dining facilities, one buffet-style and one where meals are made to order, as well as several à la carte stops around campus. Students say their rural location feels safe. A junior reports that the SPoT (Safe Place to Talk), which "does a lot of programs to promote safe sex and understanding of sexual assault and mental health awareness," is proving to be an effective source of support.

Social life is mostly on campus, and activities include live bands, trivia contests, dinners, and dances. "There are tons of events hosted by clubs all the time," says a chemistry major. Students of legal age may drink on campus, but students say the drinking and party culture is low-key, especially with no Greek life. Students enjoy a number of traditions, including Lobsterfest at the start of the year, Madrigal Dinner during the holidays, and Mountain Day, on which classes are canceled for the day and students attend outdoor activities at Raystown Lake ("Food, carnival games, kayaking, Slip 'N Slides, and the president's dog with a GoPro on—it is a great time," says a junior). Each year, students also take part in the "storming of the arch," in which "freshmen attempt to run into an arch defended by the rugby teams," explains a student, a feat that no first-year class has yet accomplished. Huntingdon (population 7,000) provides the basic necessities, as well as several restaurants, a movie theater, and a Mayfest street fair. Community service is popular, as are road trips to Penn State (40 minutes away), Baltimore, Philadelphia, and Pittsburgh.

> "Juniata makes it super affordable and possible for every student to go abroad."

The Juniata Eagles' 22 varsity teams compete in Division III. The women's volleyball team has dominated the Landmark Conference, winning 15 consecutive championships and the 2022 national title. Men's volleyball and women's field hockey are strong too. Students are also active in club and intramural sports; the men's and women's rugby clubs and intramural basketball are among the most favored.

Although students sometimes complain about the limitations of attending a small college in a small town, most seem excited to be part of such an inviting academic institution. Those seeking "big football games, raging frat parties, and a vibrant urban setting" should look elsewhere, a senior observes. However, "if you are more interested in an intensive and personal academic environment with an extremely tight-knit and supportive community, then Juniata is the place for you."

Overlaps

Allegheny,
Susquehanna,
Ursinus,
Elizabethtown,
Muhlenberg,
College of Wooster,
Dickinson,
University of
Pittsburgh

If You Apply To ›

Juniata: Early decision, early action I and II, regular decision. SATs or ACTs: optional. Accepts the Common Application with supplement.

Kalamazoo College

1200 Academy Street, Kalamazoo, MI 49006

Kalamazoo College is a small liberal arts school that opens up the world to its students—literally. An impressive 61 percent of students study abroad thanks to the ingenious K-Plan, a curriculum that allows them to study abroad for up to three academic terms. And if you need an extra boost to round out that résumé, there is an extensive career development program.

Kalamazoo College (also known as K) may be a small school in America's heartland, but it pays to send the majority of students abroad during their four years—making it a launching pad to the world. In addition to international education, the school's K-Plan emphasizes teaching, internships, and independent, faculty-guided research. Students are exposed to a demanding academic schedule and high expectations from faculty, but they say it's well worth the challenge. "Students at K really care about their studies," says an international and area studies major. "We enjoy writing, we enjoy discussion, and we enjoy critical thinking and inquiry."

Life on K's wooded, 60-acre campus centers on the Quad, a green lawn where students ponder their destinies and play ultimate Frisbee with equal ease. With its rolling hills, Georgian architecture, and brick-laid streets, the campus has the quaint look more typical of historic New England than of the nearby city of Kalamazoo, which, with surrounding communities, has 335,000 residents. Newer campus facilities include a $17 million natatorium and a 30,000-square-foot fitness and wellness center.

Founded in 1833 and formerly associated with the American Baptist Churches, Kalamazoo is the oldest private college in Michigan. Many first-years begin the year with a LandSea trip, which features three weeks of climbing, rappelling, canoeing, and backpacking in the mountains of the Adirondacks. By the end, they're convinced they can survive anything, including the rigors of a Kalamazoo College education and the long Michigan winters. Once on campus, they pursue a liberal arts curriculum that includes language proficiency, a first-year writing seminar, sophomore and senior seminars, as well as a senior individualized project—directed research, a creative piece, or a traditional thesis—basically anything that caps off each student's education in some meaningful way.

> **"Kalamazoo College does study abroad so well that it seems ridiculous not to take advantage."**

After their sophomore year, most of K's undergrads meet life's challenges with suitcase in hand, studying wherever their heart takes them, often for the regular tuition price. The college offers three-, six-, and nine-month immersive study abroad programs that are available to all students, regardless of major; almost all credit earned during study abroad transfers back to K. "Kalamazoo College does study abroad so well that it seems ridiculous not to take advantage of this opportunity," cheers a biology major. "They make it financially accessible and ensure that you won't fall behind by going abroad." Sixty-one percent of students study abroad via 56 programs offered in 29 countries.

Back on campus, students say the accelerated pace of K's three 10-week terms can make things stressful, but one senior reflects that the academic environment "has taught me to manage my time better and to ask for help when I need it." The natural sciences are exceptionally good, and interdisciplinary programs in international and area studies, community and global health, and critical ethnic studies are also strengths. Biology, chemistry, psychology, and business are the most popular majors,

Website: www.kzoo.edu
Location: Small City
Private
Total Enrollment: 1,219
Undergraduates: 1,219
Male/Female: 44/56
Financial Aid: 98%
Pell Grant: 30%
Expense: Pr $ $ $
Student Loans: 64%
Average Debt: $ $ $
Applicants: 3,334
Accepted: 80%
Enrolled: 26%
Grad in 6 Years: 76%
Returning Freshmen: 85%
Academics: ✐ ✐ ✐
Social: ☎ ☎ ☎
Q of L: ★ ★ ★
Admissions: (800) 253-3602
Email Address: admission@kzoo.edu

Strong Programs:
Natural Sciences
International and Area Studies
Community and Global Health
Critical Ethnic Studies
Biology
Chemistry
Psychology
Business

and students praise K's language departments. Biochemistry is now available as a major. Professors, rated highly for their enthusiasm and accessibility, give students lots of individual attention. "Professors come here to teach because they want to be engaged in conversations with students," attests a biology and anthropology/sociology major. Seventy-one percent of students participate in career development programs like internships, externships, and K-Trek trips to visit industries around the country.

> *Seventy-one percent of students participate in career development programs like internships and K-Trek trips to visit industries around the country.*

"K students are social justice–oriented, academically focused, a bit hippie, and overall a very supportive community," muses a junior. Sixty-five percent of students come from Michigan and 4 percent from foreign nations. The student body is 16 percent Hispanic/Latino, 6 percent Asian American, 5 percent Black, and 6 percent multiracial. Many students crave more diversity on campus. The administration says it is continuing efforts to educate students on intercultural understanding, and the campus has a decidedly progressive tone. Merit scholarships averaging $32,200 are available to qualified students. Athletic scholarships are not available.

Sixty percent of students live on campus. "The dorms are not huge but are big enough to live comfortably with another person," an economics and political science major explains. With so many students away each term thanks to the study abroad program, a certain instability pervades all activities, from athletics to student government to living groups in the co-ed residence halls, where suites hold one to six students. Dorms are divided by class year, and three dorms are available for first-year students.

> **"K students are social justice–oriented, academically focused, [and] a bit hippie."**

Dining services get mixed reviews, but students give good ratings to campus safety. While there are no Greek organizations, 10 living/learning houses offer a more community-oriented atmosphere, including family-style dinners. For those who tire of campus life, "Off-campus housing is both cheap and located close to campus, so it is a popular option," reports a sophomore.

K's campus is always buzzing with social activities like movies, concerts, speakers, and other events. Parties, often hosted by athletic teams in off-campus houses, are limited to the weekends, and students agree that the atmosphere is pressure-free when it comes to alcohol. Students look forward to the Monte Carlo casino night, homecoming, and the Day of Gracious Living, a spring day where, without prior warning, classes are canceled and students can choose to head to the beach, work on volunteer projects, or relax on campus. "It's a day where everyone can just stop for a minute and put down the books and laptops to go outside and enjoy living," explains a math major. (One popular T-shirt: "The end of learning is gracious living.") About two-thirds of students get involved in the community through service-learning courses and student-led cocurricular activities, working with local partners to address issues such as neighborhood development, sustainability, prison reform, and migrant rights. "The local music and art scenes are huge in Kalamazoo, with many free performances all year and Art Hop every month," says a senior. In addition to the typical collection of restaurants, theaters, and bars, K students benefit from the physical proximity of Western Michigan University, where they may use the library or attend cultural events. Lake Michigan's beaches and Chicago's urban playground are easy road trips for students with cars.

> *On the Day of Gracious Living, classes are canceled and students head to the beach, work on volunteer projects, or relax on campus.*

For those who equate college with athletics, K has something to offer—even if it's not nationally televised games or tens of thousands of screaming fans. The Kalamazoo Hornets have a long-standing rivalry with Hope College, culminating in the football teams' annual competition for the Wooden Shoes trophy. Kalamazoo has an outstanding men's tennis team, which has won the Michigan Intercollegiate Athletic Association (MIAA) conference championship 86 (!) times, most recently in 2022. The men's and women's swimming and soccer squads are also competitive. K offers intramural volleyball, soccer, and basketball, as well as several club sports.

Overlaps

Hope, College of Wooster, Albion, University of Michigan, Michigan State, U of I at Urbana–Champaign, Grand Valley State, Western Michigan

Kalamazoo College is best suited for those "looking for a place where everyone is really enthusiastic about learning and thrives in that kind of environment," says one student. K's academic terms may be fast-paced and the workload demanding, but students are given the flexibility to pursue their interests through individualized projects and off-campus exploration. The result, says a senior, is a student body defined by "open-minded, global citizens."

If You Apply To ›

Kalamazoo: Early decision I and II, early action, regular decision. SATs or ACTs: optional. Accepts the Common Application with optional writing supplement.

University of Kansas

1502 Iowa Street, Lawrence, KS 66045

Often overlooked because of its heartland location, KU has the sophistication of the leading Big Ten universities but is much easier to get into. Stereotypes of Kansas to the contrary, Lawrence is not flat as a pancake. Offers a solid slate of professional schools and an honors program that is among the nation's best. Jayhawk basketball is legendary.

Despite its conservative Midwest location, the University of Kansas is a welcoming oasis of progressive activism and tolerance. The school courts extremely dedicated students with an impressive honors program that has helped raise its academic profile. With sound academics and extracurriculars, winning athletics, and a stellar social life, the University of Kansas has a bounty of opportunities for motivated Jayhawks. "KU prides itself on offering opportunities to students that they can't get anywhere else in our region of the U.S.," says a business analytics major.

The 1,000-acre campus is set atop Mount Oread—a hill that was once a crossing point for pioneer wagon trains—and spreads out on rolling green hills overlooking river valleys. Many of the buildings are made of indigenous Kansas limestone and are famed for their red roofs. But the real beauty of the campus lies in its landscape, particularly the breathtaking autumn foliage. The Dole Institute of Politics is home to one of the world's largest congressional archives and a World Trade Center memorial. A massive $350 million expansion of the campus's Central District features an integrated sciences building, a student union, a 550-bed residence hall, and a 700-bed apartment complex, among other facilities.

> "[KU offers] opportunities to students that they can't get anywhere else in our region of the U.S."

Prospective KU freshmen may apply to the schools of Architecture & Design, Business, Engineering, Journalism and Mass Communications, Music, and Professional Studies, and to the College of Liberal Arts & Sciences. Those not admitted to one of the professional schools will automatically be considered for admission to the College, where 51 percent of the undergraduate population is enrolled. Students wishing to enter the schools of Education and Human Sciences, Health Professions, Nursing, Pharmacy, and Social Welfare must pass prerequisite courses and meet the schools' entry requirements. As part of their degrees, all KU undergraduates must complete the university-wide KU Core curriculum, which spans the entire undergraduate experience and culminates in a required capstone experience that varies by major.

Website: www.ku.edu
Location: Small City
Public
Total Enrollment: 21,996
Undergraduates: 16,535
Male/Female: 47/53
Financial Aid: 71%
Pell Grant: 20%
Expense: Pub $ $
Student Loans: 50%
Average Debt: $ $
Applicants: 15,275
Accepted: 92%
Enrolled: 29%
Grad in 6 Years: 66%
Returning Freshmen: 85%
Academics: ✐ ✐ ✐ ✐
Social: 🕿 🕿 🕿 🕿
Q of L: ★ ★ ★ ★
Admissions: (785) 864-3911
Email Address: adm@ku.edu

Strong Programs:
Architecture
Design
Education
Geology

Some of the most notable undergraduate programs offered by KU's 14 schools include architecture, design, education, geology, journalism, music, social work, and health-related majors. The School of Journalism and Mass Communications perpetuates the legacy of famed journalist William Allen White, and the School of Engineering has significantly expanded its resources and facilities, most recently with the opening of the interdisciplinary Earth, Energy, and Environment Center. Psychology, finance, journalism, marketing, and nursing are the most popular majors. Accelerated bachelor's/master's programs in several fields, ranging from environmental studies/urban planning to history of art, allow students to earn two degrees in five years. Citing budget issues, the university has eliminated its long-standing undergraduate humanities program.

"The academic climate is very flexible and supportive," says a microbiology major. "It's rigorous but not to the point of being unbearable." Forty-four percent of all undergraduate classes have fewer than 20 students, and while teaching assistants do teach some classes, students often have access to leading professors early on. "My calculus course freshman year was taught by the head of the math department—showing that there isn't a time at KU where your academics and instruction are not made a top priority," says an architecture major. The Office of Student Affairs, run by its own vice provost, wins praise for its academic advising and for its help with internships, disability services, and extracurriculars. Career services receive high ratings too.

Incoming freshmen can apply to the highly selective University Honors Program, which provides more than 1,600 academically motivated students with in-depth courses, specialized advising, early enrollment, and financial support for opportunities like research projects. Twenty-nine percent of undergrads leave U.S. borders for 165-plus KU-administered study abroad programs in more than 70 countries, including Brazil, Costa Rica, the Czech Republic, Italy, Japan, South Africa, and South Korea. KU provides five region-specific area studies programs and supports instruction in 38 languages.

The 1,000-acre campus is set atop Mount Oread and spreads out on rolling green hills overlooking river valleys.

"It's rigorous but not to the point of being unbearable."

"Proud and passionate. These two words invoke to me what it means to be a Jayhawk," says one student. Sixty-three percent of undergrads are from Kansas, and most of the rest are fellow Midwesterners (many from Chicago), although 4 percent are international. Black students account for 4 percent, Hispanics/Latinos 9 percent, Asian Americans 6 percent, and multiracial students 5 percent. KU has a history of progressive attitudes, but conservative views are well represented on campus too. KU grants four-year renewable merit scholarships to eligible freshmen, and athletes vie for more than 300 full and partial scholarships in 18 varsity sports. For Pell-eligible students who also meet certain academic criteria, the KU Pell Advantage program provides a combination of scholarships and grants to fund students' tuition and fees.

The University Honors Program provides more than 1,600 students with in-depth courses, specialized advising, and early enrollment.

Twenty-five percent of Kansas students live in KU residence halls, scholarship halls, or on-campus apartments. Most students live off campus in Lawrence apartments, which are considered expensive only by Kansas standards. Students take their meals at 16 dining locations across campus, ranging from residential dining centers to retail cafés, coffeehouses, and snack shops. "The food is a good mix of different cuisines and is also healthy and nutritious," says a junior. One student explains, "KU SafeRide provides transportation for late at night, while Lawrence police and university police constantly patrol the streets." Additionally, the Sexual Assault Prevention and Education Center conducts training on consent and bystander intervention.

The Greek system, which attracts 19 percent of the men and 26 percent of the women, is a conspicuous force in the social scene but doesn't control it. According to an accounting major, "The party culture is whatever students want to participate in (big, small, or none at all)," and a psychology major cautions, "KU is strict about alcohol on campus, especially in the residence halls." About 500 organized groups keep things lively; other activities include movies, poetry readings, game nights, cultural events, and concerts. Scholarship halls, residence halls, and other student groups also sponsor large campus parties and events. The university's bus system is much appreciated by tenderfeet, especially because that great big hill seems to double in size during the cold, windy winters.

With its myriad boutiques, restaurants, and bars and its active music scene, Lawrence is a favored destination for off-campus fun, and students also enjoy getting involved in the community through KU's Center for Community Outreach. "Lawrence is *the* American college town," asserts one enthusiastic Jayhawk. "Period." Topeka, the state capital, and Kansas City are each less than an hour's drive, and the area is also served by Amtrak.

KU varsity teams—the only ones in the nation that carry the name Jayhawks, who were antislavery pioneers in the 1850s—compete in the rough-and-tumble Big 12 Conference. The men's basketball team, a mainstay of March Madness, has won more conference titles than any other Big 12 team and defeated the North Carolina Tar Heels for the national title in 2022. James Naismith,

> **"Lawrence is *the* American college town. Period."**

who invented basketball, was KU's first coach—and the only one with a losing record. Women's volleyball and men's and women's track and field are also competitive. Students take part in about 30 sports clubs and 30 intramural sports, the most popular of which is—you guessed it—basketball, which signs up more than 125 teams. Sand volleyball, soccer, and tennis are other student favorites.

Jayhawk traditions certainly run deep. The school year kicks off with Hawk Week, the official welcome for new students. To demonstrate their loyalty to the Jayhawks, thousands of students show up for the first men's and women's basketball practices of the season. This nocturnal tradition is lovingly labeled "Late Night in the Phog"—an allusion to the fieldhouse named after the late, great basketball coach Forrest "Phog" Allen. The traditional "Rock Chalk Jayhawk" KU cheer and steam whistle signaling the end of every class period are enough to bring a pang of nostalgia to the heart of even the most grizzled Kansas alum. "The Rock Chalk chant is widely recognizable, creating a sort of bond between all Jayhawks, past and present," says one student.

With more than 200 undergraduate fields of study and a history that dates to 1865, Kansas's reputation (the nonbasketball one) continues to grow. Comprehensive study abroad programs, a distinctive honors program, and a robust sense of school spirit are just some of the reasons students choose to be Jayhawks. And as a satisfied senior points out, "You can't be a Jayhawk anywhere else."

The traditional "Rock Chalk Jayhawk" KU cheer can bring a pang of nostalgia to the heart of even the most grizzled Kansas alum.

Overlaps

Indiana University, University of Missouri, University of Oregon, Michigan State, SUNY–Buffalo, Kansas State, University of Arkansas, University of Nebraska–Lincoln

If You Apply To ›

Kansas: Early action, rolling admissions. SATs or ACTs: optional. Accepts the Common Application with supplement. Apply to particular school or program.

University of Kentucky

100 Funkhouser Building, Lexington, KY 40506

The state of Kentucky is better known for horses and hoops than for higher education, but its flagship public university, located in the heart of the Bluegrass, is working to change that. The University of Kentucky is always a championship contender on the basketball court, and its programs in business, engineering, health, and equine sciences are just as competitive. About a third of students come from out of state, mostly from Illinois, Indiana, Ohio, Tennessee, and Georgia.

UK's location in the heart of one of the finest horse-breeding areas makes it a natural place for the Gluck Equine Research Center.

While the University of Kentucky Wildcats grab the most headlines, the university's claims to excellence stretch into outstanding medical and premedical programs, scientific research involving both professors and students, and a social calendar packed with enough Southern tradition to make even the most composed debutante's head spin. Over the last decade, UK has undergone a more than $2.3 billion campus transformation, much of it focused on student life, including more than $450 million in high-tech residence halls and the Gatton Student Center, complete with dining and a state-of-the-art fitness center. UK is a national leader in efforts to support first-generation college students and has established a dedicated living/learning community for them.

"I've had many professors whose lectures made me excited to go to class."

The University of Kentucky was founded in 1865 as the state's land grand university, and its campus contains a mixture of old and new, with traditional redbrick buildings that date back to the late 1890s and modern designs using contemporary glass and concrete. The well-maintained grounds are organized around comfortable parklike spaces influenced by Frederick Law Olmsted's design. The campus contains a vast amount of mature trees and lawns set in a natural arrangement of open spaces, typical of the great land grant universities. Of course, UK's location in the heart of one of the finest horse-breeding areas in the world makes it a natural place for the Gluck Equine Research Center, a headquarters for research into horse diseases.

UK's general education program, known as the UK Core, comprises the equivalent of 30 credit hours in 10 course areas that address four broad learning outcomes. Freshmen are encouraged but not required to take an academic orientation class called UK101, designed to help them adjust to college life. Students not ready to declare a major may test the academic waters in "Exploratory Programs" in a particular college. Business, engineering, and health, especially nursing and premed programs, tend to be UK's strongest fields, but several unique programs stand out. The equine science and management major prepares students for a wide range of careers in the horse industry by teaching both science and business concepts. Students studying prevet and animal sciences at UK will find coveted slots reserved for them at Auburn University and Tuskegee in the advanced veterinary medicine program, at in-state tuition rates. UK's Gaines Center for the Humanities is unusual in its study of public higher education, and the Patterson School of Diplomacy and International Commerce is one of the smallest yet most respected schools of its type in the country. The fledgling Lewis Honors College is housed in a dedicated quad of residence halls.

"Southern hospitality abounds."

The academic climate is laid-back, but students shouldn't expect easy As. Thirty-eight percent of classes have fewer than 20 students, but lower-level "monster" science classes are common, and one student describes them as "extremely large and not at all personalized." When it comes time for course registration, a marketing major says students "have difficulty if they are freshmen because most of them have to take the same classes, and sometimes they don't get the right times—or the classes at all." It's hard to complete the engineering, health, business, and architecture programs in four years, students say. Term-time internships, known as co-ops, also complicate—but enliven—the picture. The university has bolstered its advising services in order to provide more personalized attention and to better coordinate career and academic services. Teaching assistants and full professors teach about the same number of freshman classes, and students praise UK's faculty. "I've had many professors whose lectures made me excited to go to class," says a communication sciences and disorders major. Seventeen percent of students study abroad in more than 200 available programs, including 52 that are directed by UK faculty.

"UK students are typically self-assured, slightly competitive, and outgoing," says a psychology major, and according to a classmate, "Southern hospitality abounds."

UK undergraduates hail from all 120 Kentucky counties and more than 100 countries; 32 percent are from out of state and 2 percent are international. The student body is predominantly white; Black students account for just 7 percent of undergrads, Hispanics/Latinos 6 percent, Asian Americans 4 percent, and multiracial students 4 percent. Diverse political views are represented on campus, but a senior says UK is "not really a politically charged university." Merit scholarships averaging $8,800 are offered to qualified students, as are more than 500 athletic scholarships.

The university has modernized all its residence halls and opened 14 new ones in recent years. Dorms are located on two parts of the campus—north and central—and offer suite-style rooms, with no more than four students sharing a bathroom. "Students get really nice amenities, like Tempur-Pedic mattresses, granite countertops, two sinks, and full-size closets," reports a student. The only downside of such plush accommodations, students say, is the cost. Students are not required to live on campus, but 28 percent do so. Dining services get good reviews, and a communication major says, "There are so many options from sit-down, buffet-style to specialty cafés

Students not ready to declare a major may test the academic waters in "Exploratory Programs" in a particular college.

"In Kentucky, basketball is like a second religion."

to fast food," as well as "worry-free zones" for students with dietary restrictions. The Green Dot Bystander Intervention program, designed to prevent sexual assault and domestic violence on college campuses, originated at the University of Kentucky and has been adopted by hundreds of colleges and universities across the country.

On campus, students enjoy movies, presentations, seminars, concerts, and athletic events. Twenty-three percent of Kentucky men and 33 percent of the women go Greek, and fraternities and sororities offer numerous on-campus social activities, as well as opportunities for volunteer work in the community. Students are not allowed to have alcohol on campus, except for special events that have been registered with the university. Students collaborate to mount one of the largest student-run philanthropies anywhere: DanceBlue. The yearlong fund-raising effort culminates in a 24-hour, no-sleeping dance marathon that benefits a local children's cancer clinic and pediatric cancer research. Among the highlights of any student's career at UK are two one-month periods—one in the fall, one in the spring—when students spend afternoons at Keeneland Race Track enjoying the tradition of Kentucky horse racing.

DanceBlue, a 24-hour, no-sleeping dance marathon, is one of the largest student-run philanthropies anywhere.

Despite the limited diversity on campus, Lexington abounds with a multitude of ethnic eateries, as well as theaters, shops, and nightspots. The downtown area is within walking distance of campus. "Downtown Lexington has a great social scene, so lots of students will venture off campus for concerts, restaurants, festivals, farmers markets, etc.," says a senior. When it's time for a road trip, UK students head to Cincinnati or Louisville (one hour away) or to Atlanta or Chicago (six hours).

The best road-trip destinations, of course, are anywhere there's a steamy, noisy gym and a basketball team ready to do battle with UK's always-solid Wildcats. Home games at the legendary Rupp Arena—what one student calls "a magical experience"—are consistently packed by the Big Blue Nation. "In Kentucky, basketball is like a second religion," agrees another true-blue Wildcat fan. Football and women's basketball draw crowds too. The school fields 21 Division I teams in all, most of which compete in the Southeastern Conference (SEC). Intramurals range from soccer and basketball leagues to dodgeball tournaments and hot-shot contests.

"The culture of UK is unique because it has the competitive energy of the SEC, but it's not an overly Greek-focused campus and it does a great job of supporting every interest," comments a senior. Indeed, students here find plenty of solid opportunities, from specialties in equine and animal science to support for first-generation students to serious school pride. Whether it's screaming themselves hoarse for five guys hitting the hardwood or for four-legged equines racing around an oval, for many students, the mix of collegiate craziness and old-world Southern hospitality found at the University of Kentucky is just what they want.

Overlaps

Indiana University, University of Louisville, Miami University (OH), Ohio State, University of Tennessee Knoxville, West Virginia University

Kenyon College

Ransom Hall, Gambier, OH 43022

Kenyon is a vintage liberal arts college plunked down in the middle of the Ohio countryside. More mainstream than Oberlin, more serious than Denison, and more selective than Wooster, Kenyon is best known for English and a small but distinguished drama program. Located in a tiny village where faculty and staff are the main residents. Swimming and diving teams make huge splashes.

The oldest private college in Ohio, Kenyon College provides students with an accessible and pure liberal arts experience that rivals those of leading East Coast institutions. Students here are proud of what they see as setting Kenyon apart from other liberal arts colleges. "The one thing that unites us all is that we are passionate about something," explains one student. "Whether it be drama, physics, writing, activism—Kenyon students care!" Though highly selective, the college continues to build on its reputation as a supportive academic environment.

Kenyon's 1,000-acre campus sits on a hillside overlooking a scenic view of river, woods, and fields in a secluded village of roughly 2,500 residents. Old Kenyon, the college's original building, dating from 1826, is said to be the first collegiate Gothic building in America, and the campus is on the National Register of Historic Places. The campus also boasts a 500-acre nature preserve, featuring hiking trails and extensive perennial gardens. The 98,000-square-foot, LEED Gold–certified Chalmers Library opened in 2021.

The hallmark of Kenyon's academic philosophy is a fierce devotion to the liberal arts and sciences. While there is no core curriculum at Kenyon, all students must have proficiency in a second language and complete requirements in quantitative reasoning. A bevy of academic counselors, including upperclassmen and professors, help ensure that freshmen stay on the right track. The culmination of each student's coursework at Kenyon is the senior exercise, which may take the form of a comprehensive examination, an integrative paper, a research project, a performance, or some combination of these. Approximately 12 percent of students graduate with departmental honors.

> **"Whether it be drama, physics, writing, activism—Kenyon students care!"**

English, a nationally renowned subject at Kenyon since the 1930s, is the most popular major, and it, along with the department of dance, drama, and film (which turned out the likes of Allison Janney and Paul Newman), sets the tone of campus life. Kenyon is the home of the *Kenyon Review*, a prestigious literary quarterly that offers internships to a few lucky students, and is a school about which alum E. L. Doctorow said, "Poetry is what we did at Kenyon, the way at Ohio State they played football." John Green, the giant of young adult fiction, is also an alum. Economics, psychology, political science, and biology round out the list of popular majors, and the modern languages and literatures, physics, and mathematics and statistics departments are also strong. Political science draws many undecided majors with its yearlong introductory class, Quest for Justice. The Integrated Program in Humane

Website: www.kenyon.edu
Location: Rural
Private
Total Enrollment: 1,875
Undergraduates: 1,868
Male/Female: 46/54
Financial Aid: 45%
Pell Grant: 9%
Expense: Pr $ $ $ $
Student Loans: 33%
Average Debt: $
Applicants: 7,601
Accepted: 37%
Enrolled: 21%
Grad in 6 Years: 89%
Returning Freshmen: 91%
Academics: ✏ ✏ ✏ ✏
Social: ☎ ☎ ☎
Q of L: ★ ★ ★
Admissions: (800) 848-2468
Email Address: admissions@kenyon.edu

Strong Programs:
English
Drama
Film
Modern Languages and
   Literatures
Physics
Mathematics and Statistics
Political Science
Economics

Studies concentration, the school's oldest interdisciplinary program, is also popular. Opportunities for independent study abound, such as a unique farming program that places students on nearby farms for fieldwork each week. Preprofessional opportunities include 3–2 engineering programs with several universities and high access to graduate programs in law, business, and medicine.

"Despite the academic rigor of many classes and departments at Kenyon, I have never felt competitive with my fellow students," says a psychology major. Classes are small, and even the larger introductory courses use a two-part format in which students meet for lectures one week and split up for discussion sections with the professor the next. "Kenyon's professors are active researchers and exemplary teachers," says a math major. "They are passionate about their fields, and they love getting their students excited about the material as well." Many profs live close to campus, which enhances the close-knit environment. On-campus summer research scholarships in the sciences and humanities provide opportunities for collaborative research for aspiring scientists, scholars, and doctors. Forty-three percent of Kenyon students study abroad, choosing from nearly 200 programs in 50 countries, including Kenyon-sponsored programs in England and Italy.

The 98,000-square-foot, LEED Gold–certified Chalmers Library opened in 2021.

> **"[Professors] love getting their students excited about the material."**

Twelve percent of students are Ohioans, one-third hail from New England and Mid-Atlantic states, and 10 percent come from abroad. Black students account for 3 percent of the student body, Hispanics/Latinos 7 percent, Asian Americans 4 percent, and multiracial students 5 percent, and the college is actively working to increase diversity. The liberal, friendly student body is politically engaged, especially when it comes to social justice issues, and a sophomore says, "Students at Kenyon thrive on open conversation and do not silence opinions that contradict theirs." Kenyon meets the full demonstrated financial need of admitted students and awards merit scholarships averaging $14,800, but only 9 percent of incoming freshmen qualify for Pell Grants. Newman's Own Foundation Scholarships guarantee a loan-free education for 25 selected students with the greatest need who bring the qualities of creativity, community service, and leadership to Kenyon.

The men's swimming team has won 34 national titles, and the women's team has claimed 24, most recently in 2022.

All students live on campus, with housing guaranteed for four years. Freshmen start in five dorms at the north end of campus, and most move to the south end the next year. Renovations and expansions are always in the works, but students say some accommodations still need improving. Rooms are selected via a sometimes harrowing housing lottery. Everyone, including those in the apartments with kitchens, must buy the unlimited meal plan. "Kenyon is in an isolated area of Ohio and is generally very safe," a senior says.

Given the school's rural location, social life happens on campus, with more than 150 student clubs and a Greek system that draws 20 percent of the men and 19 percent of the women. The frats throw lively parties that are open to all, and a senior says, "Every student performance—sports games, public presentations, music recitals, art shows—is incredibly well attended." With its deli, market, coffeehouse, inn, restaurant, couple of bars, bank, and post office, Gambier is at least quaint, even if it is a bit of a

> **"[Kenyon] is a quirky school that can be extremely rewarding to attend."**

culture shock for urbanites. Students enjoy buying real maple syrup, fresh bread, and cheese from Amish farmers with stands on the main street on Saturdays. There are a few more options 10 minutes away in Mount Vernon, to which the college runs a daytime shuttle bus, and two small ski areas lie near campus. Columbus and Ohio State are a 45-minute drive south, and those seeking adventure farther from home sometimes road-trip to Cleveland (home of the Rock and Roll Hall of Fame), Cincinnati, Chicago, or even Canada.

Kenyon remains defined by its traditions, the most hallowed of which is renewed each year as incoming freshmen sing college songs to the rest of the community from the steps of Rosse Hall. Departing seniors sing the same songs at graduation. On Matriculation Day each October, after a formal ceremony, freshmen sign a book that contains the signatures of virtually every Kenyon student since the early 1800s. Summer Sendoff is an outdoor concert celebrating the end of spring semester classes.

Kenyon's varsity teams are known as the Lords and the Ladies. Men's and women's tennis and soccer are consistently competitive in the North Coast Athletic Conference, but the flagship sport is definitely swimming. Kenyon's swimming and diving teams dominate Division III competition, with the men's team having won 34 national titles and the women's team claiming 24, most recently in 2022. The annual hockey game against Denison and soccer games against Ohio Wesleyan draw large crowds. Club and intramural sports attract 30 percent of the students and sponsor everything from ultimate Frisbee to ballroom dance.

Kenyon students are liberal, global thinkers who are as devoted to one another as they are to their studies and their traditions. The *Kenyon Review*, the legend of alumnus Paul Newman, and national-championship swimming give the college a distinctive identity. As one sociology major advises, "It can be tough at times dealing with the location or the intense academics, but if students embrace Kenyon, it is a quirky school that can be extremely rewarding to attend."

Overlaps

Swarthmore, Williams, Hamilton, Oberlin, Grinnell, Wesleyan, Macalester, Colby

If You Apply To ›

Kenyon: Early decision I and II, regular decision. Accepts the Common Application. Please consult Kenyon's website for the most up-to-date information regarding standardized test requirements.

Knox College

2 East South Street, Galesburg, IL 61401

This friendly and progressive Illinois college was among the first in the nation to admit Black students and women. Offers a strong creative writing program, exceptional sciences, and a real-world atmosphere. More mainstream than Beloit and Grinnell and smaller than Illinois Wesleyan. With a hugely diverse student body of about 1,100, Knox offers an unusual degree of personal attention, even by the standards of small colleges.

Website: www.knox.edu
Location: Small City
Private
Total Enrollment: 1,129
Undergraduates: 1,129
Male/Female: 43/57
Financial Aid: 96%
Pell Grant: 35%
Expense: Pr $ $
Student Loans: 65%
Average Debt: $ $ $

With the unconventional Prairie Fire as its emblem, Knox College has long made a name for itself by breaking away from the conventions of the day. Founded by abolitionists in 1837 as the Knox Manual Labor College, this liberal arts college has a tradition of debate that extends beyond the Lincoln–Douglas event that occurred here in 1858. And through a warm, supportive academic community and emphasis on "putting knowledge into practice through real-world experiences," the college continues to foster a strong sense of individualism.

Located in the heart of the Midwest—midway between Chicago and St. Louis—the 82-acre campus has spacious, tree-lined lawns and a dynamic mixture of architecture that reflects the 164-year span of construction dates of existing buildings. Old Main, constructed in 1857, is a National Historic Landmark and the only building remaining from the 1858 Lincoln–Douglas debates. Recent campus projects include the Whitcomb Art Center, which features a variety of art studios and workshops, and major renovations to the Umbeck Math and Science Center.

Students say the academic relationships at Knox are infused with a spirit of cooperation and equality. Knox operates on an honor system that allows students to take tests unproctored in any public area. Beyond the classroom, students, faculty, and administrators make decisions on boards together, each with identical voting power. As part of Knox's Blaze a Trail first-year experience program, incoming students participate in new student orientation and take First-Year Preceptorial, a small seminar taught by professors from across the college that emphasizes critical analysis, writing, and class discussion. They may also join an optional living/learning community associated with their Preceptorial course.

> "Due to how intimate our campus is, the quality of instruction is very meaningful and sincere."

All Knox students apply their learning to a real-world experience of their choice, such as independent research or creative work, an internship, community service, or study abroad, which serves as a capstone experience in their junior or senior year. What's more, through Knox's Power of Experience program, every student receives funding of at least $2,000 to support these experiences. The general education curriculum, known as Elements, spans coursework in the arts, sciences, humanities, and social sciences, through which students learn how to communicate in a second language, in numbers and symbols, and with people of diverse backgrounds. Creative writing and biology are among the school's strongest programs; the college's biannual literary magazine, *Catch*, has won several national and international awards, while biology attracts lots of research grant money. Other popular majors include psychology, business and management, and anthropology and sociology, and the theater and computer science departments are also notable. Knox offers 3–2 or 3–4 programs in engineering, nursing, medical technology, law, and architecture, as well as a cooperative program with the George Washington University School of Medicine and Health Sciences. Newer majors include journalism, public policy, and data science, and a minor in Spanish translation and interpretation is now available.

Knox's three-term system packs a great deal of studying into a short period, but students are only required to take three courses per term, which keeps the coursework "very manageable," according to a biology major. Eighty percent of classes have fewer than 20 students, and a political science and economics major says, "Due to how intimate our campus is, the quality of instruction is very meaningful and sincere." Immersive terms give students the option of engaging in a hands-on exploration of a single field of study for an entire term; available subjects include clinical psychology, studio art, repertory theater, business start-ups, and fieldwork and community-building at the off-campus Green Oaks prairie restoration site. For those interested in service, Knox was the first college in the country to establish an official Peace Corps Preparatory Program. Knox also offers more than 100 study abroad and off-campus programs around the world, and about half of students participate. Students praise Knox's academic advising system for helping them navigate the multitude of options.

"Knox students are inquisitive and like to challenge themselves," comments an art history major. "Everyone picks up new hobbies and passions at Knox." Forty-two percent of students come from Illinois, and an impressive 16 percent hail from foreign countries. While Knox is not a hotbed of

> "Everyone picks up new hobbies and passions at Knox."

political protest, students here tend to be progressive and engaged in current events, and a commitment to diversity is evident across campus. Black students make up 7 percent of the student body, Asian Americans 4 percent, Hispanics/

(continued)

Applicants: 3,038
Accepted: 71%
Enrolled: 13%
Grad in 6 Years: 75%
Returning Freshmen: 83%
Academics: ✎ ✎ ✎
Social: ☎ ☎ ☎
Q of L: ★ ★ ★
Admissions: (800) 678-KNOX
Email Address: admission@ knox.edu

Strong Programs:
Creative Writing
Biology
Theater
Computer Science
Psychology
Business and Management
Anthropology and Sociology

Through Knox's Power of Experience program, every student receives funding of at least $2,000 to support real-world experiences, such as internships.

Latinos 14 percent, and multiracial students 6 percent. Socioeconomically, 35 percent of freshmen qualify for Pell Grants, and a quarter of undergrads are first-generation college students. Merit scholarships averaging $28,900 are available, but athletic scholarships are not.

Eighty-six percent of students reside in campus digs. Most freshmen live in single-sex suites, and a senior describes the dorms as "nothing to write home about" but adds that the apartments and townhouses for upperclassmen are more comfortable. Those who move off campus must obtain permission, which can be difficult. Dining services get good reviews, especially because the staff will "work with students to create new recipes and bring new products to Knox," explains a French and history major. Students rate campus safety as strong.

Seven percent of men and 5 percent of women go Greek, and weekends are filled with on-campus club activities, cultural events, and fraternity parties, although all parties must be registered and alcohol-free. Students warn that the administration is quick to deal with underage drinkers. Annual events include the Lincoln Fest music festival and International Fair, but a junior says Flunk Day, which had its 100th anniversary in 2022, is "the crown jewel of all Knox traditions." At 7:00 on a spring morning, Old Main's bell rings, seniors bang pots and pans, and classes are canceled to make way for lawn games, inflatables, food trucks, karaoke, and other rollicking festivities.

Galesburg is a small Midwestern railroad town, and the Amtrak station makes travel easy and relatively cheap. At one time, this city of about 30,000 was a center of abolitionism, and the honorary degree that the college bestowed on then-presidential candidate Abraham Lincoln was his first. Now, Knox students devote more than 80,000 hours of service to the community every year.

"Galesburg has its fair share of locally owned businesses [and] lots of green space."

"Galesburg has its fair share of locally owned businesses, restaurants, bars, etc., as well as lots of green space," reports a sophomore. Nearby Lake Storey offers boating, water slides, and nature trails, and students looking for more excitement can travel to Peoria, about 50 miles southeast, or Chicago, about 200 miles northeast.

Prairie Fire athletics' 20 Division III teams generate a reasonable degree of enthusiasm, boosted by the school mascot, a fox named—you guessed it—Blaze. The men's and women's soccer teams are strong, both having recently earned Midwest Conference titles. Every fall, the football team endures lots of "hard Knox" against archrival Monmouth to bring home the highly prized Bronze Turkey trophy, a throwback to the time when the game was played on Thanksgiving Day. About a quarter of students participate in intramural and club sports; basketball, volleyball, and ultimate Frisbee are the most popular.

As a Knox student, "You go to school in a small town in the Midwest, where the winters are bitter and the fall and spring are all too short," muses a junior. "But despite these challenges, Knox students focus their pride on their academics and the quality of their campus experience." The result is a close-knit community, an emphasis on hands-on learning, and an open-minded atmosphere fostered by Knox's notably diverse student body. "There is a strong sense of 'we are all in this together,'" concludes a junior, "and that gives us a unity that is pretty unique."

If You Apply To ›

Knox: Early decision, early action I and II, regular decision. SATs or ACTs: optional. Accepts the Common Application with supplement.

Lafayette College

Easton, PA 18042

Geographically close to Lehigh but closer kin to Colgate and Hamilton and boasting a strong global orientation, including for engineering. Compare to Bucknell, Union, Swarthmore, and Trinity (CT), which also offer engineering. Attracts relatively preppy, athletic students who work hard and play hard. One of the smallest institutions to play Division I sports.

Lafayette College has become one of the small elite liberal arts colleges with a huge presence abroad. A national leader in undergraduate faculty-mentored research, it ranks among the top colleges in study abroad participation, and its liberal arts curriculum mixes nicely with engineering in a small college atmosphere. Says one satisfied junior, "Lafayette is a place that believes that we can be leaders, scholars, athletes, and activists and that we don't have to choose just one."

Founded in 1826 and named for the famous Marquis, Lafayette is situated on College Hill, a stately hill in Easton, Pennsylvania, just an hour and a half west of New York City and even closer to Philadelphia. The campus has an eclectic blend of architectural styles and more than 125 species of trees. Open, flexible learning and workspaces are a common theme in many Lafayette buildings, including the Skillman Library and the Acopian Engineering Center, which stays open all night and weekends. The $75 million, high-tech Rockwell Integrated Sciences Center is the largest capital project in the school's history.

A Common Course of Study includes a first-year seminar and courses in lab science, social sciences, mathematics, humanities, writing, global and multicultural proficiency, and a foreign language. "Classes are tough, and you have to put in the effort to succeed in most," reports a neuroscience major, but the atmosphere is "not competitive." Economics, mechanical engineering, neuroscience, government and law, and biology are among the most popular majors; nearly half of Lafayette's students major in STEM fields. Students in the four-year engineering and international studies dual-degree program earn two degrees in an engineering field and foreign language of their choice in addition to completing an international internship or study abroad experience. Programs in visual and performing arts have grown with the opening of the Williams Art Campus. The Dyer Center for Innovation and Entrepreneurship provides hands-on, multidisciplinary opportunities for collaboration in the liberal arts and engineering. Sixty-two percent of classes have fewer than 20 students. "Lafayette professors are really team players," says a sophomore. "They make time in their schedules to meet with students and help support us." The EXCEL program pays students who take research positions with faculty.

About 60 percent of Lafayette students pack their bags for study abroad programs offered in more than 50 countries. Options include several semester-long, faculty-led programs as well as short-term, faculty-led programs for credit during the January and May interim terms. Even engineering students are encouraged to explore foreign cultures; programs led by Lafayette faculty in Bonn, Germany, and Madrid, Spain, allow them to study abroad for a semester while maintaining normal progress toward their degrees. A government and law major comments, "There's a strong alumni network, and the Career Center does good work connecting students with alumni."

"Lafayette students are go-getters who care about the world around them," says an engineering studies major, and a chemical engineering major adds, "The majority of students are wealthy." Seventy-three percent of students are from out of state,

> **"Lafayette professors are really team players."**

Website: www.lafayette.edu
Location: Small City
Private
Total Enrollment: 2,706
Undergraduates: 2,706
Male/Female: 51/49
Financial Aid: 61%
Pell Grant: 10%
Expense: Pr $ $ $
Student Loans: 39%
Average Debt: $ $
Applicants: 8,262
Accepted: 41%
Enrolled: 23%
Grad in 6 Years: 90%
Returning Freshmen: 91%
Academics: ✐ ✐ ✐ ✐
Social: 🏆 🏆 🏆 🏆 🏆
Q of L: ★ ★ ★
Admissions: (610) 330-5100
Email Address: admissions@lafayette.edu

Strong Programs:
Economics
Mechanical Engineering
Neuroscience
Government and Law
Biology
Engineering and International Studies
Visual and Performing Arts

and another 8 percent are drawn from abroad. Black students account for 5 percent of the student body, Hispanics/Latinos 8 percent, Asian Americans 4 percent, and multiracial students 3 percent. A fairly diverse range of political views are represented on campus. Around 20 to 40 incoming freshmen receive merit-based Marquis Scholarships worth half tuition, while 10 to 15 top achievers are awarded full-tuition Marquis Fellowships. About 100 to 150 smaller merit-based Marquis scholarships are available as well, and athletes vie for nearly 150 scholarships in 11 of the school's 23 varsity sports. Lafayette guarantees to meet the full demonstrated need of admitted students, and it eliminates loans for students from families with annual incomes less than $150,000. Just 10 percent of freshmen qualify for Pell Grants, but administrators say increasing that number is a priority.

Lafayette ranks among the top colleges in study abroad participation, including among engineering students.

Ninety-three percent of students live on campus, and housing is guaranteed for all four years. Possibilities include Greek houses as well as independent dormitories and college-owned apartments with a variety of living and eating arrangements. Housing is chosen via a lottery system, but most get into the dorm of their choice. Ruef and South College are more social, while Watson Hall and Kirby House are quieter, students say. Campus dining facilities get mostly positive reviews, and students report that options for those with dietary restrictions are adequate. One student remarks, "Lafayette does not ignore the fact that sexual assault happens on campus, but rather works to continuously bring up the issue in order to put a stop to it."

Greek life attracts 21 percent of the men and 27 percent of the women. All sororities and some fraternities are dry, at least on campus; most parties occur off campus. "Greek organizations are definitely more prominent on campus than we would like

"There's a strong alumni network, and the Career Center does good work."

to admit," confides a senior. The arts program brings a range of performers to campus, and the most important nonathletic event of the year is Lafchella, a music and food festival featuring student bands and popular musical acts. The 1,000 Nights dance for freshmen and the 100 Nights dance for seniors mark the number of days remaining until graduation.

For students with cars or those willing to hop a bus or train, the bright lights of Philadelphia and New York beckon on weekends; for a change of pace, there is also hiking the Appalachian Trail. Blue-collar Easton "gets a bad rap, but is really nice," says a senior. "A lot of restaurants on the hill, lots of nice shops, great health and beauty salons. I really like Easton." Students look forward to Easton's annual garlic and bacon festivals. From College Hill and Downtown to the South Side, the city also offers plenty of opportunities for volunteer work in schools, prisons, rehabilitation centers, hospitals, and environmental sites under the auspices of Lafayette's Landis Center for Community Engagement.

Lafayette eliminates loans for students from families with annual incomes less than $150,000.

Division I sports add flavor to the Lafayette experience. The Leopards play in the Patriot League, and the field hockey, men's soccer, and men's basketball teams regularly vie for conference titles. The annual football game against nearby Lehigh is intense—dating to 1884, it's the most-played rivalry in college football. An extensive recreational program draws one-quarter of the students, buoyed by 32 club sports, several intramurals, and the massive Kirby Sports Center.

Students seeking close contact with professors, research opportunities, and a global outlook—and who aren't afraid of some serious study—might take a look at Lafayette. A freshman shares this anecdote: "I was once studying in a lounge area when a student I never met before saw my textbooks, explained that he had taken the course the year before, and proceeded to give me his number in case I had any questions throughout the semester." For those who desire a tight-knit, supportive community, that just about says it all.

Overlaps

Bucknell, Colgate, Union, Wellesley, Bowdoin, Hamilton, Swarthmore, Lehigh

Lake Forest College

555 North Sheridan Road, Lake Forest, IL 60045

A small, selective, private college in the Chicago area, Lake Forest generally attracts friendly, middle-of-the-road students. In the exclusive town from which the school takes its name, students can babysit for corporate CEOs at night and get internships at their corporations during the day. Large numbers of Foresters also study abroad.

Located just 30 miles north of the downtown Loop, Lake Forest College offers excellent programs in business, communication, and psychology, along with abundant opportunities for study abroad and professional internships at Chicagoland organizations such as the Chicago Blackhawks, the Chicago Board of Trade, and the Shedd Aquarium. Academic improvements at Lake Forest are drawing attention, and the school is shedding its image as a haven for spoiled rich kids; applications are up, and the school is attracting high-caliber students from across the nation and 80 countries.

Lake Forest was founded by Presbyterians in 1857 as an alternative to Methodist-oriented Northwestern University. With its mixture of century-old Gothic and modern glass structures, the college's 107-acre campus is storybook beautiful. Located on Chicago's North Shore in a wealthy, quiet suburb of 19,000, the campus has three contiguous parts divided by natural wooded ravines: North, Middle, and South. Each has a mix of residence halls and academic buildings.

> "The professors here know my name, they know what I struggle with, and they know my strengths."

The state-of-the-art Donnelley and Lee Library offers a 24-hour computer lab, "smart" classrooms, and collaborative workspaces. A $20 million expansion and renovation of Brown Hall, housing the social science, math, computer science, and data science departments, was completed in 2021.

General education requirements include the First-Year Studies Program, featuring "very small classes designed to help freshmen integrate into the college," says an English major. "These courses are writing intensive and offer a variety of opportunities, including trips to Chicago for plays and museum visits." Students also complete two credits in each of three liberal arts areas (humanities, social and natural sciences, and math), two cultural diversity courses, and a senior studies capstone course.

Students say Lake Forest's best and most popular majors include business, finance, communication, biology, neuroscience, psychology, and English. An entrepreneurship and innovation minor has proven popular as well. Accelerated and dual-degree programs—including three-year degree programs in philosophy and communication and dual-degree programs in law, engineering, pharmacy, accounting, and international studies—are available. Academic self-starters benefit from the self-designed major program, which allows undergrads to create their own majors outside the boundaries of traditional disciplines.

The academic climate at Lake Forest encourages collaboration. "The small class sizes allow for a lot of group discussion, group projects, and peer mentoring," says

Website: www.lakeforest.edu
Location: Suburban
Private
Total Enrollment: 1,653
Undergraduates: 1,640
Male/Female: 42/58
Financial Aid: 95%
Pell Grant: 40%
Expense: Pr $ $
Student Loans: 60%
Average Debt: $ $ $ $
Applicants: 4,358
Accepted: 64%
Enrolled: 15%
Grad in 6 Years: 73%
Returning Freshmen: 87%
Academics: ✍ ✍ ✍
Social: 🐘 🐘 🐘 🐘
Q of L: ★ ★ ★
Admissions: (847) 735-5000
Email Address: admissions@lakeforest.edu

Strong Programs:
Business
Communication
Psychology
Finance
Biology
Neuroscience
Entrepreneurship and
  Innovation

a biology major. "It's not uncommon to find an entire class sitting in a study room going over material for an upcoming exam." Foresters especially enjoy the large doses of individual attention that they receive from the faculty. "The professors here know my name, they know what I struggle with, and they know my strengths," confirms a psychology major. The Career Advancement Center offers symposia, workshops, and résumé clinics, and students benefit from the college's proximity to downtown Chicago, just an hour away by train. Many pursue term-time internships in the city's business district, known as the Loop, or at nonprofits and other organizations in surrounding communities.

Forty percent of students study abroad; students can apply their financial aid packages to approved semester-long programs.

Study abroad is integral to the Lake Forest experience, and 40 percent of students travel via more than 200 programs offered in approximately 70 nations. Students can apply their financial aid packages to approved semester-long programs. Each year, about 40 students become Richter Apprentice Scholars, living together, working in a 10-week paid research assistantship during the summer before their sophomore year, and taking part in a weekly student/faculty colloquium. "Absolutely try to do research with your professors," urges a communication major. "It is the most rewarding thing you can get involved with."

Fifty-seven percent of Lake Forest students hail from the Land of Lincoln, and 16 percent come from abroad. According to a sophomore, Foresters are usually "open-minded, amiable, and able to get along with others." Black students make up 4 percent of the student body, Hispanics/Latinos 18 percent, Asian Americans 5 percent, and multiracial students 3 percent. Students say political debate is usually

"The whole place is beautiful, and it feels like you live tucked away in a safe haven."

mild. One-third of the student body graduated from private high schools, but competitive financial aid packages are helping to bring more students from less-advantaged backgrounds to Lake Forest. The proportion of Pell-eligible freshmen has increased to 40 percent. The college awards numerous merit scholarships averaging $27,900 but does not offer athletic awards.

Sixty-nine percent of students live in the dorms, which they are required to do through their junior year. An English major says, "Different halls attract different people. I preferred living in the older buildings because they felt homier than the new buildings, which felt more like a hotel." Housing selection for upperclassmen is prioritized by seniority and GPA, "so there's a definite incentive to do well in your classes," says a senior. A fair number of students commute from home, and many seniors choose to stay on campus due to high rents in the surrounding area. Everybody eats in the central dining hall, where food is prepared to order at pizza, pasta, stir-fry, and other stations, and helpings are unlimited. A senior says, "We have regular programming events and student panels dedicated to educating the campus on sexual assault."

The proportion of Pell-eligible freshmen has increased to 40 percent.

Most social life is campus-based. Some students complain that, as a communication major explains, "the social environment can be similar to high school because the college is so small" and students tend to form cliques. The Campus Entertainment Committee mixes things up by booking movies, comedians, and big-name bands, while the Garrick Players put on several productions per year. The school's three fraternities and five sororities attract 10 percent of the men and 13 percent of the women, respectively, and though they don't have houses, their parties are open to all. Students say the party culture is relatively low-key, and underage students caught drinking on campus are strictly penalized. Everyone enjoys the semiformal Winter Ball, the annual Forester Day of Service, the Spring Concert, and the Drag Show lip-synch contest planned by PRIDE.

The town of Lake Forest is wealthy and mostly residential, and one student says, "The town is actually in a forest, so the whole place is beautiful, and it feels like you live tucked away in a safe haven." There's a commuter train station five minutes away, and the Lake Michigan beach is just as close. The college also offers a weekend shuttle service to local malls and movie theaters, though a car is helpful. Several student organizations are devoted to community service, and Greek organizations sponsor blood drives, bake sales, and car washes. One program sends students to the Appalachian Mountains in Virginia and Tennessee every spring break to help local townspeople repair substandard housing.

Division III Foresters athletics have begun to draw more attention from students. Men's basketball, women's tennis, and softball have been competitive in the Midwest Conference in recent years. Club and intramural sports programs draw 39 percent of students; lacrosse, rugby, and indoor soccer are especially popular.

Although Lake Forest's small size may feel confining to some, most students appreciate the college's collaborative atmosphere, increasing diversity, and healthy school pride. "Lake Forest takes very good care of its students by providing challenging academics, comfortable living, lots of entertainment, and a small-town feel with access to a big city," concludes a senior. "What more could anyone want?"

If You Apply To ›

Lake Forest: Early decision I and II, early action I and II, regular decision. SATs or ACTs: optional (test-optional applicants must have an admissions interview). Accepts the Common Application with supplement.

Lawrence University

711 East Boldt Way, Appleton, WI 54911

One of three small colleges in the nation that combine the liberal arts with a first-rate music conservatory (Bard and Oberlin are the others), and music of all kinds shapes the campus culture. Lawrence is half the size of Oberlin and comparable to Beloit and Grinnell, though Lawrence's personality is more mainstream than the others. Occupies a scenic bluff in northeastern Wisconsin.

Lawrence University is an unpretentious school that can appeal to both the left and right side of students' brains. For those with an analytical bent, there is Lawrence's uncommon physics program. More creative types can take advantage of the school's renowned Conservatory of Music. "I came to Lawrence because I found no other school where I could seriously study music and academics," says a senior. It's this eclectic, individualized approach to learning that attracts interested and interesting students from around the world. "Lawrence is, to me, founded on the idea that academics can be rigorous while also fun," muses a government major.

Lawrence's campus sits on a wooded bluff above the Fox River, perfect for long walks, jogging, or simply meditating underneath the trees. The pristine 88-acre campus reflects several architectural styles of the past 175 years, including Classical Revival, 1920s Georgian-inspired, and 1950s and 1960s institutional, unified by their limestone color. The award-winning Wriston Art Center and the Conservatory's Shattuck Hall of Music (both designed by Lawrence graduates) bring contemporary architectural touches to the campus.

One of the first coeducational colleges established in the nation, Lawrence was founded in 1847 to educate German immigrants and Native Americans and was named after an early benefactor. While coeducation was shocking enough, innovators at Lawrence didn't stop there. Nearly 80 years ago, administrators introduced

Website: www.lawrence.edu
Location: Small City
Private
Total Enrollment: 1,463
Undergraduates: 1,463
Male/Female: 46/54
Financial Aid: 99%
Pell Grant: 24%
Expense: Pr $ $
Student Loans: 62%
Average Debt: $ $
Applicants: 2,907
Accepted: 75%
Enrolled: 18%
Grad in 6 Years: 79%
Returning Freshmen: 89%
Academics: ✐ ✐ ✐ ✐
Social: ☎ ☎ ☎

Qualified students can be paired with alumni who are conducting research at tier-one universities for 10-week summer research assistantships.

the First-Year Studies program, a required two-term course that focuses primarily on the great works of art, music, science, and literature of both Western and non-Western origin and gives all incoming students a shared intellectual experience. General education requirements at Lawrence include First-Year Studies, distribution requirements, and diversity, foreign language, and writing-intensive courses. All seniors—in all degree programs—are required to produce a final project demonstrating proficiency in their major field of study. As a linguistics major explains, the senior project means that "while everyone is working on something different, the whole senior class is engaged in meaningful discussions and exposed to unique challenges."

At the school's Conservatory of Music, the instrument collection includes an 1815 Broadwood piano identical to Beethoven's own Broadwood and a Guarneri violin. There are first-rate jazz ensembles along with classical and world music programs. The college offers a bachelor of music degree within its liberal arts environment, and students may opt to complete a five-year, double-degree program to earn both a bachelor of music and a bachelor of arts in another field. "Music is the unifying theme at Lawrence," says one student. "Almost everybody plays it or studies it or likes to listen to it and talk about it." Economics is the most popular major, followed by biology, psychology, English, and government. The highly regarded physics department offers 3–2 engineering options with Columbia, Rensselaer, and WashU in St. Louis. Cooperative degrees in forestry and environmental studies, law, occupational therapy, and public health are also offered with such institutions as Duke, Marquette, and the Medical College of Wisconsin. New minors include health and society, statistics and data science, and creative writing.

> **"[It's] easy to connect and work closely with professors for a more personalized and thorough learning experience."**

Small classes—79 percent have fewer than 20 students—make it "easy to connect and work closely with professors for a more personalized and thorough learning experience," says a geology major. Because of the three-term calendar, the academic climate is fast-paced and intense but also "extremely collaborative," a sophomore says. "As long as you stay on top of reading and notes, it is not overwhelming."

Students are encouraged to spend at least one term of their college career off campus, and 40 percent of undergrads do so. The university is known for its London Centre, which allows students to take classes "across the pond" while taking advantage of the city's many cultural activities. Other off-campus programs include a Francophone seminar in Dakar, Senegal, and a marine biology term in the Cayman Islands. In all, more than 50 international programs are available in more than 25 countries. About 65 percent of students participate in research opportunities, especially those in the sciences. The Lawrence University Research Fellows program pairs qualified students with Lawrence faculty or with alumni who are conducting research at tier-one universities across the country for 10-week research assistantships during the summer.

> **"[Lawrentians are] forward-thinking, caring, and quirky."**

A senior describes Lawrentians as "forward-thinking, caring, and quirky." Twenty-four percent of students hail from Wisconsin, and another quarter come from Illinois and Minnesota. At 12 percent, the international population is sizable and represents more than 45 countries. Black students make up 5 percent of the student body, Asian Americans 5 percent, Hispanics/Latinos 11 percent, and multiracial students 5 percent. The political climate on campus is liberal and usually "calm," according to a sophomore. There are no athletic scholarships, but top achievers vie for merit scholarships averaging $29,500 each.

All but 4 percent of students live on campus, as four-year residency is required with few exceptions. "There are tons of options for housing: dorms, theme houses, group houses, lofts, etc.," explains a junior. On-campus students have a choice of meal plans and report that the food is diverse, healthy, and friendly to those with dietary restrictions. "Some of our produce comes from a student-run garden right across the street from the dining hall," says one student. In an effort to enhance campus safety, all on-campus parties hosted by student groups must be attended by at least one member who has been trained in bystander intervention.

The student-run Great Midwest Trivia Contest, held since 1966, is the longest-running trivia contest in the nation.

Social life at Lawrence is mostly campus-based and as varied and eclectic as the students. Greek life attracts a modest 8 percent of the men and 6 percent of the women; students say the party culture tends to be laid-back. "Lawrence students aren't the kind to party every weekend, but we're also not the kind to never party at all," opines a sophomore. Thanks to the Conservatory, students can almost always count on there being some kind of concert or performance on any given day. The Winter Carnival and President's Ball, held in January, and LU-aroo, a student-organized music festival in the spring, are favorite annual traditions. The student-run Great Midwest Trivia Contest takes place during January each year; held since 1966, it's the longest-running trivia contest in the nation. Octoberfest is also a big weekend event, held in conjunction with the city of Appleton, which draws people in from nearby cities.

Relations between Lawrence and Appleton are good. "The town is safe and has lots to do," says a student, including "cafés, restaurants, shops, nightlife, performing arts, and farmers markets." Downtown Appleton is just one block from campus, but the nearest grocery store is a five-minute drive; the school provides regular shuttles to help students get around. Volunteerism is popular, and students regularly take part in activities such as tutoring at local schools. The best road trips are to Milwaukee (two hours), Green Bay (half an hour), and Chicago (four hours). Weekend seminars are held at Björklunden, the college's 441-acre estate on the shores of Lake Michigan.

"I've always felt that this school is a hidden gem."

And what would a Midwest fall Saturday be without football? The Division III Lawrence Vikings draw good crowds almost every weekend. Baseball and men's and women's ice hockey, cross-country, and basketball are among the most competitive teams. The sparkling recreation center helps students fend off midwinter blues. Participating in a rousing game of intramural broomball, a variation of ice hockey played in shoes with brooms and kickballs, is a must for students, even if all you do is watch. Ultimate Frisbee is a popular club sport.

With an outstanding liberal arts curriculum, knowledgeable and caring faculty, an administration that treats students like adults, and a charming country setting, Lawrence University is easily one of the best little-known schools in the country. "Lawrence really does provide the tools and opportunities necessary to become an effective leader. I've always felt that this school is a hidden gem," remarks a film studies major. And for students with a musical ear, Lawrence's symphony of offerings strikes just the right chord.

Overlaps

St. Olaf, Macalester, Oberlin, DePauw, Grinnell, Ripon, Beloit, Knox

If You Apply To ›

Lawrence: Early decision, early action I and II, regular decision. SATs or ACTs: optional. Accepts the Common Application with supplement. Music applicants must audition and complete additional requirements.

Lehigh University

27 Memorial Drive West, Bethlehem, PA 18015

Built on the powerful combination of business, engineering, and the humanities, Lehigh occupies a middle ground between techie havens such as Drexel and Rensselaer and liberal arts/engineering institutions such as Bucknell and Union. By graduation, students are primed for the global job market. Hillside campus means that students get plenty of exercise. A wrestling powerhouse.

Website: www.lehigh.edu
Location: Small City
Private
Total Enrollment: 6,404
Undergraduates: 5,374
Male/Female: 54/46
Financial Aid: 60%
Pell Grant: 19%
Expense: Pr $ $ $
Student Loans: 46%
Average Debt: $
Applicants: 14,107
Accepted: 46%
Enrolled: 23%
Grad in 6 Years: 87%
Returning Freshmen: 94%
Academics: ✍ ✍ ✍ ✍
Social: 🏮 🏮 🏮
Q of L: ★ ★ ★ ★
Admissions: (610) 758-3100
Email Address: admissions@
lehigh.edu

Strong Programs:
Arts and Engineering
Computer Science and
    Business
Environmental Engineering
Integrated Business and
    Engineering
Finance
Mechanical Engineering
Industrial and Systems
    Engineering
Accounting

From the College of Arts and Sciences to the College of Business, Lehigh University combines the academic resources of a large research university with the collegial atmosphere of a much smaller institution. Since Lehigh's founding in 1865, much of its reputation has rested on its consistently strong engineering program, and the school has invested millions of dollars in recent years to enhance critical academic programs such as nanotechnology, biotechnology, bioscience, and optoelectronics. With the university's robust approach to experiential learning, students are well prepared for life after college. Says one engineering major, "Lehigh students have the know-how to jump right into the workforce and tackle any challenges that they may face."

Grand old oaks shade the buildings on Lehigh's 1,600-acre campus, which is tucked into the side of an eastern Pennsylvania mountain. The university spreads out over three contiguous campuses: the main Asa Packer Campus, named for Lehigh's businessman founder; the Goodman Campus, named for a donor; and the Mountaintop Campus, which formerly housed the research laboratory of now-defunct Bethlehem Steel. Architectural styles range from ivy-covered collegiate Gothic, including the historic Linderman Library, built in 1878, to modern glass and steel. Several construction projects are in the

> **"[The Mountaintop research] programs are really cool."**

works as part of the university's 10-year campus expansion plan; the $145 million Health, Science, and Technology Building (the university's largest facility, at 200,000 square feet) and the Business Innovation Building were completed in 2022.

Distribution requirements are divided into four domains—the mathematical sciences, the natural sciences, the social sciences, and the arts and humanities. First-years take an Evolution Seminar that focuses on the transition to college life. Additionally, some degrees include a mandatory internship or capstone project. Finance, mechanical engineering, industrial and systems engineering, and accounting are the most popular majors. Lehigh is big on connecting traditionally separate disciplines, so students interested in interdisciplinary study will find a wealth of options, including majors in arts and engineering, computer science and business, and environmental engineering and minors in engineering leadership and sustainable development. "I love the flexibility that I have had with my major, and it is really cool that I have been able to study both engineering and psychology," says a senior. The College of Health, offering undergraduate degrees in community and global health and population health, enrolled its first class in fall 2020. Several dual-degree options are available, such as a dental program with the University of Pennsylvania.

Lehigh prides itself on offering innovative special programs. The Technical Entrepreneurship Capstone program brings engineering, business, and arts students together to design and make products for sponsoring companies. The IDEAS (Integrated Degree in Engineering, Arts, and Sciences) and Integrated Business and Engineering programs offer four-year honors curricula that allow students to blend two focus areas into a single course of study. Lehigh's Office of Creative Inquiry sponsors several interdisciplinary initiatives, among them the Mountaintop program, which gives roughly 175 students a chance to work in teams with faculty mentors on cutting-edge projects during the summer. Recent Mountaintop projects include a Stormwater Smart Campus, Zero Hunger College, and 3-D Concrete Printing. "Take part in the Mountaintop research over the summer," urges a psychology major. "It's really fun to be on campus then, and the programs are really cool." Co-ops allow students to spend eight months working for a major-related company—and getting paid to do so—while still graduating in four years. Twenty-eight percent of students participate in more than 250 study abroad options offered in more than 60 countries. Faculty-led programs during winter and summer breaks are available in about a dozen countries, including China, the Czech Republic, and Ghana.

> The $145 million Health, Science, and Technology Building (the university's largest facility) was completed in 2022.

Lehigh students are ambitious, and many pursue double majors and multiple extracurriculars, but the atmosphere is by no means cutthroat. "From group projects to late-night study groups in Linderman Library, I have always been able to find a classmate to help me in a variety of subjects," says a journalism major. Forty-nine percent of undergraduate courses enroll fewer than 20 students, and a finance and economics major says, "Professors at Lehigh are as good as they get when it comes to professional experience and the research they are involved in." Students praise the wide range of services made available to them, including career counseling. "Career services is especially good at bringing large numbers of employers at a time to campus," says one junior. "Our placement numbers speak for themselves."

> "Professors at Lehigh are as good as they get when it comes to professional experience."

According to an accounting major, "Everybody here is determined to succeed and have a good time doing it." Twenty-six percent of Lehigh's students come from Pennsylvania, and many others hail from other Northeastern states; 8 percent come from more than 30 foreign countries. Black students account for 5 percent of the population, Hispanics/Latinos 10 percent, Asian Americans 9 percent, and multiracial students 4 percent. As for the political atmosphere, a mechanical engineering major reports, "Political opinions are rarely expressed on campus." Merit scholarships averaging $15,200 are awarded annually, and athletes vie for more than 200 scholarships in 25 sports.

> The Mountaintop program gives 175 students a chance to work in teams with faculty mentors on cutting-edge projects during the summer.

Fifty-nine percent of Lehigh students live on campus; first- and second-year students are required to do so. Accommodations are described as "decent." Many upperclassmen choose to live in apartment-style dorms, Greek houses, and off-campus apartments. Campus dining receives above-average reviews for taste and variety. Students note that the Office of Gender Violence Education and Support has done much to educate the campus community, including rallies and prevention-awareness training, and a chemical engineering major comments, "In general, campus is really safe as long as you use basic city smarts."

An active Greek scene (20 percent of the men join fraternities and 25 percent of the women belong to sororities) fuels the campus social life. "Students who live off campus often host parties, and it creates a really great social scene," says one student. Although students agree that a drinking and party culture does exist, according to a finance major, "There isn't pressure from anyone to become involved in those activities." Plenty of on-campus social options are available too, says a business information systems major: "Lehigh After Dark events are always a huge hit and range from midnight breakfast bars and a massive carnival to massage therapy sessions and bingo nights." Favorite traditions include the Founder's Day celebration as well as bed races, the Turkey Trot, and other spirit activities during the week leading up to the

> "In general, campus is really safe as long as you use basic city smarts."

big football game against Lafayette. Locally and nationally, students volunteer roughly 65,000 hours each year.

The bustling campus has helped revive Bethlehem, a once-great steel town in the heart of the Lehigh Valley, just five minutes from campus. "Bethlehem is a hidden gem," says a junior. "There is always something to do, whether that's seeing a show at the Steel Stacks or grabbing a bite to eat downtown." Students look forward to the city's Musikfest in early August, a 10-day music festival that attracts more than one million people and showcases nearly every musical style. For those with wheels, Philadelphia is 50 miles to the south and New York City is 75 miles to the east. Skiers will appreciate the close proximity of the Poconos in the winter, while sun worshippers can enjoy the nearby Jersey Shore in the early fall and late spring.

The Division I Lehigh Mountain Hawks field a number of competitive teams. Lehigh's wrestling program is a powerhouse, having brought home numerous Eastern Intercollegiate Wrestling Association championships. Women's basketball is a recent Patriot League champion; other solid programs include softball and men's basketball, soccer, cross-country, and lacrosse. Fans flock to the annual Lehigh versus Lafayette football game, which was first played in 1884 and is the longest-standing rivalry in college football. "LeLaf is huge!" cheers a junior. About 65 percent of students participate in the extensive intramural and club sports programs. The Goodman Campus provides first-class practice and playing facilities for Lehigh's varsity and recreational sports teams alike.

Lehigh students proudly juggle rigorous classes and a packed extracurricular calendar in an environment that is well-balanced rather than intense. "Lehigh is in the Goldilocks zone," explains an economics major. "It is just small enough that it is easy to find and form a comfortable and intimate community, but big enough that everyone can explore any and all of their interests." With abundant opportunities and plenty of support, students here expect to succeed.

The annual Lehigh versus Lafayette football game was first played in 1884 and is the longest-standing rivalry in college football.

Overlaps

Tulane, William & Mary, Northeastern, Wake Forest, Boston College, Villanova, Bucknell, Drexel

If You Apply To ›

Lehigh: Early decision I and II, regular decision. Accepts the Common Application. Apply to particular colleges. Please consult Lehigh's website for the most up-to-date information regarding standardized test requirements.

Lewis & Clark College

Portland, OR 97219

The West Coast's leader in international and study abroad programs. Politically liberal, but not as far out as crosstown neighbor Reed. With Mount Hood visible in the distance (sometimes), there is a wealth of outdoor possibilities. Located in suburban Portland, within easy reach of the bustle of downtown.

Website: www.lclark.edu
Location: City Outskirts
Private
Total Enrollment: 3,038
Undergraduates: 2,008
Male/Female: 36/64
Financial Aid: 98%

The 19th-century explorers Lewis and Clark struck out from Middle America to find where the trail ended, and their travels took them to Portland, a lush, green paradise by the Willamette River. The college that bears the explorers' names encourages students to explore too. Since establishing its first overseas study programs in 1962, the college has sent thousands of students around the world to gain global perspectives in their fields of study. Back on campus, opportunities for academic exploration, research, and urban adventures abound. Without a doubt, Lewis & Clark students receive, as one junior puts it, "an excellent, hands-on education."

Lewis & Clark, which produced its first graduates in 1873, boasts a gorgeous campus perched atop fir-covered bluffs overlooking the river. The campus is an old estate, complete with elaborate gardens, fountains, and pools, where cement is almost nonexistent and the roads are paved with cobblestones. The 50,000-square-foot Howard Hall, built as part of the college's commitment to sustainable development, earned a gold certification from the U.S. Green Building Council. Lewis & Clark draws 100 percent of its power from renewable sources.

Lewis & Clark requires that all students achieve competency in a foreign language and international studies; 55 percent of students fulfill these requirements by studying abroad for a semester or more. The college offers more than 30 study abroad programs each year, many of which are faculty-led, on six continents. Students may also study in a number of American cities. In addition to the international studies and language requirements, students must complete courses in creative arts; culture, power, and identity; historical perspectives; natural sciences; and physical education and well-being. A required, two-semester first-year seminar helps ease new students into college life.

> **"[Classes] are fairly small and intimate, allowing you to have close connections with your professors."**

Not surprisingly, one of the most popular majors at Lewis & Clark is international affairs; others include psychology, biology, economics, sociology and anthropology, and English. Students seeking advanced degrees may take advantage of a 4–1 B.A./M.A.T. program in collaboration with Lewis & Clark's Graduate School of Education and Counseling, a 3–3 B.A./J.D. program or a 3–1 B.A./M.S.L. program with Lewis & Clark Law School, and 3–2 programs in engineering. The Center for Community and Global Health offers premed and other health professions advising. Honors programs are available in most departments. The Rogers Summer Science Research Program teams students and faculty on research projects ranging from the evolution of spider venom to cybersecurity analysis. The Bates Center for Entrepreneurship encourages collaboration with faculty, mentors, and outside professionals to reframe problems using entrepreneurial thinking.

Academically, "Classes are a mix in terms of difficulty, student participation, and amount of work," reports a student double majoring in psychology and rhetoric and media studies. Freshmen and graduating seniors get priority in the registration process, helping ensure graduation in four years. For those who plan out their requirements with their academic advisors but are unable to finish in four years, the college commits to paying for an additional semester of study. Professors get high marks for being knowledgeable and passionate. "The class sizes at L&C are fairly small and intimate, allowing you to have close connections with your professors," explains a sociology and anthropology major.

"Students here are socially conscious, motivated, and involved," says an international affairs major. Eleven percent of undergrads hail from Oregon, and many of the rest are West Coasters seeking an emphasis on the liberal arts; the college is also a haven for well-off Easterners who see L&C as an escape from the social claustrophobia of the typical prep school scene. Four percent of students are drawn from foreign countries. The campus is politically active and predominantly left-leaning. A senior reports that a student movement to change the school's name on the grounds that it "glorifies colonizers and genocide" has been a hot-button issue of late. The student body is 5 percent Asian American, 2 percent Black, 12 percent Hispanic/Latino, and 9 percent multiracial. The Office of Equity and Inclusion aims to promote and expand campus diversity. Non-need-based financial aid awards average $24,900, but there are no athletic scholarships.

Lewis & Clark's residency requirement keeps students on campus for two years; 71 percent of all undergraduates stay in campus housing, which is described as convenient. "The most common room is a double, but there are also quads and singles, all of which have sufficient room for their respective residents," reports a student. Owing to the college's hilltop location, lucky dorm residents have views of Mount St. Helens, Mount Hood, or the Portland skyline—at least when they are not fogged in.

(continued)

Pell Grant: 21%
Expense: Pr $ $ $
Student Loans: 49%
Average Debt: $ $
Applicants: 5,519
Accepted: 79%
Enrolled: 15%
Grad in 6 Years: 73%
Returning Freshmen: 86%
Academics: ✐ ✐ ✐
Social: ☎ ☎ ☎
Q of L: ★ ★ ★
Admissions: (503) 768-7040
Email Address: admissions@lclark.edu

Strong Programs:
International Affairs
Psychology
Biology
Economics
Sociology and Anthropology
English
Education

Fifty-five percent of students fulfill an international studies requirement by studying abroad for a semester or more.

Students involved in performing arts, multicultural engagement, outdoor pursuits, and other programs can join living/learning communities. Dining halls cater to different diets, offering vegetarian and vegan options at every meal, and "the food can be tasty, but not always," says a student. L&C is located in a residential section of Portland, but safety is still a priority—residence halls have card-swipe entry systems and door alarms, and campus security officers are on duty 24 hours a day.

Fun-seekers at Lewis & Clark rely primarily on programs offered through Student Activities, such as on-campus movies, contests, dances, improv nights, and talent shows; there is no Greek life. Yearly events include the Fall Ball and Spring Fling dances, the International Fair, and the Suntan and Sunburn music festivals. Students 21 and older are permitted to consume alcohol on campus, and students report that alcohol policies prioritize student safety. "There is not a huge party culture on campus, but it manifests in smaller kick-backs," says a senior.

The neighborhood immediately surrounding the college is pleasant, affluent suburbia, which means a few stores, restaurants, and bars. Students get involved in community service through a variety of campus organizations. The activity of Portland—mostly on Hawthorne Boulevard in the southeast section, and in the Pearl District or on 23rd Street in the northwest quadrant—is 15 minutes away on the city's public transit system or the free campus shuttle service, the Pioneer Express. On the weekends and during breaks, College Outdoors sponsors trips to Mount Hood (great skiing, about an hour distant), the eastern Oregon high desert (two hours), or the coastal beaches (an hour and a half). Seattle and Vancouver, BC, three- and six-hour drives, are favorite road trips, as are San Francisco and Las Vegas when there's more time.

> **"There is not a huge party culture on campus, but it manifests in smaller kick-backs."**

Pioneer teams compete in the Division III Northwest Conference, and the most successful teams include men's basketball and men's and women's tennis, cross-country, and rowing. Lewis & Clark has a well-organized intramural program. Ultimate Frisbee, basketball, and volleyball are student favorites. The L&C speech and debate team has won multiple national titles in recent years.

Lewis & Clark's many outdoor enthusiasts and champions of social causes thrive in the college's laid-back atmosphere. Students are knowledge-seeking pioneers—ones who would make the school's namesakes proud. "Students here look outside their lives and experiences in order to find something greater," says a senior. "We constantly question and search for the answers."

If You Apply To ›

Lewis & Clark: Early decision, early action, regular decision. SATs or ACTs: optional. Accepts the Common Application.

Louisiana State University

1146 Pleasant Hall, Baton Rouge, LA 70803

In the state famous for Mardi Gras, students come to LSU for a great time as well as a good education. Finding the former is a no-brainer. The latter can be had in business, engineering, and life sciences fields. Administrators are trying to make LSU a more serious place with higher admissions standards and less underage drinking. Aging, flood-prone library contrasts with Taj Mahal–like facilities for football and other sports. Only university in the country with a live tiger residing on campus.

From abundant azaleas and Japanese magnolias and the smell of Cajun cuisine to the sororities' stately mansions and the "huge and legendary" rivalries with Alabama and Florida, few schools evoke the spirit of the South like Louisiana State University in Baton Rouge. The university offers solid programs in business, engineering, and the life sciences, and the academic profile of its students continues to rise, bolstering LSU's strong sense of community and school pride. "We care so much about our university and everything that we do on *and* off the field," enthuses a junior. "Geaux Tigers!"

LSU sits on 2,000 acres along the banks of the Mississippi River on the grounds of a former plantation. Most of the 250 buildings are Italian Renaissance in style, with tan stucco walls and red tile roofs. Lakes and sprawling oak trees dot the landscape, helping to diffuse the strong sun and temper Louisiana's legendary humidity. Recent campus projects include an $85 million expansion of the lavish student recreation center, paid for by hefty student fees, and Azalea and Camellia halls, two new suite-style residential buildings.

Founded in 1853, LSU was once an open-admissions university for state residents, but standards have gone up over the years, and with them the caliber of students. Students must complete a broad core curriculum with coursework in English composition, analytical reasoning, social sciences, humanities, natural sciences, and the arts. Entry-level classes can be large, but 42 percent of all undergraduate courses enroll fewer than 20 students. Especially motivated students may opt to join the Ogden Honors College to enjoy smaller class sizes, live in the Laville Honors House, and produce a senior thesis.

> "Overall the professors here at LSU love their material and are dedicated to teaching."

LSU students choose from more than 75 undergraduate degrees and tend to focus on practical majors that will help them get into graduate school or find jobs after graduation. To that end, popular majors include biological sciences—typical for premeds—as well as kinesiology, psychology, mass communication, and business. LSU's programs in landscape architecture, engineering (especially petroleum), physics, computer science, English, and music are highly regarded. Given LSU's location and history as a federal sea grant college, its offerings in coastal environmental science and ecology are notable as well. The renowned, multidisciplinary LSU Center for Internal Auditing was the first university-based internal auditing training program to be established. Professors are lauded for their enthusiasm and skill behind the lectern. "Overall the professors here at LSU love their material and are dedicated to teaching," one student says. Research opportunities abound and include the President's Future Leaders in Research Program, which provides undergraduates the chance to work side by side with professors in a research setting, such as a lab or in the field, to learn what a career in that area might be like. Undergrads interested in study abroad can choose from nearly 400 programs ranging in length from one week to one year.

Seventy-three percent of LSU Tigers are Louisiana natives, and 1 percent come from abroad. Black students make up 16 percent of the undergraduate student body, Asian Americans 5 percent, Hispanics/Latinos 8 percent, and multiracial students 2 percent. A political science major describes the political climate on campus as "very moderate for a Southern school." LSU's tuition is below the national average, but in the face of dwindling support from the state, the university has passed more and more of the cost of education on to students in the form of fees—such as a "student excellence fee"—that function like de facto tuition. Thousands of merit scholarships are available, averaging $6,100, and LSU hands out more than 450 athletic scholarships each year in 21 sports. The Pelican Promise Scholarship provides additional financial aid to low-income, Pell-eligible, in-state students.

Website: www.lsu.edu
Location: City Center
Public
Total Enrollment: 29,736
Undergraduates: 25,204
Male/Female: 45/55
Financial Aid: 94%
Pell Grant: 30%
Expense: Pub $ $
Student Loans: 45%
Average Debt: $ $
Applicants: 36,561
Accepted: 71%
Enrolled: 27%
Grad in 6 Years: 69%
Returning Freshmen: 83%
Academics: ✍ ✍
Social: ☎ ☎ ☎ ☎ ☎
Q of L: ★ ★ ★
Admissions: (225) 578-1175
Email Address: admissions@lsu.edu

Strong Programs:
Business
Engineering
Landscape Architecture
Physics
Computer Science
English
Music
Coastal Environmental Science

Given LSU's location and history as a federal sea grant college, its offerings in coastal environmental science and ecology are notable.

Thirty-one percent of students live on campus. Over the past decade, the university has invested more than $150 million in housing facilities, with more than 70 percent of the undergraduate housing either newly constructed or renovated. Twenty-two percent of first-year students choose to live in 10 residential colleges organized by academic interest. Meals at the dining halls receive average reviews, but a number of "delicious and inexpensive" eateries lie within easy reach of campus. Although crime can be a concern in Baton Rouge, a senior reports, "Campus safety is a priority, and our police department has increased night patrolling and self-defense classes since my first year." LSU also provides a transit system so that students don't have to walk alone after dark.

With nearly 500 student clubs, tailgating during football season, and the many nearby bars in Tigerland, social life at LSU "is never-ending," enthuses a student. "LSU, of course, is a party school," comments a junior. "It is part of the Tiger pride and culture." Fifteen percent of the men and 24 percent of the women go Greek. The administration has instituted several policy changes related to Greek life, including a ban on hard alcohol at all on- and off-campus Greek events, in hopes of reducing binge drinking, hazing, and other problems. "LSU has made an effort to educate and encourage victims and bystanders of hazing to speak out," says a senior. As for traditions, everyone looks forward to homecoming and annual festivals such as Groovin', a free concert featuring a big-name artist. "Our Memorial Tower plays our alma mater every day at noon, and everyone loves to stop and listen to it," cheers an English major. Road trips to New Orleans and the Florida beaches are common during spring break.

> **"LSU, of course, is a party school. It is part of the Tiger pride and culture."**

Tiger football is king in Baton Rouge—witness the 102,000-seat Tiger Stadium, the $28 million renovated locker room that the *New York Times* described as "a purple-and-gold mash-up of a first-class airplane cabin and a sci-fi space station," and Mike the Tiger, the live tiger mascot that lives in a 15,000-square-foot habitat adjacent to the football stadium. "Football season at LSU is by far the best college football experience in the world," boasts a senior. The rowdy LSU contingent at away games has earned a reputation worthy of English soccer fans. Many students follow the team (and the fun) to Oxford, Mississippi (home of Ole Miss), or Auburn, Alabama (home of the Auburn Tigers). The hard-charging women's basketball team claimed the national title in 2023, as did men's track and field in 2021. Tiger baseball is a dynasty, having brought home multiple Southeastern Conference titles. Men's basketball, women's gymnastics, and women's soccer are also strong. As for recreational sports, intramural soccer, flag football, and softball are popular.

LSU's trees and traditions date back 170 years, but the school continues to evolve in its efforts to attract a more academically motivated student body. The university is focused on the goals of learning, discovery, diversity, and engagement, and though it may be a while before its academic profile matches its athletic prowess, that's what administrators say they are aiming for. In the meantime, students are happy to *laissez les bons temps rouler*!

Overlaps

University of Tennessee Knoxville, Auburn, University of Arkansas, Clemson, Oklahoma State, University of Louisiana, Southeastern Louisiana, Texas A&M

If You Apply To ›

LSU: Rolling admissions. SATs or ACTs: optional. Accepts the Common Application with supplement. Application allows students to utilize preferred name, gender pronouns, and self-identified gender.

Loyola University Maryland

4501 North Charles Street, Baltimore, MD 21210

Vintage Jesuit school with a rigorous liberal arts curriculum, caring faculty, and a strong sense of community. Baltimore location a plus for those with "I don't want to miss anything" attitude. Same size as Providence, smaller than BC, Fordham, and other Roman Catholic schools in urban settings. No varsity football, but top-ranked lacrosse teams evoke plenty of school spirit.

Four U.S. universities bear the name of St. Ignatius of Loyola, founder of the Society of Jesus (Jesuits), but this one is the granddaddy of them all. Founded in 1852 (and the one that laid claim to www.loyola.edu), Loyola University Maryland combines the virtues of a residential campus with ready access to a major city on the Amtrak corridor. Loyola jumped up from "college" to "university" status in 2009 and, with a "big enough but not too big" feel, manages to strike a balance between real-world experience and the traditional Jesuit ideals of academic excellence, a liberal arts curriculum, and *cura personalis* (a.k.a. care of the whole person).

Loyola's Evergreen campus, the home to undergraduates, sits on 80 green and wooded acres in a mixed residential area in northern Baltimore, about 15 minutes from the heart of the city. (Campuses in Timonium and Columbia, Maryland, house graduate students.) The academic Quad features the largest collection of collegiate Gothic buildings in Baltimore, including the Alumni Memorial Chapel with its lovely stained-glass windows. Architectural variety is provided by the Tudor-style Humanities Center, built in 1896; the contemporary Sellinger School of Business and Management, with its five-story glass facade; and the LEED Gold–certified Fernandez Family Center for Innovation and Collaborative Learning, which opened in 2021.

> **"[The Messina program] makes new students feel like they are a part of the Loyola community."**

Undergraduate academics at Loyola are organized around the triumvirate of the School of Education, the Sellinger School of Business and Management, and Loyola College of Arts and Sciences. Consistent with Jesuit academic tradition, Loyola students pursue a core curriculum that encourages critical thinking across the liberal arts and sciences. Among the requirements are a course in ethics and the choice of one diversity-designated course—with a focus on global or domestic diversity or justice awareness. Messina is the university's first-year living/learning program, in which students enroll in two linked seminar classes, one in the fall and one in the spring, focused on one of four themes: The Visionary, Self and Other, Stories We Tell, and The Good Life. The courses are taught by their core advisor, and students benefit from additional Messina resources, including an upper-class peer mentor (called an "Evergreen") and special programs, events, and excursions. "It makes new students feel like they are a part of the Loyola community and realize how many people care about them here," says a biology major.

The business program, which consists of nine majors ranging from accounting to sustainability management, is strong, as are most of the humanities. Business administration, psychology, biology, and communication are the most popular majors. Other strong areas, students say, include education, speech-language-hearing sciences, and engineering. A new major has been added in forensic studies. Students describe the academic program at Loyola as challenging but supportive. "Students are generally not competing against each other for the best grades, but rather tend to work together on projects or while studying," says a senior. Teaching

---

Website: www.loyola.edu
Location: City Outskirts
Private
Total Enrollment: 4,130
Undergraduates: 3,729
Male/Female: 43/57
Financial Aid: 96%
Pell Grant: 19%
Expense: Pr $ $
Student Loans: 62%
Average Debt: $ $ $ $
Applicants: 9,286
Accepted: 84%
Enrolled: 12%
Grad in 6 Years: 81%
Returning Freshmen: 88%
Academics: ✍ ✍ ✍
Social: ☎ ☎ ☎
Q of L: ★ ★ ★
Admissions: (410) 617-5012
Email Address: admission@loyola.edu

Strong Programs:
Business Administration
Accounting
Sustainability Management
Education
Speech-Language-Hearing Sciences
Engineering
Psychology
Biology

Students praise their professors' emphasis on teaching and getting to know students. "I cannot imagine what it would be like not to have a professor know my name," says a senior.

Each summer, 10 to 12 undergraduates are selected to work side by side with faculty from the six natural and applied science departments to conduct research in the students' area of interest and participate in seminars. For top students, the Honors Program provides an interdisciplinary route through a more ambitious core curriculum. A whopping two-thirds of the students study abroad in their choice of more than 25 countries, usually for a semester during their junior year. Venues range from Bangkok, Dubai, and Singapore to Cape Town, Glasgow, and, of course, Rome. Loyola students are encouraged to do community service while abroad and to submit an Immersion Research Project upon return. "I studied in Cork, Ireland, and it was one of the highlights of my college experience!" cheers a senior.

First-year students benefit from an upper-class peer mentor (called an "Evergreen").

> "I cannot imagine what it would be like not to have a professor know my name."

Students at Loyola tend to be, in the words of one senior, "fairly preppy." Twenty-six percent of undergraduates hail from Maryland, and 2 percent come from other countries. Black students represent 8 percent, Hispanics/Latinos 12 percent, Asian Americans 3 percent, and multiracial students 4 percent. Sixty percent of undergrads describe themselves as Catholics; there are fewer than 10 Jesuits on the faculty. "Religion has a huge impact on campus," says one non-Catholic, who adds, "As a Christian, I love the fact that I can openly talk about my religion and that others accept my beliefs." Students cite women's and LGBTQ rights, immigration reform, homelessness, and hunger as popular causes on campus. Merit awards average $21,400, and Loyola offers about 150 athletic scholarships.

The business program, which consists of nine majors ranging from accounting to sustainability management, is strong.

Loyola students enjoy the spacious, modern residence halls, which are located west of the main campus and are connected by a pedestrian bridge spanning Charles Street. "One of the perks of Loyola's housing is that there are only a few traditional dorms," explains a psychology major. "Loyola has mostly apartment-style living," and it's possible to live in an apartment or suite with a kitchen and bathroom as early as freshman year. Not surprisingly, 75 percent of students live on campus. The main dining facility is Boulder Garden Café, but other options range from the Reading Room to Starbucks. Campus security is not an issue. "We are in a relatively dangerous part of the city," says an accounting major, "but the Loyola police do a good job to make us all feel safe on campus."

> "The passion for service runs very strong through the veins of Loyola."

Loyola has no fraternities or sororities, but given the proximity to Baltimore, this arrangement is just fine with students. "Most of Loyola's social life takes place off campus," says a student. "Bars and clubs are very close to campus, and the penalties for throwing a party in your room are pretty steep." That's not to say that on-campus life is monastic. "The campus is always buzzing with things like concerts and festivals," says an English major. The undisputed high point of the social calendar is Loyolapalooza, the spring festival held on the last weekend before final exams to celebrate the academic year. Students gather on the Quad for a concert, games, and food. A close second is the annual Black Student Association Fashion Show in the spring.

The undisputed high point of the social calendar is Loyolapalooza, the spring festival held on the last weekend before final exams.

Baltimore is a city where urban problems have been well documented. For students at Loyola, this means that community service, in which 64 percent of students get involved, plays a prominent role in campus life. "The passion for service runs very strong through the veins of Loyola," says a senior. The Center for Community, Service, and Justice connects students with opportunities ranging from one-time volunteer activities to semester-long service-learning courses. The city of Baltimore also offers an abundance of sights, including the famed Inner Harbor, with its many restaurants and museums, as well as major league sports. Loyola's neighbors include numerous other colleges and universities, including Johns Hopkins and Towson University. "Loyola students do not regard Baltimore as a 'college town' per se, but it has plenty of young-adult neighborhoods and pockets of entertainment," reports an accounting major. Washington, D.C., an hour away by train, is a frequent weekend destination.

Loyola eschews varsity football, but the Greyhounds compete in the Division I Patriot League in eight men's and nine women's sports. Befitting the school's Maryland location, both the men's and women's lacrosse teams are consistently strong. Men's soccer and golf have also been successful in recent years. For those with more modest athletic ambitions, Loyola sponsors 25 club sports teams and more than 20 intramural events, as well as 40 outdoor adventure trips each year. Flag football, volleyball, ultimate Frisbee, and soccer are especially popular. The state-of-the-art Fitness and Aquatic Center features a well-equipped fitness center, a rock-climbing wall, a 14-lane pool, and other amenities.

Some Loyola denizens lament the absence of football and the dearth of on-campus parties, but such complaints seem a small price to pay for four years as part of a close-knit community that takes its humanistic, academic, and social values seriously. "We care for each other, and our Jesuit mission rings true in our day-to-day lives," says a senior. A classmate adds, "The good food, residence halls, and location don't hurt either."

> **Overlaps**
>
> **Creighton, Villanova, Santa Clara, St. Joseph's, Fairfield, Providence, Boston College, Fordham**

If You Apply To ›

Loyola: Early action, regular decision. SATs or ACTs: optional. Accepts the Common Application.

Loyola Marymount University

I LMU Drive, Suite 100, Los Angeles, CA 90045

LMU is a Roman Catholic university known for its strategic L.A. location and world-class programs in film and television, business, engineering, and communication. Big international emphasis in film and theatre arts. Compare to Chapman, Santa Clara, and University of San Diego. To take full advantage of L.A., access to a car is highly beneficial.

At Loyola Marymount University, one of the largest Roman Catholic universities on the West Coast, students are treated to ideal weather year-round, a vast array of internship opportunities, and an academic lineup that includes solid programs in film and television, liberal arts and sciences, and business. "LMU is more than an academic institution," says a junior. "It is a community dedicated to helping students grow and thrive."

Established in 1911, LMU occupies a 142-acre campus perched on a bluff overlooking the Pacific Ocean and Marina del Rey in Westchester, a peaceful residential neighborhood of Los Angeles. Campus architecture is a mix of modern and a modified Spanish Colonial Revival style, with orange-tiled roofs. The university is sponsored by three religious orders: the Society of Jesus (Jesuits), the Religious of the Sacred Heart of Mary, and the Sisters of St. Joseph of Orange. Campus highlights include the 24-hour Hannon Library, the $110 million, LEED Gold–certified Featherston Life Sciences Building, and the new Fitzpatrick Pavilion, boasting high-tech production and screening spaces for the film school. A downtown campus houses the law school.

Website: www.lmu.edu
Location: Suburban
Private
Total Enrollment: 9,295
Undergraduates: 6,859
Male/Female: 46/54
Financial Aid: 88%
Pell Grant: 10%
Expense: Pr $ $
Student Loans: 47%
Average Debt: $ $ $
Applicants: 19,045
Accepted: 46%
Enrolled: 18%

(continued)

Grad in 6 Years: 79%
Returning Freshmen: 90%
Academics: ✐ ✐ ✐
Social: ☎ ☎ ☎
Q of L: ★ ★ ★
Admissions: (310) 338-2750
Email Address: admission@
  lmu.edu

Strong Programs:
Film and Television Production
Journalism
Entrepreneurship
Computer Science
Engineering
Theatre Arts
Marketing
Psychology

Film students have the chance to study in Bonn, Germany, and produce their own documentaries that are exhibited at festivals.

LMU offers 55 baccalaureate majors and 59 minors in six colleges and schools. The general education requirements (known as the Core Curriculum) are designed to encourage intellectual breadth, tackling themes such as faith and reason; ethics and justice; culture; art and society; and science, nature, and society. Incoming students may take part in a number of programs designed to support the transition to college, including a first-year seminar and an honors program.

The most popular programs include marketing, psychology, communication studies, finance, and political science; these are also some of the university's best. Other strong programs include film and television production, journalism, entrepreneurship, computer science, engineering, and theatre arts. Students in the School of Film and Television have access to a number of resources, including a student-run production office, a television stage, and a film soundstage with a professional green screen

> "Professors truly know their students and take a personal interest in their learning."

(for those cool CGI effects!). They also benefit from the program's strong international emphasis, including the chance to study in Bonn, Germany, and produce their own documentaries that are exhibited at festivals in Germany and the U.S. Those in the Seaver College of Science and Engineering take part in national competitions to build rockets and race eco-friendly cars. New academic offerings include majors in information systems and business analytics, statistics and data science, and international relations and minors in international documentary production and business law. Thanks to its hip Los Angeles locale, LMU offers experience-hungry students a plethora of internships, including stints at Disney and Warner Bros. LMU offers more than 60 exchange, semester, and short-term study abroad options on six continents in a wide range of disciplines; 41 percent of students participate during their time at LMU.

Like nearby Tinseltown, LMU manages to be both competitive and relaxed. "LMU students generally care about their academic performance and seek challenges where they can," observes an economics major. Fifty-five percent of classes have fewer than 20 students, and while academic rigor and quality of instruction vary by program, students say teacher-student interaction is commonplace. "Professors truly know their students and take a personal interest in their learning," says a junior.

LMU undergraduates hail from 48 states and 85 foreign countries; 59 percent come from California and 10 percent from abroad. "Students at LMU generally enjoy Los Angeles, care about social justice, and enjoy the sunshine and involved community at school," says a senior. About 37 percent of students are Catholic. Black students represent 7 percent of the student body, Hispanics/Latinos 23 percent, Asian Americans 10 percent, and multiracial students 8 percent. A dance major says LMU attracts "an interesting mix of liberal and conservative students," and students report that the political atmosphere is occasionally divisive. Merit scholarships averaging $12,100 are available for qualified students, and the athletically inclined vie for 245 athletic scholarships in 13 sports.

It's a tradition for your friends to toss you into Foley Fountain on your birthday.

About half of LMU students live on campus. Many first-years choose to participate in themed living/learning communities, including those dedicated to specific academic disciplines, first-generation students, and Ignatian leadership. The university offers a variety of dining options, but students complain that meals are "hit or miss" and "too expensive." Students describe campus security as good, and one student comments, "LMU does a good job of informing students about sexual consent."

The social life at LMU takes place "both on and off campus," says one student. Student organizations and clubs frequently host activities, and Greek life influences the scene too, attracting 16 percent of the men and 25 percent of the women. Students say there is little pressure to drink. "If students want to drink, they can find alcohol," says a freshman. "Those that don't want to, don't have to." Everyone looks forward to Fallapalooza, an outdoor music festival that kicks off the school year, and it's a tradition for your friends to toss you into Foley Fountain on your birthday. The university's Jesuit heritage promotes a commitment to community service, and about 70 percent of students take part, volunteering more than 200,000 hours of service every year in after-school programs, homeless shelters, health clinics, and other settings. The area of Westchester is "definitely not a college town," groans a sophomore. Fortunately, Marina del Rey and Santa Monica are a short car or bus ride away, and it's only a mile to the beach. "Since L.A. is a big city, there are plenty of places for a college student to eat, shop, and find entertainment." Popular road trips include San Diego, Santa Barbara, and Las Vegas.

> **"[Students] care about social justice and enjoy the sunshine and involved community at school."**

Back on campus, LMU's varsity teams compete in the Division I West Coast Conference. The men's soccer, women's beach volleyball, and softball teams are nationally competitive and recently won conference titles. The Lions' rivalry with nearby Pepperdine always draws a huge crowd, and the basketball team's annual pep rally—LMU Madness—"is a pretty big event," says a student. Intramurals and club sports are popular and include flag football, billiards, lacrosse, and rugby, among others. LMU's debate team is a standout too, regularly placing at the top in national and international tournaments.

With its dynamic mix of solid academics, Jesuit and Marymount traditions, and thriving social life, LMU offers students substance and style. "We're very friendly, with a gorgeous campus," says a student. Whether you're a budding scientist or a future filmmaker, Loyola Marymount University may be worth a look.

<aside>

Overlaps

Chapman, Santa Clara, University of San Diego, University of Southern California, UCLA, Cal Poly–San Luis Obispo, UC Santa Barbara, NYU

</aside>

If You Apply To ›

LMU: Early decision I and II, early action, regular decision. Accepts the Common Application with supplement. Applicants to animation, dance, music, production (film and television), studio arts, and theatre arts are required to submit a portfolio or audition. Please consult LMU's website for the most up-to-date information regarding standardized test requirements.

Loyola University New Orleans

6363 St. Charles Ave., Box 89, New Orleans, LA 70118

Of the four Loyolas in the nation, this is the only one where you can go to Mardi Gras and then study the music you heard the next morning in class. New Orleans (a.k.a. NOLA) is an ideal setting for this Roman Catholic, Jesuit university with strengths in business, communication, science, and the arts. NOLA is the most freewheeling Deep South city, and campus politics are mainly liberal.

Loyola University New Orleans is a liberal arts school founded in 1904 by the Society of Jesus (Jesuits) that continues to enhance its rich tradition through extensive service-learning programs, increasing admissions standards, and a renewed commitment to diversifying the student body. "Social justice is at the heart of the education and life here," says a senior. The university has capitalized on its unique NOLA setting to develop excellent programs in environmental studies, entrepreneurship, and artistic and creative fields, with a preprofessional bent.

The school's attractive and well-kept 22-acre main campus, in the University section of Uptown New Orleans, mixes Tudor, Gothic, and modern structures. It

<aside>

Website: www.loyno.edu
Location: City Center
Private
Total Enrollment: 3,755
Undergraduates: 3,033
Male/Female: 33/67
Financial Aid: 99%
Pell Grant: 43%

</aside>

(continued)

Expense: Pr $
Student Loans: 73%
Average Debt: $ $ $
Applicants: 7,455
Accepted: 78%
Enrolled: 16%
Grad in 6 Years: 59%
Returning Freshmen: 81%
Academics: ✑ ✑ ✑
Social: ☎ ☎ ☎
Q of L: ★ ★ ★
Admissions: (800) 456-9652
Email Address: admit@loyno
.edu

Strong Programs:
Business
Communication
Environmental Studies
Digital Filmmaking
Music Industry Studies
Finance
English
Neuroscience

Loyola's majors in digital filmmaking, graphic design, jazz studies, and popular and commercial music are increasingly sought-after.

overlooks acres of Audubon Park and, beyond, the mighty Mississippi River. Two blocks up St. Charles Avenue, Loyola's Broadway campus has an additional four acres. The renovated Monroe Hall features state-of-the-art science labs, high-tech design studios, recording and production facilities, and a seventh-floor greenhouse. The Monroe Library houses approximately 500,000 volumes, an art gallery, and the Pan-American Life Student Success Center.

The Loyola Core involves distribution requirements designed to develop skills in critical thinking, effective communication, quantitative reasoning, information literacy, and ethical reasoning. In addition to taking a First-Year Seminar that introduces them to college-level work and the Jesuit tradition of "thinking critically, acting justly," incoming students are assigned a "success coach" who provides academic guidance and helps instill life skills. Other aspects of Loyola's comprehensive first-year experience include a series of lectures and panel discussions, educational excursions, service-learning projects, and a peer mentoring program.

The School of Communication and Design, whose students do well in national competitions, wins praise, as does virtually any program in the College of Music and Media, including majors in digital filmmaking, graphic design, jazz studies, and popular and commercial music that are increasingly sought-after in a city where these creative professions are defining specialties. Indeed, music industry studies is one of the most popular majors, along with psychology, mass communication, biology, and management. Loyola's urban and electronic music production major is the first of its kind in the country, and students make use of state-of-the-art broadcast and recording studios. Environmental studies, finance, English, neuroscience, and premed advising are also strengths, and a minor in New Orleans studies is available. New and fast-growing majors include nursing and public health.

> **"I have connected on a personal level with every professor I've had here."**

Loyola's academic climate is said to be challenging, supportive, and vibrant. Forty-nine percent of undergraduate classes have fewer than 20 students, and while students report that the quality of teaching varies by department, most faculty make an effort to get to know their students. "I have connected on a personal level with every professor I've had here," says an English major. Regarding counseling services, a senior explains, "Unlike many universities, Loyola does not limit how many sessions a student can have every semester or academic year."

The University Honors Program, open to students in all majors, gives high-achieving students access to small seminars, collaborative research projects with faculty, social activities, and other special opportunities. Twenty-one percent of undergraduates exercise their wings in study abroad programs available in more than 50 countries, from Mexico and India to Belgium and South Korea. With the help of the service-learning office, 26 percent of students make service part of their studies, and Loyola is a top producer of Peace Corps and Teach for America volunteers. Many students invest their sweat equity in the Loyola University Community Action Program, a student-led coalition of several organizations that take on issues such as hunger and homelessness. Seventy percent of students take advantage of internship opportunities.

Given Loyola's academic strengths, the student body is an interesting mix of creative types, social justice activists, and career-minded preprofessionals. Forty-five percent of Loyola undergraduates are Louisiana natives, and many of the remaining students are from the Southeast; 3 percent are international. Twenty-one percent are Hispanic/Latino, 20 percent are Black, 3 percent are Asian American, and 5 percent are multiracial. Religion—specifically Roman Catholicism—has a significant influence on campus; 38 percent of students are Catholic. Daily mass is voluntary, but many students attend. Ten other religions are also represented on campus, and the political atmosphere is largely liberal. Students are particularly active in advocating for women's rights and LGBTQ- and gender-related issues. Loyola awards merit scholarships averaging $22,300 each year and roughly 120 athletic scholarships in nine sports. About a third of undergrads are first-generation college students, and 43 percent of freshmen are Pell-eligible.

Many Loyola students commute from home or off-campus apartments; 54 percent of undergraduates reside on campus. The transition to college is eased by Themed Living Communities, which house classmates together in a common living space within one of the residence halls. Campus dining in the Orleans Room is described as adequate, and a junior comments, "It's a great benefit to have Tulane University across the street because we can use their dining facilities as well." Iggy's Cupboard is a free, student-run food pantry designed to address the issue of food insecurity on campus. According to a senior, "This is a very safe campus."

Loyola is a top producer of Peace Corps and Teach for America volunteers.

"Loyola gives us lots of cool things to do on campus," a philosophy major says, including musical performances, sporting events, and Third Friday—a different themed party or festival held the third Friday of every month with free food, music, and games. Fraternities and sororities are rarities at Jesuit schools, but they make themselves felt at Loyola, with 12 percent of the men and 13 percent of the women choosing to belong. Major annual events include the "Sneaux Day" that blankets Loyola's

"Loyola takes [New Orleans's] party spirit and uses it to uplift the campus community."

front lawn with artificial snow, the musical event Christmas at Loyola, and a crawfish boil in the spring. Loyola even takes the week of Mardi Gras off as a holiday and allows students to register overnight visitors so they can attend the festivities. With so much bustling nightlife in the surrounding city, students report that not much underage drinking happens on campus. "New Orleans is such an exciting city to go to college in," cheers a theatre arts major. "It has a super-cool culture of local shops and businesses"—not to mention the seemingly endless bars, clubs, restaurants, and live music venues.

The Wolf Pack's 18 teams compete in the NAIA Division I, most as members of the Southern States Athletic Conference, and the men's basketball team won the NAIA national championship in 2022. Other competitive teams include women's basketball and women's golf. Loyola's wellness program offers a range of fitness classes, intramurals, club sports, and other recreational activities for jocks and non-jocks alike. Basketball, flag football (no real pigskins at Loyola), volleyball, and rugby are popular pastimes.

Students at Loyola know how to pull together and draw strength from their faith as well as from the distinctive culture of New Orleans. Whether they're working closely with caring professors or relaxing with friends amid the Big Easy's boundless energy, students are satisfied with their choice. "Loyola is jubilant and celebratory like no other place," concludes a political science major. "New Orleans loves to party, and Loyola takes that party spirit and uses it to uplift the campus community."

Overlaps

Rider, Valparaiso, Stetson, Seattle Pacific, Lipscomb, Xavier University of Louisiana, Tulane, Morehouse

If You Apply To ›

Loyola: Early action, regular decision. SATs or ACTs: not considered. Accepts the Common Application with supplement. Audition, portfolio, and/or interview required for admission to the College of Music and Media.

Macalester College

1600 Grand Avenue, St. Paul, MN 55105

A small school that punches well above its weight, Macalester offers an internationalist and multiculturalist view of the world. One of only a handful of leading liberal arts colleges in a metropolitan setting. Carleton has a bigger national reputation, but Mac has the progressive capital city of St. Paul and a distinctive Scottish flavor. Eighty-one percent of the student body hails from outside Minnesota.

Website: www.macalester.edu
Location: City Center
Private
Total Enrollment: 2,201
Undergraduates: 2,201
Male/Female: 43/57
Financial Aid: 85%
Pell Grant: 25%
Expense: Pr $ $ $ $
Student Loans: 61%
Average Debt: $ $
Applicants: 9,046
Accepted: 31%
Enrolled: 21%
Grad in 6 Years: 90%
Returning Freshmen: 96%
Academics: ✐ ✐ ✐ ✐ ½
Social: 🍷 🍷 🍷
Q of L: ★ ★ ★ ★
Admissions: (651) 696-6357
Email Address: admissions@
  macalester.edu

Strong Programs:
International Studies
Geography
Economics
Mathematics
Statistics
Computer Science
Media and Cultural Studies
Biology

Founded in 1874, Macalester College is an international island in the heart of the Great Plains. Liberal describes both its curriculum and its politics. Students here advocate for all sorts of issues with local, national, or international import—from LGBTQ rights and immigration policy to divestment from fossil fuels. Mac students come to the school "deeply caring about a social justice issue," says one student, "and throughout their years at Mac, their passions expand and deepen." Bagpipes are heard frequently on campus, opening formal events and leading all major processions as a stirring reminder of the college's historic Scottish roots. Says one senior, "Bagpipes are like the Macalester anthem."

Macalester takes its name from a Scotsman named Charles Macalester, an advisor to Abraham Lincoln and other U.S. presidents. The college is located in a friendly, family-oriented neighborhood in St. Paul, Minnesota, one mile from the Mississippi River, which divides St. Paul from Minneapolis. Summit Avenue, a tree-lined street with the longest, best-preserved stretch of Victorian homes in the nation, forms the campus's northern boundary. The self-contained, 53-acre campus is arranged around 136-year-old Old Main, a splendid Victorian structure listed on the National Register of Historic Places. The unifying theme is red brick, the better to set off the octagonal Weyerhaeuser Chapel, constructed of black glass. Other notable facilities include the Janet Wallace Fine Arts Center (a.k.a. "J-Wall"), a $32 million theater and dance building and favorite study spot described by a student as a "supercool building" complete with "art studios where you can see ceramics students at the pottery wheel late into the night."

> **"We love discussing political and social issues—sometimes to a fault."**

Mac's general education requirements span the liberal arts and sciences and include at least two courses that address cultural diversity, in the United States and internationally. Every student also completes a seminar-style First-Year Course and, in their senior year, a capstone experience, such as an independent research project, performance, artistic work, or other original work. In addition to international studies, Mac's academic strengths include geography, economics, math, statistics, computer science, and media and cultural studies. Eleven foreign languages are offered, including Arabic, Portuguese, and Russian. The most popular majors are economics, biology, mathematics, and computer science. Science facilities include an observatory and labs for electronic instrumentation and laser spectroscopy.

A sophomore says, "We take our studies seriously and, as a result, conversations continue outside of the classroom because that's how much of an impact they've had on us." Mac emphasizes small class sizes, working together to handle the challenging workload, and interdisciplinarity. "Students and professors can work across academic disciplines to publish papers and pursue projects," explains a history and English double major. Teaching and personal relationships are paramount, with professors often having students over for dinner or dishing off passes on the intramural basketball court.

The late Kofi Annan, former UN secretary general and class of '61, typified one of Macalester's hallmarks: internationalism, not just in its curriculum and its student body but also in its emphasis on international, off-campus experiences. An impressive 57 percent of students go abroad to complete traditional coursework, independent research, and internships, choosing from 90 exchange and partner programs on six continents. Fifty-two percent conduct undergraduate research, often in stipend-supported positions with Mac professors during the summer. Before graduation, more than three-quarters of the students complete an internship, usually in the Twin Cities area, and almost all students get involved in volunteer work.

An impressive 57 percent of students go abroad to complete traditional coursework, independent research, and internships.

An economics major says Mac students tend to fall "somewhere between the quirky intellectual and the globe-trotting activist," adding, "We love discussing political and social issues—sometimes to a fault." Nineteen percent of Macalester students hail from Minnesota, and the rest come from every state, the District of Columbia, and nearly 100 other countries—the proportion of international students is substantial, at 13 percent. Five percent of domestic students are Black, 10 percent are Hispanic/Latino, 8 percent are Asian American, and 8 percent are multiracial. Merit scholarships averaging $17,200 are available to eligible students; there are no athletic scholarships. Macalester guarantees to meet 100 percent of the demonstrated financial need of all admitted students, including international students.

Freshmen and sophomores are required to live in college housing; 62 percent of all students dwell in college-owned digs, which include traditional residences with single or double rooms as well as suites for upperclassmen. "Some of the first-year halls are a bit old, but they have so much character and community that it doesn't matter!" enthuses a geography major.

"Students dot the lawns playing Frisbee, soccer, or cricket—yes, cricket!"

Junior and senior residents of the Interfaith House and the Veggie Co-op prepare their own meals, while other students enjoy vittles in the campus center. "It's really easy to hate on Café Mac, the one dining hall here," says a junior, "but honestly the food here is much better than people give it credit for." Students praise campus security and the college's proactive approach to sexual assault awareness. "We are constantly holding dialogues, having discussions, bringing in outside speakers, and addressing policy about this growing issue," reports a junior.

Given the proximity of a major metropolitan area, much of Mac's social life takes place in the city, although there are plenty of events on campus organized by the student-backed Program Board and other student clubs for those loath to leave. "There is no Greek life at Mac, so the parties normally happen off campus," notes a sophomore. Popular annual events include Founders Day, Winter Ball, Springfest, and the Brain Bowl football game against in-state rival Carleton. There are about a dozen other colleges and universities in town, and the Twin Cities are an excellent place to live, with plenty of bookstores, coffee shops, restaurants, bars, and movie theaters, plus dance and jazz clubs and professional sports teams. Public transportation makes it relatively easy to get around. The Mall of America is nearby, though Mac students tend to tire of it quickly. For those with wheels, the best road trips include Chicago, Madison, and Duluth—and Bemidji, Minnesota, "to see Babe the Blue Ox," according to a senior.

Macalester guarantees to meet 100 percent of the demonstrated financial need of all admitted students.

Competitive Division III Scots teams include baseball, football, women's water polo, and men's and women's soccer, cross-country, and track and field. Macalester has one of the oldest competitive debate programs in the nation, and the mock trial program is highly ranked nationally. About 60 percent of the students compete in intramural and club sports, including dodgeball, rugby, and ice hockey. "Whenever the weather's nice, students dot the lawns playing Frisbee, soccer, or cricket—yes, cricket!" says one student.

Overlaps

Carleton, Grinnell, Oberlin, Brown, Middlebury, St. Olaf, Vassar, Kenyon

Macalester pairs high-powered scholarship with global perspectives informed by its Scottish heritage. The skill and diversity of the student body are rising. Students here appreciate their freedom to grow within a supportive community. "We are all encouraged to explore ourselves, and we are all encouraged to find our passions and commit to them," says one student. "It is what binds us all."

If You Apply To ›

Macalester: Early decision I and II, early action, regular decision. SATs or ACTs: optional. Accepts the Common Application with supplement.

University of Maine

Orono, ME 04469

A sleeper choice for out-of-staters amid better-known public universities such as UMass, UNH, and UVM. Not coincidentally, UMaine is the least expensive—and easiest in admission—of the four. A popular marine sciences program flourishes here, as does engineering. UMaine is a global leader in the development of offshore wind power. Offers a solid honors program and one of the top varsity hockey programs in the nation. Aggressively recruiting out-of-state students.

Website: www.umaine.edu
Location: Rural
Public
Total Enrollment: 8,757
Undergraduates: 7,878
Male/Female: 50/50
Financial Aid: 97%
Pell Grant: 27%
Expense: Pub $ $
Student Loans: 73%
Average Debt: $ $ $ $
Applicants: 14,329
Accepted: 96%
Enrolled: 16%
Grad in 6 Years: 59%
Returning Freshmen: 76%
Academics: ✐ ✐
Social: ☎ ☎ ☎ ☎
Q of L: ★ ★ ★
Admissions: (207) 581-1561
Email Address: umaine admissions@maine.edu

Strong Programs:
Marine Sciences
Engineering
Business

At the University of Maine, nearly 8,000 undergraduates help themselves to a range of strong academic programs at a reasonable cost. As the state's flagship university, UMaine attracts top students to its marine sciences program. A friendly, medium-sized student body and an emphasis on undergraduate learning help create a cozy atmosphere that warms up the long Maine winters. A biology major boasts, "We're competitive, we're focused on groundbreaking technology in our academics, and above all, we're focused on taking care of each other."

Situated on an island between the Stillwater and Penobscot rivers, UMaine's campus covers 660 acres, centered on a large, tree-shaded grass mall. Architectural themes range from English academic to contemporary. Newer facilities include the Innovative Media Research and Commercialization Center, which contains a computer-driven 3-D router, a video production lab, and rich-media classrooms, and the Emera Astronomy Center, home to the state's largest planetarium. The $78 million Ferland Engineering Education and Design Center opened in 2022.

> "We're focused on groundbreaking technology in our academics."

As Maine's only public research university, UMaine (founded in 1865) offers nearly 100 undergraduate majors and academic programs. The university is divided into the College of Education and Human Development; the College of Engineering; the College of Liberal Arts and Sciences; the College of Natural Sciences, Forestry, and Agriculture; and the Honors College (which now enrolls about 750 students)—as well as the Maine Business School. Specific general education requirements vary from college to college, though all students must demonstrate writing proficiency and earn credits in physical or biological science, human value and social context, math (including statistics and computer science), and ethics. A capstone experience, such as a poster presentation or service project, is also mandatory.

UMaine's engineering programs are some of the strongest and most demanding on campus. Other best bets include business, forestry, earth and climate sciences, and nursing. Marine sciences undergrads can spend a semester by the sea at UMaine's prominent Darling Marine Center, and UMaine's Climate Change Institute is renowned. The most popular majors include management, finance, marketing, and psychology. The university offers 23 accelerated programs that allow students to earn both a bachelor's and master's degree in just five or six years, in fields as diverse as botany, information systems, and special education. Students describe the academic climate as cooperative and usually relaxed. Forty-one percent of all classes have fewer than 20 students, making it relatively easy to interact with professors. "I didn't know professors could be so attentive, intelligent, and dedicated to building their students' knowledge," attests a biology major.

(continued)

Forestry
Earth and Climate Sciences
Nursing
Management
Finance

Research is a key part of an undergraduate education at UMaine and is woven into many areas of the curriculum, as is real-world experience. First-year students looking for exposure to research in their first semester can select one of 30 optional, one-credit Research Learning Experiences in scientific fieldwork, graphic design, market research, and more. UMaine's Explorations program lets first-year students work with professionals in different areas before declaring their degree choices, and the First-Year and Transfer Center is the go-to resource for new students seeking academic or personal support. SPIFFY, the student investment club, manages a $3.2 million, real-money portfolio. UMaine students may choose from hundreds of study abroad programs in more than 60 countries.

Marine sciences undergrads can spend a semester by the sea at UMaine's prominent Darling Marine Center.

Most undergrads hail from Maine and other parts of New England (making them immune to the frigid temperatures). "The common thread among UMaine students is their kindness," explains a senior. "In the winter, students will go around scraping the snow off other students' cars, even if they don't know them." Faced with a declining youth population in Maine, the university has been working hard to lure out-of-state students with several programs, including the Flagship Match program, which allows them to pay the same in-state tuition they would pay at their home flagship university. Such efforts are paying off—out-of-state enrollment is up to 39 per-

"In the winter, students will go around scraping the snow off other students' cars."

cent, nearly double what it was eight years ago. Racial diversity still has a long way to go: Black students account for 2 percent of the student body, Asian Americans 2 percent, Hispanics/Latinos 5 percent, and multiracial students 4 percent. International students add 2 percent. Students describe the political climate as balanced, with both sides of the aisle well represented. Merit scholarships average $8,000 a year for qualified students, and 190 athletic scholarships are available in 10 sports.

Thirty-five percent of UMaine students live on campus; the rest seek shelter in Orono, nearby Bangor, or the sparsely populated area in between. Dorms are co-ed; some have gyms, computer labs, or apartment-style suites. First-years may opt to join one of eight living/learning communities organized around themes like nursing, engineering, and honors. "First-year residence halls are very well kept and have plenty of room," reports a student. Meal options in the three main dining halls receive average reviews. "Campus feels incredibly safe to me," says one student. "The dorms are very well-secured and can only be accessed with our student ID cards."

The Flagship Match program allows students to pay the same in-state tuition they would pay at their home flagship university.

Despite—or possibly because of—UMaine's relatively isolated location, the campus pulses with social life; more than 200 student groups and organizations plan plays, carnival nights, concerts, and comedy hours, with a different activity offered each night. Fraternities draw 15 percent of men, while sororities sign up 10 percent of women. Between local bars and clubs and frequent parties at Greek and off-campus houses, the party scene at UMaine is lively but, according to a senior, "not overwhelming if it's not your style." Underage drinking on campus, though prohibited, is common. Everyone looks forward to Maine Day, held the week before spring finals, when classes are canceled for the day so students can do service projects in the morning, followed by a campuswide cookout with games and a concert.

A nursing major says the midsized town of Orono and the surrounding area have much to offer: "cute shops, cozy libraries, indoor and outdoor ice skating, music stores, bowling, movie theaters, a variety of restaurants, and vibrant museums." Buses to Bangor, a fair-sized city 10 minutes away, run every 15 to 20 minutes. UMaine students tend to be outdoor enthusiasts, and popular road trips include Acadia National Park, skiing at Sugarloaf, L.L. Bean's 24-hour store in Freeport, and the real-life Mount Katahdin, which appears on L.L. Bean's logo. Those seeking big-city adventures enjoy Boston, four hours away, or Montreal, with its lower drinking age.

> "[The party scene is] not overwhelming if it's not your style."

UMaine is the state's only Division I school, and athletic events are a big part of student life. Ice hockey reigns supreme, especially when rivals Boston College, Boston University, or New Hampshire are in town, and the Black Bears are perennial champions. Women's field hockey and basketball have claimed America East conference titles in recent years. Men's and women's track and field are also competitive. The popular intramural and club sports programs cover more than 35 sports, from swimming and sailing to kickball and broomball (ice hockey with a dodgeball and a broom, played with shoes instead of skates).

UMaine is a medium-sized school with a small-school atmosphere. Combine the state's natural beauty with an increased emphasis on top-quality facilities and more intimate student/faculty interaction, and it's no surprise that this campus draws more die-hard "Maine-iaks" each year—more and more of them from other states.

Overlaps

University of Rhode Island, Montana State, University of Wyoming, University of Idaho, North Dakota State, University of New Hampshire, University of Vermont, University of Southern Maine

If You Apply To ›

Maine: Early action, rolling admissions. SATs or ACTs: optional. Accepts the Common Application with supplement.

Manhattanville College

2900 Purchase Street, Purchase, NY 10577

One of the few small liberal arts colleges in the NYC area, Manhattanville occupies a former estate (complete with a castle) and is a quick train ride into Manhattan. Strong programs include education, psychology, and nursing, and the distinctive Portfolio System has been rebooted for modern times. Sixty-one percent of students are women and 29 percent are Hispanic/Latino.

Website: www.mville.edu
Location: Suburban
Private
Total Enrollment: 1,647
Undergraduates: 1,289
Male/Female: 39/61
Financial Aid: 87%
Pell Grant: 37%

Founded in 1841 by the Sisters of the Sacred Heart as an all-women's boarding school, Manhattanville College today is a private, nondenominational, coeducational, liberal arts college with a mission to "educate students to be ethical and socially responsible leaders in a global community." Manhattanville has overhauled its signature Portfolio System, which had been the college's calling card since 1971. Now known as ATLAS, the new system is currently offered as an optional certificate program in which students set goals, reflect on their academic and cocurricular experiences, and showcase their work in e-portfolios. But ATLAS is just one way Manhattanville encourages individuality and personal growth. Personal attention is another.

Manhattanville College pulled up stakes from its original location on Houston Street in New York City in the 1950s for a 125-acre estate in Purchase, New York. The estate is located in wealthy Westchester County, near the town of White Plains—home to several major corporations and just 28 miles from the excitement of the Big Apple. Overlooking the central Quadrangle, which was designed by Central Park architect Frederick Law Olmsted, is the focal point of the campus: Reid Castle, a 19th-century replica of a Norman castle. The President's Cottage, built in 1860, has been converted into a modern Center for Design Thinking complete with a high-tech fabrication lab with 3-D printers.

Manhattanville's general education program, called GenEd 20, requires course-work in math, science, fine arts, social science, humanities, global studies, and a second language. Freshmen take a first-year seminar focused on ethics and social responsibility and two semesters of first-year writing. Seminar professors serve as faculty mentors, and all incoming students are also assigned academic advisors and peer mentors to help ease the transition to college life.

The college's strongest offerings include education, business (especially management and finance), and psychology, while communication studies and performing arts are also popular. Manhattanville's School of Education boasts a near-perfect pass rate for the New York State Teaching Exam. Enrollment in the recently established School of Nursing and Health Sciences is growing rapidly, and the school has added a new major in radiologic

"Professors always want to get the best out of you and challenge you."

technology. A popular major in sport studies prepares students for a wide range of careers, such as sports business management, sport psychology, physical education, and sports journalism. Art and design programs are enhanced by the proximity of New York City's many museums and galleries. Students may choose from a bevy of five-year bachelor's/master's degree programs in several fields, cross-register for courses at neighboring Purchase College, SUNY, or opt to design their own major. Manhattanville has eliminated majors in American studies; Asian, Middle Eastern, and North African studies; French; and world religions.

Undergraduates enjoy regular access to professors, especially since 77 percent of classes have fewer than 20 students. "Professors always want to get the best out of you and challenge you in different ways to prepare you for whatever career path you choose," explains a senior. Students give high praise to the academic support services offered by the Academic Resource Center, the Writing Center, the Center for Student Accommodations, and the Valiant Learning Support Program. Qualified freshmen may apply for the Castle Scholars Honors Program for a more intensive curriculum. The college has more than 100 study abroad options in 30 countries, but only about 3 percent of students participate. Fifty-nine percent get involved in undergraduate research. The Center for Career Development helps secure internship placements at more than 350 locations in and beyond the New York Metro area, such as MasterCard, the Metropolitan Museum of Art, and U.S. Senate offices.

A communication studies major characterizes Manhattanville students as "diverse, friendly, and chill," and a classmate adds that there is a "strong New York Latino-based community where everyone accepts each other's diversity." Indeed, most undergraduates (74 percent) are New Yorkers, and Hispanics/Latinos represent the largest minority group, at 29 percent. Black students make up 11 percent of the student body, Asian Americans 2 percent, and multiracial students 2 percent; 3 percent of undergrads come from overseas. Students describe themselves as politically aware, and a senior says, "Our president has held open-school conferences for all students to gather and discuss pressing issues." Thirty-seven percent of freshmen are eligible for Pell Grants. While there are no athletic scholarships, hundreds of merit scholarships averaging $20,000 are awarded to qualified students.

(continued)

Expense: Pr $
Student Loans: 85%
Average Debt: $
Applicants: 2,971
Accepted: 83%
Enrolled: 9%
Grad in 6 Years: 61%
Returning Freshmen: 73%
Academics: ✏️ ✏️ ✏️
Social: ☎ ☎ ☎
Q of L: ★ ★ ★
Admissions: (914) 323-5464
Email Address: admissions@mville.edu

Strong Programs:
Education
Business Management
Finance
Psychology
Communication Studies
Performing Arts
Nursing
Sport Studies

Enrollment in the recently established School of Nursing and Health Sciences is growing rapidly.

About half of Manhattanville's students live on campus in one of four residence halls, which have lounges, communal kitchens, and laundry rooms. Freshmen are assigned rooms that are "spacious and very comfortable" according to a student, while upperclassmen hoping to score coveted singles or suites enter a lottery that a senior describes as "a little *Hunger Games*-ish." Campus dwellers can choose from three different meal plans and can use their meal cards at the main dining hall, the Pub (a deli-type eatery), and vending machines. "The meals are pretty consistent, but it isn't Mom or Dad's homemade cooking," a junior says. Students report feeling safe on campus, and one notes, "The school as a whole has been promoting more awareness" of campus sexual assault.

The student programming board is working to improve the campus social life with weekend events such as dance parties, gaming tournaments, comedy and talent shows, movies, plays, and concerts. With no fraternities or sororities, off-campus parties are often hosted by sports teams and usually open to all, although students say Manhattanville is no party school. Every spring, students look forward to Quad Jam, an all-day concert and carnival. Another favorite tradition is Red Madness, "a giant pep rally where all the athletic teams compete for who has the best dance routine," explains a sophomore. There's also a Fall Fest'ville and an International Bazaar, in which students give cultural performances and share ethnic foods.

Manhattanville students contribute 30,000 hours of community service each year through more than 60 local and global programs. The college's hometown, Purchase, "is not a college town. It is an affluent area with mansions all over," a junior says. Students frequently take the school's free bus to White Plains to enjoy a variety of restaurants, bars, and shops, and as one student points out, "Manhattanville is only 30 miles from New York City, so students can also go to the city for fun." Road trips include Rye Beach in the warmer months and upstate New York or Vermont for skiing in the winter.

"[Students are] diverse, friendly, and chill."

Manhattanville has invested heavily in athletics in hopes of increasing its visibility, although some students complain of a continuing lack of school spirit. Even so, Valiant teams (inspired by a 15th-century quote, "To the valiant of heart, nothing is impossible") hold their own in the Division III Skyline Conference. Men's tennis is a recent conference champion, and men's and women's ice hockey, soccer, volleyball, and basketball have also been competitive. Intramural and club sports, ranging from indoor soccer and floor hockey to eSports tournaments, draw about a quarter of the students.

"Manhattanville really feels like a close-knit community," a junior says. The familial atmosphere can get claustrophobic at times, but for those wishing to be part of a close but growing community where values matter, Manhattanville may be worth a look.

Overlaps

Mercy, Pace, Manhattan College, Marist, Iona, Purchase (SUNY), St. John's University (NY), Sacred Heart

If You Apply To ›

Manhattanville: Early action, rolling admissions. SATs or ACTs: optional. Accepts the Common Application with supplement. Auditions are required for performing arts applicants. Portfolios are recommended for visual arts applicants.

Marquette University

Milwaukee, WI 53201

Marquette is an old-line Roman Catholic, Jesuit university situated near the heart of downtown Milwaukee. Service learning is a major emphasis. The student body is mainly from the southern Wisconsin/northern Illinois corridor and is 60 percent Catholic. Relatively inexpensive, in keeping with its middle- and working-class roots. Compare to Saint Louis University and Loyola of Chicago.

At Marquette University, students practice what they preach. The college experience at this Roman Catholic institution includes an emphasis on personal growth, civic responsibility, and community service. The university continuously seeks new and innovative ways to strengthen its traditions and values drawn from the Society of Jesus (Jesuits), while at the same time expanding its global focus and connecting students with practical, real-world experiences. Service learning, which helps students put classroom theories to the test through volunteer work, is a cornerstone of campus life, helping to shape well-rounded students who graduate ready, as the school puts it, to "be the difference" in the world.

> "The professors I've had have really instilled the idea of teamwork."

Marquette, which opened its doors in 1881 and takes its name from the 17th-century Jesuit explorer Jacques Marquette, occupies more than 90 acres of "concrete with interludes of grass and trees" just a few blocks from the heart of downtown Milwaukee. While offering the advantages of an urban setting, its campus does have plenty of open spaces suitable for throwing everything from a Frisbee to a barbecue. Although most of the buildings are relatively modern, the campus is the site of the St. Joan of Arc Chapel, which was built in France 600 years ago and later transported to Wisconsin. It is said to be the only medieval structure in the Western Hemisphere dedicated to its original purpose. More recent additions include an 890-bed residence facility and a 47,000-square-foot athletic research center.

The Marquette Core Curriculum is structured in three parts. Foundations courses ground students in the theology, philosophy, and rhetoric of a Jesuit perspective. Discovery courses encourage an interdisciplinary approach, as students take four courses all centered around a chosen theme, such as Crossing Boundaries and Exploring the Unknown. A final Culminating course helps students reflect on and apply what they've learned in the Core. Students who want to get a head start on the Marquette experience in a close-knit group can opt to participate in the five-week Emerging Scholars Program, which offers credit and noncredit courses.

The most popular majors at Marquette include biomedical sciences, nursing, psychology, and exercise physiology. Engineering programs and the social welfare and justice major are well regarded, as are more specialized majors in operations and supply chain management and bioinformatics. Through an affiliation with the Milwaukee Institute of Art and Design, two fine arts minors are available in studio art and graphic design. Marquette has its own art museum and an active theatre program. New majors are available in environmental science and statistical science. Marquette's highly popular service-learning courses, which draw more than 1,000 students every semester, connect participants with service opportunities in more than 130 community agencies. Overall, about three-quarters of Marquette students take part in some type of community service experience prior to graduation.

> "If you use your street smarts and the campus resources in place, you are entirely safe."

Website: www.marquette.edu
Location: City Center
Private
Total Enrollment: 9,927
Undergraduates: 7,360
Male/Female: 43/57
Financial Aid: 99%
Pell Grant: 21%
Expense: Pr $
Student Loans: 56%
Average Debt: $ $ $ $
Applicants: 16,270
Accepted: 86%
Enrolled: 12%
Grad in 6 Years: 81%
Returning Freshmen: 89%
Academics: ✍ ✍ ✍
Social: ☎ ☎ ☎
Q of L: ★ ★ ★
Admissions: (414) 288-7302
Email Address: admissions@marquette.edu

Strong Programs:
Social Welfare and Justice
Engineering
Operations and Supply Chain Management
Bioinformatics
Biomedical Sciences
Nursing
Psychology
Exercise Physiology

Forty-nine percent of classes have fewer than 20 students, and students report little difficulty getting into the ones they want. One student says, "Marquette is pretty collaborative. The professors I've had have really instilled the idea of teamwork." The school's Jesuit influence is felt in the classroom, and the Manresa project, named for the Spanish town where St. Ignatius spent a year praying about his vocation, helps professors incorporate Ignatian teaching into their classes—focusing particularly on community-based learning and service, social justice, and personal reflection on faith and vocation.

Thirty percent of Marquette students travel each year for study abroad programs offered in more than 45 countries, which include 33 short-term, faculty-led options. The flagship Sibanye Cape Town service learning program in South Africa is especially popular; participants combine their studies at the University of the Western Cape with two full days of volunteer work per week in areas like education, public health, and economic development. The university is also home to the Les Aspin Center for Government in Washington, D.C., which allows students to take courses while participating in an internship with a federal government agency. Twenty-one percent of students assist faculty members with their research, and approximately 260 top freshmen per year join the University Honors Program, which offers enhanced core courses, small seminars, and an optional living/learning community.

> *Service-learning courses, which draw more than 1,000 students every semester, connect participants with service opportunities in community agencies.*

Most of the undergraduate student body is from the Midwest, 34 percent from Wisconsin itself; 2 percent come from foreign countries. In general, Marquette boasts a friendly collection of traditional, middle-class students. Student religious organizations are active, and students, faculty, and staff can attend mass every day of the week. Catholics are understandably predominant in the student body, at 60 percent, but religious practice is left to the individual. According to one sophomore, "We are the type of students who love debate, and love the free-flowing exchange of ideas." Black students make up 4 percent of the student body, Hispanics/Latinos 16 percent, Asian Americans 6 percent, and multiracial students 3 percent. Marquette's successful Educational Opportunity Program enables low-income, disadvantaged students to have the benefit of a college education. Merit scholarships averaging $16,600 are available, as are athletic scholarships in 16 sports.

> **"A quick bus ride can take you to some of the most booming social spots in Milwaukee."**

Forty-one percent of Marquette students make their home on campus; residency is required for freshmen and sophomores, except for commuters who live within 30 miles with a parent or guardian. All but two residence halls are co-ed, and there are more than 400 university-owned apartments (which come with a separate electric bill). Within the residence halls are six living/learning communities organized around academic and cultural interests. "Marquette has many dining halls, considering the size of the campus, and one is open 24/7," notes a junior. Regarding security on this urban campus, a senior says, "If you use your street smarts and the campus resources in place, you are entirely safe. We have student shuttle services, a police department, blue-light emergency phones, mobile applications, and everything else in place to keep you safe." The LGBTQ+ Resource Center supports students with an interest in LGBTQ and gender identity issues, and students are required to take yearly online training on sexual violence prevention.

> *A majority of students participate in roughly two dozen intramural sports and 44 club teams.*

Social life takes place both on and off campus. While Milwaukee is hardly a college town, students say there are many good things about being there, including major-league baseball and basketball, plenty of concerts and festivals, and a spate of new downtown developments. "A quick bus ride can take you to some of the most booming social spots in Milwaukee," says a junior. An old advertising slogan once claimed that "Milwaukee Means Beer," and few Marquette students would disagree. Students report that Marquette is stricter than most universities in enforcing the drinking age, especially in the dorms. Fraternities and sororities attract 3 percent of the men and 9 percent of the women. A well-loved tradition is the Miracle on Westowne Square, the annual lighting of the campus Christmas tree and accompanying mass.

The Golden Eagles Division I men's basketball and women's volleyball teams are highly competitive in the Big East Conference. A majority of students participate in roughly two dozen intramural sports and 44 club teams. Sports fans will be impressed with Milwaukee's Fiserv Forum, close to campus and home to Marquette basketball and the NBA's Milwaukee Bucks. Nature lovers can head to Lake Michigan, a 40-minute walk from campus, or to Kettle Moraine, a glaciated region ideal for hiking and cross-country skiing. Chicago is only 95 miles away.

Students at Marquette are engaged not only in their own personal growth but also in the betterment of their local and global communities through service. Students say it's the supportive, familial atmosphere that makes them excited about those goals and that makes Marquette what it is. Confirms a senior, "Marquette students really are a community. Everyone supports everyone else."

If You Apply To ›

Marquette: Rolling admissions. SATs or ACTs: optional. Accepts the Common Application.

University of Mary Washington

1301 College Avenue, Fredericksburg, VA 22401

Situated in historic Fredericksburg, Mary Washington could easily be mistaken for one of Virginia's elite private colleges. A public liberal arts and sciences college, it offers just as much history and tradition albeit for a much lower price. Unusual program in historic preservation. Named for George Washington's mother and formerly a women's college, it is still about two-thirds female.

Strolling among the University of Mary Washington's elegant buildings of red brick with white columns has led more than one pleased parent to declare, "Now this is what a college should look like." Indeed, for an aura of history and tradition, few schools stack up to this small college in Fredericksburg, a site of Civil War action and the boyhood town of George Washington. "Tradition is at the heart of UMW and is one of the many things that instills a sense of community here," says a junior.

The campus features classical Jeffersonian buildings, sweeping lawns, brick walkways, and breathtaking foliage. "Seeing the trees change all around campus is so satisfying," opines a first-year student. If the campus architecture reminds some people of the University of Virginia, it's no accident: UMW was the all-female branch of that august institution before going co-ed in 1970 and cutting its ties in 1972. The campus has undergone a spate of renovations in the last few years, including a $24 million overhaul of Seacobeck Hall, a longtime dining facility that now houses the College of Education; a significant expansion of the Jepson Science Center; and major revamps of two of the university's oldest residence halls, Willard Hall and Virginia Hall, both of which house first-year students.

Website: www.umw.edu
Location: Small City
Public
Total Enrollment: 3,222
Undergraduates: 3,100
Male/Female: 35/65
Financial Aid: 77%
Pell Grant: 17%
Expense: Pub $ $ $
Student Loans: 55%
Average Debt: $ $ $
Applicants: 5,042
Accepted: 82%
Enrolled: 15%
Grad in 6 Years: 68%
Returning Freshmen: 83%

Mary Washington has gained a reputation as one of the premier public liberal arts and sciences colleges in the country. The core curriculum, which emphasizes a strong liberal arts focus, has been updated to include a diverse and global perspectives requirement, a digital-intensive course requirement, a "Beyond the Classroom" component (a faculty-supervised experience such as research, a community engagement course, study abroad, or an internship), and an "After UMW" component focused on professional and career development. In addition to pledging to uphold the university's honor code, incoming students must take a discussion-based first-year seminar, in which classmates live together and receive dedicated advising. Nearly every major requires students to complete a capstone project or experience or to take a senior-level intensive seminar.

Mary Washington's program in historic preservation is solid: "It's pretty unique and has great local partners for internships," says a senior. Among the sciences, biology and chemistry are the clear favorites. The noteworthy international affairs program benefits from the university's proximity to Washington, D.C., and geography, education, theatre, and women's and gender studies are also strengths. Popular majors include business administration, psychology, biology, English, and communication and digital studies.

The close ties between students and faculty are a great source of pride at Mary Washington, and an economics major describes the academics as "rigorous and hands-on." Sixty-one percent of classes have fewer than 20 students, and instructors are said to be intelligent and accessible. "I never imagined that I would find such a highly engaged and compassionate set of professors my first year of college," says one student. Students are encouraged to take on research projects of their own design, and science students are eligible for a 10-week summer research program. Eleven percent of students participate in the university's honors program. Several departments offer grants for work abroad or in the U.S., and about 20 percent of students study abroad in their choice of more than 30 countries. The college's location, roughly an hour from both Washington, D.C., and the state capital, Richmond, is a handy asset for the budding politicos who seek internships every year. A large majority of students continue on to jobs after graduation rather than graduate school.

Incoming students take a discussion-based first-year seminar, in which classmates live together and receive dedicated advising.

At Mary Washington, an unusually strong sense of community characterizes everything from academics to campus life. "Students are self-motivated by the excitement of learning something new," comments a theatre major. Ninety percent of students are from Virginia, and just 1 percent arrive from abroad. Black students make up 8 percent of the student population, Hispanics/Latinos 11 percent, Asian Americans 4 percent, and multiracial students 5 percent. "Our James Farmer Multicultural Center is a great place for students to learn more about different cultures and take part in social justice activities," says a senior. Students report that, politically, the campus is heavily liberal. Eligible undergraduates receive merit awards averaging $3,700, but there are no athletic scholarships.

"Seeing the trees change all around campus is so satisfying."

Mary Washington has a two-year residency requirement, and all told, 53 percent of students live in university housing. The residence halls offer a variety of living arrangements, including singles, suites, gender-neutral options, and first-year living/learning clusters. "The freshman dorms are really nice and kept up," says a student. Dining services draw mostly unenthusiastic reviews. "We have good support programs through the Office of Title IX," observes a sophomore, "and there seems to be a general consensus among students that UMW is a safe place."

The favorite tradition is Devil-Goat Day, an all-day competition pitting odd- and even-year classes against each other.

"The social life is rather slow, and the campus on the weekends is pretty quiet," reports a political science major, but student involvement in the more than 150 active campus clubs is high. There is no Greek life (aside from a couple of off-campus frats not recognized by the university), but parties can occasionally be found both on and off campus, generally thrown by sports teams. "Campus policies regarding alcohol are never punitive and always educational," says a senior. Other student organizations offer special events each Friday, and volunteering is a big part of campus life. Traditions matter here, beginning with Eagle Gathering, a welcome ceremony where new students light candles and sing the alma mater. The annual Multicultural Fair draws thousands of residents and vendors from the local community to campus. Third-year students anticipate Junior Ring Week, during which they receive their class rings. The favorite tradition is Devil-Goat Day, an all-day competition pitting odd- and even-year classes against each other in events such as sumo wrestling, jousting, and the Velcro wall.

> **"Students are self-motivated by the excitement of learning something new."**

Small and friendly, nearby Fredericksburg "has a relaxed social atmosphere. Students are always hanging out downtown at coffee shops or by the Rappahannock River on nice days," according to a senior. While it lacks some of the nightlife of a larger city, there are historic homes to visit, museums, bookstores, a mall, the Central Park shopping plaza, and plenty of restaurants. For dance clubs and bars, students drive to Richmond or D.C. Also an hour's drive away is the scenery of the Chesapeake Bay, due east, and the Blue Ridge Mountains, due west.

Mary Washington doesn't have a football team, but its 21 Division III Eagles sports teams fly high in the Coast-to-Coast Athletic Conference. Men's and women's soccer, tennis, and swimming are top performers; the men's swim team has won four individual national championships. About 30 percent of students use the 76-acre sports and field complex, complete with an Olympic-size pool, for more than 20 club sports and a variety of intramurals, ranging from ultimate Frisbee and soccer to indoor Wiffle ball.

"Students looking for an easy pass and wild parties should look elsewhere," advises one student. Instead, the University of Mary Washington offers a first-rate liberal arts and sciences education, the feel of a private school, and a public school price tag. A junior concludes, "UMW is such a positive environment, full of kind individuals who share the goal of communal success."

Overlaps

New College of Florida, St. Mary's College of Maryland, Massachusetts College of Liberal Arts, UNC Asheville, SUNY–College at Geneseo, William & Mary, College of Charleston, Elon

If You Apply To ›

Mary Washington: Early decision, early action, regular decision. SATs or ACTs: optional. Accepts the Common Application with supplement. Application includes optional question about gender identity.

University of Maryland

College Park, MD 20742

The name says Maryland, but the location says Washington, D.C. Students in College Park can jump on the Metro just as they do at American or Georgetown. Maryland, the state's flagship campus, is nothing if not big, and savvy students will look to programs such as the Honors College and living/learning communities for some personal attention.

Website: www.umd.edu
Location: Suburban
Public
Total Enrollment: 36,340
Undergraduates: 28,344
Male/Female: 51/49
Financial Aid: 55%
Pell Grant: 15%
Expense: Pub $ $
Student Loans: 38%
Average Debt: $ $ $
Applicants: 50,146
Accepted: 52%
Enrolled: 23%
Grad in 6 Years: 88%
Returning Freshmen: 96%
Academics: ✐ ✐ ✐
Social: ☎ ☎ ☎
Q of L: ★ ★ ★
Admissions: (800) 422-5867
Email Address: applymaryland
@umd.edu

Strong Programs:
Engineering
Computer Science
Criminology and Criminal
    Justice
Business
Journalism
Information Science
Finance
Economics

The Heritage
Community, a
complex with two new
residence halls and
a dining facility, was
completed in 2022.

For good luck on exams, University of Maryland students rub the nose of Testudo, the school's terrapin mascot. But even without touching the storied statue, most students here feel lucky to be at a diverse school that offers a multitude of programs, from living/learning communities to special opportunities for freshmen, that make it feel smaller and more personal, despite its daunting size. "With hundreds of different student organizations," says a senior, "students will always be able to find their niche."

Maryland's 1,340-acre campus embraces an array of architectural styles, including the Georgian brick buildings ringing the oak-lined mall at the heart of the campus. The 17,950-seat Xfinity Center hosts Terrapin basketball games and special university events. The $152 million Iribe Center for Computer Science and Engineering features six floors of specialized, high-tech labs. Construction on the Heritage Community, a complex with two new residence halls and a dining facility, was completed in 2022.

Maryland, which dates to 1856, has earned a strong reputation for its engineering, computer science, and criminology and criminal justice departments, as well as the Smith School of Business and Merrill College of Journalism. The most popular majors are computer science, information science, finance, economics, and biological sciences. Newer undergraduate majors include immersive media design, human development, and biocomputational engineering. General education requirements entail a

> "The FIRE program has really sparked and encouraged my interest in research."

number of distribution areas, including professional writing, oral communication, diversity, and others. Students must also take an "i-Series" course that emphasizes "broad, analytical thinking about significant issues." For students at the extremes of the academic spectrum, there are departmental honors programs and the Honors College, as well as an intensive educational development and tutoring program. Students participating in individual studies can combine established majors and create their own programs.

Maryland's academic climate is "more collaborative than competitive," according to one student. Lower-level courses tend to be large and impersonal ("easy to hide in, even easier to skip"), but the corresponding weekly discussion sections led by teaching assistants offer personal attention. The situation improves by junior year, when classes of 20 to 40 students become the norm. "Professors are clearly well versed in their fields," says a biochemistry major, "but there is some expectation for students to teach themselves material." The university is putting more emphasis on helping students make timely progress toward their degrees. A two-day orientation, seminars, and course clusters are offered for freshmen, and 60 percent of freshmen participate in more than 25 living/learning programs that provide experiential learning opportunities in more intimate settings. The First-Year Innovation and Research Experience (FIRE) program allows qualified freshmen to join faculty-led research groups for research and mentorship experiences. One participant comments, "The FIRE program has really sparked and encouraged my interest in research." Internships in nearby Washington, D.C., and Baltimore are plentiful, and 22 percent of undergrads study abroad in dozens of countries, such as Costa Rica, Israel, and Sweden.

Seventy-five percent of undergraduates are Maryland natives, while New York and New Jersey are also well represented; 3 percent hail from foreign nations. Diversity is more than just a buzzword: 12 percent of students are Black, 10 percent are Hispanic/Latino, 20 percent are Asian American, and 5 percent are multiracial. Major social and political issues on campus revolve around greater awareness of racial and LGBTQ+ issues. Qualified undergrads receive merit awards averaging $7,000, and athletes vie for nearly 430 scholarships in 20 sports.

Thirty-seven percent of students live on campus in single-sex or co-ed dorms; freshmen are guaranteed housing. While many juniors and seniors seek off-campus accommodations, those who stay on campus all four years will find that their digs improve as they gain seniority—upperclassmen have the option of on-campus apartments and suites. Even so, the quality of the dorms varies significantly based on their age, and a senior says, "The dorms are a gamble for a lot of money." Dining services get much better reviews. Campus safety features include front desks in the dorms that are staffed 24/7 and walking and riding escort services to transport students after dark. "The area has its rough spots but it is constantly becoming safer," a sophomore says.

The university's reputation as a haven for those who prefer partying to studying is changing as students with better credentials apply, but there is still always something happening in the dorms and at local pubs. Students enjoy frequent school-sponsored concerts, movies, speakers, and Terps After Dark events, as well as the traditional football and basketball games and off-campus fraternity parties. "Social life is epic here," raves a history and education double major. Fourteen percent of men and 19 percent of women go Greek, but they don't dominate the tone of campus life. As for drinking, "They say no tolerance and in recent years, there have been crackdowns. As a result, policies have increased in effectiveness," says one student.

"Terrapin pride runs rampant around here."

Art Attack is a favorite annual event in which local artists share their crafts and national touring artists perform an evening concert. Other popular events include homecoming and Maryland Day, where "the campus mall basically turns into something that resembles a state fair," explains a junior. When Maryland's suburban campus feels too small, a few bucks and a few minutes on the Metro (Washington's subway system) brings Terrapins into downtown D.C. at a hare's pace; downtown Baltimore is a 40-minute drive.

Division I sports are a big deal here, and in a bow to the importance of television revenue, the Terrapins compete in the predominately Midwestern, 14-member Big Ten Conference. Despite the football team's disappointing record on the Big Ten stage, the Terrapins continue to achieve success: men's and women's lacrosse, women's basketball, and baseball have claimed conference titles recently. Basketball fans are intrepid and not always civilized, turning out en masse to disparage opponents. "Students here have a lot of school spirit," a junior says. "Terrapin pride runs rampant around here." Around two dozen intramurals and more than 45 club sports draw roughly a quarter of the students.

The University of Maryland's overwhelming size is both a blessing and a curse for the increasingly capable undergraduates here. On one hand, "the diversity of the student body and the opportunities afforded are infinite," a sophomore says. On the other, largeness can translate into crowded dorms, big classes, parking problems, and other hassles. Still, most students agree that the university's range of academic programs, advantageous location near the nation's capital, and persistent school spirit make the Maryland experience worthwhile.

Overlaps

Penn State, University of Michigan, University of Delaware, UMBC, Ohio State, Rutgers, George Washington, Virginia Tech

If You Apply To ›

Maryland: Early action, regular decision. Accepts the Common Application with supplement. Students who do not meet academic standards may submit additional information for consideration. Please consult Maryland's website for the most up-to-date information regarding standardized test requirements.

University of Maryland, Baltimore County

Baltimore, MD 21250

A midsized public university with the feel of a private. Strategically located in a suburban setting between Washington, D.C., and Baltimore, UMBC invests heavily in learning communities and other efforts to ensure that its undergraduates thrive. Nationally known for its selective Meyerhoff Scholars Program and a chess team that routinely bests its Ivy League competition. Working on its commuter reputation.

Website: www.umbc.edu
Location: Suburban
Public
Total Enrollment: 10,676
Undergraduates: 9,144
Male/Female: 55/45
Financial Aid: 84%
Pell Grant: 28%
Expense: Pub $ $
Student Loans: 43%
Average Debt: $ $
Applicants: 11,093
Accepted: 81%
Enrolled: 23%
Grad in 6 Years: 70%
Returning Freshmen: 87%
Academics: ✐ ✐ ✐
Social: ☎ ☎ ☎
Q of L: ★ ★ ★
Admissions: (410) 455-2292
Email Address: admissions@ umbc.edu

Strong Programs:
Biological Sciences
Psychology
Computer Science
Information Systems
Engineering
Bioinformatics
Theatre
Visual Arts

Since its founding in 1966, the University of Maryland, Baltimore County, has allowed students to take charge of their academic world. Students here are given access to academic and social resources and a thriving research agenda usually reserved for those attending mammoth public institutions or pricey private colleges. "At UMBC, there is a high level of attention, effort, and care put into the educational program," remarks a senior. What's more, the school fields a killer chess team that regularly keeps competitors in check. UMBC encourages exploration and expects students to support one another and the community at large. It's your move.

UMBC's 500-acre suburban campus is located between D.C. and Baltimore, offering students access to an array of cultural attractions including restaurants, art galleries, specialty shops, and museums. In the past decade, the university has invested more than $420 million in new facilities and landscaping, including a LEED Gold–rated performing arts and humanities building, a 6,000-seat athletics arena and event center, the Interdisciplinary Life Sciences Building, the Center for Well-Being, and more than 3,000 trees.

All students must complete general foundation requirements, which include courses in the arts and humanities, foreign language, social science, math, and biological/physical science. The university offers a number of programs designed to help first-year students ease into college life. In addition to orientation programs, First-Year Seminars allow students to partner with faculty members to explore course material in an intimate, active learning environment. Students focus on creative and critical-thinking skills and written and oral communication and take part in faculty and peer critiques. Additional mentoring is available to those who may be at risk for not completing their degrees.

> **"All of my professors have shown a personal interest in my growth."**

UMBC's most popular programs are also its strongest, including biological sciences, psychology, computer science, information systems, and engineering. Programs in bioinformatics, theatre, and visual arts are also well regarded. The individualized study major gives students a chance to create their own majors drawing on a wide range of disciplines. Students can also take advantage of established interdisciplinary programs in Asian studies, Africana studies, and global studies. Forty-four percent of classes have fewer than 20 students, and students say the environment is more cooperative than competitive. "All of my professors have shown a personal interest in my growth," adds a history major.

The Alex. Brown Center for Entrepreneurship (established with a donation from the eponymous investment banking firm) sponsors programs and courses to inspire entrepreneurial thinking among students and faculty. Budding researchers may compete for undergraduate research awards of up to $1,500 through the Provost's Office and present their work at Undergraduate Research and Creative Achievement Day. Thanks to the highly selective Meyerhoff Scholars Program, which addresses the shortage of diversity in the sciences and engineering, UMBC graduates more Black undergrads who go on to earn Ph.D.s in the natural sciences and engineering than any other American institution. Each year, the Shriver Center connects nearly 1,000 UMBC students with service-learning opportunities, while the Career Center places 2,000 students in internships, co-ops, and research positions. Roughly 5 percent of students participate in study abroad programs available in 60 countries worldwide.

UMBC students are "hardworking and honest," says an information systems major, and they tend to put academics first. Ninety-three percent of students hail from Maryland, while 4 percent come from abroad. Black students account for 21 percent of the student body, Hispanics/Latinos 9 percent, Asian Americans 23 percent, and multiracial students 5 percent. Politically, the student body leans liberal, but the campus is not a hotbed of activism. UMBC awards merit scholarships worth an average of $7,100 and athletic scholarships in 17 sports.

Thirty-three percent of students live in campus housing, which is guaranteed for incoming freshmen who apply by the deadline. Residential facilities receive average reviews. Several living/learning communities connect students with similar interests and house them together in the residence halls; some of the options include the Center for Women in Technology, Intercultural Living Exchange, Honors College, and Discovery Scholars. Students say off-campus housing is plentiful and cheap, although parking on campus can be a chore. Campus dining options include a dining hall and the Commons, which offers a variety of fare, including international cuisine. As for security, "campus is safe," says a student, "and you can call for an escort if you're feeling unsafe walking around."

Social life can be slow on campus, but a junior advises, "There's almost always something happening at UMBC if you look hard enough," including game nights, movies, student club events, and other activities. Only 3 percent of the men and 5 percent of the women go Greek, and you're unlikely to

> **"We're honestly kind of nerdy, but we're proud of it."**

find any alcohol-fueled toga parties here. "UMBC is not a place where alcohol and partying dictates who is cool," says a junior. Those looking for a livelier party scene head to University of Maryland's flagship campus in College Park or Towson University. The highlight of the social calendar is Quadmania, a weekend festival in the spring with games, carnival rides, food trucks, and a show by a big-name comedian or pop star. For more urban adventures, downtown Baltimore is 10 minutes away and Washington, D.C., 40 minutes.

The UMBC Retrievers compete in Division I and field a number of competitive teams, including men's basketball, men's lacrosse, and women's volleyball. Men's and women's swimming and diving and women's softball have captured multiple America East conference titles in recent years. The men's basketball team earned a footnote to history in 2018 by becoming the first number 16 seed in the NCAA tournament to upset a number 1 seed (sorry, Virginia!). UMBC is a perennial collegiate chess powerhouse and regularly makes the Final Four of College Chess; the university lures talented players with a bevy of scholarships. The Mock Trial team beat Yale to win the American Mock Trial Association national championship in 2021. Intramurals and club sports sign up about a quarter of the students, with soccer, basketball, and ultimate Frisbee drawing the most participants. The Retriever Activities Center, which boasts a gymnasium, cardio and weight-training spaces, fitness studios, an indoor pool, and tennis courts, recently underwent a $28 million renovation.

Freeman Hrabowski, the dynamic president who drove UMBC's growth for three decades, has now retired, but his vision is no doubt secure. Unlike the gargantuan University of Maryland at College Park, UMBC capitalizes on its small size by providing students with intimate learning communities, solid academics, and ample resources on a manageable scale. It's a combination that appeals to a certain kind of student, according to a biology major: "We're honestly kind of nerdy, but we're proud of it because students at UMBC are involved in super interesting things and go on to have interesting careers."

UMBC's Meyerhoff Scholars Program graduates more Black undergrads who go on to earn Ph.D.s in STEM fields than any other American institution.

The Mock Trial team beat Yale to win the American Mock Trial Association national championship in 2021.

Overlaps

SUNY–Binghamton, George Mason, UC Riverside, Miami (OH), North Carolina State, Johns Hopkins, University of Maryland, Towson

University of Massachusetts Amherst

Amherst, MA 01003

A liberal mecca in cosmopolitan and scenic western Massachusetts, UMass boasts strong study abroad programs and an international flavor. Management and engineering are also strong. In addition to the resources of a major research university, offers ready access to privates Amherst, Hampshire, Mount Holyoke, and Smith via the Five College Consortium. Lack of big-time sports makes for a lower national profile than the likes of Michigan or UNC.

A leading flagship and land grant university with more than 150 years of tradition, the University of Massachusetts Amherst offers students a dizzying array of majors, extracurriculars, and social opportunities in a top college town, plus a strong honors program. UMass's membership in the Five College Consortium makes it a good choice for students who want to take advantage of the extensive resources and programs of a large research university while also getting a taste of the small-school atmosphere and intellectual rigor of four elite private colleges—all without emptying their wallets.

UMass's sprawling 1,463-acre campus is centered on a pond full of ducks and swans, while architectural styles range from colonial to modern. The school is located on the outskirts of Amherst, a city that combines the energy of a bustling cosmopolitan center with the quaintness of an old New England town while also catering to college life. UMass's library system is the largest of any public institution in the Northeast. The campus has undergone a spate of recent construction, including the 70,000-square-foot Isenberg Business Innovation Hub, the Worcester Dining Commons, and a major renovation of the Student Union.

> **"[Amherst] is a lively— if small—college town."**

UMass offers more than 110 undergraduate degree programs, and among them, management, engineering, and computer science are top-ranked. Psychology, biology, public health sciences, and computer science are the most popular majors. Nursing, accounting, finance, and sport management also draw praise. New offerings include a major in public policy. Students seeking to stand out from the masses might consider the interdisciplinary major in social thought and political economy or the bachelor's degree in individual concentration, a design-it-yourself major. The Exploratory Track Program places undeclared first-years into one of seven academic advising tracks, based on the interests and academic strengths demonstrated in their admissions applications.

All undergraduates must complete courses in writing, basic mathematics and analytic reasoning, the biological and physical world, the social world, U.S. and global diversity, and an integrative experience. The writing requirement includes a freshman course taught in sections of 15 or fewer. Commonwealth Honors College offers qualified students special courses and sponsors interdisciplinary seminars, student gatherings, service projects, and a $192 million, 1,500-bed residential complex that includes nine classrooms and space for gathering, advising, and program

Website: www.umass.edu
Location: Small Town
Public
Total Enrollment: 25,119
Undergraduates: 22,466
Male/Female: 49/51
Financial Aid: 88%
Pell Grant: 21%
Expense: Pub $ $ $ $
Student Loans: 62%
Average Debt: $ $ $
Applicants: 42,540
Accepted: 66%
Enrolled: 18%
Grad in 6 Years: 84%
Returning Freshmen: 91%
Academics: ✍ ✍ ✍ ½
Social: ☎ ☎ ☎ ☎
Q of L: ★ ★ ★
Admissions: (413) 545-0222
Email Address: mail@ admissions.umass.edu

Strong Programs:
Management
Engineering
Computer Science
Nursing
Accounting
Finance
Sport Management
Psychology

administration. UMass offers 300 study abroad programs in more than 65 countries worldwide and typically sends about 24 percent of its undergrads globe-trotting. The Center for Student Business provides one of the most imaginative programs at UMass, allowing students to staff and manage seven campus businesses, learning how to work with others and resolve conflicts professionally.

UMass's intellectual and political climate is extraordinarily fertile for a large state university, and the school lends considerable research might to the Five College Consortium. This special alliance allows students to attend UMass and take courses (for no extra charge) at the other four consortium schools: Amherst College, Hampshire, Mount Holyoke, and Smith. Typically, 30 to 40 percent of the roughly 7,000 courses offered through the consortium are taken at UMass. The university is "definitely competitive," says a student. Twenty-seven percent of undergraduates participate in hands-on research with faculty. Full professors teach most courses, although some of the larger courses are broken down into smaller sections with graduate-level teaching assistants; overall, 46 percent of all undergraduate classes have fewer than 20 students. "I have had some amazing, out-of-this-world professors," says a junior, "and some abysmal ones." Academic and career counseling receive mixed reviews, and it is usually up to students to pursue career help.

The Center for Student Business allows students to staff and manage seven campus businesses.

"We have nerds, jocks, theater buffs, hippies, and future CEOs," says a senior. Seventy-seven percent of undergrads are in-staters, while 7 percent hail from more than 80 foreign countries. Five percent of UMass students are Black, 12 percent are Asian American, 9 percent are Hispanic/Latino, and 4 percent are multiracial. The university has established cultural centers on campus, providing activities and support for students from different backgrounds, but racial equity is still an issue, students report. "There are always rallies about better programs and aid for minorities," says a senior. Merit scholarships averaging $6,300 are handed out each year, and athletes vie for 400 athletic scholarships in 21 sports.

"We have so many resources. If we don't have what you want, we'll give you the opportunity to create it!"

UMass has one of the largest on-campus housing systems in the country. Sixty percent of students are housed among seven residential areas. The Residential First-Year Experience assigns first-years to living/learning communities with peers who share common interests and experiences. Many freshmen end up in the Southwest Area, a "huge, city-like complex" with five high-rise towers and 11 low-rise residence halls. "It is not a problem for students to get housing on campus; the only trouble is getting the housing that they want," says a student. Dining services get good reviews. A senior comments, "The campus is very self-contained, and so I have felt safe on campus even late at night." The UMatter at UMass program works to address issues of bias, sexual assault, hazing, high-risk drinking, and other community challenges.

The Residential First-Year Experience assigns first-years to living/learning communities with peers who share common interests and experiences.

UMass offers "a vast social life," says a student, with several social dorms, off-campus parties, and about 350 student organizations of all types. "Most of my social interactions occur on campus during my extracurriculars. On the weekends, we frequent the restaurants and bars in Amherst center, which is a lively—if small—college town," a chemical engineering major says. Both on campus and off, alcohol policies are strict and well enforced; off-campus parties are often registered with the university. First-time underage offenders are sent to alcohol-education programs. Eight percent of the men and 7 percent of the women belong to one of the more than three dozen fraternities and sororities, but they are somewhat out of the mainstream. The Bromery Center for the Arts brings nationally known theater, music, and dance performances to campus year-round. A free public transportation system allows maximum mobility, not only among the Five Colleges but also to nearby towns, which are graced with a number of exceptional bookshops.

Settled in the Pioneer Valley and surrounded by the Berkshire foothills, Amherst is close to good skiing, hiking, and canoeing areas. It's also 90 miles west of Boston, 150 miles north of New York City, and 25 miles south of Vermont and New Hampshire, making a car very useful (and very expensive if you get too many tickets from overzealous campus cops, students say).

Division I varsity sports are popular, especially football, men's and women's basketball, and ice hockey—to the elation of UMass fans, the men's hockey team won its first national championship in 2021. The UMass Minutemen and Minutewomen compete primarily in the Atlantic 10 Conference; women's basketball and lacrosse are recent conference champs. With approximately 40 intramural offerings and nearly 50 club sports, recreational opportunities are extensive.

UMass is big enough to offer a vast number of academic and extracurricular opportunities, though at times it can feel impersonal and overwhelming. But with special residential programs that group students with similar languages, cultures, and lifestyles, many students will easily find a home in Amherst. And as one junior cheers, "We have so many resources. If we don't have what you want, we'll give you the opportunity to create it!"

Overlaps

Indiana University, UConn, UC Santa Barbara, University of Maryland, University of Colorado Boulder, Northeastern, Boston University, Penn State

If You Apply To ›

UMass: Early action, regular decision. Accepts the Common Application. Please consult UMass's website for the most up-to-date information regarding standardized test requirements.

Massachusetts Institute of Technology

Room 3-108, 77 Massachusetts Avenue, Cambridge, MA 02139

If you're a science genius, come to MIT to find out how little you really know. No other school makes such a massive assault on the ego. Technology is a given, but MIT also prides itself on leading programs in economics, political science, and architecture, with unmatched undergraduate research opportunities. Those who don't study 24/7 can let off steam via the surprisingly extensive athletic offerings or by enjoying MIT's prime location near downtown Boston.

Website: www.mit.edu
Location: City Center
Private
Total Enrollment: 11,712
Undergraduates: 4,579
Male/Female: 52/48
Financial Aid: 65%
Pell Grant: 21%
Expense: Pr $ $ $
Student Loans: 18%
Average Debt: $ $
Applicants: 33,240
Accepted: 4%
Enrolled: 86%
Grad in 6 Years: 96%

Founded in 1861 in response to the country's rapid scientific and technological advances, the Massachusetts Institute of Technology continues to attract the brightest minds from near and far. MIT teachers and students have discovered many of the technological innovations that we take for granted, from electromagnets and radar to the decoding of the human genome. The school is a magnet for minds from Tim Berners-Lee, the Brit who invented the World Wide Web, to Noam Chomsky, the linguist and antiwar activist. Graduates have formed more than 25,000 companies that, among other things, employ a quarter of the workforce of Silicon Valley. While Harvard stuck to the English model of Oxbridge classical education, with its emphasis on Latin and Greek, MIT looked to the German system of learning based on research and hands-on experimentation. This emphasis is enshrined in the school motto—*Mens et Manus*, or Mind and Hand—as well as its muscular logo, showing a gowned scholar standing beside an ironmonger bearing a hammer and anvil. Intellect and craftsmanship pervade the classrooms, and students here are not so much taught as engaged and inspired.

MIT is located on 168 acres that extend more than a mile along the Cambridge side of the Charles River basin facing historic Beacon Hill and the central sections of Boston. The main campus of neoclassical architecture carved from limestone was designed by Welles Bosworth and constructed between 1913 and 1920. Since then, more modern designs in brick and glass have been added. The buildings have a utilitarian aura; most are even known by number instead of by name. Athletic playing fields, recreational buildings, dorms, and dining halls are closely arranged on the campus and provide a sense of unity. Sculptures and murals, including the works of Alexander Calder, Henry Moore, and Louise Nevelson, are found throughout the campus. The university's Brain and Cognitive Sciences Complex is the world's largest neuroscience center. Building W46, a 450-bed residence hall, was completed in 2021.

Whatever their major, all students must fulfill a set of General Institute Requirements consisting of a six-course "science core" that includes calculus and a lab and eight courses in the humanities, arts, and social sciences; there's also an eight-credit physical education requirement. Students have a choice of focus in the basic science offerings. A basic biology course, for example, might emphasize either genetics or the environ-

> **"Some professors really know how to engage the interest of the student."**

ment. To fill much of their science core, many students will join one of three first-year Learning Communities that offer a coherent freshman curriculum, small classes, and common meeting spaces. Among these is the Experimental Study Group, which offers flexible, small-group seminars instead of traditional lectures and emphasizes peer-to-peer teaching. Not only can these communities offer support, but they can also engage geniuses who excel on exams without attending the lectures.

Once called Boston Tech and now frequently referred to as "the 'Tute," MIT stresses science and engineering studies with a "concern for human values and social goals." Every science and engineering department is superb. The biology department is a leader in medical technology and the search for designer genes. Nevertheless, pure sciences tend to play second fiddle to the engineering fields that, along with computer science, draw the bulk of the majors. Electrical engineering and computer science are almost universally credited as tops in the nation. Students in these two areas may pursue a five-year-degree option, where they can obtain a professional master's degree upon completion of their studies. Biological engineering, chemical engineering, and mechanical engineering, physics, and the aeronautics and astronautics department are also highly praised programs. The most popular majors include computer science and engineering, electrical engineering, mathematics, and mechanical engineering.

For all of its emphasis on science and technology, MIT takes the arts and humanities as well as the social sciences—especially economics—seriously. Technology is, after all, the point where science and the humanities intersect over matters of values. Beyond that, the administration worries that engineers of the future will need first-rate technical skills coupled with a good understanding of technology's social context and marketplace. As one dean puts it, "Too many MIT graduates end up working for too many Princeton and Harvard graduates." Hence, the Sloan School of Management offers top-ranked undergraduate majors in management, business analytics, and finance. Even these programs, however, provide

> **"MIT is intense and will take you for quite a ride."**

students with a rigorous, math-based education. Perhaps to help ensure that they will be able to make their future discoveries known, students must take four communication-intensive subjects. Architecture, political science, urban studies, linguistics, graphics for modern art, and holography—and just about anything else that can be linked to a computer—are strong, and the minority who major in these subjects receive enough personal attention to make any college student envious. "Some professors really know how to engage the interest of the student," says a senior.

(continued)

Returning Freshmen: 99%
Academics: ✎ ✎ ✎ ✎ ✎
Social: ☎ ☎ ☎
Q of L: ★ ★ ★
Admissions: (617) 253-3400
Email Address: admissions@ mit.edu

Strong Programs:
Engineering
Economics
Architecture
Biology
Computer Science
Physics
Mathematics
Management

To fill much of their science core, many students join one of three first-year Learning Communities that offer a coherent freshman curriculum.

A pass/no record grading system helps freshmen adjust to "MIT brainstretching": in the first semester, freshmen receive grades of P, D, or F in all subjects they take. P means a C-or-better performance; Ds or Fs do not receive credit or appear on the permanent record. In the second semester, the Ps are replaced by A, B, or C; Ds and Fs do not receive credit and are only noted internally. Grades or not, most students set themselves a breathtaking pace. "MIT is intense and will take you for quite a ride," a biology/premed student says. "The courses demand your full attention and a lot of extra work," another adds. Sixty-nine percent of all undergraduate classes have fewer than 20 students. MIT students have access to world-renowned professors and Nobel Prize winners who carry lighter teaching loads to allow them time for research. Faculty advising is "pretty good for freshmen," one student says, but after that, "it's as good as you make it." MIT is working to bolster academic advising by hiring a team of professional "Institute Advisors" to support students from admission to graduation. The vast library system includes some one-of-a-kind manuscripts on the history of science and technology. One library is even open 24 hours a day, and "some students spend the majority of their time (awake or asleep) there," one student reports.

A pass/no record grading system helps freshmen adjust to "MIT brainstretching."

One of MIT's most successful innovations is the Undergraduate Research Opportunities Program, a year-round program that facilitates student/faculty research projects. Considered one of the best programs of its kind in the nation, it allows students to earn course credit or stipends for doing research. Ninety-two percent of students get involved with collaborative or independent research during their time at MIT. Relief from "tooling" (that is, studying) is found through the optional January Independent Activities Period, which offers noncredit seminars, workshops, and activities in fields outside the regular curriculum as well as for-credit subjects. Participation in the engineering co-op program, junior year abroad (including a major program at Cambridge University in England), or cross-registration at all-female Wellesley College are other helpful ways to get a change of pace.

"Some students spend the majority of their time (awake or asleep) [in the library]."

"The average MIT student can be characterized as having a passion and singular drive for what they really want in life," offers a chemical engineering major. While MIT somewhat justly earned an image as a "conservative, rich, white boys' school" in the past, there is certainly enough racial and ethnic variety to beat that rap today. Black students account for 7 percent of the undergraduate student body, Hispanics/Latinos 15 percent, Asian Americans a hefty 33 percent, and multiracial students 8 percent. Women now comprise 48 percent of undergraduates. To further welcome diversity, MIT's application includes an optional question regarding gender identity and sexual orientation. Just 8 percent of students are residents of Massachusetts, and 10 percent are international. MIT is need-blind in its admissions and does not consider legacy preferences; one in five students is the first in their family to attend college. Although there are no merit or athletic scholarships, MIT meets the full demonstrated financial need of all undergraduates—domestic and international. For students with family incomes less than $140,000 a year and typical assets, the Institute ensures that scholarship funding from all sources will allow them to attend MIT tuition-free.

Ninety-two percent of students get involved with collaborative or independent research.

Ninety-one percent of undergraduates live on campus, and all freshmen are required to live in the dorms. Guaranteed housing is either single-sex or co-ed; the dorms are in the middle of campus, and most of the fraternities and living groups are a mile or less away across the Charles. Meal plans are mandatory for dorms that don't have kitchens and optional for equipped quarters. Frat members feast on spreads prepared by their full-time cooks, and the Kosher Kitchen provides some refuge for others. MIT has recently increased its Title IX staffing, training programs, and educational outreach in an effort to combat campus sexual assault.

MIT's social scene is varied. There are special lectures, campus movies, dances, parties, and dorm activities, if one can escape the ubiquitous workload worming its way into the uneasy consciousness of a techie's every waking hour. The Rocket Team, the Guild of Bell Ringers, and a singing group called the Chorallaries are only a few of the diverse interests on this campus. Most on-campus drinking for 21-and-over students is relaxed and accepted, "as long as the alcohol does not result in unlawful behavior or cause any problems," a student explains. MIT's alcohol-prevention program is considered a national model, and drug-prevention initiatives are also comprehensive. The Greek scene attracts 45 percent of the men and 27 percent of the women. For those with the urge to roam, the multifaceted greater Boston metropolis sits only a few subway stops away. The student-friendly city boasts many restaurants, clubs, parks, shopping opportunities, and more than 40 other colleges.

When the MIT megabrains take a break, practical jokes, or "hacks" (described by one student as "practical jokes with technical merit"), are sure to follow. In past years, popular hacks have included disman-

"[MIT "hacks"] are practical jokes with technical merit."

tling a campus police car and reassembling its body at the top of the tower (complete with a box of doughnuts on the seat), unscrewing and reversing all the chairs in a 500-seat lecture hall, and, of course, welding shut Harvard's gates. Hacking can also involve Harry Potter–style late-night explorations by students in the tunnels and shafts that run through restricted parts of the campus, a practice that's definitely frowned on by the school.

When not studying or hacking, these engineering jocks often turn into real jocks. MIT has 33 varsity sports, the most of any Division III school. Teams are known as the Engineers with an industrious beaver named Tim (if you can't figure it out, don't bother to apply) as their mascot. The men's squash and co-ed sailing teams recently brought home national titles. Club ice hockey is popular, and even more popular is the extensive, well-organized intramural program (roughly 30 percent participate), with sports ranging from table tennis, billiards, and bowling to the more traditional basketball and volleyball. More than 35 instructional and competitive club sports are also available, and everyone has access to MIT's extensive athletic facilities.

Though students often wonder what life at a typical college would have been like, chances of survival and even satisfaction at MIT are excellent. Students are able to comprehend the incredible experience of attending one of the nation's leading academic powerhouses. A biology major puts it bluntly: "It will take you right up to what you think your limits are, and then MIT will shatter them and make you realize how great your potential is."

Overlaps

Harvard, Stanford, Princeton, Yale, Caltech, UC Berkeley, Columbia, Cornell University

If You Apply To ›

MIT: Early action, regular decision. SATs or ACTs: required. Does not accept the Common Application. Application includes optional question regarding gender identity and sexual orientation.

McGill University: See page 360.

1306 Stanford Drive, Suite 1210, Coral Gables, FL 33146

Football is a major reason UM is on the map, but it's hardly the only one. Renowned programs in marine science and music are big draws; business is also strong. Housing takes the form of a distinctive residential college system that offers living/learning opportunities. Attracts more Northerners than other leading Florida universities, with geographic reach continuing to expand.

Website: www.miami.edu
Location: Suburban
Private
Total Enrollment: 17,675
Undergraduates: 11,495
Male/Female: 46/54
Financial Aid: 73%
Pell Grant: 15%
Expense: Pr $ $
Student Loans: 33%
Average Debt: $
Applicants: 42,244
Accepted: 28%
Enrolled: 23%
Grad in 6 Years: 84%
Returning Freshmen: 93%
Academics: ✎ ✎ ✎
Social: ☎ ☎ ☎ ☎
Q of L: ★ ★ ★
Admissions: (305) 284-6000
Email Address: admission@
   miami.edu

Strong Programs:
Marine Science
Music
Business
Architecture
Latin American Studies
Nursing
Finance
Economics

Year-round sunshine and the colorful Miami culture could make even the most dedicated students forget why they are at college. But at the University of Miami, students can have their fun in the sun and get a solid education at the same time. The university, founded in 1925 when South Florida was beginning its boom, boasts a boatload of strong programs, including red-hot preprofessional offerings. Sound academics, a diverse and energetic student population, and a subtropical climate create a perfect storm that attracts talented Hurricanes from far and wide. "At UM you will find diversity, tradition, unity, and rivalry," says one senior, "while getting an exceptional education."

"At UM you will find diversity, tradition, unity, and rivalry."

Twenty minutes from Key Biscayne and Miami's beaches and 15 minutes from downtown Miami, the university's 239-acre campus is located in tranquil suburbia and features tall palms, wide lawns, flowering vines, outdoor sculptures, and even a butterfly garden. The campus, with its own lake right in the middle, is architecturally varied, from postwar, international-style structures to modern buildings, most with open-air breezeways to let in the warm winds. Recent additions include the massive, $153 million Lakeside Village, composed of 25 interconnected buildings featuring suite- and apartment-style housing for 1,100 students, recreational and dining areas, a 200-seat auditorium, and other facilities.

UM's Cognates Program of General Education requires students to take at least three courses in each of three areas of knowledge: arts and humanities, people and society, and STEM (science, technology, engineering, and math). With nine undergraduate schools and colleges and more than 180 majors and programs, UM offers a broad range of preprofessional options as well as those across the liberal arts. The university has one of the nation's top programs in marine science, and its architecture and business programs are well regarded. UM was the first American university to offer a four-year undergraduate degree in music engineering. It has also developed a unique program in jazz. Accelerated degree programs in Latin American studies, law, exercise physiology, biology, chemistry, computer science, biochemistry and molecular biology, and marine geology receive high marks. The most popular majors are nursing, finance, economics, and marketing; global health studies is one of the newest. The Foote Fellows Honors Program provides high-achieving students with more academic flexibility, opportunities for faculty-mentored research, and additional resources.

"Teaching assistants often reach out to students to help with workshops and extra study sessions."

UM's academic environment manages to be "both competitive and collaborative," says a junior. "Everyone wants to get into the best graduate programs, but they want their peers to do so as well." Fifty-one percent of undergraduate classes have fewer than 20 students, and full professors do teach first-year students. Professors "are extremely accessible through office hours, and teaching assistants often reach out to students to help with workshops and extra study sessions," explains a business management major. For a change of pace, 19 percent of students take advantage of more than 80 study abroad options in dozens of countries, including nine UM semester-on-location programs in France, the Czech Republic, South Africa, Italy, and elsewhere.

"The students at UM are culturally and academically diverse, with so many interests and passions," says one student. Fifty-three percent of UM's undergraduates come from out of state, including quite a few from the Northeast and upper Midwest, seeking respite from harsh weather. UM's student body is impressively diverse; Hispanics/Latinos account for a substantial 24 percent of the total, Black students 9 percent, Asian Americans 4 percent, and multiracial students 4 percent. International students, who represent 11 percent of undergraduates and more than 100 countries, play an integral role in the life of the university. Numerous merit scholarships, averaging $22,700, are available, as are lots of athletic scholarships. The university meets 100 percent of the demonstrated financial need of all admitted students.

UM offers a distinctive system of residential colleges, modeled after those at Oxford and Cambridge. Each residential college has a live-in faculty member who works with staff to organize seminars, concerts, dinners, social events, and lectures, including guest speakers from all walks of life to discuss current issues. Generally, students give the dorms average marks; 43 percent of undergrads live on campus, and others bunk in off-campus apartments or commute. "Housing is slightly dismal in the beginning, but you soon become so engulfed in campus life that you don't mind the dorms at all," reasons a senior. Scrounging up food on campus is easy. "Our food court is very diverse with just about every food option you can think of," says a senior. Students also report feeling safe on campus thanks to a robust security program that includes safety escorts, campus shuttles, and self-defense classes.

UM offers a plethora of social opportunities. "Miami is an incredible city, so there is always something fun to do with friends. The university is also constantly hosting activities on campus," reports a student. The student-run Rathskeller, a popular meeting place on campus, offers food, entertainment, a venue for postgame parties, and alcohol to students at least 21 years old. Campus alcohol policies are strict for underage students, but an art history major says, "The drinking and party culture on campus is not something that proves to be a massive issue." Off campus, however, frat parties and Miami's many bars, nightclubs, and festivals keep things lively. Fraternities account for 16 percent of the men, and sororities, with no housing of their own, attract 19 percent of the women. Students anticipate annual events such as International Week and SportsFest, which pits dorms against each other in sports ranging from flag football to obstacle courses. The biggest service event each year is Gandhi Day, during which hundreds of students spend the day doing community service.

Coral Gables (population 48,000) is not a college town. "We are a college in a big city," says a junior, which means access to events such as Miami's Art Basel, Ultra Music Festival, and the Miami Open, as well as professional sports teams (Dolphins, Heat, Marlins, Inter Miami CF). Those who shun sand between their toes head to Coconut Grove, Wynwood, Little Havana, or South Beach. Public transportation and the Hurry 'Canes Shuttle service run in front of the residential colleges. On-campus parking can be a problem, but most students recommend a car anyway in order to get "the full Florida effect." The best road trips are Key West, the Everglades, and, of course, UM football games against rival Florida State.

The Hurricanes compete in the Division I Atlantic Coast Conference. With its once mighty football team no longer so mighty, the most competitive teams are baseball and men's and women's diving, basketball, tennis, and track and field.

UM was the first American university to offer a four-year undergraduate degree in music engineering.

"Miami is an incredible city, so there is always something fun to do."

The biggest service event each year is Gandhi Day, during which hundreds of students spend the day doing community service.

<aside>

Overlaps

Tulane, University of Southern California, NYU, University of Michigan, University of Florida, Florida State, University of Wisconsin, University of Maryland

</aside>

Fourteen percent of students play intramural and club sports; flag football, soccer, and the scuba club are some of the most popular. The university also has a state-of-the-art recreation facility that includes an 18,000-square-foot fitness room and basketball, racquetball, squash, and tennis courts, plus an indoor pool and a juice bar.

It's hard to imagine a school in the Sunshine State without a generous allotment of fun, and UM is no exception. "Though we're not the number one party school in the nation anymore, we still really love to have a great time," observes a junior. That said, UM students these days are just as likely to search long and hard for the perfect instrumental phrase or mathematical proof as they are to scope out the perfect wave. Says one happy Hurricane, "The biggest complaint is that students don't have enough time in four years to access all the amazing things available."

If You Apply To ›

Miami: Early decision I and II, early action, regular decision. Accepts the Common Application. Apply to particular schools or programs. Music and theater applicants must audition or submit portfolio. Please consult Miami's website for the most up-to-date information regarding standardized test requirements.

Miami University (OH)

301 S. Campus Avenue, Oxford, OH 45056

Rather than disappear into the black hole of Ohio State, top students in the Buckeye state come here to feel as if they are going to an elite private university. Miami is the honors public university in one of the nation's most populous states. Twice the size of William & Mary, Miami has the same classic look but is much less selective. Miami's top draw is business, and its tenor is preppy/conservative. Bring your best clothes.

Website: www.miamioh.edu
Location: Small Town
Public
Total Enrollment: 17,516
Undergraduates: 16,576
Male/Female: 49/51
Financial Aid: 81%
Pell Grant: 11%
Expense: Pub $ $ $ $
Student Loans: 45%
Average Debt: $ $ $
Applicants: 29,990
Accepted: 89%
Enrolled: 17%
Grad in 6 Years: 83%
Returning Freshmen: 89%
Academics: ✐ ✐ ✐ ✐ ½
Social: ☎ ☎ ☎
Q of L: ★ ★ ★
Admissions: (513) 529-2531

This Miami is about 1,000 miles from South Beach, but that doesn't mean it's without sizzle. The academic kind, that is. Tucked into a corner of Ohio, Miami University takes its name from the Native American tribe that once lived in the Miami Valley region of the state. In recent decades, Miami has garnered national recognition as an excellent public university that has the traditional look and feel of a private, with a picture-perfect campus and high-caliber student body.

The university is staked out on 2,100 wooded acres in the center of an urban triangle of approximately three million people, encompassing Cincinnati and Dayton, Ohio, and Richmond, Indiana. The campus, one of the most architecturally homogeneous in the country, is dressed in the modified Georgian style of the colonial American period, and it remains as impeccably groomed as its sharply attired students.

> "The professors I have had have shaped my perspective on the world and life."

Recent construction projects include a 40,000-square-foot indoor arena at Miami's Equestrian Center. Construction on the $20 million McVey Data Science Building, designed to enhance interdisciplinary research and education, is slated for completion in 2024.

One of the oldest public universities in the country, Miami University was founded in 1809 to provide a classical liberal education and has never strayed from its central commitment to the liberal arts. All undergraduates must complete the Global Miami Plan for Liberal Education, which provides them with a background in a range of disciplines and includes requirements in intercultural competence, global perspectives, advanced writing, and experiential learning. Students must also fulfill a thematic sequence requirement by taking a series of related courses (usually three) outside their major, and they must complete a capstone experience their senior year. University Studies 101 is a one-credit course that helps integrate first-year students into the university community.

Popular majors include finance, marketing, psychology, and strategic communication. Programs in nursing, architecture, education, kinesiology, interior design, computer science, and software engineering have traditionally been strengths. A unique major in emerging technology in business and design teaches students skills in coding, design thinking, artificial intelligence, augmented reality, product management, and more. The Center for Social Entrepreneurship helps students put their creativity and business savvy to use in solving persistent social problems. Gerontology is available as a major and a minor, and the Scripps Gerontology Center is one of the oldest of its kind in the country. Motivated as they are, nearly half of Miami students graduate with a double major or minor.

In the classroom, "Miami strikes a good balance between intensity and creating a positive working environment for students," says a strategic communication major. Professors are lauded for their knowledge and willingness to help. "The professors I have had have shaped my perspective on the world and life with their excellent instruction," says a political science major. Thirty-five percent of classes have fewer than 20 students, and most are taught by full professors, though graduate students do appear behind lecterns from time to time.

The three-week Winter Term allows students to take a class, study abroad, conduct research, or participate in an internship. Forty-three percent of all undergrads head for foreign climes. Miami's Dolibois European Center in Luxembourg offers summer, semester, or yearlong study and the chance to live with a local family. Other opportunities span more than 75 countries. The Inside Washington program sends students to the nation's capital to meet with high-profile figures and complete an internship. Undergraduate research gets a lot of attention at Miami too. The Undergraduate Summer Scholars Program gives 100 students a stipend, a tuition waiver, and a project allowance to undertake a nine-week, faculty-mentored project. Each year, more than 2,000 Miami undergraduates work with professors on funded research, many starting as early as their first year. Ten percent of incoming first-year students are invited to join the Honors College, which entails more rigorous coursework, dedicated housing, a senior thesis, and other enrichment opportunities.

"Students here are ambitious, dedicated, and embody an attitude of success in the classroom and outside of it," observes a student. Racial and socioeconomic diversity are conspicuously lacking, although the university claims it is working to boost both; 3 percent of undergraduates are Black, 5 percent are Hispanic/Latino, 3 percent are Asian American, and 4 percent are multiracial, while just 11 percent qualify for Pell Grants. Six percent of students come from foreign countries, and 61 per-

> "With a party culture this pervasive, it is simply not possible to prevent underage drinking."

cent hail from Ohio. Miami has a long-standing reputation for wealth and conservatism, although a political science major reports that the student body is becoming "more evenly divided" between conservatives and liberals. Paul Ryan, the former Republican Speaker of the House of Representatives, learned his trickle-down economics here. The *New York Times* suggested that Miami appeals to Republican families as "a place unlikely to turn their children against them." Thousands of merit scholarships, averaging $11,900 each, and hundreds of athletic scholarships in 18 sports are awarded annually. The university also locks in tuition, fees, and room-and-board charges for four years.

(continued)

Email Address: admission@
miamioh.edu

Strong Programs:
Business
Nursing
Architecture
Education
Kinesiology
Interior Design
Computer Science
Software Engineering

A unique major in emerging technology in business and design teaches students skills in coding, design thinking, artificial intelligence, and more.

Fifty-eight percent of the student body call the campus home, and residence halls are said to be comfortable and well maintained. First-year students join one of more than 30 theme-based living/learning communities (LLCs) and affinity communities, which center on interests such as the arts, leadership, premedicine, and shared cultural backgrounds. "My LLC provided me with an internship, the majority of my friends, and an ever-growing network within the first month of my first semester," reports a first-year student. Campus dining options are described as diverse, healthy, and usually tasty but overpriced. Students give good ratings to campus safety, and regarding sexual assault, one student says, "Student education, victim resources, and general awareness are widespread."

Nineteen percent of the men and 29 percent of the women belong to fraternities or sororities, respectively, and the Greeks have a hard-partying reputation. Miami is known as the "Mother of Fraternities" because several national ones began here. Drinking at off-campus houses and local bars is a popular pastime, and a junior comments, "With a party culture this pervasive, it is simply not possible to prevent underage drinking." On-campus activities organized by Late Night Miami, such as movie screenings, musical performances, craft nights, and casino nights, provide a fun alternative but are not always well attended. Annual events include homecoming, Springfest, and continued rivalries with Ohio University. Miami offers more than 600 student organizations, and students log tens of thousands of hours of community service each year. Oxford (population 23,000) is a relatively quiet town with a decent bar scene, numerous restaurants, and local shops. For students who crave brighter lights and a bigger city, Cincinnati is about 35 miles away.

> "We have a public Ivy personality: we try to elevate ourselves and create a rigorous academic culture."

In the past two years, Miami's Division I RedHawks teams have won titles in synchronized skating (national championship) and field hockey, women's tennis, men's swimming and diving, and softball (Mid-American Conference championships). Men's ice hockey games draw enthusiastic crowds. Miami Mock Trial consistently performs well at the American Mock Trial Association national championships. Intramurals and more than 50 club sports attract 30 percent of the student body, and popular sports include broomball, soccer, and sand volleyball.

Miami University, with its strong emphasis on liberal arts and its opportunities for research, travel abroad, and leadership, is looked upon as a rising star among state universities. The school effectively combines a wide range of academic programs with the personal attention ordinarily found only at much smaller, upscale institutions. A senior sums it up this way: "We have a public Ivy personality: we try to elevate ourselves and create a rigorous academic culture."

Overlaps

William & Mary, Clemson, University of Delaware, University of Rhode Island, Northern Arizona, Ohio State, University of Cincinnati, Indiana University

If You Apply To ›

Miami (OH): Early decision, early action, regular decision. Accepts the Common Application with supplement. Applicants may indicate if they are first-generation students or members of the LGBTQ community. Please consult Miami's website for the most up-to-date information regarding standardized test requirements.

University of Michigan

515 East Jefferson Street, 1220 Student Activities Building, Ann Arbor, MI 48109

The most interesting mass of humanity east of UC Berkeley. U-M is among the nation's leaders in many subjects, but undergraduates must elbow their way to the front to get the full benefit. Superb honors and living/learning programs are the best bet for highly motivated students. Out-of-state families may need a second mortgage to cover pricey tuition.

One of the nation's elite public universities, Michigan offers an excellent faculty, dynamite athletics, an endless number of special programs, and the most interesting collection of students east of Berkeley. Boasting more than 640,000 living alumni, it also produces more Fulbright scholars than any other U.S. university. "Michigan is a special place because it has a deep history and reputation," says a senior. "It is an excellent school and no matter what degree you have, it is respected."

Situated on 3,207 acres, Michigan's campus is so extensive that newcomers may want to call on their GPS to find their way to class. The university is divided into two main sections. Central Campus, the heart of the university, houses most of Michigan's 19 schools and colleges. North Campus, which is two miles northeast of Central, is home to the College of Engineering; the School of Music, Theatre, and Dance; the Stamps School of Art and Design; and the Taubman College of Architecture and Urban Planning. Other campus areas include the Medical Center Complex, containing seven hospitals and 15 outpatient facilities, and South Campus, featuring state-of-the-art athletic facilities. A university bus system helps students get around. Architecturally, the main drag of campus features a wide range of styles, from the classical Angell Hall to the ultracontemporary Museum of Art addition. Recent construction includes academic facilities for the biological sciences, kinesiology, and dance programs, as well as the 105,000-square-foot Central Campus Classroom Building, which opened in 2022.

> "Michigan is a special place because it has a deep history and reputation."

Founded in 1817 in what was then the Michigan Territory, U-M offers more than 600 active degree programs, including over 280 undergraduate majors, as well as individualized concentrations. No courses are required of all first-year students at Michigan, but all undergraduates must complete some coursework in English (including composition), foreign languages, natural sciences, social sciences, and humanities. Students in the College of Literature, Science, and the Arts (LSA)—Michigan's largest school, offering the most undergraduate majors—must also take courses in quantitative reasoning and race or ethnicity.

For students with global interests, LSA's menu of 40 foreign languages includes several that can't be found at many other places, such as Dutch, Filipino, Hindi, Persian, Swahili, and Turkish. The College of Engineering and Ross School of Business are well respected, and the university's programs in health-related fields are also top-notch. Preferred admissions programs guarantee top high school students admission to Michigan's outstanding programs in architecture, business, education, information, and pharmaceutical sciences, provided they make satisfactory progress during their first years. Also worth mentioning are offerings in art, music, and musical theatre. The most popular majors are computer science, business administration, economics, and an interdisciplinary major in biopsychology, cognition, and neuroscience. New offerings include a first-of-its-kind B.S. degree in urban technology that combines urban studies with instruction in coding, digital technology, and design.

Website: www.umich.edu
Location: Small City
Public
Total Enrollment: 46,426
Undergraduates: 30,654
Male/Female: 48/52
Financial Aid: 48%
Pell Grant: 18%
Expense: Pub $ $ $ $
Student Loans: 36%
Average Debt: $ $
Applicants: 79,743
Accepted: 20%
Enrolled: 45%
Grad in 6 Years: 94%
Returning Freshmen: 97%
Academics: ✍ ✍ ✍ ✍ ✍
Social: ☎ ☎ ☎
Q of L: ★ ★ ★
Admissions: (734) 764-7433
Email Address: N/A

Strong Programs:
Engineering
Business
Architecture
Education
Art
Music
Musical Theatre
Computer Science

Students describe Michigan courses as challenging but by no means cutthroat competitive. "Academics come first, and everybody around you will be putting in the effort required to succeed," says a civil engineering major. Fifty-four percent of classes have fewer than 20 students, and one student says, "The professors here are intelligent and seem to enjoy teaching." Students report that there is excellent academic and career advising available, but only for those who seek it. The University Career Center provides individual and group career counseling/planning and works with 950 companies annually in recruiting graduating U-M students. The LSA Opportunity Hub connects LSA students with liberal arts–oriented internships, practical workshops, alumni, and employers.

Michigan's special academic programs seek to offer the best of both worlds—personalized attention and a large university setting. The First Year Experience is a themed living community, paired with an introductory course taught in the residence halls, designed to support students through the transition to college; past programming has included movie nights, ice cream socials, rock climbing, and a trip to Michigan's Upper Peninsula to learn dog sledding. The university's long-established honors program, considered to be one of the best in the nation, offers

> **"Academics come first, and everybody around you will be putting in the effort."**

qualified students honors courses and seminars, opportunities to participate in individual or collaborative research, and access to dedicated academic advisors. About 1,600 undergrads each year work outside the classroom with a small group of students and a research mentor through the Undergraduate Research Opportunities Program. Service-learning courses are plentiful, and students have the chance to study abroad in nearly 140 countries. Specific programs include a year abroad in a French or German university, a business program in Paris, summer internships in selected majors, and special short-term trips organized by individual departments.

Fifty-two percent of undergraduates hail from Michigan, and 8 percent come from abroad. The student body is notably diverse for a Midwestern state university. Black students make up 4 percent of the student body, Hispanics/Latinos 7 percent, Asian Americans 17 percent, and multiracial students 5 percent. Michigan's Program on Intergroup Relations has served as a national model for supporting diversity on college campuses, offering a variety of intergroup dialogues, courses and workshops on social justice, and community outreach programs. There are large and well-organized Jewish and LGBTQ communities here too. While the student body is more conservative today than it was a few decades ago, it is still "most noticeably liberal," says a history major, and political issues flare up from time to time on campus. Michigan is the only public university in the state that meets the full demonstrated financial need of all in-state students, and Michigan residents with family incomes of $65,000 or less qualify for the Go Blue Guarantee of four years of free tuition. At more than triple the in-state tuition rate, U-M charges out-of-state students the second-highest tuition and fees among U.S. flagship universities. Need-based financial aid is available to out-of-staters, and all applicants can vie for hundreds of merit scholarships averaging $6,100, as well as nearly 800 athletic scholarships.

Dormitories at U-M traditionally have well-defined personalities. East Quad is the home of the Residential College, the Michigan Community Scholars Program, and the Gender-Inclusive Learning Experience. North Quad is newer and the focal point for international and intercultural programming. On-campus housing is said to be mostly comfortable and well maintained, and 28 percent of students reside there. "First-years are guaranteed housing, but not every sophomore is lucky enough to secure on-campus housing, and virtually no juniors and seniors get to live in the dorms," reports a student. Alternatives include fraternity and sorority houses, a large number of college-owned and private co-ops, and plenty of off-campus rentals. Campus residents take their meals at the many dining halls located inside dorms. As for concerns about safety on campus, a student says, "Campus security is pretty good and most people I know feel safe." A Special Victims Unit of the university police deals with instances of interpersonal violence, including sexual assault.

Intramurals were invented at the University of Michigan.

Detroit is a little less than an hour away, but most students become quite fond of the picturesque town of Ann Arbor. "Ann Arbor is a quintessential college town, with a wide range of cultural opportunities and ways for students to get involved," a sophomore says. A surprising variety of visual and performing arts are offered in town and on campus. A huge art fair held each summer in Ann Arbor draws craftspeople from throughout the nation and Canada. The Huron River and many lakes and swimming holes lie only a short drive away and seem to keep the large summer-term population happy. Michigan winters, though, are known for being cold and brutal. Seven percent of the men and 16 percent of the women go Greek. As one sophomore says, "There is a large Greek party scene, and if that is what you are looking for, you won't be disappointed." Campus alcohol policies are described as "moderately effective."

"Ann Arbor is a quintessential college town."

Division I football overshadows nearly everything each fall as students gather to cheer, "Go Blue." Attending football games is an integral part of the U-M experience, students say, and the Little Brown Jug football competition with Minnesota and games against Ohio State are especially popular. Several of U-M's 29 varsity teams have brought home Big Ten championships in the past few years, among them football, men's basketball, softball, and women's golf, and the women's gymnastics team claimed the national title in 2021. Intramurals, which were invented at the University of Michigan, provide students with a more casual form of athletics, and some 30 club sports are also active. The university's Solar Car Team has won numerous American Solar Challenge competitions.

The University of Michigan strives to offer its students a delicate balance between academics, athletics, and social activities. On one hand, this is an American college with the usual interest in football and fraternities. But it's also a world-class university with a fine faculty and top-rated programs, intent on making America competitive in the 21st century. For assertive students who crave spirit and action as well as outstanding academics, Michigan is an excellent choice.

Overlaps

UC Berkeley, U of I at Urbana–Champaign, Stanford, Cornell University, Ohio State, Michigan State, UCLA, Northwestern

If You Apply To ›

Michigan: Early action, regular decision. Accepts the Common Application with supplement. Apply to particular school or program. Please consult Michigan's website for the most up-to-date information regarding standardized test requirements.

Michigan State University

250 Administration Building, East Lansing, MI 48824

Most people don't realize that MSU enrolls more full-time undergraduates than the University of Michigan. Students can find a niche in strong preprofessional programs such as hospitality business management, prevet, and education. MSU's self-contained campus is like a town unto itself, with a bus system available to get from one side to the other.

MSU is home to the $730 million Facility for Rare Isotope Beams, a new facility for nuclear physics research that was completed in 2022.

Michigan State's roots are agricultural—founded in 1855, the school pioneered the model for land grant institutions—and future farmers, plant scientists, and veterinarians still flourish here. So do those with wanderlust, thanks to study abroad programs on each of the world's seven continents. MSU's programs in natural sciences and multidisciplinary social sciences offer students the feel of a small liberal arts college and the resources of a large research university. "Resources here abound," says a senior.

The heart of the MSU campus, north of the Red Cedar River, boasts ivy-covered brick buildings, some of which predate the Civil War and are listed on the National Register of Historic Places. This area houses five colleges plus the MSU Union and 10 residence halls. Across the river are the medical complex, newer dorms, and two 18-hole golf courses. Most notably, MSU is home to the $730 million Facility for Rare Isotope Beams, a new facility for nuclear physics research that is funded in partnership with the U.S. Department of Energy and the state of Michigan and was completed in 2022. On the southernmost part of campus are farms and animal research and teaching facilities.

Michigan State students tend to be preprofessional and clear about their interests; the premed, prevet, and teacher education programs are strong, and the most popular majors include business, marketing, communication, journalism, various fields in the social sciences, and biological and biomedical sciences. Other popular options include engineering, supply chain management, environmental science, and hospitality business management; students in the latter program get real-world experience by staffing the university's hotel and conference center. To graduate, all students must satisfy university requirements in math and writing, complete a major, and take a minimum of 24 credits in the integrative studies program, which includes arts and humanities; social, behavioral, and economic sciences; and biological and physical sciences.

"You [have] the opportunity to get to know people and cultures from all over the world."

Academics at MSU get tougher as students advance through their majors, according to a junior. "Many of our courses are very competitive because they play a part in determining whether or not you are accepted into a specific program," notes a classmate. Classes are often quite large, but 24 percent enroll fewer than 20 students, and students say that, for the most part, professors are accessible and dedicated. About a quarter of undergraduates take advantage of hundreds of group-based and individual research opportunities. The Honors College offers the intimacy of a small-college atmosphere. MSU has a strong international component as well, with upward of 275 study abroad options in more than 60 countries; 25 percent of undergrads take part.

"Students here are friendly and diverse," says an elementary education major. "We also have a large international population, which is really cool because it gives you the opportunity to get to know people and cultures from all over the world." Seventy-eight percent of undergraduates are Michigan residents, and 6 percent are international. Students report that their classmates care about the world around them. Indeed, more than 2,400 alumni have served in the Peace Corps since MSU first partnered with the agency in 1961. Black students make up 7 percent of the student body, Asian Americans add 7 percent, Hispanics/Latinos constitute 6 percent, and multiracial students represent 4 percent. Scholarships are offered in 23 Division I sports, and thousands of students also receive grants and awards based on academic merit, which average $8,900 annually.

MSU requires students to live on campus for their first two years; a sophomore says the residence halls and apartment communities are "very convenient and well maintained." Those seeking a traditional college experience can bunk in one of five huge "neighborhoods," each with three to 10 residence halls plus libraries, advising and tutoring services, health services, dining halls, and recreation areas. Other living/learning programs, known by their catchy acronyms, include RISE (focus on the environment), MRULE (multiracial unity), and CORE (engineering). All of the school's 27 residence halls and apartment communities have recently been updated. MSU's dining services dish out meals at 10 dining halls, two food courts, and one food truck. "All the food is edible," says a senior.

Campus safety measures include walking escorts for those who stay late at the library, and Lansing's bus system offers discounted night-owl rates for those living farther away. Parking places on campus are in chronically short supply, and students complain about the tickets they receive as a result. After their second year, students may move off campus. Many do so because the city of East Lansing, just outside Michigan's capital, offers all the positive aspects of a large urban area (the population more than doubles when school is in session), along with the safety and community feel of a much smaller town. According to one student, "The social life at MSU is very lively on the weekends." Eleven percent of the men and 12 percent of the women join Greek organizations. Other week-

> **"The social life at MSU is very lively on the weekends."**

end alternatives include bands, dances, and comedians brought in by the University Activities Board and events held by more than 1,000 student organizations. Second-run movies are also shown in Wells Hall—free for campus dwellers and a couple of bucks for those who live off campus.

Weekends are dominated by Big Ten athletic competitions, with the MSU–Michigan rivalry especially fierce. "Our large campus is filled from end to end with individuals sporting green and white; alcohol-free tailgating is also available," says a junior. "Seeing 150,000 people in a space that usually has about 60,000 is quite an experience." (The battle with Indiana for the Old Brass Spittoon is less exciting.) The men's basketball team is consistently strong, and women's golf is a recent conference champion. After more than six decades of standing guard at Kalamazoo Street and Red Cedar Road, the legendary statue of the school's mascot, affectionately known as "Sparty," was moved indoors to protect him from the elements. However, a replica of the Spartan statue stands outside and is guarded by students when Wolverines come to town. Students are still able to paint "the Rock," a large boulder donated by the class of 1873, to advertise campus events, birthdays, anniversaries, and the like. Twenty intramurals and 27 club sports, from "spartyball" (a variation of indoor soccer) to competitive cheer, also keep students busy.

In the wake of a major sexual abuse scandal involving a former physician to athletes, administrators say they are working hard to strengthen policies and community resources to ensure that MSU continues to be a safe, respectful campus. With seemingly endless learning opportunities and an active social scene, future leaders, physicians, and financiers happily coexist here in what one student calls a "diverse, friendly, and expressive" bunch.

> *MSU offers five huge "neighborhoods," each with three to 10 residence halls plus libraries, tutoring and health services, dining halls, and more.*

Overlaps

University of Michigan, Indiana University, Purdue, Central Michigan, Western Michigan, Grand Valley State

If You Apply To ›

MSU: Early action, regular decision. SATs or ACTs: optional. Accepts the Common Application.

Middlebury, VT 05753

Set in the picturesque and ski-friendly Green Mountains of Vermont, Middlebury is a magnet for students with serious interests in environmental and international studies. Known worldwide for its summer foreign language programs. Varsity and intramural sports play a big role in campus culture, which may help explain why Middlebury was the first college to play Quadball (formerly Quidditch).

Website: www.middlebury.edu
Location: Small Town
Private
Total Enrollment: 2,937
Undergraduates: 2,858
Male/Female: 47/53
Financial Aid: 47%
Pell Grant: 19%
Expense: Pr $ $ $ $
Student Loans: 47%
Average Debt: $
Applicants: 11,906
Accepted: 13%
Enrolled: 42%
Grad in 6 Years: 94%
Returning Freshmen: 94%
Academics: ✍ ✍ ✍ ✍ ½
Social: ☎ ☎ ☎
Q of L: ★ ★ ★
Admissions: (802) 443-3000
Email Address: admissions@
    middlebury.edu

Strong Programs:
World Languages
Environmental Studies
English
International and Global
    Studies
Political Science
Architectural Studies
Economics
Computer Science

For some, Middlebury College's campus, with its picturesque sunsets, excellent skiing, and rural Vermont charm, may bring to mind a resort. Middlebury is indeed a paradise for those interested in the environment, second and third languages, and a tight-knit community. But this school's intensive workload means four years here is far from a vacation. "Middlebury is an outdoorsy school with very rigorous academics," explains an English major, and "these two personality traits counterbalance each other well," because students take their work seriously but know how to unwind too.

The college's 350-acre main campus overlooks the village of Middlebury, Vermont, which a junior describes as a "small, quaint Vermont town of 9,200 people and five stoplights." The 1,800-acre mountain campus, site of the Bread Loaf School of English,

> **"Middlebury is an outdoorsy school with very rigorous academics."**

the famed Bread Loaf Writers' Conference, and the college's Snow Bowl skiing facility, is nearby. Old Stone Row cuts across the campus, where buildings with simple lines and rectangular shapes evoke the mills of early New England. (Middlebury was founded in 1800.) Academic halls and dormitories of marble and limestone sit in quadrangles and feature views of the Adirondack and Green Mountains. Middlebury has been a leader in sustainability efforts, which include reliance on a wind turbine and systematic efforts to help students recycle. The college has achieved carbon neutrality and is working toward using 100 percent renewable energy by 2028.

Midd students take a discussion-based, writing-intensive First-Year Seminar with only 15 students; the instructor serves as advisor to those enrolled until they declare a major. In addition to satisfying distribution requirements in several liberal arts areas, students take classes in writing, cultures and civilizations, physical education, and, of course, their major. With all of these requirements, it's no wonder students and faculty become close. Students agree that the academic atmosphere is cooperative and the quality of teaching high. A neuroscience major says, "Professors exude passion about their academic area, and students definitely feed off of that enthusiasm." Thirty percent of students collaborate with faculty on research projects. During the four-week January term, students can narrow their focus to opportunities like a single intensive course or an internship.

Between June and August, Middlebury banishes English from its campus, and hundreds of students live, learn, and, ideally, think only in their chosen language. The language departments continue their excellent instruction during the school

> **"Students are generally very politically correct and care a lot about social justice."**

year; especially notable are German, Chinese, Japanese, and Hebrew. Although there is no foreign language requirement, just about everyone studies another tongue, if only to take advantage of Middlebury's schools at 37 partner universities in 16 countries around the world, from Italy and India to Chile and Cameroon. In total, there are 90 college-approved study abroad programs, and roughly 55 percent of students study internationally. Students in the interdisciplinary environmental studies major choose one of 13 areas to focus on, such as conservation psychology, creative arts, and environmental history. Other highly touted Middlebury programs include English (one of the school's most popular majors, bolstered by its connections to the Bread Loaf Writers' Conference), international and global studies, political science, and architectural studies. Economics, computer science, and neuroscience are also popular.

Students say the campus is friendly but can be cliquish, with something of a "preppy boarding school culture," according to an environmental studies major. While there a few typical groups you'll always find in large numbers at Middlebury (preppies, "outdoorsy, granola" types, and athletes), the wide range of opportunities here also means that, in the words of one sophomore, "Whatever your character, you'll find your niche." Just 5 percent of students come from within the state; 11 percent come from abroad. Seven percent of students are Asian American, 11 percent are Hispanic/Latino, 5 percent are Black, and 6 percent are multiracial. All first-year students participate in a one-day, student-run program called JusTalks, which facilitates workshops on systemic racism and other topics. "Students are generally very politically correct and care a lot about social justice," comments a junior. "Freedom of speech and controversial speakers continue to be hot topics at Middlebury." There are no merit or athletic scholarships, but the college is committed to a need-blind admissions policy and to meeting 100 percent of admitted students' demonstrated financial need. Students say the socioeconomic divide on campus can be noticeable: "It's like a true middle class doesn't exist here," remarks a junior.

Few Middlebury students live off campus (5 percent), since housing is guaranteed for four years and gets good ratings from students. First-year students live in traditional residence halls in one of two first-year clusters, which are organized based on First-Year Seminar courses and staffed by a dean. In their second year, students live in dedicated sophomore dorms. Upperclassmen can choose from a range of options, including suites, college-owned townhouses, the Environmental House (where residents cook all of their own food), and other academic interest houses. The school's three dining halls get high marks for their tasty victuals, friendly staff, and accommodations for students with dietary restrictions. "Students are allowed to swipe in and out of the dining halls as many times as they want per day," says a senior. Students say they feel safe on campus—"It's hard to feel *unsafe* in rural Vermont," reasons one sophomore—but a senior reports that "mental health services are understaffed and spread thin."

> *Just about everyone studies another tongue, if only to take advantage of Middlebury's schools at 37 partner universities in 16 countries.*

"It's hard to feel *unsafe* in rural Vermont."

"There can be a work-hard, play-hard attitude here," explains a senior, "but the 'play' means different things to different people—there are groups that party, there are groups that go hiking, etc." Indeed, Middlebury's 200-plus student organizations offer ample variety to choose from. Those who stay on campus are treated to school-sponsored dances, plays, dance performances, trivia nights, or parties at the co-ed social houses, which a sophomore describes as "casual" and "much more inclusive" than typical Greek parties at other schools. (Middlebury ousted fraternities and sororities in the mid-1990s.) Kegs are prohibited in the dorms but permitted at parties, which must be registered and also offer nonalcoholic drinks and snacks. Despite these measures, alcohol consumption is said to be common among underage students. The three-day Winter Carnival is a major annual extravaganza including parties, a bonfire with fireworks, ski races at the Snow Bowl, snow sculptures, ice-skating at an outdoor rink, and an all-school formal ball.

> *The three-day Winter Carnival is a major annual extravaganza with fireworks, ski races at the Snow Bowl, and an all-school formal ball.*

Off campus, Middlebury is "the quintessential New England town, straight out of Norman Rockwell." It has necessities such as restaurants, grocery stores,

*Middlebury's
field hockey team
has won five
consecutive national
championships.*

drug stores, hardware stores, and clothing shops, and 70 percent of students do volunteer work. "Community service is a big part of who we are here at Midd," says a sophomore. The progressive, student-friendly city of Burlington is 45 minutes away, while Montreal is a three-hour drive, Boston four, and New York City five. Snow comes early here and stays late, but Middlebury's own Snow Bowl and Rikert Nordic Center, not to mention proximity to most Vermont ski slopes, make this a paradise for ski fanatics, a breed Middlebury attracts in appropriately large numbers.

Middlebury's powerful Panthers ice hockey teams—men's and women's—draw loyal fans from across campus and the local community, especially when archrival Norwich is in town. The college offers 31 Division III varsity sports and has won recent national championships in field hockey (five consecutive titles), women's lacrosse, and women's ice hockey. Recent conference champs include women's soccer and men's golf. About half of the student body is active in the large club and intramural sports program, with rugby, water polo, crew, ultimate Frisbee, soccer, and, of course, Quadball getting the most interest.

Midd students enjoy plenty of student/faculty interaction, tight-knit friendships, and excellent recreational opportunities in a beautiful setting. Add challenging academics to the mix, and Middlebury is a comfortable yet stimulating place to spend four years, not just for writers, polyglots, and environmental enthusiasts but, says a senior, for anyone who is "academically curious and willing to work hard at whatever they do."

Overlaps

Amherst, Bowdoin, Brown, Dartmouth, Williams, Yale, Harvard, Princeton

If You Apply To ›

Middlebury: Early decision I and II, regular decision. Accepts the Common Application. Please consult Middlebury's website for the most up-to-date information regarding standardized test requirements.

Mills College: See Northeastern University, page 511.

In July 2022, Mills College in Oakland, California, finalized a merger with Northeastern University to become part of a unique bicoastal institution of higher education as Mills College at Northeastern University. Under the terms of the agreement, students who were enrolled at Mills at the time of the merger have been allowed to complete their studies at no extra cost or receive help in transferring to another college.

Under another provision of the merger, Northeastern has funded the creation of the Mills Institute, which will continue to operate on the Oakland campus and perpetuate Mills's distinctive commitment to "gender and racial justice and the advancement of women, gender nonbinary individuals, and communities of color." The first new joint program, titled Leading Social Change and open to students at both schools, was launched on the Mills campus in January 2022.

Additional information about the merger is available on the Mills College at Northeastern University website (mills.northeastern.edu).

Millsaps College

1701 North State Street, Jackson, MS 39210

Millsaps is the strongest liberal arts college in the deep, Deep South and by far the most progressive. Its largely preprofessional students typically have sights set on business, law, or medicine and are well served by location in the state capital. Usually compared to Hendrix, Rhodes, and Sewanee. About half of the students come from out of state, generally from other Southern states.

Millsaps College, founded by Methodists in 1890, was once thought of as a finishing school for well-bred Southern belles and gentlemen. Although less well-known outside the Deep South, it has long been one of the region's top liberal arts institutions. Affiliated with the United Methodist Church, Millsaps takes its motto, *Ad Excellentiam* ("toward excellence"), seriously. What characterizes the school is its focus on scholarly inquiry, spiritual growth, and community service. "Millsaps is the perfect package," says a first-year student, "strongly academic, small enough to build relationships, yet big-thinking enough to build the mind."

The college's 100-acre campus sits in the center of Jackson, on the highest point in the city. A mix of modern and traditional buildings is arranged around the Bowl, a sequestered glen surrounded by old-growth trees and shrubs that serves as a main student gathering place. Recent campus projects include the Windgate Visual Arts Center and a major remodel of the McRae Christian Center that created new classrooms for the humanities as well as a chapel for students of all faiths and backgrounds.

Under the Compass Curriculum, all students complete coursework in Foundations (covering thinking and reasoning), Communication in Humanities, Problem Solving and Creative Practice, Integrative and Collaborative Learning, Our Human Heritage, and Explorations (covering a range of liberal arts subject areas). All students take at least one business course, and a writing across the curriculum initiative ensures that every student develops writing skills. By their fourth year, students must complete the Major Experience, a capstone learning experience that may involve research, a field- or community-based course, study abroad, an internship, or an honors project.

> **"Every professor I've had has used multiple methods for presenting information."**

Millsaps offers more than 30 majors and 40 minors, including the option of a self-designed major. The Millsaps College Writing Program and creative writing are top-notch, and business is a strength. Although they enroll fewer students, the sociology/anthropology and religious studies programs are well regarded. The most popular majors are business administration, biology, accounting, and psychology. Premed-related courses, including those in biology, chemistry, and neuroscience, are strong, and the college's prehealth mentoring program pairs students with practitioners in their chosen field, allowing them to earn credit for real medical experience. Cooperative agreements allow students to opt for nursing degrees in partnership with the University of Mississippi Medical Center, the University of Alabama at Birmingham, and Vanderbilt University. Millsaps also offers a premed program with William Carey University School of Osteopathic Medicine and pre-engineering in cooperation with Mississippi State, Auburn, and Columbia universities.

"The courses are rigorous, as the professors continue to push the students' academic boundaries," says a sophomore. Most classes at Millsaps enroll fewer than 20 students, and none exceed 50. "Every professor I've had has used multiple methods for presenting information to help students understand class material," says a biology major. Each year, a few select upperclassmen join the Ford Teaching Fellows

Website: www.millsaps.edu
Location: City Center
Private
Total Enrollment: 649
Undergraduates: 631
Male/Female: 49/51
Financial Aid: 95%
Pell Grant: 40%
Expense: Pr $
Student Loans: 65%
Average Debt: $ $ $
Applicants: 2,220
Accepted: 68%
Enrolled: 15%
Grad in 6 Years: 62%
Returning Freshmen: 71%
Academics: ✑ ✑ ✑
Social: ☎ ☎ ☎
Q of L: ★ ★ ★
Admissions: (601) 974-1050
Email Address: admissions@
   millsaps.edu

Strong Programs:
Creative Writing
Business Administration
Sociology/Anthropology
Religious Studies
Biology
Accounting
Psychology
Chemistry

Program, letting them work closely with a faculty member to learn about teaching—and paying them for their time in the classroom. For-credit internships are available with local businesses, in state government offices in Jackson, and at the teaching hospital and medical center across the street from campus. The college maintains a 4,500-acre biocultural reserve in the rainforest of the Yucatán Peninsula, which hosts courses exploring ecology, archaeology, and Maya culture. Nearly 40 percent of Millsaps students study abroad in more than 50 nations, including Austria, Ghana, Scotland, Peru, and Vietnam.

"The student body at Millsaps is friendly and welcoming," opines a student. "As a transfer student, I found that the process of making new friends was easier than I expected." Half of the students now come from out of state, the majority being from other Southern states, although 3 percent arrive from foreign countries. Many Mississippians view Millsaps as a hotbed of liberalism, and students report that while there are conservatives on campus, the atmosphere is largely liberal and progressive. "Millsaps has a long history of being responsive to social issues," says a government and politics major. Indeed, Millsaps was the first college in Mississippi to voluntarily open its doors to students of color, and it recently installed gender-neutral bathrooms on campus. Black students make up 25 percent of the student body, Asian Americans 3 percent, and Hispanics/Latinos 4 percent. Forty percent of incoming first-year students are Pell-eligible. Qualified students are awarded academic merit scholarships averaging $26,400 each year, but there are no athletic awards.

Eighty-nine percent of students stay in campus housing—mostly, grouses a sophomore, because those who move off campus are subject to a 35 percent reduction in their merit-based financial aid. On-campus options include traditional, suite-style, and apartment-style halls, and a psychology major says, "Housing is average." The robust Greek system claims 51 percent of the men and 47 percent of the women; sophomore, junior, and senior men may live in one of four fraternity houses, but there is no sorority housing. "The Caf is clean and offers a large selection of food, including a vegan station," says a senior, but the quality of meals is hit or miss. "Millsaps has really emphasized sexual assault education," notes a biology major, and the issue "has been incorporated into the first-year curriculum."

"Greek life is the center of Millsaps's social life."

"Greek life is the center of Millsaps's social life," a student explains, and the fraternity houses are usually open and rocking from Wednesday through Saturday nights. Greek rush is now held after fall midterms instead of during the first hectic week of school, but that hasn't dampened the party spirit. "Campus police are very stringent" when it comes to enforcing alcohol policies, according to a senior. Major Madness is a favorite annual event, offering a week of campus entertainment and culminating in a weekend-long festival in the Bowl, with a crawfish boil, carnival games, and live music. The city of Jackson also offers a wealth of options, including professional symphony, opera, and ballet, and the city is a nexus for Mississippi's legendary blues and "roots rock" musical traditions. The "1 Campus 1 Community" program connects students with local volunteer opportunities. Easy road trips include New Orleans, Memphis, and the riverfront casinos in Vicksburg, Mississippi; closer to campus, 10 miles to the north, is a huge reservoir that is popular for weekend water sports. For students who enjoy the great outdoors, the Natchez Trace offers easy access to wooded trails and bicycling paths.

The Millsaps Majors compete in the Division III Southern Athletic Association, so the school isn't nearly as sports crazy as most Southern campuses. Men's and women's tennis, women's basketball, softball, and men's soccer have been competitive in recent years. Flag football and kickball are favorite intramural sports. Everyone benefits from the 65,000-square-foot Hall Activities Center, which has facilities for weight training, aerobics, basketball, racquetball, squash, and volleyball.

In a state renowned for the traditions of blues, barbecue, old magnolia trees, and big-time football, this small, progressive school is an anomaly. "Millsaps is a magnet for accomplished students from strong backgrounds and the kind of college not usually found in the South," remarks a junior. Small classes ensure plenty of time to get to know fellow students and faculty members. That's one tradition that never gets old.

If You Apply To ›

Millsaps: Early action, regular decision. SATs or ACTs: optional. Accepts the Common Application with supplement.

University of Minnesota

240 Williamson, 231 Pillsbury Drive SE, Minneapolis, MN 55455

Not quite as highly rated academically as the University of Michigan or the University of Wisconsin, but not nearly as expensive if you happen to be from out of state. In a university the size of Minnesota, the best bet is to find a niche, such as the honors program. Strong programs include engineering, management, and health fields. Location in the Midwest's second-largest metropolitan area means easy access to internships and other off-campus opportunities. Pack your woollies.

The University of Minnesota, like the nearby Mall of America, can be overwhelming, given its seemingly limitless variety of offerings and gargantuan size. With 150 undergraduate majors across eight colleges, plus one of the largest study abroad programs in the nation, the U of M, founded in 1851, offers an abundance of academic choices. Be warned, though—winters can be frigid, and it can take a cool customer to navigate the endless choices here.

The vast Twin Cities campus actually consists of two campuses with three main sections. The St. Paul campus encompasses the College of Food, Agricultural, and Natural Resource Sciences; the College of Biological Sciences; the College of Veterinary Medicine; and the College of Continuing Studies. The Minneapolis campus is divided by the Mississippi River into an East Bank and a West Bank that are home to the other colleges and most of the dormitories, as well as most of the fraternities and sororities. Both campuses offer a blend of traditional and modern architecture, with columned buildings seated next to sleek geometric structures. The two campuses are five miles apart and linked by a free bus service. Academic facilities are excellent, beginning with the seven-million-volume library system, one of the largest in North America. A 695-acre arboretum is used for research and teaching, and the West Bank Arts Quarter makes a lively setting for the university's art disciplines.

"The instructors have been exemplary."

Minnesota's liberal education requirements call for students in all schools and colleges to complete a set of core distribution requirements and take courses that satisfy four of five themes. The first theme, Race, Power, and Justice in the United States, was updated in the wake of the 2020 murder of George Floyd by Minneapolis police and is now required of everyone, with the aim of increasing awareness of the need for systemic societal changes. Students are free to choose which three of the remaining four themes they wish to fulfill: Civic Life and Ethics, the Environment, Global Perspectives, or Technology and Society. Freshmen must take a first-year writing course and four writing-intensive courses. The College of Science and Engineering

Website: www.twin-cities.umn .edu
Location: City Center
Public
Total Enrollment: 38,211
Undergraduates: 28,575
Male/Female: 46/54
Financial Aid: 45%
Pell Grant: 21%
Expense: Pub $ $ $ $
Student Loans: 53%
Average Debt: $ $
Applicants: 35,905
Accepted: 73%
Enrolled: 26%
Grad in 6 Years: 84%
Returning Freshmen: 92%
Academics: ✍ ✍ ✍ ✍
Social: ☎ ☎ ☎
Q of L: ★ ★ ★
Admissions: (800) 752-1000
Email Address: admissions@ umn.edu

Strong Programs:
Electrical Engineering
Mechanical Engineering

Students can choose to join one of three dozen living/learning communities, such as Design House, STEM Diversity House, and Lavender House.

A win over Michigan for custody of the Little Brown Jug or Wisconsin for Paul Bunyan's Axe is cause for celebration.

is notable for its tutorial and internship options; the electrical and mechanical engineering programs are particularly strong and well subscribed. The Carlson School of Management is well regarded and offers majors in entrepreneurial management, international business, and other areas. Theatre arts is a standout in the College of Liberal Arts. Psychology, computer science, journalism, and finance are the most popular majors.

"The classes are relatively difficult," a junior says, but "it really depends on the subject." Efforts to limit class size have been stepped up—37 percent of classes currently have fewer than 20 students—and the university is focusing more on undergraduates, bolstering academic advising and support services. Helpful teaching assistants are abundant, and professors receive high marks from most students as being approachable and knowledgeable. "The instructors have been exemplary due to their passion for the subject matter and commitment to their students," an archaeology major says.

The excellent honors program in the liberal arts college allows close contact with faculty members as well as leeway to enroll in certain graduate courses and seminars. The Undergraduate Research Opportunities Program provides scholarships of up to $1,700 for students to conduct research with faculty. Students find plenty of internship opportunities at the many corporations and government agencies in the Twin Cities area, and the university pushes its study, work, and volunteer abroad programs in nearly 100 nations. These draw 35 percent of undergrads, most of whom sign up for short-term programs.

Most U of M students are "motivated and hardworking," says a junior. Seventy-four percent of undergraduates are from Minnesota, and 6 percent hail from outside the U.S. Seven percent are Black, 5 percent are Hispanic/Latino, 12 percent are Asian American, and 5 percent are multiracial. Racial justice has been a major issue on campus since the murder of George Floyd. At the urging of student activists, the university has adjusted some of its ties with city police and committed to reviewing its campus police force and potential policy changes to support racial equity. Merit scholarships averaging $5,600 are available, as are athletic awards in all major sports.

"[Students are] motivated and hardworking."

Twenty-three percent of undergraduates live in residence halls; there are nine traditional halls and five university-run apartment facilities. Students can also choose to join one of three dozen living/learning communities, such as Design House, STEM Diversity House, and Lavender House. "The only issue is finding affordable and safe housing after freshman year," reports a journalism major, "since the cheapest available housing is in the Dinkytown houses, smack-dab in the center of a neighborhood with increasing safety issues." In response to a recent spike in crime, the campus police department has increased its patrols in the area, and the university is considering adding more street lighting and blue-light emergency response kiosks. Campus security also includes a free escort system for students. As for dining on campus, dietary restrictions are easily accommodated at the university's seven residential restaurants, but meals are said to be hit or miss. "Fresh fruit and veggies are always available," notes a junior, who also adds (lest anyone fear the campus dietitians are excessively health-obsessed), "they have the best chocolate chip cookies."

"Most social life takes place right off campus," says one student, "but there are loads of activities available on campus, such as bowling, theater, late-night activities, and movies." The 900-plus student groups and the student union's live music dance club are good places to meet people. About 12 percent of students go Greek, and "Greek organizations definitely set the tone for the party and bar scene," says a senior. "Bars, houses, apartment complexes, dorms, and even neighborhoods are separated according to Greek participation (or lack thereof)." Spring Jam, a carnival weekend put on by the Greeks each April to raise funds for charity, is a huge event, described by one student as "homecoming in spring—but better."

Here, being "under the weather" can be a good thing, as campus designers found a way to get around—or under—wet or wintry conditions by linking many of the campus buildings with tunnels. For those who love winter, happy skiers and skaters become colorful spots all over the state's white backdrop. In the spring and summer, Minnesota's famed 10,000 lakes offer swimming, boating, and fishing. The downtown areas of the Twin Cities are

> "Greek organizations definitely set the tone for the party and bar scene."

easy to get to by bus or light rail, and there are scores of good bars, restaurants, nightspots, and movie theaters. The Twin Cities are also home to six professional sports teams, many of which offer discount days for students.

This is an athletically inclined bunch of students, as Division I varsity sports and intramural competition, which can go on well past midnight, are both popular. Students always hope the current season will be one in which the gridiron Gophers take home the roses in a bowl victory, but short of that, a win over Michigan for custody of the Little Brown Jug or Wisconsin for Paul Bunyan's Axe is cause for celebration. Women's ice hockey is a perennial contender for the national championship. Men's ice hockey, baseball, and women's soccer, softball, volleyball, and track and field have all won Big Ten conference titles in recent years.

Anonymity is easy at a university of this size, but there are ample opportunities to find academic and social communities that make the campus feel smaller. Then again, size does have its virtues in the countless array of campus resources. The University of Minnesota is ideal for those who appreciate an urban setting and a good, old-fashioned, button-up-your-overcoat winter.

Overlaps

**Marquette,
University of
Minnesota Duluth,
University of
St. Thomas,
UW–Eau Claire,
UW–Madison,
University of Michigan**

If You Apply To ›

U of M: Early action, regular decision. Accepts the Common Application with supplement. Please consult U of M's website for the most up-to-date information regarding standardized test requirements.

University of Minnesota Morris

600 East 4th Street, Morris, MN 56267-2199

The plains of western Minnesota may seem an unlikely place to find a liberal arts college—and a public one at that. Morris is cut from the same cloth as Mary Washington, UNC Asheville, and St. Mary's College of Maryland. The draw: private college education at a public university price. Strong emphasis on sustainability. Remote location pushes students to Minneapolis-St. Paul for city life.

The University of Minnesota Morris is far more comprehensive than the small size of its student body might suggest. The first buildings on its 136-year-old campus were originally home to an American Indian boarding school, which was succeeded in 1910 by an agricultural school. Morris opened its doors in 1960, and since then, it has grown into a solid public liberal arts college. Morris "strives to encourage students to push their limits and go out on limbs," says an English and history double major.

The 130-acre Morris campus includes 32 traditional brick-and-mortar buildings, loosely arranged around a central mall. Two high-powered wind turbines generate

Website: www.morris.umn.edu
Location: Rural
Public
Total Enrollment: 1,114
Undergraduates: 1,114
Male/Female: 43/57
Financial Aid: 86%

(continued)

Pell Grant: 29%
Expense: Pub $ $ $
Student Loans: 68%
Average Debt: $
Applicants: 2,619
Accepted: 76%
Enrolled: 15%
Grad in 6 Years: 58%
Returning Freshmen: 78%
Academics: ✍ ✍ ✍ ½
Social: ☎ ☎
Q of L: ★ ★ ★
Admissions: (888) 866-3382
Email Address: admissions@
morris.umn.edu

Strong Programs:
Environmental Science and
Studies
Native American and
Indigenous Studies
English
Chemistry
Computer Science
Biology
Psychology
Management

*Well-regarded
programs include
environmental science,
as the Morris campus
itself serves as a study
in renewable energy.*

70 percent of the power Morris requires each day, and the campus boasts multiple solar arrays. The renovated Welcome Center is LEED Gold–certified and is the first building in Minnesota (and the first on the National Register of Historic Places) to use energy-efficient chilled-beam technology. The university has also renovated and expanded its performing arts facilities.

Everyone at Morris starts their general education requirements with the Intellectual Community seminar, which introduces students to college-level work and active interaction with faculty. Students then move on to as many as six courses under the umbrella of Skills for the Liberal Arts, along with eight courses in Expanding Perspectives. Seniors must participate in a senior seminar or capstone project, and some do both. The most popular majors are biology, psychology, management, and elementary education.

"I feel challenged but not overwhelmed, because I have a lot of support."

Other well-regarded programs include environmental science and environmental studies, as the Morris campus itself serves as a study in renewable energy; Native American and indigenous studies, which benefits from the campus's unique history; English; chemistry; and computer science.

"At Morris I feel challenged but not overwhelmed, because I have a lot of support," comments a biology and statistics major. Seventy-two percent of classes have fewer than 20 students, and students are encouraged to reach out to professors for individual help. Students say they respect professors for their knowledge and real-world experience. "The professors all do research in their field, keeping up their expertise," notes an English and theatre arts major.

Morris offers 10 to 25 service-learning courses each year, and half of the students conduct research projects with faculty. Morris's Center for Small Towns, which works with small towns, local schools, and nonprofits to address challenges specific to rural communities, provides opportunities for service projects, internships, and research. The Morris Honors Program allows high achievers to enjoy various honors courses, an honors capstone project, and a core course titled Traditions in Human Thought. Morris continues to integrate study abroad opportunities into the curriculum, offering more than 300 options for students wishing to study overseas; 43 percent of students participate by the time they graduate.

"Morris tends to be considered the 'nerdy' branch of the University of Minnesota system, and that's accurate both in terms of our interests and our achievements," observes a psychology major. Seventy-seven percent of Morris students are Minnesota residents, and 3 percent are international. The campus is more diverse than many other schools in the state: American Indians make up 10 percent, Hispanics/Latinos 7 percent, Asian Americans 2 percent, and Black students 3 percent, and 19 percent of students identify as multiracial. Both sides of the political aisle are represented on campus. Efforts to reckon with the campus's history as a Native American boarding school are drawing considerable attention, sparked by student demands to search the grounds for possible unmarked gravesites dating to that era. Honoring a policy that has been in place since 1909, a tuition waiver is available for American Indian students. Other financial incentives include the University of Minnesota Promise Scholarship, awarded to Minnesota residents with a family income that does not exceed $120,000; state residents with family incomes of $50,000 or less attend tuition-free. Merit scholarships averaging $4,900 are available, but there are no athletic awards.

Forty-eight percent of Morris students live on campus in one of the six residence halls, which offer several living/learning communities, or in an apartment complex reserved for upperclassmen. Students say the environmentally friendly Green Prairie Community residence hall is very nice, but others could use renovations. Many students opt for less expensive apartments and rental homes off campus. Dining options generally get average reviews. Morris's rural campus feels safe, according to students, and a senior says, "People are highly encouraged to speak out about sexual assault and report an incident. This speak-out approach seems to work."

There is no Greek system, but students say there's always something to do on campus, such as concerts, movies, presentations, shows, and campuswide games of Humans vs. Zombies or Hunger Games. "Being out in rural Minnesota really brings people together to make their own fun and recreation," explains a senior. The drinking age is strictly enforced on campus and in local bars. "There is a small party culture on campus. There is zero pressure to drink or do any drugs," says a computer science major. In addition, students enjoy access to about 120 student-led clubs and associations. Campus traditions include the annual Circle of Nations Indigenous Association powwow and the tug-of-war competition between the two main freshman

> **"Being out in rural Minnesota really brings people together to make their own fun."**

dorms; "Hundreds of students show up!" cheers a student. Students also look forward to the Zombie Prom in the fall and the Yule Ball, a holiday dance inspired by Harry Potter.

Morris itself is described as a "small but very friendly" town with a couple of bars, one small music venue, an ice rink, and a bowling alley. For those pining to get away, the nearest retail and restaurant chains are about 45 minutes away in Alexandria. Minneapolis-St. Paul, about three hours southeast, is also a popular destination.

The Cougars compete in the Division III Upper Midwest Athletic Conference. The women's indoor and outdoor track and field teams have claimed recent conference titles, and women's basketball, volleyball, and men's and women's soccer are also strong. Basketball, volleyball, and knocker ball (a version of soccer where participants wear large inflatable spheres and knock each other down) are among students' favorite intramurals, and men's and women's rugby and ultimate Frisbee are popular club sports. Students also use the Regional Fitness Center or hiking and biking trails to stay fit.

One of the smaller campuses in the University of Minnesota system, Morris may just epitomize the idea of "Minnesota nice," in a positive sense. Tucked away from the state's big cities, some students might find the campus isolated. But the school's location means fewer distractions—and more time for its happy students to focus on independent reading and research or just getting to know their peers. "We are the University of Minnesota's gem on the prairie," says a senior. "We have the intimacy of a private school, and the academic excellence of the state's largest educational institution, all for an affordable price."

Overlaps
St. Mary's College of Maryland, Massachusetts College of Liberal Arts, UNC Asheville, Gustavus Adolphus, St. Olaf, University of Mary Washington, University of Minnesota, University of Minnesota Duluth

If You Apply To ›

Morris: Rolling admissions. Accepts the Common Application with supplement. Please consult Morris's website for the most up-to-date information regarding standardized test requirements.

University of Mississippi

145 Martindale, P.O. Box 1848, University, MS 38677

Located in the progressive town of Oxford, Ole Miss is doing its best to put the state's problematic past behind it. Strong on public policy, international studies, and accountancy. The honors college is one of the best anywhere. Location near Faulkner's old hangouts is ideal for soaking up Southern literary traditions, and the beloved "Hotty Toddy" cheer continues to stoke school spirit, especially when Ole Miss takes on LSU and Mississippi State. Tailgating remains world class.

Website: www.olemiss.edu
Location: Small Town
Public
Total Enrollment: 16,788
Undergraduates: 14,601
Male/Female: 42/58
Financial Aid: 84%
Pell Grant: 22%
Expense: Pub $
Student Loans: 46%
Average Debt: $ $ $ $
Applicants: 19,531
Accepted: 90%
Enrolled: 20%
Grad in 6 Years: 68%
Returning Freshmen: 88%
Academics: ✐ ✐ ✐
Social: ☎ ☎ ☎
Q of L: ★ ★ ★
Admissions: (662) 915-7226
Email Address: admissions@olemiss.edu

Strong Programs:
Public Policy Leadership
International Studies
Accountancy
Pharmaceutical Sciences
Biomedical Engineering
Education
Arabic
Chinese

The University of Mississippi offers students an educational experience steeped in tradition and thick with school spirit. To be sure, some traditions have changed: a confederate monument has been moved from the main entrance to a campus cemetery, and plans are being made to create a memorial to Black Civil War soldiers. Although it originated as a reference to the wives of plantation owners, the nickname "Ole Miss" lives on as a term of affection among students and alumni. Even as Mississippi's flagship university evolves, it continues to be committed to providing a host of academic programs, including a top-notch honors college and an innovative public policy leadership major, and to supporting a vibrant campus community.

> **"It is not at all uncommon for full professors to teach freshmen."**

Founded in 1844, the University of Mississippi's central campus occupies 850 acres of rolling land in the center of Oxford. The main campus consists of 200 buildings and a mix of architectural styles, including Greek Revival, Beaux-Arts Classicism, Georgian Revival, and modern. The white-columned Lyceum, which served as a hospital during the Civil War, is the campus's oldest building and now houses administrative offices. Construction on the $175 million Duff Center for Science and Technology Innovation, the largest project in the university's history, is slated for completion in 2024.

All students must complete credit hours in English composition, mathematics, laboratory science, humanities and fine arts, social and behavioral sciences, and intercultural awareness and diversity. Approximately 75 percent of first-year students sign up for the Freshman Year Experience, a seminar-style course that helps new students transition from high school into a successful college career. The Center for Writing and Rhetoric administers two mandatory composition courses for freshmen.

Students say coursework is what you make of it and varies by program, but the atmosphere is collaborative. "The classes are definitely challenging at times," says one freshman, "but doable with the right amount of work." Accountancy is one of the university's strongest and most popular majors; the university houses the American Institute of Certified Public Accountants Library. Programs in pharmaceutical sciences, biomedical engineering, education, Arabic, and Chinese are also strengths, and integrated marketing communications, nursing, and business finance are popular. The Lott Leadership Institute is a standout that offers a public policy leadership major and an innovative curriculum that combines the systematic study of public policy with the development of leadership qualities. "The atmosphere of Lott is conducive to learning and team building," says one broadcast journalism major. "Conversational and debate classes are a change from the regular classroom, and Lott offers both." Professors are highly rated across the

> **"[Oxford is] the best college town in the nation."**

university. "It is not at all uncommon for full professors to teach freshmen and even offer tutoring to freshmen during their office hours," explains a senior.

For students who itch to have their passports stamped, Ole Miss offers numerous study abroad options, including 25 faculty-led programs, in such diverse locations as China, Greece, Ethiopia, Peru, and Thailand. Another option is the Croft Institute for International Studies, which accepts 70 students each fall. Participants study international politics, economics, and culture both in the classroom and via study abroad. Gifted students may apply for the highly competitive honors college, where they take part in small, discussion-based honors courses offered in a number of disciplines, engage in community service, complete a senior thesis, and have access to foreign study fellowships. Roughly 1,700 students from 80 majors currently participate.

"Ole Miss students are ambitious, hospitable, and well-rounded," says one public policy leadership major. Fifty-one percent of undergraduates are Mississippians and 1 percent hail from abroad. Black students make up 12 percent, Hispanics/Latinos 4 percent, Asian Americans 2 percent, and multiracial students 2 percent. "The outside view of UM is that everyone is a sorority girl or a frat guy," a mathematics major complains. "We have people of all categories and cultures." Merit scholarships averaging $11,700 are awarded annually, as are more than 250 athletic scholarships in 14 sports. The university covers tuition, room, and board for Pell-eligible Mississippi residents who meet certain academic requirements.

Twenty-eight percent of students live in the dorms, which are a hit-or-miss affair. "Some of the older dorms have seen better days," a student reports. Options include apartments, traditional residence halls, and residential colleges. Campus dining options are reported to be plentiful and tasty. "We offer several different dining halls," says a student, "some of which are all-you-can-eat and some of which are cafeteria-style."

"The Grove is a place where people come together…to support our Ole Miss Rebs."

Campus security gets a thumbs-up too. "Ole Miss is the kind of place where people look out for each other," comments a student. "We have a campus police department that works diligently to make sure the campus is safe."

The social scene is dominated by Greek life, which attracts 38 percent of the men and 49 percent of the women, although non-Greeks find plenty to enjoy as well. The Student Activities Association hosts a variety of on-campus activities each week, including movies, pageants, concerts, and multicultural events. Alcohol is forbidden from most areas of campus, and students say the school's policies are reasonably effective at curbing consumption. Campus worship organizations have a strong presence, and students can choose among 300 student groups, as well as volunteer opportunities in Oxford. One enthusiastic junior describes the city as "the best college town in the nation." Oxford has thriving arts and foodie scenes, and a senior says, "There are lots of locally owned businesses and restaurants that are unique to the area and very charming."

Famed author William Faulkner grew up here and attended the university for three semesters before dropping out, and the slew of local cultural events includes the annual Faulkner and Yoknapatawpha Conference, featuring lectures and discussions by literary scholars and critics. Although it lost out to the University of Virginia as repository of Faulkner's papers, Ole Miss operates Rowan Oak, Faulkner's home, and has a sizable collection of Faulkner materials. Blues legend B.B. King gave the university his personal record collection to help establish its Blues Archive, which is now one of the largest in the world.

The Ole Miss Rebels compete in the gauntlet known as the Southeastern Conference, where they face the likes of Alabama's Crimson Tide, the Florida Gators, and the LSU Tigers. The baseball team won the national title in 2022, and other solid teams include football, softball, and women's golf, basketball, cross-country, and rifle. School spirit is on full display, especially when LSU is in town, and teams are cheered on by the university's Landshark mascot. On game days, frenzied fans gather on the Grove—10 acres of oak and maple trees in the center of campus—for tailgating, which draws more than 100,000 loyal supporters who pitch 2,500 tents and drink from red and blue cups (no beer cans allowed). Jackets, ties, and cowboy boots are common, and food is sometimes served on silver trays. Says one happy Rebel, "The Grove is a place where people come together regardless of their differences to support our Ole Miss Rebs and share in a community that we all love." Rousing chants of the famous "Hotty Toddy" cheer can be heard throughout the football stadium just before kickoff—and just about anywhere else, for that matter. Dozens of intramural and club sports also prove to be popular diversions.

Overall, students here seem to be a contented lot, especially those in the honors college. Despite the administration's continued attempts to reconcile the school's historic roots with a 21st-century identity, it's clear that Rebel pride and the sense of community here are as strong as ever. Indeed, Ole Miss students have much to cheer about, including solid academics, game days in the Grove, and a healthy dose of school spirit.

If You Apply To ›

Ole Miss: Rolling admissions. Accepts the Common Application with supplement. Please consult Ole Miss's website for the most up-to-date information regarding standardized test requirements.

University of Missouri

230 Jesse Hall, Columbia, MO 65211

Renowned as home to one of the top journalism schools in the nation, Mizzou boasts the country's only commercial university-owned TV station, as well as a National Public Radio outlet. Also strong in agriculture, the health sciences, business, and music. Comparable in size to Iowa and Iowa State, smaller than Illinois and Indiana. Columbia offers a vibrant social scene.

In 1839, the residents of Boone County, Missouri, raised enough money to create the state university in Columbia. Today, Missouri's flagship university has evolved into a top research institution and continues to uphold the belief of its founders in the great value of higher education that is accessible to all. Having recently completed a $1.4 billion development campaign, the university continues to expand programs and facilities in ways that benefit students. It has also become a national leader in generating on-site renewable energy. "Students at Mizzou thrive on the hands-on learning approach that all of our degree programs offer, whether that's through internships, research labs, or even anchoring the news," says a junior.

The oldest public university west of the Mississippi, Mizzou occupies a 1,262-acre campus flanked by mansionlike fraternity and sorority houses and featuring 42,000 plants and trees and numerous thematic gardens. Francis Quadrangle, with 18 predominantly redbrick National Historic Landmark buildings, is the core of the campus. Central to this area are the 43-foot limestone columns of the original Academic Hall that was destroyed by fire in 1892. To the east of the Columns is the original tombstone of Thomas Jefferson, which the Jefferson family gave to Mizzou (not UVA!) in the 19th century as a symbol of his championing of state-supported education. The eastern half of the campus consists of native white limestone buildings, most notably the Memorial Union, with its striking Gothic tower.

An array of general education requirements includes courses in three content areas: social and behavioral sciences; physical, biological, and mathematical sciences; and humanities and fine arts. Two writing-intensive courses are also required, and all undergrads complete a senior-year capstone course. Full professors teach the lecture courses at Mizzou, supplemented by a weekly discussion session led by a teaching assistant to go over material presented in class. "Professors use real-world examples to tie heavy topics and theories to reality, helping us to make the connection," explains an agribusiness management major. Owing to MU's size, classes can fill up quickly, but the school guarantees the availability of coursework to complete a degree in four years.

> **"Students at Mizzou thrive on the hands-on learning approach that all of our degree programs offer."**

With more than 300 degree programs and 12 schools and colleges, Mizzou offers a comprehensive set of choices for basic and advanced study. Aspiring journalists can get hands-on experience working on the *Columbia Missourian*, the local daily paper edited by J-school faculty members and students, or at KOMU-TV, the nation's only university-owned commercial television station. KBIA, MU's National Public Radio station, is popular among journalism students and listeners alike. Agriculture is also nationally ranked, especially in the areas of agribusiness management and applied research for farm communities. The music program is noteworthy, and the College of Engineering maintains several strong undergraduate majors, including biological and civil engineering. The College of Business is competitive and features a five-year bachelor's/master's accounting program. Health sciences and psychology are other popular majors. A major in constitutional democracy prepares undergrads for careers in government, public policy, and law.

"The academic climate is relatively competitive, depending on the major," says one senior. "In my experience, there is a nice mix of classes in regards to difficulty." Committed preprofessionals will be glad to know that MU offers qualified freshmen guaranteed admission to its graduate-level programs in medicine, law, veterinary medicine, nursing, and health professions. Mizzou is also one of the leading public universities for undergraduate research. About 20 percent of students study abroad, choosing from programs in more than 40 countries. Additionally, the university sponsors Mizzou Alternative Breaks, service trips in which students work on volunteer projects in the U.S. and abroad during spring, winter, and weekend breaks.

MU offers qualified freshmen guaranteed admission to its graduate-level programs in medicine, law, veterinary medicine, and nursing.

"Mizzou's campus has a pretty Midwestern feel to it, so it's easy to talk to people and most people are generally friendly," says a senior. Seventy-nine percent of Mizzou undergraduates hail from the Show-Me State and 1 percent are international. Black students account for 6 percent of undergrads, Asian Americans 3 percent, Hispanics/Latinos 5 percent, and multiracial students 5 percent. In the years since student protests in 2015 over chronically poor race relations on campus, Mizzou has estab-

> **"I loved my residence hall experience."**

lished several scholarship and support programs designed especially for students of color, created a mandatory diversity training program for all incoming students, and initiated campuswide celebrations of cultural diversity. A student comments, "There are still scars that remain from past events involving race, but the campus has made strides to recover." Students report that both sides of the political aisle are well represented here. Merit scholarships are available averaging $8,000, and athletes may compete for roughly 250 awards in 20 Division I sports. Missouri Land Grant scholarships cover full tuition and fees for Missouri residents who qualify for Pell Grants.

(continued)

Grad in 6 Years: 73%
Returning Freshmen: 88%
Academics: ✍ ✍ ✍
Social: ☎ ☎ ☎ ☎
Q of L: ★ ★ ★
Admissions: (573) 882-7786
Email Address: mu4u@ missouri.edu

Strong Programs:
Journalism
Agriculture
Agribusiness Management
Music
Engineering
Business
Health Sciences
Psychology

Twenty-eight percent of MU students live on campus, and freshmen under age 20 are required to do so. "I loved my residence hall experience," says one sophomore. "I had a lot of space in my room and the closets were huge!" Residence halls have double rooms and are often crowded and lively. Single-sex halls, a few single rooms, and round-the-clock quiet floors are also available. About 30 percent of new students choose from among 100 Freshman Interest Groups, where 15 to 20 students with shared academic interests live in the same residence hall and enroll in three core classes together. All other undergrads living in the dorms participate in general and thematic living/learning communities. Mizzou's all-you-can-eat dining halls, coffee bars, and take-out stands offer good variety and accommodations for special needs. Student support services receive mixed reviews. "While there are mental health resources available, they don't quite live up to the efficiency and accessibility of the academic ones," says a senior.

Students say MU's social life is packed with options, including movies, the usual fraternity and sorority parties, 600-plus student organizations, shopping, eating out, and visiting great parks and hiking areas around town. Says a senior, "There is always something going on at Mizzou, whether it be a free event being put on by campus or a social event happening in Greek Town." Twenty-three percent of the men and 28 percent of the women go Greek. Mizzou is a champion of tough alcohol policies, and students have agreed to ban alcohol from all fraternities and sororities, making it one of the largest Greek systems in the nation to go dry. (The rule is lifted when alumni come home to visit!)

> "Columbia is a bustling college town that is high-energy most weekends."

"Columbia is a bustling college town that is high-energy most weekends," says one student. Students support the town by engaging in 210,000 hours of community service each year, and the community caters to them in return. Road trips to St. Louis, Kansas City, and Lake of the Ozarks offer a change of scenery.

The Missouri Tigers compete in the rough-and-tumble Southeastern Conference, and basketball and football games draw big crowds. In fact, the entire town turns out in black and gold for any football game. The women's softball and volleyball programs are strong, and the men's wrestling team won nine straight Mid-American Conference titles before moving to the Big 12 at the start of the 2021–22 season. MU's popular intramural program has nearly two dozen sports and two skill divisions, attracting more than a quarter of the student body. "My favorite traditions are our school songs that we sing at all athletic events, Tiger Walk and Senior Sendoff, and yelling 'M-I-Z' and waiting for someone to yell back 'Z-O-U,'" cheers a journalism major.

Mizzou is working hard to put its racial difficulties in the rearview mirror, support a more inclusive community, and resume its trajectory as a school on the rise. It continues to grow academically and culturally while sticking with its longtime strengths. One senior reflects, "We are a school rich in tradition, but looking to the future."

Overlaps

U of I at Urbana–Champaign, Indiana University, University of Iowa, Iowa State, University of Kansas, Kansas State

If You Apply To ›

Mizzou: Rolling admissions. Accepts the Common Application. Please consult Mizzou's website for the most up-to-date information regarding standardized test requirements.

Morehouse College: See page 36.

Mount Holyoke College

50 College Street, South Hadley, MA 01075

One of two women's colleges, along with Smith, that are members of the Five College Consortium in the scenic Connecticut River Valley of western Massachusetts. Less nonconformist than Bryn Mawr and Smith. MHC is strongest in the natural and social sciences and emphasizes leadership and professional experiences.

Mount Holyoke College pioneered women's higher education in 1837 and continues to pave the way as a gender-diverse research liberal arts institution. The students who choose Mount Holyoke value achievement, leadership, inclusivity, and tradition. While students occasionally complain about the heavy workload, most bring that challenge on themselves as they seek intellectual fulfillment within MHC's supportive, caring environment as well as hands-on professional experiences that sometimes take them far afield. "Mount Holyoke is a sisterhood," says a senior. "I have never before been surrounded by so many amazing, passionate women."

Mount Holyoke is located in the heart of New England on 800 acres of rolling hills dotted with two lakes, miles of hiking trails, and waterfalls. Modern glass-and-stone buildings stand alongside classic ivy-covered brick and sandstone structures. Campus highlights include the Japanese Meditation Garden and Teahouse, the Talcott Greenhouse, an art building with studios and a bronze-casting foundry, an 18-hole championship golf course, and an equestrian center. Recent projects include the 8,000-square-foot Fimbel Maker & Innovation Lab.

Despite changes to the campus, the curriculum at this 186-year-old institution remains rooted in the traditional liberal arts and sciences. All students must take a first-year seminar; the college offers roughly 35 seminars each fall and five in the spring, covering a wide variety of disciplines and topics, such as Herstory: Writing Your History and Disaster Science. The focus of these courses is developing skills in analysis and critical inquiry. Some also include field trips to museums or events in Boston, New York, or Washington, D.C. "First-year seminars are a great way to ease into college life," says a senior.

> **"Faculty are warm, sensitive, incredibly intelligent, and highly invested in their students."**

Chemistry is a long-standing strength at Mount Holyoke, bolstered by top-of-the-line labs, a scanning electron microscope, several nuclear magnetic resonance spectrometers, and a linear accelerator. English, economics, international relations, politics, environmental studies, and computer science are also strong. The most popular majors are psychology, biological sciences, English, and economics. Five-year dual-degree programs enable students to combine degrees from MHC with B.S. degrees in engineering from the University of Massachusetts Amherst, Caltech, or Dartmouth. Many students find the Five College Consortium one of the school's greatest assets: each year, 74 percent of Mount Holyoke students take at least one course offered through the consortium. A free bus service runs every 20 minutes between MHC and Amherst College, Hampshire, UMass Amherst, and Smith, multiplying a Mount Holyoke student's access to academic, social, and cultural opportunities. As an alternative to pursuing a minor or second major, Mount Holyoke also offers the Nexus program, which builds in opportunities for internships, off-campus research, and public presentations, along with traditional coursework. Participating students select from one of nine preprofessional tracks, such as global business, non-profit organizations, and data science.

Website: www.mtholyoke.edu
Location: Suburban
Private
Total Enrollment: 2,212
Undergraduates: 2,197
Male/Female: 0/100
Financial Aid: 66%
Pell Grant: 20%
Expense: Pr $ $ $
Student Loans: 61%
Average Debt: $ $
Applicants: 3,971
Accepted: 52%
Enrolled: 29%
Grad in 6 Years: 85%
Returning Freshmen: 91%
Academics: ✍ ✍ ✍ ✍
Social: ☎ ☎ ☎
Q of L: ★ ★ ★ ★
Admissions: (413) 538-2023
Email Address: admission@ mtholyoke.edu

Strong Programs:
Chemistry
English
Economics
International Relations
Politics
Environmental Studies
Computer Science
Psychology

"Mount Holyoke is a simultaneously intense and supportive academic environment," says an environmental studies major. "I feel challenged but not overwhelmed." Students rave about the quality of teaching and the small classes. "Faculty are warm, sensitive, incredibly intelligent, and highly invested in their students," says a psychology and education major. Although some of Mount Holyoke's intro courses have 50 or more students, 71 percent of classes have fewer than 20. The school's honor code makes possible self-scheduled, self-proctored final exams. Students say the Career Development Center's assistance with résumés, cover letters, and interview preparation is particularly effective.

Many students choose to take advantage of an optional January winter term to take a noncredit, nontraditional course or do an internship in major cities or points abroad. The Lynk curriculum-to-career experience guarantees all students funding for an internship or research opportunity, domestic or international, and offers students access to special resources, workshops, and networking opportunities with alumnae. "Lynk funding allows students to do work they want to do without sacrificing a summer of making money," cheers a sophomore. Sixty-four percent of students get involved in undergraduate research. The Weissman Center for Leadership focuses on leadership development through three core programs: the Speaking, Arguing, and Writing

"We have a multitude of traditions at Mount Holyoke that we take very seriously."

Program, which helps students hone their rhetorical skills; Leadership and Public Service, which connects students with internships and other opportunities to explore careers in public service; and Community-Based Learning, which offers 25 to 30 service-learning courses every year as well as paid positions for students to work in leadership roles as community fellows and mentors. For a change of scenery, 37 percent of MHC students spend all or part of junior year in another country. In addition to roughly 100 study abroad programs from approved partners, Mount Holyoke sponsors its own in France, China, Japan, and Costa Rica.

"Students are kind, intelligent, curious, supportive, and global," asserts an international relations major. The college attracts students from 48 states and 82 countries; 18 percent are Massachusetts natives, and a substantial 24 percent are international. Black students make up 5 percent of the student body, Asian Americans 7 percent, Hispanics/Latinas 8 percent, and multiracial students 4 percent. The LGBTQ community on campus is prominent, and students cite social justice, human rights, and transgender rights as "big issues on campus." CAUSE (Creating Awareness and Unity for Social Equality) is a large and popular campus group dedicated to community-building and student leadership. Mount Holyoke's financial aid packages meet 100 percent of applicants' demonstrated financial need. Merit scholarships are available, averaging $22,200, but there are no athletic scholarships.

Ninety-five percent of Mount Holyoke students live in the residence halls, which according to one student "all have their own personality, which makes it very difficult to choose sometimes." Most dorms are also very homey, with living rooms, TV lounges, and baby grand pianos; all serve milk and cookies (as well as healthier fare like hummus and vegetables) at 9:30 p.m. on school nights. Students from all four classes live together, and housing is guaranteed for all four years. Some residence halls also offer apartment-style living. Meals in the Blanchard Community Center, the main destination for student life and dining, and campus security both get positive reviews.

"There is a unique bond and desire for empowerment on campus."

Social life on campus is described as "mellow" and inclusive, consisting of low-key parties, plays, concerts, speakers, and cultural events. "A cappella is the football of Mount Holyoke—we have six different groups who perform every semester and have significant followings in the student body," notes a senior. The Mount Holyoke College V8s (Victory Eights) are the oldest continuing female collegiate a cappella group in the United States. Students seeking a more "traditional" party scene typically head to UMass or other Five College schools. A computer science major says South Hadley (population 18,000) is "a bit isolated for people who really enjoy city life." The South Hadley Center has eateries, a pub, shops, and a movie theater. Road trips to Boston, Vermont, and New York City are popular, when students can find the time.

"We have a multitude of traditions at Mount Holyoke that we take very seriously," comments a politics and religion major. Each class has a color and a mascot, and class spirit is huge, especially for the annual Junior Show and Convocation. Every fall on Mountain Day, students wake up to ringing bells, classes are canceled (even the library is closed), and everyone treks up Mount Holyoke to picnic and see the foliage. "In the spring we have Pangy Day (short for Pangynaskeia, or 'cultivating the total world of women'), where students wrap a maypole, snuggle baby goats, and hang out in the sun with friends," explains a senior. The *Mount Holyoke News* is the oldest continuously running college newspaper in the country. Community service is an important emphasis, and 30 percent of students regularly volunteer.

In addition to academic pursuits, Division III Lyons athletics, such as crew, riding, field hockey, and lacrosse, are popular. The college encourages athletic participation with six competitive club sports and a state-of-the-art fitness center, although intramurals are not offered. Mount Holyoke's Model United Nations team frequently brings home top honors.

Mount Holyoke's diverse student body makes for a globally aware community, and its identity as a women's college nurturing future leaders promotes a culture where deep, personal relationships are the norm. Academic excellence and easy access to New York and Boston provide a small college atmosphere that's infused with art and culture. As one senior explains, "There is a unique bond and desire for empowerment on campus."

The Mount Holyoke College V8s (Victory Eights) are the oldest continuing female collegiate a cappella group in the U.S.

Overlaps

Smith, Wellesley, Barnard, Bryn Mawr, Scripps, Brown, Vassar, Tufts

If You Apply To ›

MHC: Early decision I and II, regular decision. SATs or ACTs: optional. Accepts the Common Application with supplement. Accepts applications from students who are female, transgender, and nonbinary.

Muhlenberg College

2400 Chew Street, Allentown, PA 18104

There is a definite Muhlenberg type: ambitious, studious, and preprofessional. Muhlenberg is strong in premed, prelaw, pre-anything. Has a more humble, middle-class persona than more upscale Dickinson and Lafayette and boasts a nurturing atmosphere. Takes its Lutheran values seriously, but less than 5 percent of students are Lutheran, while one-third are Jewish and another third are Roman Catholic.

Muhlenberg College is a small liberal arts school founded on solid Lutheran roots that takes pride in fostering a strong sense of community among undergraduates from a broad range of religious backgrounds. With ample opportunities for hands-on learning and lots of support, the school continues to attract the best and brightest to its preprofessional programs, including its top premed program. Put simply, says one senior, "Muhlenberg believes in students and their ability to learn."

Website: www.muhlenberg.edu
Location: Small City
Private
Total Enrollment: 2,028
Undergraduates: 2,007

Muhlenberg offers four honors programs that provide early opportunities for internships, undergraduate research, and service learning.

Muhlenberg was established in 1848 and named after the founder of the Lutheran Church in America. Set on 82 parklike acres, the 'Berg campus is a combination of older Gothic stone structures and newer buildings in a variety of architectural styles. The campus boasts a lovely chapel, the high-tech Trexler Library, a 40-acre biological field station and wildlife sanctuary, and a 64-acre arboretum with more than 300 species of wildflowers, broadleaf evergreens, and conifer trees. The Baker Center for the Performing Arts features a dramatic 45-foot glass outer shell and a variety of performance spaces. The Fahy Commons for Public Engagement and Innovation, a 20,000-square-foot, energy-efficient facility housing the Office of Community Engagement, the Innovation & Entrepreneurship Program, and other academic spaces, opened in spring 2023.

Muhlenberg's popular First-Year Seminars are small, writing- and discussion-intensive courses capped at 15 students. Recent offerings include Mutual Aid and Pandemic Solidarity, The Idea of Wilderness, and Probability and Quantum Weirdness. All students complete two additional writing-intensive courses, a two-course diversity and global engagement requirement, and a capstone experience in their major.

Muhlenberg's reputation rests on its premedical program, which continues to attract large numbers of students. Majors in biology, public health, and neuroscience are available, as are competitive early-acceptance programs in medicine with Temple and Boston University, a 3–4 optometry program with SUNY College of Optometry, and a 3–4 dentistry program with the University of Pennsylvania. The college's theater arts program is a national draw, and some alumni have gone on to star on Broadway. Science lab equipment at Muhlenberg is cutting-edge, and a comprehensive science major allows for a sampling of it all. The Living Writers course, offered once every three years, has brought a number of noted authors to campus, including Neil Gaiman, Jonathan Franzen, and Zadie Smith. Theater is Muhlenberg's most popular major, followed by psychology, business administration, and media and communication.

"The Career Center's team has helped me since freshman year."

Students describe the academic climate as serious, challenging, and encouraging. Seventy-six percent of courses have fewer than 20 students, promoting a cooperative environment. "Muhlenberg professors go out of their way to make a positive and memorable learning experience for their students," cheers a junior. Advising is strong here too, and students may take advantage of programs like Alumni Week, which is organized around conversations and workshops with alumni in all industries. "The Career Center's team has helped me since freshman year to figure out what I want to do after Muhlenberg," says a media and communication senior.

The college offers four honors programs that provide early opportunities for internships, undergraduate research, and service learning: the Muhlenberg Scholars Program, the Dana Scholars Program, the RJ Fellows Program, and the Shankweiler Scholars Program. Each program requires a culminating project or seminar in the senior year; 20 percent of students participate. Students speak highly of the college's array of service-learning course offerings, and 27 percent of undergrads conduct research with faculty. Muhlenberg sends study groups to Washington, D.C., and there is a semester-long program at the Jewish Theological Seminary in New York City. Those seeking international experiences may study abroad via 130 programs in countries around the globe; 60 percent do so, often in short-term, faculty-led programs in January and May.

"Muhlenberg is basically the golden retriever of colleges: everyone is so sweet and friendly, but we are also hardworking and dedicated to our studies," muses a public health major. Muhlenberg draws 31 percent of its students from Pennsylvania and many from adjacent New Jersey and New York, as well as 1 percent from foreign nations. Black students account for 5 percent of the student body, Hispanics/Latinos

10 percent, Asian Americans 3 percent, and multiracial students 3 percent. Many students cite increasing the diversity of the student body and faculty as a top concern on this left-leaning campus. "There is an open political dialogue where students are encouraged to express their views without worry of backlash," says a junior. Merit scholarships averaging $21,500 are available, but athletic scholarships are not.

Muhlenberg encourages students to live on campus and guarantees housing to all undergraduates, so 86 percent of students live in campus residences. "Freshmen are required to live in one of three dorms, which is actually nice because it brings them all together in one area of campus," explains a senior. Upperclassmen praise the Muhlenberg Independent Living Experience townhouses and other suite-style options. Two dorms, Robertson and South, house 140 students in single, air-conditioned rooms overlooking Lake Muhlenberg. First-years choose from a seven- or five-day meal plan, and students rave about the food, the staff, and even the dining-hall ambiance. "Our recently renovated Wood Dining Commons is a cross between a ski lodge and Hogwarts," cheers one student. "There's even a fireplace!" Campus safety receives good ratings.

"Muhlenberg is basically the golden retriever of colleges: everyone is so sweet and friendly."

Most social life at Muhlenberg takes place on campus, and students say there's something to fit every interest. The Muhlenberg Activities Council provides comedians, current movies in the Red Door Café, live music, escape rooms, and bingo nights. Hillel is among the largest of the more than 130 student organizations, as are the theater and dance associations. Allentown offers a decent variety of restaurants, bars, and minor-league sports, and a senior comments, "Muhlenberg's relationship with the surrounding community is definitely growing." Students get involved by volunteering as tutors and with groups such as Habitat for Humanity and America Reads. City buses stop on campus for trips to Allentown proper, area malls, and other local activities. Students also venture to Philadelphia (60 miles) for nightlife and cheesesteaks, New York City (95 miles) for clubbing and theater, and farther out to Baltimore or Washington, D.C. Outdoorsy students can pick up the Appalachian Trail for a little hiking.

A favorite tradition is the candlelight ceremony during freshman orientation where freshmen write down their college goals.

Twenty percent of Muhlenberg men and 21 percent of the women pledge their undergraduate years to fraternities and sororities, respectively, and according to a junior, "Greek life is thriving if you want it but not thrust upon you in any way." Students report that the school takes its policies against underage drinking seriously. Big social events include homecoming, West Fest in the fall, East Fest in the spring, the Scotty Wood basketball tournament, and Midnight Breakfast, when faculty and staff serve late-night breakfast to students before finals. A favorite tradition is the candlelight ceremony during freshman orientation where freshmen write down their college goals, to be reopened the day before graduation.

"Wood Dining Commons is a cross between a ski lodge and Hogwarts."

For the athletically inclined, the Muhlenberg Mules compete in the Division III Centennial Conference. Football, softball, and men's soccer have brought home conference titles in the last few years. Students say any contest against Johns Hopkins draws crowds. Muhlenberg's Life Sports Center offers a pool, a basketball court, other all-purpose courts, and a jogging track. Soccer, volleyball, and basketball are the most popular intramurals, while ultimate Frisbee is the most popular club sport.

"It is an unspoken expectation on campus to hold the door for the person behind you, even if they are at a farther distance than would usually warrant such a gesture," explains a student. Small gestures of kindness are just one way in which Muhlenberg earns its reputation as a "community that cares"—it also offers students a warm, intimate academic milieu and plenty of support. It's a winning formula.

Overlaps

Franklin & Marshall, Gettysburg, Ithaca, Lafayette, Skidmore, Dickinson, Syracuse, Emerson

University of Nebraska–Lincoln

1410 Q Street, Lincoln, NE 68588

Everybody knows Cornhusker football, but in other areas, Nebraska, the smallest public university in the Big Ten, flies under the radar. With less than a third of undergrads coming from out of state, has a corner on the market for Nebraskans. Business administration, psychology, and advertising and public relations top the list of majors. Given the state's demographic makeup, diversity is a challenge.

Website: www.unl.edu
Location: City Center
Public
Total Enrollment: 21,002
Undergraduates: 18,435
Male/Female: 50/50
Financial Aid: 77%
Pell Grant: 26%
Expense: Pub $
Student Loans: 55%
Average Debt: $ $
Applicants: 17,775
Accepted: 81%
Enrolled: 33%
Grad in 6 Years: 66%
Returning Freshmen: 80%
Academics: ✍ ✍ ✍
Social: ☎ ☎ ☎ ☎
Q of L: ★ ★ ★
Admissions: (800) 742-8800
Email Address: admissions@unl.edu

Strong Programs:
Animal Science
Journalism
Actuarial Science
Early Childhood Education
Business Administration
Psychology
Advertising and Public Relations
Nutrition, Exercise, and Health Science

On crisp fall weekends, when spirits are high and the Big Red football arcs through the air, Huskers cheer and paint the town of Lincoln red and white in a show of appreciation for their alma mater. In fact, on home-game Saturdays, the stadium is the third largest "city" in the state, holding 5 percent of the population. Away from the stadium, students at the University of Nebraska–Lincoln have more reasons to cheer, with notable programs ranging from software engineering to digital humanities to PGA golf management.

Nebraska, chartered in 1869 as a land grant institution, spreads across two main campuses. The East Campus is home to the College of Agricultural Sciences and Natural Resources and the College of Law. Most entering students end up on the larger City Campus, surrounded by the bustle of downtown Lincoln and home to seven undergraduate colleges: architecture, arts and sciences, journalism and mass communications, business, fine and performing arts, engineering, and education and human sciences. On City Campus, the architectural style ranges from the modern Sheldon Art Gallery designed by Philip Johnson to the architecture building, which is on the National Register of Historic Places. There are also several grassy malls, an arboretum, and a sculpture garden. A third campus location, the Innovation Campus, serves as a research and technological hub where students can test their skills with real-world tools and projects.

> "For a university this big, I think that the professors do a good job of making students feel valued."

Nebraska's 30-credit general education program, known as Achievement-Centered Education, is required of students in all majors and includes a senior-year capstone course. To help freshmen get oriented, Big Red Welcome combines a new student convocation with entertainment, information booths, and food in a carnival setting. Nebraska's College of Agricultural Sciences and Natural Resources is known for its outstanding programs in animal science, food science and technology, and agribusiness. Journalism, actuarial science, and early childhood education are also traditional strengths. The school of music's opera program has received national attention, and the Johnny Carson School of Theatre and Film offers four undergrad degrees, including a B.F.A. in emerging media arts. The most popular majors are business administration; psychology; advertising and public relations; and nutrition, exercise, and health science.

"The workload is fairly intensive, if you want to get good grades," remarks an accounting major. Although many classes are large, 34 percent have fewer than 20 students. Graduate students teach some freshman courses, but top professors can be found inside the classroom too. "For a university this big, I think that the professors do a good job of making students feel valued," says a prenursing student. "It is hard to be recognized in classes with 100 students, but I don't think that the quality of teaching is any less. And there are always office hours for students."

The University Honors Program offers qualified students challenging coursework, research opportunities, and faculty mentors. The FYRE (First-Year Research Experience) program pairs freshmen who have federal work-study awards with faculty members for up to five hours of collaborative research per week. Also, the UCARE (Undergraduate Creative Activity and Research Experience) program provides stipends for more than 400 students each year to participate in one-on-one research with a professor after freshman year. The Raikes School of Computer Science and Management is a highly selective honors program that focuses on a curriculum in technology, business, and real-world projects and awards scholarships to participants. Study abroad opportunities are available in more than 70 countries and include nearly 40 faculty-led programs; 19 percent of students take part. Career Services shows students how to make a professional résumé, holds mock interviews, and hosts potential employers, among other activities.

The UCARE program provides stipends for more than 400 students each year to participate in one-on-one research with a professor.

A junior says Nebraska students' "social etiquette and values are high, embodying 'Nebraska Nice,'" adding, "The political climate is more liberal than the state as a whole." Seventy-three percent of undergraduates hail from in state, and 5 percent come from abroad. Asian Americans make up 4 percent of the student body, Black students 3 percent, Hispanics/Latinos 8 percent, and multiracial students 3 percent. Many students say diversity—or the lack

"Social etiquette and values are high, embodying 'Nebraska Nice.'"

thereof—is an issue, but one notes, "I feel like my institution has really made an effort to expand diversity." Merit scholarships are available, with an average award of $7,900, in addition to more than 500 athletic scholarships in 19 sports.

Thirty-eight percent of students live in the university's single-sex or co-ed residence halls, and there's usually no trouble getting a room. "Most of the dorms are up-to-date and are pretty sizable, but there are a few that are smaller," explains a science education major. "There are options, however, for suite-style dorms that are available to everyone, including freshmen." Freshmen must live on campus, and many students move off campus after their sophomore year. Students praise the 28 living/learning communities offered for first-years with common academic interests who live and take classes together. "I was a member of a learning community my freshman year, and it helped make the campus seem smaller and less intimidating," recalls a nutrition and dietetics major. Dining facilities "always have a wide variety of food selections." As for security, a junior says, the campus feels safe and "the university does trainings all the time about sexual assault."

Students praise the 28 living/learning communities offered for first-years with common academic interests who live and take classes together.

"A lot of the social life starts on campus but then moves off," says a communication studies major. "You meet people on your floor or in a club, and then you hang out and go out off campus." Fraternity and house parties, 500-plus student organizations, concerts and theater performances, the movies, eating out, visiting coffee shops and bars, and road trips to Omaha or Kansas City are just some of the activities that keep students busy. For

"Lincoln is a great college town, especially during football season!"

many, the fall semester revolves around football weekends and postseason bowl games. Fraternities draw 21 percent of the men, and sororities attract 26 percent of the women. They offer both social events and a chance to get involved in the Lincoln community. Homecoming, Greek Week, the spring concert, and the Big Event (a major community service occasion) are among the most anticipated campus events.

"Lincoln is a great college town, especially during football season!" exclaims one business administration major. Another student points out that the "thirty bars within a two-minute walk of campus" are appreciated by those of age, given the school's dry campus. Town/gown relations are good and "the community is always eager for students to return in the fall," according to one premed student. Pachyderm enthusiasts will be delighted by the Nebraska Museum of Natural History's outstanding collection of prehistoric elephant skeletons. Beyond the town's sidewalks are miles of flat trails and plains, ideal for biking and cross-country skiing.

The Cornhuskers have a reputation as a Big Ten powerhouse in a number of sports. Women's bowling is a recent national champion, while baseball and softball have brought home conference titles. Men's and women's hoopsters frolic in the 15,500-seat Pinnacle Bank Arena. The annual Black Friday bowl game against the University of Iowa is shaping up to be quite the football rivalry. And who hasn't heard of the classy Nebraska football fans and their hardworking mascot Herbie Husker? "Lincoln, Nebraska, is a very special place to be on game day," boasts a junior. "Win or lose, the fans are always there." Intramural sports are popular too, with flag football and basketball drawing the most participants; more competitive students can choose from 38 club sports.

At Nebraska, future agricultural experts mingle with techno whizzes, while teachers in training brush elbows with advertising mavens. Whether studying overseas, immersing themselves in internships, launching start-ups, or going wild on Saturday afternoons, students here know how to make the most of their time. Cheers one happy Husker, "UNL is rooted in tradition, kindness, and Husker pride!"

Overlaps

University of Kansas, Iowa State, University of Minnesota, University of Iowa, University of Missouri, University of Nebraska Omaha, University of Nebraska at Kearney, Creighton

If You Apply To ›

Nebraska: Rolling admissions. SATs or ACTs: optional. Accepts the Common Application.

New College of Florida

5800 Bay Shore Road, Sarasota, FL 34243

Note to readers: As this edition of the *Fiske Guide* goes to press, New College of Florida, one of the most respected and innovative institutions in U.S. higher education, is facing an existential crisis. The governor of Florida is moving to reshape this public "honors college" in the image of a private Christian college that would, among other things, abolish diversity, equity, and inclusion efforts and impose a new core curriculum reflecting right-wing political and social principles. Caveat emptor.

Website: www.ncf.edu
Location: Small City
Public
Total Enrollment: 642
Undergraduates: 615
Male/Female: 32/68
Financial Aid: 97%
Pell Grant: 28%
Expense: Pub $
Student Loans: 37%
Average Debt: $

The mere existence of New College of Florida is proof that it's possible to find success by marching to your own drummer. This school has done away with grades and GPAs, and the laid-back student body and rigorous academic program "proves to students that learning can be a self-directed, fun, and productive experience," a sophomore says. But New College is not stopping there: the school plans to bolster student scholarships, enhance student life with new facilities, and double its enrollment by 2028. It's just one more move this fast-rising college is making in pursuit of a national reputation.

New College began in 1960 as an alternative private college for academically talented students, but when inflation threatened its existence in the mid-1970s, it offered its campus to the University of South Florida. In 2001, it became a freestanding unit of the state university system and was designated as the honors college for the state of Florida. New College's 110-acre campus is adjacent to Sarasota Bay and consists of historic mansions from the former estate of circus magnate Charles Ringling, abutting modern dorms designed by I. M. Pei. The central quad is filled with palm trees, and sunsets over the bay are spectacular.

All undergraduates must complete at least ten courses in the Chart Your Course curriculum, including classes in humanities, social sciences, natural sciences, math, writing, civic literacy, and diverse perspectives. Students have a great deal of flexibility to choose courses that focus on specific skills that they're interested in developing, ranging from problem-solving and ethical reasoning to teamwork and intercultural competence. The academic calendar is organized around two 14-week semesters separated by a monthlong January Interterm, during which students devise and carry out their own research, conduct group projects, or pursue short-term internships. Each semester, students work out a "contract" with their advisor and reflect on their progress. They also receive narrative performance evaluations instead of grades. The seven semester-long contracts and three independent study projects lead to an area of concentration, capped by a senior thesis or project that students must defend in an oral examination—excellent preparation for the majority of students who eventually go on to graduate or professional school.

> "[New College proves that] learning can be a self-directed, fun, and productive experience."

New College doesn't offer the specialized courses of a large university, but there's still plenty to choose from across the academic spectrum. Anthropology, psychology, biology, and computer science win raves, and many students also gravitate to environmental studies, marine biology, and economics. Academic programs are constantly changing to best suit student needs, and new offerings include areas of concentration in statistics, creative writing, and urban studies. The library makes up for its small size—fewer than 300,000 volumes—with a language lab, digital collections, and an interlibrary loan program with the entire state university system of Florida. "For a small college with limited resources, we have an incredibly thought-provoking and challenging curriculum," says one student. A dual-degree program in engineering with the University of Florida enables students to earn both a bachelor's and a master's degree in five years. In addition, the Cross-College Alliance expands students' options by allowing them to take courses at any of the four other institutions of higher education in Sarasota.

Courses are rigorous, but the focus on individual development and the lack of grades negate any competitive airs, and a philosophy and religion major says the academic climate is "open, intimate, and encouraging." Graduate students and teaching assistants don't lead classes here, and 92 percent of classes have fewer than 20 students. A psychology major says, "Professors will push you out of your comfort zone but be there to support you the whole time." The shape of any student's program depends heavily on the outlook of his or her faculty advisor, and students say advising—both academic and career—is readily available. All disciplines provide the opportunity for original research; the college's Pritzker Marine Biology Research Center is a highlight,

> "Professors will push you out of your comfort zone but be there to support you the whole time."

boasting a 12,000-gallon research tank and other facilities for research on aquatic ecosystems. Students may also conduct field research around the globe. Thirteen percent of students study abroad in programs offered in roughly 50 countries.

In keeping with the revolution theme, students on this relatively cosmopolitan campus tend to be, in the words of one sophomore, "barefoot hippies"—creative liberal types with '60s nuances and social habits. "New College does not produce cookie-cutter graduates," asserts a senior. "We are intellects, activists, and sometimes a little self-righteous." Students rally around issues that run the gamut from women's and

(continued)

Applicants: 1,650
Accepted: 74%
Enrolled: 13%
Grad in 6 Years: 66%
Returning Freshmen: 79%
Academics: ✐ ✐ ✐ ✐
Social: ☎ ☎ ☎
Q of L: ★ ★ ★
Admissions: (941) 487-5000
Email Address: admissions@ncf.edu

Strong Programs:
Anthropology
Psychology
Biology
Computer Science
Environmental Studies
Marine Biology
Economics

Each semester, students work out a "contract" with their advisor, reflect on their progress, and receive narrative performance evaluations.

LGBTQIA+ rights to food justice and commercialism. Hispanics/Latinos account for 18 percent of the student body, Asian Americans 4 percent, Black students 4 percent, and multiracial students 5 percent; another 2 percent come from foreign countries. Seventy-nine percent of undergrads hail from Florida, although the college is attempting to attract more out-of-state students by offering them automatic scholarships ranging from $44,000 to $80,000 over four years, depending on academic standing. All admitted Florida residents are guaranteed automatic scholarships too, ranging from $4,000 to $24,000 over four years. The college covers full tuition and fees for in-state and out-of-state students who qualify for Pell Grants. There are no athletic awards.

Eighty-one percent of students live in campus housing; students wishing to live off campus must apply for permission. The newest residence halls, built to LEED environmental standards, feature lodge and apartment-style accommodations. Thirty-nine percent of students join various living/learning communities, with themes like Global Village, Health and Wellness, and Outdoor Adventure. Students report that campus dining options are satisfactory, even for the school's sizable vegan population. Students feel secure on campus, and a political science major says, "We have a very sex-positive campus that encourages education on how to recognize and prevent sexual assault."

> "We are intellects, activists, and sometimes a little self-righteous."

The campus social scene, sans Greek life, is laid-back and "can range from dance parties, fashion shows, and game nights to listening to NPR under the stars in Palm Court," says a sophomore. Each semester, students vote on themes for "walls"—small, school-sanctioned parties held every weekend, often with quirky themes, like the Bob Ross wall, where students attempt to follow along with videos of the public television artist painting. A multitude of student organizations also keep students busy, from the New College Student Alliance (the student government) to "Cloud Watching Club (it is what it sounds like)," says a student, adding, "It's a small campus, so it's easy to become involved in new activities." The COUPs (Center of the Universe Parties) are "blow-out-of-proportion" social gatherings that occur during Halloween, Valentine's Day, and graduation. Students also flock to Dance Collective performances at the end of each semester and Queer Pride Week, in which students host events centered on LGBTQIA+ history, awareness, and pride.

Sarasota offers little more than "beaches and old people," according to one sophomore, although 24 percent of students get involved in volunteer work through more than 30 local community organizations. The Ringling Museum of Art and the Asolo State Theater adjoin the campus, and many New College instrumentalists perform with the Sarasota Orchestra, the city's professionally led symphony orchestra. The open road to Tampa, Gainesville, Key West, Orlando, New Orleans, Atlanta, and even Washington, D.C. ("to protest stuff"), beckons when Sarasota becomes too quiet.

> "The beaches are gorgeous—white sand and blue water."

New College is definitely no haven for jocks; it fields no varsity teams, although its co-ed sailing team is nationally competitive. Roughly 8 percent of students take advantage of club sports, such as rowing, swimming, tennis, and powerlifting. The nearby ocean is a major draw. "The beaches are gorgeous—white sand and blue water," says a student.

Without a Greek scene, grades, or massive football games, New College of Florida is definitely not your typical Southern institution. But the eccentricity doesn't impede students' academic motivation; in fact, it encourages an atmosphere that celebrates learning for the sake of curiosity, persistence, and thoughtfulness—whether the subject at hand is biology, bread baking, psychology, or origami. Major growth is on the way, growth the administration hopes will boost New College's national profile while at the same time opening up even more opportunities for students to succeed in their own way.

The college covers full tuition and fees for in-state and out-of-state students who qualify for Pell Grants.

"Walls" are small, school-sanctioned parties held every weekend, often with quirky themes, like the Bob Ross wall.

Overlaps

Reed, Prescott, Evergreen State, Dickinson, College of the Atlantic, St. Mary's College of Maryland, University of Minnesota Morris, University of South Florida

If You Apply To ›

New College: Early action, rolling admissions. SATs or ACTs: required. Accepts the Common Application with supplement.

University of New Hampshire

Grant House, 3 Garrison Avenue, Durham, NH 03824

UNH is a public university that looks and feels like a private college, and for out-of-staters, its cost of attendance hits the pocketbook with similar force. Draws more than half of its students from outside New Hampshire, with little racial or ethnic diversity. Well known for engineering, space science, and life science programs—especially marine biology—and its business school is nationally ranked. UNH's focus is sharply on undergrads.

Students at the University of New Hampshire know how to get their hands dirty, and this solid public institution provides them with countless opportunities to do just that. Founded as a land grant college in 1866, UNH's research mission has grown dramatically in recent years, yet the university remains a moderate-sized institution that emphasizes undergraduate instruction. Unlike many large research universities, faculty members teach all students, including first-years, and generally value teaching as much as they do their research. A love of the outdoors is a must, as is the ability to withstand long, cold winters. As they say around here, "Every day is a great day to be a Wildcat!"

The university's wide-open, grassy Durham campus is home to a mix of modern facilities and ivy-covered brick buildings. The sprawling lawns are surrounded by nearly 3,000 acres of farms, fields, and woods. During the past few years, UNH has invested in large-scale construction projects, including new residence halls, a physics building, and a veterinary diagnostic lab, as well as expansions of multiple academic buildings. An $86 million expansion and renovation of the bioscience building is slated for completion in late 2023.

The university's core curriculum, the Discovery Program, includes general education requirements that apply across the board and mandate coursework in biological science; physical science; historical perspectives; world cultures; social science; fine and performing arts; humanities; and environment, technology, and society. First-year writing is also mandatory as part of a four-course writing intensive requirement, as is a class in quantitative reasoning. All first-years take an Inquiry course involving an experiential learning component, and all seniors complete a capstone experience.

> **"Many [professors] participate in research and include students as research assistants."**

Interdisciplinary programs enhance UNH's emphasis on traditional academic offerings. A dual major allows students to pair a degree in sustainability with any other major, and minors range from leadership to green real estate to microbrewing. Engineering and business are among the most respected programs. The Paul College of Business and Economics is nationally ranked, offering a spate of majors and boasting one of the first student-run angel investment funds. Students entering Paul College participate in the First-Year Innovation and Research Experience, working in teams to develop business plans with guidance from peer advisors and alumni mentors. The marine, estuarine, and freshwater biology major is considered stellar, enhanced by UNH's proximity to the ocean and a brackish bay. Ocean engineering,

Website: www.unh.edu
Location: Small Town
Public
Total Enrollment: 12,617
Undergraduates: 11,201
Male/Female: 43/57
Financial Aid: 86%
Pell Grant: 17%
Expense: Pub $ $ $ $
Student Loans: 76%
Average Debt: $ $ $ $
Applicants: 20,150
Accepted: 87%
Enrolled: 16%
Grad in 6 Years: 77%
Returning Freshmen: 87%
Academics: ✎ ✎ ✎
Social: 🎭 🎭 🎭 🎭
Q of L: ★ ★ ★ ★ ★
Admissions: (603) 862-1360
Email Address: admissions@unh.edu

Strong Programs:
Engineering
Business Administration
Sustainability
Marine, Estuarine, and
    Freshwater Biology
Nursing
Homeland Security
Psychology
Communication

nursing, bioengineering, homeland security, and a preveterinary advising program are also strengths. The most popular majors are business administration, psychology, mechanical engineering, and communication.

Students agree that the level of academic intensity varies by school and college, but the atmosphere is always busy. "On a normal day, I see students studying and working everywhere around campus, indoors and outdoors (when the weather permits)," says a business administration major. Classes are relatively small, with just 16 percent enrolling 50 or more students, and teaching assistants only facilitate discussion sections or labs. "We have world-class professors, many of whom participate in research and include students as research assistants," says a senior, and a junior notes that professors are accessible and "easy to speak to."

Research experience is a key emphasis at UNH, and 34 percent of undergraduates get involved with research projects before they graduate. The Hamel Center for Undergraduate Research provides more than 100 research awards each year for students to work closely with faculty on original projects. It also publishes *Inquiry*, UNH's online undergraduate research journal, and hosts the Undergraduate Research Conference, which showcases the scholarly work of more than 1,800 students annually. Additional opportunities include conducting research on NASA partner projects or at the Isle of Shoals Marine Laboratory, which provides an offshore research setting six miles off the coast. Twenty-one percent of students broaden their horizons through more than 250 approved study abroad and exchange programs. The Semester in the City internship program sends civic-minded students to live together and work within social change organizations in Boston. And for the especially motivated, the invitation-only University Honors Program features small classes, personal mentoring, and optional honors-themed housing.

> "U Day is a great way to [get involved early on]."

While UNH is New Hampshire's flagship public institution, it has long been popular with out-of-staters, who make up 53 percent of its undergraduates; international students add another 1 percent. As for racial and ethnic diversity, UNH has a long way to go. Black students account for just 1 percent of the student population, Asian Americans 3 percent, Hispanics/Latinos 4 percent, and multiracial students 2 percent. "We have diversity coalitions for many minorities to try and enhance the cultural diversity of campus," reports a psychology major. Politically, students are "engaged and vocal," says a senior. UNH's published tuition and fees, both in-state and out-of-state, are among the highest of any flagship university in the country. To ease the pain, the university offers hundreds of merit scholarships, averaging $7,000, and 215 awards are available for gifted athletes. The Granite Guarantee program gives free tuition to qualifying New Hampshire residents from low-income families.

Fifty-three percent of Wildcats live in the school's co-ed residence halls; all undergrads are guaranteed housing, and accommodations are said to be generally comfortable. Most upperclassmen live off campus or in the two on-campus apartment complexes. More than a dozen themed living areas are available and are an increasingly popular option. Campus dining receives rave reviews, and students also give high ratings to campus safety. UNH is a national leader in efforts to prevent sexual assault on campus. In addition to its student-praised training programs and support services, UNH established the Prevention Innovations Research Center to develop evidence-based prevention strategies and policies.

UNH offers more than 250 student organizations covering just about any interest. "Get involved early on, as that will help you become acclimated to the campus," advises a social work and women's studies major. "U Day is a great way to do that." Service organizations are popular, and 52 percent of students get involved with

---

First-year students entering Paul College work in teams to develop business plans with guidance from peer advisors and alumni mentors.

Students celebrate the first Wildcats goal of each ice hockey game by throwing a large fish onto the ice.

community service activities. The Campus Activities Board organizes weekend social events including dances, movies, bingo, and gatherings at local coffeehouses, and favorite annual events include homecoming and concerts in the fall and spring. Greek groups claim 14 percent of the men and 12 percent of the women. The party culture at UNH is lively, but Greek parties are subject to the university's no-tolerance alcohol policy, which evicts underage students caught with alcohol more than once from on-campus housing.

Less than a five-minute walk from campus is the beautiful little town of Durham, which caters to the student clientele. Its Main Street is lined with restaurants and coffeehouses, a grocery store, an ice-cream parlor, and a few bars, which have been divided into separate sections (for legal consumers of alcohol and everyone else). The free Wildcat Transit bus system takes students to cities throughout the state, and the on-campus Amtrak station makes weekend escapes to Boston and Portland, Maine, easy—if students can find time off. (The school's nickname is the University of No Holidays, since an exceptionally generous winter break limits the number of days off during other seasons.)

> "You really have the chance to make your experience here whatever you want it to be."

The White Mountains are popular with outdoor enthusiasts, and late nights at L.L. Bean have also become commonplace. Every four years, New Hampshire takes the spotlight when the state holds the nation's earliest presidential primary, making UNH a frequent destination for political candidates.

UNH has 20 Division I athletic teams, of which ice hockey is a fan favorite. Students celebrate the first Wildcats goal of each game by throwing a large fish onto the ice, and during games against its rival, the University of Maine, students wear white to "white out" the stadium. Men's soccer and women's swimming and diving are recent America East conference champions, and other solid teams include football and men's and women's skiing. Club and intramural sports enlist 26 percent of the student body. Broomball—played with brooms, balls, and sneakers on the ice—is very popular, as are activities organized by the Outing Club, including skiing, camping, fishing, and hiking. The Northeast Passage program offers adaptive recreation programs for students and community members with disabilities.

New Hampshire's only major public university offers a huge variety of programs in a beautiful natural setting. That's one reason it attracts so many students from out of state. Another reason, a junior says, is that between smaller class sizes, community-oriented dorms, and welcoming student organizations, "You will feel like you're part of a very tight-knit community, even though there are 11,000 undergrads on campus, and you really have the chance to make your experience here whatever you want it to be."

The Northeast Passage program offers adaptive recreation programs for students and community members with disabilities.

Overlaps

University of Maine, University of Rhode Island, University of Vermont, UMass Amherst, UConn, Plymouth State, UMass Lowell, Merrimack

If You Apply To ›

New Hampshire: Early action, regular decision. SATs or ACTs: optional. Accepts the Common Application. Additional materials required for applicants to music, theatre, and studio art programs.

A public liberal arts institution in the mold of UNC Asheville or William & Mary. Also offers business, education, and engineering. With 95 percent of the students homegrown Garden Staters, TCNJ enjoys little draw beyond Jersey. On the other hand, it is now the state's second most selective institution, after a certain super-selective school up the road in Princeton. A smaller, more personal alternative to Rutgers.

Website: www.tcnj.edu
Location: Suburban
Public
Total Enrollment: 6,929
Undergraduates: 6,693
Male/Female: 43/57
Financial Aid: 47%
Pell Grant: 18%
Expense: Pub $ $ $ $
Student Loans: 62%
Average Debt: $ $ $ $
Applicants: 10,392
Accepted: 62%
Enrolled: 23%
Grad in 6 Years: 87%
Returning Freshmen: 92%
Academics: ✍ ✍ ✍ ✍
Social: ☎ ☎ ☎
Q of L: ★ ★ ★
Admissions: (609) 771-2131
Email Address: tcnjinfo@tcnj.edu

Strong Programs:
Elementary Education
Special Education
Business Administration
Finance
Psychology
Biology
Marketing
Nursing

The College of New Jersey is an up-and-coming public institution with special focus on undergraduates, an emphasis more commonly found at private schools. TCNJ offers professors focused on teaching and the encouragement of undergraduate research, as well as a campus reminiscent of that of nearby Princeton University—without the Ivy League price tag. Founded in 1855 as a teachers' college, it strives to provide students with opportunities in a host of other fields. The small size makes for closeness among students and faculty. Says one student, "TCNJ is really big on the 'community' feel."

TCNJ is set on 289 wooded and landscaped acres in suburban Ewing Township, six miles from Trenton. The picturesque Georgian colonial architecture centers on Quimby's Prairie, surrounded by the original academic buildings of the 1930s. A flock of Canada geese makes its home in one of the two campus lakes. Campus Town, a 12-acre, $120 million complex adjacent to the campus, features 612 apartments for upperclassmen, a campus gym, and retail shops and restaurants. The college recently completed the STEM Complex, a $96 million project that added the 89,000-square-foot STEM Building and renovated existing science and engineering facilities.

Liberal Learning, TCNJ's general education program, requires coursework centered on three fundamental areas: intellectual and scholarly growth, broad areas of human inquiry, and civic responsibility. Freshmen participate in several programs to prepare them for college life and academics, including a summer reading program, welcome week, and a First Seminar course, in which they take a small seminar on a topic outside of their intended major and spend their first year living with their classmates in the same residence hall. Freshmen must also perform at least eight hours of community service. All seniors complete a capstone requirement that varies by major.

"TCNJ is really big on the 'community' feel."

Consistent with the school's origins as a teachers' college, education programs are well regarded; elementary and special education are particular favorites among students. Early childhood and elementary education majors may pursue the urban education option, which prepares them to teach in urban schools and allows them to complete both a bachelor's and a master's degree in five years. The business school is strong, as are the natural sciences. Other popular majors include finance, psychology, biology, marketing, and nursing. Students in the engineering school can choose from eight majors, ranging from biomedical engineering to integrative STEM education. The college also offers a seven-year B.S./M.D. degree program with Rutgers New Jersey Medical School and a seven-year B.S./O.D. degree with SUNY College of Optometry.

Academically, TCNJ is competitive and getting more so. "The academic climate is somewhat intense," confides a sophomore. "Some students and professors try to downplay the competitive nature, but overall it's pretty driven." An honors program is available for those who wish to challenge themselves with even more rigorous academics. Forty-two percent of undergraduate classes have fewer than 20 students. The college has no teaching assistants, and faculty members generally get high marks, though quality is said to vary by department. "My professors are very passionate about their work and field of study," says a psychology major. Seventy-three percent of undergrads complete internships before they graduate. TCNJ offers foreign study programs in more than 15 countries, including South Africa, the Czech Republic, and Chile, and preapproved partner programs give students access to dozens of other countries around the globe. Twenty-two percent of students get their passports stamped to study, intern, or volunteer overseas. As part of the MUSE (Mentored Undergraduate Summer Experience) program, nearly 100 students spend eight weeks assisting faculty mentors with research and creative projects.

Freshmen take a First Seminar course, a small seminar on a topic outside of their intended major.

The typical TCNJ student is "overly book smart," according to one junior. The school has no cap on out-of-state admissions, but only 5 percent of TCNJ's students are non-Jerseyans, including the less than 1 percent who are international. The college has aggressively recruited students of color, and today, Black students account for 6 percent of undergraduates, Hispanics/Latinos 17 percent, Asian Americans 11 percent, and multiracial students 2 percent. "If

"If you don't leave this school very well educated in political correctness, then you were obviously unconscious."

you don't leave this school very well educated in political correctness, then you were obviously unconscious," says a marketing major, who praises the school for its diversity. Merit scholarships averaging $4,800 are available to qualified students. The Educational Opportunity Fund Promise Award covers full tuition and other expenses and provides specialized academic support services for qualifying New Jersey residents from disadvantaged backgrounds.

Dorm housing is only guaranteed for freshmen and sophomores; overall, 46 percent of students live on campus. "Most of the dorms are really nice," says a student, "but a few are older and outdated." Freshmen hang their hats in one of seven residence halls; after that, they can enter the lottery to secure spots in traditional residence halls, townhouses, or the Campus Town apartments. Many upperclassmen opt for nearby off-campus apartment complexes, which are plentiful. For meals, students head to 10 dining locations. The Anti-Violence Initiatives office encompasses training, counseling, and peer education efforts aimed at preventing sexual assault on campus.

As part of the MUSE program, nearly 100 students spend eight weeks assisting faculty mentors with research and creative projects.

Although suburban Ewing (population 37,000) doesn't really cater to students, funky New Hope, Pennsylvania, and preppy Princeton, New Jersey, are nearby; restaurants, bars, movie theaters—and, this being New Jersey, many malls—are within a short drive. Road trips to Philadelphia and New York, each about an hour away and accessible by train, are also highly recommended. Alcohol policies are strictly enforced; students 21 and over can enjoy adult beverages at the campus restaurant, Traditions, which also features a stage area for performances. Twenty-one percent of the men and 21 percent of the women belong to fraternities and sororities, which provide many of the off-campus parties. Campus programming includes dances, concerts, and movies. TCNJers look forward to several annual events, including homecoming, a Family Fest Day, and—the springtime favorite—Senior Week.

The College of New Jersey's 21 varsity teams (the Lions) are the pride of the New Jersey Athletic Conference and make frequent appearances in national Division III tournaments. Men's and women's cross-country and women's track and field, lacrosse, and softball have all taken home recent conference titles. Students rally around the football and basketball squads, especially when archrival Rowan comes to town. The college also offers 14 intramural and 24 club sport programs.

The College of New Jersey is one of the few public liberal arts colleges with reasonable tuition and a location that offers a relaxed suburban haven within shouting

Overlaps

**Villanova,
St. Joseph's,
Ramapo College
of New Jersey,
SUNY–Geneseo,
Christopher
Newport,
Rutgers, Rowan,
William & Mary**

distance of big-city opportunities. Not just for teachers anymore, TCNJ prides itself on the personal attention it devotes to students craving both professional preparation and a well-rounded education.

If You Apply To ›

TCNJ: Early decision I and II, regular decision. Accepts the Common Application. Art applicants must submit portfolio. Music applicants must audition. Please consult TCNJ's website for the most up-to-date information regarding standardized test requirements.

New Jersey Institute of Technology

University Heights, Newark, NJ 07102

One of the few public polytechnic universities in the Northeast. Within New Jersey, NJIT occupies a middle ground between the behemoth Rutgers and smallish Stevens Institute, and 90 percent of undergrads are state residents. Primarily offers engineering, computing, architecture, design, and business, and co-op option is popular. At three to one, NJIT's gender ratio is skewed toward males.

Website: www.njit.edu
Location: City Center
Public
Total Enrollment: 8,845
Undergraduates: 7,287
Male/Female: 75/25
Financial Aid: 77%
Pell Grant: 34%
Expense: Pub $ $ $ $
Student Loans: 54%
Average Debt: $ $ $
Applicants: 11,578
Accepted: 69%
Enrolled: 17%
Grad in 6 Years: 74%
Returning Freshmen: 88%
Academics: ✎ ✎ ✎
Social: ☎
Q of L: ★ ★
Admissions: (973) 596-3300
Email Address: admissions@njit.edu

Strong Programs:
Computer Science
Mechanical Engineering
Information Technology
Civil Engineering
Business

The New Jersey Institute of Technology provides a solid STEM education that prepares students for a future in an ever-changing global workplace. NJIT's challenging programs emphasize education, research, service, and (not surprisingly) economic development. The combination is enticing—as is the price tag, relative to the top-tier private technical institutes that are some of NJIT's closest competitors.

Founded in 1881 by local industrialists in what was then a thriving industrial center, NJIT's urban 48-acre campus is dotted with more than 40 buildings of diverse architectural styles, ranging from Elizabethan Gothic to contemporary design. More recent additions include the $110 million Wellness and Events Center and the 10,000-square-foot Makerspace, which gives students hands-on design and manufacturing experience with top-of-the-line tools and technology. Some of New Jersey's greatest cultural institutions are just blocks away, including the Newark Museum, Symphony Hall, and the New Jersey Performing Arts Center.

To graduate, students must fulfill general education requirements in areas ranging from college writing and cultural literacy to computer science and math. All freshmen take First Year Seminar, a course that introduces them to university life, and all seniors complete a capstone seminar. NJIT is composed of five schools and colleges plus the Dorman Honors College, offering more than 50 undergraduate majors. Computer science, mechanical engineering, information technology, and civil engineering are the most popular majors. Students earning their B.S. in business choose from five concentrations, from marketing to innovation and entrepreneurship. NJIT offers the only undergraduate forensic science program in the state, as well as prehealth and prelaw programs with an emphasis on technology. New majors are available in financial technology, data science, and materials engineering.

> **"Students here are certainly intelligent and come off as nerds."**

While some say the atmosphere can be low-pressure in certain fields, most agree that the workload across the board is demanding. Thirty percent of classes have fewer than 20 students; most don't exceed 40. Professors are given average to high marks. One computer science major offers this assessment: "I would say 10 percent of the professors I would never want to take again, 70 percent were fine, and 20 percent were incredible." Since most have worked in their industry, they can provide job information and networking opportunities. Academic advising isn't always as helpful as it could be, says a sophomore, "especially for transfer students," but career services receive positive reviews.

(continued)

Forensic Science
Architecture
Design

Perhaps NJIT's most-favored academic option is the co-op program, which enables students to earn course credits outside of the classroom while gaining paid work experience at tech companies and other organizations. Top freshman applicants are offered a spot in the Honors College, and they can stay as long as they keep their grades up; about 700 undergraduates in all majors are enrolled. Perks include a dedicated honors dorm, research opportunities, and acceptance into the accelerated premed and other prehealth programs. Study abroad is an option, but with their packed schedules, few students find time for it. In the midst of this heavily male-dominated campus, the Murray Center for Women in Technology offers scholarships, networking opportunities, and resources to help female students and faculty alike advance in their chosen fields.

NJIT offers the only undergraduate forensic science program in the state.

As New Jersey's comprehensive technological public university, NJIT attracts a wide range of students with different interests. But a few things bring them together, says a digital design major: "We are friendly and diverse, and most of us love technology and video games." In-state residents represent 90 percent of the undergraduate student body, and international students add 6 percent. Nine percent of undergrads are Black, 22 percent are Hispanic/Latino, 23 percent are Asian American, and 3 percent are multiracial. One student praises the Educational Opportunity Program, saying, "If it weren't for them, I would not be here. They make it easy to be a minority." Thirty-four percent of incoming freshmen receive Pell Grants. The university awards merit scholarships averaging $15,100 to qualified students, and roughly 120 athletic scholarships are also available.

"Ten percent of the professors I would never want to take again…and 20 percent were incredible."

About 700 undergrads in all majors enroll in the Honors College; perks include a dedicated honors dorm and research opportunities.

NJIT's five residence halls accommodate 21 percent of the students. "Housing is pretty standard," reports a student. "You have a choice of suite-style or communal-style as a freshman." Upperclassmen move into on-campus fraternity or sorority houses or nearby off-campus apartments. Meals in Highlander Commons, the main dining hall, receive average reviews. Because of its urban location, safety is always a consideration at NJIT, but "public safety officers are always around," says an electrical engineering major. A sophomore adds, "The school supports speaking up about sexual assault," and provides ample resources for those who need them.

Newark is hardly a college town, yet it is undergoing a gradual urban renaissance, and several good restaurants are within walking distance. "Newark has something of a social scene during the day; at night, a trip to Jersey City or New York City is usually a better bet," explains a senior. Forty percent of students regularly volunteer in the community. On campus, 5 percent of the men and 5 percent of the women join the Greek system. HackNJIT, a 24-hour hackathon, is always well attended, and the Student Activities Council plans events like laser tag, arcade days, and movie nights. One of the best annual campus events is Spring Fest, which features bands, intramural games, carnival rides, and a semiformal. Diwali, the Indian festival of lights, and Chinese New Year also give undergrads pause to party. Another option is the beach, an hour away. Most students agree that the administration's strict alcohol policies are effective.

Overlaps

Rensselaer, Case Western Reserve, Virginia Tech, Colorado School of Mines, Stevens Institute of Technology, Rutgers, Rowan, College of New Jersey

NJIT students take pride in their athletic prowess, and the school is a member of the Division I America East Conference, competing mainly against Northeastern schools like SUNY–Stony Brook and University of Maryland, Baltimore County. Among NJIT's 17 varsity Highlanders teams, men's and women's basketball and tennis, men's soccer, and baseball are some of the most competitive. Soccer, basketball, and racquetball are the favorites when it comes to intramurals, and ice hockey, ultimate Frisbee, and bowling are some of the most active club teams.

"Students here are certainly intelligent and come off as nerds, but everyone has their own niche," says a biomedical engineering student. NJIT students choose their school because they want a top-notch technological education without the topflight price tag. Academics are the priority here; if the social life is less than electrifying, students don't mind. After all, they know highly skilled jobs will beckon after graduation. Getting through is a challenge, but there's ample compensation available for NJIT alums in the technologically dependent workplaces of today—and tomorrow.

If You Apply To ›

NJIT: Early action I and II, rolling admissions. Accepts the Common Application. College of Architecture and Design applicants must submit portfolio of creative work. Please consult NJIT's website for the most up-to-date information regarding standardized test requirements.

University of New Mexico

Albuquerque, NM 87131

UNM gives new meaning to cultural diversity. Studies related to Hispanic and Native cultures are strong, and in a land of picture-perfect sunsets, photography is a big deal. Even the mascot—Lobos—is Spanish. Technical programs are fueled by government labs in Albuquerque and Los Alamos, while the business school produces an outsized percentage of New Mexico's commercial elite.

Website: www.unm.edu
Location: City Center
Public
Total Enrollment: 14,515
Undergraduates: 11,379
Male/Female: 42/58
Financial Aid: 74%
Pell Grant: 42%
Expense: Pub $
Student Loans: 43%
Average Debt: $
Applicants: 14,026
Accepted: 65%
Enrolled: 33%
Grad in 6 Years: 51%
Returning Freshmen: 68%
Academics: ✐ ✐ ✐
Social: ☎ ☎ ☎
Q of L: ★ ★ ★
Admissions: (505) 277-8900
Email Address: unmlobos@
unm.edu

The University of New Mexico's heritage stretches back to 1889 when New Mexico wasn't even a state, and the university's strengths are still rooted in the rich history of the American Southwest. New Mexico excels in areas such as Latin American and Southwest studies. Lest you think it is a typical state school, consider that many students are commuters or of nontraditional age. UNM also boasts the state's only law, medical, and architecture and urban planning schools.

Seated at the foot of the gorgeous Sandia Mountains in the lap of Albuquerque, the beautifully landscaped campus sports both Spanish and Pueblo Indian architectural influences, with lots of patios and balconies. The duck pond is a favorite spot for sunbathing, and the mountains, which rise majestically to the east, are visible from virtually any point on campus. Newer facilities include the $25 million McKinnon Center for Management.

UNM offers more than 4,000 courses in 12 colleges and schools, running the gamut from arts and sciences, education, and engineering to management, fine arts, and the allied health fields. Academic and general education requirements vary, but the core curriculum mandates courses in English, humanities, social and behavioral sciences, physical and natural sciences, math, fine arts, and a second language.

"[The academic climate is] very laid-back and depends on what field of study you are going into."

Those reluctant to specialize can spend a few semesters in the broad University College, which offers bachelor of liberal arts and bachelor of integrative studies degrees. The Honors College awards a bachelor of arts in interdisciplinary liberal arts. The Tamarind Institute, a nationally recognized center housed at UNM's

College of Fine Arts, offers training, study, and research in fine-art lithography. Anthropologists may explore one of New Mexico's many archaeological sites, and engineers may join in major solar-energy projects. Other solid programs include Native American studies, Chicana and Chicano studies, and Latin American studies. Students may also minor in Navajo language.

The academic climate is "very laid-back and depends on what field of study you are going into," according to a senior. Students are quick to help one another study, and competition for grades is the exception rather than the rule. Fifty-one percent of classes have fewer than 20 students. As for professors, "I would have to give them a B," says a student. "There have been some very good ones and some that were very knowledgeable but didn't know how to teach." Freshman Learning Communities and academic coaching help ease the transition from high school to the college environment. Many classes are offered in late afternoon and evening sessions, and about half of the student body takes advantage of these after-hours options. Study abroad programs around the world beckon to 18 percent of undergrads.

By virtue of its location, UNM gives new meaning to cultural diversity, even though the vast majority (87 percent) of students are state residents. High enrollment of students of color—50 percent Hispanic/Latino, 6 percent Native American, 4 percent Asian American, 3 percent Black, and 4 percent multiracial—reflects this cultural diversity. Two percent of undergraduates are from overseas. UNM hosts a number of centers and student groups, such as El Centro de la Raza and Nations at UNM, that support diversity and cultural activities. "Students here are pretty chill," says a journalism major. "We hang out and stuff, but for the most part we are focused on school." The state-funded New Mexico Opportunity Scholarship covers the full cost of tuition and

> **"People here are serious and accepting, which makes UNM a comfortable environment."**

required fees for all in-state residents, regardless of income. Merit and athletic scholarships are available as well, and 42 percent of freshmen qualify for Pell Grants.

UNM has traditionally been a commuter school (and parking is a perennial complaint), although first-year students coming from outside a 30-mile radius of campus are required to live in the residence halls. Currently, a scant 7 percent of students (including 21 percent of freshmen) live on campus. Students say they are happy with the variety of food available to them, and good lighting, an escort service, and police who patrol around the clock help them feel safe.

"Social life takes place both on and off campus," a junior says. Alcohol, though banned from UNM residence halls, is readily available, according to most students, especially at Greek parties. Just 3 percent of the men and 3 percent of the women join the Greek system. Other students find their fun off campus in Albuquerque's clubs and restaurants. For the more socially conscious, the university sponsors Spring Storm, an outing of roughly 1,000 students who volunteer around the city on a Saturday. Annual social events include Welcome Back Days in the fall and Nizhoni Days, a weeklong celebration of Native American culture. Each spring, the whole campus turns out for a four-day fiesta with food and live music.

Albuquerque—sometimes referred to as ABQ—is New Mexico's largest city (with 560,000 residents), and it offers a variety of cultural attractions, including the nation's largest hot air balloon festival, a growing artists' colony, and concert tours to charm the ears. Santa Fe is an hour away. Those with cars take advantage of the state's natural attractions: the Sandias, the Carlsbad Caverns, and superb skiing in Taos, as well as excellent hiking and camping opportunities. For the historically inclined, numerous Spanish and Native American ruins are within an easy drive.

The UNM Lobos (Spanish for "wolves") compete in the Division I Mountain West Conference, and the men's football and basketball squads usually draw crowds. The women's cross-country team is a regular contender for the national

(continued)

Strong Programs:
Latin American Studies
Native American Studies
Business
Studio Art
Anthropology
Engineering
Chicana and Chicano Studies
Navajo Language

The state-funded New Mexico Opportunity Scholarship covers the full cost of tuition and required fees for all in-state residents.

Annual social events include Nizhoni Days, a weeklong celebration of Native American culture.

Overlaps

Arizona State, CU Boulder, Eastern New Mexico, Highlands, New Mexico State, University of Texas at El Paso

title. Recreational and intramural sports are popular; students flock to flag football, volleyball, soccer, and basketball.

UNM offers a sun-drenched location that satisfies—precisely because its academic climate is as relaxed as the rolling desert dunes. "People here are serious and accepting," says a senior, "which makes UNM a comfortable environment."

If You Apply To ›

UNM: Rolling admissions. SATs or ACTs: optional. Does not accept the Common Application.

New York University

22 Washington Square, New York, NY 10012

From safety school to global brand, NYU's rise has been breathtaking. The siren song of Greenwich Village now extends to the Tandon School of Engineering in Brooklyn, degree-granting campuses in Abu Dhabi and Shanghai, and a dozen global academic centers around the world. Major draws include the renowned Tisch School of the Arts and the best undergraduate business school north of Penn.

With the world at its doorstep, New York University invites its student body to jump right in. Firmly planted in the heart of Greenwich Village, one of the most eclectic and energizing neighborhoods in New York City, NYU has set its sights on becoming the world's first truly global university. Its growing student body, burgeoning new facilities, and multiple opportunities for high-level internships and research projects have made it a top option for a rising number of students. "Our dorms are like city apartments, and our walk to class is on city sidewalks and across busy streets," says a business and political economy major. "Going to NYU prepares students to live and work in the real world."

It doesn't get more real world than the venue that NYU has called home since its founding in 1831. NYU has campuses and centers throughout the city but is primarily situated on Washington Square. Trendy shops, galleries, clubs, bars, and eateries crowd neighboring blocks; SoHo, Little Italy, and Chinatown are just blocks away. Academic buildings—both modern and historic—blend with 19th-century brick townhouses surrounding Washington Square Park (the closest thing NYU has to a quad). NYU's library is one of the largest open-stack facilities in the country, with millions of volumes. Kimmel Center for University Life houses meeting space for hundreds of student organizations, plus areas for the frequent recruitment fairs and lectures from national and international leaders. It also holds the Skirball Center for the Performing Arts' 860-seat theater, which is the largest performing arts facility south of 42nd Street. The brand-new, $1.2 billion Paulson Center is a massive, 735,000-square-foot multiuse facility on Mercer Street. Completed in spring 2023, the complex features classrooms, practice and performance spaces for the drama and music programs, a world-class sports center complete with a six-lane pool, housing for 400 freshmen and 42 faculty members, dining facilities, a Commons for meet-ups and studying, and more.

The city scene is central to the NYU experience. So, too, is the wide range of academic programs. Under the College Core Curriculum, freshmen and sophomores take courses including foreign language, expository writing, foundations of

> **"It's common for students to take on difficult courseloads, along with a job or internship."**

Website: www.nyu.edu
Location: City Center
Private
Total Enrollment: 49,397
Undergraduates: 27,645
Male/Female: 42/58
Financial Aid: 57%
Pell Grant: 18%
Expense: Pr $ $ $
Student Loans: 36%
Average Debt: $ $
Applicants: 95,517
Accepted: 13%
Enrolled: 49%
Grad in 6 Years: 87%
Returning Freshmen: 94%
Academics: ✑ ✑ ✑ ✑ ½
Social: ☎ ☎ ☎
Q of L: ★ ★ ★
Admissions: (212) 998-4500
Email Address: admissions@nyu.edu

Strong Programs:
Film and Television
Visual and Performing Arts
Business
Economics
Journalism

contemporary culture, and foundations of scientific inquiry. The language offerings go beyond the typical Spanish-French-German—among the choices are Arabic, Cantonese, Hindi, Modern Irish, Swahili, and Tagalog—and NYU operates a language exchange program with Columbia University as well. The Tisch School of the Arts trained such famed artists as Martin Scorsese, Spike Lee, Donald Glover, and Maggie Rogers, and current undergrads continue to win many national student filmmaker awards. Tisch also boasts excellent drama, dance, photography, and television departments, and it's not uncommon to see students who haven't yet finished B.F.A. degrees performing in Broadway shows.

(continued)

Politics
Global Liberal Studies
Nursing

Wall Street's future bull and bear wranglers hang out at the Stern School of Business, where they benefit from unique interdisciplinary majors such as business and political economy and business, technology, and entrepreneurship. The Leslie eLab also provides space for aspiring entrepreneurs.

"At NYU, studying away is not a matter of 'if,' but 'where.'"

Another favorite department among students (and the New York corporations who recruit them after graduation) is accounting, known for its high job-placement rate. In the College of Arts and Science, economics, English, journalism, history, politics, and global liberal studies win highest marks from students. The Tandon School of Engineering, the Steinhardt School, the Silver School of Social Work, the College of Nursing, and the School of Professional Studies offer a bevy of career-based programs, including engineering, education, media, nutrition, and real estate. Steinhardt's offerings in music, music theatre, and music business are notable. Across the university, the most popular majors are business, nursing, economics, and theatre. The Gallatin School of Individualized Study provides flexible schedules and freedom from requirements for those wishing to engage in independent study or develop their own programs. For those tempted to linger around the Village for more than four years, there's a seven-year dental program and several five-year bachelor's/master's programs.

The $1.2 billion Paulson Center is a massive multiuse facility that features classrooms, a world-class sports center, housing for 400 freshmen, and more.

Finding a cheap New York apartment may be easier than sailing through NYU's challenging academics. Regardless of major, everyone is very focused on career preparation—it's never enough to just concentrate on your classes. "It's common for students to take on difficult courseloads, along with a job or internship," explains a film and television major. Despite the university's mammoth size, 63 percent of classes taken by undergraduates have fewer than 20 students. Graduate students might lead foreign language sections, writing workshops, and the recitations that accompany lectures, but students still say teaching is usually top-notch and professors are reasonably accessible. "Surprisingly, most of our introductory courses are taught by really great and well-known professors," says one student.

"[NYU students enjoy] one of the most vibrant social scenes on the planet."

Point to a spot on a world map and you'll likely hit a country hosting undergraduates from NYU, which sends more of them abroad than any other school. "At NYU, studying away is not a matter of 'if,' but 'where,'" says a junior. In addition to its campuses in Abu Dhabi and Shanghai, the university has 12 academic sites in cities from Buenos Aires and Prague to Sydney and Tel Aviv, as well as exchange agreements with universities in other locations throughout the world. More than half of NYU undergrads study abroad, sometimes as early as their freshman year through the university's Liberal Studies Core. Locally, internships range from jobs on Wall Street to assignments with film industry giants. The career center is "amazingly personal and well run," says an econ major, and has thousands of listings for on-campus jobs, full-time jobs, and internships. Students qualifying for freshman honors seminars study in small classes under top faculty and eminent visiting professors. An annual undergraduate research conference at the College of Arts and Science gives students the chance to present findings from their research.

It's not uncommon to see students who haven't yet finished B.F.A. degrees performing in Broadway shows.

An international politics major says NYU students are "high-achieving individuals, cosmopolitan, independent, self-driven, and confident." Thanks in part to the university's investment in student housing, 51 percent of undergraduates now come from outside New York State, including a substantial 24 percent from outside the United States. In-staters hail primarily from the city and nearby suburbs. Black students make up 8 percent of undergrads, Asian Americans 19 percent, Hispanics/Latinos 17 percent, and multiracial students 4 percent. On this generally liberal campus, social justice, immigration policy, the Israeli-Palestinian conflict, and rights of all kinds—LGBTQ, animal, human, and workers'—are important, students say. Although most financial aid is need-based, merit awards averaging $18,600 are available; athletic scholarships are not.

Whereas NYU students once had to fend for themselves in New York's outrageous housing market, the university now guarantees four years of housing to all freshmen (and most transfers) who seek it. More than 20 residence halls, ranging from old hotels to a converted monastery, provide a wide range of accommodations. Most rooms have private baths and are larger, cleaner, newer, and better equipped than many city apartments, enticing 40 percent of students to stay on campus. "Housing is lovely although expensive, like everything else in Manhattan," opines a senior. Freshmen are housed largely in freshman residence halls, many of which have themed floors, and rooms are assigned by lottery each spring. The university provides free shuttle buses to dorms that are farther uptown or downtown. The dining halls offer extensive choices—from wraps to sushi to a dedicated kosher eatery. "The dining halls really try to accommodate everyone," says one student. Of course, downtown's array of ethnic restaurants also offers a variety of food at cheap prices.

"We graduate at Yankee Stadium, which is incredible."

Because NYU is large and fairly decentralized, the Student Resource Center helps students navigate university resources and services. The university's Wellness Exchange provides students with a hotline that connects them with professionals who can help them address daily challenges or crises they may encounter, and S.P.A.C.E. (Sexual Misconduct Prevention, Assistance, Counseling, and Education) provides comprehensive resources and support. Students also meet with academic advisors—usually professors in their major department—at least once a semester. For concerned parents and students, NYU hosts a series of workshops on keeping safe, and programs like the NYU Trolley and Safe Ride Van Service provide door-to-door service for students until 3:00 a.m. "I always feel safe," says a linguistics major. "I can't walk more than one block without seeing an NYU security officer or an NYPD car just patrolling the area."

NYU's social life is divided between the campus and the city. "Students can be found all over the Village and NYC enjoying one of the most vibrant social scenes on the planet," enthuses a romance languages and psychology major. Many students march in the city's Halloween Parade, which takes over the Village, while most fall and spring weekends find a city-sponsored street fair somewhere nearby. On campus, there are concerts, movies, fraternity and sorority events (only 1 percent of the men and 3 percent of the women go Greek), and more than 300 clubs and organizations. Underage students caught with alcohol in public areas in the dorms may lose their housing. The rest take their chances with the notoriously strict bouncers at bars and clubs around Manhattan. The springtime Strawberry Festival includes free berries, cotton candy, outdoor concerts, and carnival amusements. The Violet Ball, a dinner/dance held each fall in the atrium of Bobst Library, offers an excuse to get dressed up. "We graduate at Yankee Stadium, which is incredible," cheers a senior.

While sports have not traditionally been a big emphasis at NYU, successful Violets programs include women's golf (recent national champions), volleyball, and basketball, as well as men's and women's fencing and swimming and diving, all of which compete in Division III. Roughly one-third of undergrads participate in intramural sports, which include flag football, bowling, and indoor cricket.

The heartbeat of New York City thumps day and night; NYU students thrive on all that energy and know how to capture it in their studies and social lives. "To be an NYU student is to be part college student, part New Yorker," a senior says. "Don't come here if you're not up to working hard and moving fast."

If You Apply To ›

NYU: Early decision I and II, regular decision. Accepts the Common Application. Portfolio or audition required for some programs. Please consult NYU's website for the most up-to-date information regarding standardized test requirements.

University of North Carolina Asheville

I University Heights, Asheville, NC 28804

Located in a picturesque mountain setting outside the progressive and arts-minded city from which it takes its name, UNC Asheville is North Carolina's contribution to the tradition of "public liberal arts" colleges. With 2,700 full-time, degree-seeking students, it is about half the size of William & Mary and somewhat smaller than Mary Washington. By Southern standards, a progressive university in a progressive city.

The University of North Carolina Asheville offers all of the perks that are generally associated with pricier private institutions: rigorous academics, small classes, and a beautiful setting. And it does it for a fraction of the cost. This public liberal arts and sciences university continues to integrate experiential learning into its traditional curriculum, emphasizing undergraduate research, internships, and service-learning experiences. According to a mass communication major, "We definitely lean into the culture of being a mountain school, a smaller school, and a liberal arts school."

Located in the heart of North Carolina's gorgeous Blue Ridge Mountains, the 360-acre campus lies in the middle of one million acres of federal and state forest near the tallest mountain in the East and the most heavily visited national park in the country. The campus was built in the 1960s when the university, whose origins go back to 1927, joined the UNC system. Much of the brick architecture reflects the style of that decade, although many of the

> **"We definitely lean into the culture of being a mountain school."**

buildings have been added within the past several years, including a high-tech science and multimedia building. The Botanical Gardens at Asheville, adjacent to the main campus, features thousands of native plants and trees and serves as a wildlife refuge and study center for biology students. The STEAM Studio, located just off campus, brings together science, engineering, and art students in one collaborative, state-of-the-art makerspace. Completed in 2021, a major renovation of Owen Hall, housing the art, art history, and new media departments, earned LEED Silver certification.

Asheville's general education curriculum, the Liberal Arts Core, is required of all undergraduates. In addition to first-year and senior-capstone liberal arts seminars, students must take courses in eight areas spanning the humanities, sciences, and mathematics, as well as two Diversity Intensives, one of which must focus on U.S. racial and ethnic diversity. The most popular majors at Asheville are psychology, environmental studies, mass communication, health and wellness promotion, and

Website: www.unca.edu
Location: Small City
Public
Total Enrollment: 2,749
Undergraduates: 2,749
Male/Female: 42/58
Financial Aid: 85%
Pell Grant: 34%
Expense: Pub $
Student Loans: 58%
Average Debt: $
Applicants: 4,550
Accepted: 82%
Enrolled: 16%
Grad in 6 Years: 65%
Returning Freshmen: 75%
Academics: ✍ ✍ ✍ ✍
Social: ☎ ☎ ☎
Q of L: ★ ★ ★ ★
Admissions: (828) 251-6481
Email Address: admissions@
  unca.edu

Strong Programs:
Atmospheric Sciences
Visual Arts

UNC Asheville is a global source of information for climate and atmospheric sciences.

biology. Students can take advantage of Asheville's strengths as a global source of information for climate and atmospheric sciences and as a center of digital imaging, music, and fine arts and studio crafts. "UNC Asheville is a very environmentally friendly, artsy school," says a management major. A joint B.S. degree in engineering (with a concentration in mechatronics) with North Carolina State University is the only such program in the state and is one of the fastest-growing majors.

Courses are challenging, but "UNC Asheville is laid-back and slower paced, which might be different for students who are used to competition and a faster-paced lifestyle," comments an economics major. Fifty-nine percent of all classes have fewer than 20 students, and a number of them have service-learning components. As a French and political science double major points out, "Our faculty's mentorship and close relationships are especially evident in undergraduate research." Research is indeed a key emphasis here: Asheville founded the National Conference on Undergraduate Research and has hosted the conference five times. About 60 percent of Asheville students will have an undergraduate research experience by graduation. The UNC Asheville honors program offers special courses—as well as cultural and social opportunities—to motivated students who can make the grade. Study abroad is an option too, and 10 percent of students participate in programs available in more than 50 countries. "Career advising is strong and they constantly reach out to students about future plans," cheers a senior.

The head count at Asheville has risen steadily over the past decade, but only 11 percent of students come from out of state and another 1 percent from abroad. (The state limits its out-of-state admits to 18 percent.) Asheville has shed its early reputation as a hippie haven, but students still value individualism: "We encourage everyone to be themselves and pursue their own interests," says a psychology major. Currently, the student body is 5 percent Black, 9 percent Hispanic/Latino, 2 percent

"Our faculty's mentorship and close relationships are especially evident in undergraduate research."

Asian American, and 5 percent multiracial, but Asheville is making special efforts to bring more students from underrepresented groups to campus. Students say the campus is home to a strong LGBTQ community, and a substantial number of transfer students add their own brand of diversity. Students tend to be progressively minded, and issues of environmental sustainability and racial and gender equity get particular attention on campus. Thirty-four percent of current freshmen are Pell-eligible. Asheville offers more than 200 athletic scholarships, as well as merit scholarships averaging $2,300.

Forty-six percent of the students live in the residence halls, which offer single and double rooms as well as suite-style options. "Housing is very nice and convenient but expensive," says a junior. Residential learning communities offer special residential and academic options for students with similar interests, such as the Cloud (for computer science and atmospheric sciences majors) and the Transfer Learning Community (for transfer students). For meals, students may eat dining-hall fare or grab something quick at retail outlets around campus, including local cuisine. A sophomore says, "Our campus security is excellent. We have an on-campus police force that patrols regularly around campus."

Campuswide events include the Turning of the Maples in October (featuring apple cider, maple cookies, and pumpkin bowling on the quad).

Social life at Asheville is fairly low-key. Greek life is not an influential presence, with only 2 percent of the men and 1 percent of the women joining up. Most parties take place off campus, especially since RAs tightly monitor underage drinking in the dorms. "There is no tolerance for unsafe, underage, or unwise drinking," says a student. There are more than 60 student organizations, including the student newspaper, the *Blue Banner*. Several campuswide events bring the school together each year, including the Turning of the Maples in October (featuring apple cider, maple cookies, and pumpkin bowling on the quad), homecoming, and a spring lawn party.

During Greenfest, explains a student, the campus community gathers to "do outdoor service work on campus and attend informative talks about environmental issues and other events like a farm-to-table dinner."

The city of Asheville, long a haven for artists and an increasingly popular retirement destination, offers a tame but inviting nightlife, with popular hangouts like the Orange Peel, the Grey Eagle, and Isis Music Hall, and the city has been named Beer City USA several times. Asheville is also home to a bevy of street performers, outdoor music festivals, and live entertainment events. For the many

"We have a great rivalry with Western Carolina."

Asheville students with a hankering for the great outdoors, the university is surrounded by the Blue Ridge Mountains and the Smokies, where students can hike and rock climb; water buffs can go rafting and kayaking on the nearby rivers. Preorientation wilderness trips and urban excursions help build friendships among freshmen. Those with cars can head to Greenville and Charlotte, one and two hours away, respectively. Real big-city action takes extra effort, though, since Atlanta is a four-hour trek.

The Division I Bulldogs boast Big South Conference teams in 16 sports. Men's and women's basketball, men's tennis, and women's swimming and diving are among the most successful. "We have a great rivalry with Western Carolina," says a health and wellness major. Intramurals and club sports are at least as popular as the varsity sports (especially ultimate Frisbee, soccer, and eSports), as are outdoor adventure trips and the on-campus challenge course and bike shop.

"Everyone who works here is dedicated to the student experience in some way," says a senior. "That means you won't be a number." Indeed, all the ingredients for a superior college experience lie in wait at Asheville: strong academics, dedicated professors, and an administration that continues to push for excellence. It's a place to get the kind of liberal arts education usually associated with private colleges—but at the cost of a public university.

Overlaps

Furman, College of Wooster, New College of Florida, St. Mary's College of Maryland, Christopher Newport, William & Mary, University of Mary Washington, Elon

If You Apply To ›

UNC Asheville: Early decision I and II, rolling admissions. Accepts the Common Application with supplement. Please consult UNC Asheville's website for the most up-to-date information regarding standardized test requirements.

University of North Carolina at Chapel Hill

BEST BUY

Jackson Hall, CB 2200, Chapel Hill, NC 27599

Close on the heels of UVA as the South's most prestigious public university. With 82 percent of the spots in each incoming class reserved for in-staters, admission is selective but not impossible for out-of-staters who aren't 6'9" with a 43-inch vertical jump. But they keep trying by the thousands. Chapel Hill is a quintessential college town that is morphing into a medium-sized city.

Welcome to "the Southern part of heaven," a place where the sky is Carolina blue and the academics are red-hot. As the flagship campus of the state university system, the University of North Carolina at Chapel Hill has earned its place among the South's most prestigious universities. The atmosphere here is a unique brand of Southern, a rowdy mixture of hard work, sports fanaticism, progressive social values, and traditions that seems to attract bright, serious, and fun-loving students from everywhere.

Website: www.unc.edu
Location: Small Town
Public
Total Enrollment: 26,450
Undergraduates: 18,917

(continued)

Male/Female: 40/60
Financial Aid: 53%
Pell Grant: 21%
Expense: Pub $
Student Loans: 35%
Average Debt: $
Applicants: 53,776
Accepted: 19%
Enrolled: 45%
Grad in 6 Years: 92%
Returning Freshmen: 97%
Academics: ✍ ✍ ✍ ✍
Social: ☎ ☎ ☎ ☎
Q of L: ★ ★ ★ ★
Admissions: (919) 966-3621
Email Address: unchelp@
   admissions.unc.edu

Strong Programs:
Communication and Media
   Studies
Business Administration
Chemistry
Sociology
English
Global Studies
Philosophy
Biology

Undergraduate research is prevalent in all disciplines, and many students present their findings at professional conferences or publish results in academic journals.

Chartered in 1789, UNC was the first public university in the United States to open its doors, and North Carolinians still take pride in Carolina's identity as "the University of the people." UNC's gorgeous and comfortable campus occupies 730 acres lush with trees and lawns and brick-paved walkways. The architecture ranges from Palladian, Federal, and Georgian to postmodern, with red brick the prevailing motif. The Old Well, the university's symbol, stands at the northern end of the campus.

The university's recently implemented IDEAs in Action general education curriculum places greater emphasis on the first-year experience, interdisciplinary learning, undergraduate research, and out-of-class experiences like internships and study abroad. The curriculum centers on developing skills in nine "focus capacities"—categories of courses that range from quantitative reasoning to ethical and civic values. In their first year, students take a College Thriving course, which eases the transition to college life. They also choose either a First-Year Seminar on a specialized topic, such as the Poetic Roots of Hip-Hop, or a First-Year Launch course, like Econ 101 or Bio 101, which provides an introduction to a major. Required, cross-disciplinary Ideas, Information, and Inquiry courses, which focus on broad themes like Health and Happiness, are team-taught by faculty members from three different fields to expose students to diverse academic perspectives.

"I don't feel a sense of competition at all."

Chapel Hill offers more than 75 undergraduate degree programs. Some of the strongest are communication and media studies, business administration, chemistry, sociology, English, global studies, and philosophy. Other popular majors include biology, psychology, economics, and political science. The university has developed a broad range of opportunities to help students become entrepreneurial, including an entrepreneurship minor and the Carolina Challenge, a student-run competition that awards up to $50,000 in prizes each year for the best business plan. Computer science and neuroscience are some of the fastest-growing majors. Biomedical and health sciences engineering, a joint-degree program with North Carolina State University, is the only option for those seeking an engineering major.

"Although this is a prestigious university, I don't feel a sense of competition at all," says one sophomore. Academic and social life are governed by a student-run honor system. Forty-one percent of classes enroll fewer than 20 students, and access to registration is based on seniority. If you get closed out of a class, "be persistent," advises a first-year. The Carolina faculty is, for the most part, top-notch. Professors keep regular office hours, and a history major says, "The majority of professors go out of their way to help students and make sure that they are learning everything they possibly can." Regarding career preparation, a senior cheers, "Our career services department on campus puts effort into each and every student."

Undergraduate research is prevalent in all disciplines, and many students present their findings at professional conferences, publish results in academic journals, and win fellowships to support summer research in the United States and abroad. For those tired of the classroom rush, Research Triangle Park, a nearby research and corporate community and home of the National Humanities Center, employs many students as research assistants. UNC offers more than 400 study abroad programs in approximately 70 countries, in which 43 percent of students participate. Summer School, including the two-week "Maymester," provides undergraduates with diverse course options, some with off-campus travel or research opportunities not possible during the academic year. One-third of the students are involved in community service, many through a service-learning program for which they receive academic credit. Additionally, UNC's honors program is nationally recognized.

"Our career services department on campus puts effort into each and every student."

"Carolina students are proud to attend this school, and they bleed Carolina blue," says one Tar Heel. Out-of-state admission is extremely tough; by statute, 82 percent of first-year undergraduates must be North Carolina residents. Five percent of all undergrads come from foreign countries. Big social and political issues on campus include multiculturalism, gender roles, and religious issues. Black students account for 9 percent of the student body, Asian Americans 12 percent, Hispanics/Latinos 10 percent, and multiracial students 5 percent. Women outnumber men on campus 3 to 2. UNC awards a limited number of highly competitive academic scholarships, along with more than 600 athletic scholarships in 26 sports. What's more, the university is need-blind in admissions and commits to meeting the full demonstrated financial need of all admitted students—one of only two public universities in the U.S. to do so (see also University of Virginia). The Carolina Covenant program, which has served as a national model to universities seeking to increase socioeconomic diversity, offers scholarships, grants, and work-study as well as extensive mentoring and other support to qualifying students who are at or below 200 percent of the poverty level, giving eligible low-income students the chance to graduate debt-free.

> **"Carolina students are proud to attend this school, and they bleed Carolina blue."**

Forty-six percent of undergraduates live in university housing, which "is an invaluable part of the experience," according to one student. Housing on the north side of campus offers old and recently renovated dorms; the south side offers several new housing options, which are a 15-minute hike from academic buildings (not to worry—there's a free campus shuttle). "The pickiest of the picky could be happy with Carolina dining services," says a first-year. Campus security is praised for its constant presence. "Sexual assault has become a very visible issue in the sense that people are more willing to talk about it," comments a sociology major, adding that the university has "taken steps to address the issue." UNC has also been busy in recent years taking down statues and renaming buildings associated with slavery.

The university is need-blind in admissions and commits to meeting the full demonstrated financial need of all admitted students.

"'College town' in the dictionary should show a picture of Chapel Hill," boasts one senior. Franklin Street, the main drag in town that runs across the northern boundary of campus, offers ethnic restaurants, ice-cream parlors, coffeehouses, vegetarian eateries, bakeries, a dance club, a generous supply of bars, and the Varsity movie theater. Fraternities and sororities may account for only 14 percent of the men and 14 percent of the women, but they exert an influence far beyond their numbers. "Fraternities are a social hub, and many students flock to their off-campus parties," confirms one student. Between Greek life and other campus-sponsored activities, "There are always five or six things happening on any given day," says a political science major. FallFest kicks off the school year with an emphasis on the idea that you don't have to drink to have fun. The annual Carolina Jazz Festival and Halloween Celebration on Franklin Street are always, shall we say, raucous. The North Carolina Literary Festival is held biannually. And, as a senior explains, "We also have other fun traditions: students taking a sip from the Old Well, climbing up the Bell Tower, and streaking before finals (though we're not supposed to talk about that last one)."

> **"'College town' in the dictionary should show a picture of Chapel Hill."**

Student and alumni enthusiasm for Tar Heel athletics is legendary, and the word "popular" doesn't do justice to the basketball games. A contest between Tar Heel hoopsters and NC State makes any Carolina fan's heart beat faster, but Duke takes the prize as the most reviled of all devils. The Tar Heels, national runners-up in 2022, play in the 21,750-seat Smith Center, named for the late coach Dean Smith, one of the winningest college basketball coaches of all time. Women's field hockey has won four national championships in the last five years, and women's lacrosse claimed the national title in 2022. Men's and women's soccer and tennis are also

The annual Halloween Celebration on Franklin Street is always, shall we say, raucous.

highly competitive. Extensive intramural and club sports programs draw heavy participation; intramural basketball and soccer alone each boast rosters of more than 200 teams. Those who crave fresh air can take advantage of the Outdoor Education Center's mountain bike trails, rope courses, and one of the longest double zip lines on the East Coast.

As a popular saying goes, "If God is not a Tar Heel, why is the sky Carolina blue?" It's a cute turn of phrase but also points to the passion that is well-known in these parts. As one of the best college buys in the country, UNC at Chapel Hill gives students everything they want, both academically and socially. Despite efforts by Philistine forces in the state legislature to meddle in campus affairs for political purposes, North Carolina's flagship university, with its 234-year history, continues to sustain an atmosphere of extreme pride, a love of tradition, and monumental school spirit. One first-year, full of that school spirit, says, "Southern hospitality blended with a high level of thinking, an overwhelming dose of friendliness and pep, and a spectacularly gorgeous campus make Chapel Hill my favorite place in the world."

Overlaps

University of Virginia, Duke, UC Berkeley, UCLA, University of Michigan, North Carolina State, Vanderbilt, Appalachian State

If You Apply To ›

UNC at Chapel Hill: Early action, regular decision. Accepts the Common Application with supplement. Please consult UNC at Chapel Hill's website for the most up-to-date information regarding standardized test requirements.

University of North Carolina Wilmington

Wilmington, NC 28403

Still overshadowed by Chapel Hill and the other biggies in the strong UNC system but making a name for itself. Strong in marine biology and other sciences. You won't see the Seahawks in the NCAA Final Four anytime soon, but you will be able to get to know your professors. Students tend to think of themselves as "hardworking beachgoers," and only 12 percent hail from outside North Carolina.

Website: www.uncw.edu
Location: Small City
Public
Total Enrollment: 12,941
Undergraduates: 11,670
Male/Female: 37/63
Financial Aid: 60%
Pell Grant: 21%
Expense: Pub $
Student Loans: 60%
Average Debt: $ $
Applicants: 15,792
Accepted: 68%
Enrolled: 23%
Grad in 6 Years: 72%
Returning Freshmen: 83%
Academics: ✑ ✑

At the University of North Carolina Wilmington, students enjoy extensive undergraduate research opportunities, a slate of solid sciences, and a close-knit community of like-minded individuals who like their modern academics mixed with a bit of old-fashioned Southern charm. The university's close proximity to the ocean provides motivated students with ample opportunities for fun in the sun and a natural lab for the school's stellar marine biology program. Whether diving into the sea or into their studies, UNCW students are filled with school spirit.

Founded as Wilmington College in 1947, UNCW moved to its present location in the heart of New Hanover County in 1961. The 660-acre campus is only minutes from Wrightsville Beach and historic downtown Wilmington and features Georgian architecture and designated conservation areas. These conservation areas are significant zones of natural beauty with their longleaf pines, oaks, dogwoods, and native magnolias. Notable campus landmarks include the clock tower, the Leutze Hall portico, Chancellor's Walk, and the Campus Life complex, which serves as the hub of the university community. After sustaining $140 million in damage caused by Hurricane Florence in 2018, the university has been moving forward with a spate of new construction to add and enhance academic and residential facilities. Four new residence halls and a dining hall have opened since 2020.

UNCW's University Studies curriculum requires students to complete coursework in three main categories—Foundations, Building Competencies, and Approaches and Perspectives—and to complete one approved Explorations Beyond the Classroom experience, such as an internship or a study abroad program. Freshmen benefit from a slate of special programs, including a required two-day orientation and a first-year seminar. Each seminar is limited to 25 students and has a Seahawk "link": older students who help with the transition into UNCW life. About a third of incoming freshmen sign up for learning communities, taking courses together related to an academic or personal interest. "My learning community was a safe space to explore college with built-in buddies!" recalls a junior.

Some of the most popular majors are nursing, business administration, communication studies, psychology, and biology. The university's strengths lie in the natural sciences, especially marine biology, chemistry, ecology, and other disciplines that form the core of the marine sciences. "Our university places a large emphasis on lab and fieldwork," says one geography major.

"Our university places a large emphasis on lab and fieldwork."

Outside of the sciences, UNCW offers solid programs in film studies and creative writing. Newer offerings include majors in respiratory therapy, digital arts, and coastal engineering. Freshmen are taught by full professors, and a social work major says, "Professors work hard to engage students and help students succeed, even during challenging times." Enrollments in introductory courses sometimes swell to more than 100, but 45 percent of all classes have fewer than 20 students.

A hallmark of the UNCW student experience is the Experiencing Transformative Education through Applied Learning program, which places students in hands-on learning opportunities, such as directed independent study, undergraduate research, internships, and service-learning projects, requiring them to integrate the theories, ideas, and skills they have learned in new contexts. Research opportunities include Undergraduate Research and Creativity Fellowships, which award up to $3,000 for innovative research. For those yearning to experience new vistas, the UNC system offers 1,000 approved study abroad trips in more than 50 countries; 20 percent of students participate. Students in the UNCW Honors College engage in living/learning communities, advanced coursework, and experiential seminars; honors students also complete a senior honors capstone research project.

According to a marketing major, UNCW students are "hardworking beachgoers. Every student here is hardworking and motivated but enjoys a little time off as well." Eighty-eight percent of undergrads are native to North Carolina, and 1 percent are international. Lack of diversity is a frequent student complaint. Black students represent 5 percent of the student body,

"How much better can a social scene get than the beach?"

Hispanics/Latinos 8 percent, Asian Americans 2 percent, and multiracial students 4 percent. Students describe a "relaxed" balance of liberal and conservative political views. "We're a coastal school, so many students are passionate about clean-water programs and recycling," reports a senior. Outstanding students can vie for merit scholarships averaging $3,200, as well as more than 200 athletic scholarships. Under UNCW's Support Opportunity Access Responsibility program, high-achieving students from low-income families may receive grants and scholarships equaling the cost of in-state tuition and fees, in addition to federal loans or work-study funding if needed.

All freshmen and sophomores (except commuters who live at home with a parent or guardian) are required to reside on campus. Options range from traditional freshman dorms to sophomore suites and apartments for upperclassmen. Most students who move off campus stay within a mile or so of the school. Campus eateries include Wagoner Hall, Dub's Café, the Shore, the Hawks Nest food court, and

(continued)

Social: ☎ ☎
Q of L: ★ ★ ★
Admissions: (910) 962-3243
Email Address: admissions@ uncw.edu

Strong Programs:
Marine Biology
Chemistry
Ecology
Film Studies
Creative Writing
Nursing
Business Administration
Communication Studies

A required first-year seminar is limited to 25 students and has a Seahawk "link": an older student who helps with the transition into UNCW life.

The sea kayaking and paddleboarding trips organized by Seahawk Adventures are favorite diversions.

the Hub; students give the food positive reviews. A public health major comments, "The quality of the meals at UNCW is high—they are always tasty and fill me up." Students praise campus police for keeping the area secure and the CARE office for helping to combat sexual assault on campus.

When it comes to social life, a junior asks, "How much better can a social scene get than the beach?" Indeed, the beach is the place to be for many popular events, such as the Beach Blast party the first week of school. Students also look forward to homecoming, the Dub Idol and Hawk It Out singing and dance competitions, and the annual oozeball mud volleyball tournament. Additionally, "UNCWeekends puts something on every weekend for students both on and off campus," says a public health major. Fraternities and sororities attract 5 percent of the men and 7 percent of the women, respectively. The party scene is far from raucous, students report, and underage drinkers face stiff penalties if caught. Downtown Wilmington is "a very scenic and beautiful city," says a student, and offers its share of restaurants, bars, and shops. "From the many bars to the many beaches, we have hundreds of social spots to hang out," boasts a senior. Road trips include jaunts to Myrtle Beach, the Outer Banks, Washington, D.C., and the Appalachian Mountains.

UNCW fields 19 varsity teams that compete in Division I. Recent Colonial Athletic Association conference champions include men's and women's golf, men's tennis, and baseball. "Seahawk basketball is huge!" raves one freshman. Club and intramural sports are also popular, especially flag football, basketball, and soccer, and the sea kayaking and paddleboarding trips organized by Seahawk Adventures are other favorite diversions.

Despite complaints of limited parking and the lack of football, students at the University of North Carolina Wilmington seem to be a happy lot. "Everyone here always seems to be in a good mood and goes out of their way to speak to and help others," says a senior. "Maybe it's the Southern charm in us, but whatever it is, it sure helps make this laid-back college an awesome place to attend."

Overlaps

Appalachian State, UNC Charlotte, North Carolina State, UNC Greensboro, East Carolina, UNC at Chapel Hill, University of South Carolina, College of Charleston

If You Apply To ›

UNC Wilmington: Early action, regular decision. Accepts the Common Application with supplement. Please consult UNC Wilmington's website for the most up-to-date information regarding standardized test requirements.

North Carolina State University

Box 7103, Raleigh, NC 27695

Although NC State may lack the high national profile of neighbors Duke and UNC at Chapel Hill, it is a powerhouse in North Carolina's Research Triangle and beyond—just ask the thousands of graduates who have moved into jobs in the area. Engineering, business, and biology are the most popular programs. Location in the state capital a big plus. Compare to Clemson and Virginia Tech.

Whether you're looking for a stellar education or a top-rated basketball program, North Carolina State University offers students the benefits of a large school—highly regarded professors, a diverse student body, and plenty to do on weekends—while making sure that no one feels left out. Says an electrical engineering major, "There is definitely a place for everyone here, since there are so many avenues to explore."

Website: www.ncsu.edu
Location: City Center
Public
Total Enrollment: 28,945
Undergraduates: 23,285

The 2,137-acre campus, which dates to 1887, consists of redbrick buildings, brick-lined walks, and cozy courtyards dotted with pine trees. There is no dominant style but more of an architectural stream of consciousness that reveals a campus that has grown and changed with time. Holladay Hall has been designated as a historic site by the Raleigh City Council, while the ultramodern Hunt Library features a game lab, visualization studio, and digital production suites. For amusement, you can always stroll over and watch its robotic book retrieval system in action. NC State's Centennial Campus, a 1,227-acre, public-private research campus, is home to the $150 million Fitts-Woolard Hall, housing several engineering programs. The $45 million Wellness and Recreation Center boasts a 48-foot-tall climbing wall, top-of-the-line training equipment, and a teaching kitchen for students to learn about nutrition and practice healthy cooking.

General education requirements cover a broad range of liberal arts disciplines in addition to coursework that reflects interdisciplinary perspectives, develops writing skills, examines diversity and inclusion in the U.S., and engages students in-depth in an area that is clearly distinct from their major. An Exploratory Studies program provides guidance and counseling for incoming students to introduce them to possible majors. "The academic climate is a mixture of healthy competitiveness and teamwork/support," says an economics major. Many classes are large, but faculty get high grades for being accessible and helpful during office hours. A biology major comments, "As with any university, NC State employs some outstanding faculty and some less-than-stellar professors who are more effective in the laboratory than in the lecture hall."

> **"The academic climate is a mixture of healthy competitiveness and teamwork/support."**

NC State excels in the professional areas of engineering, architecture, business, agriculture, and the sciences, which are among the largest and the most demanding divisions. Not surprisingly, given its location in the heart of textile country, the university also boasts the largest and one of the best textiles programs in the nation. Engineering tops the list of most popular majors, followed by business, biological sciences, and agriculture. The College of Humanities and Social Sciences is the second largest school in the university, and solid nontechnical areas include communication, English, international studies, and social work. Notable programs are also available in genetics, forest management, biomedical engineering, sport management, and turfgrass science.

An important feature of NC State's approach to education is the cooperative education program, through which students in all schools can alternate semesters of on-site work with traditional classroom time. Twenty-seven percent of students conduct undergraduate research. The university benefits greatly from its relationships with private industry through the state's high-tech Research Triangle Park, located nearby, as well as from cooperative ties with Duke and UNC at Chapel Hill. NC State offers approximately 400 study abroad programs in more than 50 countries, in which 17 percent of undergrads participate. In the University Scholars program, academic standouts live together and participate in weekly activities such as cultural events, honors classes, and outdoor recreation trips. Students in the University Honors Program take small seminars and complete a capstone project, and they can join a dedicated living/learning community.

NC State's star continues to rise as it becomes more selective. One student says the student body, a.k.a. Wolfpack, consists mainly of "hardworking and humble" North Carolinians; consistent with state mandates, 89 percent are in-state students, and 3 percent are international. Six percent of undergraduates are Black, 7 percent are Hispanic/Latino, 8 percent are Asian American, and 4 percent are multiracial. Conservatism among students is not uncommon, but in general, according to a junior, "political and social activism are not widespread among the student body."

(continued)

Male/Female: 50/50
Financial Aid: 63%
Pell Grant: 19%
Expense: Pub $
Student Loans: 49%
Average Debt: $ $
Applicants: 32,893
Accepted: 47%
Enrolled: 32%
Grad in 6 Years: 85%
Returning Freshmen: 94%
Academics: ✍ ✍ ✍ ½
Social: ☎ ☎ ☎
Q of L: ★ ★ ★
Admissions: (919) 515-2434
Email Address: undergrad-admissions@ncsu.edu

Strong Programs:
Engineering
Architecture
Business
Agriculture
Textiles
Biological Sciences
Communication
English

NC State's Centennial Campus is home to the $150 million Fitts-Woolard Hall, housing several engineering programs.

Jocks and sports fans are visible, and the university offers 329 athletic scholarships in 23 sports. Those with outstanding academic qualifications can compete for merit scholarships averaging $4,800. The Pack Promise guarantees that every North Carolina resident admitted to NC State with a family income at or below 150 percent of the federal poverty level will receive an aid package that meets 100 percent of their demonstrated financial need.

Thirty-four percent of students live on campus, which is a requirement for freshmen, who choose between hall-style and suite-style accommodations. Twenty-nine percent of students opt to reside in the school's 15 Living and Learning Villages, where they can live and socialize with others who share their interests, such as entrepreneurship and women's empowerment. "Not very many people stay on campus after their freshman year, and only then is it hard to get a room—in the off-campus apartments," reports a chemistry major. The dining halls feed all freshmen and anyone else who cares to join the meal plan, and the food gets positive reviews. Campus safety also receives good ratings.

The 29 fraternities and 20 sororities attract 11 percent of the men and 14 percent of the women. The Greek scene provides much of the entertainment, but parties in dorms and at off-campus apartments are also popular. Alcohol policies are enforced, and if you're thinking about grabbing a brew, "don't try unless you're 21," warns a senior. A junior says, "There are always countless free events going on campus: concerts, festivals, free movies, or outdoor activities." Packapalooza, "a huge block party on Hillsborough Street with a free concert at the end," kicks off the academic year, and Wolfstock, a concert on the last day of classes in the spring, closes it. Public transportation affords easy access to downtown, with its shops, restaurants, theaters, and night spots. Many students also like to head to the beach, which is about two hours away, or to the mountains for hiking or skiing, which is about a three-and-a-half-hour trip. Volunteering is popular too.

> "[Packapalooza is] a huge block party on Hillsborough Street with a free concert at the end."

Students love to cheer on their Division I Wolfpack teams, which do well in baseball, football, wrestling, women's gymnastics, and men's and women's swimming and diving. But needless to say, basketball reigns supreme—playing in the high-powered Atlantic Coast Conference. Some ardent NC State fans storm nearby Hillsborough Street following game-day victories, especially those over archrival UNC at Chapel Hill. Indeed, the annual State versus Carolina football game always packs the stadium, and the never-ending call to "Beat Carolina!" permeates the campus year-round. Club sports and intramurals also thrive; offerings include cricket, flag football, disc golf, and, for the exceptionally agile, trampoline dodgeball.

North Carolina State has moved well beyond its origins as a land grant school focusing on agriculture and engineering. It has attracted a dedicated and friendly student body lured by an emphasis on learning beyond the classroom and inspired by the university's "Think and Do" slogan. NC State works well for those who can shoot hoops and for those who can calculate the trajectory of the same three-point shot.

If You Apply To ›

NC State: Early action, regular decision. Accepts the Common Application with supplement. Applicants to studio-based majors must submit a portfolio and additional essay. Please consult NC State's website for the most up-to-date information regarding standardized test requirements.

Northeastern University

360 Huntington Avenue, Boston, MA 02115

Northeastern is synonymous with preprofessional education and hands-on experience. By interspersing co-op jobs with academic study, students can help finance their education while getting a leg up on the job market—domestic and global. Aided by a huge spike in applications and an ambitious building program, NU has transformed itself from blue-collar urban into Boston chic. With students always coming and going, campus life can be uneven.

Long known for its co-op program and hands-on learning experiences, Northeastern University has become one of the region's top-tier institutions. More selective than ever, NU has added lavish new facilities and recruited big-name professors while continuing to combine liberal arts requirements with up to 18 months of challenging work placements. "The school has encouraged and empowered me to explore the world through research and study abroad," cheers one mechanical engineering major, "experiences that will stay with me forever."

Northeastern's 73-acre campus is an unlikely oasis located in the heart of Boston, just minutes away from Fenway Park, shopping centers, nightclubs, cafés, Symphony Hall, and the Museum of Fine Arts. The campus's green spaces are interspersed with brick walkways, sculptures, and outdoor art. Older buildings are utilitarian gray brick, while newer structures are modern glass and brick. During inclement weather, students can be found navigating the underground tunnel system that connects many campus buildings. No longer a commuter college, NU has had the rare luxury for

> **"Professors want to make sure that you are as attractive as possible to potential employers."**

an urban institution of having erstwhile parking lots available for new construction. The state-of-the-art Interdisciplinary Science and Engineering Complex furthers NU's emphasis on applied—or, to use the local jargon, "use-inspired"—research. In recent years, NU has assembled a network of eight satellite campuses, including London, Vancouver, and most recently Portland, Maine.

Northeastern's core curriculum (known as NUpath) embraces writing-intensive instruction, mathematical/analytical thinking, and comparative understanding of religions and cultures. Students must take part in a first-year learning community, integrated experiential learning, and a capstone experience in their major. Woven into the Northeastern experience is its signature co-op program—which dates to 1909 and is the second oldest in the country—that places students in full-time positions related to their major and personal interests. Students have the option to complete up to two co-ops, each four to six months in length, if they seek to graduate in four years (roughly two-thirds of students go this route), or to complete up to three co-ops if they enroll in the university's traditional five-year bachelor's degree programs. Working with a specialized co-op advisor, students may choose from more than 2,900 established co-op employer partners located in more than 146 countries, or they may propose their own co-op. Destinations range from non-profits in Boston to a digital advertising agency in the Czech Republic, a children's occupational therapy center in Uganda, or even an Antarctic research station. Faculty members and dedicated co-op advisors prepare students for their co-ops with a special course beforehand, check in with them while they are out in the field, and organize academic reflection on the experience afterward. "Professors want to make sure that you are as attractive as possible to potential employers," says a political science major.

Website: www.northeastern.edu
Location: City Center
Private
Total Enrollment: 32,403
Undergraduates: 20,235
Male/Female: 47/53
Financial Aid: 70%
Pell Grant: 13%
Expense: Pr $ $ $
Student Loans: 50%
Average Debt: $ $ $
Applicants: 75,244
Accepted: 18%
Enrolled: 33%
Grad in 6 Years: 91%
Returning Freshmen: 97%
Academics: ✐ ✐ ✐
Social: ☎ ☎
Q of L: ★ ★
Admissions: (617) 373-2200
Email Address: admissions@
northeastern.edu

Strong Programs:
Architecture
Journalism
Business and Marketing
Engineering
Social Sciences
Health Professions
International Business

NU's undergraduate programs are divided among seven colleges and schools: the College of Arts, Media, and Design; the D'Amore-McKim School of Business; the Khoury College of Computer Sciences; the College of Engineering; the Bouvé College of Health Sciences; the College of Science; and the College of Social Sciences and Humanities. The Explore Program offers experiential learning opportunities and academic advising to help undeclared students learn about potential majors and careers. Students with diverse interests may select from a slew of combined majors that cross disciplines, such as information science and cognitive psychology, political science and communication studies, and international affairs and cultural anthropology. Architecture and journalism are strengths, and the most popular majors fall under the categories of business and marketing, engineering, social sciences, and health professions. The well-regarded international business program features an "expat year," in which students spend one semester studying at an overseas university and six months working at an international co-op. Health sciences students may pursue a six-year doctor of pharmacy degree, and several "PlusOne" programs allow students to earn a master's degree by completing an additional year of study.

> "I feel extremely safe on campus even though it is in the middle of the city."

> *Working with a co-op advisor, students may choose from more than 2,900 established co-op employer partners in more than 146 countries.*

Under the Dialogue of Civilizations program, faculty members take more than 1,200 students abroad each summer. Overall, 17 percent of students work or study abroad. High-achieving first-year students may be invited to join the honors program to pursue more challenging coursework and live together in dedicated housing. In 2022, Northeastern absorbed struggling Mills College, a women's college in Oakland, California, to form a unique "bicoastal" institution of higher education. Under the terms of the merger, Northeastern is funding the creation of a Mills Institute that will continue to operate on the Oakland campus and perpetuate Mills's distinctive commitment to "gender and racial justice and the advancement of women, gender nonbinary individuals, and communities of color." The first new joint program, titled Leading Social Change and open to students at both schools, was launched on the Mills campus in January 2022.

Northeastern students tend to be academically and professionally driven. "Very quickly, we are sent out into the real world to really understand what we are doing and where we want to go," muses a political science and international affairs major. "This causes us to mature quite quickly." Northeastern was founded in 1898 as a YMCA educational program to serve local students from diverse socioeconomic backgrounds. These days, only 23 percent of undergraduates are from Massachusetts, and just 13 percent qualify for Pell Grants. Consistent with Northeastern's efforts to promote a global culture, 14 percent come from overseas. Asian Americans comprise 18 percent of the student body, Hispanics/Latinos 10 percent, Black students 5 percent, and multiracial students 6 percent. Merit scholarships averaging $14,500 are awarded annually, as are nearly 300 athletic scholarships.

> "You are pushed to meet new people and develop networking skills."

> *Several "PlusOne" programs allow students to earn a master's degree by completing an additional year of study.*

Forty-seven percent of NU undergraduates live in university-owned housing. Most first-years and sophomores live on campus, unless a co-op or study abroad program takes them away from Boston. After that, university housing is limited and offered on a space-available basis, so most upperclassmen rent privately owned apartments near campus. The dining halls offer "a lot of options and good food," according to students, who also speak highly of NU Public Safety: "I feel extremely safe on campus even though it is in the middle of the city," says one senior. Another adds, "All Northeastern students go through sexual assault and diversity training that gives us the tools to deal with these issues while on campus, as well as during study abroad and even during our co-op experiences."

When it comes to Northeastern's social scene, "Most of the social life happens off campus," one student says. Hundreds of clubs and activities abound, but the continuous flow of students on and off the campus for co-ops tends to be disruptive. "I may see a friend one quarter in class and then not again for six months. It's hard to stay connected," a student explains. The upside of this, says an engineering student, is that "you are pushed to meet new people and develop networking skills." Fraternities and sororities attract 9 percent of NU men and 16 percent of women, respectively. Regular traditions include Springfest, an annual concert that draws the likes of Chance the Rapper and MisterWives, and the annual Underwear Run during Parent Weekend in the fall, when students run through the city at night in their underwear or wacky costumes. Boston is, of course, the "ultimate college town" and offers a seemingly endless array of concerts, museums, clubs, and eateries. In the winter, students head to the ski slopes of Vermont, and in balmier weather, they're off to the beaches of Cape Cod and the North Shore.

For the annual Underwear Run during Parent Weekend in the fall, students run through the city at night in their underwear or wacky costumes.

Northeastern fields 19 Division I varsity teams (the Huskies) as part of the Colonial Athletic Association and the Hockey East Association. The biggest sports series of the year is the Beanpot Hockey Tournament ("Hockey is king here at Northeastern"), which pits Northeastern against rival teams from Boston College, Boston University, and Harvard. "It is all about bragging rights and pride, and

"Hockey is king here at Northeastern."

the fans from the schools make it fun," reports a student. One T-shirt reads, "No—we don't want to B.U.," epitomizing the competitive nature of the sports teams in the Boston area. NU's men's and women's ice hockey and men's basketball teams are recent conference champions, and the fleet-footed men's and women's track and cross-country teams regularly leave their opponents blinking in the dust. The recreation program offers more than 30 intramural options, and with 50-plus club teams, Northeastern is well represented in nonvarsity competition with other schools.

Northeastern is a school on the rise. It has moved well beyond its origins as an open admissions commuter school and—through aggressive fund-raising, an ambitious building program, and unabashed marketing—adapted its century of experience with co-op education to the emerging global economy. Northeastern students tend to be serious about their studies but learn to wear many hats. "We are employees at co-op, students in class, friends and roommates in our free time," explains one denizen. "We balance work and play while still meeting deadlines." Northeastern students graduate with a broad reservoir of experiences that they know will serve them well once they start scouring those job listings—both in the U.S. and around the world.

Overlaps

University of Southern California, NYU, Boston College, Boston University, George Washington, UC Berkeley, Columbia, Cornell University

If You Apply To ›

Northeastern: Early decision I and II, early action, regular decision. Accepts the Common Application. Studio art applicants must submit portfolio. Please consult Northeastern's website for the most up-to-date information regarding standardized test requirements.

1801 Hinman Avenue, P.O. Box 3060, Evanston, IL 60208

The Big Ten is not the Ivy League, and NU has more school spirit than its high-powered Eastern counterparts. Much more preprofessional than its nearby rival University of Chicago or any of the Ivies except Penn, NU is comparable to Duke and Stanford with an academic culture that encourages interdisciplinary work. World-renowned in journalism. Suburban setting on the shore of Lake Michigan, with easy access to Chicago.

Website: www.northwestern.edu

Location: Suburban

Private

Total Enrollment: 18,711

Undergraduates: 8,350

Male/Female: 47/53

Financial Aid: 60%

Pell Grant: 21%

Expense: Pr $ $ $ $

Student Loans: 28%

Average Debt: $ $ $ $

Applicants: 47,636

Accepted: 7%

Enrolled: 63%

Grad in 6 Years: 95%

Returning Freshmen: 99%

Academics: ✍ ✍ ✍ ✍ ✍

Social: ☎ ☎ ☎

Q of L: ★ ★ ★

Admissions: (847) 491-7271

Email Address: ug-admission@northwestern.edu

Strong Programs:
Journalism
Radio/Television/Film
Theater
Engineering
Music
Education
Chemistry
History

On Sunday nights before finals begin at Northwestern University, students are encouraged to let off steam with a campuswide "primal scream." The ear-shattering event illustrates two big themes at NU: students work really hard, but they also know how to let loose and enjoy themselves. This elite, top-tier university, the only private school in the Big Ten, boasts some of the most well-respected preprofessional programs in the country. Plus, Northwestern is ideally located just outside of Chicago. "I love being at a place where I can learn and have a great social life," says one student.

Northwestern, founded in 1851 by a group of Methodist ministers and businessmen to serve the former Northwest Territory (hence the name!), is situated on 231 acres about a dozen miles north of the Chicago Loop. An eclectic mix of stone buildings with abundant ivy, the leafy campus is set off from the town of Evanston and runs for a mile along the shore of Lake Michigan. Students migrate between the North Campus (techy) and the South Campus (artsy). The newer buildings are located adjacent to a 14-acre lagoon, part of an 85-acre lakefill addition built in the '60s. This area provides students with a prime location for picnicking, fishing, running, cycling, or just daydreaming. Recent campus additions include the 96,000-square-foot Ryan Fieldhouse, part of a larger $270 million sports complex.

Half of Northwestern's undergraduates are enrolled in arts and sciences, while the other half are spread out among five professional schools, all with national reputations. Indeed, students tend to identify more strongly with their school than with Northwestern as a whole. The Medill School of Journalism, the only such program at a top private university, sends student reporters out with iPads and video cameras as well as spiral notebooks. The curriculum integrates multimedia techniques with the study of "audience understanding" and features internships at dozens of top newspapers, magazines, and television stations across the nation. There's also a four-year accelerated B.S.J./M.S.J. program. A dazzling electronic studio centralizes Medill's state-of-the-art broadcast newsroom and the communication school's radio/TV/film department. The School of Communication also houses a notable program in theater. The McCormick School of Engineering and Applied Science is strong in all aspects of engineering and pairs students with clients with practical problems. Five-year co-op options are available. The School of Music wants students who can combine conservatory-level musicianship with high-level academics; it offers a five-year program from which students emerge with two B.A. degrees. The School of Education and Social Policy is the only school of its kind in the country and competes with Vanderbilt for education majors. Students and faculty members alike are encouraged to range across traditional disciplinary barriers—a policy that has led to the creation of some entirely new fields such as materials science—and students are free to switch schools once they are enrolled.

> **"I love being at a place where I can learn and have a great social life."**

Consistent with this approach, students say the university's best programs include the Integrated Science Program and Mathematical Methods in the Social Sciences, a selective program that gives students the technical skills to move into various areas of the social sciences. Strong arts and sciences departments include chemistry and history, although the humanities as a group are less strong. The social sciences (especially economics, psychology, and political science), journalism, neuroscience, engineering, and visual and performing arts enroll the most majors. Each of the undergraduate schools determines its own general education requirements, but broad outlines are similar. Each school requires a graduate to have coursework in "the major domains of knowledge"—science, mathematics and technology, individual and social behavior, historical studies, values, the humanities, and the fine arts. Incoming students take part in Wildcat Welcome, a weeklong orientation designed to ease the transition into college life.

Students tend to identify more strongly with their school than with Northwestern as a whole.

Unlike most schools on a 10-week quarter system, Northwesterners take four (not three) courses each quarter, except in engineering, where five are permitted. "Students tend to be supportive and collaborative," says a senior, but "the academics are rigorous and will take some adjustment from high school." Virtually all undergraduate courses are taught by regular faculty members. Introductory courses are larger than most, but 76 percent of all undergraduate classes have fewer than 20 students. "The quality of

"Many students are overachievers. Many are goal- and career-oriented."

teaching at Northwestern depends on the department and the professor," confides a senior, "but overall I would say it's very high quality." The Office of Undergraduate Research helps students apply for research assistantships and faculty-mentored independent projects, often with the support of grants. About a third of students take a break from campus through their choice of 150 study abroad programs in 50 countries.

Upon graduating, NU students tend to pursue business fields like consulting and finance, with technology, education, and communication distant followers. "Many students are overachievers," comments a social policy major. "Many are goal- and career-oriented." Twenty-five percent of undergraduates hail from Illinois, and 10 percent come from overseas. Students of color represent a sizable contingent of the student body, with Asian Americans accounting for 20 percent, Black students 6 percent, Hispanics/Latinos 14 percent, and multiracial students 7 percent. There are no academic merit scholarships, but NU does guarantee to meet the full demonstrated need of every admit and has eliminated need-based loans from its financial aid packages. It also offers hundreds of scholarships for its athletes.

Fifty-five percent of undergraduates reside in university housing, mostly in double rooms, although there are also singles, triples, and suites. "Housing varies significantly in quality at Northwestern," reports a journalism and political science major, and a classmate adds, "The nicer dorms on campus are competitive to get into." Several residential colleges, in areas like engineering, commerce and industry, and communication, bring students and faculty members together during faculty "firesides" or simply over meals. Fraternities and sororities also have their own houses. Most upperclassmen move off campus, but a senior cautions, "Housing in Evanston is expensive." Students can choose to eat at any one of six residential dining halls or a variety of restaurants and cafés on campus. "There is always at least one option for halal, kosher, vegan, vegetarian, gluten-free, or allergen-free needs," says a sophomore. Students generally feel safe on campus, but crime has been a concern in Evanston, especially after dark.

Unlike most schools on a 10-week quarter system, Northwesterners take four (not three) courses each quarter.

Much of the social life at NU is centered on the Greek system, with 30 percent of the men and 39 percent of the women joining up. Some students say finding a social niche can be tough, especially for those who aren't involved in

Dillo (Armadillo) Day is a popular end-of-the-year music festival with big-name artists, food trucks, and a beer garden.

Greek life, athletics, journalism, or theater. The school's alcohol policy is stiff but not always effective, "like the vast majority of campuses nationwide," says a student. The student government and Activities and Organizations Board sponsor an array of campuswide events, including theater productions, concerts, and movies. The 30-hour Dance Marathon and Dillo (Armadillo) Day, an end-of-the-year music festival with big-name artists, food trucks, a beer garden, and art installations, are popular annual events. Another tradition is upheld when representatives of student organizations slip out in the dead of night to paint their colors and slogans on a centrally located rock. In all, there are more than 500 student organizations, ranging from an African drum and dance ensemble to Adshop, an advertising agency that lets students hone their marketing skills by promoting local businesses. Suburban Evanston is "the restaurant haven of Chicago's North Shore," says a junior. A short stroll off campus brings you to the town's myriad restaurant options, trendy bars, and coffee shops with space to plug in a laptop and study, but most businesses close by 10 p.m. For culture or a night out, of course, Chicago is right across the border.

Football and tailgate parties are a traditional way of bringing alumni back and rousing the students to support the smallest and only private school in the Division I Big Ten. The Wildcats football team's trip to the 1996 Rose Bowl remains the stuff of legend.

"Housing varies significantly in quality at Northwestern."

In the last few years, women's lacrosse and softball have brought home Big Ten championship titles. As far as facilities, NU is on par with many schools its size and larger, with the beautiful Norris Aquatics Center/Henry Crown Sports Pavilion and the Nicolet Football and Conference Center used for conditioning of varsity athletes. The student-sponsored intramural program provides vigorous competition among teams from dorms and rival Greek groups, and 38 club sports are an option too. Northwestern also boasts one of the winningest debate teams in the country.

Northwestern occupies a unique niche in U.S. higher education. It has the academics of the Ivies, the spirited atmosphere of the Big Ten publics, and, along with Duke, Stanford, and perhaps Vanderbilt, combines success in Division I sports with quality instruction. Northwestern students bask in their school's balance of challenging academics, preprofessional bent, and myriad opportunities to get off campus to learn and let loose.

Overlaps

Columbia, U Penn, Stanford, Duke, Brown, Yale, WashU in St. Louis, University of Michigan

If You Apply To ›

Northwestern: Early decision, regular decision. Accepts the Common Application with supplement. Please consult Northwestern's website for the most up-to-date information regarding standardized test requirements.

University of Notre Dame

220 Main Building, Notre Dame, IN 46556

The Holy Grail of higher education for many Roman Catholics. ND's heartland location and 80-percent-Catholic enrollment make it a bastion of solid education and equally solid values, religious and otherwise. Offers business, science, architecture, and engineering in addition to the liberal arts. ND's personality is much closer to Boston College or Holy Cross than Georgetown. Only school ever ranked #1 in both football and graduation rates.

Founded in 1842 by the French priest Edward Sorin from the Congregation of Holy Cross, the University of Notre Dame has come a long way from its fledgling days in a rustic log cabin. While described as "a Catholic academic community of higher learning," its students need not be affiliated with the Roman Catholic Church (though about 80 percent are). Notre Dame takes pride in fostering a culture that values open discussion of religious, spiritual, and social issues, and it appeals to non-Catholics who are committed to social justice or seek a broadly spiritual dimension to their education. A soft spot for football doesn't hurt either.

With 1,250 acres of manicured quads, twin lakes, and woods, the university offers a peaceful setting for studying. The lofty Golden Dome that rises above the ivy-covered Gothic and modern buildings and the old brick stadium, where Knute Rockne made the Fighting Irish almost synonymous with college football, are national icons. The university recently completed a $1.1 billion construction spree that added 20 new buildings in less than a decade, including several new aca-

> "The workload is very demanding. It requires the student to have very good time-management skills."

demic buildings and residence halls. The nine-story Duncan Student Center overlooks the football stadium and boasts a career services center, dining facilities, a fitness center with a massive rock-climbing wall, and premium stadium seating for football VIPs. Notre Dame's $13 billion endowment is the largest of any of the country's Catholic colleges and universities.

Liberal education is more than just a catchphrase at Notre Dame. No matter what their major, students must take the First Year of Studies, one of the most extensive academic and counseling programs of any university in the nation. The core of the program is a one-semester writing-intensive university seminar limited to 20 students per section. The remainder of each freshman's schedule is reserved for the first of a comprehensive list of general education requirements covering writing and mathematics, natural science, theology, philosophy, history, social science, and fine arts. Academic and peer advisors are assigned to each student, as are tutors if necessary. Administrators are quick to point out that, due in part to the success of the first-year support program, a whopping 98 percent of freshmen make it through the year and return for sophomore year.

In the College of Arts and Letters, highly regarded departments include English, theology, and philosophy. Physics and chemistry are tops in the College of Science, bolstered by the first-rate equipment in the Nieuwland and Jordan Science Halls. Within the engineering school, chemical engineering rules, while the Mendoza College of Business's accountancy program is ranked among the nation's best. Another standout is the School of Architecture's five-year undergraduate degree program, in which students spend their entire junior year in Rome. The most popular majors overall are finance, economics, political science, and neuroscience and behavior. Students describe the academic climate as fairly competitive but not cutthroat by any measure. "The workload is very demanding," says a senior. "It requires the student to have very good time-management skills." Sixty percent of classes enroll fewer than 20 students, and students praise faculty members for being dynamic, personable, knowledgeable, and accessible. "The professors here care a great deal about their students, and it shows," says a biology major.

Notre Dame offers a variety of special academic programs and options. One of the most popular is the Program of Liberal Studies, in which students study art, philosophy, literature, and the history of Western thought within their Great Books seminars. The Summer Comprehensive Grant program awards up to $5,000 to students wishing to spend their summer focusing on independent research. Roughly 70 percent of undergrads take part in Notre Dame's extensive

Website: www.nd.edu
Location: Small Town
Private
Total Enrollment: 12,802
Undergraduates: 8,933
Male/Female: 52/48
Financial Aid: 48%
Pell Grant: 12%
Expense: Pr $ $ $
Student Loans: 42%
Average Debt: $ $ $
Applicants: 23,642
Accepted: 15%
Enrolled: 58%
Grad in 6 Years: 96%
Returning Freshmen: 98%
Academics: ✍ ✍ ✍ ✍
Social: ☎ ☎ ☎
Q of L: ★ ★ ★
Admissions: (574) 631-7505
Email Address: admissions@ nd.edu

Strong Programs:
English
Theology
Physics
Chemical Engineering
Accountancy
Architecture
Finance
Economics

Due in part to the success of the first-year support program, a whopping 98 percent of freshmen return for sophomore year.

international study program, which includes opportunities at the university's Global Gateways in London, Dublin, Rome, Beijing, and Jerusalem.

With a predominantly lay board of trustees and faculty, Notre Dame remains committed to "the preservation of a distinctly Catholic community," and it has a more self-consciously Catholic identity than any other major research university, including Boston College and Georgetown. The president and several other top administrators are priests of the Congregation of Holy Cross, and each dorm has its own chapel with daily masses, though attendance is not required. The main social issues discussed on campus include abortion; gender, racial, and LGBTQ issues; and faith. Black students make up 4 percent of the undergraduate student body, Hispanics/Latinos 12 percent, Asian Americans 5 percent, and multiracial students 6 percent. Despite its relative cultural homogeneity, Notre Dame recruits from all over the country; 87 percent of the students are from states outside of Indiana, and 6 percent hail from other countries. Competitive merit awards, averaging $15,500, are offered to students with outstanding high school records, and the university meets 100 percent of accepted students' demonstrated financial need. The Division I powerhouse deals out hundreds of athletic scholarships as well.

> **"The dorm culture is a unique part of ND's personality."**

Seventy-eight percent of ND students live on campus, which is required for their first three years. For their freshman year, students are assigned to a residence hall, mixed among the other classes, and they are encouraged to stay in the same one until graduation. Since ND has never had Greek organizations, the single-sex dorms become surrogate fraternities and sororities that breed a similar spirit of community and family. "The dorm culture is a unique part of ND's personality," comments a sophomore. Notre Dame has been co-ed since 1972, and parietal rules (midnight on weekdays, 2 a.m. on weekends) are still strictly enforced—and the subject of many student complaints. Students eat in the North or South dining halls or take their pick from 26 other restaurants, cafés, and to-go locations. As for safety, "The campus is self-contained and well-lit," reports a student.

ND's social life isn't as rambunctious as it once was, thanks to policies that forbid alcohol at campus social events. The rules relating to alcohol in the dorms are a bit more relaxed. For those who choose not to indulge, there are several groups dedicated to good times without alcohol. Most activities take place on campus and include parties, concerts, and movies. A popular event is the An Tóstal (Gaelic for "the pageant") festival, which comes the week before spring finals and guarantees to temporarily relieve academic anxiety with silly games, free food, giveaways, music, and other activities. The annual Notre Dame Forum brings internationally known speakers to campus to address timely topics like sustainability and the Catholic Church's sex abuse crisis. Students are involved in the community through volunteer work—more than 10 percent of grads enter public service positions. The best outlet for culture is nearby Chicago, about 90 minutes away. South Bend, with a metro area population of 325,000, offers plenty of opportunities for entertainment as well.

> **"Notre Dame football is massive."**

Notre Dame competes in the Division I Atlantic Coast Conference (ACC) for all sports except football and ice hockey. There's nothing like Notre Dame football, with its proud gridiron heritage and legends from Knute Rockne and the Gipper right on down to more recent greats such as Joe Montana. ND's name may be French, but the spirit of the Fighting Irish reigns supreme and has regained its former glory under head coach Brian Kelly. "Notre Dame football is massive," cheers a sophomore. It wasn't intentional—at least that's what they say—but the giant mosaic of Jesus Christ on the library lifts his hands toward the heavens as if to signal yet

Students in the School of Architecture's standout five-year undergraduate degree program spend their entire junior year in Rome.

The giant mosaic of Jesus Christ on the library lifts his hands toward the heavens as if to signal yet another Irish touchdown.

another Irish touchdown. Tailgate parties are celebrated events, occurring before and after the game. Aside from football, Notre Dame offers a solid all-around athletic program. Men's soccer and men's cross-country have brought home recent ACC championships, and the co-ed fencing program won its second consecutive national title in 2022. Die-hard jocks who weren't recruited for varsity teams will find plenty of company in ND's very competitive club and intramural sports. The Bookstore Basketball Tournament, the largest 5-on-5, outdoor hoops tournament in the world with more than 700 teams competing, lasts for a month.

From administrators to students, everyone here is considered part of the "Notre Dame family." Traditions are held in high esteem. For those looking for high-quality academics, a friendly, caring environment with a Catholic bent, and an excellent athletic scene, ND could be an answer to their prayers.

If You Apply To ›

ND: Early action, regular decision. Accepts the Common Application. Please consult Notre Dame's website for the most up-to-date information regarding standardized test requirements.

Oberlin College

38 E. College Street, Oberlin, OH 44074

The college that invented nonconformity. From the Underground Railroad and coeducation to global learning and the modern peace movement, Obies have long been in the forefront. As at Grinnell and Reed, Oberlin's curriculum is less radical than its students. Oberlin is especially strong in the sciences, and its music conservatory is among the nation's best. The annual Drag Ball is quintessential Oberlin.

New and contrasting ideas are a way of life at Oberlin College, a liberal arts school where nonconformity is a cherished tradition and student activism continues to make occasional headlines. Tucked away in a small Ohio town and dating to 1833, Oberlin was a stop on the Underground Railroad, and it was the first American college to adopt a policy to admit students of color and the first to grant undergraduate degrees to women in a coeducational program. That pioneering spirit has not faded. With diverse academic challenges ranging from cinema studies to neuroscience, Obies thrive on higher thinking and exploring their myriad talents. As one junior puts it, "Students here don't sit around during their free time; there's always another activity to be doing, a book to read, a lecture to go to."

Oberlin's attractive 440-acre campus features a mix of Italian Renaissance buildings (four designed by Cass Gilbert), late 19th- and early 20th-century organic stone structures, and some less interesting 1950s barracks-type dorms. The buildings rise over flatlands typical of the Midwest, which do little to stop brutal winter winds. The Allen Memorial Art Museum, sometimes mentioned in the same breath **"We're all pretty quirky, all pretty dorky."** as those at Harvard and Yale, is one of the loveliest buildings on campus, with a brick-paved, flower-laden courtyard and a fountain. The Oberlin College Science Center offers state-of-the-art classrooms, a science library, and laboratory space. Work is underway on the $140 million Sustainability Infrastructure Project, which will convert the entire campus to geothermal heating and cooling with the goal of achieving carbon neutrality by 2025.

(continued)

Email Address: college
.admissions@oberlin.edu

Strong Programs:
Music
Biology
Chemistry
Environmental Studies
Neuroscience
Creative Writing
Dance
Economics

There are no academic requisites for freshmen at Oberlin, but general education requirements include proficiency in writing and math and coursework in arts and humanities, natural sciences and math, social and behavioral sciences, and cultural diversity. Students must also participate in three January terms, during which they pursue monthlong projects, traditional or unique, on or off campus. About 40 different First-Year Seminar classes are available every semester, with enrollment limited to 14 students each, and although optional, almost all freshmen sign up because "it's a great way to make friends," says a student. "It also introduces you to the Oberlin academic experience."

Oberlin's Conservatory of Music occupies a well-deserved spot among the nation's most prominent performance schools; the voice, violin, and technology in music and related arts programs are especially praised. It is the oldest continuously operating music conservatory in the country, and Oberlin is one of only a handful of liberal arts colleges with a conservatory (see also Bard and Lawrence). The conservatory boasts 150 practice rooms, a substantial music library, and Steinway pianos—one of the world's largest collections. It enrolls about a fifth of Oberlin undergrads, who must audition to gain acceptance. Each year, about 40 students enter the Double Degree Program, which allows them to earn both a B.M. and a B.A. in five (or fewer) years; these students must be admitted to both the college and the music conservatory.

> "There are more protests, awareness and advocacy groups, and campaigns here than I can keep track of."

Oberlin has been a leader among liberal arts colleges seeking to promote their science offerings; biology and chemistry are two of the college's strongest departments, and environmental studies and neuroscience are well regarded. The creative writing and dance departments are notable, and students also flock to economics, politics, psychology, and computer science. Interdisciplinary and self-created majors, such as Africana, East Asian, Russian, Jewish, and gender studies, are popular—not surprisingly at such a liberal school. For those with more technical inclinations, 3–2 engineering degrees are offered in partnership with Case Western Reserve, WashU in St. Louis, Columbia, and Caltech. One of Oberlin's more unusual offerings is ExCo, an experimental college that offers students and interested townsfolk the chance to teach and learn together. Most classes are taught by students, and topics can range from community organizing to knitting to salsa dancing and much more.

The $140 million Sustainability Infrastructure Project will convert the entire campus to geothermal heating and cooling.

Oberlin's students are as serious about their schoolwork as they are about politics, justice, and other social causes, and heavy workloads are the norm. "Oberlin is academically rigorous but not competitive between students," says a junior. Seventy-seven percent of classes have fewer than 20 students, and a math and economics double major says, "I always love how much passion the professors bring because it makes classes more engaging." Most departments offer group and individual independent study opportunities and invite selected students to pursue demanding honors programs, especially during their senior year. Sixty-six percent of students conduct undergraduate research, and a whopping 80 percent of students study, intern, or do service work abroad in Oberlin-directed programs in Italy, Spain, and the UK or more than 90 other affiliated programs.

Oberlin students are—in a word—*passionate*. "We're all pretty quirky, all pretty dorky. Oberlin students love learning and love talking about the things they're passionate about," says a politics and history major. Eighty-two percent of undergraduates are from states outside of Ohio, primarily from the Mid-Atlantic states, and 11 percent come from abroad. But achieving diversity in rural Ohio has been a challenge: Black students account for 6 percent of the student body, Asian Americans 5 percent, Hispanics/Latinos 8 percent, and multiracial students 8

> "Social life is based a lot around live music."

percent. Merit scholarships averaging $23,000 are available to qualified students, and Oberlin promises to meet students' full demonstrated financial need—though a mere 8 percent of incoming freshmen are eligible for Pell Grants. For all its talk of nonconformity, Oberlin is also a model of political correctness. "Though the student body is homogeneously liberal," says a junior, "there are more protests, awareness and advocacy groups, and campaigns here than I can keep track of." A popular annual event is the Drag Ball, in which half the student body comes in full drag. "It's very Oberlin, because it's all about challenging social norms," says a student.

Ninety-one percent of Oberlin students live in campus housing, including several program houses focusing on various foreign languages and cultural backgrounds. For five dollars, students can rent up to two original works from the college's art museum to decorate their rooms. A small number of upperclassmen are allowed to live off campus every year, and those who wish to do so must try their luck in a random lottery. Students may eat in any of five dining halls and cafés. Appetizing alternatives to institutional fare can be found at the six co-ops that

"Oberlin is the epitome of a liberal arts school."

comprise the Oberlin Student Cooperative Association, a nearly $3-million-a-year corporation run entirely by students. Regarding safety, students say they feel safe on campus but report that the administration's handling of sexual assault cases needs improvement to better support survivors.

Social life, like so much of the Oberlin experience, is lively and eclectic. "Social life is based a lot around live music—we go to a lot of concerts, and parties usually book at least one campus band," says a junior. The midnight Organ Pump concerts in Finney Chapel each semester combine serious classical music with musical oddities, such as the school police blotter performed as Anglican chant. Several house parties, plays, movies, and conservatory performances are planned each week. And since there's no Greek system, nothing is exclusive. "The open-mindedness of the student body extends to social life, so while people do drink and do drugs, there is little pressure to partake if that's not your thing," comments a senior.

The small town of Oberlin offers some good restaurants and local shops, although they tend to close early. "There's only really two square blocks of downtown," says one student, "but within it is basically everything that you need." When the urge to wander strikes, Cleveland is only 30 miles away. Although relations between ultraprogressive Oberlin and the town are sometimes uneasy, Obies are always enthusiastic about giving back to the community through volunteer activities at local schools, hospitals, and nursing homes.

The Division III Yeomen and Yeowomen (medieval terms for people who own and cultivate land that hearken back to the college's founding motto of "Learning and Labor") appear to be building a loyal fan base: the women's cross-country team is a perennial powerhouse, and men's cross-country and women's track and field have claimed North Coast Athletic Conference championships in recent years. As for intramural and club sports, 30 percent of students compete, and ultimate Frisbee and Quadball (formerly known as Quidditch) are consistent favorites.

Oberlin may be small, but its emphasis on global learning, undergraduate research, and a vibrant liberal arts education helps it burst those statistical seams. Students are more likely to discuss local poverty than the quality of cereal choices in the dining halls, and they can be found playing a Steinway or plugging away at astronomy. One Obie sums it up this way: "Oberlin is the epitome of a liberal arts school, and that is reflected in all of the ways students customize their learning experiences, from the topics they choose for papers and projects to how they demonstrate that they care about current events."

Overlaps

Kenyon, Vassar, Carleton, Macalester, Northwestern, Reed, Lawrence, Wesleyan

Occidental College

1600 Campus Road, Los Angeles, CA 90041

Oxy is a streetwise cousin to the more upscale and suburban Claremont Colleges. Plentiful internships and study abroad give Oxy students real–world perspectives. Opportunities for undergraduate research are abundant. Oxy's innovative diplomacy and world affairs program features internships with UN agencies. Strong focus on diversity and social justice.

Website: www.oxy.edu
Location: City Outskirts
Private
Total Enrollment: 1,964
Undergraduates: 1,964
Male/Female: 42/58
Financial Aid: 76%
Pell Grant: 15%
Expense: Pr $ $ $
Student Loans: 55%
Average Debt: $ $ $
Applicants: 6,495
Accepted: 38%
Enrolled: 22%
Grad in 6 Years: 83%
Returning Freshmen: 92%
Academics: ✐ ✐ ✐ ✐
Social: ☎ ☎ ☎
Q of L: ★ ★ ★ ★
Admissions: (800) 825-5262
Email Address: admission@ oxy.edu

Strong Programs:
Economics
Diplomacy and World Affairs
Psychology
Biology
Urban and Environmental Policy
Politics
Chemistry
Media Arts and Culture

Founded in 1887, Occidental College is one of a handful of small colleges located in a big city, in this case La La Land. But unlike the sprawling and impersonal City of Angels, Oxy emphasizes a strong sense of community and a decidedly diverse student population. Notable attendees include former president Barack Obama. "Students dream big at Oxy," says a senior. "Whether a student wants a career in Hollywood or on Wall Street, everyone knows that it starts in the classroom."

Set against the backdrop of the San Gabriel Mountains, Oxy's self-contained Mediterranean-style campus is a secluded enclave of flowers and trees between Pasadena and Glendale, minutes from downtown Los Angeles. The McKinnon Center for Global Affairs features a two-story, LED-lit wall of sculpted glass with embedded interactive screens that display a shifting array of student and faculty research and coursework. Newer campus additions include a state-of-the-art music production center and an $18 million aquatic center.

Inside this urban oasis resides a thriving community of high achievers who don't for a moment believe that the liberal arts are dead or even wounded. Required first-year cultural studies seminars include topics in human history and culture,

"Students dream big at Oxy." with an emphasis on writing skills, and are limited to 16 students each. In addition, all Oxy students must show proficiency in a foreign language and complete coursework in world cultures, fine arts, the preindustrial era, science, and math. In their final year, all students complete a senior comprehensive, or "comp," such as a project, paper, or exam that shows mastery in their field.

Many of Occidental's academic departments are excellent; economics, diplomacy and world affairs, psychology, biology, urban and environmental policy, politics, and chemistry are among the strongest and most popular majors. The media arts and culture major, which offers concentrations in critical media and media production, is solid; students learn both theory and production skills and enjoy access to internships in L.A.'s film and entertainment industries. There are also 3–2 engineering programs with Caltech and Columbia University and a 4–2 biotechnology program with Keck Graduate Institute (of the Claremont Colleges). Academics at Oxy are challenging, but the atmosphere is not competitive. Faculty members are readily available in and out of the classroom, and students say the teaching, in general, is excellent. Sixty-seven percent of classes have fewer than 20 students, and as academic advisors are responsible for about four students per class (16 total), personal relationships develop quickly. "Professors' office doors are always open for students if they need help in class or in life," confirms a senior.

Oxy encourages diverse learning experiences through independent study, internships, and study abroad. The college boasts an unusual UN program that allows students to intern with UN-related organizations while also taking classes and living in Manhattan for a semester. The Campaign Semester, offered every two years, gives students a chance to work full-time on political campaigns and then return to campus for a seminar where they reflect on their experiences. About two-thirds of students study abroad or pursue international research or internships in programs offered in more than 50 countries. The Summer Research Program supports more than 100 student research projects in the sciences, social sciences, and humanities every summer, and many students publish and present their work.

In their final year, all students complete a senior comprehensive, or "comp," such as a project, paper, or exam.

"Students at Oxy are generally creative, smart self-starters and politically and socially engaged/opinionated," says a sociology major. Perhaps not surprisingly, students tend to be liberal, and the raging social concerns are "racial and social inequalities, environmentalism, and gender issues," according to one student. Forty percent of the students are from California, and 6 percent hail from foreign nations. Black students make up 5 percent of the population, Hispanics/Latinos 16 percent, Asian Americans 13 percent, and multiracial students 11 percent. Merit scholarships are doled out to qualified students each year—averaging $13,400—but there are no athletic scholarships.

"Students at Oxy are generally creative, smart self-starters."

Unlike many of its peers, Occidental stopped pursing wealthy applicants years ago and started investing in grants and scholarships for lower-income students of color. The college now meets the full demonstrated financial need of admitted students. The Barack Obama Scholars Program provides top achievers who have demonstrated serious commitment to public service with a four-year scholarship covering the full cost of attendance, as well as funding for three summer experiences, such as internships or service projects.

The residence halls are small—almost all house fewer than 150 students—and co-ed by floor or room. Seventy-eight percent of students live on campus, but what you get depends on your luck in the housing lottery. Freshmen live together in five dedicated first-year halls, and students are required to live on campus and purchase a meal plan until their senior year, when they can opt to move off campus. Special-interest housing, like Multicultural Hall, Food Justice House, and Queer House, is popular. "The food is fresh and yummy!" cheers a student. "It's always changing and they bring in locally sourced produce." Resources related to sexual assault include the Project SAFE student group, which a senior says "has been absolutely wonderful in creating a safe and respectful campus."

The Campaign Semester, offered every two years, gives students a chance to work full-time on political campaigns.

While the bustle of L.A. often beckons on weekends, the Oxy campus provides its share of fun too, whether it be a "basketball game, concert, dance, or party," says one student. Greek organizations attract 12 percent of the men and 21 percent of the women, but they are neither selective nor exclusive; students choose which to join rather than being chosen, and the frats must invite everyone to their functions. As for alcohol, "like most other colleges, there is underage drinking even though this is illegal," says a junior.

"We are pushed to take our writing and critical thinking to the next level."

Dance Production—a decades-old tradition in which student dancers perform works by student choreographers—sells out both performances each year. Other big events include Apollo Night (a talent contest) and the Fall Fest and Spring Fest concerts, featuring big-name performers. You may want to keep your birthday a secret, or on that unhappy day, a roaring pack of your more sadistic classmates will carry you out to the middle of campus and mercilessly toss you in the Gilman Fountain. It's a tradition, after all.

A student characterizes the surrounding neighborhood of Eagle Rock as "a quaint little community with an eclectic combination of 'ma and pa' restaurants and plenty of hole-in-the-wall stores." Community outreach is important at Occidental and dates back to the mid-1960s, when the college opened its Community Literacy Center and one of the country's first Upward Bound programs for underserved students. A majority of Oxy students participate in some kind of community project, most through the Center for Community Based Learning. When students become weary of the social life in the "Oxy fishbowl," they head for the bars, restaurants, museums, and theaters of downtown Los Angeles and Pasadena, where, one student notes, "You can find almost anything except snow." But the ski slopes of the San Gabriel Mountains are not far away, and neither is Hollywood nor the beautiful beaches of Southern California. A car (your own or someone else's) is practically a necessity, though the college runs a weekend shuttle service to Old Town Pasadena and other popular spots. The weather is warm and sunny, but the air is sometimes thick with that infamous L.A. smog.

Oxy's 20 sports teams (the Tigers) compete in Division III. Men's and women's cross-country and track and field, women's lacrosse, and women's soccer are some of the most competitive teams. Oxy's 125-year-old football rivalry with Pomona–Pitzer ended in 2020 when the college discontinued the sport. The school's *Io Triumphe* ("Hurrah, O Triumph") nonsense chant, a tradition since 1905, has been mocked for nearly a century by rival Redlands, which made up a gibberish chant of its own in 1921. Oxy's small recreational sports program offers intramural soccer and basketball along with seven club sports; rugby and ultimate Frisbee are popular.

Occidental's creative, motivated, and diverse students are not here for the bright lights and beautiful people of Los Angeles; those are just fringe benefits. Instead, students are drawn to this intimate oasis of learning by professors who hate to see anyone waste one whit of intellectual potential. "We are pushed to take our writing and critical thinking to the next level," says a sociology major. And students here are only too happy to live up to these lofty expectations.

Overlaps

Carleton, Colorado College, Macalester, Pomona, Reed, Scripps, Pitzer, University of Southern California

If You Apply To ›

Oxy: Early decision I and II, regular decision. Accepts the Common Application with supplement. Please consult Oxy's website for the most up-to-date information regarding standardized test requirements.

Oglethorpe University

4484 Peachtree Road NE, Atlanta, GA 30319

Small wonder that brochures for Oglethorpe trumpet Atlanta as the college's biggest drawing card. In a region where most liberal arts colleges are in sleepy towns, Oglethorpe has the South's most exciting city at its fingertips. Highly diverse student body and extensive financial aid. Oglethorpe Idea stresses broad academic values, while interdisciplinary Core Program gives shape to the curriculum.

Website: www.oglethorpe.edu
Location: Suburban
Private
Total Enrollment: 1,361
Undergraduates: 1,361

Founded in 1835, Oglethorpe University is named for the visionary founder of the state of Georgia, James Edward Oglethorpe. His idealism is well captured in the school's motto, *Nescit cedere* (He does not know how to give up), and in its ambition to become the first-choice university for high-achieving students in a region where it faces tough competition from much bigger names. Even as it continues to increase enrollment, the university remains committed to the Oglethorpe

Idea and to connecting students with real-world experiences. Says a junior, "Although few outside of the Southeast have heard of it, this school provides a top-notch education."

Oglethorpe's 118-acre campus is strategically located in Brookhaven, one of Atlanta's safest and most popular inner suburbs, with a picturesque Gothic campus that gives a traditional college feel. The heavily wooded, slightly rolling terrain is perfect territory for walks or long runs, and the beautiful campus has served as the backdrop for numerous movies and TV shows. Oglethorpe's academic buildings and some residence halls are in the English Gothic style. Newer facilities include the Cousins Center for Science and Innovation, featuring laboratory-classrooms and workshops.

The university's guiding principle is the Oglethorpe Idea—a philosophy based on the conviction that education should help students make a life, a living, and a difference. All students take the sequenced, interdisciplinary Core Curriculum program at the same point in their college careers, providing them with a model for integrating information and gaining knowledge. In

"The diversity is one of my favorite things about our campus."

addition to requiring several liberal arts and sciences courses that help develop students' ability to reason, read, and speak effectively, the core asks them to reflect on and discuss matters fundamental to understanding who they are and what they ought to be.

Oglethorpe's most popular majors—business administration, biology, communication studies, and psychology—are some of its strongest, along with English, accounting, film and media studies, theater, and preprofessional advising for a variety of health and medical fields. Minors in urban leadership and nonprofit management are specialties. The art department offers tracks in film production, medical and scientific illustration, and photography. Aspiring engineers may take advantage of dual-degree programs with Auburn, Georgia Tech, and other universities, and future teachers can enroll in a dual-degree program with Mercer. The school also offers cross-registration with other schools in the Atlanta area.

"I have never breezed through a class," says an art history major. "The academics are so rigorous." Oglethorpe's faculty may be demanding, but they're also friendly and helpful. "They really do care for you intellectually and personally," says one junior. Classes are generally small—60 percent have fewer than 20 students. The Compass advising program guides students through all aspects of their first year, while the "A_LAB" (Atlanta Laboratory for Learning) coordinates opportunities like internships, research, service, and study abroad. Seventeen percent of students sign up for a wide variety of study abroad programs, including short-term and faculty-led options. Sophomores and juniors interested in producing an independent honors thesis can apply for admission to the Honors Program.

What's an Oglethorpian like? "We tend to be open-minded, thoughtful, and intellectual," explains one student. Most come from public schools and 79 percent are Georgians; 10 percent hail from abroad. Oglethorpe prides itself on being one of the first Georgia colleges to admit Black students. Currently, 25 percent of students are Black, 5 percent are Asian American, and 12 percent are Hispanic/Latino. Socioeconomic diversity is also strong, with 39 percent of freshmen receiving Pell Grants. "The diversity is one of my favorite things about our campus," cheers a senior. Notably, every admitted student who completes the FAFSA form receives a $500 grant, regardless of financial need. Merit scholarships are also available, averaging $27,800. In an effort to earn more national name recognition, Oglethorpe's Flagship 50 program pledges to match the in-state tuition rate of each U.S. state's flagship institution for incoming freshmen who meet certain academic requirements.

Forty-seven percent of Oglethorpe's students live on campus—and most love it. "The dorms are big and have nice furniture," says an accounting major. Most

(continued)

Male/Female: 37/63
Financial Aid: 99%
Pell Grant: 39%
Expense: Pr $
Student Loans: 72%
Average Debt: $ $ $
Applicants: 2,277
Accepted: 81%
Enrolled: 22%
Grad in 6 Years: 58%
Returning Freshmen: 79%
Academics: ✐ ✐ ✐
Social: ☎ ☎ ☎
Q of L: ★ ★ ★
Admissions: (404) 364-8307
Email Address: admission@ oglethorpe.edu

Strong Programs:
Business Administration
Biology
Communication Studies
Psychology
English
Accounting
Film and Media Studies
Theater

Sophomores and juniors interested in producing an independent honors thesis can apply for admission to the Honors Program.

rooms are suites with private bathrooms, and some singles are available. Meals in the Petrel's Nest dining hall get average reviews. The Healthy Campus Task Force promotes healthy lifestyles, tackling issues ranging from eating disorders to preventing sexual assault.

The Flagship 50 program pledges to match the in-state tuition rate of each U.S. state's flagship institution for incoming freshmen.

The social scene on campus is active for a small school. "Our Student Government Association sponsors events like bubble soccer, food truck Fridays, Bob Ross art night, and more," explains a human resource management major. Students of legal drinking age are allowed to have alcohol on campus. Fraternities and sororities, which claim 11 percent of the men and 13 percent of the women, throw parties that draw big numbers. "Greek parties are really fun but much less raucous/drug-infused than parties at other schools like UGA and Georgia Tech," opines one senior. The campus celebrates its origins once a year during Oglethorpe Day. Named after a 1742 battle in which James Oglethorpe defeated Spanish troops in southern Georgia, the annual Battle of Bloody Marsh is a tug-of-war game between students and faculty. Each holiday season brings a particularly unique tradition: the Boar's Head Ceremony celebrates a medieval scholar who halted a stampeding wild boar by ramming his copy of Aristotle down the animal's throat.

It's rumored that Oglethorpe barflies do more hopping than Georgia bullfrogs, and bars, clubs, and cafés abound within 10 minutes of campus. Students can also find excitement on the campuses of the dozen or so other colleges in the area or in downtown Atlanta. "There are always city events like free yoga that are just a short MARTA ride away!" enthuses a junior. Atlanta proper offers everything you can imagine—arts, professional sports (including basketball's Hawks, football's Falcons, and baseball's Braves), and entertainment (ride the Great American Scream Machine at Six Flags). Oglethorpe always has a big contingent going to Savannah for St. Patrick's Day and to New Orleans for Mardi Gras, and sunny Florida beckons too.

> "[SGA] sponsors events like bubble soccer, food truck Fridays, Bob Ross art night, and more."

Oglethorpe's mascot, the Stormy Petrel, is a sea bird that flies in the face of storms. (James Oglethorpe was inspired by them on his first visit to Georgia in 1733.) Oglethorpe fields 16 Division III varsity sports. The men's golf team is a powerhouse, making regular NCAA Tournament appearances, and men's soccer and tennis are recent Southern Athletic Association champions. Men's and women's basketball games against cross-city rival Emory are popular. Intramural sports attract about 10 percent of the student body. The Georgia landscape makes possible a plethora of outdoor activities, including hiking at nearby Stone Mountain and boating or swimming in Lake Lanier (named for Georgia poet Sidney Lanier—Oglethorpe Class of 1860).

Though Oglethorpe is still working to achieve widespread name recognition, its diverse and growing group of students get all the attention they need from a caring faculty on a close-knit campus. And being in a large city like Atlanta provides anything else that might be lacking, ranging from great nightlife to internships and postgraduate employment with big-name corporations. In a sea of large Southern state schools, Oglethorpe stands out as a place where students come first.

Overlaps

Agnes Scott, Birmingham–Southern, Hendrix, Emory & Henry, Austin College, Millsaps, Mercer, Berry

If You Apply To ›

Oglethorpe: Early action, rolling admissions. Accepts the Common Application with supplement. Application includes optional questions on gender identity and preferred pronouns.

The Ohio State University

Student Academic Services Building, 381 West Lane, Columbus, OH 43210

The biggest school in the Big Ten, Ohio State competes for top students not only with Michigan and Wisconsin but also with two other fine Ohio publics, Miami and Ohio U. Operates the mother of all college sports programs, which consistently racks up national titles and spills over into undergraduate wellness programs. Check out the top-notch honors program. Columbus, the capital of Ohio, is booming.

Envision a campus with 53,000 full-time students and too many opportunities to count. What might come to mind is The Ohio State University (and don't forget the "The"—it's trademarked), located in the heart of the state's capital, offering 15 colleges and 12,000 courses in more than 200 undergraduate majors. If those numbers aren't staggering enough, consider the fact that OSU has 36 varsity sports, 20 intramural sports, nearly 60 sports clubs, and the third largest campus in the nation. It also has an operating budget larger than that of the state of Delaware. While students cite the school's size as both a blessing and a curse, all seem to agree that at OSU, the sky is the limit for those with a desire to sample its academic and other resources.

"Classes demand a lot of attention, independence, and self-advocacy on the part of the student."

This megauniversity stands on 1,665 acres in the middle of the city, just two miles north of downtown Columbus. "One part of the campus maintains a nostalgic air while another is relatively modern," observes a student. The grounds are nicely landscaped, and a centrally located lake provides a peaceful setting for contemplation and a break from all the surrounding activity. OSU's rich array of academic resources includes 12 libraries with eight million volumes. Across the Olentangy River from campus is a teaching and research farm associated with the College of Food, Agricultural, and Environmental Sciences. The Recreation and Physical Activity Center (RPAC) is the nation's largest facility dedicated to student fitness, wellness, and recreation. Since 2016, eight new residence halls, a dining hall, and a recreation facility have been added to the campus's North district.

Launched in 2022, Ohio State's new general education curriculum reduces the number of required credits in order to give students more flexibility to pursue minors or second majors. The university's commitment to liberal arts learning remains strong: all undergrads must satisfy requirements that include courses in writing, math, data analysis, arts and humanities, historical studies, social and behavioral science, and diversity. Some of the school's most celebrated departments include business, engineering, neuroscience, dance, and design; political science and education are also

"Social life is never-ending."

strong. OSU is internationally known for pioneering work in computer graphics and animation. The African American and African studies program offers one of the most extensive offerings of African languages of any U.S. university. Furthermore, the university has the nation's only ABET-accredited program in welding engineering and the nation's first undergraduate program in data analytics. The majors that enroll the most students include finance, psychology, communication, and biology. A personalized study program enables students to create their own majors.

Freshmen may take advantage of numerous first-year programs, including the First Year Success Series, covering topics like study skills and career exploration, and pre-enrollment programs like Buckeyes First (for first-generation students). Once the academic year is underway, they experience a variety of class formats and sizes, ranging from intimate freshman seminars to large lectures; overall, one-third of

Website: www.osu.edu
Location: City Center
Public
Total Enrollment: 53,025
Undergraduates: 42,905
Male/Female: 50/50
Financial Aid: 80%
Pell Grant: 18%
Expense: Pub $ $
Student Loans: 46%
Average Debt: $ $
Applicants: 58,180
Accepted: 57%
Enrolled: 25%
Grad in 6 Years: 88%
Returning Freshmen: 94%
Academics: ✍ ✍ ✍ ½
Social: ☎ ☎ ☎ ☎
Q of L: ★ ★ ★
Admissions: (614) 292-3980
Email Address:
    askabuckeye@osu.edu

Strong Programs:
Business
Engineering
Neuroscience
Dance
Design
Political Science
Education
Finance

undergraduate classes have fewer than 20 students. "Classes demand a lot of attention, independence, and self-advocacy on the part of the student," comments a sport industry major. Teaching assistants hold smaller recitation sections of large lecture courses and deal on a personal level with students. Class sizes generally whittle down as students continue in their fields of study. At such a large institution, the quality of instruction can vary greatly, and students report this to be the case.

OSU's honors program allows selected students to learn from top professors in small classes averaging about 25 students each. "The whole system of honors classes, priority scheduling, honors housing, and cocurricular activities really adds to the overall experience at OSU," a biology major says. Twenty-four percent of undergraduates participate in research opportunities coordinated by the Office of Undergraduate Research and Creative Inquiry. Columbus affords students access to internships with the state government, Fortune 500 companies, and major tech and research organizations, including the IBM Analytics Solutions Lab and Battelle. About 20 percent of students study abroad through 200 programs offered in more than 50 countries.

"Most students are extremely well-mannered, ambitious, open-minded, and obsessed with the Buckeyes," says a loyal sophomore. Seventy-five percent of Ohio State's undergraduates hail from Ohio, and most out-of-staters come from Illinois, Pennsylvania, California, New York, and New Jersey. Seven percent come from foreign countries. The student body is 8 percent Black, 5 percent Hispanic/Latino, 9 percent Asian American, and 4 percent multiracial. Several programs aim to attract and retain students of color, including a statewide Young Scholars Program that begins working with students when they start the seventh grade. As for politics, a public policy analysis major opines, "OSU is not a particularly politically involved campus." Qualified students compete for merit scholarships averaging $7,100, and hundreds of athletic scholarships go to talented athletes each year. The Ohio State Tuition Guarantee sets and freezes rates for tuition, fees, and room and board for in-state freshmen in each entering class for four years.

The residence halls, which house 32 percent of the Ohio State masses, are located in three areas: North, South, and Olentangy (that is, those closest to the Olentangy River). Freshmen and sophomores are required to live in residence halls unless they are commuting from home, and freshmen are scattered among each of OSU's 42 residence halls. A senior advises, "Make sure to look into the Scholars Program, which puts you in a learning community for four years with other people who have the same major or professional goals." Campus residents may choose from four meal-plan options, and the food gets mostly positive reviews. Buckeyes ACT is a comprehensive program intended to combat sexual misconduct and relationship violence on campus.

"As hard as students may work during the school week, everything stops on game day."

OSU is a bustling place on weekends. "Social life is never-ending," cheers one student. With nearly 1,400 student organizations to choose from, it's hardly difficult to find something to get involved with. Various social events are planned within residence hall communities. The student union runs eateries, a tavern, movies, and other activities. Six percent of OSU men and 13 percent of the women join fraternities and sororities. "Greek organizations do not dictate social life on campus," says a junior, and most partying happens off campus.

Such a large student market has, of course, produced a strip of bars, fast-food joints, convenience stores, bookstores, vegetarian restaurants, and you-name-its along the edge of the campus on High Street, and downtown Columbus is just a few minutes away. The fine public transportation system carries students throughout this capital city. "It's really easy to access all kinds of cool stuff downtown, as all students get free bus passes," explains a sophomore. Columbus boasts a symphony orchestra, a ballet, and professional hockey and soccer teams; OSU's D-Tix program offers students discounted or free tickets to cultural and sporting events. The city's central location in the state makes it easily accessible to Cleveland and Cincinnati. Outdoor enthusiasts can ski in nearby Mansfield, canoe and sail on the Olentangy and Scioto rivers, hike the city's 19 metro parks, or camp in nearby Hocking Hills.

Ohio State operates arguably the most lavish—and successful—college sports program in the nation. The Buckeyes field 16 men's, 17 women's, and three co-ed varsity teams, from golf to gymnastics to riflery. (A buckeye, incidentally, is a small, shiny nut that falls from Ohio's official state tree.) Recent national champions include women's ice hockey, synchronized swimming, and dance and co-ed pistol, while Big Ten champs include men's and women's tennis and women's swimming and diving. "Football is somewhat like religion," says one student. "As hard as students may work during the school week, everything stops on game day." Rivalries abound, although the annual gridiron contest with "That Team Up North" (Michigan's Wolverines) gets the most heated; preparations for the big game include "crossing out every letter M on all campus signs with red tape," explains a fervent fan. Many students take advantage of an extensive roster of club sports and an ambitious intramural program that boasts a dozen basketball courts and 26 courts for handball, squash, and racquetball.

OSU's sheer size is sometimes overwhelming to be sure, but students here seem to thrive on the challenge and excitement of a big university, not to mention Buckeye spirit. For those who really want to be Buckeyes, be prepared to jump in with both feet and be assertive about your goals. "Knowing what you want is great, but to get it, you'll need to work hard," warns one student. "Because if you want it, there are likely hundreds of other people who want it too."

If You Apply To ›

OSU: Early action, regular decision. Accepts the Common Application with supplement. Please consult OSU's website for the most up-to-date information regarding standardized test requirements.

Ohio University

Chubb Hall 120, Athens, OH 45701

OHIO is roughly one-third the size of Ohio State and plays up its homey feel compared to the cast of tens of thousands in Columbus. The Honors Tutorial College is a draw for top students who want to work closely with faculty. Communication and journalism top the list of prominent programs, and learning communities are plentiful. OHIO is not in the Big Ten, but the Mid-American Conference generates excitement.

With top-notch programs in journalism, business, and engineering, Ohio University has become a competitive public research institution without shedding its small-town roots. Faculty interests range from dinosaur anatomy to rural diabetes rates. Students here love to hit the town for fun but are quick to hit the books as well. Those who choose to attend OHIO receive ample returns, says a senior, including "a quality education, lifelong friends, supportive faculty, and a beautiful campus."

Established in 1804 as the first institution of higher learning in the old Northwest Territory, Ohio University is located in Athens, which lies about 75 miles southeast of Columbus, the state capital, and was named after the ancient center of learning in Greece. Encircled by winding hills, the campus features neo-Georgian

Website: www.ohio.edu
Location: Small Town
Public
Total Enrollment: 17,487
Undergraduates: 14,262
Male/Female: 44/56
Financial Aid: 89%
Pell Grant: 30%
Expense: Pub $ $ $

(continued)

Student Loans: 66%
Average Debt: $ $ $
Applicants: 21,733
Accepted: 89%
Enrolled: 19%
Grad in 6 Years: 67%
Returning Freshmen: 81%
Academics: ✎ ✎ ✎
Social: ☎ ☎ ☎ ☎
Q of L: ★ ★ ★
Admissions: (740) 593-4100
Email Address: admissions@
ohio.edu

Strong Programs:
Communication Studies
Journalism
Business
Engineering
Nursing
Education
Management
Marketing

architecture, tree-lined redbrick walkways, and white-columned buildings all clustered on "greens," which are like small neighborhoods. Long walks are especially nice during the fall foliage season. In an effort to improve campus sustainability, all new construction and renovation projects over $2 million follow standards for LEED Silver or higher certification. The state-of-the-art, $76 million Chemistry Building was completed in 2021.

The BRICKS general education curriculum, launched in fall 2021, involves two writing-intensive foundations courses, a standard set of distribution requirements, and an upper-level capstone course, and it incorporates interdisciplinary, intercultural, and hands-on learning. Students enroll in nine undergraduate colleges and one center, and the Scripps College of Communication contains five distinct schools: journalism, information and telecommunication systems, communication studies, media arts and studies, and visual communication. OHIO's most popular majors are nursing, management, marketing, and psychology. The highly regarded journalism program offers tracks in news and information and strategic communication in addition to an emphasis on learning to use current and emerging technology. Nursing and education are also strengths.

> **"[With learning communities] you can make connections in your program in your very first class."**

OHIO students work hard, but a communication major says the academic environment is "open and inviting." Freshmen are often taught by full professors with TAs handling study sessions. OHIO supports more than 250 learning communities, in which 98 percent of first-year students participate; some have a residential component, but most do not. "Learning communities are paired with a professor in your area of study, so you can make connections in your program in your very first class," explains a journalism major. Classes of 100-plus students do exist, but 38 percent of undergraduate classes have fewer than 20 students, and faculty make themselves as available as possible. "The professors are more than willing to help you learn if you are willing to ask," says a junior.

One of the advantages of an Ohio University education, and something that sets the school apart from run-of-the-mill state institutions, is the Honors Tutorial College. Founded in 1972, it's the nation's first multidisciplinary, degree-granting honors program modeled on the tutorial method used in British universities, notably Oxford and Cambridge. Ranked as one of the best programs on campus, it is highly selective: only around 60 to 70 freshmen are accepted into it every year. Students pursue an individualized curriculum in their major field and spend much of their time in one-on-one weekly tutorials with profs. Special opportunities abound for those not in the honors college too. A separate OHIO Honors Program, open to students in all colleges, offers challenging small-group seminars and the option to complete honors projects in traditional classes. Co-op programs are available for engineering students, and nearly anyone can earn credit for an internship. The Provost's Undergraduate Research Fund provides financial support for undergraduate research, and students showcase about 850 research and creative projects at the university's annual Student Research Expo. The Office of Global Opportunities offers worldwide destinations for anywhere from one week to one year; 11 percent of students study abroad.

Students in the Honors Tutorial College pursue an individualized curriculum and spend much of their time in one-on-one tutorials with profs.

"Students at Ohio University are accepting, motivated, and enthusiastic about being Bobcats," says a communication studies major. Eighty-five percent of undergraduates are Ohioans, and 1 percent are international. Students express a desire for greater diversity on campus: "While we do have a strong Multicultural Center, they are representing such a small population of students," says a senior. Just 5 percent of undergraduates are Black, 4 percent are Hispanic/Latino, 1 percent are Asian American, and 4 percent are multiracial. The student body's liberal leanings are pronounced in comparison to the conservatism of southeast Ohio. The OHIO Signature Awards program provides merit scholarships and need-based grants for outstanding students, and the athletically gifted can vie for nearly 250 scholarships. The "OHIO Guarantee+" initiative sets fixed rates for each incoming class for tuition, housing, dining, and most other fees that are guaranteed not to increase for four years. It also provides students with individualized graduation plans to ensure that they graduate on time—or OHIO will cover the cost of additional courses.

Forty-two percent of students live in campus housing. Five LEED-certified residence halls have been built in recent years. Juniors and seniors usually move to nearby apartments or rental houses. Both campus dining halls have been renovated and receive positive reviews; one location now accepts food stamps. A senior comments, "There has been increasingly more transparency from my school about sexual assault, but there can always be more help and more awareness for this issue and for the [survivors]."

> The "OHIO Guarantee+" initiative ensures that students graduate on time—or OHIO will cover the cost of additional courses.

Campus social life includes guest speakers and performers, plays, midnight movies, and other events. Only about 9 percent of the men and 12 percent of the women choose to participate in Greek life. The administration has attempted to curtail underage drinking with a strict alcohol policy, and many students complain that OHIO's traditional party-school image overshadows the school's academic quality, but an accounting major concedes that "there is definitely a large party atmosphere." Students look forward to university-sponsored events such as homecoming and the International Street Fair, as well as unsanctioned events like the so-called fest season in Athens. "We are known for our street fests," says a journalism major. "Almost every Saturday in the spring has a party on a street." Court Street is dotted with bars and clubs, and the city's fabled Halloween celebration is a huge block party that draws people from all over the Midwest. Volunteer opportunities, such as Habitat for Humanity and a local homeless shelter, are available through the Campus Involvement Center. Students also love to hike and camp at the nearby state parks and national forest or trek to Columbus for shopping.

> "There is definitely a large party atmosphere."

Division I sports are a big draw at OHIO. The Bobcats field 16 varsity teams, and men's basketball is a recent Mid-American Conference champion. The Bobcat football team makes regular bowl game appearances, and the baseball, women's basketball, volleyball, and softball teams are competitive too. The university also boasts a nationally ranked forensics team. Twenty-four intramural and 32 club sports draw 17 percent of the students; popular choices include flag football, rugby, and soccer.

Students say Ohio University has much to offer, from quality professors to a vibrant social life and a sense of community. "We are always looking out for one another," says a sophomore, "and we all love Athens—it has a special place in our hearts."

Overlaps
Ohio State, Miami (OH), University of Cincinnati, Penn State, West Virginia University, Colorado State, Kent State, Bowling Green State

If You Apply To ›

OHIO: Early action, rolling admissions. SATs or ACTs: optional. Accepts the Common Application with supplement. Honors Tutorial College applicants must interview. Visual and performing arts applicants must submit portfolio or audition.

Ohio Wesleyan University

South Sandusky Street, Delaware, OH 43015

OWU serves up the liberal arts with a popular side dish of business-related programs. Has expanded campus housing in recent years as part of efforts to enhance the residential experience. Attracts middle-of-the-road to liberal students with preprofessional aspirations. Offers a variety of research, travel, and internship programs, notably New York Arts and Wesleyan in Washington.

Website: www.owu.edu
Location: Small City
Private
Total Enrollment: 1,332
Undergraduates: 1,332
Male/Female: 45/55
Financial Aid: 99%
Pell Grant: 31%
Expense: Pr $ $
Student Loans: 70%
Average Debt: $ $ $ $
Applicants: 3,573
Accepted: 74%
Enrolled: 14%
Grad in 6 Years: 64%
Returning Freshmen: 79%
Academics: ✍ ✍ ✍ ½
Social: 🐦 🐦 🐦 🐦 🐦
Q of L: ★ ★ ★
Admissions: (800) 922-8953
Email Address: owuadmit@
owu.edu

Strong Programs:
Business Administration
Zoology
Botany
Microbiology
Psychology
Communication
Exercise Science
Education

Ohio Wesleyan University is a small school with a big commitment to providing its students with a well-rounded education. Established in 1842 and traditionally affiliated with the United Methodist Church, OWU has instituted what it calls an indefinite "pause" in its relationship with the denomination in response to the church's decision in 2019 to strengthen its ban on LGBTQ clergy and same-sex marriages. As the *Fiske Guide* goes to press, discussions are ongoing. Hallmarks of an OWU education include strong preparation for graduate and professional school, a solid grounding in the liberal arts, real-world experience, and an emphasis on having fun outside the classroom.

Situated in the center of the state and on the outskirts of Columbus, OWU's spacious 200-acre campus is peaceful and quaint. Several buildings are on the National Register of Historic Places. The architecture ranges from Greek Revival to colonial to modern, with brick academic buildings on one side of a downtown thoroughfare that runs through the campus and dormitories and fraternities on the other side.

> **"Professors want to see their students thrive and help them every step of the way."**

Stately University Hall, with its majestic spire and bell tower, is the main campus landmark and houses the president's office and the 1,100-seat Gray Chapel, home to the largest Klais organ in the United States. In a significant expansion of campus housing, the university has opened four duplexes for living/learning communities, renovated a first-year residence hall, and built a new apartment village for seniors that opened in 2021.

To graduate, OWU students must take an interdisciplinary first-year seminar, as well as coursework in the social sciences, natural sciences, arts, humanities, cultural diversity, and foreign language. Students must also pass three mandatory writing classes to sharpen their written communication skills, but these aren't burdensome. In fact, more than a quarter of students find time to complete double or triple majors. The most popular majors are psychology, zoology, business administration, communication, and exercise science. Preprofessional education has always been Ohio Wesleyan's forte, especially in business; the curriculum also includes majors in education, nutrition, and data analytics, and the highly popular zoology, botany, and microbiology majors are interesting alternatives to the traditional premed route. Nursing, dentistry, optometry, veterinary medicine, law, and public administration round out the list of preprofessional offerings. The Woltemade Center for Economics, Business, and Entrepreneurship caters to budding entrepreneurs, and the music and fine arts programs offer both professional and liberal arts degrees. Classes are small, with 72 percent enrolling fewer than 20 students, and an economics and psychology major says, "Professors want to see their students thrive and help them every step of the way."

All students are required to participate in the OWU Connection, supplementing their major with interdisciplinary learning, global perspectives, service learning, and practical experiences; students may fulfill these expectations by choosing from a number of pathways, such as special courses, study abroad, internships, and independent projects. Students seeking financial support for such endeavors may apply for a Theory-to-Practice Grant. The honors program offers qualified students one-on-one tutorials and a chance to conduct research with faculty members in areas of mutual interest. Students who desire careers in public policy and service may choose to pursue a semester-long internship through the Wesleyan in Washington program, while others may join the New York Arts program to spend a semester in Manhattan in apprenticeships with working professionals in the arts and creative industries. Thirty percent of students study abroad, and the university's travel-learning courses, which append one to two weeks of travel to a regular semester-long class, are particularly popular.

The university's travel-learning courses, which append one to two weeks of travel to a regular semester-long class, are particularly popular.

Sixty-one percent of students come from Ohio and 7 percent are international. Students agree that diversity could be improved but is valued on campus; Black students make up 6 percent of the student body, Hispanics/Latinos 6 percent, Asian Americans 3 percent, and multiracial students 5 percent. Liberals and conservatives are well represented on campus, and hot topics include racial, gender, and sexual equality. Merit scholarships averaging $30,400 are available for qualified students.

Eighty-six percent of OWU students live in university-sponsored housing. All but one of the dorms are co-ed, and rooms are mostly doubles or apartment-style, four-person suites. All fraternities offer a residential option, and there is a Panhellenic House for women in sorori-ties. "We have small-living units or SLUs, which are essentially themed houses," says a senior. "The members of these houses do house projects every semester for the

"Because of the high amount of volunteering that OWU students do in Delaware, we have a fairly good relationship."

campus and are an extremely important part of the OWU community." Students enjoy numerous culinary choices, from 24/7, all-you-can-eat in the main dining hall to snacks from the college grocery store, although the price of meals is a common complaint. The Department of Public Safety operates the SafeRide program, where student employees use an OWU-branded vehicle to safely provide passage for other students at night.

"There are many social events on campus to keep students busy and entertained. The school hosts many functions, like laser tag or roller-skating or different events with free food," says a sophomore. Does the buttoned-down seriousness of recent years mean that OWU has forsaken its heritage of raucous partying? Administrators certainly hope so. Part of OWU's commitment to mend its partying ways includes dry rush for all fraternities and an armband policy at parties. Still, Greek membership attracts 25 percent of men and 19 percent of women. "There is definitely pressure to drink, because so many people do it every weekend," says one student. Among OWU's best-loved traditions are homecoming in the fall and the President's Ball in December. Day on the Jay, held at the beginning of the year and again at the end of the spring semester, is a carnival-like celebration with games, inflatables, and plenty of free food.

Day on the Jay is a carnival-like celebration with games, inflatables, and plenty of free food.

The city of Delaware (population 42,000) is "adorable," says one junior. "There are several small shops and restaurants that are also relatively diverse from Greek to Cajun to just regular pizza and burger joints." The Little Brown Jug, one of harness racing's Triple Crown events, takes place each autumn, bringing thousands of people to the city. Sixty-five percent of students are involved in service, either through mission trips or local service projects like Habitat for Humanity, Delaware Reads, and the Delaware County Humane Society. "Because of the high amount of volunteering that OWU students do in Delaware, we have a fairly good relationship with the town," one student says. Ohio's capital and largest city, Columbus, is only

30 minutes away by car and offers many internship and job opportunities. Lakes, farms, and even ski slopes are within a few hours' drive.

OWU's Division III Battling Bishops are a North Coast Athletic Conference powerhouse. Men's soccer, men's basketball, field hockey, and men's and women's track and field are among the strongest teams. Sports fever carries over into intramural and club sports (40 percent of students take part); ultimate Frisbee, rugby, basketball, and soccer draw the most enthusiasm.

Ohio Wesleyan offers a solid liberal arts education focused not on bells and whistles, but on practical, career-related experience. "Ohio Wesleyan is a place where the education goes well beyond the classroom," says one student. "The family atmosphere and the opportunities that the college provides you enrich the entire college experience."

If You Apply To ›

OWU: Early decision, early action, regular decision. SATs or ACTs: optional. Accepts the Common Application with supplement.

University of Oklahoma

1000 Asp Avenue, Room 127, Norman, OK 73019

Tops among public universities in attracting National Merit Scholars, OU is strong in engineering and geology-related fields. Check out the nationally recognized Honors College and the growing variety of living/learning options. Football aside, OU has traditionally lacked the visibility of rival UT Austin. Counseling services are a national model.

The University of Oklahoma has more to boast about than its powerhouse football program. Founded in 1890, OU has capitalized on its Great Plains location by cultivating strengths in petroleum and geological engineering, meteorology, and the history and culture of the American West. It has also worked to make itself, in the words of a first-year student, "a large university with a small-town vibe" by capping the size of freshman comp courses and establishing residential colleges. Couple that with a genuine friendliness among the student body, and it's easy to understand this favorite saying: "Sooner born and Sooner bred, when I die, I'll be Sooner dead!"

Located about 20 miles south of Oklahoma City, OU's 3,500-acre Norman campus features tree-lined streets and predominantly redbrick buildings. Many are historic in nature and built in the Cherokee Gothic or Prairie Gothic style. The Norman campus is home to 16 colleges; six medical and health-related colleges are located on the OU Health Sciences Center campus in Oklahoma City, and programs from colleges on both campuses are also offered at OU's Schusterman Center in Tulsa. The Sam Noble Oklahoma Museum of Natural History houses more than 10 million artifacts, including the oldest work of art ever found in North America—a lightning bolt painted on an extinct bison skull—and the largest Apatosaurus on display in the world. Newer facilities include the 75,000-square-foot Gallogly Hall, the university's first LEED Gold–certified building, which houses the biomedical engineering program.

> "Professors do a great job of engaging students and making the material easy to understand."

OU's general education requirements consist of coursework in symbolic and oral communication (including English composition), natural science, social science, and arts and humanities. Freshmen must take a First-Year Experience course, choosing one of three options: Gateway to Belonging at OU, Global Perspectives and Engagement, and Ethical Leadership Development. Students must also complete at least one upper-division course outside of their major. Most OU first-years start out in University College before choosing among OU's degree-granting colleges.

The most popular majors include nursing, psychology, accounting, and finance. The Gallogly College of Engineering offers aerospace, civil, mechanical, and environmental engineering, among others. The Mewbourne College of Earth and Energy provides programs in geology, geophysics, and paleontology, and its petroleum engineering program ranks among the best in the nation. OU is home to the largest school of meteorology in the country and the National Weather Center. In the Dodge Family College of Arts and Sciences, the natural sciences, notably chemistry, are strong. The Price College of Business, OU's second-largest college, offers a dozen majors, including energy management, entrepreneurship and venture management, and healthcare business. Other well-recognized programs at OU include history of the American West and Native American studies majors and a minor in Constitutional studies. The Rainbolt College of Education's rigorous teacher-certification program, Teacher Education Plus, incorporates field experience, mentoring, and instruction from 63 full-time faculty.

"I have never had a course that is impossible," comments a psychology major, "but I have also never been in a class that requires little effort." Study groups are common, and students recommend University College's academic tutoring and advising services. OU has worked to address large classes and is one of the nation's few public universities to cap first-year English comp courses at no more than 19 students;

"OU offers the classic college experience."

overall, 49 percent of undergraduate classes have fewer than 20 students. In the past two decades, increased private support has allowed OU to create significantly more endowed faculty positions, helping the school attract and retain talented professors. "Professors do a great job of engaging students and making the material easy to understand and fun to learn," says one sophomore. OU's recently expanded advising service offers support on topics ranging from financial and mental health issues to life skills.

The rigorous Honors College offers 2,200 students small classes with outstanding faculty members, independent study options, and opportunities to apply for competitive funded research programs, including the Honors Research Assistant Program. Students across the university compete for Undergraduate Research Opportunities Program grants of up to $1,000 to support faculty-mentored research and creative work. Study abroad opportunities are available in 80 countries, including programs at OU's study centers in Italy and Mexico. Students are often able to apply their financial aid to study abroad, and special scholarships are available for qualified students as well.

OU is home to the largest school of meteorology in the country and the National Weather Center.

A nursing major says OU students create a "lively, energetic, young, and studious" atmosphere on campus. Sixty percent of undergraduates hail from the Sooner state, and 3 percent come from abroad. Black students account for 5 percent, Asian Americans 7 percent, Hispanics/Latinos 13 percent, American Indians 3 percent, and multiracial students 9 percent. A meteorology major describes the political climate as "open and accepting," with greater diversity of views than one tends to find in the rest of the very red state. Qualified students receive scholarships based on academic merit, with awards averaging $3,000, and there are also more than 250 athletic scholarships in 17 sports. OU offers a variety of special aid programs aimed at making the university more affordable for low-income students.

About a third of OU undergraduates live on campus, and the university is making living/learning communities a major focus. The residence halls and Cross

(continued)

Strong Programs:
Petroleum Engineering
Geology
Meteorology
Chemistry
Energy Management
Entrepreneurship and Venture
   Management
History of the American West
Native American Studies

Village are mostly occupied by first-year students, who can choose to live on specific academic floors or at the Honors College. Residential colleges modeled after those at Yale and Oxford also serve as living/learning communities and are the preferred option, along with the OU Traditions Square apartment community, for upperclassmen. Come mealtime, one student says, "Eating at the Caf is like eating dinner with the whole freshman class every night." Students say they feel safe on campus and praise programs like OU Advocates and required trainings for their efforts in sexual assault prevention.

The OU social scene is vibrant and well balanced with on-campus activities and off-campus fun. Twenty-seven percent of men and 34 percent of women go Greek. Although the dorms and Greek houses are dry, off-campus fraternity parties are the highlight of weekends at OU. The "three-strikes" alcohol policy "has greatly cut down on alcohol incidents" on campus, says one student. Campus Corner, located right across the street from campus, is another source of nightlife, with several res-

"I consider game days an all-day festival."

taurants and bars, as well as coffee shops and boutiques. Norman, population 128,000, is Oklahoma's third-largest city, and Oklahoma City is just 20 minutes away. OU's annual day of volunteering, the Big Event, sends more than 5,000 students into the community for a day of service. Favorite traditions include the University Sing talent show, tailgating, and, of course, the annual road trip to Dallas for the OU–Texas football game.

OU is known for successful Division I athletics and is capitalizing on that reputation by moving to the Southeastern Conference in 2025. Sooner football has brought home the Big 12 Conference title six times since 2015. "Every football game day, the town swells to over 500,000 people, and I consider game days an all-day festival," says a letters major. The softball and women's gymnastics teams captured national titles in 2022, and the men's gymnastics and men's and women's basketball teams make regular NCAA Tournament appearances too. Recreational and intramural programs attract 16 percent of the undergraduate population, and flag football and basketball are especially popular.

"OU offers the classic college experience," says a senior. Indeed, students at Oklahoma have a lot to brag about. "The educational opportunities are top-notch," says one junior, and "a student can come from anywhere and find that they are part of something special." If you're searching for a school with plenty of spirit and a feeling of family, OU may be worth a look—sooner, rather than later.

Overlaps

UT Austin, Texas A&M, University of Kansas, CU Boulder, Texas Christian, Oklahoma State, Texas Tech, Baylor

If You Apply To ›

OU: Early action, regular decision. Accepts the Common Application with supplement. Please consult OU's website for the most up-to-date information regarding standardized test requirements.

Olin College of Engineering

1000 Olin Way, Needham, MA 02492

Olin opened its doors in 2002 with an innovative project-based curriculum and a commitment to turning out "technologists with soul." Already an elite institution that competes with Caltech and MIT. Every enrolled student gets a hefty merit scholarship. Located in Needham, near Babson and Wellesley, on the outskirts of Boston.

In the mid-1990s, leaders of the F. W. Olin Foundation began daydreaming about what "state-of-the-art" engineering education for the 21st century would look like. Two decades and $470 million later they have their answer: the Franklin W. Olin College of Engineering. This elite engineering school aims to turn out farsighted graduates who are not only technically competent but who can "come up with innovative ideas and products." The curriculum is project-based, and students become as comfortable in the machine shop as in labs and classrooms. The founders also decided that, rather than gradually building up the quality and reputation of their new school, they would invest in excellence from the get-go. By offering every enrolled student a half-tuition scholarship worth more than $110,000 over four years, Olin has succeeded in luring superbright students away from Caltech, MIT, and other engineering highfliers. Sure, the college lacks the rich tradition and reputation for research of more established institutions. But that doesn't seem to bother the more than 350 students who have latched on to perhaps the best deal in U.S. higher education.

"There's no real feeling of anything but the friendliest competition."

Olin's 70-acre campus is located adjacent to Babson College in a pleasant suburb less than 15 miles west of Boston. The campus design is an innovative blend of the traditional and futuristic. Five buildings curve around a central green space, creating a sense of community and echoing the design of the traditional New England college. The classrooms make use of state-of-the-art instructional media, and there are plenty of meeting and public spaces to encourage the kind of collaboration called for in modern-day engineering.

Olin's innovative curriculum emphasizes science and engineering, as well as business and entrepreneurship. Students choose from three majors—electrical and computer engineering, mechanical engineering, or a self-designed major in engineering with a concentration, such as bioengineering, computing, design, robotics, or sustainability. In addition, students must complete 30 credits of math and science and 28 credits of arts, humanities, social sciences, and entrepreneurship. The course catalog is thin, especially in liberal arts subjects, but students can and do take courses at nearby Babson, Wellesley, and even Brandeis.

The hands-on nature of Olin's curriculum means that students start engineering right away with relatively simple projects, building mechanical systems intended to mimic animals or insects that hop in the first-semester Design Nature course. They then progress to more sophisticated challenges like Principles of Integrated Engineering, in which they build a project involving electronic, mechanical, and software components (such as an automatic cake decorator or a light-seeking flower pot). Concern for "engineering design" is built into every subject. Each student also completes one of two options—SCOPE (Senior Capstone Program in Engineering) or ADE (Affordable Design and Entrepreneurship)—for a yearlong, team-based senior capstone project, in which they apply their knowledge to solving real-world problems, in partnership with outside organizations or communities.

"We're all engineers, but we have social skills!"

Courses are rigorous, but working in teams and across disciplines is the norm for faculty as well as students. "We work very hard, and we work a lot," says one senior, "but there's no real feeling of anything but the friendliest competition." Grading starts after the first semester. Forty-eight percent of all classes have fewer than 20 students, and all are led by professors, with whom students are on a first-name basis. Prospective faculty members must go through an extensive interview and audition process, and once hired, none are ever granted tenure. Like their students, many of them have been lured from the likes of MIT because they like the challenge of helping to create what one of them termed "the model of engineering for the future." A sophomore explains, "The professors value feedback from the

Website: www.olin.edu
Location: Suburban
Private
Total Enrollment: 360
Undergraduates: 360
Male/Female: 48/52
Financial Aid: 100%
Pell Grant: 13%
Expense: Pr $ $ $
Student Loans: 49%
Average Debt: $
Applicants: 907
Accepted: 18%
Enrolled: 56%
Grad in 6 Years: 97%
Returning Freshmen: 100%
Academics: ✑ ✑ ✑ ✑ ✑
Social: ☎ ☎ ☎
Q of L: ★ ★ ★ ★ ★
Admissions: (781) 292-2222
Email Address: info@olin.edu

Strong Programs:
Engineering
Electrical and Computer
   Engineering
Mechanical Engineering

Every enrolled student receives a half-tuition scholarship worth more than $110,000 over four years.

students very highly—courses are often altered halfway through the semester with suggestions from the students."

First-year students participate in an interactive, weeklong orientation program that includes team-building exercises, meetings, and meals with faculty and advisors, as well as a trip into Boston. The college also encourages students to engage in "Passionate Pursuits" by enabling them to pursue personal interests via independent projects, for which they receive nondegree academic credit and, often, funding. A sampling of student projects includes rock climbing, guitar making, marathon training, gelato making, and Bhangra (Indian folk dancing). Olin offers several direct-exchange options, as well as preapproved programs at approximately 40 institutions around the world; 26 percent of students study away from campus. Eighty-five percent conduct research with faculty members.

The hands-on curriculum means that students start engineering right away with relatively simple projects in the first-semester Design Nature course.

"We're all engineers, but we have social skills!" asserts a senior. Only 14 percent of students hail from Massachusetts, and 7 percent come from abroad. Black students represent a mere 3 percent of the student body, Asian Americans 20 percent, Hispanics/Latinos 11 percent, and multiracial students 12 percent. Students appreciate the balanced male/female ratio as "very uncommon" for an engineering school, and according to a sophomore, "Students are generally liberal but not particularly active in promoting political issues." To make sure that it selects students who are a good fit for Olin's unique approach to engineering, the admissions office invites 225 to 250 applicants to attend one of three "candidates' weekends" in the spring, where they learn about the school, take part in team projects such as building a weight-bearing bridge out of Styrofoam, and go through a 25-minute interview with a team that may include faculty, staff, students, and alumni. About 125 to 135 of these students are accepted, and about 40 are placed on a waiting list. In addition to awarding half-tuition scholarships, Olin guarantees to meet 100 percent of any remaining demonstrated financial need for all enrolled domestic students.

"Olin is pretty quirky, and we like to think we're different—passionate, weird, and doing fun things."

All students live on campus in Olin's two residence halls, first-years and sophomores in doubles in West Hall and upperclassmen in either doubles or suites in East Hall. Meal options in Olin's sole dining hall get average reviews. Olin operates with a student-designed honor system that makes for unlocked rooms and take-home exams. "You can leave your laptop in the lounge, and it won't walk off," says a senior. Campus security is good and "students do feel physically safe," says one student. An electrical and computer engineering major adds that students have been "urging more action from the administration" when it comes to responding to the issue of sexual assault.

When students aren't laboring over the latest Modeling and Simulation of the Physical World assignment, they tend to congregate on campus for fun. "There are parties in the residence halls, and the Student Activities Committee hosts some sort of schoolwide event every weekend," says a junior. There are no Greek organizations, and students say the social scene does not revolve around alcohol. "The campus alcohol policies are quite reasonable," says a student, "relying largely on student responsibility." The student orchestra has no conductor—or, as the joke goes, "not even a semiconductor." When the campus scene grows tiresome, students often travel to nearby Babson (on foot) or Wellesley (by shuttle bus) to mingle. Aside from frequent visits to Boston, students enjoy road trips to Vermont or the beaches of Maine.

The student orchestra has no conductor—or, as the joke goes, "not even a semiconductor."

The surrounding town of Needham "isn't a great college town but does have some good restaurants," says a sophomore. Students take advantage of volunteer opportunities, and the college organizes community-oriented events, such as a charity auction where students offer up everything from original artwork to haircutting services. Campus traditions, however, are few and far between. "I think our healthy disregard for tradition makes life a little more interesting," says a senior, adding, "We do have a traditional spring formal and an academic exposition at the end of each semester."

Although Olin does not offer varsity sports, two competitive club sports are available: soccer in the fall and ultimate Frisbee in the spring. In addition, "pick-up leagues have evolved for soccer, Frisbee, football, and basketball," says a junior, and students are allowed to participate in intramural sports at Babson and Wellesley. Many students join extracurricular project teams that participate in competitions like Formula SAE, SAE Baja, and robotic sailing.

For those who have what it takes, Olin College offers a top-notch engineering degree at a bargain price. Olin students have watched their school grow up and blossom before their eyes, frequently taking part in shaping its innovative approach to engineering education. Students here value interdisciplinary, project-based instruction, and the importance of "learning to learn," and they graduate inspired to shake up the workforce. As one junior comments, "Olin is pretty quirky, and we like to think we're different—passionate, weird, and doing fun things."

Overlaps

MIT, Stanford, Caltech, Harvey Mudd, UC Berkeley, Yale, Carnegie Mellon, Rose–Hulman

If You Apply To ›

Olin: Regular decision. Accepts the Common Application with supplement. Please consult Olin's website for the most up-to-date information regarding standardized test requirements.

University of Oregon

1585 E 13th Ave, Eugene, OR 97403-1226

A flagship university of manageable size in a great location, UO is notable for its emphasis on the undergraduate educational experience in and out of the classroom. Liberal arts are more than just a slogan, and programs in the sciences, business, and communication are strong. Splashy sports program plays a big—faculty members say too big—role in shaping the vibrant campus life and culture. Lagging state funding assures that it lacks the academic range of larger flagship universities.

Blend two vegetarians, one track star, one fraternity brother, two tree huggers, three hikers, and one conservative. What have you got? Ten UO students. Sure, the joke's hokey, but its offbeat humor is typical of the laid-back, slightly eccentric attitude that prevails here in Eugene, where bicycling is the main form of transportation, recycling is a requirement, and littering is déclassé. As the most accessible of the West Coast flagship universities, the University of Oregon attracts brainy students who are proud of their quirky ways.

UO's buildings date from as early as 1876 and are surrounded by the university's lush 295-acre arboretum-like campus, which boasts more than 4,000 trees representing nearly 500 species. Many academic buildings were built before World War II and represent a blend of classical styles, including Georgian, Second Empire, Jacobin, and Lombardic. Construction on the ultramodern, $1 billion Knight Campus for Accelerating Scientific Impact (funded in part by a $500 million donation from UO alum and Nike cofounder Phil Knight and his wife) is ongoing. The first phase, a 160,000-square-foot, glass-and-steel facility, opened to students and researchers in 2020, and the second phase is set to begin in 2023.

Website: www.uoregon.edu
Location: Small City
Public
Total Enrollment: 20,562
Undergraduates: 17,165
Male/Female: 44/56
Financial Aid: 69%
Pell Grant: 22%
Expense: Pub $ $ $ $
Student Loans: 42%
Average Debt: $ $
Applicants: 31,558
Accepted: 93%
Enrolled: 16%
Grad in 6 Years: 74%

(continued)

Returning Freshmen: 87%

Academics: ✏️ ✏️ ✏️ ½

Social: ☎ ☎ ☎

Q of L: ★ ★ ★ ★

Admissions: (800) 232-3825

Email Address: uoadmit@
   uoregon.edu

Strong Programs:

Journalism

Design

Education

Business

Music

Dance

Architecture

Environmental Studies

First-Year Interest Groups help new students develop close working and advising relationships with faculty members and other students.

Oregon's academic calendar is organized by quarters, and its general education program consists of standard distribution requirements, as well as one course exploring difference, inequality, and agency in the U.S. and one course on global perspectives. Each summer, the university offers IntroDUCKtion to new students, featuring opportunities for orientation, registration, and advisement. First-Year Interest Groups (FIGs) help new students develop close working and advising relationships with faculty members and other students. Each FIG consists of 20 freshmen who take three courses together around a common theme, such as Going Green and Path to Global Citizenship.

Due to chronically low state funding, UO has a relatively modest array of academic offerings for a major research university. UO's professional schools—journalism, design, education, law, business, and music and dance—are highly regarded, and

> **"The academic climate at the University of Oregon is collaborative yet challenging."**

considered to be more accessible to entry-level students than similar programs elsewhere. The most popular majors include business administration, psychology, general social science, and human physiology. The College of Design is the home of sought-after programs in architecture, landscape architecture, and interior architecture—the state's only accredited degrees in these fields. In the College of Arts and Sciences, environmental studies is strong, and the science departments enjoy advanced resources and research opportunities in fields like nanotechnology, optogenetics, and neuropsychology. Pine Mountain Observatory, a field-study resource for astronomy and physics students located high in the Cascade Mountains, and the Oregon Institute of Marine Biology give students a chance for hands-on studies in their major. Newer offerings include a major in bioengineering and minors in commerce and society, science communication, and Black studies.

"I would say that the academic climate at the University of Oregon is collaborative yet challenging," says an accounting major. "Above all else, it is what you make of it." Thirty-five percent of classes have fewer than 20 students. The quality of instruction varies, and it's not uncommon to find teaching assistants handling some of the teaching duties, but a math major says most professors are knowledgeable and will "check in on students' progress." A senior adds that it is possible to find "supportive and encouraging mentors" among the faculty.

Highly motivated undergraduates may apply to the Clark Honors College, a small liberal arts college with its own four-year curriculum that includes a senior thesis and opportunities for exclusive research assistantships. Student-run community internship programs provide credit for community volunteer work. One-quarter of undergrads study or complete internships abroad during their time at UO, and more than 300 programs are offered in more than 90 countries.

Only 54 percent of undergraduates are native Oregonians, largely because the university has increasingly relied on revenue from full-paying outsiders to balance the budget. "There are a lot of people from California," says a freshman,

> **"There are a lot of people from California [and] a lot of artsy hipsters."**

and "a lot of artsy hipsters." International students account for 3 percent of the student body. Asian Americans represent 7 percent, Black students 3 percent, Hispanics/Latinos 15 percent, and multiracial students 9 percent. "The political climate is skewed liberal all across campus," notes a sophomore. Numerous merit scholarships worth an average of $7,100 are awarded to qualified students, as are roughly 250 athletic scholarships in 20 sports. The PathwayOregon program covers tuition and fees for Pell-eligible Oregonians.

Twenty-seven percent of UO students live in the university's 10 residence halls, which are a mix of traditional halls and modern high-rises. Freshmen are required to reside on campus. A student says of the rooms, "They are pretty small, but I love the cozy feeling." There are a number of thematic living arrangements, including the Global Scholars Hall, the Clark Honors College, and Kalapuya Ilihi Hall, which is named for the native inhabitants of the Willamette Valley and offers communities for Native American and indigenous studies, social activism, art and design, and media and social action. Students can choose from five meal plans, and 14 dining venues serve up fresh, diverse menus. "The food on campus is actually amazing," says a sophomore. Students say they feel secure on campus, but some cite the growing homeless population just off campus as a safety concern. Even so, a senior reports, "There is a ride service called Duck Rides that can pick you up within a five-mile radius of campus and bring you back to your residence hall or off-campus apartment for free, no questions asked, to ensure students' safety."

Thirteen percent of UO men and 16 percent of the women join Greek organizations, which provide living space, interesting social diversions, and a wealth of leadership and community service opportunities. "The university plays host to a variety of concerts, culture nights, film viewings, guest lecturers, sporting events, and dances," a journalism major says. Students 21 and over may have alcohol in their rooms, but only with the doors closed. A junior says, "There are large parties happening around

Everyone looks forward to the biannual Street Faire that brings local vendors to campus in the fall and the spring.

"[At football games] thousands of students whoop and holler and scream their lungs out."

campus most nights of the week for people who would like to spend their time on such activities," but there is no pressure to do so. Everyone looks forward to the biannual Street Faire that brings local vendors to campus in the fall and the spring. "There is great food, local businesses, and artists, and everyone on campus gets to enjoy something different," explains a psychology major. Other major events include the Willamette Valley Music Festival, where big-name artists perform for students on campus, and, of course, every home football game, where "thousands of students whoop and holler and scream their lungs out" for their Ducks.

Eugene (population 175,000) offers plenty of popular hangouts and is, according to one enthusiastic student, "the best college town ever! Everything about Eugene is based around the Ducks!" The one drawback to all this fun is Oregon's weather: it rains and rains from late fall through spring. Still, the moist climate rarely dampens enthusiasm for the many expeditions available through the university's well-coordinated outdoor program, from rock climbing to skiing. An hour to the west, the rain turns to mist on the Pacific Coast; an hour to the east, it turns to snow in the Cascade Mountains. Those who stick around all year are rewarded with green, sunny summers.

UO's official mascot is a whimsical yellow-and-green likeness of Donald Duck.

UO's official mascot is a whimsical yellow-and-green likeness of Donald Duck. The athletic program is financially independent of the university, and the Ducks continue to dominate their Division I athletic rivals. The women's program made NCAA history by becoming the first to win national titles in women's cross-country, indoor track, and outdoor track in the same season—the "triple crown." Football, men's track and field and golf, and women's basketball have had impressive successes as well. Duck fans love cheering on their teams, especially during the annual football game against archrival Oregon State, a grudge match that has been playing out since 1894. Intramurals are another time-honored pastime here, and roughly 44 percent of students take part.

A recent University of Oregon Orientation Week T-shirt sported a picture of a duck and a simple exhortation: "Let your future take flight." UO offers ample opportunities for those with lofty ambitions to succeed. Indeed, UO's accessible academics, expert faculty, and abundance of social activities confirm that UO is all it's quacked up to be.

Overlaps

University of Arizona, CU Boulder, UCLA, UW–Madison, University of Maryland, University of Washington, Oregon State, Cal Poly–San Luis Obispo

Oregon State University

Corvallis, OR 97331

The biggest dilemma facing the typical 18-year-old Oregonian is whether to be a Beaver or a Duck. Choose Duck and hang with the ex-hippies in cosmopolitan Eugene. Choose Beaver and get small-town life with professional programs in business, engineering, and life sciences in Corvallis. Strong STEM focus, along with global emphasis.

Website: www.oregonstate.edu
Location: Small City
Public
Total Enrollment: 21,906
Undergraduates: 18,676
Male/Female: 53/47
Financial Aid: 63%
Pell Grant: 21%
Expense: Pub $ $
Student Loans: 52%
Average Debt: $ $
Applicants: 23,219
Accepted: 91%
Enrolled: 21%
Grad in 6 Years: 68%
Returning Freshmen: 86%
Academics: ✑ ✑ ✑
Social: ☎ ☎ ☎
Q of L: ★ ★ ★
Admissions: (541) 737-4411
Email Address: osuadmit@
    oregonstate.edu

Strong Programs:
Business
Engineering
Forestry
Natural Resources
Marine Biology
Oceanography
Climate Science
Agricultural Sciences

Once known as Moo U, there's much more to Oregon State University than fruits and vegetables. One of the most accessible West Coast public universities, OSU is strong in many departments, including biotechnology, forestry, and engineering. As a land grant university founded in 1858, OSU offers abundant research opportunities and co-op work experiences, especially for students in STEM fields. Says one satisfied student, "Anyone would be lucky to be at Oregon State."

Located in the pristine but rainy Willamette Valley, OSU's campus is a mix of older buildings and more modern structures. In addition to the 500-acre main campus, OSU owns 13,000 acres of forestland near campus and numerous agricultural tracts throughout Oregon. Thousands of azalea and rhododendron bushes welcome springtime on campus with their colorful blooms, and summers are unfailingly sunny. Newer facilities include the eco-friendly, $65 million Oregon Forest Science Complex.

OSU's extensive Baccalaureate Core requires courses in a variety of areas, including skills; perspectives; and difference, power, and discrimination. One writing-intensive course is required as well. Perhaps the core's most innovative facet is its "synthesis" requirement, in which upperclassmen take two interdisciplinary courses on global issues in the modern world. The level of academic pressure varies by major, but even those in the various honors programs say they don't feel overworked. Although classes can be large, a senior says, "Professors make sure to get to know each individual and work with them, so that we as students gain the most from our education."

"The best way to describe students at Oregon State? Two words: 'Go Beavs!'"

OSU's College of Liberal Arts ranks with business and engineering as the largest on campus, but there are many more preprofessionals than poets. With the exceptions of history and English, the liberal arts—including such standard fare as sociology, economics, and philosophy—play second fiddle to more practical, technical fields. The business school offers some of the finest business-related programs in the state, and majors in forestry, natural resources, marine biology, oceanography, climate science, and engineering are strong drawing cards. Even though agriculture doesn't lure as many students as it used to, those who do come find excellent programs, including agricultural sciences, animal sciences, and food science and technology. Computer science, business administration, mechanical engineering, and psychology are among the most popular majors.

Students in the Honors College participate in small seminars with top professors and hands-on research, culminating in a senior thesis. The university's small-town location makes it difficult to find much career-oriented part-time employment, and internships are hard to come by. (OSU operates on a quarter system.) Students in almost all majors, however, can participate in the cooperative education program, which allows them to alternate terms of study with several months of work in a relevant job. About a quarter of undergraduates get involved in research. The 6 percent who choose a semester abroad may select from 200 study abroad programs or research and internship opportunities in 70 countries around the world.

"The best way to describe students at Oregon State? Two words: 'Go Beavs!'" cheers a senior. Indeed, school spirit runs high on this friendly campus, where most students are "well-rounded and chill but diligent," says a biohealth sciences major. Sixty-four percent of undergraduates are from Oregon, and 5 percent hail from foreign countries. Just 2 percent are Black, 12 percent are Hispanic/Latino, 8 percent are Asian American, and 7 percent are multiracial. The Office of Diversity and Cultural Engagement sponsors several cultural resource centers, conferences, social justice retreats, and other diversity initiatives to support students from underrepresented backgrounds. Students report that the campus is split fairly evenly between liberals and conservatives. Merit scholarships averaging $8,700 are awarded annually, as are nearly 350 athletic awards in 17 sports. The Bridge to Success program allows roughly 3,000 in-state students per year to attend the university tuition-free.

> *In addition to the 500-acre main campus, OSU owns 13,000 acres of forestland near campus.*

> **"People in the valley don't tan, they rust."**

Freshmen are expected to live in college housing, though fraternity pledges have the option of living in their houses. Co-ed and single-sex options are available in the dorms, which house 18 percent of the students. "I loved living in my hall because it is where I made many friends; however, I much prefer living off campus because it is not as expensive," a student says. In addition to standard rooming situations, several living/learning communities in areas like engineering, outdoor adventure, and the environment are also options. "Dining on campus is great, and so are the eateries just off campus: reasonably priced, with different styles and cuisines," says a mechanical engineering major. Campus security gets good reviews too.

> *To fulfill the "synthesis" requirement, upperclassmen take two interdisciplinary courses on global issues in the modern world.*

Eleven percent of the men and 13 percent of the women join fraternities and sororities, and Greek events offer a social scene but don't dominate campus life. Administrative efforts to make Greek parties safer include a ban on hard alcohol, a training program for students who wish to serve as sober party monitors, and a medical amnesty policy. Favorite campus traditions include the All-University Sing (featuring musical numbers staged by fraternity and sorority members) and the Dam Jam music festival in the spring. As for Corvallis (population 60,000), a senior says, "Corvallis is a little dry when it comes to outings, but OSU's clubs and activities make up for that." A popular student activity is complaining about the Willamette Valley weather: "People in the valley don't tan, they rust," warns one native. One reward for all the rain, however, is the abundance of flowers that bloom in all colors and shapes each May. Beautifully rugged beaches are less than an hour away, and some of the best skiing in the country can be found in the Cascade Mountains, two hours east. Hiking and rafting are nearby too, and camping on the coast provides more good times.

Cheering for Beavers athletic teams claims a lot of students' time and energy here, as does participation in 40 intramural leagues and 40 club sports. Benny Beaver, the school's former (and somewhat benign) mascot, has been replaced by a more aggressive beaver that students have dubbed the "angry beaver." Baseball, men's soccer, and men's and women's basketball are highly competitive in the Pac-12 Conference and on the national stage. Oregon State's rivalry with the University of Oregon dates back to 1894, and one student says, "Games between OSU and U of Oregon are a big part of every season."

While still a leader in agricultural education, OSU has expanded its reputation as a university that prepares students for successful futures in ever-evolving scientific, technical, and business fields. OSU doesn't scream for attention. Instead, it's

Overlaps
Colorado State, Washington State, University of Nebraska–Lincoln, Oklahoma State, Iowa State, University of Oregon, University of Washington, Cal Poly–San Luis Obispo

content to be a "nice" college, in "a safe and pleasant little town," where professors are "helpful" and, even if everyone doesn't know your name, they'll let you stand under their umbrella whenever the skies open up.

If You Apply To ›

Oregon State: Early action, regular decision. SATs or ACTs: optional. Accepts the Common Application with supplement. Applicants have the option of identifying their gender, preferred name, and sexual orientation.

University of the Pacific

3601 Pacific Avenue, Stockton, CA 95211

The university's name dates from a time when there were no other universities near the Pacific. Still the only small, independent university in California north of L.A., it offers an eye-popping array of programs for an institution its size, including business, engineering, pharmacy, and education. The student body is just as diverse.

Website: www.pacific.edu
Location: Suburban
Private
Total Enrollment: 5,282
Undergraduates: 3,152
Male/Female: 47/53
Financial Aid: 73%
Pell Grant: 37%
Expense: Pr $ $
Student Loans: 64%
Average Debt: $ $
Applicants: 10,901
Accepted: 79%
Enrolled: 9%
Grad in 6 Years: 66%
Returning Freshmen: 85%
Academics: ✏️ ✏️ ✏️
Social: ☎ ☎ ☎
Q of L: ★ ★ ★ ★
Admissions: (209) 946-2211
Email Address: admission@ pacific.edu

Strong Programs:
Engineering
Business
Education
English
International Relations
Prepharmacy

University of the Pacific was established in 1851 by Methodist ministers as California's first institution of higher education. Perhaps that's why it looks like 175 acres of New England plunked down in California wine country. With its stately combination of red brick and ivy, it could be mistaken for an East Coast liberal arts college. But instead of a blanket of snow, Pacific is surrounded by the lush greenery of the San Joaquin Valley. On campus, this increasingly competitive bastion of learning offers its 3,200 undergrads a solid and diverse academic program and scores of things to do when not hitting the books.

With majestic evergreens and flowering trees complementing collegiate Gothic buildings, Pacific is home to six undergraduate schools and the College of the Pacific, the university's liberal arts and sciences division. There is also a school of law in Sacramento and a superlative school of dentistry in San Francisco. A biological sciences building provides 56,000 square feet of space for the biological sciences department. Newer facilities include Calaveras Hall, an apartment-style residence hall for sophomores.

The university-wide general education program has three components: the Pacific seminars, the breadth program, and fundamental skills. All students complete three Pacific Seminars, starting with a two-course sequence (What Is a Good Society? and Topical Seminars on a Good Society) in their first year, followed by What Is an Ethical Life? in their senior year. In addition, students must complete six to nine courses in the breadth program and must demonstrate competence in writing, math, and reading. Strong offerings abound in the schools of engineering and business (with specialty concentrations in arts and entertainment management, business law, and entrepreneurship). The sciences, education, English, and international relations are also strong. A freshman says, "The best academic departments tend to be prepharmacy, predentistry, and the health, exercise, and sport science programs, because they do an astounding job of preparing students for their future professions." Students may also design their own majors with faculty approval.

Students report that the academic atmosphere is relaxed. "Instead of students who do whatever it takes to be at the head of the class, everyone works

> **"The faculty members are very accessible and always willing to help."**

together," says an international relations major. Forty-two percent of the undergraduate classes have fewer than 20 students, and teaching assistants teach labs only. "The faculty members are very accessible and always willing to help," says one sophomore. The university guarantees graduation in four years (assuming the student follows all university guidelines), or it will pay for the extra schooling. Students are also guaranteed to have the opportunity for some type of experiential learning, and a number of internship and co-op programs are available. An extensive study abroad program offers 200 choices in dozens of countries; international relations and global studies majors are required to spend at least one semester abroad.

(continued)

Health, Exercise, and Sport Science

Pacific students are "genuinely nice and friendly," says one freshman. Eighty-seven percent of undergraduates are California residents, and 8 percent hail from foreign countries. As for ethnic diversity, Asian Americans account for 35 percent, Black students 4 percent, Hispanics/Latinos 25 percent, and multiracial students 4 percent. The school is middle-of-the-road to conservative, though politics in general play a small role on campus. "We're very open to all political, religious, sexual orientations, etc.," says a senior. Though not unusually expensive by national standards, the university price tag can seem steep when compared to the University of California system. So Pacific has stepped up efforts to compete, using merit scholarships, which average $21,500 annually, as well as athletic scholarships in several sports. Thirty-seven percent of freshmen qualify for Pell Grants.

Pacific offers strong specialty concentrations in arts and entertainment management, business law, and entrepreneurship.

"You instantly feel like you are surrounded by very friendly and loving people."

Freshmen and sophomores are required to live on campus, and 46 percent of all undergrads make their home on campus. "Housing is generally pretty clean and the sense of community is felt all across the halls," says one student. With three meal plans, two dining halls, and one fast-food-type facility, residents are well fed. A senior reports, "Campus security is pretty effective."

"The social life happens on campus, whether it is at sporting events, going to events for different fraternities, sororities, or clubs, or simply playing games out on the UC Lawn," says a student. Just 2 percent of the men and 1 percent of the women go Greek, and the majority of Greek houses are designated substance-free. "I only recently attended my first party where there was alcohol," one student says. "There was no pressure for me to drink." Students caught violating the alcohol policy must take an online course in alcohol education. Other social opportunities are offered by the Residence Hall Association, intramural and club sports, conservatory and drama/dance programs, campus movies, and more than 170 student clubs. Annual campus festivities include the Lip Sync competition during homecoming, the popular Fall Festival, Diversity Week, and International Spring Festival. For weekend excitement, Pacific students love to hit the road: within about two hours, they can be skiing, shopping in San Francisco, or surfing in Monterey. Stockton itself (population 322,000) offers shopping and plenty of fast-food joints, as well as numerous volunteer opportunities.

Students are guaranteed to have the opportunity for some type of experiential learning, such as an internship, co-op, or study abroad.

Pacific dropped football long ago, but the Tigers field a number of other competitive Division I teams. The women's volleyball team makes regular NCAA Tournament appearances, and men's and women's basketball and water polo are also strong. The university also sponsors a solid speech and debate team.

Pitted against the state's immense public university system, Pacific stands out for offering major university opportunities in a small-college setting. The administration is striving to place more focus on its student body, which is becoming more top-notch and diverse. A political science major says, "When you come here, you instantly feel like you are surrounded by very friendly and loving people."

Overlaps

UC Davis, UC Berkeley, UCLA, Caltech, UC San Diego, UC Santa Barbara, University of Southern California

University of Pennsylvania

1 College Hall, Philadelphia, PA 19104

An Ivy League institution in name, Penn has more in common with places like Georgetown and Northwestern—where the liberal arts share center stage with preprofessional programs. At Penn, that means business, engineering, and nursing. Penn has something else other Ivies don't: school spirit. It's a good idea to apply early decision if Penn is your first choice.

Website: www.upenn.edu
Location: City Center
Private
Total Enrollment: 21,677
Undergraduates: 9,631
Male/Female: 46/54
Financial Aid: 43%
Pell Grant: 19%
Expense: Pr $ $ $
Student Loans: 20%
Average Debt: $ $
Applicants: 56,332
Accepted: 6%
Enrolled: 73%
Grad in 6 Years: 96%
Returning Freshmen: 98%
Academics: ✍ ✍ ✍ ✍ ✍
Social: ☎ ☎ ☎
Q of L: ★ ★ ★
Admissions: (215) 898-7507
Email Address: info@
  admissions.upenn.edu

Strong Programs:
Business
Engineering
Nursing
Communication
Anthropology
Management and Technology
Cognitive Science
Biological Basis of Behavior

Benjamin Franklin would be proud of the way the university he helped create has surged in recent years. Once relegated to the bottom rungs of the Ivy League (and often confused with Penn State), the University of Pennsylvania is now the first choice for top students who see no conflict between high-level academics and having a life. The undergraduate College of Arts and Sciences—once on the university's back burner—is now central not only to its undergraduates, but also to three other undergraduate schools that tap into its programs and course offerings. With a distinguished history that dates to 1740, Penn established the nation's first medical school, the first business school, the first journalism curriculum, and the first psychology clinic, and it is a pioneer in service learning and service research. In her inaugural address, a former president paid tribute to Franklin as "the ultimate visionary and pragmatist. Franklin thought education should be for the body as well as for the soul—that it should enable a graduate to be a breadwinner as well as a thinker, that it should produce socially conscious citizens as well as conscientious bankers and traders."

"Penn" is the university's traditional informal name. In recent years "UPenn" has also emerged as a nickname; although this alternative is used more by outsiders than by students themselves, it is gaining currency. Penn's campus is situated in a tree-shaded, self-contained, 299-acre nest called University City, which is adjacent to downtown Philadelphia. Its 218 buildings range from Victorian Gothic to postmodern. There are very old structures, such as College Hall, and newer ones, such as Wharton's Huntsman Hall and Skirkanich Hall, home to Penn's bioengineering programs. New College House West, a $163 million, 450-bed undergraduate residential house, opened in 2021.

> "[Professors] are tops in their field and have developed a great teaching style."

Penn's reputation has traditionally been wrapped up with its 12 graduate schools, especially the prestigious Wharton School of Business; the Annenberg School of Communication; and the well-known law, medical, and veterinary schools. (Penn claims to be the first university in the country to offer both undergraduate and graduate studies.) Three of the four undergraduate schools—engineering, nursing, and the undergraduate division of Wharton—are also professionally oriented and offer an education that's hard to beat anywhere. The undergraduate College of Arts and Sciences (a.k.a. "The College") has come into its own in recent years and provides students with high-quality instruction as well as the chance to run into a Nobel laureate here and there.

Finance is among the most popular undergrad majors, followed by economics and nursing. Penn's anthropology department ranks with Chicago's as tops in the country, while the management and technology program is also outstanding. Penn has earned applause in the field of cognitive and computer sciences because of its special program linking psychology, linguistics, and computers with philosophy. Another popular crème-de-la-crème interdisciplinary major, biological basis of behavior, combines psychology, biology, and anthropology. Students are allowed to design their own individualized majors, and they can hop from school to school—undergraduate or graduate—in doing so. Students in the Vagelos Program in Life Science and Management pursue studies in both the College of Arts and Sciences and the Wharton School, exposing them to research and development, biotech start-ups, managed care, and other related issues.

At the Wharton School (named after the 19th-century industrialist who founded it), the Joseph Wharton Scholars program emphasizes breadth in the arts and sciences. Another added plus that comes with a Penn undergraduate education is the opportunity for early entry (submatriculation) into the university's graduate programs. Juniors may apply to any master's program (continuing into the Wharton M.B.A. program is especially popular) and begin completing graduate requirements during their senior year. Penn offers no co-op programs and discourages full-time internships for credit, remaining true to the Ivy League belief that learning should be based in academic settings. Thirty percent of students explore more exotic classrooms by studying abroad at Penn's programs in Italy, Scotland, Japan, China, and Nigeria, among others. Freshmen are encouraged but not required to participate in a seminar program that explores various areas of academic interest, and also in the Penn Reading Project, which involves student and faculty discussion of a common text.

> **Penn is now the first choice for top students who see no conflict between high-level academics and having a life.**

> **"Penn is a competitive university but is also intellectually stimulating."**

Two-thirds of undergraduate classes have fewer than 20 students, and while professors at Penn take their research responsibilities seriously, they are surprisingly accessible to freshmen. "Most departments have fantastic professors who are tops in their field," says one student, "and have developed a great teaching style." The academic program at Penn is well supplemented by its huge and busy library, which houses more than six million volumes.

Despite all the preprofessional programs, Penn never lets its undergraduates stray too far from the liberal arts. The general education requirements in the College of Arts and Sciences mandate that students take at least one course in each of seven "sectors": society; history and tradition; arts and letters; living world; physical world; humanities and social sciences; and natural sciences and mathematics. Students must also complete one course in each of six "foundational approaches" areas, including writing, foreign language, quantitative data analysis, formal reasoning and analysis, cross-cultural analysis, and cultural diversity in the U.S. Strict academic policies and demanding professors exacerbate the academic pressure. "Penn is a competitive university," says one nursing major, "but is also intellectually stimulating."

> **Students are allowed to design their own individualized majors, and they can hop from school to school—undergraduate or graduate—in doing so.**

> **"Penn students have historically been extremely involved with the local community."**

Thousands of faculty and students give expression to Benjamin Franklin's adage that service to humanity is "the great aim and end of all learning." To wit, Penn is a national leader in service learning and service research. Students work with local public school students as part of academic coursework in disciplines as diverse as history, anthropology, and mathematics. There are tons of opportunities to volunteer—from tutoring to Big Brothers Big Sisters to the Ronald McDonald House. "Penn students have historically been extremely involved with the local community and have taken the experiences they've had in the neighborhood with them to the real world," an economics and history double major says.

Nineteen percent of Penn undergraduates are Pennsylvania natives, and 13 percent are international. "There are all kinds of people with all kinds of personalities, interests, and backgrounds," says a student, "all of which makes Penn a vibrant place to live and study." Eight percent of undergrads are Black, 10 percent are Hispanic/Latino, 26 percent are Asian American, and 5 percent are multiracial. Penn admits students regardless of need—and meets full demonstrated need with loan-free financial aid packages—but does not offer any merit or athletic scholarships. Outreach programs target hundreds of schools and thousands of students from low- and middle-income families in an effort to improve socioeconomic diversity.

Fifty-eight percent of all undergraduates live on campus and enjoy a wide range of living options in Penn's 13 co-ed "College Houses." The Quad, home to three of the 13 houses, seems to be the hot spot, described as "well maintained and incredibly comfortable." Most College Houses offer living/learning programs for those who want to be surrounded by others with the same interests. Some upperclassmen move to the apartment-style accommodations in three high-rises across campus, but most head to nearby off-campus houses and apartments—"for the freedom, plus it's a lot cheaper," a junior says. Meal plans are required for freshmen, and the food isn't all that bad for institutional fare. "The best kept secret on campus is the kosher cafeteria," a finance and management major says.

Undergraduates may work hard during the week, but in contrast to typical Ivy League achievers, they leave it behind them on weekends. "Social life at Penn centers around frats," a junior explains. "Parties freely serve alcohol to underage drinkers," according to another student, despite school policies dictating otherwise. More than two dozen fraternities attract 20 percent of the men, while sororities claim 21 percent of the women. The frats' exclusive claim to the houses along Locust Walk, the main artery on campus, has been undone: after some controversy, it was determined that non-Greeks, too, must be able to live at the social nexus of the campus. Two big annual events at Penn are Spring Fling, a weekend "nothing short of absolutely incredible fun," and Hey Day, a century-old tradition where juniors, donning Styrofoam hats and thin wooden canes, march down Locust Walk to officially become seniors, taking chomps out of each other's hats as they go.

Downtown Philadelphia is only a few minutes away by foot, Lyft, or public transportation. Penn is located in the western part of town, once considered to be dangerous, but nowadays, as a senior explains, "There are a wealth of cultural resources at the tip of your fingers, and more and more students are able to find jobs in the Philadelphia area after graduation." Students frequent sporting events, malls, South Street ("a miniature Greenwich Village"), and, of course, myriad bars and clubs. The city is home to several other colleges, and a student says, "There is a lot of social intermingling among the schools, and university students dominate the nightlife." Road trips include New York City, Washington, D.C., Atlantic City, and even Maine and Florida.

Penn is more sports-minded than most Ivy schools, and Division I football is the biggie. The team has grown accustomed to sitting on the top of the Ivy League and has sparked a widespread boost in school spirit. Tickets are free for those with a student ID. The Penn–Princeton rivalry is always a crowd-pleaser. At the end of the third quarter of each home game, everyone in the stands begins belting out the lyrics of the Penn fight song, and when they get to "Here's a toast to dear old Penn," the students shower the field with burnt toast, "a moment that makes all Penn students proud," according to a senior. Aside from football, solid Quakers

Hey Day is a century-old tradition where juniors march down Locust Walk to officially become seniors.

"There are a wealth of cultural resources at the tip of your fingers."

Division I football has sparked a widespread boost in school spirit; the Penn–Princeton rivalry is always a crowd-pleaser.

teams include men's and women's basketball, men's lacrosse, and women's field hockey and fencing. A bevy of intramurals and nearly 40 club sports bring thousands of less-seasoned athletes out to play each year, and all types of athletes benefit from the swanky track and weight-lifting facilities. Each spring, Penn hosts the prestigious Penn Relays, a track-and-field extravaganza that attracts the nation's best track athletes.

While its students work hard, Penn lacks the intellectual intensity of some of the other top Ivies, and you can detect preprofessional undercurrents. But most accept it for what it is: a first-rate university where you can live a relatively normal life. Penn is one Ivy League university where no one apologizes for having fun. Says one sophomore, "There is a great balance between academics and social activities, which is rare in such highly competitive institutions."

If You Apply To ›

Penn: Early decision, regular decision. Accepts the Common Application with supplement. Please consult Penn's website for the most up-to-date information regarding standardized test requirements.

Pennsylvania State University

201 Old Main, University Park, PA 16802

With a student body the size of a small city, Penn State is strong in fields from meteorology and business to film and television. The 1,800-student Schreyer Honors College is one of the nation's elite programs. Although its athletic programs have tended to grab most of the headlines (not always positive), Penn State remains one of the premier public universities academically.

Living it up with nearly 40,000 fellow full-time undergraduates in what sportswriters have long dubbed Happy Valley is probably not for the faint of heart. But those who can muster the energy to take advantage of Penn State's legendary school spirit and to navigate its vast sea of academic options will be rewarded with stellar programs in engineering, the sciences, and other fields appropriate to a land grant university.

With an eclectic architectural mix, including white-columned brick, stone, and some modern apartments, Penn State, which was founded in 1855, continues to experience growth as major renovation and expansion projects proceed. New facilities and renovations are constantly underway. The $144 million Chemical and Biomedical Engineering Building is among the newer additions to campus. "Penn State just keeps growing and improving itself," says one student.

Penn State's general education requirements consist of 45 credits that include several communications and quantification courses as well as humanities, arts, natural sciences, social and behavioral sciences, and health and physical education courses. The incorporation of critical-thinking skills has been a priority in redesigning the general curriculum. In addition, undergrads

"**Your academic experience is completely what you make it.**"

must enroll in courses on U.S. and international diversity. One helpful program offered to freshmen is LEAP (Learning Edge Academic Program), which gives new students the benefit of a big university while making it seem small. Students in LEAP take a team approach by taking classes and living together. About 1,800 of the university's best and brightest are invited to participate in the Schreyer Honors College,

Website: www.psu.edu
Location: Small City
Public
Total Enrollment: 45,752
Undergraduates: 39,353
Male/Female: 53/47
Financial Aid: 42%
Pell Grant: 22%
Expense: Pub $ $ $ $
Student Loans: 55%
Average Debt: $ $ $ $
Applicants: 78,508
Accepted: 58%
Enrolled: 19%
Grad in 6 Years: 85%
Returning Freshmen: 93%
Academics: ✏ ✏ ✏ ✏ ½
Social: ☏ ☏ ☏ ☏ ☏
Q of L: ★ ★ ★
Admissions: (814) 865-5471

(continued)

Email Address: admissions@
psu.edu

Strong Programs:
Meteorology
Business
Film and Television
Engineering
Forensic Science
Nutrition and Family Studies
Computer and Information
    Sciences
Food Sciences

*The Schreyer Honors
College offers
opportunities for
research and an
honors thesis, as well
as honors options
in regular courses.*

which offers opportunities for research and an honors thesis, as well as honors options in regular courses.

The most popular majors at Penn State fall under the categories of engineering, business, computer and information sciences, and social sciences. The university maintains strong programs in the scientific and technical fields such as earth sciences, engineering, forensic science, and life sciences, as well as nutrition and family studies. The meteorology program boasts alumni worldwide, including the founder of AccuWeather, an internationally renowned private forecasting firm. The College of Information Sciences and Technology is designed to prepare students for the digital age. The College of Agricultural Sciences has extensive facilities that include huge livestock barns. Its food sciences program is one of the best in the nation. Dairy products from the school's cows are sold at an on-campus store, and courses are offered in the production of its famous ice cream. Students can choose from more than 160 undergraduate majors and more than 190 graduate fields spread over 24 locations statewide, including the College of Medicine and Dickinson Law, both located near Harrisburg, and Penn State Law on the University Park campus. Combined undergraduate/graduate degree options are available, as are engineering co-op programs, distance learning, and student-designed majors.

"Penn State students are active, fun, and open-minded."

"The one thing about Penn State is that your academic experience is completely what you make it," counsels one student. Some of the intro-level lecture courses draw up to 400 students at University Park, yet most students seem to agree that classes are excellent and require your full attention. Students report that professors are accessible and engaging—when they are teaching; grad students frequently take on that responsibility. For cramming outside of class, the Penn State library system contains 8.6 million volumes. Roughly 16 percent of students study abroad through nearly 300 summer, semester, and full-year programs offered in roughly 50 countries.

"Penn State students are active, fun, and open-minded," says one student. Fifty-nine percent of undergraduates are residents of Pennsylvania, with 10 percent hailing from foreign nations. More than half of Penn State's undergrads who finish at University Park began their education at one of the university's 19 undergraduate campuses across the state. Many students note that race and diversity issues can be pronounced on a campus that is still pretty homogeneous for a public university: Asian Americans make up 7 percent of the undergrad population, Black students 4 percent, Hispanics/Latinos 8 percent, and multiracial students 4 percent. A whopping 695 athletic scholarships are available in 29 varsity sports, as are thousands of merit awards, averaging $5,000.

Freshmen must live in the dorms, which students say are comfortable and located near classroom buildings and dining facilities. Overall, 25 percent of students live on campus; the rest find a home off campus, often in downtown apartments. "I loved living in the dorms," reports one

"I loved living in the dorms. I think it's part of the whole college experience."

public relations major. "I think it's part of the whole college experience and I made some great friends along the way." The meal plan operates on a point system where you pay for what you eat. Stand for State is a comprehensive bystander intervention program covering sexual assault, drug and alcohol use, acts of bias, and mental health concerns.

"Social life at Penn State is huge," says a freshman. Seventeen percent of men and 20 percent of women go Greek. Partying at Penn State mostly happens at fraternities, but the administration has been focusing on measures to increase student safety and reduce dangerous drinking, hazing, and sexual assault, including imposing new rules for social events sponsored by Greek organizations. Greek Chapter Scorecards track conduct violations and disciplinary actions, as well as academic performance, community service hours, and philanthropic fund-raising efforts, for every Greek chapter on campus. For social alternatives, the HUB (the campus union building) offers nonalcoholic entertainment, and more than 1,000 student organizations keep students busy too. Favorite annual events include the mid-July arts festival, the Dance Marathon, and, of course, homecoming.

University Park students take advantage of the picturesque and peaceful locale by engaging in outdoorsy activities, including skiing and snowboarding at a nearby slope, and sailing, canoeing, hiking, and renting cabins in Stone Valley. State College offers restaurants, bars, and cultural events such as symphonies, theatrical shows, and ballets, while the Bryce Jordan Center hosts top-notch performers. The town may be small, but according to a biochem major, "a majority of the students get involved in community service to maintain and constantly improve town relations."

Penn State was once viewed as the model of how the values of big-time football and academic excellence could coexist, but this image took a major hit a decade ago with the conviction of a former assistant football coach as a sexual predator. Since then, new leadership, governance, and other changes have sought to put the scandal in the rearview mirror. When thousands of alumni converge to cheer on their Nittany Lions (named after a type of local mountain lion) in blue and white, the festivities include tailgating replete with pregame parties and postgame revelry. As a member of the Big Ten, Penn State's foes include Michigan and Ohio State, both of which make great road trips. Nittany Lions teams have won 80 national team championships in a wide variety of sports; the men's wrestling team has brought home 10 national titles in the last 13 years. Men's lacrosse and men's and women's soccer are recent conference champions. There are three large gyms, a competitive-size pool, an indoor ice rink, and an extensive program of intramural and club sports for the recreational athlete, including a large angler's club.

After a period of agonizing soul-searching about what led to its football scandal a decade ago and more recent Greek life troubles, Penn State's sense of pride and community spirit have reasserted themselves. As one proud Lion explains, "Imagine a family of 40,000—the excitement, compassion, and sense of belonging."

The men's wrestling team has brought home 10 national titles in the last 13 years.

Overlaps

University of Pittsburgh, Temple, University of Maryland, University of Delaware, Rutgers, Indiana University of Pennsylvania, Ohio State

If You Apply To ›

PSU: Early action, rolling admissions. Accepts the Common Application with supplement. Apply to particular school or program. Please consult Penn State's website for the most up-to-date information regarding standardized test requirements.

Pepperdine University

24255 Pacific Coast Highway, Malibu, CA 90263

With stunning views of the Pacific Ocean, Pepperdine boasts what is arguably the most beautiful campus setting in American higher education. Proximity to L.A., only 35 miles away, contributes to its growing popularity. Pepperdine describes itself as a "Christian university," and students come ready to embrace its conservative Christian emphasis.

Website: www.pepperdine.edu
Location: Suburban
Private
Total Enrollment: 6,361
Undergraduates: 3,427
Male/Female: 42/58
Financial Aid: 93%
Pell Grant: 19%
Expense: Pr $ $ $ $
Student Loans: 44%
Average Debt: $ $ $
Applicants: 11,855
Accepted: 53%
Enrolled: 16%
Grad in 6 Years: 83%
Returning Freshmen: 93%
Academics: ✍ ✍ ✍
Social: ☎ ☎
Q of L: ★ ★ ★ ★
Admissions: (310) 506-4392
Email Address: admission-seaver@pepperdine.edu

Strong Programs:

Business Administration

Communication

Public Relations

Psychology

Marketing

Economics

Biology

Sports Medicine

Students are required to attend Seaver 200—"faith exploration gatherings" similar to chapel—10 times each semester.

Given its picturesque surroundings, it's easy to confuse Pepperdine University with a Southern Californian resort. Surrounded by the beautiful seashore, Pepperdine University might seem like paradise for students seeking sunshine rather than studies at this conservative Christian university, though students take their work and their worship seriously. "The philosophy of the school is that God and the academic experience must be married," says a senior communication major. "This creates an intimate learning environment that prides itself on moral integrity and a high academic standard." Business and communication are the most blessed programs, though other departments deserve recognition too. Undergrads praise their educational opportunities, the strength of their school's spiritual community, and the vast sandy beaches beckoning below their hilltop campus.

There's no denying that Pepperdine's location, nestled in the Santa Monica Mountains about 35 miles northwest of Los Angeles, is a strong selling point. The 830-acre Malibu campus, to which the school moved from L.A. in 1972, overlooks

"The philosophy of the school is that God and the academic experience must be married."

the Pacific Ocean and features fountains, hillside gardens, mountain trails, and a 20-minute walk to the beach. Spanish revival architecture—cream-colored stucco buildings topped with red ceramic tile roofs—dots the landscape. The Phillips Theme Tower, a 125-foot-tall white stucco cross, stands 345 feet above sea level on the outskirts of campus, reminding students and faculty of the school's Christian heritage.

Pepperdine was founded in 1937 by George Pepperdine, a lifelong member of the conservative Churches of Christ who established a hugely successful retail auto parts company and became concerned that too many young people were losing their religious faith when they entered college. The church's continued influence on the school pervades many aspects of campus life, from the prohibition of overnight dorm room visits by members of the opposite sex to the requirement that students attend Seaver 200—"faith exploration gatherings" similar to chapel—10 times each semester. Drinking is officially prohibited on campus too. Though restrictions like this would drive the average American kid up a wall, most Pepperdine students like what one calls the "highly moral" atmosphere. "In comparison to other schools, Pepperdine students generally have a more religious foundation and thus have high standards of moral integrity," opines a student.

The academic programs of Seaver College, Pepp's undergraduate school, aim to provide students a "traditional liberal arts curriculum based on a Christian worldview." Individual classes are demanding, as is the required General Education program, which includes a first-year seminar and courses in English composition, speech and rhetoric, math, a foreign language, Western culture, world civilizations, laboratory science, fine arts, literature, and human institutions and behavior. Students must also take three religion courses. Faculty members are said to be accessible and responsive—not surprising when 71 percent of classes have fewer than 20 students. One student says professors "demand a lot from their students and expect a high standard and quality of work."

The business administration department is unequivocally the strongest and most popular at Pepperdine, and it tends to set the tone on campus. Those seeking advanced business education can enroll in a B.S./M.B.A. program that allows them to earn a bachelor's degree in business administration from Seaver College and an M.B.A. from the university's graduate business school in five years. The communication department, with majors including advertising, public relations, and journalism, is also highly touted and boasts radio and television broadcasting studios. Psychology, marketing, economics, biology, and sports medicine are also popular. Dual-degree engineering programs are available in partnership with the University of Southern California and Washington University in St. Louis. The well-organized

Career Center allows students to sign up for job fairs, interviews, and individual and group career-counseling sessions. Sophomores interested in international culture may spend a year at Pepperdine's own facilities in Buenos Aires, Florence, Heidelberg, Lausanne, or London. Locations for summer study have included East Africa, the Galapagos Islands, Madrid, and Oxford. Roughly 80 percent of Pepperdine's undergraduates participate in short- and long-term study abroad programs.

One might expect students at this religiously oriented school to be politically conservative, and a good portion are. Many come from well-to-do California Republican families; there are also quite a few wealthy international students. Students joke that there's never a shortage of Porsches and BMWs on campus, but there is a shortage of places to park them. "I think students who are struggling financially would have a difficult time fitting in," confesses an advertising major. Overall, 49 percent of undergraduates are California natives, and 9 percent come from abroad. Hispanics/Latinos account for 17 percent of the students, Asian Americans 13 percent, Black students 4 percent, and multiracial students 8 percent. The Republican influence is felt far and wide. Pepperdine has received millions of dollars from conservative donors, including the late Pittsburgh financier Richard Mellon Scaife. Nevertheless, one student says, "Pepperdine tends to shy away from political activism." The university awards merit scholarships averaging $13,200 to top achievers, in addition to about 325 athletic scholarships in 14 sports.

> "[Professors] demand a lot from their students and expect a high standard and quality of work."

Sixty-five percent of undergraduates live on campus. A senior declares that Pepperdine's residence halls are "comfortable, convenient, and really quite nice." Rooms are assigned on a first-come, first-served basis, and the housing stock consists of 25 dorms, including the newer, suite-style Seaside Residence Hall. First-year students are typically assigned to suites with bathrooms, living rooms, and four double bedrooms. Some consider these arrangements crowded, but a junior says they "connect freshmen instantly to seven suitemates and friends." Despite the above-average cost of living in the Malibu area, many upperclassmen choose to live off campus. As for dining in the campus's 11 venues, a senior says, "The meals are just OK." Some students express a desire for greater transparency regarding incidents of campus sexual harassment and assault, reporting that the administration "has tried to hide certain cases without sharing them with the student body."

Sophomores may spend a year at Pepperdine's own facilities in Buenos Aires, Florence, Heidelberg, Lausanne, or London.

Some say flashy student vehicles fit into the small, very wealthy community of Malibu better than the students themselves. Because the social scene in Malibu is pretty slack, with a 10 p.m. noise curfew and high price tags for everything, students typically head to L.A., Hollywood, Westwood, and Santa Monica for fun. "For a large proportion of students, academics and their social lives take priority over religious matters," says a public relations major. "Parties on weekends are well attended and probably draw a larger portion of students than church on Sunday." Seventeen percent of the men and 31 percent of the women join one of five national fraternities or eight national sororities, which are playing a larger role in social life. Along with student government, they sponsor dances, movies, and other typical college activities, including the occasional illicit drink. "Pepperdine enforces a 'dry' campus," says one student. The Tyler Campus Center serves as the main social center, and annual events including Songfest, Waves Weekend, and Midnight Madness draw crowds.

> "Parties on weekends are well attended."

Sports receive a lot of attention at Pepperdine. The Waves compete in the Division I West Coast Conference. Competitive teams include men's golf (national champs in 2021), women's golf, men's and women's tennis, and women's beach

Overlaps

Baylor, Loyola Marymount, Santa Clara, Southern Methodist, University of San Diego, Chapman, Westmont, Wheaton (IL)

volleyball. Ten club and intramural sports keep students busy, as does the physical education department, with classes in everything from surfing to ballet. A tennis pavilion and recreation center serves varsity jocks and weekend warriors alike.

Pepperdine has taken up the challenge of trying to marry the Christian focus of a Bible college with the academic rigor of a secular university—all in a location not known for the strength of its moral fiber. Students love to tease their well-manicured university with T-shirts proclaiming, "Pepperdine. 8-month party. 60K cover charge." But most seem to think the solid, values-oriented education they receive is worth the stiff price tag.

If You Apply To ›

Pepperdine: Early action, regular decision. Accepts the Common Application. Fine arts applicants must submit portfolio. Performing arts applicants must audition. Please consult Pepperdine's website for the most up-to-date information regarding standardized test requirements.

University of Pittsburgh

4227 Fifth Avenue, Alumni Hall, Pittsburgh, PA 15260

As its home city has risen in stature, Pitt has become a hot commodity along with next-door neighbor Carnegie Mellon. A state-related university in the mold of the University of Cincinnati—not the state flagship, but strong in a host of preprofessional programs, especially in health fields. Curiously, Pitt is among the nation's best in philosophy. Admissions is rolling, so apply early.

Pittsburgh has joined the ranks of the most livable cities in the United States. The University of Pittsburgh has matured, too, becoming a formidable public research institution. The school offers numerous opportunities for students pursuing medical, engineering, and business careers but leaves a great deal of room for exploration in the liberal arts. Students are encouraged to be individuals and carve out their own academic niche, either with multiple majors or with certificate programs. "The great thing about Pitt is they are always adding and adapting programs to fit the students' needs and interests," says a junior.

Pitt began as a tiny, private educational academy in the Allegheny Mountains in 1787. Oh, how times have changed. The university, which became state-related in 1966, is adjacent to Carnegie Mellon and is now part of the landscape of shops, museums, and galleries that make up Oakland, the heart of Pittsburgh's educational and medical center. Spacious, light-filled, contemporary buildings and generic modern office buildings make up the Pitt campus, but the architectural focal point is the fabled 42-story, neo-Gothic academic building, appropriately called the Cathedral of Learning, a national historic landmark. The stately and towering cathedral, with its unique Nationality Rooms, attracts 30,000 visitors annually. And contrary to images you may hold of inner-city Pittsburgh, the campus adjoins a 456-acre city park. Construction on the new, 270,000-square-foot Campus Recreation and Wellness Center is slated for completion in 2024.

Academic requirements in the Dietrich School of Arts and Sciences include writing, quantitative and formal reasoning, and foreign languages, as well as coursework

> **"With the rigorous material and courseload comes a lot of support from faculty and staff."**

Website: www.pitt.edu
Location: City Center
Public
Total Enrollment: 26,462
Undergraduates: 19,188
Male/Female: 44/56
Financial Aid: 48%
Pell Grant: 17%
Expense: Pub $ $ $ $
Student Loans: 59%
Average Debt: $ $ $ $
Applicants: 34,656
Accepted: 67%
Enrolled: 21%
Grad in 6 Years: 84%
Returning Freshmen: 93%
Academics: ✏ ✏ ✏ ½
Social: ☎ ☎
Q of L: ★ ★
Admissions: (412) 624-7488
Email Address: pitt.admissions@pitt.edu

in the humanities, social and natural sciences, and foreign cultures. First-year students undergo an extensive orientation before the fall term starts, take a one-credit freshman studies seminar, and complete a course on anti-racism. Pitt offers guaranteed admission into a wide variety of graduate programs for outstanding freshman applicants. The Outside the Classroom Curriculum is an optional cocurricular program in which students participate in activities in 10 goal areas, such as leadership development, sense of self, service to others, and arts appreciation, in order to round out their college experience.

(continued)

Strong Programs:
Engineering
Nursing
Rehabilitation Science
Bioengineering
Philosophy
Business
Biological Sciences
Psychology

With 16 undergraduate, graduate, and professional schools and more than 100 undergraduate majors across its five-campus system, Pitt rightfully claims to accommodate students with diverse needs. The engineering and nursing schools are excellent and attract high-caliber students. Premed students can watch transplants at the famed University of Pittsburgh Medical Center, one of the world's leading organ transplant centers. The rehabilitation science major prepares students for Pitt's highly competitive physical therapy program, which is tops in the country; bioengineering is also a strength. The most popular majors include engineering, business, biological sciences, psychology, and computer and information sciences. The interdisciplinary politics and philosophy major is a unique offering.

Coursework at Pitt is described as intensive but manageable; a chemistry major says, "With the rigorous material and courseload comes a lot of support from faculty and staff, so it all ends up balancing out." Forty-two percent of classes have fewer than 20 students, and a senior says the atmosphere is "incredibly collaborative." Pitt faculty members are often at the top of their fields, leading the way in areas like astronomical discoveries and medical advances.

The academically motivated can pursue a distinctive, research-focused bachelor of philosophy degree from the excellent University Honors College. Pitt is one of the top 10 institutions in the nation in terms of annual research support awarded by the National Institutes of Health. Forty-six percent of undergrads pursue research projects, facilitated by the university's 400 centers, institutes, laboratories, and clinics. For those who want to travel, the university boasts study abroad options in 42 countries; 29 percent of undergrads participate. **"Bars tend to be big here."** Closer to home, Pitt is a partner with Carnegie Mellon and Westinghouse Electric Company in the Pittsburgh Supercomputing Center. Students praise the Career Center's internship guarantee program, which places students in local internships after they've completed a set of workshops and other requirements.

The Career Center's internship guarantee program places students in local internships after they've completed a set of workshops and other requirements.

Sixty-six percent of undergraduates are from Pennsylvania, including a substantial number from the Pittsburgh area, and 4 percent hail from 52 other countries. Black students account for 5 percent of the student body, Asian Americans 14 percent, Hispanics/Latinos 6 percent, and multiracial students 5 percent. "From the Black Action Society to the Rainbow Alliance, there is an organization or group for students of any identity and background at Pitt," says a junior. When it comes to political and social issues, students say the campus is "very vocal" but also respectful. Pitt offers merit awards averaging $9,400 to incoming freshmen, and more than 250 athletic scholarships are available in 19 varsity sports. Pell Grant recipients benefit from the Pitt Success Pell Match Program, which matches the federal grant dollar for dollar.

PITT ARTS provides students with low-cost tickets to attend cultural events in the city.

While student housing may have been scarce in the past, Pitt continues to increase the amount of on-campus living space and guarantees housing for three years. Forty-two percent of students live on campus in 25 co-ed and single-sex dorms with all kinds of rooming situations, from singles to seven-person, apartment-style suites. Students say the quality varies and some options are overpriced. Living/

learning communities are popular, with 17 options for first-years and nine for upperclassmen. Hungry students may choose from nearly 20 dining spots; the food gets average marks. Campus safety is bolstered by a consistent police presence, and a sophomore notes, "The administration has shown that they're receptive and responsive to student concerns about issues like sexual assault."

Within minutes of Pitt's campus are shops, parks, museums, professional sporting events, and performing arts venues, and PITT ARTS provides students with low-cost tickets to attend cultural events in the city. The university also grants students fare-free access to city buses. "Exploring the city has been one of my favorite parts of my Pitt experience. There's so much more to do and see outside of Oakland," says a senior. Another adds that, for students of age, "Bars tend to be big here." On campus, students have more than 600 clubs and organizations to choose from, and 10 percent of the men and 12 percent of the women belong to the Greek system. "Greek life is small on campus, so they don't take over the scene like at other schools," says one senior. Favorite annual events include Cathedral Ball, a dance held before fall finals, and Bigelow Bash, a spring concert that brings recognizable performers like T-Pain and MisterWives to campus. Adjacent Schenley Park offers jogging trails and facilities for outdoor recreation. Ski slopes and mountain trails are not far away, and road trips to Penn State and Philadelphia, Boston, and New York City are popular.

> **"The Pitt vs. Penn State game is always a highlight each year."**

The Pitt Panthers compete in the Division I Atlantic Coast Conference, and men's soccer, football, and women's volleyball have taken home recent championships. "The Pitt vs. Penn State game is always a highlight each year," cheers a junior. Approximately 22 percent of undergrads take part in intramurals and club sports; basketball, football, soccer, and volleyball are the most popular.

Pitt is a large university made to feel small. Its flexibility in adapting to students' needs and its commitment to community breed a kind of loyalty and pride that students say can't be found elsewhere. Case in point, one senior declares, "I have two separate friends who have our unofficial slogan, 'Hail to Pitt,' tattooed on them." Now *that's* commitment.

Overlaps

Penn State, Ohio State, University of Michigan, Purdue, University of Maryland, Northeastern, Rutgers, Carnegie Mellon

If You Apply To ›

Pitt: Rolling admissions. Accepts the Common Application with supplement. Please consult Pitt's website for the most up-to-date information regarding standardized test requirements.

Pitzer College: See page 152.

Pomona College: See page 154.

Presbyterian College

503 S. Broad Street, Clinton, SC 29325

A South Carolina liberal arts college that competes head-to-head with Wofford for students who want their education served up with plenty of personal attention. Business programs complement the focus on liberal arts. Lacks the urban allure of Furman or Oglethorpe, but Scottish heritage adds flavor. About two-thirds of PC students are from South Carolina.

Consistent with the school's founding by clergyman William Plumer Jacobs way back in 1880 to educate orphans, Presbyterian College students live up to the motto *Dum Vivimus Servimus* ("While we live, we serve."). Virtually all students volunteer while at PC. Increasingly, they are also logging research hours in the lab, traveling to far corners of the world, and trying out potential careers through internships. At the same time, they continue to pursue personal, spiritual, and academic growth in a liberal arts environment.

The Presbyterian campus sits on 240 acres in the South Carolina piedmont. The redbrick buildings are largely Georgian in style, with tall, white columns and lots of shade trees. Many structures are listed on the National Register of Historic Places, including the campus's most recognizable building, Neville Hall. The campus resembles Thomas Jefferson's University of Virginia, with buildings grouped around three plazas just perfect for reading, studying, or throwing a Frisbee. New apartment-style housing for seniors was recently completed.

Presbyterian's curriculum emphasizes the traditional liberal arts, with a range of required courses, as well as experiential learning: all students either study abroad, conduct independent research, or complete an internship before graduation. The required Compass program extends from freshman through senior year, beginning with a First-Year Exploration course that focuses on critical thinking, academic skills, and personal exploration of vocation and calling. Sophomores take a course that helps them explore potential career paths. Students must also develop an electronic portfolio and participate in a senior capstone course.

> **"[The coursework] is not so intrusive that it devours all of a student's time."**

"The coursework is intense at times but is not so intrusive that it devours all of a student's time," says a political science major. An honor code holds students accountable for their behavior and creates an atmosphere of mutual respect. Classes are small, with 70 percent enrolling fewer than 20 students, encouraging personal relationships with faculty. "My professors have been so much more than just teachers to me—they have become my friends, travel partners, mentors, and role models," enthuses an English and history double major. The most popular majors are business administration, biology, psychology, and history. These are also some of PC's strongest programs, along with English and music. Computational biology is an unusual offering. Aspiring engineers can take advantage of dual-degree programs with Auburn, Clemson, Georgia Tech, and other institutions. High-achieving students desiring a degree in pharmacy can apply to the Early Entry Pre-Pharmacy Program, which allows them to earn a doctorate degree in six years through the PC School of Pharmacy.

Options for off-campus study, in which 20 percent of students partake, include semester-long exchange programs as well as highly popular, short-term Maymester trips led by faculty to destinations such as Australia, Greece, South Africa, India, and, of course, Scotland. For eight weeks each summer, 10 to 25 Summer Fellows receive stipends to live on campus, undertake independent research guided by

Website: www.presby.edu
Location: Small Town
Private
Total Enrollment: 1,154
Undergraduates: 923
Male/Female: 50/50
Financial Aid: 89%
Pell Grant: 30%
Expense: Pr $
Student Loans: 58%
Average Debt: $
Applicants: 1,964
Accepted: 71%
Enrolled: 16%
Grad in 6 Years: 61%
Returning Freshmen: 76%
Academics: ✍ ✍ ✍
Social: ☎ ☎ ☎
Q of L: ★ ★ ★ ★
Admissions: (864) 808-1880
Email Address: admissions@presby.edu

Strong Programs:
Business Administration
Biology
Psychology
History
English
Music
Computational Biology
Prepharmacy

faculty, and present the findings of their work. Fifteen percent of all undergrads get involved in research.

While less than 10 percent of students are Presbyterian, the campus atmosphere is distinctively Christian. "Our students practice servitude and Christian love in their daily lives," a senior says. Thirty percent of undergraduates hail from states outside South Carolina, and 3 percent come from nations abroad. Minorities are a small but increasing presence on campus: Black students make up 18 percent of the population, Hispanics/Latinos 6 percent, Asian Americans 1 percent, and multiracial students 5 percent. Politically, reports a senior, "PC seems to be split between both major political parties." Merit scholarships worth an average of $19,900 are handed out to eligible students, as are roughly 100 athletic awards.

The Early Entry Pre-Pharmacy Program allows high-achieving students to earn a doctorate in six years through the PC School of Pharmacy.

Ninety-five percent of Presbyterian students live on campus, where accommodations range from traditional rooms with hall baths to suites and apartments, and quality is said to vary. Housing selection is based on academic standing: in each class, students with the most credits and the best grades get to choose first. "It's more incentive to study hard and have a good GPA so you can live where you want to live," explains a business administration major. The two dining facilities on campus, a buffet-style dining hall and a food court, receive mixed reviews. "The Sunday buffet is awesome—after church, people from the community pay to eat in our cafeteria," says an English major. A senior notes that the campus feels safe and the school's strict honor code means that "you can trust your neighbors at PC."

"PC is Southern, classic, timeless, and fun!"

Thirty-three percent of PC's men and 38 percent of the women join Greek groups, and "social life is very active," says one student. "Fraternity Court is the popular spot on weekend nights." The school has taken a firm stand against underage and unsafe drinking: all frat parties must be registered and attended by sober party monitors, while staff check IDs and distribute under-21 wristbands at the door. For alternatives, the Student Activities Board hosts movie nights, coffeehouses, art nights, and other events on campus, and many students join clubs. Owing to PC's aforementioned motto, Student Volunteer Services is the largest organization on campus, routinely sending students to local orphanages, nursing homes, schools, and other facilities where their time and talents can be helpful. Favorite annual traditions include Shuckin' and Shaggin', an oyster roast and dance in the fall, and Spring Fling, a weekend carnival. Students also look forward to the Christmas at PC concert and to the outdoor graduation ceremony under the oaks, complete with bagpipes. As for the surrounding area, "Clinton is not a very active town," states a business administration major, so students usually head to Greenville, Spartanburg, or Columbia (all within an hour's drive) when they want to get off campus for a bite to eat or shopping. PC is equidistant from South Carolina's mountains and beaches, providing many opportunities to enjoy the outdoors.

The college's mascot is the Blue Hose, a reference to the stockings of their Scottish ancestors.

PC's 19 varsity sports teams compete in Division I. The college's mascot is the Blue Hose, a reference to the stockings of their Scottish ancestors. (While some students wear kilts during athletic events, most constrain such enthusiasm, says a junior.) Men's tennis is a recent Big South Conference winner, and other strong programs include women's wrestling, tennis, and basketball and men's soccer. Recreational sports are divided into three divisions, depending on how competitive you are. All students may take advantage of PC's 31-acre recreational facility, with lighted softball, football, and soccer fields, volleyball courts, a basketball court, a track, and an amphitheater.

Presbyterian College students take pride in the school's history and traditions, including its very own tartan. PC's church affiliation keeps students focused on service and on bettering the broader world, adding dimension to their classroom experiences. One Blue Hose sums it up this way: "PC is Southern, classic, timeless, and fun!"

Overlaps

Wofford, Anderson, Furman, Charleston Southern, Berry, Birmingham–Southern, Sewanee, Oglethorpe

Prescott College

220 Grove Avenue, Prescott, AZ 86301

With its commitment to environmental studies, sustainability, and social justice in a liberal arts context, Prescott attracts students who love the outdoors and are looking for an alternative college experience. Unique academic calendar. Has ready access to northern Arizona and southern Utah, the nation's most exotic outdoor playground. College of the Atlantic is the only remotely comparable college in the *Fiske Guide*. If you loved Outward Bound, consider Prescott.

Future *Hunger Games* contestants take note: this tiny outpost in the wilderness of central Arizona is a perfect spot for the nature lover who seeks adventure, wants to learn survival skills, and likes studying outdoors. Where else but Prescott College could you major in adventure education or take courses like Backcountry Skiing and Avalanche Training, Ecopsychology, and Barrio Pedagogy? Before any Prescott student sets foot in a classroom, they head to the outback for three weeks of hiking and camping, or to the town of Prescott for service-learning, research projects, and field trips. Wilderness Orientation and Community-Based Orientation offer an introduction to everything Prescott stands for: hands-on experience, personal and social responsibility, cooperative living, and stewardship of the environment.

> "You can interact with your coursework in a way that's more meaningful to you."

Founded in 1966 and still the only private liberal arts college in Arizona, Prescott retains the air of a 1960s commune. Surrounded by national forest, the college's "campus" consists of a two-block-long handful of buildings in the small town of Prescott. The architectural style of the campus ranges from the historic to the modern. The largest of the college's buildings is the Crossroads Center, an all-green building, which houses the library, computer labs, classrooms, conference centers, and the Crossroads Café. The administrative building was once a convent; its chapel is now used for meetings, art shows, and performances.

Prescott's requirements for graduation are characteristically unorthodox. Instead of grades, faculty members give narrative evaluations, although students may elect to receive grades. And rather than accruing credits, students design individualized "degree plans" that outline the competence (major) and breadth (minor/concentration) areas they will pursue, and the Senior Project (thesis) they will complete to demonstrate competence (graduate). Students must obtain two levels of writing certification (college level and thesis level) and math certification, showing knowledge of college-level algebra. Students also take a set of required interdisciplinary Core Curriculum courses, which are cotaught by faculty from multiple fields. Prescott's personal touch even extends to graduation, a unique experience where a faculty member speaks about each student personally and then the student speaks on their own behalf.

> "Prescott's campus has no borders. There are so many opportunities to go abroad or be out in the field."

Prescott bills itself as a college "for the liberal arts and the environment," and students tend to envision themselves becoming teachers, researchers, park rangers,

Website: www.prescott.edu
Location: Small City
Private
Total Enrollment: 543
Undergraduates: 310
Male/Female: 37/63
Financial Aid: 68%
Pell Grant: 43%
Expense: Pr $
Student Loans: 69%
Average Debt: $ $ $
Applicants: 147
Accepted: 99%
Enrolled: 25%
Grad in 6 Years: 43%
Returning Freshmen: 75%
Academics: ✐ ✐ ✐
Social: ☎ ☎
Q of L: ★ ★ ★
Admissions: (877) 350-2100
Email Address: admissions@ prescott.edu

Strong Programs:
Environmental Studies
Adventure Education
Education
Psychology and Human
   Development
Cultural and Regional Studies
Arts and Letters

wilderness guides, social activists, and the like. To design their degree plans, students start by selecting an area of study: adventure education, arts and letters, cultural and regional studies, education, environmental studies, psychology and human development, and sustainable community development. Those with eclectic interests can opt for interdisciplinary studies to blend courses from multiple areas. Each area of study offers several concentrations. In the standout environmental studies program, for instance, concentrations cover impressive breadth and depth, ranging from earth science and marine studies to natural history and ecology. Adventure education, in which students learn everything from alpine mountaineering to sea kayaking, is also a specialty. The teacher preparation program offers students teaching credentials in elementary and secondary education. Several programs have accelerated pathways in which undergrads can earn a master's degree tuition-free. Prescott does not offer a comprehensive program in advanced math, chemistry, physics, or foreign languages other than Spanish.

Before setting foot in a classroom, students head to the outback for three weeks of hiking and camping, or to the town of Prescott for service-learning.

"People are inspired to work hard because their projects reflect their passions, not because they're worried about getting an A," observes one senior. A human consciousness major adds, "Because you're not cramming for the next test (I never took one here), you can interact with your coursework in a way that's more meaningful to you." There's no tenure track at Prescott, and publishing and research take a backseat to teaching, although students warn that the quality of instruction can be inconsistent. With virtually all classes enrolling fewer than 20 students, the academic atmosphere is intimate, to say the least.

Prescott's academic calendar consists of two 16-week terms, each of which is divided into four blocks. During each block, students pursue intense immersion in just one course for four weeks, a model designed to allow maximum flexibility for fieldwork, community-based studies, and outdoor learning. Students may spend a block in the backcountry of Baja California or the alpine meadows of Wyoming, for example, or in a local service clinic. Students can even take a one-month rafting trip down the Colorado River for credit. Though Prescott does not offer a traditional study abroad program, students are encouraged to take courses in marine biology and cultural studies at the Kino Bay Center for Cultural and Ecological Studies in Mexico, as well as a social justice course in Kenya; about half of Prescott students have an international experience by the time they graduate. "Prescott's campus has no borders," says a sustainable community development major. "There are so many opportunities to go abroad or be out in the field." Paid internships are available through partnerships with AmeriCorps and other organizations.

"There is a 'hippie' stereotype of PC students, but I think that image is slowly shifting."

"There is a 'hippie' stereotype of PC students, but I think that image is slowly shifting," remarks a senior. Environmental issues still predominate among the liberal student body. Despite the challenges of low retention and graduation rates, Prescott's unconventional approach continues to entice students well beyond Arizona. Prescott's Changemaker Scholarship is bringing in more students by awarding guaranteed tuition scholarships worth up to $16,000 per year to every incoming undergraduate who enrolls in a degree program. Currently, 62 percent of undergraduates are out-of-staters; less than 1 percent come from other countries. The minority population is small but growing, with Black students making up 3 percent of the total, Hispanics/Latinos 5 percent, Asian Americans 2 percent, American Indians 2 percent, and multiracial students 3 percent. Pell Grant recipients represent 43 percent of incoming freshmen.

Adventure education, in which students learn everything from alpine mountaineering to sea kayaking, is a specialty.

Thirty-four percent of full-time undergrads call the on-campus housing units—a grouping of eight-person townhouses known as the Village—home. The vast majority of students fend for themselves in the town of Prescott, a rapidly growing community of approximately 47,000 where almost everything is accessible by bicycle. The college assists with the apartment hunt by providing lists of available properties and by cosigning leases when necessary. The Crossroads Café, the only dining facility, draws praise for being tasty and fresh. "Omnivores, vegetarians, vegans, and gluten-free folk all love the food in the café," cheers one student. Additionally, "The café staff offer cooking lessons throughout the semester. There's also free community lunch every Wednesday."

Social life at Prescott is informal, often consisting of small, "mellow" off-campus parties. With fewer than 20 student organizations and no strong traditions to speak of, students say the campus doesn't offer much in the way of a social scene. "If you love the outdoors, Prescott is great. Do not come here for a social experience," advises an adventure education major. As for the townsfolk, students describe them as "a mix of artists, activists, students, locals, retirees, and ranchers." Those looking for nightlife can hit Whiskey Row, the town bar scene, or drive to Flagstaff (90 minutes) or Phoenix (two hours).

The college offers just one sport—cycling—which has won titles in road cycling, mountain biking, and cyclocross. For other sports, students often participate in city leagues. "Our school has bike jousting, juggling, barefoot soccer, ultimate Frisbee, and capoeira—none of which involve competing against other schools," says one student.

Prescott may not have the huge campus or financial resources that are typically associated with larger schools; however, the small classes and specialized programs appeal to a student who would not be interested in your "typical" college. As a senior explains, "Our passion and dedication to education springs from a deep inner desire to effect positive change in the world."

If You Apply To ›

Prescott: Rolling admissions. SATs or ACTs: optional. Accepts the Common Application with supplement.

Princeton University

110 West College, Princeton, NJ 08544

Princeton is the smallest of the Ivy League's Big Three, which means more attention from faculty and plenty of opportunity for rigorous independent work. Offers engineering but no business major. The affluent suburban location contrasts with urban New Haven and Cambridge. Residential college system modeled on Yale's provides a support network and a social alternative to long-standing eating clubs. Generous financial aid program covers full tuition, room, and board for about one-quarter of undergraduates.

Princeton occupies a distinctive niche among America's superelite universities. It is a major research university with a world-class corps of professors who, in the absence of lots of graduate and professional students, lavish their attention on a relatively modest number of undergraduates. Princeton has an engineering school as well as programs in applied science, architecture and public planning, public policy, and an Entrepreneurial Hub near campus, but it is basically an "arts and sciences university." The academic atmosphere across campus is dominated by commitment to the liberal arts—with a carefully structured set of core requirements and a heavy emphasis on independent study, including a mandatory senior thesis. A sophomore says,

(continued)

Expense: Pr $ $ $
Student Loans: 17%
Average Debt: $
Applicants: 37,601
Accepted: 4%
Enrolled: 78%
Grad in 6 Years: 98%
Returning Freshmen: 96%
Academics: ✐ ✐ ✐ ✐ ✐
Social: ☎ ☎ ☎
Q of L: ★ ★ ★
Admissions: (609) 258-3060
Email Address: uaoffice@
   princeton.edu

Strong Programs:
Mathematics
Philosophy
Architecture
Economics
History
Computer Science
Engineering
Public and International Affairs

Two new residential colleges, Yeh College and New College West, opened in 2022, and a third is slated for completion in 2026.

"What sets Princeton students apart is that they come here not just for an excellent education, but they come to share knowledge with others."

For better or worse, Princeton has been known as a bastion of exclusivity, although its undergraduates are now just as racially and ethnically diverse as any other Ivy League school. Still, university leaders are looking to make Princeton's particular brand of high-powered undergraduate liberal arts education available to an even more diverse group of students. Sensitive to faculty complaints that Princeton enrolls too many bright students whose main claim to fame is that they have learned to work the system, the admissions office is on the lookout for more students with demonstrated intellectual curiosity—including more STEM majors, creative types, and high-ability/low-income students. The administration has made major investments in the sciences, engineering, and creative and performing arts to enhance these efforts. Established in 2021, the Emma Bloomberg Center for Access and Opportunity provides all students with mentorship and academic enrichment opportunities. Two of the center's programs aimed at supporting first-generation, low-income, and other underrepresented students include the Freshman Scholars Institute, which offers an academic and social introduction to Princeton over the summer before classes start, and the Scholars Institute Fellows Program that covers all four years.

> **"[Princeton students] come to share knowledge with others."**

Cloistered in a secluded but upscale New Jersey town, Princeton's architectural trademark is Gothic, from the cavernous and ornate university chapel to the four-pronged Cleveland Tower rising majestically above the treetops. Interspersed among the Gothic are examples of colonial architecture, most notably historic Nassau Hall, which served as the temporary home of the Continental Congress in 1783 and has defined elegance in academic architecture ever since. A host of modern structures, some by leading American architects Robert Venturi, Frank Gehry, and I. M. Pei, add variety and distinction to the campus, but the ambiance is still quintessential Ivy League at its best. The outstanding library facilities embrace five million volumes and provide 500 private study carrels for seniors working on those mandatory theses; there are another 700 enclosed carrels in other parts of the campus. Princeton's campus is self-contained, but those who venture outside its walls will find the surroundings quite pleasing. One side of the campus abuts quaint Nassau Street, which is dominated by chic (and pricey) boutiques and restaurants, as well as coffee shops and more affordable eateries. The other side of campus ends with a huge man-made lake that was financed by Andrew Carnegie so that Princetonians would not have to forgo crew. Two new residential colleges, Yeh College and New College West, opened in 2022, and a third, Hobson College, is slated for completion in 2026. A new art museum designed by Sir David Adjaye, renowned designer of the National Museum of African American History and Culture in Washington, D.C., is expected to open in 2024.

Princeton became the model for American-style liberal arts colleges after John Witherspoon was lured from the University of Edinburgh to become president in 1768. Today, Princeton is distinctive in its modest scale and its emphasis on undergraduates. Each student's Princeton experience begins with a week of orientation; each year, 800 students participate in Outdoor Action, a few days of wilderness activities immediately preceding orientation. All first-year students are also assigned a faculty advisor. Seventy-five percent of undergraduate classes have fewer than 20 students. With fewer graduate students to siphon off resources or consume faculty time than at large research universities, undergraduates get the lion's—or should we say Tiger's!—share of both; at last count, 70 percent of Princeton's department heads taught introductory

> **"I can open the newspaper and read my professor's article."**

undergraduate courses. An economics major says, "I can open the newspaper and read my professor's article or turn on the TV and see him giving a speech, then go to a lecture to hear him speak, then go to his office to speak with him one-on-one." Two-thirds of new students work closely with senior faculty members by participating in the optional Freshman Seminar program, choosing from more than 75 options offered annually, ranging from the Physics of Music to the Search for Life in the Universe. Lovers of literature can study with poet Paul Muldoon, and nearly every other department has a few stars of its own. "We have some of the most brilliant professors in the world here," confirms a junior. Senior professors lead at least one or two of the small discussion groups that accompany each lecture course.

Every student must fulfill distribution requirements in culture and difference, epistemology and cognition, ethical thought and moral values, historical analysis, literature and the arts, social analysis, quantitative and computational reasoning, and science and engineering. Students also take a first-year writing seminar and must demonstrate proficiency in a language other than English. During their junior year, liberal arts students work closely with a faculty member of their choice in completing two junior papers—about 30 pages of independent work each semester in addition to the normal courseload. Princeton also requires every graduate to complete a senior thesis—an enterprise that serves as a culmination of their work in their field of concentration. As a result, "seniors develop close personal relationships with their thesis advisors," says one student. Alumni often cite the thesis as one of their best experiences at Princeton.

> **"Seniors develop close personal relationships with their thesis advisors."**

Naturally, given Princeton's small size, the number of courses offered is smaller than at other Ivies, but students still have many high-quality options. Princeton's math and philosophy departments are among the best in the nation, and architecture, economics, history, public policy, English, physics, molecular biology, and romance languages are right on their heels. As part of a major effort to become a national center in the field of molecular biology, the university supports a sizable laboratory for teaching and research. Princeton is one of the few top liberal arts universities with equally strong computer science and engineering programs, most notably chemical, mechanical, electrical, and aerospace engineering. Operations research and financial engineering is one of the fastest-growing majors. One of Princeton's best-known programs is the prestigious Princeton School of Public and International Affairs (formerly named after Woodrow Wilson), which offers a multidisciplinary, policy-focused major for undergraduates. The university renamed the school in 2020, after years of student protests over former president Wilson's strong advocacy of racial segregation. Sixty-one percent of students study abroad in 100-plus programs offered in more than 40 nations. For those wishing to postpone their entry into the university in favor of an international experience, Princeton's Bridge Year program covers the full cost of one-year service abroad programs in Bolivia, India, Indonesia, and Senegal.

> *Princeton requires every graduate to complete a senior thesis—an enterprise that serves as a culmination of their work in their field of concentration.*

> **"The courses are very challenging and rigorous, but perhaps because of that, people are very cooperative."**

"The courses are very challenging and rigorous," a junior reports, "but perhaps because of that, people are very cooperative. They realize that no one can really succeed alone." The university honor code, unique among the Ivies, allows for unproctored exams. A limited number of courses can be taken on the pass/fail option. Although the faculty gets high ratings for its academic advising, students are rather cool on the university's nonacademic counseling programs.

"Our students are tight-knit, extremely hardworking, highly cooperative, and supportive of one another's activities," says an economics major. Nineteen percent of undergraduates are New Jersey residents, and 12 percent are international. Black students account for 8 percent of the student body, Hispanics/Latinos 11 percent, Asian Americans 23 percent, and multiracial students 7 percent. While diversity is present, the social atmosphere can be somewhat stratified. "As an African American, I can say that even the African Americans are subdivided based on economics, place of origin, and whether you went to public or private school," explains one senior. Although students report that there can be a general air of apathy around campus, administrators are quick to point to the numerous political organizations on campus as evidence of students' interest in political and social issues. Princeton undergraduates, both domestic and international, are admitted to the university without regard to their financial need, and those who qualify for aid receive generous support that covers their full demonstrated need. In fact, Princeton was the first university in the U.S. to replace loans with grants for all aid recipients. Effective fall 2023, students from families with annual incomes of less than $100,000 do not pay tuition, room, or board and also receive grants of $4,050 per year to assist with the cost of books and personal expenses. Most students from families with annual incomes of less than $150,000 only pay $12,500 per year.

In an attempt to improve campus life and broaden the social options, Princeton has grouped its dorms into eight residential colleges, each with its own dining hall, faculty residents, and an active social calendar. Under this system, nearly all students live and dine with their residential college unit for all four years. Just 6 percent of undergraduates live off campus. The university's turn-of-the-century Gothic dorms may look like crosses between cathedrals and castles, but students say conditions on the inside are sometimes less glamorous. Some halls offer apartment- and suite-style layouts.

Princeton's eating clubs are its most firmly entrenched bastions of tradition. Run by students and unaffiliated with the school, they line Prospect Avenue, and have, for more than a century, assumed the dual role of weekday dining hall and weekend fraternity. Of the 11, five admit members through an open lottery, but the others still use a controversial selective admissions process called bicker (because of the wrangling over whom to admit), to the chagrin of the administration and most students. While many of the clubs opened their doors to women back when Princeton went co-ed, two of the oldest and most exclusive—the Ivy Club and the Tiger Inn—remained all-male until 1991, when a court decision compelled them to admit women. Now, all the clubs are co-ed.

"Virtually all social life takes place on campus, both at the eating clubs and at dorm parties."

Catering exclusively to upperclassmen, the eating clubs provide a secure sense of community for their members. More than half of all sophomores join one of the clubs at the end of the year, becoming full-fledged members by the fall of their junior year. Annual dues vary; the most expensive is the Ivy Club, which charges its members nearly $12,000 a year. Financial aid covers eating costs for those who qualify and want to join. Unfortunately, the social options for those who choose not to join may feel limited. All too often the upper-level eating clubs steal the thunder from college-sponsored social events. As a result, "the underclassmen spend too much time pining for the day when they, too, can join the closest thing Princeton has to cliques," says one student. Some opt for life in independent dormitories or join the handful of Greek fraternities and sororities (not sanctioned by the administration) that have sprung up on campus over the past few years and have become feeders to particular eating clubs.

"Virtually all social life takes place on campus, both at the eating clubs and at dorm parties," says a sophomore. Princeton has the oldest licensed college radio station in the nation, plenty of journalistic opportunities, a prestigious debating and politics society (Whig-Clio) whose ranks have included James Madison and Aaron Burr, and a plethora of arts offerings. McCarter Theatre, adjacent to campus, houses Princeton's Triangle Club, which counted Jimmy Stewart and Brooke Shields as members. The roundup of annual campus events includes lawn parties in the fall and spring and an international festival. Each year about 60 percent of students engage in volunteer activities such as tutoring, working in soup kitchens, or helping the elderly. Few students complain about boredom, and many praise the affluent town of Princeton for the parks, woods, bike trails, and, most important, the quiet and safety it offers students. Students rarely venture much farther than New York or Philadelphia, each one hour away (in opposite directions) on the train.

Athletics are a big deal at Princeton, both varsity and intramural. Several of the Tigers' 38 Division I teams have claimed recent Ivy League conference titles, among them football, men's soccer and cross-country, and women's basketball, lacrosse, rowing, fencing, and golf. Women's rugby is the newest addition to the varsity roster. Dozens of club and intramural sports are available, ranging from archery to ballroom dancing to handball, and the eating clubs and residential colleges offer recreational athletic programs too. Every spring students compete in the annual dodgeball tournament.

Princeton's unofficial motto is "Princeton in the nation's service and the service of humanity," and the oft-repeated notion that with privilege comes responsibility lives on as part of its culture. It's easy to be humbled at Princeton. Even the most jaded students must be awed and inspired when they think of those who've traversed the campus paths before them. While some may find the ambiance too insular, not many turn down membership in this very rewarding club.

Princeton's 11 eating clubs are its most firmly entrenched bastions of tradition.

Overlaps

Harvard, Stanford, Yale, MIT, Columbia, University of Pennsylvania

If You Apply To ›

Princeton: Single choice early action, regular decision. Accepts the Common Application. Applicants must submit a graded, written paper, preferably from an English, social studies, or history class. Please consult Princeton's website for the most up-to-date information regarding standardized test requirements.

Principia College

Elsah, IL 62028

Prin is a tiny college in a tiny town about an hour from St. Louis. All students, faculty, and staff are practicing Christian Scientists. Prin is mainly liberal arts, though one of its most popular programs is business administration. Sixty percent of students study abroad. Campus tenor is similar to places like Pepperdine and Wheaton (IL).

Students come to Principia College with a common bond—Christian Science. They shun smoking, drinking, drugs, and sex in favor of God and learning. Prin graduates are culturally, spiritually, and intellectually well-rounded, the product of a liberal arts education that promotes critical thinking and a broad worldview. As the only college anywhere for Christian Scientists, Prin, founded in 1912 with the goal of "serving the Cause of Christian Science" (but with no formal ties to the Boston-based

Website: www.principiacollege.edu
Location: Rural
Private
Total Enrollment: 315

Sixty percent of Principia students participate in the five or six study abroad programs the school organizes each year.

church), attracts a lot of international students. The historic campus is reminiscent of Harry Potter's Hogwarts, but the fictional school of wizardry never had a woolly mammoth to unearth as Prin once did. Says one senior, Prin "has a warm, calm, and cozy atmosphere that reminds me of a second home."

Principia's 2,600-acre campus, on limestone bluffs above the mighty Mississippi River, is a designated National Historic Landmark. The dominant architectural influences are colonial American, Tudor, and medieval, and many buildings—including most student housing—were designed by California architect Bernard Maybeck. A contemporary of Frank Lloyd Wright, Maybeck urged Principia trustees to bring the college to its current spot when they relocated from St. Louis in 1935. The College Chapel, whose bells ring out hymns every Sunday evening, is the symbolic center of campus. An $18 million renovation of the college's main administrative and student services building was completed in 2021.

In addition to coursework in their major, students must complete a broad range of distribution requirements in the arts, humanities, social sciences, and natural sciences, as well as two physical education courses. All freshmen participate in a first-year experience program their first semester, and all seniors must complete either a capstone course or a major-related internship.

"Most classes take advantage of group work in small teams."

Of the 25 majors offered, the most popular are sociology, studio art, business administration, mass communication, and educational studies. Students say environmental studies, political science, and religious studies are also strong. A dual-degree program in engineering science is available, in conjunction with the University of North Dakota.

Academics are challenging, but students can count on each other and their professors for help. "Most classes take advantage of group work in small teams, and this helps you develop teamwork, leadership, and collaborative skills," says a senior. Most professors receive high marks. "Due to the small classroom style, faculty members are extremely accessible," says a business administration major. Sixty percent of Principia students participate in the five or six study abroad programs the school organizes each year. Each program enrolls 18 to 22 students, and sites are determined by academic subject and focus. Recent locations have included Croatia, Malawi, Nepal, and Scotland. Others participate in a prairie restoration program, gather data for the study of the Mississippi River's aquatic life, or build solar cars to be entered in races around the world.

"We are all Christian Scientists who strive to be the most moral people we can be," says one junior. The minority population is minuscule—3 percent of students are Black, 7 percent are Hispanic/Latino, 2 percent are Asian American, and 2 percent are multiracial. Still, an impressive 24 percent of students arrive from abroad, and only 15 percent are from Illinois. One international student says, "I've found that diversity positively impacts me. I've learned that there are more good things that bind us than negative things that divide us as human beings." Principia does not accept any governmental financial aid, so Pell Grants and the typical federal loans are not available to students, but the school does offer merit scholarships averaging $24,500, grants, and private, institutionally funded loans. No athletic scholarships are available.

All students live on campus, except for the few who are married or live locally with their parents. "The housing at Principia is superb, in the form of large, historical houses rather than the typical dormitory," says a senior. Students are expected not to be in wings where the opposite sex lives during "house hours" every night. Freshmen live in two modernized Maybeck houses with upperclassmen resident advisors trained to help new students adjust to college life. "Each house has its own sense of culture and traditions, and houses have brother-sister relationships as well as rivalries," explains a business administration and mass communication major. A sit-down pub and restaurant on campus provides a nice alternative to traditional dining-hall fare. "Dining facilities are improving, but vegetarians and vegans are still struggling," reports a junior. Students agree that they feel safe on campus, citing the rural location and a strong security presence.

In addition to eschewing alcohol, tobacco, and drugs, students are also asked to sign a pledge of abstention from premarital and extramarital sexual relationships. "Those who sign the contract are committed to those morals for religious reasons," a political science major says. "It's a wonderful thing not to have to deal with alcohol on campus," adds a senior. It goes without saying that Greek organizations are nonexistent; instead of partying, students keep busy at school-sponsored concerts, movies, dances, or intramural sporting events that pit one house against another. "Prin is remote enough where people stay on campus during the weekends to attend our awesome social events," says one student. Each house organizes its own annual celebration, international students show off their native cuisines at the Whole World Festival, and everyone looks forward to Spring Formal. The Public Affairs Conference

"We are all Christian Scientists who strive to be the most moral people we can be."

is the oldest student-run event of its type, bringing in big-name speakers to give talks, lead workshops, and provide networking opportunities to students. "Elsah is not a college town," says a junior, complaining that "not much has changed" since the town was founded in 1853. Stores, restaurants, and movie theaters are about 20 minutes away in Alton, and St. Louis is about an hour's drive.

Principia's Panthers compete in Division III, and men's and women's soccer, men's rugby, and women's beach volleyball are especially competitive. Thirty percent of students play intramural and club sports; the men's rugby and women's lacrosse club teams are strong. Campus athletic facilities include a four-court indoor tennis center, a field house with gym and pool, and outdoor courts and running trails.

Prin students embrace the conservative environment at their Christian Scientist school. Gone are the pressures that take hold of most college students, and a political science major says it "promotes character development and personal growth." A strong international presence and study abroad opportunities give students a taste of what lies beyond this quaint rural campus, but in the meantime, a junior says, students enjoy the comfort of Prin's "supportive community of like-minded thinkers."

Overlaps

Wheaton (IL), Pepperdine, Northwestern, Purdue, William & Mary

If You Apply To ›

Principia: Rolling admissions. Please consult Principia's website for the most up-to-date information regarding standardized test requirements. Accepts the Common Application. Only college in the world that admits only Christian Scientists.

Providence College

Providence, RI 02918

Strong Roman Catholic atmosphere makes Providence more comparable to Notre Dame than to nearby Boston College or Holy Cross. Liberal arts emphasis rooted in a required two-year interdisciplinary Western Civilization sequence, though more than a third of the students eventually opt for business disciplines. Friars athletic teams do well in small but high-profile Big East Conference. No fraternities or sororities, but Providence is a vibrant college town.

Website: www.providence.edu
Location: City Outskirts
Private
Total Enrollment: 4,262
Undergraduates: 4,060
Male/Female: 45/55
Financial Aid: 74%
Pell Grant: 17%
Expense: Pr $ $ $
Student Loans: 63%
Average Debt: $ $ $ $
Applicants: 11,129
Accepted: 58%
Enrolled: 16%
Grad in 6 Years: 89%
Returning Freshmen: 92%
Academics: ✍ ✍ ✍
Social: ☎ ☎ ☎
Q of L: ★ ★ ★
Admissions: (401) 865-2535
Email Address: pcadmiss@
providence.edu

Strong Programs:
Marketing
Finance
Accountancy
Management
Biology
Psychology
Education
Chemistry

As the nation's only college or university operated by the Dominican Friars, Providence College, founded in 1917, wears its Roman Catholic and Dominican identities on its sleeve. Nearly 70 percent of students are Catholic, friars in habits walk the campus grounds, crucifixes adorn the walls of classrooms and offices, and St. Dominic Chapel stands tall in the heart of the campus. The school's mission is grounded in these identities, as it aims to "provide an education for the whole person—body, mind, and soul—that bridges the common divides between matter and spirit, God and creation, faith and reason." Students here enjoy solid offerings in the sciences and liberal arts—including a unique and rigorous two-year Western Civ course—and a tight-knit community of like-minded men and women.

Located only an hour's drive from Boston and just a few hours' drive from New York City, Providence College's 105-acre campus is situated in Rhode Island's capital city. The campus boasts open spaces, beautiful lawns, and student-centered facilities. The traditional brick and stone academic buildings, residence halls, and campus chapel coexist with several contemporary structures.

> **"[Students are] preppy, white, Catholic, and generally upper middle class."**

The college recently completed a massive, five-year campus transformation project that added several new facilities, among them the Ruane Center for the Humanities, a four-level addition to the Science Complex, and the $30 million Ryan Center for Business Studies.

The heart of Providence's Core Curriculum is a sequence of seminar-based classes that comprise the Development of Western Civilization (DWC). This 16-credit course spans students' freshman and sophomore years and introduces them to the seminal ideas and primary texts in history, literature, theology, and philosophy, as well as the music and visual arts that shaped the Western world and other civilizations. Aside from DWC, students take additional coursework in theology, philosophy, natural science, social science, quantitative reasoning, and fine arts, and they must demonstrate proficiency in intensive writing, oral communication, diversity, and civic engagement.

Providence comprises four schools: arts and sciences, business, professional studies, and continuing education. The noteworthy School of Business draws 38 percent of the students and offers some of the most popular majors, include marketing, finance, accountancy, and management. All School of Business majors share a common set of core courses to ensure that business graduates have a broad understanding of all essential business disciplines. Biology, psychology, and education are also popular choices, and the chemistry program is strong. Providence has added majors in health policy and management and environmental biology. The college also offers a combined degree program with the New England College of Optometry, which allows for completion of the B.A. and doctorate in seven years.

"The academic climate at Providence College is rigorous but supportive," says a junior. Fifty-five percent of the undergraduate classes have fewer than 20 students and are taught by tenured or junior faculty. A Spanish and global studies double major says, "Professors here go the extra mile for their students. They are enthusiastic and available to us." The Liberal Arts Honors Program offers students of high academic ability and initiative a more in-depth and rigorous version of PC's core curriculum, and small, seminar-style honors courses are offered in virtually all areas. Students have ample opportunity for experiential learning through internships and faculty-directed laboratory or field research. PC's Center for Global Education sends 40 percent of students to their choice of more than 40 countries, including Argentina, Italy, New Zealand, and South Africa.

Eleven percent of PC's undergraduates come from Rhode Island, and the remainder are mostly from the Northeast. Most students are "preppy, white, Catholic, and generally upper middle class," according to a sophomore. Just 1 percent are international. Black students account for 4 percent of the student body, Hispanics/Latinos 10 percent, Asian Americans 1 percent, and multiracial students 3 percent. Many students are vocal about social and political issues, particularly when it comes to religion and race. "We have a lot of outspoken liberals and closet Republicans at PC," observes a senior. The lack of racial diversity on campus draws near-universal concern: "I think it is felt

> **"We have Division I school spirit but in a small-school atmosphere."**

very strongly among the minority students that we need more diversity on campus, even with all of our cultural clubs," says a junior. Merit scholarships averaging $20,600 are available to qualified students, and gifted athletes may vie for more than 100 awards.

Seventy-six percent of students live in the dorms, where conditions are said to be adequate and well maintained, if not spacious. Options include eight traditional halls, five apartment buildings, and a suite-style residence. Many seniors move off campus into the surrounding neighborhoods. Campus dining is "good and constantly getting better," says a global studies major. "We have a good line of communication between administration and students, and I feel as if PC has implemented all that they can to keep students safe," says an English major.

A junior says the social life is varied and, "There are free events for students to attend almost every day of the week, including weekends." Absent a Greek presence, students find other ways to let off steam. Annual traditions include a spring concert featuring top national acts and Civ Scream, held at midnight on the eve of Western Civ finals: "The entire sophomore class circles around the quad and screams to let out their frustration over Civ. People do crazy things and it is always something to remember," says a student. And although the college is located in "kind of a run-down area," an English major says the city of Providence "is full of opportunities," including a mall, a movie theater, and a cultural district with all sorts of shops and eateries. Owing to the college's strong Catholic identity, community service and volunteer work are popular pastimes. The city is also home to six other colleges, which enhances the social scene. Popular road trips include treks into Boston and New York City.

The Providence Friars field 19 varsity teams, most of which play in the competitive Division I Big East Conference (hockey is part of the Hockey East Association). Highly ranked teams include men's and women's ice hockey, basketball, soccer, and cross-country, as well as women's field hockey. "Basketball and hockey games are very important to PC students because we can show our school spirit," says a sophomore. Students get especially rowdy when rivals UConn and URI are in town. A majority of students get involved in intramurals and club sports, with flag football, softball, rugby, and lacrosse proving to be particularly popular.

Providence College appeals primarily to those students who want to challenge themselves academically without compromising their faith. Despite frequent

The Liberal Arts Honors Program offers students of high academic ability a more in-depth and rigorous version of PC's core curriculum.

Owing to the college's strong Catholic identity, community service and volunteer work are popular pastimes.

Overlaps

Holy Cross, Fairfield, Stone Hill, Villanova, Loyola University Maryland, Boston College, Fordham, Notre Dame

complaints about the length and rigor of the Western Civ requirement and the lack of diversity, students here seem content with what the college has to offer and are proud to be part of the PC community. "PC is preppy and a great place to be," says a senior. "We have Division I school spirit but in a small-school atmosphere."

If You Apply To ›

Providence: Early decision I and II, early action, regular decision. SATs or ACTs: optional. Accepts the Common Application with supplement.

University of Puget Sound

1500 North Warner, Tacoma, WA 98416

Ask anyone in Tacoma about Puget Sound and they'll tell you that UPS (the college, not the package service) delivers solid liberal arts programs with a touch of business. Within easy reach of the Sound and Mount Rainier, the university specializes in all things Asia, including a nine-month university-sponsored trip. Compare to Whitman and Willamette.

Website: www.pugetsound.edu
Location: Small City
Private
Total Enrollment: 2,084
Undergraduates: 1,835
Male/Female: 43/57
Financial Aid: 100%
Pell Grant: 18%
Expense: Pr $ $ $
Student Loans: 50%
Average Debt: $ $
Applicants: 5,025
Accepted: 88%
Enrolled: 9%
Grad in 6 Years: 74%
Returning Freshmen: 88%
Academics: ✍ ✍ ✍ ½
Social: ☎ ☎ ☎
Q of L: ★ ★ ★ ★
Admissions: (253) 879-3211
Email Address: admission@ pugetsound.edu

Strong Programs:
Asian Studies
Psychology
Politics and Government
Economics
Business

A strong curricular emphasis on global awareness, supportive faculty, and a relatively laid-back atmosphere have raised the profile of the University of Puget Sound, transforming it from a regional liberal arts college in Tacoma to an undergraduate institution with national reach. The school's first-rate Asian studies program continues to draw students interested in cultural studies, Pacific Rim economics, and international travel, and the UPS community is as close-knit as ever. "People don't come here because they have heard of us before," says one contented senior. "They come here because they visit and they don't want to leave."

Founded by Methodists in 1888 to bring higher education to the region, Puget Sound is cradled by the Cascade Range and the rugged Olympics, with easy access to the urban energy of Seattle and the natural beauty of Mount Rainier. The 97-acre campus boasts carefully maintained lawns, native fir trees, and plenty of other greenery, thanks to the moist climate. Most buildings, with distinctive arches and porticos, were built in the 1950s and '60s. Additional facilities include an athletics and aquatics center and a 3,850-square-foot Sculpture House, with facilities for welding, woodwork, and painting.

> **"Students at Puget Sound are definitely outdoorsy. Lots of Birkenstocks and plaid."**

Puget Sound students must complete a core curriculum that includes a freshman seminar in writing and rhetoric, and another in scholarly inquiry and research; they must also demonstrate foreign language proficiency and take a course on knowledge, identity, and power. In their first three years at Puget Sound, students also study five Approaches to Knowing—fine arts, humanities, math, natural sciences, and social sciences. An upper-level capstone course, Connections, challenges traditional disciplinary boundaries and examines the benefits and limits of an interdisciplinary approach to learning.

After navigating UPS's requirements, students may pursue a B.A., B.S., or B.M. (bachelor of music) degree. Some of the most popular majors are psychology, politics and government, economics, business, biology, international political economy, and neuroscience. "I would recommend the environmental policy and decision-making classes; you're often able to go on field trips with professors and working professionals," notes a senior. The university has developed a reputation as a jumping-off point to Asia—both literally and figuratively. Its curriculum stresses two of the fastest-growing fields in the region: Asian studies and Pacific Rim economics. Nearly one-third of Puget Sounders take at least one Asian studies course, and once every two years, there's a nine-month, school-sponsored trip through Japan, Thailand, Korea, India, China, and Nepal, where participants study art, architecture, politics, economics, and philosophy. In all, more than 100 study abroad programs are available in more than 40 nations; 32 percent of students participate. Other special offerings include a classics-based honors program, the Business Leadership Program, and residence-based humanities programs.

(continued)

Students say that while their peers are academically motivated and coursework can be challenging, the atmosphere at Puget Sound is "generally very relaxed and enjoyable, with professors always encouraging lots of interaction from students," explains a history major. Sixty-eight percent of classes have fewer than 20 students. "I have been so well taken care of by our professors, and I see them as instructors but also mentors," says a psychology major. Students also praise the plentiful opportunities for undergraduate research, which recently have ranged from examining bacteria on lizard eggs to summer fieldwork studying graffiti in Europe. Advising, which includes both academic and peer advisors, and career services receive positive reviews.

"Students at Puget Sound are definitely outdoorsy," says a Hispanic studies junior. "Lots of Birkenstocks and plaid. Politically liberal, for the most part." Most come from western states, with 29 percent hailing from Washington; less than 1 percent come from abroad. Black students make up only 3 percent of the student body, Hispanics/Latinos 12 percent, Asian Americans 8 percent, and multiracial students 9 percent. According to a junior, "There is a big push for more diversity on campus," and students are also concerned with LGBTQ rights, gender equality, and environmental issues. There are no athletic scholarships, but merit awards averaging $21,400 are doled out annually.

The first-rate Asian studies program continues to draw students interested in cultural studies, Pacific Rim economics, and international travel.

Sixty-six percent of Puget Sound students live on campus, and freshmen and sophomores are required to do so. First-year students all live together, and after that students may live in Greek chapter housing, pursue a single room in the dorms, or apply for one of 60 university-owned houses, many

"The vibe is laid-back, but purposeful at the same time."

of which focus on themes like outdoor leadership and music. "The surrounding neighborhood is happy to rent out houses to students who choose to live off campus their junior and senior years," reports a computer science major. Aside from the main campus dining area, students can chow down at three campus cafés and the Cellar, and meals get good reviews for freshness and variety. "We have a strong security team that takes sexual assault very seriously and has been good at communicating with the campus about situations that have happened," comments a junior.

Twenty-five percent of Puget Sound men and 24 percent of the women go Greek, though fraternities and sororities don't dominate the social scene and all Greek parties are alcohol-free. "Social life at UPS is fairly intimate. In my experience, people tend to hang out more off campus on the weekends, at people's houses and such," a philosophy major says. Popular school-sponsored activities include the Log Jam BBQ and club fair that kicks off the school year, the Foolish Pleasures festival of short student-produced films, and the Lumbershoot music festival in the spring (a play on Seattle's Bumbershoot). An active Hawaiian student organization sponsors a luau each spring, with "great food and lots of traditional dances." The Repertory Dance Group and Puget Sound Outdoors are among the most popular campus organizations. A few Tacoma bars and restaurants are within walking distance, and a

Students may apply to live in one of 60 university-owned houses, many of which focus on themes like outdoor leadership and music.

junior says the university is working "to give students pipelines to the local community through volunteering and social justice programs, free and discounted museum passes, and more." With the mountains and beaches so close—Seattle is 30 minutes away by car, Portland two hours south, and Vancouver, British Columbia, three hours north—road trips are de rigueur. That's especially true during ski season, and the school rents out all the necessary equipment.

Students are fond of saying that Puget Sound's Division III varsity teams, the Loggers, "Kick Axe." Solid teams include football, men's and women's soccer (recent Northwest Conference champs), women's crew, and women's volleyball. The school's archrival is Pacific Lutheran University; "football and basketball games against PLU are a big deal and always packed," says a fan. About half of the students sign up for intramural and club sports.

Don't let UPS students' slacker-chic clothes and casual demeanor fool you. Puget Sound means serious study for students seeking immersion in the liberal arts and the natural beauty of the outdoors. As a molecular and cellular biology major explains, "The vibe is laid-back, but purposeful at the same time. People who come to this school are passionate and love to share those passions with others."

Overlaps

Lewis & Clark, Whitman, Willamette, Reed, Pomona, Pacific Lutheran, Seattle University, University of Oregon

If You Apply To ›

Puget Sound: Early decision, early action, regular decision. SATs or ACTs: optional (test-optional applicants must submit two short-answer essay questions). Accepts the Common Application with supplement.

Purdue University

475 Stadium Drive, West Lafayette, IN 47907

Purdue is Indiana's STEM university—with side helpings of business, health professions, and liberal arts. Compare to Kansas State and Big Ten rival Michigan State. Does better than most large universities in giving students hands-on opportunities such as internships and co-ops—and resisting tuition increases. Flight technology and aerospace—and turning out future astronauts—are longtime specialties.

Successful Indiana colleges typically have three things in common: a solid agricultural program, a powerhouse basketball team, and a conservative student body. Purdue University has all of these—plus one of the nation's strongest engineering programs, and the distinction of having awarded more bachelor's degrees in the field than any other institution. Purdue is also home to the nation's first computer science department, and its programs in pharmaceutical sciences, nursing, and management are top-notch. Budding classicists, dramatists, and literary critics might want to look elsewhere, but those seeking small-school friendliness with big-school spirit may be very happy to join the ranks of Boilermakers.

Purdue, founded in 1869 and named for its first major donor, is the main attraction in the small industrial town of West Lafayette, where the population triples when students return each fall. The campus features redbrick and limestone buildings arranged around lush shaded courtyards. Newer facilities include the $64 million STEM Teaching Lab, which provides multidisciplinary laboratory classrooms for up to 15,000 undergraduates. Purdue is also home to Amazon's first ever brick-and-mortar location, where students can have textbooks shipped overnight for no cost.

Website: www.purdue.edu
Location: Small City
Public
Total Enrollment: 42,322
Undergraduates: 35,470
Male/Female: 58/42
Financial Aid: 55%
Pell Grant: 14%
Expense: Pub $
Student Loans: 39%
Average Debt: $ $ $
Applicants: 59,173
Accepted: 69%
Enrolled: 25%
Grad in 6 Years: 83%
Returning Freshmen: 92%

Students apply to and enroll in one of Purdue's 10 colleges, and academic requirements vary by school and major. Typically, they include English, math, a lab science, and foreign language proficiency. Management is the most popular major, followed by mechanical engineering, computer science, and industrial engineering. Students flock to the five-year engineering co-op program, one of the most competitive on campus, because it marries classroom study with paid, real-world work. Additionally, Purdue offers a strong undergraduate program in professional flight technology, which includes hands-on training at the university's own airport. Purdue has produced more than 20 astronauts, including pioneers Neil Armstrong and Gus Grissom. A four-year program in retail management is available in partnership with the Fashion Institute of Technology (FIT) in New York. For those seeking to save money on their degree and pursue their post-graduation plans sooner, Purdue offers more than 20 "Degree in 3" programs in the Colleges of Liberal Arts and Education, through which students can earn a bachelor's degree in three years; options range from communication and history to sociology and special education.

> **"I've had some teachers who were phenomenal at connecting with the students."**

"The academic climate is fairly competitive and intense," says a sophomore. Despite the university's size, 38 percent of classes have fewer than 20 students and many freshman classes are seminar-style, taught by graduate students and academic advisors who help answer students' questions and provide career advice. "I've had some teachers who were phenomenal at connecting with the students and having them understand the concepts," one student confides, "and other teachers act like they are presenting to an empty room." About a third of undergrads study abroad, and options are available for students in all majors in more than 60 countries. Undergraduates also participate in more than 2,000 research projects each year.

"The students here are very academically focused and driven," says a junior. "They have fun and relax on weekends, but everyone knows the reason we are here is to get a degree to be successful in the future." Half of Purdue's undergraduates hail from Indiana, although there is a healthy proportion of international students, at 11 percent. Just 2 percent are Black, 12 percent are Asian American, 6 percent are Hispanic/Latino, and 4 percent are multiracial. A tuition freeze has been in place since 2013, helping to keep costs down. Thousands of merit scholarships averaging $5,400 are awarded annually; athletes vie for nearly 250 scholarships in 18 sports. The Purdue Promise program grants financial assistance and specialized academic and leadership coaching to eligible Indiana residents from lower-income backgrounds.

Forty-one percent of students live in Purdue's residence halls. Almost all freshmen live on campus, though they aren't required to, and Harrison Hall is said to be a good pick for newbies. "Some are definitely nicer than others," a sophomore admits. "Many of them still do not have air-conditioning." The notion of a "co-ed dorm" here means that men and women share a lobby. Most upperclassmen find housing just off campus. Those

> **"[Purdue has] an awesome sense of community. Boiler Up!"**

with a grumbling stomach are treated to tasty options on campus. "Our food is fantastic," cheers one junior. "It's all-you-can-eat." Walking and riding escorts and a visible security presence help students feel safe.

"The social life typically takes place on campus," reports one philosophy major. Alcohol is prohibited in dorms, and "people have been kicked out of the residence halls for being caught with alcohol," says a sophomore. Still, as at other schools, underage students can find ways to get served. Greek life draws 15 percent of Purdue men and 19 percent of the women and offers many social opportunities.

(continued)

Academics: ✍ ✍ ✍ ½
Social: ☎ ☎ ☎
Q of L: ★ ★ ★
Admissions: (765) 494-1776
Email Address: admissions@purdue.edu

Strong Programs:
Professional Flight Technology
Aeronautical and Astronautical Engineering
Agriculture
Computer Science
Pharmaceutical Sciences
Nursing
Management
Mechanical Engineering

Purdue offers a strong undergraduate program in professional flight technology and has produced more than 20 astronauts.

But there are other options, too, including sports games and more than 1,000 student organizations, ranging from the BBQ society to professional development clubs. "Outside of class, you can do anything from skydiving, paintball, choir, rock climbing, salsa dancing—anything. It's up to you," encourages a senior mechanical engineering major.

As far as college towns go, West Lafayette "would not exist if it weren't for Purdue," one student says. Another adds, "The surrounding area has a good social scene for those 21 [and over], with excellent bars and nightlife. There are also many great nearby restaurants within walking distance for all students." Harry's Chocolate Shop—a bar, not a candy store—is a longtime student favorite. Chicago and Indianapolis are favored weekend destinations for students with cars, and each spring, a week of fun and parties leads up to the Grand Prix go-kart races. Students also look forward to the Bug Bowl, an annual event sponsored by Purdue's entomology department, including cricket-spitting and cockroach races.

Purdue's "Boilermaker" moniker was coined by a sportswriter in 1891 describing how "the Burly Boiler Makers from Purdue" defeated Wabash College's football team 44–0. Boilermaker pride manifests itself at Division I games of all types, especially when the opposing team is Indiana University, known derisively as "that school down south," in the annual struggle for the Old Oaken Bucket. Every year, the winner adds a link to a chain on the bucket in the shape of either an "I" or "P." Men's and women's basketball, golf, and swimming and diving are among the most competitive sports on campus. Thirty-one club sports and more than 35 intramurals are a big draw for those looking for friendly competition. Solar car racing and Rube Goldberg machine contests are some of the more popular activities among STEM students.

Purdue drew national headlines several years ago with its acquisition of for-profit Kaplan University and plans to create a "mega-university" known as Purdue Global, but the project has been slow to take off. In the meantime, happy Purdue students continue to discover that learning is fun when academics are mixed with real-world experience and a healthy dose of school spirit. "Purdue has great academic programs, incredible organizational and social opportunities, and an awesome sense of community," says one enthusiastic sophomore. "Boiler Up!"

If You Apply To ›

Purdue: Early action, regular decision. SATs or ACTs: required. Accepts the Common Application with supplement. Apply to particular schools or programs.

Queen's University: See page 362.

Quinnipiac University

275 Mount Carmel Avenue, Hamden, CT 06518

Aggressive expansion of programs and facilities has put Quinnipiac on the map of comprehensive New England colleges with a preprofessional bent. Less selective than Fairfield and Ithaca, with more dual-degree options. Business and health sciences are big attractions. Best known to the general public for its political polling and hockey prowess. Midway between NYC and Boston.

Over the last three decades, Quinnipiac University has grown from a small liberal arts college of 2,000 full-time undergraduates to a full-fledged university with 6,000 undergrads, three dozen graduate programs, and nine academic divisions spread out over three campuses—a massive expansion that has helped increase the school's national prominence. With enrollment now leveling off and its strengths in health, business, and communications well established, the university has begun to carve out a niche for itself as a place where talented, preprofessional undergraduates can get on a fast track to advanced degrees and jump-start their careers.

Quinnipiac's 250-acre Mount Carmel campus sits adjacent to Sleeping Giant State Park, with its 1,700 acres of hiking and walking trails, 90 minutes from New York City and two hours from Boston. The university was founded in 1929 as a business school and took its name from the local Quinnipiac Native Americans. Traditional New England red brick dominates, and a large central quad is surrounded by the library, the student center, the admissions and financial aid office, and academic buildings. The three-building Evans College of Arts and Sciences Center features a spacious quad that overlooks Clark's pond and its family of resident swans. The 250-acre York Hill campus is just across Whitney Avenue and features the cozy Rocky Top Student Center, which resembles a European ski lodge and boasts panoramic views of the region. The 104-acre North Haven campus, located four miles from the Mount Carmel campus, serves as home to the Center for Medicine, Nursing, and Health Sciences, the School of Law, and the School of Education.

> "A lot of students come here for a very specific program or a dual degree."

Quinnipiac's liberal arts philosophy is evident in its general education curriculum, which includes foundational courses in the sciences, social sciences, humanities, fine arts, writing, and intercultural understanding, as well as a capstone requirement in the senior year. All freshmen take a First-Year Seminar designed to help them practice critical thinking and inquiry.

Quinnipiac offers nearly 60 undergraduate majors; the newest include business analytics, data science, and sustainability and environmental policy. The most popular majors include nursing, health science studies, finance, and marketing. The School of Business's programs in entrepreneurship and finance are strong, while students in the School of Communications benefit from solid offerings in journalism and film, television, and media arts. Quinnipiac owns several media outlets, including a student-run radio station and television station. Seventeen engineering labs accommodate majors in civil, industrial, software, and mechanical engineering. Irish studies is a noteworthy minor; the university's Ireland's Great Hunger Institute houses one of the world's largest collections of art and literature dealing with the Great Irish Famine. A spate of combined undergraduate/graduate degree programs are available in such fields as business, communications, law, and social work; the entry-level physician assistant, physical therapy, and occupational therapy combined degree programs are particular specialties. The university's career-oriented student body makes the most of these opportunities: nearly a third of undergrads stay at Quinnipiac to complete an advanced degree in their chosen profession.

"Students will find courses challenging but reasonable," says a junior. Fifty-one percent of all classes have fewer than 20 students, and "there are no massive lecture halls," says one journalism major. There are no teaching or graduate assistants, either; all classes are taught by professors. "Professors are knowledgeable and have real-world experience that will help prepare you for your future career," notes a nursing major. Each school and college provides its own career development center, which students rate highly for assisting with internship and job placements.

Highly motivated students may enroll in the Honors Program, which features special seminars, close relationships with professors, and a slew of enrichment and

Website: www.qu.edu
Location: Suburban
Private
Total Enrollment: 7,759
Undergraduates: 5,985
Male/Female: 38/62
Financial Aid: 97%
Pell Grant: 15%
Expense: Pr $ $
Student Loans: 65%
Average Debt: $ $ $ $
Applicants: 15,720
Accepted: 88%
Enrolled: 11%
Grad in 6 Years: 80%
Returning Freshmen: 87%
Academics: ✍ ✍ ✍
Social: ☎ ☎ ☎
Q of L: ★ ★ ★ ★
Admissions: (203) 582-8600
Email Address: admissions@ qu.edu

Strong Programs:
Entrepreneurship
Finance
Journalism
Film, Television, and Media Arts
Nursing
Health Science Studies
Marketing
Engineering

Irish studies is a noteworthy minor; the university houses one of the world's largest collections of art and literature dealing with the Great Irish Famine.

The university is home to the renowned Quinnipiac Polling Institute, a national survey that polls registered voters about issues of public concern.

leadership opportunities. Internships and clinical experiences abound: communications students may elect to spend their summer on production sets or on-air in Los Angeles, while political science majors have the opportunity to assist elected officials at the state capital or in Washington, D.C. The university is home to the renowned Quinnipiac Polling Institute, a national survey that polls registered voters about political races, state and national elections, and issues of public concern. Study abroad options include a highly popular semester program at University College Cork in Ireland; 35 percent of students take part in programs offered in 32 countries across the globe. "With so many different ways to go abroad (semester program, 10-day service trip, three- or six-week seminar), there is no reason not to take advantage and explore the world," urges a physical therapy major.

"A lot of students come here for a very specific program or a dual degree, which makes them very focused on maintaining high grades," observes a biomedical sciences major. Most students come from the Northeast, and a senior reports, "Quinnipiac has a reputation for recruiting affluent students." Twenty-eight percent

"Party culture is present, but it is not over the top."

of undergrads hail from Connecticut, and 3 percent are international. The student body is 4 percent Black, 10 percent Hispanic/Latino, 4 percent Asian American, and 3 percent multiracial. Political and social issues aren't a huge concern on campus, students say. Qualified undergraduates receive merit awards averaging $21,800, and gifted athletes vie for more than 200 athletic scholarships in 21 sports.

On-campus housing is required for incoming freshmen and guaranteed for three years; 59 percent of students reside in school-owned housing. Most freshmen and sophomores live on the Mount Carmel campus, while upperclassmen live on the York Hill campus in suite-style accommodations or in nearby houses or an apartment complex owned by the university. About a quarter of the students join the 19 available living/learning communities. Students are required to purchase a meal plan; food options at the main dining hall (Café Q) and the Bobcat Den get average reviews. Campus security maintains a visible patrol on campus, and an occupational therapy major says, "Students are required to learn about sexual assault during their freshman orientation, and it's a serious topic that is reinforced throughout their time here."

Nothing brings out the Bobcat faithful like the annual hockey match versus rival Yale.

The Quinnipiac social scene is bustling. The campus hosts a variety of events, including guest speakers, comedians, craft nights, and film screenings; there are also roughly 150 student clubs to whet the appetite. Twelve percent of the men and 22 percent of the women join fraternities and sororities, which do not have dedicated housing. "Party culture is present," especially among Greek groups and sports teams, notes a senior, "but it is not over the top." Quinnipiac is a "wet" campus—students 21 or older are allowed to possess alcohol in the dorms—but underage drinkers face stiff penalties. Two annual concerts, Fall Fest and Wake the Giant, bring big headlining performers to campus.

When students tire of the campus scene, they trek into surrounding towns in search of fun. Hamden offers the usual mix of chain restaurants, movie theaters, and

"It's a rite of passage to hike Sleeping Giant State Park at least once during your time here."

bowling alleys, and the university provides a free shuttle to New Haven (home of Yale University), where students enjoy the food and nightlife. Seventy-five percent of students choose to get involved in the local community through volunteer work. The great outdoors beckon too. "It's a rite of passage to hike Sleeping Giant State Park at least once during your time here," says an English major.

The Quinnipiac Bobcats field 21 Division I teams—seven for men and 14 for women—and most compete in the Metro Atlantic Athletic Conference. Men's and women's ice hockey play in the powerful Eastern College Athletic Conference, and field hockey competes in the Big East. Women's rugby is a recent national champion, while conference champs include women's golf, women's basketball, and baseball. Nothing brings out the Bobcat faithful like the annual hockey match versus rival Yale. "The Yale rivalry is fierce, and student pride comes alive," says a student. Intramurals are popular, and the club sports program offers 20 sports, ranging from eSports to women's figure skating.

Expanding academics, flexible degree options, and increased selectivity are all part of the university's continuing mission to attract bright students. It's an expensive gamble that administrators and students feel will pay off. "There are more resources here than I can think of," says one satisfied student. "Any student who wants to succeed will succeed."

Overlaps

Sacred Heart, Fairfield, Marist, Syracuse, Hofstra, Ithaca, Providence, Villanova

If You Apply To ›

Quinnipiac: Early decision, early action, regular decision. SATs or ACTs: optional (required for some programs). Accepts the Common Application. Apply to particular program.

Randolph College

2500 Rivermont Avenue, Lynchburg, VA 24503

Co-ed since 2007, Randolph College pursues its traditional mission of strong liberal arts through a unique and creative new curriculum. Students concentrate on two courses at a time and take a break on Wednesdays for special enrichment activities, academic and otherwise. Males now make up more than a third of undergrads. Suburban location on the James River is rich in history, though of limited appeal to most students.

With rich traditions, cozy dorms, and challenging, seminar-based classes, Randolph College, named for early 19th-century politician John Randolph, has preserved the best elements of its past while evolving into an institution that remains relevant today. Its innovative TAKE2 curriculum makes Randolph the only college in the country where students take only two courses at a time, allowing for more in-depth immersion in coursework as well as more free time to pursue other educational opportunities. The college, which started out in 1891 as Randolph–Macon Women's College, offers students a place to be themselves. "Fitting in isn't what Randolph is about," says a sophomore. "One of our mottoes is 'Be an Original,' and you can see that throughout the school."

The college's 100-acre campus sits in the historic neighborhood of Lynchburg, on the banks of the James River. A brick wall built around the campus's perimeter in 1930 has become a symbol of the school for faculty, staff, and students, who fondly refer to their time at Randolph as being spent "behind the Red Brick Wall." Graceful old redbrick buildings are covered with purple wisteria and linked by glass corridors called trolleys; the surrounding trees burst into riotous bloom each spring. Main Hall, dating from 1893, houses dorm rooms, classrooms, and faculty and administrative offices. The Maier Museum of Art has one of the best college collections of American art in the country.

Launched in fall 2021, Randolph's TAKE2 curriculum divides the academic year into four seven-week sessions. During each session, students take just two courses.

> "Professors know what interests you."

Website: www.randolphcollege.edu
Location: Suburban
Private
Total Enrollment: 534
Undergraduates: 470
Male/Female: 38/62
Financial Aid: 100%
Pell Grant: 48%
Expense: Pr $
Student Loans: 79%
Average Debt: $ $ $ $
Applicants: 1,161
Accepted: 94%
Enrolled: 13%
Grad in 6 Years: 56%
Returning Freshmen: 72%
Academics: ✎ ✎ ✎
Social: ☎ ☎
Q of L: ★ ★ ★ ★
Admissions: 800-745-7692

(continued)

Email Address: admissions@
randolphcollege.edu

Strong Programs:
English
Studio Art
Chemistry
Economics
Biology
History
Psychology
Sport and Exercise Studies

Class periods are extended to allow more time for hands-on activities and group interaction. No classes are held on Wednesdays, giving students a midweek break to rest, study, or engage in extracurriculars, field trips, volunteer work, or internships. General education requirements cover traditional liberal arts subjects such as artistic expression, human experience, culture and identity, social and natural science, and writing. Incoming students take the First-Year Seminar, which examines how to maximize academic success. Every major culminates in a senior-year capstone experience, with an honors option available for highly motivated students.

Biology, history, psychology, and sport and exercise studies are some of the most popular majors at Randolph. Programs in English, studio art, chemistry, and economics are also well regarded. A program in American culture combines classroom study with guest speakers and travel to important historic or cultural sites; past topics have included Reproductive Justice in Virginia, The Struggle for Native Lands in the American West, and Working for the Weekend. SUPER (Step Up to Physical Science and Engineering at Randolph) is an immersive STEM scholarship program for first-year students that includes a two-week residential academic program in the summer and specialized academic services and mentoring.

According to a senior, the workload at Randolph is "just heavy enough to promote academic growth, but still reasonable enough to keep you sane." The student-run Honor System has been in effect for more than 130 years. Since 94 percent of classes enroll fewer than 20 students, and there are no teaching assistants, it's easy for students to form friendships with their professors. "Professors know what interests you," says a senior, "and are always open to helping out with finding jobs or internships."

All Randolph students are eligible to apply for a $2,000 RISE grant, which they can use to fund research, international travel, and other academic pursuits. The eight-week Summer Research Program is "a fantastic opportunity for students to

"We have a number of secret societies, clubs, and other social organizations."

work with a faculty member on a topic that they are passionate about," explains a history major; in addition to conducting research, participants attend a series of seminars with guest speakers, present their findings at a closing symposium, and get paid a stipend. Thirty-three percent of students study abroad. Randolph's two-week, faculty-led summer study seminars are a popular option; recent seminars have taken students to Italy, Iceland, and Korea. More than half of Randolph students secure off-campus internships, with organizations from the Chicago Lyric Opera to the National Gallery in London.

Seventy-five percent of Randolph students hail from Virginia, and 86 percent graduated from public schools; 4 percent are international. Students of color have a notable presence, with Black students accounting for 20 percent of the student body, Hispanics/Latinos 10 percent, Asian Americans 2 percent, and multiracial students 6 percent. Socioeconomic diversity is strong, with 48 percent of freshmen qualifying for Pell Grants. Students report that the political atmosphere is largely liberal. Randolph has reduced its sticker price by more than 30 percent, hoping to attract applicants who might otherwise be deterred by high published prices. Merit scholarships averaging $12,800 per year are available, but there are no athletic awards.

Its innovative new TAKE2 curriculum makes Randolph the only college in the country where students take only two courses at a time.

Seventy-eight percent of Randolph students live in the dorms, which a global studies major calls "pretty nice and comfy," although students gripe about the lack of air-conditioning in some dorms. Main Hall, a.k.a. "the Hilton," is the largest dorm, and its central location makes it the most convenient. After the first year, housing is selected by lottery, and college-owned apartments across the street from campus are the preferred option among upperclassmen. As for campus dining, a biology major says, "The actual dining hall is very nice; the food is mediocre at best." Security officers patrol continuously and take pride in knowing students by name.

"The real social scene is inside the Red Brick Wall," says a sophomore. "We have a number of secret societies, clubs, and other social organizations." The Randolph Programming Board makes sure no one is bored by hosting comedians, bands, and other entertainers, as well as talent shows and outdoor parties. Randolph's close-knit community can get too close at times (a junior warns, "You may learn things about your personal life from other people before you knew them yourself"), so students occasionally escape to other nearby colleges like Hampden–Sydney, Washington and Lee, and the University of Virginia, for those seeking frat parties and football. Underage drinkers face consequences, in accordance with the honor code. There is no Greek life, but sports teams and other organizations offer a low-key party scene.

A program in American culture combines classroom study with guest speakers and travel; past topics have included Reproductive Justice in Virginia.

The town of Lynchburg (population 80,000) hosts two other colleges and has a shopping mall and some retail chains like Target and Barnes & Noble, but is otherwise "less than exhilarating," says a biology major. Most bars and clubs in the area are 21 and over, and the restaurants, stores, and movie theaters are closed by 10 p.m. Thankfully, the college's coffee bar satisfies students' caffeine cravings.

"Students still value respect and responsibility."

"We also have a lot of hiking and recreation options that are close by and affordable," offers a junior. Students often get involved in the local community via volunteering.

Randolph's WildCats compete in Division III, and the school's top rival is the University of Lynchburg. Recently, the women's tennis team has been most competitive, along with men's soccer, basketball, and track and field. But more than athletic contests, students look forward to Randolph traditions, such as the Even/Odd class rivalry, Ring Week (in which a freshman anonymously decorates the door of a junior and leaves small gifts all week, culminating in a scavenger hunt for their class ring), and the Pumpkin Parade (during which sophomores present lit jack-o'-lanterns to seniors, who show them off in an evening parade). The Never-Ending Weekend each fall includes both a formal and the annual Tacky Party, for which tasteless attire is de rigueur.

From going co-ed to expanding cocurricular opportunities to redesigning its academic calendar in support of a more balanced college experience, Randolph College is working hard to live up to its motto *Vita abundantior* (the life more abundant). Through all these changes, a student explains, Randolph's "core dynamic and value system" have remained the same: "Students still value respect and responsibility."

Overlaps

Berry, Bridgewater, Hendrix, Oglethorpe, Eckerd, Millsaps, Wells, Centre

If You Apply To ›

Randolph: Early action, regular decision. SATs or ACTs: optional. Accepts the Common Application with supplement.

University of Redlands

1200 East Colton, P.O. Box 3080, Redlands, CA 92373

If you like the thought of palm trees against a backdrop of snow-covered peaks, Redlands may be your place. As a "university," Redlands is double the size of Occidental and Whittier. The distinctive Johnston Center for Integrative Studies, an alternative living/learning program, makes an odd contrast to the buttoned-down preprofessionalism of the rest of Redlands.

Website: www.redlands.edu
Location: Suburban
Private
Total Enrollment: 2,371
Undergraduates: 2,201
Male/Female: 40/60
Financial Aid: 90%
Pell Grant: 32%
Expense: Pr $ $ $
Student Loans: 68%
Average Debt: $ $ $ $
Applicants: 3,738
Accepted: 83%
Enrolled: 17%
Grad in 6 Years: 70%
Returning Freshmen: 81%
Academics: ✍ ✍ ✍
Social: ☎ ☎ ☎
Q of L: ★ ★ ★
Admissions: (800) 455-5064
Email Address: admissions@
   redlands.edu

Strong Programs:
Education
Music
Communication Sciences and
   Disorders
Health, Medicine, and Society
Business
Psychology
Environmental Studies
Biology

The Johnston Center
is an experimental
living/learning
community where
students create their
own course of study.

Amid the dozens of gigantic and well-known universities in the state of California stands the University of Redlands. With its innovative, alternative living/learning option and strong preprofessional emphasis, this versatile school, founded in 1907, is one of higher education's better-kept secrets, and a place where students receive all the personal attention and intellectual stimulation they could want. As a public policy and political science major explains, the combination of "free-spirited" individualism and career-oriented professionalism means that "we definitely have two different vibes on campus," but Redland students share a sense of passion for what they're pursuing.

The University of Redlands's 160-acre campus, covered in majestic oak trees, is designed around "The Quad," a large grassy area surrounded by a group of dorms that face one another. The two main landmarks are the Memorial Chapel and the Administration Building. Redlands's facilities are a mixture of older, historical columned buildings and more modern, renovated ones. The view from campus can only be described as breathtaking. Mountain ranges form the backdrop, and neighboring Big Bear Lake and Arrowhead ski resorts give endless getaway opportunities. Also nearby are the San Gorgonio Wilderness and Joshua Tree National Park.

Redlands's most distinctive attribute is the Johnston Center for Integrative Studies, an experimental living/learning community within the College of Arts and Sciences where students create their own course of study and are assessed by professor and self-evaluations rather than grades. The Johnston Center was established in 1969 to function as an alternative college within a traditional setting. With about 200 participants, it's one of the university's largest programs and offers unusual academic freedom: there are no departments, majors, or distribution requirements. Instead, students design contracts with professors for their entire plan of study. At the beginning of each course, students make up the syllabus by consensus and then set their own research and writing goals. Each student develops four-year goals—which are reviewed by a student/faculty board for direction and breadth—within one or more broad areas: the social sciences, behavioral sciences, humanities, and fine and performing arts. One student explains, "Johnston Center students tend to be independent thinkers, self-motivated, and [don't] take classes just because they have to." Recent participants have designed degrees such as food in society, urban agriculture, and social behavior across cultures.

"Interaction with professors is common and camaraderie is abundant."

Aside from Johnston, Redlands is noteworthy among liberal arts institutions in that it also offers preprofessional programs. The school of education and the music conservatory provide strong career training, as does the excellent program in communication sciences and disorders. A minor in spatial studies is bolstered by Redlands's graduate program in geographic information science. Premed/prehealth and prelaw students receive advising on requirements for graduate school, and 3–2 engineering degrees with Columbia University and WashU in St. Louis are available. Redlands has emerged as a national leader in science curriculum reform with innovative interdisciplinary offerings like the health, medicine, and society program, which combines the study of natural science, medical humanities, public policy, global health, and more. Business administration is the most popular major, and the university also offers solid majors in global business and theater business. Psychology, environmental studies, and biology are popular, too, and Redlands now offers a Peace Corps prep program for those interested in volunteer work abroad. Regardless of major, all students must take a first-year seminar, participate in 80 hours of community service, and complete a capstone requirement, such as an internship or academic research, in order to graduate.

"I love Redlands's small, discussion-based classes," says a Johnston Center student. "Education becomes a conversation, and students' original ideas are not only allowed but encouraged." Fifty-eight percent of classes have fewer than 20 students, meaning "interaction with professors is common and camaraderie is abundant," says a psychology and Spanish double major. Professors are said to be very accessible outside of class, too, even occasionally coming by the dorms for "fireside chats." With its 4–4–1 calendar, Redlands affords students the option to take one intensive course each May, and some use this time to study abroad. Students may embark on Redlands's signature program in Salzburg, Austria, or choose from more than 70 other options worldwide; 48 percent study abroad. The Redlands Four-Year Graduation Promise guarantees that if incoming students are unable to graduate in four years with the help of faculty advising, Redlands will cover the cost of additional courses needed for graduation.

"Redlands has a very personal, small-town sort of feeling," says a sophomore. "Everyone is so friendly and supportive." Seventy-one percent of undergraduates come from within the state, creating a mellow, Southern California atmosphere on campus; 2 percent hail from abroad. The climate is a definite plus, with temperatures rarely below 50 degrees. Hispanics/Latinos represent 40 percent of undergrads, Asian Americans 5 percent, Black students 4 percent, and multiracial students 7 percent. "Our school has grown more diverse and more politically active in my four years here," reports a senior, and the student body leans liberal. Redlands annually awards a variety of academic scholarships and talent scholarships in art, creative writing, music, and theater, but there are no athletic scholarships.

Sixty-seven percent of students live in the residence halls and on-campus apartments, most of which are co-ed. Students enjoy their food at The Table at Irvine Commons, the Launch Kitchen, or the Plaza Café & Market, part of the Hunsaker University Center, which has a "town square" atmosphere. Students praise Redlands's safety and its approach to sexual assault prevention; says one, "My school has taken measures to protect students by being very transparent with them."

"The party culture on campus is not all-encompassing, but it isn't dormant," reports a senior, and while alcohol is accessible, students say they don't feel pressured to drink. Local fraternities and sororities claim 11 percent of the men and 19 percent of the women, respectively, and their generally well-controlled parties are open to all. Students look

> **"The party culture on campus is not all-encompassing, but it isn't dormant."**

forward to the Spring Fest concert every year. The nearby city of Redlands offers a variety of coffee shops and restaurants, and students are highly involved in the local community. Road trips to Los Angeles, Palm Springs, and San Diego are common.

The University of Redlands sponsors 21 intercollegiate Bulldog teams, all of which consistently vie for spots among the top of the Division III Southern California Intercollegiate Athletic Conference (SCIAC). Football, baseball, and men's and women's soccer, golf, and track and field are competitive. Games against rival Occidental always draw crowds, and the "Och Tamale" school chant—a string of complete gibberish invented in 1921, supposedly in mockery of Oxy's own Latinesque nonsense chant—is a beloved school tradition ("Och tamale gazolly gazump!"). Half of students participate in at least one intramural or club sport, and weekend adventurers strike out on regular excursions organized by Outdoor Programs.

The University of Redlands is a lot of different things to a lot of different people. With nearly 180 full-time faculty members, it manages to be a liberal arts college, a pre-professional institute, and an alternative school all in one. The Johnston Center is clearly a path to travel for the innovative individualist, but even those who don't join Johnston can find what they want and need at Redlands, including a strong sense of community.

The "Och Tamale" school chant—a string of complete gibberish invented in 1921— is a beloved school tradition ("Och tamale gazolly gazump!").

Overlaps

Loyola Marymount, University of the Pacific, University of San Diego, Hamline, Drake, Chapman, Whittier, California Lutheran

If You Apply To ›

Redlands: Early decision, early action, regular decision. SATs or ACTs: optional. Accepts the Common Application with supplement. Application includes optional questions on gender identity. Applicants to music program must audition.

3203 S.E. Woodstock Boulevard, Portland, OR 97202

Reed is a West Coast counterpart to Grinnell or Oberlin, mixing nonconformist students with a traditional and rigorous curriculum. Sends huge numbers of grads on for Ph.D.s. Students who were square pegs in high school often find Reed a square hole. Annual springtime Thesis Parade epitomizes Reed's culture of quirky intellectualism.

Website: www.reed.edu
Location: City Outskirts
Private
Total Enrollment: 1,511
Undergraduates: 1,511
Male/Female: 42/58
Financial Aid: 57%
Pell Grant: 11%
Expense: Pr $ $ $ $
Student Loans: 47%
Average Debt: $
Applicants: 7,010
Accepted: 44%
Enrolled: 16%
Grad in 6 Years: 74%
Returning Freshmen: 87%
Academics: ✍ ✍ ✍ ✍ ½
Social: ☎ ☎ ☎
Q of L: ★ ★ ★ ½
Admissions: (503) 777-7511
Email Address: admission@ reed.edu

Strong Programs:
Psychology
Biology
English
Physics
Mathematics
Comparative Race and Ethnic Studies

Reed College is one of the most intellectual colleges in the country. It's the place where the late Steve Jobs—cofounder of Apple—attended for a semester before dropping out to reshape the world and where students complain that the library, which closes its doors at midnight on Fridays and Saturdays, shuts down too early. Students receive lengthy and detailed commentaries from professors on their work, which fosters continued dialogue and eliminates grade inflation. "Reed is the absolute best place for someone who likes to think, to read, to question, and to work," says a student. "It's a community of scholars."

Located in Southeast Portland, Reed's 116-acre campus boasts rolling lawns, winding lanes, a canyon creek, and protected wetlands. Two thousand majestic arbors shade a mix of original campus buildings, constructed of brick, slate, and limestone in the Tudor Gothic style, as well as lodges in the homey Northwest Timber style and some more modern facilities, such as the Performing Arts Building. Recent construction includes the $27 million, LEED Platinum–certified Trillium residence hall ("it's like living in an IKEA," quips a student) on the north end of campus.

> **"Reed is the absolute best place for someone who likes to think, to read, to question, and to work."**

Founded in 1908 and named for a pair of Oregon pioneers, Reed emphasizes personal freedom and responsibility, especially through its Honor Principle. Nevertheless, the curriculum and academic requirements are remarkably traditional. First-year students must complete Humanities 110, a yearlong interdisciplinary course focused on society and culture from the ancient Mediterranean to pre- and post-colonial Mexico to the Harlem Renaissance. The course, which has been taught for 80 years, was updated in 2018 to make it "less Eurocentric and more inclusive," according to a junior. Designed to create a shared intellectual experience for new students, the class draws on instruction from 25 professors, including some of Reed's most senior and distinguished faculty in a range of fields. Students must also take courses in three "breadth" areas: arts and literature; social sciences; and natural, mathematic, and psychological sciences. Seniors must submit a research-based thesis to graduate. On the due date, just after spring classes have ended, seniors march from the library steps to the

> **"[Professors] want to be at Reed, meaning that their top priority is teaching."**

registrar's office in the Thesis Parade. This marks the beginning of Renn Fayre (originally "Renaissance Fayre"), a weekend-long celebration that involves a feast prepared by alumni, a softball tournament, live music, and fireworks.

Academically, "the atmosphere is not competitive because the emphasis is not on grades," explains an anthropology major, but "a lot of the work expected from students matches graduate-level courses." Reed's most popular majors include psychology, biology, English, physics, and math. A major in comparative race and ethnicity studies draws from sociology, anthropology, history, and the arts. Dual-degree (3–2) programs are offered in engineering and forestry/environmental science. Students take full advantage of the range of academic options, which often keep them tethered to their computers and study carrels. You'll never find a TA at the lectern or leading a group discussion here, so students rarely attend class unprepared for the lively intellectual banter that typically ensues between inquiring and active minds. A psychology major comments that professors "want to be at Reed, meaning that their top priority is teaching." Reed has improved its retention and graduation rates considerably in the last decade or two by becoming more selective in admissions, increasing on-campus housing for a stronger residential community, and bolstering student support services, including a popular peer tutoring program.

Despite Reed's small size—73 percent of the courses taken by undergraduates have fewer than 20 students—the school offers excellent research opportunities in the liberal arts and sciences. Budding physicists and environmental scientists can work with college staff at the 250-kilowatt Triga nuclear reactor after passing an Atomic Energy Commission examination. "It's grueling, but physics here is legendary," says a junior. Reed also has a tradition of respect for calligraphy that, among other things, inspired Steve Jobs to build first-rate graphics into Apple computers and, in the process, shape the look of every computer that followed. Fifty-two exchange programs attract 20 percent of each graduating class, taking students to their choice of 23 countries, from Germany and China to Ecuador and Russia. Reed also offers domestic exchange programs with Howard, Sarah Lawrence, and the Woods Hole Oceanographic Institute. Three-quarters of Reed's grads go on to graduate school, and a quarter eventually earn Ph.D.s.

"Students who attend Reed are ridiculous, silly, cerebral, passionate, critical, and questioning," says one observant Reedie. "If we have one thing in common, we are people whose lives center on learning." While Reed's quirky brand of intellectualism attracts students from across the country, the student population draws heavily from California; only 8 percent of Reedies are in-staters. Nine percent hail from other nations. Eight percent are Asian American, 11 percent are Hispanic/Latino, 1 percent are Black, and 10 percent are multiracial. "The Multicultural Resource Center provides resources—guest speakers, lecturers, Tuesday Talks, and more—to keep diversity an ongoing discussion on campus," says an English major. A junior adds, "Reed has a prominent queer population." As for the political climate, an anthropology major remarks, "The campus is very left-leaning, and there is pressure to meet social expectations to be politically correct." All financial aid at Reed is need-based, and the school covers 100 percent of admitted students' demonstrated need, but just 11 percent of first-year students are Pell-eligible.

About 80 percent of Reed students live on campus in comfortable rooms, some of which feature such homey touches as fireplaces or balconies. Reed's "neighborhood" housing model groups residence halls into distinct neighborhoods with specific programming, like workshops and social events. First-year students live together in designated neighborhoods, sophomores select neighborhoods based on their interests, and juniors and seniors live in upper-division neighborhoods. There are six language houses (French, German, Russian, Spanish, Chinese, and Arabic), each of which is staffed with a native speaker. First-years and sophomores are guaranteed housing; upperclassmen seeking a taste of post-college independence must contend with Portland's pricey rental market. In the Commons dining hall, a student says, "The food is surprisingly good and diverse, and the kitchen is happy to help with any particular dietary needs." Campus security receives positive reviews, and as part of the school's strategy to prevent campus sexual assault, a junior explains, "Conversations about consent are woven into the culture of Reed."

"On campus, there are always small parties, or plays, or giant Student Union (SU) dances, or fire-dancing shows, or bands playing," says one student. Past themes for SU dances have included Disco Ball, Beyoncé Ball, and Selena Ball. Students describe Reed's drug and alcohol policies, guided by the college's Honor Principle, as effective

First-year students must complete Humanities 110, a yearlong interdisciplinary course that draws on instruction from 25 professors.

"[Our] traditions are…hard to explain. You've got to see them to believe them."

Three-quarters of Reed's grads go on to graduate school, and a quarter eventually earn Ph.D.s.

and well enforced, but something of a drug culture persists on campus—although in a pressure-free way. "I have never been pushed to use substances I am not comfortable using," says a junior. Students look forward to Paideia ("education" in Ancient Greek), a weeklong program of both practical and wacky noncredit classes before spring semester begins. Past Paideia offerings have ranged from personal finance to mushroom identification to burlesque. "Other traditions are...hard to explain," muses a junior. "You've got to see them to believe them."

"Portland, Oregon, is one of the coolest, weirdest places in America, so of course it's a good social scene," raves a senior. The city boasts a diverse range of live music, literary events, and film screenings, as well as an eclectic array of shops, bars, and restaurants. Many students get involved in community service projects organized by SEEDS (Students for Education, Equity, and Direct Service). The mammoth Powell's bookstore downtown is about a 15-minute drive, and Oregon's coastal beaches, mountains, or high desert are all about two hours away—although finding time for road trips can be a challenge. The school also owns a ski cabin on Mount Hood that sleeps 15.

The closest thing Reed has to a school mascot is the Doyle Owl, a 300-pound concrete sculpture that dorm residents regularly plot to steal from one another. While Reed doesn't have varsity athletics, club teams in basketball, rugby, soccer, and ultimate Frisbee do compete with other clubs in the area. A variety of intramural and recreational sports are available for the less competitive, such as mountaineering, rowing, and curling.

Reed attracts seriously intellectual, unconventional students, but it is not without a sense of humor—the school's unofficial, tongue-in-cheek slogan is "Atheism, Communism, Free Love." If you're a lover of learning who prefers to start Saturday nights with your nose in a book and end them at an all-school dance party, this Portland school is definitely worth a look.

Overlaps

Amherst, Carleton, Lewis & Clark, Pomona, Swarthmore, Oberlin, NYU, UC Berkeley

If You Apply To ›

Reed: Early decision I and II, early action, regular decision. Accepts the Common Application with supplement. Please consult Reed's website for the most up-to-date information regarding standardized test requirements.

Rensselaer Polytechnic Institute

110 Eighth Street, Troy, NY 12180

If you can spell Rensselaer, you've already got a leg up on many applicants. RPI is one of the nation's great technical universities—along with Caltech, Harvey Mudd, and MIT—and one of the most innovative. The beauty of RPI is the chance for hands-on learning and synergy between technology, management, and entrepreneurship. School spirit soars when Division I hockey teams take the ice.

Website: www.rpi.edu
Location: Small City
Private
Total Enrollment: 6,704
Undergraduates: 5,564
Male/Female: 69/31
Financial Aid: 87%

It would be an exaggeration to say that technology has divine status at Rensselaer Polytechnic Institute, though the school's conversion of a Gothic chapel into a computer lab does hint in that direction. Even if it's not deified, technology remains omnipresent at this school, which pioneered the teaching of calculus via computer in the early '90s. RPI's Artificial Intelligence Multiprocessing Optimized System is the most powerful supercomputer housed at a private university, and the school is hiring new faculty to support research and educational efforts in artificial intelligence and data analytics. Students attend class in high-tech studio classrooms where they work on team projects and collaborate to solve real-world problems. Recent investments in residential life, off-campus learning opportunities, and career services continue to raise RPI's profile at home and abroad.

Set high on a bluff overlooking Troy, New York, Rensselaer's 275-acre campus mixes modern research facilities and classical, ivy-covered brick buildings dating to the turn of the 20th century. The cutting-edge Shirley Ann Jackson, Ph.D. Center for Biotechnology and Interdisciplinary Studies (named for the renowned physicist and former president of RPI) houses more than 400 researchers in biotechnology and related disciplines who work in such areas as regenerative medicine, bioinformatics, biocatalysis, and metabolic engineering.

In order to graduate, students must complete distribution requirements and attain "data dexterity," a requirement that administrators describe as "proficiency in using diverse data sets to define and solve complex real-world problems." An initiative called The Arch requires all students to live on campus and attend a full academic semester the summer between their sophomore and junior year. The summer semester offers more than 210 courses,

> **"Who better to learn from than those who have written the book?"**

in addition to field trips, pop-up courses, career development workshops, and other activities. In their junior year, all students undertake a semester-long off-campus experience, such as an internship, co-op, research, or study abroad program.

Founded in 1824 by landowner and philanthropist Stephen Van Rensselaer, RPI made its reputation as one of the nation's premier engineering schools and continues to excel in traditional favorites such as mechanical and aeronautical engineering, as well as newer specialties like biomedical and environmental engineering. Architecture, computer science, and information technology are also strengths. RPI's Lally School of Management combines elements of a business school with the latest technical applications. Entrepreneurship is one of its specialties; budding entrepreneurs from all majors may participate in a support system for start-up companies. RPI is a national leader in the study and application of digital media and offers B.S. degrees in electronic arts and games and simulation arts and sciences. Majors in the humanities and social sciences are limited, and their quality is directly related to their applicability to technical fields. Students with long-term professional goals may take advantage of accelerated B.S./M.B.A. programs in engineering and business administration or science and business administration.

"The workload does get pretty intense," says one junior, "but everybody helps each other out to be as relaxed and prepared as possible." Eighty-three percent of Rensselaer's full-time students are undergraduates, a high percentage for a top engineering school; because of this, RPI has worked hard to ensure that classes are smaller and more attention is paid to individual needs. Fifty-four percent of classes enroll fewer than 20 students. "Two of my freshman courses were taught by CEOs of successful companies," says an information technology major. "Who better to learn from than those who have written the book?" Students also give high ratings to the drop-in tutoring services offered by the Advising and Learning Assistance Center. About half of all undergrads work on research projects with faculty members. For students who can't wait to start working, popular co-op programs help them earn both money and credit. Study abroad programs are available in more than 15 countries on four continents.

Thirty-one percent of RPI students are New Yorkers, and 15 percent are international. RPI is fairly diverse, with Asian Americans comprising 18 percent of the student body, Black students 5 percent, Hispanics/Latinos 11 percent, and multiracial students 5 percent. "Students at RPI are hardworking, passionate, determined, and intelligent—as well as slightly nerdy," says an architecture major. RPI is far from a center of political activism; students say they're more focused on academics. "Politics? Not so much on this campus," remarks a student. The biggest campus issue may be choosing the Grand

---

(continued)

Pell Grant: 18% .
Expense: Pr $ $ $
Student Loans: 44%
Average Debt: $
Applicants: 17,484
Accepted: 53%
Enrolled: 8%
Grad in 6 Years: 87%
Returning Freshmen: 89%
Academics: ✍ ✍ ✍ ✍
Social: ☎ ☎ ☎
Q of L: ★ ★ ★
Admissions: (518) 276-6216
Email Address: admissions@ rpi.edu

Strong Programs:
Engineering
Architecture
Computer Science
Information Technology
Business
Electronic Arts
Games and Simulation Arts and Sciences

In their junior year, all students undertake a semester-long off-campus experience, such as a co-op, research, or study abroad program.

Marshal, who oversees a boisterous weeklong carnival celebrating campus elections, during which professors are barred from giving tests. Merit scholarships averaging $23,000 are available, as are athletic scholarships for men's and women's ice hockey.

Fifty-seven percent of students live in university housing; freshmen and sophomores are required to live in the residence halls, where they are supported by a team

"Hockey at RPI equals insanity."

of faculty and peer advisors intended to create smaller, more tightly knit student communities. Housing selection is a sometimes fraught process, but a freshman reasons, "Even though you may not get your preferred room, RPI's worst room is far above average." Most upperclassmen choose to move into less expensive off-campus apartments. Meals served in the four campus dining halls get average reviews. A senior notes that RPI's recent restructuring of Title IX procedures "has made sexual assault a conversation people are really starting to have." The school's Safe Ride ride-sharing service provides safe transportation for students coming home from a late-night study session or a night on the town.

Sixteen percent of men and 12 percent of women go Greek. With the implementation of stricter rules regulating Greek life and alcohol, an architecture major reports, "Greek groups don't set the tone for social life as much as they used to." Alcohol is not allowed in Greek housing or residence halls, but an on-campus pub serves beer and wine to those 21 and over. For alternatives, an environmental engineering major explains, "The RPI Union will consistently pump out events for students throughout the week and on weekends," such as live entertainment, concerts, and movies. With more than 200 student clubs and organizations, a mechanical engineering major says, "Whether you are into dancing, coding, playing video games, playing sports, modifying cars, or going on outdoor trips, there are plenty of social groups that offer what you are looking for."

Free shuttle buses run regularly from campus to downtown Troy, a former hub of the industrial revolution. "Troy is not a college town," says a senior, "but it does have good places to eat and some beautiful parks." Rensselaer has helped generate eco-

"The curriculum and the attitudes of the students reflect a professional development–oriented culture."

nomic growth in Troy by investing in the downtown area, and students frequently get involved with community service projects. Movie theaters are within easy reach, and for a taste of bigger-city nightlife, Albany is a half-hour drive. For more adventurous excursions, the Berkshires, Catskills, Adirondacks, Lake Placid, New York City, and Boston are popular destinations.

The athletic scene at Rensselaer revolves around hockey, hockey, hockey—the school's only teams playing in Division I. One of the biggest weekends of the year is Big Red Freakout, when all festivities center around cheering on the beloved Big Red. "Hockey at RPI equals insanity," one student says. "If you go to one hockey game all season, go to the men's hockey season opener. The place is packed with rowdy RPI students who scream and chant in unison." Twenty-one varsity teams compete in Division III, and the men's and women's basketball and women's field hockey teams are most successful. There are many intramural sports to choose from, but the most popular may be the D-level hockey team (meaning "I really don't know how to play this," explains a junior).

After nearly 200 years, Rensselaer is still providing cutting-edge technology to students constantly wondering how things work. Computer geeks and video game junkies aren't the only ones who will find a home here. RPI students work hard, but they don't seem to mind. Says an industrial and management engineering major, "The curriculum and the attitudes of the students reflect a professional development–oriented culture with emphasis on initiative, hands-on experiences, networking, and career readiness."

One of the biggest weekends of the year is Big Red Freakout, when all festivities center around cheering on the beloved Big Red hockey team.

Overlaps

Northeastern, Cornell University, Carnegie Mellon, Georgia Tech, Rochester Institute of Technology, Purdue, Caltech, MIT

University of Rhode Island

14 Upper College Road, Kingston, RI 02881

URI is a smallish alternative to UConn and UMass. With Boston, Providence, and vacation hot spot Newport within easy reach, there is plenty to do. Strong programs include engineering, marine sciences, nursing, and pharmacy. Enrollment and faculty ranks have been on the rise in recent years. Nearly half of URI's students are out-of-staters.

No longer an unabashed party school, the University of Rhode Island has earned a reputation for challenging academics with an emphasis on innovation and interdisciplinary learning. URI offers an environment in which students engage in service learning, do research with top faculty, and find a much heavier emphasis on alternative styles of learning. "Our college is an amazing place to learn, prosper, and have fun," boasts one sophomore.

URI was chartered as a land grant school in 1888, and its 1,200-acre campus is located in the small town of Kingston. Surrounded by farmland and only six miles from the coast, it is also within easy driving distance of cities such as Providence—the Renaissance City and home to Brown, the Rhode Island School of Design, and several other colleges and universities—Boston, and New York. The main academic buildings at URI, a mixture of modern and "old New England granite," surround

> **"Students here are involved and outgoing."**

a central quad on Kingston Hill. At the foot of Kingston Hill lie the athletic buildings and agricultural fields. Dozens of construction projects have been completed in the last five years, including a $150 million facility for the College of Engineering.

New students initially enroll in the University College, which offers academic and career guidance, as well as advice on fulfilling general education requirements. All new students take URI 101, a one-credit course intended to acquaint them with support services, cocurricular activities, academic majors, and career options. After a year or two in University College, students choose more specialized colleges, such as the well-regarded College of Pharmacy, which offers a six-year Pharm.D. program. The engineering, business, and marine sciences departments are also strong, and the most popular majors include nursing, psychology, kinesiology, and communication studies. The five-year international engineering dual-degree program combines degrees in engineering and a foreign language with a year abroad for language immersion and an engineering internship. Students can earn up to four academic credits during the Winter J Term session in January.

Academic intensity at URI tends to vary by program. Professors receive generally good marks for their teaching, but their accessibility can be hit or miss. "At times, it can be difficult to work with faculty," says a marine affairs major, who encourages students to "find a professor or faculty member who is invested in you and your studies." Forty percent of classes enroll fewer than 20 students. The Academic Enhancement Center, along with its Writing Center, provides peer tutorials, course-specific collaborative learning projects, supplemental instructional sessions, and special programs for high-risk students.

Website: www.uri.edu
Location: Small Town
Public
Total Enrollment: 14,494
Undergraduates: 12,768
Male/Female: 43/57
Financial Aid: 84%
Pell Grant: 23%
Expense: Pub $ $ $ $
Student Loans: 73%
Average Debt: $ $ $ $
Applicants: 25,105
Accepted: 76%
Enrolled: 17%
Grad in 6 Years: 70%
Returning Freshmen: 85%
Academics: ✐ ✐ ✐
Social: ☎ ☎ ☎ ☎
Q of L: ★ ★ ★
Admissions: (401) 874-7000
Email Address: admission@ uri.edu

Strong Programs:
Engineering
Marine Sciences
Nursing
Pharmacy
Business
Psychology
Kinesiology
Communication Studies

URI offers international exchange programs with universities in such diverse locales as Chile, France, Korea, and Norway, as well as domestic exchange programs with state colleges and universities. Twenty percent of undergraduates participate in the 200-plus available programs in more than 70 countries. Students interested in research can collaborate on projects with multidisciplinary teams of faculty through established research partnerships, such as the Partnership for the Coastal Environment. URI's Honors Program draws about 900 students with an honors colloquium and expanded research opportunities. The Center for Student Leadership Development offers a minor in leadership studies, as well as conferences, retreats, and workshops.

Although URI gives preference to in-state students who meet certain requirements, 47 percent of undergrads come from states outside Rhode Island, and another 1 percent arrive from foreign countries. "Students here are involved and outgoing," one junior says. Five percent of the student body is Black, 11 percent is Hispanic/Latino, 3 percent is Asian American, and 3 percent is multiracial. "There is no doubt about it that URI is a predominantly white institution," says one student of color, "but diversity comes in many shapes and forms. We are diverse when it comes to socioeconomic status, nationality, sexual orientation, political affiliation, gender, and many other ways." The university has been investing in resources to support diversity in recent years, and a senior says, "URI has great women's services as well as LGBTQ services." The academic profiles of the incoming class have risen steadily over the past 10 years, in large measure due to the Centennial and Merit Scholarship Programs for outstanding freshmen. Merit awards average $5,800, and athletes vie for scholarships in 16 sports.

> **"We are 10 minutes from the beach and 30 minutes from Providence."**

Though most freshmen live on campus, 59 percent of all undergraduates choose to find off-campus digs near the beach. The majority of residence halls have recently been renovated, and the Brookside Apartments residence hall has added 500 beds for upperclassmen. "Some of the freshman dorms are gorgeous," one student reports, although "housing isn't the best aspect of URI." About 80 percent of freshmen participate in living/learning communities in a variety of disciplines. Dining options include two dining halls, and students say the staff is accommodating of various dietary needs. "Campus security does rounds around campus throughout the night," notes a student.

Greek life attracts 22 percent of the men and 27 percent of the women. The campus coffeehouse hosts open-mic nights, and more than 120 student organizations provide a variety of activities. The student newspaper that covers it all has one of the most original names anywhere: *The Good Five Cent Cigar* (as in, "what this country needs is a really good five-cent cigar," a quip uttered by U.S. vice president Thomas R. Marshall in 1914). Given the small size of the state, a fair number of students choose to head home on weekends. As for Kingston, it's a sleepy New England college town of 6,400; students get involved in the community through clubs or URI 101, which requires volunteer work. "There is nothing in Kingston," complains one student, "but we are 10 minutes from the beach and 30 minutes from Providence." Wakefield and Newport, both nearby, offer more entertainment, and fun road trips include Boston (90 minutes) and New York City (four hours).

Division I sports are big at Rhode Island, and basketball games are especially exciting. Midnight Madness (the team's first sanctioned practice of the year) is always well attended, and URI fans love it when the Rams defeat archrival Providence College. Recent Atlantic 10 conference champs include men's basketball, soccer, and track and field, as well as women's rowing. URI also offers 17 club sports and more than a dozen intramurals. A favorite student tradition is oozeball, an April volleyball tournament played in about two feet of mud. As befits the school's locale, sailing draws much interest, and the club team regularly produces All-Americans.

URI offers students a large-school feel in a small state. Consistent efforts by the administration to invest in campus upgrades and new educational opportunities have paid off, as evidenced by the changing face of the student body and their accomplishments. Students here work hard to achieve good grades and lay the foundation of lifelong learning.

If You Apply To ›

URI: Early action, regular decision. Accepts the Common Application. Please consult URI's website for the most up-to-date information regarding standardized test requirements.

Rhode Island School of Design

2 College Street, Providence, RI 02903

The nation's best-known art and design school, RISD sits on a hillside adjacent to Brown. The campus offers easy access to downtown Providence, but it can't match the location of rival Parsons in New York's Greenwich Village. Offers 16 undergraduate majors in architecture, fine arts, and design. Industrial design is a specialty, and athletics are quirky.

Founded in the late 19th century by a group of activist women to address the country's need for more artisans and craftsmen, Rhode Island School of Design has grown into a premier arts incubator. It's a place where today's artists and designers gather to share ideas and create tomorrow's masterpieces and architectural icons. In fact, the cofounders of Airbnb, Brian Chesky and Joe Gebbia, met and developed their creative instincts here. RISD (pronounced "Rizdee") grants degrees in virtually every design-related topic, and like the varied curriculum, the students and their creations are as diverse as the colors on an artist's palette. The one thing everyone here shares is an intense workload and a highly competitive spirit. "RISD students are masochists," says one freshman.

Though you might expect an art school like RISD to occupy funky, futuristic buildings, the predominant look here is colonial New England. Set on the upgrade of College Hill, RISD is located at the edge of Providence's beautifully preserved historic district, adjacent to Brown University. Many campus buildings date from the 1800s and early 1900s; the mostly redbrick-and-white-trim group includes converted homes, a bank, and even an old church. Perhaps RISD's most prized facility is the RISD Museum, a superlative collection of roughly 100,000 works that includes everything from Roman and Egyptian art to works by Monet, Matisse, and Picasso.

"RISD students are masochists."

While RISD looks traditionally New England on the outside, behind those historic walls lies something else entirely. First-year students take a common curriculum called Experimental and Foundation Studies, which acclimates them to RISD's approach to studio learning and group critiques. In addition to courses in their major, students must complete coursework in the liberal arts (theory and history of

Website: www.risd.edu
Location: Small City
Private
Total Enrollment: 2,576
Undergraduates: 2,044
Male/Female: 33/67
Financial Aid: 36%
Pell Grant: 15%
Expense: Pr $ $ $
Student Loans: 46%
Average Debt: $ $ $ $
Applicants: 4,742
Accepted: 19%
Enrolled: 56%
Grad in 6 Years: 86%
Returning Freshmen: 95%
Academics: ✍ ✍ ✍ ✍
Social: ☎ ☎
Q of L: ★ ★ ★ ★
Admissions: (401) 454-6300
Email Address: admissions@risd.edu

(continued)

Strong Programs:
Illustration
Industrial Design
Graphic Design
Architecture
Film/Animation/Video
Painting

art and design; literature; and history, philosophy, and social sciences) and a final-year project to graduate.

The most popular majors include illustration, industrial design, graphic design, architecture, film/animation/video, and painting. Students may choose to supplement their degrees with one of six concentrations in computation, technology, and culture; drawing; theory and history of art and design; history, philosophy, and the social sciences; literary arts and studies; and nature-culture-sustainability studies. The Nature Lab allows for examining, exploring, and understanding patterns, structures, and interactions of design in nature. RISD also offers cross-registration and a dual-degree option with Brown, for students seeking more diverse courses.

Hands-on studio courses abound at RISD, and 84 percent of classes have fewer than 20 students. "The academic atmosphere is competitive because we are passionate, and collaborative because we need others' input for our work to be successful," explains a textiles major. Though highly selective, RISD will sometimes take a chance on students who did not perform well in high school by the usual academic criteria but who make up for that with special artistic talent. Still, while students at RISD don't "hit the books" in the traditional sense, the in-studio workload is considerable, and students warn that organizational and time-management skills are essential. Teaching here is said to be generally good, although it can be a mixed bag. "For the most part, I have had positive and supportive professors, but I have also had professors who lacked a sense of criticality," reports a senior.

The 21-week European Honors Program in Rome offers studio work with visiting artists, special study tours, and immersion in Italian culture.

During RISD's Wintersession, five weeks between the first and second semesters, students are encouraged to take courses outside their major. Each year, about 40 juniors and seniors venture to Rome for the 21-week European Honors Program, which offers self-directed studio work with RISD faculty and visiting artists, special study tours, immersion in Italian culture, and a chance to savor the likes of Michelangelo, Bernini, and Caravaggio firsthand. An international exchange program provides opportunities to study abroad at approved art institutions in 25 countries worldwide. In all, 12 percent of students study overseas.

RISD students (referred to as "RISDoids") come to Providence to form a distinctly urban mix of styles and personalities. "We are the lost misfits who have found each other," says a senior. A mere 4 percent of students are native Rhode Islanders, not surprising given the state's small size, while an impressive 33 percent hail from foreign countries. The racial makeup of the campus is fairly mixed, with Asian Americans representing 23 percent of the student body, Black students 4 percent, Hispanics/Latinos 9 percent, and multiracial students 6 percent. Students say the campus is liberal, open-minded, and inclusive. Some complain about the skewed male/female ratio, since "sometimes there is not even one male-identifying person in the classroom," according to an illustration major. Socioeconomic disparities can be a concern as well; one senior remarks, "I cannot afford to be as elaborate in my projects as most people can, wasting materials and going all out, but I find other ways." Tuition and fees here are steep, and although the school has been increasing its need-based financial aid, it does not guarantee to meet students' full need. Merit and athletic scholarships are nonexistent.

> **"A RISD party is usually a group of five to seven friends drinking wine… and cooking together."**

The co-ed club ice hockey team, called the Nads, inspires RISDoids to holler "Go Nads!"

Sixty-five percent of undergraduates reside on campus, and all RISD housing is gender inclusive. Freshmen live together in a group of co-ed dorms known as the Quad. "All on-campus housing is well maintained, comfortable, and damn luxurious for dorms, with plenty of security," says one film major. "It's just grossly overpriced." Most upperclassmen move off campus to nearby apartments, many of which occupy floors of restored homes; RISD also owns an apartment building and some renovated colonial and Victorian houses. All boarders buy the meal plan, but campus dining receives mixed reviews. Some students criticize the administration for handling sexual assault cases too lightly.

Despite a student body that looks like it could have been plucked from the streets of New York's Greenwich Village, RISD is not the place to come for a wild and funky nightlife. "Given the high level of commitment at RISD, there is not a large social life," laments an architecture major. "Many students are consumed by their studios, working until very late." The Tap Room inside Memorial Hall went dry years ago, but students 21 and over are allowed to drink alcohol within their private rooms in upper-class housing. There is no Greek life, and a painting major comments, "A RISD party is usually a group of five to seven friends drinking wine, listening to good music, and cooking together." Students head to Brown for more adventuresome parties, and Providence provides some social outlets as well. Though RISD isn't much for traditions, one big annual event is the Artists' Ball, a festive October dance party featuring eclectic and over-the-top student-made costumes. When claustrophobia sets in, students can flee to the RISD farm, a 33-acre recreation area on the shores of nearby Narragansett Bay. Boston and New York City are one and four hours away by train, respectively.

> **"If you are a student who thrives under pressure…then RISD is the place for you."**

Though jocks are an endangered species at RISD, recreation opportunities are plentiful and, shall we say, unique. There is no intercollegiate sports program in the ordinary sense, though there is a co-ed club ice hockey team, called the Nads (which, of course, inspires RISDoids to holler "Go Nads!") and a mascot named Scrotie (use your imagination). The school also boasts strong men's and women's cycling teams that compete at the varsity level. Other recreational sports range from soccer and ultimate Frisbee to sailing and skiing.

"If you are a student who thrives under pressure, under constraints that are meant to fortify your critical skills, then RISD is the place for you," says one senior. Indeed, students come to RISD committed to their crafts, and most march to the beat of their own drums as they rush from studio courses to gallery openings to exhibitions. Students here can be confident that their endless studio hours are starting them on the path to future success.

Overlaps

Maryland Institute College of Art, School of the Art Institute of Chicago, Pratt Institute, Parsons School of Design, Carnegie Mellon, Cornell University, Cooper Union, NYU

If You Apply To ›

RISD: Early decision, regular decision. SATs or ACTs: optional. Accepts the Common Application with supplement. Portfolio with 12–20 examples of recent visual work plus two art assignment responses required.

Rhodes College

2000 North Parkway, Memphis, TN 38112

Goes head-to-head with Sewanee for the top spot in the pecking order of mid-South liberal arts colleges, with Rhodes the more progressive of the two. While Sewanee has a gorgeous rural campus, Rhodes has Memphis and its red-hot music scene. Natural and social sciences head the list of solid programs, and undergraduate research opportunities are plentiful. Strong honor system.

Website: www.rhodes.edu
Location: City Center
Private
Total Enrollment: 1,997
Undergraduates: 1,978
Male/Female: 41/59
Financial Aid: 93%
Pell Grant: 16%
Expense: Pr $ $
Student Loans: 44%
Average Debt: $ $
Applicants: 5,318
Accepted: 57%
Enrolled: 20%
Grad in 6 Years: 85%
Returning Freshmen: 94%
Academics: ✍ ✍ ✍ ½
Social: ☎ ☎ ☎
Q of L: ★ ★ ★ ★
Admissions: (901) 843-3700
Email Address: adminfo@
  rhodes.edu

Strong Programs:
Economics
English
International Studies
History
Chemistry
Business
Biology
Psychology

The Search for Values in the Light of Western History and Religion sequence has been part of the Rhodes curriculum for more than 75 years.

Since 1848, Rhodes College has been instilling the timeless values of truth and honor in Southern sons and daughters, and today increasing numbers of students from the rest of the country are discovering its charms. The school's honor code means exams are not proctored and backpacks are left unattended in the cafeteria. Its small size gives everyone an opportunity to take on leadership roles in campus clubs and organizations, and people are generally friendly. Throw in the college's proximity to Memphis's world-famous Beale Street, barbecue, and the blues, and it makes for a winning combination.

Rhodes was founded as a Presbyterian school in Clarksville, Tennessee, and it moved to its 100-acre campus in Memphis in 1925. Located in the residential midtown section of the city, Rhodes sits across from a 175-acre park housing the city's largest art museum, a golf course, and the Memphis Zoo, which has two giant pandas. Whether new or old, all campus buildings are Gothic in style, constructed of Arkansas fieldstone with leaded-glass windows and slate roofs. Thirteen of the original buildings are on the National Register of Historic Places.

The Rhodes general education curriculum features highly regarded three-course sequences known as The Search for Values in the Light of Western History and Religion, and Life: Then and Now. The Search sequence has been part of the Rhodes curriculum for more than 75 years. To receive a Rhodes degree, students must select one of the two sequences and demonstrate proficiency in 12 areas that form the foundation of the liberal arts,

"[Professors are] amazing sounding boards, mentors, and friends."

such as written communication, mathematical reasoning, and multicultural perspectives. A yearlong first-year seminar designed to ease the academic and social transition to Rhodes is also required of freshmen.

Rhodes is especially strong in the natural and social sciences, thanks to labs with state-of-the-art equipment. Business, biology, psychology, and neuroscience enroll the most students, but economics, English, international studies, history, and chemistry are also well respected. Aside from traditional lecture-style classes, the college offers seminars, honors programs, one-on-one Directed Inquiry tutorials, and interdisciplinary majors. Rhodes also participates in a dual-degree program for engineers with Washington University in St. Louis. "The academic climate at Rhodes is vigorous," says a political science and French major. "Many of our classes are challenging, and it is nearly impossible to get by without making an active effort." Sixty-nine percent of classes have fewer than 20 students, which means professors are more than talking heads. "Professors are helpful and encourage you to really think about your future," comments a junior. "They're amazing sounding boards, mentors, and friends."

Students who can't find what they want on campus may tap into a variety of study abroad programs around the world, and 75 percent do so. The Buckman International Fellows program offers summer internships in Madrid, Hong Kong, and Johannesburg. A partnership with St. Jude Children's Research Hospital lets students conduct research there in the summers and continue their projects during the next school year; half of Rhodes students take part in undergraduate research, often with the support of fellowships.

"Students at Rhodes are personable, high achieving, and well rounded," says a business major. Like Davidson and Hendrix, Rhodes tends to attract white, Southern, middle- and upper-middle-class students, although diversity is inching upward. Students hail from 45 states; 29 percent of students are Tennessee natives, and 6 percent are international. Black students represent 9 percent of the student body, Asian Americans 7 percent, Hispanics/Latinos 6 percent, and multiracial students 5 percent. The political atmosphere is "relatively liberal," comments a senior, but "political persuasions are not so overwhelming that they define the college as an institution." Eligible students receive scholarships based on academic merit, and the average award is $27,000. There are no athletic scholarships.

Sixty-five percent of Rhodes students live on campus, where all dorms are air-conditioned and clean. Freshmen live in Glassell or Williford, and upperclassmen vie for rooms in the East and West Village apartments during the yearly lottery. Twenty percent of first-year students opt to join living/learning communities. Students eat in the Refectory, known as "the Rat" (presumably not a commentary on the menu), or the Lynx Lair; the former has hot food lines and the latter offers fare such as wraps, sandwiches, and burgers, along with a well-stocked salad bar. "Our two campus dining facilities serve very edible food," reports one student, "and there is typically something for all tastes, preferences, and lifestyles." Students give good ratings to general campus safety. One student reports, "The school has made some policy changes regarding sexual assault and the protection of sexual assault victims, but there is still a lot of work that needs to be done."

Fraternities draw 24 percent of the men and sororities sign up 34 percent of the women. "The majority of campus social life revolves around partying and Greek life," says a biology major. Chartered buses provide rides to off-campus parties, many of which are sponsored by the Greeks, though independents are welcome to attend. Despite campus policies prohibiting underage drinking, students say those who are determined

> "The majority of campus social life revolves around partying and Greek life."

A partnership with St. Jude Children's Research Hospital lets students conduct research there in the summers.

can usually find booze—if not at parties, then in other students' rooms. In April, everyone looks forward to the three-day Rites of Spring concert and to the preceding Rites of Play carnival, which brings underprivileged kids to campus for a day of food, fun, and games.

Lively and energetic Memphis has its fair share of college students, with three other four-year institutions in the area and a number of community colleges as well. There are plenty of clubs and bars, along with live music and arts organizations, volunteer opportunities, and internships. "Service is an integral part of the Rhodes experience," a student says, and more than 80 percent of students get involved in community service.

Rhodes fields 11 women's and 10 men's varsity Lynx teams, which compete in Division III. The women's lacrosse team has won six straight Southern Athletic Association conference titles, and women's golf and men's track and field have also been successful in recent years. About a quarter of all students participate in intra-murals and club sports, the most popular being five-on-five basketball and crew, respectively. The Bryan Campus Life Center boasts squash and racquetball courts and a suspended indoor track. Rhodes's mock trial team holds the record for con-secutive appearances in the national championship tournament (33).

Rhodes College students relish the school's solid academics and rich Southern tradition. The school's reputation is rising, within and outside the Southeast, and it is slowly becoming more diverse. What hasn't changed is the friendly vibe on campus and the eagerness of students, faculty, and staff to welcome you to the community.

Overlaps

Centre, Sewanee, Furman, Hendrix, Trinity University (TX), Vanderbilt, Tulane, WashU in St. Louis

If You Apply To ›

Rhodes: Early decision I and II, early action, regular decision. Please consult Rhodes's website for the most up-to-date information regarding standardized test requirements. Accepts the Common Application.

Rice University

6100 Main Street MS-17, Houston, TX 77251

One of the few top private colleges making serious efforts to keep tuition affordable. Rice is outstanding in engineering, architecture, the natural sciences, and music, and it is a national leader in entrepreneurship studies. With nearly 4,200 undergraduates, Rice is smaller than many applicants realize but plans to expand to 4,800 by 2025. In lieu of Greek life, Rice has a residential college system like Yale and Princeton.

Website: www.rice.edu
Location: City Center
Private
Total Enrollment: 7,828
Undergraduates: 4,150
Male/Female: 52/48
Financial Aid: 57%
Pell Grant: 17%
Expense: Pr $ $
Student Loans: 20%
Average Debt: $
Applicants: 29,544
Accepted: 9%
Enrolled: 44%
Grad in 6 Years: 92%
Returning Freshmen: 97%
Academics: ✍ ✍ ✍ ✍ ✍
Social: ☎ ☎ ☎
Q of L: ★ ★ ★ ★
Admissions: (713) 348-7423
Email Address: admission@
 rice.edu

Strong Programs:
Engineering
Architecture
Music
Physics and Astronomy
Computer Science
Kinesiology
Biosciences
Economics

Founded in 1912 by Texas cotton mogul William Marsh Rice, Rice University has stayed true to its mission of providing unsurpassed programs in natural sciences, engineering, the arts, and humanities—with a price tag most families can afford. With its top-notch programs in the liberal arts and sciences and huge endowment (used to tamp down tuition), Rice is a good deal among top schools. It is the dominant university in the Southwest and second only to Duke in the entire South. Thanks to an aggressive growth plan, a nearly $2 billion building campaign, and generous financial aid, enrollment is soaring as the university continues to attract more and more top talent from around the country.

> **"[Students create] a caring and supportive atmosphere."**

Rice was modeled after such disparate institutions as progressive, low-tuition Cooper Union and the more traditional Princeton University. Today, Rice boasts plenty of distinctive characteristics all its own. The predominant architectural theme of the campus, situated three miles from downtown Houston, is Spanish Mediterranean. A particular standout is the colorful Duncan Hall, designed by British architect John Outram. Newer facilities include the Brockman Hall for Opera, which features a 600-seat, European-style opera theater. But Rice's buildings are less notable than its trees—4,600 of them at last count, with the entire campus officially designated as an arboretum. About half of the trees are live oaks, with branches that spread high and wide and provide an unbroken canopy of shade from the searing Houston sun.

Rice has traditionally excelled in the natural sciences and engineering, and students majoring in these areas still dominate the student body. Architecture here is one of the finest undergraduate programs in the nation, and the physics and astronomy department works closely with NASA. Programs in computer science, engineering, kinesiology, and biosciences are popular, and economics and music are highly regarded. Business is only available as a minor; an entrepreneurship minor, offered jointly through the School of Engineering and Rice's well-established graduate business program, is also an option. Rice has a long tradition of encouraging double and even triple majors in such seemingly opposite fields as electrical engineering and art history. Under the area-major program, students can draw up proposals for independent interdisciplinary majors. All freshmen participate in a freshman writing program that is tailored, in part, to individual disciplines. Other distribution requirements are flexible: students take three courses each in the humanities, social sciences, and applied sciences/mathematics, choosing the courses that interest them most.

> **"The professors are so invested in my learning."**

Courses are challenging, but for the most part, says a senior, "Students are almost always willing to help each other, creating a caring and supportive atmosphere." Everyone operates under the honor system, and most exams go unsupervised. Class size rarely presents a problem; 70 percent have fewer than 20 students. Faculty members receive high marks, and full professors often teach freshmen. "One of my favorite things about Rice is how the professors are so invested in my learning," says a kinesiology major. Under the Mellon Fellow program, selected humanities and social sciences majors may work with a faculty mentor on an academic project that offers a summer research stipend. Sixty-eight percent of undergrads complete at least one research experience by the time they graduate. About a quarter of students participate in 150 study abroad programs offered in 60 countries.

Students describe their classmates as friendly and quirky, and a senior says Rice students are "intellectual, but not navel-gazing." Rice was founded to serve "residents of Houston and the state of Texas," and 41 percent of undergraduates still hail from the Lone Star State. Most of the out-of-staters are transplanted from California, Florida, the Northeast, and other Southern states; 12 percent come from other countries. Twenty-eight percent of undergraduates are Asian American, 16 percent are Hispanic/Latino, 8 percent are Black, and 5 percent are multiracial. "The political climate at Rice is pretty liberal, especially for a Texas school," notes an engineering major.

Rice practices need-blind admissions (although it is need-aware for international students) and guarantees to meet the full demonstrated need of every admit. Merit scholarships averaging $18,700 are available to qualified students, and about 250 athletic scholarships are awarded each year. The ambitious Rice Investment financial aid program makes tuition free for low-income and middle-class students. Undergraduates with an annual family income of up to $140,000 receive full-tuition grants, and those whose annual family income does not exceed $75,000 also qualify for grants that cover room, board, and mandatory fees. Additionally, students with family incomes between $140,000 and $200,000 are awarded half-tuition grants, and need-based loans have been eliminated for all students who qualify for the Rice Investment. A junior points out that "Rice has improved low-income accessibility by training faculty and staff on how to support first-generation and low-income students."

> "While Rice students can write algorithms and social commentary, they still know how to throw a good party."

Rice's founder did not approve of elitist organizations, which means fraternities and sororities are no-nos. Their functions are largely assumed by the 11 residential colleges, Rice's version of dorms, which 69 percent of students currently call home—although the university's expansion plans include opening a 12th residential college and increasing the number of students living on campus by about one-third, to 3,525. The housing system is based on the British residential college model. Every undergraduate is assigned to a residential college in their first year, and they remain a member of that college for all four years—even if they choose to live off campus at any time. Students praise the residential college system for giving everyone a sense of belonging to a relatively small community. The quality of housing "varies from OK to super nice," according to one senior. Each residential college is connected to a "servery" (a.k.a. dining hall), and students can eat anywhere they please. "There's a wide variety of options, so you can be as indulgent or as healthy as you want," says a senior. Another student comments that "Campus security is about as good as it can be in a big city like Houston." Among Rice's efforts to combat the issue of sexual assault on college campuses is a mandatory five-week, one-credit Critical Thinking in Sexuality course taken by all incoming freshmen.

Social life is campus-based and revolves around the residential colleges, which frequently host themed, campuswide parties as well as private gatherings. "While Rice students can write algorithms and social commentary, they still know how to throw a good party," boasts one junior. Students 21 and over are allowed to have alcohol on campus. Other student organizations host activities like shows, dinners, and dances too. Halloween brings a massive naked run, but the favorite annual tradition by far is Willy Week, which features a variety of festivities put on by the residential colleges, a university-wide water-balloon fight, and the highly anticipated Beer Bike, a relay race in which co-ed teams must speed around

The physics and astronomy department works closely with NASA.

Sixty-eight percent of undergrads complete at least one research experience by the time they graduate.

Undergraduates with an annual family income of up to $140,000 receive full-tuition grants.

a bicycle track and chug water ("which used to be beer, before the drinking law changed," a student explains).

Houston has a bustling nightlife, but you'd better bring a car to enjoy it. The light-rail system makes it easier to get to the city, but it's still a challenge to get around—even with free transportation passes. The city offers ample opportunities for internships and volunteerism; 40 percent of students get involved in service learning. Galveston's beaches on the Gulf of Mexico are only 45 minutes away, and heading for New Orleans, especially in February, can make a great weekend trip.

Ardent football fans abound at Rice; tearing down the goalposts after home victories remains a happy Owls tradition. Baseball is a powerhouse, and women's volleyball and tennis are strong too. All teams compete in the Division I Conference USA. Rice students go really wild for intramurals, which pit the residential colleges against each other—75 percent participate.

William Marsh Rice never lived to see the fruits of his bequest (sadly, he was chloroformed by his valet in an ill-fated conspiracy to claim his estate), but he would certainly be proud of the eponymous university that he created. "Rice is a welcoming place with an openness to new ideas and a willingness to explore," says an economics major. As the university grows, it remains to be seen whether it will be able to maintain the close relationships with faculty and the intimate quality of the residential experience that has made it special. But when students venture outside the campus for the last time, their Rice diplomas open doors to the corporate world. And thanks to Rice's efforts to keep tuition affordable, their wallets haven't been emptied.

Overlaps

Stanford, Duke, University of Chicago, Cornell University, Vanderbilt, Harvard, Yale, MIT

If You Apply To ›

Rice: Early decision, regular decision. Please consult Rice's website for the most up-to-date information regarding standardized test requirements. Accepts the Common Application with supplement. Music applicants must audition. Architecture applicants must submit portfolio.

University of Richmond

28 Westhampton Way, Richmond, VA 23173

Offers students a preprofessional climate rooted in the liberal arts. Though located in the South, there are plenty of Yankee and international voices on UR's forward-looking campus. Business and a unique school for leadership studies are featured offerings, along with a strong global emphasis, but working to diversify its strengths and reputation beyond business. Compare to Bucknell but with urban proximity, or to Emory.

Website: www.richmond.edu
Location: Suburban
Private
Total Enrollment: 3,450
Undergraduates: 2,970
Male/Female: 47/53
Financial Aid: 66%
Pell Grant: 17%
Expense: Pr $ $ $ $

Students at the University of Richmond enjoy a healthy mix of Southern ambiance and intellectual rigor that includes small classes, close friendships, and lots of teamwork. A force for progressive liberal arts and sciences, UR describes itself as "a private university for the public good." It was a pioneer in leadership studies and continues to expand its international emphasis. Under its unique coordinate system, a holdover from the days of single-sex education, men and women take advantage of separate student governments, traditions, and dean's offices for advising and support.

UR's 350-acre campus is nestled amid rolling hills about 15 minutes from downtown Richmond, the state capital. The campus, notable for its stately pines and redbrick collegiate Gothic buildings, wraps around a 10-acre lake. Established in

1830, the university moved in 1914 to its present location on former plantation land. Students and faculty involved in the Race and Racism Project research and document the university's complex history with race, and plans are in the works to memorialize a burial ground of enslaved people that was recently rediscovered on the campus. Recent additions to campus include the Well-Being Center, housing student health and counseling services as well as an organic café, mind-body studio, and meditation and yoga rooms.

All Richmond undergraduates complete general education requirements in communications (including writing and a foreign language) and in six other fields: historical studies, literary studies, natural science, social analysis, symbolic reasoning, and visual and performing arts. Everyone takes a First-Year Seminar in the fall and spring of their first year, with faculty drawn from across the university, on topics ranging from bioethics to constitutional law.

Richmond's more than 60 academic majors include cross-disciplinary majors such as philosophy, politics, economics, and law (PPEL) that combine coursework from the School of Arts and Sciences, Business School, and Law School. Business administration is the most popular major—UR boasts a top undergraduate business school, which is also

"My anthropology professor from my freshman year has been like my second mom."

known for its accounting program—but the university is actively building up its other offerings, especially in the sciences. Popular options include biology, political science, and psychology. An interdisciplinary major in health studies focuses on health policy, global health, and epidemiology. The Jepson School of Leadership Studies, founded in 1986, draws on the liberal arts to educate students about how they can best serve society. About half of UR students take the foundation leadership course. UR is at the forefront of the movement called "digital humanities," and the Digital Scholarship Lab allows students to mine huge databases in order to generate new knowledge. A new major in Africana studies has been added.

Students describe the academic climate as intense but collaborative. Classes are usually small; 74 percent have fewer than 20 students. Richmond students enjoy close relationships with professors and the absence of teaching assistants in the classroom. "My anthropology professor from my freshman year has been like my second mom for the last three years," says a senior, adding, "I know it's hard to believe, but every student here has at least one professor that they have this special kind of mentorship with." Students are also enthusiastic about the Office of Alumni and Career Service's career-related programs, such as Spider Road Trips, which take students to major cities to learn firsthand about various industries and network for potential jobs and internships.

The Richmond Guarantee offers traditional undergrads guaranteed funding of up to $5,000 for at least one summer research or internship experience. Eighty percent of undergrads study abroad for credit, choosing from 70 programs at partner universities worldwide. About 16 percent of sophomores participate every year in what one student calls the "especially sought-after" Sophomore Scholars in Residence program, a

"The newest apartments are way nicer than anything I will be able to afford after school."

living/learning program that combines a yearlong interdisciplinary course, a group capstone project in the spring, and various opportunities for community-based activities and domestic or international travel.

"Students are generally very friendly," says an environmental studies major, but "the overall culture at UR can feel cliquey." Nearly half of UR students hail from the Northeast, and only 18 percent are Virginians. International students account for 9 percent of the undergraduate population. Seven percent of students are Black, 7 percent are Asian American, 10 percent are Hispanic/Latino, and 4 percent are multiracial. The Student Center for Equity and Inclusion works to support multicultural,

(continued)

Student Loans: 39%
Average Debt: $ $
Applicants: 13,955
Accepted: 29%
Enrolled: 22%
Grad in 6 Years: 89%
Returning Freshmen: 91%
Academics: ✍ ✍ ✍ ½
Social: ☎ ☎ ☎
Q of L: ★ ★ ★
Admissions: (804) 289-8640
Email Address: admission@ richmond.edu

Strong Programs:
Business Administration
Leadership Studies
Philosophy, Politics,
    Economics, and Law
Accounting
Health Studies
Biology
Political Science
Psychology

An interdisciplinary major in health studies focuses on health policy, global health, and epidemiology.

LGBTQ, and first-generation students and foster inclusion on campus. A political science major comments, "Students in nonelection years are generally apathetic and are not very politically involved." Despite its high sticker price, UR prides itself on being accessible, mainly because it practices need-blind admissions and guarantees to meet the full demonstrated financial need of domestic applicants. The Richmond Scholars program awards merit scholarships equivalent to full tuition, room, and board to 25 top students in every entering class, while Presidential Scholarships, worth one-third of tuition, are given to up to 80 incoming students. Division I athletes vie for nearly 250 athletic scholarships.

Although Richmond does not have an on-campus housing requirement, 85 percent of undergraduates live on campus all four years. First-year students typically live in traditional doubles; suite- and apartment-style options are available after that. "The newest apartments are way nicer than anything I will be able to afford after school," says a senior. First-years can apply for the Richmond Endeavor living/learning program, which combines two academic courses with advising from a faculty mentor and a peer advisor. The Heilman Dining Center offers hot entrées as well as made-to-order paninis, pizza, pasta, and such; seven retail dining locations provide other options. "I am convinced that the dining center offers the best brunch in Richmond," cheers one gourmand. Students say they generally feel safe at UR, and initiatives like the Spiders for Spiders peer network are educating students on how to "prevent potentially bad situations and listen to survivors [of sexual violence] in the proper ways," according to a senior.

> "Fraternities host 'lodges,' which are on-campus events that are essentially huge dance parties."

Students agree that Richmond is "a very social campus" with plenty of options for entertainment during the week and on weekends. Nonresidential fraternities and sororities attract 17 percent of men and 25 percent of women, and they throw most of the parties. "Fraternities host 'lodges,' which are on-campus events that are essentially huge dance parties that are open to any student who attends UR," explains a junior. The Campus Activities Board sponsors regular movie nights, karaoke, and concerts. First-year students have Proclamation Night for women and Investiture for men, during which they sign the honor code and write a letter to themselves, which is returned to them to open at the start of their senior year. Other traditions include the Ring Dance, a soiree for junior women at the elegant Jefferson Hotel, and a candlelight graduation celebration by the lake.

Eager to shed its past image as a privileged enclave, UR has made a strong commitment to the city of Richmond. Seventy-nine percent of students volunteer outside of class in programs coordinated by the Center for Community Engagement. The city boasts good restaurants, art galleries, beautiful historic neighborhoods, and plenty of internship opportunities at local corporations and government agencies. For those wishing to get away, Williamsburg, Virginia Beach, and Washington, D.C. are not far, and nature buffs also like the river and the nearby backpacking, thanks to the proximity of the Blue Ridge Mountains.

The school's 17 varsity teams spin their webs in Division I. The Spiders are members of the Atlantic 10 Conference, with the exception of football, men's lacrosse, and women's golf, which play in the highly competitive Colonial Athletic Association, Southern Conference, and Patriot League, respectively. The women's swimming and diving team is a perennial contender for the conference title. Other recent conference champs include men's basketball, men's cross-country, and women's lacrosse. Football Saturdays find throngs of students throwing tailgate parties. More than 30 club sports offer various levels of competition, as do a variety of intramurals.

Students at Richmond certainly find plenty of programs to like. From first-of-their-kind academic programs to innovative out-of-classroom learning and networking opportunities, Richmond is working hard to push its vision of preprofessional education shaped by commitments to the liberal arts, leadership, and community involvement.

If You Apply To ›

Richmond: Early decision I and II, early action, regular decision. Accepts the Common Application. Please consult Richmond's website for the most up-to-date information regarding standardized test requirements.

Ripon College

300 Seward Street, P.O. Box 248, Ripon, WI 54971

Located where the Republican Party was born in 1854, Ripon is more middle-of-the-road than Beloit and Lawrence and similar in atmosphere to places like DePauw and Knox. With about 800 students, Ripon is the smallest of the five. Strengths are science, education, and communication. Required Catalyst curriculum focuses on developing real-world professional skills. Sixty-eight percent of students are in-staters.

Everything about Ripon College is small, aside from perhaps its academic ambitions. The school is in a tiny Wisconsin town, and there are just under 800 students, meaning "if you don't go to class, your professor will know," a freshman says. Winter brings bitter cold and lots of snow, but the warmth of personal relationships with peers and professors helps to compensate for the frigid temperatures. "Ripon is a school where you're surrounded by familiar faces," says a computer science and theater major. "It's impossible to get lost on this campus."

Ripon's 250-acre campus sits in a town of 7,800, about 20 miles west of Highway 41 between Fond du Lac and Oshkosh. It features tree-lined walks, wetlands, prairie, and woods, and a mixture of 19th- and 20th-century architecture lends a majestic feel. The Willmore Center, the campus's main health and wellness facility, has been fully renovated.

Ripon's Catalyst curriculum calls for students to complete five required seminar courses. Two courses in the first year and two in the sophomore year focus on developing basic academic skills that will prepare students for the Applied Innovation Seminar their junior year, in which they work in small teams with a faculty member to research, develop, and present solutions to large questions facing society. "The Catalyst curriculum enhances skills that employers are looking for,"

> "Ripon is a school where you're surrounded by familiar faces. It's impossible to get lost."

explains a sophomore. All Ripon students graduate with a concentration in applied innovation, and their academic transcripts attest that they have acquired skills in oral communication, writing, critical thinking, collaboration, quantitative reasoning, information literacy, interdisciplinary integration, and intercultural competence. In addition to the Catalyst courses, most students complete a senior seminar or thesis in their major.

A politics and government major describes the academic climate as "moderately relaxed" and the workload as "very reasonable." Ripon students delight in their small classes, 57 percent of which have fewer than 20 students, and report that student-initiated study groups are common. "Professors are able to give each student a great amount of personalized attention," cheers a mathematics and physics major. "Office hours are the best at Ripon—make use of them."

Website: www.ripon.edu
Location: Small Town
Private
Total Enrollment: 790
Undergraduates: 790
Male/Female: 51/49
Financial Aid: 100%
Pell Grant: 35%
Expense: Pr $ $
Student Loans: 85%
Average Debt: $ $ $ $
Applicants: 2,486
Accepted: 80%
Enrolled: 10%
Grad in 6 Years: 60%
Returning Freshmen: 72%
Academics: ✏ ✏ ✏
Social: ☎ ☎ ☎
Q of L: ★ ★ ★
Admissions: (800) 947-4766
Email Address: adminfo@ripon.edu

Strong Programs:
Sciences
Education
Communication
Exercise Science
Psychology
Biology
History
Business Management

Ripon's strengths include the sciences, education, and communication; the most popular majors are psychology, communication, biology, history, and business management. Students also give high marks to exercise science and the premed and health sciences advising program. Newer offerings include minors in creative writing and museum studies. Motivated students with AP credits—or just the stamina to take an extra class each term—may finish in three years, thanks to Ripon's accelerated degree program. A 3–2 dual-degree program in engineering with WashU in St. Louis is another option, as is a 3–3 law program with multiple partner universities. About 15 percent of students take terms away from campus, in the U.S. or abroad, through 30 programs organized by Ripon or partner providers.

All Ripon students graduate with a concentration in applied innovation.

Ripon students are generally "laid-back, friendly, and positive people," says a student. Sixty-eight percent come from Wisconsin, and most of the rest hail from elsewhere in the Midwest. Two percent come from foreign nations. Black students account for 4 percent of the student body, Asian Americans make up 2 percent, Hispanics/Latinos add 9 percent, and multiracial students represent 3 percent. The college organizes a student diversity conference every April and other programs to support diversity and inclusion on campus. The town of Ripon's claim to fame is its status as the birthplace of the Republican Party, founded on February 28, 1854, to be exact, three years after the college. These days, a senior comments, the campus is "rather unusual in that there is a fairly equal split between Republicans and Democrats." The school offers merit scholarships worth an average of $26,100 but no athletic awards. Thirty-five percent of incoming freshmen are eligible for Pell Grants. The Access Ripon College program covers full tuition and room and board, without loans, for qualified students of low-income families.

"The Catalyst curriculum enhances skills that employers are looking for."

Ninety-two percent of Ripon students live on campus, since they must petition to live off campus. Freshmen are housed together; students may choose co-ed or single-sex halls, with doubles, singles, or suites. Students complain that some facilities need renovations or repairs. "A prospective student should not expect a state-of-the-art or modern living experience at Ripon," cautions a senior. Ripon has two main dining areas—the Commons, with a traditional hot-food line and made-to-order options, and the Spot, a pub-style hangout. The college recently switched to a new food service provider, and a psychobiology major reports that "the quality of food has improved." Campus security receives good ratings and, according to a psychology major, most students "feel comfortable and safe" reporting incidents of sexual harassment or assault.

At the start of each year, all the churches in Ripon come together to host a home-cooked potluck dinner for students.

Social life is mainly concentrated on campus. Twenty-four percent of the men join fraternities and 24 percent of the women pledge sororities. Members of Greek life are grouped together in the dorms and host parties in their rooms or lounges, where alcohol is permitted for those of age, but one student likens this to "having a party at your parents' house. You're allowed to do it, but you're constantly being watched." Underage drinkers face fines. Campus hangouts like The Spot and The Nest offer live music, comedy, game nights, art shows, and poetry readings. Favorite annual traditions include homecoming and the Springfest concert and carnival. The best road trips include nearby Oshkosh and Appleton or even Milwaukee and Madison. Chicago is a three-hour drive.

"Downtown Ripon offers many great restaurants, little shops, and a movie theater," says a freshman, but most places close down early. About 81 percent of students get involved in community service in the local area, and at the start of each year, all the churches in Ripon come together to host a home-cooked potluck dinner for students. Though Ripon's winters can be bitterly cold, the college's location means that frozen lakes and a blanket of snow are a natural part of the winter landscape, and cross-country and downhill skiing, tobogganing, and ice skating are regular diversions. There is even some fervent cheering for dogsled and iceboat races. And when it's not winter ("for one month during the year," quips one student), nearby Green Lake offers boating, fishing, and other water sports.

Ripon's varsity teams (the Red Hawks) compete in Division III, and matches against Beloit and Lawrence usually draw excited crowds; the Lawrence–Ripon rivalry is one of the oldest in Wisconsin. Men's and women's basketball and track and field have claimed recent Midwest Conference titles. Intramural sports are popular, especially indoor soccer, sand volleyball, basketball, badminton, and cornhole. Ripon also boasts nationally ranked Ethics Bowl and Business Ethics Bowl teams.

Ripon College offers a strong grounding in the liberal arts, along with a peaceful, quaint, historical, and friendly community where you'll be much more than a number. "I am on a first-name basis with our dean and president, and it's not because I'm in trouble," a junior says. Though being at such a small place can be stifling, Ripon students aren't complaining. "We are interactive. We are tight-knit. We are a community," one student says. "We are Ripon."

> ### Overlaps
> **St. Norbert, Carroll University, Carthage, Coe, Knox, Marquette, DePauw, Beloit**

If You Apply To ›

Ripon: Rolling admissions. SATs or ACTs: optional. Accepts the Common Application with supplement.

University of Rochester

Rochester, NY 14627

The name may conjure up an urban public university, but Rochester, located in an up-and-coming city, is a quality private university in the orbit of Carnegie Mellon, Case Western Reserve, Johns Hopkins, and WashU in St. Louis. The university has a scientific bent and a penchant for churning out premeds. Music is another strength. Innovative Take Five and e5 programs reward ambitious students with a tuition-free fifth year to explore new interests or pursue entrepreneurial projects.

The University of Rochester is not afraid of change. This distinguished private university implemented its unique Rochester Renaissance Plan in the mid-1990s, and since then it has never looked back. The plan included reducing class size; making new investments in the library, classrooms, and computer networking facilities; and launching a curriculum that eliminates entry-level general education courses to allow students to design their own paths. Today, ever-expanding academic opportunities ensure that students have freedom to explore while getting plenty of hands-on experience in the process.

Founded in 1850, the University of Rochester occupies a snug 90-acre campus, which nestles up to a bend in the Genesee River two miles south of downtown Rochester. One student acknowledges that the university lives under "perpetually gray (read: winter) skies," but finds comfort that "it's great for winter sports or studying or even sleeping late on a snowy Saturday." Although a few buildings are modern—the Wilson Commons student center designed by I. M. Pei, for example—most of the older structures come in Greek Revival and Georgian colonial styles. There is an aesthetically pleasing contrast between old and new, and the Eastman Quadrangle, with the library and original academic buildings, adds to Rochester's stately look.

Website: www.rochester.edu
Location: Suburban
Private
Total Enrollment: 10,139
Undergraduates: 6,238
Male/Female: 49/51
Financial Aid: 74%
Pell Grant: 19%
Expense: Pr $ $ $ $
Student Loans: 51%
Average Debt: $ $ $
Applicants: 19,543
Accepted: 41%
Enrolled: 20%
Grad in 6 Years: 86%
Returning Freshmen: 91%
Academics: ✍ ✍ ✍ ✍

Social: ☎ ☎ ☎
Q of L: ★ ★ ★
Admissions: (585) 275-3221
Email Address: admit@
admissions.rochester.edu

Strong Programs:
Music
Engineering
Optics
Business
Psychology
Computer Science
Economics
Premed

Optics has long been a strength, and Rochester's Institute of Optics awards about half of all optics degrees in the U.S.

There are no general education subject requirements at Rochester, but academic offerings are designed to expose students to the full range of liberal arts. The curriculum—appropriately but unimaginatively known as the Rochester Curriculum—focuses on three classic divisions of learning: humanities and arts; social science; and natural science, mathematics, and engineering. Students choose a major from one of these areas and also complete a cluster of three courses in each of the remaining two divisions. Orientation Rochester-style is a week long and includes a fall festival called Yellowjacket Weekend, designed to help new students "become fully integrated in the university community."

The university's 200 degree programs span the standard fields of study, but Rochester takes special pride in its famed Eastman School of Music, which is open to undergraduates. It also excels in the engineering and scientific fields,

"[The weather is] great for winter sports or studying or even sleeping late on a snowy Saturday."

including biomedical engineering. Optics has long been a strength—naturally, given that the city of Rochester is home to Kodak, Xerox, and Bausch & Lomb. The university's Institute of Optics, the nation's first center devoted exclusively to the subject, is a leader in basic optical research and theory, and it awards about half of all optics degrees in the U.S. The most popular majors include business, psychology, computer science, mechanical engineering, and economics. Rochester's Combined Degree Programs offer simultaneous admission to both undergraduate and graduate degree programs in medicine, public health, engineering, and education.

Students admit the academics are challenging but describe the atmosphere as helpful. "There are many study spaces used primarily for group work, and many professors explicitly encourage working together on assignments and projects," says a brain and cognitive science major. Eighty percent of classes have fewer than 20 students. Professors are praised for their skills behind the lectern as well as their passion. "Teaching is dynamic—incorporating guest speakers, videos, lecture slides, and discussions," notes one senior. Students also highly rate the Greene Center for Career Education and Connections for its vigorous preparation of seniors for the job market.

For students whose educational ambitions can't be realized in just four years, two innovative programs offer up to an extra year of study at no extra cost. The Take Five Scholars Program allows students to spend an additional semester or year—tuition free—exploring interests outside their major or a topic they wish to study in greater depth. The Experiential-Five (e5) Program extends the same offer but with an entrepreneurial focus: e5 students pursue internships, undertake special projects, develop entrepreneurial plans, or launch a start-up. Both programs involve a competitive application process where students propose a course schedule, an action plan, and a faculty advisor.

Overall, 77 percent of Rochester students get involved in undergraduate research programs; opportunities include Research and Innovation Grants, which provide

"Many professors explicitly encourage working together on assignments and projects."

funding of up to $4,500, and the *Journal of Undergraduate Research*. Students selected for the Senior Scholars Program undertake a capstone project that can range from a piece of scholarly research to a work of artistic creativity. More than 70 Rochester-sponsored study abroad programs are available in over 40 countries, and 30 percent of students take part.

"Students can be intense," says an economics major. "Most of the people here are high achievers, go-getters, and hard workers." Thirty percent hail from New York State. Many also come from New England, and there's been a large jump in the numbers from Florida, the Midwest, California, and overseas, with 25 percent coming from foreign countries. Asian Americans make up 14 percent of the student body, while Black students account for 5 percent, Hispanics/Latinos 7 percent, and multiracial students 4 percent. A senior says, "There is always an active dialogue" about current social and political issues. Eligible undergraduates receive merit scholarships averaging $15,700. The Rochester Promise initiative offers free tuition to eligible graduates of local city high schools.

First-years and sophomores are required to live on campus, and 90 percent of all undergrads choose to do so all four years. "Dorms are comfortable, modern, high-tech, very generously sized, and well maintained," a senior says. New students are assigned to rooms—usually doubles—and upperclassmen can usually get suites or apartments through the lottery. In addition to a variety of co-ed and single-sex options, special-interest floors are available for enthusiasts of music, computers and technology, anime, green space, and interclass living. Fare served in the dining halls receives high ratings from students, as does campus safety. "Security officers patrol all the time," says one student, "and if ever you feel unsafe, they will pick you up and take you where you need to go, any time of the day."

Twenty percent of the men and 26 percent of the women go Greek, and fraternities contribute heavily to the social life of Greeks and independents alike by sponsoring parties and concerts. Students of legal age are allowed to drink in designated areas of the campus, but students agree that Rochester is not much of a party school. "While there are many things to do in the city of Rochester, it seems that most of the social life occurs right on campus," observes one student. UR has its own set of movie theaters, and

> "Most of the people here are high achievers, go-getters, and hard workers."

a cappella concerts always draw a crowd. Favorite annual events include Meliora Weekend during homecoming, the holiday Boar's Head Dinner, and a spring fling known as Dandelion Day. Wilson Day is an annual day of community service that places incoming students in more than 50 agencies throughout the city of Rochester to paint houses, landscape, and play bingo in nursing homes.

Many students take the free campus shuttle into the greater Rochester area, where they may entertain themselves on the beaches of Lake Ontario, in the International Photography Museum at the Eastman House, or at the Rochester Philharmonic Orchestra. An unofficial Rochester tradition calls for each student to eat a "garbage plate" at Nick Tahou's, an infamous local dive, before graduating. In addition to frequent ski trips, favored out-of-town destinations include Niagara Falls, about 70 miles west, and, for the more venturesome, Toronto, 125 miles farther westward.

The 23 varsity sports are coming of age at Rochester, and Yellowjacket teams compete in the Division III University Athletic Association. Rochester athletic teams have captured recent conference or regional championships in men's soccer and basketball, women's field hockey and softball, and men's and women's swimming and diving. About a quarter of students participate in intramurals each semester. If intramural competition isn't your bag, Rochester has group fitness classes and a sports complex complete with lighted rooftop tennis courts, a Nautilus fitness center, an eight-lane pool, and an indoor track.

In the past, students bemoaned the fact that their university didn't have a wider academic reputation, but that has changed, thanks in part to the Rochester Renaissance Plan. Improvements have been made in the curriculum, the facilities, and just about anywhere you look on campus. Rochester seems to be winning its battle for a spot among the nation's leading private universities. Now if they could only do something about all that snow.

The Take Five Scholars Program allows students to spend an additional semester or year—tuition free—exploring interests outside their major.

Wilson Day is an annual day of community service that places incoming students in more than 50 agencies throughout the city.

Overlaps

Cornell University, NYU, Tufts, Carnegie Mellon, Boston University, Case Western Reserve, Johns Hopkins, WashU in St. Louis

If You Apply To ›

Rochester: Early decision, regular decision. SATs or ACTs: optional. Accepts the Common Application with supplement. Musicians apply directly to the Eastman School of Music.

Rochester Institute of Technology

60 Lomb Memorial Drive, Rochester, NY 14623

RIT is the largest of New York's major technological universities. The school is strong in anything related to computing, art and design, and engineering. In the city built by Kodak (remember them?), photography, imaging science, and film and animation are among the tops in the country. National leader in serving deaf and hard-of-hearing students. More relaxed feel than most technical schools.

Website: www.rit.edu

Location: Suburban

Private

Total Enrollment: 14,911

Undergraduates: 12,733

Male/Female: 66/34

Financial Aid: 74%

Pell Grant: 30%

Expense: Pr $ $

Student Loans: 73%

Average Debt: $ $ $ $

Applicants: 21,683

Accepted: 71%

Enrolled: 21%

Grad in 6 Years: 71%

Returning Freshmen: 88%

Academics: ✐ ✐ ✐

Social: ☎ ☎ ☎

Q of L: ★ ★ ★

Admissions: (585) 475-6631

Email Address: admissions@ rit.edu

Strong Programs:

Computer Science

Art and Design

Engineering

Photography

Imaging Science

Film and Animation

Industrial Design

Game Design and Development

Unlike many liberal arts colleges that prefer that students test the academic waters before deciding on a major or future job plans, Rochester Institute of Technology focuses on career-oriented and technology-based academics from the get-go. And unlike many big universities where the academic luminaries shine from research-oriented graduate schools, RIT's spotlight is very definitely on undergraduates. Established in 1829, RIT is more accessible than many of its closest competitors too. Students who are geared up and ready to "go professional" will be more than satisfied with RIT's extensive co-op program.

While the town of Rochester may sometimes seem like a reluctant host to weekend fun-seekers, it can hardly deny that it is, in fact, a college town; RIT shares the city with six nearby colleges. Its main campus, located on 1,300 suburban acres six miles from downtown Rochester, has its own distinctive style—redbrick buildings with sharp, contemporary lines. A MAGIC Spell Studios facility housing a state-of-the-art production studio for the RIT MAGIC (Media, Arts, Games, Interaction, and Creativity) Center recently opened.

> "RIT makes me want to work harder, without making me feel like I won't succeed."

RIT's general education program offers students considerable flexibility. The number of required liberal arts credits has been reduced and more than 80 academic minors have been added within the past few years. Unlike many universities, RIT allows freshmen to schedule significant coursework in their majors early on, and spreads out liberal arts requirements over a more extended period. Those who are unsure of their academic path may enroll in University Exploration or any of the university's college-based exploration options before deciding on a major.

RIT specializes in carving out niches for itself with unusual programs, and majors are offered in more than 200 fields, from basic electrical and chemical engineering to packaging science and bioinformatics. Fortunately, applicants narrow the range of choices to a manageable size by applying to one of nine undergraduate colleges: Art and Design; Saunders College of Business; Golisano College of Computing and Information Sciences; Gleason College of Engineering; Engineering Technology; Health Sciences and Technology; Liberal Arts; Science; or the National Technical Institute for the Deaf. RIT is a leader in providing access and support services for deaf and hard-of-hearing students. Many hearing students choose to learn sign language as well.

Predictably, majors in engineering and engineering technology are among the most popular at RIT, particularly mechanical engineering and electrical engineering; computer science and game design and development also enroll high numbers of students. Photography is a signature program, and the film and animation and industrial design programs are well regarded. The College of Art and Design offers excellent programs in ceramics, furniture design, glass, and metals and jewelry design, and students have the run of Bevier Gallery, where visiting artists provide firsthand instruction. Dozens of accelerated dual-degree options allow students to earn a bachelor's degree and a master's degree in five years. Undergraduates being the school's top priority, classes are kept relatively small—49 percent have fewer than 20 students—and the faculty develops new academic programs to fit career needs. A biology major says, "Professors have a passion for what they teach, and it shows."

Students come to RIT to prove themselves, both in the classroom and through real-world experiences, so it's no surprise that students' schedules are demanding. "RIT makes me want to work harder, without making me feel like I won't succeed," says a biomedical engineering major. Through RIT's co-op program, more than 4,500 juniors and seniors each year take one to two terms away from campus for full-time, paid positions that give them practical experience in their field, key networking opportunities with potential employers, and, often, inspired ideas to bring back to campus. The Simone Center for Student Innovation and Entrepreneurship helps students learn how to take

"Whatever quirk you have, bring it here, because it makes us fun."

an idea from conception to commercialization through coursework, consulting opportunities, and workshops. Students showcase their research and creative projects every year during Imagine RIT. Although 600 study abroad programs are available in more than 60 countries, including RIT's global campuses in China, Croatia, Kosovo, and the United Arab Emirates, only 2 percent of students find time to go abroad.

RIT students are quirky and comfortable in their own skin. "People wear bathrobes to class and knit during lectures and do interpretive dances on the quad," says a junior. "Whatever quirk you have, bring it here, because it makes us fun." Forty-nine percent of undergraduates are from New York State, the remainder coming largely from New Jersey, Pennsylvania, and Connecticut; 5 percent are international. Five percent of students are Black, 9 percent Hispanic/Latino, 11 percent Asian American, and 5 percent multiracial. "The male-to-female ratio is still not where it should be," says one woman, "but this is a tech school, and 2 to 1 really isn't that bad." The large number of deaf students helps create a unique atmosphere. Politically, students tend to be aware of global issues, if not overtly active in them. RIT admits students without regard to financial need and offers merit scholarships averaging $14,600 to eligible students, but there are no athletic scholarships.

Half of RIT students live on campus; freshmen are required to live in the dorms, while upperclassmen sign up for the numerous campus apartments on a first-come, first-served basis. RIT offers a variety of special-interest houses and lifestyle floors, including "mainstream" floors where both deaf and hearing students live. Those who choose to live off campus take advantage of areas serviced by the school shuttle bus. Vegetarians, vegans, and carnivores alike will find on-campus meal options to be reasonably diverse. Campus security is "all over campus all of the time," says one student.

RIT's buzzing campus may seem at odds with its sedate suburban, semirural surroundings, and students say there's not much within walking distance of the campus. Downtown Rochester has more to offer, including minor league baseball, farmers markets, museums, and bookstores, and students also take road trips to Buffalo, Syracuse, and Canada. For those without transportation, there's always something to do on campus, courtesy of the more than 300 student clubs and organizations, including a fine jazz ensemble and chorus that perform regularly. Just 3 percent of the men and 2 percent of the women choose to go Greek. "Party culture is minimal here but available for anyone looking for it," reports a senior. Brick City Homecoming, FreezeFest, and SpringFest are favorite annual celebrations.

RIT fields 21 Division III athletic teams. In addition, the Tigers men's and women's ice hockey teams compete in Division I, and both have won conference titles in recent years. Men's lacrosse captured the national title in 2021; men's swimming and diving, track and field, and cross-country and women's volleyball are also competitive. Approximately half of RIT undergrads participate in more than a dozen intramural sports.

RIT students are dedicated and career-oriented, yet they don't take themselves too seriously, which gives this demanding techie school a surprisingly relaxed feel. And best of all, says an imaging science major, thanks to an abundance of co-op education opportunities, "we graduate with lots of lab/field/hands-on experience." Indeed, self-motivated and focused, RIT students have their eyes on the future and are well prepared to meet it.

Overlaps

Rensselaer, Northeastern, Drexel, Penn State, SUNY–Stony Brook, SUNY–Buffalo, Worcester Polytechnic, Syracuse

If You Apply To ›

RIT: Early decision I and II, regular decision. SATs or ACTs: optional. Accepts the Common Application with supplement. Applicants to art, design, and film and animation programs must submit portfolio.

Rollins College

1000 Holt Avenue, Box 2720, Winter Park, FL 32789

The oldest postsecondary institution in Florida, Rollins is the marriage of a liberal arts college and a graduate business school that operates under the mantra of "applied liberal arts." A haven for out-of-staters who want their ticket punched to Orlando, with its abundant entertainment and professional opportunities. Strong Greek system and world-class water-skiing. Australian studies a specialty.

Website: www.rollins.edu
Location: Suburban
Private
Total Enrollment: 2,472
Undergraduates: 2,139
Male/Female: 40/60
Financial Aid: 92%
Pell Grant: 17%
Expense: Pr $ $ $
Student Loans: 50%
Average Debt: $ $ $
Applicants: 8,049
Accepted: 51%
Enrolled: 13%
Grad in 6 Years: 71%
Returning Freshmen: 83%

Move over, Mickey Mouse. Hold up, Harry Potter. You're not the only attractions in central Florida. For students looking to hit the books under the ever-present Florida sunshine, there's also Rollins College. Located in a quiet suburb of Greater Orlando, Rollins, which was founded in 1885 and named after a benefactor, offers students plenty of places to have fun and gain hands-on career experience. "Rollins is close to hundreds of internships and job opportunities just waiting for the next ambitious student," says one satisfied senior.

Capitalizing on its location along the shores of Lake Virginia, Rollins's 80-acre campus combines the natural beauty of the lakeside with consistent, Spanish Mediterranean architecture. The Bush Science Center is a state-of-the-art, LEED-certified facility featuring 19 research labs, 18 student/faculty lounges, and 15 instructional labs. Lakeside Neighborhood, a recently built apartment-style residential complex for upperclassmen, boasts such luxurious amenities as full-size beds, in-unit laundry machines, a café, a gym, and an outdoor pool.

The general education curriculum, known as Rollins Foundations in the Liberal Arts, seeks to help students develop skills relevant to any major or career, while preparing them for global citizenship and responsible leadership. Students are required to demonstrate competency in foreign language, mathematical thinking, writing, ethical reasoning, and health and wellness. First-year students must take a fall-semester Rollins College Conference course, a small class of no more than 15 students, led by a professor-advisor who is assisted by two upperclassmen peer mentors. Students also complete five Foundations classes, linked seminar courses that use an interdisciplinary lens to examine one of five themes: Cultural Collisions, Enduring Questions, Environments, Identities, and Innovation. The final Foundations class is an interdisciplinary capstone that requires students to conduct original research on a global issue, which they present to the campus community at the Foundations Summit.

The most popular of Rollins's nearly 40 undergraduate majors include international business, communication studies, business management, psychology, computer science, and English. Economics and biology draw large numbers too. A minor in Australian studies is a particular specialty and involves travel Down Under. The chemistry department turned out a Nobel Prize winner, and the Annie Russell Theatre hosts productions staged by the well-known theater department. A 3–2 accelerated management program allows qualified freshmen to gain guaranteed admission to Rollins's top-ranked Crummer Graduate School of Business, leading to B.A. and M.B.A. degrees in five rather than six years. Accelerated bachelor's/master's programs are also available in human resources, public health, pre-engineering, applied behavior analysis and clinical science, liberal studies, and teaching.

"The academic climate is vigorous, conversation-based, and challenging but with proper academic assistance from faculty," says a public policy and political economy major. Students tend to form close relationships with professors, especially since there are no teaching assistants here, and the professors "only want to see you succeed and find your passion," according to one student. Rollins offers many opportunities to collaborate on research with faculty or pursue independent projects, participate in internships, and volunteer through service-learning classes. About 70 percent of all undergrads study abroad at least once while at Rollins, taking off for programs in more than 50 countries all over the world. Seven percent sign up for the challenging, four-year Honors curriculum, which culminates in researching, writing, and defending a senior thesis.

> "The academic climate is vigorous, conversation-based, and challenging but with proper academic assistance."

Rollins has had a reputation for attracting, in the words of one student, affluent and "entitled students who don't work hard or give back." While some students still fit that mold, a sophomore says, most are "kind, welcoming, ambitious, committed to public service, and politically/civically engaged." Students report that both sides of the political aisle are well represented on campus, but the atmosphere doesn't usually get heated. Fifty-three percent of Rollins undergraduates are from Florida, and 9 percent hail from outside the United States. The student body is 4 percent Black, 17 percent Hispanic/Latino, 4 percent Asian American, and 5 percent multiracial. Merit scholarships average $24,700 for qualified students, and more than 230 athletic scholarships are up for grabs.

Sixty-eight percent of the college's students live on campus in spacious co-ed dorms. "Dorms are really nice," a student says, and feature "big rooms and hardwood floors." Another adds that, for those who prefer to live off campus, "there are plenty of houses and apartments near the campus that can be rented at a reasonable cost." Six dining facilities are located throughout campus, including a nautically themed, pub-style restaurant that treats diners to views of the lake, and the food receives positive reviews. A senior says, "Campus security is top of the line and super friendly."

(continued)

Academics: ✐ ✐ ✐
Social: ☎ ☎ ☎ ☎
Q of L: ★ ★ ★
Admissions: (407) 646-2161
Email Address: admission@ rollins.edu

Strong Programs:
Theater
International Business
Communication Studies
Business Management
Psychology
Computer Science
English
Economics

An interdisciplinary capstone requires students to conduct original research on a global issue, which they present at the Foundations Summit.

The Greek scene claims 22 percent of the men and 28 percent of the women, so there's always a party somewhere—often off campus. The administration has clamped down on social excesses, with party monitors checking IDs and a student activity director attending each on-campus party. Penalties for underage drinking are strictly enforced. "There is so much more to social life here than partying," insists a junior, especially through the college's more than 100 student organizations tailored to just about any interest. Students can paddleboard, sail, or wakeboard on Lake Virginia between classes, and there are also movies on Mills Lawn or "dive-in" movies at the pool, lip-synch contests, and live bands in the campus center. Fox Day in the spring is "a sacred tradition"—the president cancels classes for the day by placing a fox statue on the front lawn, and people head for the beach, hit the theme parks, or relax on campus.

"Winter Park isn't a typical college town," says one student. "It is one of the oldest cities in Florida, has a charming restaurant and shopping street known as Park Avenue, and is family friendly." Every freshman participates in SPARC, Rollins's annual day of service held during orientation, and many students volunteer with community partners such as Habitat for Humanity and local schools. "Community service is a big part of the Rollins experience," comments a math and computer science major. Orlando's offerings include entertainment complexes and theme parks such as Walt Disney World, Epcot Center, Universal CityWalk, and Islands of Adventure. Popular road trips include Cocoa Beach, Miami, and Tampa.

"Students can expect to find a safe haven [and] a real college experience."

Athletics are an integral part of campus life. Division II Tars teams (a nickname for 18th-century sailors) have claimed 23 national championships and more than 95 Sunshine State conference titles. The water ski team is a perennial national powerhouse. Other competitive teams include men's and women's soccer and women's lacrosse, softball, and golf. Intramural sports are popular, too, with more than 20 leagues and events during the school year. Club sports teams have been formed for everything from eSports and wakeboarding to volleyball and dance.

Rollins students enjoy sand and sun, as well as a diverse academic climate. As the oldest recognized college in the state of Florida, Rollins offers a rich legacy and smooth-as-silk Southern character. Says one senior, "Students can expect to find a safe haven [and] a real college experience," not to mention plenty of practical career preparation.

Overlaps

Furman, Rhodes, Sewanee, Elon, College of Charleston, University of Miami (FL), Stetson, Eckerd

If You Apply To ›

Rollins: Early decision I and II, regular decision. SATs or ACTs: optional. Accepts the Common Application with supplement.

Rose–Hulman Institute of Technology

5500 Wabash Avenue, Terre Haute, IN 47803

Rose–Hulman provides that rare combination of technical education and personal attention. Only Caltech, Clarkson, and Harvey Mudd offer comparable intimacy and a technical academic environment. Nearby Indiana State and Saint Mary-of-the-Woods help mitigate the skewed gender ratio. RHIT is among the few engineering schools that encourage study abroad and boast significant athletic opportunities.

Rose–Hulman Institute of Technology may not be as well known as Caltech, MIT, or even Carnegie Mellon, but it was the first private college to offer an undergraduate degree in chemical engineering, and it continues to innovate today. If you can handle the lopsided male/female ratio and the limited list of majors (all in engineering, mathematics, and the sciences, with the exception of international studies), Rose–Hulman offers an outstanding technical background and bright prospects for future employment. Students are smart and motivated, and they love using their computers for work and play. "We are all dorks," says a senior. "Some of us just hide it better than others."

Established in 1874 and co-ed since 1995, Rose–Hulman is the oldest private engineering school west of the Alleghenies. Its benefactors were Chauncey Rose, an entrepreneur who brought the railroad to Indiana, and the Hulman family, who owned the Indianapolis Motor Speedway for 74 years and gave their fortune to the school in 1971. The 250-acre campus includes numerous trees, rolling hills, and a lake. The Kremer Innovation Center features a variety of high-tech engineering labs. Completed in 2021, a new $29 million academic building houses flexible classrooms, design studios, state-of-the-art science labs, and collaborative workspaces.

> **"The professors don't hold our hands but also won't let us crash and burn."**

General education requirements at Rose–Hulman include math, physics, chemistry, and humanities and social sciences. In the first quarter, freshmen must take a Foundations for Success course that covers such topics as time management and study skills. Students in any major can enroll in multidisciplinary senior capstone projects, often completing projects for outside organizations.

"Being on a quarter system, the academics are fast-paced and challenging but still manageable," explains a junior, especially because students are so willing to work together. Forty-eight percent of classes have fewer than 20 students. Mechanical engineering, computer science, electrical engineering, and computer engineering are the most popular majors. Chemical and civil engineering, math, and physics are also strong, and the school's optical engineering major is uncommon at the undergraduate level. A major in engineering design gives students a chance to work on projects with real clients through all phases of the design process. Regardless of which discipline you choose, odds are you'll find faculty members willing to help. "The professors don't hold our hands but also won't let us crash and burn," says a mechanical engineering major. "They believe in learning by trial and error but have always been there for support."

Since only a handful of graduate students are enrolled, teaching assistants don't teach classes, and opportunities to get involved with faculty research abound. The Interdisciplinary Research Collaborative gives selected students the chance to pursue ongoing research projects for 10 weeks during the summer. The ESCALATE living/learning community introduces freshmen to the principles of entrepreneurial and business success. Rose–Hulman is increasing its emphasis on global education, and students have the option of enrolling in international studies as a second major, designed to complement their primary major. The school also offers exchange programs and a number of courses that combine traditional on-campus coursework with a two- to three-week trip at the end of the quarter. Still, with their demanding schedules, only 3 percent of students go abroad. When it comes time to start the job search, Rose–Hulman students are in good hands. "Career services works with every student individually to assist them in finding the right job for them," cheers a senior. "They helped me make lots of decisions when I had multiple offers at hand."

At Rose–Hulman, says a chemical engineering major, "You'll find a lot of students who enjoy video games, *Star Wars*, Marvel movies, board games, or other similar pastimes." Thirty-four percent of undergrads are Indiana natives, and 9 percent

Website: www.rose-hulman.edu
Location: Suburban
Private
Total Enrollment: 2,073
Undergraduates: 2,058
Male/Female: 75/25
Financial Aid: 100%
Pell Grant: 12%
Expense: Pr $ $
Student Loans: 54%
Average Debt: $ $ $ $
Applicants: 4,536
Accepted: 77%
Enrolled: 18%
Grad in 6 Years: 86%
Returning Freshmen: 91%
Academics: ✎ ✎ ✎
Social: ☎
Q of L: ★ ★
Admissions: (800) 248-7448
Email Address: admissions@ rose-hulman.edu

Strong Programs:
Chemical Engineering
Civil Engineering
Mathematics
Physics
Optical Engineering
Mechanical Engineering
Computer Science
Electrical Engineering

Rose–Hulman's optical engineering major is uncommon at the undergraduate level.

come from abroad. Black students make up 5 percent of the student body, Asian Americans 7 percent, Hispanics/Latinos 5 percent, and multiracial students 6 percent. "Diversity is increasingly celebrated at this school," reports a student. Political and social issues don't usually play a big role in campus life. Merit scholarships are available, averaging $20,200, but there are no athletic awards.

Sixty-two percent of students live on campus; freshmen and sophomores are guaranteed rooms in the residence halls. "We're allowed to do almost anything to the rooms, like add lofts or decks to gain space," says a civil engineering major. (At an engineering school, would you expect anything less?) Most upperclassmen move into Greek houses or find other off-campus digs. For meals, there's a traditional cafeteria as well as two restaurant-style dining facilities. "To be blunt, no college food will ever be good," reasons a senior, "but Rose–Hulman genuinely offers the best college food I have had." The campus and the surrounding area are safe, according to students.

The town of Terre Haute (population 60,000) has some restaurants and bars, a mall, a couple of Starbucks locations, and two movie theaters, but generally, it's "sleepy and lacking in nightlife," says a physics major. Various groups, including the Greek organizations and Habitat for Humanity, help the town out with service projects. There are eight fraternities and three sororities, which draw 34 percent of the men and 27 percent of the women, respectively. Fraternity parties are a staple of weekend social life. When it comes to drinking, a civil engineering major reports, campus policies emphasize safety, and "the only places where alcohol is actively discouraged are the freshman halls." Everyone looks forward to Greatest Floor (a 24-hour competition between residence halls), basketball games against DePauw, and the homecoming bonfire. "Freshmen build up and guard the bonfire the week preceding homecoming while upperclassmen try to sabotage it," explains a junior. Students say the best weekend excursions are road trips to Chicago, Cincinnati, Indianapolis, or St. Louis, all within a few hours' drive.

Varsity teams (the Fightin' Engineers) play in Division III; football, men's and women's soccer and track and field, and women's golf are some of the strongest teams. Competitive tech teams like the Rocketry Club, Human Powered Vehicle Team, Team Rose Motorsports, and Cyber Defense Team are strong, but if you're envisioning Rose–Hulman students as pasty-faced lab dwellers, you're misinformed. About half of the student body participates in 19 club sports and 30 intramurals, with basketball, volleyball, and ultimate Frisbee the most popular.

Students committed to careers in engineering or the sciences will find a top-flight education at this Midwestern technical school. While Rose–Hulman "doesn't have that big-school pride" so common in this part of the country, students say the "charming and homey" community feel created by the intimate classes and the school's small size more than makes up for that. "Everyone is just so gosh darn polite here," gushes a freshman. "Students are friendly and kind and cooperative, as opposed to competitive."

Everyone looks forward to Greatest Floor (a 24-hour competition between residence halls) and the homecoming bonfire.

"You'll find a lot of students who enjoy video games, *Star Wars*, Marvel movies, [and] board games."

Overlaps

Harvey Mudd, Olin College of Engineering, Kettering, Lawrence Tech, Milwaukee School of Engineering, Clarkson, Colorado School of Mines, Purdue

If You Apply To ›

Rose–Hulman: Early action, regular decision. Accepts the Common Application. Please consult Rose–Hulman's website for the most up-to-date information regarding standardized test requirements.

Rutgers–The State University of New Jersey

65 Davidson Road, Piscataway, NJ 08854

One of only nine American universities founded during the Colonial period, Rutgers is the dominant public university in the Garden State. Originally chartered as Queens College but subsequently renamed for Revolutionary War hero and benefactor Henry Rutgers. Everything is available: engineering, business, pharmacy, the liberal arts, and the nation's largest women's college. Well known as the birthplace of football.

Proud of traditions that extend back to its founding in 1766, this flagship public university of New Jersey likes to compare itself to a city with multiple neighborhoods, each with its own particular identity. With roughly 45,500 full-time undergraduate students spread across three regional campuses in New Brunswick, Newark, and Camden, Rutgers is all about choice. Choices between more than 120 undergraduate majors and 4,000-plus courses. Choices about which of the more than 800 student organizations catch your fancy. Even choices about which of its many libraries, computer labs, and student centers to frequent. "Rutgers is a place that gives students opportunities to do and be whatever they want," says a senior.

Seventy-five percent of full-time undergraduates (more than 34,000) enroll in Rutgers–New Brunswick, which is itself a collection of five residential sub-campuses strung out along the Raritan River and linked by a free university bus system that allows students to move easily among the various units for classes, housing, and social life. The historical core is the College Avenue campus, which boasts architectural gems dating to the American Revolution and is home to the huge

> **"The sense of community in classes is very strong."**

School of Arts and Sciences. In addition to the football stadium, the Busch campus hosts the engineering and pharmacy schools, while Cook offers a bucolic setting for the School of Environmental and Biological Sciences. Douglass, with its Georgian colonial architecture, is home to the Douglass Residential College, the largest women's college in the country. Livingston, with its extensive array of solar panels, is home to the business school, the basketball arena, and a movie theater.

Among the more than 120 undergraduate majors offered at Rutgers–New Brunswick, the most popular include psychology, computer science, biological sciences, information sciences, and human resources management. Perhaps surprisingly, philosophy is internationally renowned. Students universally praise fine arts, agricultural sciences, business, mathematics, and the six-year pharmacy program. The "incredible resources and opportunities" at Douglass Residential College make the women and gender studies major a good bet, according to an English major. Workloads vary across disciplines, and students generally find them ambitious but manageable. "The sense of community in classes is very strong," says one senior. "Students like to help each other out, and professors understand that you are at Rutgers to do more than take classes." Faculty members all have office hours, and first-year students are taught by regular professors. As at any big state university, classes can be large, although 48 percent have fewer than 20 students. A sophomore reports that "even in those 200-person lecture halls, my professors know my name and are super flexible when it comes to finding time to meet with struggling students."

In an effort to reverse the perennial exodus of New Jersey high school superstars from the state, Rutgers offers a wide range of special academic programs, including the state-of-the-art (and highly selective) Honors College, whose members pursue specialized courses, fulfill service requirements, and complete a cumulative capstone

Website: www.rutgers.edu
Location: Small City
Public
Total Enrollment: 43,185
Undergraduates: 34,361
Male/Female: 50/50
Financial Aid: 64%
Pell Grant: 26%
Expense: Pub $ $ $ $
Student Loans: 54%
Average Debt: $ $ $
Applicants: 43,161
Accepted: 68%
Enrolled: 24%
Grad in 6 Years: 84%
Returning Freshmen: 94%
Academics: ✍ ✍ ✍ ✍
Social: ☎ ☎ ☎
Q of L: ★ ★ ★
Admissions: (732) 932-4636
Email Address: admissions@ugadm.rutgers.edu

Strong Programs:
Philosophy
Fine Arts
Agricultural Sciences
Business
Mathematics
Pharmacy
Women and Gender Studies
Psychology

project during their senior year. Interdisciplinary living/learning communities offer live-in faculty that draw students with common interests ranging from various cultural and ethnic identities to meteorology. Biology students have the run of the 360-acre Rutgers Ecological Preserve and Natural Teaching Area, and the Aresty Research Center supports students seeking to engage in research early in their undergraduate career. Entering students have the option of a research-based first-year seminar where they work closely with a faculty member. A junior singles out the Road to Wall Street Program that "provides finance majors with one-on-one mentoring with people currently working on Wall Street." Rutgers is home to more than 175 specialized research centers and institutes dedicated to topics ranging from ancient Roman art to mountain gorillas. Rutgers also offers undergraduate study abroad in more than 30 countries, from France and Greece to Thailand. As for career, health, and other student support services, an English major reports, "The services are strong, but students have to reach out for them."

Interdisciplinary living/learning communities offer live-in faculty that draw students with common interests.

Although the administration has been attempting to increase the number of out-of-staters, 84 percent of Rutgers–New Brunswick students hail from the Garden State. Nevertheless, the student body reflects the substantial diversity of the state itself, with a good mix of students from cities, suburbs, farms, and seaside communities, and students take pride in their heterogeneity. "Our diversity spans interests, race, gender, class, sexual orientation, religion, and politics," says a management major. "It is the best part of Rutgers." Students of color account for just over half of undergraduates, including 7 percent Black, 14 percent Hispanic/Latino, 31 percent Asian American, and 4 percent multiracial. Nine percent of undergrads come from abroad. Nearly 500 students receive athletic scholarships in 22 sports; merit scholarships average $8,800.

"[Professors] are super flexible when it comes to finding time to meet with struggling students."

On-campus housing in New Brunswick typically accommodates 36 percent of full-time students and is readily available on all five sub-campuses. "The rooms are large, and every room comes with a microwave and fridge/freezer combination," reports a music education major. Other on-campus housing options include apartment complexes with kitchens and living rooms. "We have four dining halls, and there are many cafés and food vendors on campus that accept meal swipes," notes one sophomore. "Most people can find a place they are happy eating at regularly." In part because of its Office for Violence Prevention and Victim Assistance, Rutgers has become a national leader in confronting sexual assault on campus. The university also offers a special dormitory for students who are trying to overcome addictions to drugs and alcohol. "The university is generally safe," says an urban planning major. "Access to emergency services is easy and plentiful."

Rutgers is home to more than 175 specialized research centers and institutes.

Social life happens both on and off campus. The Greek scene is located off campus near College Avenue, and a sophomore notes, "Only 11 percent of students are involved in Greek life, so we are definitely not 'go Greek or go home.' People party in apartments, bars, houses, and dorms, and there is no single party culture." Another reports, "The RAs are really effective about enforcing alcohol policies." Each sub-campus has its own student center with such diversions as pinball machines, pool tables, bowling alleys, and a snack bar, and the Rutgers University Programming Association sponsors films, performances, and other events. As a major city, New Brunswick offers an array of nearby restaurants and theaters. For those who want to hit the road for fun, New York City and Philadelphia are each only about an hour's drive or train ride, and students flood the Jersey Shore in springtime.

Given that Rutgers likes to remind the world that it was the birthplace of college football, homecoming is a big deal.

Funky social rituals include Hot Dog Day, which features rides and free hot dogs, and Beats on the Banks, which brings a major rapper or other artist to campus. Given that Rutgers likes to remind the world that it was the birthplace of college football, homecoming is a big deal—with tailgate parties in the stadium parking lot, tons of food (including roast pigs and whole sides of beef), continuous music, and thousands of revelers. Students participating in the Homecoming Bed Races decorate twin beds on wheels and race them down College Avenue for charity. An annual 24-hour dance marathon, which raises money for a children's cancer charity, is another proud tradition.

Varsity, intramural, and club sports fill whatever gap is left by the social scene. In an effort to move from relative athletic obscurity to instant national prominence, Rutgers in 2014 became the 14th (sic) member of the powerhouse Big Ten, which appreciated its proximity to New York City and other East Coast media markets. The Scarlet Knights compete in nine men's and 13 women's Division I sports, and men's and women's basketball and lacrosse, men's wrestling, and women's soccer, rowing, and field hockey are nationally ranked. "Rutgers likes to pretend that Penn State is our rival, even though they don't care about us," confesses a management major. "So that is fun." Nonvarsity athletes can take their pick of more than 50 club sports and dozens of intramural leagues and tournaments.

> **"We are definitely not 'go Greek or go home.'"**

Rutgers has the usual abundance of people and programs characteristic of a large state university coupled with loyal support from the state's legislature and private sector and tuition that is relatively affordable. Students express irritation about the bus system ("not enough buses," "they leak when it rains"), but most appreciate the fact that, as a public land grant university, Rutgers offers them a huge range of professional and other academic options from which to choose. An exercise science major concludes, "Students at Rutgers have the whole world at their fingertips."

> ### Overlaps
> Penn State, University of Maryland, Michigan State, Ohio State, University of Minnesota, College of New Jersey, NYU, Boston University

If You Apply To ›

Rutgers: Early action, regular decision. Does not accept the Common Application. Apply to particular school. Arts applicants must interview, audition, or submit portfolio. Please consult Rutgers's website for the most up-to-date information regarding standardized test requirements.

University of St Andrews: See page 377.

College of Saint Benedict and Saint John's University

37 South College Avenue, St. Joseph, MN 56374

The College of Saint Benedict (CSB) and Saint John's University (SJU) are throwbacks to the way colleges were 50 years ago: women and men on separate campuses and copious amounts of school spirit. Founded by Benedictines, with monastic communities still active on both campuses. Eighty percent of students are from Minnesota, but global perspectives and study abroad are big emphases.

Remember when women's colleges had nearby brother schools, when dorms were single-sex, and when visitors of the opposite gender were only welcome at certain times? Doesn't ring a bell? Well, you might ask your grandparents. Or you could visit the College of Saint Benedict and Saint John's University. These two single-sex campuses—all-female CSB and all-male SJU—are five miles apart and have their own presidents, but they share a common heritage and mission: students and faculty

Website: www.csbsju.edu
Location: Small Town
Private
Total Enrollment: 3,084
Undergraduates: 3,048

(continued)

Male/Female: 50/50
Financial Aid: 100%
Pell Grant: 21%
Expense: Pr $ $
Student Loans: 72%
Average Debt: $ $ $ $
Applicants: 3,246
Accepted: 90%
Enrolled: 27%
Grad in 6 Years: 75%
Returning Freshmen: 85%
Academics: ✐ ✐ ✐
Social: ☎ ☎ ☎
Q of L: ★ ★ ★
Admissions: (800) 544-1489
Email Address: admissions@
    csbsju.edu

Strong Programs:
Global Business Leadership
Political Science
Nursing
Music
Chemistry
Environmental Studies
Accounting
Psychology

The environmental studies program is enhanced by access to the area's natural resources and one of the largest solar farms in the upper Midwest.

join together in a shared liberal arts education, guided by Benedictine principles. The schools' small sizes and respect for tradition give rise to a tight-knit community.

Founded in 1857 by what is now one of the largest men's Benedictine monasteries in the world, Saint John's now operates as an independent entity. It occupies 2,600 pristine acres in rural Minnesota, an area filled with forests, lakes, and the wide-open spaces perfect for outdoorsy types. The two colleges are connected by a free and frequent shuttle bus. Alongside a 137-year-old quadrangle erected by monks is a strikingly modern church designed by Marcel Breuer. Saint Benedict, established in 1913 by Benedictine sisters, is a cohesive 800-acre campus comprised of redbrick buildings and cobblestone walks. Together, the colleges have invested millions in facilities in recent years, including a major renovation of the SJU library that added a Learning Commons.

> **"Everyone is playing a critical role in the learning process."**

Saint Benedict and Saint John's share a joint academic program through which students take classes together on both campuses. The core curriculum, known as the Integrations Curriculum, aims to give students a cohesive, interdisciplinary, and hands-on education. It features components like a first-year seminar, experiential learning such as study abroad or service learning, and an electronic portfolio that ties together students' four years.

The global business leadership program prepares students to be leaders in a global economy and is the most popular major, followed by accounting, psychology, and biology. Programs in political science, nursing, music, and chemistry are also well regarded. The interdisciplinary environmental studies program is enhanced by access to the area's natural resources and one of the largest solar farms in the upper Midwest. The theology program benefits from abundant resources, including the Hill Museum & Manuscript Library, one of the foremost microfilm collections of centuries-old handwritten manuscripts. "Many of the classes are flipped classrooms or centered on discussion, so everyone is playing a critical role in the learning process," says a chemistry major. Very few classes have more than 30 students, and some fill up fast. The small classes encourage a community atmosphere and strong student/faculty ties. "Faculty members encourage students to ask them questions and will go out of their way for the success of their students," says a nursing major.

For those seeking respite from Minnesota winters, which can start in November and occasionally run until April, the colleges offer faculty-led, semester-long international study programs in 15 countries on six continents. Each program is limited to about 30 students, and 43 percent of students take part.

> **"Study abroad is a big part of our culture here."**

Numerous shorter trips are also offered during semester and summer breaks. "Study abroad is a big part of our culture here," says a biology major, "and your scholarships will transfer over to your study abroad, making it affordable." The McNeely Center for Entrepreneurship provides classes, coaching, and assistance to budding entrepreneurs from a range of disciplines. The program's Entrepreneurial Scholars travel to Silicon Valley and China/Hong Kong, and all of them start their own entrepreneurial ventures. Undergraduate research is becoming more prevalent at CSB/SJU (24 percent of students participate), and there is an endowed summer research program in the health and medical areas. Exceptional first-year students are invited to join the colleges' honors program, and upper-class students may also apply.

"Students value community and look out for each other," says a sophomore. "We all share a sense of brotherhood and sisterhood." Forty-six percent of students, known as "Bennies" and "Johnnies," are Roman Catholic, 80 percent are from Minnesota, and most are white. Black students constitute 4 percent of the student body, Hispanics/Latinos 9 percent, and Asian Americans 3 percent. International students account for 3 percent of the student population. A senior notes that despite the homogeneity on campus, the schools offer "a lot of programming events encouraging students to learn about diversity." Politically, a junior says, "We encompass all viewpoints, from ultraconservative to ultraliberal." In an effort to become more inclusive, CSB and SJU have both adopted policies allowing for the admission of transgender students. Merit scholarships averaging $24,000 are available, but there are no athletic scholarships.

Through a four-year residential program, virtually all students live on campus; seniors wishing to move off campus must apply for permission. "The progression to nicer housing as you get older is a rite of passage," says a senior. The residence halls are staffed partly by members of the monastic communities, but students aren't made to feel like a nun is watching their every move. On-campus apartments, such as Flynntown, provide a more independent living area for juniors and seniors. Students can choose from four dining halls on either campus, and most report the fare to be tasty and diverse. Campus security gets good reviews, and a sophomore says, "We have bystander intervention training programs on a variety of concerns, such as eating disorders and domestic violence."

The Joint Events Council organizes regular weekday and weekend social events, including student performances, comedians, magicians, and concerts. Students 21 and older are allowed to consume alcohol in their rooms or at SJU's on-campus pub, Brother Willie's, named after a deceased brother known as the Night Abbot who dispensed spiritual and worldly wisdom to students studying late in the residence halls. Underage drinkers face stiff penalties if caught. There are no fraternities or sororities, and parties tend to be small affairs. Each year, students look forward to the Festival of Cultures, the Maple Syrup Festival, the Fruit at the Finish Triathlon, the Senior Farewell, and spring break trips involving community service. Also popular is the annual Pines music festival, which welcomes the spring with a day of concerts featuring popular Christian musicians. Says a sophomore, "Off campus, there are many things to do in St. Cloud and also in St. Joseph, such as parties, coffee shops, restaurants, shopping, and movies." Seventy-four percent of students engage in community service, often through Campus Ministry programs. St. Cloud is a few minutes away, and the Twin Cities are 70 miles southeast.

The CSB Bennies field 11 Division III teams, and the SJU Johnnies boast 12. The football team is a perennial powerhouse, and its rivalry with St. Thomas is as strong as ever. Curiously enough, a team of guys known as the Rat Pack gets students psyched up for games. Men's golf, women's volleyball, and softball make regular national tournament appearances, and the men's basketball, track and field, and baseball teams are recent conference champs. Nonvarsity students can participate in a variety of club and intramural sports, and activities like kayaking and indoor rock climbing, offered through the Outdoor Leadership Center, are popular year-round.

Students who attend CSB/SJU revel in the schools' small-town setting, their traditions, and the grounding that comes from their shared Benedictine values. Perhaps more than anything, they treasure the community spirit that allows them to grow both individually and together. "We have a strong sense of school pride and alumni connection," says one happy student. "Once a Bennie or a Johnnie, always a Bennie or a Johnnie."

> *SJU's on-campus pub, Brother Willie's, is named after a deceased brother who dispensed spiritual and worldly wisdom to students.*

> **"Once a Bennie or a Johnnie, always a Bennie or a Johnnie."**

Overlaps

University of St. Thomas, Gustavus Adolphus, St. Olaf, Augsburg, St. Catherine, Luther, Augustana (IL), Hobart and William Smith

If You Apply To ›

St. Benedict and St. John's: Early action I and II, regular decision. SATs or ACTs: optional. Accepts the Common Application with supplement. CSB accepts applications from students who consistently live and identify as women, regardless of the gender assigned to them at birth. SJU accepts applications from students who consistently live and identify as men, regardless of the gender assigned to them at birth.

St. John's College

Annapolis Campus: 60 College Avenue, Annapolis, MD 21401
Santa Fe Campus: 1160 Camino Cruz Blanca, Santa Fe, NM 87505

Books, books, and more books is what you'll get at St. John's—from Thucydides to Tolstoy, Euclid to Einstein. St. John's attracts smart, intellectual, and nonconformist students who like to talk (and debate) about books and ideas. Easy to get in, not so easy to graduate. One of the few institutions with two coequal campuses. Students admitted to one can spend time at the other. St. John's is a croquet powerhouse.

Annapolis

Website: www.sjc.edu
Location: Small City
Private
Total Enrollment: 540
Undergraduates: 473
Male/Female: 53/47
Financial Aid: 95%
Pell Grant: 19%
Expense: Pr $
Student Loans: 79%
Average Debt: $ $
Applicants: 967
Accepted: 53%
Enrolled: 27%
Grad in 6 Years: 66%
Returning Freshmen: 81%
Academics: ✎ ✎ ✎ ✎ ½
Social: ☎ ☎ ☎
Q of L: ★ ★ ★ ★
Admissions: (800) 727-9238
Email Address: annapolis
 .admissions@sjc.edu

Strong Programs:
The Great Books Program
Liberal Arts and Sciences

Santa Fe

Website: www.sjc.edu
Location: Small City
Private
Total Enrollment: 411
Undergraduates: 355
Male/Female: 51/49
Financial Aid: 97%
Pell Grant: 23%
Expense: Pr $
Student Loans: 57%

With no majors, departments, or professors (in the traditional sense), and a combined total of fewer than 1,000 students on its two campuses, St. John's College is about as far from the typical postsecondary experience as you can get. Or maybe it's much closer to what college used to be in the "good old days"; the Annapolis campus traces its roots to King William's School—the Maryland colony's "free" school—founded in 1696. More than two centuries later, in 1964, St. John's opened a second campus in Santa Fe, New Mexico, to facilitate a doubling of enrollment and offer its superserious students a change of scenery. While the campuses may be a thousand miles apart, the Johnnies who populate them share an all-consuming quest for knowledge in the classical tradition. Their true teachers are the Great Books, about 200 of the most influential works of Western civilization. "Students at St. John's College aspire to join the great conversations that began in the primeval forests and have expanded to what we think we know today," says a sophomore. "We appreciate the value of tradition and its role in education."

Physically, the two St. John's campuses are more than just two time zones from one another. The colonial brick structures of the small urban campus in Annapolis, where the central classroom building dates from 1742, are squeezed into the city's historic district.

"We appreciate the value of tradition and its role in education."

With the Maryland state capitol and the U.S. Naval Academy in the neighborhood, this campus exudes old-world charm, and its location at the confluence of the Severn River and the Chesapeake Bay allows students to participate in sailing, crew, and individual sculling. The Santa Fe campus sits on 250 landlocked acres in the sun-drenched capital of New Mexico, just two and a half miles from downtown. The adobe-style buildings reflect Spanish and Native American traditions, and their perch in the Sangre de Cristo Mountains offers beautiful views of the city below. Students at St. John's in Santa Fe can get back to nature in nearby state and national forests, which offer hiking, mountain biking, kayaking, snowboarding, and skiing. Students may attend both campuses during their academic careers, and about 10 percent do so.

The St. John's curriculum, known as "the program," has every student read the Great Books in roughly chronological order. All students major in liberal arts, discussing the books in seminars, writing papers about them, and debating the riddles of human existence that they raise. Classes are led by tutors, who would be tenured professors anywhere else, but here are just the most advanced students. In a snub to the general trend in American academia toward more and more specialization, each tutor is required to teach any subject within the curriculum. As a group, the tutors help students divine wisdom from each other and from great philosophers, writers, scientists, and thinkers, from Thucydides and Tolstoy to Euclid and Einstein to Austen, Woolf, and Du Bois. "Because St. John's is not a research institution, the tutor's only job is teaching and engaging with students," says one junior. Both campuses follow a curriculum that would have delighted 19th-century English poet and educator Matthew Arnold, who argued that the goal of education is "to know the best which has been thought and said in the world."

There are no registration or scheduling hassles at St. John's; the daily course of study is mapped out before students set foot on campus. The curriculum includes four years of mathematics, two years of ancient Greek and French, three years of laboratory science, two years of music, and, of course, four years of Great Books seminars. Freshmen study the Greeks, sophomores advance through the Romans and the Renaissance, juniors cover the 17th and 18th centuries, and seniors do the 19th and 20th centuries. Readings are from primary sources only: math from Euclid and Ptolemy, physics from Maxwell, psychology from Freud, and so on. The assumption is that the Great Books can stand on their own, representing the highest achievements of human intellect. Importantly, juniors and seniors also take seven-week electives, called preceptorials, where they study a book or topic one-on-one with a tutor. Electives include in-depth courses in computer science that may involve building a simple computer or, in typical St. John's fashion, delving into Richard Feynman's writings on the nature of computer language. In their final semester, seniors write a 20- to 60-page critical essay on a topic of their choice and must pass an hour-long oral examination by a committee of three tutors.

> **"Our class conversations carry over into the dining hall, the quad, the common rooms."**

"There is a real sense of community and a collaborative feel to all of the academic work we do," says one sophomore. "Our class conversations carry over into the dining hall, the quad, the common rooms, and coffee shop." While there are no multiple-choice tests and no formal exams, courses are rigorous with a heavy load of reading every week and lots of writing. Since everyone's doing the same thing, there's a lot of pressure not to slack off. St. John's prefers that all eight semesters be completed in residence—meaning no heading off campus for internships, study abroad programs, or the like, unless it's during the summer break. Some St. John's students find they need a year off between the sophomore and junior years to decompress; some switch from Annapolis to Santa Fe or vice versa, and the six-year graduation rate at both campuses is relatively low. In recent years the college has expanded mental health services to offer unlimited counseling to all students, both on campus and via telehealth services.

A fifth of St. John's students are transfers from more conventional colleges—a true act of devotion, since St. John's requires everyone to begin as freshmen. Though the reasons students choose St. John's are never simple, the common thread is a fierce love of learning. One Santa Fe student says, "Most students on campus identify as avid readers and also take a keen interest in the arts and outdoor activi-

> **"We don't have any Greek organizations (besides study groups for reading ancient Greek!)."**

ties." The vast majority of students at both campuses are out-of-staters; international students represent 15 percent of the student body in Annapolis and 16 percent in Santa Fe. In Annapolis, 5 percent are Hispanic/Latino, 5 percent are Asian American, 2 percent are Black, and 7 percent are multiracial, while in Santa Fe those groups account for 9 percent, 1 percent, 1 percent, and 5 percent, respectively. One student reports that students are "more interested in political philosophy and theory" than in actually engaging in political or social activism. St. John's lowered its sticker price by about 33 percent in 2019 and has since implemented a tuition freeze in an effort to make the school more affordable for students from low- and middle-income families. Limited merit scholarships are available, but not for athletic prowess.

Seventy percent of students in Annapolis and 70 percent of those in Santa Fe live in the college's co-ed dorms; freshmen and sophomores are required to reside on campus. In Annapolis, the six "historic" residence halls are arranged around a central quad, while the two modern halls face College Creek. (Students warn that "historic" is code for "old,"

(continued)

Average Debt: $$$
Applicants: 456
Accepted: 63%
Enrolled: 42%
Grad in 6 Years: 72%
Returning Freshmen: 66%
Academics: ✏️ ✏️ ✏️ ✏️ ½
Social: ☎ ☎ ☎
Q of L: ★ ★ ★ ★
Admissions: (800) 331-5232
Email Address:
   santafe.admissions@sjc.edu

Strong Programs:
The Great Books Program
Liberal Arts and Sciences

The St. John's curriculum, known as "the program," has every student read the Great Books in roughly chronological order.

In their final semester, seniors write a 20- to 60-page critical essay and must pass an hour-long oral examination.

and complain about erratic heating and cooling and a lack of hot water for morning showers.) In Santa Fe, the dorms are small, modern units clustered around courtyards. Most students get singles or divided double rooms. Upperclassmen typically live off campus in apartments and group houses. Meals at both campuses get average reviews.

"With the amount of reading and thinking done here, students most definitely need to find ways to have well-rounded lives. There are pick-up sports, dance groups, musical ensembles, and many other interest-based clubs to participate in," says one student. A senior adds, "We don't have any Greek organizations (besides study groups for reading ancient Greek!)." Drinking is a favored release for Johnnies, who have, of course, read Plato's *Symposium* and are familiar with the likes of François Rabelais ("Drink constantly. You will never die."). Still, hard liquor is not allowed on campus, and parties and kegs must be registered. And although college-sponsored events are patrolled to prevent underage drinking, youngsters tip their share of brew at smaller dorm gatherings. According to one student, only those who are extremely rowdy or disruptive are reported to the dean's office to face penalties. Road trips to Washington, D.C., Baltimore, New York, and Assateague State Park are options for Annapolis students with cars. In Santa Fe, nearby blues and jazz clubs are popular, though one student cautions that the town shuts down around 9 p.m.

> **Popular annual events on both campuses include the Arc party, held to celebrate the sophomores' completion of the Old Testament.**

Popular annual events on both campuses include Lola's, a casino night sponsored by the senior class; the Arc party, held to celebrate the sophomores' completion of the Old Testament; and Reality, a three-day festival of food, games, and general debauchery thrown for the seniors the weekend before commencement. "Sometimes we wear togas," hints a junior. Intercollegiate club teams in crew, sailing, fencing, and croquet are available in Annapolis. The croquet match against The Naval Academy each spring for the Annapolis Cup is the occasion for a genteel lawn party to which the Midshipmen don crisp croquet white while the Johnnies sport uniforms that have ranged from kilts to Viking clothing. Annapolis students relish their intramural teams, with names like the Druids and the Spartans. Santa Fe offers one intercollegiate sport—archery—and a handful of club sports. The nearby Rio Grande and Chama rivers offer excellent white-water canoeing, kayaking, and rafting, while the Hueco Tanks area offers rock climbing and bouldering; the Taos Ski Valley and Ski Santa Fe are excellent in the winter months. The Outdoor Programs Office organizes trips and makes athletic equipment available for use.

"Sometimes we wear togas."

Students at St. John's are as passionate about learning as their peers at other schools are about basketball rivalries or blowout parties. And while those larger colleges and universities try desperately to grow and change, St. John's cherishes its traditions—including the mandate that seniors wear formal academic dress to their oral examinations, which are open to the public. As one happy Johnnie reflects, "A heated discussion about Plato on the grassy knoll is the type of sight that reminds me why I love this place."

Overlaps

Reed, University of Chicago, Bard, Kenyon, University of Maryland, Columbia, William & Mary, Princeton

If You Apply To ›

St. John's: Early decision, early action, regular decision. SATs or ACTs: optional. Accepts the Common Application with supplement. Apply to one campus only.

St. John's University and College of St. Benedict: See page 613.

St. Lawrence University

Canton, NY 13617

St. Lawrence is perched far back in the North Country, closer to Ottawa and Montreal than to Syracuse. The remote Adirondack location breeds camaraderie, and St. Lawrence students have a special bond similar to that at places like Dartmouth and Whitman. Compare to Allegheny and Hobart and William Smith. Environmental studies is the crown jewel: Where else can you live, learn, and work in a Mongolian-style yurt?

St. Lawrence University attracts snow lovers who place equal value on their experiences inside and outside the classroom. Its upstate New York location in St. Lawrence County offers quick access to both pristine ski slopes and rugged hiking trails—and to the bright lights of Ottawa and Montreal. A flood of construction has helped to make the campus almost as breathtaking as the natural beauty that surrounds it. And intimate classes mean it's as easy to form friendships with faculty members as it is with fellow students.

Hiking trails, a river, and a university-owned golf course surround St. Lawrence's 94 buildings, which sit on a 1,000-acre tract; facilities are clustered, so even the most distant buildings are only a 10-minute walk from one another. Many buildings date from the late 19th century. Over the past two decades, the school has invested hundreds of millions of dollars to beautify its campus with infrastructure and buildings that emphasize sustainability. The LEED Gold–certified Johnson Hall of Science supports the biology, chemistry, biochemistry, neuroscience, and psychology programs.

> **"The LINC program connects sophomores with alumni working in their field of interest."**

St. Lawrence, founded in 1856 by members of the progressive Universalist Church, offers a classical liberal arts education, placing a premium on small classes and team teaching. The general education curriculum consists of courses in several liberal arts and science disciplines as well as diversity and environmental literacy requirements. Everyone participates in the two-semester First-Year Program (FYP), which emphasizes critical-thinking, research, and communication skills. Students enroll in an FYP course based on academic interest and live with their classmates in the same residential community. FYP professors also serve as academic advisors. "This program creates an instant living and learning community the moment you step on campus, and students within FYPs become like family," says one student. Optional Sophomore Seminars involve intensive advising, teas and coffees with professors, and ample volunteer and hands-on learning opportunities, including course-related field trips.

Economics is the most popular major, followed by business in the liberal arts (an unusual major that rejects the notion of business as a stand-alone area of study), psychology, government, and biology. Programs in conservation biology, statistics, and global studies are notable, and befitting St. Lawrence's location, Canadian studies is also a specialty. Students in the signature environmental studies program are encouraged to pursue combined majors that integrate the study of environmental issues with substantial study in one of 10 other fields, such

> **"There is a very lively party culture at St. Lawrence."**

as geology, psychology, English, or sociology. Courses demand that students pay attention and keep up with their work, but students say competition is hardly a concern. Since there are no teaching assistants, full professors teach even the introductory courses and make themselves available for extra help; 63 percent of all classes have fewer than 20 students. "My professors are always looking for new ways to challenge students," comments a biology and physics double major.

Website: www.stlawu.edu
Location: Small Town
Private
Total Enrollment: 2,240
Undergraduates: 2,220
Male/Female: 46/54
Financial Aid: 97%
Pell Grant: 23%
Expense: Pr $ $ $ $
Student Loans: 67%
Average Debt: $ $ $
Applicants: 5,217
Accepted: 57%
Enrolled: 20%
Grad in 6 Years: 80%
Returning Freshmen: 89%
Academics: ✍ ✍ ✍
Social: ☎ ☎ ☎
Q of L: ★ ★ ★
Admissions: (315) 229-5261
Email Address: admissions@stlawu.edu

Strong Programs:
Environmental Studies
Conservation Biology
Statistics
Global Studies
Canadian Studies
Economics
Business in the Liberal Arts
Psychology

In an effort "to make the world our classroom," St. Lawrence encourages students to spend time away from campus. Sixty-one percent do so, and while some participate in one of the school's international programs in more than 20 countries, others choose the nearby Adirondack Semester near Tupper Lake, about an hour from campus. Under this program, offered each fall, a small group of students live and study in a yurt village in a park, where they learn wilderness survival skills and take courses on topics such as environmental philosophy and nature writing. The St. Lawrence University Fellowship Program offers housing and $4,000 stipends to selected students for summer research. Internships are popular, too, with 73 percent of students taking part. Students give high ratings to the Center for Career Excellence, especially its Laurentians Investing in Networking and Careers (LINC) mentorship program. "The LINC program connects sophomores with alumni working in their field of interest," explains a participant.

Students enroll in a First-Year Program course based on academic interest and live with their classmates in the same residential community.

Students here are "outdoorsy, community-oriented, and athletic," says a chemistry major. Thirty-seven percent of Laurentians are New Yorkers, and 9 percent are international. Diversity can be a challenge in the North Country, and just 3 percent of students are Black, 6 percent are Hispanic/Latino, 2 percent are Asian American, and 2 percent are multiracial. Politically, the campus is "liberal but not aggressively so," reports a senior. The university awards merit scholarships averaging $23,000 to top students and hands out 44 athletic scholarships for Division I men's and women's ice hockey.

"You can rent out gear for free from the Outdoor Program."

Virtually all students live on campus, and seniors definitely have it best, with access to "spacious townhouses that sit along the golf course," says a sophomore. Everyone else makes do in the "adequate" residence halls, which have mostly double rooms. Fourteen theme houses and two theme floors are also an option. The main dining hall is said to be "satisfactory" most of the time, with accommodations for vegans, vegetarians, and other special diets and themed dinners served up once a month. The university's rural campus is "generally very safe," says a senior. Students credit the administration with actively working to improve how it handles mental health and sexual assault on campus, including implementing a 24-hour mental health hotline.

Befitting St. Lawrence's location, Canadian studies is a specialty.

University-sponsored social activities include a campus pub, first-run movies each week, and the student-run Java Barn music venue—a great place to hear a live band or attend an open-mic night. With 12 percent of the men and 15 percent of the women joining fraternities and sororities, Greek groups are a presence but not a dominant force in campus social life. Students 21 and over are permitted to drink on campus. "There is a very lively party culture at St. Lawrence," says a history major, but students report that alcohol policies are effective and parties rarely get out of hand.

The most popular pastimes include skiing, hiking, kayaking, and generally making the most of St. Lawrence's Adirondack backyard.

The "charming" town of Canton doesn't offer much in the way of nightlife, but it does have a selection of bars, restaurants, and shops and a twice-weekly farmers market; Potsdam, 10 minutes away, offers more. Ottawa and Montreal, where there's better shopping and dining (and the drinking age is lower, too), are easily accessible for weekend road trips. But students say the most popular pastimes include skiing, hiking, rock climbing, kayaking down the Grasse River (when it's not frozen over), and generally making the most of St. Lawrence's Adirondack backyard. "You can rent out gear for free from the Outdoor Program, which allows students to try new things without having to worry about expenses," cheers a junior. Favorite annual traditions include Peak Weekend in the fall, when students, faculty, and staff summit all 46 of the Adirondack High Peaks, and Titus Weekend, when students host a "rail jam" on campus and then head to nearby Titus Mountain to celebrate the winter season with skiing, music, and other festivities.

In varsity sports, the Division I Skating Saints hockey teams are the top draw, especially when the opponent is archrival Clarkson. Solid Division III teams include men's and women's lacrosse, men's soccer, and men's and women's cross-country and track and field; the squash, alpine skiing, and co-ed riding teams are strong too. The golf course doubles as a running route in warmer weather and a cross-country ski trail during the winter. About half of the students participate in 25-plus club sports and a variety of intramurals; available sports range from club hockey to ultimate Frisbee, co-ed soccer, and an annual fall quadathlon.

St. Lawrence makes up for frigid winters with the warmth of a close-knit, caring community. As the frenzied pace of construction winds down and academic standards and career preparation are ratcheted up, St. Lawrence is a school on the rise, especially for those wanting to get back to nature. "St. Lawrence is always looking for ways to improve," comments a junior. "There are always new things being added to the St. Lawrence student experience."

If You Apply To ›

St. Lawrence: Early decision, regular decision. SATs or ACTs: optional. Accepts the Common Application with supplement.

Saint Louis University

221 North Grand Boulevard, St. Louis, MO 63103

SLU is a pleasant oasis amid the bustle of midtown St. Louis, and both the campus and the surrounding neighborhood have been spiffed up in recent decades. In addition to strengths in premed and entrepreneurship, SLU has an unusual specialty in aviation science. Competes with Loyola Chicago and Marquette for bragging rights among Midwestern Jesuit institutions.

Within sight of St. Louis's famed Gateway Arch, the historical gateway to the American West, sits Saint Louis University, which in 1818 became the first university established west of the Mississippi River. The school's academic atmosphere is shaped by the tradition of its founders, the Society of Jesus (Jesuits); administrators ensure that each student receives personal care and attention and expect graduates to contribute to society and lead efforts for social change. Students, in turn, find an atmosphere where their faith is encouraged. SLU offers students many nationally recognized programs, from health sciences to business and, of course, theology. "SLU is the type of university that prepares the whole person to go out into the world," says a freshman.

The SLU campus features pedestrian walkways, lush greenery, fountains, and sculptures, as well as signature Saint Louis University arched gateways at all entrances. Cupples House, a beautiful old mansion in the middle of campus, houses 19th-century furniture and an art gallery—and is just a short walk from the modern Busch Student Center. The center is home to a bookstore, eateries, lounges, and conference facilities. Numerous campus renovations and additions have been undertaken in recent years, including the $50 million Interdisciplinary Science and Engineering Building.

> "SLU is the type of university that prepares the whole person to go out into the world."

In keeping with SLU's strong Jesuit commitment to education in the broadest sense, all undergrads must complete core curriculum requirements in philosophy,

Website: www.slu.edu
Location: City Outskirts
Private
Total Enrollment: 10,665
Undergraduates: 6,628
Male/Female: 37/63
Financial Aid: 88%
Pell Grant: 19%
Expense: Pr $ $
Student Loans: 57%
Average Debt: $ $ $
Applicants: 15,047
Accepted: 70%
Enrolled: 17%
Grad in 6 Years: 80%
Returning Freshmen: 89%
Academics: ✍ ✍ ✍
Social: ☎ ☎
Q of L: ★ ★ ★
Admissions: (314) 977-2500

(continued)

Email Address: admission@
slu.edu

Strong Programs:
Health Sciences ·
Business
Philosophy
Theology
Flight Science
Engineering
Nursing
Exercise Science

SLU offers degree programs in aviation management and flight science, a legacy of the days when St. Louis was an aviation hub.

theology, cultural diversity, communication, mathematics, science, and other foundational disciplines. First-year students participate in summer orientation and a Fall Welcome program before classes begin. The most popular majors are nursing, exercise science, health sciences, and biology. Many students take advantage of premed advising, and five- and six-year direct entry programs allow students to earn advanced degrees in occupational therapy, athletic training, and physical therapy. Business and entrepreneurship majors benefit from the Chaifetz Center for Entrepreneurship, which offers innovation challenges, competitions, and networking events like Billicon Valley. Philosophy and theology are outstanding programs, and SLU attracts scholars from around the globe with one of the world's most complete microfilm collections of Vatican documents. SLU is also home to America's first certified college of aviation and offers degree programs in aviation management and flight science, a legacy of the days when St. Louis was an aviation hub. (Remember Charles Lindbergh's "Spirit of St. Louis"?) Engineering offerings are solid too.

The academic climate at SLU is competitive, and one student says, "This school sets high standards for its students, thereby creating opportunities for a good learning environment." Forty percent of undergraduate classes have fewer than 20 students, but the quality of teaching varies greatly, students say. About a third of SLU undergrads study outside of the United States in more than 50 approved programs across the globe. In Madrid, Spain, SLU has one of the largest and most charming American campuses in Europe. The Micah Program is a living/learning program integrated around themes of peace, justice, and service—it takes its name from the biblical prophet Micah, who spoke out against social injustice in ancient Israel.

SLU students tend to be "friendly and pretty laid-back," says a senior, but "most take school seriously." Many undergraduates come from private, religiously affiliated high schools; 22 percent are Roman Catholic. Thirty-seven percent hail from the Show-Me State, while 4 percent come from abroad. Black students constitute 7 percent of the student body, Asian Americans 13 percent, Hispanics/Latinos 8 percent, and multiracial students 5 percent.

"This school sets high standards for its students."

Consistent with SLU's Jesuit heritage, human rights and inclusion are prominent issues of debate. The school offers athletic scholarships as well as merit scholarships worth an average of $22,000.

Fifty-four percent of undergraduates live on campus, and about half of the freshmen take part in residential learning communities centered on a specific theme or interest. Upperclassmen can move into spacious courtyard-style apartments, but many opt for less expensive apartments off campus. "The dorms are sufficient," one student says. "They're nothing to brag about." Meals at the university's 20 on-campus dining locations are reportedly tasty, with vegetarian, vegan, halal, and gluten-free options available. Students say they feel safe on campus thanks to an active public safety department and the continuing improvement of surrounding neighborhoods.

Atlas Week is a celebration of diversity that includes the Parade of Nations, cultural performances, speakers, and the Billiken World Festival.

Social life at SLU includes campus events, such as movies in the Quad, dances, and Greek parties, and the plethora of restaurants and coffee shops in St. Louis, as well as movie theaters, museums, bars, sporting events, and nightlife. A student says, "The social life is very active. Students know how to juggle personal with academic lives." Greek life at SLU—unusual for a Jesuit institution—claims 11 percent of the men and 25 percent of the women. Students say most parties take place in off-campus apartments or at an off-campus fraternity house, and despite the rules limiting alcohol on campus, it's common in the apartments. Homecoming in the fall and the VIBE concert in the spring feature bands, club-sponsored booths, and vendors. Atlas Week is a weeklong celebration of diversity that includes the Parade of Nations, cultural performances, speakers, and the Billiken World Festival. True to tradition, Sunday evening mass is usually packed with students of all beliefs, and more than 80 percent of students participate in community service and outreach projects. Road trips to Kansas City, Chicago, and schools like the University of Illinois and Indiana University are also popular.

SLU has no varsity football team, but other Billiken squads more than compensate for this deficit. (A billiken was a charm doll and a common good-luck charm in the early 1900s. A popular sportswriter of the time said the charm resembled the then-football coach, and the name stuck.) Teams compete in the Division I Atlantic 10 Conference, and the Billiken's men's soccer, basketball, and baseball teams and women's soccer, basketball, and volleyball teams are the most competitive. For weekend warriors, the Simon Recreation Center boasts a 40-meter pool, six racquetball courts, and loads of equipment. Sand volleyball and flag football are popular intramural sports.

Saint Louis University is winning students' devotion and increasing its national visibility by offering a slew of strong programs. The Jesuit education prepares students to work for a more just and humane world. "SLU is a good choice for its relatively moderate-sized classrooms, its dedication toward a Jesuit mission, and its enjoyable learning environment," says a senior.

If You Apply To ›

SLU: Early decision I and II, early action, regular decision. SATs or ACTs: optional. Accepts the Common Application with supplement. Apply to particular programs.

St. Mary's College of Maryland

St. Mary's City, MD 20686

A public liberal arts institution of the same breed as Mary Washington, UNC Asheville, and much larger William & Mary. The college's historic but sleepy environs are 90 minutes from D.C. and Baltimore on Maryland's western shore. With the Chesapeake Bay close at hand, St. Mary's College is a haven for sailors and nature enthusiasts. Maryland's public honors college is a well-kept secret beyond the state's borders.

Thirty-one years ago, St. Mary's College of Maryland was just another public college, albeit one with a gorgeous waterfront campus in the oldest continuously inhabited English settlement in the New World. In 1992, the state of Maryland decided to make St. Mary's College its public honors college—and the rest, as they say around here, is history. Students can easily design their own majors, undertake independent research projects, or work closely with professors to investigate whatever interests them.

St. Mary's College has never been connected with any religious denomination and takes its name from its founding in 1840 in St. Mary's City, the original capital of Maryland. The campus sits on a peninsula in southern Maryland where the Potomac River meets the Chesapeake Bay. Not surprisingly, it has an excellent center for estuary research, as well as a strong working relationship with the Chesapeake Biological Laboratory; the school even has its own marina right on the St. Mary's River, with a shoreline that gets beautiful sunset views. Architectural

Website: www.smcm.edu
Location: Rural
Public
Total Enrollment: 1,497
Undergraduates: 1,473
Male/Female: 42/58
Financial Aid: 88%
Pell Grant: 18%
Expense: Pub $ $ $ $
Student Loans: 59%
Average Debt: $ $
Applicants: 2,872
Accepted: 77%

(continued)

Enrolled: 17%
Grad in 6 Years: 73%
Returning Freshmen: 85%
Academics: ✍ ✍ ✍ ✍
Social: ☎ ☎ ☎
Q of L: ★ ★ ★ ★
Admissions: (240) 895-5000
Email Address: admissions@
smcm.edu

Strong Programs:
Biology
Anthropology
Chemistry
Biochemistry
English
Music
Psychology
Environmental Studies

All seniors complete a capstone requirement, usually in the form of a yearlong research project known as the St. Mary's Project.

styles range from colonial to modern buildings, though the land on which the campus is built belongs to a 1,100-acre national historic landmark, commemorating Maryland's first colonial settlement. For that reason, students may step over archaeological digs as they stroll to class. The new Performing Arts Center, featuring a 700-seat auditorium, a 125-seat recital hall, studios, classrooms, and rehearsal spaces, opened in 2022.

The college's core curriculum, known as LEAD (Learning through Experiential and Applied Discovery), emphasizes hands-on experience and career development alongside breadth in the liberal arts. Entering students take a writing-intensive, discussion-focused First Year Seminar. They may choose from two dozen topics—ranging from The Attention Economy to The War on Science—taught by professors from every discipline at the college. To fulfill gen-ed requirements, students can select a Core Inquiry, a set of linked classes that explores a theme, such as Public and Environmental Health, Climate, or Justice, from different disciplinary perspectives. Students also progress through a series of courses over their four years on leadership, teamwork, and career development. Additionally, the Honors College Promise guarantees that every student will have access to a research, internship, or study abroad experience. All seniors complete a capstone requirement, usually in the form of a yearlong research project known as the St. Mary's Project.

> **"Seize the opportunity to go abroad, because SMCM is very helpful."**

Biology is among the most popular majors and also one of the more difficult programs; students can spend time on the college's research boat when they tire of the lab. Students also sign up in droves for psychology, environmental studies, and economics. Anthropology, chemistry, biochemistry, and English are traditional strengths, and the standout music department includes prize-winning pianist Brian Ganz. The college recently launched new majors in business administration and management, performing arts, and marine science. Aside from the 23 established majors (which include eight cross-disciplinary study areas), more freethinking types may design their own majors.

"Because of the nature of an honors college, all students who attend St. Mary's are academically focused, and there is a common goal to succeed," explains a senior. Sixty-seven percent of classes have fewer than 20 students, and professors are said to be accessible and well respected. "Professors at St. Mary's are always engaged in research and like to involve students in the process," says a psychology major.

St. Mary's College offers study abroad semesters at Fudan University in China, James Cook University in Australia, Sciences Po in France, and Stellenbosch University in South Africa, among others, as well as short-term study tours in several other countries. Forty percent of students study internationally. "Seize the opportunity to go abroad," recommends a psychology major, "because SMCM is very helpful with making sure you have the materials and info you need." The Washington Program places students in top summer internships with the government, nonprofits, and think tanks in Washington, D.C., and also offers mentoring from alumni.

> **"It's virtually impossible to graduate without knowing how to sail."**

Ninety-three percent of undergraduates come from Maryland, which gives the campus a homegrown feel; less than 1 percent come from foreign countries. Students acknowledge that campus diversity, while growing, has a long way to go. Black students account for 11 percent of the student body, Hispanics/Latinos 8 percent, Asian Americans 4 percent, and multiracial students 5 percent. A sociology major comments that politically conservative students "might have a tough time fitting in." St. Mary's College is more expensive than other publics in Maryland but much less expensive than the private liberal arts colleges with which it also competes. Qualified students receive merit scholarships worth an average of $4,500. There are no athletic awards.

Campus housing is guaranteed for all four years, but students report that facilities are in need of updates. Eighty-two percent of full-time students live on campus. Most residence halls are co-ed, although open (gender-neutral) housing is available; apartments and townhouses are reserved for upperclassmen. Off-campus housing options include old farmhouses and riverside cottages for rent. "The Great Room (our cafeteria) is one of the best parts about living on campus and one of the reasons you frequently see seniors still on unlimited meal plans," cheers a senior. Regarding campus safety, a student says, "I feel incredibly safe as a woman on my campus, and the Title IX office takes things really seriously here."

St. Mary's College doesn't have fraternities or sororities, and its secluded peninsular location means there's little nightlife off campus, but one senior confirms, "The fun that happens on campus is more than enough to make up for that!" The student-run Programs Board organizes events like concerts, comedians, and costume parties, and for the culture-hungry, there are also theaters, an art gallery, lectures, and films on campus. Students report that the party scene is limited and alcohol policies are strictly enforced. The St. Mary's River offers a wealth of outdoor activities. "Most days if we aren't in class, you'll find us paddleboarding, sailing, kayaking, swimming, or just studying on the docks. On nice days, there's a summer-camp atmosphere to it all," says one student. Another adds, "It's virtually impossible to graduate without knowing how to sail." The waterfront also becomes the focus of campuswide activities, including the bamboo boat race held each fall, Bay-to-Bay Service Day and the Bottom County music festival in April, and the end-of-year World Carnival.

Campuswide activities on the waterfront include the Bottom County music festival in April and the end-of-year World Carnival.

The college fields 21 varsity Seahawks teams, most of which compete in the Division III United East Conference; men's soccer and women's lacrosse are among the most successful. The college also boasts a nationally ranked sailing program. About a quarter of the students take part in recreational sports; floor hockey, dodgeball, and soccer are favorite intramurals, while rugby, ultimate Frisbee, and equestrian are the most popular club sports.

St. Mary's College has worked hard to establish itself as one of the nation's premier public liberal arts colleges. Though its small size and remote location can feel confining to some, students leave with a solid grounding in the liberal arts—and the close bonds that they forge with friends during peaceful days on the St. Mary's River. For those looking to be part of an intellectual community in a small-town setting, St. Mary's College just might be a place to set sail.

Overlaps

Beloit, Dickinson, Guilford, University of Mary Washington, UNC Asheville, UMBC, Washington College, William & Mary

If You Apply To ›

St. Mary's: Early decision, early action, regular decision. SATs or ACTs: optional. Accepts the Common Application with supplement.

Saint Michael's College

One Winooski Park, Colchester, VT 05439

Liberal arts college founded by Edmundites located near a top college town with breathtaking views of the Adirondack and Green mountains. Cheerful, service-oriented academic community with most students being New Englanders. Proximity to Burlington helps make for vibrant social scene. Easy access to Montreal and to some of the best skiing and snowboarding in the East.

Website: www.smcvt.edu
Location: Small City
Private
Total Enrollment: 1,437
Undergraduates: 1,395
Male/Female: 46/54
Financial Aid: 99%
Pell Grant: 28%
Expense: Pr $ $
Student Loans: 71%
Average Debt: $ $ $ $
Applicants: 2,359
Accepted: 86%
Enrolled: 16%
Grad in 6 Years: 78%
Returning Freshmen: 86%
Academics: ✐ ✐ ✐
Social: 🍺 🍺 🍺 🍺
Q of L: ★ ★ ★
Admissions: (800) 762-8000
Email Address: admission@smcvt.edu

Strong Programs:
Business
Psychology
Education
Biology
Environmental Science
Religious Studies
Neuroscience
Prepharmacy

Saint Michael's College carries the distinction of being the only Edmundite institution of higher learning in the world. The college was established by the Society of Saint Edmund, a group of Roman Catholic country priests who took Saint Edmund, Archbishop of Canterbury, as their patron and spiritual inspiration. The Society maintains an on-campus presence to this day, and the influence of the patron saint can be found in the college's dedication to meaningful residential experiences, comprehensive liberal arts, and social justice. A junior says, "Saint Michael's teaches students to go out into the world and work to make it a better place."

Founded in 1904, Saint Michael's sits on 440 acres overlooking Vermont's Green Mountains and the Winooski River. Just five minutes from Burlington, the campus features redbrick architecture, themed gardens, a central quad, a 340-acre natural area, and even a working farm. To the east, Mount Mansfield—Vermont's tallest peak—provides a spectacular backdrop. The Dion Family Student Center and Quad Commons residence hall overlook the mountains and use geothermal heating and cooling, among other green technologies.

Under the core curriculum, all students take four courses: First-Year Seminar, Fundamental Philosophical Questions, Study of Christian Traditions and Thought, and Junior Seminar. Seniors complete a capstone project as part of a senior seminar in their major. Students also meet requirements in the areas of Intellectual Exploration (liberal arts and sciences), Edmundite Tradition, and Professional Competencies, which encourage experiential learning.

Saint Michael's offers a plethora of solid programs, including business, psychology, education, biology, environmental science, and religious studies. Neuroscience is a top draw, too, and new majors in public health and equity studies have been added. A 3–2 engineering program with nearby University of Vermont and a prepharmacy program

"My classroom experiences have ranged from OK to legitimately transformative."

are popular, and a 4+1 Masters in Teaching program allows education majors to earn a master's degree and teaching license in just one additional year. Students may also take advantage of cross-registration options with Champlain College.

"My classroom experiences have ranged from OK to legitimately transformative," says an English major. "Most of the time, it just feels like I'm getting a good education." Sixty percent of classes have fewer than 20 students, and many are taught in a discussion-based format. Students praise professors for their knowledge and willingness to make themselves available. "Professors are very devoted to the success of their students," observes a senior, and student support services generally receive favorable reviews.

The Honors Program inducts 14 percent of undergraduates, who take specialized core courses and a colloquium, live in honors housing, and complete a senior honors project in their major. A hefty 31 percent of Saint Michael's students take part in undergraduate research, and each year, about 50 students receive stipends for full-time work as research partners with faculty during the summer. More than

100 study abroad options include such far-flung locales as Argentina, Ghana, India, Tanzania, and Denmark; 36 percent of undergraduates participate.

On campus, says a senior, "I always see people smiling and being generous and helpful to others." Just under half of the student body is Catholic. Black students account for only 2 percent of the student body, Hispanics/Latinos 6 percent, Asian Americans 2 percent, and multiracial students 2 percent. Typically, about 15 percent come from Vermont and 4 percent from foreign countries. Student organizations like the Diversity Coalition and Martin Luther King Jr. Society put on events throughout the year to support inclusion on campus. The political atmosphere is heavily liberal, and a senior identifies "white privilege, white supremacy, and gun control" as hot-button issues. The college offers merit awards averaging $23,900 to qualified students, and a limited number of athletic scholarships are available in 18 of the college's 21 varsity sports.

Students are required to spend all four years on campus in the residence halls, which a sophomore says "creates a sense of community among the different classes." All first-year students are housed in living/learning communities organized around four main themes: leadership, service, wellness, and approaches to transition. Residence

"[Burlington] consists of young people and entrepreneurs, offering a fun atmosphere."

halls include traditional dorms with double and single rooms, suites with shared living spaces, townhouses, and apartment-style accommodations. Campus dining options include an unlimited meal plan at the Green Mountain Dining Room; meals are said to be "decently good" but repetitive. Students report feeling safe on campus, and while there have been instances of sexual assault, says one student, the school "always informs us of what steps they are taking to protect the community and hold those who were responsible accountable."

Socially, says a sophomore, "There's a good mix of hanging out on campus, going downtown, and going skiing or hiking with friends." Despite the lack of Greek life, there is a reliably lively party scene. Apart from senior housing, the campus is dry, and students describe a no-pressure, safety-oriented attitude toward drinking. The Residential Initiative Program delivers a slew of alternative weekend options. Campuswide activities include comedians, coffeehouse music and poetry performances, and talent shows. Every Friday and Saturday night, the college hosts the Weekend Grilling Program, which provides free food between 11 p.m. and 1 a.m. Fall and spring concerts are popular campus events, and students relish the annual P-Day (Preparation Day) tradition, which is "a time for students to relax before finals" with free food, bouncy houses, lawn games, a movie screening, and live music, according to an English major. Popular excursions "are to downtown Burlington or to the mountains and great outdoors like Mount Mansfield or Camel's Hump," says one student. Montreal, just 90 minutes away, is a popular weekend trip.

Nearby Burlington (population 45,000) is "a great college town, as it contains two other colleges: UVM and Champlain," a sophomore says. "The area consists of young people and entrepreneurs, offering a fun atmosphere to eat, shop, and go out." Saint Michael's students receive a free bus pass that will take them downtown, and the Saint Michael's Cultural Pass gives students unlimited access to performances at Burlington's Flynn Theater for little or no cost. An unrestricted (and deeply discounted) season pass to Sugarbush Ski Resort is available as well. Seventy percent of students get involved in at least one service program through MOVE (Mobilization of Volunteer Efforts) over the course of their college careers; "Volunteering is a huge aspect of life at Saint Michael's," confirms one student.

Saint Michael's fields 21 Division II sports, the majority of which compete in the Northeast-10 Conference. Competitive Purple Knights teams include alpine skiing, men's and women's lacrosse and ice hockey, and men's basketball. Club and

Overlaps

Saint Anselm, Stonehill, Salve Regina, Merrimack, Assumption University, Providence, St. Lawrence, Holy Cross

intramural programs draw 40 percent of students and include the Adventure Sports Center, which organizes about 75 outings per semester, including sea kayaking, rock and ice climbing, white-water rafting, and other outdoor pursuits.

Saint Michael's College attracts students who appreciate the unique vision inspired by Saint Edmund so many years ago—not to mention the beautiful Vermont setting—and who want to use their education for the betterment of the world. An English major reflects, "St. Mike's is a weird mash-up of progressive, traditional, humble, compassionate people who just want to be good for the world and do the right thing."

St. Olaf College

1520 St. Olaf Avenue, Northfield, MN 55057

Grounded in strong Lutheran traditions, St. Olaf boasts a religiously diverse student body, strong academics, and a global orientation. Has more of a Midwestern feel than crosstown rival Carleton, but is a leader among liberal arts colleges in the percentage of students who study abroad. The St. Olaf Choir is world famous. With about 2,900 students, St. Olaf is on the big side of small.

Website: wp.stolaf.edu
Location: Small Town
Private
Total Enrollment: 2,948
Undergraduates: 2,948
Male/Female: 42/58
Financial Aid: 75%
Pell Grant: 22%
Expense: Pr $ $
Student Loans: 63%
Average Debt: $ $
Applicants: 6,494
Accepted: 47%
Enrolled: 24%
Grad in 6 Years: 85%
Returning Freshmen: 91%
Academics: ✍ ✍ ✍ ✍
Social: 🎭 🎭 🎭
Q of L: ★ ★ ★ ★
Admissions: (800) 800-3025
Email Address: admissions@stolaf.edu

Strong Programs:
Biology

St. Olaf College's home is Northfield, Minnesota, which bills itself as the city of "Cows, Colleges, and Contentment." Founded in 1874 by Norwegian Lutheran immigrants and affiliated with the Evangelical Lutheran Church in America, St. Olaf provides a solid liberal arts education and plenty of opportunities to study abroad. One Ole describes her peers at St. Olaf as "Minnesota nice" (not, by the way, a characteristic inherited from the not-so-nice 11th-century Norwegian king who became the school's namesake). "I wanted a school with an atmosphere of hard work, but without demoralizing competitiveness, and that is what I've found at St. Olaf," remarks a satisfied senior.

St. Olaf's meticulously landscaped 350-acre campus is located on Manitou Heights, overlooking the Cannon River valley and the town of Northfield (population 21,000). More than 10,000 trees, native prairie, and a wetlands wildlife area surround the 34 native limestone buildings that form the campus. Holland Hall, built in 1925, was modeled on the Mont-Saint-Michel monastery in France. Regents Hall of Natural and Mathematical Sciences, a 200,000-square-foot science center, earned the prestigious LEED Platinum rating. A new 300-bed residence hall and townhouse-style residences housing 140 students opened in 2022.

> "I wanted a school with an atmosphere of hard work, but without demoralizing competitiveness."

In addition to distribution requirements in a range of liberal arts subjects, St. Olaf's core curriculum includes an OLE Experience in Practice requirement that asks students to engage in significant hands-on learning, whether through an independent research project, study abroad, an internship, or other faculty-led coursework or experiences. All first-year students complete a first-year seminar and a writing and rhetoric course, requirements that can be fulfilled either by taking individual courses or by signing up for a Conversation Program—an interdisciplinary, team-taught program that brings together students and faculty for a critical exploration of specific topics within their historical, cultural, and social contexts. Programs include Enduring Questions, American Conversations, Asian Conversations, Environmental Conversations, and Race Matters. These signature one- to two-year programs "take care of a ton of general requirements, but they are extremely rigorous," cautions one freshman. Two additional programs—the Science Conversation and the Public Affairs Conversation—are open to sophomores and upperclassmen, respectively.

(continued)

Economics
Psychology
Mathematics
Music
Dance
Chemistry
Norwegian

Biology, economics, psychology, and mathematics are the most popular majors and some of the school's best. The music department draws high praise; it offers many performance opportunities with eight school choirs and seven instrumental ensembles. The St. Olaf Choir performs in major venues around the nation and can be heard singing with the Minnesota Orchestra. Dance and chemistry are also notable, and, not surprisingly, Norwegian is a specialty. The Center for Integrative Studies allows students to form their own majors.

Academically, Oles (pronounced "Oh-lees") have their work cut out for them, but they say the atmosphere on campus is supportive and encouraging. Students hold faculty members in high regard for their engaging approaches to teaching. "The professors really show care and concern for each individual student's learning," says a quantitative economics major. Fifty-two percent of the classes have fewer than 20 students, and instructors reportedly have as many as 10 hours of open-office time a week. The Piper Center for Vocation and Career receives high ratings, especially for its Connections Program trips, which take students to major cities nationwide to network with alumni. "I had the chance to go on the San Francisco trip and we visited alums at Google, Apple, Cisco, and several start-ups," says a junior.

In the last quarter century, St. Olaf has cultivated an international agenda for its students and faculty, and it consistently ranks among the top baccalaureate liberal arts colleges in the country for the percentage of students who study abroad. Seventy-three percent of students participate. In addition to approved partner and exchange programs, St. Olaf offers as many as 100 study abroad programs in more than 40 countries, including St. Olaf's faculty-led Global Semester and Environmental Science in Australia and New Zealand programs. Research opportunities are available in all disciplines, and are especially robust in the sciences; about half of the students take advantage of them.

The OLE Experience in Practice requirement asks students to engage in significant hands-on learning, such as independent research or an internship.

"The professors really show care and concern for each individual student's learning."

"We work hard for what we want and don't give up when things get tough," comments a sophomore. "Oles are a very tenacious bunch." Forty-three percent of students hail from Minnesota, and 10 percent come from overseas. Asian Americans make up 6 percent, Hispanics/Latinos 8 percent, Black students 3 percent, and multiracial students 4 percent, and the college is actively recruiting more students from diverse backgrounds. Nineteen percent of students are Lutheran; chapel services, though not mandatory, are held daily. Most students are high achievers from Midwestern public schools, drawn in part by hundreds of merit scholarships, which average $19,700 each year. St. Olaf has a tradition of meeting the full demonstrated need of all admitted students.

Ninety percent of undergrads reside in on-campus housing or in college-owned houses available off campus. All first-years live together in four dedicated dorms, where Junior Counselors on each floor plan fun community activities; upperclassmen enjoy suite-style layouts. Students eat in one large, modern dining hall and rave about the meals: "The food is way better than I ever thought college food could be," cheers a vocal performance major. They can also use their meal plans at neighboring Carleton's two dining halls (and vice versa). Students give good ratings to campus safety and report that efforts to educate the community about campus sexual assault have been effective.

The four-day Christmas Festival features televised choir concerts and hearty Scandinavian food in the dining hall.

St. Olaf's social life takes place mostly on campus, and weekend spots include a student-run nightclub called the Pause (beloved for its pizza and live entertainment) and a coffeehouse, the Cage. The fine arts department provides many music, theater, and dance performances. "St. Olaf is a dry campus, meaning no alcohol, but the policy isn't strictly enforced," explains a senior, and while there are no fraternities or sororities, a low-key party scene can be found. The Student Activities Committee sponsors frequent dances, speakers, and cultural events, covered by student fees and at-the-door ticket sales. The most talked-about annual event, which has been running for more than 100 years, is the four-day Christmas Festival, during which five choirs and the St. Olaf Orchestra combine in televised concerts celebrating Christmas—and the college dining hall serves hearty Scandinavian food.

"Northfield is a pretty active small town with festivals, live music, and other activities," says a political science and economics major. The town also offers a decent number of coffee shops, cafés, and bars, as well as two breweries; Froggy's and the Contented Cow are favorite hangouts. Each September, the locals reenact the failed 1876 attempt by Jesse James to rob the town bank. "Students are actively involved in community mentor, volunteer, and outreach programs," reports a student. For those seeking a taste of city life, buses leave regularly for the twin cities of Minneapolis and St. Paul, less than an hour's drive, where one can experience a shopper's paradise at the huge Mall of America.

"Oles are a very tenacious bunch."

St. Olaf has outstanding Division III athletic programs. The Oles men's soccer, men's and women's cross-country, and swimming and diving teams are consistently competitive in the Minnesota Intercollegiate Athletic Conference, and the Nordic and Alpine skiing teams have achieved national success. The St. Olaf football team battles rival Carleton for the honor of having the statue in the town's square face the winning campus. The chorus of St. Olaf's fight song is "Um! Yah! Yah!" which has become a popular chant on campus. Students can also take their pick of more than 25 club sports and 20 intramurals; broomball—ice hockey played with brooms instead of sticks and shoes rather than skates—is the sport of choice in the winter. The men's and women's ultimate Frisbee club teams are nationally competitive.

For those yearning for a school where spirituality and scholarship exist on the same exalted plane, St. Olaf could be the right place to spend four years. It's a school where students work hard, are encouraged by good teachers, toughened by Minnesota winters, and nourished by strong moral values and community spirit.

Overlaps

Gustavus Adolphus, Macalester, Luther, Carleton, Grinnell, University of St. Thomas, Lawrence, Augustana (IL)

If You Apply To ›

St. Olaf: Early decision I and II, early action, regular decision. SATs or ACTs: optional. Accepts the Common Application with supplement. Music applicants must submit additional application.

University of San Diego

5998 Alcalá Park, San Diego, CA 92110

With a panoramic view of the Pacific Ocean, USD is riding a wave of popularity enhanced by its sun-drenched location. Not to be confused with its UC counterpart across town, USD is now a popular alternative to Roman Catholic peers the University of San Francisco and Santa Clara. Strong in business, engineering, and study abroad.

Students at the University of San Diego have many reasons to cheer: a beatific oceanside campus, a rich Roman Catholic heritage centered around ethical conduct and compassionate service, and an array of superb academics. "USD is becoming more and more competitive, and the academic programs continue to get better," says one freshman. "There has never been a better time to come to USD than right now."

Founded in 1949, USD occupies 180 acres on a mesa overlooking San Diego's Mission Bay and is only two miles north of downtown San Diego. The buildings are designed in 16th-century Spanish Renaissance architectural style in a nod to San Diego's Catholic heritage and the Universidad de Alcalá in Spain. In a fitting architectural juxtaposition, at one end of campus is the Joan B. Kroc (of McDonald's fame) Institute for Peace and Justice; at the other end is the Jenny Craig Pavilion, featuring facilities where you can work off your Big Macs. Newer additions include the Learning Commons, which houses the Honors Program, the Writing Center, flexible classrooms, and collaboration rooms.

USD's core curriculum focuses on integrating knowledge and experiences from different disciplines. The core encompasses Competencies, such as writing and critical thinking; Foundations courses in theology, philosophy, ethics, and diversity and inclusion; and Explorations courses in five general liberal arts areas. A fourth component, Integrative Learning, is the focus of the first year, when new students join one

> **"[My LLC] really enabled me to find out more about myself and what I am passionate about."**

of five living/learning communities (LLCs): Cultivator, Collaborator, Advocate, Illuminator, and Innovator. In addition to taking a fall-semester course related to the theme of their LLC and living together with their classmates in the residence halls, first-years also have access to a "scholastic assistant," an older student who serves as a mentor and organizes out-of-class activities. Students describe the LLCs as integral to their transition to college life. "Being a part of programs such as these really enabled me to find out more about myself and what I am passionate about," says a communication studies major.

USD offers more than 60 degree programs—an impressive number given its relatively small student body—across seven schools: business, leadership and education sciences, law, nursing and health science, arts and sciences, engineering, and peace studies. Some of the most popular undergraduate majors include business administration, finance, marketing, behavioral neuroscience, accountancy, communication studies, and psychology. Engineering is a traditional strength. Forty percent of classes have fewer than 20 students, but none exceed 50, which allows for classroom discussions and collaborative projects. "The workload is substantial, but it is also feasible," says a political science major. Professors are said to be knowledgeable and accessible. Career services receive good ratings, especially when it comes to finding internships.

The Honors Program offers small classes and a core curriculum of innovative courses to qualified students. More than 200 students across the university present research projects at USD's annual undergraduate research conference. Those who overdose on Southern California's ubiquitous blue skies and sunshine may take part in USD's robust study abroad program, which sends students to live and study in their choice of more than 30 countries and more than 80 programs, including a permanent program at the University of San Diego Madrid Center in Spain. Nearly half of all undergrads participate in yearlong, semester, summer, or intersession programs.

At USD, a business major says, "I have never yet met a person who doesn't put their heart and soul into their work." Fifty-nine percent of undergrads hail from the Golden State, 6 percent are international, and many come from affluent

Website: www.sandiego.edu
Location: City Center
Private
Total Enrollment: 7,106
Undergraduates: 5,481
Male/Female: 44/56
Financial Aid: 76%
Pell Grant: 19%
Expense: Pr $ $
Student Loans: 46%
Average Debt: $ $
Applicants: 14,326
Accepted: 53%
Enrolled: 15%
Grad in 6 Years: 80%
Returning Freshmen: 92%
Academics: ✍ ✍ ✍
Social: ☎ ☎ ☎ ☎
Q of L: ★ ★ ★ ★
Admissions: (800) 248-4873
Email Address: admissions@sandiego.edu

Strong Programs:
Engineering
Business Administration
Finance
Marketing
Behavioral Neuroscience
Accountancy
Communication Studies
Psychology

First-year students join one of five living/learning communities (LLCs): Cultivator, Collaborator, Advocate, Illuminator, and Innovator.

backgrounds. "Low-income students would have a hard time here because students engage in expensive activities outside of class," remarks a senior. Black students account for 3 percent of the student body, Hispanics/Latinos 23 percent, Asian Americans 8 percent, and multiracial students 8 percent. Thirty-eight percent of students are Catholic, and there is a healthy conservative presence on campus, but one freshman notes, "The university is making a big push toward acceptance and understanding of all people and beliefs." The school offers merit awards averaging $19,300 to qualified students, and there are more than 100 athletic awards.

Forty-two percent of undergraduates live on campus, and all but commuters are required to do so for both their first and second year. Residence halls are a mix of singles, doubles, triples, and limited quads, with singles and doubles representing the majority of the units. Apartments range from one room to four bedrooms. When the dinner bell rings, students have plenty to cheer about. "Meals are delicious," says one junior. "Dining facilities are nice, clean, and a hot place to be at all hours of the day." Campus security is excellent, students say, with officers on duty around the clock. "A huge sexual assault awareness task force has done a lot of good things after a few accusations in the past few years," according to a senior.

And how about the campus social scene? "Mission Beach, where most upperclassmen live, has a vibrant social scene. Many USD students congregate in the area on weekends," a finance major explains. For those who choose to eschew the sand and waves, USD offers a slate of on-campus activities, including movies, concerts, and mass (lest you forget, USD is a Catholic university). The Greek scene attracts 18 percent of the men and 30 percent of the women. Alcohol is allowed only in designated areas for those students of legal age, and "this policy is heavily enforced by the RAs," says a marketing major. Downtown San Diego has plenty to offer, including a bevy of bars, eateries, and shopping centers. The USD community is big on giving back, too, via more than 300,000 hours of service each year. Popular road trips include Las Vegas and Big Bear. Back on campus, students enjoy annual festivals such as International Week and Greek Week, the Alcalá Bazaar, and the Olé Music Fest.

> **"I have never yet met a person who doesn't put their heart and soul into their work."**

USD sponsors 17 Division I intercollegiate teams and is a member of the West Coast Conference for all sports except football, which competes in the Pioneer League. Students are especially rowdy when the Torero basketball team takes on rival Gonzaga. Football, men's golf, women's volleyball and basketball, and men's and women's tennis have been competitive in recent years. Sixteen percent of students participate in intramural and club sports; among the most popular are ultimate Frisbee, dodgeball, soccer, and lacrosse.

Don't underestimate USD—this small, friendly institution offers a rich variety of academic programs, and its students seem to understand that they are living out their college careers in one of the most beautiful spots in the country. As a sophomore reflects, "The great thing about USD is you can get a great education in a challenging academic environment and in one of the most beautiful cities in the nation."

Overlaps

Loyola Marymount, Pepperdine, Santa Clara, University of San Francisco, Gonzaga, UC San Diego, UCLA, UC Santa Barbara

If You Apply To ›

USD: Regular decision. SATs or ACTs: not considered. Accepts the Common Application.

University of San Francisco

2130 Fulton Street, San Francisco, CA 94117

Talk about prime real estate: USF is next door to the legendary Haight–Ashbury district, down the street from Golden Gate Park, and within five miles of the Pacific Ocean. Though USF is a Jesuit institution, just a fifth of its students are Roman Catholic. Asia Pacific studies is a standout, along with preprofessional offerings. Big emphasis on service learning.

Founded by the Society of Jesus (Jesuits) in 1855, the University of San Francisco has evolved to reflect the energy and freewheeling spirit of the city that it calls home. Its culturally diverse collection of undergraduates feast on nursing, biology, business, and other academic challenges in a liberal arts setting that encourages them to use their knowledge and experiences to change the world for the better.

USF's 55 well-kept acres, spotted with beautiful basilica-type buildings and modern facilities, are, as one student puts it, "wedged into the heart of San Francisco." The campus stands atop one of San Francisco's seven hills, adjacent to Golden Gate Park, overlooking San Francisco Bay and the city skyline. The Lone Mountain East residence hall, housing 600 sophomores in apartment-style units, opened in 2021.

The 44-unit Core Curriculum requires students to take courses in six major categories: foundation of communication; math and sciences; humanities; philosophy, theology, and ethics; social sciences; and visual and performing arts. All students take at least one Community Engaged Learning class to build local relationships and volunteer in the community. Optional first-year seminars give students insights

> "Internships and service learning are definitely big parts of the education here at USF."

into unique topics and a taste of the city through excursions and other enrichment activities; recent topics include the ethics of artificial intelligence and the immigrant experience in the Bay Area. The Muscat Scholars Program supports incoming first-generation students in their transition to college life, and the Black Achievement Success and Engagement initiative provides a rigorous scholars program, resource center, living/learning community, and full-tuition scholarship for Black-identified students.

Undergraduates at USF choose from more than 100 majors, minors, and interdisciplinary concentrations. The university places a strong emphasis on its preprofessional programs in nursing, science, communications, and business. By enrollment, nursing, psychology, finance, and marketing are the most popular majors. Biology, data science, entrepreneurship and innovation, and hospitality management are also strengths. In the School of Nursing's Simulation Lab, nursing students interact with state-of-the-art mannequins, including adult, pediatrics, and obstetrics, that simulate symptoms and conditions specific to real-life patients and scenarios. The Center for Asia Pacific Studies enhances interdisciplinary majors with an Asian focus, as does the Asian studies program. The visual arts program provides courses in art education, graphic and fine art, drawing, painting, art history, and museum studies. Newer majors include engineering, which offers concentrations in electrical and computer, environmental, and sustainable civil engineering. Accelerated, three-year bachelor's degree options are available in 21 majors, as are dual-degree bachelor's/master's programs in several preprofessional fields.

Some of the preprofessional majors are quite demanding, and "competition for internships and leadership opportunities can get intense," says an advertising major. But students agree that the climate in the classroom is generally more relaxed

Website: www.usfca.edu
Location: City Center
Private
Total Enrollment: 7,722
Undergraduates: 5,728
Male/Female: 35/65
Financial Aid: 87%
Pell Grant: 28%
Expense: Pr $ $
Student Loans: 58%
Average Debt: $ $ $ $
Applicants: 22,372
Accepted: 71%
Enrolled: 9%
Grad in 6 Years: 76%
Returning Freshmen: 86%
Academics: ✎ ✎ ✎
Social: ☎ ☎ ☎
Q of L: ★ ★ ★ ★
Admissions: (415) 422-6563
Email Address: admission@usfca.edu

Strong Programs:
Nursing
Communications
Biology
Data Science
Entrepreneurship and Innovation
Hospitality Management
Psychology
Finance

All students take at least one Community Engaged Learning class to build local relationships and volunteer in the community.

and collaborative. Forty-three percent of undergraduate classes have fewer than 20 students, and according to a junior, "All USF professors are active in their field" and able to bring real-world experience into the classroom.

"Internships and service learning are definitely big parts of the education here at USF," says one senior. Nearby Silicon Valley is a boon for those seeking research or internship opportunities in the tech sector, banking and finance firms, biotech companies, arts organizations, and nonprofits. USF is the official host of the Human Rights Film Festival, which is integrated into the curriculum. The four-year Honors College, open to students in all majors, offers small interdisciplinary seminars, lectures from visiting scholars and artists, and opportunities to apply for funding to conduct research or travel abroad. The "distinctively Jesuit" St. Ignatius Institute living/learning community allows students to study the great books of Western civilization and spend a semester or year studying abroad in Oxford, England. Overall, the university offers more than 100 study abroad programs in 45 countries. "USF also has a partnership with UC San Francisco, so a lot of people are able to do research at the various UCSF campuses," notes a junior.

> **"USF students are very open-minded and adventurous."**

"USF students are very open-minded and adventurous," comments a senior. Fifty-eight percent of undergraduates are from California, and 11 percent hail from abroad. About 20 percent identify as Catholic. Asian Americans account for 27 percent of the population, Black students 7 percent, Hispanics/Latinos 21 percent, and multiracial students 10 percent. A sociology major points to "socioeconomic advancement for marginalized communities, environmental and social justice, and LGBTQ+ positivity and acceptance" as popular causes on campus. Admission is need-blind, and USF offers merit scholarships averaging $19,600, as well as athletic scholarships.

For the traditional Night Howl in the fall, new students gather in front of Gleeson Library and howl at the moon for good luck.

Forty-five percent of undergrads live in on-campus housing, which is guaranteed for the first two years. After that, most students brave San Francisco's budget-busting rental market, which "can be a struggle," says a senior, especially if you don't have a parent or guardian who can cosign a lease. On-campus students say the dining facilities offer a range of vegan, vegetarian, and other choices. "Campus safety officers are constantly roaming the campus making sure that the students are safe," reports a student. And while students say sexual assault has not been a big problem on campus, "USF encourages a lot of dialogue" on the issue.

More than 100 student clubs and organizations provide numerous events and social activities. The College Players is the oldest continuously performing college theater group in the West. Fraternities attract 5 percent of the men and sororities draw 10 percent of the women, although they don't have houses. The school's zero-tolerance policy on underage drinking is strictly enforced. The traditional Night Howl occurs at the end of first-year orientation in the fall: new students gather by the wolf sculpture in front of Gleeson Library and "howl at the moon for good luck," explains a sophomore. In the spring, the Donaroo music festival, which brings big-name performers to campus, is the highlight of the school social calendar. But USF's greatest social asset is undoubtedly its location, and most socializing takes place off campus. San Francisco is a cosmopolitan city where students can take advantage of reliable public transportation, including the famous cable cars, to get to a variety of attractions, ranging from Chinatown and the beach to museums and the symphony. "Living in a city like San Francisco, there is no reason to constrict oneself to the confines of a campus, with so many concerts, bars, nightclubs, and other happenings going on literally every single night of the year," says a senior.

> **"Living in a city like San Francisco, there is no reason to constrict oneself to the confines of a campus."**

Varsity athletics provide a popular diversion as well, and the Division I USF Dons compete in the West Coast Conference. Men's soccer and women's cross-country are perennial powerhouses. The university sponsors 22 club and intramural sports; the club volleyball, boxing, and judo teams are nationally competitive. Students make ample use of the Koret Health and Recreation Center, which touts an Olympic-size swimming pool, exercise and weight rooms, and a variety of playing courts.

In line with its Jesuit tradition, the core mission of USF is to provide a solid liberal arts and preprofessional education that develops students holistically, promotes the common good, and creates "a more humane and just world." Students complain about the "notoriously expensive" cost of living in San Francisco and ever-rising tuition rates, but those who can swing it take advantage of the cosmopolitan setting to get involved and make the most of their time here. "Students at USF truly care about learning and we desire to achieve great things in life," says a kinesiology major. "I haven't met a student who doesn't want to change the world."

If You Apply To ›

USF: Early decision, early action, regular decision. SATs or ACTs: optional. Accepts the Common Application with supplement.

Santa Clara University

500 El Camino Real, Santa Clara, CA 95053

Santa Clara is a selective midsized California university now drawing increased national attention. Gorgeous Silicon Valley campus is within easy reach of San Francisco, and the large endowment also contributes to an air of prosperity. A well-developed core curriculum keeps students focused on basic academic and other values. Offers engineering and business in addition to the liberal arts.

Steeped in history and tradition, Santa Clara University was founded by the Society of Jesus (Jesuits) in 1851 with a mission that emphasizes a commitment to academics and the community. The class schedule is based on 10-week quarters, classes stay small and intimate, and the curriculum focuses on an expanding global society. "Santa Clara's personality is warm, friendly, inquisitive, and passionate about social justice," says a marketing major. Add to that the infinite opportunities for networking and internships in Silicon Valley, and Santa Clara offers a well-rounded educational experience.

SCU's old-world charm includes 106 acres complete with lush green lawns, palm trees, and luscious rose gardens, accented by authentic Spanish architecture. The Mission Gardens, replete with olive trees, are a beautiful escape from the pressures of school. The famous classic mission church was rebuilt in 1926 in the design of the six previous churches that were destroyed by seemingly biblical disasters ranging from fires to floods. The Sobrato Campus for Discovery and Innovation, a massive $300 million facility housing the university's STEM programs, opened in 2021.

> "If you want to be a big fish in a small pond, SCU is a great choice."

The Core Curriculum is designed to express the school's "most basic values." It prescribes courses in three broad categories—Knowledge, Habits of Mind and Heart (skills), and Engagement with the World. The Core Pathways program supplements

Website: www.scu.edu
Location: Small City
Private
Total Enrollment: 7,663
Undergraduates: 5,773
Male/Female: 52/48
Financial Aid: 73%
Pell Grant: 9%
Expense: Pr $ $ $
Student Loans: 38%
Average Debt: $
Applicants: 16,848
Accepted: 54%
Enrolled: 17%
Grad in 6 Years: 91%
Returning Freshmen: 94%
Academics: ✍ ✍ ✍
Social: ☎ ☎ ☎ ☎
Q of L: ★ ★ ★ ★

(continued)

Admissions: (408) 554-4700
Email Address: admission@
scu.edu

Strong Programs:
Finance
Economics
Marketing
Environmental Science
Environmental Studies
Public Health Science
Bioengineering
Computer Science and
Engineering

the major and core curriculum by offering 24 sets of courses with innovative common themes across disciplines, such as design, hunger and poverty, justice and the arts, and values in science and technology; students choose one Pathway and complete three or four courses. It culminates in an integrative Pathway Reflection Essay. All first-year students are members of a Residential Learning Community (RLC) and take two-quarter sequences of Critical Thinking & Writing and Cultures & Ideas linked to their RLC. Students must complete a requirement that involves community service, and most majors require a capstone experience or senior project.

In addition to liberal arts, Santa Clara offers preprofessional programs in engineering and business. Engineering students can opt for a dual-degree program that allows them to get a bachelor's and master's degree in five years. The Leavey School of Business is renowned along the West Coast, with finance, economics, and marketing all strong.

"Our school is quite posh."

In the College of Arts and Sciences, communication and psychology remain popular. Other notable majors include environmental science, environmental studies, public health science, bioengineering, and computer science and engineering.

While courses are challenging, students say the quarter system gives them more control over the intensity of their workload. "Every 10 weeks you can change your workload to something that fits best for you," explains a public health science major. Small classes—38 percent enroll fewer than 20 students—taught by full professors allow plenty of time for one-on-one interaction. Students in all fields opt to engage in research supervised by a faculty member, much of it subsidized by grants. "It's very easy to get research or TA positions," says an economics major. "If you want to be a big fish in a small pond, SCU is a great choice."

For students looking for more of a challenge, the honors program places 65 to 70 selected freshmen in seminar-style classes, and an endowed scholarship sponsors one student's junior year at Mansfield College, Oxford University. The LEAD (Leadership, Excellence, and Academic Development) Scholars Program invites students whose parents did not attend college to join a small community of peers who work closely with faculty and staff to cultivate leadership skills. The study abroad program is extensive, with options in 42 countries on every continent except Antarctica, and 28 percent of undergrads study internationally during their four years. Those seeking professional experience find ample assistance at the Career Center, which offers mock interviews, résumé edits, cover letter help, goal-setting, and more. "I cannot stress enough how much of a perk Silicon Valley is for going to SCU," enthuses a sophomore. "Internship opportunities are endless."

The Sobrato Campus for Discovery and Innovation, a massive $300 million facility housing the university's STEM programs, opened in 2021.

According to a psychology major, Santa Clara students are "very driven and 'go, go, go' all the time." Thirty-five percent of undergraduates are Roman Catholic, and religion, while not intrusive, is a force in many aspects of campus life. The campus ministry provides counseling and opportunities for spiritual development, and many students are active in local volunteer organizations. Fifty-six percent of undergraduates hail from California, 6 percent come from foreign countries, and the rest are from 48 states. The student body on this liberal campus is almost evenly split between public school graduates and alumni of religiously affiliated or other private schools. Twenty percent of the students are Asian American, 3 percent are Black, 18 percent are Hispanic/Latino, and 9 percent are multiracial, but socioeconomically, the school is much less diverse, with just 9 percent of incoming first-year students receiving Pell Grants. "Our school is quite posh," concedes an accounting major. "Being located in the heart of Silicon Valley, there is a lot of luxury." Merit-based academic awards averaging $16,300 and 200 athletic scholarships are available to those who qualify. The Johnson Scholars

"[Students are] very driven and 'go, go, go' all the time."

Program rewards up to 10 outstanding incoming students with four-year, full-tuition scholarships and special opportunities to develop leadership skills.

Almost all freshmen and sophomores live on campus before packing up and heading for shared houses or apartments for the last two years; 53 percent of all undergrads reside in campus housing. All first-year students, including commuters, participate in one of the nine Residential Learning Communities, living in themed dorms and taking courses with students who share similar academic or social interests. The campus offers one central dining hall. "Everything is made fresh," says an environmental science major, "and we have a killer salad bar for those who like their veggies." Students give good ratings to campus safety. "I think people feel safe on and around campus because of the location," reports a junior.

Santa Clara ended its support of fraternities and sororities, but Greek organizations and a lively off-campus party scene persist, albeit independently. On-campus social life is led by the nearly 200 student organizations that coordinate events, making it "easy to join in on the fun," says a senior. The Bronco is a sports and recreation area where students can hang out, play billiards, and enjoy a late-night meal. Fall Concert, the Global Village celebration, the Gonzaga basketball game, and the Love Jones talent show are favorite annual events. The town of Santa Clara is mostly residential. For those who want to bask in the sun, Santa Cruz is only 20 miles away. San Francisco lies within 45 minutes, and other short road trips include Napa Valley, Monterey, and Palo Alto.

The Santa Clara Broncos compete in Division I; men's and women's soccer and basketball, women's volleyball, men's tennis, and baseball are among the more successful programs. Women's soccer recently claimed the national title. Fourteen intramural and 17 club sports draw the enthusiastic participation of a third of the undergraduates. "Every patch of grass usually has someone either chucking a Frisbee or kicking a ball around," says a political science major.

Santa Clara University is a warm place in every sense of the word. The physical setting is comfortable and scenic. More important, the SCU community gives meaning to the traditional Jesuit ideals of infusing morality and ethics into strong and coherent academics. Students say they are reminded of all this daily by their school's nickname: "Claradise."

The honors program places 65 to 70 selected freshmen in seminar-style classes.

Overlaps

Loyola Marymount, UC Berkeley, UCLA, University of San Diego, University of Southern California, Boston College, Cal Poly–San Luis Obispo, UC Davis

If You Apply To ›

SCU: Early decision I and II, early action, regular decision. Accepts the Common Application with supplement. Please consult Santa Clara's website for the most up-to-date information regarding standardized test requirements.

Sarah Lawrence College

1 Mead Way, Bronxville, NY 10708

A free-spirited sister of East Coast alternative institutions like Bard and Bennington where individualism reigns supreme. Though co-ed, women significantly outnumber men. Strong in the humanities and visual and performing arts, Sarah Lawrence takes its inspiration from the Oxford University tutorial system. Nationally known for creative writing and filmmaking. Full of quirky, headstrong intellectuals who hop the train to New York City with ease.

Every student designs his or her own program of study, and almost no subject is out of bounds.

Sarah Lawrence College attracts creative, curious, and highly motivated individuals who are both critical thinkers and devotees of independent learning. They love literature and the arts and take pride in their academic prowess. Indeed, freedom and exploration are valued more highly than any tradition here. Yet students also appreciate the things that have always been constants here, such as the emphasis on small classes and one-on-one conferences with professors. As a senior studying theater and sociology attests, what makes Sarah Lawrence stand out is that "students are given full agency and autonomy over their education."

Established in 1926 and named after the wife of a founder, Sarah Lawrence sits on a quaint, 44-acre tract in the city of Yonkers called Lawrence Park West, a wealthy Westchester County community close to the village of Bronxville, where even the public library boasts Oriental rugs and fireplaces. On campus, the prevailing architectural theme is English Tudor, including the mansion from the founder's converted estate. The landscape is hilly and green, with more than a hundred types of trees and abundant rock outcroppings. Because the school's founders believed that there should be as little physical separation as possible between life and work, many classrooms, dormitory suites, and faculty offices are all housed in the same buildings. Though its holdings are small—fewer than 350,000 volumes—the cozy library is charming. The Barbara Walters Campus Center (named for one of the school's most famous alumna) provides space for student organizations, socializing, campus dining, and community events.

> **"The professors are all integrated almost as colleagues into the work we are doing."**

Regardless of what they choose to focus on, all students at Sarah Lawrence become intimately acquainted with the written word; writing begins in the first year and continues relentlessly "across the curriculum" for the next three. General education requirements include credits in at least three of four academic areas, leaving lots of room for students to dabble in whatever strikes their fancy. Though there are formal grades, more important is the student's portfolio of work, accompanied by in-depth, written evaluations from professors, filed twice a year. To ease the transition to college, all first-years take a First-Year Studies seminar, choosing from more than 30 topics. The professor of their chosen course becomes their "don," the person who very often guides their academic development throughout their four years.

Despite challenging academics, a senior says, "Competition between students is low because everybody's course of study is so individualized." Indeed, every student designs his or her own program of study, and almost no subject is out of bounds. Writing, literature, filmmaking, and visual and performing arts are among the college's traditional strengths, and other popular concentrations include foreign languages, biology, and computer science. Aspiring psychologists—also a significant group on campus—may participate in fieldwork at the college's Early Childhood Center. The premed program, more structured than other offerings, places nearly all eligible graduates into medical school.

Classes are intimate, with 88 percent of them enrolling fewer than 20 students. Most students take three courses per semester, and professors meet one-on-one with their students weekly or biweekly, in a system modeled after Oxford University's tutorials, so there's no time to slack off—or fall behind. "The quality of instruction is very high because the professors are all integrated almost as colleagues into the work we are doing," says a political economy student. Perhaps because of the college's emphasis on personal relationships with professors, even the registration process requires deep thought: students interview teachers to ensure that courses fit into their academic plans and that the professor is someone they respect and want to study with.

> **"[Students are] progressive, a little bohemian, and critical of the status quo."**

All students at Sarah Lawrence conduct research as part of their one-on-one work with professors. Ninety percent of all courses include this research, known as "conference work." The Sarah Lawrence Center for the Urban River is a facility on the banks of the Hudson River that affords research opportunities for students pursuing environmental and social sciences. Students are encouraged to study abroad, and the college runs its own semester, yearlong, and summer study abroad programs in such locales as Oxford, London, Paris, Havana, Shanghai, and Tokyo. Forty-seven percent of students undertake some sort of international experience. Those interested in service learning may participate in the Intensive Semester in Yonkers, in which they take three classes in Yonkers centered on the history of the city and community empowerment, while also working with local nonprofit organizations.

Professors meet one-on-one with their students weekly or biweekly, in a system modeled after Oxford University's tutorials.

A creative writing student describes Sarah Lawrence students as "progressive, a little bohemian, and critical of the status quo." Eighteen percent of undergrads are natives of New York State—the bulk from nearby New York City—and 7 percent come from abroad. Five percent of students are Black, 4 percent Asian American, 9 percent Hispanic/Latino, and 6 percent multiracial. Many students come from upper-class families, and a senior comments, "It can be difficult for students from working-class backgrounds and first-generation college students" to find their place on campus. Political and social issues ranging from racism and human rights to climate change attract much attention here, and students are "more than happy to start a protest," says one student. A sophomore remarks, "I can't think of a time when I met a conservative on campus." Merit scholarships averaging $24,200 are available to qualified students.

"I really recommend the health and wellness services at our school."

Seventy-eight percent of students live in the "eclectic" campus housing, which is available to all full-time students. Campus food receives fair reviews, and there are plenty of options for students with special dietary needs. Campus security is strong, and students report that sexual harassment and assault policies and support services are effective. "I really recommend the health and wellness services at our school," says a junior. "They bring therapy dogs to campus. When I had COVID, they checked on me every single day, and the nurses really care."

With a plethora of student organizations hosting on-campus activities, and the school's proximity to New York City, social life is varied and active. Theater fans and aspiring actors flock to discounted Broadway shows, and clubs, bars, museums, and concert halls also beckon. Not surprisingly, Greek life has never been part of the Sarah Lawrence scene. College policies require party hosts who serve alcohol to register, and a dance and literature student says party culture is "not a defining part" of campus life. Favorite traditions include the annual screening of *The Princess Bride* on the lawn during orientation week, fall and spring formals, and midnight breakfast, served during the last week of each semester. Students also look forward to Sleaze Week, "a week dedicated to gender expression, including educational activities, guest speakers, movie screenings, and more, ending with a dance, the Sleaze Ball," explains a senior.

Favorite traditions include the annual screening of **The Princess Bride** *on the lawn during orientation week.*

The Sarah Lawrence Gryphons, named for a mythical figure that is part lion, part eagle, field 16 teams that compete in the Division III Skyline Conference. Women's tennis is a recent conference champ, and women's soccer, women's swimming, and men's basketball are also competitive. "We have very unofficial rivalries with Vassar and Bard—more ironic than not," claims a senior. The intramural program revolves around one-day invitational events—squash matches, dodgeball tournaments, fitness challenges—rather than league play.

Sarah Lawrence offers a close-knit community for writers, artists, and creative thinkers in a lush setting just outside the hustle and bustle of Manhattan. "The

Overlaps

Bard, Vassar, Skidmore, Mount Holyoke, Oberlin, NYU, Barnard, Fordham

education students get at Sarah Lawrence is unlike any other. You can truly have it all here," says a writing student. "You can play sports and perform in the theater. You can study botany and poetry at the same time. I think everyone could benefit from the Sarah Lawrence education."

If You Apply To ›

Sarah Lawrence: Early decision I and II, early action, regular decision. SATs or ACTs: optional. Accepts the Common Application.

Scripps College: See page 157.

Seattle University

Seattle, WA 98122

Unlike the University of Washington, Seattle U is a stone's throw from downtown and within walking distance of the waterfront. Jesuit tradition guarantees a nurturing environment and student growth both academically and in community service. Transitioning to a national institution but remains true to its humble roots. Out-of-staters are drawn as much by the city of Seattle as by the university itself.

Although Seattle has cultivated a reputation based largely on software, Starbucks lattes, and perpetually gray skies, the city is also home to Seattle University, a vibrant institution founded by the Society of Jesus (Jesuits) in 1891 that attracts 4,200 undergraduates to its urban campus. With strong preprofessional programs and a commitment to social and spiritual engagement, SU continues to express its mission to empower leaders for a just and humane world.

SU's campus, bordered by busy city streets, is a 50-acre urban sanctuary in the heart of Seattle. The university's diverse buildings are united by a recurring theme of red brick and light-filled atriums. The Chapel of St. Ignatius is a prize-winning building designed by Steven Holl around the concept of a "gathering of different lights." New buildings are designed to meet environmentally friendly standards, and energy efficiency and sustainability are top priorities for renovations. Special areas like the Ethnobotanical Garden and Japanese American Remembrance Garden highlight native plants and local history. The James Tower Clinical Nursing Lab is a state-of-the-art training facility for the school's many nursing students. The $100 million Center for Science and Innovation opened in 2021.

> **"Professors are more than willing to get students connected with opportunities in the area."**

The 60-credit University Core Curriculum introduces all students to the "unique tradition of Jesuit liberal education" and aims to develop the whole person for a life of service, provide a foundation for questioning and learning in any major or profession, and provide a common intellectual experience to all SU students. The core features seminars in writing, quantitative reasoning and creative expression, humanities, social sciences, and natural sciences, as well as coursework in philosophy and theology. Freshmen complete a first-year seminar built around a central theme or problem (enrollment is limited to 19 students), and seniors must complete

Website: www.seattleu.edu
Location: City Center
Private
Total Enrollment: 5,796
Undergraduates: 4,151
Male/Female: 38/62
Financial Aid: 92%
Pell Grant: 21%
Expense: Pr $ $
Student Loans: 74%
Average Debt: $ $
Applicants: 8,539
Accepted: 82%
Enrolled: 14%
Grad in 6 Years: 75%
Returning Freshmen: 85%
Academics: ✏ ✏ ✏
Social: ☎ ☎ ☎
Q of L: ★ ★ ★ ★
Admissions: (206) 220-8040
Email Address: admissions@ seattleu.edu

Strong Programs:
Nursing

a capstone course. In addition, the writing-across-the-curriculum initiative requires all sophomores to submit a writing sample for assessment.

SU students choose from more than 60 undergraduate degree programs. SU's most popular majors are also some of its best: nursing, finance, marketing, and accounting. The B.S. degree in diagnostic ultrasound is a particular specialty, and criminal justice, engineering, computer science, and biology are also strengths. A six-year, dual-degree program in business and law is also available. "Being on the quarter system is conducive to fostering academic growth as a community because students are aware that there is no time to slack off," notes a sophomore. Sixty-two percent of classes have fewer than 20 students, making professors easily accessible.

(continued)

Finance
Marketing
Diagnostic Ultrasound
Criminal Justice
Engineering
Computer Science
Biology

More than 200 service-learning courses are offered each year, and 80 percent of students perform community service during their time at SU. Motivated students may enroll in the University Honors program, which offers three concurrent classes in every term. The program makes extensive use of the seminar format and focuses on the history of ideas, with tracks in Intellectual Traditions; Society, Policy, and Justice; and Innovations. According to a strategic communications major, "Many of our majors require some sort of internship, and professors are more than willing to get students connected with opportunities in the area." When students want to escape Seattle's dreary skies and near-constant drizzle, they can take part in the university's study abroad program. Fifteen percent of students pack their bags for programs offered in 55 nations around the world, including China, France, Greece, Japan, and Sweden. SU also sends approximately 20 students to the National Conference for Undergraduate Research each year as part of a robust undergraduate research program.

Nursing is popular, and the B.S. degree in diagnostic ultrasound is a particular specialty.

"Everyone at this school believes in making the world a better place in their own way," comments a communication and media major. Twenty-three percent of undergraduates are Roman Catholic. Forty-four percent hail from Washington, and 9 percent are from other nations. Black students constitute 4 percent of the student body, Asian Americans 23 percent, Hispanics/Latinos 14 percent, and multiracial students 9 percent. The university, like its host city, has a reputation for progressive liberalism. "We're all feminists, agents against racism, and allies," says a sophomore, adding, "As a queer student, I feel more than safe—I feel embraced." Merit scholarships worth an average of $24,200 are awarded annually, and athletes vie for more than 250 scholarships.

"We're all feminists, agents against racism, and allies."

Forty-nine percent of SU students live in university housing. First-year students are assigned to one of eight theme communities, which focus on common interests like social change and advocacy, creative expression, and global exploration. Students are required to live on campus through their sophomore year; after that, housing is not guaranteed. A biology major says, "The surrounding area is very expensive, so most students who move off campus share bedrooms in apartments or townhouses." Dining options, on the other hand, get rave reviews for being local, seasonal, organic, sustainable, made to order, and, in the words of one student, "delicious, Instagram-ready food." Students report feeling safe on campus, day and night.

More than 200 service-learning courses are offered each year.

With more than 175 student clubs and organizations, there are plenty of opportunities to socialize on campus. Consistent with Jesuit tradition, there are no fraternities or sororities, and one student says, "Not a whole lot of drinking occurs on campus." Instead, students head off campus to enjoy Seattle's vibrant nightlife. "We are right next to Capitol Hill, which is the famous arts district/nightlife neighborhood," explains a sophomore. "Everything is walkable." Students can take advantage of the city's ubiquitous coffeehouses, eateries, shops, and concert venues. Everyone anticipates the annual Quadstock festival. "For one Saturday during spring quarter, the campus turns into a huge block party, with live music, games, and food," says a senior; Talib Kweli, Smallpools, and Saint Motel have been recent headliners.

Overlaps

Gonzaga, Santa Clara, Creighton, University of the Pacific, Loyola Marymount, University of Washington, University of Western Washington, University of Oregon

SU's Redhawks compete in the Western Athletic Conference (and Division I). Men's and women's soccer and softball have been competitive in recent years. Basketball, baseball, and soccer games against the University of Washington draw crowds. Intramural and club sports sign up 30 percent of students; popular options include flag football, softball, crew, and cycling.

With its emphasis on the liberal arts, civic engagement, and Jesuit principles, SU affords students an experience "which focuses on educating the entire person," according to one junior. For those students who are not averse to hard work and overcast skies, Seattle University might be an inspired choice—just be sure to pack a parka.

If You Apply To ›

Seattle: Early action, regular decision. SATs or ACTs: optional. Accepts the Common Application. Application includes optional question about gender identity.

Skidmore College

815 North Broadway, Saratoga Springs, NY 12866

Founded in 1903 as a "young women's industrial club," now co-ed Skidmore College still excels in the fine and performing arts that were then deemed proper for young ladies. But little else remains the same, most notably strength in the life sciences. Compare to Connecticut College, Vassar, and Wheaton (MA). Unique wooded campus gives the feel of living in a forest.

Website: www.skidmore.edu
Location: Small City
Private
Total Enrollment: 2,650
Undergraduates: 2,650
Male/Female: 41/59
Financial Aid: 53%
Pell Grant: 12%
Expense: Pr $ $ $ $
Student Loans: 39%
Average Debt: $ $
Applicants: 11,176
Accepted: 31%
Enrolled: 21%
Grad in 6 Years: 84%
Returning Freshmen: 90%
Academics: ✍ ✍ ✍ ✍
Social: ☎ ☎ ☎
Q of L: ★ ★ ★
Admissions: (800) 867-6007
Email Address: admissions@ skidmore.edu

Skidmore College serves up solid academics with a decidedly nontraditional flair. These politically liberal and free-spirited students seem a happy lot, thanks to small classes and accessible faculty members. "The college has a charm, sort of like a summer camp," says a junior. Thanks to an emphasis on interdisciplinary learning, students can "have diverse interests and be able to dabble in anything," a senior says.

In 1961, as enrollment surged, Skidmore traded its Victorian campus in the heart of Saratoga Springs for 750 acres on the northwest edge of town. Since then, the campus has grown to more than 50 buildings on 1,200 acres, and the student body has doubled in size (men were welcomed in 1971). While contemporary in style, the new buildings on Skidmore's Jonsson campus reflect the Victorian heritage of the school's original Scribner campus. Covered walkways connect the residential, academic, and social centers, and the prevailing views are of surrounding mountains, woods, and fields. Increasingly concerned with sustainability, the college has implemented geothermal heating and cooling in half of its buildings and generates 20 percent of its power from a nearby hydroelectric dam and its own solar array. Skidmore's newest facility, the 100,000-square-foot Tisch Center for Integrated Sciences, will house all of the college's science and math programs as well as 68 research and teaching labs; the North Wing opened in 2020, the East Wing in 2022, and the full project is slated for completion in 2024.

Skidmore's First-Year Experience includes a classwide summer reading project and a choice from among more than 40 Scribner Seminars. These seminars are typically capped at 16 students and taught by professors who also serve as mentors and advisors. Seminar topics are broad and varied, in keeping with Skidmore's 44 majors;

> "The college has a charm, sort of like a summer camp."

recent offerings include Bad Science, Japanese Popular Culture, and Environmental Advocacy. Students in each seminar receive guidance and support from an upper-class peer mentor, and themes raised in the summer reading crop up again during the year in campuswide programming.

The most popular majors at Skidmore are English, business, psychology, political science, economics, and studio art; the most popular minor is media and film studies. Not coincidentally, students say these are some of the college's best programs as well, along with performing arts. Nearly one-third of students major in the physical and life sciences. Students in biology, environmental science, environmental studies, and geoscience courses may conduct fieldwork in the college's 300-acre North Woods, a natural laboratory. Skidmore augments liberal arts and sciences offerings with preprofessional majors in business, education, health and human physiological sciences, and social work, not to mention a bevy of cooperative and dual-degree programs in engineering, business administration, accounting, finance, physical and occupational therapy, and nursing, offered in conjunction with such institutions as Clarkson, Dartmouth, Syracuse, and others.

(continued)

Strong Programs:
Performing Arts
Life Sciences
English
Business
Psychology
Political Science
Economics
Studio Art

"Skidmore is a very collaborative working environment. Professors challenge students to constantly improve communication skills by working with other students and submitting work in both written and oral forms," explains a sophomore. "The professors have a huge passion for whatever they're studying," adds a senior. "They are always accessible." Seventy-three percent of classes have fewer than 20 stu-

"Professors challenge students to constantly improve communication skills."

dents, enhancing that accessibility. Students speak highly of the 120 approved off-campus study options in 45 countries, especially Skidmore-run programs in France, England, New Zealand, and Spain. Forty-eight percent of students spend at least one semester off campus. Skidmore's Summer Collaborative Research Program provides roughly 80 students a funded opportunity to work individually with faculty mentors for up to 10 weeks on original research in disciplines ranging from biology to business. Internships are popular, too, with 85 percent of students doing at least one during their college years, often with funding from the school.

"Skidmore has a very diverse student body in terms of sexual, religious, geographic, and gender identities. There is also a diverse field of interests," says a student. Students are generally well-off. They hail primarily from New York (32 percent), New England, and New Jersey; 9 percent come from foreign countries. Asian Americans constitute 6 percent of the student body, Hispanics/Latinos 10 percent, Black students 5 percent, and multiracial students 5 percent. Limited awards for academic merit—up to six annually in music and up to 14 annually in math and science (each worth $60,000 over four years)—are available, although there are no athletic scholarships. Additionally, the college commits to meeting the full demonstrated financial need of all enrolled students.

Eighty-five percent of students do at least one internship, often with funding from the school.

Eighty-seven percent of Skidmore students live in the dorms, and most students get singles after freshman year. Dorms are integrated by class and co-ed by floor or suite, with kitchenettes and lounges on every floor. "Housing is great. It's guaranteed all four years, and the on-campus apartments are unbelievably nice," says a student. Most buildings have carpeting, air-conditioning, and cozy window seats. Some upperclassmen move to apartments—whether on campus in the Northwoods Village Apartments or the Sussman Village Apartments, or off campus in Saratoga Springs. The Murray-Aikins Dining Hall provides students with fresh food choices in a state-of-the-art facility. "I have friends come and visit me from other schools and demand to be sneaked into our dining hall," boasts a freshman.

"Most of the social life revolves around campus clubs and organizations," reports a chemistry major. "Since we don't have Greek life, we don't have the stereotypical

Skidmore's more traditional activities include Winter Carnival, the National College Comedy Festival, Spring Fling, and Fun Day.

party scene on campus." Skidmore's more traditional activities, which have continued even after a half century of coeducation, include Club Fair, Winter Carnival, the National College Comedy Festival, Spring Fling, Earth Day, and Fun Day (part of senior week) in the spring, with games and an inflatable obstacle course on the college green. Newer traditions include a student-run tribute concert; the Big Green Scream, which ushers in the men's and women's basketball seasons; and Pack the Rink, which marks the beginning of the men's ice hockey season.

The nearby Adirondacks and Green Mountains make Skidmore a haven for backpackers, skiers, and members of the popular Outdoors Club. The old resort town of Saratoga Springs, with its healing waters, antique shops, and eateries, offers plenty of culture, including the Saratoga Performing Arts Center, the country's oldest thoroughbred racetrack, and annual Victorian Streetwalk and Chowderfest events. Saratoga is also the summer home of the New York City Ballet, the Lake George Opera, and the Philadelphia Orchestra. Students reach out to the community through BenefAction, a volunteer group connected to several local agencies and schools. The best road trips include Albany, New York City, Boston—and especially Montreal, where you don't need a fake ID to hit the bars at 18.

Skidmore's men's and women's varsity teams (the Thoroughbreds) compete in Division III; the men's and women's basketball and tennis teams have claimed Liberty League championships in recent years. The riding program has won eight Intercollegiate Horse Show Association national championships. About 20 club and intramural sports are available as well.

Skidmore continues to win the hearts of motivated students with gorgeous scenery; caring faculty; and its flexibility, openness, and receptivity to change and growth. Students here are also a bit quirky, says a sophomore, "wearing shorts in the winter, for example." They're more likely to cheer on the fall of a foreign dictator than a goal by the lacrosse team. The point is, there's room for—and encouragement of—all types of students.

Overlaps

Vassar, Colgate, Hamilton, Bates, Oberlin, Connecticut College, Wheaton (MA), Bowdoin

If You Apply To ›

Skidmore: Early decision I and II, regular decision. SATs or ACTs: optional. Accepts the Common Application.

Smith College

College Lane, Northampton, MA 01063

The furthest left-leaning of the nation's leading women's colleges. Liberal Northampton provides sophisticated social life, and membership in the Five College Consortium adds depth and breadth all around. With a total enrollment of about 2,600, Smith is one of the largest top women's colleges, strong in the sciences and the arts, and the first women's college to offer engineering. Compare to Bryn Mawr.

Website: www.smith.edu
Location: Small City
Private
Total Enrollment: 2,895
Undergraduates: 2,554
Male/Female: 0/100

Heaven only knows what Sophia Smith would think of the women's college she founded in 1871 with the hope it would be "pervaded by the Spirit of Evangelical Christian Religion." There are still Evangelicals at Smith, but today they join the rest of their schoolmates in crusading against racism, classism, sexism, and homophobia. Though the all-female school remains strongly committed to its liberal arts mission, it is also focused on placing women at the forefront of science and technology. Students here have the opportunity to become leaders in the male-dominated field of engineering or pursue interdisciplinary fields such as landscape studies or the study of women and gender. "Smith has an open curriculum, a great college town, and a very strong science program," says one sophomore.

Smith is in the small city of Northampton, an artsy and politically progressive oasis within an hour's drive of the Berkshire Mountains. The 147-acre campus resembles a medieval fortress from the front gate, but inside it sparkles with many gardens, Paradise Pond, and a plant house. Buildings cover a range of styles from late 18th century to modern, and the college has successfully retained its historic atmosphere while keeping facilities up-to-date. The college's science and engineering building, Ford Hall, earned LEED Gold certification and boasts a myriad of high-tech equipment, including two electron microscopes. Smith's four libraries house one of the largest collections of any liberal arts college in the country. The new, state-of-the art main library, designed by Maya Lin (of Vietnam Veterans Memorial fame) to replace the historic Neilson Library, opened in 2021.

> **"Smith has an open curriculum [and] a great college town."**

With the exception of at least one writing course, Smith women have unusual freedom to plan a course of study. They must take half of their credits outside of their major, and first-year students can take small seminars on topics such as Rebellious Women and Pandemics in Fact and Fiction. Students can expand their academic options by registering for courses at any of the other Five College Consortium member schools: Amherst, Hampshire, Mount Holyoke, and UMass Amherst.

Psychology is among the most popular majors on campus, followed by computer science, government, biological sciences, engineering, and English. Four in 10 Smith women major in science and thereby enjoy numerous opportunities to assist professors with their research. The Picker Engineering Program, the country's first women-only, accredited engineering program, offers an ambitious engineering curriculum taught within the full depth and breadth of the liberal arts. Administrators hope the program will lead to greater gender parity in engineering. Those who complete it are highly sought-after: recent graduates have headed to prestigious graduate programs at Cornell, Harvard, MIT, Princeton, and other colleges; received highly competitive National

> **"[Smithies are] women who know what they want and know how to get things done."**

Science Foundation fellowships; or been quickly snatched up by employers. Smith's art history department is among the best in the nation and enjoys access to the college's superb museum. Dance and music are notable as well. Landscape studies, which focuses on the relationship between humans and natural and built environments, is a first-of-its-kind undergraduate program among liberal arts colleges.

Be ready to hit the books with your newfound sisters at Smith. Coursework is described as "very intense and very difficult," although the atmosphere is "not too competitive because we all want to grow together," according to one student. Students generally refrain from discussing grades, choosing instead to focus on helping each other. Smith's student-run honor system, which covers everything from exams to library checkout, is widely praised and enforced. All courses are taught by professors, and 68 percent of them have fewer than 20 students. Students seem to be pleased with the quality of teaching. "My professors have all been accessible and supportive as well as open-minded and articulate," says a sophomore.

Qualified students may enter the Smith Scholars program and embark on one or two years of independent study or extra college research for full credit. The STRIDE program allows freshmen and sophomores to become paid research assistants to professors. Students are also enthusiastic about the opportunity to take part in Smith's well-known study abroad program, which sends 40 percent of the junior class to a number of countries for at least a semester. The Praxis program allows each student

---

(continued)

Financial Aid: 62%
Pell Grant: 18%
Expense: Pr $ $ $
Student Loans: 54%
Average Debt: $
Applicants: 6,064
Accepted: 30%
Enrolled: 37%
Grad in 6 Years: 91%
Returning Freshmen: 95%
Academics: ✎ ✎ ✎ ✎ ½
Social: ☎ ☎ ☎
Q of L: ★ ★ ★ ★
Admissions: (413) 585-2500
Email Address: admission@ smith.edu

Strong Programs:
Engineering
Art History
Dance
Music
Landscape Studies
Psychology
Computer Science
Government

Four in 10 Smith women major in science and thereby enjoy numerous opportunities to assist professors with their research.

to participate in at least one summer internship funded by the college. About 120 older students are enrolled in the groundbreaking Ada Comstock Scholars program for women returning to college.

Smithies are "women who know what they want and know how to get things done," says a government major. Twenty-one percent of undergraduates hail from Massachusetts, and 14 percent come from abroad. Black students account for 6 percent of the student body, Asian Americans 10 percent, Hispanics/Latinas 13 percent, and multiracial students 5 percent. Nobody disputes that Smith is a liberal place, with social issues of the day dominating conversations, though some students are surprised to find themselves in such a freewheeling atmosphere. With an endowment of more than $2 billion, Smith has deeper pockets than many of its competitors. And though it's got a hefty price tag, the school meets the full demonstrated financial need of admitted students and has replaced loans with grants in all need-based financial aid packages. It also offers a limited number of merit-based awards that average $35,700 annually.

> *About 120 older students are enrolled in the groundbreaking Ada Comstock Scholars program for women returning to college.*

Housing at Smith, which consists of 40 houses (not dorms), is universally adored, and is home to 95 percent of students. "The house system builds strong community, and each house has its own traditions," a student explains. Each house accommodates from 12 to 100 students and functions as a self-governing unit, responsible for everything from visiting hours to weekend parties and concerts. The atmosphere is less that of a sorority than of an extended family.

> **"My professors have all been accessible and supportive as well as open-minded and articulate."**

Classes are mixed in each house, and first-year students easily mingle with seniors. Alternative options include food cooperatives, language-themed housing, and an apartment complex. There are several dining locations on campus open at specific times for breakfast, lunch, and dinner on the weekdays and brunch and dinner on the weekends, and the food gets good reviews. Some houses even have family-style Thursday dinners to which students invite faculty members.

You will not be greeted with a rocking social scene at Smith, but there are plenty of parties to be had and great places to visit. "The student organizations on campus are pretty good at organizing events like movie nights and sundae parties," says a senior. The five-college system sponsors a free bus service that runs to the other four campuses of the consortium, which offer a broad range of social and cultural opportunities. In addition, each house throws an average of two parties a semester. For special weekends, a whole fraternity may be invited from Dartmouth or another nearby college, an arrangement that is only slightly more civilized than the typical college bar scene. Students say the alcohol policies are getting stricter, and IDs are checked and hands are stamped at campus parties. Smith also offers time-honored traditions like Mountain Day in the fall, when the president cancels class for a day of hiking and bonding, complete with brown-bag lunches.

> *On Mountain Day in the fall, the president cancels class for a day of hiking and bonding, complete with brown-bag lunches.*

Northampton, known as NoHo after New York City's SoHo neighborhood, is a college town of about 30,000 that is known for its freewheeling culture and funky bohemianism. The town is home to multiple subcultures and is generally tolerant of everyone. "Northampton is one of my favorite places," says a senior. "It's small and artsy, has multiple venues for music and dance, a dance club, bowling alley, and a lot of great restaurants. There is never a lack of nightlife."

> **"The house system builds strong community."**

The Community Service Office assists student volunteers with finding long-term placements and short-term projects in Northampton, the surrounding communities, and on campus. The New England countryside has numerous special charms, including ski slopes only an hour away. The best road trips are to Boston (two hours) or New York City (three hours).

Smith has a long tradition of success in Division III athletics; the college was the first women's college to join the NCAA and still places a premium on recruiting strong athletes. The Pioneer crew, basketball, soccer, and field hockey teams are competitive in the New England Women's and Men's Athletic Conference. Smith's multimillion-dollar sports complex features indoor tennis and track facilities and a six-lane swimming pool. Interhouse competitions include everything from kickball to inner-tube water polo to rugby.

"It can be hard to adapt to the environment of a women's college," acknowledges one senior. "But it's been the most valuable thing I've ever done." The strict evangelism is long gone, and today's Smith women are far from Sophia Smith wannabes. But her namesake and spirit live on at this eclectic, open-minded institution where women don lab coats, power suits, combat boots, and even white dresses at graduation. This "community of close, intelligent, interesting, and compassionate women" readies them to be and do just about anything.

If You Apply To ›

Smith: Early decision I and II, regular decision. SATs or ACTs: optional. Accepts the Common Application with supplement. Accepts applications from students whose birth certificates reflect their gender as female or who identify as female.

University of the South (Sewanee)

735 University Avenue, Sewanee, TN 37383

Easily mistaken for an Oxford or a Cambridge plunked down in the highlands of Tennessee. Traditions loom large at Sewanee, including its honor code and the wearing of "class dress" and academic gowns. Affiliated with the Episcopal Church, it is more buttoned-down than Davidson and Rhodes and continues to have old-line Southern feel. English, environmental studies, prebusiness, and study abroad programs are standouts. If you have a horse, bring it along.

Tradition is respected at University of the South, known simply as Sewanee, after its location. A group of southern Episcopal bishops, many of whom later fought in the Confederate military, founded the school in 1857, envisioning it as a distinguished center of learning for the region. Before Sewanee could open, its campus buildings and endowment were lost to the Civil War. Anglican parishes in England gave money to restart the school, and Oxford and Cambridge donated the library's first volumes. Sewanee opened its doors for its first convocation in 1868, with nine students and four professors. The Roberson Project on Slavery, Race, and Reconciliation, established in 2017, explores the university's historical ties to slavery and the ongoing impacts of racial injustice. Many Sewanee traditions remain alive and well—including calling academic semesters Advent and Easter—even as the school emphasizes inclusivity and a broader national appeal.

Sewanee is located atop Tennessee's Cumberland Plateau, between Chattanooga and Nashville. The atmosphere is like "attending Oxford in England," a freshman says, "only with mountains!" Stately English Gothic buildings are carved from beige-and-pink sandstone native to the region, and each has plenty of space, as the school spreads out over a 13,000-acre forested plot fondly known as "the Domain." Particularly noteworthy structures are St. Luke's and All Saints' Chapel, and Convocation Hall, built in 1886. Recent additions

Website: www.sewanee.edu
Location: Small Town
Private
Total Enrollment: 1,791
Undergraduates: 1,724
Male/Female: 47/53
Financial Aid: 97%
Pell Grant: 12%
Expense: Pr $ $
Student Loans: 40%
Average Debt: $ $ $
Applicants: 4,162
Accepted: 60%
Enrolled: 19%
Grad in 6 Years: 80%
Returning Freshmen: 90%
Academics: ✍ ✍ ✍ ✍
Social: ☎ ☎ ☎

(continued)

Q of L: ★ ★ ★ ★
Admissions: (800) 522-2234
Email Address: admiss@
sewanee.edu

Strong Programs:
English
Environmental Studies
Psychology
Economics
Politics
International and Global
Studies

include the Wellness Commons, housing the Wellness Center, a fitness facility, and a mini bookstore.

As part of Sewanee's general education program, students pursue seven learning objectives in their first two years: Reading Closely, Understanding the Arts, Seeking Meaning, Exploring Past and Present, Observing and Experimenting, Cross-Cultural Comprehension, and Encountering Perspectives. An optional Finding Your Place course enhances the first-year experience with lectures, discussions, service opportunities, and field trips before classes begin in the fall. All students take a writing-intensive course, and in keeping with European tradition, Sewanee seniors must pass comprehensive exams in their majors to earn their diplomas.

Psychology, economics, politics, and English are the most popular majors, along with international and global studies, an interdisciplinary program with faculty from 14 departments. The strength of Sewanee's English department is nationally recognized, thanks in part to a bequest from playwright Tennessee Williams. The *Sewanee Review*—the oldest continuously published literary quarterly in the United States—and the Sewanee Writers' Conference enhance the department's reputation. The sciences are also strong, especially variations on environmental studies, given the campus's rich natural setting. The Integrated Program in the Environment encompasses six majors and six minors that incorporate coursework in the natural and social sciences, humanities, and fine arts; the program also offers cooperative master's programs with Duke and Yale. Premed and preprofessional programs are highly regarded; students applying to medical, dental, and veterinary schools enjoy high acceptance rates. Although Sewanee does not offer a business major, its economics and finance majors can be paired with a prebusiness program that offers special experiential learning opportunities and a business minor with finance, managerial, and international tracks.

> **"The professors here are top-notch and have absolutely made my experience."**

Students report that the coursework is challenging and intensive, but the atmosphere breeds camaraderie. "Students will frequently hole up in the library or in a classroom together studying for tests or writing essays," explains a sophomore. Fifty-seven percent of courses enroll fewer than 20 students, and the faculty receives rave reviews. "The professors here are top-notch and have absolutely made my experience," cheers a politics major. Most professors wear black academic gowns when they teach, as do many members of Sewanee's signature honor society, the Order of the Gown. The "class dress" tradition encourages students to dress appropriately for class; sweatpants, gym shorts, and pajamas are definitely frowned upon, and it's not unheard-of for some students to don dresses, skirts, jackets, or ties. Administrators say students and professors voluntarily observe these traditions to demonstrate their commitment to teaching and learning. Sewanee also takes its honor code very seriously. Violations—such as lying, cheating, or stealing—usually result in suspension. Sewanee is "steeped in tradition that almost all students abide by, no matter how archaic," a sophomore says.

Sewanee spreads out over a 13,000-acre forested plot fondly known as "the Domain."

The Sewanee Pledge initiative promises three benefits to all undergraduates: funding for a summer internship or research opportunity; access to a semester-long study abroad program at no additional tuition cost; and a graduation guarantee that provides an additional year of study tuition-free to students who are unable to complete a single major within four years. Overall, 28 percent of students study abroad in their choice of more than 200 approved programs; the Sewanee Semester in Spain and short-term summer programs tend to draw the most interest.

> **"[Sewanee is] steeped in tradition that almost all students abide by, no matter how archaic."**

Twenty-two percent of Sewanee's students are Tennessee natives, though many of the rest come from the Southeast; 4 percent are international. Southern culture is strong here and the atmosphere can be quite familial—almost a quarter of entering freshmen are legacies. Still, one senior argues, Sewanee students are not simply a "large group of privileged preps." The student body is 19 percent Episcopalian and overwhelmingly Christian, although students of all faiths are welcomed. Students of color have a small but growing presence on campus, with Black students making up 4 percent of the student body, Asian Americans 1 percent, Hispanics/Latinos 5 percent, and multiracial students 3 percent. Both sides of the political aisle are represented on campus, and students say debates are civil and healthy. Each year, the school hands out merit scholarships averaging $21,900, and socioeconomic diversity is gradually rising. Sewanee has expanded its financial aid program, promising to meet the full demonstrated financial need of all students.

The Integrated Program in the Environment encompasses six majors and six minors and offers cooperative master's programs with Duke and Yale.

Virtually all Sewanee students live in the dorms, and students report that while the quality of the facilities varies, the community atmosphere is tight-knit and enjoyable. McClurg Dining Hall serves a wide variety of food and accommodates students' requests. Life on the mountain is peaceful and "students most always feel safe and secure," according to one junior. Students receive training in alcohol and sexual misconduct intervention strategies.

Fraternities and sororities are a huge deal here, with the vast majority of students—51 percent of the men and 69 percent of the women—signing up. The university enforces an open-door policy for on-campus events, which makes Greek parties more inclusive here than at many other schools. "Greek life rules the social scene, but university-funded programs help keep life from becoming one long frat-a-thon," remarks a student.

"University-funded programs help keep life from becoming one long frat-a-thon."

Drinking is a fact of life, but a sophomore reports that with a medical amnesty policy and other measures, "the main focus is safety." Annual Fall and Spring Party weekends draw alumni and friends back to campus, and students also enjoy the Perpetual Motion dance performances and Sewaneeroo music festival. Popular road trips include Atlanta, Nashville, and Chattanooga, so it helps to have a car. Nearby lakes, waterfalls, and caverns also offer rafting, hiking, camping, and other active day trips.

The equestrian team regularly ranks among the top teams in the country.

Varsity sports are popular at Sewanee, where the Tigers compete in Division III. Football is probably the favorite sport on campus—games are important social events. While a once-popular cheer dating to the 1890s ("Sewanee, Sewanee, leave 'em in the lurch. Down with the heathens and up with the Church. Yea, Sewanee's right!") isn't often heard at games nowadays, the YSR acronym ("Yea, Sewanee's right!") persists, usually being shouted at the end of the school's alma mater and other moments that call for a burst of school spirit. The men's and women's tennis teams dominate the Southern Athletic Association, each winning several conference titles in the last decade, and men's and women's golf and swimming and diving have also been successful. The equestrian team regularly ranks among the top teams in the country. About two-thirds of students participate in intramurals, club sports, and the Outing Program, which sponsors outdoor adventures like caving and kayaking as well as trips to the Rio Grande for canoeing and to Colorado for Alpine mountaineering.

Sewanee's small size means it offers students plenty of opportunity to really make a difference. The rich traditions tap into the university's long history and give the campus a life and personality all its own. "Having a campus as lush and unique as Sewanee has made it an extremely special place," muses a senior, "and helps foster positive attitudes from everyone around."

Overlaps

Davidson, Rhodes, Furman, Washington and Lee, Wake Forest, University of Tennessee Knoxville, University of Georgia, University of Virginia

If You Apply To ›

Sewanee: Early decision I and II, early action, regular decision. SATs or ACTs: optional. Accepts the Common Application.

Columbia, SC 29208

Among public flagship universities in the South, USC struggles against the image of being one giant step behind UNC at Chapel Hill. The university boasts one of the top international business programs in the nation. Criminal justice is also a specialty. Unlike Clemson, USC is in a major city. Check out the Honors College, which is one of the best anywhere.

Website: www.sc.edu
Location: City Center
Public
Total Enrollment: 35,471
Undergraduates: 25,634
Male/Female: 44/56
Financial Aid: 75%
Pell Grant: 19%
Expense: Pub $ $
Student Loans: 54%
Average Debt: $ $ $
Applicants: 42,045
Accepted: 62%
Enrolled: 15%
Grad in 6 Years: 78%
Returning Freshmen: 87%
Academics: ✍ ✍ ✍
Social: ☎ ☎ ☎
Q of L: ★ ★ ★
Admissions: (803) 777-7700
Email Address: admissions-ugrad@sc.edu

Strong Programs:
International Business
Criminal Justice
International Studies
Global Studies
Psychology
Nursing
Exercise Science
Biological Sciences

Whether it's football or international business, students at the University of South Carolina are game—after all, they're the Gamecocks and, like their mascot, they've got plenty of fighting spirit. Students love to cheer on the school's football and basketball teams, especially if the opponent is longtime rival Clemson. South Carolina is working hard to give its campus a more cosmopolitan feel through academic programs with a strong global focus and initiatives such as the Student Council on Diversity and Inclusion.

South Carolina's main campus is located in the heart of Columbia (population 138,000), which also happens to be the state capital. Government buildings and downtown businesses are within an easy walk, allowing students to secure internships or even part-time jobs during the school year. The old section of the campus, which dates to the school's 1801 founding, includes the glorious oak-lined Horseshoe; 10 of its 19th-century

> **"The courses are challenging and the environment is laid-back."**

buildings are now listed in the National Register of Historic Places. The $250 million Innovista complex integrates public and private sector research in high-tech facilities. The massive, $210 million Campus Village complex, housing 1,800 students, a dining facility, and academic support spaces, is set to open in fall 2023.

Regardless of the program in which they enroll, students must complete the Carolina Core, a series of distribution requirements that includes courses in problem solving, writing, foreign language, global citizenship and multicultural understanding, and scientific literacy (among others). USC has been a national leader in developing initiatives to support the first-year transition, such as the required three-hour University 101 seminar. According to one student, University 101 is "an incredible class. You learn about student skills, time management, all the resources at USC, and have a ton of fun." To build community, there's the Freshman Reading Experience, in which entering students read the same book before coming to campus then discuss it in small groups upon arrival.

South Carolina offers a slew of undergraduate degree programs; business is popular, as are psychology, nursing, exercise science, biological sciences, and criminal justice. With South Carolina's coastal economy depending on foreign trade, the university

> **"Students share notes, study together, and help out others."**

has developed a top-notch international business program, as well as notable majors in international studies and global studies. Students in the journalism and mass communications program benefit from an excellent film library right on campus, while budding marine scientists may study and do research at a 17,000-acre facility about three hours away. Art students, neglected at many universities, here have access to the latest cameras, editing stations, and computers, as well as pottery kilns and other necessary equipment. Musicians enjoy a four-level building with a music and performance library, rehearsal rooms, recording studios, and a 250-seat lecture hall. The English program benefits from sizable collections of research material on F. Scott Fitzgerald and Ernest Hemingway. An unusual minor in medical humanities gives doctors-to-be an introduction to the ethical, cultural, legal, economic, and political factors that affect medical practice today.

"For the most part, the courses are challenging and the environment is laid-back," says one senior. A classmate adds, "Students share notes, study together, and help out others." Forty percent of undergraduate classes have fewer than 20 students, and the quality of teaching is generally high: "All my professors are passionate about what they teach and do a great job of sharing their passion with us," one student says. Unlike many honors programs that focus on lower-division education, USC's Honors College provides curricular and research opportunities across all four years. About 600 courses are available annually through the Honors College, which serves more than 2,000 students. Nineteen percent of undergraduates study, intern, volunteer, or conduct independent research abroad, taking advantage of programs offered in more than 60 different countries.

USC draws students from all 50 states and more than 100 countries; 60 percent of undergrads are in-staters and 3 percent are international. Nine percent of students are Black, 4 percent are Asian American, 5 percent are Hispanic/Latino, and 4 percent are multiracial. "It is the norm to be involved with at least two or three student organizations and to be very active on campus," says one student. Another cites education funding and LGBTQ rights as hot-button issues. The university awards merit scholarships averaging $6,100 and more than 400 athletic scholarships. The Gamecock Guarantee promises to cover tuition and fees for low-income South Carolina residents who are the first in their family to attend college.

With South Carolina's coastal economy depending on foreign trade, USC has developed a top-notch international business program.

> **"The engineering students build a 30-foot-tall tiger and burn it to the ground before the big [Clemson] game."**

All first-year students live on campus in nearly two dozen living/learning communities, ranging from academic fields like business and engineering to special interests like sustainability and leadership. "I loved living on campus," recalls one junior. "It was so easy to walk to class from my residence hall." After the first year, housing can be expensive and difficult to get, students say, and only 31 percent of all undergrads reside on campus. Dining options range from fast-food stands to all-you-can-eat lines, with plenty of vegetarian and healthy choices—and, of course, some junk food too. "You will never go hungry," promises one student. Students report feeling safe while roaming campus.

All first-year students live on campus in nearly two dozen living/learning communities.

"Most social life takes place off campus," says a psychology major. "We have cool bars and restaurants close to campus that are geared toward younger people." Twenty-five percent of South Carolina's men and 31 percent of the women go Greek, and their chapters provide much of the weekend social life on campus. Despite school policies, some underage students "sneak [alcohol] in, and are not bothered if they behave themselves," says a speech/language pathology major. Still, concerned about binge and underage drinking, administrators have increased funding for alternative activities, such as films, dance performances, theatrical productions, concerts, and comedy shows. And with more than 400 student groups on campus, everyone should be able to find a niche. Downtown Columbia offers more theaters, a comedy club, a performing arts center, and Five Points, a strip boasting several bars. Outdoorsy types appreciate the beaches an hour and a half away, as well as the mountain ranges four hours north for hiking, skiing, and camping.

Fall football weekends are always a big deal at South Carolina, which competes in the Division I Southeastern Conference. The enduring rivalry with the Clemson Tigers is one of the oldest and most colorful in college sports, with festivities beginning weeks in advance; their annual game (the Palmetto Bowl) has been played for more than a century. "We do an annual Tiger Burn, where the engineering students build a 30-foot-tall tiger and burn it to the ground before the big game," says one Gamecock. "That's really fun!" Winter weekends welcome another of USC's strong

Overlaps

University of Houston, UMass Amherst, University of Missouri, University of Nebraska–Lincoln, University of South Florida, Auburn, University of Tennessee Knoxville, Clemson

sports, basketball, played in the 342,000-square-foot Colonial Center. The women's basketball team elated fans by bringing home the national title in 2017 and again in 2022. USC's baseball and women's golf, soccer, and softball teams are competitive too. Students can also choose from dozens of club and intramural sports or dip into the indoor and outdoor pools at the Strom Thurmond Fitness and Wellness Center, which also features an indoor track, basketball and racquetball courts, and a climbing wall.

School spirit remains as strong as ever at South Carolina's flagship university, but the pace of change is picking up. Yet even as its academic focus grows increasingly global, USC has a more personal feel than many state universities, thanks to its special emphasis on student support and diversity of all types. Perhaps that's why Gamecocks say no place could be finer.

If You Apply To ›

South Carolina: Early action, regular decision. Accepts the Common Application with supplement. Please consult South Carolina's website for the most up-to-date information regarding standardized test requirements.

University of Southern California

University Park, Los Angeles, CA 90089

USC's old handle: "The University of Spoiled Children." USC's new handle: highly selective West Coast university with preeminent programs in cinematic arts and business. The region's only major private university that just happens to have a top football team. L.A.'s answer to NYU with way more Heisman Trophies.

Website: www.usc.edu
Location: City Center
Private
Total Enrollment: 42,631
Undergraduates: 20,206
Male/Female: 49/51
Financial Aid: 63%
Pell Grant: 21%
Expense: Pr $ $ $ $
Student Loans: 32%
Average Debt: $ $
Applicants: 71,031
Accepted: 13%
Enrolled: 41%
Grad in 6 Years: 92%
Returning Freshmen: 96%
Academics: ✑ ✑ ✑ ½
Social: ☎ ☎ ☎
Q of L: ★ ★ ★
Admissions: (213) 740-1111
Email Address: admitusc@ usc.edu

Once dismissed as little more than an academic bastion of privilege, the University of Southern California has come into its own as a West Coast destination for students seeking the advantages of study in a center for the arts, technology, communication, and international trade. The school's lush campus and prime Los Angeles location has led to a flood of applicants, making it continually tougher to win admission. Students cheer on national championship teams and give high marks to the Trojan alumni network as well. Often accused of being elitist, USC, founded in 1880, continues to populate the next generation of Los Angeles business leaders.

USC's University Park campus has an unmistakably upscale vibe and offers a mix of traditional ivy-covered and modern structures, arranged around fountains and reflecting pools, well shaded from the Southern California sun. Sitting on 226 parklike acres, just minutes from downtown Los Angeles, USC is a veritable urban oasis. Newer additions to campus include the $700 million, 2,700-bed USC Village, a student housing project as well as a neighborhood revitalization effort that includes eight residential colleges, a Gothic-style dining hall, and two dozen retail stores.

> **"[We have] the flexibility to take classes from different professional schools."**

USC's Core Curriculum, aimed at sharpening critical thinking and communication skills, requires nine courses: six general education, two intensive writing, and one diversity. Students with high GPAs and test scores may choose the Thematic Option—a.k.a. the "Traumatic Option"—in place of regular general education courses. The 200 or so who do get smaller classes with some of the university's best teachers and a handpicked group of writing instructors. Freshmen may also join one of the school's Learning Communities, groups of 20 students with common academic interests, such as business, medicine, technology, or languages. Each community takes four common courses during the first year and meets with a dedicated faculty mentor and staff advisor three to six times a semester. The First Generation Plus Student Success Center serves as a resource hub supporting first-generation, undocumented, former foster youth, and transfer students.

USC offers undergraduates the chance to pursue degrees not only in the Dornsife College of Letters, Arts, and Sciences, but also at any of its 20 professional schools and schools of the arts—an advantage that students appreciate. "The flexibility to take classes from different professional schools really highlights the emphasis here on interdisciplinary studies," says a cinema and media studies major. In fact, USC strongly encourages students to pursue double majors or a combination of majors and minors in unrelated academic fields, which means business majors may minor in bioethics, or Russian and art history majors may study the music industry or business too. Majors in business, social sciences, visual and performing arts, engineering, and communication are strong and enroll the most students. The cinematic arts, film, and television production major is first-rate, and architecture is highly regarded. The progressive degree program allows students to apply to a master's-level program during their junior year; depending on the field, one can earn a bachelor's and master's degree in as little as 10 semesters.

The academic climate is challenging, and students report that while there is some "friendly competition," their classmates are mostly supportive of each other. Sixty-two percent of undergraduate classes enroll fewer than 20 students, but the quality of teaching varies, especially in some introductory courses for freshmen, which can be huge. Advising and career services get mixed reviews. An English major says, "My biggest support system at USC has been my professors, and they are normally my first line of defense when I need advice." The Discovery Scholars program honors original research and creativity among undergraduates, and the Global Scholars program singles out students who

> "My biggest support system at USC has been my professors."

excel both at home and abroad. USC offers more than 50 semester- and yearlong study abroad programs in nearly 30 countries, in addition to several short-term options offered during summer and winter breaks and the May term.

USC students are perhaps best characterized by a sense of "ambitious drive," says one senior. Most pride themselves on their ability to maintain decent grades along with an active social life. About half of USC undergrads come from within the state, and 12 percent come from foreign countries. This left-leaning campus is racially diverse, with Black students making up 6 percent of the student body, Hispanics/Latinos 17 percent, Asian Americans 24 percent, and multiracial students 6 percent. Hundreds of merit scholarships, averaging $17,800, are awarded each year, as are about 375 athletic awards. USC also meets 100 percent of students' demonstrated financial need and is need-blind in its admissions. Undergraduates from families with annual incomes of $80,000 or less qualify for free tuition.

Thirty-five percent of USC undergrads live on campus. All freshmen are housed in residential colleges, which are led by faculty masters in residence and serve as a hub for social life. Since swimming pools, tennis courts, carpeting, microwaves, refrigerators, and air-conditioning are just some of the luxuries to be found in USC dorms, not to mention the USC Village, it's no wonder more upperclassmen would like to stay on campus. But because there isn't enough space for everyone, students typically move after their first year to fraternity and sorority houses or apartments, which are just a short walk away. Dining halls offer plenty of options, including an international buffet in the Parkside complex. Some nearby areas are rather rough, but thanks to USC's police department, which regularly patrols the campus and surrounding neighborhood, most students say they've never felt unsafe. "USC has

(continued)

Strong Programs:
Business
Social Sciences
Visual and Performing Arts
Engineering
Communication
Cinematic Arts, Film, and
    Television Production
Architecture

USC strongly encourages students to pursue double majors or a combination of majors and minors in unrelated academic fields.

All freshmen are housed in residential colleges, which are led by faculty masters in residence and serve as a hub for social life.

made sure that, with regard to sexual assault, all students know where to seek help and access tools to deal with this issue," notes a senior.

The on-campus social scene revolves around activities organized by student clubs, fraternity parties on "The Row," sporting events, the annual Springfest concert, and the *Los Angeles Times* Festival of Books in the spring. Ten percent of the men and 12 percent of the women go Greek. Several fraternities have severed ties with the university following the enactment of new rules imposed in the wake of a series of sexual assault accusations stemming from fraternity parties. Though L.A. is hardly a college town in any traditional sense, it does offer an endless variety of bars, clubs, shopping, and cultural experiences. As a junior points out, "The entire Los Angeles area is full of fun things to do if you're willing to hop on a train or take an

> **"[L.A.] is full of fun things to do if you're willing to hop on a train or take an Uber."**

Uber." Whether you're looking for an internship at a law firm or a movie studio, you want to learn to surf, or you're eager to check out a new band before they get signed to a major label, L.A. delivers. Famous Venice Beach is just a few miles from USC's campus, and in the winter months, students can reach the San Gabriel Mountains (and its ski resorts) in less than an hour (by car, not by skis). USC students are also active in the community, tutoring in 10 local schools through the Joint Educational Project.

Along with UCLA, USC will move to the Big Ten Conference in 2024. For now, Trojan athletics compete in the Division I Pac-12 Conference and have won 134 team national championships in 17 men's and women's sports, including women's beach volleyball in 2021 and 2022. Two of USC's biggest schoolwide traditions center on the ol' pigskin. The first is Troy Week—the week leading up to the UCLA game—which culminates with the Conquest pep rally and concert in the middle of campus. Then there's the Weekender, when USC students take off en masse for northern California to see their beloved Trojans face off against Stanford or Berkeley. Throngs of USC undergrads, alumni, and fans gather in San Francisco's Union Square for a huge pep rally, featuring the band, cheerleaders, and university personalities.

USC is a university on the move, though its progress has recently been marred by well-publicized scandals involving athletics, admissions, and sexual abuse. "We are drawing an academically competitive and involved student body," says a geography and communication major. Pack your sunscreen, flip-flops, and some assertiveness, and you'll fit right in. Shrinking violets, on the other hand, should probably look elsewhere.

Along with UCLA, USC will move to the Big Ten Conference in 2024.

Overlaps

Stanford, UCLA, UC Berkeley, NYU, Northwestern, Boston University, Cornell University, UC San Diego

If You Apply To ›

USC: Early action, regular decision. Accepts the Common Application. Please consult USC's website for the most up-to-date information regarding standardized test requirements.

Southern Methodist University

P.O. Box 750181, Dallas, TX 75275

SMU is best known for business, the performing arts, and an abundance of school spirit. Go-getter mentality is pervasive, and students benefit from internships and other opportunities in nearby Dallas. Picture-book campus on the city outskirts adds to its appeal. Methodist, but mainly in name.

Southern Methodist University is looking beyond its long-standing characterization as a training ground for the business elite of Dallas. Admissions standards are on the rise, and recent years have brought an updated curriculum that emphasizes interdisciplinary study, a new residential model, and, in the words of one senior, "tons of new campus buildings." The highly regarded Cox School of Business sets the no-nonsense tone for SMU's success-driven academic climate. Although founded in 1911 by what is now the United Methodist Church, SMU is nondenominational; 8 percent of students are Methodist, and all faiths are welcomed.

SMU's well-landscaped campus is situated in the toney suburb of University Park, located "five minutes from downtown Dallas and within 30 minutes of everything else," according to one student. Flower beds, fountains, and neatly trimmed lawns surround stately brick buildings, most of them collegiate Georgian. Dallas Hall, with its four-story rotunda, is the centerpiece. The Meadows Museum houses one of the finest collections of Spanish art outside Spain, and SMU is the only private college in the country to host a presidential library on its main campus, the George W. Bush Presidential Center. The recently opened Ford Hall for Research and Innovation serves as an interdisciplinary research hub for faculty, students, and industry partners to collaborate on complex problems.

> "Some of my professors have practically been my life coaches."

The Common Curriculum combines coursework in a range of disciplines with hands-on experiences and is designed to prepare students to be flexible, lifelong learners in a rapidly changing world. Students say they find ample time to explore their interests. "There is a lot of room to double or even triple major," explains a biology and math major. The Office of Engaged Learning supports students who wish to undertake capstone-level projects on campus or abroad, such as extended research, service projects, internships, and entrepreneurial start-ups; participants can apply for fellowships of up to $2,000.

Students hail the Cox School of Business (including its Caruth Institute for Entrepreneurship) and the Meadows School of the Arts, which turns out professional artists, actors, singers, and dancers, as SMU's strongest suits. Some of the most popular fields of study are finance, economics, biology, accounting, and applied physiology and sport management, an interdisciplinary program that teaches the biological basis of health while offering the business skills needed in the health and fitness industries. Engineers have access to top-of-the-line research labs and an extensive co-op program, thanks to the proximity of hundreds of high-tech companies, including AT&T and Texas Instruments. The Tower Center for Political Studies focuses on international relations and comparative politics, while the Tate Lecture Series gives students a chance to interact with national and international figures, such as Smithsonian Institution leader Lonnie G. Bunch III, *New York Times* columnist David Brooks, and author and television producer Padma Lakshmi. As for the humanities, English and history are particularly strong, and SMU publishes *Southwest Review*, the third-oldest continuously published literary quarterly in the nation. SMU was the first university in the South to offer a major in human rights.

> "There's a big go-getter mentality all throughout campus."

SMU prides itself on small classes; 55 percent of undergraduate courses have fewer than 20 students. "Some of my professors have practically been my life coaches," says an advertising major. "They've helped me excel in classes and prepare for interviews. They've provided recommendation letters and answered my emails at two in the morning. They never stop caring for their students." Most classes are taught by full-time faculty, and teaching assistants provide extra help. The student-staffed Altshuler Learning Enhancement Center offers tutoring and workshops.

Website: www.smu.edu
Location: City Outskirts
Private
Total Enrollment: 9,355
Undergraduates: 6,727
Male/Female: 50/50
Financial Aid: 74%
Pell Grant: 20%
Expense: Pr $ $ $
Student Loans: 29%
Average Debt: $ $ $ $
Applicants: 15,685
Accepted: 53%
Enrolled: 19%
Grad in 6 Years: 82%
Returning Freshmen: 91%
Academics: ✐ ✐ ✐
Social: ☎ ☎ ☎ ☎
Q of L: ★ ★ ★ ★
Admissions: (800) 323-0672
Email Address:
  ugadmission@smu.edu

Strong Programs:
Business
Visual and Performing Arts
Engineering
English
History
Finance
Economics
Biology

The Tate Lecture Series gives students a chance to interact with national and international figures, such as David Brooks and Padma Lakshmi.

The top 10 percent of each incoming class is invited to join the University Honors Program, which features small seminars on topics not offered broadly. Study abroad programs take 26 percent of undergrads around the world; faculty-led options are available in 14 locations. Each year, 20 to 25 exceptional incoming students are named President's Scholars and awarded full-tuition scholarships as well as opportunities to study abroad and participate in an annual retreat in Taos. Employers in the Dallas area offer a whopping 4,400 internships and learning opportunities to SMU students every year.

A marketing major describes SMU students as passionate and driven to succeed, adding, "There's a big go-getter mentality all throughout campus." Forty-three percent of undergraduates are from the Lone Star State, and 4 percent come from outside of the U.S. Hispanics/Latinos account for 14 percent of the student body, Asian Americans 8 percent, Black students 5 percent, and multiracial students 4 percent. SMU has a long ways to go in shedding its traditional image as a bastion of privilege; many students come from affluent families, and despite slowly increasing racial and socioeconomic diversity, a student comments, "We still need to improve." A senior reports that, politically, there is a "pretty good mix" of views on campus. SMU offers merit scholarships averaging $31,100, as well as roughly 250 athletic scholarships in 17 sports.

Fifty-two percent of undergrads live on campus; first- and second-year students are required to live in one of 11 Residential Commons, each of which has a resident faculty member, intended to integrate academic, residential, and social experiences.

"Boulevarding on game days is the most fun tailgating experience in the South!"

SMU Service House residents engage in community service in disadvantaged neighborhoods across Dallas. All residence halls are co-ed by floor, and options include single and double rooms, some with their own bathrooms. The traditional, all-you-can-eat meal plans include dining dollars that can be used at the two main dining halls and at on-campus fast-dining options like Chick-fil-A, Cinco Taco, and Panera Bread. "Now that I live off campus, I actually miss the food in the SMU dining halls," says a student. Campus security is said to be strong, and students praise the Not On My Campus campaign aimed at raising awareness of the issue of sexual assault.

When the weekend comes, the more than 200 student groups sponsor speakers and other diversions. "Social life at SMU is vibrant both on and off campus," says a sophomore. Thirty-six percent of the women join sororities, and 24 percent of the men pledge fraternities. "Greek organizations have off-campus parties, since SMU is technically a dry campus," notes a senior. Dallas has plenty to offer in terms of social life: "Whether it's exploring the Deep Ellum and Bishop Arts districts or going out in Uptown, we never get bored here," says a management major. Hundreds of students volunteer with more than 70 nonprofits in the greater Dallas area, and service trips over spring break are popular too. Highlights of the campus calendar include Perunapalooza, a birthday carnival in honor of the Mustang mascot (a pony). Students mark the end of the fall semester with the Celebration of Lights featuring holiday lights and carols at Dallas Hall. Favorite road trips are to Austin, with its abundance of restaurants, bars, and live music, and South Padre, Texas, a popular spring break spot with a great beach.

Football games are a big deal here—after all, this is Texas—and SMU students get riled up for the annual battle against Texas Christian University for possession of the Iron Skillet. For home games, students inject a dose of madness into their Methodism through Boulevarding, which features lavish tents, family activities, music, and food on the main quad. "Boulevarding on game days is the most fun tailgating experience in the South!" cheers an environmental studies major. When basketball season arrives, students camp out with their friends to get tickets, and

"The Mob" spirit group packs into the student section of Moody Coliseum. The SMU Mustangs compete in the Division I American Athletic Conference with considerable success. Men's golf, tennis, and swimming and diving and women's rowing are recent conference champions. About a third of the students participate each year in club sports and the intramural program, which offers more than 18 individual and team sporting activities.

"SMU is a relatively small school that has a big school feel," says a senior. "We still have a blast before home football games, we have big parties, and we have incredible school spirit." Although known for its striking campus and success-oriented students, SMU offers solid preprofessional training along with an active social life and ample opportunities to give back to the city of Dallas. The result is an environment where future industry moguls, problem solvers, performers, and artists alike can find space to grow.

Overlaps

Vanderbilt, Texas Christian, University of Southern California, Wake Forest, University of Miami (FL), UT Austin, Baylor, Tulane

If You Apply To ›

Southern Methodist: Early decision I and II, early action, regular decision. Accepts the Common Application with supplement. Please consult Southern Methodist's website for the most up-to-date information regarding standardized test requirements.

Southwestern University

1001 E. University Avenue, Georgetown, TX 78626

The oldest institution of higher education in Texas, Southwestern is one of its top liberal arts colleges. Compare to more conservative Austin College and much larger Trinity University. Southwestern prides itself on individual attention and down-to-earth friendliness, with emphasis on interdisciplinary and inquiry-based learning. Participation in the Paideia program adds spice to the learning environment.

In a state known for political conservatism and an assumption that bigger is better, Southwestern University stands out like a monadnock. Small and agile, it pursues a flexible and innovative brand of teaching and learning in a culture where the liberal arts are not always appreciated. "You learn to express and defend your opinions," says one student. "I learned how to think."

Founded in 1840, five years before Texas became a state, Southwestern sits on 700 acres at the edge of the rolling Texas Hill Country, although the city of Austin has expanded to meet Georgetown. The Texas limestone buildings, built in the Romanesque style, date from the early 20th century, and there are plenty of lush lawns and towering oak trees. Southwestern's commitment to sustainability includes an agreement with the city of Georgetown that allows it to use 100 percent wind power for the campus's electrical needs. The university recently sold two valuable properties and is using the funds for a slate of renovation and construction projects, including a new, mixed-use first-year residence hall, an on-campus football stadium, and more.

> "You learn to express and defend your opinions."

To graduate, Southwestern students must complete a First-Year Seminar and satisfy requirements in several liberal arts areas, as well as language and culture, social justice, fitness and recreational activity, and a capstone experience. All students participate in the Paideia program, which gives them a chance to explore interests that

Website: www.southwestern.edu
Location: Suburban
Private
Total Enrollment: 1,480
Undergraduates: 1,480
Male/Female: 46/54
Financial Aid: 99%
Pell Grant: 26%
Expense: Pr $ $
Student Loans: 55%
Average Debt: $ $ $
Applicants: 4,757
Accepted: 51%
Enrolled: 15%
Grad in 6 Years: 73%
Returning Freshmen: 81%
Academics: ✐ ✐ ✐ ½
Social: ☎ ☎ ☎

(continued)

Q of L: ★ ★ ★
Admissions: (512) 863-1200
Email Address: admission@
    southwestern.edu

Strong Programs:
Psychology
Communication Studies
Biology
Business
Studio Art
Environmental Studies
Sociology

may fall outside their major and see how different disciplines are interconnected. A sociology and English double major explains, "It's nice to be able to get a taste of how others may see and understand the world in various other disciplines." The university has bolstered academic advising, assigning every incoming student to a professional academic advisor, followed by a faculty or staff advisor after their first year.

The most popular majors are also some of Southwestern's strongest: psychology, communication studies, biology, and business, which is taught as one of the liberal arts. In the Sarofim School of Fine Arts, where pottery is a specialty, student work approaches graduate-level quality. Environmental studies and sociology are also strengths. Political science and STEM majors alike benefit from SU's proximity to Austin, the state capital and a hub of tech innovation. Interdisciplinary minors are available in data science, health studies, and design thinking. The university offers three preprofessional programs in engineering, law, and health.

"We are constantly being challenged to take what we learn in class and apply it to more difficult problems," says a senior. Sixty-seven percent of SU classes have fewer than 20 students, and professors are appreciated for their willingness to help students with course concepts and research opportunities. Academic support and career services are highly praised as well, from departmental student mentors, such as the SCI Guides in the natural sciences, to the comprehensive resources offered by the Center for Career and Professional Development, including one-on-one counseling, alumni panels, and campuswide internship and job fairs. "I definitely feel prepared for life after college because everything is a process that has been put in motion since I arrived my first semester," says a junior.

> **"We are constantly being challenged to take what we learn in class and apply it to more difficult problems."**

SU encourages undergraduate research (about half of the students participate), and each year holds a symposium to showcase students' scholarly endeavors. The King Creativity Fund provides grants to support up to 20 "innovative and visionary projects" each academic year. Twenty-one percent of Southwestern's students choose to study in a foreign land, and SU hosts faculty-led programs in England, Spain, Peru, and Argentina, among others. The university also sponsors an internship program in Washington, D.C., and an arts apprenticeship program in New York City.

Eighty-seven percent of Southwestern students come from Texas, and many are the first in their families to go to college. The university is affiliated with the United Methodist Church, and 8 percent of students are Methodist. Hispanics/Latinos are the largest minority group at SU, making up 27 percent of the student body; Black students add 5 percent, Asian Americans 4 percent, and multiracial students 5 percent. One percent come from foreign countries. Students describe a sometimes volatile mix of conservative and liberal political views on campus. "The CDSJ (Coalition for Diversity and Social Justice) is a fantastic umbrella organization that has a place for everyone to get involved and be an activist on and off campus," says a computer science major. Eligible students receive scholarships based on academic performance, averaging $24,700 annually; talent awards are also available for fine arts majors, though there are no athletic scholarships.

All students participate in the Paideia program, which gives them a chance to explore interests that may fall outside their major.

Sixty-four percent of SU students live in the residence halls, where the number of stars definitely improves as you get older—juniors and seniors usually get apartment-style facilities with their own bedrooms, bathrooms, and kitchens. Meals at the central, all-you-can-eat Mabee Commons dining hall are getting "somewhat better than what they'd been in recent years," according to a senior. Students do enjoy the nearby Cove's coffee bar and late-night grill. Students can also swipe their "Pirate cards" at pizzerias and other local merchants. Students say they generally feel safe on campus, but the administration's handling of sexual assault cases has been a hot-button issue.

Almost all the social life at Southwestern takes place on campus. "Wednesday, Friday, and Saturday nights are the main party nights, but there is always something going on," says one student. The school sponsors frequent activities like retro game nights, carnival nights, and free concerts. Southwestern has a strong Greek system, drawing 24 percent of the men and 33 percent of the women, "but you do not have to be Greek to have a fabulous social life," says a sociology major. Students 21 and older are permitted to consume alcohol in designated areas on campus. Annual traditions include the spring concert on the mall and Late Night Breakfast, in which "faculty and staff serve students breakfast during finals week while karaoke and other fun stuff happens!"

Political science and STEM majors alike benefit from SU's proximity to Austin, the state capital and a hub of tech innovation.

Georgetown (population 75,000), the county seat, caters mainly to families, but things are getting more exciting thanks to the expanding bar and restaurant options, weekly farmers markets, and live music on Friday evenings. The city's historic downtown and the popular Blue Hole swimming area are both within walking distance of campus, and students enjoy bike trails along the San Gabriel River. "Georgetown offers a lot of natural beauty," says a communication major. Fifty-nine percent of students get involved in the community through service-learning and volunteer work. The bars and clubs of Austin's Sixth Street are just a half hour away, and San Antonio, College Station, Dallas, and Houston aren't that much farther.

"You do not have to be Greek to have a fabulous social life."

The Southwestern Pirates field 20 Division III varsity sports. The school is a member of the Southern Collegiate Athletic Conference; women's tennis and men's golf are recent conference champions. Men's tennis, women's soccer, and women's volleyball are also competitive. The university reintroduced football in 2013 and wasted little time in claiming a conference title. Games against archrival Trinity in San Antonio always draw crowds. Sixty percent of students compete in 18 intramural and club sports, with flag football, basketball, sand volleyball, and pickleball being the most popular.

With its emphasis on in-depth and student-centered learning, Southwestern is doing its best to push the frontiers of liberal arts instruction in the 21st century. "SU allows you to continue to grow and challenge yourself in a safe and accepting atmosphere," says a freshman. In a state where things tend to be huge and overwhelming, Southwestern University is out to show that good things can come in small packages.

Overlaps

Centre, Allegheny, Kalamazoo, Hendrix, Wheaton (MA), Trinity University (TX), Baylor, Austin College

If You Apply To ›

Southwestern: Early decision, early action, regular decision. SATs or ACTs: optional (test-optional applicants must interview. Test scores required for consideration for competitive scholarships). Accepts the Common Application with supplement.

Spelman College: See page 38.

Stanford University

Stanford, CA 94305-3005

If you're looking for an Eastern counterpart to Stanford, think Duke with a touch of MIT mixed in. Stanford's big-time athletics, preprofessional feel, and laid-back atmosphere set it apart from Ivy League competitors. In contrast to the hurly-burly of Bay Area rival Berkeley, Stanford's aura is upscale, spacious, and green. Bring your bike and a pair of sunglasses, and leave your ego behind.

Website: www.stanford.edu
Location: Suburban
Private
Total Enrollment: 16,552
Undergraduates: 7,645
Male/Female: 49/51
Financial Aid: 84%
Pell Grant: 20%
Expense: Pr $ $ $
Student Loans: 13%
Average Debt: $
Applicants: 55,471
Accepted: 4%
Enrolled: 80%
Grad in 6 Years: 96%
Returning Freshmen: 98%
Academics: ✍ ✍ ✍ ✍ ✍
Social: ☎ ☎ ☎ ☎
Q of L: ★ ★ ★ ★ ★
Admissions: (650) 723-2091
Email Address: admission@
stanford.edu

Strong Programs:
Computer Science
Engineering
International Relations
Public Policy
Earth Systems
Communication
Biology
Marine Science

Stanford built its academic reputation around science and engineering, fields conducive to American ingenuity and industry.

You might think the only difference between Stanford and the Ivy League is a couple hundred extra sunny days each year. You'd be wrong. From the red-tiled roofs to the lush greenery and California vibe, Stanford is a world away from the Gothic intellectual vibes of the Ivies. Virtually all the great Eastern universities began as places to ponder human existence and the meaning of life, with European institutions as their models. Stanford, by contrast, built its academic reputation around science and engineering, fields conducive to American ingenuity and industry, and only later cultivated excellence in the humanities and social sciences. In this sense, Stanford is, without a doubt, the nation's first great "American" university. Now one of the most super-selective universities in the country—turning down 24 of every 25 applicants—Stanford has begun to increase the size of its entering classes and intends to expand its dormitories and number of faculty proportionately until it reaches a new comfort level.

The differences between Stanford and other institutions it competes against for the country's top high school seniors are evident everywhere, from the architecture to the curriculum. The school's mission-style buildings look outward to the world at large, rather than inward to ivy-covered court-yards. And unlike its Colonial-era predecessors, Stanford—founded in 1885 by Leland and Jane Stanford in memory of their son Leland Jr.—has been co-ed from the beginning. During its centennial, the school became the first U.S. university to successfully launch a billion-dollar capital campaign; today Stanford's endowment is $36 billion. Some architectural critics say the campus looks like the world's biggest Mexican restaurant, even though Frederick Law Olmsted, designer of New York City's Central Park, planned many of the buildings. The campus stretches from the foothills of the Santa Cruz Mountains to the edge of Palo Alto in the heart of Silicon Valley, smack in the middle of earthquake country. The campus is nationally recognized as "bicycle friendly" and is outfitted with 12 miles of bike lanes, 19,000 bike parking spaces, and free bike repair stations.

> "People are always working together on projects and assignments."

Stanford requires students to complete one course in Thinking Matters and 11 in a series called Ways of Thinking/Ways of Doing, which includes aesthetic and interpretive inquiry, social inquiry, scientific analysis, formal reasoning, applied quantitative reasoning, engaging diversity, ethical reasoning, and creative expression. Stanford also requires writing and rhetoric courses and one year of a foreign language. More than 200 optional, small-group Introductory Seminars are available to freshmen and sophomores, covering topics like The Data Scientist as Detective and The Global Refugee Crisis, in which about half of students enroll; one student credits these courses with helping freshmen "develop relationships with really engaging professors."

Computer science is the most popular major on campus, followed by human biology, economics, symbolic systems, and engineering, especially mechanical engineering. Stanford has developed a spate of interdisciplinary programs, notably international relations, public policy, and earth systems; the latter is an interdisciplinary environmental science major. The Haas Center for Public Service offers more than 130 service-learning courses in a wide range of disciplines, while the well-regarded communication department offers paid positions at various California media outlets. The Stanford Hopkins Marine Station is located on a mile of coastland in Pacific Grove, next to the Monterey Bay Aquarium, and offers courses in marine and biological sciences.

Don't let Stanford's California location fool you into thinking studying is optional—it's more like a full-time job. "People are always working together on projects and assignments. This might be because it is intense, and many students do take on a heavy workload," one student says. Students sometimes compare themselves to ducks: they look peaceful on the surface, but they're paddling like mad underneath. Stanford's faculty ranks among the best in the nation, with impeccable credentials, and most departments boast a nationally known name or two. Class sizes are generally small, with 68 percent enrolling fewer than 20 students, and 93 percent are taught by faculty, as opposed to graduate students. "Overall, professors do seem to care about the students. They are definitely accessible, almost all having open office hours," says one computer science major.

For students inclined to study abroad, programs are offered at Stanford's campus in Cape Town, South Africa, as well as several other locations around the globe, including Australia, Chile, Japan, and Germany. Forty-eight percent of each graduating class takes advantage of these programs. Closer to home, the Stanford-in-Washington program allows 60 students to live, study, and intern in the nation's capital each quarter, and a similar program is offered in New York City. The Summer Research College is designed to create community among undergraduates engaged in full-time summer research on campus, and there are three honors programs. Three-quarters of students undertake independent study projects with faculty. For those seeking additional academic support, the Schwab Learning Center—named after alum Charles Schwab—offers services for students with learning disabilities and ADHD.

> **"[Professors] are definitely accessible, almost all having open office hours."**

Stanford students may be Olympic champions and future Rhodes scholars, but students say there isn't a sense of elitism on campus. One notes, "People are a bit quirky, but everyone is generally happy and easy to get along with." Thirty-five percent are from California, while international students represent 11 percent of the population. More than half of undergraduates identify as students of color: Asian Americans account for 25 percent, Hispanics/Latinos 18 percent, Black students 7 percent, and multiracial students 10 percent. Students on this liberal campus are keen to be heard, and recent hot topics include "divestment from Israel, divestment from fossil fuels, and race relations," according to one senior. Admissions are need-blind, and the university guarantees to meet the full demonstrated financial need of every domestic admit. Academic scholarships are based on need (meaning no merit awards), and Stanford has eliminated parent contributions for families with annual incomes below $150,000. The university also awards hundreds of athletic scholarships every year.

The campus is outfitted with 12 miles of bike lanes, 19,000 bike parking spaces, and free bike repair stations.

Freshmen must live on campus, and Stanford guarantees housing for four years; 97 percent of students stay on campus, in part because of the lack of affordable off-campus options in extraordinarily expensive Silicon Valley. As students gain seniority, a lottery system decides where they'll live. "Junior year I lived in an old faculty mansion for 30 students that had a Thai chef," one student says. The multimillion-dollar Governor's Corner complex includes all-oak fixtures, homey rooms with views of the foothills, microwave ovens in the kitchenettes, and Italian leather sofas in the lounges. Dorm dwellers must sign up for a meal plan. "Campus security is quite good. We have an AlertSU program that texts emergency messages to the school whenever there is any sort of security violation, and Stanford is extremely well-lit at night," says a freshman.

> **"People are a bit quirky, but everyone is generally happy and easy to get along with."**

Like most things at Stanford, social life and activities vary a great deal, although most take place on campus, with a constant lineup of events and performances. Greek organizations claim 15 percent of the men and 16 percent of the women and provide their share of happy hours and weekend bashes, which are open to all. Underage drinking happens, but is kept under control. As one freshman puts it, "Party culture is not exclusively Greek, and social life is not exclusively partying." As tradition goes, Full Moon on the Quad occurs at the first full moon of the fall quarter, during which freshmen can become "true Stanford students" by kissing a senior at midnight on the quad. The Viennese Ball is a February event that may make you wish you'd taken ballroom dancing lessons, and Halloween finds students partying at the Mausoleum, the Stanfords' final resting place.

The Haas Center for Public Service offers more than 130 service-learning courses in a wide range of disciplines.

Halloween finds students partying at the Mausoleum, the Stanfords' final resting place.

Palo Alto "has a few fun hangouts and is slightly overpriced," a political science major says, and students love to seek refuge in the outdoors—nearby hills are perfect for jogging and biking. Trips to the Sierra Nevada mountains (four hours away) or to the Pacific Coast (45 minutes) are popular, as are jaunts to San Francisco, Los Angeles, or the Napa Valley.

The Stanford Cardinals have a proud athletic tradition that has made it a perennial winner of the Division I Directors' Cup, which recognizes the best overall collegiate athletic program in the country. The women's water polo, women's golf, and men's gymnastics teams captured national championships in 2022. The baseball team has been to the College World Series, and the football team has become a powerhouse. Men's water polo and women's volleyball, swimming and diving, and soccer are also standouts. The annual contest against Pac-12 archrival Cal (Berkeley) is dubbed the "Big Game." The marching band proudly revels in its raucous irreverence, to the delight of students and the dismay of conservative types. For those not drawn to varsity play, Stanford offers 31 club sports and 20 intramural activities, and its vast sports complex includes 26 tennis courts, two gymnasiums, a stadium, an 18-hole golf course, and four swimming pools.

> "Party culture is not exclusively Greek, and social life is not exclusively partying."

Stanford University's sunny demeanor and infectious West Coast optimism offer an appealing alternative to the gloom and gray weather that seem to hang over some of its East Coast counterparts, with the same high-caliber academics and deep athletic traditions that have made them great. One student muses, "There is a very innovative and individualistic personality that is also a collective culture on campus."

Overlaps

Harvard, Princeton, Yale, MIT, Brown, Duke, Columbia, University of Chicago

If You Apply To ›

Stanford: Single choice early action, regular decision. Accepts the Common Application with supplement. Please consult Stanford's website for the most up-to-date information regarding standardized test requirements.

State University of New York

As the second-largest comprehensive university system in the country (after its California State counterpart), the State University of New York provides its 370,000 students with a lavish buffet of educational opportunities, from optometry, fashion, and ceramics to space-age Ph.D.s in nanoscale engineering and everything in between.

The statistics of SUNY (pronounced "SOOney") are awesome. SUNY has an annual operating budget of billions, greater than the gross national product of many countries and larger than the budget of more than a dozen American states. The system encompasses 64 campuses across New York and 21,000 acres of property. It has some 326,000 undergraduates, more than 4,350 undergraduate majors, and 33,000 faculty members. Every year SUNY's colleges and universities award about 91,000 degrees (74,000 of them to undergraduates), ranging from associate's to Ph.D.s in thousands of academic fields. And it boasts nearly 3 million living alumni.

Not only does this scale and breadth make SUNY a microcosm of all that American higher education has to offer, but its universities have long been among the most affordable in the U.S. Under New York State's Excelsior Scholarship program, the first of its kind in the country, in-state students from households earning up to $125,000 qualify for free tuition at any of the state's two- and four-year institutions.

These statistics are all the more remarkable considering that until 1948, the State of New York had no state university at all. That year, the legislature created the State University of New York around a cluster of 29 institutions, the best of which focused on the training of teachers, to handle the flow of returning World War II veterans.

A "gentleman's agreement" not to compete with the state's private colleges, which for generations had enjoyed a monopoly on higher education in New York, hindered SUNY's movement into the liberal arts. Not until Nelson A. Rockefeller became governor in 1960, and made its expansion a priority, did the State University begin its dramatic growth.

SUNY has since evolved into a vast knowledge network consisting of 14 University Centers and doctoral-granting institutions (think research universities, medical schools, specialized colleges of environmental science and veterinary medicine, and the like); 13 four-year Arts and Sciences Colleges (think liberal arts institutions, offering both undergraduate and graduate programs); seven Technology Colleges, offering both two- and four-year degrees in specialized fields; and 30 locally sponsored Community Colleges.

Consistent with this ambitious enterprise, system leaders have made a concerted effort to recognize and enhance student diversity and to make students of all backgrounds feel welcome. The Office of Diversity, Equity, and Inclusion has helped increase enrollment of students of color. Nevertheless, a slight majority of the student body—53 percent—continues to be white. Fifteen percent of students are Hispanic/Latino, 10 percent are Black, 8 percent are Asian American, and 3 percent are multiracial. SUNY has launched numerous initiatives to increase retention and graduation rates among underrepresented students and is now turning its attention to faculty—to the support of historically underrepresented faculty of color in general and of women faculty of all races in STEM fields. SUNY's definition of diversity is sweeping and covers not only race and ethnicity but also religion, sexual orientation, gender identity and expression, age, and socioeconomic status.

Prospective students apply to SUNY via the system's ApplySUNY portal or the Common App, selecting the campuses where they wish to be considered. Levels of selectivity inevitably vary widely across an institutional network of this size: most SUNY Community Colleges operate on an open-enrollment basis, while SUNY's "U-centers" and specialized programs are among the most competitive public institutions in the nation. Students who earn associate's degrees in a two-year SUNY program are guaranteed the chance to continue their education at a four-year institution (though not necessarily at their first choice). In-state undergraduates pay the same tuition at all SUNY institutions and comparable, if varying, fees. Rates at the Community Colleges are lower and vary. For the roughly 17,000 out-of-state students, who make up 5 percent of the student body, tuition and fees at a SUNY school currently run between $10,700 and $26,700, depending on the type of institution—well within range of other leading public flagships such as UC Berkeley and the University of Michigan.

Mainly for political reasons, the State University of New York chose not to follow the model of other states and build a single, flagship campus like an Austin or a Chapel Hill. Instead, it created four University Centers with undergraduate, graduate, and professional schools—one in each corner of the state. Although each of them considers itself to be a comprehensive university, there has been a certain degree of specialization from the beginning: Albany is strongest in education and public policy, Binghamton is best known for undergraduate arts and sciences, Stony Brook is noted for its hard sciences, and Buffalo maintains a strong reputation in the life sciences and geography. In January 2022 the state formally designated both Stony Brook and Buffalo as joint flagships of the SUNY system. Critics charge that the decision to forgo a dominant flagship campus for so many decades has diminished SUNY's chances of achieving national prominence, and that the lack of big-time, Division I football and famous Ph.D. programs has affected its reputation. That said, others maintain that somewhere in the labs and libraries of these public powerhouses are lurking the Nobel Prize winners of this century.

SUNY's 13 Arts and Sciences Colleges vary in size and character. Many were founded historically as teachers' colleges and have successfully made the transition into public liberal arts colleges on the small, New England model. They range from Potsdam, the northernmost SUNY campus and one of the oldest colleges in the United States, to Purchase, a suburban campus in Westchester County that specializes in the visual and performing arts, to Old Westbury on Long Island, which began as an experimental institution to serve minority students, older women, and others who had been "bypassed" by more traditional institutions.

The seven Technology Colleges lack the academic prominence of their Arts and Sciences peers, but they play a key role in serving state and regional demand for vocational training by delivering a wide variety of two- and four-year programs. Five of them (Alfred State, Canton, Cobleskill, Delhi, and Morrisville) are concerned primarily with agriculture but also have programs in engineering, nursing, medical technology, data processing, and business administration. Farmingdale offers an extensive range of programs, from ornamental horticulture to aerospace technology. Maritime, founded in 1874, is the oldest maritime academy in the United States.

A little-known feature of the SUNY system is that five of its state-funded programs are lodged in private institutions—four at Cornell University (agriculture and life sciences, human ecology, industrial and labor relations, and veterinary medicine) and one at Alfred University (ceramics). Even though they are attending a private institution, students in these programs pay much lower SUNY-level tuition rates.

Like their peers around the country, SUNY's 30 Community Colleges have traditionally enjoyed a lower profile, but a growing emphasis on vocationalism and the soaring costs of higher education have brought them back into favor. It used to be that students looked to New York's Community Colleges for terminal degrees that could readily apply to the marketplace. Now, a growing number of students who otherwise would have been packed off to a four-year college are saving money by staying home for the first two years and then transferring within the SUNY system to a four-year college—or even a University Center—to get their bachelor's degrees. More than half of SUNY's Community Colleges offer on-campus housing.

Following are full-length descriptions of SUNY's four University Centers (the University at Albany, Binghamton University, the University at Buffalo, and Stony Brook University) as well as two of the Arts and Sciences Colleges best known beyond New York's borders (Purchase College and the College at Geneseo).

SUNY–University at Albany

1400 Washington Avenue, Albany, NY 12222

Like the rest of the SUNY system, University at Albany is much better than its relative anonymity would suggest. Strong in anything related to public policy, including criminal justice and social welfare. Study abroad programs in Europe and Asia are also strengths. Only 7 percent of undergrads are from outside the Empire State. Campus is a living reminder of just how bad 1960s architecture could be.

Website: www.albany.edu
Location: Suburban
Public
Total Enrollment: 13,950
Undergraduates: 11,787
Male/Female: 46/54
Financial Aid: 90%
Pell Grant: 42%
Expense: Pub $
Student Loans: 66%
Average Debt: $ $
Applicants: 21,265
Accepted: 68%
Enrolled: 21%
Grad in 6 Years: 65%
Returning Freshmen: 83%
Academics: ✍ ✍ ✍ ✍
Social: ☎ ☎ ☎
Q of L: ★ ★ ★
Admissions: (518) 442-5435
Email Address:
  ugadmissions@albany.edu

Strong Programs:
Public Policy and Management
Social Welfare

Founded in 1844 to train teachers, UAlbany offers a bevy of outstanding programs in arts and sciences, business administration, and preprofessional programs, and it is placing increased emphasis on technology. Study abroad is solid too, but—consistent with its location in the state capital—it's the university's public policy programs that truly shine.

Designed by Edward Durrell Stone, who also designed the Kennedy Center and Lincoln Center, UAlbany's main uptown campus is stark, modern, and suburban. Almost all the original academic buildings are clustered in the center of the campus, while students are housed in symmetrically situated quads so similar in appearance that it usually takes a semester to figure out which one is yours. (Hint: the quads are named for periods in New York history—Indian, Dutch, Colonial, State, and Freedom—and progress clockwise around the campus. Got it?) The downtown campus primarily houses the university's public policy programs, and the health sciences campus is home to public health programs and research centers. A spate of construction projects has changed the face of the uptown campus over the past decade, and a $180 million Emerging Technology and Entrepreneurship Complex, located adjacent to the main campus, opened in 2021.

> "Our school has a vibrant social life on and off campus."

UAlbany's general education program consists of 30 credits of distribution requirements, through which students must demonstrate competency in advanced writing, oral discourse, information literacy, and critical thinking. In addition, all freshmen take a required introductory seminar. For the career-minded, most of UAlbany's preprofessional programs are among the best of any SUNY branch. Students in the public policy and management, social welfare, and criminal justice programs may take advantage of their proximity to the state government to participate in internships. Psychology, communication, and criminal justice are popular majors, and undergrads are clamoring for admittance to the university's business administration program, which is especially strong in accounting. Students can sign up for one of more than 30 B.A./M.A. programs or opt for a six-year law degree in conjunction with UAlbany Law School. The New York State Writers Institute is the least traditional of UAlbany's offerings and has enhanced the university's reputation in creative writing. The College of Emergency Preparedness, Homeland Security, and Cybersecurity is the first of its kind in the nation.

The academic climate is challenging, and courses tend to be demanding. Classes can be large, but 25 percent enroll fewer than 20 students. Students form study groups to help one another through the coursework, and professors are always available to offer support. "The quality of teaching is excellent overall," a physics major says. "There are some superstar professors and a bad apple here and there, but usually very good instructors." Qualified students can take part in the Honors College, which allows freshmen and sophomores to enroll in up to six introductory courses that have been designed by distinguished faculty. The courses emphasize research, service learning, and a creative component. Senior honors students design and complete a yearlong research or creative project. About 12 percent of students take advantage of UAlbany's superior offerings in foreign study, which include programs in 40 countries, plus hundreds of other options available through the SUNY system.

According to a sophomore, "A great many students come from New York City and Long Island, and it can be difficult for western and upstate New Yorkers as well as out-of-state students to fit in." Just 4 percent of undergraduates come from states outside New York, and another 3 percent come from foreign countries. Black students make up 21 percent of the student body, Hispanics/Latinos 18 percent, Asian Americans 9 percent, and multiracial students 4 percent. "This campus is friendly and welcoming of individuals of every race and sexual orientation," says a sociology major. UAlbany makes available merit scholarships, averaging $4,200, and roughly 200 athletic scholarships in 18 sports. Forty-two percent of first-year students are Pell-eligible. Thanks to New York State's Excelsior Scholarship program, in-state residents whose annual household income does not exceed $125,000 qualify for free tuition.

Forty-eight percent of students live in university housing; freshmen and sophomores are required to live in dorms, where the rooms are described as small but "satisfactory." Each floor is divided into four- to six-person suites. Living/learning communities allow incoming freshmen who share similar interests or majors to live together in the same residence hall and take some courses together. Many students move off campus because "the transportation system to and from campus is convenient and the cost of apartments is as cheap or cheaper than living on campus," explains a junior. Students on the main campus take their meals at the Indian or State quads or at the recently remodeled Campus Center, while most downtowners live and eat at Alumni Quad. "The Advocacy Center for Sexual Violence is a fantastic resource for students and is quite effective," says a sophomore.

"You can find an outlet here for even the most obscure interest."

"Our school has a vibrant social life on and off campus," says a senior. "There are multiple clubs and events on campus, and downtown Albany also has a good social scene, such as clubs and restaurants." Students have more than 250 clubs and organizations to choose from, many of which are involved in community service. While most people are serious about their work, a UAlbany weekend starts on Thursday night for many, with off-campus parties or barhopping about town. Students warn that alcohol policies forbidding underage drinking are strict and well enforced. Fraternities and sororities attract just 1 percent of the men and 1 percent of the women, yet they have become the school's main party-throwers. Parkfest is a huge all-school concert that brings in well-known as well as up-and-coming bands.

(continued)

Criminal Justice
Business Administration
Creative Writing
Emergency Preparedness, Homeland Security, and Cybersecurity
Psychology
Communication

Honors College courses designed by distinguished faculty emphasize research, service learning, and a creative component.

The Student Association owns and operates Dippikill, a wilderness retreat described as UAlbany's "own little Walden" in the Adirondacks.

The natural resources of the upstate region keep students busy skiing and hiking, and the Student Association owns and operates Dippikill, a wilderness retreat described as UAlbany's "own little Walden" in the Adirondacks. Treks to Montreal and Saratoga are also popular.

As for varsity sports, most Great Danes teams play in the Division I America East Conference. The men's and women's indoor and outdoor track and field teams have dominated the conference, claiming dozens of championships in recent years. Men's and women's lacrosse, men's soccer, and women's basketball are also highly competitive. Intramurals and club sports engender a great deal of student enthusiasm, and participation numbers in the thousands.

The University at Albany is not the concrete, sterile diploma mill it may appear to be. It's a place of opportunity for those willing to put in the hours and hard work. As one veteran cautions, "You can find an outlet here for even the most obscure interest, but this is not a school that will educate you when you're not looking."

Overlaps

**SUNY–Stony Brook,
SUNY–Binghamton,
SUNY–Stony Brook,
SUNY–Plattsburgh,
SUNY–Buffalo,
SUNY–New Paltz,
SUNY–Oneonta,
College of Saint Rose**

If You Apply To ›

SUNY–Albany: Early action, regular decision. Accepts the Common Application with supplement. Please consult SUNY–Albany's website for the most up-to-date information regarding standardized test requirements.

SUNY–Binghamton University

P.O. Box 6001, Binghamton, NY 13902-6000

If 100,000 screaming fans on a Saturday afternoon tickles your fancy, head 200 miles southwest to Penn State. Binghamton has become one of the premier public universities in the Northeast because of its outstanding academics and commitment to undergraduates. It is writing the rules on how to integrate global awareness and international experiences into undergraduate study.

Website: www.binghamton.edu
Location: Suburban
Public
Total Enrollment: 16,200
Undergraduates: 13,966
Male/Female: 48/52
Financial Aid: 77%
Pell Grant: 27%
Expense: Pub $
Student Loans: 52%
Average Debt: $ $
Applicants: 39,533
Accepted: 44%
Enrolled: 18%
Grad in 6 Years: 84%
Returning Freshmen: 91%
Academics: ✑ ✑ ✑ ✑ ½
Social: ☎ ☎ ☎

Since its founding in 1946, Binghamton University has offered a private-school experience at a public-school price, even for out-of-staters. With more than 450 clubs and an emphasis on small classes—87 percent of those taken by undergraduates have fewer than 50 students—it's no wonder that students who apply here are also considering schools such as Cornell and NYU. Binghamton offers an intellectually challenging environment with an emphasis on global experiences, including education abroad opportunities in more than 100 countries, area studies programs that focus on specific regions of the world, and the unique Languages Across the Curriculum program. "The biggest complaint," muses one student, "is the one thing that no one can change: the weather."

Binghamton's campus sits on 930 acres of open grassy space and includes a nature preserve, trails, fountains, and a pond. The oldest buildings date from 1958, so the prevailing architectural style is modern and "functional." Some students say that, from the air, the circular campus bears a striking resemblance to the human brain, but administrators insist that's merely a coincidence. A slew of renovations and construction, including two residential communities, science and technology buildings, a major renovation of the University Union, and the addition of a $60 million baseball stadium complex has given the campus an up-to-date feel. A 13-acre Health Sciences Campus, located a short drive from the main campus, includes the School of Pharmacy and Pharmaceutical Sciences building; the Health Sciences Building, which opened in 2021; and a new research facility for the pharmacy school that is slated for completion in fall 2023.

Students apply to one of the university's five schools with undergraduate programs: the Decker College of Nursing and Health Sciences, the Harpur College of Arts and Sciences, the College of Community and Public Affairs, the School of Management, and the Thomas J. Watson College of Engineering and Applied Science (named for the founder of IBM). Regardless of the school they choose, students face the same general education requirements, which span four categories: language and communication, creating a global vision, liberal arts (including sciences, mathematics, aesthetics, and humanities), and physical activity and wellness. The Student Transition and Success program provides first-year students with peer mentors and assistance in exploring experiential learning opportunities and career paths.

> "Students are usually self-motivated and cooperative."

Popular majors include integrative neuroscience, psychology, economics, biological sciences, and accounting. Business administration and engineering majors are strong, and minors in global studies and health and wellness studies are well regarded. More than 50 combined bachelor's/master's degree programs are available, and the pharmacy school offers guaranteed acceptance to its Pharm.D. program to academically eligible incoming students. Students have the option to design their own majors via the Individualized Major Program in Harpur College. Binghamton's academic reputation is enhanced by a tough grading policy, which includes pluses and minuses as well as straight letter grades, and Fs on the transcripts of failing students rather than no credit. "Students are usually self-motivated and cooperative," says a sophomore. "Beating the test is usually more important than beating other students." According to a biology major, "There are some great teachers here and some not so great. All faculty members, however, have made themselves very accessible."

Binghamton operates student exchanges with universities around the world and directly sponsors more than 50 study abroad programs in locations as diverse as the UK, Costa Rica, India, Ghana, South Korea, and Australia. "Study abroad at Binghamton is huge!" says an English major. Twenty-two percent of students study abroad at some point in their undergraduate careers. Undergraduate research is also emphasized here (39 percent of students participate), and the invitation-only First-Year Research Immersion program involves enriched courses taught by teams of faculty from multiple STEM disciplines. Faculty-supervised independent research, often culminating in a senior honors thesis, is common in Harpur College. The Source Project allows first-year students to conduct original research in social sciences and the humanities. The Binghamton University Scholars Program is a four-year honors program offering special seminars and leadership training to exceptional students, along with opportunities for experiential learning and junior- and senior-year capstone projects.

The Student Transition and Success program provides first-year students with peer mentors.

Although Binghamton offers a top-notch liberal arts and sciences education, word of its excellence has been slow to cross state lines: only 7 percent of undergraduates come from states beyond the Empire State, and another 4 percent hail from foreign nations. By other measures, though, Binghamton's student body is rather diverse: Black students make up 5 percent of the total, Hispanics/Latinos 13 percent, Asian Americans 16 percent, and multiracial students 4 percent. "The biggest social and political issues on campus relate to social equality," a student reports. "Students at Binghamton are very proactive, and we hold meetings that raise questions and provoke ideas." The university has taken several steps in recent years to create a more inclusive campus environment, including the establishment of an LGBTQ center and the addition of a vice president for diversity, equity, and inclusion. Binghamton offers merit scholarships and grants worth an average of $8,800,

> "Study abroad at Binghamton is huge!"

(continued)

Q of L: ★ ★ ★ ★
Admissions: (607) 777-2171
Email Address: admit@ binghamton.edu

Strong Programs:
Area Studies
Foreign Languages
Business Administration
Engineering
Integrative Neuroscience
Psychology
Economics
Biological Sciences

as well as roughly 300 full or partial athletic scholarships in 21 sports. Under the state's Excelsior Scholarship program, New York residents from families earning $125,000 or less per year qualify for free tuition.

About half of Binghamton's students live in the residence halls, most of which have traditional double rooms with bathrooms down the hall or suites with common rooms and shared bathrooms. As one student explains, "Binghamton models the housing system after Oxford. We have six different residential communities, comprised of two to five buildings each. This makes a rather large university seem smaller and more comfortable." One community consists of two apartment-style buildings for upperclassmen. Each community is led by a collegiate professor who helps link students' residential and academic experiences, and each has its own set of traditions. Dining halls have plenty of options, and students report feeling safe while trekking around the university grounds. "The university works hard to make our campus feel like a home; students have enough to worry about, and safety does not need to be one of those things," a senior says.

When the weekend comes, Binghamton students know how to let off steam. On campus, a senior says, "The options are endless: bowling, concerts, performances, Late Nite Binghamton, sports, and much more." Late Nite Binghamton brings free movies, games, a coffee bar, and other nonalcoholic fun to campus, from 8 p.m. until 1 a.m. every Friday and Saturday. Frat parties occur off campus; 15 percent of the men and 16 percent of the women go Greek. One student emphasizes that Greek Life is "not something that defines you at this school." While some underage students manage to find alcohol, any caught violating the school's policy "will be taken care of accordingly," says a senior. Annual campus traditions include Stepping on the Coat (to celebrate the arrival of warm weather), the Spring Fling carnival, and Senior Days.

> **"Binghamton models the housing system after Oxford. We have five different residential communities."**

Binghamton itself is "far from the most exciting place on earth, but the community is still alive and has its own distinct pulse," according to a biomedical engineering major. The downtown area offers restaurants and bars, and "many students volunteer with local groups, such as food drives and mentoring children," says a nursing major. Popular road trips include Ithaca, for parties at Ithaca College and Cornell, and Syracuse, for Destiny USA, as well as Cortland and Oneonta, about an hour away by car. The toughest part about going away, students gripe, may be finding a parking space when you return.

Binghamton teams compete in Division I, but the school doesn't field a football squad. As a result, perhaps the most significant rivalry is with Cornell in men's lacrosse. Women's basketball, volleyball, and softball and men's cross-country, tennis, and baseball are competitive in the America East Conference. Binghamton's debate team is among the best in the nation, and computer science students excel in the FAA National Design Competition. Intramurals, club sports, and fitness programs attract about 80 percent of the student body.

With a four-year graduation rate that is among the highest of any public university, Binghamton has a reputation for an excellent education at a reasonable price that continues to draw smart New Yorkers to its vibrant and growing campus. Despite the hubbub of city life, the university maintains a cozy feel. Says one happy senior, "When you walk on the campus, you instantly feel at home and a huge sense of camaraderie."

The invitation-only First-Year Research Immersion program involves enriched courses taught by teams of faculty from multiple STEM disciplines.

Annual campus traditions include Stepping on the Coat (to celebrate the arrival of warm weather).

Overlaps

Clemson, Miami (OH), UC Santa Barbara, UC Santa Cruz, William & Mary, Boston University, Cornell University, NYU

If You Apply To ›

SUNY–Binghamton: Early action, regular decision. Accepts the Common Application with supplement. Please consult SUNY–Binghamton's website for the most up-to-date information regarding standardized test requirements.

SUNY–University at Buffalo

15 Capen Hall, Buffalo, NY 14214

The largest and most academically comprehensive of SUNY's four university centers, Buffalo is also one of the system's two flagship universities, along with Stony Brook. Majority of students come from Western New York and New York City, and a high percentage commute from home. Working to set itself apart with the visibility that comes from big-time Division I sports, including football. Great place for poets.

As part of the mammoth State University of New York system, the University at Buffalo is working hard to ensure it gets noticed. Very few universities share UB's strength in medicine, engineering, and computer science, and the university is one of the world's leading supercomputer sites. Its resources are large enough to warrant three campuses: North, South, and Downtown. In addition to the sciences, the former private university offers strong professional schools, including a top-ranked school of pharmacy. "As large as we are, we have a very diverse and welcoming atmosphere," says a senior.

UB traces its heritage to 1846 when it was founded as a private college, led by future U.S. president Millard Fillmore, that evolved into a large university and in 1962 became part of the newly established SUNY system. (UB recently removed Fillmore's name from some campus landmarks due to his support as U.S. president of the Fugitive Slave Act of 1850.) The university's North Campus, home to most undergraduate programs, stretches across 1,100 acres in the suburbs just outside the city line and boasts buildings designed by world-renowned architects such as I. M. Pei. Meanwhile, the South Campus, along Main Street, favors collegiate ivy-covered buildings and is the home of the schools of architecture, pharmacy, nursing, and public health, as well as UB's highly rated dentistry program. The university provides connecting bus service—known as the UB Stampede—between the North and South campuses. UB's six main libraries, which are the most comprehensive in the SUNY system, hold more than four million volumes and the James Joyce Collection, the largest Joyce collection in the world. The university continues building and renovating at a steady pace, and the new One World Café, an international eatery with seating for more than 500 students situated at the heart of the North Campus, opened in 2022.

> **"As large as we are, we have a very diverse and welcoming atmosphere."**

The general education program, known as the UB Curriculum, includes a small-group UB Seminar for all new students; required coursework in diversity, writing, math, and natural sciences; Pathways that allow students to explore interests thematically; and a Capstone e-portfolio aimed at integrating their learning. "First-year seminars and classes help make the college transition a successful and enjoyable one," says a sociology major. The engineering and business management schools are nationally prominent, and architecture is solid. Occupational and physical therapy programs are also quite good, while the English department is notable for its emphasis on poetry. Well-known poets visit the campus frequently, and students not only compose and read poetry, but study the art of performing it as well. Music, geography, and French are well regarded, but other humanities vary in quality. Of UB's 140-plus undergraduate majors, some of the most popular are psychology, social sciences, engineering, business administration/marketing, and nursing. The university offers more than 55 combined bachelor's/master's degrees (such as a five-year business administration B.S./M.B.A.) and numerous interdisciplinary

---

Website: www.buffalo.edu
Location: Suburban
Public
Total Enrollment: 27,056
Undergraduates: 19,750
Male/Female: 55/45
Financial Aid: 59%
Pell Grant: 35%
Expense: Pub $ $
Student Loans: 59%
Average Debt: $ $
Applicants: 30,750
Accepted: 70%
Enrolled: 20%
Grad in 6 Years: 74%
Returning Freshmen: 83%
Academics: ✐ ✐ ✐ ✐
Social: ☎ ☎
Q of L: ★ ★
Admissions: (716) 645-6900
Email Address:
   ub-admissions@buffalo.edu

Strong Programs:
Engineering
Business
Architecture
Occupational and Physical
   Therapy
English
Music
Geography
French

majors, as well as opportunities for self-designed majors. Seven percent of undergrads study abroad, choosing from more than 1,000 options available through the SUNY system.

Students agree that the academic atmosphere in most disciplines at UB is competitive. "Success through hard work and innovative thinking is really stressed," says an occupational therapy major. "You are measured against your peers in many classes and labs." Class sizes can get quite large, which can be an adjustment for first-years, but 34 percent of all undergraduate courses have fewer than 20 students. At a school where graduate education and research get lots of the attention, the faculty are often experts in their field, but, an international business major says, "Students oftentimes do not build relationships with professors." Given the sheer size of the school and the multitude of opportunities, a junior says, "It's easy to get lost or confused." UB's Finish in 4 program seeks to alleviate these challenges and help students graduate on time, in part by expanding course availability and curricular plans. Students say the Career Design Center is the most helpful of UB's student support services. Students accepted into the UB Honors College enjoy smaller classes, priority class registration, faculty mentors, and specialized advising.

UB offers more than 55 combined bachelor's/master's degrees (such as a five-year business administration B.S./M.B.A.).

"Students like to be involved but at the same time are very studious," says one senior. "They also like to party." Eighty-seven percent hail from New York State, and 14 percent come from nations outside the U.S. Black students account for 9 percent of the student body, Hispanics/Latinos 8 percent, Asian Americans 17 percent, and multiracial students 3 percent. The campus is socioeconomically diverse as well, with 35 percent of entering first-years qualifying for Pell Grants. UB's considerable efforts in increasing awareness of diversity include the Intercultural and Diversity Center and the Office of Equity, Diversity, and Inclusion. Campus politics tend to lean left. Merit scholarships averaging $4,000 are offered to the top incoming students, and athletes compete for nearly 300 athletic scholarships. In-state residents qualify for free tuition under the state's Excelsior Scholarship program, provided their family's annual income is $125,000 or less.

> "Success through hard work and innovative thinking is really stressed."

In-state residents qualify for free tuition under the state's Excelsior Scholarship program if their family's annual income is $125,000 or less.

Thirty percent of students live on campus in traditional residence halls or apartments for upper-class students; the rest commute from home or find less expensive apartments nearby. Most of the on-campus dwellers reside on the North Campus. Gender-inclusive housing is available for students who wish to live in a mixed-gender housing environment. Students have a smorgasbord of dining choices ranging from three dining halls to more than 35 food courts, restaurants, and snack stops, including local favorite Tim Hortons. "Everything is clean, well organized, with great service, and fantastic food," cheers a junior. Students report that security on campus is adequate and sexual assault cases are "definitely not taken lightly."

Oozefest is a massive mud-volleyball tournament that draws students, faculty, staff, and alumni.

"The social life is really split between on and off campus," explains a social sciences major. School-sponsored events and activities organized by the more than 400 student organizations keep students busy during the week. Alcohol is allowed on campus for students 21 and over. The university recently enacted new anti-hazing and oversight regulations for the Greek system, to which 1 percent of UB men and 2 percent of women belong. Many students gravitate to the downtown area on the weekends; "Downtown Buffalo is super fun and young," says a sophomore. Friday night happy hour centers on beer and the chicken wings that spread the fame of Buffalo cuisine. Also popular are the Albright-Knox Art Gallery, with its world-renowned collection of modern art, and the Triple-A baseball Bisons, who play downtown. The two major pro teams, the Buffalo Bills (football) and the Sabres (hockey), are both top draws.

The winters are cold in Buffalo, but students can take refuge inside a series of enclosed elevated walkways that connect most of the North Campus academic buildings. The flip side is that the outlying areas of the city offer great skiing, skating, and snowmobiling—and the ski club even offers free rides to the slopes. Having a car might be a good idea, but students warn that parking can be a problem on campus. Although most students are content to stay in Buffalo, those who want a change of scenery can drive to Niagara Falls, just a few minutes away, or to Rochester, Cleveland, or Toronto, where the drinking age is lower. "The best road trip is 10 minutes to Canada," says an anthropology and geology double major.

> **"Downtown Buffalo is super fun and young."**

UB has been trying to enhance its visibility by getting its name on the sports pages. It is the only major SUNY unit to field a Division I football team; fans pack into the school's 30,000-seat football stadium. The Bulls men's and women's basketball teams are the most successful, often making NCAA tournament appearances. Men's and women's track and field and women's swimming are also competitive. Intramural sports are popular, especially soccer and Oozefest—a massive mud-volleyball tournament that draws students, faculty, staff, and alumni. "Oozefest is probably our number-one tradition," says a senior. "Tons of teams sign up, dress in costume, and start playing early in the morning."

At a university as large as UB, students find that they often have to take more initiative with their education, but students here say they appreciate UB's huge range of academic programs, research resources, social events, and people to meet. Yes, students are exposed to the long Buffalo winters, but they also get exposed to some top-notch professors. Says one satisfied senior, "UB is a school that provides people from all walks of life the opportunity to obtain a quality education and experience diversity firsthand."

<table>
<tr><td>

Overlaps

University of Pittsburgh, University of Iowa, SUNY–Stony Brook, Rutgers, UC Irvine, SUNY–Albany, SUNY–Binghamton, Cornell University

</td></tr>
</table>

If You Apply To ›

University at Buffalo: Early action, rolling admissions. Please consult UB's website for the most up-to-date information regarding standardized test requirements. Accepts the Common Application with supplement.

SUNY–College at Geneseo

1 College Circle, Geneseo, NY 14454

Geneseo is a preferred option for New Yorkers who want the feel of a private liberal arts college at a public-school price. It is similar in scale to Mary Washington and William & Mary in Virginia, much smaller than Miami of Ohio. Offers business and education in addition to the liberal arts and sciences. Less than 5 percent of the students come from outside New York.

The SUNY–College at Geneseo offers a serious academic environment at an affordable price. This public institution attracts high achievers who "tend to be friendly, liberal, and hardworking," says a junior. Responsive, attentive professors help compensate for the long winters and somewhat isolated location. Excellent preprofessional programs have been making it harder to win admission to this most pastoral campus of the State University of New York system.

Geneseo sits in the scenic Genesee Valley of western New York. Founded as a public teacher training college in 1871, it became part of the emerging SUNY system

<table>
<tr><td>

Website: www.geneseo.edu
Location: Small Town
Public
Total Enrollment: 4,327
Undergraduates: 4,290
Male/Female: 36/64
Financial Aid: 83%

</td></tr>
</table>

(continued)

Pell Grant: 25%

Expense: Pub $

Student Loans: 65%

Average Debt: $

Applicants: 9,103

Accepted: 74%

Enrolled: 15%

Grad in 6 Years: 76%

Returning Freshmen: 83%

Academics: ✍ ✍ ✍ ½

Social: ☎ ☎ ☎

Q of L: ★ ★ ★ ★

Admissions: (585) 245-5571

Email Address: admissions@ geneseo.edu

Strong Programs:
Biology
Physics
Geography
Education
Business Administration
Accounting
Psychology
Communication

New and rapidly growing majors include data analytics, sustainability studies, and neuroscience.

in 1948. The surrounding community has been designated a National Historic Landmark Community. An elementary education major calls the town "small and inviting" and says the historic storefronts and nearby forests and rolling hills make for "beautiful scenery." Campus architecture ranges from Gothic to modern, and recent campus improvements include an outdoor sports stadium and an ongoing renovation of the Milne Library, expected to be completed in 2024.

General education requirements include two courses each in the natural sciences, social sciences, and the arts; one course each in humanities, Western civilization, other world civilizations, American history, and mathematics; and foreign language proficiency. All first-year students take a writing seminar in a small class, focusing on a theme related to the instructor's discipline. Popular majors include psychology, communication, business administration, and accounting. Biology, physics, geography, education, and business (especially accounting) are strengths. New and rapidly growing majors include data analytics, sustainability studies, and neuroscience. Cooperative programs with other SUNY campuses in physical therapy, optometry, engineering, and other fields allow students to finish their graduate degrees a year ahead of schedule.

> **"Many professors are welcoming and willing to answer questions and interact with students."**

"Geneseo is challenging but never unreasonable," says a sophomore. Thirty-five percent of the classes have fewer than 20 students, and the quality of teaching is said to be generally high, especially in upper-level courses. "Many professors are welcoming and willing to answer questions and interact with students," says an accounting major. Top students are invited to join the prestigious Edgar Fellows scholarship program, which includes a $2,000 annual scholarship, five honors courses designed specifically for the program, and an opportunity to complete a senior thesis or a research, creative, or service project. Forty-one percent of all undergrads undertake research projects. The acclaimed Geneseo Opportunities for Leadership Development program, which is open to all students, seeks to prepare students for college and community leadership roles via workshops and symposia. Twenty-six percent of students study abroad, usually during the summer, and the college offers nearly 70 programs in more than 40 nations; through other SUNY campuses, students have access to more than 1,000 programs.

Ninety-eight percent of Geneseo students are from New York State, and 1 percent come from abroad. Asian Americans make up 4 percent of the student body, Hispanics/Latinos 9 percent, Black students 3 percent, and multiracial students 1 percent. Geneseo is "a blue school in a red town," according to a junior, but the political climate doesn't usually get heated. "Students tend to care about each other and treat each other with respect," says a senior. Geneseo offers merit scholarships averaging $3,000 each to qualified first-year students, but no athletic awards. New York State's Excelsior Scholarship grants free tuition to in-state students whose families earn up to $125,000 in annual income.

Forty-nine percent of Geneseo students live in the residence halls and townhouses, where 17 living/learning communities are available for interested students. Rooms are guaranteed for four years, although most upperclassmen choose to move off campus. The Red Jacket Dining Complex has been renovated, and a senior reports, "The quality of meals has been improving every semester." Students say that, given its small-town location, the campus is safe, and an English major notes that Geneseo has "stepped up its educational resources on sexual consent for incoming students."

> **"Hockey is huge here."**

"We do not have a huge nightlife like you would have on a larger campus, but there is a very charming Geneseo social scene," says a psychology major. "There are a lot of activities on campus as well as great festivals and events in the town itself."

Fraternities and sororities, which draw 17 percent of the men and 21 percent of the women, set the social tone and host most of the parties. "Greek life is a loud, influential minority," says one student. If Greek life doesn't appeal, students can get involved in any of the more than 180 student organizations or partake in college-sponsored late-night activities at the College Union. Students are active in the community, volunteering thousands of hours of service each year through annual days of service, events like Relay For Life, and numerous student groups. Students also look forward to annual fall and spring festivals, GREAT Day (a celebration of student research and creative work), and monthly multicultural club dinners and shows.

Adjacent to campus, the town of Geneseo's Main Street has more than 60 shops, restaurants, and cafés. A campus shuttle takes students to a nearby Wegmans supermarket and Walmart. Outdoorsy types appreciate the nearby Letchworth State Park, often referred to as the "Grand Canyon of the East"; rowers enjoy beautiful Conesus Lake, only a 10-minute drive from campus. Popular road trips include Rochester, 30 miles north, and Buffalo, 60 miles west; don't forget your hat, mittens, and parka!

Almost half of Geneseo students participate in recreational sports; broomball is the most popular intramural, while rugby is the most popular club sport. Geneseo's varsity teams, the Knights, compete in Division III. Men's ice hockey and women's basketball are nationally competitive, while men's and women's cross-country and swimming and diving are perennial conference champions. Ice hockey, though, stirs up the most school spirit: "Hockey is huge here," confirms a senior.

The SUNY–College at Geneseo offers students the best of two worlds. Given its size, professors can provide the kind of personal attention normally seen only at private liberal arts colleges; because of its public status, all that attention comes at a bargain price. These factors have made it more difficult to get in—and, it turns out, getting in is only half the battle. "Students are very serious about their education," says a sophomore. "Once you are here, you must work hard."

The acclaimed Geneseo Opportunities for Leadership Development program, which is open to all students, offers workshops and symposia.

Overlaps

SUNY–Binghamton, Ithaca, Syracuse, SUNY–Buffalo, University of Rochester, Mary Washington, William & Mary, SUNY–Albany

If You Apply To ›

SUNY–Geneseo: Early decision, regular decision. SATs or ACTs: optional. Accepts the Common Application with supplement. Theater and music applicants must audition. Arts applicants must submit a portfolio.

Purchase College, SUNY

735 Anderson Hill Road, Purchase, NY 10577

One of the few public institutions that has a strong arts specialty. The visual and performing arts are signature programs, but many students also come to Purchase for a robust range of liberal arts offerings, from environmental studies and psychology to film and creative writing. Proximity to NYC enhances academic and social opportunities. Eclectic campus life offers funky traditions and an active music scene.

Purchase College, SUNY is a dream come true for aspiring artists of all kinds—an academic environment that provides a strong sense of community, yet celebrates individuals for their unique talents and contributions. The liberal arts are well supported here, too, with a growing number of academic opportunities. Purchase's location just 30 miles north of New York City is ideal for its creative, socially conscious students, who take full advantage of the endless cultural and professional opportunities the city has to offer. A literature major says, "There's a raw energy

Website: www.purchase.edu
Location: Suburban
Public
Total Enrollment: 3,221
Undergraduates: 3,152
Male/Female: 40/60

Almost all the faculty members in the School of the Arts are professionals who perform or exhibit regularly in the New York metropolitan area.

that exists on campus—in the students and professors—that I don't think many other colleges have."

Set on a 500-acre wooded estate in an area of upscale Westchester County's most scenic suburbia, Purchase has a campus described by one student as "sleek, modern, ominous, and brick." The college, founded in 1967 to serve as a "cultural gem" in the SUNY system, has earned a national reputation for its instruction in music, dance, theater, and visual arts. Almost all the faculty members in the School of the Arts are professionals who perform or exhibit regularly in the New York metropolitan area, and the spacious, dazzling facilities here rank among the best in the world. The college also boasts the Neuberger Museum, one of the largest public college museums. The four-theater Performing Arts Center is huge, and dance students, whose building contains a dozen studios, whirlpool rooms, and a "body-correction" facility, may never again work in such splendid and well-equipped surroundings.

Mingling with highly motivated and talented performers and artists can make some students in the School of Liberal Arts and Sciences feel a little out of place, and the academic atmosphere reportedly varies between programs. "Dancers, actors, visual artists, and music students pull the most weight as far as campus life is concerned," opines a student. Even so, about 60 percent of Purchase students pursue liberal arts degrees. Environmental studies, biology, film, creative writing, and new media have strong reputations, and psychology, playwriting and screenwriting, and communication are other popular choices. An arts management major offered through the School of the Arts prepares students to develop, manage, and produce artists and performers.

> **"There's a raw energy that exists on campus—in the students and professors."**

Regardless of their chosen school or degree program, all Purchase students complete the same core curriculum, which requires coursework in eight knowledge areas spanning the arts, humanities, sciences, and health and wellness. When they arrive in the fall, most new students take an introductory First-Year Seminar. Students in the liberal arts and sciences complete a senior project, which is often research-based, while those in the arts divisions undertake a senior recital or show. Purchase students tend to be serious about their own personal achievements, and, with 72 percent of classes enrolling fewer than 20 students, professors are said to be accessible and friendly. "The professors are engaged, extremely qualified, and very interested in our education," says a student. Faculty members lead short-term study abroad programs during the summer on such topics as art history and language in Italy and political theater in Prague; affiliated programs in the SUNY system provide access to hundreds of other options.

One student describes Purchase students as "artsy, creative, hippies, gay, vegans, and open-minded, liberal activists." Another adds, "Purchase is a very judgment-free zone, and we are proud of that." Eighty-two percent of students are from New York State, most from New York City and Westchester and Rockland counties. Others are from Long Island, New Jersey, and Connecticut; 2 percent are international. Black students account for 12 percent of the student body, Hispanics/Latinos 25 percent, Asian Americans 4 percent, and multiracial students 6 percent. Thirty-six percent of freshmen are eligible for Pell Grants. In addition to need-based aid, merit scholarships averaging $3,300 are awarded each year on the basis of academic achievements, auditions, and portfolios. New York residents from families whose annual incomes are below $125,000 can attend Purchase tuition-free under the state's Excelsior Scholarship program.

Sixty-one percent of Purchase students live on campus, and a student explains, "There are older and newer dorms and their condition definitely reflects their age." Options are improving, however, with a 300-bed residence hall that recently opened, and plans are in the works to renovate some of the older facilities. With quirky names like Wayback, Farside, and Fort Awesome, the dorms at least sound like fun places to live. Housing in the surrounding suburbs is expensive and hard to find, so many students commute from home. The dining facilities are said to offer decent fare, and the college has expanded its resources and educational programming related to student safety.

The campus is a neighbor to the world headquarters of major corporations like IBM and PepsiCo, and the town of Purchase is by no means student-oriented. A campus shuttle takes students to nearby White Plains and Port Chester, and to the Metro North station where they can catch a train to the Big Apple. The school has been working in recent years to strengthen campus life, and students say those efforts are paying off. A senior explains, "Most excitement takes place on campus, so you never have to leave, but being so close to the city is a huge benefit!" A lively music scene brings indie and up-and-coming bands to campus throughout the year, and the Performing Arts Center regularly hosts student, faculty, and guest performances. New York artists and celebrities also visit for lectures, performances, and other events. With about 50 active clubs on campus, there is usually something going on in the Student Center (a.k.a. "the Stood"). Fraternities and sororities are definitely out. Purchase is not without its traditions, although even these tend to be unconventional: Fall Ball ("a giant drag show"), Zombie Prom ("a literal prom where people use fake blood and wear tattered clothes like zombies"), and the Culture Shock music festival ("carnival rides, food trucks and vendors, petting zoos, and performances by famous people").

> **"[Purchase is the] fun, weird cousin of the SUNY schools."**

Purchase fields 17 varsity sports that compete in the Division III Skyline Conference. The few competitive Panthers teams include men's basketball, men's and women's tennis, and volleyball. Intramural and club sports draw about 30 percent of students and range from the typical basketball and soccer to the not-so-typical Nerf club and circus skills club.

As the "fun, weird cousin of the SUNY schools," as one senior puts it, Purchase is a perfect place to study the arts and still be able to indulge in academics of all kinds, or vice versa. "It's a great place to come and devote yourself to your craft," says a senior. Indeed, the opportunity that Purchase offers for a personalized, diverse education is unique within the SUNY system.

With quirky names like Wayback, Farside, and Fort Awesome, the dorms at least sound like fun places to live.

Overlaps

SUNY–New Paltz, CUNY–Hunter, SUNY–Albany, NYU, Skidmore, Pace, Syracuse, Ithaca

If You Apply To ›

SUNY–Purchase: Early action, rolling admissions. SATs or ACTs: optional. Accepts the Common Application with supplement. Apply to particular school or program. Auditions held for acting, dance, and music. Portfolios required for art and design, creative writing, film, and theater design/technology.

SUNY–Stony Brook University

118 Administration Building, Stony Brook, NY 11794

Strategically located 60 miles east of New York City, Stony Brook is one of the academic leaders of the SUNY system. The natural sciences, engineering, and health fields are the major drawing cards. Situated in the lap of Long Island luxury, Stony Brook offers easy access to beachfront playlands. Still caters mainly to students from the New York tristate area.

The WISE (Women in Science and Engineering) program provides mentoring and research experiences during the freshman year.

As one of two flagship universities in the SUNY system, Stony Brook aims to be the model of a student-centered research university. Its three Undergraduate Colleges provide a small college community experience with all the assets of a leading research university. Since its founding in 1957, the public university has made a name for itself with its top-notch programs in the hard sciences. It has also become known for the high quality of its professors and its challenging but supportive learning environment.

The school's location on Long Island's plush North Shore is a powerful drawing point. Sitting on 1,040 wooded acres just outside of the small, picturesque village of Stony Brook, and only 90 minutes from New York City and half an hour from the beaches of the South Shore, the campus is a conglomeration of redbrick buildings interspersed with several modern brick and concrete designs. Campus beautification and sustainability are priorities, and grass and trees have replaced much of the uninspiring campus concrete. Recently completed construction includes two residence halls and a dining facility.

The Stony Brook Curriculum is based on a series of learning outcomes and is organized into four categories: Demonstrate Versatility, Explore Interconnectedness, Pursue Deeper Understanding, and Prepare for Lifelong Learning. Students also take one class fulfilling a Respect Diversity and Foster Inclusiveness requirement. All freshmen—residents and commuters alike—enter the university as members of one of three Undergraduate Colleges. Each college has its own faculty director, as well as both academic and residential advisors. Freshmen participate in theme-based academic and cocurricular programs, which include two small seminar courses.

"[In the spring, we have] Strawberry Fest, where there are different strawberry-themed foods for us to try."

Coming of age in the high-tech era, Stony Brook quickly became known for its science departments. Facilities are extensive, and the science faculty includes a number of internationally known researchers. The comprehensive university hospital and research center make health science and nursing strong. The hospital, which has been ranked among the nation's best for teaching, attracts grants and offers many opportunities for research programs for undergrads as well as graduate students. Biology is the most popular major, followed by psychology, health science, and business management. Engineering, geology, marine vertebrate biology, physics, economics, and anthropology are also strengths. Stony Brook boasts the first and only school of communication and journalism in the SUNY system. The art program benefits from a fine arts building, complete with studios and a reference library, that complements Stony Brook's beautiful five-theater Staller Center for the Arts and 5,000-square-foot Zuccaire Gallery. The Grammy-winning Emerson String Quartet is in residence in the music department. A major in creative writing and literature has been introduced, as have minors in professional writing and film and screen studies.

Students spend a lot of time studying, and the coursework is difficult, but "students aren't overly competitive," says a junior. "In my experience, they've preferred to support one another." Classes are often large, with 23 percent enrolling more than 50 students. A health science major comments, "Professors are always attentive to students, especially those who reach out for extra help."

An Undergraduate Research and Creative Activities program offers undergraduates the opportunity to work on research projects with faculty members from the time they are freshmen until they graduate. The WISE (Women in Science and Engineering) program encourages women entering the university as freshmen to pursue study in the sciences, engineering, and mathematics. The program provides mentoring from women professors in these fields, as well as research experiences during the freshman year. About 3 percent of students take advantage of Stony Brook's study abroad programs (England, France, Italy, Japan, and Madagascar are just some of the possibilities), while others choose established internships in the fields of policy analysis, political science, psychology, foreign language, or social welfare. University Scholars is a four-year honors program for students who rank at the top of the incoming freshman class that offers specialized support, programming, and events.

"The majority of the students here are hardworking, ambitious, and well equipped to handle life," says a chemistry major. Eighty-four percent of Stony Brook undergraduates hail from New York, and a good portion commute from Long Island homes; 10 percent arrive from foreign countries. The student body is 6 percent Black, 14 percent Hispanic/Latino, 32 percent Asian American, and 3 percent multiracial. "There isn't much public display of political or social discontent on campus," says a sophomore. Merit scholarships averaging $5,400 are given out each year, in addition to nearly 200 athletic scholarships. Thirty-nine percent of freshmen receive Pell Grants. As at other SUNY schools, in-state students at Stony Brook whose families earn $125,000 or less in annual income enjoy free tuition under the state's Excelsior Scholarship program.

> **"Professors are always attentive to students, especially those who reach out for extra help."**

Stony Brook, which has one of the largest residential programs in the SUNY system, has a slew of robust facilities that provide students access to state-of-the-art fitness centers, computing centers, and big-screen TVs. Forty-seven percent of undergrads live in university housing. While residential freshmen must take a meal plan, upperclassmen who live in suites on campus either opt for a flexible food-service plan or pay a nominal fee to cook for themselves. Kosher and vegetarian food co-ops keep interested students well supplied with cheap eats. The university's Walk Service Program escorts students around campus at night. "We sit through so many sexual assault lectures and workshops and online courses, and it has honestly helped," says one student. "I found it comforting that everyone had to go through this and understand it."

> *Stony Brook has one of the largest residential programs in the SUNY system; 47 percent of undergrads live in university housing.*

At Stony Brook, a biology and Spanish major says, "The social life is secondary. Academics are the heart and soul of this school." Because many students go home on the weekends, students say the party scene is low-key. The university has fairly strict policies on alcohol consumption, and "the policies are as effective as possible with young students in college," a student reports. The fledgling Greek system draws just 2 percent of the men and 2 percent of the women. Current and classic movies are screened during the week, and student organizations coordinate other entertainment in the form of frequent concerts, plays, and other performances. Annual traditions include the Wolfieland carnival at the start of the school year and the homecoming football game. "In the spring, we have Earthstock, a celebration of nature and recycling, and Strawberry Fest, where there are different strawberry-themed foods for us to try," explains a biomedical engineering major. The Roth Pond Regatta, featuring cardboard boat races, is another big social event.

> **"Everyone wants to support each other in their endeavors."**

"Stony Brook is a wealthy residential town that cannot be categorized as a 'college town,'" one student says. Nearby Port Jefferson offers small shops and interesting restaurants. Beachcombing on the nearby North Shore, or on the Atlantic Ocean shore of Long Island, and heading into New York City are popular ways to pass the weekends. Having a car on campus is helpful, but many students make do with trains, and a station is conveniently located at the edge of campus.

Stony Brook's 18 Division I teams compete in the America East Conference, except for football, which hits the gridiron in the Colonial Athletic Association, and women's tennis. The nationally ranked Seawolves women's lacrosse team has dominated the conference in recent years, and other conference champs include women's basketball, women's soccer, and baseball. Intramurals, ranging from soccer and flag football to handball and table tennis, provide one of the school's greatest rallying points, and students are also active in more than 40 club sports.

> ### Overlaps
> **Rutgers, UConn, University of Pittsburgh, Georgia Tech, UC San Diego, SUNY–Binghamton, NYU, SUNY–Buffalo**

Though Stony Brook is not old enough to have ivy-covered walls, it does offer some of the best academic opportunities in the SUNY system. Students tout their school's diversity and creativity, as well as the feeling of hospitality that pervades campus life. Says a freshman, "There is a strong sense of community here, and everyone wants to support each other in their endeavors."

If You Apply To ›

SUNY–Stony Brook: Regular decision. Accepts the Common Application with supplement. Please consult Stony Brook's website for the most up-to-date information regarding standardized test requirements.

Stetson University

421 N. Woodland Boulevard, DeLand, FL 32723

The oldest private university in Florida, Stetson keeps company with the likes of Baylor and Furman among prominent Deep South institutions. Established the state's first schools of business, law, and music. Business and music are traditionally the strongest programs. Feels more like a small college than a university.

Website: www.stetson.edu
Location: Small City
Private
Total Enrollment: 3,750
Undergraduates: 2,777
Male/Female: 43/57
Financial Aid: 98%
Pell Grant: 45%
Expense: Pr $ $
Student Loans: 61%
Average Debt: $ $ $
Applicants: 9,260
Accepted: 92%
Enrolled: 7%
Grad in 6 Years: 64%
Returning Freshmen: 72%
Academics: 🖋 🖋 🖋
Social: 🐳 🐳 🐳
Q of L: ★ ★ ★
Admissions: (386) 822-7100
Email Address: admissions@
   stetson.edu

Strong Programs:
Accounting
Professional Sales
Finance
Entrepreneurship
Music

Stetson University, founded in 1883 and named for the maker of the famed 10-gallon hat, draws students from around the Southeast and Northeast with its small size and emphasis on liberal learning. Once a bastion of conservatism, the school has become more liberal and ecumenical since cutting ties with the Southern Baptists in the 1990s. With top-notch business programs and strengths in music, health sciences, and digital arts, this private Florida university continues to attract students who aren't afraid to wear a variety of hats during their stay.

Located halfway between Orlando and Daytona Beach, Stetson's 185-acre campus features mainly brick structures in styles from Gothic to Moorish to Southern colonial. While some modern buildings are scattered about, the theme is decidedly Southern, complete with royal palms and oak trees. The Carlton Union Building, home to dining services and student activities, has been completely renovated, and the $19 million Brown Hall for Health & Innovation opened in 2022.

Stetson has three undergraduate colleges and schools—music, business administration, and arts and sciences—and its general education requirements apply to all of them. All entering students take a First Year Seminar, which allows them to work closely with Stetson faculty to ease the transition to college. Freshmen who are undecided on a major participate in the Discovery program, and all students take a Junior Seminar that focuses on personal and social responsibility. Seniors in the College of Arts and Sciences must complete a faculty-mentored capstone research or creative project, while music students perform a senior recital. Business students take a strategic management course and complete two experiential learning activities, such as internships or leadership opportunities. Additionally, all students must pass four writing or writing-enhanced courses in order to graduate. The Stetson Promise guarantees that if students can't graduate in four years, the university will cover a semester of tuition.

> **"The professors constantly encourage you to take on more projects and research."**

Stetson is known for its business program, particularly majors in accounting, professional sales, finance, and entrepreneurship. Would-be money managers benefit from the award-winning Roland George Investments program, where they oversee a portfolio worth $6 million in stocks and bonds. Students who hope to work for themselves can tap into the Prince Entrepreneurship Program, which connects them with successful business owners, while the Family Enterprise Center was one of the first in the nation in educating students for work in family businesses. The most popular majors are health sciences, psychology, finance, political science, and biology. The digital arts program is well regarded, and Russian, East European, and Eurasian Studies is a surprising strength. Stetson's music school is notable (ahem) for choral music and public performances in addition to academic programs in theory, composition, and performance. Aspiring lawyers may take advantage of a 3+3 accelerated B.A./J.D. program or a 4+3 direct admission program with Stetson's College of Law.

"I lived on campus all four years because I loved how connected it made me."

"Stetson has a positive, well-balanced academic climate," says a computer science major. Seventy-one percent of classes have fewer than 20 students, and group work is common in many disciplines. Professors are always willing to help, and many have worked in the field they are teaching before stepping in front of the lectern. "The professors constantly encourage you to take on more projects and research, if you are interested, and push you within their classes," says an English major.

Students with wanderlust can choose from more than 100 faculty-led, exchange, or affiliate programs, and international internships are an option too; 20 percent of undergrads typically study abroad. Stetson's honors program incorporates international study, community service, and a senior colloquium and also allows students to create their own majors. The Stetson Undergraduate Research Experience program awards funding to students for summer research or creative projects with faculty members, and original student work is celebrated at the annual Stetson Showcase.

Would-be money managers in the Roland George Investments program oversee a portfolio worth $6 million in stocks and bonds.

"The majority of Stetson students are academically minded and community driven," says a health sciences major. Seventy percent of Stetson Hatters are native Floridians, and 6 percent hail from foreign countries. Black students constitute 11 percent of the student body, Hispanics/Latinos make up 19 percent, Asian Americans add 2 percent, and multiracial students represent 6 percent.

"[DeLand is an] adorable, small Southern town."

Many come from affluent families, but 45 percent of current freshmen are Pell-eligible. Students of all faiths and backgrounds are welcomed on campus, and the university has two chaplains (Pentecostal and Buddhist) as well as a professionally staffed Hillel House. Students describe a mix of political views on campus. Merit scholarships and non-need-based grants averaging $26,400 are awarded each year, and Stetson also hands out athletic scholarships in 17 sports.

Sixty percent of undergrads live in the residence halls, since everyone is required to do so through junior year, except for commuters who live at home. "I lived on campus all four years because I loved how connected it made me to my campus and my peers," comments a senior. Stetson's traditional, buffet-style cafeteria is known as the Commons, and students say the meals are usually satisfactory, with sufficient accommodations for those with dietary restrictions. Campus safety receives good ratings. "The campus is well lit at night, and Public Safety is very present," reports a psychology major.

The women's beach volleyball program has taken home six Atlantic Sun Conference titles in recent years.

"Greek organizations are usually the place to find parties or connections to party life," says a junior, adding that "music organizations also offer a type of subculture partying." Fraternities attract 23 percent of the men and sororities draw 19 percent of the women, but students say that tightened alcohol policies have pushed most partying off campus to nearby apartments or bars. The Council for Student Activities offers plenty of on-campus alternatives, bringing in big-name acts, and students also get involved in more than 100 student organizations. Students look forward to annual homecoming events, including a comedy show, a talent show, Greenfeather (aimed at promoting community service), and tailgating. Ninety-two percent of students participate in volunteer activities, often through service-learning courses. When your birthday rolls around, it's best to don your bathing suit—it's a popular tradition for fellow students to toss you into the midcampus Holler Fountain.

As for the "adorable, small Southern town" of DeLand (population 39,000), it boasts "shops, galleries, and cafés," but only a handful of bars, so students often head to Orlando (40 minutes from campus) or Daytona Beach (20 minutes) to eat out, shop, or dance the night away. In addition to the omnipresent beaches, Blue Spring and DeLeon Springs offer canoeing and nature watching. Popular road trips include Miami for clubbing and the Keys for camping.

The women's beach volleyball program has been the standard-bearer for Stetson's Division I Hatters, taking home six Atlantic Sun Conference titles in recent years. Women's tennis won the conference championship in 2022, and other solid teams include men's and women's basketball, baseball, and softball. The football team competes in the Pioneer Football League against the likes of Butler, Dayton, and Davidson. The Hollis Wellness Center offers a variety of fitness facilities, and roughly 20 percent of students participate in club and intramural sports, ranging from ultimate Frisbee and surfing to flag football and pool battleship.

Stetson students tip their hats to the one-on-one attention freely given at this small Sunshine State university with a strong sense of what it is. "Stetson is very much a 'what can we do for our students' school," explains a junior. "This comes from the faculty relationships with students and the large amount of resources they give us." After four years spent enjoying great weather and forming close friendships with peers and professors, students emerge with solid academic foundations for future work or study.

Overlaps

Baylor, Furman, Baldwin Wallace, Butler, John Carroll, Loyola University New Orleans, University of Redlands, Valparaiso

If You Apply To ›

Stetson: Early decision, early action I and II, regular decision. SATs or ACTs: optional. Accepts the Common Application with supplement. Application includes optional fields for gender identity and preferred pronouns.

Stevens Institute of Technology

1 Castle Point Terrace, Hoboken, NJ 07030

Stevens ranks with Clarkson and Worcester Polytechnic among East Coast technical institutes that offer intimacy and personalized education. Youth-oriented Hoboken is a major plus and an easier commute to Manhattan than most places in Brooklyn. Co-op program is a popular option. Plan to work hard.

Website: www.stevens.edu
Location: Small City
Private
Total Enrollment: 6,825
Undergraduates: 4,025
Male/Female: 70/30

At Stevens Institute of Technology, students accept intense classwork, all-nighters, and trips to the Big Apple as givens. The school is located just across the Hudson River from Manhattan, which means that students have the cultural, athletic, and gastronomic resources of New York City at their fingertips. Engineering and the sciences set the tone on campus—and even business, arts, and humanities programs are taught through the lens of technology—but students seem prepared to take on the challenge of balancing work and play.

An eclectic mix of architectural styles compose Stevens's 55-acre campus. Many of the residence halls and administrative buildings are redbrick; classroom and lab facilities range from traditional, ivy-covered brownstones to modern glass-and-steel structures. The ABS Engineering Center houses five labs designed for robotics, naval engineering, structural engineering, hydraulics, and other research. The new, nearly $275 million University Center Complex boasts two residential towers housing 1,000 students in suite-style accommodations; a university center with space for dining, fitness, student clubs, and events; and outstanding views of Manhattan's skyline. The largest project in the school's history, the complex nearly doubled the number of beds available for on-campus housing.

Stevens was created in 1870 through the will of 19th-century inventor Edwin Stevens. It is organized into four schools—the Schaefer School of Engineering and Science, the School of Business, the College of Arts and Letters, and the School of Systems and Enterprises—and offers 35 majors. Most programs require calculus, chemistry, physics, and humanities courses. All entering students are required

> **"Stevens students are competitive by nature and push each other in every class."**

to participate in the Freshman Experience, which is a sequence of two common courses: Writing and Communication and Knowledge, Nature, Culture. Most seniors take a yearlong capstone course culminating in a team-based senior design project.

Engineering has long been king of the hill at Stevens; programs in biomedical, chemical, civil, computer, electrical, and naval engineering are all highly regarded, as is the major in mechanical engineering, not surprising since the program dates to the school's founding. Business programs are growing in number and popularity and include a major in quantitative finance, rare at the undergraduate level. Other notable majors include computer science, cybersecurity, business and technology, music and technology, and visual arts and technology. A five-year co-op program allows engineering and science students to incorporate full-time internships into their studies. Students describe the academic climate as challenging and "frenetic" but also supportive. "It's very tech-oriented, with a lot of hands-on group work," says a mechanical engineering major, adding, "It's not for the faint of heart." Thirty-eight percent of classes have fewer than 20 students, and students agree that, despite a few professors more interested in their research than their teaching, the quality of instruction is above average. "Professors are often able to provide industry insight," comments a senior.

Professional practice is an important part of the Stevens environment, with nearly all students participating in cooperative education, internships, or mature research and design projects. The Pinnacle Scholars Program, which invites top students to participate in faculty-guided research or an international experience during the summer, comes with a stipend of up to $5,000, the option to pursue an accelerated master's degree, and other benefits. Hundreds of short- and long-term study abroad and exchange programs are available, although few students find the time to take advantage of them. Men vastly outnumber women, but one junior sees this as an advantage: "As a female at Stevens, I feel this has actually helped me with holding my own and 'vying with the boys,' as I call it. It does not faze me to be the only girl in a group project." The Lore-El Center for Women's Leadership offers events ranging from health and wellness activities to leadership conferences and professional dinners with successful women in industry. Stevens has an active on-campus recruiting program with major corporations, start-up firms, and government organizations. A junior reports, "Stevens has plenty of staff to help students out with career advising and mental health services."

"Stevens students are competitive by nature and push each other in every class," says a biology major. Sixty-five percent of the students at Stevens are from

---

(continued)

Financial Aid: 96%
Pell Grant: 18%
Expense: Pr $ $ $
Student Loans: 71%
Average Debt: $ $ $ $
Applicants: 11,320
Accepted: 53%
Enrolled: 18%
Grad in 6 Years: 87%
Returning Freshmen: 93%
Academics: ✎ ✎ ✎
Social: ☎ ☎
Q of L: ★ ★ ★ ★
Admissions: (201) 216-5194
Email Address: admissions@ stevens.edu

Strong Programs:
Mechanical Engineering
Biomedical Engineering
Computer Engineering
Quantitative Finance
Computer Science
Cybersecurity
Business and Technology
Music and Technology

Business programs are growing in number and popularity and include a major in quantitative finance, rare at the undergraduate level.

New Jersey; many others come from the greater New York City area, and 2 percent hail from foreign nations. Eighteen percent of undergraduates are Asian American, 15 percent are Hispanic/Latino, just 2 percent are Black, and 4 percent are multiracial. Politics don't usually receive much attention on campus. In addition to need-based financial aid, qualified students receive merit-based scholarships that average $20,200. The Clark Scholars and Stevens ACES programs seek to attract more students from underrepresented backgrounds to STEM fields.

Thirty-two percent of undergraduates live in housing provided by Stevens, while others find their own off-campus apartments. Meals in the main dining hall are "a lot better than your average cafeteria food," remarks a senior. Students say campus security officers are visible and friendly, and a sophomore notes that a bystander intervention campaign "has been very effective because students are more inclined to report a Title IX violation."

Twenty-one percent of Stevens men join fraternities, and 29 percent of the women pledge sororities. "People like to party here, but they keep it in check," says a quantitative finance major. "Greek houses follow campus policies regarding alcohol and usually hold registered parties where bouncers check IDs." An Entertainment Committee plans weekly events, from comedy nights to hypnotists and musical guests. The student-run TechFest is a favorite annual event highlighted by a big-name musician. Greenwich Village, Times Square, and the bright lights of Broadway are just 15 minutes away on the PATH train, while Hoboken offers popular pubs and clubs right next to campus. Road trips, often taken by train, include Yankee Stadium in the Bronx and Six Flags Great Adventure near Trenton. Beaches and ski slopes are both within a 90-minute drive.

"People like to party here, but they keep it in check."

Students cheer enthusiastically when the Division III Stevens Ducks take the pool, field, and court. Most teams compete in the Middle Atlantic Conference and most are competitive: 13 men's and women's teams brought home conference titles in 2022, and the men's volleyball team is a recent national championship winner. For those without the time or talent to play at the varsity level, there are intramural and club teams in everything from basketball, soccer, and flag football to archery, crew, and bowling.

Stevens's urban location and relatively small size can make for fun times, but the emphasis here is on hard work and innovation. Stevens graduates go on to make a dent in the world; notable alums include Nobel Laureate Frederick Reines, who detected the subatomic world of the neutrino; Alexander Calder, world-renowned sculptor of mobiles; and Marques Brownlee, well-known YouTuber and tech influencer. "Stevens is a hub for future innovators," concludes an electrical engineering major. "The curriculum and the services are all meant to prepare students for impactful careers in technology-based fields."

Overlaps

Rensselaer, Northeastern, Worcester Polytechnic, Lehigh, Carnegie Mellon, Rutgers, Rochester Institute of Technology, Clarkson

If You Apply To ›

Stevens: Early decision I and II, regular decision. Accepts the Common Application with supplement. Please consult Stevens's website for the most up-to-date information regarding standardized test requirements.

Susquehanna University

Selinsgrove, PA 17870

Susquehanna offers a refreshing alternative to the cookie-cutter education at many small colleges. Its innovative core curriculum emphasizes personal development and requires students to spend at least two weeks learning off campus. Best known for its business program, and big on study abroad. With a more down-to-earth atmosphere than at upscale competitors like Bucknell and Dickinson, it is a national leader in promoting socioeconomic diversity.

"Susquewho?" That's the question many students ask when they're first introduced to this undergraduate institution in rural central Pennsylvania. While it may not be a household name, Susquehanna University is earning a reputation as an innovator. Friendly faculty, personal attention, and an increasing emphasis on community make SU a good place to expand your mind. The university's off-campus study requirement makes it an ideal choice for those looking to see more of the world too.

Susquehanna's campus is beautiful and serene, set on 325 lush acres in the small town of Selinsgrove on the Susquehanna River. Most of the 94 buildings on campus are brick, with Georgian the predominant architectural style. Selinsgrove Hall, built in 1858, and Seibert Hall, built in 1901, are on the National Register of Historic Places. A 14-acre, 12,000-panel solar array supplies nearly a third of the campus's electricity.

Susquehanna's Central Curriculum emphasizes coursework in five areas: Richness of Thought (fine arts and math); Natural World; Human Interactions (history, sociology, ethics, and language); Intellectual Skills (writing, oral presentation, and teamwork); and Connections (an off-campus, cross-cultural experience matched with diversity classes). All first-year students must complete a summer Common Reading assignment based on a specific theme, participate in an orientation pro-

> **"The Career Development Center does a lot of work with alumni networking and workshopping."**

gram, and take a Writing and Thinking course as well as a First-Year Seminar that helps them make the transition to college-level work. Finally, all students take a capstone course or practicum in their major that usually involves an extensive research or creative project.

The prestigious Weis School of Business attracts the most Susquehanna students, thanks in part to the fact that it guarantees all of its students an international internship and offers a semester-long London Program exclusively for business majors. Communication studies, psychology, creative writing, and accounting are other popular majors, and biology and music are solid. Susquehanna is increasingly recognized for its science programs, especially biochemistry, environmental science, and biomedical sciences. New options include minors in sustainability management and church music. SU students may also pursue 3–2 engineering degrees in partnership with Case Western Reserve, Columbia, and WashU in St. Louis.

Fifty-four percent of classes at SU have fewer than 20 students, and student/faculty interaction is one of Susquehanna's strong points. Students describe academics as challenging, and a senior says, "Professors expect students to be active, visit their office hours, and ask questions." Students enjoy a bevy of support services too. "The Career Development Center does a lot of work with alumni networking and workshopping to help students get ready for their professional life," says a publishing and editing major. Counseling and Psychological Services has added staff and increased hours, and a senior comments, "They offer a ton of availability and services for all types of needs."

Website: www.susqu.edu
Location: Rural
Private
Total Enrollment: 2,107
Undergraduates: 2,107
Male/Female: 44/56
Financial Aid: 100%
Pell Grant: 25%
Expense: Pr $ $
Student Loans: 80%
Average Debt: $ $ $ $
Applicants: 4,688
Accepted: 88%
Enrolled: 12%
Grad in 6 Years: 71%
Returning Freshmen: 87%
Academics: ✍ ✍ ✍
Social: ☎ ☎ ☎
Q of L: ★ ★ ★ ★
Admissions: (570) 372-4260
Email Address: suadmiss@susqu.edu

Strong Programs:
Business Administration
Biology
Music
Communication Studies
Psychology
Creative Writing
Accounting
Biomedical Sciences

To fulfill their curricular Connections requirement, students utilize the GO (Global Opportunities) program, which requires them to study away from campus for at least two weeks and to reflect on their experiences when they return. Students choose from more than 130 options—a third of which are semester-long programs—on six continents; about 95 percent of students study abroad, while the remaining 5 percent head to locations across the U.S. As a senior explains, "The goal is for students to experience a new culture before they graduate, and this requirement adds to the culture of diversity at Susquehanna." Most students also complete internships as a crucial part of their education and future job searches. For about 7 percent of students, the academic experience is defined by the Susquehanna Honors Program. The four-year program entails a sequence of special courses and projects, off-campus opportunities like conferences and other events, and an optional living/learning community.

About 95 percent of students study abroad, while the remaining 5 percent head to locations across the U.S.

At Susquehanna, observes a sociology major, "Students are warm and personable, and they're easy to get along with." Sixty-three percent of SU students are from Pennsylvania, and the majority attended public high school; 1 percent of students are international. Six percent are Black, 7 percent are Hispanic/Latino, 2 percent are Asian American, and 3 percent are multiracial; diversity education is an area of emphasis on campus. A political science major describes the political climate as "relatively tame," and the campus is rather moderate. Merit scholarships averaging $33,000 are available for resident Einsteins, but there are no athletic scholarships.

"Students are challenged to take initiative with their learning."

All Susquehanna students are required to live on campus, except for the 10 percent who are commuters. First-year students are assigned to four traditional residence halls. After the first year, students partake in a lottery system to choose from a variety of options, including suites, townhouses, on-campus apartments, and Greek houses. One student says food in the main cafeteria "can be hit or miss, but when it's good, it's good." Students report that the campus feels secure, and a sophomore adds, "Campus Safety, the Violence Intervention and Prevention Center, and our Green Dot bystander training program help make campus a safer place and promote a safer culture."

"Social life at Susquehanna is very active" and mostly campus-based, explains a student. Charlie's, the school coffeehouse, offers activities like open-mic, trivia, and football-and-wings nights, while Trax, the on-campus nightclub, serves alcohol to those of age. Seventeen percent of the men and 23 percent of the women belong to fraternities and sororities, respectively, but Greeks and parties do not dominate the social scene. Homecoming, Spring Concert, and Spring Carnival are the big annual events. Favorite campus traditions include a Thanksgiving dinner at which faculty members serve students "the best meal of the year," a candlelight Christmas service, and Senior Hike, when the university president leads seniors to the top of nearby Mount Mahanoy.

Favorite campus traditions include a Thanksgiving dinner at which faculty members serve students "the best meal of the year."

Outside the university, Selinsgrove is "small and quaint," with several restaurants and stores. SU was originally founded in 1858 to prepare students for the ministry, and the university's commitment to the community has remained strong. Each year, 69 percent of the student population volunteers on significant community service projects. In the surrounding countryside, "it's not uncommon to see an Amish family go by in their horse and buggy," says a student. Students head outdoors to kayak, hike, and picnic at the Susquehanna River and nearby state parks. For those with cars, Penn State is an hour away.

The Susquehanna River Hawks field 23 Division III teams, plus cheerleading. Men's and women's track and field, men's basketball, and women's cross-country and softball all boast recent Landmark Conference titles. Students also enjoy a diverse recreational sports program consisting of 10 club sports and a variety of intramurals. The crew, equestrian, and ice hockey clubs sign up the most students, while flag football, co-ed soccer, and cornhole are among the most popular intramurals.

Overlaps

Gettysburg, Juniata, Muhlenberg, Ursinus, Washington and Jefferson, Bucknell, Dickinson, University of Scranton

At Susquehanna, "Students are challenged to take initiative with their learning" in a friendly, open environment, says a senior. From interning with local organizations to taking classes on the other side of the globe, the firsthand exposure to diverse experiences and perspectives that SU students receive makes Susquehanna worthwhile—and a name worth learning.

If You Apply To ›

Susquehanna: Early decision, early action I and II, regular decision. SATs or ACTs: optional. Accepts the Common Application with supplement. Creative writing, graphic design, and studio art applicants must submit portfolio. Music applicants must audition.

Swarthmore College

500 College Avenue, Swarthmore, PA 19081

Don't mistake Swarthmore for a miniature version of an Ivy League school. Swat is more intellectual (and liberal) than its counterparts in New Haven and Cambridge. The college's honors program gives hardy souls a taste of graduate school, which is where legions of Swatties invariably end up. Geekier than Wesleyan, more grounded than Reed, and more collaborative than just about anywhere.

Swarthmore College's leafy green campus may be just 11 miles from Philadelphia, but students often don't have the time or the inclination to make the jaunt. That's because they have opted for one of the country's most self-consciously intellectual undergraduate environments. Swatties are bright, hardworking, and eclectic in their interests, and campus life is fabled for its intensity. But the intensity doesn't come from huge amounts of coursework (à la Yale) as much as the self-imposed drive of talented students who want to do lots of things simultaneously—from academics to social protests to rugby—and do them well. "Swat is a truly intellectual place where people love ideas with all of their hearts," a philosophy major says.

Swarthmore was founded in 1864 by the liberal Hicksite branch of the Religious Society of Friends (Quakers) in Philadelphia and named after a 17th-century English manor house that was a center of the early Quaker movement. Swarthmore's 425-acre suburban campus is a nationally registered arboretum, distinguished by rolling wooded hills. Multistory buildings with natural stone exteriors from local quarries,

"Swat is a truly intellectual place."

shaped roofs, and cornices are the norm, fostering a quiet, collegiate atmosphere. The Wister Education Center and Greenhouse is LEED Gold–certified and includes classrooms, exhibit areas, and greenhouse space. The $120 million Singer Hall, housing biology, engineering, and psychology programs as well as state-of-the-art labs and classrooms, was completed in 2021.

Students are required to take three courses in each of the college's three divisions—humanities, natural sciences and engineering (unusual for a liberal arts college), and social sciences—and at least two of the three must be in different departments. Swatties must also demonstrate foreign language competency, fulfill a physical education requirement (which includes a swimming test), and take three writing courses from at least two divisions. Optional first-year seminars emphasize close interaction with faculty members; about 86 percent of students participate. The most popular majors are economics, computer science, biology, mathematics, and

Website: www.swarthmore.edu
Location: Suburban
Private
Total Enrollment: 1,643
Undergraduates: 1,643
Male/Female: 50/50
Financial Aid: 54%
Pell Grant: 22%
Expense: Pr $ $ $
Student Loans: 26%
Average Debt: $
Applicants: 13,012
Accepted: 8%
Enrolled: 45%
Grad in 6 Years: 94%
Returning Freshmen: 95%
Academics: ✍ ✍ ✍ ✍ ✍
Social: ☎ ☎ ☎
Q of L: ★ ★ ★ ★
Admissions: (610) 328-8300
Email Address: admissions@ swarthmore.edu

Strong Programs:
Economics
Computer Science
Biology

political science, and students also give high marks to majors in visual and performing arts. Cross-registration is offered with nearby Bryn Mawr, Haverford, and Penn.

Freshmen at Swarthmore are graded on a pass-fail system for their first semester, there is no class rank or dean's list, and there is a big emphasis on group projects. A freshman explains, "While the courses are generally very challenging, the environment of Swat is not competitive at all. You will often see students reminding each other of assignments, giving each other tips on how to succeed, and studying in the library together." Indeed, the administration has encouraged a spirit of collegiality by sprinkling small lounges and cappuccino bars around the dorms and academic spaces. Class sizes are intimate as well, with 76 percent enrolling fewer than 20 students. "All the classes are taught by professors, many of them world-class, and they are always accessible and very, very friendly," says a classics and fine arts double major. Aside from teaching, Swarthmore professors also serve as advisors, and students are also assigned to Student Academic Mentors, who shepherd them through the first year on campus.

Swarthmore is among the top five institutions in the nation for the proportion of graduates who go on to earn Ph.D.s, at 22 percent.

Undertaken by 18 percent of Swat's students, the acclaimed two-year honors program features small seminars or independent study and collaborative relationships between students and professors. Setting it apart from any other program in the United States are the written and oral examinations, which are reviewed by external faculty at the end of the senior year and gauge the students' ability to hold their own with experts in the field. One student describes honors as "like a pre-Ph.D. program"; indeed, Swarthmore is among the top five institutions in the nation for the proportion of graduates who go on to earn Ph.D.s, at 22 percent. Thirty-nine percent of Swarthmore students study abroad in countries such as France, Japan, Poland, and Spain. Roughly two-thirds of students get involved with faculty-guided research or independent creative projects. A sophomore adds, "We have a great group of networked alumni who are always willing to help students, especially with externships, in which students stay with their Swat alum host family one week before winter break and shadow them."

"Ultimately, we are all nerds here," a history major says. "Each of us in our own way has found a place where our passionate, geekiest interests are validated, appreciated, and celebrated by our fellow Swatties." Swarthmore is home to a diverse student body; 6 percent are Pennsylvania residents and 16 percent are international. Eight percent of students are Black, 17 percent Asian American, 14 percent Hispanic/Latino, and 9 percent multiracial.

"[Professors] are always accessible and very, very friendly."

Consistent with its Quaker roots, Swarthmore encourages students to be as educated as possible on issues of cultural, racial, and socioeconomic pluralism, and the entire community is brought into decisions on issues such as socially responsible investments and the pay scale of campus workers. The college banned fraternities and sororities in 2019 in response to student protests over allegations of sexist and racist activities by the two fraternities that existed at the time. Liberals far outnumber conservatives, students say, but students on both sides are keen to stand up for issues they are passionate about. Swarthmore is need-blind in its admissions and meets 100 percent of admitted students' demonstrated financial need. In an effort to reduce the burden of debt, the college joined the ranks of schools that have replaced loans with grants in their financial aid packages. In addition, every student receives a $700 credit at the start of each academic year to fund the purchase of textbooks from the campus bookstore.

For the McCabe Mile, participants take a break from studying for midterms by running 18 laps around the basement stacks of the McCabe Library.

Ninety-six percent of undergraduates live on campus, and housing is guaranteed for all four years. "The dorms each have their own personality," says a senior, "and for the most part they are quite comfortable and well maintained." Dining options are said to be diverse and plentiful, if not always gourmet level, and a handful of local eateries are also covered by the meal plan. Campus safety personnel are "quick to respond in any circumstance," and a sophomore says, "We have a *very* active Title IX office that works on prevention and resolution equally."

Most social life at Swarthmore takes place on campus, and it often begins late, since students hit the books until 10 or 11 p.m. and then head out for fun. "In order to receive funding from the Social Affairs Committee, an event has to be open to all members of campus," explains an economics major. "Because of this regulation, you don't have to worry about getting in to a party or having to pay for most events." The college allows students of legal age to have alcohol on campus, and one student says, "Campus police are not disciplinarians. They want students to be safe." Annual traditions include the McCabe Mile, where participants take a break from studying for midterms by running 18 laps around the basement stacks of the McCabe Library, and Primal Scream, where everyone screams at midnight the night before final exams.

Students' biggest complaints include lack of sleep and too much work, self-imposed or otherwise. When not studying, Swatties are often volunteering in Philadelphia or the nearby smaller city of Chester. The Eugene Lang Center for Civic and Social Responsibility has made Swarthmore a national force in the area of service learning. "Swarthmore is characterized by a genuine will to do good in the world," an engineering major says. The village of Swarthmore, known as the "'Ville," has some stores, a pizza parlor, and a Chinese restaurant. Students say there's not much in the way of off-campus social activity. For that, they hop from the on-campus train station into downtown Philadelphia, where many temptations await, including concerts, dance clubs, museums, and four professional sports teams. The King of Prussia mall, with a movie theater and department stores, isn't far either.

> **The Eugene Lang Center for Civic and Social Responsibility has made Swarthmore a national force in the area of service learning.**

> "Our passionate, geekiest interests are validated, appreciated, and celebrated by our fellow Swatties."

With Swarthmore's focus on academics, athletics aren't a high priority. The school scrapped its football program because the need to recruit enough males to remain competitive in the increasingly intense Division III environment was undermining efforts to recruit students with other interests and talents. Men's basketball and swimming have won Centennial Conference championships in recent years. Other competitive Garnet teams include men's and women's soccer and tennis. Any victory over archrival Haverford will have Swatties swelling with pride. Intramurals and club sports are available, and the women's rugby team's annual Prom Dress Rugby match against Ursinus is a beloved event. In the Crum Regatta, student-made boats float in nearby Crum Creek—Swarthmore's answer to the America's Cup.

Swarthmore is a place where the administration supports the student body completely, and students are given a voice in a variety of issues ranging from faculty hiring decisions to making campuswide policies. Students who want to take an active role in their education beyond the classroom door may find the right fit here. Says a student, "We really are dedicated to learning just because we like to learn, not because we want the A."

Overlaps

Amherst, Bowdoin, Carleton, Pomona, Williams, Wesleyan, Yale, Brown

If You Apply To ›

Swarthmore: Early decision I and II, regular decision. Accepts the Common Application with supplement. Please consult Swarthmore's website for the most up-to-date information regarding standardized test requirements.

Syracuse University

900 South Crouse Avenue, Syracuse, NY 13244

Syracuse defines itself as a research university that takes undergraduates seriously. World renowned in communications, its signature program, Syracuse is also strong in architecture, management, the arts, and public affairs. The university has been a national leader in promoting socioeconomic diversity. Basketball provides solace during snowy winter nights.

Website: www.syracuse.edu
Location: Small City
Private
Total Enrollment: 18,177
Undergraduates: 14,072
Male/Female: 45/55
Financial Aid: 82%
Pell Grant: 18%
Expense: Pr $ $ $
Student Loans: 53%
Average Debt: $ $ $ $
Applicants: 39,682
Accepted: 59%
Enrolled: 16%
Grad in 6 Years: 82%
Returning Freshmen: 91%
Academics: ✍ ✍ ✍
Social: ☎ ☎ ☎
Q of L: ★ ★ ★
Admissions: (315) 443-3611
Email Address: orange@syr.edu

Strong Programs:
Communications
Television, Radio, and Film
Architecture
Management
Life Sciences
Sport Management
Visual and Performing Arts
Geography

Anyone who has watched college sports on TV is familiar with the bright-orange color associated with Syracuse University. They've seen the screaming fans and the stadium overflowing with cheering hordes. But beyond all the athletic fanfare is passion of another sort: Syracuse has set out to become a thriving, student-centered research university. In recent years, the university has launched academic programs and research initiatives in emerging areas such as global enterprise technology, bio-enabled science, and artificial intelligence, and it has invested in new faculty hires. By fostering close working relationships between students and faculty, expanding course offerings, and pouring loads of money into facility upgrades, Syracuse has made its former reputation as an academic assembly line with killer sports teams a distant memory.

The Syracuse campus is located on a hill overlooking the city of Syracuse in central New York State. The character and mixture of architectural styles depict a continuously changing campus, which is grassy, full of trees, and bordered by residential neighborhoods. Fifteen of the university's 140 buildings are listed in the National Register of Historic Places. Many schools and colleges have restructured facilities to accommodate more faculty/student research. Recent construction projects include a $118 million renovation of the JMA Wireless Dome (formerly called the Carrier Dome) and a major renovation and expansion of the Schine Student Center in the heart of campus.

> **"I have yet to meet a professor who is unwilling to go out of their way to help their students."**

General education requirements vary by school and college, but several of them subscribe to the Arts and Sciences core requirements, which include coursework in the sciences, math, social sciences, humanities, and contemporary issues. All entering first-year students participate in a one-credit seminar course on issues of identity, belonging, and student success, in addition to a writing seminar. All students also take at least one course that fulfills an inclusion, diversity, equity, and accessibility requirement.

The S. I. Newhouse School of Public Communications is undoubtedly the superstar of Syracuse's academic programs, offering eight majors and opportunities for dual majors. Journalism and the television, radio, and film major are two of the school's strengths. Additionally, Syracuse's programs in architecture, management, life sciences, sport management, and visual and performing arts, especially drama, are popular and well regarded. Also well-known is the Maxwell School of Citizenship and Public Affairs, whose faculty members teach sought-after undergraduate courses in economics, history, political science, international relations, and other social sciences. The College of Arts and Sciences is the largest college at Syracuse and offers recognized programs in geography, writing and rhetoric, philosophy, and chemistry.

A civil engineering major says that "each school at Syracuse has its own academic climate, and some are more competitive than others," but students can expect challenging coursework across the board. Classes are usually small; 64 percent have fewer than 20 students. "Some professors go above and beyond to teach material, while others stick to the old PowerPoint presentations," says a senior, but another student adds that, despite different approaches to teaching, "I have yet to meet a professor who is unwilling to go out of their way to help their students."

Teaming with NASA, the university has a $3 million virtual aerospace engineering facility—one of three in the nation—where students have helped design a reusable space launch vehicle. Syracuse students have also participated in NASA's reduced-gravity student flight programs. The university offers an honors program for a small number of the most motivated students, and a large portion of students participate in undergraduate research. Thirty-nine percent study abroad via Syracuse's centers in England, France, Italy, Spain, and Chile, as well as more than 100 other programs in 60 countries. Syracuse's centers in Los Angeles and New York City offer semester-long programs for those pursuing careers in the entertainment industry.

Thirty-one percent of undergrads are from New York State, and most of those hail from New York City and Long Island; 13 percent are international. The number of students of color has been steadily increasing, with Black students now representing 7 percent of the student body, Asian Americans 7 percent, Hispanics/Latinos 11 percent, and multiracial students 4 percent.

Syracuse has study abroad centers in England, France, Italy, Spain, and Chile.

"People [in my learning community] were my ultimate support system."

Administrators say that Syracuse has invested more funds in scholarships that primarily benefit underrepresented students, and that it remains committed to admissions policies that have made the school a national leader in promoting socioeconomic diversity. The university's reputation took a hit in the spring of 2019 following racist and antisemitic incidents on campus. Since then, reports a student, "Syracuse has made immense strides in bringing minority voices to the forefront of the conversations on diversity issues." Athletes are well supported with 438 athletic scholarships in 16 sports. Merit scholarships average $12,000.

Fifty-three percent of undergraduates live in university housing, which is described as comfortable and well maintained. Students are required to live on campus for their first two years; all first-years reside in residence halls on North Campus. South Campus offers apartment-style facilities. More than two dozen living/learning communities and theme housing are popular options among first-year students. "I was in the engineering learning community, where I met my closest friends," says a senior. "These people were my ultimate support system." The campus offers 20 eateries, including five residential dining centers. As for safety, the university provides a transport/escort service for students studying late on campus and 24/7 on-site security in all campus housing.

The "painters" are famous at Syracuse— groups of students who each paint a letter of the school's name on their bare chests for home games.

Twenty-one percent of men belong to fraternities, and 45 percent of women join sororities. "Greek Life definitely plays a huge role on this campus. I have never felt pressured to drink, however," a student says. Students 21 and over spend many an evening barhopping on Marshall Street, a lively strip near campus. Orange After

"On game days we're all bleeding orange."

Dark puts on late-night activities like movie nights, bowling, and laser tag. Students also enjoy the annual Juice Jam, Mayfest, and Martin Luther King Jr. celebrations.

Students generally enjoy the city of Syracuse, which offers a variety of off-campus retreats, including an excellent art museum, a professional theater, a resident opera company, a symphony, and a string of movie theaters and restaurants. The city's Armory Square is flanked with coffee shops, upscale boutiques, clubs, and eateries. Many students are involved in the community through internships and volunteer work. If students tire of the life in Syracuse, several quaint country towns, complete with orchards, lakes, and waterfalls, are nearby, as are multiple ski resorts. Destiny USA, about 10 minutes away, is the country's sixth-largest shopping center and has an 18-theater cinema and indoor go-kart track. Popular road trips include Skaneateles Lake, Ithaca, Niagara Falls, Montreal, and Rochester.

"Whether you are a socialite who loves Greek life or a nerd who loves science, on game days we're all bleeding orange," says one senior. The Syracuse Orange football team rocks the spacious JMA Dome, cheered on by their fruit-inspired mascot, Otto the Orange, and 50,000 fans. Men's soccer were national champions in 2022. Men's and women's basketball are consistently strong, and a lively Duke–Syracuse basketball rivalry has been established. Men's lacrosse and cross-country have claimed recent Atlantic Coast Conference titles. The "painters" are famous at Syracuse—they are groups of students who each paint a letter of the school's name on their bare chests and run through rain, sleet, or snow to each home game. Syracuse extends its enthusiasm for sports to more than 60 club and intramural programs as well.

From special academic partnerships with NASA to opportunities to study abroad or volunteer right at home, students at Syracuse know they've got something special. The wintry climate may be cold and snowy, but the ubiquitous bright-orange paraphernalia all over campus is enough to warm anyone. "Orange is more than a color—it is a way of life," says a physics and political science double major. "Syracuse students are all in."

If You Apply To ›

Syracuse: Early decision I and II, regular decision. Accepts the Common Application. Apply to particular program; can apply to single, dual, or combined programs. Applicants to art and architecture programs must submit portfolio. Applicants to drama and music programs must audition. Please consult Syracuse's website for the most up-to-date information regarding standardized test requirements.

University of Tennessee Knoxville

Knoxville, TN 37996

UT is in the middle of the pack among its Southeastern rivals—behind Florida, U of Georgia, and UNC; ahead of Alabama, Arkansas, and Ole Miss. As the only major public university in Tennessee, UT comes close to being all things to all students. Strong in business, engineering, and architecture. One of the few Southern flagship universities located in a major city.

Website: www.utk.edu
Location: City Center
Public
Total Enrollment: 27,734
Undergraduates: 23,852
Male/Female: 46/54
Financial Aid: 51%
Pell Grant: 19%
Expense: Pub $ $ $
Student Loans: 50%
Average Debt: $ $
Applicants: 29,909
Accepted: 75%
Enrolled: 26%
Grad in 6 Years: 72%

Students at the University of Tennessee put a premium on school spirit, athletics, and academics—typically in that order. In the fall, boisterous fans pack into one of the nation's largest on-campus football stadiums to watch the Volunteers play against national powerhouses like Alabama, Arkansas, and Florida. Also competitive is the SEC-dominating women's basketball team. "Bleeding orange is the only way to go!" cheers one happy Volunteer. Amid this excitement, it's easy to forget that UT also prides itself on a number of strong academic programs.

Set in the foothills of the Great Smoky Mountains, UT, whose roots date to 1794, is in the heart of east Tennessee's urban hub. The 910-acre campus has an array of architectural styles ranging from Gothic to Georgian to modern. Particularly noteworthy is the Hodges Library—the largest one in the state—built in the shape of a ziggurat. The university has spent approximately $1 billion in the last eight years on new construction, renovations, and landscaping improvements. Streets that once ran through the center of campus have been transformed into landscaped pathways, and several parking lots have been replaced by grassy lawns. Other recent projects include a $167 million student union, a $114 million science building, and the $129 million Zeanah Engineering Complex—the largest academic building on campus, opened in 2021.

UT's general education requirements are fairly extensive and include courses in written and oral communications, quantitative reasoning, arts and humanities, cultures and civilizations, social sciences, and natural sciences, plus a foreign language or multicultural studies. Many strong academic programs are in preprofessional fields, most notably business (particularly supply chain management), architecture, engineering, and nursing. On the liberal arts side, biology, psychology, kinesiology, and sustainability are popular majors. The modern foreign languages and literatures major allows students to combine a concentration in a language, such as German, Spanish, or Japanese, with one in international business.

"Some classes are harder than anything I could imagine and some require little effort."

Academic competition varies, as does course difficulty. "Some classes are harder than anything I could imagine and some require little effort," says one junior. Large lectures are commonplace, and students report occasional problems with registration because preference is given to seniors. Even so, the university has bolstered academic advising, tutoring, and career services in recent years, and graduation rates have been on the rise. Professors receive mixed reviews: "I have had some really good professors and some mediocre ones," a supply chain management major says.

UT is the managing partner of Oak Ridge National Laboratory—the federal government's largest nonweapons lab, located a few miles away—which enhances science and technology offerings, and involves 350 students and faculty in disciplines as diverse as English and physics. About 9 percent of undergraduates are members of the university-wide Chancellor's Honors program, and most of UT's colleges also offer honors tracks. UT established the Haslam Scholars program for 15 of the university's top students; selection criteria include scholastic achievement, leadership potential, and special talents. Haslam scholars enjoy such benefits as study groups mentored by top UT faculty, a study abroad experience, and research support. Twenty percent of students study abroad during their four years, selecting from programs in more than 60 countries on six continents. The most popular options are short-term, faculty-led programs that provide students the opportunity to study under the guidance of a faculty member during the summer terms.

UT students are "levelheaded but tend to get a little crazy on the weekends," says a student. Seventy-one percent of undergraduates are homegrown Tennesseans, and 3 percent are international. Enrollment of students of color remains low—Black students account for 5 percent of undergrads, Hispanics/Latinos 5 percent, Asian Americans 4 percent, and multiracial students 4 percent—but the university has hired a vice chancellor

"[Students are] levelheaded but tend to get a little crazy on the weekends."

for diversity and engagement to promote and improve campus diversity. Financial aid opportunities have been generous, with thousands of merit scholarships available (averaging $6,100) and 260 athletic scholarships in 20 sports.

Twenty-seven percent of UT students live on campus. Although a few older buildings remain, the university built several new residence halls as part of a recent multiphase housing development plan. Each of the dorms has a residence hall association, which for a token fee provides checkout of sports equipment, games, cooking utensils, and other useful items. Freshmen may choose from 14 living/learning communities, where they collaborate with peers on shared academic interests. Remote alarm units and the LiveSafe mobile app allow students to report a crime from anywhere on campus, and the university has developed comprehensive sexual assault awareness and prevention programs.

Students say that the social life is "very important" and active both on and off campus. Greek life is popular—18 percent of the men and 31 percent of the women

UT is the managing partner of Oak Ridge National Laboratory, which involves 350 students and faculty in diverse disciplines.

Cumberland Avenue (a.k.a. The Strip), a few blocks away, offers a lively variety of bars and eateries.

join up. The social calendar is dotted with numerous major events, including homecoming, the Carnicus and All Sing skit and singing competitions, and Knoxville's Dogwood Arts Festival. True to their name, Volunteers also like to get involved in community service projects. Cumberland Avenue (a.k.a. The Strip), a few blocks away, offers a lively variety of bars and eateries. But nothing compares to the sea of orange that engulfs the campus on Saturday afternoons in the fall. More than 100,000 people jam the football stadium to see the Volunteers (a term dating to the Mexican–American War) take on their Southeastern Conference rivals. Denizens liken football in Knoxville to religion, and according to one, "'Alabama' is a four-letter word" in these parts. UT has claimed 23 team national championships and more than 200 team SEC titles in its history. Recent conference champs include baseball, men's basketball and tennis, and women's soccer and swimming and diving. The intramural program attracts roughly a quarter of undergraduates, and the most popular sports are flag football, indoor and outdoor soccer, basketball, and softball.

With its athletic prowess well established, administrators and students are hoping that UT can develop a comparable reputation for its academics. In its quest to climb the ranks of public research universities, UT is transforming its campus with a spate of new construction and ever-increasing academic resources. In the meantime, many will find the growing opportunities here at the "Big Orange" to be well worth the squeezing.

If You Apply To ›

UT: Early action, regular decision. SATs or ACTs: required. Accepts the Common Application. Additional essay required for nursing program applicants. Audition required for music applicants.

University of Texas at Austin

P.O. Box 8058, Austin, Texas 78713

UT Austin is on anybody's list of the top 10 public universities in the nation, and the Plan II liberal arts honors program is one of the country's most renowned academic programs anywhere. Though it is also the capital of Texas, Austin ranks among the nation's best college towns—a progressive enclave in a conservative state. Boot camp for aspiring political types and tech entrepreneurs in the Lone Star State and beyond. Super-competitive admissions for out-of-staters. Where else can you spend time watching bats?

Website: www.utexas.edu
Location: City Center
Public
Total Enrollment: 48,333
Undergraduates: 38,062
Male/Female: 43/57
Financial Aid: 45%
Pell Grant: 26%
Expense: Pub $ $
Student Loans: 41%
Average Debt: $

The University of Texas at Austin has come a long way from where it began in 1883 as a small school with only one building, eight teachers, two departments, and 221 students. Today, the campus is a Texas-sized home to more than 38,000 full-time undergraduates. From its extensive academic programs to its powerful athletic teams to its location in one of the nation's ultimate college towns, UT Austin has everything a Longhorn could ask for. "Our university is a diverse community with amazing opportunities for success," says a junior.

A 400-acre oasis near downtown Austin, replete with rolling hills, trees, creeks, and fountains, the campus features buildings ranging from "old, distinguished" limestone structures to contemporary Southwest architecture. The fabled UT Tower is adorned with a large clock and chimes (a lifesaver for the disorganized) and is illuminated in Longhorn orange after big athletic wins. From the steps of the Tower, one can see the verdant Austin hills and the state capitol. The outstanding library system holds more than 10 million volumes located in 17 different libraries across campus. New facilities include the 184,000-square-foot Thomas Energy Engineering Building, which opened in 2022.

All undergraduates complete a 42-hour core curriculum that requires coursework in English composition, humanities, American and Texas government, American history, social sciences, math, science and technology, and visual and performing arts. Entering freshmen are expected to participate in a small-group community their first semester and take a First-Year Signature Course, which is usually taught by a senior professor and introduces them to academic discussion and analysis of issues from an interdisciplinary perspective.

The list of academic strengths at UT Austin is daunting. Undergraduate offerings in accounting, advertising, architecture, communication, finance, marketing, radio-television-film, and social work are first-rate. Engineering and computer science programs are excellent and continue to expand. The English department is huge (nearly 60 tenure-track professors), and students give it high marks. UT's McDonald Observatory, based in West Texas, boasts one of the world's largest telescopes.

> **"There are many rigorous majors that have accelerated courses or competitive programs."**

Students say the academic climate is competitive and demanding. "There are many rigorous majors that have accelerated courses or competitive programs," says a student. Many UT classes are quite large—24 percent enroll more than 50 students—and smaller sections fill up quickly. UT is a research university, so the professors are often busy in the laboratories. They do, however, have office hours. "My professors are above and beyond my expectations," says a psychology major. "Their own interest in their topics is obvious, and the determination to aid the students is admirable."

The Plan II liberal arts honors program, a national model, is one of the oldest honors programs in the country and one of the best academic deals anywhere. It offers qualified students a flexible curriculum, top-notch professors, small seminar courses, and individualized counseling, and provides them with all of the advantages of a large university in a small-college atmosphere. Business, communication, engineering, liberal arts, and natural sciences honors programs are also available. Being in the capital city should have its advantages, and it does. Nearly 200 UT undergrads work for lawmakers in the Texas Legislature, only a 10-minute walk from campus. Internships with the likes of Apple, Meta, and Tesla in the city's rapidly expanding tech sector (nicknamed Silicon Hills) are just as popular. Engineering majors can alternate work and study in the co-op program. The Sanger Learning Center offers sessions with learning specialists, peer tutoring, coaching on public speaking, and other academic help. Study abroad options are available in 100 countries, and roughly 30 percent of UT undergrads head to foreign locales during their four years, one of the highest percentages among U.S. public universities.

UT students are "intelligent, involved, and proactive in their education," says a senior. Given the university's stellar academic profile, it's no surprise that admission here has become exceedingly difficult for out-of-staters. Ninety percent of UT undergraduates are Texans, and 4 percent hail from outside the U.S. Historically, UT has been integral in the careers of big-time (conserva-

> **"My professors are above and beyond my expectations."**

tive) Texas politicians, but the liberals are not exactly hiding out on this huge campus. Issues such as human rights, gun control, and abortion can get students on both sides pretty riled up here. Hispanic/Latino students account for 27 percent of undergrads, Asian Americans 24 percent, Black students 5 percent, and multiracial students 4 percent. The university offers special welcome programs, social and educational events, and peer mentoring for students of color and first-generation

(continued)

Applicants: 66,043
Accepted: 29%
Enrolled: 47%
Grad in 6 Years: 88%
Returning Freshmen: 96%
Academics: ✑ ✑ ✑ ✑ ½
Social: ☎ ☎ ☎ ☎
Q of L: ★ ★ ★ ★
Admissions: (512) 475-7399
Email Address: admissions@ austin.utexas.edu

Strong Programs:
Business
Architecture
Communication
Radio-Television-Film
Social Work
Engineering
Computer Science
English

Internships with the likes of Apple, Meta, and Tesla in the city's rapidly expanding tech sector (nicknamed Silicon Hills) are popular.

students. It also awards merit scholarships averaging $4,000, as well as hundreds of athletic scholarships. In addition, UT Austin provides full-tuition scholarships to in-state undergraduates whose families make $65,000 or less per year, and smaller awards to those with incomes of $125,000 or less.

University housing, which accommodates only 18 percent of undergrads, ranges from functional to plush. "Most of the dorms are old," says a student, "but they have nice facilities." Residence halls offer a variety of living options based on common social and educational interests. Apartments and condos close to campus are lovely—and very expensive. More reasonably priced digs can be found in other parts of town. But be forewarned: UT life requires lots of walking, especially for commuters, though free shuttle stops are scattered about. As for food, there is a wide variety of options, including healthy, vegetarian, kosher, and vegan fare. Security can be a concern (Austin is an urban area, after all), but students report feeling safe on campus, thanks to active and highly visible campus police.

The Texas Union sponsors movies and social events, and its Cactus Café is a popular venue for musical acts. It also boasts the world's only collection of orange-topped pool tables in its arcade and bowling alley. For those more interested in octaves than eight balls, the Performing Arts Center has two concert halls that attract nationally known performers. There are also more than 1,300 student organizations from which to choose. Eleven percent of the men and 17 percent of the women go Greek. Annual festivals include 40 Acres Fest, a sprawling carnival of the campus organizations. And Texas Independence Day provides an occasion for celebration in March.

> **UT Austin provides full-tuition scholarships to in-state undergraduates whose families make $65,000 or less per year.**

> **"[Austin] has a great live music scene and is beautiful."**

As the state capital, Austin is hardly a typical college town, but it is one of the best. "I love it," exclaims a junior. "It has a great live music scene and is beautiful." Nightlife centers on nearby Sixth Street, full of bars, restaurants, and buskers of all types, and the well-known music scene that features everything from blues to jazz to rock to folk, as well as the Austin City Limits and South by Southwest festivals. Along with live music, bat-watching is one of Austin's most popular activities—the city is known as "Bat City" after the colony of Mexican free-tailed bats that lives under the Congress Avenue Bridge in the spring and summer. It's the largest urban bat colony in North America. Halloween draws an estimated 80,000 costumed revelers to Sixth Street (and sometimes up its lampposts). When the weather gets too muggy (quite often in spring and summer), students head for off-campus campgrounds, lakes, and parks. The most popular road trips are to San Antonio or Dallas. For spring break, students travel to Padre Island, if not New Orleans.

> **The Longhorns won their second consecutive Directors' Cup, awarded to the best overall collegiate athletics program in the country, in 2022.**

Athletics are as vital as oxygen for most Texans, so it shouldn't come as a shock that the annual operating expenses of UT Austin's athletic department exceed $200 million—or that the university announced plans to join the lucrative Division I Southeastern Conference in 2025. For now, the university competes in the Big 12, and the Longhorns won their second consecutive Directors' Cup, awarded to the best overall collegiate athletics program in the country, in 2022. Students especially look forward to the annual Texas–Oklahoma rivalry football game played in the Cotton Bowl Stadium in Dallas. "Football games pull the student body together and give us a chance to show our school spirit," says one student. Bevo XV, the famed UT mascot, is the latest in a long line of live longhorn steer mascots who have at various times been known to bolt loose from their handlers, rip their shirts, and, on one memorable occasion, lie down in the end zone during a game. Basketball and baseball are also popular; the baseball program has many alumni in the major leagues, and the annual spring game between UT's baseball alumni and the current college squad is

> **"Football games pull the student body together and give us a chance to show our school spirit."**

quite a contest. The men's indoor track and field, men's golf, women's tennis, and women's rowing teams all won national titles in the 2021–22 academic year. UT's extensive intramural and club sports program rounds up 22 percent of students and offers weekend athletes access to the same great facilities that the big-time jocks use.

UT Austin may seem overwhelming because of its imposing size, but students say the school spirit and sense of community found here make it feel smaller. UT prides itself on having one of the most reasonably priced tuitions in the country for a flagship public research university. It also offers one of the best all-around educational experiences a student could ask for, especially if you make it into Plan II.

If You Apply To ›

UT Austin: Regular decision. Does not accept the Common Application. Apply either to institution as a whole or particular program. Certain departments have additional requirements. Please consult UT Austin's website for the most up-to-date information regarding standardized test requirements.

University of Texas at Dallas

Richardson, TX 75080

A rising star in the Lone Star State, UT Dallas is now the most selective of the regional campuses of the UT system. Has put on a full-court press to attract top students in science, technology, and business. Good living conditions and a serious honors program. Football here is of the flag variety. Less selective than Texas Tech and Texas A&M.

The University of Texas at Dallas was founded in 1961 as a graduate research center to service the local tech industry, especially in the areas of space sciences and astrophysics. It did not begin awarding undergraduate degrees until 1975, and it waited until 1990 to admit its first freshman class. Since that time, the university has continued to grow and hone its chops as a four-year university with an emphasis on engineering, mathematics, the sciences, and the management of new technologies. "UTD is a young, vibrant, and promising institution," raves one senior. "Even freshmen have the chance to create new organizations and traditions, work in real labs with full professors, and be in contact with top administrators." Although the university may not fit the typical Texas "frats and football" mold, students here still find plenty of reasons to cheer.

UT Dallas is situated on 650 rolling acres in the Dallas suburb of Richardson. Most buildings are positioned around a central mall that features a variety of blooming trees, low flower beds, fountains, and reflecting pools. The predominant architectural style is modern, and many buildings are interconnected by a series of glass sky bridges. The Natural Science and Engineering Research Laboratory is playfully referred to as the "mermaid building" for its iridescent blue, green, and magenta shingles, which resemble fish scales. The Engineering and Computer Science West building features makerspaces and exposed electrical, mechanical, and HVAC systems that serve as teaching tools. Recent additions to campus include the $101 million Sciences Building.

> "Even freshmen have the chance to create new organizations and traditions."

To graduate, UT Dallas students must complete a general education curriculum consisting of coursework across a broad range of liberal arts and science disciplines. As part of the school's Orbit program for student success, all freshmen take

Website: www.utdallas.edu
Location: Suburban
Public
Total Enrollment: 23,720
Undergraduates: 17,997
Male/Female: 56/44
Financial Aid: 73%
Pell Grant: 24%
Expense: Pub $ $ $
Student Loans: 33%
Average Debt: $
Applicants: 18,838
Accepted: 87%
Enrolled: 25%
Grad in 6 Years: 74%
Returning Freshmen: 88%
Academics: ✍ ✍ ✍
Social: ☎ ☎ ☎
Q of L: ★ ★ ★
Admissions: (972) 883-2270
Email Address: admission@ utdallas.edu

a small-group Freshmen Seminar, learn about campus resources, and receive peer mentoring. In addition, all students complete the required Comets to the Core project, which puts students from different majors into small groups to propose multifaceted solutions to a global problem selected by the UTD community, such as water crises or childhood poverty.

UTD boasts highly respected programs in speech, language, and hearing sciences; information technology and systems; biomedical engineering; and neuroscience. STEM fields account for more than half of UTD's 56 undergraduate degree programs, and students praise virtually all of the university's programs in the hard sciences and technology, especially engineering and computer science. The innovative School of Arts, Technology, and Emerging Communication, which blends humanities with science and technology, offers a popular B.A. degree as well as concentrations in animation and games, critical media studies, and emerging media arts. The Jindal School of Management offers a solid menu of business programs, and a handful of majors in the social sciences and humanities are available as well. Some of UTD's most popular majors include computer science, biology, psychology, and mechanical engineering. A major in business analytics and a minor in African American and African diaspora studies were recently added. More than 40 undergraduate programs offer a fast-track option that allows qualified seniors to take graduate courses as they work toward earning a master's degree in less time.

Students say that while the academic climate is collaborative, courses can be grueling. A healthcare studies major counsels, "Our courses are rigorous but definitely doable with studying and asking for help when you need it." Twenty-seven percent of undergraduate classes enroll more than 50 students. "Most professors, especially STEM professors, will take time out of their day to answer your questions, and they do a great job of providing resources to their students," says a mechanical engineering major.

Qualified students may take part in the Wildenthal Honors College, which houses eight programs that grant students access to personal mentoring and special social and academic opportunities. The program is valuable because it "gets smaller groups together to form real communities and resource networks," according to one junior. The Undergraduate Research Program provides stipends for students to pursue short-term research proposals. Study abroad options are available in nearly 60 countries, and roughly 3 percent of undergrads go overseas. The McDermott Scholars program offers a full ride plus stipends for international travel, field trips, and other benefits; approximately 25 freshmen are selected every year.

> "Most professors, especially STEM professors, will take time out of their day to answer your questions."

Given the student body's heavy interest in STEM fields, one student says, "UTD would best fit a nerd." Ninety-one percent of undergraduates hail from the Lone Star State and 4 percent from abroad. Black students account for 6 percent of the student body, Asian Americans add 39 percent, Hispanics/Latinos represent 18 percent, and multiracial students make up 4 percent. When it comes to political and social issues, a sophomore says, "UTD seems politically quieter than other universities." The university hands out merit scholarships averaging $12,100 each year, but no athletic scholarships. UTD covers full tuition and mandatory fees for Texas residents whose families earn $65,000 or less per year. The Academic Bridge Program helps more than 130 high-potential students from underserved schools make the transition to college-level academics with personal advising, mentoring, and tutoring.

Twenty-two percent of undergrads live on campus in suite-style residence halls and apartment-style housing. "Dorms are some of the best dorms I've seen at any university," says one student. Freshmen can choose to participate in a living/learning community (LLC); options range from management and engineering to

More than 40 undergraduate programs offer a fast-track option that allows qualified seniors to take graduate courses.

first-generation and social sciences. LLC students live in the same residence hall, attend classes together, and participate in various group activities. A bevy of dining options are available, including choices for the health conscious. Students rate campus security highly.

Students say the social scene is slowly heating up. "On campus, clubs and sports are the main channels for social life," explains a cognitive science major. The growing Greek system attracts 5 percent of the men and 6 percent of the women. A math major describes the party scene as "very low-key and generally off campus," and the university is said to be "fairly strict" when it comes to enforcing alcohol policies. Popular traditions include Weeks of Welcome, homecoming, and the annual Oozeball tournament (that's mud volleyball, for the uninitiated). Richardson is "definitely not a college town, but the surrounding community is pleasant and relaxed," says a senior. Students frequent the Northside restaurants across the street from campus and get involved with the locals through volunteering and community service projects. When it's time for off-campus fun, many make the short trip to downtown Dallas, which is "lively, artsy, and sophisticated," according to a molecular biology major.

> **"UTD is driven, talented, smart, quirky, and has eclectic interests."**

UTD may be one of the few places in Texas where football isn't considered a way of life. In fact, you won't find football listed among the university's 17 varsity sports, but you will find a co-ed eSports team. Nevertheless, the UT Dallas Comets are regular contenders in the Division III American Southwest Conference, winning recent titles in baseball, women's golf, and women's tennis. Temoc, the student-designed official mascot, is a blue-skinned comet in human form (try spelling it backward!). The chess team is a juggernaut, having made 18 appearances in the President's Cup (the "final four" of college chess). About 10 percent of students take part in intramural and club sports. Popular activities include flag football, basketball, spikeball, and soccer, and students are enjoying a recently built cricket field.

UTD appeals to those students seeking challenging coursework, access to undergraduate research and top-notch facilities, and administrators who value their input. "Sure, UTD is a relatively new university, but there is enough tradition to be proud of," reasons a biomedical engineering major, who adds, "UTD is driven, talented, smart, quirky, and has eclectic interests that truly make the university interesting once you get to know it." Indeed, students here aren't bound by tradition—they're creating it.

> *You won't find football listed among the university's 17 varsity sports, but you will find a co-ed eSports team.*

Overlaps

Georgia Tech, Iowa State, CU Boulder, UC Santa Barbara, University of Maryland, Texas Tech, UT Austin, Texas A&M

If You Apply To ›

UT Dallas: Rolling admissions. Accepts the Common Application. Please consult UT Dallas's website for the most up-to-date information regarding standardized test requirements.

Texas A&M University

College Station, TX 77843

Coming to A&M is like joining an elite club with 62,000 full-time members. In addition to fanatical school spirit, Texas A&M offers leading programs in the natural sciences, engineering, and business. To succeed in this mass of humanity, students must find their academic niche. The student body is 95 percent Texan, and out-of-staters should be prepared for major culture shock.

Known for top-notch science and engineering programs and unsurpassed school spirit, Texas A&M opened in 1876 as the state's first public institution of higher education: a land grant college with a military training focus. Today, this school of more than 50,000 full-time undergrads boasts a massive endowment and innumerable traditions. When they're not studying for rigorous classes, Aggies may be found at Midnight Yell before each home and away football game or yelling—as the saying around campus goes, "Aggies don't cheer, we yell!"—for their teams at other high-energy athletic events.

Texas A&M occupies the largest university campus in the country in terms of acreage (5,200)—something made obvious to students every time they walk to class.

> "[Undergraduate research is] as easy as emailing a professor and starting that conversation."

The campus combines historic brick buildings from the turn of the 20th century with new, modern facilities and is pulled together by a heavy cover of live oak trees. The campus is in a constant state of flux, as renovations and new construction take place on a regular basis, including the 118,000-square-foot, high-tech Innovative Learning Classroom Building. Aggie Park, a 20-acre, $35 million project featuring an outdoor amphitheater, a performance pavilion, a lake, and some 600 freshly planted trees, was completed in 2022.

The general education requirements are standard, but incoming Aggies can expect some heavy coursework. They must also fulfill an international and cultural diversity requirement and demonstrate computer literacy and proficiency in a foreign language. While Texas A&M is best known for its agriculture, engineering, and veterinary medicine colleges, the university is cultivating a strong liberal arts program and an even stronger business school. Psychology, biomedical sciences, mechanical engineering, and communication tend to be the most popular majors. Aggies stand by their science programs and have done outstanding research in oceanography and animal science. Technical programs of virtually all kinds are heartily supported, especially nuclear, space, and biotechnical research.

Students generally agree that while academics are taken seriously here, the climate is, in the words of a junior, "definitely collaborative." Teaching assistants and grad students are often found behind lecterns, and 28 percent of classes have more than 50 students. Some professors prioritize research over teaching, and a bio-

> "No matter who you are, you'll be greeted with a smile and a 'Howdy!'"

medical sciences major rates the quality of instruction as "mostly excellent, sometimes only sufficient." Undergraduate research is, unsurprisingly, important here, and getting involved is "as easy as emailing a professor and starting that conversation," says a biomedical engineering major. Highly motivated students also recommend the University Honors Program as a good way to make friends and enjoy perks like "priority registration, access to smaller classes with better professors, and networking with the brightest minds here at Texas A&M," according to one participant. Studying, working, and volunteering sometimes take students far from Aggieland—A&M is a leader among American public universities in sending students abroad. Roughly one-third of undergrads study internationally during their four years, mostly in short-term programs; more than 100 faculty-led programs are available, along with hundreds of other options through partnerships and exchange programs worldwide.

Ninety-five percent of undergraduates are from Texas, and just 1 percent come from other countries. Aggies are known for their friendliness. Says one, "From your first tour on campus to the day you graduate, no matter who you are, you'll be greeted with a smile and a 'Howdy!'" Black students make up just 2 percent of the student body, Asian Americans 10 percent, Hispanics/Latinos 25 percent, and multiracial students 4 percent. The campus is decidedly conservative, and a senior comments that "not many rallies or political protests are organized here." Athletes

Technical programs of virtually all kinds are heartily supported, especially nuclear, space, and biotechnical research.

compete for hundreds of scholarships, while scholars vie for thousands of merit awards averaging $4,800. In-state students can lock in their tuition rate for four years, but out-of-staters are subject to tuition increases.

A&M's single-sex and co-ed dorms range from cheap and not-so-comfortable to expensive and cushy (with private bathrooms and in-unit laundry machines), but they accommodate only 22 percent of undergrads. A communication major recommends the university's freshman living/learning communities as a chance to "meet people with similar interests as you" and because "applying for one can help guarantee a spot to live on campus." Most upperclassmen live in the numerous apartments and houses in College Station or its twin city, Bryan, and the university runs an extensive bus system throughout the community. Dining halls, fast-food chains, snack shops, and food trucks are all over campus. "I'm never afraid on campus that my things will get stolen or that I will be in danger," says a nonprofit management major. Students report that the "Step In. Stand Up." campaign has done much to raise awareness about sexual harassment and assault.

A&M is a leader among American public universities in sending students abroad.

When it comes to social life, a junior advises, "It is imperative that you join a student organization in order to make A&M feel a little smaller and to really find your niche and purpose." With more than 1,100 student-led clubs and organizations to choose from, students should have little trouble doing so. Greeks attract 6 percent of the men and 15 percent of the women, and students say that, with such a large student body, neither Greek life nor partying define the social scene.

"It is imperative that you join a student organization in order to make A&M feel a little smaller."

Students appreciate the amenities of the surrounding area, especially in the Northgate district, which offers ample restaurants and bars. "College Station is a model college town," asserts a senior. When the school empties out for holidays, the town does too. Students are actively involved in the community, and the Big Event, which draws thousands of Aggies each year, is the nation's largest student-run, one-day community service event. Those seeking a getaway can drive an hour and a half to either Houston or Austin, and the beaches of the Gulf Coast beckon.

Texas A&M is practically synonymous with tradition. Boasts one senior, "You could write a book—and many have—about all the traditions we have here." Favorites include the Twelfth Man, in which all students stand for the entirety of every football game as a symbol of their loyalty and readiness to take the field, and Aggie Muster, held in more than 300 locations around the world to remember alumni who died within the year. There's also the 400-plus member Fightin' Texas Aggie Band and the senior "boot line" at the end of the football halftime performance. The fabled Corps of Cadets is one of the largest uniformed leadership training programs in the country, with about 2,100 cadets. Although this is just a fraction of the student body, the Corps remains the single most important keeper of the spirit and traditions of Aggieland. Yet another ritual: thousands of seniors join hands and meander through the campus visiting favorite spots for the last time during the Elephant Walk each spring (akin to elephants wandering away from their herds before they die).

Football fans rock Kyle Field with cries of "Gig 'em, Aggies," or "Hump it, Ags," after every Aggie touchdown.

Athletics, whether on the varsity level or for recreation, are at the top of almost anyone's list here. The school's 20 varsity teams compete in the ultracompetitive Division I Southeastern Conference (SEC), where they line up against powerhouses such as Alabama and LSU. Since joining the SEC in 2012, Texas A&M has won four national titles and 28 conference championships. Football fans rock Kyle Field with cries of "Gig 'em, Aggies," or "Hump it, Ags," and after every Aggie touchdown, fans kiss their dates. Basketball, flag football, racquetball, and soccer are among the most popular sports in the well-organized and extensive intramural program. Aggie jokes abound, much to the irritation of A&M students, who don't take too kindly to being the object of ridicule. Example: "How do you get a one-armed Aggie out of a tree?" "Wave."

Overlaps

UT Austin, UC Berkeley, University of Michigan, UNC at Chapel Hill, UCLA, UT Dallas, University of Houston, Baylor

With undergraduate enrollment increasing by 25 percent in just eight years, students express concerns that the university may be getting too large: "There are simply too many students here for the campus and the community to sustain them," remarks a senior, "and our school identity is becoming diluted because of overpopulation." Texas A&M is undeniably gargantuan, yet it is also self-consciously familial. "A great school will challenge and nurture you to become an individual who is ready to conquer any problem in the world—and that right there is Texas A&M," says one satisfied biology major. With varied educational opportunities and memorable traditions worth cheering (that is to say, "yelling") about, it's no wonder students here are so devoted to their "Aggie Family."

If You Apply To ›

Texas A&M: Early action (engineering only), regular decision. Does not accept the Common Application. Apply to particular schools or programs. Primarily committed to state residents. Please consult Texas A&M's website for the most up-to-date information regarding standardized test requirements.

Texas Christian University

TCU Box 297013, Fort Worth, TX 76129

The personalized private alternative to Texas-sized state universities. Tuition is less, and the student body less affluent, than that at archrival SMU. Though affiliated with the Disciples of Christ, TCU goes lighter on religion than, say, Baylor. Strengths include business, communication, and the fine arts. Strong sense of community and school spirit.

Website: www.tcu.edu
Location: Suburban
Private
Total Enrollment: 11,620
Undergraduates: 10,019
Male/Female: 39/61
Financial Aid: 83%
Pell Grant: 12%
Expense: Pr $ $
Student Loans: 36%
Average Debt: $ $ $ $
Applicants: 19,782
Accepted: 54%
Enrolled: 24%
Grad in 6 Years: 83%
Returning Freshmen: 91%
Academics: ✑ ✑ ✑
Social: ☎ ☎ ☎
Q of L: ★ ★ ★
Admissions: (800) TCU-FROG
Email Address: frogmail@tcu.edu

You know a school has spirit (if that's the right word) when its students paint themselves purple to cheer raucously for a spiky toad. Although outsiders might be baffled by such a display, Texans know these folks are TCU fans cheering for the home team (officially known as the Texas Christian University Horned Frogs) at a Saturday afternoon football game. There's a true sense of school spirit and solidarity here. And while TCU is more selective than rivals Southern Methodist and Baylor, it has a reputation for being more accessible.

The spacious 302-acre campus is kept in almost perfect condition and features tree-lined walkways and grassy areas. Nearby is a lovely residential neighborhood not too far from the shops and restaurants of downtown Fort Worth. The campus, which dates to 1873, boasts an eclectic mix of architecture, ranging from neo-Georgian to contemporary. Notable facilities include the Hays Business Commons and the acoustically perfect, 700-seat Van Cliburn Concert Hall, part of the recently built, $53 million TCU Music Center.

> **"My advisor is so eager to help. I think he really enjoys giving me advice."**

Students choose their majors from 114 disciplines, with the core curriculum embodying the base of the liberal arts education. The core emphasizes critical thinking and is divided into three areas: essential competencies; human experience and endeavors; and heritage, mission, vision, and values. There are first-year seminar courses, along with a student orientation and Frog Camp (an optional summer camp that emphasizes team building and school spirit). TCU's standout programs are business, nursing, biology, strategic communication, education, and fine arts. The most popular majors are nursing, finance, communication studies, and marketing. In the Neeley School of Business, selected upperclassmen manage a $1.75

million investment portfolio. The university also offers an innovative dance program with a ballet major, a strong theatre internship program, and majors in ranch management and comparative race and ethnic studies.

"TCU is home to many students who are high achievers," says a sophomore. "However, it is not as competitive a climate as other universities." Classes are often small, with 41 percent enrolling fewer than 20 students, and many professors take on the role of mentors, as do academic advisors. "My advisor is so eager to help," says a student. "I think he really enjoys giving me advice."

Top achievers may be invited to join the honors college, living together in the honors dorm their first year and pursuing individual research opportunities as part of their honors thesis senior year. "Honors classes are focused more on critical thinking, ethics, and human connections rather than definitions and formulas," explains one participant. Globally minded students can travel to 20 countries to study abroad in their pick of more than 50 programs, including faculty-led options; 38 percent do so. Career services, which are specific to each college, get high marks, and students also recommend getting involved with leadership opportunities offered through the Leadership & Student Involvement office.

"Students at TCU are the friendliest people you will ever meet!" cheers a social work major. The student body is fairly homogeneous; 46 percent are from Texas, many from affluent, conservative families. Black students account for 5 percent of the student body, Hispanics/Latinos 16 percent, Asian Americans 2 percent, and multiracial students 4 percent; 5 percent of students are international. Lack of diversity is a top concern among students, but a junior notes that TCU has been "taking a lot more interest in diversity and inclusion efforts within everything from recruitment and admissions to first-year experience programs." This is hardly an activist campus,

"TCU is full of rah-rah school spirit."

and although TCU is affiliated with the Christian Church (Disciples of Christ), the atmosphere is not overtly religious. TCU provides merit awards averaging $19,500 and more than 300 athletic scholarships.

Forty-nine percent of the student body lives on campus. Dorm life offers a good experience, with up-to-date facilities and helpful staff. "TCU works to make such an amazing community that I would live in Milton, my freshman dorm, forever if I could," enthuses a biology major. Most juniors and seniors, however, move off campus, and fraternity and sorority members may live in their Greek houses after their first year. Campus meals receive average reviews, except for Sunday brunch. "No one misses Sunday brunch," says a salivating finance major. "Lobster macaroni and cheese, chocolate fountains, pastries, mountains of fruit, I could go on for days." An evening transportation service, Froggy Five-O, takes you wherever you want to go on campus, and students say they feel safe. The annual, weeklong It's On Us campaign works to raise awareness of sexual assault, and a senior says, "I am proud of TCU for addressing it head-on."

Greek life is important at TCU; 43 percent of the men and 57 percent of the women join Greek organizations. They party in the esprit de corps tradition, but there's plenty of fun left on campus and in Fort Worth to keep the non-Greek Frogs hopping, such as movie nights, concerts, food trucks, and sports games. "Alcohol violations are a big deal," says a student, and involve a three-strike system. Students look forward to the annual fall concert that brings big-name acts to campus, and the traditional lighting of the Christmas tree (featuring carols, hot chocolate, cookies, Santa, reindeer, and even fireworks) is always a special event. "Fort Worth is cultured and has plenty of things to do," says a senior. "The stockyards let you get in touch with the inner country in you, and no one should miss a visit to Billy Bob's, the world's largest honky-tonk." Dallas is only 45 minutes to the east; other road trips include Austin, San Antonio, the Gulf Coast, and Shreveport, Louisiana.

(continued)

Strong Programs:
Business
Nursing
Biology
Strategic Communication
Education
Dance
Theatre
Finance

Honors students live together in the honors dorm their first year and pursue an honors thesis senior year.

The Horned Frog football team finished the 2022 season as runner-up to Georgia in the national championship.

TCU fields 22 varsity athletic programs, which compete in the tough Big 12 Conference. The Horned Frog football team finished the 2022 season as runner-up to Georgia in the national championship. The annual grudge match against Southern Methodist for the Iron Skillet always draws lively crowds. Baseball, men's tennis, and women's soccer have claimed conference titles in recent years. Intramural and club sports are popular with students as well.

From its student-friendly admissions process to its dedication to supporting and developing students once they hop onto campus, TCU is an accessible university offering a personalized educational experience. The school's warm students have no shortage of purple pride. As one junior says, "TCU is full of rah-rah school spirit and a student body that never fails to say, 'Go Frogs!'"

If You Apply To ›

TCU: Early decision, early action, regular decision. Accepts the Common Application. Optional Freedom of Expression question allows space for any information not included elsewhere in application. Please consult TCU's website for the most up-to-date information regarding standardized test requirements.

Texas Tech University

Lubbock, TX 79409

A child of the remote West Texas plains, Texas Tech is emerging from the large shadow of Texas A&M as one of the state's top research universities. It takes big-time sports to be on the map in Texas, and the Red Raiders have taken up the challenge. Bills itself as smaller and more personal than UT or A&M.

Website: www.ttu.edu
Location: City Center
Public
Total Enrollment: 33,412
Undergraduates: 28,935
Male/Female: 51/49
Financial Aid: 66%
Pell Grant: 22%
Expense: Pub $ $
Student Loans: 50%
Average Debt: $ $ $
Applicants: 33,756
Accepted: 68%
Enrolled: 29%
Grad in 6 Years: 63%
Returning Freshmen: 85%
Academics: ✏ ✏ ✏
Social: ☎ ☎ ☎
Q of L: ★ ★ ★
Admissions: (806) 742-1480
Email Address: admissions@ttu.edu

Texas Tech University has come a long way from its humble beginnings. It opened its doors in 1925 in the West Texas city of Lubbock with fewer than 1,000 students enrolled in four schools: agriculture, engineering, home economics, and liberal arts. Today, Tech hosts 29,000 full-time undergraduates, hundreds of academic programs, and schools of medicine and law, and it aspires to become a leading research university on the national level. "We are enjoying increasing emphasis on undergraduate research, service learning and community engagement, personal and professional ethics, and internationalization," administrators say.

Tech's 1,839-acre campus features expansive lawns, impressive landscaping, and Spanish Renaissance–style red-tile-roofed buildings. The school has completed more than $1 billion in construction projects in recent years, including the Sports Performance Center and an honors residence hall. Tech also has a slew of other facilities around Texas, such as a 16,000-acre agricultural facility and research farm.

The university's 10 undergraduate colleges and schools boast more than 150 degree programs. Tech's comprehensive general education requirements span all of the colleges and schools, and most majors involve a capstone course as well. The College of Agricultural Sciences and Natural Resources "has the strongest financial foothold on campus, with the largest endowment," says an economics major. "Within the College of Human Sciences lies the department of personal financial planning, the best of its type in the country." Mechanical engineering, marketing, communication studies, biology, and management are some of the most popular majors, and the education,

> **"Tech students want to learn and excel and push those around them to do the same."**

animal science, wind energy, and music programs are also well regarded. The university studies major, which allows students to build their own interdisciplinary major by combining any three existing areas of study, is a popular option.

Despite Tech's massive size, 76 percent of classes have fewer than 50 students. As at many large research universities, a junior reports, academic rigor and quality of instruction "really depend on the teacher and the level of the class." Graduate assistants may lead discussion sections or labs, but they aren't the main force at the lectern. An optional one-credit freshman seminar helps with the transition from high school to college.

The Program in Inquiry and Investigation (known as Pi Squared) is a two-semester course that prepares interested freshmen to conduct undergraduate research. Between 350 and 400 outstanding first-year students enroll in Tech's Honors College every year, where they sit on committees, help with recruiting, make decisions about course content, and evaluate faculty. They can also work on research projects, either independently (with a professor's guidance) or as part of a student/faculty team. Those yearning to leave the hardscrabble plains of West Texas may study abroad in more than 50 countries; Tech also has its own campuses in Spain and Costa Rica. About 20 percent of students go abroad, an impressive figure boosted by the requirement that all undergrads enrolled in the Whitacre College of Engineering must have an international experience lasting at least six weeks.

"Tech students want to learn and excel and push those around them to do the same," says a student. The Tech student body is largely homegrown; 91 percent hail from the Lone Star State and 2 percent come from foreign nations. Black students account for 6 percent of the undergraduate population, Hispanics/Latinos 29 percent, Asian Americans 3 percent, and multiracial students 4 percent. The university sponsors frequent discussion series and workshops on the issues of diversity, inclusion, and racial equity. According to a public relations major, "A majority of students identify as Republican." Tech offers merit scholarships worth an average of $4,500, as well as more than 350 athletic awards in 17 varsity sports. Elite chess players can vie for a handful of scholarships as well. The Red Raider Guarantee offers free tuition and fees to qualified freshmen who are Texas residents and whose families earn less than $65,000 per year.

Only 24 percent of the students at Tech live in the dorms, mainly freshmen who are required to do so. "The dorms are the ultimate college experience," enthuses one senior. Co-ed, single-sex, and quiet study dorms are available, as are 18 living/learning communities. Dining options are plentiful, and a junior says, "Whether you're a vegetarian or on a protein diet, you'll eat well here." About 50 restaurants in the area also take the university's Tech Express debit card. A safe-ride shuttle service helps students feel safe, and the Risk Intervention and Safety Education office is working to prevent sexual violence and support personal wellness on campus.

"The dorms are the ultimate college experience."

More than 500 student organizations offer plenty of activities to keep students busy on campus. Thirteen percent of the men pledge fraternities and 18 percent of the women join sororities, so a sizable contingent heads to the parties at Greek Circle, although students say Greek groups don't dominate the social scene. Since so many students live off campus, that's where most of the weekend action is. "Most partying happens at places like bars or house parties, and never on campus," explains a junior. The Depot District is a popular destination, as most bars and clubs admit anyone 18 and over.

Annual traditions include homecoming, complete with a bonfire and chili cook-off; the Carol of Lights during the first weekend in December; and Arbor Day, when hundreds of students fan out across campus to plant flowers and trees for the spring. The city of Lubbock (population 260,000) offers numerous opportunities to get involved with the community through work with the Boys & Girls Clubs

(continued)

Strong Programs:
Agriculture
Personal Financial Planning
Education
Animal Science
Wind Energy
Music
Mechanical Engineering
Marketing

All undergrads enrolled in the Whitacre College of Engineering are required to have an international experience lasting at least six weeks.

Annual traditions include homecoming, complete with a bonfire and chili cook-off.

of America, United Way, animal shelters, or Bible study at local churches. Popular road trips include any of the four nearby lakes (for picnicking, boating, or camping), skiing in New Mexico (four hours away), and anywhere the Red Raiders are playing, especially if it's against the University of Texas Longhorns.

The Division I Red Raiders compete in the Big 12 Conference, and the men's basketball and baseball; men's and women's track and field, tennis, and golf; and women's soccer teams are among the school's best. When the football team takes the field, the Masked Rider, replete with red and black cape and cowboy hat, motivates the crowd by galloping up and down the sidelines, and "fans throw tortillas on the field at kickoff," says a sophomore. The university's livestock and meat-judging teams have won several national championships in recent years. Intramural and club sports, which attract about half of the undergraduates, include everything from the typical soccer and flag football to paintball and roller hockey.

Texas Tech has come a long way over the past 98 years in carving out its own niche. Students should come prepared for the heat, the relative isolation of the West Texas Plains, and the effort it often takes to be more than a number at any school of this size. Those who do, says a public relations major, will be rewarded by a strong sense of community and school pride: "Everyone is friendly here at Texas Tech because we're all part of something bigger than ourselves."

Overlaps

Texas A&M, Texas State, UT Austin, Oklahoma State, University of Arkansas, UT Dallas, UT San Antonio, University of Houston

If You Apply To ›

Texas Tech: Rolling admissions. Does not accept the Common Application. Please consult Texas Tech's website for the most up-to-date information regarding standardized test requirements.

University of Toronto: See page 364.

University of Toronto: See page 364.

Trinity College

300 Summit Street, Hartford, CT 06106

Long known for both its quality academics and its well-to-do students, Trinity is shaking up its admissions practices and emerging as a national leader in efforts to diversify its student body. Abundant community-based learning and service opportunities take imaginative advantage of the school's troubled urban setting. Trinity joins Lafayette, Smith, Swarthmore, and Union as a small liberal arts college that offers engineering.

Website: www.trincoll.edu
Location: City Center
Private
Total Enrollment: 2,113
Undergraduates: 2,106
Male/Female: 51/49
Financial Aid: 49%
Pell Grant: 15%
Expense: Pr $ $ $ $
Student Loans: 48%

For students at Trinity College, the learning experience doesn't stop at the campus borders. At first glance, the small liberal arts college and the large, gritty city of Hartford, Connecticut, seem like an uneasy match. But instead of insulating itself from outside problems, Trinity takes advantage of its surroundings by using Hartford as its classroom. At the college's downtown Liberal Arts Action Lab, community partners team up with students and faculty to research and propose solutions to problems facing the city. On campus, academic standards continue to rise, and students graduate with a strong liberal arts background. "Students are the priority here," says one senior.

Trinity was founded in 1823 by Connecticut Episcopalians as an alternative to Congregationalist Yale. Splendid Gothic-style stone buildings behind wrought-iron fences decorate Trinity's 100-acre campus. The large, grassy quadrangle is perfect for tossing a Frisbee or relaxing on warm spring and fall afternoons. Along with revitalizing the neighborhood that surrounds it, Trinity's campus is undergoing its own revitalization. Newer facilities include the Gruss Music Center, the Crescent Center for Arts and Neuroscience, and several athletic fields. Classroom facilities in some of the college's original buildings have recently been renovated, and the Crescent Street Townhouses provide accommodations for 340 upperclassmen.

Trinity's general education requirements include distribution courses across the liberal arts and sciences, as well as demonstrated proficiency in writing, mathematics, and a foreign language. The First-Year Seminar emphasizes writing, speaking, and critical thinking; the seminar instructor serves as students' academic advisor. Six Gateway programs give selected freshmen a chance to study in-depth topics from interdisciplinary perspectives through a three-semester sequence of courses. Offerings include InterArts, Interdisciplinary Science, Community Action, Humanities, Global Health Humanities, and Cities, which one student calls "phenomenal—very challenging and rewarding." A global engagement requirement can be completed by coursework or study abroad.

Popular majors at Trinity include economics, political science, psychology, biology, and modern languages. Human rights studies is notable, and students say the school's small but accredited engineering program is strong. That department sponsors the Firefighting Home Robot Contest, the largest public robotics competition in the U.S., open to entrants of any age, ability, and experience. Accelerated bachelor's/master's degree programs are available in American studies and neuroscience. Through the BEACON program, biomedical engineering students can take courses at UConn, the UConn Health Center, and the University of Hartford while conducting research at three area health centers. Trinity's close ties to the community also are apparent in the curriculum; students can take courses on urban development and the history of the city of Hartford, or choose from service-learning courses that incorporate opportunities to work with more than 80 local community service organizations.

> "The academic climate is rigorous but not overly competitive."

Faculty/student collaboration is a tradition at Trinity. Two-thirds of students work with professors on research and scholarly papers, and many students join their mentors to present findings at symposia. "The academic climate is rigorous but not overly competitive," says a senior. Seventy percent of classes have fewer than 20 students. Students say that professors have high expectations of them, and most go the extra mile to provide support.

More than half of the students seek internships in government (including the Legislative Internship Program at the nearby state capital), nonprofit organizations, and businesses in Hartford (the insurance capital of the world). Trinity's study-away program, in which 62 percent of students take part, includes Trinity's own international program sites in nine cities, ranging from Cape Town to Vienna to Shanghai, as well as more than 90 approved and affiliated programs. Trinity's Global Start program offers selected first-year students the chance to spend their first semester studying in Costa Rica. Other enticing choices include the Trinity/La MaMa Urban Arts program in New York City and the Washington Semester in D.C.

Trinity has retreated from its ill-conceived policy of consistently increasing freshman enrollment, a practice that undermined the academic quality of entering students and strained faculty resources. Although the school has had a reputation for enrolling, in the words of a sophomore, "prep school students from privileged families," it is moving away from its traditionally heavy penchant for New England boarding school grads, seeking to diversify the student body. Seventeen percent of Trinity students are Connecticut natives; an increasing number come from

(continued)

Average Debt: $ $ $
Applicants: 5,603
Accepted: 38%
Enrolled: 25%
Grad in 6 Years: 85%
Returning Freshmen: 91%
Academics: ✍ ✍ ✍ ✍
Social: ☎ ☎ ☎ ☎
Q of L: ★ ★ ★
Admissions: (860) 297-2180
Email Address: admissions.office@trincoll.edu

Strong Programs:
Human Rights Studies
Engineering
American Studies
Neuroscience
Economics
Political Science
Psychology
Biology

Six Gateway programs give selected freshmen a chance to study in-depth topics, such as Global Health Humanities, from interdisciplinary perspectives.

California, and 13 percent are international. Asian Americans currently account for 4 percent of the student body, Hispanics/Latinos 9 percent, Black students 6 percent, and multiracial students 3 percent. Although no one would mistake the campus for a political hotbed, students remain aware of global issues and local concerns. Athletic scholarships are not available and merit awards are limited, but Trinity does provide special financial packages to replace student loans for students with the most need. The college also guarantees to meet students' full demonstrated need for four years.

Eighty-six percent of Trinity's students live in the co-ed dorms. Freshmen are assigned housing based on their First-Year Seminar and grouped into "nests" of 60 to 75 students, aimed at creating a more intimate sense of community. Students report that meals at Mather, Trinity's dining hall, are adequate, with options for those with special tastes and needs, and the à la carte and grab-and-go items at the Bistro and the Cave provide alternatives. "Campus safety officers are always around to make sure our students feel safe," says a senior.

"The social life revolves around on-campus activity," a sophomore says. Students praise the Trinity College Activities Council, which brings in comedians and musical performers and organizes parties, study breaks, and community service days. "The campus dances are very popular with the entire student body," says a senior. The Underground Coffeehouse and the Bistro's weekly comedy nights are also student favorites. But the action on Thursday, Friday, and Saturday nights is mostly at the Greek houses (25 percent of the men and 21 percent of the women join up). An effort by the administration to force the single-gender organizations to go co-ed was abandoned after houses failed to attract members of the opposite sex and alumni donors with Greek ties pulled back. Students say alcohol is not hard to come by, but "the campus policies on alcohol are fairly severe on underage drinkers and abusers," says a student. Spring Weekend brings bands to campus for a three-day party outdoors. Popular road trips include Montreal, Boston, New York City, and the beaches and mountains of Maine.

> **"The campus dances are very popular with the entire student body."**

Trinity's location in Hartford has been problematic; some students describe the surrounding area as "scary" and "a terrible college town." In part because the state of Connecticut has not done a good job of investing in its cities, downtown Hartford does not attract visitors from outside the city, and the administration worries about urban problems, such as drugs. Even so, one philosophy major says things are improving: "Hartford has a terrific assortment of restaurants, ranging from cheap but delicious ethnic fare to upscale, parent-friendly places." A college-sponsored "culture van" takes students downtown to catch a show at the Bushnell or visit the Wadsworth Atheneum, the nation's oldest public art museum. A professional soccer team and a citywide bike-share program were recently introduced. Many see the city's troubles as offering "unique opportunities for internships, mentoring, and community service," according to a sophomore. The Office of Community Service and Civic Engagement helps coordinate such opportunities, and students have created and run organizations that provide housing, tutoring, meals, and other services to youth, families, and senior citizens.

> **"[Hartford offers] unique opportunities for internships, mentoring, and community service."**

Trinity's Bantams compete in Division III, and thanks to its international recruits, both men's and women's squash are powerhouses (the men's team has won 17 national titles in the last 24 years). Other solid programs include men's ice hockey, football, and women's lacrosse. Homecoming typically brings Wesleyan or Amherst to campus for a football game, which gets underway after Trinity students

Service-learning courses incorporate opportunities to work with more than 80 local community service organizations.

A college-sponsored "culture van" takes students downtown to catch a show at the Bushnell or visit the Wadsworth Atheneum.

Overlaps

Colby, Boston College, Connecticut College, Wesleyan, Boston University, Brown, Tufts, Holy Cross

burn the opposing school's letter on the quad. About half of the students take part in the intramural and club sports programs.

With its dual emphasis on traditional liberal arts education and civic engagement, Trinity aims to prepare students to be independent thinkers ready to make a difference both locally and globally. And students here have taken their civic responsibility to heart. At Trinity, an English major says, "Students are pushed to reshape the way they think and tackle challenges to make an impact in their community."

If You Apply To ›

Trinity College: Early decision I and II, regular decision. SATs or ACTs: optional. Accepts the Common Application with optional essay supplement that encourages applicants to write about their interest in Trinity.

Trinity College Dublin: See page 381.

Trinity University

One Trinity Place, San Antonio, TX 78212-7200

One of the few quality Southwestern liberal arts colleges in a major city. Trinity is twice as big as nearby rivals Austin College and Southwestern University and offers a diverse curriculum that includes business, education, and engineering in addition to the liberal arts. San Antonio runs neck and neck with Austin as the most desirable city in Texas.

Trinity University is a small school with big bucks. Thanks to that liquid that gushes out of the Texas soil, Trinity has one of the nation's largest educational endowments at a school its size. The wealth is used unashamedly to lure capable students with bargain tuition rates and to entice talented professors from around the nation. The result? A student body composed of smart, ambitious men and women, and a stellar faculty. Students here enjoy challenges but still manage a laid-back Texas attitude. "It's friendly, warm, personal, engaged, and academically stimulating," a senior says.

Trinity was founded in 1869 in a small central Texas town just after the end of the Civil War. In 1952, the school moved to its current location, a residential area about three miles from downtown San Antonio, one of the most beautiful cities in the Southwest. The 125-acre campus, filled with the Southern architecture of O'Neil Ford, is located on what was once a rock quarry. Everything fits the school's aesthetically pleasing and somewhat well-to-do image, from the uniform redbrick buildings to the stately pathways that wind along gorgeous green lawns and through immaculate gardens spotted with Henry Moore sculptures. Trinity's most dominant landmark is Murchison Tower, which rises in the center of campus and is visible from numerous vantage points throughout San Antonio. The newly constructed Dicke Hall houses the English and religion departments as well as support programs for the humanities.

> "[Trinity is] friendly, warm, personal, engaged, and academically stimulating."

Trinity's general education curriculum, called Pathways, contains five signature curricular elements: the First-Year Experience, Core Capacities, Approaches to Creation and Analysis, Interdisciplinary Clusters, and Experiential Learning. Trinity

Website: www.trinity.edu
Location: City Center
Private
Total Enrollment: 2,601
Undergraduates: 2,471
Male/Female: 47/53
Financial Aid: 98%
Pell Grant: 16%
Expense: Pr $ $
Student Loans: 46%
Average Debt: $ $ $ $
Applicants: 9,626
Accepted: 34%
Enrolled: 20%
Grad in 6 Years: 79%
Returning Freshmen: 92%
Academics: ✑ ✑ ✑
Social: ☎ ☎ ☎
Q of L: ★ ★ ★
Admissions: (800) 874-6489
Email Address: admissions@trinity.edu

has a highly praised education department, with a five-year master of arts in teaching program, and a good advising program for students interested in health professions. Trinity's business-related programs are some of its best and most popular; the engineering, neuroscience, psychology, and political science programs are strong too. Business administration, economics, accounting, and biology enroll the most students. Budding journalists and advertisers can try their hand at broadcasting through internships with the communication department's television and radio stations. The five-year accounting program allows students to serve an internship with the big four accounting firms in offices around the nation while earning a salary and receiving college credit. The Languages Across the Curriculum program features classes such as business, history, and anthropology taught in languages that include Chinese, German, Spanish, and Russian.

"The academic climate at Trinity is both rigorous and casual," comments a finance and business analytics major. "The coursework is not easy, but the creativity and autonomy that faculty give to students in class is great." Classes at Trinity are small: 65 percent have fewer than 20 students. According to a junior, "Professors always hold office hours for students to come in and talk or ask questions." A team of professional academic advisors work with incoming first-year students until they declare their majors, at which point students are assigned to a faculty advisor within their department. Forty-five percent of students participate in research projects with faculty mentors, while 37 percent study abroad in programs offered in more than 50 countries.

A team of professional academic advisors work with incoming first-year students until they declare their majors.

Seventy-five percent of Trinity undergraduates are Texans, and 4 percent are international. The school is fairly diverse ethnically; Hispanics/Latinos account for 22 percent, Asian Americans 8 percent, Black students 4 percent, and multiracial students 4 percent. Students report that the campus leans liberal politically, but the atmosphere is generally accepting rather than ostracizing. "Everyone feels the need to stay civil and calm, for the most part," observes a senior. Merit scholarships averaging $24,900 are available to academically gifted students; there are no athletic scholarships.

Students are required to live on campus through their junior year. In fact, 81 percent of the students live in the residence halls, which one student describes as "fantastic, with walk-in closets, private balconies, suite-style rooms, and a cleaning service." Residence halls are co-ed by suite, with one single-sex residence hall that is off-limits to freshmen. A university-owned apartment complex is an option for upperclassmen, but most seniors find their own places off campus. Campus dining is "delicious," according to a student. "I've been eating on campus for four years and I'm still not sick of the food." A junior says students feel safe and "the university police are constantly monitoring the campus."

"The creativity and autonomy that faculty give to students in class is great."

With more than 100 clubs hosting events every weekend, there is plenty of activity to keep students busy. The university sponsors an excellent lecture series that brings notable politicians and public figures to campus. Beer and wine may be consumed on campus by those of legal age in upper-class residence halls. Seventeen percent of the men and 28 percent of the women join the local fraternity and sorority organizations, which hold parties in Greek houses just off campus. "The parties are more like kick-backs rather than a rager type of vibe," explains a sociology major. For first-year students, the school year commences with the traditional Tower Climb, where they climb to the top of the school's bell tower to shake the president's hand and see a knockout view of San Antonio. Students look forward to the Tigerfest dance in the fall and the Chocolate Festival, where student clubs compete to create the best chocolate dessert. They also anticipate Fiesta, a weeklong, annual celebration of San Antonio's mixed culture that features bands, dancing, food, and drink.

For the traditional Tower Climb, first-year students climb to the top of the school's bell tower to shake the president's hand.

San Antonio, with its famed River Walk replete with interesting restaurants, receives a well-deserved thumbs-up from students. It doesn't hurt that the city is home to several other colleges. "San Antonio is a great place to be, because there are so many things to do. That being said, you need a car to get almost anywhere," says one student. Students frequent the many outdoor shops and cafés in the historic Pearl district, as well as cultural and musical attractions and touristy hangouts such as Six Flags and SeaWorld. Students get involved in city life by contributing more than 88,000 hours of community service every year. Residents of the HOPE Hall living/learning community spend two hours a week volunteering with organizations that serve the city's homeless population; "Being part of HOPE Hall grounded and humbled me," says one participant. The city's beautiful, warm weather provides plenty of activities for the students year-round, but there are also many fun road trips. The funky state capital of Austin is 90 miles north, and students can also road-trip to the Texas Gulf Coast and the Hill Country.

> **"Trinity's strong sense of community as well as its San Antonio roots provide a great culture."**

Trinity's varsity sports teams compete in the Division III Southern Collegiate Athletic Conference. The Tigers men's and women's soccer teams are perennial conference champions, and the baseball team is nationally competitive. Students enjoy a variety of intramural and club sports; flag football signs up the most athletes. Country line dancing and outdoor recreation trips are popular too.

A big state and big money give students at this small university many of the advantages of a larger school, from strong preprofessional offerings and accomplished professors to plentiful research opportunities. But a senior says it's Trinity's emphasis on people and the rich heritage of its location that make it a special place: "Trinity's strong sense of community as well as its San Antonio roots provide a great culture."

<table>
<tr><td>

Overlaps

Austin College, Southwestern, Colorado College, Furman, Lafayette, Macalester, Skidmore, Denison

</td></tr>
</table>

If You Apply To ›

Trinity University: Early decision I and II, early action, regular decision. Accepts the Common Application with supplement. Please consult Trinity's website for the most up-to-date information regarding standardized test requirements.

Truman State University

100 East Normal, Kirksville, MO 63501

Widely regarded as Missouri's de facto honors college, Truman has more in common with private institutions than with nondescript regional publics. Occupies a public ivy niche like Miami of Ohio and William & Mary. Rural setting encourages strong focus on academics, including lots of undergraduate research. Less than a quarter of the students are from out of state, mainly from Illinois.

Truman State University, Missouri's only public liberal arts college, attracts high achievers from across the Show-Me State. Founded in 1867 as a regional teacher training institution, the school became a statewide university in 1985 and 11 years later took the name of the only Missourian to serve as a president of the United States. Indeed, since shifting to a liberal arts and sciences mission, Truman has worked to become a "public ivy" on the order of Miami University (OH) or William & Mary. True, the small town of Kirksville, Missouri, is no Williamsburg, Virginia—or even Oxford, Ohio. But the school's relative isolation makes it easier to concentrate on

Website: www.truman.edu
Location: Rural
Public
Total Enrollment: 3,425
Undergraduates: 3,186
Male/Female: 40/60
Financial Aid: 89%

(continued)

Pell Grant: 19%
Expense: Pub $
Student Loans: 49%
Average Debt: $ $
Applicants: 4,068
Accepted: 61%
Enrolled: 27%
Grad in 6 Years: 72%
Returning Freshmen: 84%
Academics: ✍ ✍ ✍
Social: ☎ ☎ ☎
Q of L: ★ ★ ★
Admissions: (660) 785-4114
Email Address: admissions@
truman.edu

Strong Programs:
Nursing
Education
Accounting
Business Administration
Biology
Exercise Science
Psychology

academics. "Truman is a fairly inexpensive school that has an amazing reputation," an accounting major states. "This brings students who are extremely hardworking but also want an affordable education."

Truman is located in the northeastern corner of Missouri, about 200 miles from both Kansas City and St. Louis. The flower-laden campus includes approximately 40 buildings on 210 acres, many of which are Georgian in style—in fact, the oldest portion of the campus, dating to 1873, is modeled on Thomas Jefferson's design for the University of Virginia. The Robison Planetarium and Multimedia Theater is one of the campus's newest facilities.

Truman's revamped general education curriculum—The Dialogues—emphasizes practical skills and experiences alongside breadth in the liberal arts and sciences.

> **"[Small classes allow] for complex and mature discussions of course material."**

Highlights of the curriculum include a common experience for incoming freshmen, consisting of a Self and Society seminar and the Truman Symposium, as well as a requirement that seniors take a capstone course in their major. In addition, all students are encouraged to complete at least one hands-on learning experience, such as study abroad, an internship, or undergraduate research. First-year students participate in Truman Week, a five-day program designed to help them adjust to college life.

The most popular major is business administration; biology, exercise science, and psychology round out the list of programs with the highest enrollment. An interdisciplinary studies major allows students to combine coursework from two or more disciplines to create a specialized major. Nursing is a traditional strength, and there are also solid five-year programs for students interested in education or accounting, which culminate in the awarding of bachelor's and master's degrees. New majors in social issues advocacy and music business are now available.

Students describe a competitive but rewarding academic climate. Classes rarely have more than 50 students, which makes access to top-notch professors the norm and "allows for complex and mature discussions of course material," explains a sophomore. Students praise the career center, and a freshman notes, "There are tons of seminars to talk about practical ways to improve your hirability."

> *The Honors Scholar Program requires students to complete at least five rigorous courses of their choosing in a range of disciplines.*

Students seeking to challenge themselves beyond the regular curriculum can sign up for the Honors Scholar Program, which requires them to complete at least five rigorous courses of their choosing in a range of disciplines. Study abroad opportunities are available via roughly 500 programs in more than 65 countries around the world; 22 percent of students participate. Forty percent of students conduct independent research or collaborate with faculty members on research projects, and Truman typically sends one of the largest delegations of undergraduates to the annual National Conference on Undergraduate Research.

"I would call Truman a nerd school," says a physics and mathematics double major. "Nearly everyone at Truman is there to learn first, so education and work take priority over almost everything else." Seventy-eight percent of Truman students are native to Missouri, and 8 percent hail from abroad. Hispanic/Latino students represent 3 percent of the student body, Asian Americans 3 percent, Black students 3 percent, and multiracial students 4 percent. A political science major categorizes the low-key political climate as "slightly left of center." Merit scholarships are available to qualified students; the average award is $6,400. The school also hands out nearly 300 athletic scholarships. Additionally, the Truman Access Grant provides funding to a limited number of students who have unmet need after their federal financial aid and Truman scholarship award have been packaged.

> **"I would call Truman a nerd school. Nearly everyone at Truman is there to learn first."**

Thirty-nine percent of Truman students live on campus in the residence halls, and an exercise science major says, "Considering these are college dorms, I think they are more than just acceptable." Students say it's easy to get a room, but most students move off campus after their sophomore year. "The meals at the dining hall are surprisingly good, and the menu is constantly rotating," cheers an accounting major. Students report feeling safe on their rural campus. Mental health on campus and a culture of stress have been concerns at Truman, but the administration has invested in counseling services and created campuswide wellness initiatives in response. A nursing major comments, "Whether it's being more lenient about canceling for snow days/poor weather, urging professors to be understanding of students' mental health barriers, or even just promoting positive mental health, Truman has made an incredible change in how it approaches the topic of mental health."

Social life at Truman is robust, according to students. "Because of Truman's semi-isolated location, the Student Activities Board brings in various musicians, comedians, YouTube stars, speakers, and performers to campus for free," explains a freshman. The Greek system plays an integral part in Truman's social life—22 percent of men and 19 percent of women sign up—but there are also 200 other student organizations to choose from. Since the campus is dry, says an exercise science major, "Most parties take place off campus, where they're hosted by Greek organizations, athletic teams, or one of the five bars in town." Students also venture out on road trips to St. Louis, Kansas City, various destinations in Iowa, and Quincy, Illinois. Everyone looks forward to homecoming and Oktoberfest (featuring free root beer) in the fall and the Final Blowout carnival in the spring, with wacky games, inflatables, free food, and prizes. Campuswide games of Humans vs. Zombies, played once per semester, are another social highlight.

> "Truman has made an incredible change in how it approaches the topic of mental health."

The town of Kirksville (population 17,600) grows on you, say students. "All of the essentials of a college town are present, including a Walmart, a bowling alley, a good movie theater, and a beautiful state park," a business administration major says. Two-thirds of students take advantage of various opportunities to get involved in volunteer work and service learning. The Big Event is a popular one-day service event that brings more than 1,500 campus volunteers to Kirksville. Truman hosts 12 service organizations, which provide thousands of hours of service every year.

When not exercising their academic muscles, Truman's Bulldogs, members of the Great Lakes Valley Conference, are succeeding in the pool and on the playing field. The men's and women's swim teams have won multiple Division II titles, and the football, men's and women's basketball, and women's track teams are also competitive. The success of the Forensics Team, the school's longest-running cocurricular activity and winner of several state titles, speaks for itself. Roughly a quarter of the students participate in the 20 intramural events offered per semester, which include everything from basketball and soccer to pickleball and baggo.

"With some of the highest admissions standards of any public university in the state, Truman has a distinct culture of academic excellence," says a student. Indeed, Truman offers challenging academics, pursued within a close-knit community. Though its rural Missouri location can feel isolating, its affordable price is certainly worth considering.

> The success of the Forensics Team, the school's longest-running cocurricular activity and winner of several state titles, speaks for itself.

Overlaps

SUNY–Geneseo, Creighton, Bradley, College of New Jersey, University of Minnesota Morris, Miami (OH), University of Missouri, Saint Louis University

If You Apply To ›

Truman State: Rolling admissions. Accepts the Common Application with supplement. Please consult Truman's website for the most up-to-date information regarding standardized test requirements.

Tufts University

Bendetson Hall, Medford, MA 02155

One of the smallest and most undergraduate-focused of the major research universities, Tufts is known for its global focus and emphasis on civic engagement. Strengths run the gamut from classics and philosophy to engineering and international relations. Located just outside student-friendly Boston, it has more in common with Brown than any other Ivy. Compare to other top urban schools such as Georgetown, Northwestern, and WashU. The Experimental College lets students take nontraditional courses for credit.

Website: www.tufts.edu
Location: City Outskirts
Private
Total Enrollment: 12,001
Undergraduates: 6,509
Male/Female: 45/55
Financial Aid: 37%
Pell Grant: 11%
Expense: Pr $ $ $ $
Student Loans: 27%
Average Debt: $ $ $
Applicants: 31,198
Accepted: 11%
Enrolled: 51%
Grad in 6 Years: 94%
Returning Freshmen: 97%
Academics: ✑ ✑ ✑ ✑ ½
Social: ☎ ☎ ☎
Q of L: ★ ★ ★ ★
Admissions: (617) 627-3170
Email Address: undergraduate
.admissions@tufts.edu

Strong Programs:
Engineering
International Relations
Classics
Philosophy
Child Study and Human
   Development
Biology
Computer Science
Economics

Once considered a backup for those who couldn't get into an Ivy, Tufts University, founded in 1852 by Universalist businessman Charles Tufts, isn't a safety school anymore. Applications are up dramatically, propelling Tufts into the ranks of the more selective schools in the country. With its strong academics, high-achieving student body, and attractive setting, some might say that not all that much more separates Tufts from its illustrious neighbors, Harvard and MIT, than a few stops on the T. Says one senior, "Tufts is a school for people who aren't afraid to speak their mind but are also open to having someone change their mind."

Tufts's 150-acre, tree-lined campus on Walnut Hill overlooks the heart of nearby Boston and is a striking scene. The main campus, with its brick and stone buildings, sits on the Medford/Somerville boundary. Medford, the fifth-oldest city in the country, was a powerful shipbuilding center during the 19th century. Somerville lies adjacent to the Tufts campus, and in 1776, the first American flag was raised on its Prospect Hill. Notable campus facilities include the LEED Gold–certified Science and Engineering Complex.

Undergraduate teaching is what attracts students to Tufts. They get highly personalized attention from faculty, and they enjoy wide freedom to pursue independent study and to complete research and internships for credit. Tufts students also get a healthy diet of traditional academic fare. For liberal arts students, distribution requirements include a World Civilization course in addition to art, English and foreign languages, social sciences, humanities, natural sciences, and math. Engineers

> **"Professors are willing to sit with you and explain topics…or give you general advice on life."**

must take eight courses in the arts, humanities, and social sciences, with one of those fulfilling a writing requirement. The most popular majors include biology, computer science, international relations, and economics. Tufts also boasts strong classics and philosophy departments, and there is an excellent child study and human development program. Newer interdisciplinary programs, such as data science, civic studies, and human factors engineering (or engineering psychology) are growing in popularity. With the university's acquisition of the School of the Museum of Fine Arts in Boston, students can earn a B.F.A. in interdisciplinary studio art or pursue a five-year program that combines the B.F.A. with a B.A. or B.S. degree in another field within the School of Arts and Sciences.

Tufts has two popular programs in which students who need a break from being on the receiving end of knowledge can develop and teach courses. The first, the Experimental College, annually offers more than 100 nontraditional, full-credit courses on topics ranging from Pharmacology and Therapeutics to The Ethics of Voluntourism that are taught by students, faculty, and outside lecturers. The second, Freshman Explorations seminars, are taught by two upperclassmen and a faculty member who doubles as an advisor; these courses are a way for freshmen to get to know each other and ease into the college experience.

"The academics are tough but rewarding," says one junior, and students agree that the atmosphere is supportive. Sixty-three percent of classes have fewer than 20 students, and most courses are taught by full professors. "Professors are willing to sit with you and explain topics you don't understand, give recommendations on research opportunities, or give you general advice on life," says an economics and international relations double major.

For those looking to get off campus, Tufts offers the Washington Semester, exchanges with Swarthmore and Spelman, and cross-registration at a number of Boston schools. Forty-five percent of undergrads study abroad. Students may choose to spend their summer at Tufts's overseas campus in Talloires, France, embark on a semester or year abroad at one of nearly 200 preapproved programs, or select one of Tufts's own full-immersion programs in 10 locations around the globe. The Institute for Global Leadership includes the popular, interdisciplinary Education for Public Inquiry and International Citizenship (EPIIC) program. The yearlong intensive experience revolves around a theme and includes a weekly colloquium, international symposium, and a research project or internship. Recent EPIIC themes have been Race and International Relations and China and the World.

Students may choose to study abroad at one of Tufts's own full-immersion programs in 10 locations around the globe.

"Most Tufts students are excited about what they are learning and very friendly," says a senior. Twenty-six percent of undergrads hail from Massachusetts; California, New York, and New Jersey are also well represented. The university's reputation in international relations attracts a respectable number of international students (11 percent) and Americans living abroad. Asian Americans make up 16 percent of the population, Hispanics/Latinos 9 percent, Black students 5 percent, and multiracial students 7 percent. The campus is largely liberal, and many students are enthusiastically engaged in social and political issues, to the point that student activism itself has become a hot-button topic. "The level of social activism has caused a fissure in the student body between those who are fighting for a cause and those who channel their energies elsewhere," remarks a senior. No merit or athletic scholarships are available, and while the school does meet the full demonstrated financial need of all admits, just 11 percent of incoming freshmen qualify for Pell Grants.

"Partying at a frat is just as acceptable as staying in with your roommate and watching Netflix."

Seventy-one percent of students live on campus. Accommodations in the Uphill and Downhill (the two quads joined by a great expanse of grass and trees) campus dorms vary from long hallways of double rooms to apartment-like suites, old houses, and co-ops—and a good-natured rivalry exists between the two areas. Freshmen and sophomores must live on campus in the dorms, while upperclassmen compete in a lottery or move to apartments just a short walk from campus. "When you're a freshman, go all-freshman housing. Nothing is more special than a community of all freshmen where everyone's looking for a niche to fit in," a student advises. All first-years are required to have the unlimited meal plan, and students give dining services good reviews. The campus police department is said to be effective, and a chemical engineering major reports that an ongoing dialogue is "pushing the administration in the right direction for handling sexual assault on campus, and positive changes have been made."

A good-natured rivalry exists between the Uphill and Downhill areas of campus.

"If you have something that you uncontrollably geek about... then Tufts is the place for you."

According to a senior, "Partying at a frat is just as acceptable as staying in with your roommate and watching Netflix." Tufts has earned a national reputation for its programs to promote the "responsible" use of alcohol and has revised multiple policies governing the Greek system, including delaying rush until sophomore year. Currently, 6 percent of the men and 12 percent of the women join fraternities and sororities. "Drinking is a significant part of life at Tufts," admits a sophomore, "but it's not overwhelming." University-sponsored activities include concerts, plays (Aidekman Arts Center stages 15 to 20 productions each year), and free movies on weekend nights. Several a cappella groups thrive at Tufts, and a favorite student group is the Tufts Dance Collective, where "groups of students practice goofy dances all semester" and put on two shows per year that draw big crowds. Other major campus events include homecoming and Halloween on the Hill, the latter of which is a carnival for children in the community, as well as Spring Fling, an outdoor concert that helps students relax before final exams.

While suburban Medford may not be exciting for those of college age, the T metro system extends to the Tufts campus, so it's easy to make a quick jaunt to "student city" (a.k.a. Boston) for work or play. Davis Square in Somerville is even closer and provides plenty of restaurants, nightlife, and music stores. The largest student organization by far, with more than 1,000 students, is the Leonard Carmichael Society, the umbrella group for volunteer activities ranging from adult literacy and blood drives to work with the homeless and victims of domestic violence.

Tufts fields 29 teams in the Division III New England Small College Athletic Conference (NESCAC). The Jumbos men's soccer, men's lacrosse, women's basketball, and softball teams are competitive nationally. Sixteen percent of students play in intramural and club sports. The Tufts Sabermetrics team, which grew out of the Experimental College, is a national powerhouse in competitions that apply sophisticated statistical techniques to the sport of baseball.

Tufts is experiencing a modern-day renaissance. This, along with a swelling applicant pool, makes Tufts a much hotter school than it was just a few years ago. And its proximity to Boston, an intellectual and educational mecca, makes it even more attractive. "If you have something that you uncontrollably geek about and love to be able to share that passion," says a senior, "then Tufts is the place for you."

Overlaps

Dartmouth, University of Chicago, Brown, Harvard, Wesleyan, Georgetown, Northwestern, WashU in St. Louis

If You Apply To ›

Tufts: Early decision I and II, regular decision. Accepts the Common Application with supplement. Portfolio required for applicants to School of the Museum of Fine Arts. Application includes optional gender identity field. Please consult Tufts's website for the most up-to-date information regarding standardized test requirements.

Tulane University

6823 St. Charles Avenue, New Orleans, LA 70118

The map may say that Tulane is in the South, but it has the temperament of an East Coast institution. Similar number of undergraduates as Emory and Vanderbilt among leading Southeastern universities. Tulane has developed a strong emphasis on interdisciplinary research and community service, both academic and practical. High achievers can shoot for the honors program.

Website: www.tulane.edu
Location: City Center
Private
Total Enrollment: 11,857
Undergraduates: 7,746
Male/Female: 39/61

Once a staid, genteel choice for students seeking a traditional education, Tulane University has rebranded itself with a focus on interdisciplinary research, scholarship, and community service. It now attracts service-minded students from all 50 states who choose from more than 150 service-learning opportunities, many of them existing courses that were revamped to include a service-learning component after Hurricane Katrina, which devastated Louisiana in 2005. Tulane promises a solid education to those who are ready to take up residence in the Big Easy. "Tulane students have to be adventurous," remarks a junior. "Prospective students should only apply if they're looking to pursue a rigorous academic culture with a strong sense of community service."

Tulane is unusual in that it was created as a public medical college in 1834 but then privatized in 1884 thanks to the beneficence of businessman Paul Tulane. The school's 110-acre campus is located in an attractive residential area of uptown New Orleans, about 15 minutes from the French Quarter and the business district. Tulane's administration building, Gibson Hall, faces St. Charles Avenue, where one of the nation's last streetcar lines still clatters past mansions. Across the street is Audubon Park, a 385-acre spread where students jog, walk, study, or watch the sun set over the Mississippi River—a popular way to unwind on Fridays. The buildings of gray limestone and pillared brick, separated by southern live oak trees, are modeled after the neocollegiate/Creole mixture indigenous to Louisiana institutional-type structures. One particular point of pride is the university's 13 Tiffany windows, one of the largest collections anywhere.

Tulane remains committed to its mission as a major research university that emphasizes undergraduate opportunities. All undergrads enroll in the Newcomb-Tulane College, which coordinates academic experiences and support. Students complete a rigorous set of core curriculum requirements that includes a service-learning course as well as a public service project,

"Students can really tailor their curriculum to their interests."

which can take the form of a research project, internship, study abroad program, or honors thesis. Several programs help freshmen make the transition from high school to college, such as TIDES (Tulane InterDisciplinary Experience Seminars), where students connect with a peer mentor and take a small-group course on topics as varied as yoga, J. R. R. Tolkien, and New Orleans cemetery architecture. Some TIDES courses have associated residential learning communities that encourage closer bonding with classmates.

Together, five schools—architecture, business, liberal arts, public health and tropical medicine, and science and engineering—offer more than 75 undergraduate majors. The most popular include business, public health, social sciences, and biological sciences. Tulane's strength lies in the natural sciences, environmental sciences, architecture, and the humanities; international programs in general and Latin American studies in particular are especially strong. The Stone Center for Latin American studies offers more than 150 courses taught by 70 faculty members. An interdisciplinary program in political economy (economics, political science, and philosophy) stands out among the social sciences and is very popular with prelaw students. Environmental studies majors benefit from the ByWater Institute, where faculty members and students work together to study and preserve Louisiana's waterways and coast.

"Since students can really tailor their curriculum to their interests, people are usually pretty diligent about their studies," observes a mathematics and sociology double major. Sixty-one percent of classes have fewer than 20 students; graduate instructors teach some beginning-level classes in English, foreign languages, and math. "Professors here work hard to ensure that all of their students feel supported and are learning the material," says a political science major. Each year the university's highly acclaimed honors program invites about 700 outstanding students to partake in accelerated courses taught by top professors. Tulane offers more than 100 study abroad programs in 40 nations, including one-semester programs in locations such as Thailand to study community public health and Senegal to study international development. In addition, Tulane's Junior Year Abroad program in the UK is one of the country's oldest and most prestigious programs. One-third of undergrads study internationally during their time at Tulane.

(continued)

Financial Aid: 69%
Pell Grant: 8%
Expense: Pr $ $ $
Student Loans: 31%
Average Debt: $ $ $
Applicants: 45,525
Accepted: 10%
Enrolled: 46%
Grad in 6 Years: 86%
Returning Freshmen: 94%
Academics: ✍ ✍ ✍ ½
Social: ☎ ☎ ☎ ☎
Q of L: ★ ★ ★
Admissions: (800) 873-9283
Email Address: undergrad
.admission@tulane.edu

Strong Programs:
Natural Sciences
Environmental Sciences
Architecture
International Studies
Latin American Studies
Political Economy
Business
Public Health

Across the street is Audubon Park, a 385-acre spread where students jog, walk, study, or watch the sun set over the Mississippi River.

Tulane manifests a somewhat Southern feel in a sophisticated and cosmopolitan institution. "Tulane students are willing to try new things, experiment, and work toward the betterment of their community," says an anthropology major. Nine percent of undergraduates are Louisiana residents, and 5 percent come from outside the U.S. Despite the diversity of its host city, Tulane's student body is fairly homogeneous: 5 percent are Black, 8 percent are Hispanic/Latino, 5 percent are Asian American, 5 percent are multiracial, and a mere 8 percent of freshmen qualify for Pell Grants. A senior reports that Tulane "is working to improve diversity, but there's a lot left to be done." The university awards hundreds of merit scholarships, averaging $20,700, and 140 athletic scholarships.

Fifty-two percent of students live on campus; nonlocal freshmen and sophomores must do so. Many upperclassmen opt to move off campus, and one confides that some of the dorms "are in rough shape." The recently opened Dining Room at the Commons is the university's main dining facility, offering 10 meal stations with rotating menus. A monthly farmers market and food trucks that accept the school's meal plan enhance students' options. Tulane has beefed up its counseling staff and programming to combat sexual assault, and a late-night shuttle service transports students safely to and from campus. "We are situated in a quite safe and residential area of New Orleans," notes an international relations major.

> "Tulane is a mixture of New Orleans soul, Southern hospitality, and college student swagger."

Social life at Tulane goes almost without saying. Fraternities and sororities are a presence—23 percent of the men and 52 percent of the women join—but do not dominate the social life, and there are more than 200 student organizations on campus. "My absolute favorite Tulane tradition is Crawfest, our student-run music festival that has over 10 tons of crawfish, several musical performances, and so much more," cheers a junior. Though you're supposed to be 21 to enjoy the bar scene in the cafés and clubs that dot the French Quarter, a sophomore explains that "alcohol is accessible." Playing host to about 130 festivals every year, "New Orleans itself never stops partying!" boasts a student. Mardi Gras is such a celebration that classes are suspended for two days and students from all over the country pour in to celebrate. Road-trip destinations include the Gulf Coast, Austin, Houston, and the Florida panhandle.

While schoolwork is taken seriously at Tulane, so are sports. Women's volleyball, men's and women's basketball, and men's and women's tennis are solid, and the baseball team has a big following. The university fields 16 Green Wave teams that compete in the Division I American Athletic Conference. Club and intramural sports are big, and students can also opt for weight work, squash, or swimming, among other options, at the Reily Student Recreation Center.

Rich in tradition, Tulane is a forward-looking school where the possibilities seem endless. And like its hometown, it is an energetic melting pot of interests and activity. As one senior puts it, "Tulane is a mixture of New Orleans soul, Southern hospitality, and college student swagger." Those seeking a dynamic, service-oriented education in a vibrant city need look no further. *C'est si bon!*

Overlaps

Brown, Duke, Emory, George Washington, Northwestern, Vanderbilt, University of Michigan, Louisiana State

If You Apply To ›

Tulane: Early decision, early action, regular decision. Accepts the Common Application with supplement. Please consult Tulane's website for the most up-to-date information regarding standardized test requirements.

800 South Tucker Drive, Tulsa, OK 74104

Tulsa is a modestly priced private university in an area of the country dominated by large and less expensive public universities. Smaller than Texas Christian and WashU but larger and with a more diverse curriculum than Colorado School of Mines. With a technical orientation rooted in Oklahoma oil, Tulsa is struggling to "reimagine" the relationship between vocationalism and the liberal arts. One unlikely strength: English literature.

The University of Tulsa is a small, private university with a technical bent and a growing international reputation. Known for its engineering and science programs, including petroleum engineering and geosciences, Tulsa is doubling down on its strengths in STEM fields while simultaneously overhauling its approach to the liberal arts. With its emphasis on undergraduate research and hands-on work experience stronger than ever, TU attracts students from across the country and around the world.

TU's 210-acre campus is just three miles from downtown Tulsa, and there's a striking view of the city's skyline from the steps of the neo-Gothic McFarlin Library. The university's more than 90 buildings run the architectural gamut from 1930s-vintage neo-Gothic to contemporary, all variations on a theme of yellow Tennessee limestone dubbed "TU stone." The Lorton Performance Center is TU's showcase facility for the performance arts. The Helmerich Center for American Research houses the Gilcrease Library and Archive, which features among its 100,000 holdings the Bob Dylan Archive.

In 2019, TU launched an ambitious five-year effort to rethink the role of the liberal arts in professional education. After some apparent initial false starts involving controversial cuts to liberal arts offerings, the trustees voted in January 2020 to encourage students to "earn a combined major and minor in the liberal arts and professional studies." The goal is to "enable a combined liberal arts/ professional studies degree to be a norm for students and a differentiator for TU." Tulsa has also continued to close or consolidate "a number of academic programs that had low enrollment or outcomes that did not meet student expectations," including theater, music, philosophy, and religion.

"I have had a high-paying internship ever since my freshman year."

In addition to its well-established and internationally recognized petroleum engineering and geosciences programs, TU offers solid majors in computer science, nursing, biochemistry, psychology, and accounting. Tulsa is one of 77 schools in the nation that trains America's Cyber Corps, the first line of defense against computer hackers and terrorists, and in 2021 the university added a B.S. degree in cybersecurity. The English department has some impressive resources at its disposal in McFarlin Library's special collections, which boast letters, manuscripts, and other materials by 19th- and 20th-century authors; notable items include a stained necktie that once belonged to James Joyce and more than 50,000 items representing the late Nobel laureate V. S. Naipaul's life and work. Students in the international engineering/science and language program earn both a B.S. in engineering or science and a B.A. in a foreign language in five years. Mechanical engineering, finance, computer science, and management are the most popular majors.

Courses are rigorous, and students say the workload can be heavy, but classmates are always willing to help one another out. Sixty-one percent of classes enroll fewer than 20 students, and professors are praised for being approachable and accommodating of student needs. "One time I was struggling with a lab, so I went to talk to

Website: www.utulsa.edu
Location: City Outskirts
Private
Total Enrollment: 3,382
Undergraduates: 2,598
Male/Female: 51/49
Financial Aid: 98%
Pell Grant: 28%
Expense: Pr $
Student Loans: 38%
Average Debt: $ $ $
Applicants: 5,958
Accepted: 75%
Enrolled: 13%
Grad in 6 Years: 73%
Returning Freshmen: 82%
Academics: ✍ ✍ ✍
Social: ☎ ☎ ☎
Q of L: ★ ★
Admissions: (918) 631-2307
Email Address: admission@ utulsa.edu

Strong Programs:
Petroleum Engineering
Geosciences
Computer Science
Nursing
Biochemistry
Psychology
Accounting
Mechanical Engineering

my professor," recounts a sophomore. "He ended up clearing all of his meetings for the afternoon so he could redo the entire lab with me step by step. These types of things are not uncommon at TU." Students also give high ratings to the university's academic support resources, including workshops, subsidized tutoring sessions, and grad students who serve as academic counselors, helping with goal setting, study tips, and time-management skills. The CaneCareers Job Placement Guarantee promises that if students who complete an online professional development program are not subsequently employed or enrolled in graduate school within six months of graduation, the university will cover the cost of tuition for one semester in one of TU's master's degree programs.

The Gilcrease Library and Archive features among its 100,000 holdings the Bob Dylan Archive.

Honors students take exclusive seminars, complete a thesis or advanced project, develop portfolios, and can live together in an honors house. The Tulsa Undergraduate Research Challenge offers outstanding opportunities to conduct cutting-edge research with faculty mentors and has produced dozens of national scholarship winners. "There is a wide variety of research here in all academic departments, so there is something for everyone," cheers a chemistry major. Twelve percent of students study abroad for a semester, short term, or summer; short-term programs include a nursing and technology course in Scotland, an athletic training course in Ireland, and a tropical biology course in Costa Rica. "Tulsa puts high emphasis on the vital role summer internships can play in one's academic career," says an enthusiastic senior. "I have had a high-paying internship ever since my freshman year."

"TU is a very academic school that recruits students who care about their grades."

"TU is a very academic school that recruits students who care about their grades," comments a freshman. Fifty-three percent of Tulsa's students are from Oklahoma; most others are from the Midwest and Southwest, with many hailing from Texas and Missouri. Seven percent are international. The student body is 8 percent Black, 10 percent Hispanic/Latino, 7 percent Asian American, 3 percent American Indian, and 10 percent multiracial. Students describe the campus as "moderately liberal," and a junior says TU is "not a hotbed for political activism." A bevy of merit and athletic scholarships are available for qualified students.

TU offers well-established and internationally recognized petroleum engineering and geosciences programs.

Sixty-eight percent of students reside in campus housing; most freshmen and sophomores are required to do so, and while some upperclassmen move off campus, many choose to stay because of the school's six luxury apartment villages. A marketing major says, "Our worst dorms are nicer than the newest dorms on many state school campuses." The Student Union food court was recently renovated, and students can also choose from cafeteria and bar-and-grill options, but many students describe the cafeteria food as, simply, "bad." Students give administrators credit for adopting a more transparent approach to the issue of sexual assault. "We are always informed when an assault is reported," notes a media studies major.

The social life at TU is surprisingly robust, if not raucous, thanks to hundreds of student organizations and a healthy Greek life. The university sponsors regular social events, and students enjoy simply hanging with friends at small gatherings too. The Greek organizations claim 22 percent of TU men and 23 percent of the women, and the frats host registered parties that are limited to a preauthorized guest list. Student-initiated policies govern drinking on campus and are well enforced. Campus traditions include the ringing of the college's cupola bell by each senior after his or her last final exam. Other big events include the homecoming bonfire and football game and the Springfest concert.

"Tulsa is such a vibrant city and is booming every day."

Nearby parks, lakes, and a huge recreational water park please outdoor enthusiasts. Downtown Tulsa offers symphony, ballet, opera, museums, and an annual St. Patrick's Day celebration. "Tulsa is such a vibrant city and is booming every day," says a senior, who recommends the Brookside and Cherry Street districts and concerts at Cain's Ballroom. Sixty-two percent of students take active part in community service opportunities coordinated through the True Blue Neighbors program, volunteering time with groups like Habitat for Humanity, Reading Partners, and the Community Food Bank of Eastern Oklahoma. The Bricktown section of Oklahoma City and nearby casinos, along with more distant Dallas, St. Louis, and Kansas City, are popular road trips.

In Oklahoma, sports are important, to say the least. The Division I Golden Hurricanes compete in the American Athletic Conference in 17 intercollegiate sports. Students get riled up when the football team is pitted against rivals Oklahoma and Oklahoma State, and when the basketball team suits up against Memphis and SMU. Men's and women's tennis, track and field, and cross-country are also competitive, as is the softball team. Many students take advantage of TU's club sports and intramural offerings; the most popular by far is flag football.

Even as it strives to rethink its academic philosophy and programs, TU continues to emphasize hands-on learning experiences and professional preparation. How well the university's new "combined liberal arts/professional studies" approach will work out remains to be seen. Students can be forgiven if they are not sure exactly what sort of education they are signing up for.

If You Apply To ›

Tulsa: Early action, rolling admissions. Accepts the Common Application with supplement. Please consult Tulsa's website for the most up-to-date information regarding standardized test requirements.

Union College

807 Union Street, Schenectady, NY 12308

Union is split down the middle between liberal arts and engineering. That means its center of gravity is more toward the technical side than places like Lafayette, Trinity, and Tufts, but less so than Clarkson and Rensselaer. Big commitment to undergraduate research. Schenectady is less than exciting, but there are outdoor getaways in all directions. Relatively anonymous because it does not fit into conventional categories.

Founded in 1795, Union College is one of the oldest nondenominational liberal arts colleges in the country. Its name reflects the founders' desire to create a welcoming, unifying academic community open to the region's diverse religious and national groups. More than 225 years later, Union is known for its interdisciplinary studies and its study abroad programs. Engineering and the liberal arts go hand-in-hand here. Undergraduate research has deep roots at Union, starting in the mid-20th century when a chemistry professor began involving students in his colloid chemistry investigations. Today, "Union is constantly thinking of ways to better the students' experience," says one satisfied student.

Union's 100-acre campus sits on a hill overlooking Schenectady, which played a pivotal role in the Industrial Revolution as a transportation and manufacturing center. The campus was designed in 1813 by French architect and landscaper Joseph Jacques Ramée, whose vision took shape in brownstone and red brick, with plenty of white arches, pilasters, and lacy green trees. The campus plan also includes eight acres of formal gardens and woodlands. The eye-catching, 16-sided Nott Memorial, a National Historic Landmark described as "a feat of high Victorian Gothic," is a

Website: www.union.edu
Location: Small City
Private
Total Enrollment: 2,065
Undergraduates: 2,065
Male/Female: 55/45
Financial Aid: 77%
Pell Grant: 14%
Expense: Pr $ $ $ $
Student Loans: 53%
Average Debt: $ $ $ $
Applicants: 7,470
Accepted: 47%
Enrolled: 16%
Grad in 6 Years: 85%

(continued)

Returning Freshmen: 91%
Academics: ✍ ✍ ✍ ✍
Social: ☎ ☎ ☎
Q of L: ★ ★ ★
Admissions: (518) 388-6112
Email Address: admissions@
union.edu

Strong Programs:
Geology
Computer Science
English
History
Economics
Mechanical Engineering
Biology
Neuroscience

*Eighty percent
of all Union
students conduct
undergraduate
research en route
to their degrees.*

meeting, study, and exhibition center. After a two-year expansion and renovation, the interdisciplinary Science and Engineering Center has been transformed into a state-of-the-art, fully integrated complex; the $100 million project was the largest in the school's history.

To fulfill Union's general education requirements, students take core courses in their first and second years that promote reading, writing, and analytical skills, including a required interdisciplinary First-Year Preceptorial. They also take courses spread among social science, humanities, linguistic and cultural competency, quantitative and mathematical reasoning, and natural and applied science or engineering. All students must complete a senior thesis or senior seminar paper in order to graduate.

Among Union's most popular majors are economics, mechanical engineering, biology, and neuroscience. Students also flock to strong programs in geology, computer science, English, and history; the latter department is home to Union's most esteemed lecturer, Stephen Berk, whose course on the Holocaust and Twentieth-Century Europe is a hot ticket. Each year, about 50 incoming freshmen are named Union Scholars. The designation extends the First-Year Preceptorial to two terms and gives students access to independent study projects, departmental honors programs, and expanded study abroad options. Eighty percent of all Union students conduct undergraduate research en route to their degrees, and each spring Union cancels classes one afternoon for the Steinmetz Symposium, so that students can present scholarly projects to their peers and professors in a professional conference atmosphere.

> "Union is constantly thinking of ways to better the students' experience."

Interdisciplinary study is the norm at Union, with established programs in bioengineering, Latin American and Caribbean studies, law and public policy, and Russian and Eastern European studies, to name a few. The college's Kelly Adirondack Center, 10 minutes from campus, features the 15,000-item Adirondack Research Library and is a boon to students interested in environmental research and stewardship. The educational studies program allows aspiring teachers to complete courses and fieldwork required for secondary school certification in a variety of subjects, along with a strong liberal arts grounding. The Leadership in Medicine program, a joint program with Clarkson University's Union Graduate College and Albany Medical College, gives students the opportunity to earn a bachelor's degree, an M.S. in health management or an M.B.A. in health systems administration, and a medical degree in eight years.

"Union's culture is built around the relationships between students and faculty," says a sophomore. "We are very lucky to have stellar professors who are always looking to be active in the lives of their pupils." Sixty-nine percent of classes have fewer than 20 students, and students can expect to see full professors at the lecterns rather than teaching assistants. Union operates on a trimester system, which means thrice-a-year exams and a late start to summer jobs—but also the opportunity to concentrate on just three courses a term. More terms also means more opportunities for independent study and internships, either in the state capital of Albany, 20 minutes away, or in Washington, D.C. By the time graduation rolls around, nearly 60 percent of students have studied abroad, many of them in faculty-led, three-week "mini terms" during winter or summer break.

> "[We] have stellar professors who are always looking to be active in the lives of their pupils."

Thirty percent of Union students are New Yorkers and 10 percent are international. Four percent of students are Black, 9 percent are Hispanic/Latino, 6 percent are Asian American, and 3 percent are multiracial, but the school has been working to boost these numbers. A senior describes the political climate as "rather balanced," and a sophomore says, "I find that there is a great amount of privilege at our school." Union awards hundreds of merit scholarships averaging $16,700, and it meets the full demonstrated financial need of admitted students, but it does not offer athletic scholarships.

Ninety-two percent of Union students live on campus. The Minerva house system (named after the Roman goddess of wisdom) is aimed at getting students and faculty members to contribute to Union's social, residential, and intellectual life—and, students say, at decreasing the influence of the Greek system, which draws 24 percent of the men and 33 percent of the women. "The dorms are fine, pretty typical, but the apartments for seniors and all the theme houses are very nice," reports a student. Students recommend West, which is co-ed by room and thus very social, as well as Fox and Davidson, where freshmen and sophomores live in suites. Dining options consist of four main eating areas, and the quality of meals "really depends on the day," says a freshman. "Campus police watch out very closely for the safety of students," says a sociology major.

"The majority of social life is on campus," says a student. "There are Minerva events and on-campus movies as well as typical fraternity parties." Campus events also include comedians, concerts, and speakers. Despite these alternatives and strictly enforced alcohol policies, most students agree that "Greek life dominates," as one student asserts. Favorite annual traditions include the lobster bake (each student gets their own crustacean) and Springfest, an outdoor concert. An unofficial student tradition is to do a lap around the Nott Memorial—sans clothing.

"The apartments for seniors and all the theme houses are very nice."

Off campus, Schenectady, whose name derives from the Mohawk word for "the place beyond the pines," is an old-line industrial city that a freshman says is a decent—if not great—college town. A sophomore adds, "There are essentially no college-town amenities—like bookstores—in walking distance. You need a car." What Schenectady lacks can be found in Saratoga Springs, which boasts restaurants, jazz clubs, horse racing, and Skidmore College, or in the nearby Adirondacks and Catskills. Popular road trips include Boston, Montreal, New York, and the ski slopes of nearby Vermont. Students are trying to help Schenectady rebound, through on-campus tutoring programs for local schoolchildren and work with groups like the YMCA and the Boys & Girls Clubs. There's also a service project during freshman orientation.

Union's athletic teams (the Dutchmen) compete in Division III, aside from men's and women's ice hockey, both of which are Division I. Baseball and men's basketball are recent Liberty League conference champions, and women's basketball, lacrosse, and soccer are also solid. Intramural and club sports include teams in everything from volleyball and broomball to ultimate Frisbee and fly-fishing.

Union's mission has been constantly evolving for more than two centuries, and it continues to adapt to meet the needs and interests of students and faculty. It retains its commitment to a strong core liberal arts curriculum while acknowledging the increasing effects of globalization and technology. Union College has plenty to offer—a small, friendly place full of eager intellectual exchange.

Overlaps

Bates, Lafayette, Hamilton, Skidmore, Trinity College (CT), Colgate, University of Vermont, Rensselaer

If You Apply To ›

Union: Early decision I and II, early action, regular decision. SATs or ACTs: optional. Accepts the Common Application.

Ursinus College

Box 1000, Collegeville, PA 19426

Ursinus is the smallest of the cohort of eastern Pennsylvania liberal arts colleges that includes Franklin & Marshall, Lafayette, and Muhlenberg. The plus side is more attention from faculty and more emphasis on independent and outside-the-box learning. The setting is small town, but Philly is within arm's reach.

Website: www.ursinus.edu
Location: Suburban
Private
Total Enrollment: 1,530
Undergraduates: 1,530
Male/Female: 52/48
Financial Aid: 98%
Pell Grant: 19%
Expense: Pr $ $ $
Student Loans: 78%
Average Debt: $ $ $ $
Applicants: 3,818
Accepted: 83%
Enrolled: 14%
Grad in 6 Years: 72%
Returning Freshmen: 85%
Academics: ✍ ✍ ✍
Social: ☎ ☎ ☎
Q of L: ★ ★ ★
Admissions: (610) 409-3200
Email Address: admission@ursinus.edu

Strong Programs:
Environmental Studies
English
Politics
International Relations
Biology
Applied Economics
Health and Exercise Physiology
Psychology

Although it is a secular institution, Ursinus College, founded in 1869, takes its name from a 16th-century German Calvinist, Zacharias Ursinus, who directed that students should "examine all things and keep what is good." In recent years, Ursinus has reinvigorated its liberal arts roots—expanding its offerings and restructuring its core curriculum to emphasize questions of human existence and to prepare students "not simply to make a living, but to make a life of purpose." What hasn't changed is the close-knit feel of the school. "Ursinus's culture is one of inquisitive learning through experimentation and discussion with peers that brings students together in a small campus atmosphere," muses a senior.

Ursinus is located in Collegeville, about 25 miles west of Philadelphia and 10 miles from the green, rolling hills of Valley Forge National Park. Buildings on the 170-acre campus are mostly constructed of Pennsylvania fieldstone; many have had their interiors upgraded and their exteriors preserved and restored. Actors and dancers benefit from rehearsal and exhibition space in the Kaleidoscope Performing Arts Center. Newer additions include the 42,500-square-foot Innovation and Discovery Center.

Ursinus's core curriculum, called Quest: Open Questions Open Minds, is intended to engage students in deep inquiry and reflection on four central themes: identifying personal values, living in communities, understanding the world, and making life-shaping decisions. The core begins with the Common Intellectual Experience—a two-semester course taken in the first year that explores works ranging from Plato to Hindu scripture to Ta-Nehisi Coates. Additional components include interdisciplinary coursework, an experiential learning project (an independent research or creative project, an internship, study abroad, student teaching, or civic engagement), and a Core Capstone course in the senior year.

"Many Summer Fellows end up extending their research into honors research senior year."

Students choose among more than 30 majors, with the most popular being biology, applied economics, health and exercise physiology, psychology, and neuroscience. Environmental studies is strong, providing students access to the college's organic farm and the Whittaker Environmental Research Station. Ursinus also offers solid programs in English, politics, and international relations. Classes are small—64 percent have fewer than 20 students—and students are mostly pleased with the quality of teaching, especially since there are no teaching assistants. According to a psychology and international relations double major, the academic climate is "rigorous in some disciplines and very laid-back in others, but mostly the professors expect a high level of work and motivation from the students."

Each year, 70 to 80 rising juniors and seniors get fellowships from the school to fund full-time summer research projects with a faculty member. "Many Summer Fellows end up extending their research into honors research senior year," explains a senior. The Parlee Center for Science and the Common Good aims to help students understand and explain the ethical, political, and cultural impacts of their scientific work, offering a speaker series, a student fellows program, internships, and summer research opportunities. The U-Imagine Center for Integrative and Entrepreneurial Studies and the Melrose Center for Global Civic Engagement offer similar programming. Eighteen percent of Ursinus students study abroad, both in programs designed and run by the college and in affiliate programs. The Philadelphia Experience places selected students in a residence hall in Philadelphia for a semester to take courses with Ursinus faculty, along with their choice of an internship or independent research project.

"Our students have many different interests," says an applied economics major. "A football player may also be in the men's a cappella group. A theater star may also do honors biology research." Fifty-eight percent of students are from Pennsylvania and less than 1 percent are from foreign countries, with most others hailing from New York, New Jersey, and other Mid-Atlantic and New England states. Black students make up 8 percent of the student body, Asian Americans 4 percent, Hispanics/Latinos 8 percent, and multiracial students 4 percent. Both sides of the political aisle are represented on campus, and a freshman describes the atmosphere as "calm," with students "discussing their opinions together." Non-need-based scholarships and grants averaging $31,800 are available each year, but no athletic scholarships are offered.

> *The Philadelphia Experience places selected students in Philadelphia for a semester to take courses and do an internship or research project.*

Ninety-one percent of students at Ursinus live in college housing, which adds to the feeling of community. Upperclassmen quickly grab the Main Street houses, a string of Victorian-era homes comprising the Residential Village across the street from campus, while freshmen are clustered in BPS and BWC (short for Beardwood-Paisley-Stauffer and Brodbeck-Wilkinson-Curtis, respectively), which have generously sized rooms. Reimert Hall is the party dorm. Student-run special interest housing is available, too, for those who

"Everyone—the students, professors, and staff— is so friendly and open."

share social or academic interests. At the main dining hall, Wismer, "the meals are actually good ninety-nine percent of the time," says a freshman, and "they have options that are vegan and vegetarian and food that is free of seven main allergens as well." A junior reports, "Campus Safety is always seen around campus mingling with students and gaining their respect and trust."

Much of the social life occurs on campus, including performances, themed cuisine nights, and craft nights organized by the student activities board. Greek life draws 4 percent of the men and 8 percent of the women, and parties hosted by fraternities and sports teams are a popular weekend diversion. Registered on-campus parties are monitored by student "social hosts" who check IDs and make sure things don't get out of hand. "A lot of drinking goes on," reports a junior. Homecoming is a favorite tradition in the fall, and in the spring, students look forward to the annual Bear Bash concert and Airband, "a big charity lip-synching and performing event," says an English major. Sixty-five percent of students perform regular volunteer work.

> *The annual women's Prom Dress Rugby encounter with Swarthmore is always a big hit.*

The town of Collegeville is just 10 blocks long—and Ursinus takes up five of those—but a politics major says it offers "a few good bars and restaurants to entertain students." Frequent school-sponsored shuttles take students to the shops, restaurants, sporting events, and festivals of Philadelphia, less than an hour away. Many students with cars escape to the Jersey Shore during warmer months.

Ursinus students love their Division III sports. For those seeking post-collegiate careers in coaching, Ursinus is a well-known stepping stone to those positions, thanks in part to a tight network of loyal alumni who tap each other for opportunities. The Bears field strong teams in men's and women's basketball, men's lacrosse, women's swimming, and field hockey. Intramural and club sports draw 40 percent of students, and the annual women's Prom Dress Rugby encounter with Swarthmore is always a big hit.

Ursinus may not be in the center of a big metropolitan area, and it doesn't offer big-time sports, but the college compensates for its lack of size with the feeling that students, faculty, and staff are one big family. "The special thing about Ursinus is the people," says a biology major. "Everyone—the students, professors, and staff—is so friendly and open and just wants you to succeed."

Overlaps

Muhlenberg, Washington College, Allegheny, Washington and Jefferson, Wheaton (MA), Gettysburg, Temple, Drexel

University of Utah

Salt Lake City, UT 84112

One of the oldest universities west of the Mississippi, the University of Utah sits in the region's only major city. Science and professional programs such as business and engineering are traditional strengths. Has positioned itself as a more accessible alternative to California's public higher education system—with plenty of academic opportunities and school spirit to go around. Applications have doubled in the last decade, and out-of-state enrollment is on the rise.

Website: www.utah.edu
Location: Small City
Public
Total Enrollment: 27,167
Undergraduates: 20,294
Male/Female: 52/48
Financial Aid: 71%
Pell Grant: 19%
Expense: Pub $
Student Loans: 38%
Average Debt: $
Applicants: 18,302
Accepted: 95%
Enrolled: 29%
Grad in 6 Years: 67%
Returning Freshmen: 87%
Academics: ✍ ✍ ✍
Social: ☎ ☎ ☎
Q of L: ★ ★ ★
Admissions: (801) 581-8761
Email Address: admissions@utah.edu

Strong Programs:
Engineering
Business
Entrepreneurship
International Studies
Social Work
Dance
Computer Science
Psychology

In addition to being the flagship institution of the state's higher education system, the University of Utah is a major national scientific research center. Founded in 1850, the university is unusual in its ability to offer students the advantages of living in a city while at the same time maintaining a connection with nature. Utah has increased its focus in recent years on the undergraduate experience, beefing up academic programs and building new residential facilities, including a $51 million student life center. Applications have surged as a result, and students say enthusiasm for their school is higher than ever. "We have the school spirit, the drive to transform the world, and the resources and connections needed for students to succeed," cheers one senior.

Set in the foothills of the Wasatch Mountains near the shores of the Great Salt Lake, the university enjoys a picturesque location a half-hour drive from "the greatest snow on earth." Occupying 1,500 well-landscaped acres with nearly as many different kinds of trees as undergraduates, the campus doubles as the state's arboretum. The university's structures range from historic 19th-century buildings to state-of-the-art modern facilities. A spate of new construction continues, including the recently completed Kahlert Village, a 992-bed freshman residential complex.

Utah students choose from a comprehensive academic menu, including more than 100 undergraduate majors, and the U does not skimp on general education requirements. Students must take classes in writing, American institutions, math, statistics, and intellectual explorations, which include two courses in the humanities, sciences, social sciences, or fine arts, as well as fulfill international and diversity course requirements. Utah is renowned for its research in biomedical engineering, and majors in business administration, entrepreneurship, international studies, and social work are strong. The Lassonde Entrepreneur Institute offers training to budding entrepreneurs, 400 of whom get to reside in the $45 million Lassonde Studios, featuring the sort of pods and shared spaces characteristic of high-tech workplaces. An unusual major in quantitative analysis of markets and organizations was developed jointly by the business school and the department of economics. Programs in ballet and modern dance are also well regarded. Students interested in video game development or digital animation may pursue a major in computer science with an entertainment arts and engineering emphasis or a major in games. The most popular majors include psychology, communication, kinesiology, and nursing.

> "Much of the social life is recreational."

The academic climate can be challenging, but in general "the workload is fairly manageable," according to one sophomore. Introductory courses often enroll hundreds of students, with smaller discussion sections led by graduate student teaching assistants. Overall, 41 percent of classes have fewer than 20 students. Students report that the quality of teaching varies by department, but for the most part, says a business major, "professors care about what they teach their students and want them to learn." The LEAP (Learning Engagement Achievement Progress) learning community involves a two-semester sequence of courses led by faculty and peer advisors; 10 percent of freshmen participate. Those seeking a more challenging curriculum and the chance to write a thesis may apply to the Honors College.

The MUSE (My Utah Signature Experience) Project is an advising program that helps coordinate unique learning experiences that range from lunchtime lectures with distinguished professors to internships and service projects for any interested undergraduate. The state government–backed USTAR (Utah Science Technology and Research) initiative has enhanced opportunities for collaborative student/faculty research, in which 32 percent of undergraduates get involved, often with the support of research grants. Eleven percent of students study abroad via some 500 programs offered in more than 50 countries around the globe.

The state government–backed USTAR initiative facilitates collaborative student/faculty research, in which 32 percent of undergrads get involved.

Utah's students are a mostly middle-class, fairly homogeneous lot; 65 percent of undergraduates are from Utah, and nearly all attended public schools. A growing number of students are arriving from out of state, especially Californians who feel shut out by the higher education system in their home state; 6 percent come from abroad. Black students make up just 1 percent of the student population, Asian Americans 6 percent, Hispanics/Latinos 14 percent, and multiracial students 6 percent. Students describe their fellow Utes as "friendly" and "supportive" and say the political climate is diverse and sometimes polarized. A substantial percentage of Utah students

"People are here to learn, and there is a strong focus on research and advancement."

are Mormon, and according to a junior, "the influence of the Church of Jesus Christ of Latter-day Saints in Utah" is a hot-button issue on campus. Utah offers merit scholarships averaging $8,400 and more than 400 athletic scholarships in 18 sports.

Only 15 percent of students live on campus, but those who do seem to be pleased with the housing facilities, many of which were built to accommodate visitors during the 2002 Olympics. Off-campus apartments within walking distance of the campus are plentiful. Students are also generally satisfied with the food, though edibility varies based on which campus eatery you choose. At lunchtime, local food trucks usually line up around the Marriott Library plaza, a popular gathering place. Students report feeling safe on campus, and the university has increased the number of staff dedicated to Title IX issues.

Utah has had a reputation as a commuter school, but students say that is changing, and the on-campus social scene is becoming livelier with the influx of out-of-state students. Participation in Greek life is an increasingly popular option; currently, 7 percent of the men and 9 percent of the women join fraternities and sororities. "From lectures, concerts, dance performances, and late-night Crimson Nights parties, there is something for everyone," a student says. Students also look forward to Redfest, which brings major musical acts to campus every spring.

The co-ed skiing team has won the national championship four times since 2017.

Utah's proximity to the mountains means that "much of the social life is recreational," according to one junior. Favorite road trips take students to Las Vegas, Lake Powell, and nearby ski resorts (with slopeside bus service available from the school). Salt Lake City isn't exactly a college town, but a junior says, "The nightlife in SLC downtown is great if you are over 21." Adjacent to campus, the Latter-day Saints Institute of Religion sponsors dances and other social activities with a decidedly conservative bent. There are also centers for other faiths, notably Jewish and Roman

Catholic. Cultural activities include the respected Utah Symphony, several dance companies, opera, and, of course, the Mormon Tabernacle Choir.

Utes teams compete in the Division I Pac-12 Conference, and football and basketball bring students together in the MUSS—Mighty Utah Student Section—where cheers are loudest during the "Holy War" rivalry football game against Brigham Young. The co-ed skiing team has won the national championship four times since 2017. Men's basketball and women's gymnastics, softball, and volleyball also make regular NCAA Tournament appearances. In addition to the university's dozens of club sports and intramurals (canoe battleship, anyone?), the Outdoor Adventure Program offers backpacking, river running, mountain biking, and skiing trips.

Students say that academic quality, diversity, and the residential experience are all on the rise at Utah. "People are here to learn, and there is a strong focus on research and advancement," says a family, community, and human development major. It's also one of the few places where you can find nationally recognized professional programs within easy reach of nationally recognized skiing.

If You Apply To ›

University of Utah: Early action, rolling admissions. Accepts the Common Application with supplement. Application includes optional fields for gender identity and sexual orientation. Please consult Utah's website for the most up-to-date information regarding standardized test requirements.

Vanderbilt University

2305 West End Avenue, Nashville, TN 37240

Strongest and most selective of schools that still find a way to blend Southern hospitality with modern, cutting-edge academics in an urban setting. Vandy has become more diverse in recent years, geographically and otherwise. More selective than Emory and now comparable to Duke and Rice among leading schools south of the Mason–Dixon line. One of the few major universities where both academics and athletics are top-notch.

Once a quiet, conservative school in the heart of the South known as a preferred choice for Atlanta and Birmingham elites, Vanderbilt University has diversified its student body and brought a more cosmopolitan atmosphere to campus. Coats, ties, and pearls may be giving way to Commodore fan gear at football games these days, but the university continues to succeed in marrying Old South gentility with modern attitudes. The result is a relaxed, friendly culture that makes the rigorous academic environment easier to handle. "Students looking for a balance between great academics and a solid social life need to look at Vandy," counsels a history major.

Established in 1873 by railroad and shipping magnate Cornelius Vanderbilt, the university's 340-acre tract in Nashville is an arboretum and includes Peabody College, the central section of which is listed on the National Register of Historic Places. On the main campus, art and sculptures dot the landscape, and architectural styles range from Gothic to modern glass and brick. The Sarratt Student Center serves as a social hub, with a movie theater, Rand Dining Hall, a pub, and offices for student organizations. Two new residential colleges have opened in the last two years and a third is slated for completion in 2023.

Undergraduates choose one of four schools—College of Arts and Science, School of Engineering, Blair School of Music, or Peabody College of Education and Human Development—but everyone takes their core liberal arts courses in the College of Arts and Science, where the writing program is a standout. Immersion Vanderbilt, a graduation requirement, calls for every undergraduate to undertake an immersive learning experience (such as internships, fieldwork, or performances) culminating in a final project. Optional first-year Commons Seminars allow students to explore various topics in small groups with close faculty interaction; recent offerings have included everything from Alzheimer's Disease for the Next Generation to Adaptive Fashion Design and Production.

Engineering, education, and music are particular strengths at Vandy. Popular majors include economics; medicine, health, and society; human and organizational development; computer science; engineering (especially mechanical); and biological sciences. Education majors who enroll at Peabody College are required to double major, usually in a liberal arts field. Many students interested in financial careers declare an economics major and pursue a business minor. The university recently launched a new interdisciplinary major in climate studies.

"The academic climate of Vanderbilt is absolutely collaborative."

"The academic climate of Vanderbilt is absolutely collaborative," an elementary education major says. "It provides the academic rigor I was hoping for without any of the cutthroat aspect I was afraid would accompany such an academically challenging school." Sixty percent of courses have fewer than 20 students, and in the classroom, Vanderbilt students abide by the school's honor system, which dates from 1875. The system governs all aspects of academic conduct and makes it possible for professors to give unproctored exams. Students rave about the faculty. "Many professors go out of their way to encourage students to get involved with research and internship opportunities," comments a junior.

Internship opportunities abound in Nashville, particularly in state government, health-care management, the tech sector, and, of course, the music industry. Sixty-three percent of students, from all four undergraduate schools, participate in research, and many copublish articles. The campus is home to more than 100 interdisciplinary centers and institutes. Vanderbilt's study abroad program typically attracts about 40 percent of students and offers the chance to spend a summer, a semester, or a year on one of seven continents via more than 120 programs. The optional "Maymester" allows students to spend four weeks on a single project, helpful for double majors or those who'd like to embark on a short-term internship or overseas trip.

Ten percent of undergraduates are in-state residents, and 10 percent are international, coming from more than 50 countries. Asian Americans account for 17 percent of the student body, Black students 11 percent, Hispanics/Latinos 11 percent, and multiracial students 6 percent. Students report that a diverse mix of political views are represented on campus. "I would not describe Vanderbilt as an activist campus per se, but in my two years there have been several rallies and protests," observes an English major.

"Many professors go out of their way to encourage students to get involved with research and internship[s]."

Vanderbilt employs a need-blind admissions process, meets full demonstrated need for all admitted students, and offers loan-free financial aid packages for students with demonstrated need. In addition to need-based aid, the university awards approximately 250 full-tuition merit scholarships, complete with summer stipends, to top admitted students through three signature merit scholarship programs. It also awards 245 athletic scholarships.

Seventy-nine percent of Vanderbilt undergraduates live on campus. All first-year students live together in 10 Commons houses and take part in Vanderbilt Visions,

---

(continued)

Academics: ✎ ✎ ✎ ✎
Social: ☎ ☎ ☎ ☎
Q of L: ★ ★ ★ ★
Admissions: (800) 288-0432
Email Address: admissions@vanderbilt.edu

Strong Programs:
Engineering
Education
Music
Economics
Medicine, Health, and Society
Human and Organizational Development
Computer Science
Biological Sciences

Every undergraduate undertakes an immersive learning experience (such as internships, fieldwork, or performances) culminating in a final project.

a living/learning initiative designed to foster a sense of community among new students. Each first-year is assigned to a Visions group, which has about 18 students, a faculty advisor, and an upper-class peer mentor. In addition to meeting with their group once a week during the fall semester, students have opportunities to get to know the faculty who live in the various Commons houses. Students also compete in the Commons Cup. A junior explains, "You and your house compete in intramurals, sustainability, community service, and academics over the course of the whole year." Six residential colleges for upper-class students are available as well. Other options for older students include 10-person townhouses, six-room suites, theme dorms, and school-owned apartments.

Vanderbilt has more than 20 dining facilities that "always provide a delicious array of options," according to a junior, and all campus residents are required to buy a meal plan. The Taste of Nashville program allows students to use their meal money at two dozen local restaurants. Students report feeling safe on campus, thanks to an active security department that "watches out for Vanderbilt students and keeps us safe." As for sexual assault awareness and prevention, one student says Vanderbilt "is facing this issue head-on," especially through the efforts of the Project Safe Center.

Thirty-three percent of the women and 27 percent of the men join the Greek system; while many Greek parties are open to the entire campus, the effort to encourage mixing between the groups is not always successful. "Fraternities and sororities start the social scene," a senior says, "but certainly don't encompass all aspects of Vanderbilt's social life." The first-year Commons campus is dry, but of-age students are allowed to have alcohol elsewhere on campus, although open containers are banned in public and kegs are also taboo. As at many colleges, one student says, "underage students can find loopholes." Students get involved in more than 475 student organizations. Favorite Vanderbilt traditions are the Commodore Quake and Rites of Spring music festivals, as well as Founders Walk at the end of move-in weekend, where new incoming students walk through campus while upperclassmen welcome them with cheers.

Vanderbilt's proximity to Music City USA provides plenty of diversions. "Nashville is so much fun," cheers one senior. "The list of excellent restaurants, bars, shopping, and live music venues is endless." Country music fans won't want to miss the Hall of Fame. Beyond Nashville's borders are the Great Smoky Mountains and state parks with picnic facilities, beautiful lakes, and skiing in the winter. The best road trips are to Memphis (home of Elvis), New Orleans (for Mardi Gras), and Louisville (for the Kentucky Derby). Students also engage in the local community through a variety of service-oriented programs. Alternative Spring Break, which takes students to more than 30 service sites across the country for volunteer work during spring break, is Vandy's largest student-run organization.

Vanderbilt may be the smallest—and the only private—institution in the competitive and football-crazy Division I Southeastern Conference, but there is no shortage of enthusiasm among Commodore fans. Vandy reconfigured its athletic program some years ago in an effort to cut costs. Instead of losing ground (as many feared), the programs have thrived. The baseball team is a perennial contender for the national title, while the men's golf and women's soccer teams are recent conference champs. The Vanderbilt Aerospace Club has won NASA's annual Student Launch Challenge, an eight-month-long rocketry competition, several times in recent years. There are 30-plus club sports for weekend jocks, as well as more than 40 intramural sports leagues.

Vanderbilt sits squarely among the top universities in the nation and has capitalized on its unique blend of Southern charm and scholarly achievement to

The university recently launched a new interdisciplinary major in climate studies.

"Nashville is so much fun."

During Founders Walk, new incoming students walk through campus while upperclassmen welcome them with cheers.

Overlaps

Duke, Northwestern, Rice, University of Pennsylvania, Yale, Harvard, Emory, WashU in St. Louis

attract students from around the country and beyond. Four years here do carry a steep before-financial-aid sticker price; witness a tongue-in-cheek campus slogan, "Vanderbilt: It Even Sounds Expensive." But for many, investing in a Vanderbilt education is money well spent.

If You Apply To ›

Vanderbilt: Early decision I and II, regular decision. Accepts the Common Application with supplement. Apply to particular school or program. Audition required for music applicants. Please consult Vanderbilt's website for the most up-to-date information regarding standardized test requirements.

Vassar College

Poughkeepsie, NY 12604

It is hard to imagine that Vassar once considered picking up and moving to Yale in the 1960s rather than become a co-ed institution. Half a century after admitting men, still on its ancient and picturesque campus, Vassar is a thriving, highly selective, avant-garde institution where traditional strengths in the fine arts and humanities are matched by robust offerings in the natural and social sciences. At the forefront of national efforts to promote socioeconomic diversity in elite schools.

Are you a scientist who composes music in your spare time? Or perhaps an actor who enjoys dissecting Plato and Aristotle? If so, you may feel at home at Vassar, a distinguished liberal arts college just 70 miles north of New York City. Once known as the most liberal of the Seven Sisters, and still a bastion of the left, Vassar prides itself on curricular flexibility, tolerance, and diversity. "Vassar could be categorized as a liberal and artsy school," says a junior. "Students here are smart but not necessarily rule-abiding."

Founded in 1861 by a brewer named Matthew Vassar, the college sits just outside Poughkeepsie, New York. Its 1,000-acre campus includes two lakes and plenty of trees. Daffodils bloom in the spring, and foliage is omnipresent in the fall. Encircled by a fieldstone wall, the campus also boasts an astronomical observatory with one of the largest telescopes in the Northeast,

> "Students here are smart but not necessarily rule-abiding."

a state-of-the-art physics building, a farm with an ecological field station, and an art center with 21,000 works, from Ancient Egyptian to modern times. The architecture is predominantly neo-Gothic, with buildings also designed by notables such as Marcel Breuer, Eero Saarinen, and James Renwick.

Vassar has no core curriculum and no distribution requirements. Indeed, academic flexibility is paramount. That said, all students must choose one first-year writing seminar from nearly 50 courses taught across the curriculum, as well as one course that requires significant quantitative analysis. Students must also demonstrate intermediate-level proficiency in a foreign language and can opt to study one of the 20 languages taught at Vassar.

The most popular majors include political science, psychology, economics, and biology. The biology building houses two electron microscopes, while music students are spoiled by a grand collection of Steinway pianos sprinkled across the campus. Drama, film, art, neuroscience, English, and international studies are also traditional strengths. Regardless of their course of study, students find the academic

Website: www.vassar.edu
Location: Small City
Private
Total Enrollment: 2,491
Undergraduates: 2,491
Male/Female: 38/62
Financial Aid: 60%
Pell Grant: 20%
Expense: Pr $ $ $ $
Student Loans: 53%
Average Debt: $
Applicants: 10,884
Accepted: 20%
Enrolled: 31%
Grad in 6 Years: 93%
Returning Freshmen: 94%
Academics: ✑ ✑ ✑ ✑ ½
Social: ☎ ☎ ☎
Q of L: ★ ★ ★ ★
Admissions: (845) 437-7300
Email Address: admissions@ vassar.edu

Strong Programs:
Drama
Film
Art

climate rigorous. "Vassar students are always trying to do their personal best—they're seeking to engage more deeply with each subsequent assignment and each subsequent semester," says a senior. Small classes and tutorials are the norm, and exams are given under an honor system. Since Vassar has no graduate students or research-only faculty, all classes are taught by professors. "I'm really happy with the balance Vassar professors strike between research and teaching, because of how well they know both their fields and how to teach them," muses an environmental studies major.

Each year, 45 percent of students study abroad via 200 programs offered in more than 60 countries. Vassar allows students to use their financial aid packages to support study away from campus. Also highly regarded is the college's Undergraduate Research Summer Institute, which offers stipends for students to work one-on-one with faculty members on scientific projects, either on or off campus. The Ford Scholars program offers opportunities for student/faculty collaboration in the humanities and social sciences. Most students participate in some sort of off-campus internship or community-based fieldwork for credit during the academic year. "Vassar's Career Development Office is deft at leveraging the tremendous alumni network to find students opportunities at all grade levels," says a media studies major.

> **"I'm really happy with the balance Vassar professors strike between research and teaching."**

According to an economics major, Vassar attracts "curious, creative, and socially conscious people" who generally share progressive points of view. Vassar's LGBTQ community is visible and active, and a biology major notes, "People usually introduce themselves with their gender pronouns." Twenty-two percent of students are native New Yorkers and 8 percent are international. Asian Americans make up 13 percent of the student body, Black students 4 percent, Hispanics/Latinos 11 percent, and multiracial students 8 percent. The school's ALANA Center supports students of color and other ethnic and cultural groups. Vassar has been a leader among elite private schools in promoting socioeconomic diversity on campus; despite this, one senior comments, "The vibe can still feel pretty rich/entitled at times." Although the college does not award merit or athletic scholarships, it does offer need-blind admissions for first-year applicants who are U.S. citizens or permanent residents and guarantees to meet the full demonstrated financial need of admits; it also eliminates or reduces loans for students from low-income households.

Vassar has no core curriculum and no distribution requirements.

Housing is guaranteed for four years, and 96 percent of students live on campus, where there's an eclectic mix of nine dorms. All but one are co-ed. "Some dorms are really modern and sparkling," says a junior. "Others have a vintage college feel, with traditional wood paneling, trim, and floors." The word is that Lathrop is the best dorm for freshmen, but no halls are reserved strictly for first-year students. Seniors favor the college-owned townhouses (five-person suites) and the four-person Terrace Apartments, both with kitchens and living rooms. Campus dining has improved considerably, students say, with recent renovations, expanded options, and late-night hours. Students report that their open campus feels safe, and a psychology major says, "Conversations about consent in all realms of college life are common, and there are multiple systems in place to report sexual assault and help survivors."

> **"We are not a dry campus, as our founder did brew beer."**

Absent a Greek system, social life revolves around campus films, lectures, concerts, and small parties hosted in senior apartments or townhouses. "We are not a dry campus, as our founder did brew beer," quips a biology major; parties must be registered with campus security. Performing arts groups provide an important

Vassar allows students to use their financial aid packages to support study away from campus.

social outlet too. "Between student theater, a cappella, comedy troupes, slam poetry, dance groups, and more, students can go see high-quality performances multiple times every weekend," says an economics major. The city of Poughkeepsie has undergone a renaissance in recent years and features the world's longest elevated pedestrian bridge (212 feet tall and 1.28 miles long, in case you're wondering). Restaurants and shops are within walking distance of campus, and malls and movie theaters aren't much farther away, but a junior says, "Poughkeepsie is not explored by students as much as it should be." In warmer weather, Mohonk State Park offers hiking and other outdoor diversions. Also close by are Franklin D. Roosevelt's Hyde Park (for history) and the Culinary Institute of America (for gourmet meals prepared by students). For those feeling more adventurous, New York City is easily reached by train.

Students can still unwind after a hard day of classes with afternoon tea in the Rose Parlor of historic Main Building.

True to its heritage as one of the Seven Sisters, traditions are big at Vassar. "The year starts with Serenading—a time when the freshmen pay tribute to the seniors by singing them songs," one student explains. On Founder's Day in May, the entire community celebrates Matthew Vassar's birthday with music, carnival rides, food, and a day out on the grass. Fireworks and a movie cap off the festivities. "Founder's Day is easily the most highly anticipated day of the year," says a senior. And students can still unwind after a hard day of classes with afternoon tea in the Rose Parlor of historic Main Building.

Vassar's Division III varsity squads (the Brewers) compete in the Liberty League. Competitive teams include men's volleyball and women's basketball, field hockey, soccer, and rugby. Intramural sports are offered at two levels, competitive and recreational, and there are also club sports; 45 percent of students participate. Teams face off in everything from basketball and soccer to ultimate Frisbee, sailing, and spikeball.

While Vassar continues to offer a menu of high-quality liberal arts courses emphasizing interdisciplinary connections, the college has also embraced technology and diversity, helping to create an atmosphere where individual passions shine. Says one contented Brewer, "We take the time to enjoy college for what it is—a serious, but not too serious, time of life for learning and development."

Overlaps

Brown, Wesleyan, Pomona, Amherst, Tufts, Swarthmore, Bowdoin, Yale

If You Apply To ›

Vassar: Early decision I and II, regular decision. Accepts the Common Application with supplement. "Your Space" section of application allows candidates room to show something else about themselves. Please consult Vassar's website for the most up-to-date information regarding standardized test requirements.

University of Vermont

194 South Prospect Street, Burlington, VT 05401

For an out-of-stater sizing up public universities, there could hardly be a more appealing place than UVM. The size is manageable, Burlington is a fabulous college town, and Lake Champlain and the Green Mountains are on your doorstep. UVM feels like a private university, but, alas, it is also priced like one. Attracts a mix of party animals and serious scholars.

Website: www.uvm.edu
Location: Small City
Public
Total Enrollment: 12,468
Undergraduates: 10,779
Male/Female: 37/63
Financial Aid: 89%
Pell Grant: 15%
Expense: Pub $ $ $ $
Student Loans: 59%
Average Debt: $ $ $ $
Applicants: 25,559
Accepted: 64%
Enrolled: 18%
Grad in 6 Years: 77%
Returning Freshmen: 88%
Academics: ✍ ✍ ✍ ½
Social: ☎ ☎ ☎ ☎ ☎
Q of L: ★ ★ ★ ★ ★
Admissions: (802) 656-3370
Email Address: admissions@
  uvm.edu

Strong Programs:
Animal Science
Biology
Biomedical Engineering
Data Science
Food Systems
Business Administration
Psychology
Environmental Studies

With its beautiful setting, wide academic offerings, and abundance of clubs and cocurricular pursuits, the University of Vermont draws students from across the state and around the country. And, says a math major, they're not all granola types with a penchant for soy milk and snowboarding. While it's a public school, UVM's academics, research opportunities, and price tag are more akin to those of a private institution. Generous financial aid packages, investment in infrastructure, and a growing emphasis on hands-on learning experiences are helping to ensure that Vermont remains both affordable and relevant amid increasing competition from schools of both types.

Chartered in 1791, UVM was the fifth college to be established in New England. UVM's picturesque campus sits on the shores of Lake Champlain in Burlington, virtually a stone's throw from the Canadian border.

> **"Professors do an excellent job of combining curricula with a sense of purpose."**

Architectural styles range from colonial to high Victorian Gothic and functional modern; the oldest structures, in the center of the campus, are recognized on the National Registry of Historic Places. Recent additions to the campus include a state-of-the-art, $104 million STEM complex, a residential complex, and an integrated arts center.

UVM began as a private university but attained quasi-public status in 1862 with the passage of the Morrill Land-Grant College Act and a merger with a public agricultural college. Today, UVM's seven undergraduate colleges and schools set their own curricula grounded in the liberal arts. All students across the university must take general education courses in quantitative reasoning, sustainability, and diversity, and all first-year students must fulfill a three-credit foundational writing and information literacy requirement.

Some of the most popular majors include business administration, psychology, environmental studies, and political science. Animal science, biology, biomedical engineering, data science, and food systems are also strengths. Premed, nursing, and prevet students benefit from the research and teaching capabilities of Vermont's fine medical school in the heart of campus, as well as from a seven-year program with the vet school at Tufts. Nearly 40 accelerated master's programs allow undergrads to begin working toward advanced degrees. How tough is the academic environment? "It really depends on the course of study that you choose," says one student. Forty percent of classes enroll fewer than 20 students, and professors are said to be accessible and supportive. A junior says, "Professors do an excellent job of combining curricula with a sense of purpose. Everything we do here is worthwhile."

Special programs for first-years include four-day TREK programs, in which students, led by upper-class mentors, go hiking or biking, do community service, or take a leadership skills development course before classes start. In the College of

> **"Many UVM students like to be outdoors in all seasons."**

Arts & Sciences, students are enthusiastic about the First-Year Seminar program, which places first-years together in groups of 10 to 15 in a writing-intensive, discussion-oriented seminar taught by a professor who is also each student's advisor. Students in the Honors College write a senior thesis, and an environmental studies major notes, "There are lots of opportunities for undergraduates to get involved in professors' research because we have a relatively small population of grad students." Through the Vermont Legislative Research Service, undergraduate public policy students provide state legislators with policy briefs on current issues. Eighteen percent of all undergrads go abroad; UVM offers 500 options in nearly 70 countries.

"Many UVM students like to be outdoors in all seasons," reports a public communication major, and they tend to be highly involved in extracurriculars. Twenty-five percent of UVM undergraduates are native Vermonters and 2 percent are international. Hispanics/Latinos make up 5 percent of the student body, Asian Americans 3 percent, Black students 1 percent, and multiracial students 3 percent. The lack of racial and other diversity is a common complaint, and social justice and environmental issues also receive attention on campus. "Student activism is very frequent here, and there are constantly conversations about how we can make the university a better place," observes a community and international development major. The university offers merit scholarships averaging $15,900 and more than 250 athletic awards in 20 sports. The Catamount Commitment covers tuition and fees for qualifying in-state students from low-income families.

Sixty-seven percent of UVM undergrads live in campus housing; they are required to do so for their first two years. All students living on campus are affiliated with a residential learning community, with options ranging from Outdoor Experience to Leadership and Social Change to the popular Wellness Environment. "Living in the res hall is a ton of fun, and it's an awesome environment to meet new people," says an animal science major. Students express appreciation for the university's efforts to serve local, organic, and sustainable options at four dining halls and several retail and café locations. A political science and history major notes, "At UVM, we talk about sexual assault, and because of that, we have a high level of reporting when compared to other schools."

Through the Vermont Legislative Research Service, public policy students provide state legislators with policy briefs on current issues.

"Student activism is very frequent here."

Just 5 percent of UVM men and 6 percent of women join Greek groups, so when the weekend comes, college-sponsored movies, dances, craft nights, and coffeehouses help keep things lively. Students enjoy the Fallfest, Winterfest, and Springfest concerts every year, and the Naked Bike Ride is a notable biannual tradition, according to a senior: "On the last day of classes each semester, hundreds of people gather at midnight to run or bike naked around a campus green."

Much of the fun also happens on nearby ski slopes, mountain trails, and waterways, and in Burlington itself, especially the Church Street pedestrian mall, where the music scene draws top talent and is always bustling. "You can spend your Friday night at a gourmet restaurant, an off-Broadway theater production, or barhopping around town, and still be atop a mountain skiing the very next morning," says a junior. Indeed, the energetic downtown boasts symphonies, art galleries, chic shopping, and lively bars and restaurants, and Lake Champlain is only five minutes away. Forty-four percent of students volunteer in the local community, often through service-learning courses. As much as they love their little city, students do look forward to getting out of town. A favorite road trip is Montreal—90 minutes away—with its even bigger music scene and a drinking age of 18. The Outing Club is one of UVM's most popular student organizations, as the nearby Green Mountains, White Mountains, and Adirondacks offer prime hiking, backpacking, and rock climbing.

All students living on campus are affiliated with a residential learning community, such as the popular Wellness Environment.

UVM fields a number of highly competitive Division I Catamount ("cat of the mountains") teams. The men's ice hockey team is the school's pride and joy, having ranked as high as second nationally. Students get access to tickets before the general public, a nice perk, since games are always sold out. There is no football team, but men's and women's soccer and lacrosse and men's basketball are competitive. The ski team is a perennial powerhouse, winning 37 Eastern Intercollegiate Ski Association titles. Thirty percent of students participate in dozens of intramural and club sports, with broomball, ice hockey, and soccer proving to be popular, along with less traditional options like canoe battleship and eSports.

Students at UVM may be laid-back, but they're also curious, caring, open-minded, active, and willing to work hard. They view extracurricular involvement as critical to the undergraduate experience, and at UVM they find abundant opportunities to engage both inside and outside the classroom. Says one junior, "It's hard to describe the energy that ignites everything we do."

Overlaps

University of Colorado Boulder, UConn, UMass Amherst, University of New Hampshire, St. Lawrence, SUNY–Binghamton, Syracuse, Northeastern

Villanova University

800 Lancaster Avenue, Villanova, PA 19085

Set in an upscale suburb, Villanova is becoming increasingly popular as Philadelphia's answer to Boston College. As at BC, about 70 percent of the students are Roman Catholic (compared with about half at Georgetown). The troika of business, engineering, and nursing are popular at 'Nova. Downtown Philadelphia is a quick hop away by train.

Website: www.villanova.edu
Location: Suburban
Private
Total Enrollment: 8,192
Undergraduates: 6,812
Male/Female: 45/55
Financial Aid: 47%
Pell Grant: 12%
Expense: Pr $ $ $ $
Student Loans: 47%
Average Debt: $ $ $ $
Applicants: 24,410
Accepted: 25%
Enrolled: 28%
Grad in 6 Years: 92%
Returning Freshmen: 96%
Academics: ✐ ✐ ✐
Social: ☎ ☎ ☎
Q of L: ★ ★ ★
Admissions: (610) 519-4000
Email Address: gotovu@
villanova.edu

Strong Programs:
Finance
Engineering
Nursing
Economics
Social Sciences
Biology
Communication

Villanova University takes pride in its Augustinian heritage, emphasizing intellectual, professional, and spiritual growth as a path to "transforming hearts and minds." The school has all the trappings of a vintage Roman Catholic university, from strong academics to deeply rooted traditions and rivalries, and students firmly dedicated to their faith and service to others. Says one junior, "There are times I walk out of a class at Villanova and just have to stop for a second to take it all in and appreciate what an amazing opportunity I've been afforded."

Founded in 1842 by the community-focused Order of Saint Augustine, Villanova's lush campus of more than 260 acres is situated along Philadelphia's suburban Main Line. Old stone buildings, well-kept lawns, and secluded, tree-lined walkways are a reminder of the campus's historical roots, while several newer buildings are LEED certified. Recent construction includes a major project that has transformed 14 acres of parking lots and asphalt into a bustling area featuring new residence halls, eateries, a bookstore, and a performing arts center, all linked to the campus core by a pedestrian bridge.

> **"Villanova professors go the extra mile for their students."**

Undergraduates may enroll in the College of Liberal Arts and Sciences, the Villanova School of Business, the College of Engineering, or the Fitzpatrick College of Nursing. All students follow a liberal arts core curriculum. First-year students take the yearlong Augustine and Culture Seminar (ACS) and are housed with their ACS classmates or in optional themed learning communities in the residence halls. In the first semester, they read works from the ancient, medieval, and Renaissance periods—ranging from the Greeks and Saint Augustine to the Middle Ages and Shakespeare. In the second semester, students explore works from the Early Modern, Enlightenment, Romantic, Modernist, and Contemporary eras.

Finance, engineering, nursing, and economics are both strong and popular at Villanova, as are the social sciences, biology, and communication programs. Additional undergraduate programs include majors in gender and women's studies and Arab and Islamic studies, as well as minors in global health, counseling, and business law and corporate governance. Forty-two percent of undergraduate classes have fewer than 20 students. "The courses are rigorous and are often discussion-oriented and reading- and writing-intensive," says one communication major. Another student says, "Villanova professors go the extra mile for their students through office hours, research, and personal conversations." An honors program is available to about 300 students. Forty percent of students study abroad each year;

communication and computer science students can apply for semester-long internships at the Vatican in Rome.

"The students who attend Villanova are passionate and devoted," says a sophomore. "They care about their work, but, more importantly, they care about their community." Many are from the East Coast, and 22 percent hail from Pennsylvania; 2 percent come from foreign countries. Black students account for 6 percent of the student body, Hispanics/Latinos 10 percent, Asian Americans 7 percent, and multiracial students 4 percent. "We're not an extremely political campus," one student muses, "although social justice issues like poverty, hunger, and homelessness are all big issues." Merit scholarships are available, averaging $28,300, as are more than 200 athletic scholarships in 24 sports.

First-years in the yearlong Augustine and Culture Seminar read works ranging from the Greeks and Saint Augustine to the Contemporary eras.

Housing on campus is guaranteed for three years, and 83 percent of undergraduates call the residence halls home. "Rooms are great at Villanova," says one senior. "My first and second year I had a sink in my room so I didn't have to walk down the hall to wash my face or brush my teeth." Freshmen live primarily on the South Campus Circle, while upperclassmen choose residence halls on the main campus or apartment-style housing on West Campus via lottery system. Most seniors move to houses and apartments in the surrounding neighborhoods. The university offers more than a dozen campus eateries, which serve everything from pizza to Chinese food, wraps, and vegetarian and vegan menus. "Food at Villanova is delicious," says a student. "Tons of variety with so many options I sometimes don't know which one to choose."

"I have never had a dull weekend at Villanova because there is always something going on. If you are looking to party, you can. If you are looking to just chill, you can do that too," a student explains. Weekend social life centers around campus events and parties, some sponsored by Greek groups, which claim 17 percent of the men and 19 percent of the women. Students

"The students who attend Villanova are passionate and devoted."

get together with friends at the student center on Fridays and Saturdays for Late Night at Villanova events, such as comedians, bands, open-mic nights, and dance parties. Juniors and seniors tend to spend evenings at bars along the local Main Line or in Philadelphia, just 12 minutes away by train. The city's entertainment and cultural opportunities include museums and pro sports, as well as events at numerous other colleges and universities, from La Salle and Temple to Drexel, Penn, and St. Joseph's.

Despite the tough courses, a senior says, "Everyone works hard, plays hard, and still finds time to give back to the community." Indeed, Villanova students volunteer roughly 250,000 hours of service each year. About 400 students participate in service trips over the fall and spring breaks, volunteering for projects like building houses and assisting victims of natural disasters. Each fall, Villanova hosts the largest annual student-run Special Olympics event in the world, drawing thousands of athletes, coaches, and volunteers from across campus and the local community.

Each fall, Villanova hosts the largest annual student-run Special Olympics event in the world.

When they are not out socializing or serving their community, Villanova students are cheering for the men's basketball team, which has brought home two Division I national championships in recent years. Men's and women's cross-country, women's swimming and diving, and softball are competitive in the Big East Conference. Club sports and intramurals are a big draw, and popular activities include basketball, flag football, soccer, and men's ice hockey.

Despite the changes in the world around it, Villanova continues its devotion to its students, community, and strong traditions, both academic and spiritual. The administration has set its sights on making Villanova one of the premier Roman Catholic institutions, up there with Notre Dame, Georgetown, and Boston College. While taking pride in tradition, it recognizes that its continuing improvements to campus facilities and ongoing development of educational and cocurricular programs will help its students remain competitive in the workplace and the world beyond.

Overlaps

Boston College, Fordham, Georgetown, Lehigh, Notre Dame, Northeastern, University of Pennsylvania, University of Virginia

If You Apply To ›

Villanova: Early decision I and II, early action, regular decision. Accepts the Common Application. Apply to a particular school or program. Please consult Villanova's website for the most up-to-date information regarding standardized test requirements.

University of Virginia

P.O. Box 400160, Charlottesville, VA 22904

Is it Thomas Jefferson? The Romanesque architecture? The Charlottesville air? Whatever it is, students nationwide go gaga for UVA, where competition for out-of-state admission has hit Ivy League levels. Relatively small for a top-notch public flagship, UVA combines old-line conservatism with high-quality academics and a social scene that is spirited in multiple senses of the word. Charlottesville is a big small town with plenty of culture, just over two hours from D.C.

Website: www.virginia.edu
Location: Small City
Public
Total Enrollment: 22,833
Undergraduates: 16,337
Male/Female: 44/56
Financial Aid: 45%
Pell Grant: 12%
Expense: Pub $ $ $ $
Student Loans: 35%
Average Debt: $ $
Applicants: 47,971
Accepted: 21%
Enrolled: 39%
Grad in 6 Years: 94%
Returning Freshmen: 97%
Academics: ✎ ✎ ✎ ✎ ✎
Social: 🍺 🍺 🍺 🍺
Q of L: ★ ★ ★ ★ ★
Admissions: (434) 982-3200
Email Address: undergrad admission@virginia.edu

Strong Programs:
Commerce
Engineering
Global Studies
Sociology
Economics
Biology
Computer Science
Psychology

Easily one of the most prestigious public schools in the nation, the University of Virginia is known to all in Charlottesville as Mr. Jefferson's University. Not just any Mr. Jefferson, mind you, but *the* Mr. Jefferson, author of the Declaration of Independence. Of all his accomplishments, Jefferson was arguably proudest of UVA—he even asked that his epitaph speak to his role in creating the university in 1819 rather than his presidency of the United States. This legacy has come under increasing scrutiny recently in light of growing public awareness of some of Jefferson's racist views and ownership of hundreds of slaves. In response, the university has sought to "contextualize" its Jeffersonian legacy and remove the names of persons who supported the Confederate cause from places of honor on campus.

Located just east of the Blue Ridge Mountains in central Virginia, UVA's campus (the "Grounds") is dotted with historic buildings designed by Jefferson himself and still in use today. At the core is Jefferson's "academical village," with majestic white pillars and extensive brickwork. The village rises around a rectangular terraced green, known as the Lawn, which is flanked by two rows of identical one-story rooms reserved for undergraduate student leaders. Ten pavilions, five on either side of the Lawn, each feature a different style; all of them open onto a colonnaded walkway. Behind the buildings are public gardens, while the Rotunda, a half-scale model of the Roman Pantheon, overlooks the Lawn and stands as a symbol of the Enlightenment belief in secularism and freedom. Countering all this Jeffersonian stateliness is the abstract Memorial to Enslaved Laborers, created in 2020 to honor the 4,000 enslaved people who built and sustained UVA.

> **"Our honor code is more than just some words scribbled on paper—it's a way of life."**

UVA isn't just an elite public school; it holds its own against the best private schools as well, especially in the areas of business, engineering, and global studies. Sociology and the life sciences draw praise as well. The most popular majors are commerce, economics, biology, computer science, and psychology. The vast majority of incoming freshmen enroll in the College of Arts and Sciences, but undergraduates may also enroll in the schools of Engineering, Nursing, or Education and Human Development. After their second year, about 350 students are accepted into the McIntire School of Commerce, UVA's undergraduate business school. Not surprisingly, competition for these spots is tough. A five-year program for aspiring teachers yields a B.A. from the College of Arts and Sciences and a Master of

Teaching degree from UVA's Curry School of Education and Human Development. The Batten School of Leadership and Public Policy trains students for public service careers in both domestic and international arenas and offers a five-year bachelor/master of public policy. Students who qualify for the Distinguished Majors program may pursue independent study during their third and fourth years.

Students agree that the workload at UVA is "intense but manageable," in the words of a commerce major. Virginia requires students in arts and sciences to complete the College Curriculum, which features three categories of coursework: Engagements (a yearlong sequence of small first-year seminars), Literacies (language, rhetoric, computation, and data analysis), and Disciplines (21 credits in a range of liberal arts areas). Although 52 percent of classes enroll fewer than 20 students, lower-level classes can be huge, with as many as 500 people. A senior explains that, especially in upper-level courses, "Most professors are willing to schedule appointments as you might need and are excited to connect with their students." Special programs for freshmen include University Seminars, which are taught by some of the university's best faculty and limited to 18 students in order to encourage interactive learning and intensive discussion.

Highly capable students may win admission to the Echols Scholars program, which allows about 200 top-entering freshmen the chance to pursue academic exploration without the constraints of distribution or major-field requirements. Echols students also live together for their first year. The Rodman Scholars program in the School of Engineering and Applied Science selects its members based on top academic performance and leadership. An intensive two-week January term

> "Students at UVA generally are fairly serious about academics, competitive, and very motivated."

provides additional opportunities for research seminars, interdisciplinary coursework, and study abroad. Thirty percent of undergrads go abroad to study, conduct research, or intern in their choice of more than 65 countries. UVA boasts the highest four-year graduation rate of any public university, at 89 percent.

Students instituted Virginia's notable honor system in 1842 after no one owned up to shooting a professor on the Lawn. The residence halls, student council, and Judiciary Committee remain student-run to this day—and they really put the brakes on lying, cheating, or stealing. And don't take the policies lightly—breaching the codes means a swift dismissal from campus. (An "informed retraction" process offers the possibility for such students to take responsibility for their offense and make amends with a two-semester Honor Leave of Absence.) After a number of controversial cases recently, discussions continue about the appropriateness of the single-sanction system. But rest assured, some form of the honor code will remain integral to the culture here. A classics major says, "Our honor code is more than just some words scribbled on paper—it's a way of life and a bond of trust between you, your peers, and faculty."

Sixty-eight percent of undergraduates are Virginians, and 4 percent are international. Admission for out-of-staters gets tougher every year, and many of those students come from New York, New Jersey, Pennsylvania, and Maryland. Seven percent of UVA students are Black, 17 percent are Asian American, 7 percent are Hispanic/Latino, and

> "The drinking culture extends to many organizations outside of Greek life."

6 percent are multiracial. "Students at UVA generally are fairly serious about academics, competitive, and very motivated," says a junior, who adds that due to the underrepresentation of various groups, "the culture can sometimes feel exclusive." Students describe a mix of political views on campus but say the student body leans liberal. Race and systemic racism are perennial hot-button issues "because of our historical origins," explains a student of color. "Founded by a slave owner, built by

UVA's campus (the "Grounds") is dotted with historic buildings designed by Thomas Jefferson himself and still in use today.

The Batten School of Leadership and Public Policy offers a five-year bachelor/master of public policy.

slaves, serviced by slaves, closed to women and people of color until the 20th century." A training program on implicit bias is required of all incoming freshmen. UVA is one of only two public universities in the nation that practices need-blind admissions and meets 100 percent of all admitted students' demonstrated financial need (see also UNC at Chapel Hill), although achieving socioeconomic diversity remains a challenge. The school hands out hundreds of athletic scholarships each year, along with merit awards worth an average of $6,300 each. In-state students from families with incomes of less than $80,000 attend tuition-free.

Thirty-eight percent of students at Virginia live on campus, including about 800 who bunk in the three residential colleges: Brown College at Monroe Hill, Hereford College, and International Residential College. Hereford's contemporary architecture has been described by the *New York Times* as "proudly, almost defiantly modern," in contrast to most of the other campus buildings. First-year residence halls are said to be the nicest on campus, and freshmen get first pick for housing. Fifty-four top seniors win the honor of living in spartan rooms along the Lawn, and among the outer set of rooms, called the range, students can visit room #13, which was occupied for a semester by Edgar Allen Poe in 1826 before he was suspended for nonpayment of tuition. "Most upperclassmen live off Grounds, and there is a chaotic rush to get good housing beginning as early as September of the year prior," complains a junior. Meal plans are required for first-years and campus fare receives decent reviews.

After being at the center of a broad national debate about the extent of drinking and sexual violence on college campuses, especially at fraternities, UVA has in recent years initiated and updated several programs aimed at education and prevention. "Our administration is increasing the normalcy of talking about sexual assault, and I do think it is helping," reflects a junior. As for general safety, a student reports, "We have campus police, Charlottesville police, and an Ambassadors watch program all looking out for the safety of students."

"Almost everything here is a tradition."

Students say the UVA social scene is dynamic and varied. Fraternities draw 31 percent of Virginia's men, and sororities sign up 31 percent of women; Greek parties happen off campus. Mr. Jefferson founded UVA as a place where students could come together to "drink from the cup of knowledge," and now that fraternity rush is dry and parties must have guest lists, there's less quaffing of other brews going on. Still, determined Virginians haven't stopped metamorphosing into Rowdy Wahoos when the sun goes down—the nickname comes from a school cheer about a fish that can drink twice its weight. One senior observes that "the drinking culture extends to many organizations outside of Greek life as well." For nondrinkers and those under 21, the student-run University Programs Council and nearly 900 clubs and other organizations offer movies, concerts, social hours, and other booze-free options. Most students are "highly involved" in multiple extracurriculars.

"Almost everything here is a tradition," remarks one student. Favorites include Lighting of the Lawn, featuring a cappella performances and an orchestrated light show on the Rotunda that kicks off the holiday season, and Foxfield, in which students dress up and host catered parties prior to attending a steeplechase horse race each April. Jackets and ties also come out for football games, a relic of when UVA was all male and gridiron contests were an opportunity to meet women. Streaking the Lawn is a rite of passage, students say. We would like to tell you more about the various secret societies, but we can't—for one thing, they're secret!

"Our rivalry with Virginia Tech is hilarious."

As for Charlottesville (population 46,000), it's "the perfect college town," says an anthropology major, and often a pleasant surprise for those coming from larger urban areas. There are restaurants and bars; gorgeous vineyards and wineries; and plenty of shops, theaters, and other cultural attractions. Students congregate at the Corner, a commercial strip adjacent to campus boasting several popular bars. They also immerse themselves in community service in the area; UVA's nationally recognized Madison House coordinates the activities of a host of volunteer groups. Outdoorsy folks can hike, bike, ski, and sightsee in the nearby Blue Ridge Mountains, or simply daydream while strolling Skyline Drive. Popular road trips include Washington, D.C., Richmond, and anywhere the Cavaliers are playing football, basketball, or soccer.

Big-time Atlantic Coast Conference basketball has long been an integral part of UVA life, and the men's team claimed the national championship title in 2019. The Cavaliers field a number of other competitive Division I teams as well: women's swimming and diving, women's rowing, men's lacrosse, and men's tennis are all recent national champions. Competitions get especially heated when Virginia Tech's Hokies come to town. A junior comments, "Our rivalry with Virginia Tech is hilarious and an excellent way to bond two very different people together as peers." There are also dozens of intramural sports leagues or tournaments, in everything from flag football to inner-tube water polo, and more than 65 club sports.

"UVA is an institution that has always been known for its academic excellence and quirky traditions," comments a government major. "To be a Wahoo is something that is unique and to be treasured." The social life is as vigorous as the academics are rigorous, and the friendships that are formed here last far beyond the college years—much as Mr. Jefferson's legacy, complicated as it is, continues to be felt on campus long after his death.

> ## Overlaps
>
> **UCLA, UC Berkeley, University of Michigan, UC Santa Barbara, University of Florida, Virginia Tech, U Penn, William & Mary**

If You Apply To ›

UVA: Early decision, early action, regular decision. Accepts the Common Application. Please consult UVA's website for the most up-to-date information regarding standardized test requirements.

Virginia Tech

Blacksburg, VA 24061

Offers a unique blend of high tech and Southern hospitality. Engineering has always been its calling card, but business and architecture are popular. Admission is competitive for out-of-state applicants. Blacksburg is a nice college town, but far from the population centers near the coast. Hokie Nation loves its football team. Compare to Clemson, Georgia Tech, and Purdue.

Officially known as the Virginia Polytechnic Institute and State University, Virginia Tech is a land grant university that offers a slate of solid academic programs, competitive Division I athletics, and storied traditions. Engineering, business, and architecture attract top students from around the country who are proud to be part of the "Hokie Nation." A senior says, "Even in a school with 34,000 students, I feel like I'm in a small town with 200 people. Everyone here is so friendly."

Its campus, set on a plateau in the scenic Blue Ridge Mountains, occupies 3,000 acres and comes complete with a duck pond, hiking trails, and a 250-year-old plantation that operates as a museum. Students enjoy unlimited outdoor recreation thanks to the proximity of the Jefferson National Forest, the Appalachian Trail, the scenic Blue Ridge Parkway, and the majestic old New River. The campus

> **Website:** www.vt.edu
> **Location:** Small Town
> **Public**
> **Total Enrollment:** 34,448
> **Undergraduates:** 28,929
> **Male/Female:** 57/43
> **Financial Aid:** 58%
> **Pell Grant:** 16%
> **Expense:** Pub $ $ $
> **Student Loans:** 47%

(continued)

Average Debt: $ $ $
Applicants: 42,054
Accepted: 56%
Enrolled: 28%
Grad in 6 Years: 87%
Returning Freshmen: 92%
Academics: ✏ ✏ ✏
Social: ☎ ☎ ☎
Q of L: ★ ★ ★ ★
Admissions: (540) 231-6267
Email Address: admissions@
   vt.edu

Strong Programs:
Engineering
Business
Hospitality and Tourism
   Management
Architecture
Industrial Design
Animal Science
Forestry
Meteorology

The five-year architecture program is considered one of the nation's best.

buildings are an attractive mix of gray limestone structures, colonial-style brick, and modern cement buildings, and the campus continues to undergo renovations and additions.

Virginia Tech is best known for its first-rate technical and professional training. For undergrads with an appetite for engineering, Tech has programs for every taste, including aerospace, chemical, computer, mining, ocean, and more. The Pamplin College of Business, which offers a notable major in hospitality and tourism management, is also prominent. The five-year architecture program is considered one of the nation's best, and the industrial design major is strong too. The most popular majors include engineering (especially mechanical), biology, business information technology, and finance. Though no longer Tech's centerpiece, the College of Agriculture and Life Sciences remains strong, especially in animal science. Students in the College of Natural Resources and Environment can choose from solid majors in forestry, meteorology, sustainable biomaterials, and wildlife conservation. The humanities tend not to fare as well in the university's high-tech environment, although internationally known poet Nikki Giovanni, who teaches creative writing and advanced poetry, is a bright spot. The university also has a tradition of excellence in the performing arts, and the school's theater group has won numerous awards.

"Even in a school with 34,000 students, I feel like I'm in a small town."

A junior describes the academic climate as "rigorous, but very encouraging." The general education program, known as Pathways, requires students to take coursework in several liberal arts areas and gives students the option of pursuing interdisciplinary Pathways minors or hands-on learning experiences, like research or study abroad, to fulfill their gen-eds. Introductory class size tends to be large—sometimes well into the hundreds. Most of the big lecture classes are taught by full-time faculty, though discussions and grading are generally handled by teaching assistants. A senior says, "For the most part, my professors seemed to really care about what I was pursuing and how I was learning, not just performing." The roughly 1,700 students who participate in the Honors College are guaranteed access to top faculty and research opportunities.

The nationally acclaimed Small Business Institute enables faculty-led groups of business majors to work with local merchants, analyze their problems, and make suggestions on how to increase profits. Each year, about 500 students (mostly engineers) take advantage of Tech's co-op program, getting paid for real-world work experience. The Corps of Cadets, a tradition since the university's founding in 1872, offers a unique opportunity for students who wish to combine leadership training with an academic major. The 1,100 Cadets who enroll follow a structured military lifestyle, living together in the Corps' dedicated residence halls and wearing uniforms to class. In addition to choosing between a military/ROTC track and a citizen-leader track, Cadets can earn a minor in leadership. Sixty-nine percent of undergrads conduct research, and for the 28 percent who aspire to study abroad, Tech offers more than 200 programs in 60 nations around the globe.

According to a senior, Virginia Tech students are "down-to-earth, reasonable, and fun people." Seventy-seven percent of undergraduates call Virginia home, and 5 percent arrive from abroad. Not surprisingly, the admissions office is inundated with out-of-state applicants, which means stiff competition for the slots available to non-Virginians. Tech's relative isolation from major cities is a drag on minority recruitment: Black students represent 5 percent, Hispanics/Latinos 9 percent, Asian Americans 12 percent, and multiracial students 5 percent. "For a school in southwest Virginia, the political climate on campus is refreshingly balanced," says a sophomore. Students looking at pricey Northeastern technical schools will find Tech a real bargain. The university hands out 472 athletic scholarships, in addition to thousands of merit awards averaging $4,100. The Funds for the Future program aims to offset tuition increases for low-income undergraduates.

Freshmen and the Corps of Cadets are required to live on campus, but overcrowding has been an issue in recent years as enrollment continues to increase. "You need to look for housing early," warns a student. Currently, 32 percent of all undergrads reside on campus. After their first year, most students move into nearby off-campus apartment complexes. Dining services receive enthusiastic reviews for variety, taste, and options for special diets. "Virginia Tech offers many classes to learn how to protect yourself and make yourself knowledgeable about the issue of sexual assault," notes a sophomore.

Important annual events include the Ring Dance (when juniors receive their school rings) and the Corps of Cadets military ball.

Leisure-time favorites include bowling and billiards in the student center, club activities, and school-sponsored plays, concerts, arts and crafts fairs, and dances. Thirteen percent of the men and 19 percent of the women join fraternities and sororities, and students say Greek groups do not dominate social life. Some of the most important annual events include the Ring Dance (when juniors receive their school rings) and the Corps of Cadets military ball. Service is a big emphasis, and many students get involved in the local com-

"[The academic climate is] rigorous, but very encouraging."

munity. "Blacksburg has many great restaurants within walking distance of campus, as well as a discount movie theater and the farmers market every weekend," says a neuroscience major. For real big-city action, Washington, D.C., and Richmond are four and three hours away by car, respectively. Given that the school is nestled in the Blue Ridge Mountains, hiking, biking, caving, and water sports are popular pastimes too.

Virginia Tech competes in the Division I Atlantic Coast Conference, and the football team's multiple appearances in postseason bowl games have cheered alumni and hiked applications. The annual big game pits the Hokies against the Cavaliers of the University of Virginia. Men's wrestling and men's and women's basketball and track and field have also performed well in recent years. Tech's extensive recreational program boasts more than 40 intramural and 30 club sports, with everything from football to horseshoes and underwater hockey—a recent rage.

Virginia Tech encourages students to "invent the future," and that's just what today's citizens of the Hokie Nation aim to do. By taking advantage of Tech's particular blend of high-tech learning and Southern hospitality, students have countless opportunities to gain industry experience, travel abroad, and spend four years with like-minded peers.

Overlaps

Clemson, Georgia Tech, Purdue, University of Virginia, University of Colorado Boulder, Texas A&M, James Madison, Penn State

If You Apply To ›

Tech: Early decision, early action, regular decision. Accepts the Common Application with supplement. Music applicants must audition. Please consult Virginia Tech's website for the most up-to-date information regarding standardized test requirements.

Wabash College

301 West Wabash, Crawfordsville, IN 47933

Wabash and Hampden–Sydney in Virginia are the last of the all-male breed. With steady enrollment and plenty of money in the bank, Wabash sees no reason to change. Intense bonding is an important part of the Wabash experience, and few co-ed schools can match the loyalty of Wabash alumni. The Gentleman's Rule says it all.

Website: www.wabash.edu
Location: Small Town
Private
Total Enrollment: 837
Undergraduates: 837
Male/Female: 100/0
Financial Aid: 99%
Pell Grant: 20%
Expense: Pr $
Student Loans: 74%
Average Debt: $ $ $ $
Applicants: 1,635
Accepted: 62%
Enrolled: 21%
Grad in 6 Years: 83%
Returning Freshmen: 85%
Academics: ✍ ✍ ✍ ½
Social: ☎ ☎
Q of L: ★ ★ ★
Admissions: (800) 345-5385
Email Address: admissions@
wabash.edu

Strong Programs:
Chemistry
Biology
English
Religion
Rhetoric
Theater
Economics
Political Science

Wabash College was founded in Indiana in 1832 by transplanted Ivy Leaguers who shared the Enlightenment's optimistic view of human nature and envisioned a "classical and English high school rising into a college as soon as the wants of the country demand." Their vision proved to be 20/20. All-male Wabash has not only prospered but also remained true to its conservative academic and social traditions, including the Gentleman's Rule of self-responsibility that students continue to live by. "Wabash College has a culture that has not changed for 50 years. It can be a hard school to fit into if you do not meet the status quo, but it also is a brotherhood," says a junior.

> **"Wabash prides itself on being very competitive; the classroom atmosphere can be intense."**

The 94-acre Wabash campus is characterized by redbrick, white-columned, Georgian-style buildings (three are originals from the 1830s). Located in the heart of Crawfordsville, a small town of about 16,000, Wabash is surrounded by grass and tall trees that are part of the gorgeous Fuller Arboretum. Recent campus projects include the 3,400-seat Little Giant Stadium, completed in 2021 to accommodate football games, track meets, and other large events.

The Wabash educational program has certainly proved itself over the years. This small college has amassed an impressive list of alumni: executives of major corporations, doctors, lawyers, and a large number of Ph.D.s. Wabash alumni are typically faithful to their school in the form of generous donations. On a per-capita basis, the school's $420 million endowment makes it one of the wealthiest in the nation. General education requirements include courses from a wide variety of fields—natural and behavioral sciences, literature and fine arts, mathematics, and language studies. All freshmen participate in a community service project during orientation and take a tutorial in the fall that is designed to focus them on reading, writing, and class participation, followed by a colloquium titled Enduring Questions in the spring. All seniors must complete comprehensive examinations in their final semester, consisting of two days of written exams in their major and an hour-long oral exam on their overall liberal arts experience.

> **"[Students] demonstrate a strong desire to fight the stigma around mental health."**

Economics, rhetoric, political science, and history draw the most majors at Wabash, and high accolades go to the chemistry, biology, and English departments. Religion, rhetoric, and theater are traditional strengths, and newer majors include environmental studies and philosophy, politics, and economics (PPE). Those who can't satisfy their high-tech interests at Wabash can opt for a 3–2 program in engineering with Columbia, Washington University in St. Louis, or Purdue.

"Wabash prides itself on being very competitive; the classroom atmosphere can be intense at times, and the workload is pretty heavy," says a religion major. Seventy-four percent of classes have fewer than 20 students, and a financial economics major explains, "Students have the ability to form professional relationships with their professors and often obtain help outside of the classroom when needed." Students roundly praise the Quantitative Skills Center and the Writing Center for their assistance with classwork, as well as career services for connecting them with internships, jobs, and influential alumni. A peer educator program called Supplemental Instruction offers further support with coursework. Ninety-two percent of students participate in at least one internship during their time at Wabash.

Paid, full-time research positions with faculty are a popular summertime pursuit at Wabash, particularly among students in the sciences. About half of the students study abroad via semester-long programs offered by third-party providers as well as cross-cultural immersion-learning courses at Wabash that include short-term travel components—at no extra cost to students. WabashX initiatives provide hands-on experience in four interdisciplinary fields: democracy and public discourse; global health; innovation, business, and entrepreneurship; and digital arts and human values. Participating students engage in such opportunities as academic summits, internships, consulting projects, volunteer work, and travel abroad. They also enjoy access to dedicated coworking space in the Fusion 54 center in downtown Crawfordsville, where they can interact with local business leaders.

WabashX initiatives provide hands-on experiences such as academic summits, internships, consulting projects, volunteer work, and travel abroad.

"Most guys at Wabash are just your everyday kind of dude," muses a classics and religion double major. "We tend to mostly like sports and hanging out with friends." Most come from public high schools in Indiana, but 21 percent come from other states, and 4 percent hail from foreign countries. Black students represent 4 percent of the student body, Hispanics/Latinos 10 percent, Asian Americans 1 percent, and multiracial students 4 percent. A biology major

"Every day is for the boys, and it's fantastic to be a part of."

reports that "the student body tends to lean right" but politics generally don't play a large role in student life. Merit awards averaging $30,300 are available to qualified students. Applicants who enroll under Wabash's early decision plan are guaranteed an internship after their sophomore year and may qualify for a scholarship covering future tuition increases if they maintain a certain GPA.

For housing, the college offers five residence halls, two lodges, two duplex-style townhomes, and 10 fraternity houses; all students are required to live on campus all four years. Dorm residents must eat in the dining hall. "Nine times out of 10, the food is good, but that one time can really stand out," says a sophomore. Wabash addresses the topics of sexual assault and gender-based violence during new student orientation and leadership development activities throughout the year. The college has beefed up counseling and mental health services in recent years, and a senior says students "demonstrate a strong desire to fight the stigma around mental health."

The surrounding town of Crawfordsville leaves much to be desired. With few options off campus, the school's 10 fraternities tend to dominate the social scene: 59 percent of the students join up. "Greek organizations *are* the social life on campus. No one else throws parties," says a sophomore. Many students say there is a noticeable divide between fraternity brothers and "independents." As for drinking on campus, students say that policies are generally loose, as long as students are behaving responsibly, which is to say in a gentlemanly fashion. Weekend trips to Purdue and Indiana University are also popular. Traditions are taken seriously at Wabash, from homecoming to not passing beneath certain archways on campus. Chapel Sing, where freshmen compete to see who can best sing the lengthy school song, is a favorite ritual, but undoubtedly the biggest is the school's long-standing rivalry with DePauw, which dates to 1890 and is capped off every year by the football game that decides who gets to keep the prized Monon Bell. Wabash has won 10 of the last 13 rivalry games.

The school's 10 fraternities tend to dominate the social scene: 59 percent of the students join up.

That competitive spirit extends to all of the Little Giants (so named because the 1904 football team was performing above its weight) Division III athletic programs.

The wrestling team is a perennial contender for the national title and was the national runner-up in 2022, while the football, basketball, and track and field teams have recently won North Coast Athletic Conference titles. About half of the students participate in intramural and club sports, including basketball, dodgeball, football, soccer, and softball.

Traditions have not changed much since the school's founding back in the 1830s and still play an important part in the lives of the men at Wabash. Some students complain about the lack of women and culture in the surrounding area, but many are happy with the college's intensive, rigorous programs and expanding opportunities for interdisciplinary study and hands-on experiences. "Wabash is a brotherhood through and through," says a satisfied junior. "Every day is for the boys, and it's fantastic to be a part of."

If You Apply To ›

Wabash: Early decision, early action, regular decision. SATs or ACTs: optional. Accepts the Common Application with supplement.

Wake Forest University

Winston-Salem, NC 27106

Wake Forest's Baptist heritage and Winston-Salem location give it a more down-home flavor than Duke or Emory. But take out your magnifying glass and you'll also find one of the nation's most innovative institutions. It was Wake, not Brown or Tufts, that became the first leading private university to go test-optional for the SAT and ACT back in 2008. Holds its own in big-time Atlantic Coast Conference sports with schools five times its size. The strong Greek system dominates the social scene.

Long one of the top private schools in the Southeast, Wake Forest has transformed its regional recognition into a national reputation. The university is best known for basketball, but its solid academics are worthy of a look as well. Students work hard, hence the nickname "Work Forest," but the university's size and strong Greek system means it's also easy to establish close friendships. "Wake Forest is the best of both worlds," says a political science major. "Academics are challenging, and you're surrounded by motivated and intelligent peers. At the same time, students pride themselves on being social."

Located in the Central Piedmont region of North Carolina, Wake Forest was founded in 1834 by the North Carolina Baptist Convention in Wake Forest, near Raleigh. It moved to Winston-Salem in 1956 and in 1986 replaced formal ties to the Baptists with a "fraternal" relationship. The university's 340-acre campus features flowers, wooded trails, and stately magnolias. There are more than 40 Georgian-style buildings constructed of old Virginia brick with granite trim. The campus is bordered by the lush, 148-acre Reynolda Gardens annex, which features a formal garden, greenhouses, and one of the first collections of Japanese cherry trees in the U.S. Wake Downtown is a 115,000-square-foot, STEM-focused space adjacent to Wake's School of Medicine in downtown Winston-Salem. Newer additions include the 180,000-square-foot Wake Forest Wellbeing Center, housing fitness and recreation facilities as well as offices for student health services.

To graduate from Wake Forest, students must complete a standard distribution of liberal arts courses, in addition to taking an introductory first-year seminar and satisfying a cultural diversity requirement. The most popular programs include finance, communication, economics, psychology, and politics and international affairs; the School of Business is highly regarded. Wake has an unusual number of interdisciplinary centers and programs for an institution of its size. The innovative Center for Entrepreneurship sponsors programs such as Startup Lab, which allows students to develop business concepts into commercial ventures with the help of seed capital. The Interdisciplinary Arts Center brings together students, faculty, and staff for arts collaborations with subject matter ranging from romance languages to neuroscience.

Students agree that courses at Wake Forest are rigorous, but a history and psychology double major says, "I have been impressed by how collaborative Wake students are." Fifty-seven percent of undergraduate classes have fewer than 20 students. Faculty members get high marks; graduate assistants teach some labs and health classes, but otherwise professors are at the lectern. "I've been told by professors, department heads, and academic advisors that their first goal for me is that I learn the material and have enriching experiences while at school," says a physics major. "It's very refreshing to have faculty who put the emphasis on this rather than grades." The Office of Personal and Career Development takes a four-year approach to helping students prepare for future careers.

> **"It's very refreshing to have faculty who put the emphasis on [enriching experiences] rather than grades."**

Undergraduates at Wake Forest have plenty of opportunities to participate in faculty-mentored research, and Richter Scholarships fund select independent study or research projects that involve travel away from campus. The Pro Humanitate Institute allows students to put their skills and knowledge to work helping the community; the center takes its name from the school's motto, which means "In Service to Humanity." Exceptionally able students may qualify for the Honors in Arts and Sciences distinction by taking three or more honors seminars during their first three years. The Wake Washington Center gives selected undergraduates the chance to live, study, intern, and network in the nation's capital for a semester. And for those who wish to spread their wings internationally, Wake Forest's residential study centers in Copenhagen, London, Vienna, and on the Grand Canal in Venice beckon. Wake Forest offers more than 400 semester, summer, and yearlong study abroad programs in more than 70 countries worldwide; 75 percent of undergrads participate.

"Students at Wake Forest are highly driven above all else," says a senior. Eighty percent of undergraduates hail from outside North Carolina, including 9 percent who come from foreign countries. "Students tend to be very conservative," says a sophomore, and a senior adds, "We are not a politically active school." The university's move to de-emphasize the SAT and ACT was one of its many efforts to boost lagging diversity, but success has been limited. Currently, Black students make up 6 percent of the undergraduate population, Asian Americans add 4 percent, Hispanics/Latinos contribute 8 percent, and multiracial students represent 5 percent. Although the university meets 100 percent of admitted students' demonstrated financial need, it is weak on socioeconomic diversity, with a mere 10 percent of freshmen qualifying for Pell Grants. Merit scholarships averaging $10,600 are awarded to eligible students, in addition to about 170 athletic scholarships.

> **"Students at Wake Forest are highly driven above all else."**

Seventy-six percent of students live on campus, as they are required to do for their first three years. In addition to all-gender restrooms across campus, the university now offers gender-neutral housing options and has increased the size and visibility of its LGBTQ Center. Dining options have improved recently, students

(continued)

Email Address: admissions@wfu.edu

Strong Programs:
Business and Enterprise
  Management
Finance
Communication
Economics
Psychology
Politics and International Affairs

Startup Lab allows students to develop business concepts into commercial ventures with the help of seed capital.

say: "There are two standard cafeterias, as well as a Starbucks, Chick-fil-A, Moe's, Subway, and other options." One student complains, "Campus security could be better. There is a fair amount of crime in certain areas of campus." Students say sexual assault is not a prevalent issue, but the Safe Office is an effective resource for those who need it.

Thirty-four percent of men and 61 percent of women go Greek, and Greek life dominates the social scene. Fraternities and sororities do not have houses on campus, but they throw open parties in dorm lounges or in off-campus houses. "Other organizations, such as Student Union, make a huge effort to bring other social options, such as concerts, movies, and events, to campus," says a student. The school's honor code helps to keep rowdy behavior in check; as one student cautions, "If you are caught with alcohol, and you are under 21, there are strict consequences." Everyone enjoys the annual homecoming festivities, and after the Demon Deacons score big athletic victories, students roll the quad in toilet paper to celebrate. Other favorite events include a midnight concert by the school orchestra every Halloween, with members in full costume, and Lilting Banshees comedy troupe shows. Another Wake Forest tradition is Hit the Bricks, an eight-hour relay race benefitting cancer research that runs along the brick pathways of Hearn Plaza. Popular road trips are to the beach or the mountains; Chapel Hill, Durham, and Raleigh are each 100 miles away, and Atlanta and the Washington/Baltimore areas are about a five-hour drive.

> **"We are a small school with big school spirit."**

The city of Winston-Salem is rich in culture, with a symphony, a Christmastime "Moravian love feast," film festivals, multiple art museums, a thriving arts district, and the well-known University of North Carolina School of the Arts. It's also home to the corporate headquarters of another Southern specialty: Krispy Kreme Doughnuts. "Winston is a very suburban town with a lot of young families and a Southern feel," a student says. The town also has a strong music scene, with live bands playing regularly at downtown venues. Popular volunteer activities include Project Pumpkin, a trick-or-treat night on campus for underprivileged children.

Wake Forest sports teams became known as the Demon Deacons after a major victory over Duke in 1922 when, in the words of the editor of the school newspaper, they "fought like demons." Basketball is the undisputed king at Wake Forest—think Chris Paul and Tim Duncan—and is perennially strong in the rough-and-tumble Division I Atlantic Coast Conference. Other solid teams include men's and women's soccer, men's tennis, baseball, and women's golf. Of course, virtually any contest against in-state rival UNC at Chapel Hill is guaranteed to get students excited. Intramural and club sports are also offered—soccer, basketball, and floor hockey are some of the most popular—and according to a senior, "Fun supersedes talent."

A spirit of engagement pervades the Wake Forest experience, as well as an underdog mentality when compared with competitors that are bigger, slightly more famous, or located in places like Chapel Hill or Atlanta instead of Winston-Salem. The Deacs always punch above their weight. As one student puts it, "We are a small school with big school spirit."

If You Apply To ›

Wake Forest: Early decision I and II, regular decision. SATs or ACTs: optional. Accepts the Common Application with supplement.

P.O. Box 9000, Asheville, NC 28815

Among a handful of schools where students combine academics, community engagement, and on-campus work that helps keep tuition down. Roots in the culture of Appalachia combine with a strong international and social justice orientation to give Warren Wilson its distinctive flavor. Setting in the mountains of western North Carolina is tough to beat. Campus atmosphere ranges from liberal to far-out alternative.

Warren Wilson is a small liberal arts college flush with engaging little quirks. It promotes global perspectives while maintaining its roots in Appalachian culture. It puts students to work (including on the campus farm) and makes service learning a central part of the educational experience. The school is also at the forefront of the "green" movement and has fully divested its endowment from fossil fuels. "My school is wild," says a senior. "It is a big old 'take that' to the status quo. It is a group of people who are going to change the world."

Founded by the Presbyterian Church in 1894 as the Asheville Farm School, Warren Wilson College initially provided formal schooling for "mountain boys." In 1967, it transformed into a four-year, co-ed liberal arts college that, while still maintaining its Presbyterian heritage, welcomes students of all backgrounds. WWC is located 15 minutes from downtown Asheville in the lush Swannanoa Valley of the Blue Ridge Mountains. Its 1,132-acre campus features formal gardens, fruit and vegetable gardens, a 300-acre farm, and approximately 25 miles of hiking trails. Consistent with campus culture, the wood-and-stone buildings are small in scale and built in an architectural style that emphasizes natural earth tones accented by extensive stonework by traditional Appalachian stonemasons. The campus is home to one of the most important Cherokee archaeological sites in the Southern Appalachian Mountains, dating from as early as 5000 B.C.

> **"My school is wild. It is a big old 'take that' to the status quo."**

The signature feature of the WWC curriculum is its unique three-part education program, which combines liberal arts coursework, community engagement, and campus work. To graduate, students must perform significant community service; they volunteer with more than 100 community organizations tackling issues like food security, homelessness, education, and the environment. Warren Wilson is also one of only nine four-year colleges in the nation that requires all residential students to work on campus—a practice that helps keep tuition down. To fulfill their work requirement, students choose to spend either eight or 16 hours every week working in crews that range from blacksmithing, carpentry, and recycling projects to IT services, tutoring, and photography, as well as keeping the college farm going. To meet general education requirements, WWC students take a broad range of liberal arts courses aimed at developing four core competencies: foundational knowledge and skills, critical inquiry, effective communication, and "civic identity values." All first-year students enroll in the writing-intensive First-Year Seminar, which includes introductory service-learning experiences that take students and faculty off campus weekly. In addition, every undergraduate major requires a culminating capstone project.

Students may choose from 20 majors, 33 minors, and more than 25 concentrations. Some of the most popular majors are environmental studies, psychology, creative writing, sociology/anthropology, and art. Students give high marks to the social work major and the natural sciences, especially biology and conservation biology. Accelerated 3–2 and 3–3 programs are available in pre-environmental management, preforestry, prelaw, and pre-M.B.A., and the integrative studies major allows

Website: www.warren-wilson.edu
Location: City Outskirts
Private
Total Enrollment: 794
Undergraduates: 714
Male/Female: 34/66
Financial Aid: 98%
Pell Grant: 33%
Expense: Pr $
Student Loans: 66%
Average Debt: $ $
Applicants: 1,146
Accepted: 77%
Enrolled: 25%
Grad in 6 Years: 45%
Returning Freshmen: 66%
Academics: ✍ ✍ ✍ ½
Social: ☎ ☎ ☎ ☎
Q of L: ★ ★ ★ ★ ★
Admissions: (800) 934-3536
Email Address: admit@warren-wilson.edu

Strong Programs:
Social Work
Biology
Environmental Studies
Psychology
Creative Writing
Sociology/Anthropology
Art
Outdoor Leadership

students to develop and complete individually designed majors. The popular outdoor leadership major prepares students to lead outdoor adventure education programs, focusing on both technical skills like backpacking and rock climbing and interpersonal skills like leadership and counseling. Appalachian studies, a minor within the global studies program, serves as a catalyst for local cultural activities, including numerous musical groups. And where else does the music department offer you the choice of "finger-picking" or "flat-picking" guitar?

A biology major says Warren Wilson's study-serve-work program is "challenging and fulfilling, but it requires commitment from the student in order to get the most out of it." Classes are small, and a freshman says, "Our faculty members are highly accessible, and many of them live on campus." An honors track is open to high-achieving students in several majors. Internship opportunities are available in all programs, and 53 percent of students study abroad during their time at WWC. Faculty-led programs involve a semester-long course on campus, followed by two to three weeks on an international "field experience." Qualified students may also study for a semester or two in countries such as China, Finland, Germany, Japan, and South Korea. The Center for Integrated Advising and Careers provides every incoming student with an Integrated Advising Coach, which one senior calls "an integral addition to student success."

> **"[Students are] laid-back and at the same time buzzing with excitement and passion."**

Warren Wilson students are "laid-back and at the same time buzzing with excitement and passion," explains a biology major. "We all care deeply about something, which makes for a chill but intense culture." Thirty-nine percent of students hail from North Carolina, and 4 percent are international. Black students account for 5 percent, Hispanics/Latinos 8 percent, Asian Americans 1 percent, and multiracial students 5 percent. Progressive political views and social justice concerns are big on campus, and hot-button issues include hiring more diverse faculty and staff members and "embedding racial equity curriculum into every academic department," reports a student. Upon graduation, most students go into service professions, such as teaching or working for environmental or other nongovernmental organizations. The first step for some is into the Peace Corps, for which the school offers a special advising program. Thirty-three percent of freshmen are Pell-eligible, and merit scholarships averaging $19,200 are available. Under the school's North Carolina Free Tuition Plan, all North Carolina residents who qualify for federal or state need-based financial aid will have the rest of their tuition covered by the college for all four years.

Eighty-nine percent of students live in the dorms, which an environmental studies major describes as "adequate." The 36-bed, LEED Platinum–certified EcoDorm incorporates solar heating and natural ventilation and is made of hardwoods milled on campus. Other theme housing options are also available. Students have one main dining hall and three cafés to choose from; the vegetarian and vegan fare at Cowpie is said to be particularly tasty. Students say they feel safe

> **"[Party culture] consists of gatherings of friends around a campfire, in a dorm, or in one of the pastures on campus."**

on campus, and the Center for Gender and Relationships provides advocacy, support, and education regarding diverse gender identities and campus sexual assault.

In the absence of Greek organizations, students create plenty of ways to have fun and blow off steam on campus. The outdoor program is the largest on campus and sponsors weekly hiking, camping, skiing, or other excursions. "Party culture on campus is minimal and primarily consists of gatherings of friends around a campfire, in a dorm, or in one of the pastures on campus," explains a senior. Students 21 and over who wish to imbibe must bring their own beer to parties. Popular events include the student-run Warren Wilson Circus and homecoming, which features live bluegrass music, a barbecue, and dancing. On Work Day, classes are canceled so

Warren Wilson is one of only nine four-year colleges in the nation that requires all residential students to work on campus.

Appalachian studies, a minor within the global studies program, serves as a catalyst for local cultural activities.

students and faculty can work together on campus projects and enjoy a pig roast, courtesy of the campus farm crew.

"[Asheville's] downtown scene is amazing for the relatively small size of the town," says a student. Museums, cafés, theaters, music clubs, and the symphony are only 15 minutes away. A transportation crew provides rides into town for grocery runs and special events. Thanks to the college's service requirement, students take an active role in the community through volunteer work. WWC sponsors short-term service projects during vacation breaks, and popular road trips include Atlanta and the beaches of South Carolina.

In a state famed for its rabid sports fans, many Warren Wilson students are decidedly nonchalant about athletics, and sports have not been a big emphasis here. Nevertheless, the college has been accepted as a provisional member of the NCAA's Division III and has added tennis and lacrosse programs. Currently competing in the U.S. College Athletic Association, the Fighting Owls boast strong men's and women's basketball, soccer, and cross-country teams. The varsity cycling and mountain biking teams are nationally competitive. Intramural and club sports are options as well.

Success at Warren Wilson is measured not only by grades but also by community service and a sense of stewardship. "One of the most beautiful things about Wilson is that it is a college where I can help pull a calf during a winter calving season in a beautiful valley, then head up to my Latin American Cinema class," says a global studies major. Those who aren't afraid to get their hands dirty will see this small liberal arts college as a valuable place that combines the notion of thinking globally with acting locally.

> *Upon graduation, most students go into service professions, such as teaching or working for environmental or other nongovernmental organizations.*

Overlaps

Evergreen State, Guilford, College of the Atlantic, Bard, Bennington, Eckerd, Reed, Brevard

If You Apply To ›

Warren Wilson: Early decision, early action, rolling admissions. SATs or ACTs: optional. Accepts the Common Application with supplement. Application includes fields to indicate preferred name, gender, and gender pronouns.

University of Washington

1410 N.E. Campus Parkway, Seattle, WA 98195

UDub wows visitors with its sprawling parklike campus in hugely popular Seattle. Washington is tougher than University of Oregon for out-of-state admission but not as hard as UC heavyweights Berkeley or UCLA. In addition to breathtaking views, location near both the coast and mountains makes for strong marine and environmental studies programs.

The University of Washington has cemented its reputation as a solid research institution, and its 30,000 full-time undergraduates benefit from traditional strengths in business, health, and natural sciences. Students here understand that size and its consequent anonymity are the prices that must be paid for the wealth of opportunities that await them, although First-Year Interest Groups and a four-year honors program help make the university feel smaller. Those looking for an extra-personal touch might want to investigate UW's campuses in Tacoma and Bothell, where average class sizes are smaller. But if the Seattle campus is your focus, one senior hints, just "learn to work the system."

Washington's Seattle campus blends Gothic architecture and the lush, green landscape of the Pacific Northwest. It features a number of distinctive landmarks.

Website: www.washington.edu
Location: City Center
Public
Total Enrollment: 42,604
Undergraduates: 29,515
Male/Female: 43/57
Financial Aid: 60%
Pell Grant: 21%
Expense: Pub $ $
Student Loans: 30%

New facilities include the $100 million, state-of-the-art Health Sciences Building.

Red Square sits atop the Central Plaza parking garage and features the Broken Obelisk, a 26-foot-high steel sculpture gifted to the university by the Virginia Wright Fund. All of the university's energy comes from renewable resources (including, of course, hydropower), and, despite campus growth, UW has reduced its overall energy use. New facilities include the $100 million, state-of-the-art Health Sciences Building.

Undergraduates in both professional and liberal arts programs must fulfill standard, university-wide distribution requirements in order to graduate. Individual schools and colleges also have their own requirements. Freshmen are given special attention via the First-Year Interest Group (FIG) program, which offers a chance to meet, discuss, and study with other first-years who have similar interests. Each FIG consists of 20 to 25 students who share a cluster of classes (which fulfill graduation requirements), and includes a weekly seminar led by a junior or senior peer advisor.

"All of my best experiences and opportunities have been through the Honors Program."

Many of Washington's diverse undergraduate strengths correspond with its excellent graduate programs. The competitive business major, for example, benefits from the university's highly regarded business school and is one of the most popular undergraduate majors, along with psychology, biology, communication, and biochemistry. Students majoring in public health, pharmacy, and nursing profit from access to facilities and faculty at the medical school, an international leader in cancer and heart research, cell biology, and organ transplants. English and drama are traditional strengths in the humanities. Also recommended for undergraduates are marine biology, environmental studies, architecture, and most engineering programs, especially computer science (which is tops in the country in producing female graduates), human centered design and engineering, and bioengineering. Reflecting the focus on natural resources in Washington's economy, the program in fisheries is excellent, as are earth and atmospheric sciences, including oceanography.

UW follows a quarter system, which means academics are challenging and fast-paced. A common complaint about the university is "having to apply to a major. It is already hard to get into UW, but then once you do, you might not even get into your desired major," explains a senior—and this tends to create a hypercompetitive atmosphere. Entry into preprofessional and STEM-related programs is particularly difficult, and students say you might want to have a backup plan. Twenty-six percent of undergraduate classes have more than 50 students. "Faculty members often compensate for large class sizes by making themselves extremely accessible," says a public health major, and many professors are tops in their field.

For those interested in skirting the masses, UW's Honors Program offers small classes on interesting subjects taught by fine professors. "All of my best experiences and opportunities have been through the Honors Program: from scholarships, to the Honors Living Learning Community in the residence halls, to Honors-specific study abroad courses," cheers a sophomore. Fourteen percent of all undergraduates study abroad via more than 90 faculty-led programs as well as options at more than 70 partner institutions across the globe. A program in experiential learning encourages students to find internships, and a variety of classes give students the opportunity to volunteer as part of their coursework. In addition, 30 percent of undergrads conduct faculty-mentored research.

"The residence halls are really new and nice facilities for the most part."

Sixty-seven percent of undergraduates are state residents, and although the university has traditionally preferred to keep its focus on the home folks, it now has a notably large proportion of international students, at 14 percent. It also has an unusually large population of students over the age of 25. The student body is 27 percent Asian American, 9 percent Hispanic/Latino, 3 percent Black, and 8 percent multiracial. The campus, like its host city, is politically liberal. Students, says a senior, "are go-getters and active in the world around them." Merit-based scholarships averaging $4,000 per year are available to high-achieving students, and the university also doles out nearly 450 athletic scholarships. The Washington College Grant provides free or reduced tuition for in-state students from low- and middle-income families who meet certain requirements. The grant is funded in part by a statewide tax on Washington-based businesses like Amazon and Microsoft that depend on highly skilled workers.

Thirty-one percent of students live in the school's 12 co-ed dorms, including 69 percent of freshmen. "The residence halls are really new and nice facilities for the most part. The main drawback is that they are pretty expensive," says a junior. Most students live off campus in Seattle or other parts of King County. Each dorm has its own cafeteria and fast-food line based on a debit card system. The Husky Union Building also offers a dining hall, espresso bar (don't forget, this is Seattle!), writing center, sun deck, and lounges. Regarding campus safety, a freshman cautions, "Since campus is in an urban area, you really have to be careful at night."

"The social life at UW is disconnected," says a senior, due to the large commuter population and the diverse social options that draw students into the city every weekend. On campus, the social scene tends to be defined by the Greeks and the 1,000-plus student organizations that sponsor various activities. Thirteen percent of the men and 12 percent of the women join a combined total of 65 fraternities and sororities. Alcohol is allowed on campus for students 21 and over but marijuana is not (despite being legal in the state of Washington), and students report that policies are strictly enforced. One tradition everyone looks forward to is Dawg Daze in the fall,

> **"Since campus is in an urban area, you really have to be careful at night."**

which "consists of 200-plus events to welcome first-year students and returning students from their summer vacations," explains a communication major. Sooner or later most students hit "the Ave," University Way, where shops and restaurants await them. Two new light-rail stations, one at either side of campus, or a 10-minute bus ride connect students to a full array of urban offerings in Seattle. The Seattle Center and other venues host outstanding operas, symphonies, touring shows, and major league sports.

But who needs pro sports with Washington's Division I Huskies around? Husky Fever breaks out on every football weekend, and the stands are always packed for UW's team, especially when Washington State comes to town to vie for the coveted Apple Cup. Women's rowing won a national championship in recent years, while volleyball, men's rowing, and men's golf have claimed Pac-12 conference titles. UW offers more than 35 club sports and 30 intramural leagues, in which 30 percent of students compete. More than anything else, the great outdoors defines the University of Washington. The campus offers breathtaking views of Lake Washington and the Cascade and Olympic mountains. Outdoor pastimes for students include boating, hiking, camping, and skiing, all found nearby, and Canada is close enough for road trips to Vancouver. The weather is consistently temperate, and natives insist that the city's reputation for rain is undeserved. Then again, the sports stadium has an overhang to protect spectators from showers.

"UW gives you a reality check that you're not as smart or as special as you think you are, and then shows you all the potential that you still have and gives you the guidance and tools to be successful," says a junior. While some students will not appreciate the occasionally impersonal academics, many students can overlook these obstacles for the big picture of the up-and-coming University of Washington—one that takes in more than just the beautiful scenery.

First-Year Interest Groups, which consist of 20 to 25 students, benefit from a weekly seminar led by a junior or senior peer advisor.

Overlaps

UC Berkeley, UCLA, UT Austin, U of I at Urbana–Champaign, University of Michigan, University of Oregon, UC San Diego, UC Santa Barbara

Washington and Jefferson College

60 South Lincoln Street, Washington, PA 15301

Premed Central would be as accurate a name as any for W&J, which has one of the nation's highest proportions of students who go on to medical school. Law school and business school are also popular destinations, and undergraduates in all fields pack their bags to conduct independent research in far-flung locales through the innovative Magellan Project. The Greek system dominates social life.

Website: www.washjeff.edu
Location: Small Town
Private
Total Enrollment: 1,134
Undergraduates: 1,134
Male/Female: 51/49
Financial Aid: 99%
Pell Grant: 31%
Expense: Pr $ $
Student Loans: 82%
Average Debt: $ $ $ $
Applicants: 3,150
Accepted: 84%
Enrolled: 12%
Grad in 6 Years: 71%
Returning Freshmen: 78%
Academics: ✍ ✍ ✍
Social: ☎ ☎ ☎
Q of L: ★ ★
Admissions: (724) 223-6025
Email Address: admission@ washjeff.edu

Strong Programs:
Business Administration
Chemistry
English
Communication Arts
Economics
Biological Physics
Accounting
Psychology

Wannabe doctors and lawyers would be well-advised to give Washington and Jefferson College a look. This small Pennsylvania college, founded in 1781 by Presbyterian ministers, is renowned for its preprofessional programs, and graduates are almost guaranteed acceptance into medical or health-related graduate programs. At the same time, the college's curriculum is growing more interdisciplinary and international in scope and putting more emphasis on independent student work. Classes remain small here and, despite the somewhat rural location, students enjoy an active social life thanks to a hearty Greek scene and the nearby city of Pittsburgh.

The campus, like the student body, is tight-knit: more than 50 buildings sit on 65 acres in a small town about 30 miles outside of Pittsburgh. W&J is the 11th-oldest college in the country and houses the eighth-oldest college building, which was built in 1793. The school got its name following the merger shortly after the Civil War of two colleges whose names you can probably guess. The prevailing architectural style is traditional colonial/Georgian, though modern structures have been added at a rapid pace during the past two decades.

> "Because it is such a small campus, you know everyone in your academic field."

Graduation requirements call for students to take a range of liberal arts and sciences courses and demonstrate proficiency in writing, speaking, reading, quantitative reasoning, foreign language, and use of information technology. Every first-year student enrolls in a first-year seminar selecting from 25 options, many of which involve college-sponsored trips to major East Coast cities and some of which are linked to living/learning communities. All graduating seniors take part in a capstone experience.

Given that W&J is a magnet for students who plan to pursue M.D.s, J.D.s, and M.B.A.s, some of the school's most popular majors are business administration, accounting, psychology, political science, and biology. Chemistry, English, communication arts, economics, and biological physics are also strong. An entrepreneurship minor gives students the chance to interact with founders of Fortune 500 companies, and the interdisciplinary computing and information studies major offers five concentrations, in big data, computer science, digital media, interaction design, and web and mobile technologies. A thematic major allows students to design their own course of study. Rare among liberal arts colleges are the 3–4 programs with the Pennsylvania Colleges of Optometry and Podiatry. More technically minded students can take advantage of 3–2 engineering programs with Case Western Reserve, Columbia, and WashU in St. Louis.

W&J's formula for success starts with individual attention in small classes; 81 percent of classes have fewer than 20 students, and a sophomore says, "Professors don't just read off a slide, they actually teach and engage in discussion." Students agree that the academic climate is tough, especially for those on the premed and prelaw tracks, but as a business major points out, "Because it is such a small campus, you know everyone in your academic field very well. This makes it very easy to work with others on a problem you have or on a project." In addition to faculty advisors and peer mentors, a Student Success Consultant meets with students one-on-one to guide them through their first year. More than 70 percent of students do internships, and a robust alumni mentorship program ensures that every W&J student who wants an alumni mentor and career coach will have one.

An entrepreneurship minor gives students the chance to interact with founders of Fortune 500 companies.

The Magellan Project provides funding for approximately 100 freshmen, sophomores, and juniors to put their liberal arts education to work each year through self-designed summer research projects or internships that involve domestic or international travel. Past projects have studied sea turtle rehabilitation in Australia and early childhood education in Denmark. "The Magellan Project is by far the best opportunity that W&J offers," enthuses one participant. The Washington Fellows Program is an honors program that provides participating students a bevy of special opportunities to interact with distinguished faculty, alumni, and guests. During the January intersession, students find brief apprenticeships in prospective career areas, take a short-term tour abroad, or engage in nontraditional coursework. Twelve percent of students study abroad, and the Office of Study Abroad offers about 40 approved semester- and year-abroad options in more than 20 countries.

W&J students describe their classmates as "goal-oriented" and "willing to help others." Sixty-nine percent of students hail from Pennsylvania and many are from neighboring states in the Northeast; 1 percent are international. Eight percent of students are Black, 5 percent are Hispanic/Latino, 2 percent are Asian American, and 5 percent are multiracial.

"The Magellan Project is by far the best opportunity that W&J offers."

Students report an even split between liberals and conservatives on campus and a "respectful atmosphere regarding political issues." Students get something of a bargain if they win an academic scholarship, which averages $30,200. The college does not award athletic scholarships.

Students can live in either co-ed or single-sex dorms, and 89 percent of students live on campus. Housing is guaranteed for four years, and students say the freshman dorms are "adequate," but the choices get better with academic rank and include suite-style and apartment options for upperclassmen. Campus meals get mostly positive reviews. "The dining facilities have become healthier and offer more options for students with dietary needs," comments a biology major. W&J has launched bystander awareness training and a student group of peer advocates to help educate the community on preventing sexual violence.

The Magellan Project provides funding for self-designed summer research projects or internships that involve domestic or international travel.

The active Greek scene draws 21 percent of the men and 29 percent of the women, and chapter parties are said to be "very inclusive and welcoming" of non-Greeks. The Student Activity Board has worked to offer more on-campus events, such as free movies, cultural events, and Big Bingo, "a huge bingo event with epic prizes," explains a senior. At the HUB, students enjoy big-screen televisions, Netflix, pool tables, and a student-run café that gives away free food and milkshakes every weekend. George & Tom's snack bar has become a favorite hangout with a stage for comedy and musical acts. There are also numerous student organizations to join, from the equestrian club to the student theater company. During the course of the year, Democracy Day, the Spring Street Fair, and Spring Concert are the most popular events.

Not all students share the administration's appreciation for "the unique characteristics of the western Pennsylvania milieu." Many complain that there is nothing to do in Washington, a former steel/mining town of 13,000, now hit by hard times. While relations with the locals can be a bit strained, students try to assuage this by actively volunteering in the community. One student says, "Most people just make the drive to Pittsburgh," which is 30 minutes away; the University of Pittsburgh and Penn State are popular destinations for more diverse social opportunities.

Just about anyone has a shot at the Division III varsity sports at W&J, where the teams are known, naturally, as the Presidents. Recent Presidents' Athletic Conference champions include baseball and women's lacrosse. Twenty-four percent of students participate in intramural and recreational sports, with flag football, basketball, and softball attracting the most interest.

With expanding academic options and the freedom to self-design experiences abroad, W&J is opening more and more doors for students. Students praise the education they receive and the school's close-knit environment. As one sophomore sums up, "If you want to get into med school, law school, or grad school, W&J is a great launching pad."

Overlaps

Allegheny, College of Wooster, Juniata, Knox, Ursinus, Penn State, University of Pittsburgh, Duquesne

If You Apply To ›

W&J: Early decision, early action, regular decision. SATs or ACTs: optional. Accepts the Common Application with supplement.

Washington and Lee University

Lexington, VA 24450

The ninth oldest university in the U.S., tradition-bound W&L is one of the most selective small colleges in the South, rivaled only by Davidson. W&L supplements the liberal arts with strong programs in business and journalism. Picture-postcard campus is three hours from Washington, D.C. Honor System thrives, but diversity has a long way to go. Greeks dominate the social scene.

Website: www.wlu.edu
Location: Small City
Private
Total Enrollment: 2,225
Undergraduates: 1,847
Male/Female: 49/51
Financial Aid: 54%
Pell Grant: 10%
Expense: Pr $ $ $ $
Student Loans: 32%
Average Debt: $ $
Applicants: 6,614
Accepted: 19%
Enrolled: 39%
Grad in 6 Years: 94%
Returning Freshmen: 96%
Academics: ✐ ✐ ✐ ✐ ½
Social: ☎ ☎ ☎

Washington and Lee University, which shares the town of Lexington, Virginia, with the Virginia Military Institute, has always epitomized Southern gentility. The Fancy Dress Ball is a highlight of each year, the Honor System is revered, and the long-standing "Speaking Tradition" ensures at least casual communication between members of the W&L community when they pass one another on the well-manicured grounds. But this is not your grandfather's W&L. Nearly four decades after women were first admitted, today's atmosphere is a little less 19th century and a little more 21st century—as befits one of the South's leading liberal arts colleges. Says a senior, "Each individual walks away with a unique sense of what it means to be an honorable, thoughtful, civilized participant in a global society."

> "Everyone here has succeeded in the past and everyone wants to keep doing it."

Founded in 1749, W&L is named after George Washington, whose donation to the school in 1796 saved it from dire financial straits, and Robert E. Lee, who was president of the college from 1865 until his death in 1870. After an agonizing year-long discussion, university trustees voted in 2021 to retain Lee as part of the school's name. In doing so, they issued a statement deploring "the university's past veneration of the Confederacy" and the fact that it once owned slaves. They also stripped Lee's name from the campus chapel (his burial site), canceled the annual Founder's

Day celebration on his birthday, and announced a number of steps designed to "expand diversity and inclusion." W&L's wooded campus sits atop a hill of lush green lawns, sweeping from one national landmark to another. The Colonnade is the school's most iconic group of buildings—stately redbrick structures with white Doric columns—and the prevailing architectural style is Greek Revival, although the physical face of the campus is changing. The school also boasts the $13.5 million Ruscio Center for Global Learning and the Elrod University Commons, which contains a dining hall, movie theater, and bookstore.

General education requirements account for one-third of a student's coursework and include a first-year writing seminar and courses in literature, fine arts, history, philosophy, religion, science and math, social science, foreign language, and physical education. The Spring Term is a single, four-week experience intended to offer students and faculty more innovative approaches to teaching and learning. Many use the term to study abroad; 51 percent of students spend time overseas at some point, traveling to destinations in more than 40 countries.

Although a standard liberal arts program remains the foundation of W&L's curriculum, the university offers excellent preprofessional programs, particularly in business and accounting, through the Williams School of Commerce, Economics, and Politics, as well as in journalism and engineering. Economics, politics, history, biochemistry, and neuroscience are popular choices as well. The Shepherd Program for the Interdisciplinary Study of Poverty and Human Capability offers a minor in poverty studies that requires students to complete an eight-week summer internship with an organization focused on poverty-related issues.

"Students don't compete much with each other, but they work very hard to improve themselves and their grades," explains a business and sociology double major. "Everyone here has succeeded in the past and everyone wants to keep doing it." Classes are small—77 percent have fewer than 20 students—and there are no teaching assistants. Says one student, "There are department heads teaching intro-level

> **"There are department heads teaching intro-level classes and senior seminars."**

classes and senior seminars, and since these classes are small all the way through, the quality of teaching is excellent." Well-qualified students can apply for the Summer Research Scholars Program, which offers students paid fellowships for assisting professors in research or doing their own; nearly half of undergrads conduct research. The famous Honor System lends a relaxed feeling to the otherwise rigorous academic climate. Tests and final exams are taken without faculty supervision; doors remain unlocked, laptops stay on desks, and library stacks are open 24 hours a day. Counseling and career services are highly praised. "The career counselors make an effort to get to know each student on an individual basis to position students for success," says a junior.

Seventeen percent of W&L students are native Virginians, and students from northeast of D.C. are well represented; international students make up 5 percent of the population. Amid ongoing and uphill efforts to increase diversity of all types, Black students currently account for 4 percent of the student body, Hispanics/Latinos 7 percent, Asian Americans 4 percent, and multiracial students 5 percent. Though the atmosphere is still more traditional than at most leading liberal arts colleges, the days of rock-ribbed conservatism are gone. Middle-of-the-road is perhaps the best way to describe the political leanings of today's student body. A sophomore notes, "Students are generally civil in discussing their various opinions."

W&L's Johnson Scholarship Program awards merit scholarships covering tuition, room, and board to approximately 10 percent of each entering class. Johnson Scholars also receive funding of up to $7,000 to support summer experiences like internships and research projects. As a Division III school, W&L does not offer

(continued)

Q of L: ★ ★ ★ ★

Admissions: (540) 458-8710

Email Address: admissions@wlu.edu

Strong Programs:
Business Administration
Accounting
Journalism
Economics
Politics
History
Biochemistry
Neuroscience

Under the famous Honor System, doors remain unlocked, laptops stay on desks, and library stacks are open 24 hours a day.

athletic scholarships. The university guarantees to meet the full demonstrated financial need—without loans—of all admitted students, and for those whose families earn less than $125,000 annually, the W&L Promise program provides full-tuition grants. With these initiatives, socioeconomic diversity is slowly increasing, but only 10 percent of first-years are Pell-eligible and the majority of students still come from wealthy backgrounds. A senior observes, "There are challenges for lower-income students due to implicit expectations, such as appearances and social expenses." Despite such challenges, a first-generation student urges, "We need diverse students at Washington and Lee, and the support system from the university is in place to welcome them."

For students whose families earn less than $125,000 annually, the W&L Promise program provides full-tuition grants.

Seventy-six percent of students reside on campus, as they are required to do for their first three years. Students spend their first year in recently renovated, co-ed dorms. Many sophomores move into Greek houses or theme houses, while upperclassmen opt for apartment- and townhouse-style accommodations. First-year students must purchase a meal plan, and dining options get good reviews. Students say the Honor System, campus security personnel, and thorough training programs on preventing and responding to sexual assault contribute to their feelings of safety on campus.

"We have the largest percentage of Greek students in the nation."

"We have the largest percentage of Greek students in the nation, so Greek life definitely sets the tone for the social scene," explains a junior. "Our parties are very inclusive: anyone is allowed to walk into any house on campus when there is a party happening." Seventy-five percent of the men and 71 percent of the women take part in Greek life. A lot of creative energy goes into fraternity bashes, which often feature live bands, although the formal Fancy Dress Ball (a.k.a. "$100,000 prom") and the Black Ball, sponsored by the Student Association for Black Unity, also draw raves. While underage drinking is banned in the dorms, students insist that their peers "like to party and drink." Friday Underground, a weekly coffeehouse with free food, coffee, and student performances, has proven to be a popular social alternative. W&L's mock political convention for the party out of power, held every four years, has predicted past presidential nominees with uncanny accuracy.

The Outing Club, the largest student organization on campus, organizes day trips in the Appalachian Mountains throughout the year.

The school's scenic location in the midst of the Appalachian Mountains means an abundance of activities for nature lovers, including hunting, fishing, camping, mountain biking, skiing, and tubing on the rivers. The Outing Club, the largest student organization on campus, organizes day trips throughout the year and lengthier excursions during school breaks. Lexington, a "quiet, friendly town that has much history to offer," also offers a few bars, two movie theaters, and several restaurants. Washington, D.C., Richmond, Charlottesville, and Roanoke are easily reached by car for weekend trips.

W&L offers 24 varsity sports at the Division III level, and most teams participate in the Old Dominion Athletic Conference. In recent years, the Generals have taken home conference championships in football, men's and women's swimming and tennis, and women's field hockey, golf, lacrosse, riding, and volleyball. The university sponsors approximately 25 club and intramural sports, ranging from a nationally competitive club rugby team to skiing and fly-fishing.

"Washington and Lee is an institution with a lot of history, but per our motto, we are 'not unmindful of the future,'" says an English major. A sense of history and tradition does indeed pervade the campus, from the liberal arts curriculum to the time-tested Honor System, even as the university attempts to minimize the legacy of Robert E. Lee. W&L continues to focus on preparing students to succeed in a more globally interconnected world. According to a biology major, one thing remains constant: "W&L is a tight-knit community with trust and honor at the forefront."

Overlaps

Williams, Amherst, Swarthmore, Pomona, Wellesley, Davidson, Middlebury, William & Mary

Washington College

300 Washington Avenue, Chestertown, MD 21620

Washington College is one of the oldest schools in the country. Small liberal arts college with strengths in creative writing, American history, and environmental science. The college has George Washington rather than Thomas Jefferson as its *éminence grise*. Chestertown is small and quaint, so students make their own fun. Best known for the annual Sophie Kerr Prize—worth more than $68,000 to a graduating senior.

Chartered in 1782 in the closing days of the American Revolution, Washington College was the first college to be established in the newly independent United States, and the first to adopt a thoroughly secular mission: educating citizens, patriots, and leaders for the new democracy. It takes its name from George Washington, who never slept in any of its dorms but who did make a modest founding grant of 50 guineas and served as a trustee. His spirit looms over the campus as strongly as that of "Mr. Jefferson" at UVA. One of the first things freshmen do upon arrival is sign the Honor Code (WC students cannot tell lies). The college is now focused on increasing the quality of its academic programs and becoming more affordable for students of limited financial means.

Washington College sits on 112 acres adjacent to downtown Chestertown, a quiet community of 5,100 on the Chester River on the eastern shore of Chesapeake Bay. Most buildings are redbrick, Georgian-style structures connected by old brick walkways and enhanced by large shade trees. The historic heart of the campus is the green where commencement is held and where a bronze statue of You Know Who keeps watch. The Gibson Center of the Arts, the Toll Science Center, and the Hodson Commons mix large expanses of glass with traditional red brick. The college has invested millions in renovations and new facilities in recent years; renovations to two residence halls, Reid and Minta Martin, were completed in 2022.

> **"Classes are challenging and require a high level of work in order to excel."**

First-year students begin their studies with a required First-Year Seminar course in which they develop their reading, writing, research, discussion, and presentation skills. In addition to standard distribution requirements, students must also complete a senior capstone experience that, depending on their major field, can take the form of a comprehensive exam, thesis, scientific research project, theatrical production, or portfolio of writing or artwork.

While the most popular majors include business management, biology, psychology, political science, and economics, the college's signature academic strengths are English literature and creative writing. Regardless of their disciplines, all students are expected to develop writing proficiency, and the college offers a four-year integrated approach to nurturing good writers. The school has a long-standing tradition of bringing writers such as Alice McDermott, Mark Doty, and Tim O'Brien to campus. The Rose O'Neill Literary House is a cultural hub where

Website: www.washcoll.edu
Location: Small Town
Private
Total Enrollment: 1,004
Undergraduates: 1,004
Male/Female: 42/58
Financial Aid: 99%
Pell Grant: 25%
Expense: Pr $ $
Student Loans: 74%
Average Debt: $ $ $
Applicants: 2,893
Accepted: 70%
Enrolled: 13%
Grad in 6 Years: 71%
Returning Freshmen: 84%
Academics: ✍ ✍ ✍
Social: ☎ ☎ ☎
Q of L: ★ ★ ★
Admissions: (410) 778-7700
Email Address:
   wc_admissions@washcoll.edu

Strong Programs:
English and Creative Writing
History
American Studies
Environmental Science and
   Studies
Business Management
Biology
Psychology
Political Science

students can discuss poetry and literature over a cup of tea and freshly baked cookies. Seniors from all disciplines may submit writing portfolios to vie for the Sophie Kerr Prize. Named after a popular American writer of the early 20th century, it is the largest undergraduate literary prize in the country and inevitably gives the school its annual 15 minutes of fame in the national media. The 2022 winner took home a check for $68,292.

Not surprisingly, WC is also a wonderful place to study history and American studies. The Starr Center for the Study of the American Experience, located in the old Custom House on the Chester River, helps students study the culture of the Native Americans who once populated the area, trace the Revolutionary War campaigns in the Chesapeake region, and explore the area's maritime heritage from aboard *Sultana*, a reproduction 18th-century schooner. WC also takes advantage of its rural setting and nearby waterways to offer a strong program in environmental science and studies. The Center for Environment & Society promotes stewardship of the area's natural resources, including a Chesapeake Semester that offers hands-on experience in the watershed and a trip to Costa Rica for comparative study. The River and Field Campus, located 10 minutes from the college's main campus, is a 7,400-acre living laboratory for avian research, local farming, and other environmental research. The college now offers a major in data science. A 3–2 dual-degree program in environmental studies is available with Duke University, as is a 3–2 engineering program with Columbia.

"The dining hall has greatly improved during my time here."

With the exception of a few introductory classes, students report that all of their instruction comes from full professors who are easily accessible, and 84 percent of classes have fewer than 20 students. "Professors make an effort to explain material from several perspectives so that all students understand and can engage in it," says a biology major. WC operates on a four-credits-per-course basis, with three hours of classes and students expected to work on their own for the fourth. "Classes are challenging and require a high level of work in order to excel," comments an environmental science major. Every freshman is assigned to a Peer Mentor, an older student who is trained to help them adjust to the academic and other sides of college life.

The Presidential Fellows program offers special academic opportunities to the top 20 percent of entering freshmen. One-third of WC students study abroad in programs offered in more than 30 countries. Short-term, faculty-led options are available during summer and winter breaks. The school's location 75 miles east of Washington, D.C., affords excellent access to internships, which 65 percent of students pursue. In recent years, WC students have interned at the National Archives, the U.S. Congress, and the Smithsonian. A political science major notes, "The Center for Career Development helps students connect with alumni in the workforce, find jobs, and even prepare for interviews."

"Students at Washington College are warm and welcoming," states an English and sociology major. Forty-two percent of students at Washington are from Maryland, and 3 percent hail from other countries. Black students represent 10 percent of the student body, Hispanics/Latinos 8 percent, and Asian Americans 3 percent. Students describe the campus as left-leaning, and according to an English and history major, a prominent issue of late has been "working to make the campus more inclusive" for students of color and LGBTQ+ students. Merit scholarships averaging $34,000 annually are available; there are no athletic scholarships. The Washington Scholars program awards full scholarship funding to high-achieving, high-need students.

"We love our namesake!"

All students are guaranteed on-campus housing for all four years, and 83 percent take up the offer. Rooms are assigned through a lottery with numbers based on class

The Rose O'Neill Literary House is a cultural hub where students can discuss literature over a cup of tea and freshly baked cookies.

Every freshman is assigned to a Peer Mentor, an older student who is trained to help them adjust to college life.

year. A sophomore reports that "not all dorms are created equal, but none of them are completely unacceptable." The newest dorm, Corsica, is among the choicest in a cluster of dorms located on what students call the "Western Shore," overlooking the athletic fields. Meals at the dining hall are all-you-can-eat, and a senior claims, "The dining hall has greatly improved during my time here," in terms of quality and options for vegans and vegetarians. Students give decent ratings to campus safety and efforts to raise awareness about sexual assault.

According to a sophomore, WC's social life is "slow-paced compared to other schools." There are occasional off-campus house parties, but the sleepy nature of Chestertown means that most social life takes place on campus, much of it coordinated by the school's 100 student organizations. The Student Events Board sponsors concerts, film series, open-mic nights, silent discos, bonfires, and other entertainment. Seven percent of the men belong to fraternities and 12 percent of the women to sororities. The Crab Feast, put on by the frères of Phi Delta Theta, is popular, as is the May Day celebration, which gives students an excuse to strip to their birthday suits at midnight and scamper around the quad. By far the biggest social event of the year is the formal Birthday Ball in February in honor of You-Know-Who's birthday. "We love our namesake!" cheers an English major. Students 21 and over are allowed to imbibe on campus, and students say alcohol policies are focused on student safety. A junior says, "Chestertown is quirky and charming, with historic buildings, music, food, art, and boutique shopping," but students seeking more active nightlife head for Annapolis, Baltimore, Philadelphia, or Washington, D.C.

WC's Shoremen and Shorewomen compete in the Division III Centennial Conference. Men's and women's rowing and the co-ed sailing team are nationally competitive, while men's soccer won a recent conference title. Students turn out in huge numbers for the annual War on the Shore, when the men's lacrosse team takes on its biggest rival, Salisbury University. Thirty-five percent of students participate in intramural and club sports; equestrian, eSports, dance, and soccer are popular offerings. Held once a month, Outdoor Adventure trips, like rock climbing, cycling, and crabbing and fishing charters, are widely anticipated.

After managing to be around for more than 240 years without making much of a splash beyond Chesapeake Bay, Washington College now seems bent on creating a niche for itself in academic areas where it has a comparative advantage, especially creative writing, American history, and the environment. Students describe WC as a "small, tight-knit community" bound by the classic values of a small liberal arts college. George would probably approve.

Held once a month, Outdoor Adventure trips, like rock climbing and crabbing and fishing charters, are widely anticipated.

Overlaps

Allegheny, Muhlenberg, Ursinus, Goucher, Transylvania, St. Mary's College of Maryland, University of Delaware, University of Maryland

If You Apply To ›

Washington College: Early decision, early action, regular decision. SATs or ACTs: optional. Accepts the Common Application.

Washington University in St. Louis

Campus Box 1089, One Brookings Drive, St. Louis, MO 63130-4899

Half a step behind Northwestern, on the shoulder of Vanderbilt, and a half step ahead of Emory, you'll find Washington University in St. Louis. No institution plays the rankings game with more zest—note the tiny acceptance rate due in part to favoring early decision and denying strong applicants who appear bound elsewhere. Core strength in the biological sciences with a halo effect from its top-ranked medical school; also elite in business. Preprofessional orientation, yet encourages exploration.

Website: www.wustl.edu
Location: City Outskirts
Private
Total Enrollment: 14,769
Undergraduates: 7,323
Male/Female: 48/52
Financial Aid: 50%
Pell Grant: 17%
Expense: Pr $ $ $
Student Loans: 25%
Average Debt: $
Applicants: 33,634
Accepted: 13%
Enrolled: 45%
Grad in 6 Years: 94%
Returning Freshmen: 96%
Academics: ✎ ✎ ✎ ✎ ½
Social: ☎ ☎ ☎ ☎
Q of L: ★ ★ ★ ★
Admissions: (800) 638-0700
Email Address: admissions@wustl.edu

Strong Programs:
Biology
Chemistry
Business
Engineering
Architecture
Design
Biomedical Engineering
Philosophy-Neuroscience-Psychology

Though it's always been well recognized regionally, Washington University in St. Louis long ago established itself as a truly national institution—with a friendly, relaxed Midwestern feel that differentiates it from the high-strung Eastern Ivies. Applications have skyrocketed, and with a hefty $12.3 billion endowment, strong preprofessional programs, and an emphasis on research, it's not hard to see why. An architecture major says, "WashU is a high-end, collaborative research institution dedicated more to the growth of its students than the growth of its own personal brand."

WashU was founded in 1853 and given its name to honor George Washington and his service to the country. Its 169-acre campus adjoins Forest Park, one of the nation's largest urban parks. Buildings are constructed in the collegiate Gothic style,

"WashU is a high-end, collaborative research institution."

mostly in red Missouri granite and white limestone, with plenty of climbing ivy, gargoyles, and arches. The state-of-the-art Knight and Bauer Halls are home to the Olin Business School and include classrooms designed to enhance student and faculty interaction. As part of a major construction initiative on the east end of campus, the university built four new academic and multiuse facilities for arts and engineering, expanded the campus art museum, and added a new dining pavilion and the Sumers Welcome Center.

Undergraduates enroll in one or more of WashU's five divisions—arts and sciences, architecture, art, business, or engineering. General education requirements vary by school and program. The university's offerings in the natural sciences, particularly biology and chemistry, have long been notable, especially among those on the premed track. Bio majors benefit from efforts to integrate undergraduate research into activities at WashU's outstanding medical school, which provides significant opportunities to conduct advanced laboratory research with faculty. WashU's business, engineering, architecture, and design programs are traditional strengths as well, and biomedical engineering has become a specialty. Double majors are encouraged, and interdisciplinary majors, such as philosophy-neuroscience-psychology and business and computer science, are growing rapidly.

Each academic division offers options for incoming freshmen to acclimate to the university environment and explore their options. In Arts & Sciences, for instance, students may take first-year seminars on diverse topics, such as The Secret Lives of Plants and Introduction to Memory Studies. Similarly, the Olin Business School's Foundations of Business Course, taught by senior faculty, focuses on a different topic each week. Students in the Beyond Boundaries program take team-taught, cross-disciplinary courses on a range of topics across the university's five divisions in their first year, before moving into the division of their choice as sophomores. Those seeking even broader horizons may study in their choice of more than 50 different countries, and 30 percent do so, often through faculty-led programs during the summer. Students report that it's easy to get involved with WashU's extensive research projects. "When I declared my psychology major, I was handed a stack of papers with about 45 different research opportunities (in the psych department alone!)," a sophomore enthuses.

Students agree that while academics are rigorous, the university's collaborative atmosphere is a major factor that sets it apart from its Ivy League competitors. "It's not a competitive culture or a weed-out school," comments an English and political science major. Those who are struggling will find plenty of help from teaching assistants (who conduct review sessions), academic advisors, study groups, and even a 24-hour peer counseling service called Uncle Joe's. Sixty-five percent of classes have fewer than 20 students, and undergrads have uncommon access to one-on-one mentoring relationships with top faculty. A junior says, "My professors are highly knowledgeable and largely able to convey their knowledge to students clearly."

Students in the Beyond Boundaries program take team-taught, cross-disciplinary courses in their first year.

"Most WashU students are really passionate about something but are rarely pretentious about it," says a junior. Eighty-two percent of undergraduates are out-of-staters, with a large contingent from Eastern states like New York and New Jersey, and another 7 percent are international. Black students account for 9 percent, Hispanics/Latinos 11 percent, Asian Americans 19 percent, and multiracial students 6 percent. "The Center for Diversity and Inclusion has become like a second home to me because of the great study space and the opportunities to have necessary dialogues with excellent professionals and fellow students," says a sophomore. Students are engaged in social and political issues, especially racial justice and renewable energy, and tend to be moderate but left-leaning.

"It's not a competitive culture or a weed-out school."

A limited number of academic scholarships averaging $33,300 are awarded each year, but there are no athletic scholarships. As part of its efforts to become more socioeconomically diverse, WashU adopted a need-blind admissions policy for domestic first-year applicants in 2021. The university has also replaced loans with grants for students from families with incomes below $75,000, in addition to awarding them more than $3,500 in grants to offset costs like the purchase of a personal computer. WashU meets the full demonstrated financial need of admitted students, and in recent years, it has doubled the proportion of freshmen who qualify for Pell Grants (17 percent). For Pell-eligible students from Missouri and Southern Illinois, the WashU Pledge covers the full cost of attendance for four years. A sophomore notes that, socially, "A person who is from a low-income background may have a difficult time fitting in due to the 'spending' culture at WashU."

Those who are struggling will find plenty of help from advisors, study groups, and even a 24-hour peer counseling service called Uncle Joe's.

Seventy-two percent of WashU students live in campus housing, including the co-ed dormitories known as residential colleges. "The rooms are larger than your average dorm room, and we have Tempur-Pedic mattresses," boasts a student. "If that doesn't qualify us as best housing, I don't know what would." Freshmen and most sophomores live on the "South 40" (40 acres located on the south end of the main campus); freshmen are guaranteed rooms, and gender-inclusive housing is available as an option. Upperclassmen may live in university-owned apartments, and some choose true off-campus digs in the nearby neighborhoods of University City and Clayton, where apartments are reasonably priced. Meal plans may be used in any of the dining centers, which students say are excellent. "Dining Services offers a wealth of options, with international cuisine, vegetarian, gluten-free, dairy-free, kosher, halal, and more available at each and every dining location," cheers a junior. Students give good ratings to campus safety, and a sophomore says, "Students are very well educated on all the resources available to address the issue of sexual assault."

"My professors are highly knowledgeable and largely able to convey their knowledge to students clearly."

"The social life is as abundant as each student makes it," says a junior, with ample options both on and off campus. WashU students pride themselves on being able to balance work and play, and on weekends, movies, fraternity parties, and concerts tear them away from their books. Every spring, the whole campus turns out for the century-old Thurtene Carnival, the oldest student-run philanthropic festival in the country. Student groups—especially fraternities and sororities, which attract 18 percent of the men and 12 percent of the women—build booths, sell food, and put on plays; profits are donated to a children's charity. Four student-led cultural shows—Diwali, Lunar New Year Festival, Black Anthology, and Carnaval—are always well attended. Another big event is WILD (Walk In Lay Down), held at the beginning and end of the academic year. Everyone brings blankets and inflatable couches to the main quad, assumes a horizontal position, and listens to big-name bands. Alcohol policies emphasize safe and responsible drinking, and students say that, in that regard, they are effective.

WashU offers robust recreational options because of its location abutting Forest Park: a golf course, an ice-skating rink, a zoo, a lake with boat rentals, art and history museums, an outdoor theater, and a science center are all within a short walk. So too are the restaurants, bars, shops, and galleries of the Delmar Loop. The St. Louis Blues and Cardinals attract pro hockey and baseball fans, and the city is also home to the addictive Ted Drewes frozen custard. The school runs a free shuttle service to parts of St. Louis not within walking distance and offers a Metro Pass for free access to the city's bus and light-rail systems. "St. Louis is often described as the largest small town you will ever visit or the smallest big city you will ever see," says a sophomore. "I appreciate St. Louis because there is plenty to do without it being overwhelming." Community service programs such as Each One Teach One, in partnership with the city's schools, attract a sizable number of students. The best road trips include Chicago, Nashville, Memphis, and Lake of the Ozarks, as well as Columbia, Missouri—home of the University of Missouri.

"I appreciate St. Louis because there is plenty to do without it being overwhelming."

The WashU Bears compete in Division III, and the men's indoor track and field team won the national championship in 2022. Men's and women's soccer and outdoor track and field, men's basketball, and women's cross-country have claimed University Athletic Association conference titles in recent years. About half of the students compete in 40 club sports or play intramural sports, ranging from badminton, racquetball, and flag football to pocket billiards and ultimate Frisbee.

Word among high school counselors is that most students don't get admitted to selectivity-conscious WashU through regular admissions—you are either locked in through early admissions or cherry-picked off the waitlist. But however they get there, students find WashU both academically challenging and personally supportive. As one senior reflects, "The atmosphere is not only about learning academically, but growing as a person."

Overlaps

Northwestern, Duke, Vanderbilt, Rice, Johns Hopkins, Yale, U Penn, University of Michigan

If You Apply To ›

WashU: Early decision I and II, regular decision. Accepts the Common Application with supplement. Apply to one of five undergraduate schools. Portfolio is required for applicants to College of Art and recommended for applicants to College of Architecture. Please consult WashU's website for the most up-to-date information regarding standardized test requirements.

Wellesley College

Wellesley, MA 02481

There is no better recipe for popularity than first-rate academics and a postcard-perfect campus on the outskirts of Boston. That formula keeps Wellesley atop the women's college pecking order—along with superb programs in economics and the natural sciences. Among leading women's colleges, only Barnard accepts a lower percentage. Just over half of undergraduates are students of color.

Wellesley College is not just the best women's college in the nation—it's one of the best colleges in the nation, period. With a history dating to 1870 and an alumnae roster that includes Hillary Rodham Clinton, Diane Sawyer, the late Madeleine Albright, and Madame Chiang Kai-shek, Wellesley should be at the top of the list for high achievers who are seeking the benefits of an all-women's college. Wellesley women excel in whatever field they choose, including traditional male bastions like economics and the sciences. "Wellesley is an energetic and serious place," says a senior. "When you come on campus, you can just feel that we're doing very important work here."

Nestled in a Boston suburb, the Wellesley campus, one of the most beautiful anywhere, occupies 500 rolling acres of cultivated and natural areas, including Lake Waban. Campus buildings range in architectural style from Gothic (with stone towers and brick quadrangles) to state-of-the-art science, arts, and sports facilities. A 22-acre arboretum and botanical garden features a wide variety of trees and plants. The Davis Museum houses 11 galleries, a cinema, and a café. The five campus libraries, which include an academic art library, boast more than a million volumes. Several facilities have been renovated under the Wellesley Campus Renewal Plan, including the student services building, studio art and performance spaces, and the Science Center.

> **"You can just feel that we're doing very important work here."**

Wellesley has distribution requirements that include units in language and literature; visual arts, music, theater, film, and video; social and behavioral analysis; epistemology and cognition; religion, ethics, and moral philosophy; historical studies; natural and physical science; and mathematical modeling and problem-solving. In addition, students must take a first-year writing class, a foreign language, and a course on multiculturalism.

With its hefty $2.9 billion endowment (the largest among the nation's all-female colleges and universities) and lavish facilities, Wellesley offers a top-of-the-line educational experience. Some of the most popular majors are economics, political science, psychology, computer science, and biological sciences. Economics is known as the powerhouse; in fact, Wellesley has produced most of the country's high-ranking female economists. Biology is also strong, and students in biochemistry work with faculty on DNA research. Nearly two dozen interdepartmental majors are available in fields ranging from peace and justice studies to chemical physics to a notable program in international relations. Anything Wellesley women find lacking in their curriculum can probably be found at MIT, where they have full cross-registration privileges. Wellesley students can also take courses at nearby Babson College, Brandeis University, and Olin College of Engineering.

"Wellesley has a reputation for being competitive, but I find that's not entirely true," observes a mathematics major. "Most students are open to collaboration and willing to support each other." Under the honor system, students may take their finals, unsupervised, at any time during exam week. Class sizes are almost always

---

Website: www.wellesley.edu
Location: Suburban
Private
Total Enrollment: 2,381
Undergraduates: 2,381
Male/Female: 0/100
Financial Aid: 58%
Pell Grant: 22%
Expense: Pr $ $ $ $
Student Loans: 38%
Average Debt: $
Applicants: 7,665
Accepted: 16%
Enrolled: 49%
Grad in 6 Years: 92%
Returning Freshmen: 97%
Academics: ✍ ✍ ✍ ✍ ✍
Social: ☎ ☎ ☎
Q of L: ★ ★ ★ ★
Admissions: (781) 283-2270
Email Address: admission@wellesley.edu

Strong Programs:
Economics
Biology
Biochemistry
International Relations
Peace and Justice Studies
Political Science
Psychology
Computer Science

small. Professors are highly respected and make themselves readily available. "My professors have always been engaging," says a biochemistry major. "I never thought a class like Integrated Biophysical Chemistry could be discussion heavy." First-years (as they are exclusively called here) have both faculty advisors and peer mentors. Students give rave reviews to Wellesley's recently revamped career services, which "place emphasis on establishing connections," according to an econ major, but complain that the counseling center is understaffed. In an effort to alleviate first-year students' stress about grades as they adjust to Wellesley's rigorous atmosphere, the college employs a shadow-grading policy, in which their first-semester grades do not appear on their academic transcripts.

Seventy-seven percent of students conduct undergraduate research or independent study, and grants from private foundations have allowed Wellesley to add innovative programs, including independent research tutorials for advanced science students and fellowship funding for joint student/faculty projects. Half of the students study abroad through 180 approved programs, including Wellesley-run programs in France and Germany. Through the Albright Institute, 40 students each year are chosen to be Albright Fellows, attending classes with both Wellesley and visiting professors, then completing a funded summer internship abroad; past Fellows have interned with the U.S. State Department, the European Union Chamber of Commerce, and the Human Rights Education and Monitoring Center.

> **"I never thought a class like Integrated Biophysical Chemistry could be discussion heavy."**

What are Wellesley women like? A sophomore says, "Think Beyoncé: empowered, smart, and driven." Only 16 percent of students are from Massachusetts, and although the Northeast is the best represented geographical area, students come from every state and more than 85 countries; 14 percent are international. Eight percent are Black, 22 percent are Asian American, 15 percent are Hispanic/Latina, and 6 percent are multiracial. "Wellesley is very LGBTQIA+ friendly," reports a neuroscience major, and a psychology major adds, "We are liberal and very outspoken about racism, different forms of sexism and misogyny, cultural clashes, etc." All financial aid awards are based on need—meaning no merit scholarships—but admissions for U.S. citizens and permanent residents are need-blind, and Wellesley meets the full calculated need of admitted students. Wellesley has also eliminated loans for families with incomes below $100,000 per year (with typical assets) and has reduced loans for others.

Residence life at Wellesley is a step ahead of most institutions. Virtually every student lives on campus, and residence halls feature high-ceilinged living rooms, hardwood floors, fireplaces, walk-in closets, kitchenettes with microwaves, and even grand pianos. First-years are housed in the same halls as upperclasswomen, and juniors and seniors are generally granted single rooms. Peer tutors also live in each hall and are trained to tutor in specific subjects, as well as in study skills and time management. Meal cards are valid in all dining halls and at the campus snack bar, which is stocked with everything from milk and flour to Twinkies. "We have a dining hall that is vegetarian and kosher, as well as one that is nut-free," says a sophomore. Campus security is strong, and a junior notes, "Sexual assault cases are minimal on campus, but students have access to a number of resources for sexual education and reporting."

> **"Think Beyoncé: empowered, smart, and driven."**

Wellesley's social scene tends to be quiet, although as a sophomore explains, "All of the student organizations have to host at least one all-campus event every semester, meaning there is always a dance, mixer, cultural show, or movie being shown." The Lulu Chow Wang Campus Center, referred to affectionately as "the

> *Wellesley has produced most of the country's high-ranking female economists.*

> *Half of the students study abroad through 180 approved programs, including Wellesley-run programs in France and Germany.*

Lulu," is a hub of activity day and night, with its student-run pub, Café Hoop, and coffeehouse. The closest thing Wellesley has to sororities are nonresidential societies, which sometimes host parties, for arts and music, literature, Shakespeare, politics, and general lectures. Service is also a key component of the Wellesley community, dating back to the college's inception. Wellesley's motto, *Non ministrari sed ministrare*, translates to "Not to be served, but to serve."

Wellesley is chock-full of traditions, the most endearing of which include Flower Sunday (where first-years are paired with older students in a welcome ceremony), step-singing (an all-campus sing-along on the chapel steps), Spring Weekend (with a big-name band and comedian), and a hoop-rolling contest by seniors in their graduation robes. The winner of this contest will supposedly be the first in her class to achieve her goals, whatever they may be, and she gets off to a flying start when her classmates toss her in the lake. The lake is also the site of Lake Day, when students take a break from classes to enjoy a festival held on the lawn.

Wellesley's "Scream Tunnel" is legendary among Boston Marathon runners.

The town of Wellesley is an upper-crust Boston suburb without many amenities for students. "Be forewarned," cautions a student, "Wellesley is a snobby town of rich people." Still, when it comes to weekend fun, Wellesley is in a prime location. Not even half an hour away, Boston attracts students with all manner of social opportunities. Cambridge—with Harvard Square, MIT frat parties, and

"Wellesley is very LGBTQIA+ friendly."

lots of clubs and cafés—is accessible by an hourly school shuttle that runs on weekdays and weekends. There is also a commuter rail station located a short walk from campus. Cape Cod, Providence, and the Vermont and New Hampshire ski slopes are close by car.

Many students balance their academic schedule with Division III athletics, intramurals, and club sports. The rowing team is a perennial contender for the national title. Other top Blue teams include swimming and diving, soccer, and volleyball. The big athletic rival is Smith College, another of the Seven Sisters group of great women's colleges. The sports center, named the Nannerl Keohane Sports Center in honor of Wellesley's 11th president (who went on to run Duke), offers an Olympic-size pool; squash, racquetball, and tennis courts; dance studios; a weight room; and an indoor track. Harvard's Head of the Charles crew race and the Boston Marathon—Wellesley's "Scream Tunnel" is legendary among runners worldwide—share honors as the most popular spectator sports of the year.

When it comes to academics, Wellesley women are serious. Their school is competitive with all but the top three Ivies. Many of them enjoy the traditions of the school and appreciate the idyllic atmosphere for contemplation but know they are poised to dominate whatever field they enter. "Female empowerment isn't served with dinner, and we don't get confidence boosts for dessert," muses one student. "But somehow, after just a few years here, all my ideas about what's actually possible and how much I'm truly capable of have changed."

If You Apply To ›

Wellesley: Early decision I and II, regular decision. Accepts the Common Application with supplement. Accepts applications from students who live as women and consistently identify as female, as well as students who were assigned female at birth and identify as nonbinary. Current students participate on admissions board. Please consult Wellesley's website for the most up-to-date information regarding standardized test requirements.

Wells College

Aurora, NY 13026

Founded in 1868 by Henry Wells of stagecoach fame, Wells is a small liberal arts college that shares the fabled "waves of blue" of Cayuga Lake with much larger Cornell. A family atmosphere is its hallmark, right down to the dinner bell that calls everyone to the evening meal. Big on interdisciplinary study and internships during the frosty January term. A model of socioeconomic diversity.

Website: www.wells.edu
Location: Rural
Private
Total Enrollment: 335
Undergraduates: 335
Male/Female: 39/61
Financial Aid: 99%
Pell Grant: 61%
Expense: Pr $
Student Loans: 92%
Average Debt: $ $ $ $
Applicants: 2,167
Accepted: 68%
Enrolled: 9%
Grad in 6 Years: 55%
Returning Freshmen: 46%
Academics: ✍ ✍ ✍
Social: ☎ ☎
Q of L: ★ ★ ★ ★
Admissions: (315) 364-3264
Email Address: admissions@ wells.edu

Strong Programs:
Sociology and Anthropology
Education
Women's and Gender Studies
Biology
Psychology
Business
English
Book Arts

Wells College moved beyond its origins as a women's college in 2005 when it began accepting men, but it has by no means abandoned its storied history. Whether it's riding to graduation in an old Wells Fargo stagecoach or showing off in the annual Odd-Even basketball game between freshmen and sophomores, the tradition of Wells is apparent at every turn. Enrollment has been fairly stable over the last decade, and with only 335 students, anonymity is nonexistent and close relationships with professors and peers come with the territory.

Most of the buildings on Wells's 365-acre campus, which is listed on the National Register of Historic Places, are old, massive, and covered with ivy—the way college ought to look, you might say. The lakeside location affords beautiful sunsets as well as boating and fishing opportunities for those looking for a break from academics. The renovated Sommer Student Center boasts a game room, student lounge, and pub.

Wells's recently revamped core curriculum combines a solid grounding in the liberal arts with hands-on experiences. Freshmen take a college writing course and a class that introduces them to the Wells environment. In addition to a number of distribution requirements, students take courses aimed at developing real-world skills like financial literacy and personal wellness. Students also undertake two experiential learning activities, one of which must be off campus, such as internships, study abroad, service-learning projects, or student teaching. Additionally, all students complete a senior capstone project in their major.

> "There is always someone there to help you achieve your goals."

The most popular majors include biology, psychology, business, and English; students also give high marks to sociology and anthropology, education, and women's and gender studies. Majors in inclusive childhood education and sustainability have recently been added, and there's an unusual minor in book arts. Individualized majors are an option for students whose needs are not met by established programs. There are also dual-degree programs in education with the University of Rochester; in business administration with Clarkson University; in engineering with Clarkson and Columbia; and in pharmacy with SUNY–Binghamton. For a change of pace, students may cross-register for up to four courses at Cornell University or Ithaca College.

"The academic climate is very collaborative in the sense that there is always someone there to help you achieve your goals," says a psychology major. Eighty-three percent of classes enroll fewer than 20 students, giving students easy access to faculty, and most courses are discussion-based, with the professor present to moderate and focus the conversation. The student-run collegiate association enforces the honor system, and take-home and self-scheduled tests are the rule rather than the exception. Wells uses a semester calendar with elements of the 4–1–4 plan, with internships, research, and study abroad taking place in January. Foreign study draws 30 percent of students; the college's flagship program in Florence, Italy, is especially popular.

"Wells students are polite and humble, and they are led by a sense of being one community," says a business major. Seventy-six percent of Wells students are state residents, while 1 percent are international. Black students make up 10 percent of the student body, Hispanics/Latinos 18 percent, Asian Americans 2 percent, and multiracial students 3 percent. Courses, workshops, and a support network for new students help to educate the campus on the importance of multiculturalism. Liberal social and political views are prominent, and women's rights, LGBTQ rights, and immigration policies are key topics of discussion. Wells practices need-blind admissions and has reduced its sticker price by about 25 percent. A notably high portion of freshmen—61 percent—qualify for Pell Grants. Numerous merit scholarships are awarded each year, but not for athletics.

All students are guaranteed college housing, and only 9 percent live off campus. There are plenty of single rooms, though first-years are typically assigned to doubles, and substance-free and single-sex options are available. "Some of the dorms at Wells are old, but that is what makes them special—they add a nice touch," says a junior. Some residences have bay windows and winding staircases, while others offer lake views. Meals are served in a magnificent Tudor-style dining hall with two working fireplaces, but the food gets lukewarm reviews. Security is "extremely reliable," says one student.

The college's flagship study abroad program in Florence, Italy, is especially popular.

"Traditions are the backbone of Wells College."

Though there are no Greek organizations at Wells, the school doesn't need them, given its bevy of other traditions. "Traditions are the backbone of Wells College," confirms a junior. For example, bells are rung every evening to announce dinner and also to celebrate the first snowfall of the season. Additionally, tea and coffee are served every Wednesday afternoon. Though the long dresses and china cups have long since disappeared, tea is still a great time to hang out with friends, faculty members, and staff, as well as a welcome break from long afternoon seminars. On the last day of classes, there's a celebration around the sycamore tree, where sophomores present roses to seniors. Then, the president of the college and her staff serve breakfast to the graduating class.

"Social life at Wells happens in the dining hall, at club/org meetings and events, and at athletic games," explains a computer science major. "However, there is little to do on campus when clubs and organizations aren't hosting anything." Students say the campus party scene is very low-key and alcohol policies are well enforced. The town of Aurora has a popular bar and grill and a hotel—and that's about it. "It's a small village, not a college town at all," says a student, but the residents are friendly and on good terms with students, especially since many student clubs participate in community service. Those looking for a more traditional college party scene head 30 miles south to Ithaca College and Cornell. Auburn and Syracuse are good for shopping, while New York City and Montreal offer shows and other big-city perks. Given the beautiful, hilly terrain, Wells students also enjoy camping in the warmer months and cross-country or downhill skiing in the winter, especially with the slopes of Greek Peak less than an hour away.

Tea and coffee are served every Wednesday afternoon, a great time to hang out with friends, faculty members, and staff.

Varsity teams at Wells compete in Division III, and since the school is so small, virtually anyone interested gets the chance to play. The Express men's and women's volleyball and swimming teams have been the most competitive. A fledgling intramural program offers kickball, dodgeball, and ultimate Frisbee, and dance is a popular club sport. Anyone may use the golf course and the college's tennis courts, while the field house offers a pool and other exercise equipment.

Along with its abundant traditions and close-knit atmosphere, Wells has retained what one student calls a "liberal, progressive, feminist, and independent" spirit, which most students say suits them just fine. "I believe the classes are good, the community is wonderful, and Wells really prepares you for life," says one student. "I already feel more independent having studied at Wells."

Overlaps

Ithaca, Hartwick, Albion, Keuka, Nazareth College, Canisius, College of Saint Elizabeth, SUNY–Albany

Wesleyan University

45 Wyllys Avenue, Middletown, CT 06459

Usually compared to Amherst or Williams, Wesleyan is really more like Swarthmore. The key differences: Wesleyan is twice as big and a little more streetwise. Wes students are progressive, politically minded, and fiercely independent. Multicultural specialties like ethnomusicology and East Asian studies add spice to the scene. New York and Boston are both two hours away but not easily accessible on public transportation.

Website: www.wesleyan.edu
Location: Small City
Private
Total Enrollment: 3,364
Undergraduates: 3,232
Male/Female: 44/56
Financial Aid: 45%
Pell Grant: 13%
Expense: Pr $ $ $ $
Student Loans: 34%
Average Debt: $ $
Applicants: 13,067
Accepted: 19%
Enrolled: 36%
Grad in 6 Years: 91%
Returning Freshmen: 95%
Academics: ✍ ✍ ✍ ✍ ✍
Social: ☎ ☎ ☎
Q of L: ★ ★ ★
Admissions: (860) 685-3000
Email Address: admission@
  wesleyan.edu

Strong Programs:
Film Studies
East Asian Studies
Economics
Neuroscience and Behavior
English
Music
Astronomy
Molecular Biology and Biochemistry

Whether they're engrossed in academics, debating and demonstrating over social issues, or engaged in community service, Wesleyan students seem to do things with a passion and intensity that helps set this school apart from tamer institutions. "There's an energy on this campus; for me, it's a spirit of creativity and political energy," a sophomore explains. In recent years, a significant number of Wesleyan alumni have gone on to make their mark in the high-tech world and the entertainment industry, including *Hamilton* creator Lin-Manuel Miranda, whose earlier Broadway hit, *In the Heights*, had its origins as a sophomore theater production.

Diversity at Wesleyan begins with the campus architecture. The nucleus of this stately university is a century-old row of lovely brownstones that look out over the football field. The rest of the buildings can be described as "eclectic" and range from mod-looking dorms of the '50s and '60s to the beautiful and modern Center for the Arts. Dozens of Wesleyan-owned wood-frame houses serve as senior residences that look freshly plucked from Main Street, USA. The Gordon Career Center is situated in the heart of the campus and features a multi-purpose career commons. Founded in 1831 when Methodists teamed up with local citizens, Wesleyan likes to describe itself as "a small college with university resources." The libraries have more than a million volumes, practically unheard-of at a school this size. Whenever you happen to walk past the brightly lit, glass-walled study room of Sci-Li (the science library), you're apt to see numerous students huddled over their books. A remodeled Public Affairs Center and a new art gallery are under construction, scheduled for completion in 2024.

> "Professors don't claim to know everything and appreciate students challenging their perspectives."

Wesleyan's curriculum ensures the relevance of liberal arts education in the 21st century by offering seminars for first-year students and clustering courses to help students reach their academic objectives. Students are expected to take a minimum of three courses in each of three areas—humanities and the arts, social and behavioral sciences, and natural sciences and mathematics. Wesleyan students can choose from among nearly 50 majors, in addition to a number of minors and certificate programs. At the end of their freshman year, students may apply to major in one of Wesleyan's competitive, interdisciplinary colleges, including the College of Letters (European literature, history, and philosophy), the College of Social Studies (history, government, political and social theory, and economics), and the Science in Society Program (which allows students to do advanced work in a science discipline while studying science and medicine through a philosophical, sociohistorical lens). Other interdisciplinary colleges offering linked majors include the College of the Environment, the College of Integrative Sciences, and the College of Educational Studies. The first-rate College of Film and the Moving Image enjoys an international reputation and recently completed construction of the $27 million Basinger Center for Film Studies. The College of East Asian Studies, another strength, offers advanced language courses and study abroad with a focus on cultural fluency, and it boasts an authentic Japanese tea room.

The College of East Asian Studies offers advanced language courses, study abroad, and an authentic Japanese tea room.

Wesleyan's most popular majors—economics, psychology, government, English, and neuroscience and behavior—are also some of its strongest. Music, astronomy, molecular biology and biochemistry, American studies, and earth and environmental sciences are also standouts. But even the smaller departments attract attention. Ethnomusicology, including African drumming and dance, is a stunning specialty; students can be found reclining on the wide, carpeted bleachers at the World Music Hall or watching a dozen musicians play the Indonesian gamelan. The math department emphasizes problem-solving in small groups rather than interminable lectures dedicated to theory. Undergraduates in the sciences and psychology work alongside faculty in their research laboratories and frequently earn the opportunity to publish in scientific journals. Students can also take advantage of dual-degree programs in engineering with Dartmouth, Caltech, and Columbia.

Despite Wesleyan's rigorous academics and heavy workload, students say the supportive atmosphere makes for a relatively relaxed feel. The university has used its wealth to attract highly rated faculty members who are expected to be scholar-teachers: academic superstars who juggle groundbreaking research, enthusiastic lectures, and personal student attention at the same time—and they seem to pull it off. "Professors don't claim to

"Inclusion—both on and off campus—is always the goal of student activism."

know everything and appreciate students challenging their perspectives," says a senior. Wesleyan strives to keep its classes small, and 73 percent of the courses have fewer than 20 students. "With popular classes, you have to be persistent, but you can get in," a history major says. If beseeching is not your style, studying abroad may be a temporary tonic to registration headaches. Programs are available in all areas of the world, and 43 percent of students typically take part. Internships are popular too.

Wesleyan's excellent reputation and strong recruiting network attract students from all over, ensuring the mash-up of viewpoints that makes it such a vital place. "Students at Wes are progressive and adventurous," muses a neuroscience and behavior major. "We're always willing to have a conversation and explore something new." Just 9 percent of undergraduates are Connecticut natives, and 11 percent hail from foreign nations. The student body is 6 percent Black, 11 percent Hispanic/Latino, 8 percent Asian American, and 7 percent multiracial. Students are mostly liberal and vocal about hot social and political issues. "Inclusion—both on and off campus—is always the goal of student activism," says a government major. Wesleyan meets the full demonstrated need of all admitted students, most of whom are admitted on a need-blind basis, and has a policy of waiving any loan obligation for most families with incomes below $120,000 per year.

Faculty members are scholar-teachers: academic superstars who juggle groundbreaking research, enthusiastic lectures, and personal student attention.

For housing, most freshmen are consigned to singles or doubles in the campus dorms. Students say the Butterfield complex is the choice for quiet study, while Clark Hall is where the party people go. Housing is guaranteed for four years, and upperclassmen who want to live off campus must apply for permission (very few do). "The housing system at Wesleyan is really unique. It's based on a system of progressive independence, so every year you have more freedom and more responsibility," explains a student. Upperclassmen enjoy townhouses for four or five students, as well as college-owned houses and apartments. Campus dining gets good reviews:

"Vegetarians love Wesleyan and so do meat eaters. There is an option for everyone," one student says. Students report feeling safe on campus and say the university has taken an active role in sexual assault prevention.

Greek membership is nominal, with just 2 percent of men and 2 percent of women joining up. After controversy over their single-sex status, some Greek groups have gone co-ed, and two former fraternities have turned into co-ed literary societies. Wesleyan's enforcement of the drinking age is relaxed compared with most schools. Consistent with the university's encouragement of independence, students bear a large part of the responsibility for policing themselves. "There is definitely a drinking/party culture, but there is absolutely no pressure to participate," says one senior. Activities abound from comedy performances to a cappella groups, films, plays, bands, lectures, parties, and events planned by the nearly 300 student groups. "Most students stay on campus for weekends and other social events," a junior says. Major events on the social calendar include WesRave, a silent dance party on Foss Hill, and the Spring Fling outdoor festival. Uncle Duke Day and Zonker Harris Day are two events with a more psychedelic, '60s flavor, in which students pay tribute to the infamous *Doonesbury* characters. And who could forget Undies in Olin, when "students strip to their underwear in Olin Library during admitted student tours in the spring," says a senior.

> **"Students strip to their underwear in Olin Library during admitted student tours in the spring."**

Middletown is a small city within easy driving distance of Hartford and New Haven, but it is off the beaten track of steady public transportation (like trains). It has undergone a renaissance in recent years, and students cheer the myriad ethnic restaurants available. "Middletown isn't a bad place for college," says a student. "There are bars on Main Street that cater to a college crowd. Plus, there is a diverse collection of restaurants, which is great for when the family comes to visit." Wes students contribute a great deal of time to community service and help maintain a peaceful, beneficial relationship with the town. And Wesleyan's rural surroundings afford the much-appreciated opportunity to jog through the countryside, swim at nearby Wadsworth Falls, or pick apples in the local orchards. Good road trips include New York and Boston, each two hours away, and decent ski areas and beaches just under an hour away.

The Wesleyan Cardinals compete in the Division III New England Small College Athletic Conference (NESCAC) and field 30 varsity teams. The women's tennis team is a frequent contender for the national title. Men's basketball won the NESCAC title in 2022, and baseball and men's and women's lacrosse are also strong. Annual encounters with "Little Three" rivals Williams and Amherst lure even the most bookwormish student out of the

> **"This is a place that encourages and supports multifaceted learning."**

library and into the heat of the action. Recreational sports are popular: 41 percent of students compete in four intramural and 19 club sports. The ultimate Frisbee club (the "Nietzsch Factor," named after a former star player's dog, not a misspelling of the philosopher) almost always trounces challengers. Athletics are enhanced by a complex that comes complete with a 200-meter indoor track, a fitness center, and a 50-meter pool.

The key to Wesleyan's success seems to be the fostering of an intellectual milieu where independent thinking and an appreciation of differences are omnipresent. As a junior puts it, "At Wesleyan, you're not solely a STEM kid or a student of history; this is a place that encourages and supports multifaceted learning." Indeed, the Wesleyan experience means liberal learning in a climate of individual freedom—a freedom that requires motivated students who stay on task despite the laid-back atmosphere. Abundant opportunities are open to students willing to take advantage of them, which is precisely what these doers do.

West Virginia University

P.O. Box 6009, Morgantown, WV 26506

Surrounded by the likes of Ohio, Pennsylvania, and Virginia, West Virginia has traditionally exported its best students to other states for college. But WVU also attracts its share of out-of-staters, some drawn to its one-of-a-kind forensics program. The honors program is a must for top students, and the university has solid programs in professional fields ranging from health sciences to engineering.

West Virginia University earned the right to be the state's flagship land grant university in the wake of the Civil War by being the only one in the state to offer research and doctoral-degree programs. WVU has expanded to offer more than 130 undergraduate majors, approximately 480 student organizations, and 18 intercollegiate varsity athletic programs, not to mention leading research in petroleum and natural gas engineering, forensic science, and rural health. With solid academic programs and a lively social scene, the school has become an increasingly popular choice for scholars, researchers, and athletes, as well as party animals.

WVU is situated in the picturesque mountains of north-central West Virginia, a few miles from the Pennsylvania border and overlooking the Monongahela River. A driverless rail system connects the campus's three areas—the older downtown, the more modern Evansdale, and the health sciences area. Ten of the ivy-covered Morgantown

> **"Certain classes and a segment of the student population create a competitive climate."**

buildings, dating mainly from the 19th century, are listed on the National Register of Historic Places; many of their interiors have been restored or renovated. Reynolds Hall, a 186,000-square-foot business and economics complex featuring academic, residential, and recreational space, opened in 2022.

All WVU students must complete the General Education Foundations program, which consists of coursework in eight areas: English, science and technology, mathematics and quantitative skills, society and connections, human inquiry and the past, artistic expression, global and diversity studies, and a special focus area drawing on a subject of personal interest. For many students, fulfilling the special focus area requirement leads to a minor or even a second major. All incoming students take a First-Year Seminar that covers study skills, university and community support services, goal setting, and career planning.

West Virginia's degree programs span 14 colleges and schools, the best of which are engineering (particularly energy-related) and the allied health sciences (medical technology, physical therapy, nursing, and occupational therapy). The most popular majors are exercise physiology, biology, psychology, nursing, criminology, engineering, and business. WVU was the first school in the nation to offer a degree in forensic science and is the only one to offer it at the bachelor's, master's, and doctoral levels. Additional programs of note include undergraduate majors in strategic communications, management information systems, health informatics and information management, physics, and—for those interested in children's theater—puppetry. Thirty-five percent of undergraduate classes have fewer than 20 students,

Website: www.wvu.edu
Location: Small City
Public
Total Enrollment: 22,320
Undergraduates: 18,031
Male/Female: 48/52
Financial Aid: 79%
Pell Grant: 23%
Expense: Pub $
Student Loans: 61%
Average Debt: $ $ $
Applicants: 17,074
Accepted: 90%
Enrolled: 28%
Grad in 6 Years: 63%
Returning Freshmen: 81%
Academics: ✐ ✐
Social: ☎ ☎ ☎ ☎
Q of L: ★ ★ ★
Admissions: (304) 293-2121
Email Address: N/A

Strong Programs:
Engineering
Health Sciences
Forensic Science
Exercise Physiology
Biology
Psychology
Nursing
Criminology

and students say the difficulty of WVU academics depends largely on the classes they take. "Certain classes and a segment of the student population create a competitive climate," explains a senior. The Honors College offers small classes, special housing, and early registration to the top 5 percent of WVU students. Study abroad programs are available in more than 70 countries through a variety of faculty-led, partner, and exchange options.

Reynolds Hall, a business and economics complex featuring academic, residential, and recreational space, opened in 2022.

WVU students describe their classmates as friendly, helpful, boisterous, and "sometimes rowdy." Though WVU attracts students from all U.S. states and more than 100 countries, its appeal is primarily regional. Fifty-five percent of undergraduates are in-staters, and 3 percent are international; sizable contingents arrive from western Pennsylvania, Maryland, and New Jersey. Black students represent 3 percent of undergrads, Hispanics/Latinos 4 percent, Asian Americans 2 percent, and multiracial students 6 percent. The university offers thousands of merit scholarships, worth an average of $4,700, and hundreds of athletic awards.

Twenty-two percent of WVU's undergraduates live on campus. Most dorms are co-ed; the older ones are known for their character, while the newer residential complexes in Evansdale have larger rooms and luxuries like air-conditioning. Living/learning communities are available in areas ranging from forensics and creative arts to innovation and the environment. "Off-campus housing is plentiful, but rent is high because demand is high," cautions a senior. Students complain that meals in the four main dining halls are "incredibly overpriced" and parking on campus can be difficult, although the local Morgantown Mountain Line buses take students to all university housing for free. Despite "frequent events highlighting awareness for women's issues, particularly sexual assault," a sophomore says, many students feel that the university has been doing a "less-than-satisfactory job addressing individual cases once they have been brought to light."

"Little else can compare to singing 'Country Roads' with the student body."

Morgantown is a small city of 30,000 with a college-town feel and plenty of community service opportunities. "This town revolves around the university and provides so much for the students," says a senior. The school has worked hard to curtail underage drinking, banning alcohol in the dorms and placing restrictions on Greek parties and rush activities, although students report that these efforts haven't slowed down the off-campus party scene. WVU also banned five fraternities from campus for at least 10 years for failing to comply with new rules. Roughly 6 percent of the men and 5 percent of the women go Greek. Social life on campus often centers on the free food, movies, bands, and comedians offered Thursday through Saturday by the school-sponsored Up All Night program. The annual Welcome Week offers hundreds of activities, including a free FallFest concert, and Mountaineer Week showcases the customs of Appalachia. For those with cars, road trips to Pittsburgh, Columbus, and Washington, D.C., are quick and easy.

The cricket club team has won several national championships, most recently in 2022.

With no major sports teams to cheer for, West Virginians are passionate about their Mountaineers. "Every football game is a festival in some way," says a senior, and a sophomore adds, "Little else can compare to singing 'Country Roads' with the student body" after every home victory. West Virginia also fields competitive Division I Big 12 teams in men's and women's basketball and soccer, along with women's gymnastics and men's wrestling. Intramural and club sports are popular, especially basketball, flag football, and dodgeball. The cricket club team has won several national championships, most recently in 2022. Students also enjoy easy access to nearby hiking, white-water rafting, and skiing.

"To those looking from the outside, WVU might seem to be a lax, rural, Appalachian university—after all, our reputation as a 'party school' precedes us," muses a mechanical and aerospace engineering double major. "However, on campus,

Overlaps

Fairmont, James Madison, Marshall, Penn State, Ohio State, Towson, University of Delaware, University of Maryland

it is apparent that the vast majority of programs are rigorous and active." As WVU grows, its self-proclaimed mission is evolving to be more student-centered. At the same time, the university continues to be dedicated to academic preparation and research that will improve the lives of citizens not only in West Virginia, but across the globe.

If You Apply To ›

West Virginia: Rolling admissions. Accepts the Common Application with supplement. Please consult West Virginia's website for the most up-to-date information regarding standardized test requirements.

Westmont College

Santa Barbara, CA 93108

A Christian liberal arts college, Southern California style. Westmont academics are taught from an unapologetically Christian perspective, but overall climate is more laid-back than at other evangelical powerhouses like Wheaton (IL) and Gordon. Nationally known for kinesiology. Almost everyone gets financial aid, but cultural homogeneity is an issue. Shorts and sandals are the norm, and the worldly temptations of Santa Barbara's surf and sand lurk only five minutes away.

Westmont College prides itself on offering students a strong grounding in the liberal arts while remaining faithful to its motto, *Christus Primatum Tenens* ("Christ holding preeminence"). Unlike many Christian colleges, Westmont has never had ties to any particular Protestant denomination and sees itself as part of a worldwide evangelical tradition embracing a range of theological perspectives. Faculty members, all practicing Christians, take pride in presenting competing lifestyles and value systems as a way to challenge and nurture students' faith. "The school's culture is that of a Christian community," says a chemistry major. "It is very cheerful and kind, and there are many hugs!"

Founded in 1937, Westmont sits on a former estate nestled in the foothills of the Santa Ynez Mountains along the Pacific Coast. The campus, which has been periodically evacuated in recent years due to Old Testament–like wildfires and flooding, boasts a Mediterranean-style residence, gardens, and buildings crafted of sandstone and other local natural materials. A senior characterizes the academic climate as "fostering a 'we're-all-in-this-together' attitude." All classes are taught by regular faculty members, who are described by one psychology major as "interactive, attentive, and highly empathetic." Students have good things to say about Westmont's career advising and other support services; the psychological counseling center has added staff and expanded its hours.

> "[Students are] generally laid-back, friendly, outdoorsy, and bubbly."

Westmont requires all students to undertake an extensive general education program grounded in the Christian liberal arts tradition. The program includes courses in biblical literature and history, standard distribution requirements, and a skills component that includes writing- and speech-intensive courses and foreign language. With their Christian heritage under their belts, students then undertake one of two "Compassionate Action" options aimed at applying their faith to society. Most majors include a capstone or senior seminar course, in which seniors reflect on what they have learned over the previous four years.

Website: www.westmont.edu
Location: Small City
Private
Total Enrollment: 1,229
Undergraduates: 1,229
Male/Female: 39/61
Financial Aid: 96%
Pell Grant: 14%
Expense: Pr $ $
Student Loans: 65%
Average Debt: $ $ $ $
Applicants: 2,351
Accepted: 79%
Enrolled: 20%
Grad in 6 Years: 73%
Returning Freshmen: 85%
Academics: ✍ ✍ ✍
Social: 🕿 🕿 🕿
Q of L: ★ ★ ★ ★
Admissions: (800) 777-9011
Email Address: admissions@ westmont.edu

Strong Programs:
Kinesiology
Economics and Business
English

The Augustinian Scholars Program offers four-year scholarships to 60 incoming freshmen, who engage in seminars on Christian intellectual traditions.

One of Westmont's most popular majors is kinesiology—the interdisciplinary study of the art and science of human movement or, as Westmont faculty like to put it, "God's greatest creation: the human body." The economics and business major, which requires students to study abroad twice, is a noteworthy draw. Students rate English, chemistry, and biology as strong, and psychology is a popular choice. The religious studies department boasts a number of respected scholars, which is a good thing, since so many of their courses are required for graduation. Music is well-funded and strong, as is art, which focuses on the fine arts and art history. Newer majors include engineering and data analytics.

Thirty percent of students engage in undergraduate research independently or with a professor. Students present their work at biannual Research Symposia. The Augustinian Scholars Program offers generous four-year scholarships to 60 incoming freshmen, who engage in seminars that explore Christian intellectual traditions and higher education as a Christian calling. A semester-long program in social entrepreneurship based in downtown Santa Barbara involves project-based internships. Westmont prides itself on fostering global perspectives; 51 percent of students receive academic credit for foreign study, often in programs led by Westmont faculty. Students returning from time abroad can earn a minor in global studies by taking additional seminar and research courses.

A sophomore describes fellow students as "generally laid-back, friendly, out-doorsy, and bubbly." Most Westmont students come from California (69 percent) or other Western states, mainly from middle- and upper-middle-class Christian homes. "Since Christianity is integrated into the curriculum, and there is chapel three times each week, you'd have a rough time fitting in if you were not Christian," says a biology major. Two percent of students come from outside the United States. Hispanics/Latinos make up 20 percent of students, Asian Americans 7 percent, and multiracial students 7 percent, while Black students account for just 2 percent. Many students lament that cultural and socioeconomic diversity is relatively low, and one

"Christianity is integrated into the curriculum, and there is chapel three times each week."

says, "Minorities from more diverse communities may have a hard time adjusting." The campus political climate is usually low-key, although a junior notes that there have been some "small demonstrations against the college's position on LGBTQ+ relationships." Westmont is generous with its financial aid. Merit scholarships average $25,800 per year, and athletic scholarships are available as well.

The dorms at Westmont are clean, well-maintained, and conveniently located. The Global Leadership Center, where every room has its own bathroom, gives priority to seniors and students who engage in leadership and study abroad programs. All students are required to live on campus for all four years, with only a few exceptions. Westmont has a single all-day dining facility, imaginatively known as the Dining Commons, where, as a communication major puts it, "the food is pretty good as far as cafeteria food goes." Fridays are "Farm Fresh," featuring veggies from the campus's own garden, managed by students minoring in environmental studies. Students give the college high ratings for campus safety.

Through the student-run Potter's Clay program, students spend spring break working on service projects in Ensenada, Mexico.

Consistent with their Christian values, almost all Westmont students engage in community service projects. Through the student-run Potter's Clay program, students spend their spring break working with contractors, doctors, and other professionals in Ensenada, Mexico. The Urban Initiative sends teams to work with local nonprofit organizations in U.S. cities. On campus, the Westmont Activities Council sponsors intramurals, dances, and other events. "People at Westmont are usually conservative, so socializing may look like going swing dancing or to a movie rather than to a party," says a chemistry and biology major. Alcohol is banned on campus, but a communication major says that "students are allowed to drink off campus if they are of legal age." A campus shuttle allows ready access to Santa Barbara's many options, ranging from coffee shops and shopping to hiking, surfing, and beach volleyball. Westmont traditions include the annual Spring Sing musical skit competition between dorms and the Fringe Festival featuring theater, dance, and films directed and performed by students.

Athletics at Westmont are low-key, but the school's seven men's and eight women's varsity teams (the Warriors) do well in competition with eight other Christian colleges in the NAIA Golden State Athletic Conference. Baseball, men's and women's basketball and track and field, and women's volleyball are among the more successful teams. Popular intramural and club sports include rugby and ultimate Frisbee.

Westmont students laugh at their stereotypes ("drinking smoothies from the local Blenders store") and occasionally bristle at the chapel requirements ("more a burden than a time with God"), but most welcome these as part of the fabric that makes Westmont's friendly, close-knit, and caring community possible. "While it is very easy to stay within the walls of comfortableness," observes one senior, "there are plenty of opportunities to push the limits of your comfort zone, whether through global travel or local mission work."

If You Apply To ›

Westmont: Early action I and II, rolling admissions. Accepts the Common Application with supplement. Applicants must agree to Community Life Statement. Please consult Westmont's website for the most up-to-date information regarding standardized test requirements.

Wheaton College (IL)

501 College Avenue, Wheaton, IL 60187

Wheaton is at the top of the academic heap in evangelical education, challenged only by Pepperdine (with its Malibu digs) and traditional competitors such as Gordon and Calvin. Students must not only follow Wheaton's stringent code of conduct but also affirm their personal faith in Jesus Christ. Wheaton's low tuition makes it relatively affordable. The worldly temptations of Chicago hover less than an hour away.

Wheaton College combines academic rigor and evangelical orthodoxy with a firm commitment to the liberal arts, preparing students "to build the church and benefit society worldwide 'For Christ and His Kingdom.'" It is one of only two evangelical schools in the *Fiske Guide* with an admissions process that requires students to be professing Christians (see also Gordon College), and its Community Covenant prohibits the use of alcohol, tobacco, and drugs. Though most adolescents would chafe under such restrictions, Wheaties take it all in stride. "There's an emphasis on tradition and culture," says an elementary education major. "We are openly Christian, and students on this campus are really passionate and really kind and caring."

Wheaton was founded in 1860 by evangelical abolitionists and was a stop on the Underground Railroad. Today the college is nondenominational, and its verdant, 80-acre campus is an oasis of sorts in the midst of one of Chicago's oldest and most established suburbs. The castle-like Blanchard Hall, completed in 1927, keeps watch over the community from atop the front campus hill; when couples get engaged, they climb to the top of the tower to share their news by ringing the bell. Nearby sits Billy Graham Hall, which houses a museum and the college archives,

Website: www.wheaton.edu
Location: Suburban
Private
Total Enrollment: 2,430
Undergraduates: 2,200
Male/Female: 43/57
Financial Aid: 94%
Pell Grant: 22%
Expense: Pr $
Student Loans: 58%
Average Debt: $ $ $
Applicants: 1,963
Accepted: 88%
Enrolled: 32%
Grad in 6 Years: 88%

making it a hub for research on American evangelicalism. (The late evangelist was a Wheaton alumnus.) A $62 million expansion of the Armerding Center for Music and the Arts has added a 648-seat concert hall, among other performing arts spaces.

Sporting one of the largest endowments among the nation's evangelical schools, Wheaton offers students a generous bevy of programs and facilities. General education requirements ("Christ at the Core") include a broad array of thematic coursework, as well as a first-year seminar, an advanced seminar, and a senior capstone experience. Business and economics is Wheaton's most popular major, followed by communication, English, and applied health sciences. Biblical and theological studies, philosophy, theater, and music are considered strengths. Motivated students may opt for 3–2 dual-degree programs in nursing and engineering or choose from 11 accelerated, five-year master's degree programs ranging from teaching and theology to Old Testament archaeology. In the classroom, there's an emphasis on teamwork, and a biology major calls the atmosphere "serious but collaborative." The quality of teaching varies, but students get "the benefit of Christian professors who provide a stimulating intellectual experience in light of the Christian faith," according to one junior.

Students have the opportunity to participate in research at Argonne National Laboratory, just down the road, and for those seeking a truly global experience, there's study abroad in more than 30 countries; 45 percent of students partake. "Study abroad programs are quite common to the Wheaton experience," a student says, describing them as "superb and life-changing." Those concerned with social justice, a definite focus at Wheaton, may be interested in the Human Needs and Global Resources program, which sends students to developing countries for six months to work on projects such as building roads and schools. Summer study in several scientific fields is available at the Black Hills Science Station, while leadership training takes place at Honey Rock, Wheaton's campus in the Wisconsin North Woods. For incoming first-year students, the required two-week Wheaton Passage program combines on-campus orientation with an off-campus experience intended to facilitate community-building and self-discovery. Options include a wilderness track (backpacking, canoeing, rock climbing, or sea kayaking), a Northwoods track (arts and outdoor activities or equestrian training at Honey Rock), and an urban track (city adventures and urban studies in downtown Chicago or the city's Woodlawn neighborhood). A Wheaton Passage track for transfer students explores Chicago's diverse neighborhoods.

> **"[Students] encourage their peers to pursue excellence in their God-given gifts."**

"The student body is extremely motivated and high-achieving," says one student. "They desire to encourage their peers to pursue excellence in their God-given gifts." Twenty-three percent of Wheaton students hail from Illinois, and 4 percent come from overseas. Nine percent are missionary and third-culture kids. Black students comprise 3 percent of the student body, Hispanics/Latinos make up 7 percent, Asian Americans add 10 percent, and multiracial students account for 6 percent. With both conservative and liberal students represented on campus, students say the political climate is active and sometimes tense. Wheaton's Community Covenant shuns "homosexual behavior and all other sexual relations outside the bounds of marriage between a man and woman"; thus, LGBTQ issues have been controversial. "LGBTQ students struggle to find a voice or place on campus," comments a student. There are no athletic scholarships, but merit awards averaging $13,900 are awarded to qualified students. Wheaton ranks first in the country in the proportion of Pell Grants recipients who succeed in paying back their student loans.

Ninety percent of Wheaton students live in campus housing, and well-kept accommodations range from single-sex dorms with traditional double rooms and

Billy Graham Hall is a hub for research on American evangelicalism. (The late evangelist was a Wheaton alumnus.)

bathrooms down the hall to college-owned houses and apartments. Opposite-sex visitation is limited to certain hours on certain days, though "each semester, dorms are allowed two 'raids' to their opposite floor," says an education major. Everyone eats in Anderson Commons, where one student says, "everything is made from scratch." Students report feeling safe on campus. "Our Title IX coordinator on campus is an active participant in Wheaton's discourse and daily life. Besides this, Wheaton does not often acknowledge issues of sexual assault publicly or openly," remarks a senior.

The required Wheaton Passage program combines on-campus orientation with an off-campus experience like rock climbing or adventures in Chicago.

Since Wheaton lacks fraternities and sororities, and because students agree to abstain from alcohol, drugs, and tobacco, the social life revolves around other pursuits. "We have a lot of fun here, but all alcohol-free fun," says a psychology major. The College Union plans events like talent shows, roller disco, and an annual President's Ball. A junior says, "The town of Wheaton is a friendly suburb with nice restaurants and a good bike trail, but it's pretty much closed down by 9 p.m." A commuter train near campus whisks students to downtown Chicago in 45 minutes, where restaurants, blues clubs, theaters, museums, shopping, and professional sports are in abundance. Favorite traditions include Missions in

"We have a lot of fun here, but all alcohol-free fun."

Focus week, which brings missionary organizations and Christian speakers to campus, and the individual dorm floors' own traditions, one of which includes an annual root beer kegger.

Wheaton's athletic teams (the Thunder) compete in Division III; football and men's and women's basketball, soccer, and swimming are among the strongest teams. Football, basketball, and soccer games "are always exciting and well attended," says one student, especially if the opponent is Augustana College. The debate and chess teams are competitive too. Forty percent of students play intramural and club sports. And while it's not an athletic competition per se, juniors and seniors do get excited about decorating "the Bench," a reinforced concrete slab that is the subject of an ongoing and often rough-and-tumble game of keep-away.

Wheaton College remains "committed to the principle that truth is revealed by God through Christ, in whom is hidden all the treasures of wisdom and knowledge." Students believe that their school's dedication to Christianity only strengthens the bonds they develop with one another and their understanding of the broader world. "The Wheaton education is hard to duplicate," says one student. "Learning at Wheaton truly does prepare you for Christ and His kingdom."

Overlaps

Calvin, Westmont, Taylor, Gordon, Hope, Pepperdine, Biola, Baylor

If You Apply To ›

Wheaton (IL): Early action I and II, regular decision. Accepts the Common Application with supplement. Please consult Wheaton's website for the most up-to-date information regarding standardized test requirements.

Wheaton College (MA)

Norton, MA 02766

Although its address says it's in Massachusetts, Wheaton is actually closer to Providence than to Boston. But getting to either by train is quick and easy. One of the few nationally known institutions in the area that is still not super competitive. Curriculum includes interdisciplinary, hands-on, and project-based work in addition to traditional courses. Smaller than Skidmore, comparable to Connecticut College.

Website: www.wheatoncollege
.edu

Location: Suburban

Private

Total Enrollment: 1,701

Undergraduates: 1,701

Male/Female: 38/62

Financial Aid: 100%

Pell Grant: 23%

Expense: Pr $ $ $

Student Loans: 66%

Average Debt: $ $ $ $

Applicants: 3,724

Accepted: 82%

Enrolled: 16%

Grad in 6 Years: 73%

Returning Freshmen: 84%

Academics: ✍ ✍ ✍

Social: ☎ ☎ ☎

Q of L: ★ ★ ★ ★

Admissions: (508) 286-8251

Email Address: admission@
wheatoncollege.edu

Strong Programs:
Visual Art
Chemistry
Business and Management
Psychology
Biology
Economics
Political Science
Neuroscience

Sophomores undertake a required hands-on learning experience, such as a research or service project, study abroad, or an internship.

Wheaton College offers students plenty of opportunities to make their academic marks. Since 2000, more than 250 Wheaton students have received national fellowships, and the college remains among the top 10 liberal arts colleges for Fulbright scholars. Increasingly focused on experiential learning, Wheaton makes sure its students shine outside the classroom too. Says one satisfied senior, "Wheaton's commitment to supporting its students to leverage their liberal arts education and change the world permeates all aspects of life on campus."

The college was founded in 1834 by Laban Wheaton, a judge and U.S. congressman, in memory of his daughter. Established to offer high-quality education to women, Wheaton has been co-ed since 1988. The school's relatively rural location offers few distractions from intellectual pursuits. Its 400-acre campus blends Georgian brick buildings and modern structures set among beautiful lawns and shade trees. The two halves of the campus (upper and lower) are separated by Peacock Pond, which probably qualifies as the only heated duck pond on any American campus. Recent campus projects include a major renovation of the Science Center.

"People are very attuned to feminist and gender issues."

Wheaton's Compass curriculum supports a broad foundation of knowledge and shows students how to make linkages between disciplines. In their first year, all students take a reading- and writing-intensive, interdisciplinary course taught by a faculty team representing different academic fields. As sophomores, students undertake a required hands-on learning experience, such as a research or service project, a study abroad program, or an internship. In addition, throughout their four years, students pursue a Mentored Academic Pathway—a personal academic plan guided by faculty and staff advisors—and develop a portfolio reflecting on their experiences and showcasing their work.

Business and management, psychology, biology, economics, and political science are Wheaton's most popular majors. Programs in the arts are well recognized—impressive given the school's small size—and the chemistry department is also strong. Students interested in interdisciplinary study can choose majors like neuroscience or theater and English dramatic literature, or they may design their own majors. Dual-degree programs with Dartmouth, Emerson, and other institutions are available in engineering, business, communication, religion, and optometry. The Center for Global Education offers more than 100 approved study abroad programs in more than 45 countries around the world; 55 percent of students participate. One unique option sends students and a faculty member to Royal Thimphu College in Bhutan for a semester; the king of Bhutan happens to be a Wheaton alumnus.

According to a psychology major, "Critical thinking, intensive writing, and collaborative projects are part of almost every class, which allows for in-depth exploration of concepts, themes, and lessons." Fifty-eight percent of Wheaton's classes have fewer than 20 students. "Professors are open to feedback and are available to talk outside the classroom," says a junior. Aside from a faculty advisor, students get a staff mentor and two peer advisors, known as preceptors. The Filene Center for Academic Advising and Career Services gets high marks from students seeking internships—and jobs after graduation. The center awards summer fellowships ranging from $2,000 to $5,000 to students pursuing unpaid internships, research opportunities, or service projects, ensuring that, in the words of one senior, "students never have to worry about choosing between a paycheck and a professional experience."

Thirty-six percent of Wheaton students come from Massachusetts, and 5 percent hail from foreign nations. The student body is largely white and affluent; "I was often the only student in my classes without a MacBook," observes a senior. Black students account for 6 percent, Hispanics/Latinos 6 percent, Asian Americans

4 percent, and multiracial students 5 percent. Students are said to be friendly and open to differing views; politically, the campus leans left. "Wheaton's legacy as a former women's college means that people are very attuned to feminist and gender issues," explains a senior. "These are issues that students rally around." Merit scholarships averaging $27,200 are available, but there are no athletic awards.

As might be expected on this small, suburban campus, virtually everyone (96 percent) lives in one of Wheaton's dorms or theme houses. All students are guaranteed housing for four years; freshmen live in doubles or triples, and upperclassmen try their luck in the lottery system. "Housing is livable, but some of the facilities are getting old," comments a sophomore. The recently renovated dining halls are bright and spacious, and the biggest winners of all are the ducks, which thrive on the leftover bread students toss into Peacock Pond. "There's a big push for local, fresh, and organic produce," says a junior. Students say they feel safe on campus and that campus safety officers are visible and active. A film and new media studies major notes, "Many local people walk around campus, and I never feel unsafe with the openness of the campus."

> **"Theme houses and suites do throw down quite often."**

Social life at Wheaton includes dances, concerts, lectures, parties on campus, and other activities organized by the more than 100 student groups. Students unwind at the college's student center, which offers a café, dance studio, and sun deck for afternoon study breaks. There are no sororities or fraternities here, but there is a party scene, as a junior explains: "Theme houses and suites do throw down quite often." Students say they appreciate the school's "Safety Always Matters Most" approach to drinking. The biggest event of the year is Spring Weekend, featuring live bands, outdoor barbecues, and the Head of the Peacock race, where students build vessels (no boats allowed) and race them across Peacock Pond. "The winner gets to take our president on a victory lap around the pond," cheers a freshman. And it's an unofficial tradition to go for a swim in the pond at least once before graduation.

The town of Norton, just outside campus, draws students with services opportunities, such as a Big Brother Big Sister program, hospital visits, and academic tutoring, but there's little to do otherwise, students say. "It's a very quiet town, and most students stay on campus rather than venture off into Norton," says a student. Relatively convenient access to two state capitals livens up the social scene. "We're 20 minutes from Providence and 40 minutes from Boston. If you can't find something to do on the weekend, you're just looking for something to complain about," remarks a student.

> **"We text with deans, have lunch with professors, [and] coffee with advisors."**

The Wheaton Lyons compete in Division III. The Lyons nickname honors Mary Lyon, the 19th-century educational pioneer who established Wheaton's first curriculum and later founded Mount Holyoke. Recent conference champs include baseball and synchronized swimming. The athletic facility boasts an eight-lane swimming pool, a field house, and an 850-seat arena for basketball or volleyball. Popular club and intramural sports include rugby, ultimate Frisbee, soccer, and basketball.

Students at Wheaton take an active role and are involved in campus planning and college operations, as well as in their community. "We don't just have coffee in the café," says a political science major. "We text with deans, have lunch with professors, coffee with advisors, a beer with our favorite professor. These kinds of relationships are the Wheaton way. They supplement the intellectual energy and debate that takes place among students." Indeed, students here take pride in their achievements inside and outside the classroom, while striving to preserve the school's friendly, small-town feel.

For the Head of the Peacock race, students build vessels (no boats allowed) and race them across Peacock Pond.

Overlaps

Stonehill, Connecticut College, Clark, Colby, Skidmore, Mount Holyoke, Bates, Hobart and William Smith

Whitman College

345 Boyer Avenue, Walla Walla, WA 99362

Whitman has quietly established itself as one of the West's leading liberal arts colleges. Don't bother with the umbrella: Walla Walla is in arid eastern Washington. Whitman's isolation breeds community spirit and alumni loyalty. True to its liberal arts heritage, Whitman has no business program. Combines outdoorsy camaraderie with the slower pace of life in the rural Northwest.

Website: www.whitman.edu
Location: Small Town
Private
Total Enrollment: 1,524
Undergraduates: 1,524
Male/Female: 44/56
Financial Aid: 91%
Pell Grant: 14%
Expense: Pr $ $ $
Student Loans: 39%
Average Debt: $
Applicants: 5,155
Accepted: 59%
Enrolled: 16%
Grad in 6 Years: 89%
Returning Freshmen: 90%
Academics: ✍ ✍ ✍ ✍
Social: ☎ ☎ ☎
Q of L: ★ ★ ★ ★
Admissions: (509) 527-5176
Email Address: admission@
   whitman.edu

Strong Programs:
Biology
Psychology
Economics
Politics
Environmental Studies
English
Biochemistry, Biophysics, and
   Molecular Biology
Astronomy

You don't have to own a Frisbee to succeed at Whitman, but if you've got one, bring it along—you'll find a campus full of friendly students eager to toss it back to you. Though it isn't well-known outside the Pacific Northwest, Whitman offers a solid liberal arts education, along with plenty of fun for outdoorsy types. Students are down-to-earth and friendly and feel a deep loyalty to one another—and to their school.

Whitman was founded in 1882, initially under religious auspices, and named in honor of Marcus and Narcissa Whitman, missionaries who ministered to the Cayuse Indians and settlers on the Oregon Trail. (Unfortunately, they were killed by Cayuse who accused them of causing a fatal measles epidemic.) Even today, everything important is within walking distance of campus, including the main drag of Walla Walla, which once won a national Best Main Street award. The 117-acre campus, which features colonial buildings and modern facilities, sits at the foot of the Blue Mountains, surrounded by golden wheat fields and vine-

> **"Students are very immersed in their academic life."**

yards. Beyond Walla Walla (which means "many waters" in the Cayuse language) are gorgeous mountains, rivers, and forests. Newer facilities include a residence hall housing 150 sophomores and a 500-seat dining hall.

All Whitman students complete the General Studies Program, which includes both a first-year seminar and distribution requirements in various disciplines. The first-year program revolves around a two-semester sequence of courses that emphasizes analytical reading of common texts—such as Plato's *Symposium*, Darwin's *On the Origin of Species*, and Toni Morrison's *Beloved*—as well as discussion skills and effective writing. Depending on their major, all seniors must either complete a written senior thesis and oral defense or pass comprehensive written and oral exams in their major; Whitman was the first U.S. college or university to require seniors to do so.

Biology, psychology, economics, politics, environmental studies, English, and the interdisciplinary major in biochemistry, biophysics, and molecular biology are some of the best (and most popular) programs at Whitman; the school also boasts an astronomy program, unusual among small colleges. Whitman has an extensive Asian art collection, and additional coursework in Chinese language and Asian studies is available through a summer program in China. Whitman has 3–2 programs in engineering, oceanography, forestry, and environmental management, offered in partnership with institutions like Caltech, Columbia, Duke, and the University of Washington.

Seventy-one percent of classes have fewer than 20 students, fostering a collaborative atmosphere. "Students are very immersed in their academic life and follow-up conversations outside of the classroom," comments a senior. An environmental studies major reports, "Professors are extremely knowledgeable in their fields and are excited to get to know their students."

Forty-five percent of Whitman students study off campus, most packing their bags for one of the more than 80 semester- and yearlong programs that are offered in 45 countries. Short-term Crossroads courses, which are led by faculty during the summer, are another option, and financial aid packages can be applied to all approved programs. Students may also take urban studies terms within the U.S. in Philadelphia and Washington, D.C. "Semester in the West is Whitman's signature program," explains an environmental studies and politics major. "Students travel across the American West and meet with activists, environmentalists, ranchers, Native Americans, and lawmakers to discuss local issues." During the daylong Whitman Undergraduate Conference, student scholarship and creativity are celebrated with presentations, posters, and performances. Highly competitive Whitman Internship Grants award $3,000 to selected students to pursue unpaid internships.

Whitman was the first U.S. college to require seniors to complete a thesis and oral defense or pass comprehensive written and oral exams.

Thirty-two percent of students are from Washington State, and many of the rest hail from the suburbs of Western cities, notably San Francisco and Portland; 10 percent arrive from overseas. Whitties are "outdoorsy activists," says a psychology major. "Generally, students are kindhearted and authentic." The student body leans liberal, and recent activism has focused on increasing diversity on campus. Currently, 6 percent of students are Asian American, 9 percent are Hispanic/Latino, 2 percent are Black, and 7 percent are multiracial. The Intercultural Center and Glover Alston Center help support diversity and intercultural awareness on campus. There are numerous merit scholarships averaging $15,300 but no athletic awards. Whitman now meets the full financial need of students from Washington State.

"Semester in the West is Whitman's signature program."

Two-thirds of Whitman students live in campus housing; freshmen and sophomores are required to do so. In the newest residence hall, Stanton, "the accommodations feel like a resort," says a student, who adds that "the older buildings are comfortable and in good shape." A number of theme houses are available for students who share interests such as fine arts, community service, and global awareness. Meals in the main dining hall get enthusiastic reviews. "I rarely get tired of the food, and it's easy to stay healthy on the meal plan, which is a rare find at a college," cheers a psychology major. A junior reports that "Whitman security is available 24/7 to support students," and measures like safety escorts, bystander intervention training, and "sober roamers" who watch over their classmates at registered on-campus parties help keep the campus community safe.

Everyone looks forward to the annual rivalry game against Whitworth University (the "Battle of the Whits").

The social life at Whitman revolves around on-campus activities, such as theatrical productions and events held by more than 80 student clubs, as well as fraternity or off-campus house parties. Twelve percent of the men and 11 percent of the women go Greek, and according to a physics major, "Greek life at Whitman is very relaxed." When the weather is nice, students gather on Ankeny Field to study, toss a Frisbee, or relax, and watching the sun set over the wheat fields is a popular pastime. "There is a surprisingly large population that smokes marijuana socially," says a student, noting that the substance is legal for those 21 and over in the state of Washington. "It's very accepted, yet people don't feel pressured to smoke." Big annual events include the spring Renaissance Faire and the Whitsquatch music and art festival, featuring student bands and popular musicians.

"[Whitties are] outdoorsy activists. Generally, students are kindhearted and authentic."

The town of Walla Walla (population 34,000), located in an arid valley in the center of agricultural southeastern Washington, supports a symphony, community playhouse, art galleries, two rodeos, and a hot-air balloon festival, not to mention a state penitentiary. "The Walla Walla area is small and quaint—a great place to explore local wineries or try out new restaurants," says a senior. About 70 percent of students get involved in community service opportunities. Outdoor pursuits are important in this part of the country, where autumn is gorgeous, winter sporadically snowy, and spring delightfully warm. Hiking, biking, and backpacking are minutes away, and white-water rafting and rock climbing are popular on weekends. Two ski centers and other recreational areas are within an hour's drive, and Seattle (260 miles) and Portland (235 miles) offer a welcome change of scenery.

The Whitman Blues compete in Division III. Men's tennis has brought home a dozen Northwest Conference championships in recent years. Men's and women's basketball are nationally competitive, and everyone looks forward to the annual rivalry game against Whitworth University (the "Battle of the Whits"). Men's and women's swimming, women's tennis, women's golf, and baseball are solid too. The majority of students play club and intramural sports. Club lacrosse and rugby tournaments draw crowds, as does "Onionfest," a regional ultimate Frisbee tournament. Rock climbers can challenge themselves at the world-class Climbing Center.

"If you're choosing a liberal arts school in the Northwest," says a student, "choose Whitman!" Indeed, students seeking a traditional liberal arts education with a strong sense of community and a healthy dose of outdoor fun would do well to heed this enthusiastic Whittie's advice. And they don't need an umbrella.

If You Apply To ›

Whitman: Early decision I and II, regular decision. SATs or ACTs: optional. Accepts the Common Application with supplement.

Whittier College

13406 East Philadelphia Street, Whittier, CA 90608

Whittier's Quaker heritage brings a touch of the East to suburban L.A. Less selective than Occidental and the Claremont Colleges, Whittier lures ethnically and socioeconomically diverse students with a bevy of academic scholarships and a welcoming community. Whittier's functional campus lacks the opulence of the Claremonts and the panache of Pepperdine. Check out the Whittier Scholars option.

Founded in 1887 by members of the Religious Society of Friends (Quakers), Whittier College is a global training ground for a diverse student body interested in standing up for social justice and making a positive impact in the world. Whittier students can be found all around the world, studying in dozens of foreign countries. And when they return to the Whittier campus, they have access to caring faculty and classmates who "want to be liberally educated and enjoy the small-campus vibe," says a mathematics-business major.

Located just 18 miles away from downtown Los Angeles, the college, whose name is inspired by Quaker poet John Greenleaf Whittier, is perched on a hill overlooking the town of Whittier, California, with the San Gabriel Mountains rising up from the horizon. The 73-acre campus is a pleasant mixture of modern buildings tucked between the red-roofed, white-walled Spanish traditionals. Its landmark building, Deihl Hall, includes a digital audio/video computer lab for languages. A four-foot-high granite monument stands on the north campus lawn honoring Whittier's most famous alum, former president Richard Nixon. The state-of-the-art Science & Learning Center is the latest addition to campus.

Whittier offers its undergraduates two major curricular programs: the traditional Liberal Education Program and the Whittier Scholars Program. Most students take the first option, in which they fulfill distribution requirements that emphasize an interdisciplinary focus, cultural perspectives, and critical and quantitative thinking. They also choose a major from among more than 30 options, the strongest and most popular of which include business administration, psychology, political science, kinesiology, English, biology, and child development.

The second curricular option, the Whittier Scholars Program, is the college's signature program and a path taken by 12 percent of the undergraduates. They are relieved of most general requirements and start from square one with an "educational design" process. With the help of an academic advisor, Whittier Scholars carve their majors out of standard offerings by taking a bit of this and a bit of that. Recent self-designed majors have included urban community studies, cultural nutrition, and film and humanities. The program is highly regarded because of the more active role it allows students to play and the freedom it affords them in pursuing their interests.

> "[Whittier students] want to be liberally educated and enjoy the small-campus vibe."

All students, no matter which curriculum they choose, must fulfill a yearlong freshman writing requirement, choosing their preferences from a variety of seminars. First-years also attend a series of speakers who discuss topics relevant to student coursework and take part in the Exploring Los Angeles series, which includes trips to museums and cultural events. Seniors complete a capstone requirement.

Whittier ended its formal affiliation with the Quakers in the 1940s, but the prevailing spirit of community hearkens back to their traditions. A biology major says, "Whittier provides a positive learning environment where students are actively encouraged to get involved." Fifty-one percent of classes have fewer than 20 students, and freshmen are taught by full professors. "For the most part, the quality of the teaching has been very intense, but very rewarding," says a student. For those looking to add global scope to their college experience, as 47 percent of students do, semester-long and short-term study abroad options include destinations like Paris, Rome, Cape Town, and Beijing; many programs are faculty-led. What's more, every student who studies abroad in a Whittier-approved program receives an automatic Global Poet Scholarship worth $2,000.

"Students at Whittier are mostly liberal and are passionate about social justice and national politics," says a senior. Seventy-eight percent of undergraduates come from California, while 7 percent arrive from abroad. Diversity is taken seriously here. Whittier draws a good portion of students—including many commuters—from nearby communities east of Los Angeles, and the school's Latino population has grown by more than 20 percent in the last decade as local demographics have shifted. Currently, Hispanic/Latino students represent 53 percent of the student body, while Black students add 4 percent, Asian Americans 6 percent, and multiracial students 4 percent. "Tolerance is a big watchword on campus," a junior says, and the college's Office of Equity and Inclusion provides an array of resources and programming to support diversity. Forty percent of students are the first in their families to go to college, and 33 percent of incoming freshmen receive Pell Grants. In addition to need-based aid, the college awards merit scholarships averaging $26,700.

Half of Whittier students live on campus. The Turner Residence Hall entices many students with panoramic views of Los Angeles. "The first-year residence halls

(continued)

Average Debt: $ $ $ $
Applicants: 2,884
Accepted: 82%
Enrolled: 12%
Grad in 6 Years: 64%
Returning Freshmen: 82%
Academics: ✎ ✎ ✎
Social: ☎ ☎ ☎
Q of L: ★ ★ ★ ★
Admissions: (888) 200-0369
Email Address: admission@ whittier.edu

Strong Programs:
Business Administration
Psychology
Political Science
Kinesiology
English
Biology
Child Development

Every student who studies abroad in a Whittier-approved program receives an automatic Global Poet Scholarship worth $2,000.

are older with limited air-conditioning," reports a history and music major. Many freshmen choose to participate in living/learning communities organized around particular academic or social interests. Campus residents take their meals at the Campus Inn dining hall (known as the CI), where the food is said to be typical college fare. The Spot, Whittier's popular campus coffeehouse, includes a nightclub called—logically enough—the Club. Students give high ratings to campus safety.

Ten social societies (they're not called fraternities or sororities here) attract 10 percent of the men and 10 percent of the women but hardly dominate the social scene. Their dances, however, which frequently feature live entertainment, are welcomed by all. Whittier has a fairly strict alcohol policy, students say. Popular annual events include the Whittfest concert in the spring, the Midnight Breakfast served by professors during second-semester finals, and Sportsfest, which is a campuswide competition in which dorms compete in a variety of athletic, intellectual, and wacky games and events. The most important campus landmark is the Rock, which sits near the front of campus and is given a fresh coat of paint by countless aspiring artists.

For many, a favored diversion is road-tripping, everywhere from Disneyland to the California beaches. Other common destinations include Joshua Tree, San Diego, and Las Vegas. For nightlife closer to campus, Los Angeles looms large. The local community, known as Uptown Whittier, offers quaint shops, restaurants, a movie theater, and cobblestone sidewalks, and a senior calls it "a perfect place for a night on the town with friends." It's also a place for community-minded students to get involved. The Center for Engagement with Communities provides course-based service-learning internships and research, in which the majority of students participate.

"The quality of the teaching has been very intense, but very rewarding."

Johnny Poet is Whittier's pen-wielding mascot (inspired by the school's namesake). The Poets compete in Division III, where softball and men's and women's water polo are competitive. In 2022 the school eliminated its 115-year-old football program as well as men's and women's golf and men's lacrosse. Intramurals are a big draw, especially the Halloween dodgeball tournament.

The coronavirus pandemic has led to declining enrollment numbers. Nevertheless, the students at Whittier have created a supportive, intimate environment where people work together and celebrate their diversity. And with the opportunity to design their own majors, students here are active in their own education but get plenty of support along the way. Says a sophomore, "I have no doubt that I have faculty, staff, and administrators advocating for me and cheering me on."

If You Apply To ›

Whittier: Early action, regular decision. SATs or ACTs: optional. Accepts the Common Application.

Willamette University

900 State Street, Salem, OR 97301

Willamette is strategically located next door to the Oregon state capitol and 50 minutes from Portland. Bigger than Whitman, smaller than U of Puget Sound, and more civic-minded than Lewis & Clark, Willamette offers extensive study abroad enhanced by ties to Asia. Well-known in the West but is still developing a national reputation to equal that of competitors such as Lewis & Clark.

Willamette University was founded in 1842 in the Willamette Valley as the first university in the West. Students frequently take advantage of their proximity to the state's executive and legislative offices as well as a nearby hospital for internships, jobs, or off-campus learning experiences. A comprehensive study abroad program carries students to destinations around the globe. On campus, students find a more personal atmosphere than larger universities nearby and appreciate the low-key yet challenging academic milieu. One satisfied chemistry major says, "This is the place where you can grow as a student, leader, and person as you pursue your passions."

The 61-acre campus is home to abundant trees (testimony to Oregon's frequent rain), small wildlife, and occasionally steelhead salmon that splash around in Mill Stream, which runs between WU's redbrick academic buildings. The college-owned forest at Zena is a 305-acre outdoor laboratory about a 10-minute drive from campus that hosts regular student and faculty research in biology, sustainability, art, and other fields. The university's LEED Gold–certified Ford Hall features large, collaborative learning spaces and faculty offices.

All students at Willamette (pronounced "Will-AM-it") take the freshman College Colloquium seminar, study in a language other than English, and satisfy an equity, diversity, and inclusion course requirement. They also complete coursework in five liberal arts categories: math and sciences, natural sciences, social sciences, humanities, and arts. In addition, students take capstone senior seminars, often culminating in research or thesis projects. The most popular majors are economics, biology, politics, earth/environmental science, and psychology. Other particularly strong programs include exercise and health science, chemistry, Japanese studies, music, theatre, and history. The college recently added undergraduate majors in business and public health, and three combined degree programs in business (3–2 B.A./M.B.A.), law (3–3 B.A./J.D.), and data science (3–1 B.S./M.S.) integrate the liberal arts and professional education. In 2021, Willamette merged with Pacific Northwest College of Art, the region's oldest school of art and design, significantly expanding offerings in these areas.

> "Students are expected to work hard, read copious amounts, and actively contribute in class."

Academics are rigorous, but students don't compete for grades. "Students are expected to work hard, read copious amounts, and actively contribute in class," says a senior. "That being said, the climate is very collaborative." Classes are small; 75 percent have fewer than 20 students on the roster. "Professors are committed to their students as their first priority," says a math major. And for those seeking additional support, "Tutors are available in every subject, for free, and there is a writing center within which students can arrange appointments for help with papers or academic projects," reports a senior.

When students aren't reading or writing papers, undergraduate research opportunities in every discipline beckon; the university awards more than 75 undergraduate research grants each year. Half of the student body participates in a robust study abroad program that sends them to their choice of more than 45 nations, and Willamette also benefits from its colocation with the U.S. campus of Tokyo International University.

"Willamette students are positive, motivated, smart individuals," says a senior. "They want to give back, but also achieve highly." Twenty-nine percent of WU students are native Oregonians, and much of the remainder comes from Western states, notably California and Washington; less than 1 percent are international. Black students make up 2 percent of the student body, Hispanics/Latinos 14 percent, Asian Americans 5 percent, and multiracial students 8 percent. Social justice issues spark discussion on campus, and the Student Center for Equity and Empowerment supports students from underrepresented groups. Says a sophomore, "Willamette

Website: www.willamette.edu
Location: Small City
Private
Total Enrollment: 1,680
Undergraduates: 1,159
Male/Female: 42/58
Financial Aid: 99%
Pell Grant: 28%
Expense: Pr $
Student Loans: 57%
Average Debt: $ $
Applicants: 3,680
Accepted: 79%
Enrolled: 9%
Grad in 6 Years: 72%
Returning Freshmen: 86%
Academics: ✍ ✍ ✍ ½
Social: ☎ ☎ ☎
Q of L: ★ ★ ★
Admissions: (844) BEARCAT
Email Address: bearcat@willamette.edu

Strong Programs:
Exercise and Health Science
Chemistry
Japanese Studies
Music
Theatre
History
Economics
Biology

Japanese studies is a strength, and Willamette benefits from its colocation with the U.S. campus of Tokyo International University.

tends to be very involved in state and city political issues." Willamette offers talent and academic merit scholarships each year averaging $15,700; there are no athletic awards.

Fifty-seven percent of Willamette students live in campus housing, which is social and convenient to classes and parties. "Willamette's dorms are not remarkable, but they provide incredible experiences for fostering community," says a student. Students may move off campus starting junior year, and "living in Salem is quite cheap," says an upperclassman. The student-owned and -operated Bistro offers a coffeehouse atmosphere and is a popular alternative to cafeteria fare. "All of the food is fresh, local, and made on campus by staff that students grow to know personally," explains a senior. Students report that the university has taken a strong stance on responding to and educating the community about sexual assault.

Social life tends to center on campus, whether it's free movies and lectures, open-mic nights at the Bistro, dance parties (salsa or swing), or performances by the music and theatre departments. Sixteen percent of Willamette men and 13 percent of the women go Greek, but students say that Greeks don't dominate the social

"Willamette tends to be very involved in state and city political issues."

scene. When it comes to drinking, "Parties happen, but [students] are remarkably well-behaved," a student says. Annual social highlights include the Black Tie Affair formal dance, a spring music festival, and a student-run luau held by the Hawai'i Club for more than three decades. "There is a tradition of throwing your friends into Mill Stream on their birthday," says a junior.

Downtown Salem is a short walk from campus, and while students say it's no college town, it does have movies, shopping, restaurants, bars, and coffeehouses. Riverfront Park provides a pleasant place to enjoy a concert or festival in the warmer months or to go ice skating in the winter. Also nearby are the Cascade Mountains and beaches of Newport and Lincoln City (an hour's drive), skiing and snowboarding on Mount Hood or in the high desert town of Bend (three hours), and the cosmopolitan cities of Portland (50 minutes) and Seattle (about four hours north). Willamette students remain true to the school motto, "Not unto ourselves alone are we born," volunteering more than 70,000 hours each year with various community organizations.

The Willamette Bearcats compete in Division III, and men's golf and women's swimming are recent Northwest Conference champions. Men's and women's cross-country, men's soccer, and women's lacrosse are also strong. The annual football game against Linfield draws big crowds, and games against Pacific Lutheran are also well attended. Club sports range from the competitive (soccer, rugby, and ultimate Frisbee) to the recreational (badminton, volleyball, taekwondo, eSports, and more), and intramurals are another popular option.

Willamette may be the best little school you've never heard of, at least if you're from outside the California–Oregon–Washington corridor. "Willamette is unabashedly itself," says one student. "Community members from all backgrounds feel very comfortable being themselves and embracing who they are." The school's close-knit community is strengthened by its emphasis on service and by warm, supportive faculty members who push students to achieve.

If You Apply To ›

Willamette: Early decision, early action, regular decision. SATs or ACTs: optional. Accepts the Common Application. Applicants have the option of providing information about their gender and sexual identity.

P.O. Box 8795, Williamsburg, VA 23187

Founded in 1693 by royal charter and named after the reigning British monarchs at the time, William & Mary is the original "public Ivy." With 6,500 undergraduates, it is larger than Mary Washington and Richmond, smaller and more intellectual than the University of Virginia. W&M boasts one of the top graduation rates among public universities and sends one of the highest proportions of graduates on to Ph.D.s. Williamsburg, capital of the former Colony of Virginia, is more exciting for tourists than for college students.

Traditions abound at William & Mary, yet this historic university—the second-oldest in the nation after Harvard—continues to evolve. It has graduated three former U.S. presidents—Thomas Jefferson, James Monroe, and John Tyler. Rival UVA prides itself on being "Mr. Jefferson's" university, but W&M is quick to remind the Cavaliers that it educated Mr. Jefferson in the first place. "Students at William & Mary choose to attend the university for its intense academic rigor, strong sense of community, rich history, and legacy of traditions," says one senior.

A profusion of azaleas and crape myrtle adds splashes of color to William & Mary's finely manicured campus, located about 150 miles southeast of Washington, D.C. The campus is divided into three sections and includes Lake Matoaka, the oldest human-made lake in Virginia, and a wooded wildlife preserve, which is filled with trails and widely used by the science departments. The Historic Campus is a grouping of three colonial structures still in use. The oldest and most strik-ing is the Wren Building, which was constructed between 1695 and 1700 and is the country's oldest college building, and arguably one of the loveliest. The Old Campus buildings date from the '20s and '30s, and New Campus, where ground was first broken in the '60s, is home to a recreation center and the Integrated Science Complex now under construction. Crim Dell, a wooded area with a small pond spanned by an old-style wooden bridge, is one of the most romantic spots on any campus.

> "[Professors] are at W&M because they love teaching students first and foremost—and it shows."

William & Mary, which was founded as a private college and did not go public until 1906, created Phi Beta Kappa in December of 1776. The honor code, established by Thomas Jefferson in 1779, demands much from the university's students. W&M's College Curriculum includes two first-year seminars: one "big ideas" course and one reading- and writing-intensive course, both of which are offered in every academic discipline. Students must also take coursework in a range of liberal arts areas, with a particular emphasis on interdisciplinary perspectives, and fulfill requirements in global perspectives; difference, equity, and justice; and foreign language proficiency. All seniors complete a capstone project. The Charles Center for Academic Excellence facilitates honors programs, research opportunities, and interdisciplinary majors like American studies, environmental science, and women's studies.

Not surprisingly, the history department is a signature program at William & Mary, but 65 percent of students now major in STEM or computational fields. Government, biology, neuroscience/psychology, and health sciences are among the most popular majors, and business (especially accounting), economics, neuro-science, and international relations are well regarded. New options include majors in business analytics and data science. Aspiring engineers can sign up for a 3–2 pro-gram with Columbia University. W&M's innovative joint degree program with the University of St Andrews in Scotland is one of the few international undergraduate

Website: www.wm.edu
Location: Small Town
Public
Total Enrollment: 8,197
Undergraduates: 6,457
Male/Female: 42/58
Financial Aid: 50%
Pell Grant: 12%
Expense: Pub $ $ $ $
Student Loans: 31%
Average Debt: $ $
Applicants: 17,475
Accepted: 37%
Enrolled: 26%
Grad in 6 Years: 91%
Returning Freshmen: 93%
Academics: ✎ ✎ ✎ ✎ ✎
Social: ☎ ☎ ☎
Q of L: ★ ★ ★
Admissions: (757) 221-4223
Email Address: admission@ wm.edu

Strong Programs:
History
Business
Accounting
Economics
Neuroscience
International Relations
Government
Biology

joint degrees available in the U.S. "It changed my life," chirps a senior. "St Andrews is my favorite place on earth."

Academics at W&M are rigorous. "Students take their classes and the work that goes along with them seriously," reports an English major. "It is not 'cool' to do poorly in class." A notable side effect is what is generally described as a "stress culture," in which, as a senior explains, "students will try to one-up each other with their stress levels, lack of sleep, or amount of work left to do." Nevertheless, students say the prevailing culture is also one of cooperation and support. "Rather than compete for the highest grades, students are collaborative and willing to help their peers achieve their best potential," says a psychology major. Faculty members are said to be supportive as well. "Professors are passionate about their research, but they are at W&M because they love teaching students first and foremost—and it shows," says a government major. Forty-six percent of classes have fewer than 20 students, although a few introductory lectures have more than 100. Teaching assistants are used for grading or lab purposes only.

> "[Students are] curious, driven, friendly, and quirky."

Students rave about W&M's study abroad options. "There are tons of opportunities to study abroad that are fit for every student: from semester-long programs to programs over summer and winter breaks that last between two and eight weeks, and even spring break study abroad opportunities," reports a senior. Fifty-one percent of W&M's undergrads receive credit for academic globetrotting. The top 10 percent of freshmen are designated Monroe scholars and receive summer research stipends to support independent projects. Eighty-five percent of students participate in some sort of faculty-mentored research experience. Students cheer the Cohen Career Center, which helps freshmen and sophomores identify and pursue career interests.

A government major describes her fellow students as "curious, driven, friendly, and quirky," while a sophomore admires their "very endearing nerdiness." An economics major cites "a strong culture of belonging," in which, as an English major adds, "people at W&M are unafraid to be themselves." Because William & Mary is a state-supported university, 65 percent of its undergraduates are Virginians, hailing largely from wealthier counties in the northern part of the state; 5 percent are international. Competition for the nonresident spots—mostly taken by students from the Mid-Atlantic and farther north—is stiff. Despite administrative efforts to improve the situation, a lack of socioeconomic and racial diversity is both a problem and a hot-button topic on this left-leaning campus. "The student body is not diverse," says one senior. "As a first-generation and low-income student, coming to William & Mary and living in Williamsburg was a major culture shock. It is difficult to fit in." Asian Americans now account for 10 percent of the students, Hispanics/Latinos 9 percent, Black students 6 percent, and multiracial students 6 percent. Only 12 percent of incoming freshmen are Pell-eligible. Like many older colleges, W&M has begun to grapple with its historical ties to slavery, including the renaming of several buildings and restoration of the recently discovered Bray School, said to be the oldest existing schoolhouse for Black children. Merit scholarships averaging $9,600 are disbursed to qualified undergrads, and W&M has its share of eagerly recruited athletes—nearly 300 athletic scholarships are offered annually.

> "[There is] growing advocacy for, and acceptance of, mental health support services."

William & Mary recently embarked on a comprehensive 10-year plan to overhaul 80 percent of its housing and to improve dining services with, among other things, two new dining facilities—changes that students agree are long overdue. Sixty-eight percent of undergrads occupy campus housing, which is required for the first two years and guaranteed for all four. Dorms range from stately old halls with high ceilings to modern structures and are conveniently located throughout the campus.

The honor code, established by Thomas Jefferson in 1779, demands much from the university's students.

The history department is a signature program at William & Mary, but 65 percent of students now major in STEM or computational fields.

Nevertheless, "Housing is not W&M's strong suit," reports a senior. "Most dorms are outdated, and some lack air-conditioning." Special-interest housing is available—there are eight language houses—and life in a fraternity or sorority house is an option. As for campus dining, the less said the better. "The food is below average. It is probably the number one area that needs improvement," says a history major.

Students report feeling safe on campus. A finance major praises "the growing advocacy for, and acceptance of, mental health support services." Several student-led groups address issues of sexual assault. The Haven program features peers trained to talk to sexual assault survivors. The McLeod Tyler Wellness Center houses health, counseling, recreation, and other services ranging from mindfulness workshops and yoga sessions to fitness classes. It operates the Counseling Center and Student Health Center, though students claim that wait times for the former can be long.

On campus, students can enjoy the soothing voices of one of the many a cappella groups, dance the night away at fraternity parties, grab a midnight snack at the Sadler Center, or watch the latest dance or theater performance at Phi Beta Kappa Theater. Twenty percent of the men and 28 percent of the women join Greek organizations, which host most of the on-campus parties. "Greek life is an option, but it by no means dictates social life, which is nice," says a government major. A senior counsels, "Don't come to William & Mary if you're looking for a party school!" The university has strict policies against underage drinking, but students say as long as they behave safely, they stay out of trouble.

"I love the lore and the cute town."

Traditions are the stuff of which William & Mary is made. "It's honestly why I'm still here," gushes an English major. "I love the lore and the cute town." Perhaps the most cherished is the annual Yule Log Ceremony in the Wren Courtyard, where students sing carols and hear the president read a holiday story. On Charter Day, bells chime and students celebrate the distinguished history of their 330-year-old institution. Each year, freshmen walk through the Wren Building for Opening Convocation, where they're greeted by cheering upperclassmen and faculty. Four years later, as they graduate, they pass through the Wren in the other direction. Multiple secret societies are known to exist; their activities are, well, secret, but rumored to be generally philanthropic in nature.

Anyone who gets restless can always step across the street to Colonial Williamsburg to picnic, jog down Duke of Gloucester Street (a.k.a. "Dog Street"), or study in a beautiful garden. "Eventually, you don't raise an eyebrow when Colonial reenactors are behind you at the grocery store buying beer," quips one senior. Its appeal to tourists notwithstanding, Williamsburg leaves much to be desired as a college town. "It's boring," explains an English major. Nightlife is a hit-or-miss affair (mostly miss), although volunteer opportunities abound and 70 percent of students participate. Richmond, Norfolk, and Virginia Beach—a favorite springtime mecca—are about an hour's drive; Washington, D.C., and the University of Virginia are also popular road trips.

Each year, more than 500 Tribe athletes compete on 23 Division I teams. Men's and women's swimming and diving, men's cross-country, and women's tennis have been consistently competitive in recent years. Intramurals and more than 40 club sports, such as rowing and ultimate Frisbee, attract a large percentage of the student body.

William & Mary is reminiscent of the dual-faced Roman god Janus, ever mindful of its rich historical legacy but also keenly aware of new academic and cultural forces swirling about. As a place to look both ways, W&M is, as one student puts it, "happy, quirky, intelligent, and proud." A senior sums up her experience: "The academic climate can be a bit aggressive at times. But overall, I am proud to attend an institution at which academics are important."

William & Mary recently embarked on a comprehensive 10-year plan to overhaul 80 percent of its housing and to improve dining services.

At the annual Yule Log Ceremony in the Wren Courtyard, students sing carols and hear the president read a holiday story.

Overlaps

University of Virginia, UNC at Chapel Hill, Cornell University, Boston College, Georgetown, Mary Washington, University of Richmond, Virginia Tech

Williams College

Williamstown, MA 01267

Running neck and neck with Amherst on the selectivity chart, Williams sits on a campus of surpassing beauty in the foothills of the Berkshires. Making serious efforts to broaden racial, ethnic, and socioeconomic diversity, but still attracts plenty of well-toned, all-around jock-intellectuals who will one day be corporate CEOs. The campus art museum, one of the best anywhere, anchors strong arts programs. Locals hail the splendid isolation of Williamstown as a way to build community.

Website: www.williams.edu
Location: Rural
Private
Total Enrollment: 2,171
Undergraduates: 2,121
Male/Female: 48/52
Financial Aid: 48%
Pell Grant: 14%
Expense: Pr $ $ $ $
Student Loans: 34%
Average Debt: $
Applicants: 12,452
Accepted: 9%
Enrolled: 52%
Grad in 6 Years: 94%
Returning Freshmen: 97%
Academics: ✏ ✏ ✏ ✏ ✏
Social: ☎ ☎ ☎
Q of L: ★ ★ ★ ★
Admissions: (413) 597-2211
Email Address: admission@williams.edu

Strong Programs:
Studio Art
Art History
Environmental Studies
Economics
Mathematics
Biology
Computer Science
Political Science

Williams College vies with rival Amherst for possession of both the color purple—they each use it on team uniforms and in their logos—and the title of most selective liberal arts college in the United States. Nestled in a small hamlet in the Berkshires, Williams is the more isolated of the two, but students say that makes for a more intimate sense of community. "I wanted an environment where I could share ideas and debate with my friends over a meal or a late-night snack, and I've certainly found that at Williams," says a freshman. School spirit abounds, and when not gazing at the purple mountains' majesty, students at Williams are digging into their studies with fervor.

Williams was established in 1793 as a "western counterpart" to Harvard and Yale under a bequest from the estate of landowner Ephraim Williams. The college's buildings constitute a veritable *omnium-gatherum* of architectural styles, from the elegantly simple Federal design of the original West College to contemporary structures by Charles Moore and William Rawn. The brick and gray stone buildings are arranged in loosely organized quads, which are both enclosed and open to nature. Recent additions include the 113,000-square-foot, eco-friendly Wachenheim Science Center, housing the mathematics and statistics, psychology, and geosciences departments.

> **"I wanted an environment where I could share ideas and debate with my friends over a meal."**

The Williams curriculum emphasizes interdisciplinary studies and personalized teaching. Distribution requirements include at least three courses in each of the school's three divisions: languages and arts, social studies, and sciences and mathematics. Students must also fulfill requirements in writing and in quantitative and formal reasoning, pick a major from 35 options, pass four quarters of phys ed, spend at least six semesters in residence, and participate in Winter Study every January, when they may take a course, complete a research project, or travel abroad.

One of Williams's greatest strengths is in art, which benefits from the Williams College Museum of Art (one of the finest college art museums in America), the Clark Art Institute, and MASS MoCA, a nearby center for contemporary visual, performing, and media arts. Williams was one of the first liberal arts colleges to establish an environmental studies program, which is enhanced by fieldwork opportunities in the 2,600-acre, college-owned Hopkins Forest. Popular majors include economics, mathematics, biology, computer science, political science, and English. Students seeking a change of pace, especially during the bitter and blustery winter, can pack their bags for more than 250 programs, including short-term, faculty-led study tours and an innovative yearlong program organized with Oxford's Exeter College in England. About half of students study abroad.

There are only two small graduate programs at Williams—in art history and development economics—so graduate students are few and far between, and you'll never find them behind a lectern. Roughly two-thirds of Williams students sign up for courses taught in the Oxford tutorial format: two students and a faculty member meet each

"My professors always try to form personal connections with every single one of us."

week, with the students alternating who has to do independent work, like an essay, lab report, or art piece, and who gets to critique it. "Tutorials are basically all critical engagement all the time," explains a political science major, because students learn to communicate, collaborate, and defend their ideas. And while academics at Williams are rigorous, the environment is supportive. "My professors always try to form personal connections with every single one of us," says a junior. About half of the students conduct research with faculty, often in funded positions. A senior says alumni "go out of their way to help Williams students succeed" by setting them up with internships and other opportunities.

Students at Williams are accomplished. One student says, "I know people who can read Harry Potter in Latin, translate rap songs into Arabic, and sight-read 'Rocket Man' perfectly on the piano." Just 16 percent of students are in-staters and another 8 percent are international. Black students make up 5 percent of the student body, Asian Americans add 13 percent, Hispanics/Latinos represent 12 percent, and multiracial students comprise 7 percent. Politically, Williams leans left, and students say there is a small but dedicated group of student activists on campus. Many students come from affluent backgrounds, which according to a junior lends a certain "New England boarding school" vibe to campus, but Williams has a need-blind admissions process for domestic applicants, and socioeconomic diversity has been slowly increasing. All financial aid is need-based—there are no merit or athletic scholarships—and the college guarantees to meet the full demonstrated need of all admitted students. Furthermore, Williams offers all-grant financial aid packages, meaning that students who receive financial aid no longer have to borrow loans or fulfill work-study requirements.

Ninety-three percent of students live on campus; housing is guaranteed for four years, and only seniors are eligible to move out. "You can't go wrong with any housing here," says a student. First-years live in groups of 25 to 35 students each (known as "entries") along with three or four junior advisors, who serve as big siblings, mentors, and sounding boards. After the first year, students have an affiliation with one of

"I know people who can read Harry Potter in Latin [and] translate rap songs into Arabic."

four upperclassmen residential neighborhoods and enter their housing draw. Campus dining offers three dining halls with friendly staff and satisfying meals, and small co-ops are available for seniors who want to cook for themselves. In addition to required trainings and other college programming, a student says, "Multiple student groups host events throughout the year to keep up the conversation surrounding the prevention of sexual assault."

Fraternities and sororities were abolished long ago, but that hasn't stopped Williams students from partying. "The party culture is centered around athletic teams, performance groups, and cultural affinity groups," explains an economics major, and most parties are open to anyone. Drinking is a popular pastime on weekends, but most students report no pressure to imbibe. The college has taken steps to make sure that whatever drinking does go on happens safely, such as outlawing

Two-thirds of students sign up for courses taught in the Oxford tutorial format, where two students and a faculty member meet each week.

Students who receive financial aid no longer have to borrow loans or fulfill work-study requirements.

drinking games, requiring registration of parties over a certain size, and mandating availability of food and nonalcoholic beverages whenever alcohol is present. Other events like guest speakers, comedians, and concerts keep students busy, too, and favorite traditions include homecoming, Winter Carnival, and Spring Fling. The most beloved tradition is Mountain Day, held on a Friday in October. Which day it will be is a well-kept secret, broken only when the college president sends out an email canceling classes, and church bells begin tolling at 8 a.m. Students picnic on the campus's main lawn, then choose from a variety of hikes, including one to the top of Mount Greylock, where hot cider and donuts are waiting on the summit.

On Mountain Day in October, the college president cancels classes and students hike to the top of Mount Greylock.

The small village of Williamstown (population 7,800), adjacent to campus, is "sort of the quintessential New England town," says a student. The Log is a popular hangout for pizza and live performances, and students frequent a few cafés and an independent movie theater, but the town isn't exactly a hot spot for social life. The Clark Art Institute, within walking distance of campus, possesses one of the finest collections of Renoir and Degas in the nation, as well as a great library. The college theater is home to the Williamstown Theatre Festival in the summer, which often features Broadway stars. Nearby slopes and trails beckon, offering skiing, cycling, and backpacking. Civilization—in the form of Albany, New York—is just an hour's drive. Other popular destinations include New York City and Boston (both accessible by train from Albany, or three hours by car).

With 32 varsity teams and an active club sports program, athletics are more like an established religion here than an extracurricular activity. The Ephs (short for founder Ephraim) are a perennial winner of the Division III Directors' Cup, awarded annually to the school with the strongest overall athletic program. Recent New England Small College Athletic Conference champions include football, men's rowing, men's swimming and diving, and men's and women's cross-country. Williams competes against Amherst and Wesleyan in the "Little Three," and any contest with archrival Amherst ensures an especially enthusiastic crowd. After all, Amherst was founded in 1821 by a breakaway group of Williams students, along with the school's then-president. Intramurals are a popular option for those seeking less competitive athletic diversions.

It takes a special kind of student to be happy at Williams. Those who delight in the life of the mind and don't mind trading the amenities found at more urban schools for a small, intimate community will no doubt bleed purple by the time they leave. Says a senior, "I've never been more engaged in what I'm learning than here at Williams."

Overlaps

Brown, Amherst, Dartmouth, Yale, Harvard, Middlebury, University of Pennsylvania, Cornell University

If You Apply To ›

Williams: Early decision, regular decision. Accepts the Common Application with supplement. Please consult Williams's website for the most up-to-date information regarding standardized test requirements.

University of Wisconsin–Madison

702 W. Johnson Street, Suite 1101, Madison, WI 53715

Madison draws nearly a third of its students from out of state, a higher proportion than some other leading Midwestern public universities. Why brave the cold? Reasons include top programs in an array of professional fields and several innovative living/ learning programs. There's also the pleasure of life in Madison, a combination state capital/college town in the mold of Austin, Texas. Sky-high retention rates.

For 175 years, the University of Wisconsin has been guided by the Progressive-era philosophy of the "Wisconsin Idea" that the purpose of a great state university is to seek truth and apply the resulting knowledge to the benefit of the students and society as a whole. Such a philosophy has turned Wisconsin, which dates to 1848, into one of the world's leading universities—one where more than 30,000 full-time undergraduates take advantage of high-level academics and a rich array of resources. State funding is back on the rise after years of deep budget cuts, and Wisconsin remains a place where professional and other programs are outstanding. Just bring a strong desire to learn—and a very warm coat.

Described by one Madison student as "architecturally olden with a modern touch," the mainly brick campus is distinctive. It spreads out over 936 hilly, tree-covered acres and across an isthmus between two glacial lakes, Mendota and Monona. From atop Bascom Hill, the center of campus, you look east past the statue of Lincoln and the liberal arts buildings, down to a library mall that was the scene of many a political demonstration during the '60s. Farther east, you see rows of State Street pubs and restaurants and the bleached dome of the Wisconsin state capitol. On the other side of the hill, another part of campus, dedicated to the agricultural and health sciences, twists along Lake Mendota. But students from both sides of the hill congregate in the old student union, Memorial Union, where political arguments and backgammon games can rage all night. Outside on the union's veranda, students can look out at the sailboats in summer or iceboats in winter.

> **"Anyone can fit in, you just have to find your own niche."**

Distribution requirements vary among the different schools and academic departments, but they are uniformly rigorous, with science and math courses required for B.A. students, and a foreign language for virtually everyone. All students must fulfill a three-part graduation requirement in quantitative reasoning, communication, and ethnic studies. Students who prefer the academic road less traveled can opt for the Integrated Liberal Studies certificate program, which allows them to fulfill several gen eds with a series of related, interdisciplinary courses, rather than taking electives at random.

Madison's academic climate is demanding. "There are a lot of smart people studying here," notes one student. A list of first-rate academic programs at Madison would constitute a college catalog elsewhere. Some 70 programs are considered in the top 10 nationally. Some highlights include education, agriculture, communication, biological sciences, and social sciences. The most popular majors are computer science, economics, psychology, and political science. Due to overcrowding, some of the strongest fields, such as business and engineering, have more selective admissions criteria than others. Although many classes are large, 46 percent have fewer than 20 students. Professors at Madison are certainly among the nation's best, with National Academy of Science members and Guggenheim fellows scattered liberally among the departments.

While the university's size can be daunting, harried freshmen aren't left to fend for themselves. The university offers a number of first-year programs designed to ease the transition into college life. A first-year seminar encourages students to examine learning strategies; connect with faculty, staff, and peers; and become familiar with campus resources. First-Year Interest Groups (FIGs) consist of 20 first-year students who may live in the same residence hall or "residential neighborhood" and who also enroll in a cluster of three classes together. Each FIG cluster of courses has a central theme; the central or "synthesizing" course integrates content from the other two classes. After freshman year, many students participate in internships, and 21 percent choose to study abroad in programs all over the world, including France, Brazil, India, Israel, and Thailand. Forty-three percent conduct undergraduate research.

Website: www.wisc.edu
Location: City Center
Public
Total Enrollment: 42,137
Undergraduates: 31,884
Male/Female: 47/53
Financial Aid: 60%
Pell Grant: 17%
Expense: Pub $ $
Student Loans: 41%
Average Debt: $ $
Applicants: 53,829
Accepted: 60%
Enrolled: 26%
Grad in 6 Years: 89%
Returning Freshmen: 95%
Academics: ✍ ✍ ✍ ✍ ½
Social: ☎ ☎ ☎ ☎
Q of L: ★ ★ ★ ★
Admissions: (608) 262-3961
Email Address: onwisconsin@ admissions.wisc.edu

Strong Programs:
Education
Agriculture
Communication
Biological Sciences
Business
Engineering
Computer Science
Economics

First-Year Interest Groups consist of 20 first-year students who enroll in a cluster of three classes together around a central theme.

If there is a common characteristic among Madison undergraduates, it is assertiveness. "It's easy to get lost in the crowd here, so you have to be fairly strong and confident," declares one student. "No one holds your hand." The flip side is that "anyone can fit in, you just have to find your own niche." Fifty-eight percent of undergraduates hail from Wisconsin, and 10 percent are international. The school is a heartland of progressive politics, and Madison's reputation as a haven for liberals remains intact. "Students here are called liberal because they are eager and willing to change and are continually looking for newer and better ideas," explains one activist. Asian Americans make up 8 percent of the student body, Hispanics/Latinos 7 percent, Black students 2 percent, and multiracial students 4 percent. Academic merit scholarships averaging $8,300 are awarded each year, along with more than 300 athletic scholarships.

Nature enthusiasts can lose themselves in the university's 12,000-acre nature preserve.

Twenty-six percent of undergrads, mostly freshmen, reside in university housing. Dorms are either co-ed or single sex and come equipped with laundry facilities, game rooms, and lounges. Most also have a cafeteria. The student union offers two meal plans, and there are plenty of restaurants and fast-food places nearby. Escort services for those walking and those needing a ride help keep students safe on campus. A variety of programs and groups, such as U Got This! and We're Better Than That, are working to educate the community on preventing sexual assault and supporting survivors.

One old standby for social life that is still as popular as ever is the student union, which hosts bands, shows, and so forth and provides a great atmosphere in which to hang out. There are more film clubs than anyone can follow, and everyone has a favorite bar. Nine percent of the men and 8 percent of the women go Greek. "Frat parties are a very popular break from the bar scene," quips one expert on both options. Madison (a.k.a. Madtown) is an excellent college town and has been the stomping ground for many fine rock 'n' roll and blues bands on the road to fame. Volunteering is a tradition here; the university consistently tops the list for providing the Peace Corps with the most entrants of any college or university in the nation. Nature enthusiasts can lose themselves in the university's 12,000-acre nature preserve or hit nearby ski slopes.

> **"[UW–Madison is] diverse, intellectual, fashionable, and moderately hedonistic."**

The students at this Big Ten school show "tons of interest" in sports, especially hockey and football, and especially when the Badgers try to rout the University of Michigan's Wolverines. The formidable women's ice hockey and volleyball teams claimed national titles in 2021, and the school has produced its share of Big Ten champions as well, most recently in men's cross-country and ice hockey. Bucky Badger apparel, emblazoned with slogans ranging from the urbane to the decidedly uncouth, is ubiquitous. However, the much-acclaimed marching band may outdo all the teams in popularity. Recreational sports are another favorite pastime, with dozens of intramurals and more than 40 club sports offered at varying levels of competitiveness.

Despite fervent efforts in recent years by politicians with narrow and instrumentalist views of higher education to scuttle the Wisconsin Idea, Madison remains one of the best and most well-rounded flagship state universities anywhere. It is a school that students sum up as "diverse, intellectual, fashionable, and moderately hedonistic." And these are the qualities that attract bright and energetic students from everywhere. "You feel you're accepted for who you are no matter what," says one student. "It's so nice to just be yourself."

Overlaps

University of Michigan, University of Minnesota, U of I at Urbana–Champaign, Purdue, Indiana University, Ohio State, UC San Diego, University of Washington

If You Apply To ›

Wisconsin: Early action, regular decision. Accepts the Common Application. Please consult Wisconsin's website for the most up-to-date information regarding standardized test requirements.

Wittenberg University

P.O. Box 720, Springfield, OH 45501

Wittenberg is an outpost of cozy Midwestern friendliness. Less national than Denison or Wooster, Witt has plenty of old-fashioned school spirit and powerhouse Division III athletic teams. Top students should aim for the honors program, which provides a chance for independent research. Witt doles out plenty of merit scholarships to better-than-average students.

Founded in 1845 by German Lutherans, Wittenberg University remains true to its faith by emphasizing strong student/faculty relationships—and making sure that students don't get too settled in their campus comfort zone. In fact, Wittenberg requires all students to complete a community service experience before they graduate. "The campus is beautiful, it's a great school, and it's so obvious how much everyone here loves it," gushes an education major.

The Wittenberg campus is classic Midwestern collegiate, with a mixture of 1800s and Gothic-inspired buildings on 100 rolling acres in southwestern Ohio. The redbrick Myers residence hall, with picturesque white pillars and an open-air dome dating from the 19th century, stands at the center. Many of the campus's buildings are showing their age, although the recently opened $40 million Health, Wellness, and Athletics Complex features a full-size indoor turf field surrounded by a running track, among other facilities.

Launched in fall 2021, Wittenberg's Connections core curriculum emphasizes a solid liberal arts background, with coursework ranging from scientific inquiry to U.S. diversity and equity to creative process. A required First-Year Seminar in the fall helps students transition from high school to college. All students must complete one civic engagement experience, such as an academic course that incorporates volunteer work, as well as two other hands-on learning experiences, which may include research, internships, study abroad, or leadership experiences. Finally, seniors create a culminating reflection that connects their experiences over their four years.

> **"Extremely knowledgeable [professors] help with class problems or even career advice."**

Wittenberg students give high marks to the education program, which is among the most popular majors, along with biology, business, and various offerings in the social sciences. Health-related fields, especially nursing and other prehealth professional programs, are particularly well regarded. Other notable programs include music, international studies, East Asian studies, sport management, and data science. Wittenberg also offers 3–2 engineering programs with Columbia University and Case Western Reserve. The academic climate is described as "challenging but friendly," and study groups are common, according to one junior. Professors are roundly praised for their teaching styles and willingness to make themselves available outside the classroom. "Students take advantage of having professors who are extremely knowledgeable by getting help with class problems or even career advice," one senior says. Fifty-nine percent of classes have fewer than 20 students. As long as students declare their major on time and complete all courses with a C or better, the college guarantees a degree in four years—and will pay for any additional necessary courses.

The Compass program combines nine different student support services in one collaborative space in the Thomas Library and is intended, in part, to improve the college's retention and graduation rates. In addition to offering academic support,

---

Website: www.wittenberg.edu
Location: Small City
Private
Total Enrollment: 1,220
Undergraduates: 1,210
Male/Female: 48/52
Financial Aid: 97%
Pell Grant: 35%
Expense: Pr $
Student Loans: 97%
Average Debt: $ $ $
Applicants: 3,272
Accepted: 92%
Enrolled: 12%
Grad in 6 Years: 64%
Returning Freshmen: 70%
Academics: ✍ ✍ ✍
Social: ☎ ☎ ☎
Q of L: ★ ★ ★
Admissions: (937) 327-6314
Email Address: admission@wittenberg.edu

Strong Programs:
Education
Nursing
Music
International Studies
East Asian Studies
Sport Management
Data Science
Biology

Compass connects students to research, community service, and internship opportunities. A University Honors Program enrolls 13 percent of students, who conduct independent research culminating in a senior thesis, and individual departments offer ample opportunities to work on research with faculty members. In fact, 47 percent of students partake in undergraduate research. Wittenberg encourages students to take a semester or a year away from campus, and 30 percent do so, both in the U.S. and abroad. Most students pack their bags for the college's own faculty-led semesters in Germany and Costa Rica, although a multitude of other partner programs are available. Wittenberg's Local Government Management Internship Program is an option for those interested in public service.

Wittenberg requires all students to complete a community service experience before they graduate.

"Witt students are proactive," says a junior. "We are constantly championing new causes, whether through community service or fundraising. We are always on the go!" Nowadays, Lutherans represent just 11 percent of the student body. Seventy-eight percent of Wittenberg students are native Ohioans, and less than 1 percent hail from other countries. Many others are from nearby states like Indiana, Michigan, and Pennsylvania. Black students make up 10 percent of the student body, Hispanics/Latinos 6 percent, Asian Americans 1 percent, and multiracial students 6 percent. The Diversity Center houses student awareness organizations to help support underrepresented groups on campus. Students say the campus is fairly evenly split between conservatives and

"Witt students are proactive. We are constantly championing new causes."

liberals, and both groups are vocal. Wittenberg is generous in awarding merit scholarships, which average $26,200; there are no athletic scholarships. Thirty-five percent of incoming freshmen receive Pell Grants. The Wittenberg College Access Program provides special financial aid packages to academically talented students from low-income families.

Eighty-six percent of students reside on Wittenberg's hilly campus; freshmen and sophomores are required to do so. After that, most upperclassmen choose houses and apartments owned by the school in the surrounding neighborhood—the "Wittenburbs," as students like to say. "Dorms are spacious and air-conditioned," a student explains, "with options for all-girl, honors, and substance-free housing." Those in need of sustenance (perhaps to fuel all-night study sessions) select from a variety of dining options that students call "acceptable," including vegetarian and low-fat items. In an effort to mitigate sexual assault on campus, the university has implemented bystander awareness and response training programs.

The women's volleyball team dominates the North Coast Athletic Conference, winning 18 of the last 20 championships.

When not working hard at their studies, students at Wittenberg can choose among more than 100 student organizations, performing arts groups, and intramurals. Greek life is a big emphasis, with 27 percent of men and 30 percent of women belonging to fraternities and sororities. When the weekend rolls around, social life centers on parties in houses, dorm rooms, and apartments on or near campus. Greek groups, the Union Board, and the Residence Hall Association bring in guest speakers, movies, comedians, and concerts. Favorite annual events include Greek Week, homecoming ("the alumni involvement is incredible"), W Day, and Wittfest, a campus festival and concert with games, food, prizes, and socializing before finals. "It is open to the community, but all the students go," a senior says. "It resembles a carnival, and at night there's a big concert on the lawn." Springfield (population 59,000) is a struggling blue-collar city, but it's beginning to show signs of revival. The city offers movie theaters, restaurants, a brewery, a performing arts center, and plenty of service opportunities. "There are definitely some gems in Springfield, and every now and then, my friends and I like to get off campus to explore," comments a finance major. Popular road trips include Dayton (30 minutes), Columbus (45 minutes), and Cincinnati (90 minutes).

Wittenberg's athletic teams (the Tigers) are competitive in Division III, and rivalries with Allegheny, Wabash, and The College of Wooster really get students riled up, especially when the football team takes the field. The women's volleyball team dominates the North Coast Athletic Conference, winning 18 of the last 20 championships. Men's basketball, football, and women's cross-country are also competitive. Intramurals and club sports are a huge draw, too, with sports such as crew, racquetball, and rugby. Nearby state parks offer swimming, camping, biking trails, and picnics in the warmer months, and skiing in the winter.

While not as well-known as many of its bigger Midwestern brethren, Wittenberg has plenty to offer those students who decide to attend, including a solid honors program, an active Greek scene, and serious Division III athletics. And with an increased focus on student support and diversifying its academic offerings, the school is slowly extending its regional reach.

If You Apply To ›

Wittenberg: Early decision, early action, rolling admissions. SATs or ACTs: optional. Accepts the Common Application with supplement.

Wofford College

429 North Church Street, Spartanburg, SC 29303-3663

Wofford is about three-quarters the size of Furman and larger than Presbyterian. Strong in the life sciences and study abroad. Wofford is one of the smallest institutions to compete in Division I football, and Greek life dominates the traditional social scene. Diversity is a constant challenge. Where else do first-year students get their own personal librarian?

Wofford students take pride in combining a well-rounded curriculum built on traditional strengths in the sciences with career-related internships and study abroad. The college has taken bold steps to increase—and diversify—enrollment while lowering the student/faculty ratio. Students study hard under the "eyes of Old Main" and form lasting friendships with peers and faculty members. "We are bright, driven individuals who learn to utilize our skills to the best of our potential to make the world around us a better place," says a junior.

Wofford is located near the heart of Spartanburg (population 38,000), a mid-sized city in the northwest corner of South Carolina, and it is affiliated with the United Methodist Church. Founded in 1854, it's one of fewer than 200 existing American colleges that opened before the Civil War, and it still operates on its original campus, a National Historic District. Azaleas, magnolias, and dogwoods surround the distinctive, twin-towered Main Building and four original faculty homes on the 180-acre campus, which is also a nationally recognized arboretum. Recent additions to campus include the sustainably designed Chandler Center for Environmental Studies and a 150-bed residence hall.

"Wofford is very competitive in the sense that students feel pressured to excel."

Wofford requires courses in English, fine arts, foreign languages, humanities, science, history, philosophy, cultural perspectives, math, and physical education. First-years take a required Liberal Arts Seminar 101 course in the fall that hones their

Website: www.wofford.edu
Location: Small City
Private
Total Enrollment: 1,743
Undergraduates: 1,743
Male/Female: 48/52
Financial Aid: 95%
Pell Grant: 18%
Expense: Pr $ $
Student Loans: 52%
Average Debt: $ $ $
Applicants: 4,351
Accepted: 52%
Enrolled: 20%
Grad in 6 Years: 80%
Returning Freshmen: 81%
Academics: ✍ ✍ ✍
Social: ☎ ☎
Q of L: ★ ★ ★
Admissions: (864) 597-4130

(continued)

Email Address: admission@
wofford.edu

Strong Programs:
Biology
Business
English
Government
Finance
Psychology
Spanish

reading, writing, and discussion skills; recent offerings have included Confronting Climate Change, Victorian Women Behaving Badly, and Muslims in America. All first-years are also assigned a Student Success Team that includes an academic advisor, a student peer leader, a staff guide, and a personal librarian.

Traditionally, Wofford's strongest and most attractive programs have been in the life sciences, which account for about a third of its graduates. Every year, two dozen of the school's graduates go on to graduate medical or dental programs; another two dozen go on to law school. Business programs (especially when combined with a second major in Chinese, French, German, or Spanish) and English, with its emphasis on creative writing, are solid, and government is also strong. Creative writing students end by writing a novella, the best of which is given the Benjamin Wofford Prize and published in paperback. Some of the most popular majors are biology, finance, English, psychology, and Spanish. Prospective engineers may apply for 3–2 programs with Clemson or New York's Columbia University. Sixty-two percent of classes enroll fewer than 20 students, and students agree that, across the board, the workload tends to be heavy. "I would say the academic climate at Wofford is very competitive in the sense that students feel pressured to excel," says a sophomore.

"Professors encourage students to come visit their office about both class and personal concerns," says a psychology major. "Many help students secure research positions, internships, and other opportunities." Indeed, special enrichment opportunities abound at Wofford. The Presidential Seminar brings together 20 outstanding seniors from different disciplines to discuss readings from classical and contemporary essays on philosophy, politics, and the complexities of human nature. The Career Center connects students to internships, entrepreneurship opportunities, and other career services. Sixty-three percent of Wofford students participate in some form of study abroad, embarking on programs in more than 70 countries on all seven continents. Short-term, faculty-led programs are offered during the January term, while semester- and yearlong options are available through approved partners; students can often apply financial aid toward program costs. Every year, one lucky Presidential International Scholar travels around the world, all expenses paid, to study an issue of global importance for a semester.

> "I see Wofford as an institution focused on moving forward while still preserving tradition."

Fifty-seven percent of students hail from South Carolina and just 2 percent from abroad. Black students make up 7 percent of the student population, Asian Americans 2 percent, Hispanics/Latinos 5 percent, and multiracial students 4 percent. Conservative white students from middle- to upper-class backgrounds make up the majority, and students note that the low level of racial diversity has been a source of tension on campus. "Wofford's administration is a lot more liberal and encourages diversity, whereas Wofford students and alums often show distaste or frustration toward more socially liberal and inclusive endeavors," comments a student. Merit scholarships averaging $22,400 are available to qualified students, and there are also 165 athletic scholarships in 19 sports.

Creative writing students end by writing a novella, the best of which is given the Benjamin Wofford Prize and published in paperback.

Eighty-seven percent of Wofford's students live on campus, where first-years get doubles in Greene Hall and the recently renovated Marsh Hall or four-person suites in Carlisle Hall. A biology major explains, "Each year that you are at Wofford, the housing situation gets better and better, culminating in the Village—a fantastic apartment community for the seniors." About a quarter of first-years join living/learning communities so they can live with classmates who share their academic interests. A senior says meals in Wofford's three main dining facilities are "getting better each year." Campus security gets mixed reviews. "Sexual assault is an issue on Wofford's campus because most cases go unreported," says a junior, who also credits the administration with increasing the visibility of Title IX staff and resources "so more cases will be reported."

The Greek system is a huge force in Wofford's social life, enlisting 31 percent of the men and 41 percent of the women. The Greek Village features individual houses for fraternities, sororities, and multicultural organizations and serves as the social center of campus. Most Greek groups host parties every Friday and Saturday—with some kicking off the weekend on Thursday. "The school wants to shut down underage drinking, and they're cracking down on it," warns one student. The Student Affairs Committee offers campuswide events like comedians and music for those uninterested in the Greek system. "Spring Weekend is much anticipated at Wofford, as there are bands, cookouts, shaving-cream fights, and a beach volleyball tournament," says a student. Off campus, Spartanburg is home to six other colleges. Students say it's not a great college town, but there are some fun hangouts and occasional street fairs and concerts. Almost every Wofford student participates in some type of volunteer work. Terrier Play Day brings kids from the community to campus for a fair with booths and games. For a change of pace, students can head to Greenville, Atlanta, and Charlotte.

The Wofford Terriers compete in the Division I Southern Conference and have produced a number of competitive teams, including football, men's basketball, and women's volleyball; games against rival Furman always draw crowds. The school's quiz bowl and chartered financial analyst teams are nationally competitive. Students are also active in intramural, recreational, and club sports, and some of the most popular programs include Terrier Tag, soccer, basketball, and lacrosse.

A former Wofford chaplain was fond of saying, "You don't come to Wofford—you join it." And students say that's true, citing the close-knit community and intimate student/faculty relationships fostered by the school's small size. Although administrative efforts to build a more diverse, inclusive campus have been met with some resistance, the status quo here is slowly changing. "Wofford is in a period of transition currently, but I don't think that's a negative," reflects an English major. "Wofford is interested in creating citizens of our world who will foster improvement, and I see Wofford as an institution focused on moving forward while still preserving tradition."

Wofford's quiz bowl and chartered financial analyst teams are nationally competitive.

Overlaps

Furman, Presbyterian, College of Charleston, Sewanee, Clemson, University of South Carolina, UNC at Chapel Hill, Wake Forest

If You Apply To ›

Wofford: Early decision, early action, regular decision. SATs or ACTs: optional. Accepts the Common Application.

The College of Wooster

Wooster, OH 44691

Despite its status as a humble Midwestern college with fewer than 2,000 students, Wooster is renowned in academic circles around the globe. Access is relatively easy, but graduating takes work, with students completing an Independent Study project in their senior year and earning a coveted Tootsie Roll. More intellectually serious than competitors such as Denison. Prioritizes mentorship and prides itself on turning students into real scholars.

Mentored undergraduate research is the heart of a Wooster education, highlighted by the Independent Study required of all seniors.

Instead of telling students what to think, The College of Wooster focuses on teaching students how to do it themselves through what it calls its "research-based liberal arts curriculum." From the first freshman seminar to the final day when seniors hand in their theses, the college paves each student's path to independence. The emphasis here is on global perspectives, mentored research, and the heritage that stems from its origin as a college founded in 1866 by Scottish Presbyterians. The one-on-one attention from faculty makes Wooster an intellectual refuge in the rural countryside of Ohio. "Wooster is a school that really celebrates hard work," says a senior.

Located in the city of Wooster, Ohio, the college's hilltop campus is spread over 240 acres, with many campus buildings designed in the English–collegiate Gothic style and constructed of cream-colored brick. More recent buildings are trimmed in Indiana limestone or Ohio sandstone. The central arch and two towers of Kauke Hall (the central building in Quinby Quadrangle, the square around which the college grew) make it stand out. The Gault Library for Independent Study offers a private carrel for each senior in the humanities and social sciences. Completed in spring 2023, a $40 million renovation of the student center has centralized student support services, updated the dining hall, and expanded space for student clubs and relaxation.

> **"Wooster is a school that really celebrates hard work."**

What goes on behind the facades of Wooster's attractive buildings is more impressive than the structures themselves. The required First-Year Seminar in Critical Inquiry, limited to 15 students per section, introduces students to intensive writing, critical thinking, and interdisciplinary study. In addition to the first-year seminar, three semesters of Independent Study, and six cross-discipline courses, Wooster mandates coursework in writing; foreign language; global engagement; diversity, power, and privilege; social justice or religious perspectives; quantitative literacy; and seven to nine classes in the student's major.

At Wooster, "students develop specific and deep academic interests," says an English major. The most popular majors are also some of the strongest: political science, biology, psychology, communication studies, and neuroscience. Business economics and global and international studies are also strengths. The chemistry department has traditionally ranked near the top among private colleges in the number of graduates who go on to earn Ph.D.s. Several optional Pathway programs, in interdisciplinary areas such as activism and social change, entrepreneurship, and public health, allow students to explore broader academic and career interests that may or may not align with their major. To complete a Pathway, students typically take three or four courses, participate in at least one experiential learning opportunity (internships, service projects, off-campus study, etc.), and reflect on their experiences. Seventy-one percent of classes enroll fewer than 20 students, and only a few introductory courses have teaching assistants, who run review sessions and offer extra help. Students praise faculty members for their devotion to teaching, and a history major says, "Mentorship and collaboration are pervasive across campus."

Indeed, mentored undergraduate research is the heart of a Wooster education, highlighted by paid opportunities in the Applied Methods and Research Experience, APEX Fellowships, the Sophomore Research Program, and other internships. The Independent Study (IS) required of all seniors lets students explore subjects they're passionate about with one-on-one faculty guidance.

> **"The research skills you develop are second to none."**

"The research skills you develop are second to none," affirms one student. IS has become such a part of Wooster that each year seniors celebrate IS Monday—the day they turn in their projects—with a campuswide parade led by bagpipers. Completion of the IS earns you a Tootsie Roll, to eat or keep for posterity next to your diploma. "It's a day all Wooster graduates will always remember!" a senior says. The college even awards nearly $100,000 each year for student research, travel, or materials to support thesis work. The APEX (Advising, Planning, and Experiential Learning) center combines several offices related to student and career services and helps coordinate internships and study abroad. When Wooster's remote locale gets too confining, students may choose from semester-long programs in more than 60 countries worldwide, or short-term TREK programs led by Wooster faculty during spring and summer breaks; 26 percent of students participate.

Wooster awards nearly $100,000 each year for student research, travel, or materials to support thesis work.

Wooster students are "creative and independent, but not to the extent that it feels overly eccentric," says an English major. As the college's reputation spreads, it's becoming more selective. Black students constitute 9 percent of the student body, Asian Americans 4 percent, Hispanics/Latinos 6 percent, and multiracial students 4 percent. Wooster has a notable international flavor—15 percent of students hail from more than 60 foreign nations, while 33 percent come from Ohio. Politically, the campus is "overall quite liberal," says a junior. Merit awards averaging $31,300 are available, and students are admitted without regard for financial need.

All students live on Wooster's campus in 14 co-ed dorms, where rooms are small but mostly "acceptable." "Wooster is in the process of updating older dorms so they can be modern and ADA friendly," reports a communication studies major. Students seriously committed to service may apply to live in one of the college's 30 residential program houses, each of which is affiliated with a community group. Meals are served in the Lowry Center dining hall and get average reviews. When it comes to responding to the issue of campus sexual assault, a neuroscience major says, "The school is constantly improving and is transparent about its effectiveness." But in general, students say that given Wooster's location "in the middle of cornfields," safety isn't an issue.

"[Students are] creative and independent, but not to the extent that it feels overly eccentric."

Despite the school's rural location, students say they enjoy the "quaint and friendly" town of Wooster, a 10-minute walk from campus. "The downtown area offers an excellent social scene for daytime events like going to brunch, hanging out with friends, and going to the farmers market on Saturdays," says a senior. Still, the vast majority of social life is campus-based, especially at night. Visiting lecturers and student performances keep students busy on weekdays, and the Wooster Activities Crew organizes events like craft and karaoke nights, movies, and cookouts on weekends. Two major weekend hangouts on campus are the Underground, a bar and dance club that hosts well-known bands, and the Alley, featuring multipurpose activity space and free arcade games. The college has no national Greek organizations, but local "sections" draw 13 percent of the men and "clubs" attract 20 percent of the women. Students say the party scene is low-key and no one is pressured to drink alcohol. Cleveland is a one-hour drive.

Wooster's kilted bagpipe band and its Scottish dancers perform during Scot Saturdays and other big events throughout the year.

The school's Scottish heritage is on display in its kilted bagpipe band and its Scottish dancers, who perform during Scot Saturdays, Scot Spirit Day in the fall, and other big events throughout the year. "Every student leaves Wooster with a love for bagpipes," enthuses a sociology major. Other annual traditions include an outdoor music festival and the Culture Show during International Education Week in the fall. When it snows—which it does quite often in Wooster—students descend upon the Kauke arch and fill it with snow, a tradition that goes back nearly 60 years.

Wooster fields a number of competitive Division III teams. Fighting Scots basketball is a spectator favorite, especially when the opponent is rival Wittenberg. Baseball and women's soccer are recent North Coast Athletic Conference winners, and women's lacrosse has also been strong of late. Moot Court has been successful in regional and national competition. Club and intramural sports sign up students in droves; soccer, ultimate Frisbee, and rugby are particularly popular.

The College of Wooster is nationally recognized for its commitment to mentored research and its international focus. Wooster students are proud to be independent thinkers. And as a political science major explains, the college's distinctive Independent Study requirement actively shapes both the individual student experience and the campus atmosphere: "Having that big project on the horizon from the day you enroll changes the way you engage with your education, and I think that brings an element of intensity, dedication, and commitment to the academics at Wooster."

If You Apply To ›

Wooster: Early decision I and II, early action, regular decision. SATs or ACTs: optional. Accepts the Common Application.

Worcester Polytechnic Institute

100 Institute Road, Worcester, MA 01609-2280

Small, innovative, and undergraduate-oriented, WPI is anything but a stodgy technical institute. The WPI Plan is hands-on and project-based and takes a humanistic view of engineering. Emphasizes teamwork instead of competition. Global focus unusual for an engineering school. WPI is smaller than Rensselaer and has roughly the same number of undergraduates as MIT.

As a pioneer in STEM education, Worcester Polytechnic Institute has built a solid reputation, particularly for its engineering programs. But with its ever-expanding academic curriculum (including business studies), surprising devotion to music and theater, and dedication to hands-on undergraduate experiences, WPI has broadened the definition of what it means to be a techie haven. More than anything, it's WPI's intentionally humanistic approach to engineering that really sets it apart. As a mechanical engineering major explains, "We all have one common denominator that brings us together: we all love STEM and we all want to design, build, and innovate to make the world better."

WPI, established in 1865, is the third-oldest independent science and engineering school in the nation. Its compact 95-acre campus is set atop one of Worcester's "seven hills" on the residential outskirts of town and borders two parks and the historic Highland Street District, where local merchants and students come together to form the neighborhood community. Old English stone buildings complete with creeping ivy are focal points of

> **"We all want to design, build, and innovate to make the world better."**

the architecture, but modern facilities have moved in to claim their own space on the immaculately kept grounds. The $49 million Innovation Studio features high-tech classrooms, makerspaces, and labs, as well as a 140-bed residence hall. Unity Hall, a 100,000-square-foot, interdisciplinary academic and research facility that also houses several student services, opened in 2022.

WPI's curriculum remains remarkably broad and flexible for a high-powered technological university. The intent of WPI's unique educational philosophy is to build self-confidence and social skills, to nurture well-rounded students interested in using their knowledge to improve the world, and, especially, to develop teamwork. First-years have the option of signing up for a two-term Great Problems Seminar, which a junior calls "a great way to get one's feet wet with project-based learning." Standard course distribution requirements vary by major but include classes in engineering, math, and science, as well as a humanities and arts requirement. The Interactive Qualifying Project (IQP) is a distinctive requirement that has students apply technical knowledge to one of society's problems, usually working in teams of two to four students with a faculty advisor. The Major Qualifying Project (MQP) requirement serves as a capstone in which students work on a truly professional-level problem in their major course of study. Many IQPs and MQPs involve corporate, nonprofit, or government sponsors, to whom students present their research findings and recommendations.

The most popular majors are mechanical engineering, computer science, biomedical engineering, and electrical and computer engineering. Aerospace engineering and architectural engineering are traditional strengths, as are interdisciplinary programs such as interactive media and game development, and bioinformatics and computational biology. The school launched the nation's first undergraduate robotics engineering program, which has grown to include M.S. and Ph.D. programs, making it the first university to offer all three levels. WPI also offers a rare fire protection engineering combined B.S./M.S. program. Many biomedical engineering majors do their projects at UMass Medical and Tufts Veterinary, as well as at local hospitals. Math and science types can pick up middle or high school teaching credentials through the university's STEM Education Center. Creative writing, music, and drama are offered as minors, and well over 300 students participate in 30 musical and theatrical groups on campus.

An academic year at WPI consists of four terms, each lasting seven weeks, which means courses are fast-paced and intense. "I am always amazed by how much material we are able to learn in such a short period," comments a senior. When students are not completing their IQP and MQP projects, they take three courses per term. Although some introductory classes enroll more than 100 students, most classes are small—66 percent have fewer than 20 students—and students say teamwork is the norm inside and outside the classroom. Professors are praised for their approachability and willingness to establish relationships, especially when it comes to research opportunities. To further promote cooperation and cohesiveness, the only recorded grades are A, B, C, or No Record. Failing grades do not appear on transcripts, and the school does not compute GPAs or class ranks. "The grading system allows students to take more risks in their curriculum by taking harder classes when they want to," says a chemical engineering major. As of fall 2022, WPI has begun piloting an eight-year test-blind admissions policy.

"The grading system allows students to take more risks in their curriculum."

In light of the increasingly interdependent global economy, WPI offers a distinctive Global Projects Program, in which students travel to more than 50 off-campus project centers run by resident faculty advisors across the U.S. and around the world, working in teams to solve a real-world problem for a local sponsor. About 80 percent of students take advantage of the program, most of them to fulfill their IQP or MQP requirements. Every incoming freshman is eligible for a Global Project Scholarship of up to $5,000 to support participation in the program. Overall, about 75 percent of students take part in some sort of international experience before they graduate. Super motivated students can also complete Individually Sponsored Residential Projects, in which they design their own independent, off-campus study project, under the direction of a faculty member, in addition to their other project work. The co-op program enables students to take time away from the classroom to pursue paid, full-time work experience; most participants can expect to add on extra time to their degree program.

(continued)

Strong Programs:
Aerospace Engineering
Architectural Engineering
Interactive Media and Game
  Development
Bioinformatics and
  Computational Biology
Robotics Engineering
Mechanical Engineering
Computer Science
Biomedical Engineering

The Interactive Qualifying Project has students apply technical knowledge to one of society's problems, usually in teams of two to four students.

WPI established the new Center for Well-Being in 2022 to provide cohesive wellness programming and mental health support.

"Students at WPI are all nerds," says a biology and biotechnology major. "Even the most posh among us fail to hide their true inner love for STEM." Forty-five percent of degree-seeking undergraduates are Massachusetts natives, and 6 percent come from abroad. Black students account for 3 percent of the students, Hispanics/Latinos 9 percent, Asian Americans 10 percent, and multiracial students 4 percent. Men outnumber women 3 to 2. A chemical engineering major calls the student body "relatively apolitical," since "students in general are much more interested in impacting the world through science, technology, and engineering than through political activism." Merit scholarships averaging $18,300 are doled out annually, but there are no athletic scholarships.

First-year students are required to live in the university residence halls. Co-ed halls offer traditional and suite-style options, while on-campus apartments and smaller houses make for more homelike living. Upperclassmen tend to move to Greek houses or off-campus apartments; 53 percent of all undergrads live in campus housing. Students can take their meals in the main dining hall, food court, or on-campus restaurant. A junior notes, "Offices that support students dealing with sexual assault have a much greater presence than they did when I started here." WPI established the new Center for Well-Being in 2022 to provide cohesive wellness programming and mental health support to students.

Social life is usually a good mix of on- and off-campus activities. Student-organized coffeehouses, game nights, concerts, improv shows, and movies are popular, as are Greek parties. Twenty-two percent of the men join fraternities and 28 percent of the women enter sororities. On campus, "Fraternity parties are regulated, and a limit is placed on how many drinks an individual will be served," explains a junior. A century-old campus tradition is the Goat's Head Rivalry, a yearlong grudge match between the freshman and sophomore classes that includes the Pennant Rush, a rope pull next to Salisbury Pond, and a WPI trivia competition. The prize? A bronze goat's head trophy with the winning class's year engraved on it.

> **"Even the most posh among us fail to hide their true inner love for STEM."**

While not exactly a tourist destination, Worcester does offer a large number of clubs and restaurants, an art museum, and a large multipurpose arena that hosts concerts and sporting events. "WPI is placed in a rather convenient and nice location in the city," a freshman says. Several nearby colleges, including Clark and Holy Cross, provide even more social and academic opportunities. Boston and Hartford are both an hour's drive, as are ski resorts and beaches.

The WPI Engineers compete in Division III sports and field a number of strong teams. Women's rowing is a recent NEWMAC conference champion, and men's basketball advanced to the quarterfinals of the national championship in 2022. Softball, men's soccer, and men's and women's swimming and diving are also competitive. Sixty percent of the student body participate in intramural and recreational sports, with underwater hockey being a particular favorite among more than 40 club sports.

One of WPI's chants is fittingly mathematic: "*E* to the *x*, *d-y*, *d-x*, *e* to the *x*, *d-x*; cosine, secant, tangent, sine; 3.14159; *e-i*, radical, pi; fight 'em, fight 'em, WPI!" If you know what any of that stuff means, you'll fit right in.

If You Apply To ›

WPI: Early action I and II, early decision I and II, regular decision. SATs or ACTs: not considered. Accepts the Common Application.

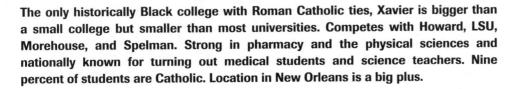

Xavier University of Louisiana

1 Drexel Drive, New Orleans, LA 70125

The only historically Black college with Roman Catholic ties, Xavier is bigger than a small college but smaller than most universities. Competes with Howard, LSU, Morehouse, and Spelman. Strong in pharmacy and the physical sciences and nationally known for turning out medical students and science teachers. Nine percent of students are Catholic. Location in New Orleans is a big plus.

As the nation's only historically Black Roman Catholic college, Xavier University of Louisiana remains committed to "the promotion of a more just and humane society." This small New Orleans university has a stellar reputation for graduating a wealth of scientists, aspiring medical professionals, and science teachers. Xavier prepares students for their chosen careers while providing a strong foundation in the liberal arts and a supportive community. Says one English major: "Xavier is where future leaders are made."

Xavier, a.k.a. XULA, was founded in 1915 by Katharine Drexel, a former Philadelphia socialite (see Drexel University) who devoted her life to the education of African Americans and Native Americans and who was canonized in 2000 by Pope John Paul II. Xavier is located near the heart of New Orleans in a quiet neighborhood dotted with bungalows. The focal point of the campus is the Library Resource Center, which, with its green roof and stately neo-Gothic architectural style, has become a landmark for those traveling by car from the New Orleans airport to the French Quarter. An enclosed campus green mutes the urban feel of the encroaching city, and yellow-brick buildings have been erected among the historic limestone structures. XULA was hard-hit in 2005 by Hurricane Katrina (much of the campus was under water), but since then it has gone on a $130 million renovation and building spree that includes the state-of-the-art Pharmacy Pavilion, the Convocation Center, and the stunning St. Katharine Drexel Chapel designed by renowned Argentine architect César Pelli.

> **"Xavier students from all over the country revel in the New Orleans culture and bond over it."**

Xavier's core curriculum, known as XCore, consists of three stages, beginning with Foundations courses in the first year that orient students to the university, basic skills like college writing, and the city of New Orleans. The second stage, Explorations, requires classes in several liberal arts categories ranging from theology and scientific reasoning to African American heritage and legacies. In the third stage, Engagements, students take two interdisciplinary seminars, each focusing on a different "big idea" or global issue, such as corporate social responsibility and food security. Finally, all students complete a senior capstone course in their major.

The university maintains its reputation as one of the most effective teaching institutions anywhere; the Center for the Advancement of Teaching and Faculty Development works to improve pedagogy across the curriculum and encourages Black students to become teachers and researchers, especially in the sciences. Sixty-nine percent of undergraduates major in a science-related field; biology and psychology are the most popular majors, along with public health sciences, chemistry (including prepharmacy), and business. "If you want to go into medicine, I would recommend Xavier," explains a student. "They have one of, if not the best, premed programs for minority students." Xavier has frequently led the nation in the number of Black alumni who graduate from medical school and in the number of undergraduates who go on to earn Ph.D.s in science and engineering—and the university has

Website: www.xula.edu
Location: City Center
Private
Total Enrollment: 3,456
Undergraduates: 2,637
Male/Female: 23/77
Financial Aid: 99%
Pell Grant: 53%
Expense: Pr $
Student Loans: 98%
Average Debt: $
Applicants: 6,575
Accepted: 95%
Enrolled: 16%
Grad in 6 Years: 48%
Returning Freshmen: 69%
Academics: ✍ ✍ ✍
Social: ☎ ☎ ☎
Q of L: ★ ★ ★
Admissions: (504) 520-7388
Email Address: apply@xula.edu

Strong Programs:
Education
Biology
Psychology
Public Health Sciences
Chemistry
Prepharmacy
Business
Political Science

announced plans to establish its own medical school. Xavier is also among the top producers of Black pharmacists and high school science teachers. Political science is a small but solid department. New programs include majors in robotics and mechatronics engineering and African American and diasporic cultures studies. In addition to the many internships available, Xavier offers cooperative education programs in all fields and study abroad programs around the world; 7 percent of students sign up for international study.

"I would describe the academic climate as competitive in terms of obtaining internships," says one student, "but collaborative as well because most students here are willing to help one another with their studies." Priests and nuns teach and help run the school, though the notably diverse faculty and staff are composed of lay-people. Forty-eight percent of classes have fewer than 20 students. "Teachers are accessible and give personalized attention," says one senior, "especially in upper-level courses." Academic and career advising are well received, and there is a strong emphasis on community service.

"Students are focused, self-motivated, driven, engaged, empowered, and very straightforward about what they want to achieve," comments a biology major. For a historically Black college, XULA's student body is quite diverse. Eighty-five percent of undergrads are Black, 2 percent are Asian American, 5 percent are Hispanic/Latino, 4 percent are multiracial, and 1 percent are white. Xavier has achieved a national reputation for its programs to reach out to local high schools to identify and nurture talented students of color. Most students come from the Deep South; 39 percent are from Louisiana, and many are second- or third-generation Xavierites. Two percent come from abroad. Frequent forums and town-hall meetings give students a chance to discuss social and political concerns. A limited number of academic awards, worth an average of $13,000, are available to qualified students, as are athletic scholarships. A substantial 53 percent of incoming freshmen are eligible for Pell Grants.

> **"Xavier is a cradle for overachieving Black students to come together and challenge each other."**

Sixty percent of Xavier students live in the contemporary-looking residence halls, three of which are single sex. Students report being mostly satisfied with, if not enthusiastic about, the campus dining options: "The dining hall gets the job done," says a student. As a major city, New Orleans experiences a fair amount of crime, so campus security is a top priority, with highly visible officers who provide rides back to the dorms after late-night study sessions.

Athletic events and activities organized by student clubs offer some entertainment on campus, and, as a junior explains, "Every Friday we have Live Music Friday, where we have music on the yard during lunchtime." Popular annual events include homecoming and Spring Fest. Otherwise, given the endless options for socializing and nightlife in New Orleans, the social scene on campus tends to be quiet. "Xavier students from all over the country revel in the New Orleans culture and bond over it," remarks a sociology major. Fraternities and sororities attract just 1 percent of the men and 5 percent of the women, and since Xavier is a dry campus, Greek parties usually happen at off-campus venues. When Mardi Gras rolls around, the university takes two days off to celebrate the holiday. As for road trips, students head to Baton Rouge, Tallahassee, Houston, and Miami.

Xavier's six Gold Rush (men's) and seven Gold Nuggets (women's) varsity sports teams compete along with the co-ed cheer team in the NAIA Division I and are enthusiastically supported, especially when the opponent is crosstown rival Dillard University. Competitive teams include men's and women's basketball (recent Gulf Coast Athletic Conference champions) and track and field, women's cross-country, and women's volleyball. The newest additions are the reestablished baseball program, which had been absent since 1960, and a newly established softball team. Those interested in recreational sports can sign up for intramural basketball, flag football, and volleyball.

"Xavier is a cradle for overachieving Black students to come together and challenge each other," opines a history major. "It is an environment that celebrates and supports high academic performance and achievement." With a mind for the future, Xavier stays true to its beginnings as a historically Black and Catholic university and to its mission of preparing students to work toward "a more just and humane society."

If You Apply To ›

Xavier: Rolling admissions. Accepts the Common Application with supplement. Please consult Xavier's website for the most up-to-date information regarding standardized test requirements.

Yale University

38 Hillhouse Avenue, New Haven, CT 06520

Yale is the middle-sized member of the Ivy League's big three: bigger than Princeton, smaller than Harvard. Its widely imitated residential college system helps Yale strike a balance between being a research university and an undergraduate college. New Haven isn't New York, but it has a relatively lively urban scene. Plan to work hard.

Founded in 1701 by Connecticut Congregationalists concerned about "backsliding" among their counterparts at a certain school in Cambridge, Massachusetts, Yale has long been recognized as one of the world's finest private universities, and one of the few Ivy League schools focused on undergraduates. Students here remain as dedicated to their studies as ever and tend to carry their achievements lightly. And thanks to Yale's residential college system, this huge research university feels like more of a home for its students. "Yale students are truly happy to be here," says a sophomore. "Everyone has a massive crush on Yale, and that makes all the difference in living and working here for four years."

Yale's campus looks like the traditional archetype—magnificent courtyards, imposing quadrangles, Gothic buildings designed by James Gamble Rogers, and Harkness Tower, a 201-foot spire once washed with acid to create its aged, stately look. Most of the residential colleges date to the 1930s. The university, which bears the name of early benefactor Elihu Yale, has increased its full-time undergraduate enrollment over the last four years and opened two new residential colleges, built in the traditional collegiate Gothic style. The Greenberg Engineering Teaching Concourse offers state-of-the-art spaces for undergraduate teaching and collaboration; together with the Yale Center for Engineering Innovation and Design and the Tsai Center for Innovative Thinking at Yale, it forms an "innovation corridor" on campus. A major renovation of the Yale Schwarzman Center student union, which includes the historic Commons dining hall, was completed in 2021.

> **"Everyone has a massive crush on Yale, and that makes all the difference."**

Inside Yale's wrought-iron gates, academic programs are superb across the board, with arts and humanities programs especially outstanding. With tradition ever-present on campus, the Puritan work ethic remains. Graduating from Yale demands

Website: www.yale.edu	
Location: Small City	
Private	
Total Enrollment: 9,275	
Undergraduates: 6,531	
Male/Female: 48/52	
Financial Aid: 56%	
Pell Grant: 20%	
Expense: Pr $ $ $ $	
Student Loans: 12%	
Average Debt: $	
Applicants: 47,240	
Accepted: 5%	
Enrolled: 71%	
Grad in 6 Years: 97%	
Returning Freshmen: 98%	
Academics: ✍ ✍ ✍ ✍ ✍	
Social: ☎ ☎ ☎	
Q of L: ★ ★ ★	
Admissions: (203) 432-9300	
Email Address: student.questions@yale.edu	
Strong Programs: Architecture	

36 courses—nine a year—rather than the 32 courses required at most other colleges. Students agree that despite all the hard work, the academic environment is not based on competition. "Students are not only willing but eager to work together to complete problem sets and study for tests," explains a junior. "Being in such a supportive environment really facilitates learning."

Although Yale has 12 professional schools and a Graduate School of Arts and Sciences, Yale College—the undergraduate arts and sciences division—remains the university's heart and soul. Virtually all professors teach undergraduates, and the professional schools' resources—especially architecture, fine arts, drama, and music—are available to them as well. Yale's superb economics department, replete with budding hedge fund managers and management consultants, offers the most popular undergraduate major, followed by political science, history, computer science, life sciences, engineering, and English. History offers one of the most demanding programs, including a mandatory 30- to 50-page senior essay. The English department is routinely at the vanguard of literary theory, while an outstanding interdisciplinary humanities major includes the study of the medieval, Renaissance, and modern periods. Most science labs and classrooms are located on Science Hill (the sciences were latecomers to all of the oldest U.S. universities and had to find space outside campus cores). Yale has spent half a billion dollars on science and engineering facilities in recent years, and nearly half of incoming students now arrive at Yale with an interest in a STEM major. The biological science departments are excellent, and its students' interests range from biomedical engineering research to preparation for medical school. Architecture and modern languages, especially French and Chinese, are first-rate, and the school's Center for the Study of Globalization is renowned as well.

> **"Professors love having undergrads in their labs as mentees."**

High-achieving freshmen with a particularly strong appetite for the humanities can enroll in Directed Studies, a yearlong, three-course program that examines the literature, philosophy, history, and politics of Western tradition. Prospective DSers, who must apply in May or June of their senior year in high school, should be prepared for some serious bonding with their books—they don't dub it "Directed Suicide" for nothing. Ninety-five percent of science and engineering majors do research with faculty members in any of the more than 800 labs on campus; many are doing their own research as early as the summer after their freshman year. "Professors love having undergrads in their labs as mentees," says a molecular, cellular, and developmental biology major. Yale's Science, Technology, and Research Scholars Program offers research and mentorship opportunities, career planning, and other specialized support for historically underrepresented students, including women, minorities, and those from economically disadvantaged backgrounds.

> *Ninety-five percent of science and engineering majors do research with faculty members in any of the more than 800 labs on campus.*

Despite its reverence for tradition, Yale doesn't require any specific courses for graduation, and it doesn't have a core curriculum. Instead, students must take two classes in humanities and arts, social sciences, and sciences, along with two courses that emphasize writing and another two that emphasize quantitative reasoning. Yale also mandates intermediate-level mastery of a foreign language. Instead of pre-registering, students spend two weeks "shopping" at the beginning of each term, sampling morsels of the various offerings before finalizing their schedules. Seventy-one percent of undergraduates take advantage of hundreds of study, internship, and research opportunities offered around the world. "Yale works hard to make study abroad affordable for every student," says a political science major. "I spent a summer abroad in Siena, Italy, and, best of all, the entire experience was covered by my Yale financial aid." The Yale in London program is popular, as are summer sessions abroad for intensive language study.

Introductory-level classes at Yale can be large lectures, accompanied by small recitation and discussion sections typically led by graduate teaching assistants, although freshman seminars are offered each year on a wide range of topics, allowing first-year students to interact with professors and peers in small groups. Upper-level seminars are small and plentiful. Of the 1,000 classes offered each semester, 71 percent have fewer than 20 students. The quality of undergraduate teaching at Yale is as high as it gets at elite schools, and "professors are extremely accessible," says one junior. Some of the most popular courses, such as John Gaddis's Cold War history class, seem more like performances, students say. Nobel laureate William Nordhaus teaches introductory economics, and James Rothman, winner of the Nobel Prize in Physiology or Medicine, lives in one of Yale's residential colleges.

Directed Studies is a yearlong, three-course program that examines the literature, philosophy, history, and politics of Western tradition.

"Yalies are passionate about the things they are involved in and fully invest themselves in those passions," observes a junior. Nevertheless, a freshman adds, "The student body is amazingly down-to-earth, especially given the insane accomplishments and talents of the students." Ninety-three percent of undergraduates are from outside of Connecticut, including many from the Northeast and 10 percent from other countries, and the student body is evenly split along gender lines. Black students make up 8 percent of students, Hispanics/Latinos 15 percent, Asian Americans 21 percent, and multiracial students 7 percent. Yalies are far less conservative than their counterparts at Harvard and Princeton, and they aren't shy about expressing their opinions. "Students are polit-

"Yale works hard to make study abroad affordable for every student."

ically active and strive to make changes they feel are necessary," says a chemical engineering major. No merit or athletic awards are available, but the university admits students without regard to financial need and meets the full demonstrated need of all its undergraduate students, who are not expected to take out loans. Families making less than $75,000 a year don't pay any portion of the cost of their child's education, and these students also receive a $2,000 grant in their first year to help cover expenses like school supplies or winter clothing.

The 14 residential colleges that serve as Yale's dorms are the focal points for undergraduate social life and central to the distinct culture of Yale. "Yale's dorms are like palaces," cheers one student. Endowed by Yale graduate Edward S. Harkness (who also began the house system at Harvard) and modeled on those at Oxford and Cambridge, Yale's colleges provide intimate living/learning communities, creating the atmosphere of a small liberal arts college within a large research university. A senior says they are "similar to the house system at Hogwarts in the Harry Potter series." Each college has a library, dining hall, "butteries" that sell late-night food, and special facilities such as a gym, photography darkroom, or small theater. All colleges also have their own head of college and dean who live in the college, as well as affiliated faculty members who can help undergraduates struggling to adapt to the rigors of life at Yale. Residential colleges organize social and cultural events, such as teas where prominent public figures meet with groups of students. The dining halls serve good meals and multiple options. A senior notes, "We have an iPhone app that tells you the menu in each dining hall each night."

The 14 residential colleges that serve as Yale's dorms are the focal points for undergraduate social life and provide intimate communities.

Much of each residential college's distinctive identity comes from its architecture. Some buildings are fashioned in a craggy, fortress-like Gothic style, while others are done in the more open colonial style, with red brick and green shutters as the prevailing motif. All colleges have their own special nooks and crannies with cryptic

"Yale's dorms are like palaces."

inscriptions paying tribute to illustrious Yalies of generations past. Freshmen in 10 of the 14 colleges live together on the Old Campus, the historic 19th-century quadrangle, before moving into their colleges as sophomores; freshmen in the other four colleges live in their college starting their first year. Students generally live in suites with a living room and single or double bedrooms, but many seniors get singles. Some upperclassmen move into New Haven, although 79 percent of students choose to stay on campus all four years. Despite New Haven's urban character, students say that they feel physically safe. A female biochemistry major adds, "There have been sexual assaults on campus, and, fortunately, the school's administration has been responding swiftly and appropriately to discipline the assailant."

In addition to identifying with their colleges, many Yale students identify strongly with extracurricular groups, clubs, and organizations, spending most of their waking hours outside class at the newspaper, radio station, or computer center. Particularly clubby are the a cappella singing groups, whose members do everything from drinking together on certain weeknights to touring together during spring break. Many of Yale's mysterious secret societies, such as Skull and Bones, have their own mausoleum-like clubhouses and issue invitations to those with the right qualifications (like being a Bush). There are also the Yale Anti-Gravity Society (jugglers), improv comedy groups, and a multitude of other organizations.

Though studying takes the lion's share of their time, students find ways to unwind. About 10 percent of Yalies belong to a fraternity or sorority, and Greek parties are open to all. "There is no pressure to get involved in a party culture," says a freshman. The undergraduate Yale Symphony Orchestra puts on an original show every Halloween that fills Woolsey Hall with students in costume. "The Halloween Show has been home to some of my favorite memories at Yale," says one student. "It is an incredible production." Each year freshmen gather for a holiday dinner that features a procession of culinary treats known as the Parade of Comestibles. The evening of the first large snowfall of the season brings the annual snowball fight on Old Campus. Each residential college mounts a spring "fun day" likely to include, in the words of a senior, "a petting zoo, free food, and bouncy castles." For the artistically inclined, there are numerous concerts and film screenings on the weekends. The Tony Award–winning Yale Repertory Theater depends heavily on graduate school talent but always brings in a few top stage stars each season and offers reduced-price student passes.

The Yale campus is in the middle of downtown New Haven (population 135,000), a once-gritty small city that is riding the crest of a resurgence that, in the words of a junior, has made it "the perfect blend of manageable quaintness and urban opportunity." Natural history and art museums on and near campus, especially the Yale University Art Gallery and the British Art Center, are excellent. The city's long-standing theatrical tradition continues at two grand old theater and concert halls a block from campus. Shops, bars, and restaurants lie within easy walking distance. Locals will swear that Pepe's on Wooster Street was the first (and best!) pizza parlor in the country, while Louis's Lunch was the first true hamburger joint. Once-testy relations between students and locals are improving. "The city definitely caters to students to make them feel welcome and safe," says a biochemistry major, and about 60 percent of Yale undergrads reciprocate by doing volunteer work in town through Dwight Hall, the largest student-run college community service organization in the country. "Community service is part of the fabric that makes Yale what it is," says a senior. "It's a major part of student life and culture." For those seeking big-city excitement, Metro North trains run almost hourly to New York, and visiting Boston is nearly as easy.

Yale fields a full complement of 34 athletic teams (the Bulldogs), which play in Division I. Recent Ivy League champions include men's basketball and golf. The co-ed and women's sailing teams claimed recent national titles. More than half the student body takes part in intramural competition among the residential colleges; the winning college gets the coveted Tying Cup. The annual Harvard–Yale football

Many of Yale's mysterious secret societies, such as Skull and Bones, have their own mausoleum-like clubhouses.

"Community service is part of the fabric that makes Yale what it is."

The undergraduate Yale Symphony Orchestra puts on an original show every Halloween that fills Woolsey Hall with students in costume.

game—known simply as The Game—is an occasion for tailgating by thousands of blue-clad students, whether it takes place in New Haven or Cambridge. Yale's Mock Trial team is consistently a top performer at national championships.

Yale is one of America's oldest institutions of higher learning, and students and graduates here take seriously the intonation, "For God, for country, and for Yale." For proof, just remember that among its alumni, Yale counts the presidents or former presidents of about 70 other colleges and universities and five U.S. presidents. As the university progresses into its fourth century, its past and former students continue to make their marks on the world. "When I meet other Yalies abroad, we can immediately connect by talking about our residential colleges, and other shared Yale traditions, such as the Halloween show," says one student. Yale has found a way to pursue world-class teaching and learning with what one senior describes as "a collegial and relaxed atmosphere that makes your four years here some of the most enjoyable times of your life."

Overlaps

Harvard, Princeton, Stanford, Columbia, Duke, MIT, University of Pennsylvania, Brown

If You Apply To ›

Yale: Single choice early action, regular decision. Accepts the Common Application with supplement. Please consult Yale's website for the most up-to-date information regarding standardized test requirements.

Index

Acknowledgments

FISKE GUIDE TO COLLEGES STAFF

Editor: Edward B. Fiske
Managing Editor: Michelle Lecuyer
Contributing Editor: Bruce G. Hammond
Response Coordinator: Julia Fiske Hogan

The *Fiske Guide to Colleges* reflects the talents, energy, and ideas of many people. Chief among them are Michelle Lecuyer, the managing editor, and Julia Fiske Hogan, the response coordinator. I am also grateful for the contributions and support of Bruce G. Hammond, my coauthor on the *Fiske Guide to Getting Into the Right College* and other books about college admissions. Thanks also to Shawn Logue, a longtime colleague, for his continuing interest in the *Fiske Guide* and his help with things technological.

One of the great joys of producing the *Fiske Guide* each year is the opportunity to work alongside the talented and dedicated members of the editorial team at Sourcebooks. They are true professionals who understand that providing college-bound students with accurate information about colleges and universities is an important mission. Among them are Dominique Raccah, Todd Stocke, Anna Michels, Kate Roddy, Olivia Turner, and Sarah Otterness. Others who played important roles were Bob Lessard, Lin Miceli, Tina George, Bret Kehoe, Nick Martinelli, Lynn Dilger, and Liz Kelsch. Thanks also to Michelle Gleeson and Alexis Brooke Redding for their thoughtful editorial suggestions. And, as always, I am grateful for the wise guidance of the college counselors who serve on the Editorial Advisory Group.

In the final analysis, the *Fiske Guide* is dependent on the contributions of the thousands of students and college administrators who took the time to answer detailed and demanding questionnaires. Their candor and cooperation are deeply appreciated. While I, of course, accept full responsibility for the final product, the quality and usefulness of the book is a testimony to their thoughtful reflections on the colleges and universities with which they are associated.

Edward B. Fiske
Chapel Hill, NC
May 2023

EDITORIAL ADVISORY GROUP

Richard Avitabile, Westport, CT
Gerimae Bassichis, Delray Beach, FL
Nancy Beane, Atlanta, GA
Sam Bigelow, Concord, MA
Carolyn Blair, Clayton, MO
Robin Boren, Englewood, CO
Lauren Cook, San Francisco, CA
Ralph Figueroa, Albuquerque, NM
Carol Gill, Mount Kisco, NY
Peggy Hoch, Palo Alto, CA
Marcia Hunt, Fort Lauderdale, FL
Marsha Irwin, San Francisco, CA
Claudia Jolivert, Coconut Grove, FL

Matt Lane, Ross, CA
Crys Latham, Washington, D.C.
Katrin Muir Lau, Houston, TX
Candice Mackey, Los Angeles, CA
Judy Muir, Houston, TX
Gay S. Pepper, Naples, FL
Jan Russell, Moraga, CA
Rod Skinner, Milton, MA
Anna Takahashi, East Palo Alto, CA
Chris Teare, Edison, NJ
Alyson Tom, Palo Alto, CA
Mark van Warmerdam, Danville, CA

COLLEGE COUNSELORS ADVISORY GROUP

Christine Asmussen, St. Andrew's–Sewanee School (TN)
Greg Birk, The American School in Switzerland
John B. Boshoven, Ann Arbor Public Schools (MI)
Claire Cafaro, Clear Directions (NJ)
Jane M. Catanzaro, College Advising Services (CT)
Ralph S. Figueroa, Albuquerque Academy (NM)
Larry Fletcher, Education Consultant (DE)
Freida Gottsegen, Education Consultant (GA)
Darnell Heywood, Columbus Academy (OH)
Susan Marrs, The Seven Hills School (OH)
Lisa Micele, University of Illinois Laboratory H.S. (IL)
Gunnar W. Olson, Kimball Union Academy (NH)
Stuart Oremus, Wellington School (OH)
Julie Rollins, Episcopal H.S. (TX)
Bruce Scher, Chicagoland Jewish H.S. (IL)

About the Authors

In 1980, when he was education editor of the *New York Times*, **Edward B. Fiske** sensed that college-bound students and their families needed better information on which to base their educational choices. Thus was born the *Fiske Guide to Colleges*. A native of Philadelphia, Fiske graduated from Wesleyan University with high honors and earned master's degrees from Columbia University and Princeton Theological Seminary. In addition to the *Fiske Guide*, he is the author of numerous books on college admissions as well as *Smart Schools, Smart Kids*, a study of current school reform efforts. Fiske left the *Times* in 1991 to pursue his interest in education in developing countries. He lived in Cambodia, New Zealand, and South Africa and wrote frequently for UNESCO, the World Bank, the Academy for Educational Development, and other international organizations. Fiske lives in Chapel Hill, North Carolina, with his wife, Helen Ladd, a professor emerita at Duke University. They are coauthors of *When Schools Compete: A Cautionary Tale, Elusive Equity: Education Reform in Post-Apartheid South Africa*, and *Handbook of Research in Education Finance and Policy*.

© Sourcebooks

Fiske Guide to Colleges 2024 is the thirteenth edition of the *Fiske Guide* that **Michelle Lecuyer** has worked on, and her seventh as managing editor. After serving in a range of editorial roles at Sourcebooks, the publisher of the *Fiske Guide*, she joined the *Fiske Guide to Colleges* staff as managing editor in 2016. Lecuyer also works as an independent writer and editor for a variety of print and online publishers. She earned a B.A. from Augustana College (IL) and an M.A. from Iowa State University. She lives near Chicago.

Invitation to Readers

The *Fiske Guide to Colleges* welcomes comments from readers on the write-ups contained in the guide, as well as suggestions regarding ways that we could better serve our readers. Please send your comments to:

Fiske Guide to Colleges
Email: editor@fiskeguide.com

Thanks for your interest in the *Fiske Guide*.

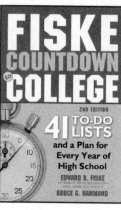

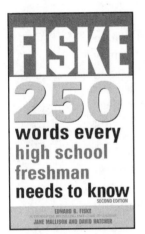

FISKE'S

College Admission Pledge
for Students

I have accepted the fact that my parents or guardians are clueless. I am serene. I will betray not a tremor when they offer opinions or advice, no matter how laughable. My soul will be light as a feather when my parents elbow their way to the front of my college tour and talk the guide's ear off. I am serene.

Going to college is a stressful time for my parents, even though they are not the ones going. I recognize that neurosis is beyond anyone's control. Each week, I will calmly reassure them that I am working on my essays, have registered for my tests, am finishing my applications, have scheduled my interviews, am aware of all deadlines, and will have everything done in plenty of time. I will smile good-naturedly as my parent asks four follow-up questions at College Night.

I will try not to say "no" simply because my parents say "yes," and I will remain open to the possibility, however improbable, that they may have a point. I may not be fully conscious of my anxieties about the college search—the fear of being judged and the fear of leaving home are both strong. I don't really want to get out of here as much as I say I do, and it is easier to put off thinking about the college search than to get it done. My parents are right about the importance of being proactive, even if they do get carried away.

Though the college search belongs to me, I will listen to my parents or guardians. They know me better than anyone else, and they are the ones who will pay most of the bills. Their ideas about what will be best for me are based on years of experience in the real world. I will seriously consider what they say as I form my own opinions.

I must take charge of the college search. If I do, the nagging will stop, and everyone's anxiety will go down. My parents have given me a remarkable gift—the ability to think and do for myself. I know I can do it with a little help from them.

FISKE'S

College Admission Pledge
for Parents

I am resigned to the fact that my child's college search will end in disaster. I am serene. Deadlines will be missed and scholarships will be lost as my child lounges under pulsating headphones or stares transfixed at an iPhone for hours at a time. I am a parent and I know nothing. I am serene.

Confronted with endless procrastination, my impulse is to take control—to register for tests, plan visits, schedule interviews, and get applications. It was I who asked those four follow-up questions at College Night—I couldn't help myself. And yet I know that everything will be fine if I can summon the fortitude to relax. My child is smart, capable, and perhaps a little too accustomed to me jumping in and fixing things. I will hold back. I will drop hints and encourage, then back off. I will facilitate rather than dominate. The college search won't happen on my schedule, but it will happen.

I will not get too high or low about any facet of the college search. By doing so, I give it more importance than it really has. My child's self-worth may already be too wrapped up in getting an acceptance letter. I will attempt to lessen the fear rather than heighten it.

I will try not to say "no" simply because my child says "yes," and I will remain open to the possibility, however improbable, that my child has the most important things under control. I understand that my anxiety comes partly from a sense of impending loss. I can feel my child slipping away. Sometimes I hold on too tightly or let social acceptability cloud the issue of what is best.

I realize that my child is almost ready to go and that a little rebellion at this time of life can be a good thing. I will respect and encourage independence, even if some of it is expressed as resentment toward me. I will make suggestions with care and try to avoid unnecessary confrontation.

Paying for college is my responsibility. I will take a major role in the search for financial aid and scholarships and speak honestly to my child about the financial realities we face.

I must help my child take charge of the college search. I will try to support without smothering, encourage without annoying, and consult without controlling. The college search is too big to be handled alone—I will be there every step of the way.

Notes